# Constitutional Law

# Constitutional Law
## Cases, Approaches, and Applications

**William D. Araiza**

VICE DEAN AND PROFESSOR OF LAW
BROOKLYN LAW SCHOOL

CAROLINA ACADEMIC PRESS
Durham, North Carolina

eBook ISBN  978-1-5310-0160-5
Print ISBN  978-1-61163-729-8
LCCN  2016935727

Carolina Academic Press, LLC
700 Kent Street
Durham, North Carolina 27701
Telephone (919) 489-7486
Fax (919) 493-5668
www.cap-press.com

Printed in the United States of America

*To my students over the years, who asked the questions that helped me learn.*

# Contents

## Part II
### The Division of Federal and State Regulatory Power

## Part III
### Substantive Rights under the Due Process Clause

**Part V**
**General Fourteenth Amendment Issues**

# Table of Principal Cases

# About This Book

Constitutional Law is far too large a topic to be comprehensively covered in a book that aspires to be a reasonable size. (Indeed, it's all too large a topic to be covered in one law school class: you will also encounter foundational constitutional law issues in courses as varied as Criminal Procedure, Administrative Law, and Property.) The challenge of learning such a sprawling topic—even the limited parts of it covered in a standard Constitutional Law class—is only increased by the demands placed on law students today to learn not just legal doctrine but skills. Quite literally, students in a modern constitutional law class have to learn not just what constitutional law is, but also how to practice it effectively.

This book attempts to meet these challenges in several ways. First, it focuses on the core "constitutional law" that is normally taught in a constitutional law survey class in most American law schools: constitutional structure (separation of powers and federalism) and Fourteenth Amendment rights (including the related issues of congressional enforcement power and "state action"). Other topics, such as constitutional criminal procedure, procedural due process, the Takings Clause, and the First Amendment, are normally covered in other classes. This book does not reproduce material that will be presented in books students will be asked to read (and purchase) for those classes.

Second, the content and structure of this book reflect its aim of teaching skills. A basic skill students need to learn is how to read a constitutional law opinion. In order to teach that skill, this book presents relatively fewer primary cases, but relatively longer excerpts of those cases. Those longer excerpts allow students to discern the structure of the justices' constitutional law argumentation, rather than simply providing isolated snippets that present the black-letter rule without adequate surrounding context. Cases and doctrinal progressions that aren't set forth in full-blown excerpts are presented in notes that provide the connective tissue between the primary cases.

Another basic skill is the use of precedent. This book is careful to retain excerpted cases' citations to cases previously presented in the book. The goal of including those citations is to allow students to refer back to those cited cases, and to reflect on how—and how well—the Court employs its own precedents.

The book's structure also reflects this focus on precedent, but also more generally on doctrinal approaches and methodologies. For example, after Chapter 1's examination of the judicial power, Chapter 2 considers other aspects of the separation of national powers, rather than moving immediately to federalism, as many books do. This was not an arbitrary choice. Judicial power cases *are* separation of power cases;

thus, Chapter 1's cases about the judicial power focus on the same concerns, adopt the same methodologies, and indeed, rely on the same cases, as Chapter 2's cases about the executive-congressional relationship. Grouping these cases together, as Part I does, allows students to find connections between different doctrines and between precedents that, at first blush, deal with different issues.

Other parts of the book reflect this same philosophy. For example, Part III's examination of modern substantive due process analysis is not organized by the various topics covered (*e.g.*, family structure, sexuality, and bodily autonomy). Instead, the cases are presented chronologically, thus giving the students to see how the Court at a given time understands and applies the due process precedents that came before.

Finally, the book's supplement aims to teach a skill that often goes unacknowledged in constitutional law books (and courses): the application of the constitutional law rules handed down by the Supreme Court. Often, books simply present the canonical Supreme Court cases on a given topic, and leave it at that. This approach often leaves students unsure what the rules announced in those cases really mean in practice. This result is unfortunate: most students' constitutional law practice will mainly consist of convincing lower courts how to apply Supreme Court caselaw.

This book's supplement acknowledges this reality by providing appellate caselaw—usually quite recent caselaw—applying those rules. That caselaw is presented in several forms: standard excerpts from opinions, notes, and problems based on cases. In addition to helping students learn how lower courts apply Supreme Court rules (and thus how to best frame legal arguments about such applications), these materials remind them that the constitutional "law" governing a particular case or entity emanates not just from the Supreme Court, but from the federal circuit or even the state courts where that case is filed or that entity is located. Of course, the supplement also plays the more traditional role of providing information about the Supreme Court's most recent cases.

The supplement also provides links to online resources that illustrate or are otherwise related to the material in the accompanying chapter. Because websites are often abandoned or assigned new URLs, this material is provided in the supplement where it can be updated annually.

# A Note on Editing

This book aspires to be a helpful and easy-to-use learning tool. That philosophy informs the editing conventions it employs.

Helping students understand how the Court uses precedent is an important aim of this book. Thus, it retains most cites to cases that have already appeared in the book. Citations to other cases are also sometimes retained, when the context would make it awkward or confusing to delete them. To promote readability, deleted citations are not marked by ellipses.

When an opinion cites a case that has already appeared in the book, a *supra.* cite is provided, but only the first time that opinion cites that earlier case. If the cited case has appeared as a full-blown excerpt, the citation will only include the year the case was decided and its chapter location. If the cited case has appeared only in a note, the citation will include the full U.S. Reports citation, in order to allow students to locate it more easily. If an opinion cites a case that appears *later* in the book, no citation is provided, on the theory that students have not yet encountered the cited case and thus cannot evaluate the Court's use of it. Pin cites (*i.e.*, cites to particular pages in the Court's opinion) are generally omitted, except (again) where the context demands they be retained.

The book has attempted to maintain the original paragraph breaks in the Court's opinions, but it sometimes deviates from that in order to promote readability (*e.g.*, to avoid one-sentence or even one-line paragraphs). The book also deviates from the Court's opinions in that it deletes brackets around letters. Thus, for example, if the Court's opinion reads as follows,

> "As we recognized in *Smith*, 'pass[ing] such a law is a red flag' of unconstitutionality."

the excerpt in the book will read

> "As we recognized in *Smith*, 'passing such a law is a red flag' of unconstitutionality.'"

Internal quotation marks are often omitted as well, unless (as with the example above) the internal quotation is integral to the Court's sentence structure.

Ellipses can reflect the deletion of a word, phrase, sentence, or sometimes an entire paragraph or section. As noted earlier, ellipses are not used to reflect the deletion of citations. Asterisks are used rather than ellipses only when ellipses are typographically inappropriate; there is no substantive significance to the use of one rather than the other. (Note, however, that in rare cases justices will use asterisks to separate parts of an opinion. This book simply reprints those asterisks.)

In short, readers can rely on this book for accurate transcriptions of the Court's language, but not for paragraph structure, transformation of a quoted word (*e.g.*, from singular to plural or from one tense to another), and use of internal quotations. Users of the book who wish to quote from the cases presented here for their own writing should consult the original versions of the cases.

# Introduction

Constitutional Law is many things. It's fascinating, and a crucial part of any American lawyer's knowledge. But it's also difficult. The issues themselves are highly complex, and that complexity is only multiplied by the vastness of the field, and the disagreement about fundamental aspects of constitutional interpretation—for example, about the proper methodology for interpreting the document.

This brief introduction can't even come close to comprehensively discussing these issues (let alone resolving them). Instead, it tries to introduce students to the topic. The hope is that this Introduction will contextualize the materials that appear in this book, so as to make them more comprehensible. In order to provide that context, this Introduction tackles several basic issues.

## 1. The Scope of the Material

Constitutional law is a vast topic. The Constitution is, simultaneously, a general blueprint for governmental structure, a guide for specific structural questions (*e.g.*, how old does one have to be in order to become President?), and a charter of rights. Indeed, as noted earlier, the topic is so broad that no one law school class aspires to cover all of constitutional law. Classes called "Constitutional Law" typically cover the materials addressed in this book: the basics of federalism and the separation of powers (including the powers of the federal courts), due process, and equal protection. Even this enumeration overstates the coverage: for example, the Due Process Clause of the Fourteenth Amendment has been understood to include, or "incorporate" as rights against state governments, most of the individual rights the Bill of Rights protects against *federal* impairment. But this book—and indeed, most courses in Constitutional Law—do not cover those Bill of Rights provisions in detail. For example, while the Fourteenth Amendment's Due Process Clause incorporates the Fourth Amendment's guarantee against unreasonable searches and seizures, you will not find a discussion of Fourth Amendment doctrine in this book, even though technically this right, in its incorporated form, is a "due process" right. For that discussion you'd need to take a class on Criminal Procedure.

But even the topics this book *does* cover comprise a vast array of issues. Does the federal government have the power to regulate water pollution? Can Congress control how administrative agencies regulate? Can the President launch missile strikes on a foreign nation without a declaration of war? Can a state ban late-term abortions?

Same-sex marriage? Can a state university engage in racial preferences? The disparate nature of these topics, and others like them, presents a daunting challenge to students seeking a coherent understanding of the material covered in a basic Constitutional Law course. Finding themes in the Court's discussion of these topics will likely be one of your major tasks during this class. But one problem we can start to resolve is the one caused by the interrelationships between the different topics you'll consider. That interrelatedness creates a classic "chicken and egg" problem—that is, you can't understand topic A until you've learned about topic B, but you can't understand topic B until you've learned topic A. In order to break out of this loop, the next part of this Introduction provides a very basic roadmap to the different areas the book covers, and notes places where an understanding of one topic will be useful to your comprehension of another.

## 2. An Overview of the Material

At a very basic level, this book covers the following topics, in the following order: (1) the separation of powers (Part I); the federal-state relationship (Part II); substantive rights under the Due Process Clause (Part III); equality rights under the Equal Protection Clause (Part IV); and congressional power to enforce the Fourteenth Amendment and the problem of Fourteenth Amendment "state action" (both in Part V).

This book thus begins with structure, before moving on to rights. But don't be fooled into thinking that structure and rights are hermetically sealed from each other. They are not. Indeed, the original drafters of the Constitution (the statesmen who gathered in Philadelphia in 1787) inserted relatively few rights into the original document. Most of the rights we think about today when we think of "constitutional rights"—*e.g.*, rights to free speech, or to be free of unreasonable searches or seizures or cruel and unusual punishment—were included as amendments to the Constitution, after the Constitution's opponents insisted on those amendments. But this is not to say the framers did not care about rights. They cared deeply. But for them, the real guarantee that the new federal government would not violate rights flowed from the structure the Constitution created—a structure of limited federal power (as Part II examines), exercised through a structure which divided up even that limited power between three branches (as Part I examines). Thus, the structure you will study in the first half of the class was understood by the framers to have concrete (and positive) implications for rights, by dividing power among competing institutions.

Your understanding of those structural materials will be assisted by realizing some basic facts. First, the federal government enjoys only those powers the Constitution grants. In other words, it does not possess a residual sovereignty to regulate whatever conduct it believes needs regulating—what is sometimes referred to as "the police power." (Note that "the police power" goes far beyond what we think about as normal police department activities). Nevertheless, those enumerated powers cover a vast amount of regulatory ground. Most of that breadth comes from one particular federal power: Congress's power, granted to it in Article I, to "regulate Commerce . . . among the several states." Over the last seventy-five years, the interstate commerce power has come be understood as granting Congress an enormous degree of power to regulate economic and social life. This has happened largely because the economy itself has become so nationally integrated that almost any conduct (say, a local sale of a loaf of bread) can be plausibly thought of as being part of a national (and even global) chain of activity. But it has also come about because, over that period, the Supreme Court has become much more accepting of Congress's use of the commerce power.

Obviously, these developments matter for purposes of the federalism materials you'll study in Part II. But they also matter for Part I's separation of powers discussion. The increased breadth of federal regulatory power has been accompanied by a growth in the federal regulatory apparatus—the alphabet soup of federal administrative agencies you may have heard of, from the Environmental Protection Agency (EPA), to the Securities and Exchange Commission (SEC), the Food and Drug Administration (FDA), and a host of others. Part I considers who controls that bureaucracy—the President (who, after all, has the power under Article II to "take Care that the Laws be faithfully executed"), or Congress, which enacted the legislation those agencies implement (and indeed, which created the agencies to begin with).

But the scope of federal power matters to the separation of powers for another reason. After all, it was the federal courts, and the Supreme Court in particular, that have come to be understood as the ultimate arbiter of the federal-state balance. As you'll see in Part II, it was the Court that blocked much (though certainly not all) of the New Deal legislation expanding federal control over the economy in the middle of the Twentieth century. More recently, in the last quarter-century the Court has reinserted itself into the federalism equation, insisting on a key role in judging whether Congress has exceeded its Article I powers (in particular, but not only, its power over interstate commerce). Part I's consideration of how the Court came to play such a crucial role in determining what the Constitution means thus has major implications for how our federal system has evolved.

Just as the separation of powers materials in Part I presuppose some knowledge of the federalism materials in Part II, so too those federalism materials presuppose some knowledge of the individual rights materials in Parts III–V. These two sets of materials are related in part because another crucial congressional power, other than the power to regulate interstate commerce, is the power to enforce the Reconstruction Amendments (the 13th, 14th, and 15th Amendments, so labeled because they were all part of the process by which the former confederate states were "reconstructed" after the Civil War). The enforcement power is discussed in Part V; the due process and equal protection rights Congress has the power to enforce are discussed, respectively, in Parts III and IV.

These materials are also related in a more fundamental way. The Fourteenth Amendment profoundly changed the relationship between the federal government and the states. With that amendment's ratification, the Constitution directly regulated how states treated their own citizens. Thus, in a very real way, Part II's focus on federalism continues into the rest of the book. Indeed, so does Part I's discussion of the power of the federal courts, since the Supreme Court has played the primary role in interpreting the Fourteenth Amendment.

Parts III and IV consider, respectively, substantive rights under the Due Process Clause and equality rights under the Equal Protection Clause. But even that straight-forward statement requires clarification. Part III's consideration of "substantive rights under the Due Process Clause" is not a complete examination of all such rights. As noted earlier, it does not examine particular Bill of Rights provisions (*e.g.*, the Fourth Amendment right against unreasonable searches) that are included, or "incorporated," within the "liberty" protected by the Due Process Clause. (However, Part III does examine the incorporation process itself.) Instead, this book's discussion of "due process" rights focuses mainly on so-called "unenumerated" rights—the rights that are not textually provided in the Bill of Rights, but that the Court has found implicit in the idea of the "liberty" due process protects: rights to family relationships, privacy, sexual autonomy, abortion, and, for a period in our history, economic liberty.

As you'll see when you read these materials, this book organizes the modern due process cases by the particular methodology the Court used to identify the existence of a due process right, and to decide whether the challenged government action violated that right. The modern Court has been unable to coalesce around a single approach to due process cases. The book presents cases illustrating the varied approaches the justices have taken to those questions.

Part IV considers equality. Unlike due process, which applies explicitly to both the federal government (through the Fifth Amendment) and the states (through the Fourteenth), the guarantee of "the equal protection of the laws" applies explicitly only to the states, via the Fourteenth Amendment's Equal Protection Clause. However, as you'll see in Part IV in a case called *Bolling v. Sharpe*, the Court has found an analogous equality guarantee to apply against the federal government, as part of the Fifth Amendment's Due Process Clause.

Beyond that wrinkle, one thing you may notice when you read the equal protection materials is that, after an initial burst of concern with racial equality in the 1870s, they turn away from serious consideration of race for decades, and toward the meaning of "equal protection" in other contexts. As you think about the Court's consideration of equal protection in those other contexts, consider the interpretive difficulty inherent in the phrase "the equal protection of the laws." What does that guarantee require? What does it mean to treat persons equally? Can courts competently decide when treating two groups differently violates equal protection, or when, instead, such differential treatment (for example, different tax rates for different types of income) is appropriate? Part IV considers these questions as applied to a variety of government classifications.

Part V concludes the book by considering two issues that apply to both due process and equal protection. First, in Chapter 17, it examines Congress's power to "enforce" the Fourteenth Amendment (both due process and equal protection). Those materials will require you to think about whether Congress may be better-placed than courts to decide what "due process" and "equal protection" mean. Chapter 18 discusses the problem of state action—that is, the requirement that parties alleging a violation of their Fourteenth Amendment rights point to some conduct by a state. In most of the due process and equal protection cases you read in Parts III and IV, the state action is obvious. But Chapter 18 highlights situations where the issue is not as clear-cut.

# 3. The Unlitigated Constitution

This casebook devotes a not-insignificant number of pages to the constitutional views of persons and institutions other than courts (in particular, Congress, the President, and, to a lesser degree, important "cause" litigators who developed long-term litigation strategies designed to achieve broad constitutional change rather than simply specific results for their clients). Nevertheless, like the vast majority of constitutional law texts, this book focuses on courts, cases, and opinions. This focus necessarily obscures many parts of the Constitution—those that courts do not speak about, either because they feel themselves incompetent or not authorized to speak on those issues, or because they are so clear that nobody litigates them. These provisions comprise important pieces of our constitutional structure. It is worthwhile spending at least a moment considering "the unlitigated constitution."

Consider, for example, the structure of the national government. While many structural issues are litigated (as noted in Parts I and II of the book), many others are so explicit as to be settled simply as a matter of text. But they still raise important questions. For example, why is the Senate constructed the way it is? As of the 2010 census, the most populous state, California, had nearly 37 million people, while the least populous, Wyoming, had fewer than 550,000. Yet both states have two senators. To the extent state population disparities reflect socially-relevant differences (urban/rural, minority/white, affluent/poorer, industrialized/agriculture or mining based), this structure locks in a bias toward certain interests. If nothing else, it locks in differences in voting power: a Californian can surely complain that her vote counts less than any other American's, and substantially less than a resident of a sparsely-populated state. These issues matter for the democratic nature of our government.

Other structural features raise different concerns. For example, our system is set up so that the President does not have to be a member of the party that controls Congress. (Indeed, such "divided government" has become common in recent decades.) Other democracies are structured differently; for example, so-called "parliamentary democracies" are structured so that the majority party in the legislature is, by definition, the party that controls the executive branch. (Thus, the British Prime Minister is always the leader of the party that controls the House of Commons.) As you'll see when you read the materials in Part I, justices explain that the framers "separated" national powers in order to discourage the tyranny that comes from concentrated power. But critics have noted a darker side to our system: the paralysis and gridlock that many Americans routinely complain about today. That system is not subject to judicial challenge—it is clearly how our government is set up. But, like these other examples, it is worth considering: after all, just because it's not litigated doesn't mean it's not "constitutional law."

Finally, consider the "state action" limitation of the Fourteenth Amendment. As you'll see, judges, lawyers and scholars have proposed ways in which this limitation should not be as absolute as it might otherwise seem. But it unquestionably exists: in some basic way, the Fourteenth Amendment only acts as a limit on governmental (*i.e.*, "state") action. To what extent does this limitation crimp the Amendment's implicit promise that all Americans would be equal, and that certain basic rights (to "life, liberty, and property") would not be impaired, except after "due process"? Does it matter that, today, corporations and other private institutions have power over individual Americans that was likely unimaginable when the Fourteenth Amendment was drafted? What does it matter if states are prevented from denying "equal protection," if private parties are free to do just that (at least in the absence of statutory regulation)? Again, the basic rule is unquestioned: the Fourteenth Amendment limits only states. What does that foregone choice by the Congress that drafted the Fourteenth Amendment mean for our conceptions of "equal protection" and "due process"?

# 4. Methods of Constitutional Interpretation

A final concept that you should be aware of as you begin your study of constitutional law is the modern debate over the proper method(s) of interpreting the Constitution. In recent decades scholars have heatedly debated the appropriateness of various interpretive methodologies. Those debates are not merely academic: judges and justices have entered those debates as well, and you'll see their reflection in the judicial opinions you read.

The first debate you'll encounter, in Part I, is between those who view the separation of powers as a doctrine calling for bright-line rules demarcating the prerogatives of the three branches, and those who apply blurrier, more fact-specific, balancing tests. Both of these approaches can claim a foundation in fundamental separation of powers principles: the Constitution unquestionably separates the legislative, executive and judicial powers, but it also calls for branches to share powers, for example when Article II makes the President Commander-in-Chief of the armed forces but gives Congress the power to declare war and provide for military forces. These countervailing principles have led to a separation of powers jurisprudence that oscillates uneasily between these two approaches.

An even more fundamental interpretive faultline is the one over "originalism." This is an interpretive methodology that, as understood today, seeks to find constitutional meaning in the original meaning of the words used in the Constitution. (Earlier versions of originalism focused on the original *intentions* of those who drafted and/or ratified the Constitution, or the original *expectations* about how a provision would be applied; however, these approaches have faded somewhat in favor of so-called "original meaning originalism.") The insight underlying originalism is straightforward:

the Constitution is comprised of words, and the standard way lawyers interpret a legal document is to inquire into what the relevant words meant at the time of enactment. Indeed, the argument goes further, and observes that the Constitution is legitimate law only because it was ratified by the American people. But what those people ratified was the words, with the meanings those words had to those people. Thus, the argument goes, the only legitimate way to give force to the Constitution as legally binding is to give effect to the original meaning of its words.

This is a powerful argument. But it encounters the response that the Constitution, as a short and often non-specific document, cannot always sensibly be interpreted solely by recourse to its "original public meaning." As a practical matter, such meaning may be difficult to uncover, given the passage of time. It may also be difficult for more fundamental reasons as well. For example, one might wonder whether one can really understand the original public meaning of a word, or a term, when the surrounding context has changed dramatically. Consider one example. One might, with effort, be able to determine what the average American thought "interstate commerce" meant in 1787. But that meaning might be inextricably enmeshed in a set of understandings about the world—*e.g.*, understandings about how much interstate trade there was in 1787, and how much commerce was in fact truly local, in the sense that isolated communities had essentially no impact on commerce across state lines. Did the meaning of "interstate commerce"—not just its application, but its actual meaning—change when the economy integrated as much as it did after the Industrial Revolution? Finally, one single "meaning" may simply not exist. The Constitution was a compromise; it is highly likely that the framers left certain provisions vague simply because there was no consensus about what they should mean.

A prominent competitor to originalism is so-called "living constitutionalism." Speaking very generally, this theory posits that constitutional meaning should evolve over time, in response to the nation's political, economic, and social evolution. Consider, for example, the Fourteenth Amendment's Equal Protection Clause. In 1868, it was highly unlikely that most Americans understood "equal protection" to require sex equality. (Early women's rights advocates did push for such a meaning, but they were a distinct minority.) When today we believe that "equal protection" includes sex equality, are we engaging in living constitutionalism? Some originalists argue that sex equality is simply an application of the Clause's original meaning, which, they say, was to abolish all arbitrary classifications. Of course, if all originalist analysis can do is posit a meaning at a very high level of generality (*e.g.*, "the original meaning of equal protection is to prohibit all arbitrary classifications"), then all of the hard work is being done at the level of applying that meaning to concrete cases. In that case, a living constitutionalist might well accept originalism, but argue that such analysis does very little to decide cases without some other interpretive tool filling in what originalism leaves undecided. And, indeed, some prominent originalists essentially agree with this critique, at least in certain cases.

As you read this book, think about these methodological disputes. While they may seem far removed from the nuts-and-bolts issues the cases decide, understanding these broader principles will help you uncover connections between the cases. It will also help you craft effective legal arguments.

# 5. Setting the Scene: The Constitutional System in 1787

English colonization of the North American continent had existed for over 150 years when the thirteen colonies declared their independence in 1776. Those colonies featured governments that would be roughly recognizable today, consisting of colonial legislatures, some type of court system, and an executive, often appointed from London.

The period after independence featured changes to those colonial governments, the implications of which influenced the framers a decade later. After independence the colonies reorganized themselves as states. They ejected royal governors, and while most of them instituted the office of "governor," those positions often held much less authority, with popularly-elected legislators taking on greater power.

The results worried many of the statesmen who gathered in Philadelphia in 1787. They expressed concern that those newly-empowered legislatures, freed from any significant check from other branches, had infringed on property and contract rights, for example, by printing currency in amounts that effectively diminished the value of debts, and even overturning court judgments on debts. (Justice Scalia discusses this phenomenon in *Plaut v. Spendthrift Farm*, excerpted in Chapter 1.) Echoes of these concerns can be seen in the Constitution's restrictions on states coining money, "making any Thing but gold and silver Coin a Tender in Payment of Debts," and "passing any ... Law impairing the Obligation of Contracts." Art. I, § 10, cl. 1. Beyond those limitations on states, the experience of all-powerful, unchecked legislative bodies convinced many framers of the importance of dividing sovereign power, in order to guard against tyranny.

At the same time, the nation's experience under the Articles of Confederation convinced many Americans of the need for a stronger central government. The Articles, under which the nation was governed during the Revolution and until the ratification of the Constitution, essentially created a league, or community, of sovereign nations. While the Articles government had the authority to act abroad, it had very little coercive authority domestically: for example, it relied on states for its tax revenue, and lacked the power to regulate commerce between the states. As a consequence, the national government was unable to act vigorously to promote economic growth and prevent trade wars between the states.

These weaknesses ultimately led political leaders to push for a convention to strengthen the central government. That movement eventually led to the Philadelphia convention, where delegates from the states reached compromises that resulted in the Constitution. When the Constitution was sent to the states for ratification, opponents of the Constitution, known as the anti-Federalists, objected that the proposed federal government would be so strong that it would threaten Americans' liberties. In response, the Constitution's proponents, known as Federalists, argued that the limited powers the document gave to the federal government reduced that risk; nevertheless, they promised to amend the Constitution to provide a set of explicit guarantees — what became the Bill of Rights.

The ratification fight in New York produced a particularly noteworthy set of arguments. Prominent Federalists — Alexander Hamilton, James Madison, and John Jay — wrote a series of essays urging ratification. Those essays, which were printed in the local press, were eventually published as *The Federalist Papers*. Throughout Parts I and II you'll see references to those essays, which are considered important insights into the Constitution's meaning.

# The Constitution of the United States of America

We the People of the United States, in Order to form a more perfect Union, establish Justice, insure domestic Tranquility, provide for the common defence, promote the general Welfare, and secure the Blessings of Liberty to ourselves and our Posterity, do ordain and establish this Constitution for the United States of America.

## Article I

Section 1. All legislative Powers herein granted shall be vested in a Congress of the United States, which shall consist of a Senate and House of Representatives.

Section 2. The House of Representatives shall be composed of Members chosen every second Year by the People of the several States, and the Electors in each State shall have the Qualifications requisite for Electors of the most numerous Branch of the State Legislature.

No Person shall be a Representative who shall not have attained to the age of twenty five Years, and been seven Years a Citizen of the United States, and who shall not, when elected, be an Inhabitant of that State in which he shall be chosen.

Representatives and direct Taxes shall be apportioned among the several States which may be included within this Union, according to their respective Numbers, which shall be determined by adding to the whole Number of free Persons, including those bound to Service for a Term of Years, and excluding Indians not taxed, three fifths of all other Persons. The actual Enumeration shall be made within three Years after the first Meeting of the Congress of the United States, and within every subsequent Term of ten Years, in such Manner as they shall by Law direct. The Number of Representatives shall not exceed one for every thirty Thousand, but each State shall have at Least one Representative; and until such enumeration shall be made, the State of New Hampshire shall be entitled to chuse three, Massachusetts eight, Rhode-Island and Providence Plantations one, Connecticut five, New-York six, New Jersey four, Pennsylvania eight, Delaware one, Maryland six, Virginia ten, North Carolina five, South Carolina five, and Georgia three.

When vacancies happen in the Representation from any State, the Executive Authority thereof shall issue Writs of Election to fill such Vacancies.

The House of Representatives shall chuse their Speaker and other Officers; and shall have the sole Power of Impeachment.

Section 3. The Senate of the United States shall be composed of two Senators from each State, chosen by the Legislature thereof, for six Years; and each Senator shall have one Vote.

Immediately after they shall be assembled in Consequence of the first Election, they shall be divided as equally as may be into three Classes. The Seats of the Senators of the first Class shall be vacated at the Expiration of the second Year, of the second Class at the Expiration of the fourth Year, and of the third Class at the Expiration of the sixth Year, so that one third may be chosen every second Year; and if Vacancies happen by Resignation, or otherwise, during the Recess of the Legislature of any

State, the Executive thereof may make temporary Appointments until the next Meeting of the Legislature, which shall then fill such Vacancies.

No Person shall be a Senator who shall not have attained to the Age of thirty Years, and been nine Years a Citizen of the United States, and who shall not, when elected, be an Inhabitant of that State for which he shall be chosen.

The Vice President of the United States shall be President of the Senate but shall have no Vote, unless they be equally divided.

The Senate shall chuse their other Officers, and also a President pro tempore, in the Absence of the Vice President, or when he shall exercise the Office of President of the United States.

The Senate shall have the sole Power to try all Impeachments. When sitting for that Purpose, they shall be on Oath or Affirmation. When the President of the United States is tried the Chief Justice shall preside: And no Person shall be convicted without the Concurrence of two thirds of the Members present.

Judgment in Cases of Impeachment shall not extend further than to removal from Office, and disqualification to hold and enjoy any Office of honor, Trust or Profit under the United States: but the Party convicted shall nevertheless be liable and subject to Indictment, Trial, Judgment and Punishment, according to Law.

Section 4. The Times, Places and Manner of holding Elections for Senators and Representatives, shall be prescribed in each State by the Legislature thereof; but the Congress may at any time by Law make or alter such Regulations, except as to the Places of chusing Senators.

The Congress shall assemble at least once in every Year, and such Meeting shall be on the first Monday in December, unless they shall by Law appoint a different Day.

Section 5. Each House shall be the Judge of the Elections, Returns and Qualifications of its own Members, and a Majority of each shall constitute a Quorum to do Business; but a smaller Number may adjourn from day to day, and may be authorized to compel the Attendance of absent Members, in such Manner, and under such Penalties as each House may provide.

Each House may determine the Rules of its Proceedings, punish its Members for disorderly Behaviour, and, with the Concurrence of two thirds, expel a Member.

Each House shall keep a Journal of its Proceedings, and from time to time publish the same, excepting such Parts as may in their Judgment require Secrecy; and the Yeas and Nays of the Members of either House on any question shall, at the Desire of one fifth of those Present, be entered on the Journal.

Neither House, during the Session of Congress, shall, without the Consent of the other, adjourn for more than three days, nor to any other Place than that in which the two Houses shall be sitting.

Section 6. The Senators and Representatives shall receive a Compensation for their Services, to be ascertained by Law, and paid out of the Treasury of the United States.

They shall in all Cases, except Treason, Felony and Breach of the Peace, be privileged from Arrest during their Attendance at the Session of their respective Houses, and in going to and returning from the same; and for any Speech or Debate in either House, they shall not be questioned in any other Place.

No Senator or Representative shall, during the Time for which he was elected, be appointed to any civil Office under the Authority of the United States, which shall have been created, or the Emoluments whereof shall have been encreased during such time; and no Person holding any Office under the United States, shall be a Member of either House during his Continuance in Office.

Section 7. All Bills for raising Revenue shall originate in the House of Representatives; but the Senate may propose or concur with amendments as on other Bills.

Every Bill which shall have passed the House of Representatives and the Senate, shall, before it become a Law, be presented to the President of the United States: If he approve he shall sign it, but if not he shall return it, with his Objections to that House in which it shall have originated, who shall enter the Objections at large on their Journal, and proceed to reconsider it. If after such Reconsideration two thirds of that House shall agree to pass the Bill, it shall be sent, together with the Objections, to the other House, by which it shall likewise be reconsidered, and if approved by two thirds of that House, it shall become a Law. But in all such Cases the Votes of both Houses shall be determined by Yeas and Nays, and the Names of the Persons voting for and against the Bill shall be entered on the Journal of each House respectively. If any Bill shall not be returned by the President within ten Days (Sundays excepted) after it shall have been presented to him, the Same shall be a Law, in like Manner as if he had signed it, unless the Congress by their Adjournment prevent its Return, in which Case it shall not be a Law.

Every Order, Resolution, or Vote to which the Concurrence of the Senate and House of Representatives may be necessary (except on a question of Adjournment) shall be presented to the President of the United States; and before the Same shall take Effect, shall be approved by him, or being disapproved by him, shall be repassed by two thirds of the Senate and House of Representatives, according to the Rules and Limitations prescribed in the Case of a Bill.

Section 8. The Congress shall have Power To lay and collect Taxes, Duties, Imposts and Excises, to pay the Debts and provide for the common Defence and general Welfare of the United States; but all Duties, Imposts and Excises shall be uniform throughout the United States;

To borrow Money on the credit of the United States;

To regulate Commerce with foreign Nations, and among the several States, and with the Indian Tribes;

To establish an uniform Rule of Naturalization, and uniform Laws on the subject of Bankruptcies throughout the United States;

To coin Money, regulate the Value thereof, and of foreign Coin, and fix the Standard of Weights and Measures;

To provide for the Punishment of counterfeiting the Securities and current Coin of the United States;

To establish Post Offices and post Roads;

To promote the Progress of Science and useful Arts, by securing for limited Times to Authors and Inventors the exclusive Right to their respective Writings and Discoveries;

*— Right*

To constitute Tribunals inferior to the supreme Court;

To define and punish Piracies and Felonies committed on the high Seas, and Offences against the Law of Nations;

To declare War, grant Letters of Marque and Reprisal, and make Rules concerning Captures on Land and Water;

To raise and support Armies, but no Appropriation of Money to that Use shall be for a longer Term than two Years;

To provide and maintain a Navy;

To make Rules for the Government and Regulation of the land and naval Forces;

To provide for calling forth the Militia to execute the Laws of the Union, suppress Insurrections and repel Invasions;

To provide for organizing, arming, and disciplining, the Militia, and for governing such Part of them as may be employed in the Service of the United States, reserving to the States respectively, the Appointment of the Officers, and the Authority of training the Militia according to the discipline prescribed by Congress;

To exercise exclusive Legislation in all Cases whatsoever, over such District (not exceeding ten Miles square) as may, by Cession of Particular States, and the Acceptance of Congress, become the Seat of the Government of the United States, and to exercise like Authority over all Places purchased by the Consent of the Legislature of the State in which the Same shall be, for the Erection of Forts, Magazines, Arsenals, dock-Yards, and other needful Buildings;—And

To make all Laws which shall be necessary and proper for carrying into Execution the foregoing Powers, and all other Powers vested by this Constitution in the Government of the United States, or in any Department or Officer thereof.

Section 9. The Migration or Importation of such Persons as any of the States now existing shall think proper to admit, shall not be prohibited by the Congress prior to the Year one thousand eight hundred and eight, but a Tax or duty may be imposed on such Importation, not exceeding ten dollars for each Person.

The Privilege of the Writ of Habeas Corpus shall not be suspended, unless when in Cases of Rebellion or Invasion the public Safety may require it.

No Bill of Attainder or ex post facto Law shall be passed.

No Capitation, or other direct, Tax shall be laid, unless in Proportion to the Census or Enumeration herein before directed to be taken.

No Tax or Duty shall be laid on Articles exported from any State.

No Preference shall be given by any Regulation of Commerce or Revenue to the Ports of one State over those of another: nor shall Vessels bound to, or from, one State, be obliged to enter, clear or pay Duties in another.

No Money shall be drawn from the Treasury, but in Consequence of Appropriations made by Law; and a regular Statement and Account of the Receipts and Expenditures of all public Money shall be published from time to time.

No Title of Nobility shall be granted by the United States: And no Person holding any Office of Profit or Trust under them, shall, without the Consent of the Congress, accept of any present, Emolument, Office, or Title, of any kind whatever, from any King, Prince or foreign State.

Section 10. No State shall enter into any Treaty, Alliance, or Confederation; grant Letters of Marque and Reprisal; coin Money; emit Bills of Credit; make any Thing but gold and silver Coin a Tender in Payment of Debts; pass any Bill of Attainder, ex post facto Law, or Law impairing the Obligation of Contracts, or grant any Title of Nobility.

No State shall, without the Consent of the Congress, lay any Imposts or Duties on Imports or Exports, except what may be absolutely necessary for executing it's [sic] inspection Laws: and the net Produce of all Duties and Imposts, laid by any State on Imports or Exports, shall be for the Use of the Treasury of the United States; and all such Laws shall be subject to the Revision and Controul of the Congress.

No State shall, without the Consent of Congress, lay any Duty of Tonnage, keep Troops, or Ships of War in time of Peace, enter into any Agreement or Compact with another State, or with a foreign Power, or engage in War, unless actually invaded, or in such imminent Danger as will not admit of delay.

## Article II

Section 1. The executive Power shall be vested in a President of the United States of America. He shall hold his Office during the Term of four Years, and, together with the Vice President, chosen for the same Term, be elected, as follows:

Each State shall appoint, in such Manner as the Legislature thereof may direct, a Number of Electors, equal to the whole Number of Senators and Representatives to which the State may be entitled in the Congress: but no Senator or Representative, or Person holding an Office of Trust or Profit under the United States, shall be appointed an Elector.

The Electors shall meet in their respective States, and vote by Ballot for two Persons, of whom one at least shall not be an Inhabitant of the same State with themselves. And they shall make a List of all the Persons voted for, and of the Number of Votes for each; which List they shall sign and certify, and transmit sealed to the Seat of the Government of the United States, directed to the President of the Senate. The President of the Senate shall, in the Presence of the Senate and House of Representatives, open all the Certificates, and the Votes shall then be counted. The Person having the greatest Number of Votes shall be the President, if such Number be a Majority of the whole

Number of Electors appointed; and if there be more than one who have such Majority, and have an equal Number of Votes, then the House of Representatives shall immediately chuse by Ballot one of them for President; and if no Person have a Majority, then from the five highest on the List the said House shall in like Manner chuse the President. But in chusing the President, the Votes shall be taken by States, the Representatives from each State having one Vote; a quorum for this Purpose shall consist of a Member or Members from two thirds of the States, and a Majority of all the States shall be necessary to a Choice. In every Case, after the Choice of the President, the Person having the greatest Number of Votes of the Electors shall be the Vice President. But if there should remain two or more who have equal Votes, the Senate shall chuse from them by Ballot the Vice President.

The Congress may determine the Time of chusing the Electors, and the Day on which they shall give their Votes; which Day shall be the same throughout the United States.

No Person except a natural born Citizen, or a Citizen of the United States, at the time of the Adoption of this Constitution, shall be eligible to the Office of President; neither shall any person be eligible to that Office who shall not have attained to the Age of thirty five Years, and been fourteen Years a Resident within the United States.

In Case of the Removal of the President from Office, or of his Death, Resignation, or Inability to discharge the Powers and Duties of the said Office, the Same shall devolve on the Vice President, and the Congress may by Law provide for the Case of Removal, Death, Resignation or Inability, both of the President and Vice President, declaring what Officer shall then act as President, and such Officer shall act accordingly, until the Disability be removed, or a President shall be elected.

The President shall, at stated Times, receive for his Services, a Compensation, which shall neither be encreased nor diminished during the Period for which he shall have been elected, and he shall not receive within that Period any other Emolument from the United States, or any of them.

Before he enter on the Execution of his Office, he shall take the following Oath or Affirmation: — "I do solemnly swear (or affirm) that I will faithfully execute the Office of President of the United States, and will to the best of my Ability, preserve, protect and defend the Constitution of the United States."

Section 2. The President shall be Commander in Chief of the Army and Navy of the United States, and of the Militia of the several States, when called into the actual Service of the United States; he may require the Opinion, in writing, of the principal Officer in each of the executive Departments, upon any Subject relating to the Duties of their respective Offices, and he shall have Power to Grant Reprieves and Pardons for Offences against the United States, except in Cases of Impeachment.

He shall have Power, by and with the Advice and Consent of the Senate, to make Treaties, provided two thirds of the Senators present concur; and he shall nominate, and by and with the Advice and Consent of the Senate, shall appoint Ambassadors, other public Ministers and Consuls, Judges of the supreme Court, and all other Officers of the United States, whose Appointments are not herein otherwise provided for, and which shall be established by Law: but the Congress may by Law vest the Appointment of such inferior Officers, as they think proper, in the President alone, in the Courts of Law, or in the Heads of Departments.

The President shall have Power to fill up all Vacancies that may happen during the Recess of the Senate, by granting Commissions which shall expire at the End of their next Session.

Section 3. He shall from time to time give to the Congress Information of the State of the Union, and recommend to their Consideration such Measures as he shall judge necessary and expedient; he may, on extraordinary Occasions, convene both Houses, or either of them, and in Case of Disagreement between them, with Respect to the Time of Adjournment, he may adjourn them to such Time as he shall think proper; he shall receive Ambassadors and other public Ministers; he shall take Care that the Laws be faithfully executed, and shall Commission all the Officers of the United States.

Section 4. The President, Vice President and all civil Officers of the United States, shall be removed from Office on Impeachment for, and Conviction of, Treason, Bribery, or other high Crimes and Misdemeanors.

### Article III

Section 1. The judicial Power of the United States, shall be vested in one supreme Court, and in such inferior Courts as the Congress may from time to time ordain and establish. The Judges, both of the supreme and inferior Courts, shall hold their Offices during good Behaviour, and shall, at stated Times, receive for their Services, a Compensation, which shall not be diminished during their Continuance in Office.

Section 2. The judicial Power shall extend to all Cases, in Law and Equity, arising under this Constitution, the Laws of the United States, and Treaties made, or which shall be made, under their Authority;—to all Cases affecting Ambassadors, other public ministers and Consuls;—to all Cases of admiralty and maritime Jurisdiction;—to Controversies to which the United States shall be a Party;—to Controversies between two or more States;—between a State and Citizens of another State;—between Citizens of different States;—between Citizens of the same State claiming Lands under Grants of different States, and between a State, or the Citizens thereof, and foreign States, Citizens or Subjects.

In all Cases affecting Ambassadors, other public Ministers and Consuls, and those in which a State shall be Party, the supreme Court shall have original Jurisdiction. In all the other Cases before mentioned, the supreme Court shall have appellate Jurisdiction, both as to Law and Fact, with such Exceptions, and under such Regulations as the Congress shall make.

The Trial of all Crimes, except in Cases of Impeachment, shall be by Jury; and such Trial shall be held in the State where the said Crimes shall have been committed; but when not committed within any State, the Trial shall be at such Place or Places as the Congress may by Law have directed.

Section 3. Treason against the United States, shall consist only in levying War against them, or in adhering to their Enemies, giving them Aid and Comfort. No Person shall be convicted of Treason unless on the Testimony of two Witnesses to the same overt Act, or on Confession in open Court.

The Congress shall have Power to declare the Punishment of Treason, but no Attainder of Treason shall work Corruption of Blood, or Forfeiture except during the Life of the Person attainted.

## Article IV

Section 1. Full Faith and Credit shall be given in each State to the public Acts, Records, and judicial Proceedings of every other State. And the Congress may by general Laws prescribe the Manner in which such Acts, Records and Proceedings shall be proved, and the Effect thereof.

Section 2. The Citizens of each State shall be entitled to all Privileges and Immunities of Citizens in the several States.

A Person charged in any State with Treason, Felony, or other Crime, who shall flee from Justice, and be found in another State, shall on Demand of the executive Authority of the State from which he fled, be delivered up, to be removed to the State having Jurisdiction of the Crime.

No Person held to Service or Labour in one State, under the Laws thereof, escaping into another, shall, in Consequence of any Law or Regulation therein, be discharged from such Service or Labour, but shall be delivered up on Claim of the Party to whom such Service or Labour may be due.

Section 3. New States may be admitted by the Congress into this Union; but no new State shall be formed or erected within the Jurisdiction of any other State; nor any State be formed by the Junction of two or more States, or Parts of States, without the Consent of the Legislatures of the States concerned as well as of the Congress.

The Congress shall have Power to dispose of and make all needful Rules and Regulations respecting the Territory or other Property belonging to the United States; and nothing in this Constitution shall be so construed as to Prejudice any Claims of the United States, or of any particular State.

Section 4. The United States shall guarantee to every State in this Union a Republican Form of Government, and shall protect each of them against Invasion; and on Application of the Legislature, or of the Executive (when the Legislature cannot be convened) against domestic Violence.

## Article V

The Congress, whenever two thirds of both Houses shall deem it necessary, shall propose Amendments to this Constitution, or, on the Application of the Legislatures of two thirds of the several States, shall call a Convention for proposing Amendments, which, in either Case, shall be valid to all Intents and Purposes, as Part of this Constitution, when ratified by the Legislatures of three fourths of the several States, or by Conventions in three fourths thereof, as the one or the other Mode of Ratification may be proposed by the Congress; Provided that no Amendment which may be made prior to the Year One thousand eight hundred and eight shall in any Manner affect the first and fourth Clauses in the Ninth Section of the first Article; and that no State, without its Consent, shall be deprived of its equal Suffrage in the Senate.

## Article VI

All Debts contracted and Engagements entered into, before the Adoption of this Constitution, shall be as valid against the United States under this Constitution, as under the Confederation.

This Constitution, and the Laws of the United States which shall be made in Pursuance thereof; and all Treaties made, or which shall be made, under the Authority of the United States, shall be the supreme Law of the Land; and the Judges in every State shall be bound thereby, any Thing in the Constitution or Laws of any state to the Contrary notwithstanding.

The Senators and Representatives before mentioned, and the Members of the several State Legislatures, and all executive and judicial Officers, both of the United States and of the several States, shall be bound by Oath or Affirmation, to support this Constitution; but no religious Test shall ever be required as a Qualification to any Office or public Trust under the United States.

## Article VII

The Ratification of the Conventions of nine States, shall be sufficient for the Establishment of this Constitution between the States so ratifying the same.

## Amendment 1 [1791]

Congress shall make no law respecting an establishment of religion, or prohibiting the free exercise thereof; or abridging the freedom of speech, or of the press; or the right of the people peaceably to assemble, and to petition the Government for a redress of grievances.

## Amendment 2 [1791]

A well regulated Militia, being necessary to the security of a free State, the right of the people to keep and bear Arms, shall not be infringed.

## Amendment 3 [1791]

No Soldier shall, in time of peace be quartered in any house, without the consent of the Owner, nor in time of war, but in a manner to be prescribed by law.

## Amendment 4 [1791]

The right of the people to be secure in their persons, houses, papers, and effects, against unreasonable searches and seizures, shall not be violated, and no Warrants shall issue, but upon probable cause, supported by Oath or affirmation, and particularly describing the place to be searched, and the persons or things to be seized.

## Amendment 5 [1791]

No person shall be held to answer for a capital, or otherwise infamous crime, unless on a presentment or indictment of a Grand Jury, except in cases arising in the land or naval forces, or in the Militia, when in actual service in time of War or public danger; nor shall any person be subject for the same offence to be twice put in jeopardy of life or limb; nor shall be compelled in any criminal case to be a witness against himself, nor be deprived of life, liberty, or property, without due process of law; nor shall private property be taken for public use, without just compensation.

## Amendment 6 [1791]

In all criminal prosecutions, the accused shall enjoy the right to a speedy and public trial, by an impartial jury of the State and district wherein the crime shall have been committed, which district shall have been previously ascertained by law, and to be informed of the nature and cause of the accusation; to be confronted with the witnesses against him; to have compulsory process for obtaining witnesses in his favor, and to have the Assistance of Counsel for his defence.

## Amendment 7 [1791]

In Suits at common law, where the value in controversy shall exceed twenty dollars, the right of trial by jury shall be preserved, and no fact tried by a jury, shall be otherwise re-examined in any Court of the United States, than according to the rules of the common law.

## Amendment 8 [1791]

Excessive bail shall not be required, nor excessive fines imposed, nor cruel and unusual punishments inflicted.

## Amendment 9 [1791]

The enumeration in the Constitution, of certain rights, shall not be construed to deny or disparage others retained by the people.

## Amendment 10 [1791]

The powers not delegated to the United States by the Constitution, nor prohibited by it to the States, are reserved to the States respectively, or to the people.

## Amendment 11 [1795]

The Judicial power of the United States shall not be construed to extend to any suit in law or equity, commenced or prosecuted against one of the United States by Citizens of another State, or by Citizens or Subjects of any Foreign State.

## Amendment 12 [1804]

The Electors shall meet in their respective states and vote by ballot for President and Vice-President, one of whom, at least, shall not be an inhabitant of the same state with themselves; they shall name in their ballots the person voted for as President, and in distinct ballots the person voted for as Vice-President, and they shall make distinct lists of all persons voted for as President, and of all persons voted for as Vice-President, and of the number of votes for each, which lists they shall sign and certify, and transmit sealed to the seat of the government of the United States, directed to the President of the Senate;—The President of the Senate shall, in the presence of the Senate and House of Representatives, open all the certificates and the votes shall then be counted;—The person having the greatest Number of votes for President, shall be the President, if such number be a majority of the whole number of Electors appointed; and if no person have such majority, then from the persons having the highest numbers not exceeding three on the list of those voted for as President, the House of Representatives shall choose immediately, by ballot, the President. But in choosing the President, the votes shall be taken by states, the representation from each state having one vote; a quorum for this purpose shall consist of a member or members from two-thirds of the states, and a majority of all the states shall be necessary to a choice. And if the House of Representatives shall not choose a President whenever the right of choice shall devolve upon them, before the fourth day of March next following, then the Vice-President shall act as President, as in the case of the death or other constitutional disability of the President — The person having the greatest number of votes as Vice-President, shall be the Vice-President, if such number be a majority of the whole number of Electors appointed, and if no person have a majority, then from the two highest numbers on the list, the Senate shall choose the Vice-President; a quorum for the purpose shall consist of two-thirds of the whole number of Senators, and a majority of the whole number shall be necessary to a choice. But no person constitutionally ineligible to the office of President shall be eligible to that of Vice-President of the United States.

## Amendment 13 [1865]

Section 1. Neither slavery nor involuntary servitude, except as a punishment for crime whereof the party shall have been duly convicted, shall exist within the United States, or any place subject to their jurisdiction.

Section 2. Congress shall have power to enforce this article by appropriate legislation.

## Amendment 14 [1868]

Section 1. All persons born or naturalized in the United States and subject to the jurisdiction thereof, are citizens of the United States and of the State wherein they reside. No State shall make or enforce any law which shall abridge the privileges or immunities of citizens of the United States; nor shall any State deprive any person of life, liberty, or property, without due process of law; nor deny to any person within its jurisdiction the equal protection of the laws.

Section 2. Representatives shall be apportioned among the several States according to their respective numbers, counting the whole number of persons in each State, excluding Indians not taxed. But when the right to vote at any election for the choice of electors for President and Vice President of the United States, Representatives in Congress, the Executive and Judicial officers of a State, or the members of the Legislature thereof, is denied to any of the male inhabitants of such State, being twenty-one years of age, and citizens of the United States, or in any way abridged, except for participation in rebellion, or other crime, the basis of representation therein shall be reduced in the proportion which the number of such male citizens shall bear to the whole number of male citizens twenty-one years of age in such State.

Section 3. No person shall be a Senator or Representative in Congress, or elector of President and Vice President, or hold any office, civil or military, under the United

States, or under any State, who, having previously taken an oath, as a member of Congress, or as an officer of the United States, or as a member of any State legislature, or as an executive or judicial officer of any State, to support the Constitution of the United States, shall have engaged in insurrection or rebellion against the same, or given aid or comfort to the enemies thereof. But Congress may by a vote of two-thirds of each House, remove such disability.

Section 4. The validity of the public debt of the United States, authorized by law, including debts incurred for payment of pensions and bounties for services in suppressing insurrection or rebellion, shall not be questioned. But neither the United States nor any State shall assume or pay any debt or obligation incurred in aid of insurrection or rebellion against the United States, or any claim for the loss or emancipation of any slave; but all such debts, obligations and claims shall be held illegal and void.

Section 5. The Congress shall have power to enforce, by appropriate legislation, the provisions of this article.

## Amendment 15 [1870]

Section 1. The right of citizens of the United States to vote shall not be denied or abridged by the United States or by any State on account of race, color, or previous condition of servitude.

Section 2. The Congress shall have power to enforce this article by appropriate legislation.

## Amendment 16 [1913]

The Congress shall have power to lay and collect taxes on incomes, from whatever source derived, without apportionment among the several States, and without regard to any census or enumeration.

## Amendment 17 [1913]

The Senate of the United States shall be composed of two Senators from each State, elected by the people thereof, for six years; and each Senator shall have one vote. The electors in each State shall have the qualifications requisite for electors of the most numerous branch of the State legislatures.

When vacancies happen in the representation of any State in the Senate, the executive authority of such State shall issue writs of election to fill such vacancies: Provided, That the legislature of any State may empower the executive thereof to make temporary appointments until the people fill the vacancies by election as the legislature may direct.

This amendment shall not be so construed as to affect the election or term of any Senator chosen before it becomes valid as part of the Constitution.

## Amendment 18 [1919]

Section 1. After one year from the ratification of this article the manufacture, sale, or transportation of intoxicating liquors within, the importation thereof into, or the exportation thereof from the United States and all territory subject to the jurisdiction thereof for beverage purposes is hereby prohibited.

Section 2. The Congress and the several States shall have concurrent power to enforce this article by appropriate legislation.

Section 3. This article shall be inoperative unless it shall have been ratified as an amendment to the Constitution by the legislatures of the several States, as provided in the Constitution, within seven years from the date of the submission hereof to the States by the Congress.

Amendment 19 [1920]

The right of citizens of the United States to vote shall not be denied or abridged by the United States or by any State on account of sex.

Congress shall have power to enforce this article by appropriate legislation.

Amendment 20 [1933]

Section 1. The terms of the President and Vice President shall end at noon on the 20th day of January, and the terms of Senators and Representatives at noon on the 3d day of January, of the years in which such terms would have ended if this article had not been ratified; and the terms of their successors shall then begin.

Section 2. The Congress shall assemble at least once in every year, and such meeting shall begin at noon on the 3d day of January, unless they shall by law appoint a different day.

Section 3. If, at the time fixed for the beginning of the term of the President, the President elect shall have died, the Vice President elect shall become President. If a President shall not have been chosen before the time fixed for the beginning of his term, or if the President elect shall have failed to qualify, then the Vice President elect shall act as President until a President shall have qualified; and the Congress may by law provide for the case wherein neither a President elect nor a Vice President elect shall have qualified, declaring who shall then act as President, or the manner in which one who is to act shall be selected, and such person shall act accordingly until a President or Vice President shall have qualified.

Section 4. The Congress may by law provide for the case of the death of any of the persons from whom the House of Representatives may choose a President whenever the right of choice shall have devolved upon them, and for the case of the death of any of the persons from whom the Senate may choose a Vice President whenever the right of choice shall have devolved upon them.

Section 5. Sections 1 and 2 shall take effect on the 15th day of October following the ratification of this article.

Section 6. This article shall be inoperative unless it shall have been ratified as an amendment to the Constitution by the legislatures of three-fourths of the several States within seven years from the date of its submission.

Amendment 21 [1933]

Section 1. The eighteenth article of amendment to the Constitution of the United States is hereby repealed.

Section 2. The transportation or importation into any State, Territory, or possession of the United States for delivery or use therein of intoxicating liquors, in violation of the laws thereof, is hereby prohibited.

Section 3. This article shall be inoperative unless it shall have been ratified as an amendment to the Constitution by conventions in the several States, as provided in the Constitution, within seven years from the date of the submission hereof to the States by the Congress.

### Amendment 22 [1951]

Section 1. No person shall be elected to the office of the President more than twice, and no person who has held the office of President, or acted as President, for more than two years of a term to which some other person was elected President shall be elected to the office of the President more than once. But this Article shall not apply to any person holding the office of President, when this Article was proposed by the Congress, and shall not prevent any person who may be holding the office of President, or acting as President, during the term within which this Article becomes operative from holding the office of President or acting as President during the remainder of such term.

Section 2. This article shall be inoperative unless it shall have been ratified as an amendment to the Constitution by the legislatures of three-fourths of the several States within seven years from the date of its submission to the States by the Congress.

### Amendment 23 [1961]

Section 1. The District constituting the seat of Government of the United States shall appoint in such manner as the Congress may direct: A number of electors of President and Vice President equal to the whole number of Senators and Representatives in Congress to which the District would be entitled if it were a State, but in no event more than the least populous State; they shall be in addition to those appointed by the States, but they shall be considered, for the purposes of the election of President and Vice President, to be electors appointed by a State; and they shall meet in the District and perform such duties as provided by the twelfth article of amendment.

Section 2. The Congress shall have power to enforce this article by appropriate legislation.

### Amendment 24 [1964]

Section 1. The right of citizens of the United States to vote in any primary or other election for President or Vice President, for electors for President or Vice President, or for Senator or Representative in Congress, shall not be denied or abridged by the United States or any State by reason of failure to pay any poll tax or other tax.

Section 2. The Congress shall have power to enforce this article by appropriate legislation.

### Amendment 25 [1967]

Section 1. In case of the removal of the President from office or of his death or resignation, the Vice President shall become President.

Section 2. Whenever there is a vacancy in the office of the Vice President, the President shall nominate a Vice President who shall take office upon confirmation by a majority vote of both Houses of Congress.

Section 3. Whenever the President transmits to the President pro tempore of the Senate and the Speaker of the House of Representatives his written declaration that he is unable to discharge the powers and duties of his office, and until he transmits to them a written declaration to the contrary, such powers and duties shall be discharged by the Vice President as Acting President.

Section 4. Whenever the Vice President and a majority of either the principal officers of the executive departments or of such other body as Congress may by law provide, transmit to the President pro tempore of the Senate and the Speaker of the House of Representatives their written declaration that the President is unable to discharge the powers and duties of his office, the Vice President shall immediately assume the powers and duties of the office as Acting President.

Thereafter, when the President transmits to the President pro tempore of the Senate and the Speaker of the House of Representatives his written declaration that no inability exists, he shall resume the powers and duties of his office unless the Vice President and a majority of either the principal officers of the executive department or of such other body as Congress may by law provide, transmit within four days to the President pro tempore of the Senate and the Speaker of the House of Representatives their written declaration that the President is unable to discharge the powers and duties of his office. Thereupon Congress shall decide the issue, assembling within forty-eight hours for that purpose if not in session. If the Congress, within twenty-one days after receipt of the latter written declaration, or, if Congress is not in session, within twenty-one days after Congress is required to assemble, determines by two-thirds vote of both Houses that the President is unable to discharge the powers and duties of his office, the Vice President shall continue to discharge the same as Acting President; otherwise, the President shall resume the powers and duties of his office.

## Amendment 26 [1971]

Section 1. The right of citizens of the United States, who are eighteen years of age or older, to vote shall not be denied or abridged by the United States or by any State on account of age.

Section 2. The Congress shall have power to enforce this article by appropriate legislation.

## Amendment 27 [1992]

No law varying the compensation for the services of the Senators and Representatives shall take effect, until an election of Representatives shall have intervened.

# Part I

# The Branches of the Federal Government

# Chapter 1

# The Judicial Power

## A. The Power "to Say What the Law Is"

This chapter considers the scope of the federal judicial power. Most constitutional "law" — at least most of what is studied in law school — is caselaw. Hence, understanding what the Constitution means requires, as a preliminary matter, understanding why and when courts possess the power to interpret the Constitution.

*Marbury v. Madison*, the first case excerpted below, is the Court's fundamental statement about the judiciary's role in saying "what the law is" — a role which, as Chief Justice Marshall explains, logically leads to the conclusion that federal courts have the power of judicial review. As you read *Marbury*, consider the reasons the Court gives for asserting this power. Consider whether those reasons provide the foundation for the limitations on the judicial power considered in the rest of this chapter. Ask yourself how Chief Justice Marshall's explanation for the power of judicial review fits in with more aggressive statements of "the *Marbury* power" in *Cooper v. Aaron*, a case you'll read after *Marbury*.

A crucial part of *Marbury* is its explanation of when a court can order the executive branch of government to take a particular action. As you'll see, Chief Justice Marshall grounds this power by distinguishing between when the executive acts pursuant to "discretion" and when it acts pursuant to legal obligation. This distinction has exceptional resonance in our system: as you read the "political question" cases and the note on the *Chevron* doctrine, consider the extent to which the Court's refusal to "say what the law is" in those cases turns on the discretion/obligation distinction.

### Note: The Scope of "the Judicial Power" and the Lead-Up to Marbury

1. Article III vests "the judicial Power of the United States ... in one supreme Court, and in such inferior Courts as the Congress may from time to time ordain and establish." Although identifying the power, Article III explains neither its scope nor its nature, other than setting forth the category of cases over which federal courts have jurisdiction. Rather, with the exception of its jurisdictional grants, the balance of Article III focuses upon other concerns, including the tenure and compensation of judges, jury trials for criminal cases and grounds for treason. This omission means

that major institutional players—most notably, the Supreme Court itself—have had to define "the judicial power."

2. The function of the judiciary became an issue in the increasingly partisan political environment that developed after George Washington left the Presidency. The final years of the eighteenth century were characterized by intense rivalry between Federalists, who then controlled the executive and legislative branches, and Jeffersonians, who eventually prevailed in the 1800 elections. Having lost at the polls to Thomas Jefferson's Republican Party,* the Federalists, during their final days in office, worked to preserve influence over the nation's governance. Central to their strategy was a plan to reconstruct the federal courts and staff them with judges sympathetic to Federalist ideology. The outgoing Federalist-controlled Congress enacted laws that reduced the size of the Supreme Court, thereby making it more difficult for the incoming administration to make appointments, and expanded the number of inferior courts and created new justice of the peace positions in the District of Columbia, with the expectation that the outgoing Adams Administration would staff these positions with party loyalists.

A primary figure in the Federalist plan was John Marshall. As President Adams' Secretary of State, Marshall was responsible for executing and delivering the commissions to the newly appointed judges. Given the predictable hostility of the Jeffersonians to the court plan, speed was essential in confirming and commissioning the new Federalist judges. While serving in the executive branch, Marshall was nominated and confirmed as Chief Justice of the Supreme Court. Despite his new position as Chief Justice, Marshall carried on as Secretary of State to oversee that process.

Notwithstanding the Federalists' best efforts, some judicial appointees had not received their commissions by the time Jefferson took office as the nation's third President. When the new President refused to deliver the outstanding commissions, one of the frustrated justice of the peace appointees attempted to force his hand. In an original action in the Supreme Court, William Marbury sought a writ of mandamus to compel Secretary of State James Madison to deliver the commissions.

3. *Marbury v. Madison* presented Chief Justice Marshall with an opportunity to resolve a controversy in a way that would give lasting shape to the Court and the Constitution. History credits Marshall with administrative skills that vastly enhanced the high court's prestige and focus. Prior to his appointment as Chief Justice, service on the Court was characterized by poor working conditions—including long and tiresome circuit-riding—that complicated the task of attracting strong legal talent. The Court's output also tended to be cumbersome and confusing, given the Justices' practice of writing individual ("seriatim") opinions instead of a single opinion for a majority of the Court. As Chief Justice, Marshall developed the format of opinions "for the Court" and successfully discouraged his colleagues from writing dissenting opinions. Marshall's organizational efforts greatly helped establish the Court as an institution, rather than simply an agglomeration of individual judges acting as free

---

* Jefferson's party is not the ancestor of today's Republican Party.

agents. As a result, it became a much stronger participant than it might have been in the project of setting the nation's fundamental political course.

None of the impressive Marshall legacy would have been possible without an adroit disposition of the *Marbury* case. At a time when the power of the judiciary was at best unclear, and the President himself had asserted that he would not be bound by a court order to deliver the commissions, the Court's position was precarious. Marshall's challenge in *Marbury* was to establish the judiciary's authority without igniting an interbranch controversy that would fatally wound the Court. Because the judiciary relies upon the executive branch for enforcement of its orders, issuing a decree that the President successfully ignored would have relegated the Court's status to that of an institution fundamentally subordinate to the other two branches. Thus, the challenge to Marshall was to assert the power of judicial review but avoid exercising it in a way that would undermine the Court's real authority.

When Marbury sued in the Supreme Court, he argued that the Court had jurisdiction to hear his claim under Section 13 of the Judiciary Act of 1789. (The Judiciary Act is a foundational federal law that created the first set of federal courts and allocated their jurisdiction, as well as the appellate jurisdiction of the Supreme Court.) As you read Chief Justice Marshall's response to his argument, consider whether you agree with how Marbury and Marshall interpreted the statute. How would the case have come out if Marshall had embraced a different interpretation?

### § 13 of the Judiciary Act of 1789

*And be it further enacted,* That the Supreme Court shall have exclusive jurisdiction of all controversies of a civil nature, where a state is a party, except between a state and its citizens; and except also between a state and citizens of other states, or aliens, in which latter case it shall have original but not exclusive jurisdiction. And shall have exclusively all such jurisdiction of suits or proceedings against ambassadors, or other public ministers, or their domestics, or domestic servants, as a court of law can have or exercise consistently with the law of nations; and original, but not exclusive jurisdiction of all suits brought by ambassadors, or other public ministers, or in which a consul, or vice consul, shall be a party. And the trial of issues in fact in the Supreme Court, in all actions at law against citizens of the United States, shall be by jury. The Supreme Court shall also have appellate jurisdiction from the circuit courts and courts of the several states, in the cases herein after specially provided for; and shall have power to issue writs of prohibition to the district courts, when proceeding as courts of admiralty and maritime jurisdiction, and writs of *mandamus*, in cases warranted by the principles and usages of law, to any courts appointed, or persons holding office, under the authority of the United States.

# Marbury v. Madison

## 5 U.S. (1 Cranch) 137 (1803)

MR. CHIEF JUSTICE MARSHALL delivered the opinion of the court.

At the last term, on the affidavits then read and filed with the clerk, a rule was granted in this case, requiring the secretary of state to show cause why a mandamus should not issue, directing him to deliver to William Marbury his commission as a justice of the peace of the county of Washington, in the district of Columbia....

In the order in which the court has viewed this subject, the following questions have been considered and decided.

1. Has the applicant a right to the commission he demands?

2. If he has a right, and that right has been violated, do the laws of his country afford him a remedy?

3. If they do afford him a remedy, is it a *mandamus* issuing from this court?

The first object of enquiry is,

1. Has the applicant a right to the commission he demands?

His right originates in an act of congress passed in February, 1801, concerning the district of Columbia.

After dividing the district into two counties, the 11th section of this law, enacts, "that there shall be appointed in and for each of the said counties, such number of discreet persons to be justices of the peace as the president of the United States shall, from time to time, think expedient, to continue in office for five years."

It appears, from the affidavits, that in compliance with this law, a commission for William Marbury as a justice of peace of the county of Washington, was signed by John Adams, then president of the United States; after which the seal of the United States was affixed to it; but the commission has never reached the person for whom it was made out.

In order to determine whether he is entitled to this commission, it becomes necessary to enquire whether he has been appointed to the office. For if he has been appointed, the law continues him in office for five years, and he is entitled to the possession of those evidences of office, which, being completed, became his property....

It is therefore decidedly the opinion of the court, that when a commission has been signed by the President, the appointment is made; and that the commission is complete when the seal of the United States has been affixed to it by the Secretary of State....

Mr. Marbury, then, since his commission was signed by the President, and sealed by the Secretary of State, was appointed; and as the law creating the office, gave the officer a right to hold for five years, independent of the executive, the appointment was not revocable; but vested in the officer legal rights, which are protected by the laws of his country.

To withhold his commission, therefore, is an act deemed by the court not warranted by law, but violative of a vested legal right.

This brings us to the second enquiry; which is,

2. If he has a right, and that right has been violated, do the laws of his country afford him a remedy?

The very essence of civil liberty certainly consists in the right of every individual to claim the protection of the laws, whenever he receives an injury. One of the first duties of government is to afford that protection. In Great Britain the king himself is sued in the respectful form of a petition, and he never fails to comply with the judgment of his court....

The government of the United States has been emphatically termed a government of laws, and not of men. It will certainly cease to deserve this high appellation, if the laws furnish no remedy for the violation of a vested legal right.

If this obloquy is to be cast on the jurisprudence of our country, it must arise from the peculiar character of the case....

Is it in the nature of the transaction? Is the act of delivering or withholding a commission to be considered as a mere political act, belonging to the executive department alone, for the performance of which entire confidence is placed by our constitution in the supreme executive; and for any misconduct respecting which, the injured individual has no remedy.

That there may be such cases is not to be questioned; but that every act of duty, to be performed in any of the great departments of government, constitutes such a case, is not to be admitted.

By the act concerning invalids, passed in June, 1794, the secretary of war is ordered to place on the pension list, all persons whose names are contained in a report previously made by him to congress. If he should refuse to do so, would the wounded veteran be without remedy? Is it to be contended that where the law in precise terms, directs the performance of an act, in which an individual is interested, the law is incapable of securing obedience to its mandate? Is it on account of the character of the person against whom the complaint is made? Is it to be contended that the heads of departments are not amenable to the laws of their country? ...

By the act passed in 1796, authorizing the sale of the lands above the mouth of Kentucky river the purchaser, on paying his purchase money, becomes completely entitled to the property purchased; and on producing to the Secretary of State, the receipt of the treasurer upon a certificate required by the law, the president of the United States is authorized to grant him a patent. It is further enacted that all patents shall be countersigned by the Secretary of State, and recorded in his office. If the Secretary of State should choose to withhold this patent; or the patent being lost, should refuse a copy of it; can it be imagined that the law furnishes to the injured person no remedy?

It is not believed that any person whatever would attempt to maintain such a proposition.

It follows then that the question, whether the legality of an act of the head of a department be examinable in a court of justice or not, must always depend on the nature of that act.

If some acts be examinable, and others not, there must be some rule of law to guide the court in the exercise of its jurisdiction....

By the constitution of the United States, the President is invested with certain important political powers, in the exercise of which he is to use his own discretion, and is accountable only to his country in his political character, and to his own conscience. To aid him in the performance of these duties, he is authorized to appoint certain officers, who act by his authority and in conformity with his orders.

In such cases, their acts are his acts; and whatever opinion may be entertained of the manner in which executive discretion may be used, still there exists, and can exist, no power to control that discretion. The subjects are political. They respect the nation, not individual rights, and being entrusted to the executive, the decision of the executive is conclusive. The application of this remark will be perceived by adverting to the act of congress for establishing the department of foreign affairs. This officer, as his duties were prescribed by that act, is to conform precisely to the will of the President. He is the mere organ by whom that will is communicated. The acts of such an officer, as an officer, can never be examinable by the courts.

But when the legislature proceeds to impose on that officer other duties; when he is directed peremptorily to perform certain acts; when the rights of individuals are dependent on the performance of those acts; he is so far the officer of the law; is amenable to the laws for his conduct; and cannot at his discretion sport away the vested rights of others.

The conclusion from this reasoning is, that where the heads of departments are the political or confidential agents of the executive, merely to execute the will of the President, or rather to act in cases in which the executive possesses a constitutional or legal discretion, nothing can be more perfectly clear than that their acts are only politically examinable. But where a specific duty is assigned by law, and individual rights depend upon the performance of that duty, it seems equally clear that the individual who considers himself injured, has a right to resort to the laws of his country for a remedy.

If this be the rule, let us enquire how it applies to the case under the consideration of the court.

The power of nominating to the Senate, and the power of appointing the person nominated, are political powers, to be exercised by the President according to his own discretion. When he has made an appointment, he has exercised his whole power, and his discretion has been completely applied to the case. If, by law, the officer be removable at the will of the President, then a new appointment may be immediately made, and the rights of the officer are terminated. But as a fact which has existed cannot be made never to have existed, the appointment cannot be annihilated; and consequently if the officer is by law not removable at the will of the President; the rights he has acquired are protected by the law, and are not resumable by the President. They cannot be extinguished by executive authority, and he has the privilege of asserting them in like manner as if they had been derived from any other source....

It is then the opinion of the court,

1. That by signing the commission of Mr. Marbury, the president of the United States appointed him a justice of peace, of the county of Washington in the district of Columbia; and that the seal of the United States, affixed thereto by the Secretary of State, is conclusive testimony of the verity of the signature, and of the completion of the appointment; and that the appointment conferred on him a legal right to the office for the space of five years.

2. That, having this legal title to the office, he has a consequent right to the commission; a refusal to deliver which, is a plain violation of that right, for which the laws of his country afford him a remedy.

It remains to be enquired whether,

3. He is entitled to the remedy for which he applies. This depends on,

1. The nature of the writ applied for, and,

2. The power of this court.

1. The nature of the writ.

Blackstone, in the 3d volume of his commentaries, page 110, defines a mandamus to be, "a command issuing in the king's name from the court of king's bench, and directed to any person, corporation, or inferior court of judicature within the king's dominions, requiring them to do some particular thing therein specified, which appertains to their office and duty, and which the court of king's bench has previously determined, or at least supposes, to be consonant to right and justice." ...

This writ, if awarded, would be directed to an officer of government, and its mandate to him would be, to use the words of Blackstone, "to do a particular thing therein specified, which appertains to his office and duty and which the court has previously determined, or at least supposes, to be consonant to right and justice." Or, in the words of Lord Mansfield, the applicant, in this case, has a right to execute an office of public concern, and is kept out of possession of that right.

These circumstances certainly concur in this case.

Still, to render the mandamus a proper remedy, the officer to whom it is directed, must be one to whom, on legal principles, such writ may be directed; and the person applying for it must be without any other specific and legal remedy.

1. With respect to the officer to whom it would be directed. The intimate political relation, subsisting between the president of the United States and the heads of departments, necessarily renders any legal investigation of the acts of one of those high officers peculiarly irksome, as well as delicate; and excites some hesitation with respect to the propriety of entering into such investigation. Impressions are often received without much reflection or examination, and it is not wonderful that in such a case as this, the assertion, by an individual, of his legal claims in a court of justice; to

which claims it is the duty of that court to attend; should at first view be considered by some, as an attempt to intrude into the cabinet, and to intermeddle with the prerogatives of the executive.

It is scarcely necessary for the court to disclaim all pretensions to such a jurisdiction. An extravagance, so absurd and excessive, could not have been entertained for a moment. The province of the court is, solely, to decide on the rights of individuals, not to enquire how the executive, or executive officers, perform duties in which they have a discretion. Questions, in their nature political, or which are, by the constitution and laws, submitted to the executive, can never be made in this court.

But, if this be not such a question; if so far from being an intrusion into the secrets of the cabinet, it respects a paper, which, according to law, is upon record, and to a copy of which the law gives a right, on the payment of ten cents; if it be no intermeddling with a subject, over which the executive can be considered as having exercised any control; what is there in the exalted station of the officer, which shall bar a citizen from asserting, in a court of justice, his legal rights, or shall forbid a court to listen to the claim; or to issue a mandamus, directing the performance of a duty, not depending on executive discretion, but on particular acts of congress and the general principles of law? ...

This, then, is a plain case for a mandamus, either to deliver the commission, or a copy of it from the record; and it only remains to be enquired,

Whether it can issue from this court.

The act to establish the judicial courts of the United States authorizes the supreme court "to issue writs of mandamus, in cases warranted by the principles and usages of law, to any courts appointed, or persons holding office, under the authority of the United States."

The Secretary of State, being a person holding an office under the authority of the United States, is precisely within the letter of the description; and if this court is not authorized to issue a writ of mandamus to such an officer, it must be because the law is unconstitutional, and therefore absolutely incapable of conferring the authority, and assigning the duties which its words purport to confer and assign.

The constitution vests the whole judicial power of the United States in one supreme court, and such inferior courts as congress shall, from time to time, ordain and establish. This power is expressly extended to all cases arising under the laws of the United States; and consequently, in some form, may be exercised over the present case; because the right claimed is given by a law of the United States.

In the distribution of this power it is declared that "the supreme court shall have original jurisdiction in all cases affecting ambassadors, other public ministers and consuls, and those in which a state shall be a party. In all other cases, the supreme court shall have appellate jurisdiction."

It has been insisted, at the bar, that as the original grant of jurisdiction, to the supreme and inferior courts, is general, and the clause, assigning original jurisdiction to the supreme court, contains no negative or restrictive words; the power remains to the legislature, to assign original jurisdiction to that court in other cases than those specified in the article which has been recited; provided those cases belong to the judicial power of the United States.

If it had been intended to leave it to the discretion of the legislature to apportion the judicial powers between the supreme and inferior courts according to the will of that body, it would certainly have been useless to have proceeded further than to have defined the judicial power, and the tribunals in which it should be vested. The subsequent part of the section is mere surplusage, is entirely without meaning, if such is to be the construction. If congress remains at liberty to give this court appellate jurisdiction, where the constitution has declared their jurisdiction shall be original; and original jurisdiction where the constitution has declared it shall be appellate; the distribution of jurisdiction, made in the constitution, is form without substance.

Affirmative words are often, in their operation, negative of other objects than those affirmed; and in this case, a negative or exclusive sense must be given to them or they have no operation at all.

It cannot be presumed that any clause in the constitution is intended to be without effect; and therefore such a construction is inadmissible, unless the words require it.

If the solicitude of the convention, respecting our peace with foreign powers, induced a provision that the supreme court should take original jurisdiction in cases which might be supposed to affect them; yet the clause would have proceeded no further than to provide for such cases, if no further restriction on the powers of congress had been intended. That they should have appellate jurisdiction in all other cases, with such exceptions as congress might make, is no restriction; unless the words be deemed exclusive of original jurisdiction.

When an instrument organizing fundamentally a judicial system, divides it into one supreme, and so many inferior courts as the legislature may ordain and establish; then enumerates its powers, and proceeds so far to distribute them, as to define the jurisdiction of the supreme court by declaring the cases in which it shall take original jurisdiction, and that in others it shall take appellate jurisdiction; the plain import of the words seems to be, that in one class of cases its jurisdiction is original, and not appellate; in the other it is appellate, and not original. If any other construction would render the clause inoperative, that is an additional reason for rejecting such other construction, and for adhering to their obvious meaning.

To enable this court then to issue a mandamus, it must be shown to be an exercise of appellate jurisdiction, or to be necessary to enable them to exercise appellate jurisdiction.

It has been stated at the bar that the appellate jurisdiction may be exercised in a variety of forms, and that if it be the will of the legislature that a mandamus should be used for that purpose, that will must be obeyed. This is true, yet the jurisdiction must be appellate, not original.

It is the essential criterion of appellate jurisdiction, that it revises and corrects the proceedings in a cause already instituted, and does not create that cause. Although, therefore, a mandamus may be directed to courts, yet to issue such a writ to an officer for the delivery of a paper, is in effect the same as to sustain an original action for that paper, and therefore seems not to belong to appellate, but to original jurisdiction. Neither is it necessary in such a case as this, to enable the court to exercise its appellate jurisdiction.

The authority, therefore, given to the supreme court, by the act establishing the judicial courts of the United States, to issue writs of mandamus to public officers, appears not to be warranted by the constitution; and it becomes necessary to enquire whether a jurisdiction, so conferred, can be exercised.

The question, whether an act, repugnant to the constitution, can become the law of the land, is a question deeply interesting to the United States; but, happily, not of an intricacy proportioned to its interest. It seems only necessary to recognize certain principles, supposed to have been long and well established, to decide it.

That the people have an original right to establish, for their future government, such principles as, in their opinion, shall most conduce to their own happiness, is the basis, on which the whole American fabric has been erected. The exercise of this original right is a very great exertion; nor can it, nor ought it to be frequently repeated. The principles, therefore, so established, are deemed fundamental. And as the authority, from which they proceed, is supreme, and can seldom act, they are designed to be permanent.

This original and supreme will organizes the government, and assigns, to different departments, their respective powers. It may either stop here; or establish certain limits not to be transcended by those departments.

The government of the United States is of the latter description. The powers of the legislature are defined, and limited; and that those limits may not be mistaken, or forgotten, the constitution is written. To what purpose are powers limited, and to what purpose is that limitation committed to writing, if these limits may, at any time, be passed by those intended to be restrained? The distinction, between a government with limited and unlimited powers, is abolished, if those limits do not confine the persons on whom they are imposed, and if acts prohibited and acts allowed, are of equal obligation. It is a proposition too plain to be contested, that the constitution controls any legislative act repugnant to it; or, that the legislature may alter the constitution by an ordinary act.

Between these alternatives there is no middle ground. The constitution is either a superior, paramount law, unchangeable by ordinary means, or it is on a level with ordinary legislative acts, and like other acts, is alterable when the legislature shall please to alter it.

If the former part of the alternative be true, then a legislative act contrary to the constitution is not law: if the latter part be true, then written constitutions are absurd attempts, on the part of the people, to limit a power, in its own nature illimitable.

Certainly all those who have framed written constitutions contemplate them as forming the fundamental and paramount law of the nation, and consequently the theory of every such government must be, that an act of the legislature, repugnant to the constitution, is void.

This theory is essentially attached to a written constitution, and is consequently to be considered, by this court, as one of the fundamental principles of our society. It is not therefore to be lost sight of in the further consideration of this subject.

If an act of the legislature, repugnant to the constitution, is void, does it, notwithstanding its invalidity, bind the courts, and oblige them to give it effect? Or, in other words, though it be not law, does it constitute a rule as operative as if it was a law? This would be to overthrow in fact what was established in theory; and would seem, at first view, an absurdity too gross to be insisted on. It shall, however, receive a more attentive consideration.

It is emphatically the province and duty of the judicial department to say what the law is. Those who apply the rule to particular cases, must of necessity expound and interpret that rule. If two laws conflict with each other, the courts must decide on the operation of each.

So if a law be in opposition to the constitution; if both the law and the constitution apply to a particular case, so that the court must either decide that case conformably to the law, disregarding the constitution; or conformably to the constitution, disregarding the law; the court must determine which of these conflicting rules governs the case. This is of the very essence of judicial duty.

If then the courts are to regard the constitution; and the constitution is superior to any ordinary act of the legislature; the constitution, and not such ordinary act, must govern the case to which they both apply.

Those then who controvert the principle that the constitution is to be considered, in court, as a paramount law, are reduced to the necessity of maintaining that courts must close their eyes on the constitution, and see only the law.

This doctrine would subvert the very foundation of all written constitutions. It would declare that an act, which, according to the principles and theory of our government, is entirely void; is yet, in practice, completely obligatory. It would declare, that if the legislature shall do what is expressly forbidden, such act, notwithstanding the express prohibition, is in reality effectual. It would be giving to the legislature a practical and real omnipotence, with the same breath which professes to restrict their powers within narrow limits. It is prescribing limits, and declaring that those limits may be passed at pleasure.

That it thus reduces to nothing what we have deemed the greatest improvement on political institutions—a written constitution—would of itself be sufficient, in America, where written constitutions have been viewed with so much reverence, for rejecting the construction. But the peculiar expressions of the constitution of the United States furnish additional arguments in favor of its rejection.

The judicial power of the United States is extended to all cases arising under the constitution.

Could it be the intention of those who gave this power, to say that, in using it, the constitution should not be looked into? That a case arising under the constitution should be decided without examining the instrument under which it arises?

This is too extravagant to be maintained.

In some cases then, the constitution must be looked into by the judges. And if they can open it at all, what part of it are they forbidden to read, or to obey?

There are many other parts of the constitution which serve to illustrate this subject.

It is declared that "no tax or duty shall be laid on articles exported from any state." Suppose a duty on the export of cotton, of tobacco, or of flour; and a suit instituted to recover it. Ought judgment to be rendered in such a case? Ought the judges to close their eyes on the constitution, and only see the law.

The constitution declares that "no bill of attainder or *ex post facto* law shall be passed."

If, however, such a bill should be passed and a person should be prosecuted under it; must the court condemn to death those victims whom the constitution endeavours to preserve?

"No person," says the constitution, "shall be convicted of treason unless on the testimony of two witnesses to the same overt act, or on confession in open court."

Here the language of the constitution is addressed especially to the courts. It prescribes, directly for them, a rule of evidence not to be departed from. If the legislature should change that rule, and declare *one* witness, or a confession *out* of court, sufficient for conviction, must the constitutional principle yield to the legislative act?

From these, and many other selections which might be made, it is apparent, that the framers of the constitution contemplated that instrument, as a rule for the government of *courts*, as well as of the legislature.

Why otherwise does it direct the judges to take an oath to support it? This oath certainly applies, in an especial manner, to their conduct in their official character. How immoral to impose it on them, if they were to be used as the instruments, and the knowing instruments, for violating what they swear to support!

The oath of office, too, imposed by the legislature, is completely demonstrative of the legislative opinion on the subject. It is in these words, "I do solemnly swear that I will administer justice without respect to persons, and do equal right to the poor and to the rich; and that I will faithfully and impartially discharge all the duties incumbent on me as according to the best of my abilities and understanding, agreeably *to the constitution*, and laws of the United States."

Why does a judge swear to discharge his duties agreeably to the constitution of the United States, if that constitution forms no rule for his government? If it is closed upon him, and cannot be inspected by him?

If such be the real state of things, this is worse than solemn mockery. To prescribe, or to take this oath, becomes equally a crime.

It is also not entirely unworthy of observation, that in declaring what shall be the *supreme* law of the land, the *constitution* itself is first mentioned; and not the laws of the United States generally, but those only which shall be made in *pursuance* of the constitution, have that rank.

Thus, the particular phraseology of the constitution of the United States confirms and strengthens the principle, supposed to be essential to all written constitutions, that a law repugnant to the constitution is void; and that *courts*, as well as other departments, are bound by that instrument.

The rule must be discharged.

## Note: Questions about Judicial Review

1. Even if it is not expressly granted by the Constitution's text or indisputably discernible from its drafting history, the power of judicial review has hardened into constitutional reality. However, over the course of two centuries the judiciary's authority has not gone unquestioned.

2. A notable example of such questioning is President Andrew Jackson's message to Congress accompanying his veto of the bill reauthorizing the Second Bank of the United States. Despite the controversy over the wisdom of having a central bank, Chief Justice Marshall appeared to have placed the Bank's constitutionality on a firm footing in his 1819 opinion in *McCulloch v. Maryland*. (*McCulloch* is presented in Chapters 3 and 4 of this book.) Nevertheless, when President Jackson vetoed the bill rechartering the Bank, he based his reasoning not just on concerns about the Bank's wisdom, but also about its constitutionality:

> It is maintained by the advocates of the bank that its constitutionality in all its features ought to be considered as settled by precedent and by the decision of the Supreme Court. To this conclusion I can not assent. Mere precedent is a dangerous source of authority, and should not be regarded as deciding questions of constitutional power except where the acquiescence of the people and the States can be considered as well settled. So far from this being the case on this subject, an argument against the bank might be based on precedent. One Congress, in 1791, decided in favor of a bank; another, in 1811, decided against it. One Congress, in 1815, decided against a bank; another, in 1816, decided in its favor. Prior to the present Congress, therefore, the precedents drawn from that source were equal. If we resort to the States, the expressions of legislative, judicial, and executive opinions against the bank have been probably to those in its favor as 4 to 1. There is nothing in precedent, therefore, which, if its authority were admitted, ought to weigh in favor of the act before me.

> If the opinion of the Supreme Court covered the whole ground of this act, it ought not to control the coordinate authorities of this Government. The Congress, the Executive, and the Court must each for itself be guided by its own opinion of the Constitution. Each public officer who takes an

oath to support the Constitution swears that he will support it as he understands it, and not as it is understood by others. It is as much the duty of the
House of Representatives, of the Senate, and of the President to decide upon
the constitutionality of any bill or resolution which may be presented to them
for passage or approval as it is of the supreme judges when it may be brought
before them for judicial decision. The opinion of the judges has no more
authority over Congress than the opinion of Congress has over the judges,
and on that point the President is independent of both. The authority of the
Supreme Court must not, therefore, be permitted to control the Congress
or the Executive when acting in their legislative capacities, but to have only
such influence as the force of their reasoning may deserve.

But in the case relied upon the Supreme Court have not decided that all
the features of this corporation are compatible with the Constitution. It is
true that the court have said that the law incorporating the bank is a constitutional exercise of power by Congress; but taking into view the whole opinion
of the court and the reasoning by which they have come to that conclusion,
I understand them to have decided that inasmuch as a bank is an appropriate
means for carrying into effect the enumerated powers of the General Government, therefore the law incorporating it is in accordance with that provision of the Constitution which declares that Congress shall have power "to
make all laws which shall be necessary and proper for carrying those powers
into execution." Having satisfied themselves that the word "necessary" in the
Constitution means "needful," "requisite," "essential," "conducive to," and that
"a bank" is a convenient, a useful, and essential instrument in the prosecution
of the Government's "fiscal operations," they conclude that to "use one must
be within the discretion of Congress" and that "the act to incorporate the
Bank of the United States is a law made in pursuance of the Constitution;"
"but," say they, "where the law is not prohibited and is really calculated to
effect any of the objects intrusted to the Government, to undertake here to
inquire into the degree of its necessity would be to pass the line which circumscribes the judicial department and to tread on legislative ground."

The principle here affirmed is that the "degree of its necessity," involving
all the details of a banking institution, is a question exclusively for legislative
consideration. A bank is constitutional, but it is the province of the Legislature
to determine whether this or that particular power, privilege, or exemption
is "necessary and proper" to enable the bank to discharge its duties to the
Government, and from their decision there is no appeal to the courts of justice. Under the decision of the Supreme Court, therefore, it is the exclusive
province of Congress and the President to decide whether the particular features of this act are necessary and proper in order to enable the bank to perform conveniently and efficiently the public duties assigned to it as a fiscal
agent, and therefore constitutional, or unnecessary and improper, and therefore unconstitutional.

Without commenting on the general principle affirmed by the Supreme Court, let us examine the details of this act in accordance with the rule of legislative action which they have laid down. It will be found that many of the powers and privileges conferred on [the Bank] can not be supposed necessary for the purpose for which it is proposed to be created, and are not, therefore, means necessary to attain the end in view, and consequently not justified by the Constitution.

What is Jackson saying in this statement? Is he saying that Congress and the President have independent authority to interpret the Constitution when enacting, vetoing, or enforcing legislation? If so, would there be times when such independent constitutional interpretation clashes with a court order? How would such a clash be resolved? Or is he also (or merely?) suggesting that Congress and the President have the authority to apply the Court's constitutional decisions to concrete situations (*e.g.*, by determining whether a national bank is "necessary" for carrying out Congress's legitimate legislative prerogatives)? Would this more modest challenge to judicial supremacy still result in conflicts?

3. A half-century after *Marbury*, the Court's determination in *Dred Scott v. Sandford*, 19 How. 393 (1857), that the federal government could not regulate slavery and that persons of African descent could not be citizens of the Union, provoked widespread defiance in the North. (*Dred Scott* is presented in Chapter 13.) Many members of the new Republican Party took the Jeffersonian position that the political branches were not bound by the Court's decision. In the 1860 presidential campaign, Abraham Lincoln argued that the Court's judgment controlled the disposition of the actual case but did not bind the government or become general law until "fully settled." In his first inaugural address, he said the following:

I do not forget the position assumed by some, that constitutional questions are to be decided by the Supreme Court; nor do I deny that such decisions must be binding in any case, upon the parties to a suit; as to the object of that suit, while they are also entitled to very high respect and consideration in all parallel cases by all other departments of the government.... At the same time, the candid citizen must confess that if the policy of the government upon vital questions, affecting the whole people, is to be irrevocably fixed by decisions of the Supreme Court, the instant they are made, in ordinary litigation between parties, in personal actions, the people will have ceased to be their own rulers, having to that extent practically resigned their government into the hands of that eminent tribunal.

As you read the rest of the materials in this chapter, look for echoes of Jackson's and Lincoln's views.

4. Subsequent challenges to judicial authority have included President Roosevelt's plan to greatly expand the size of the Supreme Court, a plan that, as discussed in Chapter 4 of this book, arose out of presidential frustration with the Court's persistent invalidation of New Deal legislation. Defiance of a different type, and from a different

place, followed the Court's determination in *Brown v. Board of Education*, 347 U.S. 483 (1954), that racially segregated education was "inherently unequal" and thus violated the Equal Protection Clause. In *Cooper v. Aaron* the Court relied on *Marbury* to reject arguments that education officials in Little Rock, Arkansas could reject the Court's constitutional interpretation if those officials believed it to be in error, at least until a federal court had ruled in a challenge to Little Rock's own segregation policy. Does *Marbury* support the Court's reasoning in *Cooper*? Is Lincoln's view reflected (ironically) in the position taken by the segregationist Arkansas officials?

## Cooper v. Aaron
### 358 U.S. 1 (1958)

Opinion of the Court by THE CHIEF JUSTICE, MR. JUSTICE BLACK, MR. JUSTICE FRANKFURTER, MR. JUSTICE DOUGLAS, MR. JUSTICE BURTON, MR. JUSTICE CLARK, MR. JUSTICE HARLAN, MR. JUSTICE BRENNAN, and MR. JUSTICE WHITTAKER.

As this case reaches us it raises questions of the highest importance to the maintenance of our federal system of government. It necessarily involves a claim by the Governor and Legislature of a State that there is no duty on state officials to obey federal court orders resting on this Court's considered interpretation of the United States Constitution. Specifically it involves actions by the Governor and Legislature of Arkansas upon the premise that they are not bound by our holding in *Brown v. Board of Education*, 347 U.S. 483 (1954). That holding was that the Fourteenth Amendment forbids States to use their governmental powers to bar children on racial grounds from attending schools where there is state participation through any arrangement, management, funds or property. We are urged to uphold a suspension of the Little Rock School Board's plan to do away with segregated public schools in Little Rock until state laws and efforts to upset and nullify our holding in *Brown v. Board of Education* have been further challenged and tested in the courts. We reject these contentions....

The constitutional rights of respondents are not to be sacrificed or yielded to the violence and disorder which have followed upon the actions of the Governor and Legislature. As this Court said some 41 years ago in a unanimous opinion in a case involving another aspect of racial segregation: "It is urged that this proposed segregation will promote the public peace by preventing race conflicts. Desirable as this is, and important as is the preservation of the public peace, this aim cannot be accomplished by laws or ordinances which deny rights created or protected by the Federal Constitution." *Buchanan v. Warley*, 245 U.S. 60 (1917). Thus law and order are not here to be preserved by depriving the Negro children of their constitutional rights. The record before us clearly establishes that the growth of the Board's difficulties to a magnitude beyond its unaided power to control is the product of state action. Those difficulties, as counsel for the Board forthrightly conceded on the oral argument in this Court, can also be brought under control by state action....

What has been said, in the light of the facts developed, is enough to dispose of the case. However, we should answer the premise of the actions of the Governor and

Legislature that they are not bound by our holding in the *Brown* case. It is necessary only to recall some basic constitutional propositions which are settled doctrine.

Article VI of the Constitution makes the Constitution the "supreme Law of the Land." In 1803, Chief Justice Marshall, speaking for a unanimous Court, referring to the Constitution as "the fundamental and paramount law of the nation," declared in the notable case of *Marbury v. Madison* (1803) [*Supra.* this chapter] that "It is emphatically the province and duty of the judicial department to say what the law is." This decision declared the basic principle that the federal judiciary is supreme in the exposition of the law of the Constitution, and that principle has ever since been respected by this Court and the Country as a permanent and indispensable feature of our constitutional system. It follows that the interpretation of the Fourteenth Amendment enunciated by this Court in the *Brown* case is the supreme law of the land, and Art. VI of the Constitution makes it of binding effect on the States "any Thing in the Constitution or Laws of any State to the Contrary notwithstanding." Every state legislator and executive and judicial officer is solemnly committed by oath taken pursuant to Art. VI, cl. 3, "to support this Constitution." Chief Justice Taney, speaking for a unanimous Court in 1859, said that this requirement reflected the framers' "anxiety to preserve it [the Constitution] in full force, in all its powers, and to guard against resistance to or evasion of its authority, on the part of a State...."

No state legislator or executive or judicial officer can war against the Constitution without violating his undertaking to support it. Chief Justice Marshall spoke for a unanimous Court in saying that: "If the legislatures of the several states may, at will, annul the judgments of the courts of the United States, and destroy the rights acquired under those judgments, the constitution itself becomes a solemn mockery...." [A] Governor who asserts a power to nullify a federal court order is similarly restrained. If he had such power, said Chief Justice Hughes, in 1932, also for a unanimous Court, "it is manifest that the fiat of a state Governor, and not the Constitution of the United States, would be the supreme law of the land; that the restrictions of the Federal Constitution upon the exercise of state power would be but impotent phrases...."

... Since the first *Brown* opinion three new Justices have come to the Court. They are at one with the Justices still on the Court who participated in that basic decision as to its correctness, and that decision is now unanimously reaffirmed. The principles announced in that decision and the obedience of the States to them, according to the command of the Constitution, are indispensable for the protection of the freedoms guaranteed by our fundamental charter for all of us. Our constitutional ideal of equal justice under law is thus made a living truth.

## Note: Post-*Cooper Challenges to the Supreme Court's Interpretive Supremacy*

Despite *Cooper*'s reaffirmation of the Supreme Court's conclusive role in constitutional interpretation, challenges to that role periodically surface. For example, during the Reagan Administration, Attorney General Edwin Meese argued in favor of distinguishing between the Constitution and the decisions of the Court interpreting the Constitution. The theory he adopted—known as "departmentalism"—argues that each branch, within its legitimate sphere of authority, ought to have the power to interpret the Constitution without necessarily deferring to the views of the Court.

Given the two-century legacy of judicial review, and notwithstanding periodic challenges to the exercise of that power, it is doubtful that institutional authority will revert to anything less than what Chief Justice Marshall depicted in 1803. A dramatic illustration of the Court's power was provided in 1974 when it ruled that executive privilege did not shield President Nixon from the legal duty to disclose tapes and documents sought by a special prosecutor in the Watergate investigation. *United States v. Nixon*, 418 U.S. 683 (1974). Unlike President Jefferson, who promised to ignore any order to deliver the judicial commissions at stake in *Marbury*, Nixon complied with the Court's order. The magnitude of the stakes at issue was made clear when he resigned shortly thereafter, recognizing the degree to which disclosure of the tapes would erode his already-weakened political position. The fact that he nevertheless turned the tapes over reveals how unacceptable it had become to defy the Court's ruling on a constitutional issue. A quarter century later, presidential candidate Al Gore accepted the Supreme Court's decision about vote recount procedures in Florida that doomed his presidential hopes, rather than insisting that Congress settle the question of how Florida's electoral votes should be allocated. *See Bush v. Gore*, 531 U.S. 98 (2000).

## *Note:* Marbury *and "the Power to Say What the Law Is"*

1. *Marbury v. Madison* is generally seen as a masterful opinion. Chief Justice Marshall was able to assert significant power for the Court vis-à-vis both the executive branch (through his analysis of whether Madison's refusal to deliver Marbury's commission was subject to judicial review) and the legislative branch (through his analysis of whether the Court had the power to declare a federal law unconstitutional). Yet he asserted this power in the context of a case in which the government won, thus avoiding a showdown with the Jefferson Administration, which had already stated it would disobey any order to deliver the commission. Indeed, he asserted this power in the course of striking down a statute that he read as granting the Court additional jurisdiction. Thus he gave the appearance of modestly declining an opportunity to assert power, even as he established the Court (and, by extension, the entire federal judiciary) as a branch co-equal to the executive and the legislature.

Still, Marshall had to resort to several questionable devices to achieve this result. His status as President Adams' Secretary of State during the relevant period made him someone deeply involved in the underlying controversy; his decision not to recuse himself was thus at least potentially questionable. Second, note that he dealt with the question of the Court's jurisdiction as the very last question. Normally, good judicial practice suggests that a court *begin* by satisfying itself that it had jurisdiction; if jurisdiction was absent, the court's duty would be to dismiss the appeal without reaching the merits. By deferring the jurisdiction question until the end, Marshall was able to establish the principle that some executive acts were amenable to judicial review. Finally, scholars since *Marbury* have criticized Marshall for adopting a contorted reading of Section 13. In their view, Section 13 was easily susceptible to a reading in which the grant of power to issue writs of mandamus applied when the Court already had jurisdiction. On this reading, Marbury still lost, but he lost because he misread the statute as conferring jurisdiction that in fact it did not. But such a reading would not have allowed Marshall to reach the constitutional question. Today it is a standard principle of statutory interpretation that a court should try to avoid interpretations that raise serious constitutional issues. By contrast, Marshall embraced such an interpretation, rejecting plausible interpretations that avoided the constitutional issue. To be sure, some of these principles may be of more recent vintage. Others, however, such as the recusal principle, were known in 1803.

2. Regardless of the merits of his analysis or his approach, Marshall's opinion in *Marbury* has achieved canonical status in American constitutional law. But how far does it really extend? Recall that Marshall argued that the power of judicial review naturally flows from a court's need to decide the case in front it. If two laws would lead to different results, then a court has to decide which law to apply; in turn, this requires a court to determine which law is superior to the other. Because the Constitution (Article III) was superior to Section 13 of the Judiciary Act, when a conflict appeared (at least to Marshall), the inherent judicial power to decide cases meant that it had the power to declare the subordinate law to be without effect.

Does this understanding of the power of judicial review support the analysis in *Cooper v. Aaron*? Recall that in that case the Court stated that "the interpretation of the Fourteenth Amendment enunciated by this Court in the *Brown* case is the supreme law of the land, and Art. VI of the Constitution makes it of binding effect on the States." Thus, non-parties to *Brown* (*e.g.*, the Little Rock School Board) were nevertheless bound by the holding in that case. Does that conclusion follow from the understanding of the power of judicial review sketched out in the previous paragraph?

But consider the counter-argument. When the Court decides a case like *Brown v. Board of Education*, everyone understands that it is deciding the larger legal issue (in *Brown*, the constitutionality of school segregation) for the entire nation, just as in *Roe v. Wade*, 410 U.S. 113 (1973), everyone understood that the Court was making a decision about abortion that applied to the entire nation. Of course, one might argue that cases like *Brown* and *Roe* theoretically only bind the parties, but that as precedent lower courts facing similar cases would be bound to apply those cases and rule in the same way. But consider the practicalities of that result. For example, in the 1950s many southern school districts made it clear they had no intention of voluntarily complying with *Brown*. If black plaintiffs had been forced to sue every school district that segregated, then resource constraints would have meant that school districts would have remained free of *Brown*'s mandate, and the right *Brown* recognized would have been left unvindicated, for years. (Class actions and similar vehicles might have mitigated this problem, but they would have been highly imperfect vehicles for achieving the complete, nationwide application of *Brown*.)

3. Ever since *Cooper*, resistance to the Supreme Court has been tainted with the scent of racism. But recall from the discussion of the *Dred Scott* case above that some-

times the shoe is on the other foot. Individual cases may have a political valence, but broader constitutional doctrines often cut in both political directions.

## B. Congressional Checks on the Judicial Power

In *Marbury v. Madison*, Chief Justice Marshall boldly characterized the judiciary's authority: "it is emphatically the province and duty of the judicial department to say what the law is." Despite Marshall's sweeping declaration, the judicial power has always been subject to limitations. Some of these limitations appear as a matter of constitutional text. Federal judges—including Supreme Court Justices—are nominated by the President and subject to confirmation by the Senate. They are also subject to impeachment; indeed at times there have been serious calls to impeach particular justices based on their rulings. Similarly, constitutional controversies have led Supreme Court appointment and confirmation processes to become highly contentious political events. Moreover, Congress has the power to commence the process of amending the Constitution to overrule unpopular Court decisions, a power it has exercised on many occasions. This section considers other congressional tools for controlling the courts: its power to limit their jurisdiction of the federal courts, and its ability to influence how they reach decisions.

As you will see after reading these materials, the Constitution gives Congress broad power over the federal courts. It has substantial control over the jurisdiction of the Supreme Court, although the outer limits of that control have not been fully tested. It also has the power to create the lower federal courts, which strongly suggests significant power over the jurisdiction of those courts as well. It also enjoys significant discretion to create non-Article III tribunals, so-called "agency courts" or "Article I courts." In the *Schor* case excerpted below, you will see that the Court usually uses a multi-factor balancing test to determine whether the delegation of judicial power to a particular Article I court has unconstitutionally intruded on the authority of Article III courts. Dissenting in *Schor*, Justice Brennan worried that this test is skewed toward allowing Congress a great deal of power to transfer jurisdiction over many cases to these non-Article III tribunals.

The picture is similar with regard to controls over the substantive law that courts must interpret. Congress has a great deal of control over the substantive law that courts must interpret; by manipulating that law Congress can, in a sense, exercise control over the core function of courts. While the Supreme Court recognizes congressional primacy over lawmaking (and thus setting the rules that courts must apply), it has imposed some outer limits. This large, but not limitless, congressional control is sketched out in the note on *United States v. Klein* and *Robertson v. Seattle Audubon Society*.

As you read this material, consider the picture of the federal courts that emerges. What do the results in these cases suggest about what the meaning of "the judicial power"?

# 1. Jurisdiction

## *Note: The Background to* Ex parte McCardle, Ex parte Yerger *and* United States v. Klein

*Ex parte McCardle*, *Ex parte Yerger*, and *United States v. Klein* all arose out of the turbulence of the Civil War and Reconstruction era. They deal with situations where Congress, dominated by Republicans anxious to reconstruct the South as a non-slaveholding society in which former confederates did not play a leading role, feared that the Court might frustrate their efforts. Congress was already warring with President Andrew Johnson due to his less ambitious reconstruction plans; indeed, that conflict led to his impeachment and near-conviction. Congress was similarly concerned that the Court might obstruct its plans; it had been only a decade since the Court had been seen as decisively favoring slaveholding interests in the 1857 *Dred Scott* case.

In this context, the challenge for the Court was to preserve both its own powers and what it viewed as the essential prerogatives of the President, while not provoking a constitutional showdown with Congress. In the cases that follow below, the Court both retreated and advanced on these issues. In so doing it established fundamental principles of congressional control over the judiciary.

## Ex parte McCardle

### 74 U.S. (7 Wall.) 506 (1868)

[McCardle was charged with libel and various other offenses for publishing newspaper articles critical of Reconstruction and the post-Civil War military government in Mississippi. McCardle unsuccessfully sought a writ of habeas corpus from a lower federal court, pursuant to an 1867 statute that permitted federal courts to grant writs of habeas to persons held by states or the federal government. (An older statute, enacted in 1789, provided habeas jurisdiction for persons held by federal officials.) Mc-Cardle then appealed to the U.S. Supreme Court, arguing that the military occupation of the South was unconstitutional. In 1868, while the case was pending, Congress passed an act repealing the 1867 law.]

THE CHIEF JUSTICE delivered the opinion of the court.

The first question necessarily is that of jurisdiction; for, if the act of March, 1868, takes away the jurisdiction defined by the act of February, 1867, it is useless, if not improper, to enter into any discussion of other questions.

It is quite true, as was argued by the counsel for the petitioner, that the appellate jurisdiction of this court is not derived from acts of Congress. It is, strictly speaking, conferred by the Constitution. But it is conferred "with such exceptions and under such regulations as Congress shall make."

It is unnecessary to consider whether, if Congress had made no exceptions and no regulations, this court might not have exercised general appellate jurisdiction under rules prescribed by itself. For among the earliest acts of the first Congress, at its first session, was the [Judiciary] act of September 24th, 1789, to establish the judicial courts of the United States. That act provided for the organization of this court, and prescribed regulations for the exercise of its jurisdiction.

The source of that jurisdiction, and the limitations of it by the Constitution and by statute, have been on several occasions subjects of consideration here. In the case of *Durousseau v. The United States,* 10 U.S. (6 Cranch.) 307, 312 (1810); *Wiscart v. Dauchy*, 3 U.S. (3 Dall.) 321 (1796), particularly, the whole matter was carefully examined, and the court held, that while "the appellate powers of this court are not given by the [Judiciary] act, but are given by the Constitution," they are, nevertheless, "limited and regulated by that act, and by such other acts as have been passed on the subject." The court said, further, that the judicial act was an exercise of the power given by the Constitution to Congress "of making exceptions to the appellate jurisdiction of the Supreme Court." "They have described affirmatively," said the court, "its jurisdiction, and this affirmative description has been understood to imply a negation of the exercise of such appellate power as is not comprehended within it."

The principle that the affirmation of appellate jurisdiction implies the negation of all such jurisdiction not affirmed having been thus established, it was an almost necessary consequence that acts of Congress, providing for the exercise of jurisdiction, should come to be spoken of as acts granting jurisdiction, and not as acts making exceptions to the constitutional grant of it.

The exception to appellate jurisdiction in the case before us, however, is not an inference from the affirmation of other appellate jurisdiction. It is made in terms. The provision of the act of 1867, affirming the appellate jurisdiction of this court in cases of *habeas corpus* is expressly repealed. It is hardly possible to imagine a plainer instance of positive exception.

We are not at liberty to inquire into the motives of the legislature. We can only examine into its power under the Constitution; and the power to make exceptions to the appellate jurisdiction of this court is given by express words.

What, then, is the effect of the repealing act upon the case before us? We cannot doubt as to this. Without jurisdiction the court cannot proceed at all in any cause. Jurisdiction is power to declare the law, and when it ceases to exist, the only function remaining to the court is that of announcing the fact and dismissing the cause. And this is not less clear upon authority than upon principle....

It is quite clear, therefore, that this court cannot proceed to pronounce judgment in this case, for it has no longer jurisdiction of the appeal; and judicial duty is not less fitly performed by declining ungranted jurisdiction than in exercising firmly that which the Constitution and the laws confer.

Counsel seem to have supposed, if effect be given to the repealing act in question, that the whole appellate power of the court, in cases of *habeas corpus*, is denied. But this is an error. The act of 1868 does not except from that jurisdiction any cases but appeals from Circuit Courts under the act of 1867. It does not affect the jurisdiction which was previously exercised.

The appeal of the Petitioner in this case must be dismissed for want of jurisdiction.

## *Note:* Ex parte Yerger *and* United States v. Klein

1. *McCardle*'s willingness to allow Congress to limit its habeas jurisdiction carried with it the potential for a serious reduction in the Court's authority. In two cases decided shortly after *McCardle*, the Court staked out limits on Congress's control over the Court.

2. In *Ex parte Yerger*, 75 U.S. 85 (1868), the Court considered the implications of *McCardle*'s decision that Congress had validly withdrawn from the Court some part of its previously-granted habeas corpus jurisdiction. *Yerger*, like *McCardle*, considered a habeas petition brought by a southerner held in custody by the military government—in this case, for murder. At the Supreme Court, the government contended that the 1868 habeas repealer act applied in *McCardle* effectively left the Court with no habeas jurisdiction. The theory was that the 1867 statute effectively repealed the original 1789 jurisdiction grant, replacing it with a new, broader, habeas jurisdiction. Thus, the argument went, when the 1867 act was itself repealed, nothing was left of the Court's habeas jurisdiction.

The Court, noting that it had already rejected this argument in *McCardle* (see the penultimate paragraph of *McCardle*, above), rejected it again. It praised the writ of habeas corpus as a crucial part of Americans' liberty. It noted that the history of habeas jurisdiction in the United States was one of gradual but steady enlargement, except for the 1868 statute at issue in *McCardle*, which it described as being passed under "peculiar" circumstances. It observed that legislation such as the 1868 statute "is unusual and hardly to be justified except upon some imperious public exigency." Based on that description, the Court then stated that "it is not to be presumed that an act, passed under such circumstances, was intended to have any further effect than that plainly apparent from its terms." Given this principle that such jurisdictional limitations are to be construed narrowly, the Court gave the 1868 statute just such a narrow reading:

> The words [of the 1868 repealer statute] are not of doubtful interpretation. They repeal only so much of the act of 1867 as authorized ... the exercise of appellate jurisdiction by this court.... They do not purport to touch the appellate jurisdiction conferred by the Constitution, or to except from it any cases not excepted by the act of 1789. They reach no act except the act of 1867.

Thus, the Court concluded that it had jurisdiction under the 1789 act to hear Yerger's appeal.

3. Three years after the Court decided *McCardle* and *Yerger*, the Court decided *United States v. Klein*, 80 U.S. 128 (1871). That case involved a law authorizing the government to seize abandoned or captured property from those who had aided, countenanced and abetted the Confederacy during the war. Pursuant to this law, the U.S. Treasury Department took possession of the late V.F. Wilson's cotton, sold it, and placed the proceeds in the U.S. Treasury.

Prior to his death, Wilson had taken advantage of a presidential proclamation offering a "full pardon," with restoration of all rights, to those who agreed to "take and keep inviolate a prescribed oath" to support the Union. After Wilson's death, Klein, the administrator of Wilson's estate, sued to recover proceeds from the sale of the cotton, claiming that the pardon had restored Wilson's rights and property. Klein won in the Court of Claims, and the government appealed to the U.S. Supreme Court. While the appeal was pending, Congress passed a statute altering the effect of a pardon. The statute declared a presidential pardon shall not be admissible in the Court of Claims to support a claim for recovery. The statute also provided that, to the extent that the Court of Claims had ruled in favor of a claimant based on a presidential pardon:

> The Supreme Court, on appeal, shall have no further jurisdiction of the cause, and shall dismiss the same for want of jurisdiction. It is further provided that whenever any pardon, granted to any suitor in the Court of Claims, for the proceeds of captured and abandoned property, shall recite in substance that the person pardoned took part in the late rebellion, or was guilty of any act of rebellion or disloyalty, and shall have been accepted in writing without express disclaimer and protestation against the fact so recited, such pardon or acceptance shall be taken as conclusive evidence in the Court of Claims, and on appeal, that the claimant did give aid to the rebellion; and on proof of such pardon, or acceptance, which proof may be made summarily on motion or otherwise, the jurisdiction of the court shall cease, and the suit shall be forthwith dismissed.

Based on this statute, the government moved to dismiss the appeal. The Supreme Court ruled the act unconstitutional:

> [The] language of the proviso shows plainly that it does not intend to withhold appellate jurisdiction except as a means to an end. Its great and controlling purpose is to deny to pardons granted by the President the effect which this court had adjudged them to have. The proviso declares that pardons shall not be considered by this court on appeal. We had already decided that it was our duty to consider them and give them effect, in cases like the present, as equivalent to proof of loyalty....

> It seems to us that this is not an exercise of the acknowledged power of Congress to make exceptions and prescribe regulations to the appellate power.

> The court is required to ascertain the existence of certain facts and thereupon to declare that its jurisdiction on appeal has ceased, by dismissing the bill. What is this but to prescribe a rule for the decision of a cause in a particular way? In the case before us, the Court of Claims has rendered judgment for the claimant and an appeal has been taken to this court. We are directed to dismiss the appeal, if we find that the judgment must be affirmed, because of a pardon granted to the intestate of the claimants. Can we do so without allowing one party to the controversy to decide it in its own favor? Can we do so without allowing that the legislature may prescribe rules of decision to the Judicial Department of the government in cases pending before it?

> We think not....

We must think that Congress has inadvertently passed the limit which separates the legislative from the judicial power.

It is of vital importance that these powers be kept distinct. The Constitution provides that the judicial power of the United States shall be vested in one Supreme Court and such inferior courts as the Congress shall from time to time ordain and establish. The same instrument, in the last clause of the same article, provides that in all cases other than those of original jurisdiction, "the Supreme Court shall have appellate jurisdiction both as to law and fact, with such exceptions and under such regulations as the Congress shall make."

Congress has already provided that the Supreme Court shall have jurisdiction of the judgments of the Court of Claims on appeal. Can it prescribe a rule in conformity with which the court must deny to itself the jurisdiction thus conferred, because and only because its decision, in accordance with settled law, must be adverse to the government and favorable to the suitor? This question seems to us to answer itself.

## Note: Jurisdiction-Stripping Statutes in the Modern Era and "Article I Courts"

1. In addition to giving Congress control over the appellate jurisdiction of the Supreme Court, Article III also strongly implies congressional power over the jurisdiction of the lower federal courts. Article III, § 1, which authorizes creation of the lower federal courts, states that "The Judicial Power of the United States, shall be vested in one supreme Court, and in such inferior Courts as the Congress may from time to time ordain and establish." Since Congress has the power to "ordain and establish" inferior federal courts, it also presumably has the power to abolish them as well as to limit their jurisdiction. However, may Congress strip the lower federal courts of their jurisdiction over an issue (*e.g.*, constitutional challenges to school prayer) and simultaneously strip the Supreme Court of its appellate jurisdiction over that issue? Over the last half-century, bills have been introduced in Congress to strip or limit federal court jurisdiction to hear constitutional claims on a number of controversial issues, including school prayer, school bussing to integrate schools and abortion. An example is a bill introduced in 1985:

> The Supreme Court shall not have jurisdiction to review, by appeal, writ of certiorari, or otherwise, any case arising out of any State statute, ordinance, rule, regulation, practice, or any part thereof, which relates to voluntary prayer, Bible reading, or religious meetings in public schools or public buildings.

> Notwithstanding any other provision of law, the district courts shall not have jurisdiction of any case or question which the Supreme Court does not have jurisdiction to review [under this law].

If this bill had passed, would it have been constitutional? Would it violate the separation of powers by unconstitutionally altering the balance of power between the branches? Would it constitute a violation of the underlying right (here, the First

Amendment right against government establishment of a religion) if the right could not be vindicated in any federal court? These are difficult questions which the Court has not conclusively answered.

In recent years, much of the controversy around jurisdiction-stripping has focused on attempts by Congress to limit the role of the federal courts in hearing habeas corpus petitions challenging the legality of the confinement of suspected unlawful combatants, most notably at Guantanamo Bay, Cuba. For the Court's most recent statement on the constitutionality of such statutes, see *Boumediene v. Bush*, 553 U.S. 723 (2008), excerpted in Chapter 2.

2. Stripping federal courts of jurisdiction over particular claims is an extreme step, as it would require that federal rights be vindicated in courts of a different sovereign, *i.e.*, state courts. But Congress need not take that extreme step in order to limit the power of federal courts. Instead, Congress may require that certain claims be adjudicated, at least initially, by adjudicators employed by an administrative agency, who do not enjoy the institutional independence or life tenure of Article III judges. The following case considers a claim that creation of such "agency courts" (also known as "Article I courts") violates the Constitution's vesting of "the judicial Power of the United States" in Article III courts.

## Commodity Futures Trading Commission v. Schor
### 478 U.S. 833 (1986)

Justice O'Connor delivered the opinion of the Court.

The question presented is whether the Commodity Exchange Act (CEA or Act), empowers the Commodity Futures Trading Commission (CFTC or Commission) to entertain state law counterclaims in reparation proceedings and, if so, whether that grant of authority violates Article III of the Constitution.

I

The CEA broadly prohibits fraudulent and manipulative conduct in connection with commodity futures transactions. In 1974, Congress ... created an independent agency, the CFTC, and entrusted to it sweeping authority to implement the CEA.

Among the duties assigned to the CFTC was the administration of a reparations procedure through which disgruntled customers of professional commodity brokers could seek redress for the brokers' violations of the Act or CFTC regulations. Thus, § 14 of the CEA provides that any person injured by such violations may apply to the Commission for an order directing the offender to pay reparations to the complainant and may enforce that order in federal district court. Congress intended this administrative procedure to be an "inexpensive and expeditious" alternative to existing fora available to aggrieved customers, namely, the courts and arbitration.

In conformance with the congressional goal of promoting efficient dispute resolution, the CFTC promulgated a regulation in 1976 which allows it to adjudicate counterclaims "arising out of the transaction or occurrence or series of transactions or occurrences set forth in the complaint." This permissive counterclaim rule leaves the respondent in a reparations proceeding free to seek relief against the reparations complainant in other fora.

The instant dispute arose in February 1980, when respondents Schor and Mortgage Services of America, Inc., invoked the CFTC's reparations jurisdiction by filing complaints against petitioner ContiCommodity Services, Inc. (Conti), a commodity futures broker.... Schor had an account with Conti which contained a debit balance because Schor's net futures trading losses and expenses, such as commissions, exceeded the funds deposited in the account. Schor alleged that this debit balance was the result of Conti's numerous violations of the CEA.

Before receiving notice that Schor had commenced the reparations proceeding, Conti had filed a diversity action in Federal District Court to recover the debit balance....

... Conti voluntarily dismissed the federal court action and presented its debit balance claim by way of a counterclaim in the CFTC reparations proceeding. Conti denied violating the CEA and instead insisted that the debit balance resulted from Schor's trading, and was therefore a simple debt owed by Schor.

After discovery, briefing, and a hearing, the Administrative Law Judge (ALJ) in Schor's reparations proceeding ruled in Conti's favor on both Schor's claims and Conti's counterclaims. After this ruling, Schor for the first time challenged the CFTC's statutory authority to adjudicate Conti's counterclaim....

[The Court of Appeals read the statute as not authorizing the CFTC to take jurisdiction over Conti's counterclaims.] We granted certiorari and now reverse.

II

... In view of the abundant evidence that Congress both contemplated and authorized the CFTC's assertion of jurisdiction over Conti's common law counterclaim, we conclude that the Court of Appeals' analysis is untenable.... We therefore are squarely faced with the question whether the CFTC's assumption of jurisdiction over common law counterclaims violates Article III of the Constitution.

III

Article III, § 1, directs that the "judicial Power of the United States shall be vested in one supreme Court and in such inferior Courts as the Congress may from time to time ordain and establish," and provides that these federal courts shall be staffed by judges who hold office during good behavior, and whose compensation shall not be diminished during tenure in office. Schor claims that these provisions prohibit Congress from authorizing the initial adjudication of common law counterclaims by the CFTC, an administrative agency whose adjudicatory officers do not enjoy the tenure and salary protections embodied in Article III.

Although our precedents in this area do not admit of easy synthesis, they do establish that the resolution of claims such as Schor's cannot turn on conclusory reference to the language of Article III. Rather, the constitutionality of a given congressional delegation of adjudicative functions to a non-Article III body must be assessed by reference to the purposes underlying the requirements of Article III. This inquiry, in turn, is guided by the principle that "practical attention to substance rather than doctrinaire reliance on formal categories should inform application of Article III." ...

## B

As noted above, our precedents establish that Article III, § 1, not only preserves to litigants their interest in an impartial and independent federal adjudication of claims within the judicial power of the United States, but also serves as "an inseparable element of the constitutional system of checks and balances." Article III, § 1 safeguards the role of the Judicial Branch in our tripartite system by barring congressional attempts "to transfer jurisdiction [to non-Article III tribunals] for the purpose of emasculating" constitutional courts and thereby preventing "the encroachment or aggrandizement of one branch at the expense of the other." To the extent that this structural principle is implicated in a given case, the parties cannot by consent cure the constitutional difficulty for the same reason that the parties by consent cannot confer on federal courts subject-matter jurisdiction beyond the limitations imposed by Article III, § 2....

In determining the extent to which a given congressional decision to authorize the adjudication of Article III business in a non-Article III tribunal impermissibly threatens the institutional integrity of the Judicial Branch, the Court has declined to adopt formalistic and unbending rules. Although such rules might lend a greater degree of coherence to this area of the law, they might also unduly constrict Congress' ability to take needed and innovative action pursuant to its Article I powers. Thus, in reviewing Article III challenges, we have weighed a number of factors, none of which has been deemed determinative, with an eye to the practical effect that the congressional action will have on the constitutionally assigned role of the federal judiciary. Among the factors upon which we have focused are the extent to which the "essential attributes of judicial power" are reserved to Article III courts, and, conversely, the extent to which the non-Article III forum exercises the range of jurisdiction and powers normally vested only in Article III courts, the origins and importance of the right to be adjudicated, and the concerns that drove Congress to depart from the requirements of Article III.

An examination of the relative allocation of powers between the CFTC and Article III courts in light of the considerations given prominence in our precedents demonstrates that the congressional scheme does not impermissibly intrude on the province of the judiciary. The CFTC's adjudicatory powers depart from the traditional agency model in just one respect: the CFTC's jurisdiction over common law counterclaims. While wholesale importation of concepts of pendent or ancillary jurisdiction into the agency context may create greater constitutional difficulties, we decline to endorse an absolute prohibition on such jurisdiction out of fear of where some hypothetical "slippery slope" may deposit us....

In the instant cases, we are ... persuaded that there is little practical reason to find that this single deviation from the agency model is fatal to the congressional scheme. Aside from its authorization of counterclaim jurisdiction, the CEA leaves far more of the "essential attributes of judicial power" to Article III courts than did that portion of the Bankruptcy Act found unconstitutional in *Northern Pipeline Constr. Co. v. Marathon Pipe Line Co.*, 458 U.S. 50 (1982). The CEA scheme in fact hews closely to the agency model approved by the Court in *Crowell v. Benson*, 285 U.S. 22 (1932).

The CFTC, like the agency in *Crowell*, deals only with a "particularized area of law," whereas the jurisdiction of the bankruptcy courts found unconstitutional in *Northern Pipeline* extended to broadly "all civil proceedings arising under title 11 or arising in or *related to* cases under title 11." CFTC orders, like those of the agency in *Crowell*, but unlike those of the bankruptcy courts under the 1978 Act, are enforceable only by order of the district court. CFTC orders are also reviewed under the same "weight of the evidence" standard sustained in *Crowell*, rather than the more deferential standard found lacking in *Northern Pipeline*.[*] The legal rulings of the CFTC, like the legal determinations of the agency in *Crowell*, are subject to *de novo* review. Finally, the CFTC, unlike the bankruptcy courts under the 1978 Act, does not exercise "all ordinary powers of district courts," and thus may not, for instance, preside over jury trials or issue writs of habeas corpus.

Of course, the nature of the claim has significance in our Article III analysis quite apart from the method prescribed for its adjudication. The counterclaim asserted in this litigation is a "private" right for which state law provides the rule of decision. It is therefore a claim of the kind assumed to be at the "core" of matters normally reserved to Article III courts. Yet this conclusion does not end our inquiry; just as this Court has rejected any attempt to make determinative for Article III purposes the distinction between public rights and private rights, there is no reason inherent in separation of powers principles to accord the state law character of a claim talismanic power in Article III inquiries.

We have explained that "the public rights doctrine reflects simply a pragmatic understanding that when Congress selects a quasi-judicial method of resolving matters that 'could be conclusively determined by the Executive and Legislative Branches,' the danger of encroaching on the judicial powers" is less than when private rights, which are normally within the purview of the judiciary, are relegated as an initial matter to administrative adjudication. Similarly, the state law character of a claim is significant for purposes of determining the effect that an initial adjudication of those claims by a non-Article III tribunal will have on the separation of powers for the simple reason that private, common law rights were historically the types of matters subject to resolution by Article III courts. The risk that Congress may improperly have encroached on the federal judiciary is obviously magnified when Congress "withdraws from judicial cognizance any matter which, from its nature, is the subject of a suit at the common law, or in equity, or admiralty" and which therefore has traditionally been tried in Article III courts, and allocates the decision of those matters to a non-Article III forum of its own creation. Accordingly, where private, common law rights are at

---

* [Ed. Note: The "weight of the evidence" standard of review has been interpreted to mean that the reviewing court must determine if the lower court acted reasonably in deciding that the evidence supported the lower court's findings. It does not authorize *de novo* review of those factfindings.]

stake, our examination of the congressional attempt to control the manner in which those rights are adjudicated has been searching. In this litigation, however, "[looking] beyond form to the substance of what" Congress has done, we are persuaded that the congressional authorization of limited CFTC jurisdiction over a narrow class of common law claims as an incident to the CFTC's primary, and unchallenged, adjudicative function does not create a substantial threat to the separation of powers.

It is clear that Congress has not attempted to "withdraw from judicial cognizance" the determination of Conti's right to the sum represented by the debit balance in Schor's account. Congress gave the CFTC the authority to adjudicate such matters, but the decision to invoke this forum is left entirely to the parties and the power of the federal judiciary to take jurisdiction of these matters is unaffected.... This is not to say, of course, that if Congress created a phalanx of non-Article III tribunals equipped to handle the entire business of the Article III courts without any Article III supervision or control and without evidence of valid and specific legislative necessities, the fact that the parties had the election to proceed in their forum of choice would necessarily save the scheme from constitutional attack. But this case obviously bears no resemblance to such a scenario, given the degree of judicial control saved to the federal courts, as well as the congressional purpose behind the jurisdictional delegation, the demonstrated need for the delegation, and the limited nature of the delegation.

When Congress authorized the CFTC to adjudicate counterclaims, its primary focus was on making effective a specific and limited federal regulatory scheme, not on allocating jurisdiction among federal tribunals. Congress intended to create an inexpensive and expeditious alternative forum through which customers could enforce the provisions of the CEA against professional brokers.... It was only to ensure the effectiveness of this scheme that Congress authorized the CFTC to assert jurisdiction over common law counterclaims. Indeed, as was explained above, absent the CFTC's exercise of that authority, the purposes of the reparations procedure would have been confounded.

It also bears emphasis that the CFTC's assertion of counterclaim jurisdiction is limited to that which is necessary to make the reparations procedure workable. The CFTC adjudication of common law counterclaims is incidental to, and completely dependent upon, adjudication of reparations claims created by federal law, and in actual fact is limited to claims arising out of the same transaction or occurrence as the reparations claim.

In such circumstances, the magnitude of any intrusion on the Judicial Branch can only be termed *de minimis*....

Nor does our decision in *Bowsher v. Synar*, 478 U.S. 714 (1986), require a contrary result. Unlike *Bowsher*, this case raises no question of the aggrandizement of congressional power at the expense of a coordinate branch....

[Our] Article III precedents ... counsel that bright-line rules cannot effectively be employed to yield broad principles applicable in all Article III inquiries. Rather, due regard must be given in each case to the unique aspects of the congressional plan at issue and its practical consequences in light of the larger concerns that underlie Article

III. We conclude that the limited jurisdiction that the CFTC asserts over state law claims as a necessary incident to the adjudication of federal claims willingly submitted by the parties for initial agency adjudication does not contravene separation of powers principles or Article III....

JUSTICE BRENNAN, with whom JUSTICE MARSHALL joins, dissenting.

Article III, § 1, of the Constitution provides that "the judicial Power of the United States, shall be vested in one supreme Court, and in such inferior Courts as the Congress may from time to time ordain and establish." It further specifies that the federal judicial power must be exercised by judges who "shall hold their Offices during good Behaviour, and [who] shall, at stated Times, receive for their Services a Compensation, which shall not be diminished during their Continuance in Office."

On its face, Article III, § 1, seems to prohibit the vesting of *any* judicial functions in either the Legislative or the Executive Branch. The Court has, however, recognized three narrow exceptions to the otherwise absolute mandate of Article III: territorial courts, courts-martial, and courts that adjudicate certain disputes concerning public rights. Unlike the Court, I would limit the judicial authority of non-Article III federal tribunals to these few, long-established exceptions and would countenance no further erosion of Article III's mandate.

### I

The Framers knew that "the accumulation of all powers, Legislative, Executive, and Judiciary, in the same hands, whether of one, a few, or many, and whether hereditary, self-appointed, or elective, may justly be pronounced the very definition of tyranny." *The Federalist* No. 46 (J. Madison). In order to prevent such tyranny, the Framers devised a governmental structure composed of three distinct branches — "a vigorous Legislative Branch," "a separate and wholly independent Executive Branch," and "a Judicial Branch equally independent." The separation of powers and the checks and balances that the Framers built into our tripartite form of government were intended to operate as a "self-executing safeguard against the encroachment or aggrandizement of one branch at the expense of the other." "The fundamental necessity of maintaining each of the three general departments of government entirely free from the control or coercive influence, direct or indirect, of either of the others, has often been stressed and is hardly open to serious question." *Bowsher*. The federal judicial power, then, must be exercised by judges who are independent of the Executive and the Legislature in order to maintain the checks and balances that are crucial to our constitutional structure.

The Framers also understood that a principal benefit of the separation of the judicial power from the legislative and executive powers would be the protection of individual litigants from decisionmakers susceptible to majoritarian pressures....

These important functions of Article III are too central to our constitutional scheme to risk their incremental erosion. The exceptions we have recognized for territorial courts, courts-martial, and administrative courts were each based on "certain exceptional powers bestowed upon Congress by the Constitution or by historical consensus." ... By sanctioning the adjudication of state-law counterclaims by a federal administrative agency, the Court far exceeds the analytic framework of our precedents....

## II

The Court states that in reviewing Article III challenges, one of several factors we have taken into account is "the concerns that drove Congress to depart from the requirements of Article III." The Court identifies the desire of Congress "to create an inexpensive and expeditious alternative forum through which customers could enforce the provisions of the CEA against professional brokers" as the motivating congressional concern here. The Court further states that "it was only to ensure the effectiveness of this scheme that Congress authorized the CFTC to assert jurisdiction over common-law counterclaims[;] ... absent the CFTC's exercise of that authority, the purposes of the reparations procedure would have been confounded." Were we to hold that the CFTC's authority to decide common-law counterclaims offends Article III, the Court declares, "it is clear that we would defeat the obvious purpose of the legislation." Article III, the Court concludes, does not "compel this degree of prophylaxis."

I disagree—Article III's prophylactic protections were intended to prevent just this sort of abdication to claims of legislative convenience. The Court requires that the legislative interest in convenience and efficiency be weighed against the competing interest in judicial independence. In doing so, the Court pits an interest the benefits of which are immediate, concrete, and easily understood against one, the benefits of which are almost entirely prophylactic, and thus often seem remote and not worth the cost in any single case. Thus, while this balancing creates the illusion of objectivity and ineluctability, in fact the result was foreordained, because the balance is weighted against judicial independence. The danger of the Court's balancing approach is, of course, that as individual cases accumulate in which the Court finds that the short-term benefits of efficiency outweigh the long-term benefits of judicial independence, the protections of Article III will be eviscerated.

Perhaps the resolution of reparations claims such as respondents' may be accomplished more conveniently under the Court's decision than under my approach, but the Framers foreswore this sort of convenience in order to preserve freedom. As we explained in *INS v. Chadha*, 462 U.S. 919 (1983):

> The choices we discern as having been made in the Constitutional Convention impose burdens on governmental processes that often seem clumsy, inefficient, even unworkable, but those hard choices were consciously made by men who had lived under a form of government that permitted arbitrary governmental acts to go unchecked.... With all the obvious flaws of delay [and] untidiness..., we have not yet found a better way to preserve freedom than by making the exercise of power subject to the carefully crafted restraints spelled out in the Constitution....

... The Framers established *three* coequal branches of government and intended to preserve *each* from encroachment by either of the others. The Constitution did not grant Congress the general authority to bypass the Judiciary whenever Congress deems it advisable, any more than it granted Congress the authority to arrogate to itself executive functions.

### III

... [The] decision today may authorize the administrative adjudication only of state-law claims that stem from the same transaction or set of facts that allow the customer of a professional commodity broker to initiate reparations proceedings before the CFTC, but the *reasoning* of this decision strongly suggests that, given "legislative necessity" and party consent, any federal agency may decide state-law issues that are ancillary to federal issues within the agency's jurisdiction. Thus, while in this litigation "the magnitude of any intrusion on the Judicial Branch" may conceivably be characterized as "*de minimis*," the potential impact of the Court's decision on federal-court jurisdiction is substantial. The Court dismisses warnings about the dangers of its approach, asserting simply that it does not fear the slippery slope, and that this litigation does not involve the creation by Congress of a "phalanx of non-Article III tribunals equipped to handle the entire business of the Article III courts." A healthy respect for the precipice on which we stand is warranted, however, for this reason: Congress can seriously impair Article III's structural and individual protections without assigning away "the *entire* business of the Article III courts." It can do so by *diluting* the judicial power of the federal courts. And, contrary to the Court's intimations, dilution of judicial power operates to impair the protections of Article III regardless of whether Congress acted with the "good intention" of providing a more efficient dispute resolution system or with the "bad intention" of strengthening the Legislative Branch at the expense of the Judiciary....

### V

Our Constitution unambiguously enunciates a fundamental principle—that the "judicial Power of the United States" be reposed in an independent Judiciary. It is our obligation zealously to guard that independence so that our tripartite system of government remains strong and that individuals continue to be protected against decisionmakers subject to majoritarian pressures. Unfortunately, today the Court forsakes that obligation for expediency. I dissent.

## *Note:* Stern v. Marshall *and the Return of Bright-Line Article III Analysis*

1. *Schor* is a notable example of one prominent methodology for analyzing separation of powers cases. That methodology relies not on bright-line rules that clearly demarcate the power of the three branches, but instead on multi-factor balancing tests that seek to ensure that no one branch intrudes excessively on the prerogatives of another. Implicit in such tests is the idea that some combination, or sharing, of powers is inherent in our constitutional system. Justice Brennan's dissent—which insisted that, aside from carefully demarcated exceptions, "private rights" could not be adjudicated by non-Article III federal tribunals—reflects the bright line approach. Later in this Part of the book you'll encounter other examples of both approaches.

2. In 2011, the Court turned away from the multi-factor approach, and toward the more bright-line methodology. *Stern v. Marshall*, 131 S.Ct. 2594 (2011), again considered the question of Article III-based limits on the jurisdiction of Article I courts, this time in the context of bankruptcy courts. Federal bankruptcy courts, which are not Article III courts, have often been the subject of cases raising this question: by their very nature, as tribunals intended to allow a consolidated resolution of all of the bankrupt party's affairs, they adjudicate a wide variety of claims. This practice leads to arguments that those courts are unconstitutionally playing the role Article III reserved for the federal courts. Indeed, one prominent bankruptcy court case, *Northern Pipeline Constr. Co. v. Marathon Pipe Line Co.*, 458 U.S. 50 (1982), was discussed in *Schor*.

*Stern* grew out of a bitter family dispute between the bankrupt party, Vickie Marshall (a celebrity better known as Anna Nicole Smith), and Pierce Marshall. Vickie married Pierce's father and eventually sued Pierce, alleging that Pierce had interfered in his father's plans to provide for Vickie in his will. After the father died, Vickie filed for bankruptcy. Pierce made a claim against her estate in the bankruptcy court, alleging that Vickie had defamed him in the press. Vickie counterclaimed, again in the bankruptcy court, alleging tortious interference with the plans Pierce's father had to provide for Vickie. The bankruptcy court ruled in Vickie's favor on her counterclaim.

Pierce appealed to federal court, arguing that the bankruptcy court could not exercise jurisdiction over Vickie's counterclaim. The Supreme Court agreed. Writing for the five-Justice majority, Chief Justice Roberts first wrestled with whether Vickie's counterclaim constituted a "public right." After a long discussion of cases dating back to the Nineteenth Century and including *Northern Pipeline* and *Schor*, the Court concluded that her counterclaim "does not fall within any of the varied formulations of the public rights exception [to the prohibition on Article I courts] in this Court's cases." He wrote that her counterclaim "is not a matter that can be pursued only by the grace of the other branches ... or one that historically could have been determined exclusively by those branches ..."

Chief Justice Roberts continued:

> In addition, Vickie's claimed right ... does not flow from a federal statutory scheme.... [and] is not completely dependent upon adjudication of a claim created by federal law.... And in contrast to the objecting party in *Schor*, Pierce did not truly consent to resolution of Vickie's claim in the bankruptcy court proceedings. He had nowhere else to go if he wished to recover from Vickie's estate.

> Furthermore, the asserted authority to decide Vickie's claim is not limited to a particularized area of the law, as in ... *Schor*.... This is not a situation in which Congress devised an expert and inexpensive method for dealing with a class of questions of fact which are particularly suited to examination and determination by an administrative agency specially assigned to that task....

Chief Justice Roberts then cautioned that the unique context of bankruptcy courts distinguished this case from those cases (presumably including *Schor)* where the agency was given the power to adjudicate claims under a statute the agency was tasked with implementing:

> We recognize that there may be instances in which the distinction between public and private rights—at least as framed by some of our recent cases—fails to provide concrete guidance as to whether, for example, a particular agency can adjudicate legal issues under a substantive regulatory scheme. Given the extent to which this case is so markedly distinct from the agency cases discussing the public rights exception in the context of such a regime, however, we do not in this opinion express any view on how the doctrine might apply in that different context.

Justice Scalia concurred, but expressed concern with what he called "the sheer surfeit of factors that the Court was required to consider in this case." He wrote, echoing Justice Brennan's dissent in *Schor*:

> Leaving aside certain adjudications by federal administrative agencies ... in my view an Article III judge is required in *all* federal adjudications, unless there is a firmly established historical practice to the contrary. For that reason—and not because of some intuitive balancing of benefits and harms—I agree that Article III judges are not required in the context of territorial courts, courts-martial, or true "public rights" cases.

Justice Breyer, joined by Justices Ginsburg, Sotomayor and Kagan, dissented. He relied heavily on *Schor*, which he described as a case where the Court:

> took a more pragmatic approach to the constitutional question. It sought to determine whether, in the particular instance, the challenged delegation of adjudicatory authority posed a genuine and serious threat that one branch of Government sought to aggrandize its own constitutionally delegated authority by encroaching upon a field of authority that the Constitution assigns exclusively to another branch.

He noted that under *Schor* "the presence of 'private rights' does not automatically determine the outcome of the question but requires a more 'searching' examination of the relevant factors" from that case. Applying those factors, he concluded that bankruptcy court adjudication of the claim at issue was constitutional. He conceded that the right at issue was private. But he noted that bankruptcy court judges "enjoy considerable protection from improper political influence." He noted the control Article III courts had over bankruptcy proceedings, in particular, the power of an Article III district court to withdraw any case from a bankruptcy court. He also concluded that the parties consented to bankruptcy court jurisdiction, arguing that Pierce had litigation options other than filing in that court. Finally, he noted the importance of allowing bankruptcy courts to exert maximum control over the bankrupt estate's litigation, in order to ensure orderly disposition of the estate's assets.

## 2. Other Means of Congressional Control over the Courts

### *Note: Congressional Power to "Prescribe Rules of Decision"*

1. Recall that *United States v. Klein*, discussed above, considered both Congress's power to strip the Supreme Court of appellate jurisdiction as well as to "prescribe rules of decision." This latter restriction has proven difficult to apply, given its seeming conflict with Congress's well-acknowledged power to legislate—that is, to "prescribe" the "rules" governing conduct, by which courts "decide" cases. The slipperiness of *Klein*'s phrase became clear in the 1992 case of *Robertson v. Seattle Audubon Society*, 503 U.S. 429 (1992). *Seattle Audubon* arose when an environmental group sued the U.S. Forest Service, alleging that its management of old-growth forests in the Pacific Northwest violated provisions of five federal environmental laws, including the Migratory Bird Treaty Act (MBTA). While the lawsuit was pending, Congress enacted a law imposing on the Forest Service requirements more lenient than those imposed by the pre-existing statutes. Most importantly, the new statute "determined and directed" that compliance with those new requirements was "adequate consideration for the purpose of meeting the statutory requirements that are the basis of" the pending lawsuits (which the statute identified by name and docket number). The Court unanimously upheld the statute against a *Klein* challenge, finding it to be simply a run-of-the-mill statutory amendment of the MBTA and the other affected statutes. The Court reached this conclusion through the following reasoning:

> We conclude that subsection (b)(6)(A) [the "determines and directs" provision] compelled changes in law, not findings or results under old law. Before subsection (b)(6)(A) was enacted, the original claims would fail only if the challenged [timber] harvesting violated none of five old provisions. Under subsection (b)(6)(A), by contrast, those same claims would fail if the harvesting violated neither of two new provisions. Its operation, we think, modified the old provisions....

> Respondents cite three textual features of subsection (b)(6)(A) in support of their conclusion that the provision failed to supply new law, but directed results under old law. First, they emphasize the imperative tone of the provision, by which Congress "determined and directed" that compliance with two new provisions would constitute compliance with five old ones. Respondents argue that "Congress was directing the subsection [only] at the courts." Petitioners, for their part, construe the subsection as "a directive [only] to the Forest Service and BLM." We think that neither characterization is entirely correct. A statutory directive binds *both* the executive officials who administer the statute *and* the judges who apply it in particular cases—even if (as is usually the case) Congress fails to preface its directive with an empty phrase like "Congress ... directs that." Here, we fail to see how inclusion of the "Congress ... directs that" preface undermines our conclusion that what Congress directed—to agencies and courts alike—was a change in law, not specific results under old law.

Second, respondents argue that subsection (b)(6)(A) did not modify old requirements because it deemed compliance with new requirements to "meet" the old requirements. We fail to appreciate the significance of this observation. Congress might have modified MBTA directly, for example, in order to impose a new obligation of complying either with the current § 2 [of the MBTA] or with subsections (b)(3) and (b)(5) [of the challenged statute]. Instead, Congress enacted an entirely separate statute deeming compliance with subsections (b)(3) and (b)(5) to constitute compliance with § 2 — a "modification" of the MBTA, we conclude, through operation of the canon that specific provisions qualify general ones. As explained above, each formulation would have produced an identical task for a court adjudicating the MBTA claims — determining either that the challenged harvesting did not violate § 2 as currently written or that it did not violate subsections (b)(3) and (b)(5).

Finally, respondents emphasize that subsection (b)(6)(A) explicitly made reference to pending cases identified by name and caption number. The reference to [those cases], however, served only to identify the five "statutory requirements that are the basis for" those cases — namely, pertinent provisions of MBTA [and the other four statutes the plaintiffs alleged were violated]. Subsection (b)(6)(A) named two pending cases in order to identify five statutory provisions. To the extent that subsection (b)(6)(A) affected the adjudication of the cases, it did so by effectively modifying the provisions at issue in those cases.

2. Thus, *Seattle Audubon* makes it clear that, at least for statutory claims (where Congress can rewrite the substantive law), Congress can in fact micromanage courts' application of law. The next case considers whether Congress can influence the workings of the judicial branch not just by changing laws, but by making the new law applicable even to cases that have reached a final judgment in the federal courts.

## Plaut v. Spendthrift Farm

### 514 U.S. 211 (1995)

Justice SCALIA delivered the opinion of the Court.

The question presented in this case is whether § 27A(b) of the Securities Exchange Act of 1934, to the extent that it requires federal courts to reopen final judgments in private civil actions under § 10(b) of the Act, contravenes the Constitution's separation of powers or the Due Process Clause of the Fifth Amendment.

### I

In 1987, petitioners brought a civil action against respondents in the United States District Court for the Eastern District of Kentucky. The complaint alleged that in 1983 and 1984 respondents had committed fraud and deceit in the sale of stock in violation of § 10(b) of the Securities Exchange Act of 1934 and Rule 10b-5 of the Securities and Exchange Commission. The case was mired in pretrial proceedings in the District Court until June 20, 1991, when we decided *Lampf, Pleva,*

*Lipkind, Prupis & Petigrow v. Gilbertson*, 501 U.S. 350 (1991). *Lampf* held that "litigation instituted pursuant to § 10(b) and Rule 10b-5 ... must be commenced within one year after the discovery of the facts constituting the violation and within three years after such violation." We applied that holding to the plaintiff-respondents in *Lampf* itself, found their suit untimely, and reinstated a summary judgment previously entered in favor of the defendant-petitioners. On the same day we decided *James B. Beam Distilling Co. v. Georgia*, 501 U.S. 529 (1991), in which a majority of the Court held ... that a new rule of federal law that is applied to the parties in the case announcing the rule must be applied as well to all cases pending on direct review. The joint effect of *Lampf* and *Beam* was to mandate application of the 1-year/3-year limitations period to petitioners' suit. The District Court, finding that petitioners' claims were untimely under the *Lampf* rule, dismissed their action with prejudice on August 13, 1991. Petitioners filed no appeal; the judgment accordingly became final 30 days later.

On December 19, 1991, the President signed the Federal Deposit Insurance Corporation Improvement Act of 1991. Section 476 of the Act ... became § 27A of the Securities Exchange Act of 1934.... It provides:

(a) Effect on pending causes of action

The limitation period for any private civil action implied under section 78j(b) of this title [§ 10(b) of the Securities Exchange Act of 1934] that was commenced on or before June 19, 1991, shall be the limitation period provided by the laws applicable in the jurisdiction, including principles of retroactivity, as such laws existed on June 19, 1991.

(b) Effect on dismissed causes of action

"Any private civil action implied under section 78j(b) of this title that was commenced on or before June 19, 1991 —

(1) which was dismissed as time barred subsequent to June 19, 1991, and

(2) which would have been timely filed under the limitation period provided by the laws applicable in the jurisdiction, including principles of retroactivity, as such laws existed on June 19, 1991,

shall be reinstated on motion by the plaintiff not later than 60 days after December 19, 1991.

On February 11, 1992, petitioners returned to the District Court and filed a motion to reinstate the action previously dismissed with prejudice. The District Court found that the conditions set out in §§ 27A(b)(1) and (2) were met, so that petitioners' motion was required to be granted by the terms of the statute. It nonetheless denied the motion, agreeing with respondents that § 27A(b) is unconstitutional. The United States Court of Appeals for the Sixth Circuit affirmed. We granted certiorari....

### III

Respondents submit that § 27A(b) violates both the separation of powers and the Due Process Clause of the Fifth Amendment. Because the latter submission, if correct, might dictate a similar result in a challenge to state legislation under the Fourteenth Amendment, the former is the narrower ground for adjudication of the constitutional questions in the case, and we therefore consider it first. We conclude that in §27A(b) Congress has exceeded its authority by requiring the federal courts to exercise "the judicial Power of the United States," U.S. Const., Art. III, §1, in a manner repugnant to the text, structure, and traditions of Article III.

Our decisions to date have identified two types of legislation that require federal courts to exercise the judicial power in a manner that Article III forbids. The first appears in *United States v. Klein* [Note *supra.* this chapter], where we refused to give effect to a statute that was said "to prescribe rules of decision to the Judicial Department of the government in cases pending before it." Whatever the precise scope of *Klein*, however, later decisions have made clear that its prohibition does not take hold when Congress "amends applicable law." *Robertson v. Seattle Audubon Soc.* [Note *supra* this chapter]. Section 27A(b) indisputably does set out substantive legal standards for the Judiciary to apply, and in that sense changes the law (even if solely retroactively). The second type of unconstitutional restriction upon the exercise of judicial power identified by past cases is exemplified by *Hayburn's Case*, 2 Dall. 409 (1792), which stands for the principle that Congress cannot vest review of the decisions of Article III courts in officials of the Executive Branch. Yet under any application of §27A(b) only courts are involved; no officials of other departments sit in direct review of their decisions. Section 27A(b) therefore offends neither of these previously established prohibitions.

We think, however, that §27A(b) offends a postulate of Article III just as deeply rooted in our law as those we have mentioned. Article III establishes a "judicial department" with the "province and duty ... to say what the law is" in particular cases and controversies. *Marbury v. Madison* [*supra.* this chapter]. The record of history shows that the Framers crafted this charter of the judicial department with an expressed understanding that it gives the Federal Judiciary the power, not merely to rule on cases, but to decide them, subject to review only by superior courts in the Article III hierarchy—with an understanding, in short, that "a judgment conclusively resolves the case" because "a 'judicial Power' is one to render dispositive judgments." By retroactively commanding the federal courts to reopen final judgments, Congress has violated this fundamental principle.

## A

The Framers of our Constitution lived among the ruins of a system of intermingled legislative and judicial powers, which had been prevalent in the colonies long before the Revolution, and which after the Revolution had produced factional strife and partisan oppression. In the 17th and 18th centuries colonial assemblies and legislatures functioned as courts of equity of last resort, hearing original actions or providing appellate review of judicial judgments. Often, however, they chose to correct the judicial process through special bills or other enacted legislation. It was common for such legislation not to prescribe a resolution of the dispute, but rather simply to set aside the judgment and order a new trial or appeal. Thus ... such legislation bears not on the problem of interbranch review but on the problem of finality of judicial judgments.

The vigorous, indeed often radical, populism of the revolutionary legislatures and assemblies increased the frequency of legislative correction of judgments....

This sense of a sharp necessity to separate the legislative from the judicial power, prompted by the crescendo of legislative interference with private judgments of the courts, triumphed among the Framers of the new Federal Constitution. The Convention made the critical decision to establish a judicial department independent of the Legislative Branch by providing that "the judicial Power of the United States shall be vested in one supreme Court, and in such inferior Courts as the Congress may from time to time ordain and establish." Before and during the debates on ratification, Madison, Jefferson, and Hamilton each wrote of the factional disorders and disarray that the system of legislative equity had produced in the years before the framing; and each thought that the separation of the legislative from the judicial power in the new Constitution would cure them....

... The essential balance created by this allocation of authority was a simple one. The Legislature would be possessed of power to "prescribe the rules by which the duties and rights of every citizen are to be regulated," but the power of "the interpretation of the laws" would be "the proper and peculiar province of the courts." *The Federalist* No. 78....

By the middle of the 19th century, the constitutional equilibrium created by the separation of the legislative power to make general law from the judicial power to apply that law in particular cases was so well understood and accepted that it could survive even *Dred Scott v. Sandford*, 19 How. 393 (1857). In his First Inaugural Address [Note *supra.* this chapter], President Lincoln explained why the political branches could not, and need not, interfere with even that infamous judgment:

> I do not forget the position assumed by some, that constitutional questions are to be decided by the Supreme Court; nor do I deny that such decisions must be binding in any case, upon the parties to a suit, as to the object of that suit.... And while it is obviously possible that such decision may be erroneous in any given case, still the evil effect following it, being limited to that particular case, with the chance that it may be over-ruled, and never become a precedent for other cases, can better be borne than could the evils of a different practice....

B

Section 27A(b) effects a clear violation of the separation-of-powers principle we have just discussed. It is, of course, retroactive legislation, that is, legislation that prescribes what the law *was* at an earlier time, when the act whose effect is controlled by the legislation occurred—in this case, the filing of the initial Rule 10b-5 action in the District Court. When retroactive legislation requires its own application in a case already finally adjudicated, it does no more and no less than "reverse a determination once made, in a particular case." *The Federalist* No. 81....

It is true, as petitioners contend, that Congress can always revise the judgments of Article III courts in one sense: When a new law makes clear that it is retroactive, an appellate court must apply that law in reviewing judgments still on appeal that were rendered before the law was enacted, and must alter the outcome accordingly. Since that is so, petitioners argue, federal courts must apply the "new" law created by § 27A(b) in finally adjudicated cases as well; for the line that separates lower court judgments that are pending on appeal (or may still be appealed), from lower-court judgments that are final, is determined by statute, see, e.g., 28 U.S.C. § 2107(a) (30-day time limit for appeal to federal court of appeals), and so cannot possibly be a *constitutional* line. But a distinction between judgments from which all appeals have been forgone or completed, and judgments that remain on appeal (or subject to being appealed), is implicit in what Article III creates: not a batch of unconnected courts, but a judicial *department* composed of "inferior Courts" and "one supreme Court." Within that hierarchy, the decision of an inferior court is not (unless the time for appeal has expired) the final word of the department as a whole. It is the obligation of the last court in the hierarchy that rules on the case to give effect to Congress's latest enactment, even when that has the effect of overturning the judgment of an inferior court, since each court, at every level, must "decide according to existing laws." Having achieved finality, however, a judicial decision becomes the last word of the judicial department with regard to a particular case or controversy, and Congress may not declare by retroactive legislation that the law applicable to that very case was something other than what the courts said it was. Finality of a legal judgment is determined by statute, just as entitlement to a government benefit is a statutory creation; but that no more deprives the former of its constitutional significance for separation-of-powers analysis than it deprives the latter of its significance for due process purposes.

To be sure, § 27A(b) reopens (or directs the reopening of) final judgments in a whole class of cases rather than in a particular suit. We do not see how that makes any difference. The separation-of-powers violation here, if there is any, consists of depriving judicial judgments of the conclusive effect that they had when they were announced, not of acting in a manner—viz, with particular rather than general effect—that is unusual (though, we must note, not impossible) for a legislature. To be sure, a general statute such as this one may reduce the perception that legislative interference with judicial judgments was prompted by individual favoritism; but it is legislative interference with judicial judgments nonetheless. Not favoritism, nor even corruption, but *power* is the object of the separation-of-powers prohibition. The prohibition is violated when an individual final judgment is legislatively rescinded for even the *very best* of reasons, such as the legislature's genuine conviction (supported by all the law professors in the land) that the judgment was wrong; and it is violated 40 times over when 40 final judgments are legislatively dissolved. . . .

C

Apart from the statute we review today, we know of no instance in which Congress has attempted to set aside the final judgment of an Article III court by retroactive legislation. That prolonged reticence would be amazing if such interference were not understood to be constitutionally proscribed....

Finally, we may respond to the suggestion of the concurrence that this case should be decided more narrowly. The concurrence is willing to acknowledge only that "*sometimes* Congress lacks the power under Article I to reopen an otherwise closed court judgment." In the present context, what it considers critical is that § 27A(b) is "exclusively retroactive" and "applies to a limited number of individuals." If Congress had only "provided some of the assurances against 'singling out' that ordinary legislative activity normally provides—say, prospectivity and general applicability—we might have a different case" [concurring opinion].

This seems to us wrong in both fact and law. In point of fact, § 27A(b) does not "single out" any defendant for adverse treatment (or any plaintiff for favorable treatment). Rather, it identifies a class of actions (those filed pre-*Lampf*, timely under applicable state law, but dismissed as time barred post-*Lampf*) which embraces many plaintiffs and defendants, the precise number and identities of whom we even now do not know....

More importantly, however, the concurrence's point seems to us wrong in law. To be sure, the class of actions identified by § 27A(b) could have been more expansive ... and the provision could have been written to have prospective as well as retroactive effect (e.g., "all post-*Lampf* dismissed actions, plus all future actions under Rule 10b-5, shall be timely if brought within 30 years of the injury"). But it escapes us how this could in any way cause the statute to be any less an infringement upon the judicial power. The nub of that infringement consists *not* of the Legislature's acting in a particularized and hence (according to the concurrence) nonlegislative fashion; but rather of the Legislature's nullifying prior, authoritative judicial action. It makes no difference whatever to that separation-of-powers violation that it is in gross rather than particularized (*e.g.*, "we hereby set aside *all* hitherto entered judicial orders"), or that it is not accompanied by an "almost" violation of the Bill of Attainder Clause, or an "almost" violation of any other constitutional provision.

Ultimately, the concurrence agrees with our judgment only "because the law before us embodies risks of the very sort that our Constitution's 'separation of powers' prohibition seeks to avoid." But the doctrine of separation of powers is a *structural safeguard* rather than a remedy to be applied only when specific harm, or risk of specific harm, can be identified. In its major features (of which the conclusiveness of judicial judgments is assuredly one) it is a prophylactic device, establishing high walls and clear distinctions because low walls and vague distinctions will not be judicially defensible in the heat of interbranch conflict.... The delphic alternative suggested by the concurrence (the setting aside of judgments is all right so long as Congress does not "impermissibly try to *apply*, as well as *make*, the law") simply prolongs doubt and multiplies confrontation. Separation of powers, a distinctively American political doctrine, profits from the advice authored by a distinctively American poet: Good fences make good neighbors....

Justice BREYER, concurring in the judgment.

I agree with the majority that §27A(b) is unconstitutional. In my view, the separation of powers inherent in our Constitution means that at least *sometimes* Congress lacks the power under Article I to reopen an otherwise closed court judgment. And the statutory provision here at issue, §27A(b), violates a basic "separation-of-powers" principle—one intended to protect individual liberty. Three features of this law—its exclusively retroactive effect, its application to a limited number of individuals, and its reopening of closed judgments—taken together, show that Congress here impermissibly tried to *apply*, as well as *make*, the law. Hence, §27A(b) falls outside the scope of Article I. But, it is far less clear, and unnecessary for the purposes of this case to decide, that separation of powers "is violated" *whenever* an "individual final judgment is legislatively rescinded" or that it is "violated 40 times over when 40 final judgments are legislatively dissolved." [majority opinion]. I therefore write separately.

The majority provides strong historical evidence that Congress lacks the power simply to reopen, and to revise, final judgments in individual cases. The Framers would have hesitated to lodge in the Legislature both that kind of power and the power to enact general laws, as part of their effort to avoid the "despotic government" that accompanies the "accumulation of all powers, legislative, executive, and judiciary, in the same hands." *The Federalist* No. 47 (J. Madison); *id.*, No. 48 (quoting T. Jefferson, *Notes on the State of Virginia*). For one thing, the authoritative application of a general law to a particular case by an independent judge, rather than by the legislature itself, provides an assurance that even an unfair law at least will be applied evenhandedly according to its terms. For another thing, as Justice Powell has pointed out, the Constitution's "separation-of-powers" principles reflect, in part, the Framers' "concern that a legislature should not be able unilaterally to impose a substantial deprivation on one person." *INS v. Chadha*, 462 U.S. 919 (1983) (opinion concurring in judgment). The Framers "expressed" this principle, both in "specific provisions, such as the Bill of Attainder Clause,"[*] and in the Constitution's "general allocation of power."

Despite these two important "separation-of-powers" concerns, *sometimes* Congress can enact legislation that focuses upon a small group, or even a single individual. See, e.g., *Nixon v. Administrator of General Services*, 433 U.S. 425 (1977).... And, *sometimes* Congress can enact legislation that, as a practical matter, radically changes the effect of an individual, previously entered court decree. Statutes that apply prospectively and (in part because of that prospectivity) to an open-ended class of persons, however, are more than simply an effort to apply, person by person, a previously enacted law, or to single out for oppressive treatment one, or a handful, of particular individuals. Thus, it seems to me, if Congress enacted legislation that reopened an otherwise closed judgment but in a way that mitigated some of the

_____

* [Ed. Note: The Bill of Attainder Clauses, one of which applies to the federal government and the other to the states, prevents laws that mandate the punishment of a particular designated person. Art. I, §§9 & 10.]

here relevant "separation-of-powers" concerns, by also providing some of the assurances against "singling out" that ordinary legislative activity normally provides — say, prospectivity and general applicability — we might have a different case. Because such legislation, in light of those mitigating circumstances, might well present a different constitutional question, I do not subscribe to the Court's more absolute statement.

The statute before us, however, has no such mitigating features. It reopens previously closed judgments. It is entirely retroactive, applying only to those Rule 10b-5 actions actually filed, on or before (but on which final judgments were entered after) June 19, 1991. It lacks generality, for it applies only to a few individual instances. See *Hearings on H.R. 3185 before the Subcommittee on Telecommunications and Finance of the House of Representatives Committee on Energy and Commerce*, 102d Cong., 1st Sess., 3–4 (1991) (listing, by case name, only 15 cases that had been dismissed on the basis of *Lampf*). And, it is underinclusive, for it excludes from its coverage others who, relying upon pre-*Lampf* limitations law, may have failed to bring timely securities fraud actions against any other of the Nation's hundreds of thousands of businesses....

The upshot is that, viewed in light of the relevant, liberty-protecting objectives of the "separation of powers," this case falls directly within the scope of language in this Court's cases suggesting a restriction on Congress' power to reopen closed court judgments....

At the same time, because the law before us *both* reopens final judgments *and* lacks the liberty-protecting assurances that prospectivity and greater generality would have provided, we need not, and we should not, go further — to make of the reopening itself, an absolute, always determinative distinction, a "prophylactic device," or a foundation for the building of a new "high wall" between the branches. Indeed, the unnecessary building of such walls is, in itself, dangerous, because the Constitution blends, as well as separates, powers in its effort to create a government that will work for, as well as protect the liberties of, its citizens. *See The Federalist* No. 48 (J. Madison). That doctrine does not "divide the branches into watertight compartments," nor "establish and divide fields of black and white." *Springer v. Philippine Islands*, 277 U.S. 189 (1928) (Holmes, J., dissenting); *see also Youngstown Sheet & Tube Co. v. Sawyer*, 343 U.S. 579 (1952) (Jackson, J., concurring) (referring to the need for "workable government"); *id.* (Frankfurter, J., concurring). And, important separation-of-powers decisions of this Court have sometimes turned, not upon absolute distinctions, but upon degree. As the majority invokes the advice of an American poet, one might consider as well that poet's caution, for he not only notes that "Something there is that doesn't love a wall," but also writes, "Before I built a wall I'd ask to know/ What I was walling in or walling out." R. Frost, Mending Wall, *The New Oxford Book of American Verse* (R. Ellmann ed. 1976)....

Because the law before us embodies risks of the very sort that our Constitution's "separation-of-powers" prohibition seeks to avoid, and because I can find no offsetting legislative safeguards that normally offer assurances that minimize those risks, I agree with the Court's conclusion and I join its judgment.

Justice STEVENS, with whom Justice GINSBURG joins, dissenting....

### III

... Correct application of separation-of-powers principles ... confirms that the Court has reached the wrong result. As our most recent major pronouncement on the separation of powers noted, "we have never held that the Constitution requires that the three branches of Government 'operate with absolute independence.'" *Morrison v. Olson*, 487 U.S. 654 (1988) (quoting *United States v. Nixon*, 418 U.S. 683 (1974) [Note *supra.* this chapter]). Rather, our jurisprudence reflects "Madison's flexible approach to separation of powers." In accepting Madison's conception rather than any "hermetic division among the Branches," "we have upheld statutory provisions that to some degree commingle the functions of the Branches, but that pose no danger of either aggrandizement or encroachment." Today's holding does not comport with these ideals.

Section 27A ... does not decide the merits of any issue in any litigation but merely removes an impediment to judicial decision on the merits. The impediment it removes would have produced inequity because the statute's beneficiaries did not cause the impediment. It requires a party invoking its benefits to file a motion within a specified time and to convince a court that the statute entitles the party to relief. Most important, § 27A(b) specifies both a substantive rule to govern the reopening of a class of judgments — the pre-*Lampf* limitations rule — and a procedure for the courts to apply in determining whether a particular motion to reopen should be granted. These characteristics are quintessentially legislative. They reflect Congress' fealty to the separation of powers and its intention to avoid the sort of ad hoc excesses the Court rightly criticizes in colonial legislative practice. In my judgment, all of these elements distinguish § 27A from "judicial" action and confirm its constitutionality. A sensible analysis would at least consider them in the balance....

### IV

The Court has drawn the wrong lesson from the Framers' disapproval of colonial legislatures' appellate review of judicial decisions. The Framers rejected that practice, not out of a mechanistic solicitude for "final judgments," but because they believed the impartial application of rules of law, rather than the will of the majority, must govern the disposition of individual cases and controversies. Any legislative interference in the adjudication of the merits of a particular case carries the risk that political power will supplant evenhanded justice, whether the interference occurs before or after the entry of final judgment. Cf. *United States v. Klein* [*supra.* this chapter]; *Hayburn's Case*, 2 Dall. 409 (1792). Section 27A(b) neither commands the reinstatement of any particular case nor directs any result on the merits....

"We must remember that the machinery of government would not work if it were not allowed a little play in its joints." *Bain Peanut Co. of Tex. v. Pinson*, 282 U.S. 499 (1931) (Holmes, J.). The three branches must cooperate in order to govern. We should regard favorably, rather than with suspicious hostility, legislation that enables the judiciary to overcome impediments to the performance of its mission of administering justice impartially, even when, as here, this Court has created the impediment. Rigid rules often make good law, but judgments in areas such as the review of potential conflicts among the three coequal branches of the Federal Government partake of art as well as science. That is why we have so often reiterated the insight of Justice Jackson:

> The actual art of governing under our Constitution does not and cannot conform to judicial definitions of the power of any of its branches based on isolated clauses or even single Articles torn from context. While the Constitution diffuses power the better to secure liberty, it also contemplates that practice will integrate the dispersed powers into a workable government. It enjoins upon its branches separateness but interdependence, autonomy but reciprocity. *Youngstown Sheet & Tube Co. v. Sawyer*, 343 U.S. 579 (1952) (concurring opinion).

… An appropriate regard for the interdependence of Congress and the judiciary amply supports the conclusion that § 27A(b) reflects constructive legislative cooperation rather than a usurpation of judicial prerogatives.

Accordingly, I respectfully dissent.

## *Note: The Emerging Picture of Article III*

The cases you've read so far reflect a grab-bag of rules governing the judicial power. If you put them together into an overall picture of Article III courts, what does it look like? Surely, that picture simultaneously reflects the courts' independence from and reliance upon the other branches. Is there anything more precise that can be said about it?

Is there any coherence to the rules the individual cases have laid down? Consider, as one example, *Plaut*. The majority refused to allow Congress to reopen cases that have proceeded to final judgment, but at the same time it recognized that Congress can establish the time which has to transpire in order for a court to arrive at that point. Does that make sense? Could Congress require that all judgments not be final for, say, 50 years, just in case it later wants to enact a new substantive rule that would allow losers to return to court and seek a different result under the new law? Or would political checks likely prevent such legislation? Does reliance on such political checks to answer this objection mean that the bright lines Justice Scalia attempts to draw in *Plaut* are in fact blurrier than he claims?

Consider also *Schor*. The Court in that case put great weight on the fact that the administrative adjudication scheme it upheld allowed Article III courts to decide questions of law. Conversely, the Court was less concerned that the agency court's *fact-findings* were subject only to deferential Article III court review. But often fact-findings are key to a plaintiff's case; thus, the power to find those facts often constitutes the practical power to decide the case, regardless of the relevant law. Indeed, Chief Justice Charles Evans Hughes once recited what has been described as the prayer of the unscrupulous bureaucrat: "Let me find the facts for the people of my country, and I care little who lays down the general principles." If this is true, then should there really be a constitutionally-significant distinction between the power of administrative courts to find facts, and to decide law?

# C. Self-Imposed Limits on the Judicial Power

Beyond congressional control over federal courts' jurisdiction lie a number of judge-made doctrines restricting the ability of courts to hear cases, and thus interpret law. These doctrines generally come under the rubric of the term "justiciability." This Chapter concludes by considering these important doctrines.

## 1. The Political Question Doctrine

An important justiciability doctrine prevents courts from deciding "political questions." As Justice Brennan notes in the next case below, the "political question" label carries with it the potential to confuse. This doctrine does not prevent the courts from deciding cases that have political implications, that deal with the political branches, or that may be politically significant. Indeed, as you will see (and as you've already seen in *Marbury* and *Klein*), the Court often injects itself into the most controversial political issues of the day. Rather, the political question doctrine prevents courts from deciding issues when the constitutional text assigns responsibility for the decision to another branch of the government, the governing constitutional rule does not contain a "judicially-manageable" legal standard, or when prudential factors (that is, common-sense concerns about the functioning of government) militate against judicial resolution of the issue. The Court does not apply these criteria in a mechanical way, for example, by requiring that a specific number of these factors be satisfied; rather, its analysis is much more fluid.

*Baker v. Carr* sets forth the basic doctrine, which is then applied in a more recent case, *Nixon v. United States*. Note the dissents in *Nixon*, and ask yourself how determinative *Baker*'s criteria really are. Also ask yourself how the political question doctrine is consistent with *Marbury*'s statement about the courts' power "to say what the law is." How does the *Chevron* doctrine—also discussed in a note after the *Nixon* case—reflect the same concerns as the political question doctrine, at the level of statutory law?

### Baker v. Carr
#### 369 U.S. 186 (1962)

[*Baker* arose out of the Tennessee General Assembly's failure to reapportion its state legislative districts between 1901 and 1961. Because of population shifts, the failure to redraw its districts meant that districts with the same number of representatives varied extensively in population. Thus, the vote of a citizen living in one county might be worth far more or less than the vote of a citizen living in another. For example, a single vote in Moore County was worth 19 votes in Hamilton County. Although reapportionment measures were introduced in the legislature during the intervening years, they were always defeated.]

MR. JUSTICE BRENNAN delivered the opinion of the Court....

## II.
## JURISDICTION OF THE SUBJECT MATTER

The District Court was uncertain whether our cases withholding federal judicial relief [in cases of malapportionment] rested upon a lack of federal jurisdiction or upon the inappropriateness of the subject matter for judicial consideration—what we have designated "nonjusticiability." The distinction between the two grounds is significant. In the instance of nonjusticiability, consideration of the cause is not wholly and immediately foreclosed; rather, the Court's inquiry necessarily proceeds to the point of deciding whether the duty asserted can be judicially identified and its breach judicially determined, and whether protection for the right asserted can be judicially molded. In the instance of lack of jurisdiction the cause either does not "arise under" the Federal Constitution, laws or treaties (or fall within one of the other enumerated categories of Art. III, § 2), or is not a "case or controversy" within the meaning of that section; or the cause is not one described by any jurisdictional statute.... [The Court found that there was jurisdiction.] ...

## IV.
## JUSTICIABILITY

In holding that the subject matter of this suit was not justiciable, the District Court relied on *Colegrove v. Green*, 328 U.S. 549 (1946), and subsequent *per curiam* cases [holding that] the federal courts ... will not intervene ... to compel legislative reapportionment. We understand the District Court to have read the cited cases as compelling the conclusion that since the appellants sought to have a legislative apportionment held unconstitutional, their suit presented a "political question" and was therefore nonjusticiable. We hold that this challenge to an apportionment presents no nonjusticiable "political question." ...

Of course the mere fact that the suit seeks protection of a political right does not mean it presents a political question. Such an objection "is little more than a play upon words." Rather, it is argued that apportionment cases, whatever the actual wording of the complaint, can involve no federal constitutional right except one resting on the guaranty of a republican form of government, and that complaints based on that clause have been held to present political questions which are nonjusticiable....

We have said that "In determining whether a question falls within [the political question] category, the appropriateness under our system of government of attributing finality to the action of the political departments and also the lack of satisfactory criteria for a judicial determination are dominant considerations." The nonjusticiability of a political question is primarily a function of the separation of powers. Much confusion results from the capacity of the "political question" label to obscure the need for case-by-case inquiry. Deciding whether a matter has in any measure been committed by the Constitution to another branch of government, or whether the action of that branch exceeds whatever authority has been committed, is itself a delicate exercise in constitutional interpretation, and is a responsibility of this Court as ultimate interpreter of the Constitution. To demonstrate this requires no less than to analyze representative cases and to infer from them the analytical threads that make up the political question doctrine. We shall then show that none of those threads catches this case.

*Foreign relations*: There are sweeping statements to the effect that all questions touching foreign relations are political questions. Not only does resolution of such issues frequently turn on standards that defy judicial application, or involve the exercise of a discretion demonstrably committed to the executive or legislature; but many such questions uniquely demand single-voiced statement of the Government's views. Yet it is error to suppose that every case or controversy which touches foreign relations lies beyond judicial cognizance. Our cases in this field seem invariably to show a discriminating analysis of the particular question posed, in terms of the history of its management by the political branches, of its susceptibility to judicial handling in the light of its nature and posture in the specific case, and of the possible consequences of judicial action. For example, though a court will not ordinarily inquire whether a treaty has been terminated, since on that question "governmental action ... must be regarded as of controlling importance," if there has been no conclusive "governmental action" then a court can construe a treaty and may find it provides the answer. Though a court will not undertake to construe a treaty in a manner inconsistent with a subsequent federal statute, no similar hesitancy obtains if the asserted clash is with state law....

*Dates of duration of hostilities*: Though it has been stated broadly that "the power which declared the necessity is the power to declare its cessation, and what the cessation requires," here too analysis reveals isolable reasons for the presence of political questions, underlying this Court's refusal to review the political departments' determination of when or whether a war has ended. Dominant is the need for finality in the political determination, for emergency's nature demands "A prompt and unhesitating obedience," *Martin v. Mott*, 12 Wheat. 19 (1827) (calling up of militia). Moreover, "the cessation of hostilities does not necessarily end the war power. It was stated in *Hamilton v. Kentucky Distilleries & W. Co.*, 251 U.S. 146 (1919), that the war power includes the power 'to remedy the evils which have arisen from its rise and progress' and continues during that emergency." But deference rests on reason, not habit. The question in a particular case may not seriously implicate considerations of finality — *e.g.*, a public program of importance (rent control) yet not central to the emergency effort. Further, clearly definable criteria for decision may be available. In such case the political question barrier falls away: "A Court is not at liberty to shut its eyes to an obvious mistake, when the validity of the law depends upon the truth of what is declared.... [It can] inquire whether the exigency still existed upon which the continued operation of the law depended." On the other hand, even in private litigation which directly implicates no feature of separation of powers, lack of judicially discoverable standards and the drive for even-handed application may impel reference to the political departments' determination of dates of hostilities' beginning and ending.

*Validity of enactments*: In *Coleman v. Miller*, 307 U.S. 433 (1939), this Court held that the questions of how long a proposed amendment to the Federal Constitution remained open to ratification, and what effect a prior rejection had on a subsequent ratification, were committed to congressional resolution and involved criteria of decision that necessarily escaped the judicial grasp. Similar considerations apply to the enacting process: "The respect due to coequal and independent departments," and the need for finality and certainty about the status of a statute contribute to judicial reluctance to inquire whether, as passed, it complied with all requisite formalities. But it is not true that courts will never delve into a legislature's records upon such a quest: If the enrolled statute lacks an effective date, a court will not hesitate to seek it in the legislative journals in order to preserve the enactment. The political question doctrine, a tool for maintenance of governmental order, will not be so applied as to promote only disorder.

*The status of Indian tribes*: This Court's deference to the political departments in determining whether Indians are recognized as a tribe, while it reflects familiar attributes of political questions, also has a unique element in that "the relation of the Indians to the United States is marked by peculiar and cardinal distinctions which exist no where else.... [The Indians are] domestic dependent nations ... in a state of pupilage. Their relation to the United States resembles that of a ward to his guardian." Yet, here too, there is no blanket rule. While "It is for [Congress]..., and not for the courts, to determine when the true interests of the Indian require his release from [the] condition of tutelage..., it is not meant by this that Congress may bring a community or body of people within the range of this power by arbitrarily calling them an Indian tribe...." Able to discern what is "distinctly Indian," the courts will strike down any heedless extension of that label. They will not stand impotent before an obvious instance of a manifestly unauthorized exercise of power.

It is apparent that several formulations which vary slightly according to the settings in which the questions arise may describe a political question, although each has one or more elements which identify it as essentially a function of the separation of powers. Prominent on the surface of any case held to involve a political question is found a textually demonstrable constitutional commitment of the issue to a coordinate political department; or a lack of judicially discoverable and manageable standards for resolving it; or the impossibility of deciding without an initial policy determination of a kind clearly for nonjudicial discretion; or the impossibility of a court's undertaking independent resolution without expressing lack of the respect due coordinate branches of government; or an unusual need for unquestioning adherence to a political decision already made; or the potentiality of embarrassment from multifarious pronouncements by various departments on one question.

Unless one of these formulations is inextricable from the case at bar, there should be no dismissal for nonjusticiability on the ground of a political question's presence. The doctrine of which we treat is one of "political questions," not one of "political cases." The courts cannot reject as "no law suit" a bona fide controversy as to whether some action denominated "political" exceeds constitutional authority. The cases we have reviewed show the necessity for discriminating inquiry into the precise facts and posture of the particular case, and the impossibility of resolution by any semantic cataloguing.

But it is argued that this case shares the characteristics of decisions that constitute a category not yet considered, cases concerning the Constitution's guaranty, in Art. IV, §4, of a republican form of government.[*] A conclusion as to whether the case at bar does present a political question cannot be confidently reached until we have considered those cases with special care. We shall discover that Guaranty Clause claims involve those elements which define a "political question," and for that reason and no other, they are nonjusticiable. In particular, we shall discover that the nonjusticiability of such claims has nothing to do with their touching upon matters of state governmental organization.

*Republican form of government*: *Luther v. Borden*, 7 How. 1 (1849), though in form simply an action for damages for trespass was, as Daniel Webster said in opening the argument for the defense, "an unusual case." [*Luther* grew out of a controversy in Rhode Island where two competing factions claimed to constitute the legitimate state government. When agents of one group entered private property to arrest the occupant for aiding the other, ostensibly rebellious, faction, the occupant sued the agents for trespass. The plaintiff's claim necessarily relied on the allegation that the agents were not agents of the legitimate state government; thus, the claim required the Court to decide which faction constituted the legitimate government.]

Chief Justice Taney's opinion for the Court reasoned as follows: (1) If a court were to hold the defendants' acts unjustified because the charter government had no legal existence during the period in question, it would follow that all of that government's actions—laws enacted, taxes collected, salaries paid, accounts settled, sentences passed—were of no effect; and that "the officers who carried their decisions into operation [were] answerable as trespassers, if not in some cases as criminals."... A decision for the plaintiff would inevitably have produced some significant measure of chaos, a consequence to be avoided if it could be done without abnegation of the judicial duty to uphold the Constitution.

(2) No state court had recognized as a judicial responsibility settlement of the issue of the locus of state governmental authority. Indeed, the courts of Rhode Island had in several cases held that "it rested with the political power to decide whether the charter government had been displaced or not," and that that department had acknowledged no change.

(3) Since "the question relates, altogether, to the constitution and laws of [the] ... State," the courts of the United States had to follow the state courts' decisions unless there was a federal constitutional ground for overturning them.

(4) No provision of the Constitution could be or had been invoked for this purpose except Art. IV, §4, the Guaranty Clause. Having already noted the absence of standards whereby the choice between governments could be made by a court acting independ-

---

* ["The United States shall guarantee to every State in this Union a Republican Form of Government."]

ently, Chief Justice Taney now found further textual and practical reasons for concluding that, if any department of the United States was empowered by the Guaranty
Clause to resolve the issue, it was not the judiciary....

Clearly, several factors were thought by the Court in *Luther* to make the question
there "political": the commitment to the other branches of the decision as to which
is the lawful state government; the unambiguous action by the President, in recognizing the charter government as the lawful authority; the need for finality in the executive's decision; and the lack of criteria by which a court could determine which
form of government was republican.

But the only significance that *Luther* could have for our immediate purposes is in
its holding that the Guaranty Clause is not a repository of judicially manageable standards which a court could utilize independently in order to identify a State's lawful
government. The Court has since refused to resort to the Guaranty Clause—which
alone had been invoked for the purpose—as the source of a constitutional standard
for invalidating state action....

We come, finally, to the ultimate inquiry whether our precedents as to what constitutes a nonjusticiable "political question" bring the case before us under the umbrella
of that doctrine. A natural beginning is to note whether any of the common characteristics which we have been able to identify and label descriptively are present. We
find none: The question here is the consistency of state action with the Federal Constitution. We have no question decided, or to be decided, by a political branch of government coequal with this Court. Nor do we risk embarrassment of our government
abroad, or grave disturbance at home if we take issue with Tennessee as to the constitutionality of her action here challenged. Nor need the appellants, in order to succeed
in this action, ask the Court to enter upon policy determinations for which judicially
manageable standards are lacking. Judicial standards under the Equal Protection Clause
are well developed and familiar, and it has been open to courts since the enactment
of the Fourteenth Amendment to determine, if on the particular facts they must, that
a discrimination reflects *no* policy, but simply arbitrary and capricious action.

This case does, in one sense, involve the allocation of political power within a
State, and the appellants might conceivably have added a claim under the Guaranty
Clause. Of course, as we have seen, any reliance on that clause would be futile. But
because any reliance on the Guaranty Clause could not have succeeded it does not
follow that appellants may not be heard on the equal protection claim which in fact
they tender. True, it must be clear that the Fourteenth Amendment claim is not so
enmeshed with those political question elements which render Guaranty Clause claims
nonjusticiable as actually to present a political question itself. But we have found that
not to be the case here....

We conclude then that the nonjusticiability of claims resting on the Guaranty
Clause which arises from their embodiment of questions that were thought "political,"
can have no bearing upon the justiciability of the equal protection claim presented
in this case. Finally, we emphasize that it is the involvement in Guaranty Clause claims

of the elements thought to define "political questions," and no other feature, which could render them nonjusticiable. Specifically, we have said that such claims are not held nonjusticiable because they touch matters of state governmental organization....

Mr. Justice Clark, concurring....

Although I find the Tennessee apportionment statute offends the Equal Protection Clause, I would not consider intervention by this Court into so delicate a field if there were any other relief available to the people of Tennessee. But the majority of the people of Tennessee have no "practical opportunities for exerting their political weight at the polls" to correct the existing "invidious discrimination." Tennessee has no initiative and referendum. I have searched diligently for other "practical opportunities" present under the law. I find none other than through the federal courts....

Mr. Justice Frankfurter, whom Mr. Justice Harlan joins, dissenting....

... Accepting appellants' own formulation of the issue, one can know this handsaw from a hawk. Such a claim would be non-justiciable not merely under Art. IV, §4, but under any clause of the Constitution, by virtue of the very fact that a federal court is not a forum for political debate.

But appellants, of course, do not rest on this claim *simpliciter*. In invoking the Equal Protection Clause, they assert that the distortion of representative government complained of is produced by systematic discrimination against them, by way of "a debasement of their votes...." Does this characterization, with due regard for the facts from which it is derived, add anything to appellants' case? ...

Manifestly, the Equal Protection Clause supplies no clearer guide for judicial examination of apportionment methods than would the Guarantee Clause itself. Apportionment, by its character, is a subject of extraordinary complexity, involving—even after the fundamental theoretical issues concerning what is to be represented in a representative legislature have been fought out or compromised—considerations of geography, demography, electoral convenience, economic and social cohesions or divergencies among particular local groups, communications, the practical effects of political institutions like the lobby and the city machine, ancient traditions and ties of settled usage, respect for proven incumbents of long experience and senior status, mathematical mechanics, censuses compiling relevant data, and a host of others. Legislative responses throughout the country to the reapportionment demands of the 1960 Census have glaringly confirmed that these are not factors that lend themselves to evaluations of a nature that are the staple of judicial determinations or for which judges are equipped to adjudicate by legal training or experience or native wit. And this is the more so true because in every strand of this complicated, intricate web of values meet the contending forces of partisan politics. The practical significance of apportionment is that the next election results may differ because of it. Apportionment battles are overwhelmingly party or intra-party contests. It will add a virulent source of friction and tension in federal-state relations to embroil the federal judiciary in them.

\* \* \*

Dissenting opinion of MR. JUSTICE HARLAN, whom MR. JUSTICE FRANKFURTER joins.

\* \* \*

[What] lies at the core of this controversy is a difference of opinion as to the function of representative government. It is surely beyond argument that those who have the responsibility for devising a system of representation may permissibly consider that factors other than bare numbers should be taken into account. The existence of the United States Senate is proof enough of that. To consider that we may ignore the Tennessee Legislature's judgment in this instance because that body was the product of an asymmetrical electoral apportionment would in effect be to assume the very conclusion here disputed. Hence we must accept the present form of the Tennessee Legislature as the embodiment of the State's choice, or, more realistically, its compromise, between competing political philosophies. The federal courts have not been empowered by the Equal Protection Clause to judge whether this resolution of the State's internal political conflict is desirable or undesirable, wise or unwise.

\* \* \*

The suggestion of my Brother FRANKFURTER that courts lack standards by which to decide such cases as this, is relevant not only to the question of "justiciability," but also, and perhaps more fundamentally, to the determination whether any cognizable constitutional claim has been asserted in this case. Courts are unable to decide when it is that an apportionment originally valid becomes void because the factors entering into such a decision are basically matters appropriate only for legislative judgment. And so long as there exists a possible rational legislative policy for retaining an existing apportionment, such a legislative decision cannot be said to breach the bulwark against arbitrariness and caprice that the Fourteenth Amendment affords. Certainly, with all due respect, the facile arithmetical argument contained in Part II of my Brother CLARK's separate opinion provides no tenable basis for considering that there has been such a breach in this instance.

\* \* \*

In conclusion, it is appropriate to say that one need not agree, as a citizen, with what Tennessee has done or failed to do, in order to deprecate, as a judge, what the majority is doing today. Those observers of the Court who see it primarily as the last refuge for the correction of all inequality or injustice, no matter what its nature or source, will no doubt applaud this decision and its break with the past. Those who consider that continuing national respect for the Court's authority depends in large measure upon its wise exercise of self-restraint and discipline in constitutional adjudication, will view the decision with deep concern.

### Note: Textual Commitments of Decisions to Other Branches

*Powell v. McCormack*, 395 U.S. 486 (1969), involved Adam Clayton Powell, Jr., who was duly elected to the United States House of Representatives but denied his seat by the House because he had allegedly engaged in misconduct. When Powell sued, the House claimed that the case should be dismissed on "political question" grounds. In the House's view, Art. I, §5 of the Constitution, which provides that "each House shall be the Judge of the Elections, Returns, and Qualifications of its own Members...," contained a "textually demonstrable commitment of the issue" to the House. As a result, the House argued that "the House, and the House alone, has power to determine who is qualified to be a member." The Supreme Court disagreed:

> Analysis of the "textual commitment" under Art. I, §5, has demonstrated that in judging the qualifications of its members Congress is limited to the standing qualifications prescribed in the Constitution. Respondents concede that Powell met these. Thus, there is no need to remand this case to determine whether he was entitled to be seated in the 90th Congress. Therefore, we hold that, since Adam Clayton Powell, Jr., was duly elected by the voters of the 18th Congressional District of New York and was not ineligible to serve under any provision of the Constitution, the House was without power to exclude him from its membership.

The Court concluded that it could decide the case without producing a "potentially embarrassing confrontation between coordinate branches of the Federal Government" or resulting in "multifarious pronouncements by various departments on one question."

How does the Court distinguish *Powell* in the following case?

## Nixon v. United States

506 U.S. 224 (1993)

CHIEF JUSTICE REHNQUIST delivered the opinion of the Court.

Petitioner Walter L. Nixon, Jr., asks this Court to decide whether Senate Rule XI, which allows a committee of Senators to hear evidence against an individual who has been impeached and to report that evidence to the full Senate, violates the Impeachment Trial Clause, Art. I, §3, cl. 6. That Clause provides that the "Senate shall have the sole Power to try all Impeachments." But before we reach the merits of such a claim, we must decide whether it is "justiciable," that is, whether it is a claim that may be resolved by the courts. We conclude that it is not.

Nixon, a former Chief Judge of the United States District Court for the Southern District of Mississippi, was convicted by a jury of two counts of making false statements before a federal grand jury and sentenced to prison.... Because Nixon refused to resign from his office as a United States District Judge, he continued to collect his judicial salary while serving out his prison sentence.

On May 10, 1989, the House of Representatives adopted three articles of impeachment for high crimes and misdemeanors....

After the House presented the articles to the Senate, the Senate voted to invoke its own Impeachment Rule XI, under which the presiding officer appoints a committee of Senators to "receive evidence and take testimony." Senate Impeachment Rule XI.... Pursuant to Rule XI, the committee presented the full Senate with a complete transcript of the proceeding and a Report stating the uncontested facts and summarizing the evidence on the contested facts.... The Senate voted by more than the constitutionally required two-thirds majority to convict Nixon on the first two articles....

Nixon thereafter commenced the present suit, arguing that Senate Rule XI violates the constitutional grant of authority to the Senate to "try" all impeachments because it prohibits the whole Senate from taking part in the evidentiary hearings.... The District Court held that his claim was nonjusticiable, and the Court of Appeals for the District of Columbia Circuit agreed. We granted certiorari.

A controversy is nonjusticiable—*i.e.*, involves a political question—where there is "a textually demonstrable constitutional commitment of the issue to a coordinate political department; or a lack of judicially discoverable and manageable standards for resolving it...." *Baker v. Carr.* But the courts must, in the first instance, interpret the text in question and determine whether and to what extent the issue is textually committed. As the discussion that follows makes clear, the concept of a textual commitment to a coordinate political department is not completely separate from the concept of a lack of judicially discoverable and manageable standards for resolving it; the lack of judicially manageable standards may strengthen the conclusion that there is a textually demonstrable commitment to a coordinate branch.

In this case, we must examine Art. I, § 3, cl. 6, to determine the scope of authority conferred upon the Senate by the Framers regarding impeachment. It provides:

> The Senate shall have the sole Power to try all Impeachments. When sitting for that Purpose, they shall be on Oath or Affirmation. When the President of the United States is tried, the Chief Justice shall preside: And no Person shall be convicted without the Concurrence of two thirds of the Members present.

The language and structure of this Clause are revealing. The first sentence is a grant of authority to the Senate, and the word "sole" indicates that this authority is reposed in the Senate and nowhere else....

Petitioner argues that the word "try" in the first sentence imposes by implication an additional requirement on the Senate in that the proceedings must be in the nature of a judicial trial. From there petitioner goes on to argue that this limitation precludes the Senate from delegating to a select committee the task of hearing the testimony of witnesses, as was done pursuant to Senate Rule XI.... Petitioner concludes from this that courts may review whether or not the Senate "tried" him before convicting him.

There are several difficulties with this position which lead us ultimately to reject it. The word "try," both in 1787 and later, has considerably broader meanings than those to which petitioner would limit it.... Based on the variety of definitions ... we cannot say that the Framers used the word "try" as an implied limitation on the method by which the Senate might proceed in trying impeachments....

The conclusion that the use of the word "try" in the first sentence of the Impeachment Trial Clause lacks sufficient precision to afford any judicially manageable standard of review of the Senate's actions is fortified by the existence of the three very specific requirements that the Constitution does impose on the Senate when trying impeachments: The Members must be under oath, a two-thirds vote is required to convict, and the Chief Justice presides when the President is tried. These limitations are quite precise, and their nature suggests that the Framers did not intend to impose additional limitations on the form of the Senate proceedings by the use of the word "try" in the first sentence.

Petitioner devotes only two pages in his brief to negating the significance of the word "sole" in the first sentence of Clause 6.... We think that the word "sole" is of considerable significance. Indeed, the word "sole" appears only one other time in the Constitution — with respect to the House of Representatives' "*sole* Power of Impeachment." The commonsense meaning of the word "sole" is that the Senate alone shall have authority to determine whether an individual should be acquitted or convicted. The dictionary definition bears this out. "Sole" is defined as "having no companion," "solitary," "being the only one," and "functioning ... independently and without assistance or interference." If the courts may review the actions of the Senate in order to determine whether that body "tried" an impeached official, it is difficult to see how the Senate would be "functioning ... independently and without assistance or interference." ...

The history and contemporary understanding of the impeachment provisions support our reading of the constitutional language. The parties do not offer evidence of a single word in the history of the Constitutional Convention or in contemporary commentary that even alludes to the possibility of judicial review in the context of the impeachment powers....

Nevertheless, Nixon argues that judicial review is necessary in order to place a check on the Legislature. Nixon fears that if the Senate is given unreviewable authority to interpret the Impeachment Trial Clause, there is a grave risk that the Senate will usurp judicial power. The Framers anticipated this objection and created two constitutional safeguards to keep the Senate in check. The first safeguard is that the whole of the impeachment power is divided between the two legislative bodies, with the House given the right to accuse and the Senate given the right to judge.... The second safeguard is the two-thirds supermajority vote requirement....

In addition to the textual commitment argument, we are persuaded that the lack of finality and the difficulty of fashioning relief counsel against justiciability. See *Baker*. We agree with the Court of Appeals that opening the door of judicial review to the procedures used by the Senate in trying impeachments would "expose the political life of the country to months, or perhaps years, of chaos." This lack of finality would manifest itself most dramatically if the President were impeached.... Equally uncertain is the question of what relief a court may give other than simply setting aside the judgment of conviction. Could it order the reinstatement of a convicted federal judge, or order Congress to create an additional judgeship if the seat had been filled in the interim?

Petitioner finally contends that a holding of nonjusticiability cannot be reconciled with our opinion in *Powell v. McCormack* [Note *supra.* this chapter]. The relevant issue in *Powell* was whether courts could review the House of Representatives' conclusion that Powell was "unqualified" to sit as a Member because he had been accused of misappropriating public funds and abusing the process of the New York courts. We stated that the question of justiciability turned on whether the Constitution committed authority to the House to judge its Members' qualifications, and if so, the extent of that commitment. Article I, § 5, provides that "Each House shall be the Judge of the Elections, Returns and Qualifications of its own Members." In turn, Art. I, § 2, specifies three requirements for membership in the House: The candidate must be at least 25 years of age, a citizen of the United States for no less than seven years, and an inhabitant of the State he is chosen to represent. We held that, in light of the three requirements specified in the Constitution, the word "qualifications"—of which the House was to be the Judge—was of a precise, limited nature.

Our conclusion in *Powell* was based on the fixed meaning of "qualifications" set forth in Art. I, § 2. The claim by the House that its power to "be the Judge of the Elections, Returns and Qualifications of its own Members" was a textual commitment of unreviewable authority was defeated by the existence of this separate provision specifying the only qualifications which might be imposed for House membership. The decision as to whether a Member satisfied these qualifications *was* placed with the House, but the decision as to what these qualifications consisted of was not.

In the case before us, there is no separate provision of the Constitution that could be defeated by allowing the Senate final authority to determine the meaning of the word "try" in the Impeachment Trial Clause. We agree with Nixon that courts possess power to review either legislative or executive action that transgresses identifiable textual limits.... But we conclude, after exercising that delicate responsibility, that the word "try" in the Impeachment Trial Clause does not provide an identifiable textual limit on the authority which is committed to the Senate....

JUSTICE STEVENS, concurring.

For me, the debate about the strength of the inferences to be drawn from the use of the words "sole" and "try" is far less significant than the central fact that the Framers decided to assign the impeachment power to the Legislative Branch. The disposition of the impeachment of Samuel Chase in 1805 demonstrated that the Senate is fully conscious of the profound importance of that assignment, and nothing in the subsequent history of the Senate's exercise of this extraordinary power suggests otherwise. Respect for a coordinate branch of the Government forecloses any assumption that improbable hypotheticals like those mentioned by JUSTICE WHITE and JUSTICE SOUTER will ever occur. Accordingly, the wise policy of judicial restraint, coupled with the potential anomalies associated with a contrary view, provide a sufficient justification for my agreement with the views of THE CHIEF JUSTICE.

JUSTICE WHITE, with whom JUSTICE BLACKMUN joins, concurring in the judgment.

... I would ... reach the merits of the claim. I concur in the judgment because the Senate fulfilled its constitutional obligation to "try" petitioner....

## II

The majority states that the question raised in this case meets two of the criteria for political questions set out in *Baker v. Carr*. It concludes first that there is "a textually demonstrable constitutional commitment of the issue to a coordinate political department." It also finds that the question cannot be resolved for "a lack of judicially discoverable and manageable standards." ...

Although *Baker* directs the Court to search for "a textually demonstrable constitutional commitment" of [exclusive] responsibility [to another branch], there are few, if any, explicit and unequivocal instances in the Constitution of this sort of textual commitment. Conferral on Congress of the power to "Judge" qualifications of its Members by Art. I, § 5, may, for example, preclude judicial review of whether a prospective member in fact meets those qualifications. See *Powell v. McCormack*. The courts therefore are usually left to infer the presence of a political question from the text and structure of the Constitution. In drawing the inference that the Constitution has committed final interpretive authority to one of the political branches, courts are sometimes aided by textual evidence that the Judiciary was not meant to exercise judicial review — a coordinate inquiry expressed in *Baker*'s "lack of judicially discoverable and manageable standards" criterion....

## A

The majority finds a clear textual commitment in the Constitution's use of the word "sole" in the phrase "the Senate shall have the sole Power to try all Impeachments." ...

... The significance of the Constitution's use of the term "sole" lies not in the infrequency with which the term appears, but in the fact that it appears exactly twice, in parallel provisions concerning impeachment. That the word "sole" is found only in the House and Senate Impeachment Clauses demonstrates that its purpose is to emphasize the distinct role of each in the impeachment process.... Giving each House "sole" power with respect to its role in impeachments effected this division of labor. While the majority is thus right to interpret the term "sole" to indicate that the Senate ought to "function independently and without assistance or interference," it wrongly identifies the Judiciary, rather than the House, as the source of potential interference with which the Framers were concerned when they employed the term "sole." ...

The majority also claims support in the history and early interpretations of the Impeachment Clauses.... What the relevant history mainly reveals is deep ambivalence among many of the Framers over the very institution of impeachment, which, by its nature, is not easily reconciled with our system of checks and balances....

The historical evidence reveals above all else that the Framers were deeply concerned about placing in any branch the "awful discretion, which a court of impeachments must necessarily have." *The Federalist* No. 65. Viewed against this history, the discord between the majority's position and the basic principles of checks and balances underlying the Constitution's separation of powers is clear. In essence, the majority suggests that the Framers' conferred upon Congress a potential tool of legislative dominance yet at the same time rendered Congress' exercise of that power one of the very few areas of legislative authority immune from any judicial review.... In a truly balanced system, impeachments tried by the Senate would serve as a means of controlling the largely unaccountable Judiciary, even as judicial review would ensure that the Senate adhered to a minimal set of procedural standards in conducting impeachment trials.

B

The majority also contends that the term "try" does not present a judicially manageable standard. It notes that in 1787, as today, the word "try" may refer to an inquiry in the nature of a judicial proceeding, or, more generally, to experimentation or investigation. In light of the term's multiple senses, the Court finds itself unable to conclude that the Framers used the word "try" as "an implied limitation on the method by which the Senate might proceed in trying impeachments." ...

It is apparently on this basis that the majority distinguishes *Powell v. McCormack*....

This argument comes in two variants. The first, which asserts that one simply cannot ascertain the sense of "try" which the Framers employed and hence cannot undertake judicial review, is clearly untenable. To begin with, one would intuitively expect that, in defining the power of a political body to conduct an inquiry into official wrongdoing, the Framers used "try" in its legal sense....

The other variant of the majority position focuses not on which sense of "try" is employed in the Impeachment Trial Clause, but on whether the legal sense of that term creates a judicially manageable standard. The majority concludes that the term provides no "identifiable textual limit." Yet, as the Government itself conceded at oral argument, the term "try" is hardly so elusive as the majority would have it. Were the Senate, for example, to adopt the practice of automatically entering a judgment of conviction whenever articles of impeachment were delivered from the House, it is quite clear that the Senate will have failed to "try" impeachments. Indeed in this respect, "try" presents no greater, and perhaps fewer, interpretive difficulties than some other constitutional standards that have been found amenable to familiar techniques of judicial construction, including, for example, "Commerce ... among the several States," Art. I, §8, cl. 3, and "due process of law," Amdt. 5.

[Justice White then concluded that the Senate had satisfied the deferential judicial review he would have imposed on the requirement that they "try" impeachments.]

JUSTICE SOUTER, concurring in the judgment.

I agree with the Court that this case presents a nonjusticiable political question. Because my analysis differs somewhat from the Court's, however, I concur in its judgment by this separate opinion.

As we cautioned in *Baker v. Carr*, "the 'political question' label" tends "to obscure the need for case-by-case inquiry." The need for such close examination is nevertheless clear from our precedents, which demonstrate that the functional nature of the political question doctrine requires analysis of "the precise facts and posture of the particular case," and precludes "resolution by any semantic cataloguing"....

Whatever considerations feature most prominently in a particular case, the political question doctrine is "essentially a function of the separation of powers," existing to restrain courts "from inappropriate interference in the business of the other branches of Government," and deriving in large part from prudential concerns about the respect we owe the political departments. Not all interference is inappropriate or disrespectful, however, and application of the doctrine ultimately turns ... on "how importunately the occasion demands an answer."

This occasion does not demand an answer. The Impeachment Trial Clause commits to the Senate "the sole Power to try all Impeachments," subject to three procedural requirements: the Senate shall be on oath or affirmation; the Chief Justice shall preside when the President is tried; and conviction shall be upon the concurrence of two-thirds of the Members present. U.S. Const., Art. I, § 3, cl. 6. It seems fair to conclude that the Clause contemplates that the Senate may determine, within broad boundaries, such subsidiary issues as the procedures for receipt and consideration of evidence necessary to satisfy its duty to "try" impeachments. Other significant considerations confirm a conclusion that this case presents a nonjusticiable political question: the "unusual need for unquestioning adherence to a political decision already made," as well as "the potentiality of embarrassment from multifarious pronouncements by various departments on one question." *Baker*. As the Court observes, judicial review of an impeachment trial would under the best of circumstances entail significant disruption of government.

One can, nevertheless, envision different and unusual circumstances that might justify a more searching review of impeachment proceedings. If the Senate were to act in a manner seriously threatening the integrity of its results, convicting, say, upon a coin toss, or upon a summary determination that an officer of the United States was simply "a bad guy," judicial interference might well be appropriate. In such circumstances, the Senate's action might be so far beyond the scope of its constitutional authority, and the consequent impact on the Republic so great, as to merit a judicial response despite the prudential concerns that would ordinarily counsel silence. "The political question doctrine, a tool for maintenance of governmental order, will not be so applied as to promote only disorder." *Baker*.

### *Note:* Chevron v. NRDC *and the Interpretation of Statutory Law*

In *Chevron USA v. Natural Resources Defense Council*, 467 U.S. 837 (1984), the Court considered how much discretion an administrative agency ought to have when interpreting a statute it has been charged with implementing. *Chevron* is not a constitutional law case *per se*, but it raises the same type of question raised in the political question context: to what extent should a court refrain from "saying what the law is"?

*Chevron* concerned the Clean Air Act, a complex regulatory statute. Part of the statute required expensive pollution control equipment for "new stationary sources" of pollution. After changing its position several times, the Environmental Protection Agency, the agency charged with promulgating regulations under the law, eventually decided that the term "stationary source" referred not to a smokestack or other single source of pollution, but rather to an entire facility, such as an entire refinery. The result of that interpretation was that if a refinery took certain smokestacks offline when adding others, the new ones did not need to include the expensive pollution control equipment, as long as the net effect of the additions and subtractions was to reduce the total amount of pollution.

The court of appeals rejected the agency's interpretation. It conceded that it could not find a clear definition or other indication of congressional intent in the statute with regard to this issue. However, it concluded that the basic goal of the statute was to clean the environment; thus, it rejected the agency's interpretation.

The Supreme Court reversed. It held that in situations of this sort, courts should first determine if the statute provides a clear answer to the interpretive question. If it does not, the court must defer to any reasonable agency interpretation. In a key part of the opinion, the Court explained the rationale for this second step:

> The power of an administrative agency to administer a congressionally created … program necessarily requires the formulation of policy and the making of rules to fill any gap left, implicitly or explicitly, by Congress." If Congress has explicitly left a gap for the agency to fill, there is an express delegation of authority to the agency to elucidate a specific provision of the statute by regulation. Such legislative regulations are given controlling weight unless they are arbitrary, capricious, or manifestly contrary to the statute. Sometimes the legislative delegation to an agency on a particular question is implicit rather than explicit. In such a case, a court may not substitute its own construction of a statutory provision for a reasonable interpretation made by the administrator of an agency.

In a footnote earlier in the opinion the Court said the following: "The judiciary is the final authority on issues of statutory construction and must reject administrative constructions which are contrary to clear congressional intent. If a court, employing traditional tools of statutory construction, ascertains that Congress had an intention on the precise question at issue, that intention is the law and must be given effect."

How does the analysis in *Chevron* relate to the political question doctrine? To *Marbury*?

## 2. The Case or Controversy Requirement

Article III, § 2, contains perhaps the most important limitation on the judicial power: the "case" or "controversy" requirement. This limitation has spawned multiple restrictions on the scope of judicial authority that go under the general heading of bans on "advisory opinions." The first case excerpted below, *Muskrat v. United States*, illustrates the Court's basic concerns with issuing advisory opinions. Subsequent subsections consider more specific requirements growing out of the "case or controversy"-based ban on advisory opinions: the requirement that a plaintiff have standing, and the requirement that a case be both ripe for adjudication and not moot.

### a. Advisory Opinions

The prohibition on advisory opinions dates back to *Hayburn's Case*, 2 U.S. (2 Call.) 409 (1792). In *Hayburn's Case*, the Court concluded that it was unconstitutional for Congress to give courts the task of advising the Secretary of War about the amount of benefits due individual Revolutionary War veterans based on their particular disabilities. Under the statute the Secretary could reject the judges' recommendations. The Court held that it such a task was "not of a judicial nature." It also held that the statute's provision that the recommendations could be overridden by the executive branch was "radically inconsistent with the independence of the judicial power." The Court's reasoning was echoed in the case below.

## Muskrat v. United States

### 219 U.S. 346 (1911)

[In 1902, Congress passed legislation setting aside certain lands for the use of Cherokee Indians. In 1904 and 1906, Congress passed laws allowing other Indians to share in the lands. By expanding the number of participants, the 1904 and 1906 laws diminished the quantity of land allocated to those who benefitted from the 1902 statute. In 1907, Congress passed a law authorizing four named individuals, including Muskrat (one of the Indians who benefitted by the 1902 statute), to bring suit challenging the 1904 and 1906 statutes.]

Mr. Justice Day delivered the opinion of the court: ...

The first question in these cases, as in others, involves the jurisdiction of the court to entertain the proceeding, and that depends upon whether the jurisdiction conferred is within the power of Congress, having in view the limitations of the judicial power, as established by the Constitution of the United States....

In 1793, by direction of the President, Secretary of State Jefferson addressed to the Justices of the Supreme Court a communication soliciting their views upon the question whether their advice to the executive would be available in the solution of important questions of the construction of treaties, laws of nations and laws of the land, which the Secretary said were often presented under circumstances which "*do not give a cognizance of them to the tribunals of the country.*" The answer to the question was postponed until the subsequent sitting of the Supreme Court, when Chief Justice Jay and his associates answered to President Washington that in consideration of the lines of separation drawn by the Constitution between the three departments of government, and being judges of a court of last resort, afforded strong arguments against the propriety of extrajudicially deciding the questions alluded to, and expressing the view that the power given by the Constitution to the President of calling on heads of departments for opinions "seems to have been purposely, as well as expressly, united to the executive departments." ...

[By] the express terms of the Constitution, the exercise of the judicial power is limited to "cases" and "controversies." Beyond this it does not extend, and unless it is asserted in a case or controversy within the meaning of the Constitution, the power to exercise it is nowhere conferred.

What, then, does the Constitution mean in conferring this judicial power with the right to determine "cases" and "controversies"? A "case" was defined by Mr. Chief Justice Marshall as early as the leading case of *Marbury v. Madison* to be a suit instituted according to the regular course of judicial procedure....

"... By cases and controversies are intended the claims of litigants brought before the courts ... for the protection or enforcement of rights, or the prevention, redress, or punishment of wrongs.... The term implies the existence of present or possible adverse parties whose contentions are submitted to the court for adjudication." ...

... [The] object and purpose of the [present] suit is wholly comprised in the determination of the constitutional validity of certain acts of Congress; and furthermore ... should a judgment be rendered in the Court of Claims or this court, denying the constitutional validity of such acts, then the amount of compensation to be paid to attorneys employed for the purpose of testing the constitutionality of the law is to be paid out of funds in the Treasury of the United States....

It is therefore evident that there is neither more nor less in this procedure than an attempt to provide for a judicial determination, final in this court, of the constitutional validity of an act of Congress. Is such a determination within the judicial power conferred by the Constitution, as the same has been interpreted and defined in the authoritative decisions to which we have referred? We think it is not. That judicial power, as we have seen, is the right to determine actual controversies arising between adverse litigants, duly instituted in courts of proper jurisdiction. The right to declare a law unconstitutional arises because an act of Congress relied upon by one or the other of such parties in determining their rights is in conflict with the fundamental law. The exercise of this, the most important and delicate duty of this court, is not given to it as a body with revisory power over the action of Congress, but because the rights of the litigants in justiciable controversies require the court to choose between the fundamental law and a law purporting to be enacted within constitutional authority, but in fact beyond the power delegated to the legislative branch of the Government. This attempt to obtain a judicial declaration of the validity of the act of Congress is not presented in a "case" or "controversy," to which, under the Constitution of the United States, the judicial power alone extends. It is true the United States is made a defendant to this action, but it has no interest adverse to the claimants. The object is not to assert a property right as against the Government, or to demand compensation for alleged wrongs because of action upon its part. The whole purpose of the law is to determine the constitutional validity of this class of legislation, in a suit not arising between parties concerning a property right necessarily involved in the decision in question, but in a proceeding against the Government in its sovereign capacity, and concerning which the only judgment required is to settle the doubtful character of the legislation in question. Such judgment will not conclude private parties, when actual litigation brings to the court the question of the constitutionality of such legislation. In a legal sense the judgment could not be executed, and amounts in fact to no more than an expression of opinion upon the validity of the acts in question. Confining the jurisdiction of this court within the limitations conferred by the Constitution, which the court has hitherto been careful to observe, and whose boundaries it has refused to transcend, we think the Congress, in the act of March 1, 1907, exceeded the limitations of legislative authority, so far as it required of this court action not judicial in its nature within the meaning of the Constitution....

The questions involved in this proceeding as to the validity of the legislation may arise in suits between individuals, and when they do and are properly brought before this court for consideration they, of course, must be determined in the exercise of its judicial functions. For the reasons we have stated, we are constrained to hold that these actions present no justiciable controversy within the authority of the court, acting within the limitations of the Constitution under which it was created....

*The judgments will be reversed and the cases remanded to the Court of Claims, with directions to dismiss the petitions for want of jurisdiction.*

## b. Standing

A fundamental—and highly contentious—aspect of the case or controversy requirement is the requirement that the plaintiff have "standing to sue." Unlike ripeness and mootness, which focus on the timing of adjudication, standing focuses on whether a plaintiff has a sufficient interest in the litigation. Standing is related to ripeness and mootness, because a case's mootness or lack of ripeness might mean that the plaintiff lacks such an interest. However, standing cases do not always involve such questions of timing.

The basic constitutional requirements for standing are that (1) the plaintiff be injured, (2) the injury be caused by the defendant, and (3) the injury be redressable by the court. The injury must be concrete, and either actually existing or imminent. The Court has also stated that the injury must be particularized; that is, it has stated a requirement that plaintiffs may not bring "generalized grievances" to courts. Moreover, as a prudential matter courts generally do not allow plaintiffs to assert the rights of third parties.

These criteria are not susceptible to easy application. The concept of "injury" is highly elastic; as you will see in the cases below, the Court accepts a wide variety of harms as Article III "injury." Causation and redressability are similarly difficult to apply with any rigor. You may already know that the legal concept of causation includes a heavy policy element, since it is possible to make a logical argument that almost any action in the world has "caused" a particular result. *Warth v. Seldin* and the note after it recount how the Court has struggled to define the degree of causation that satisfies Article III. Redressability is largely a mirror image of causation; if a defendant has caused the plaintiff's injury then usually (though not always) the court is able to fashion a remedy that makes the plaintiff whole, or "redresses" that injury.

Beyond standing requirements based on Article III there are requirements that are labeled "prudential." That term means what it says: "prudential" limits on standing are matters of policy, based in courts' sense of which plaintiffs are best suited to raise which claims. But because these limits are prudential, and not based in Article III, they may be dispensed with by Congress or the courts themselves. *Singleton v. Wulff*, excerpted after *Warth*, examines how courts consider whether to dispense with prudential standing limits. A major prudential standing limit is the bar on a plaintiff asserting the legal rights of another. (Remember, all that Article III requires is injury, causation and redressability: technically, a plaintiff can satisfy those requirements in a lawsuit claiming that someone else's legal rights have been violated.) As you will see, courts consider whether there is a special relationship between the plaintiff and the actual holder of the legal right at issue, such that it makes sense to allow such an assertion of third-party rights.

Congress can also influence the standing calculus. As you will see in *Havens Realty v. Coleman*, Congress, just like courts, can wipe away the prudential ban on plaintiffs asserting the legal rights of a third party. But Congress can do more. Perhaps surprisingly, Congress can also affect Article III standing, by creating rights, which, when deprived, constitute injury for Article III purposes. *Havens* illustrates this dynamic as well. But there are limits to Congress's influence over standing, as reflected in *Lujan v. Defenders of Wildlife*, the last standing case excerpted in these materials.

## Warth v. Seldin
### 422 U.S. 490 (1975)

Mr. Justice Powell delivered the opinion of the Court.

Petitioners, various organizations and individuals resident in the Rochester, N.Y., metropolitan area, brought this action in the District Court for the Western District of New York against the town of Penfield, an incorporated municipality adjacent to Rochester, and against members of Penfield's Zoning, Planning and Town Boards. Petitioners claimed that the town's zoning ordinance ... effectively excluded persons of low and moderate income from living in the town, in contravention of petitioners' First, Ninth, and Fourteenth Amendment rights.... The District Court dismissed the complaint.... The Court of Appeals for the Second Circuit affirmed, holding that none of the plaintiffs, and neither Housing Council nor Home Builders Association, had standing to prosecute the action.... We affirm.

I

Petitioners Metro-Act of Rochester, Inc., and eight individual plaintiffs, on behalf of themselves and all persons similarly situated, filed this action on January 24, 1972, averring jurisdiction in the District Court under 28 U.S.C. §§ 1331 and 1343. The complaint identified Metro-Act as a not-for-profit New York corporation, the purposes of which are "to alert ordinary citizens to problems of social concern; ... to inquire into the reasons for the critical housing shortage for low and moderate income persons in the Rochester area and to urge action on the part of citizens to alleviate the general housing shortage for low and moderate income persons." Plaintiffs Vinkey, Reichert, Warth, and Harris were described as residents of the city of Rochester, all of whom owned real property in and paid property taxes to that city. Plaintiff Ortiz, "a citizen of Spanish/Puerto Rican extraction," also owned real property in and paid taxes to Rochester. Ortiz, however, resided in Wayland, N.Y., some 42 miles from Penfield where he was employed. The complaint described plaintiffs Broadnax, Reyes, and Sinkler as residents of Rochester and "persons fitting within the classification of low and moderate income as hereinafter defined...." Although the complaint does not expressly so state, the record shows that Broadnax, Reyes, and Sinkler are members of ethnic or racial minority groups: Reyes is of Puerto Rican ancestry; Broadnax and Sinkler are Negroes.

Petitioners' complaint alleged that Penfield's zoning ordinance, adopted in 1962, has the purpose and effect of excluding person of low and moderate income from residing in the town. In particular, the ordinance allocates 98% of the town's vacant land to single-family detached housing, and allegedly by imposing unreasonable requirements relating to lot size, setback, floor area, and habitable space, the ordinance increases the cost of single-family detached housing beyond the means of persons of low and moderate income.... Petitioners also alleged that "in furtherance of a policy of exclusionary zoning," the defendant members of Penfield's Town, Zoning, and Planning Boards had acted in an arbitrary and discriminatory manner....

... The Rochester property owners and taxpayers—Vinkey, Reichert, Warth, Harris, and Ortiz—claimed that because of Penfield's exclusionary practices, the city of Rochester had been forced to impose higher tax rates on them and others similarly situated than would otherwise have been necessary. The low- and moderate-income, minority plaintiffs—Ortiz, Broadnax, Reyes, and Sinkler—claimed that Penfield's zoning practices had prevented them from acquiring, by lease or purchase, residential property in the town, and thus had forced them and their families to reside in less attractive environments. To relieve these various harms, petitioners asked the District Court to declare the Penfield ordinance unconstitutional, to enjoin the defendants from enforcing the ordinance, to order the defendants to enact and administer a new ordinance designed to alleviate the effects of their past actions, and to award $750,000 in actual and exemplary damages.

On May 2, 1972, petitioner Rochester Home Builders Association, an association of firms engaged in residential construction in the Rochester metropolitan area, moved the District Court for leave to intervene as a party-plaintiff. In essence, Home Builders' intervenor complaint repeated the allegations of exclusionary zoning practices made by the original plaintiffs. It claimed that these practices arbitrarily and capriciously had prevented its member firms from building low- and moderate-cost housing in Penfield, and thereby had deprived them of potential profits. Home Builders prayed for equitable relief identical in substance to that requested by the original plaintiffs, and also for $750,000 in damages. On June 7, 1972, Metro-Act and the other original plaintiffs moved to join petitioner Housing Council in the Monroe County Area, Inc., as a party plaintiff. Housing Council is a not-for-profit New York corporation, its membership comprising some 71 public and private organizations interested in housing problems....

## II

We address first the principles of standing relevant to the claims asserted by the several categories of petitioners in this case. In essence the question of standing is whether the litigant is entitled to have the court decide the merits of the dispute or of particular issues. This inquiry involves both constitutional limitations on federal-court jurisdiction and prudential limitations on its exercise. In both dimensions it is founded in concern about the proper — and properly limited — role of the courts in a democratic society.

In its constitutional dimension, standing imports justiciability: whether the plaintiff has made out a "case or controversy" between himself and the defendant within the meaning of Art. III. This is the threshold question in every federal case, determining the power of the court to entertain the suit. As an aspect of justiciability, the standing question is whether the plaintiff has "alleged such a personal stake in the outcome of the controversy" as to warrant *his* invocation of federal-court jurisdiction and to justify exercise of the court's remedial powers on his behalf. The Art. III judicial power exists only to redress or otherwise to protect against injury to the complaining party, even though the court's judgment may benefit others collaterally. A federal court's jurisdiction therefore can be invoked only when the plaintiff himself has suffered "some threatened or actual injury resulting from the putatively illegal action."

Apart from this minimum constitutional mandate, this Court has recognized other limits on the class of persons who may invoke the courts' decisional and remedial powers. First, the Court has held that when the asserted harm is a "generalized grievance" shared in substantially equal measure by all or a large class of citizens, that harm alone normally does not warrant exercise of jurisdiction. Second, even when the plaintiff has alleged injury sufficient to meet the "case or controversy" requirement, this Court has held that the plaintiff generally must assert his own legal rights and interests, and cannot rest his claim to relief on the legal rights or interests of third parties. Without such limitations — closely related to Art. III concerns but essentially matters of judicial self-governance — the courts would be called upon to decide abstract questions of wide public significance even though other governmental institutions may be more competent to address the questions and even though judicial intervention may be unnecessary to protect individual rights.

Although standing in no way depends on the merits of the plaintiff's contention that particular conduct is illegal, it often turns on the nature and source of the claim asserted. The actual or threatened injury required by Art. III may exist solely by virtue of "statutes creating legal rights, the invasion of which creates standing...." Moreover, the source of the plaintiff's claim to relief assumes critical importance with respect to the prudential rules of standing that, apart from Art. III's minimum requirements, serve to limit the role of the courts in resolving public disputes. Essentially, the standing question in such cases is whether the constitutional or statutory provision on which the claim rests properly can be understood as granting persons in the plaintiff's position a right to judicial relief. In some circumstances, countervailing considerations may outweigh the concerns underlying the usual reluctance to exert judicial power when the plaintiff's claim to relief rests on the legal rights of third parties. In such instances, the Court has found, in effect, that the constitutional or statutory provision in question implies a right of action in the plaintiff. Moreover, Congress may grant an express right of action to persons who otherwise would be barred by prudential standing rules. Of course, Art. III's requirement remains: the plaintiff still must allege a distinct and palpable injury to himself, even if it is an injury shared by a large class of other possible litigants. But so long as this requirement is satisfied, persons to whom Congress has granted a right of action, either expressly or by clear implication, may have standing to seek relief on the basis of the legal rights and interests of others, and, indeed, may invoke the general public interest in support of their claim.

One further preliminary matter requires discussion. For purposes of ruling on a motion to dismiss for want of standing, both the trial and reviewing courts must accept as true all material allegations of the complaint, and must construe the complaint in favor of the complaining party. At the same time, it is within the trial court's power to allow or to require the plaintiff to supply, by amendment to the complaint or by affidavits, further particularized allegations of fact deemed supportive of plaintiff's standing. If, after this opportunity, the plaintiff's standing does not adequately appear from all materials of record, the complaint must be dismissed.

## III

With these general considerations in mind, we turn first to the claims of petitioners Ortiz, Reyes, Sinkler, and Broadnax, each of whom asserts standing as a person of low or moderate income and, coincidentally, as a member of a minority racial or ethnic group....

In their complaint, petitioners Ortiz, Reyes, Sinkler, and Broadnax alleged in conclusory terms that they are among the persons excluded by respondents' actions. None of them has ever resided in Penfield; each claims at least implicitly that he desires, or has desired, to do so. Each asserts, moreover, that he made some effort, at some time, to locate housing in Penfield that was at once within his means and adequate for his family's needs. Each claims that his efforts proved fruitless. We may assume, as petitioners allege, that respondents' actions have contributed, perhaps substantially, to the cost of housing in Penfield. But there remains the question whether petitioners' inability to locate suitable housing in Penfield reasonably can be said to have resulted, in any concretely demonstrable way, from respondents' alleged constitutional and statutory infractions. Petitioners must allege facts from which it reasonably could be inferred that, absent the respondents' restrictive zoning practices, there is a substantial probability that they would have been able to purchase or lease in Penfield and that, if the court affords the relief requested, the asserted inability of petitioners will be removed.

We find the record devoid of the necessary allegations. As the Court of Appeals noted, none of these petitioners has a present interest in any Penfield property; none is himself subject to the ordinance's strictures; and none has ever been denied a variance or permit by respondent officials. Instead, petitioners claim that respondents' enforcement of the ordinance against third parties—developers, builders, and the like—has had the consequence of precluding the construction of housing suitable to their needs at prices they might be able to afford. The fact that the harm to petitioners may have resulted indirectly does not in itself preclude standing. When a governmental prohibition or restriction imposed on one party causes specific harm to a third party, harm that a constitutional provision or statute was intended to prevent, the indirectness of the injury does not necessarily deprive the person harmed of standing to vindicate his rights. But it may make it substantially more difficult to meet the minimum requirement of Art. III: to establish that, in fact, the asserted injury was the consequence of the defendants' actions, or that prospective relief will remove the harm.

Here, by their own admission, realization of petitioners' desire to live in Penfield always has depended on the efforts and willingness of third parties to build low- and moderate-cost housing. The record specifically refers to only two such efforts: that of Penfield Better Homes Corp., in late 1969, to obtain the rezoning of certain land in Penfield to allow the construction of subsidized cooperative townhouses that could be purchased by persons of moderate income; and a similar effort by O'Brien Homes, Inc., in late 1971.[15] But the record is devoid of any indication that these projects, or other like projects, would have satisfied petitioners' needs at prices they could afford, or that, were the court to remove the obstructions attributable to respondents, such relief would benefit petitioners. Indeed, petitioners' descriptions of their individual financial situations and housing needs suggest precisely the contrary—that their inability to reside in Penfield is the consequence of the economics of the area housing market, rather than of respondents' assertedly illegal acts.[16] In short, the facts alleged

---

15. Penfield Better Homes contemplated a series of one- to three-bedroom units and hoped to sell them—at that time—to persons who earned from $5,000 to $8,000 per year. The Penfield Planning Board denied the necessary variance on September 9, 1969, because of incompatibility with the surrounding neighborhood, projected traffic congestion, and problems of severe soil erosion during construction. O'Brien Homes, Inc., projected 51 buildings, each containing four family units, designed for single people and small families, and capable of being purchased by persons 'of low income and accumulated funds' and 'of moderate income with limited funds for down payment....' The variance for this project was denied by the Planning Board on October 12, 1971; a revision of the proposal was reconsidered by the Planning Board in April 1972, and, from all indications of record, apparently remains under consideration. The record also indicates the existence of several proposals for 'planned unit developments'; but we are not told whether these projects would allow sale at prices that persons of low or moderate income are likely to be able to afford. There is, more importantly, not the slightest suggestion that they would be adequate, and of sufficiently low cost, to meet these petitioners' needs.

16. Ortiz states in his affidavit that he is now purchasing and resides in a six-bedroom dwelling in Wayland, N.Y.; and that he owns and receives rental income from a house in Rochester. He is concerned with finding a house or apartment large enough for himself, his wife, and seven children, but states that he can afford to spend a maximum of $120 per month for housing. Broadnax seeks a four-bedroom house or apartment for herself and six children, and can spend a maximum of about $120 per month for housing. Sinkler also states that she can spend $120 per month for housing for herself

fail to support an actionable causal relationship between Penfield's zoning practices and petitioners' asserted injury.

* * *

We hold only that a plaintiff who seeks to challenge exclusionary zoning practices must allege specific, concrete facts demonstrating that the challenged practices harm him, and that he personally would benefit in a tangible way from the court's intervention.[18] Absent the necessary allegations of demonstrable, particularized injury, there can be no confidence of "a real need to exercise the power of judicial review" or that relief can be framed "no broader than required by the precise facts to which the court's ruling would be applied."

IV

The petitioners who assert standing on the basis of their status as taxpayers of the city of Rochester present a different set of problems. These "taxpayer-petitioners" claim that they are suffering economic injury consequent to Penfield's allegedly discriminatory and exclusionary zoning practices. Their argument, in brief, is that Penfield's persistent refusal to allow or to facilitate construction of low- and moderate-cost housing forces the city of Rochester to provide more such housing than it otherwise would do; that to provide such housing, Rochester must allow certain tax abatements; and that as the amount of tax-abated property increases, Rochester taxpayers are forced to assume an increased tax burden in order to finance essential public services.

"Of course, pleadings must be something more than an ingenious academic exercise in the conceivable." We think the complaint of the taxpayer-petitioners is little more than such an exercise. Apart from the conjectural nature of the asserted injury, the line of causation between Penfield's actions and such injury is not apparent from the complaint. Whatever may occur in Penfield, the injury complained of—increases in taxation—results only from decisions made by the appropriate Rochester authorities, who are not parties to this case.

But even if we assume that the taxpayer-petitioners could establish that Penfield's zoning practices harm them, their complaint nonetheless was properly dismissed. Petitioners do not, even if they could, assert any personal right under the Constitution

---

and two children. Thus, at least in the cases of Ortiz and Broadnax, it is doubtful that their stated needs could have been satisfied by the small housing units contemplated in the only moderate-cost projects specifically described in the record. Moreover, there is no indication that any of the petitioners had the resources necessary to acquire the housing available in the projects. The matter is left entirely obscure....

18. This is not to say that the plaintiff who challenges a zoning ordinance or zoning practices must have a present contractual interest in a particular project. A particularized personal interest may be shown in various ways, which we need not undertake to identify in the abstract. But usually the initial focus should be on a particular project. We also note that zoning laws and their provisions, long considered essential to effective urban planning, are peculiarly within the province of state and local legislative authorities. They are, of course, subject to judicial review in a proper case. But citizens dissatisfied with provisions of such laws need not overlook the availability of the normal democratic process.

or any statute to be free of action by a neighboring municipality that may have some incidental adverse effect on Rochester. On the contrary, the only basis of the taxpayer-petitioners' claim is that Penfield's zoning ordinance and practices violate the constitutional and statutory rights of third parties, namely, persons of low and moderate income who are said to be excluded from Penfield. In short the claim of these petitioners falls squarely within the prudential standing rule that normally bars litigants from asserting the rights or legal interests of others in order to obtain relief from injury to themselves. As we have observed above, this rule of judicial self-governance is subject to exceptions, the most prominent of which is that Congress may remove it by statute. Here, however, no statute expressly or by clear implication grants a right of action, and thus standing to seek relief, to persons in petitioners' position. In several cases, this Court has allowed standing to litigate the rights of third parties when enforcement of the challenged restriction against the litigant would result indirectly in the violation of third parties' rights. But the taxpayer-petitioners are not themselves subject to Penfield's zoning practices. Nor do they allege that the challenged zoning ordinance and practices preclude or otherwise adversely affect a relationship existing between them and the persons whose rights assertedly are violated. No relationship, other than an incidental congruity of interest, is alleged to exist between the Rochester taxpayers and persons who have been precluded from living in Penfield. Nor do the taxpayer-petitioners show that their prosecution of the suit is necessary to insure protection of the rights asserted, as there is no indication that persons who in fact have been excluded from Penfield are disabled from asserting their own right in a proper case. In sum, we discern no justification for recognizing in the Rochester taxpayers a right of action on the asserted claim.

## V

We turn next to the standing problems presented by the petitioner associations—Metro-Act of Rochester, Inc., one of the original plaintiffs; Housing Council in the Monroe County Area, Inc., which the original plaintiffs sought to join as a party-plaintiff; and Rochester Home Builders Association, Inc., which moved in the District Court for leave to intervene as plaintiff. There is no question that an association may have standing in its own right to seek judicial relief from injury to itself and to vindicate whatever rights and immunities the association itself may enjoy. Moreover, in attempting to secure relief from injury to itself the association may assert the rights of its members, at least so long as the challenged infractions adversely affect its members' associational ties. With the limited exception of Metro-Act, however, none of the associational petitioners here has asserted injury to itself.

Even in the absence of injury to itself, an association may have standing solely as the representative of its members. The possibility of such representational standing, however, does not eliminate or attenuate the constitutional requirement of a case or controversy. The association must allege that its members, or any one of them, are suffering immediate or threatened injury as a result of the challenged action of the sort that would make out a justiciable case had the members themselves brought suit. So long as this can be established, and so long as the nature of the claim and of the relief sought does not make the individual participation of each injured party indispensable to proper resolution of the cause, the association may be an appropriate representative of its members, entitled to invoke the court's jurisdiction.

* * *

B

Petitioner Home Builders, in its intervenor-complaint, asserted standing to represent its member firms engaged in the development and construction of residential housing in the Rochester area, including Penfield. Home Builders alleged that the Penfield zoning restrictions, together with refusals by the town officials to grant variances and permits for the construction of low- and moderate-cost housing, had deprived some of its members of "substantial business opportunities and profits." ... Home Builders claimed damages of $750,000 and also joined in the original plaintiffs' prayer for declaratory and injunctive relief.

As noted above, to justify any relief the association must show that it has suffered harm, or that one or more of its members are injured. But, apart from this, whether an association has standing to invoke the court's remedial powers on behalf of its members depends in substantial measure on the nature of the relief sought. If in a proper case the association seeks a declaration, injunction, or some other form of prospective relief, it can reasonably be supposed that the remedy, if granted, will inure to the benefit of those members of the association actually injured.... *Cf.* Fed. Rule Civ. Proc. 23(b)(2).

The present case, however, differs significantly as here an association seeks relief in damages for alleged injuries to its members. Home Builders alleges no monetary injury to itself, nor any assignment of the damages claims of its members. No award therefore can be made to the association as such. Moreover, in the circumstances of this case, the damages claims are not common to the entire membership, nor shared by all in equal degree. To the contrary, whatever injury may have been suffered is peculiar to the individual member concerned, and both the fact and extent of injury would require individualized proof. Thus, to obtain relief in damages, each member of Home Builders who claims injury as a result of respondents' practices must be a party to the suit, and Home Builders has no standing to claim damages on his behalf.

Home Builders' prayer for prospective relief fails for a different reason. It can have standing as the representative of its members only if it has alleged facts sufficient to make out a case or controversy had the members themselves brought suit. No such allegations were made. The complaint refers to no specific project of any of its members that is currently precluded either by the ordinance or by respondents' action in enforcing it....

A like problem is presented with respect to petitioner Housing Council. The affidavit accompanying the motion to join it as plaintiff states that the Council includes in its membership "at least seventeen" groups that have been, are, or will be involved in the development of low- and moderate-cost housing. But, with one exception, the complaint does not suggest that any of these groups has focused its efforts on Penfield or has any specific plan to do so. Again with the same exception, neither the complaint nor any materials of record indicate that any member of Housing Council has taken any step toward building housing in Penfield, or has had dealings of any nature with respondents. The exception is the Penfield Better Homes Corp. As we have observed above, it applied to respondents in late 1969 for a zoning variance to allow construction of a housing project designed for persons of moderate income. The affidavit in support of the motion to join Housing Council refers specifically to this effort, and the supporting materials detail at some length the circumstances surrounding the rejection of Better Homes' application. It is therefore possible that in 1969, or within a reasonable time thereafter, Better Homes itself and possibly Housing Council as its representative would have had standing to seek review of respondents' action. The complaint, however, does not allege that the Penfield Better Homes project remained viable in 1972 when this complaint was filed, or that respondents' actions continued to block a then-current construction project. In short, neither the complaint nor the record supplies any basis from which to infer that the controversy between respondents and Better Homes, however vigorous it may once have been, remained a live, concrete dispute when this complaint was filed.

## VI

The rules of standing, whether as aspects of the Art. III case-or-controversy requirement or as reflections of prudential considerations defining and limiting the role of the courts, are threshold determinants of the propriety of judicial intervention. It is the responsibility of the complainant clearly to allege facts demonstrating that he is a proper party to invoke judicial resolution of the dispute and the exercise of the court's remedial powers. We agree with the District Court and the Court of Appeals that none of the petitioners here has met this threshold requirement. Accordingly, the judgment of the Court of Appeals is

Affirmed.

MR. JUSTICE BRENNAN, with whom MR. JUSTICE WHITE and MR. JUSTICE MARSHALL join, dissenting.

… The Court today, in an opinion that purports to be a "standing" opinion but that actually, I believe, has overtones of outmoded notions of pleading and of justiciability, refuses to find that any of the variously situated plaintiffs can clear numerous hurdles, some constructed here for the first time, necessary to establish "standing." While the Court gives lip service to the principle … that "standing in no way depends on the merits of the plaintiff's contention that particular conduct is illegal," in fact the opinion, which tosses out of court almost every conceivable kind of plaintiff who could be injured by the activity claimed to be unconstitutional, can be explained only by an indefensible hostility to the claim on the merits. I can appreciate the Court's reluctance to adjudicate the complex and difficult legal questions involved in determining the constitutionality of practices which assertedly limit residence in a particular municipality to those who are white and relatively well off, and I also understand that the merits of this case could involve grave sociological and political ramifications. But courts cannot refuse to hear a case on the merits merely because they would prefer not to, and it is quite clear, when the record is viewed with dispassion, that at least three of the groups of plaintiffs have made allegations, and supported them with affidavits and documentary evidence, sufficient to survive a motion to dismiss for lack of standing.

I

Before considering the three groups I believe clearly to have standing—the low-income, minority plaintiffs, Rochester Home Builders Association, Inc., and the Housing Council in the Monroe County Area, Inc.—it will be helpful to review the picture painted by the allegations as a whole, in order better to comprehend the interwoven interests of the various plaintiffs. Indeed, one glaring defect of the Court's opinion is that it views each set of plaintiffs as if it were prosecuting a separate lawsuit, refusing to recognize that the interests are intertwined, and that the standing of any one group must take into account its position vis-à-vis the others. For example, the Court says that the low-income minority plaintiffs have not alleged facts sufficient to show that but for the exclusionary practices claimed, they would be able to reside in Penfield. The Court then intimates that such a causal relationship could be shown only if "the initial focus [is] on a particular project." Later, the Court objects to the ability of the Housing Council to prosecute the suit on behalf of its member, Penfield Better Homes Corp., *despite* the fact that Better Homes *had* displayed an interest in a particular project, because that project was no longer live. Thus, we must suppose that even if the low-income plaintiffs had alleged a desire to live in the Better Homes project, that allegation would be insufficient because it appears that that particular project might never be built. The rights of low-income minority plaintiffs who desire to live in a locality, then, seem to turn on the willingness of a third party to litigate the legality of preclusion of a particular project, despite the fact that the third party may have no economic incentive to incur the costs of litigation with regard to one project, and despite the fact that the low-income minority plaintiffs' interest is *not* to live in a particular project but to live somewhere in the town in a dwelling they can afford.

Accepting, as we must, the various allegations and affidavits as true, the following picture emerges: The Penfield zoning ordinance, by virtue of regulations concerning "lot area, set backs, ... population density, density of use, units per acre, floor area, sewer requirements, traffic flow, ingress and egress[, and] street location," makes "practically and economically impossible the construction of sufficient numbers of low and moderate income" housing. The *purpose* of this ordinance was to preclude low- and moderate-income people and nonwhites from living in Penfield, and, particularly because of refusals to grant zoning variances and building permits and by using special permit procedures and other devices, ... the defendants succeeded in keeping "low and moderate income persons ... and non-white persons ... from residing within ... Penfield."

As a result of these practices, various of the plaintiffs were affected in different ways. For example, plaintiffs Ortiz, Reyes, Sinkler, and Broadnax, persons of low or moderate income and members of minority groups, alleged that "*as a result*" of respondents' exclusionary scheme, they could not live in Penfield, although they desired and attempted to do so, and consequently incurred greater commuting costs, lived in substandard housing, and had fewer services for their families and poorer schools for their children than if they had lived in Penfield. Members of the Rochester Home Builders Association were prevented from constructing homes for low- and moderate-income people in Penfield, harming them economically. And Penfield Better Homes, a member of the Housing Council, was frustrated in its attempt to build moderate-income housing.

Thus, the portrait which emerges from the allegations and affidavits is one of total, purposeful, intransigent exclusion of certain classes of people from the town, pursuant to a conscious scheme never deviated from. Because of this scheme, those interested in building homes for the excluded groups were faced with insurmountable difficulties, and those of the excluded groups seeking homes in the locality quickly learned that their attempts were futile. Yet, the Court turns the very success of the allegedly unconstitutional scheme into a barrier to a lawsuit seeking its invalidation. In effect, the Court tells the low income minority and building company plaintiffs they will not be permitted to prove what they have alleged—that they could and would build and live in the town if changes were made in the zoning ordinance and its application—because they have not succeeded in breaching, before the suit was filed, the very barriers which are the subject of the suit.

## II

### *Low-Income and Minority Plaintiffs*

As recounted above, plaintiffs Ortiz, Broadnax, Reyes, and Sinkler alleged that "as a result" of respondents' exclusionary practices, they were unable, despite attempts, to find the housing they desired in Penfield, and consequently have incurred high commuting expenses, received poorer municipal services, and, in some instances, have been relegated to live in substandard housing. The Court does not, as it could not, suggest that the injuries, if proved, would be insufficient to give petitioners the requisite "personal stake in the outcome of the controversy as to assure the concrete adverseness which sharpens the presentation of issues." Rather, it is abundantly clear that the harm *alleged* satisfies the "injury in fact, economic or otherwise," requirement which is prerequisite to standing in federal court....

Instead, the Court insists that these petitioners' allegations are insufficient to show that the harms suffered were *caused* by respondents' allegedly unconstitutional practices, because "their inability to reside in Penfield [may be] the consequence of the economics of the area housing market, rather than of respondents' assertedly illegal acts."

True, this Court has held that to maintain standing, a plaintiff must not only allege an injury but must also assert a "'direct' relationship between the alleged injury and the claim sought to be adjudicated,"—that is "the party who invokes [judicial] power must be able to show ... that he has sustained or is immediately in danger of sustaining some direct injury *as the result* of [a statute's] enforcement." But, as the allegations recited above show, these petitioners have alleged precisely what our cases require—

that *because* of the exclusionary practices of respondents, they cannot live in Penfield and have suffered harm.

Thus, the Court's real holding is not that these petitioners have not *alleged* an injury resulting from respondents' action, but that they are not to be allowed to prove one, because "realization of petitioners' desire to live in Penfield always has depended on the efforts and willingness of third parties to build low- and moderate-cost housing," and "the record is devoid of any indication that ... [any] projects, would have satisfied petitioners' needs at prices they could afford."

Certainly, this is not the sort of demonstration that can or should be required of petitioners at this preliminary stage....

Here, the very fact that, as the Court stresses, these petitioners' claim rests in part upon proving the intentions and capabilities of third parties to build in Penfield suitable housing which they can afford, coupled with the exclusionary character of the claim on the merits, makes it particularly inappropriate to assume that these petitioners' lack of specificity reflects a fatal weakness in their theory of causation. Obviously they cannot be expected, prior to discovery and trial, to know the future plans of building companies, the precise details of the housing market in Penfield, or everything which has transpired in 15 years of application of the Penfield zoning ordinance, including every housing plan suggested and refused. To require them to allege such facts is to require them to prove their case on paper in order to get into court at all, reverting to the form of fact pleading long abjured in the federal courts. This Court has not required such unachievable specificity in standing cases in the past, and the fact that it does so now can only be explained by an indefensible determination by the Court to close the doors of the federal courts to claims of this kind. Understandably, today's decision will be read as revealing hostility to breaking down even unconstitutional zoning barriers that frustrate the deep human yearning of low-income and minority groups for decent housing they can afford in decent surroundings.

### III
### *Associations Including Building Concerns*

Two of the petitioners are organizations among whose members are building concerns. Both of these organizations, Home Builders and Housing Council, alleged that these concerns have attempted to build in Penfield low- and moderate-income housing, but have been stymied by the zoning ordinance and refusal to grant individual relief therefrom.

Specifically, Home Builders, a trade association of concerns engaged in constructing and maintaining residential housing in the Rochester area, alleged that "during the past 15 years, over 80% of the private housing units constructed in the Town of Penfield have been constructed by [its] members." Because of respondents' refusal to grant relief from Penfield's restrictive housing statutes, members of Home Builders could not proceed with planned low- and moderate-income housing projects, and thereby lost profits.

Housing Council numbers among its members at least 17 groups involved in the development and construction of low- and middle-income housing. In particular, one member, Penfield Better Homes, "*is* and has been actively attempting to develop moderate income housing in ... Penfield," but has been unable to secure the necessary approvals.

The Court finds that these two organizations lack standing to seek prospective relief for basically the same reasons: none of their members is, as far as the allegations show, *currently* involved in developing a *particular* project....

Again, the Court ignores the thrust of the complaints and asks petitioners to allege the impossible. According to the allegations, the building concerns' experience in the past with Penfield officials has shown any plans for low- and moderate-income housing to be futile for, again according to the allegations, the respondents are engaged in a purposeful, conscious scheme to exclude such housing. Particularly with regard to a low- or moderate-income project, the cost of litigating, with respect to any particular project, the legality of a refusal to approve it may well be prohibitive. And the merits of the exclusion of this or that project is not at the heart of the complaint; the claim is that respondents will not approve *any* project which will provide residences for low- and moderate-income people.

When this sort of pattern-and-practice claim is at the heart of the controversy, allegations of past injury, which members of both of these organizations have clearly made, and of a future intent, if the barriers are cleared, again to develop suitable housing for Penfield, should be more than sufficient. The past experiences, if proved at trial, will give credibility and substance to the claim of interest in future building activity in Penfield. These parties, if their allegations are proved, certainly have the requisite personal stake in the outcome of *this* controversy, and the Court's conclusion otherwise is only a conclusion that *this* controversy may not be litigated in a federal court.

I would reverse the judgment of the Court of Appeals.

## *Note: Applying the Injury, Causation and Redressability Requirements*

1. After *Warth*, what does the Supreme Court require before it will hold that a plaintiff meets Article III's standing requirements? In the years after *Warth*, the Supreme Court began providing an answer. In *Village of Arlington Heights v. Metropolitan Housing Development Corporation*, 429 U.S. 252 (1977), the Court considered an equal protection challenge to a municipality's zoning decision effectively prohibiting a non-profit housing developer from building a federally-subsidized racially integrated housing complex in the village. The plaintiffs were the developer and an African-American individual who testified that he would likely become a resident of the complex if it was built. The Court held that both plaintiffs had standing. As to the developer, the Court noted that the project (perhaps in contrast to the embryonic or lapsed projects in *Warth*) had advanced quite a way toward completion: among other actions, the developer had leased the land and commissioned architectural plans for

the complex. The court dismissed the village's argument that the project still had to overcome substantial hurdles other than the zoning decision, such as financing, concluding that "all housing developments are subject to some extent to similar uncertainties." As to the individual, the Court noted his testimony indicating that he worked in the defendant municipality but lived 20 miles away, and wanted to live closer to his work, and that he would probably move into the complex if it was built. The Court also noted that the complaint alleged that the individual would qualify for residence there. Given these facts, the Court held that there was "an actionable causal relationship" between the injury suffered by these two plaintiffs and the defendant's actions.

2. Questions of causation and redressability have continued to present problems for the Court. Often the causation/redressability analysis turns on assumptions, sometimes unstated, about the nature of the injury the plaintiff claims. Consider *Simon v. Eastern Kentucky Welfare Rights Organization*, 426 U.S. 26 (1976). *Simon* involved a challenge to an Internal Revenue Service (IRS) Revenue Ruling that reduced the amount of free or low-cost care hospitals had to provide in order to qualify as a charity hospital. (Charity status is desirable because it makes contributions to the hospital tax-deductible.)

The plaintiffs included several nonprofit corporations, each of which included low-income persons among its members and represented the interests of all such persons in obtaining hospital care. The named plaintiffs also included twelve people who described themselves as "subsisting below the poverty income levels established by the Federal Government and suffering from medical conditions requiring hospital services." Plaintiffs offered proof that hospitals had discriminated against them in obtaining medical care on the basis of their indigency. The complaint alleged that "by extending tax benefits to such hospitals despite their refusals fully to serve the indigent, the defendants were 'encouraging' the hospitals to deny services to the individual plaintiffs and to the members and clients of the plaintiff organizations. Those persons were alleged to be suffering "injury in their opportunity and ability to receive hospital services in nonprofit hospitals which receive ... benefits ... as 'charitable' organizations" under the Internal Revenue Code.

The Court concluded that plaintiffs lacked standing. Discussing the individual-plaintiffs' standing claims, the Court said:

> [It] does not follow from the allegation and its corollary that the denial of access to hospital services in fact results from [the IRS's] new Ruling, or that a court-ordered return by petitioner [IRS] to [its] previous policy would result in these [plaintiffs'] receiving the hospital services they desire. It is purely speculative whether the denials of service specified in the complaint fairly can be traced to [the IRS's] 'encouragement' or instead result from decisions made by the hospitals without regard to the tax implications.... It is equally speculative whether the desired exercise of the court's remedial powers in this suit would result in the availability to [plaintiffs] of such services.

Justice Brennan, joined by Justice Marshall, concurred in the judgment on a narrower ground. He criticized the majority's standing analysis:

> [The plaintiffs'] claim is not ... that they have been and will be illegally denied the provision of indigent medical services by the hospitals. Rather, ... it is that the Internal Revenue Code requires the Government to offer economic inducements to the relevant hospitals only under conditions which are likely to benefit [the plaintiffs]. The relevant injury in light of this claim is, then, injury to this beneficial interest—as [plaintiffs] alleged, injury to their 'opportunity and ability' to receive medical services. Respondents sufficiently alleged this injury and, if, as the Court ... assumes, they had made a showing sufficient to create an issue of material fact that the Government was injuring this interest, they would continue to possess standing to press the claim on the merits.

Compare *Simon* with *Northeastern Florida Chapter of the Associated General Contractors of America v. Jacksonville*, 508 U.S. 656 (1993). *Northeastern Florida* involved a contracting association's equal protection challenge to a city's program setting aside a percentage of city contracts for minority-owned businesses. (The constitutionality of such programs is discussed later in this book, in Chapter 13). The Court rejected the city's argument that the association did not have standing to seek an injunction against the program because there was no guarantee that any of the association's members would win any contracts let under a non-race-conscious system:

> When the government erects a barrier that makes it more difficult for members of one group to obtain a benefit than it is for members of another group, a member of the former group seeking to challenge the barrier need not allege that he would have obtained the benefit but for the barrier in order to establish standing. The "injury in fact" in an equal protection case of this variety is the denial of equal treatment resulting from the imposition of the barrier, not the ultimate inability to obtain the benefit.... To establish standing, therefore, a party challenging a set-aside program like Jacksonville's need only demonstrate that it is able and ready to bid on contracts and that a discriminatory policy prevents it from doing so on an equal basis.

The Court rejected the city's argument that *Warth v. Seldin*'s denial of standing to the building associations compelled a similar result in this case:

> ... [*Warth*] did not involve an allegation that some discriminatory classification prevented the plaintiff from competing on an equal footing in its quest for the benefit.... In *Warth* ... there was no claim that the construction association's members could not apply for variances and building permits on the same basis as other firms; what the association objected to were the "refusals by the town officials to *grant* variances and permits." *Warth*. The firms' complaint, in other words, was not that they could not compete equally; it was that they did not win.

3. The Court elaborated on this analysis in *Adarand Constructors, Inc. v. Pena*, 515 U.S. 200 (1995). *Adarand* involved a road builder's challenge to a federal contracting

set-aside similar to the one in *Northeastern Florida*. The Court found that Adarand (the plaintiff-road builder) had standing to request an injunction against future use of race in administration of the program:

> Adarand, in addition to its general prayer for "such other and further relief as to the Court seems just and equitable," specifically seeks declaratory and injunctive relief against any *future* use of subcontractor compensation clauses. Before reaching the merits of Adarand's challenge, we must consider whether Adarand has standing to seek forward looking relief. Adarand's allegation that it has lost a contract in the past because of a subcontractor compensation clause of course entitles it to seek damages for the loss of that contract. [As] we explained in *Los Angeles v. Lyons*, 461 U.S. 95 (1983), the fact of past injury, "while presumably affording [the plaintiff] standing to claim damages…, does nothing to establish a real and immediate threat that he would again" suffer similar injury in the future.
>
> If Adarand is to maintain its claim for forward looking relief, our cases require it to allege that the use of subcontractor compensation clauses in the future constitutes "an invasion of a legally protected interest which is (a) concrete and particularized, and (b) actual or imminent, not conjectural or hypothetical." *Lujan v. Defenders of Wildlife*, 504 U.S. 555 (1992). Adarand's claim that the Government's use of subcontractor compensation clauses denies it equal protection of the laws of course alleges an invasion of a legally protected interest, and it does so in a manner that is "particularized" as to Adarand.… [Adarand] need not demonstrate that it has been, or will be, the low bidder on a Government contract. The injury in cases of this kind is that a "discriminatory classification prevents the plaintiff from competing on an equal footing." *Northeastern Florida*. The aggrieved party "need not allege that he would have obtained the benefit but for the barrier in order to establish standing." *Id.*…
>
> It is less clear, however, that the future use of subcontractor compensation clauses will cause Adarand "imminent" injury. We said in *Lujan* that "although 'imminence' is concededly a somewhat elastic concept, it cannot be stretched beyond its purpose, which is to insure that the alleged injury is not too speculative for Article III purposes — that the injury is '*certainly* impending.'" *Lujan*. We therefore must ask whether Adarand has made an adequate showing that sometime in the relatively near future it will bid on another Government contract that offers financial incentives to a prime contractor for hiring disadvantaged subcontractors.
>
> We conclude that Adarand has satisfied this requirement. Adarand's general manager said in a deposition that his company bids on every guardrail project in Colorado. According to documents produced in discovery, the [state highway department] let 14 prime contracts in Colorado that included guardrail work between 1983 and 1990.… Statistics from the years 1983 through 1990 indicate that the [department] lets on average 1 1/2 contracts per year that

could injure Adarand in the manner it alleges here. Nothing in the record suggests that the [department] has altered the frequency with which it lets contracts that include guardrail work. And the record indicates that Adarand often must compete for contracts against companies certified as small disadvantaged businesses. Because the evidence in this case indicates that the [department] is likely to let contracts involving guardrail work that contain a subcontractor compensation clause at least once per year in Colorado, that Adarand is very likely to bid on each such contract, and that Adarand often must compete for such contracts against small disadvantaged businesses, we are satisfied that Adarand has standing to bring this lawsuit.

4. Can the analysis in *Eastern Simon* be harmonized with that in *Northeastern Florida* and *Adarand*? If the Court correctly describes the injury in the latter two cases, then why isn't Justice Brennan's description of the injury in *Simon* also correct? Given these cases, what allegations should you make in a complaint challenging government action that doesn't immediately and directly harm your client, but which makes that harm more likely? What does your answer suggest about the injury, causation and redressability requirements in standing doctrine?

## Singleton v. Wulff
### 428 U.S. 106 (1976)

Mr. Justice Blackmun delivered the opinion of the Court (Parts I, II-A, and III) together with an opinion (Part II-B), in which Mr. Justice Brennan, Mr. Justice White, and Mr. Justice Marshall joined.

[This] case involves a claim of a State's unconstitutional interference with the decision to terminate pregnancy. The particular object of the challenge is a Missouri statute excluding abortions that are not "medically indicated" from the purposes for which Medicaid benefits are available to needy persons. In its present posture, however, the case presents two issues not going to the merits of this dispute. The first is whether the plaintiff-appellees, as physicians who perform nonmedically indicated abortions, have standing to maintain the suit, to which we answer that they do....

II.

* * *

A. There is no doubt now that the respondent-physicians suffer concrete injury from the operation of the challenged statute. Their complaint and affidavits, described above, allege that they have performed and will continue to perform operations for which they would be reimbursed under the Medicaid program, were it not for the limitation of reimbursable abortions to those that are "medically indicated." If the physicians prevail in their suit to remove this limitation, they will benefit, for they will then receive payment for the abortions. The State (and Federal Government) will be out of pocket by the amount of the payments. The relationship between the parties is classically adverse, and there clearly exists between them a case or controversy....

B.[*] The question of what rights the doctors may assert in seeking to resolve that controversy is more difficult. The Court of Appeals adverted to what it perceived to be the doctor's own "constitutional rights to practice medicine." We have no occasion to decide whether such rights exist. Assuming that they do, the doctors, of course, can assert them. It appears, however, that the Court of Appeals also accorded the doctors standing to assert, and indeed granted them relief based partly upon, the rights of their patients. We must decide whether this assertion of *jus tertii* was a proper one.

Federal courts must hesitate before resolving a controversy, even one within their constitutional power to resolve, on the basis of the rights of third persons not parties to the litigation. The reasons are two. First, the courts should not adjudicate such rights unnecessarily, and it may be that in fact the holders of those rights either do not wish to assert them, or will be able to enjoy them regardless of whether the in-court litigant is successful or not. Second, third parties themselves usually will be the best proponents of their own rights. The courts depend on effective advocacy, and therefore should prefer to construe legal rights only when the most effective advocates of those rights are before them. The holders of the rights may have a like preference, to the extent they will be bound by the courts' decisions under the doctrine of *stare decisis*.... These two considerations underlie the Court's general rule "Ordinarily, one may not claim standing in this Court to vindicate the constitutional rights of some third party." *Barrows v. Jackson*, 346 U.S. 249 (1953).

Like any general rule, however, this one should not be applied where its underlying justifications are absent. With this in mind, the Court has looked primarily to two factual elements to determine whether the rule should apply in a particular case. The first is the relationship of the litigant to the person whose right he seeks to assert.... The relationship between the litigant and the third party may be such that the former is fully, or very nearly, as effective a proponent of the right as the latter. Thus in *Griswold v. Connecticut*, 381 U.S. 479 (1965), where two persons had been convicted of giving advice on contraception, the Court permitted the defendants, one of whom was a licensed physician, to assert the privacy rights of the married persons whom they advised.... A doctor-patient relationship similar to that in *Griswold* existed in *Doe v. Bolton*, 410 U.S. 179 (1973), where the Court also permitted physicians to assert the rights of their patients. Indeed, since that right was the right to an abortion, *Doe* would flatly control the instant case were it not for the fact that there the physicians were seeking protection from possible criminal prosecution.

The other factual element to which the Court has looked is the ability of the third party to assert his own right. Even where the relationship is close, the reasons for requiring persons to assert their own rights will generally still apply. If there is some genuine obstacle to such assertion, however, the third party's absence from court

---

* [This part of Justice Blackmun's opinion spoke only for four justices.]

loses its tendency to suggest that his right is not truly at stake, or truly important to him, and the party who is in court becomes by default the right's best available proponent. . . .

Application of these principles to the present case quickly yields its proper result. The closeness of the relationship is patent, as it was in *Griswold* and in *Doe*. A woman cannot safely secure an abortion without the aid of a physician, and an impecunious woman cannot easily secure an abortion without the physician's being paid by the State. The woman's exercise of her right to an abortion, whatever its dimension, is therefore necessarily at stake here. Moreover, the constitutionally protected abortion decision is one in which the physician is intimately involved. Aside from the woman herself, therefore, the physician is uniquely qualified to litigate the constitutionality of the State's interference with, or discrimination against, that decision.

As to the woman's assertion of her own rights, there are several obstacles. For one thing, she may be chilled from such assertion by a desire to protect the very privacy of her decision from the publicity of a court suit. A second obstacle is the imminent mootness, at least in the technical sense, of any individual woman's claim. Only a few months, at the most, after the maturing of the decision to undergo an abortion, her right thereto will have been irrevocably lost, assuming, as it seems fair to assume, that unless the impecunious woman can establish Medicaid eligibility she must forgo abortion. It is true that these obstacles are not insurmountable. Suit may be brought under a pseudonym, as so frequently has been done. A woman who is no longer pregnant may nonetheless retain the right to litigate the point because it is "capable of repetition yet evading review." *Roe v. Wade*, 410 U.S. 113 (1973). And it may be that a class could be assembled, whose fluid membership always included some women with live claims. But if the assertion of the right is to be "representative" to such an extent anyway, there seems little loss in terms of effective advocacy from allowing its assertion by a physician.

For these reasons, we conclude that it generally is appropriate to allow a physician to assert the rights of women patients as against governmental interference with the abortion decision, and we decline to restrict our holding to that effect in *Doe* to its purely criminal context. In this respect, the judgment of the Court of Appeals is affirmed. . . .

Mr. Justice Stevens, concurring in part. [omitted]

Mr. Justice Powell, with whom The Chief Justice, Mr. Justice Stewart, and Mr. Justice Rehnquist join, concurring in part and dissenting in part. . . .

[Prior precedent holds] that a party may assert another's rights . . . , not when there is merely some "obstacle" to the rightholder's own litigation, but when such litigation is in all practicable terms impossible. Thus, in its framing of this principle, the plurality has gone far beyond our major precedents.

[The] litigation of third-party rights cannot be justified in this case. The plurality virtually concedes, as it must, that the two alleged "obstacles" to the women's assertion of their rights are chimerical. Our docket regularly contains cases in which women, using pseudonyms, challenge statutes that allegedly infringe their right to exercise the abortion decision. Nor is there basis for the "obstacle" of incipient mootness when the plurality itself quotes from the portion of *Roe v. Wade* that shows no such obstacle exists....

### B

The plurality places primary reliance on a second element, the existence of a "confidential relationship" between the rightholder and the party seeking to assert her rights. Focusing on the professional relationships present in *Griswold, Doe* and *Planned Parenthood of Missouri v. Danforth*, 428 U.S. 52 (1976), the plurality suggests that allowing the physicians in this case to assert their patients' rights flows naturally from those three....

### C

The physicians have offered no special reason for allowing them to assert their patients' rights in an attack on this welfare statute, and I can think of none. Moreover, there are persuasive reasons not to permit them to do so. It seems wholly inappropriate, as a matter of judicial self-governance, for a court to reach unnecessarily to decide a difficult constitutional issue in a case in which nothing more is at stake than remuneration for professional services. And second, this case may well set a precedent that will prove difficult to cabin. No reason immediately comes to mind, after today's holding, why any provider of services should be denied standing to assert his client's or customer's constitutional rights, if any, in an attack on a welfare statute that excludes from coverage his particular transaction....

## Havens Realty Corp. v. Coleman
### 455 U.S. 363 (1982)

JUSTICE BRENNAN delivered the opinion of the Court....

### I

... Defendants were alleged to have engaged in "racial steering"[1] violative of §804 of the Fair Housing Act of 1968, 42 U.S.C. §3604 (Act or Fair Housing Act). The complaint, seeking declaratory, injunctive, and monetary relief, was filed in the United States District Court for the Eastern District of Virginia in January 1979 by three individuals—Paul Coles, Sylvia Coleman, and R. Kent Willis—and an organization—Housing Opportunities Made Equal (HOME).

---

1. As defined in the complaint, "racial steering" is a "practice by which real estate brokers and agents preserve and encourage patterns of racial segregation in available housing by steering members of racial and ethnic groups to buildings occupied primarily by members of such racial and ethnic groups and away from buildings and neighborhoods inhabited primarily by members of other races or groups."

At the time suit was brought, defendant Havens owned and operated two apartment complexes, Camelot Townhouses and Colonial Court Apartments, in Henrico County, Va., a suburb of Richmond. The complaint identified Paul Coles as a black "renter plaintiff" who, attempting to rent an apartment from Havens, inquired on July 13, 1978, about the availability of an apartment at the Camelot complex, and was falsely told that no apartments were available. The other two individual plaintiffs, Coleman and Willis, were described in the complaint as "tester plaintiffs" who were employed by HOME to determine whether Havens practiced racial steering. Coleman, who is black, and Willis, who is white, each assertedly made inquiries of Havens on March 14, March 21, and March 23, 1978, regarding the availability of apartments. On each occasion, Coleman was told that no apartments were available; Willis was told that there were vacancies. On July 6, 1978, Coleman made a further inquiry and was told that there were no vacancies in the Camelot Townhouses; a white tester for HOME, who was not a party to the complaint, was given contrary information that same day. . . .

The three individual plaintiffs, who at the time the complaint was filed were all residents of the city of Richmond or the adjacent Henrico County averred that they had been injured by the discriminatory acts of petitioners. Coles, the black renter, claimed that he had been "denied the right to rent real property in Henrico County." Further, he and the two tester plaintiffs alleged that Havens' practices deprived them of the "important social, professional, business and economic, political and aesthetic benefits of interracial associations that arise from living in integrated communities free from discriminatory housing practices." And Coleman, the black tester, alleged that the misinformation given her by Havens concerning the availability of apartments in the Colonial Court and Camelot Townhouse complexes had caused her "specific injury." . . .

The District Court, on motion of petitioners, dismissed the claims of Coleman, Willis, and HOME. The District Court held that these plaintiffs lacked standing. . . . Each of the dismissed plaintiffs . . . appealed, and the Court of Appeals for the Fourth Circuit reversed and remanded for further proceedings. . . . We granted certiorari. . . .

### III

Our inquiry with respect to the standing issues raised in this case is guided by our decision in *Gladstone, Realtors v. Village of Bellwood*, 441 U.S. 91 (1979). There we considered whether six individuals and the village of Bellwood had standing to sue under §812 of the Fair Housing Act. . . . [We] concluded that the village and four of the individual plaintiffs did have standing to sue under the Fair Housing Act. In reaching that conclusion, we held that "Congress intended standing under §812 to extend to the full limits of Art. III" and that the courts accordingly lack the authority to create prudential barriers to standing in suits brought under that section. Thus the sole requirement for standing to sue under §812 is the Art. III minima of injury in fact: that the plaintiff allege that as a result of the defendant's actions he has suffered "a distinct and palpable injury," *Warth v. Seldin*. With this understanding, we proceed to determine whether each of the respondents in the present case has the requisite standing.

## A

The Court of Appeals held that Coleman and Willis have standing to sue in two capacities: as "testers" and as individuals deprived of the benefits of interracial association. We first address the question of "tester" standing.

In the present context, "testers" are individuals who, without an intent to rent or purchase a home or apartment, pose as renters or purchasers for the purpose of collecting evidence of unlawful steering practices. Section 804(d) states that it is unlawful for an individual or firm covered by the Act "to represent to *any person* because of race, color, religion, sex, or national origin that any dwelling is not available for inspection, sale, or rental when such dwelling is in fact so available," (emphasis added), a prohibition made enforceable through the creation of an explicit cause of action in §812(a) of the Act. Congress has thus conferred on all "persons" a legal right to truthful information about available housing.

This congressional intention cannot be overlooked in determining whether testers have standing to sue. As we have previously recognized, "the actual or threatened injury required by Art. III may exist solely by virtue of statutes creating legal rights, the invasion of which creates standing...." Section 804(d), which, in terms, establishes an enforceable right to truthful information concerning the availability of housing, is such an enactment. A tester who has been the object of a misrepresentation made unlawful under §804(d) has suffered injury in precisely the form the statute was intended to guard against, and therefore has standing to maintain a claim for damages under the Act's provisions. That the tester may have approached the real estate agent fully expecting that he would receive false information, and without any intention of buying or renting a home, does not negate the simple fact of injury within the meaning of §804(d). Whereas Congress, in prohibiting discriminatory refusals to sell or rent in §804(a) of the Act, required that there be a "bona fide offer" to rent or purchase, Congress plainly omitted any such requirement insofar as it banned discriminatory representations in §804(d).

In the instant case, respondent Coleman — the black tester — alleged injury to her statutorily created right to truthful housing information. As part of the complaint, she averred that petitioners told her on four different occasions that apartments were not available in the Henrico County complexes while informing white testers that apartments were available. If the facts are as alleged, then respondent has suffered "specific injury" from the challenged acts of petitioners, and the Art. III requirement of injury in fact is satisfied.

Respondent Willis' situation is different. He made no allegation that petitioners misrepresented to him that apartments were unavailable in the two apartment complexes. To the contrary, Willis alleged that on each occasion that he inquired he was informed that apartments *were* available. As such, Willis has alleged no injury to his statutory right to accurate information concerning the availability of housing. We thus discern no support for the Court of Appeals' holding that Willis has standing to sue in his capacity as a tester. More to the point, because Willis does not allege that he was a victim of a discriminatory misrepresentation, he has not pleaded a cause of action under § 804(d). We must therefore reverse the Court of Appeals' judgment insofar as it reversed the District Court's dismissal of Willis' "tester" claims.

## B

Coleman and Willis argue in this Court, and the Court of Appeals held, that irrespective of their status as testers, they should have been allowed to proceed beyond the pleading stage inasmuch as they have alleged that petitioners' steering practices deprived them of the benefits that result from living in an integrated community. This concept of "neighborhood" standing differs from that of "tester" standing in that the injury asserted is an indirect one: an adverse impact on the neighborhood in which the plaintiff resides resulting from the steering of persons other than the plaintiff. By contrast, the injury underlying tester standing—the denial of the tester's own statutory right to truthful housing information caused by misrepresentations to the tester—is a direct one. The distinction is between "third-party" and "first-party" standing.

This distinction is, however, of little significance in deciding whether a plaintiff has standing to sue under § 812 of the Fair Housing Act. *Bellwood*, as we have already noted, held that the only requirement for standing to sue under § 812 is the Art. III requirement of injury in fact. As long as respondents have alleged distinct and palpable injuries that are "fairly traceable" to petitioners' actions, the Art. III requirement of injury in fact is satisfied. The question before us, then, is whether injury in fact has been sufficiently alleged.

The two individual respondents, who according to the complaint were "residents of the City of Richmond or Henrico County," alleged that the racial steering practices of petitioners have deprived them of "the right to the important social, professional, business and economic, political and aesthetic benefits of interracial associations that arise from living in integrated communities free from discriminatory housing practices." ...

Petitioners do not dispute that the loss of social, professional, and economic benefits resulting from steering practices constitutes palpable injury. Instead, they contend that Coleman and Willis, by pleading simply that they were residents of the Richmond metropolitan area, have failed to demonstrate how the asserted steering practices of petitioners in Henrico County may have affected the *particular* neighborhoods in which the individual respondents resided.

It is indeed implausible to argue that petitioners' alleged acts of discrimination could have palpable effects throughout the *entire* Richmond metropolitan area. At the time relevant to this action the city of Richmond contained a population of nearly 220,000 persons, dispersed over 37 square miles. Henrico County occupied more than 232 square miles, in which roughly 170,000 people made their homes....

Nonetheless, in the absence of further factual development, we cannot say as a matter of law that no injury could be proved. Respondents have not identified the particular neighborhoods in which they lived, nor established the proximity of their homes to the site of petitioners' alleged steering practices. Further pleading and proof might establish that they lived in areas where petitioners' practices had an appreciable effect. Under the liberal federal pleading standards, we therefore agree with the Court of Appeals that dismissal on the pleadings is inappropriate at this stage of the litigation. At the same time, we note that the extreme generality of the complaint makes it impossible to say that respondents have made factual averments sufficient if true to demonstrate injury in fact. Accordingly, on remand, the District Court should afford the plaintiffs an opportunity to make more definite the allegations of the complaint. Cf. Fed. Rule Civ. Proc. 12(e). If after that opportunity the pleadings fail to make averments that meet the standing requirements established by the decisions of this Court, the claims should be dismissed....

JUSTICE POWELL, concurring.

In claiming standing based on a deprivation of the benefits of an integrated community, the individual respondents alleged generally that they lived in the city of Richmond or in Henrico County. This is an area of roughly 269 square miles, inhabited in 1978 by about 390,000 persons. Accordingly, as the Court holds, it is at best implausible that discrimination within two adjacent apartment complexes could give rise to "distinct and palpable injury," *Warth*, throughout this vast area. This, to me, is the constitutional core of the Court's decision. "Distinct and palpable" injury remains the minimal constitutional requirement for standing in a federal court.

Although I join the opinion of the Court, I write separately to emphasize my concern that the Art. III requirement of a genuine case or controversy not be deprived of all substance by meaningless pleading. Our prior cases have upheld standing, in cases of this kind, where the effects of discrimination were alleged to have occurred only within "a relatively compact neighborhood." *Gladstone*. By implication we today reaffirm that limitation. I therefore am troubled, not by the opinion of the Court, but by the record on which that opinion is based. After nearly four years of litigation we know only what the individual respondents chose to plead in their complaint—that they live or lived within a territory of 269 square miles, within which petitioners allegedly committed discrete acts of housing discrimination. The allegation would have been equally informative if the area assigned had been the Commonwealth of Virginia.

In *Warth*, we noted that a district court properly could deal with a vague averment as to standing by requiring amendment:

"It is within the trial court's power to allow or require the plaintiff to supply, by amendment to the complaint or by affidavits, further particularized allegations of fact deemed supportive of plaintiff's standing. If, after this opportunity, the plaintiff's standing does not adequately appear from all materials of record, the complaint must be dismissed."

The Federal Rules of Civil Procedure also permit a defendant to move for a more definite statement of the claims against him....

In this case neither the District Court nor apparently counsel for the parties took appropriate action to prevent the case from reaching an appellate court with only meaningless averments concerning the disputed question of standing. One can well understand the impatience of the District Court that dismissed the complaint. Yet our cases have established the preconditions to dismissal because of excessive vagueness with regard to standing, and those conditions were not observed. The result is more than a little absurd: Both the Court of Appeals and this Court have been called upon to parse pleadings devoid of any hint of support or nonsupport for an allegation essential to jurisdiction.

Liberal pleading rules have both their merit and their price. This is a textbook case of a high price—in terms of a severe imposition on already overburdened federal courts as well as unjustified expense to the litigants. This also is a particularly disturbing example of lax pleading, for it threatens to trivialize what we repeatedly have recognized as a *constitutional* requirement of Art. III standing.

In any event, in the context of this case, as it reaches us after some four years of confusing and profitless litigation, it is not within our province to order a dismissal. I therefore join the opinion of the Court.

## Lujan v. Defenders of Wildlife
### 504 U.S. 555 (1992)

JUSTICE SCALIA delivered the opinion of the Court with respect to Parts I, II, III-A, and IV, and an opinion with respect to Part III-B, in which THE CHIEF JUSTICE, JUSTICE WHITE, and JUSTICE THOMAS join.

This case involves a challenge to a rule promulgated by the Secretary of the Interior interpreting § 7 of the Endangered Species Act of 1973 (ESA), in such fashion as to render it applicable only to actions within the United States or on the high seas. The preliminary issue, and the only one we reach, is whether respondents here, plaintiffs below, have standing to seek judicial review of the rule.

I

The ESA seeks to protect species of animals against threats to their continuing existence caused by man. The ESA instructs the Secretary of the Interior to promulgate by regulation a list of those species which are either endangered or threatened under enumerated criteria, and to define the critical habitat of these species. Section 7(a)(2) of the Act then provides, in pertinent part:

> Each Federal agency shall, in consultation with and with the assistance of the Secretary [of the Interior], insure that any action authorized, funded, or carried out by such agency ... is not likely to jeopardize the continued existence of any endangered species or threatened species or result in the destruction or adverse modification of habitat of such species which is determined by the Secretary, after consultation as appropriate with affected States, to be critical.

In 1978, the Fish and Wildlife Service (FWS) and the National Marine Fisheries Service (NMFS), on behalf of the Secretary of the Interior and the Secretary of Commerce respectively, promulgated a joint regulation stating that the obligations imposed by § 7(a)(2) extend to actions taken in foreign nations. 43 Fed. Reg. 874 (1978). The next year, however, the Interior Department began to reexamine its position. A revised joint regulation, reinterpreting §7(a)(2) to require consultation only for actions taken in the United States or on the high seas, was proposed in 1983, and promulgated in 1986, 51 Fed. Reg. 19926.

Shortly thereafter, respondents, organizations dedicated to wildlife conservation and other environmental causes, filed this action against the Secretary of the Interior, seeking a declaratory judgment that the new regulation is in error as to the geographic scope of §7(a)(2) and an injunction requiring the Secretary to promulgate a new regulation restoring the initial interpretation. The District Court granted the Secretary's motion to dismiss for lack of standing. The Court of Appeals for the Eighth Circuit reversed by a divided vote....

## II

... Over the years, our cases have established that the irreducible constitutional minimum of standing contains three elements. First, the plaintiff must have suffered an "injury in fact"—an invasion of a legally protected interest which is (a) concrete and particularized,[1] and (b) "actual or imminent, not conjectural or hypothetical." Second, there must be a causal connection between the injury and the conduct complained of—the injury has to be "fairly ... traceable to the challenged action of the defendant, and not ... the result [of] the independent action of some third party not before the court." Third, it must be "likely," as opposed to merely "speculative," that the injury will be "redressed by a favorable decision." ...

When the suit is one challenging the legality of government action or inaction, the nature and extent of facts that must be averred (at the summary judgment stage) or proved (at the trial stage) in order to establish standing depends considerably upon whether the plaintiff is himself an object of the action (or forgone action) at issue. If he is, there is ordinarily little question that the action or inaction has caused him injury, and that a judgment preventing or requiring the action will redress it. When, however, as in this case, a plaintiff's asserted injury arises from the government's allegedly unlawful regulation (or lack of regulation) of someone else, much more is needed. In that circumstance, causation and redressability ordinarily hinge on the response of the regulated (or regulable) third party to the government action or inaction—and perhaps on the response of others as well. The existence of one or more of the essential elements of standing "depends on the unfettered choices made by independent actors not before the courts and whose exercise of broad and legitimate discretion the courts cannot presume either to control or to predict," *ASARCO Inc. v. Kadish*, 490 U.S. 605 (1989) (opinion of KENNEDY, J.); *see also Simon v. E. Ky. Welfare Rights Org.* 426 U.S. 26 (1976) [Note *supra.* this chapter]; and it becomes the burden of the plaintiff to adduce facts showing that those choices have been or will be made in such manner as to produce causation and permit redressability of injury. *E.g., Warth v. Seldin* (1974) [*Supra.* this chapter]. Thus, when the plaintiff is not him-

---

1. By particularized, we mean that the injury must affect the plaintiff in a personal and individual way.

self the object of the government action or inaction he challenges, standing is not precluded, but it is ordinarily "substantially more difficult" to establish.

### III

We think the Court of Appeals failed to apply the foregoing principles in denying the Secretary's motion for summary judgment. Respondents had not made the requisite demonstration of (at least) injury and redressability.

### A

Respondents' claim to injury is that the lack of consultation with respect to certain funded activities abroad "increases the rate of extinction of endangered and threatened species." Of course, the desire to use or observe an animal species, even for purely esthetic purposes, is undeniably a cognizable interest for purpose of standing. "But the 'injury in fact' test requires more than an injury to a cognizable interest. It requires that the party seeking review be himself among the injured." To survive the Secretary's summary judgment motion, respondents had to submit affidavits or other evidence showing, through specific facts, not only that listed species were in fact being threatened by funded activities abroad, but also that one or more of respondents' members would thereby be "directly" affected apart from their "'special interest' in the subject."

With respect to this aspect of the case, the Court of Appeals focused on the affidavits of two Defenders' members—Joyce Kelly and Amy Skilbred. Ms. Kelly stated that she traveled to Egypt in 1986 and "observed the traditional habitat of the endangered nile crocodile there and intends to do so again, and hopes to observe the crocodile directly," and that she "will suffer harm in fact as the result of [the] American … role … in overseeing the rehabilitation of the Aswan High Dam on the Nile … and [in] developing … Egypt's … Master Water Plan." Ms. Skilbred averred that she traveled to Sri Lanka in 1981 and "observed the habitat" of "endangered species such as the Asian elephant and the leopard" at what is now the site of the Mahaweli project funded by the Agency for International Development (AID), although she "was unable to see any of the endangered species"; "this development project," she continued, "will seriously reduce endangered, threatened, and endemic species habitat including areas that I visited … [, which] may severely shorten the future of these species"; that threat, she concluded, harmed her because she "intends to return to Sri Lanka in the future and hopes to be more fortunate in spotting at least the endangered elephant and leopard." When Ms. Skilbred was asked at a subsequent deposition if and when she had any plans to return to Sri Lanka, she reiterated that "I intend to go back to Sri Lanka," but confessed that she had no current plans: "I don't know [when]. There is a civil war going on right now. I don't know. Not next year, I will say. In the future."

We shall assume for the sake of argument that these affidavits contain facts showing that certain agency-funded projects threaten listed species—though that is questionable. They plainly contain no facts, however, showing how damage to the species will produce "imminent" injury to Mses. Kelly and Skilbred. That the women "had visited" the areas of the projects before the projects commenced proves nothing. As we have said in a related context, "'Past exposure to illegal conduct does not in itself show a present case or controversy regarding injunctive relief ... if unaccompanied by any continuing, present adverse effects.'" And the affiants' profession of an "intent" to return to the places they had visited before—where they will presumably, this time, be deprived of the opportunity to observe animals of the endangered species—is simply not enough. Such "some day" intentions—without any description of concrete plans, or indeed even any specification of *when* the some day will be—do not support a finding of the "actual or imminent" injury that our cases require.

Besides relying upon the Kelly and Skilbred affidavits, respondents propose a series of novel standing theories. The first, inelegantly styled "ecosystem nexus," proposes that any person who uses *any part* of a "contiguous ecosystem" adversely affected by a funded activity has standing even if the activity is located a great distance away.... [The Court rejected this theory.]

Respondents' other theories are called, alas, the "animal nexus" approach, whereby anyone who has an interest in studying or seeing the endangered animals anywhere on the globe has standing; and the "vocational nexus" approach, under which anyone with a professional interest in such animals can sue. Under these theories, anyone who goes to see Asian elephants in the Bronx Zoo, and anyone who is a keeper of Asian elephants in the Bronx Zoo, has standing to sue because the Director of the Agency for International Development (AID) did not consult with the Secretary regarding the AID-funded project in Sri Lanka. This is beyond all reason. Standing is not "an ingenious academic exercise in the conceivable," but as we have said requires, at the summary judgment stage, a factual showing of perceptible harm. It is clear that the person who observes or works with a particular animal threatened by a federal decision is facing perceptible harm, since the very subject of his interest will no longer exist. It is even plausible—though it goes to the outermost limit of plausibility—to think that a person who observes or works with animals of a particular species in the very area of the world where that species is threatened by a federal decision is facing such harm, since some animals that might have been the subject of his interest will no longer exist. It goes beyond the limit, however, and into pure speculation and fantasy, to say that anyone who observes or works with an endangered species, anywhere in the world, is appreciably harmed by a single project affecting some portion of that species with which he has no more specific connection.

## B.

Besides failing to show injury, respondents failed to demonstrate redressability. Instead of attacking the separate decisions to fund particular projects allegedly causing them harm, respondents chose to challenge a more generalized level of Government action (rules regarding consultation), the invalidation of which would affect all overseas projects. This programmatic approach has obvious practical advantages, but also obvious difficulties insofar as proof of causation or redressability is concerned. As we have said in another context, "suits challenging, not specifically identifiable Government violations of law, but the particular programs agencies establish to carry out their legal obligations ... [are], even when premised on allegations of several instances of violations of law, ... rarely if ever appropriate for federal-court adjudication."

[Margin annotation: → Public Policy]

*Could only redress Secretary*

The most obvious problem in the present case is redressability. Since the agencies funding the projects were not parties to the case, the District Court could accord relief only against the Secretary: He could be ordered to revise his regulation to require consultation for foreign projects. But this would not remedy respondents' alleged injury unless the funding agencies were bound by the Secretary's regulation, which is very much an open question.... When the Secretary promulgated the regulation at issue here, he thought it was binding on the agencies. The Solicitor General, however, has repudiated that position here, and the agencies themselves apparently deny the Secretary's authority....

Respondents assert that this legal uncertainty did not affect redressability (and hence standing) because the District Court itself could resolve the issue of the Secretary's authority as a necessary part of its standing inquiry. Assuming that it is appropriate to resolve an issue of law such as this in connection with a threshold standing inquiry, resolution by the District Court would not have remedied respondents' alleged injury anyway, because it would not have been binding upon the agencies. They were not parties to the suit, and there is no reason they should be obliged to honor an incidental legal determination the suit produced.... The short of the matter is that redress of the only injury in fact respondents complain of requires action (termination of funding until consultation) by the individual funding agencies; and any relief the District Court could have provided in this suit against the Secretary was not likely to produce that action.

A further impediment to redressability is the fact that the agencies generally supply only a fraction of the funding for a foreign project. AID, for example, has provided less than 10% of the funding for the Mahaweli project. Respondents have produced nothing to indicate that the projects they have named will either be suspended, or do less harm to listed species, if that fraction is eliminated. As in *Simon*, it is entirely conjectural whether the nonagency activity that affects respondents will be altered or affected by the agency activity they seek to achieve. There is no standing.

## IV

The Court of Appeals found that respondents had standing for an additional reason: because they had suffered a "procedural injury." The so-called "citizen-suit" provision of the ESA provides, in pertinent part, that "any person may commence a civil suit on his own behalf (A) to enjoin any person, including the United States and any other governmental instrumentality or agency ... who is alleged to be in violation of any provision of this chapter." The court held that, because § 7(a)(2) requires interagency consultation, the citizen-suit provision creates a "procedural right" to consultation in all "persons" — so that *anyone* can file suit in federal court to challenge the Secretary's (or presumably any other official's) failure to follow the assertedly correct consultative procedure, notwithstanding his or her inability to allege any discrete injury flowing from that failure. To understand the remarkable nature of this holding one must be clear about what it does *not* rest upon: This is not a case where plaintiffs are seeking to enforce a procedural requirement the disregard of which could impair a separate concrete interest of theirs (*e.g.*, the procedural requirement for a hearing

Congress Can Create Injury Where it other

prior to denial of their license application, or the procedural requirement for an environmental impact statement before a federal facility is constructed next door to them). Nor is it simply a case where concrete injury has been suffered by many persons, as in mass fraud or mass tort situations. Nor, finally, is it the unusual case in which Congress has created a concrete private interest in the outcome of a suit against a private party for the Government's benefit, by providing a cash bounty for the victorious plaintiff. Rather, the court held that the injury-in-fact requirement had been satisfied by congressional conferral upon *all* persons of an abstract, self-contained, noninstrumental "right" to have the Executive observe the procedures required by law. We reject this view.

Gen. Grievance

We have consistently held that a plaintiff raising only a generally available grievance about government — claiming only harm to his and every citizen's interest in proper application of the Constitution and laws, and seeking relief that no more directly and tangibly benefits him than it does the public at large — does not state an Article III case or controversy....

... In *United States v. Richardson*, 418 U.S. 166 (1974), we dismissed for lack of standing a taxpayer suit challenging the Government's failure to disclose the expenditures of the Central Intelligence Agency, in alleged violation of the constitutional requirement, Art. I, § 9, cl. 7, that "a regular Statement and Account of the Receipts and Expenditures of all public Money shall be published from time to time." We held that such a suit rested upon an impermissible "generalized grievance," and was inconsistent with "the framework of Article III" because "the impact on [plaintiff] is plainly undifferentiated and 'common to all members of the public.'" And in *Schlesinger v. Reservists Comm. to Stop the War*, 418 U.S. 208 (1974), we dismissed for the same reasons a citizen-taxpayer suit contending that it was a violation of the Incompatibility Clause, Art. I, § 6, cl. 2, for Members of Congress to hold commissions in the military Reserves. We said that the challenged action, "standing alone, would adversely affect only the generalized interest of all citizens in constitutional governance.... We reaffirm *Levitt* in holding that standing to sue may not be predicated upon an interest of this kind." ...

To be sure, our generalized-grievance cases have typically involved Government violation of procedures assertedly ordained by the Constitution rather than the Congress. But there is absolutely no basis for making the Article III inquiry turn on the source of the asserted right. Whether the courts were to act on their own, or at the invitation of Congress, in ignoring the concrete injury requirement described in our cases, they would be discarding a principle fundamental to the separate and distinct constitutional role of the Third Branch — one of the essential elements that identifies those "Cases" and "Controversies" that are the business of the courts rather than of the political branches. "The province of the court," as Chief Justice Marshall said in *Marbury v. Madison* (1803) [*Supra.* this chapter], "is, solely, to decide on the rights of individuals." Vindicating the *public* interest (including the public interest in Government observance of the Constitution and laws) is the function of Congress and the Chief Executive. The question presented here is whether the public interest in proper administration of the laws (specifically, in agencies' observance of a particular, statutorily prescribed procedure) can be converted into an individual right by a statute that denominates it as such, and that permits all citizens (or, for that matter, a subclass of citizens who suffer no distinctive concrete harm) to sue. If the concrete injury requirement has the separation-of-powers significance we have always said, the answer must be obvious: To permit Congress to convert the undifferentiated public interest in executive officers' compliance with the law into an "individual right" vindicable in the courts is to permit Congress to transfer from the President to the courts the Chief Executive's most important constitutional duty, to "take Care that the Laws be faithfully executed," Art. II, § 3. It would enable the courts, with the permission of Congress, "to assume a position of authority over the governmental acts of another and co-equal department." We have always rejected that vision of our role....

Nothing in this contradicts the principle that "the ... injury required by Art. III may exist solely by virtue of 'statutes creating legal rights, the invasion of which creates standing.'" *Warth* (quoting *Linda R.S. v. Richard D.*, 410 U.S. 614 (1973)). Both of the cases used by *Linda R.S.* as an illustration of that principle involved Congress' elevating to the status of legally cognizable injuries concrete, *de facto* injuries that were previously inadequate in law (namely, injury to an individual's personal interest in living in a racially integrated community, *see Trafficante v. Metropolitan Life Ins. Co.*, 409 U.S. 205 (1972), and injury to a company's interest in marketing its product free from competition, *see Hardin v. Kentucky Utilities Co.*, 390 U.S. 1 (1968)).... "[Statutory] broadening [of] the categories of injury that may be alleged in support of standing is a different matter from abandoning the requirement that the party seeking review must himself have suffered an injury." Whether or not the principle set forth in *Warth* can be extended beyond that distinction, it is clear that in suits against the Government, at least, the concrete injury requirement must remain.

We hold that respondents lack standing to bring this action and that the Court of Appeals erred in denying the summary judgment motion filed by the United States. The opinion of the Court of Appeals is hereby reversed, and the cause is remanded for proceedings consistent with this opinion.

JUSTICE KENNEDY, with whom JUSTICE SOUTER joins, concurring in part and concurring in the judgment.

Although I agree with the essential parts of the Court's analysis, I write separately to make several observations.

I agree with the Court's conclusion in Part III-A that, on the record before us, respondents have failed to demonstrate that they themselves are "among the injured." ...

While it may seem trivial to require that Mses. Kelly and Skilbred acquire airline tickets to the project sites or announce a date certain upon which they will return, this is not a case where it is reasonable to assume that the affiants will be using the sites on a regular basis, nor do the affiants claim to have visited the sites since the projects commenced. With respect to the Court's discussion of respondents' "ecosystem nexus," "animal nexus," and "vocational nexus" theories, I agree that on this record respondents' showing is insufficient to establish standing on any of these bases. I am not willing to foreclose the possibility, however, that in different circumstances a nexus theory similar to those proffered here might support a claim to standing.

In light of the conclusion that respondents have not demonstrated a concrete injury here sufficient to support standing under our precedents, I would not reach the issue of redressability that is discussed by the plurality in Part III-B.

I also join Part IV of the Court's opinion with the following observations. As Government programs and policies become more complex and farreaching, we must be sensitive to the articulation of new rights of action that do not have clear analogs in our common-law tradition. Modern litigation has progressed far from the paradigm of Marbury suing Madison to get his commission, *Marbury v. Madison*, or Ogden seeking an injunction to halt Gibbons' steamboat operations, *Gibbons v. Ogden*, 22 U.S. (9 Wheat.) 1. In my view, Congress has the power to define injuries and articulate chains of causation that will give rise to a case or controversy where none existed before, and I do not read the Court's opinion to suggest a contrary view. In exercising this power, however, Congress must at the very least identify the injury it seeks to vindicate and relate the injury to the class of persons entitled to bring suit. The citizen-suit provision of the Endangered Species Act does not meet these minimal requirements, because while the statute purports to confer a right on "any person ... to enjoin ... the United States and any other governmental instrumentality or agency ... who is alleged to be in violation of any provision of this chapter," it does not of its own force establish that there is an injury in "any person" by virtue of any "violation."

The Court's holding that there is an outer limit to the power of Congress to confer rights of action is a direct and necessary consequence of the case and controversy limitations found in Article III. I agree that it would exceed those limitations if, at the behest of Congress and in the absence of any showing of concrete injury, we were to entertain citizen suits to vindicate the public's nonconcrete interest in the proper administration of the laws. While it does not matter how many persons have been injured by the challenged action, the party bringing suit must show that the action injures him in a concrete and personal way. This requirement is not just an empty formality. It preserves the vitality of the adversarial process by assuring both that the parties before the court have an actual, as opposed to professed, stake in the outcome, and that "the legal questions presented ... will be resolved, not in the rarified atmosphere of a debating society, but in a concrete factual context conducive to a realistic appreciation of the consequences of judicial action." In addition, the requirement of concrete injury confines the Judicial Branch to its proper, limited role in the constitutional framework of Government.

An independent judiciary is held to account through its open proceedings and its reasoned judgments. In this process it is essential for the public to know what persons or groups are invoking the judicial power, the reasons that they have brought suit, and whether their claims are vindicated or denied. The concrete injury requirement helps assure that there can be an answer to these questions; and, as the Court's opinion is careful to show, that is part of the constitutional design.

With these observations, I concur in Parts I, II, III-A, and IV of the Court's opinion and in the judgment of the Court.

JUSTICE STEVENS, concurring in the judgment. [omitted]

JUSTICE BLACKMUN, with whom JUSTICE O'CONNOR joins, dissenting.

I part company with the Court in this case in two respects. First, I believe that respondents have raised genuine issues of fact — sufficient to survive summary judgment — both as to injury and as to redressability. Second, I question the Court's breadth of language in rejecting standing for "procedural" injuries. I fear the Court seeks to impose fresh limitations on the constitutional authority of Congress to allow citizen suits in the federal courts for injuries deemed "procedural" in nature.

I dissent.

I

\* \* \*

A

\* \* \*

1

Were the Court to apply the proper standard for summary judgment, I believe it would conclude that the sworn affidavits and deposition testimony of Joyce Kelly and Amy Skilbred advance sufficient facts to create a genuine issue for trial concerning whether one or both would be imminently harmed by the Aswan and Mahaweli projects. In the first instance, as the Court itself concedes, the affidavits contained facts making it at least "questionable" (and therefore within the province of the factfinder) that certain agency-funded projects threaten listed species. The only remaining issue, then, is whether Kelly and Skilbred have shown that they personally would suffer imminent harm.

I think a reasonable finder of fact could conclude from the information in the affidavits and deposition testimony that either Kelly or Skilbred will soon return to the project sites, thereby satisfying the "actual or imminent" injury standard. The Court dismisses Kelly's and Skilbred's general statements that they intended to revisit the project sites as "simply not enough." But those statements did not stand alone. A reasonable finder of fact could conclude, based not only upon their statements of intent to return, but upon their past visits to the project sites, as well as their professional backgrounds, that it was likely that Kelly and Skilbred would make a return trip to the project areas....

By requiring a "description of concrete plans" or "specification of *when* the some day [for a return visit] will be," the Court, in my view, demands what is likely an empty formality. No substantial barriers prevent Kelly or Skilbred from simply purchasing plane tickets to return to the Aswan and Mahaweli projects. This case differs from other cases in which the imminence of harm turned largely on the affirmative actions of third parties beyond a plaintiff's control. *See Whitmore v. Arkansas*, 495 U.S. 149 (1990) (harm to plaintiff death-row inmate from fellow inmate's execution depended on the court's one day reversing plaintiff's conviction or sentence and considering comparable sentences at resentencing).... To be sure, a plaintiff's unilateral control over his or her exposure to harm does not *necessarily* render the harm non-speculative. Nevertheless, it suggests that a finder of fact would be far more likely to conclude the harm is actual or imminent, especially if given an opportunity to hear testimony and determine credibility.

I fear the Court's demand for detailed descriptions of future conduct will do little to weed out those who are genuinely harmed from those who are not. More likely, it will resurrect a code-pleading formalism in federal court summary judgment practice, as federal courts, newly doubting their jurisdiction, will demand more and more particularized showings of future harm....

2

... The Court also rejects respondents' claim of vocational or professional injury. The Court says that it is "beyond all reason" that a zoo "keeper" of Asian elephants would have standing to contest his Government's participation in the eradication of all the Asian elephants in another part of the world. I am unable to see how the distant location of the destruction *necessarily* (for purposes of ruling at summary judgment) mitigates the harm to the elephant keeper. If there is no more access to a future supply of the animal that sustains a keeper's livelihood, surely there is harm.

I have difficulty imagining this Court applying its rigid principles of geographic formalism anywhere outside the context of environmental claims. As I understand it, environmental plaintiffs are under no special constitutional standing disabilities. Like other plaintiffs, they need show only that the action they challenge has injured them, without necessarily showing they happened to be physically near the location of the alleged wrong. The Court's decision today should not be interpreted "to foreclose the possibility ... that in different circumstances a nexus theory similar to those proffered here might support a claim to standing."

B

A plurality of the Court suggests that respondents have not demonstrated redressability: a likelihood that a court ruling in their favor would remedy their injury. The plurality identifies two obstacles. The first is that the "action agencies" (*e.g.*, AID) cannot be required to undertake consultation with petitioner Secretary, because they are not directly bound as parties to the suit and are otherwise not indirectly bound by being subject to petitioner Secretary's regulation. Petitioner, however, officially and publicly has taken the position that his regulations regarding consultation under § 7 of the Act are binding on action agencies....

Emphasizing that none of the action agencies are parties to this suit (and having rejected the possibility of their being indirectly bound by petitioner's regulation), the plurality concludes that "there is no reason they should be obliged to honor an incidental legal determination the suit produced." I am not as willing as the plurality is to assume that agencies at least will not try to follow the law....

The second redressability obstacle relied on by the plurality is that "the [action] agencies generally supply only a fraction of the funding for a foreign project." What this Court might "generally" take to be true does not eliminate the existence of a genuine issue of fact to withstand summary judgment. Even if the action agencies supply only a fraction of the funding for a particular foreign project, it remains at least a question for the finder of fact whether threatened withdrawal of that fraction would affect foreign government conduct sufficiently to avoid harm to listed species.

* * *

## II

The Court concludes that any "procedural injury" suffered by respondents is insufficient to confer standing. It rejects the view that the "injury-in-fact requirement [is] satisfied by congressional conferral upon *all* persons of an abstract, self-contained, noninstrumental 'right' to have the Executive observe the procedures required by law." Whatever the Court might mean with that very broad language, it cannot be saying that "procedural injuries" *as a class* are necessarily insufficient for purposes of Article III standing....

The Court expresses concern that allowing judicial enforcement of "agencies' observance of a particular, statutorily prescribed procedure" would "transfer from the President to the courts the Chief Executive's most important constitutional duty, to 'take Care that the Laws be faithfully executed,' Art. II, §3." In fact, the principal effect of foreclosing judicial enforcement of such procedures is to transfer power into the hands of the Executive at the expense—not of the courts—but of Congress, from which that power originates and emanates.

Under the Court's anachronistically formal view of the separation of powers, Congress legislates pure, substantive mandates and has no business structuring the procedural manner in which the Executive implements these mandates. To be sure, in the ordinary course, Congress does legislate in black-and-white terms of affirmative commands or negative prohibitions on the conduct of officers of the Executive Branch. In complex regulatory areas, however, Congress often legislates, as it were, in procedural shades of gray. That is, it sets forth substantive policy goals and provides for their attainment by requiring Executive Branch officials to follow certain procedures, for example, in the form of reporting, consultation, and certification requirements.

The Court recently has considered two such procedurally oriented statutes. In *Japan Whaling Assn. v. American Cetacean Society*, 478 U.S. 221 (1986), the Court examined a statute requiring the Secretary of Commerce to certify to the President that foreign nations were not conducting fishing operations or trading which "diminish the effectiveness" of an international whaling convention. The Court expressly found standing to sue. In *Robertson v. Methow Valley Citizens Council*, 490 U.S. 332 (1989), this Court considered injury from violation of the "action-forcing" procedures of the National Environmental Policy Act (NEPA), in particular the requirements for issuance of environmental impact statements.

The consultation requirement of §7 of the Endangered Species Act is a similar, action-forcing statute. Consultation is designed as an integral check on federal agency action, ensuring that such action does not go forward without full consideration of its effects on listed species. Once consultation is initiated, the Secretary is under a duty to provide to the action agency "a written statement setting forth the Secretary's opinion, and a summary of the information on which the opinion is based, detailing how the agency action affects the species or its critical habitat." The Secretary is also obligated to suggest "reasonable and prudent alternatives" to prevent jeopardy to listed species. The action agency must undertake as well its own "biological assessment for the purpose of identifying any endangered species or threatened species" likely to be affected by agency action. After the initiation of consultation, the action agency "shall not make any irreversible or irretrievable commitment of resources" which would foreclose the "formulation or implementation of any reasonable and prudent alternative measures" to avoid jeopardizing listed species. These action-forcing procedures are "designed to protect some threatened concrete interest," of persons who observe and work with endangered or threatened species. That is why I am mystified by the Court's unsupported conclusion that "this is not a case where plaintiffs are seeking to enforce a procedural requirement the disregard of which could impair a separate concrete interest of theirs."

Congress legislates in procedural shades of gray not to aggrandize its own power but to allow maximum Executive discretion in the attainment of Congress' legislative goals. Congress could simply impose a substantive prohibition on Executive conduct; it could say that no agency action shall result in the loss of more than 5% of any listed species. Instead, Congress sets forth substantive guidelines and allows the Executive, within certain procedural constraints, to decide how best to effectuate the ultimate goal. The Court never has questioned Congress' authority to impose such procedural constraints on Executive power. Just as Congress does not violate separation of powers by structuring the procedural manner in which the Executive shall carry out the laws, surely the federal courts do not violate separation of powers when, at the very instruction and command of Congress, they enforce these procedures.

To prevent Congress from conferring standing for "procedural injuries" is another way of saying that Congress may not delegate to the courts authority deemed "executive" in nature. (Congress may not "transfer from the President to the courts the Chief Executive's most important constitutional duty, to 'take Care that the Laws be faithfully executed,' Art. II, § 3"). Here Congress seeks not to delegate "executive" power but only to strengthen the procedures it has legislatively mandated. "We have long recognized that the nondelegation doctrine does not prevent Congress from seeking assistance, within proper limits, from its coordinate Branches." "Congress does not violate the Constitution merely because it legislates in broad terms, leaving a certain degree of discretion to executive or *judicial actors*." ...

Ironically, this Court has previously justified a relaxed review of congressional delegation to the Executive on grounds that Congress, in turn, has subjected the exercise of that power to judicial review. *INS v. Chadha*, 462 U.S. 919 (1983). The Court's intimation today that procedural injuries are not constitutionally cognizable threatens this understanding upon which Congress has undoubtedly relied. In no sense is the Court's suggestion compelled by our "common understanding of what activities are appropriate to legislatures, to executives, and to courts." In my view, it reflects an unseemly solicitude for an expansion of power of the Executive Branch.

It is to be hoped that over time the Court will acknowledge that some classes of procedural duties are so enmeshed with the prevention of a substantive, concrete harm that an individual plaintiff may be able to demonstrate a sufficient likelihood of injury just through the breach of that procedural duty. For example, in the context of the NEPA requirement of environmental-impact statements, this Court has acknowledged "it is now well settled that NEPA itself does not mandate particular results [and] simply *prescribes* the necessary process," but "these procedures are almost certain to affect the agency's substantive decision." This acknowledgment of an inextricable link between procedural and substantive harm does not reflect improper appellate factfinding. It reflects nothing more than the proper deference owed to the judgment of a coordinate branch — Congress — that certain procedures are directly tied to protection against a substantive harm.

In short, determining "injury" for Article III standing purposes is a fact-specific inquiry.... There may be factual circumstances in which a congressionally imposed procedural requirement is so insubstantially connected to the prevention of a substantive harm that it cannot be said to work any conceivable injury to an individual litigant. But, as a general matter, the courts owe substantial deference to Congress' substantive purpose in imposing a certain procedural requirement. In all events, "our separation-of-powers analysis does not turn on the labeling of an activity as 'substantive' as opposed to 'procedural.'" There is no room for a *per se* rule or presumption excluding injuries labeled "procedural" in nature.

### III

In conclusion, I cannot join the Court on what amounts to a slash-and-burn expedition through the law of environmental standing. In my view, "the very essence of civil liberty certainly consists in the right of every individual to claim the protection of the laws, whenever he receives an injury." *Marbury v. Madison.*

I dissent.

## Note: Generalized Grievances, Particularized Interests, and Legislative Policy

1. *The Status of the Bar on Generalized Grievances.* In *Defenders of Wildlife* the Court appears to conclude that the generalized grievance bar to standing is of constitutional dimension, rather than simply a prudential bar. However, several years later, in *Federal Election Comm'n v. Akins*, 524 U.S. 11 (1998), the Court backtracked somewhat. It observed that language suggesting constitutional status for ban on the generalized grievances "invariably appears in cases where the harm at issue is not only widely shared, but is also of an abstract and indefinite nature — for example, harm to the common concern for obedience to law." The Court observed that widely shared interests are often also abstract and indefinite, but cautioned that "their association is not invariable, and where a harm is concrete, though widely shared, the

Court has found injury in fact." In *Akins* the plaintiffs challenged the Federal Election Commission's decision that a lobbying group did not come within federal disclosure laws. They alleged that the FEC's decision injured them as voters by depriving them of information they would have found useful about the group's political lobbying. Applying its understanding of the generalized grievance bar, the Court found that injury sufficient to satisfy Article III's requirements.

2. *What Constitutes a Concrete Interest?* In *Defenders of Wildlife* Justice Scalia contrasted the "procedural right" the statute allegedly bestowed on any citizen-plaintiff with what he called "the unusual case in which Congress has created a concrete private interest in the outcome of a suit against a private party for the government's benefit, by providing a cash bounty for the victorious plaintiff." Presumably, then, a majority of the *Defenders of Wildlife* Court would have accepted such a cash bounty as a sufficiently "concrete private interest" to allow any citizen-plaintiff to have Article III standing.

3. *What type of relief redresses a plaintiff's injury?* Normally when we think of a remedy that redresses a plaintiff's injury, we think of relief that either dictates how the defendant will act toward the plaintiff (most notably, an injunction directing the defendant to conduct itself or refrain from conducting itself in a particular way in its dealings with the plaintiff) or relief that operates directly to the plaintiff's benefit (for example, a damages judgment in her favor or even the statutorily-created cash bounty of the sort Justice Scalia seemed to approve in *Defenders of Wildlife*). A step beyond such a cash bounty would be the prospect of the plaintiff's successful lawsuit forcing a defendant to pay a civil penalty *to the government* as a price of violating the statute. Do such penalties redress a plaintiff's injuries even if they are not paid to him? Do they raise separation of powers concerns? In *Friends of the Earth v. Laidlaw Environmental Services*, 528 U.S. 167 (2000), the Court considered whether such indirect relief could redress a plaintiff's injury.

*Friends of the Earth* considered whether residents near a particular river had standing to sue a company that allegedly had discharged pollutants into the river beyond what the Clean Water Act allowed. That statute authorizes the Environmental Protection Agency (EPA) to sue polluters who violate their water pollution permits. But it also allows private parties to sue if the EPA declines to, or delays its decision. When a private party sues, the statute allows courts to impose, among other remedies, civil penalties against the polluter. However, those penalties are payable to the United States, rather than to private party plaintiff. In *Friends of the Earth*, the Court held that several private parties had adequately proven that the defendant's industrial activities injured them by harming their aesthetic and recreational interests in a nearby river. The Court then considered whether civil penalties payable to the federal government redressed their injury.

The Court held they did. Writing for a seven-justice majority, Justice Ginsburg reasoned that such penalties deterred firms from violating their Clean Water Act permits, making it less likely that they would discharge excess pollutants in the future, and thereby redressing the injury the plaintiffs experienced from having their recreational and aesthetic interests harmed:

We have recognized on numerous occasions that "all civil penalties have some deterrent effect." More specifically, Congress has found that civil penalties in Clean Water Act cases do more than promote immediate compliance by limiting the defendant's economic incentive to delay its attainment of permit limits; they also deter future violations. This congressional determination warrants judicial attention and respect....

It can scarcely be doubted that, for a plaintiff who is injured or faces the threat of future injury due to illegal conduct ongoing at the time of suit, a sanction that effectively abates that conduct and prevents its recurrence provides a form of redress. Civil penalties can fit that description. To the extent that they encourage defendants to discontinue current violations and deter them from committing future ones, they afford redress to citizen plaintiffs who are injured or threatened with injury as a consequence of ongoing unlawful conduct....

We recognize that there may be a point at which the deterrent effect of a claim for civil penalties becomes so insubstantial or so remote that it cannot support citizen standing. The fact that this vanishing point is not easy to ascertain does not detract from the deterrent power of such penalties in the ordinary case. Justice Frankfurter's observations for the Court, made in a different context nearly 60 years ago, hold true here as well:

"How to effectuate policy—the adaptation of means to legitimately sought ends—is one of the most intractable of legislative problems. Whether proscribed conduct is to be deterred by *qui tam* action[*] or triple damages or injunction, or by criminal prosecution, or merely by defense to actions in contract, or by some, or all, of these remedies in combination, is a matter within the legislature's range of choice. Judgment on the deterrent effect of the various weapons in the armory of the law can lay little claim to scientific basis." *Tigner v. Texas*, 310 U.S. 141 (1940).

In this case we need not explore the outer limits of the principle that civil penalties provide sufficient deterrence to support redressability. Here, the civil penalties sought by [the plaintiffs] carried with them a deterrent effect that made it likely, as opposed to merely speculative, that the penalties would redress [the plaintiffs'] injuries by abating current violations and preventing future ones—as the District Court reasonably found when it assessed a penalty of $405,800.

Justice Kennedy joined the majority opinion, but added the following caveat: "Difficult and fundamental questions are raised when we ask whether exactions of public fines by private litigants, and the delegation of Executive power which might be inferable from the authorization, are permissible in view of the responsibilities committed to the Executive by Article II of the Constitution of the United States." However, he refrained from reaching that issue, because the parties had not raised or briefed it.

---

* [Ed. Note: A *qui tam* action is a lawsuit prosecuted by an individual to recover money owed the government, in which the successful private plaintiff is awarded a portion of the money the government recovers.]

Justice Scalia, joined by Justice Thomas, dissented. He agreed with Justice Kennedy that the separation of powers issue should be reserved, but he nevertheless expressed concern about the implications of the majority's reasoning for the President's Article II power to "take Care that the Laws be faithfully executed":

> By permitting citizens to pursue civil penalties payable to the Federal Treasury, the Act does not provide a mechanism for individual relief in any traditional sense, but turns over to private citizens the function of enforcing the law. A Clean Water Act plaintiff pursuing civil penalties acts as a self-appointed mini-EPA [Environmental Protection Agency]. Where, as is often the case, the plaintiff is a national association, it has significant discretion in choosing enforcement targets. Once the association is aware of a reported violation, it need not look long for an injured member, at least under the theory of injury the Court applies today. And once the target is chosen, the suit goes forward without meaningful public control. The availability of civil penalties vastly disproportionate to the individual injury gives citizen plaintiffs massive bargaining power—which is often used to achieve settlements requiring the defendant to support environmental projects of the plaintiffs' choosing. Thus is a public fine diverted to a private interest.

> To be sure, the EPA may foreclose the citizen suit by itself bringing suit. This allows public authorities to avoid private enforcement only by accepting private direction as to when enforcement should be undertaken—which is no less constitutionally bizarre. Elected officials are entirely deprived of their discretion to decide that a given violation should not be the object of suit at all, or that the enforcement decision should be postponed. This is the predictable and inevitable consequence of the Court's allowing the use of public remedies for private wrongs.

4. In 2007 the Court decided a standing issue that involved a number of these disparate threads. In *Massachusetts v. EPA*, 549 U.S. 497 (2007), the Court considered whether Massachusetts had standing to sue the Environmental Protection Agency to compel it to begin regulating the auto emissions that are thought to cause global climate change. In support of its standing argument, the state alleged that rising sea levels caused by climate change were threatening to flood significant parts of the state.

In a 5–4 vote the Court held that the state had standing. Justice Stevens, writing for the Court, concluded that Massachusetts was "entitled to special solicitude in our standing analysis" because its interest in the litigation—concern over loss of its lands—was "quasi-sovereign" in nature. He then concluded that the state had satisfied the standard requirements of injury, causation, and redressability. With regard to injury, he cited affidavits stating that the state had already begun to lose land due to climate change-caused submersion. He then rejected the EPA's argument that the causation requirement was not satisfied because the emissions sought to be regulated caused only an insignificant part of climate change. Writing for the Court, he said that "accepting that premise would doom most challenges to regulatory action." He also questioned the premise of the EPA's argument, observing that American motor vehicles contributed heavily to the concentration of climate change gasses in the atmosphere. Finally, he concluded that the remedy—forcing the EPA to regulate these emissions—would at least slow the growth of the climate change gasses in the atmosphere. He concluded that such a slowing sufficed to establish redressability. Justice Stevens summed up his standing analysis as follows: "In sum—at least according to petitioners' uncontested affidavits—the rise in sea levels associated with global warming has already harmed and will continue to harm Massachusetts. The risk of catastrophic harm, though remote, is nevertheless real. That risk would be reduced to some extent if petitioners received the relief they seek. We therefore hold that petitioners have standing to challenge the EPA's denial of their rulemaking petition."

Chief Justice Roberts wrote for the four dissenters on the standing issue. He criticized the majority's "special solicitude" for state-plaintiffs' standing claims, arguing that it had "no basis in our jurisprudence." Applying the three requirements for standing, he questioned whether climate change could even be understood in terms of "particularized injury" the law required: "The very concept of global warming seems inconsistent with this particularization requirement. Global warming is a phenomenon harmful to humanity at large, and the redress petitioners seek is focused no more on them than on the public generally—it is literally to change the atmosphere around the world." He criticized the majority's reliance on the affidavits the state submitted, arguing that they did not identify climate change as the undisputed cause of the submergence of state lands. He also observed that claims of future land loss were highly speculative, and based on models that had significant margins of error.

Turning to causation and redressability, Chief Justice Roberts noted the small proportion of greenhouse gas concentrations caused by American motor vehicle emissions, and then observed that the actual process by which such concentrations affected the climate was complex and poorly understood. He summed up his causation analysis with the following statement: "Petitioners are never able to trace their alleged injuries back through this complex web to the fractional amount of global emissions that might have been limited with EPA standards. In light of the bit-part domestic new motor vehicle greenhouse gas emissions have played in what petitioners describe as a 150-year global phenomenon, and the myriad additional factors bearing on petitioners' alleged injury—the loss of Massachusetts coastal land—the connection is far too speculative to establish causation."

With regard to redressability, Chief Justice Roberts observed that because other nations contributed substantially to climate change it was unclear at best whether EPA regulation of domestic emissions would redress the problem. In response to the majority's argument that regulation of domestic emissions would at least slow the growth of climate change-causing gasses, he offered the following observations:

> The Court's sleight of hand is in failing to link up the different elements of the three-part standing test. What must be likely to be redressed is the particular injury in fact. The injury the Court looks to is the asserted loss of land. The Court contends that regulating domestic motor vehicle emissions will reduce carbon dioxide in the atmosphere, and therefore redress Massa-

chusetts's injury. But even if regulation does reduce emissions—to some indeterminate degree, given events elsewhere in the world—the Court never explains why that makes it likely that the injury in fact—the loss of land—will be redressed. Schoolchildren know that a kingdom might be lost 'all for the want of a horseshoe nail,' but 'likely' redressability is a different matter. The realities make it pure conjecture to suppose that EPA regulation of new automobile emissions will likely prevent the loss of Massachusetts coastal land.

Justice Scalia, writing for the same four dissenters, wrote a separate dissent on an unrelated issue.

5. Summing up his standing analysis in *Massachusetts*, Chief Justice Roberts offered the following observations about standing, and its role in maintaining an appropriate role for the federal courts:

> When dealing with legal doctrine phrased in terms of what is 'fairly' traceable or 'likely' to be redressed, it is perhaps not surprising that the matter is subject to some debate. But in considering how loosely or rigorously to define those adverbs, it is vital to keep in mind the purpose of the inquiry. The limitation of the judicial power to cases and controversies is crucial in maintaining the tripartite allocation of power set forth in the Constitution. In my view, the Court today ... fails to take this limitation seriously.

What role should courts play when a plaintiff seeks the judiciary's help in compelling government to comply with broad, programmatic legal obligations, such as an obligation to address air pollution or climate change, where benefits to the plaintiff may be incremental and long-term? Does allowing review in such cases place the court in the role of a policy-maker, rather than a protector of individual rights? Does refusing review in such cases allow the government to avoid complying with legal requirements when those requirements are broad and programmatic, and therefore do not immediately and concretely affect a particular plaintiff?

More generally, how effective is the Court's standing doctrine "in maintaining the tripartite allocation of power set forth in the Constitution" (as Chief Justice Roberts wrote in *Massachusetts*)? Concede that standing doctrine appropriately attempts to ensure that plaintiffs have a concrete stake in the litigation they commence: is that goal served by denying standing to the researchers in *Defenders of Wildlife* because they hadn't yet bought a plane ticket, or to the white tester in *Havens Realty* because, unlike his black colleague, he did not receive deceptive housing information? It's easy to criticize these results. But if there is good reason to have a standing doctrine, what it should look like?

### c. Ripeness

The "case or controversy" requirement also includes the "ripeness" doctrine. This doctrine prohibits the federal courts from considering or resolving a dispute that has not yet matured (or "ripened") into a "case" or "controversy." The modern law of ripeness derives from the Court's analysis in *Abbott Laboratories v. Gardner*, 387 U.S. 136 (1967). As with standing, *Abbott Laboratories* recognizes both a prudential and a constitutional aspect to ripeness. In particular, it asks two basic questions: (1) is the matter currently fit for judicial review, or conversely, will it be better presented for a judicial decision in the context of a particular set of facts that sharpen the issues to be decided; and (2) to what degree will delaying the issue impose hardship on the plaintiff? *United Public Workers*, the first case in this subsection, illustrates the basic concerns of the ripeness doctrine. *Abbott Laboratories* then establishes the modern test, which is applied in the final case excerpted, *Ohio Forestry Association v. Sierra Club*.

## United Public Workers v. Mitchell

### 330 U.S. 75 (1947)

Mr. Justice Reed delivered the opinion of the Court.

The Hatch Act, enacted in 1940, declares unlawful certain specified political activities of federal employees. Section 9 forbids officers and employees in the executive branch of the Federal Government, with exceptions, from taking "any active part in political management or in political campaigns." Section 15 declares that the activities theretofore determined by the United States Civil Service Commission to be prohibited to employees in the classified civil service of the United States by the Civil Service Rules shall be deemed to be prohibited to federal employees covered by the Hatch Act. These sections of the Act cover all federal officers and employees whether in the classified civil service or not and a penalty of dismissal from employment is imposed for violation. There is no designation of a single governmental agency for its enforcement....

The present appellants sought an injunction before a statutory three-judge district court of the District of Columbia against appellees, members of the United States Civil Service Commission, to prohibit them from enforcing against appellants the provisions of the second sentence of § 9(a) of the Hatch Act.... A declaratory judgment of the unconstitutionality of the sentence was also sought. The sentence referred to reads, "No officer or employee in the executive branch of the Federal Government ... shall take any active part in political management or in political campaigns."

Various individual employees of the federal executive civil service and the United Public Workers of America, a labor union with these and other executive employees as members, as a representative of all its members, joined in the suit. It is alleged that the individuals desire to engage in acts of political management and in political campaigns.... From the affidavits it is plain, and we so assume, that these activities will be carried on completely outside of the hours of employment....

None of the appellants, except George P. Poole, has violated the provisions of the Hatch Act. They wish to act contrary to its provisions and those of § 1 of the Civil Service Rules and desire a declaration of the legally permissible limits of regulation. Defendants moved to dismiss the complaint for lack of a justiciable case or controversy....

*Second.* At the threshold of consideration, we are called upon to decide whether the complaint states a controversy cognizable in this Court. We defer consideration of the cause of action of Mr. Poole until section *Three* of this opinion. The other individual employees [declare] a desire to act contrary to the rule against political activity but not that the rule has been violated....

As is well known the federal courts established pursuant to Article III of the Constitution do not render advisory opinions. For adjudication of constitutional issues "concrete legal issues, presented in actual cases, not abstractions" are requisite. This is as true of declaratory judgments as any other field. These appellants seem clearly to seek advisory opinions upon broad claims of rights protected by the First, Fifth, Ninth and Tenth Amendments to the Constitution. As these appellants are classified employees, they have a right superior to the generality of citizens, but the facts of their personal interest in their civil rights, of the general threat of possible interference with those rights by the Civil Service Commission under its rules, if specified things are done by appellants, does not make a justiciable case or controversy. Appellants want to engage in "political management and political campaigns," to persuade others to follow appellants' views by discussion, speeches, articles and other acts reasonably designed to secure the selection of appellants' political choices. Such generality of objection is really an attack on the political expediency of the Hatch Act, not the presentation of legal issues. It is beyond the competence of courts to render such a decision.

The power of courts, and ultimately of this Court to pass upon the constitutionality of acts of Congress arises only when the interests of litigants require the use of this judicial authority for their protection against actual interference. A hypothetical threat is not enough. We can only speculate as to the kinds of political activity the appellants desire to engage in or as to the contents of their proposed public statements or the circumstances of their publication. It would not accord with judicial responsibility to adjudge, in a matter involving constitutionality, between the freedom of the individual and the requirements of public order except when definite rights appear upon the one side and definite prejudicial interferences upon the other.

The Constitution allots the nation's judicial power to the federal courts. Unless these courts respect the limits of that unique authority, they intrude upon powers vested in the legislative or executive branches. Judicial adherence to the doctrine of the separation of powers preserves the courts for the decision of issues, between litigants, capable of effective determination. Judicial exposition upon political proposals is permissible only when necessary to decide definite issues between litigants. When the courts act continually within these constitutionally imposed boundaries of their power, their ability to perform their function as a balance for the people's protection against abuse of power by other branches of government remains unimpaired. Should the courts seek to expand their power so as to bring under their jurisdiction ill-defined controversies over constitutional issues, they would become the organ of political theories. Such abuse of judicial power would properly meet rebuke and restriction from other branches. By these mutual checks and balances by and between the branches of government, democracy undertakes to preserve the liberties of the people from excessive concentrations of authority. No threat of interference by the Commission with rights of these appellants appears beyond that implied by the existence of the law and the regulations. We should not take judicial cognizance of the situation presented on the part of the appellants considered in this subdivision of the opinion. These reasons lead us to conclude that the determination of the trial court, that the individual appellants, other than Poole, could maintain this action, was erroneous.

*Third.* The appellant Poole does present by the complaint and affidavit matters appropriate for judicial determination. The affidavits filed by appellees confirm that Poole has been charged by the Commission with political activity and a proposed order for his removal from his position adopted subject to his right under Commission procedure to reply to the charges and to present further evidence in refutation. We proceed to consider the controversy over constitutional power at issue between Poole and the Commission as defined by the charge and preliminary finding upon one side and the admissions of Poole's affidavit upon the other. Our determination is limited to those facts. This proceeding so limited meets the requirements of defined rights and a definite threat to interfere with a possessor of the menaced rights by a penalty for an act done in violation of the claimed restraint....

Mr. Justice Douglas, dissenting in part....

What these appellants propose to do is plain enough. If they do what they propose to do, it is clear that they will be discharged from their positions....

On a discharge these employees would lose their jobs, their seniority, and other civil service benefits. They could, of course, sue in the Court of Claims. But the remedy there is a money judgment, not a restoration to the office formerly held. Of course, there might be other remedies available in these situations to determine their rights to the offices from which they are discharged. But to require these employees first to suffer the hardship of a discharge is not only to make them incur a penalty; it makes inadequate, if not wholly illusory, any legal remedy which they may have. Men who must sacrifice their means of livelihood in order to test their rights to their jobs must either pursue prolonged and expensive litigation as unemployed persons or pull up their roots, change their life careers, and seek employment in other fields. At least to the average person in the lower income groups the burden of taking that course is irreparable injury, no matter how exact the required showing....

The declaratory judgment procedure is designed "to declare rights and other legal relations of any interested party ... whether or not further relief is or could be prayed." ... The right to hold an office or public position against such threats is a common example of its use. Declaratory relief is the singular remedy available here to preserve the *status quo* while the constitutional rights of these appellants to make these utterances and to engage in these activities are determined. The threat against them is real not fanciful, immediate not remote. The case is therefore an actual not a hypothetical one. And the present case seems to me to be a good example of a situation where uncertainty, peril, and insecurity result from imminent and immediate threats to asserted rights.

# Abbott Laboratories v. Gardner

387 U.S. 136 (1967)

Mr. Justice Harlan delivered the opinion of the Court.

In 1962 Congress amended the Federal Food, Drug, and Cosmetic Act ... to require manufacturers of prescription drugs to print the "established name" of the drug "prominently and in type at least half as large as that used thereon for any proprietary name or designation for such drug," on labels and other printed material, §502(e)(1)(B). The "established name" is one designated by the Secretary of Health, Education, and Welfare pursuant to §502(e)(2) of the Act; the "proprietary name" is usually a trade name under which a particular drug is marketed. The underlying purpose of the 1962 amendment was to bring to the attention of doctors and patients the fact that many of the drugs sold under familiar trade names are actually identical to drugs sold under their "established" or less familiar trade names at significantly lower prices. The Commissioner of Food and Drugs, exercising authority delegated to him by the Secretary, published proposed regulations designed to implement the statute. After inviting and considering comments submitted by interested parties the Commissioner promulgated the following regulation for the "efficient enforcement" of the Act:

> If the label or labeling of a prescription drug bears a proprietary name or designation for the drug or any ingredient thereof, the established name, if such there be, corresponding to such proprietary name or designation, shall accompany each appearance of such proprietary name or designation.

A similar rule was made applicable to advertisements for prescription drugs.

The present action was brought by a group of 37 individual drug manufacturers and by the Pharmaceutical Manufacturers Association, of which all the petitioner companies are members, and which includes manufacturers of more than 90% of the Nation's supply of prescription drugs. They challenged the regulations on the ground that the Commissioner exceeded his authority under the statute by promulgating an order requiring labels, advertisements, and other printed matter relating to prescription drugs to designate the established name of the particular drug involved every time its trade name is used anywhere in such material. ...

... The injunctive and declaratory judgment remedies are discretionary, and courts traditionally have been reluctant to apply them to administrative determinations unless these arise in the context of a controversy "ripe" for judicial resolution. Without undertaking to survey the intricacies of the ripeness doctrine it is fair to say that its basic rationale is to prevent the courts, through avoidance of premature adjudication, from entangling themselves in abstract disagreements over administrative policies, and also to protect the agencies from judicial interference until an administrative decision has been formalized and its effects felt in a concrete way by the challenging parties. The problem is best seen in a twofold aspect, requiring us to evaluate both the fitness of the issues for judicial decision and the hardship to the parties of withholding court consideration.

As to the former factor, we believe the issues presented are appropriate for judicial resolution at this time. First, all parties agree that the issue tendered is a purely legal one: whether the statute was properly construed by the Commissioner to require the established name of the drug to be used *every time* the proprietary name is employed. Both sides moved for summary judgment in the District Court, and no claim is made here that further administrative proceedings are contemplated. It is suggested that the justification for this rule might vary with different circumstances, and that the expertise of the Commissioner is relevant to passing upon the validity of the regulation. This of course is true, but the suggestion overlooks the fact that both sides have approached this case as one purely of congressional intent, and that the Government made no effort to justify the regulation in factual terms....

This is also a case in which the impact of the regulations upon the petitioners is sufficiently direct and immediate as to render the issue appropriate for judicial review at this stage. These regulations purport to give an authoritative interpretation of a statutory provision that has a direct effect on the day-to-day business of all prescription drug companies; its promulgation puts petitioners in a dilemma that it was the very purpose of the Declaratory Judgment Act to ameliorate. As the District Court found on the basis of uncontested allegations, "Either they must comply with the every time requirement and incur the costs of changing over their promotional material and labeling or they must follow their present course and risk prosecution." The regulations are clear-cut, and were made effective immediately upon publication; as noted earlier the agency's counsel represented to the District Court that immediate compliance with their terms was expected. If petitioners wish to comply they must change all their labels, advertisements, and promotional materials; they must destroy stocks of printed matter; and they must invest heavily in new printing type and new supplies. The alternative to compliance—continued use of material which they believe in good faith meets the statutory requirements, but which clearly does not meet the regulation of the Commissioner—may be even more costly. That course would risk serious criminal and civil penalties for the unlawful distribution of "misbranded" drugs.

It is relevant at this juncture to recognize that petitioners deal in a sensitive industry, in which public confidence in their drug products is especially important. To require them to challenge these regulations only as a defense to an action brought by the Government might harm them severely and unnecessarily. Where the legal issue presented is fit for judicial resolution, and where a regulation requires an immediate and significant change in the plaintiffs' conduct of their affairs with serious penalties attached to noncompliance, access to the courts under the Administrative Procedure Act and the Declaratory Judgment Act must be permitted, absent a statutory bar or some other unusual circumstance, neither of which appears here.

The Government does not dispute the very real dilemma in which petitioners are placed by the regulation, but contends that "mere financial expense" is not a justification for pre-enforcement judicial review. It is of course true that cases in this Court dealing with the standing of particular parties to bring an action have held that a possible financial loss is not by itself a sufficient interest to sustain a judicial challenge to governmental action. But there is no question in the present case that petitioners have sufficient standing as plaintiffs: the regulation is directed at them in particular; it requires them to make significant changes in their everyday business practices; if they fail to observe the Commissioner's rule they are quite clearly exposed to the imposition of strong sanctions....

The Government further contends that the threat of criminal sanctions for noncompliance with a judicially untested regulation is unrealistic; the Solicitor General has represented that if court enforcement becomes necessary, "the Department of Justice will proceed only civilly for an injunction ... or by condemnation." We cannot accept this argument as a sufficient answer to petitioners' petition. This action at its inception was properly brought and this subsequent representation of the Department of Justice should not suffice to defeat it.

## Ohio Forestry Association v. Sierra Club
### 523 U.S. 726 (1998)

JUSTICE BREYER delivered the opinion of the Court.

The Sierra Club challenges the lawfulness of a federal land and resource management plan adopted by the United States Forest Service for Ohio's Wayne National Forest on the ground that the plan permits too much logging and too much clearcutting. We conclude that the controversy is not yet ripe for judicial review.

I

The National Forest Management Act of 1976 (NFMA) requires the Secretary of Agriculture to "develop, maintain, and, as appropriate, revise land and resource management plans for units of the National Forest System." ... The National Forest Service, which manages the System, develops land and resource management plans pursuant to NFMA.... In developing the plans, the Service must take both environmental and commercial goals into account.

This case focuses upon a plan that the Forest Service has developed for the Wayne National Forest located in southern Ohio. When the Service wrote the plan, the forest consisted of 178,000 federally owned acres (278 sq. mi.) in three forest units that are interspersed among privately owned lands.... The Plan permits logging to take place on 126,000 (197 sq. mi.) of the federally owned acres. At the same time, it sets a ceiling on the total amount of wood that can be cut....

Although the Plan sets logging goals, selects the areas of the forest that are suited to timber production, and determines which "probable methods of timber harvest" are appropriate, it does not itself authorize the cutting of any trees. Before the Forest Service can permit the logging, it must: (a) propose a specific area in which logging will take place and the harvesting methods to be used; (b) ensure that the project is consistent with the Plan; (c) provide those affected by proposed logging notice and an opportunity to be heard; (d) conduct an environmental analysis pursuant to the National Environmental Policy Act of 1969 (NEPA) ... ; and (e) subsequently make a final decision to permit logging, which affected persons may challenge in an administrative appeals process and in court. Furthermore, the statute requires the Forest Service to "revise" the Plan "as appropriate." Despite the considerable legal distance between the adoption of the Plan and the moment when a tree is cut, the Plan's promulgation nonetheless makes logging more likely in that it is a logging precondition; in its absence logging could not take place.

When the Forest Service first proposed its Plan, the Sierra Club and the Citizens Council on Conservation and Environmental Control each objected.... The Sierra Club then brought this lawsuit in federal court ... The Ohio Forestry Association ... later intervened as a defendant....

## II

Petitioner alleges that this suit is nonjusticiable both because the Sierra Club lacks standing to bring this case and because the issues before us — over the Plan's specifications for logging and clearcutting — are not yet ripe for adjudication. We find that the dispute is not justiciable, because it is not ripe for court review.

As this Court has previously pointed out, the ripeness requirement is designed

> to prevent the courts, through avoidance of premature adjudication, from entangling themselves in abstract disagreements over administrative policies, and also to protect the agencies from judicial interference until an administrative decision has been formalized and its effects felt in a concrete way by the challenging parties. *Abbott Laboratories v. Gardner* (1967) [*Supra.* this chapter].

In deciding whether an agency's decision is, or is not, ripe for judicial review, the Court has examined both the "fitness of the issues for judicial decision" and the "hardship to the parties of withholding court consideration." *Abbott Laboratories.* To do so in this case, we must consider: (1) whether delayed review would cause hardship to the plaintiffs; (2) whether judicial intervention would inappropriately interfere with further administrative action; and (3) whether the courts would benefit from further factual development of the issues presented. These considerations, taken together, foreclose review in the present case.

First, to "withhold court consideration" at present will not cause the parties significant "hardship" as this Court has come to use that term. *Ibid.* For one thing, the provisions of the Plan that the Sierra Club challenges do not create adverse effects of a strictly legal kind, that is, effects of a sort that traditionally would have qualified as harm. To paraphrase this Court's language in *United States v. Los Angeles & Salt Lake R. Co.*, 273 U.S. 299 (1927) (opinion of Brandeis, J.), they do not command anyone to do anything or to refrain from doing anything; they do not grant, withhold, or modify any formal legal license, power, or authority; they do not subject anyone to any civil or criminal liability; they create no legal rights or obligations. Thus, for example, the Plan does not give anyone a legal right to cut trees, nor does it abolish anyone's legal authority to object to trees being cut.

Nor have we found that the Plan now inflicts significant practical harm upon the interests that the Sierra Club advances — an important consideration in light of this

Court's modern ripeness cases. *See, e.g., Abbott Laboratories.* As we have pointed out, before the Forest Service can permit logging, it must focus upon a particular site, propose a specific harvesting method, prepare an environmental review, permit the public an opportunity to be heard, and (if challenged) justify the proposal in court. The Sierra Club thus will have ample opportunity later to bring its legal challenge at a time when harm is more imminent and more certain. . . .

Nor has the Sierra Club pointed to any other way in which the Plan could now force it to modify its behavior in order to avoid future adverse consequences, as, for example, agency regulations can sometimes force immediate compliance through fear of future sanctions. *Cf. Abbott Laboratories* (finding challenge ripe where plaintiffs must comply with Federal Drug Administration labeling rule at once and incur substantial economic costs or risk later serious criminal and civil penalties for unlawful drug distribution).

The Sierra Club does say that it will be easier, and certainly cheaper, to mount one legal challenge against the Plan now, than to pursue many challenges to each site-specific logging decision to which the Plan might eventually lead. It does not explain, however, why one initial site-specific victory (if based on the Plan's unlawfulness) could not, through preclusion principles, effectively carry the day. And, in any event, the Court has not considered this kind of litigation cost saving sufficient by itself to justify review in a case that would otherwise be unripe. The ripeness doctrine reflects a judgment that the disadvantages of a premature review that may prove too abstract or unnecessary ordinarily outweigh the additional costs of—even repetitive—postimplementation litigation.

Second, from the agency's perspective, immediate judicial review directed at the lawfulness of logging and clearcutting could hinder agency efforts to refine its policies: (a) through revision of the Plan . . . or (b) through application of the Plan in practice, *e.g.*, in the form of site-specific proposals, which are subject to review by a court applying purely legal criteria. *Cf. Abbott Laboratories.* And, here, the possibility that further consideration will actually occur before the Plan is implemented is not theoretical, but real. Hearing the Sierra Club's challenge now could thus interfere with the system that Congress specified for the agency to reach forest logging decisions.

Third, from the courts' perspective, review of the Sierra Club's claims regarding logging and clearcutting now would require time-consuming judicial consideration of the details of an elaborate, technically based plan, which predicts consequences that may affect many different parcels of land in a variety of ways, and which effects themselves may change over time. That review would have to take place without benefit of the focus that a particular logging proposal could provide. Thus, for example, the court below in evaluating the Sierra Club's claims had to focus upon whether the Plan as a whole was "improperly skewed," rather than focus upon whether the decision to allow clearcutting on a particular site was improper, say, because the site was better suited to another use or logging there would cumulatively result in too many trees being cut. And, of course, depending upon the agency's future actions to revise the Plan or modify the expected methods of implementation, review now may turn out to have been unnecessary.

This type of review threatens the kind of "abstract disagreements over administrative policies," *Abbott Laboratories*, that the ripeness doctrine seeks to avoid. In this case, for example, the Court of Appeals panel disagreed about whether or not the Forest Service suffered from a kind of general "bias" in favor of timber production and clearcutting. Review where the consequences had been "reduced to more manageable proportions," and where the "factual components [were] fleshed out, by some concrete action" might have led the panel majority either to demonstrate that bias and its consequences through record citation (which it did not do) or to abandon the claim. All this is to say that further factual development would "significantly advance our ability to deal with the legal issues presented" and would "aid us in their resolution." ...

III

The Sierra Club makes one further important contrary argument. It says that the Plan will hurt it in many ways that we have not yet mentioned. Specifically, the Sierra Club says that the Plan will permit "many intrusive activities, such as opening trails to motorcycles or using heavy machinery," which "will go forward without any additional consideration of their impact on wilderness recreation." ... These are harms, says the Sierra Club, that will not take place at a distant future time. Rather, they will take place now.

This argument suffers from the legally fatal problem that it makes its first appearance here in this Court in the briefs on the merits. The Complaint, fairly read, does not include such claims....

The matter is significant because the Government concedes that if the Sierra Club had previously raised these other kinds of harm, the ripeness analysis in this case with respect to those provisions of the Plan that produce the harm would be significantly different....

... Thus, we believe these other claims that the Sierra Club now raises are not fairly presented here, and we cannot consider them....

## d. Mootness

Like ripeness, the mootness doctrine also involves a question of timing. But this doctrine applies when the claim is that a case was presented not too soon, but too late. Even though the claim may have been ripe at one point, subsequent events have rendered it "moot," or no longer a live "case or controversy." Like other justiciability doctrines, mootness reflects a combination of prudential and Article III-based concerns. *DeFunis v. Odegaard*, excerpted below, examines the foundation of the mootness doctrine, and sets forth its most important exceptions. In particular, it notes that the defendant's voluntary cessation of the offending activity will not moot the activity if nothing would prevent the defendant from restarting that activity after dismissal of the lawsuit. It also notes that a case will not be considered moot if it is "capable of repetition but evading review"—that is, if the activity is the type that usually becomes moot, but is expected to recur. Pregnancy is the classic example of such an activity: absent the "capable of repetition by evading review" exception, a legal claim that is tied to pregnancy (*e.g.*, an abortion-rights claim) will almost always become moot within nine months, thus frustrating judicial review by appellate courts.

# DeFunis v. Odegaard
## 416 U.S. 312 (1974)

PER CURIAM.

In 1971 the petitioner Marco DeFunis, Jr., applied for admission as a first-year student at the University of Washington Law School, a state-operated institution. The size of the incoming first-year class was to be limited to 150 persons, and the Law School received some 1,600 applications for these 150 places. DeFunis was eventually notified that he had been denied admission. He thereupon commenced this suit in a Washington trial court, contending that the procedures and criteria employed by the Law School Admissions Committee invidiously discriminated against him on account of his race in violation of the Equal Protection Clause of the Fourteenth Amendment to the United States Constitution.

DeFunis ... asked the trial court to issue a mandatory injunction commanding the respondents to admit him as a member of the first-year class entering in September 1971, on the ground that the Law School admissions policy had resulted in the unconstitutional denial of his application for admission. The trial court agreed with his claim and granted the requested relief. DeFunis was, accordingly, admitted to the Law School and began his legal studies there in the fall of 1971. On appeal, the Washington Supreme Court reversed the judgment of the trial court and held that the Law School admissions policy did not violate the Constitution. By this time DeFunis was in his second year at the Law School.

He then petitioned this Court for a writ of certiorari, and Mr. Justice Douglas, as Circuit Justice, stayed the judgment of the Washington Supreme Court pending the "final disposition of the case by this Court." By virtue of this stay, DeFunis has remained in law school, and was in the first term of his third and final year when this Court first considered his certiorari petition in the fall of 1973. Because of our concern that DeFunis' third-year standing in the Law School might have rendered this case moot, we requested the parties to brief the question of mootness before we acted on the petition. In response, both sides contended that the case was not moot. The respondents indicated that, if the decision of the Washington Supreme Court were permitted to stand, the petitioner could complete the term for which he was then enrolled but would have to apply to the faculty for permission to continue in the school before he could register for another term.[2] ...

In response to questions raised from the bench during the oral argument, counsel for the petitioner has informed the Court that DeFunis has now registered "for his

---

2. By contrast, in their response to the petition for certiorari, the respondents had stated that DeFunis 'will complete his third year (of law school) and be awarded his J.D. degree at the end of the 1973–74 academic year regardless of the outcome of this appeal.'

final quarter in law school." Counsel for the respondents have made clear that the Law School will not in any way seek to abrogate this registration. In light of DeFunis' recent registration for the last quarter of his final law school year, and the Law School's assurance that his registration is fully effective, the insistent question again arises whether this case is not moot, and to that question we now turn.

The starting point for analysis is the familiar proposition that "federal courts are without power to decide questions that cannot affect the rights of litigants in the case before them." The inability of the federal judiciary "to review moot cases derives from the requirement of Art. III of the Constitution under which the exercise of judicial power depends upon the existence of a case or controversy." Although as a matter of Washington state law it appears that this case would be saved from mootness by "the great public interest in the continuing issues raised by this appeal," the fact remains that under Art. III "even in cases arising in the state courts, the question of mootness is a federal one which a federal court must resolve before it assumes jurisdiction."

The respondents have represented that, without regard to the ultimate resolution of the issues in this case, DeFunis will remain a student in the Law School for the duration of any term in which he has already enrolled. Since he has now registered for his final term, it is evident that he will be given an opportunity to complete all academic and other requirements for graduation, and, if he does so, will receive his diploma regardless of any decision this Court might reach on the merits of this case. In short, all parties agree that DeFunis is now entitled to complete his legal studies at the University of Washington and to receive his degree from that institution. A determination by this Court of the legal issues tendered by the parties is no longer necessary to compel that result, and could not serve to prevent it. DeFunis did not cast his suit as a class action, and the only remedy he requested was an injunction commanding his admission to the Law School. He was not only accorded that remedy, but he now has also been irrevocably admitted to the final term of the final year of the Law School course. The controversy between the parties has thus clearly ceased to be "definite and concrete" and no longer "touches the legal relations of parties having adverse legal interests."

It matters not that these circumstances partially stem from a policy decision on the part of the respondent Law School authorities. The respondents, through their counsel, the Attorney General of the State, have professionally represented that in no event will the status of DeFunis now be affected by any view this Court might express on the merits of this controversy. And it has been the settled practice of the Court, in contexts no less significant, fully to accept representations such as these as parameters for decision.

There is a line of decisions in this Court standing for the proposition that the "voluntary cessation of allegedly illegal conduct does not deprive the tribunal of power to hear and determine the case, *i.e.*, does not make the case moot." These decisions and the doctrine they reflect would be quite relevant if the question of mootness here had arisen by reason of a unilateral change in the *admissions procedures* of the law school. For it was the admissions procedures that were the target of this litigation, and a voluntary cessation of the admissions practices complained of could make this case moot only if it could be said with assurance "that there is no reasonable expectation that the wrong will be repeated." Otherwise, "the defendant is free to return to his old ways," and this fact would be enough to prevent mootness because of the "public interest in having the legality of the practices settled." But mootness in the present case depends not at all upon a "voluntary cessation" of the admissions practices that were the subject of this litigation. It depends, instead, upon the simple fact that DeFunis is now in the final quarter of the final year of his course of study, and the settled and unchallenged policy of the Law School to permit him to complete the term for which he is now enrolled.

It might also be suggested that this case presents a question that is "capable of repetition, yet evading review," and is thus amenable to federal adjudication even though it might otherwise be considered moot. But DeFunis will never again be required to run the gauntlet of the Law School's admission process, and so the question is certainly not "capable of repetition" so far as he is concerned. Moreover, just because this particular case did not reach the Court until the eve of the petitioner's graduation from Law School, it hardly follows that the issue he raises will in the future evade review. If the admissions procedures of the Law School remain unchanged, there is no reason to suppose that a subsequent case attacking those procedures will not come with relative speed to this Court, now that the Supreme Court of Washington has spoken. This case, therefore, in no way presents the exceptional situation … which … might permit a departure from "the usual rule in federal cases … that an actual controversy must exist at stages of appellate or certiorari review, and not simply at the date the action is initiated."

Because the petitioner will complete his law school studies at the end of the term for which he has now registered regardless of any decision this Court might reach on the merits of this litigation, we conclude that the Court cannot, consistently with the limitations of Art. III of the Constitution, consider the substantive constitutional issues tendered by the parties.[5] Accordingly, the judgment of the Supreme Court of Washington is vacated, and the cause is remanded for such proceedings as by that court may be deemed appropriate.

Mr. Justice Brennan, with whom Mr. Justice Douglas, Mr. Justice White, and Mr. Justice Marshall concur, dissenting.

I respectfully dissent. Many weeks of the school term remain, and petitioner may not receive his degree despite respondents' assurances that petitioner will be allowed to complete this term's schooling regardless of our decision. Any number of unexpected events—illness, economic necessity, even academic failure—might prevent his graduation at the end of the term. Were that misfortune to befall, and were petitioner required to register for yet another term, the prospect that he would again face the hurdle of the admissions policy is real, not fanciful; for respondents warn

---

5. It is suggested in dissent that 'any number of unexpected events—illness, economic necessity, even academic failure—might prevent his graduation at the end of the term.' 'But such speculative contingencies afford no basis for our passing on the substantive issues (the petitioner) would have us decide,' *Hall v. Beals*, 396 U.S. 45 (1969), in the absence of evidence that this is a prospect of 'immediacy and reality.' *Golden v. Zwickler*, 394 U.S. 103 (1969).

that "Mr. DeFunis would have to take some appropriate action to request continued admission for the remainder of his law school education, and *some discretionary action by the University on such request would have to be taken*." Thus, respondents' assurances have not dissipated the possibility that petitioner might once again have to run the gauntlet of the University's allegedly unlawful admissions policy. The Court therefore proceeds on an erroneous premise in resting its mootness holding on a supposed inability to render any judgment that may affect one way or the other petitioner's completion of his law studies. For surely if we were to reverse the Washington Supreme Court, we could insure that, if for some reason petitioner did not graduate this spring, he would be entitled to re-enrollment at a later time on the same basis as others who have not faced the hurdle of the University's allegedly unlawful admissions policy.

In these circumstances, and because the University's position implies no concession that its admissions policy is unlawful, this controversy falls squarely within the Court's long line of decisions holding that the "mere voluntary cessation of allegedly illegal conduct does not moot a case." Since respondents' voluntary representation to this Court is only that they will permit petitioner to complete this term's studies, respondents have not borne the "heavy burden," of demonstrating that there was not even a "mere possibility" that petitioner would once again be subject to the challenged admissions policy. On the contrary, respondents have positioned themselves so as to be "free to return to [their] old ways."

I can thus find no justification for the Court's straining to rid itself of this dispute. While we must be vigilant to require that litigants maintain a personal stake in the outcome of a controversy to assure that "the questions will be framed with the necessary specificity, that the issues will be contested with the necessary adverseness and that the litigation will be pursued with the necessary vigor to assure that the constitutional challenge will be made in a form traditionally thought to be capable of judicial resolution," there is no want of an adversary contest in this case. Indeed, the Court concedes that, if petitioner has lost his stake in this controversy, he did so only when he registered for the spring term. But petitioner took that action only after the case had been fully litigated in the state courts, briefs had been filed in this Court, and oral argument had been heard. The case is thus ripe for decision on a fully developed factual record with sharply defined and fully canvassed legal issues.

Moreover, in endeavoring to dispose of this case as moot, the Court clearly disserves the public interest. The constitutional issues which are avoided today concern vast numbers of people, organizations, and colleges and universities, as evidenced by the filing of twenty-six *amicus curiae* briefs. Few constitutional questions in recent history have stirred as much debate, and they will not disappear. They must inevitably return to the federal courts and ultimately again to this Court. Because avoidance of repetitious litigation serves the public interest, that inevitability counsels against mootness determinations, as here, not compelled by the record. Although the Court should, of course, avoid unnecessary decisions of constitutional questions, we should not transform principles of avoidance of constitutional decisions into devices for side-stepping resolution of difficult cases.

On what appears in this case, I would find that there is an extant controversy and decide the merits of the very important constitutional questions presented.

## Note: Abortions Rights Claims and Mootness

A basic exception to the requirement that a claim not be moot exists when the issue is "capable of repetition yet evading review." *Southern Pacific Terminal Company v. ICC*, 219 U.S. 498 (1911). Because pregnancies normally end after nine months, abortion-rights claims are a paradigmatic example of claims that come within this exception. *Roe v. Wade*, 410 U.S. 113 (1973), exemplifies the analysis. *Roe* involved a Texas statute criminalizing abortion. Jane Roe, a pregnant woman, sought to challenge the statute. Roe claimed that she wished to terminate her pregnancy by an abortion "performed by a competent, licensed physician, under safe, clinical conditions; that she was unable to get a 'legal' abortion in Texas because her life did not appear to be threatened by the continuation of her pregnancy; and that she could not afford to travel to another jurisdiction in order to secure a legal abortion under safe conditions." By the time the case was heard by the Court, Roe was no longer pregnant. Accordingly, the state moved to dismiss her appeal on mootness grounds. The Court held that the case was not moot:

> The usual rule in federal cases is that an actual controversy must exist at stages of appellate or certiorari review, and not simply at the date the action is initiated.

> But when, as here, pregnancy is a significant fact in the litigation, the normal 266-day human gestation period is so short that the pregnancy will come to term before the usual appellate process is complete. If that termination makes a case moot, pregnancy litigation seldom will survive much beyond the trial stage, and appellate review will be effectively denied. Our law should not be that rigid. Pregnancy often comes more than once to the same woman, and in the general population, if man is to survive, it will always be with us. Pregnancy provides a classic justification for a conclusion of nonmootness. It truly could be "capable of repetition, yet evading review."

> We, therefore, agree with the District Court that Jane Roe had standing to undertake this litigation, that she presented a justiciable controversy, and that the termination of her 1970 pregnancy has not rendered her case moot.

## Note: Recent Applications of the Mootness Doctrine

1. In a different part of the *Friends of the Earth v. Laidlaw* opinion discussed in the standing materials earlier, the Court described as "stringent" the standard for judging whether a party's voluntary conduct had mooted a case. In a 2013 case, the Court found this standard satisfied. In *Already, LLC v. Nike, Inc.*, 133 S.Ct. 721 (2013), Nike, the footwear manufacturer, brought a trademark infringement suit against Already, alleging that Already had infringed on Nike's trademarks for certain of its shoe designs. While the litigation was pending, Nike issued a covenant not to sue, pledging not to sue Already under any claim that Already was infringing on Nike's trademarks

by selling "colorable imitations" of Nike's products. Nike then moved to dismiss its lawsuit with prejudice, claiming that its covenant mooted the suit. The lower courts agreed with Nike and granted its motion, and Already appealed to the Supreme Court.

The Supreme Court unanimously agreed that the suit was moot. Writing for all nine justices, Chief Justice Roberts cited the *Friends of the Earth* standard, but held that Nike's covenant not to sue had satisfied it, by comprehensively agreeing not to raise infringement claims against Already. He also noted that Already had not claimed that it was planning on introducing a shoe that might infringe Nike's trademark but would not be covered by Nike's covenant.

The Court also rejected Already's claims of other injuries that it asserted survived the issuance of Nike's covenant, concluding that those injuries did not suffice to establish Article III injury. It rejected the argument that some of Already's investors had stated an unwillingness to invest further until Nike's trademark was struck down by a court, concluding (citing *Lujan v. Defenders of Wildlife* (*supra.* this chapter)) that such injury was too speculative to satisfy Article III's requirements. The Court also rejected Already's argument that it was injured by the very fact of Nike's trademark, which Already argued made it more difficult to compete with Nike. The Court rejected this "sweeping" and "boundless" injury claim.

Justice Kennedy, joined by Justices Thomas, Alito and Sotomayor, joined the Chief Justice's opinion, but also wrote separately to stress that covenants such as Nike's in this case "ought not to be taken as an automatic means [for an infringement plaintiff] to abandon the suit without incurring the risk of an ensuring adverse adjudication."

2. In *Chafin v. Chafin*, 133 S.Ct. 1017 (2013), the Court considered whether an international child custody dispute was mooted by the departure of the child to Scotland. In *Chafin* a foreign-citizen mother removed the child from the United States after receiving a favorable court order from a federal district court, pursuant to legislation implementing an international convention on child abduction. She then received a court order in Scotland confirming the mother's custody and the child's Scottish residency. The father appealed the district court order, but the appellate court dismissed the appeal as moot, concluding that it was "powerless" to grant relief.

The Supreme Court disagreed, and found that the case still presented a live controversy. Again writing for all nine justices, Chief Justice Roberts rejected the mother's argument that the case was mooted by the legislation's stripping of authority from American courts in such situations, describing her argument as one on the merits rather than the continued existence of a case or controversy. He conceded that the Scottish court decision made enforcement of any order favorable to the father more uncertain, but noted that many live controversies featured uncertain prospects for the enforcement of a court order — for example, when an insolvent defendant is ordered to pay damages. He also noted that the parties had a live claim concerning the father's appeal of an order requiring him to pay court costs and travel expenses.

Justice Ginsburg, joined by Justices Scalia and Breyer, concurred in order to address a separate issue.

# Chapter 2

# The Distribution of National Regulatory Powers

## A. Foundational Concepts

### Note: Introduction to the Separation of Powers

1. There is no "Separation of Powers" clause in the Constitution. Rather, we draw the meaning of the separation of powers from the structure of our national government and our understanding of what the Framers contemplated in establishing three separate branches of that government within a system of checks and balances. Separation of powers is defined both by the political resolution of interbranch disputes about the allocation of power and by judicial doctrine that has evolved in the course of the Supreme Court deciding lawsuits growing out of these disputes.

2. The text of the Constitution allocates the national power among the legislative, executive, and judicial branches, in a framework providing for separation of functions as well as interlocking checks on the accretion of power. Article I assigns to Congress "All legislative Powers" vested in the federal government. Article II assigns to the President "the executive Power." Finally, Article III assigns "The judicial Power of the United States" to the Supreme Court and to such "inferior courts" as Congress may establish. This language itself reflects the Framers' interest in limiting the opportunities for any branch to accumulate too much power, which they feared would threaten a loss of liberty.

While the vesting clauses quoted above reveal an intent to distribute authority among the branches, (other provisions reflect a commitment to commingling power.) Through language requiring interaction among the branches, there results a web of interrelated functions, or checks and balances. For example, Article I begins by vesting "All legislative Powers" in Congress, but Section 7 of Article I requires that for a bill duly passed by both legislative chambers to become law it must be presented for signature or disapproved by the President. Article II, Section 1, provides that "the executive Power shall be vested in a President"; however Section 2 requires the "advice and consent" of the Senate for the President to make treaties and to appoint officers, and further states that "Congress may by Law invest the Appointment of such inferior Officers, as they think proper, in the President alone, in the Courts of Law, or in the

Heads of Departments." As Chapter 1 has already examined, Article III vests "the judicial power" in the Supreme Court and whatever lower courts Congress may create. But by its very terms, that vesting gives Congress the power to determine the structure of the federal judicial system below the Supreme Court. Indeed, as you saw in Chapter 1, Article III has been interpreted to give Congress significant power over even the Supreme Court's jurisdiction.

The vagueness of the vesting clauses, when combined with the sharing of power implied by provisions for processes such as making laws and appointing officers, means that separation of powers questions rarely yield unambiguously clear answers. The assertion of one branch's authority often either diminishes that of another branch or is dependent on the cooperation of another. The resulting tension creates political conflict but also opportunities for political accommodation. The accommodations Congress and the President have reached sometimes affect the Court's willingness to intervene in disputes that arguably are best left to the two political branches to resolve. Moreover, the Court's decisions about whether its intervention is required by the Constitution or represents an unwarranted intrusion into the domain of the political branches themselves raise separation of powers questions.

3. Much of what we have come to understand about what the Framers originally intended relates to debates about the adoption of state constitutions between 1776 and 1787. The view adopted by a number of states in their own constitutions was that separation of functions was essential to free government, because it protected liberty by avoiding the usurpation of power and tyranny by one department. At the same time, other post-independence state constitutions went in the opposite direction and gave overwhelming power to the state legislature, on the theory that, as the most representative institution, it was best-suited to govern a democracy. Many of the Framers were quite concerned by what they saw as the growth of factions and political strife in those newly-powerful legislatures.

The concept of separation of powers we attribute to the Framers is also drawn from debate among late eighteenth century political philosophers about how best to protect liberty, as well as about the challenge of adapting institutions of mixed government to the doctrine of popular sovereignty. In short, a number of competing interests and concerns were conveniently captured in the term "separation of powers." The distinct yet interdependent branches of government that became the structure proposed in the Constitution were hardly a product of one cohesive theory of government or one agreed-upon governmental framework.

The debates at the constitutional convention and during the state ratification process confirm that no consensus existed as to the precise institutional arrangement that would satisfy all proponents of such an uncertain doctrine. The Constitution itself contained no express provision for the separation of powers. James Madison, writing *The Federalist* No. 47, defended the document against criticism that it therefore did not satisfy the requirements of separation, noting that some mixing or coordination among the branches was both practically necessary and not contrary to the teachings of Montesquieu, a well-known French political theorist and champion of separated powers. The Senate, moreover, rejected amendments subsequently proposed by Madison and others intended to confirm the "principle" of separation.

In addition, early instances of interaction among the branches in the conduct of affairs, particularly those of Congress and the President, shaped the nascent governmental structures, creating models for interbranch conduct which were neither compelled by any conception of separation of powers nor derived from language in the Constitution. Instead, these early models grew out of the practical and political considerations of the day as well as a concern for efficiency. Many of the early models have lasted through time and serve to inform our understanding of separation of powers today, even if they do not necessarily flow from any essential meaning of the concept.

4. When the Court has decided separation of powers issues, it has created an inconsistent doctrine that at times seems *ad hoc*. The differences in approaches center on which sources are available to determine whether power is within the domain of the executive, legislative, or judicial branches, and whether separation or coordination is seen as the predominant value. The approaches taken by the Court reflect the tension between, on the one hand, the importance of keeping powers separated, and, on the other, the interrelatedness of powers that produces political conflict and, in turn, political accommodation, especially between Congress and the President. The opinions excerpted and discussed in this chapter reflect both of these approaches.

## Note: *The Background of the* Youngstown *Case*

The foundational modern case concerning the respective powers of Congress and the President is *Youngstown Sheet & Tube Co. v. Sawyer*, 343 U.S. 579 (1952). *Youngstown* presents the range of competing methods of analyzing separation of powers. The majority and concurring opinions reflect, respectively, formalist and functional methodologies, while the dissent emphasizes the exigencies of the circumstances and need for urgent action in the national interest. As such, the case is a microcosm of the Court's modern approaches to the separation of powers.

*Youngstown* grew out of the crisis of the Korean War. The war began when North Korea invaded South Korea in June 1950. Although Congress never declared war, it authorized the deployment of American armed forces to support what President Truman called a "police action" to resist the North's invasion. During the conflict, to avert an imminent nationwide strike of steel workers (in April 1952 the President issued an Executive Order directing the Secretary of Commerce to seize and operate most of the country's steel mills.) The Order included findings that his action was necessary to avert the national catastrophe that would inevitably result from a stoppage of steel production in wartime. The Order was not based upon any specific statutory authority. The owners of the mills sued, challenging the seizure order.

# Youngstown Sheet & Tube Co. v. Sawyer (Steel Seizure Case)

## 343 U.S. 579 (1952)

MR. JUSTICE BLACK delivered the opinion of the Court.

We are asked to decide whether the President was acting within his constitutional power when he issued an order directing the Secretary of Commerce to take possession of and operate most of the Nation's steel mills. The mill owners argue that the President's order amounts to lawmaking, a legislative function which the Constitution has expressly confided to the Congress and not to the President. The Government's position is that the order was made on findings of the President that his action was necessary to avert a national catastrophe which would inevitably result from a stoppage of steel production, and that in meeting this grave emergency the President was acting within the aggregate of his constitutional powers as the Nation's Chief Executive and the Commander in Chief of the Armed Forces of the United States....

In the latter part of 1951, a dispute arose between the steel companies and their employees over terms and conditions that should be included in new collective bargaining agreements. Long-continued conferences failed to resolve the dispute. On December 18, 1951, the employees' representative, United Steelworkers of America, C.I.O., gave notice of an intention to strike when the existing bargaining agreements expired on December 31.... The indispensability of steel as a component of substantially all weapons and other war materials led the President to believe that the proposed work stoppage would immediately jeopardize our national defense and that governmental seizure of the steel mills was necessary in order to assure the continued availability of steel. Reciting these considerations for his action, the President, a few hours before the strike was to begin, issued Executive Order 10340.... The order directed the Secretary of Commerce to take possession of most of the steel mills and keep them running. The Secretary immediately issued his own possessory orders, calling upon the presidents of the various seized companies to serve as operating managers for the United States. They were directed to carry on their activities in accordance with regulations and directions of the Secretary. The next morning the President sent a message to Congress reporting his action. Twelve days later he sent a second message. Congress has taken no action.

Obeying the Secretary's orders under protest, the companies brought proceedings against him in the District Court. Their complaints charged that the seizure was not authorized by an act of Congress or by any constitutional provisions.... The United States asserted that a strike disrupting steel production for even a brief period would so endanger the well-being and safety of the Nation that the President had "inherent power" to do what he had done—power "supported by the Constitution, by historical precedent, and by court decisions."... [The] District Court on April 30 issued a preliminary injunction restraining the Secretary from "continuing the seizure and possession of the plants."... On the same day the Court of Appeals stayed the District Court's injunction....

## II

The President's power, if any, to issue the order must stem either from an act of Congress or from the Constitution itself. There is no statute that expressly authorizes the President to take possession of property as he did here. Nor is there any act of Congress to which our attention has been directed from which such a power can fairly be implied. Indeed, we do not understand the Government to rely on statutory authorization for this seizure. There are two statutes which do authorize the President to take both personal and real property under certain conditions. However, the Government admits that these conditions were not met and that the President's order was not rooted in either of the statutes....

Moreover, the use of the seizure technique to solve labor disputes in order to prevent work stoppages was not only unauthorized by any congressional enactment; prior to this controversy, Congress had refused to adopt that method of settling labor disputes. When the Taft-Hartley Act[*] was under consideration in 1947, Congress rejected an amendment which would have authorized such governmental seizures in cases of emergency. Apparently it was thought that the technique of seizure, like that of compulsory arbitration, would interfere with the process of collective bargaining. Consequently, the plan Congress adopted in that Act did not provide for seizure under any circumstances. Instead, the plan sought to bring about settlements by use of the customary devices of mediation, conciliation, investigation by boards of inquiry, and public reports. In some instances temporary injunctions were authorized to provide cooling-off periods. All this failing, unions were left free to strike after a secret vote by employees as to whether they wished to accept their employers' final settlement offer.

It is clear that if the President had authority to issue the order he did, it must be found in some provision of the Constitution. And it is not claimed that express constitutional language grants this power to the President. The contention is that presidential power should be implied from the aggregate of his powers under the Constitution. Particular reliance is placed on provisions in Article II which say that "The executive Power shall be vested in a President ..."; that "he shall take Care that the Laws be faithfully executed"; and that he "shall be Commander in Chief of the Army and Navy of the United States."

The order cannot properly be sustained as an exercise of the President's military power as Commander in Chief of the Armed Forces. The Government attempts to do so by citing a number of cases upholding broad powers in military commanders engaged in day-to-day fighting in a theater of war.... Even though "theater of war" be an expanding concept, we cannot with faithfulness to our constitutional system hold that the Commander in Chief of the Armed Forces has the ultimate power as such to take possession of private property in order to keep labor disputes from stopping production. This is a job for the Nation's lawmakers, not for its military authorities.

---

* [Ed. Note: The Taft-Hartley Act was a major piece of labor legislation enacted by Congress in 1947.]

Nor can the seizure order be sustained because of the several constitutional provisions that grant executive power to the President. In the framework of our Constitution, the President's power to see that the laws are faithfully executed refutes the idea that he is to be a lawmaker. The Constitution limits his functions in the lawmaking process to the recommending of laws he thinks wise and the vetoing of laws he thinks bad. And the Constitution is neither silent nor equivocal about who shall make laws which the President is to execute. The first section of the first article says that "All legislative Powers herein granted shall be vested in a Congress of the United States...." After granting many powers to the Congress, Article I goes on to provide that Congress may "make all Laws which shall be necessary and proper for carrying into Execution the foregoing Powers, and all other Powers vested by this Constitution in the Government of the United States, or in any Department or Officer thereof."

... The preamble of the order itself, like that of many statutes, sets out reasons why the President believes certain policies should be adopted, proclaims these policies as rules of conduct to be followed, and again, like a statute, authorizes a government official to promulgate additional rules and regulations consistent with the policy proclaimed and needed to carry that policy into execution. The power of Congress to adopt such public policies as those proclaimed by the order is beyond question. It can authorize the taking of private property for public use. It can make laws regulating the relationships between employers and employees, prescribing rules designed to settle labor disputes, and fixing wages and working conditions in certain fields of our economy. The Constitution does not subject this lawmaking power of Congress to presidential or military supervision or control.

It is said that other Presidents without congressional authority have taken possession of private business enterprises in order to settle labor disputes. But even if this be true, Congress has not thereby lost its exclusive constitutional authority to make laws necessary and proper to carry out the powers vested by the Constitution....

The Founders of this Nation entrusted the lawmaking power to the Congress alone in both good and bad times. It would do no good to recall the historical events, the fears of power and the hopes for freedom that lay behind their choice. Such a review would but confirm our holding that this seizure order cannot stand. The Judgment of the District Court is Affirmed.

Mr. Justice Frankfurter, concurring.

Although the considerations relevant to the legal enforcement of the principle of separation of powers seem to me more complicated and flexible than may appear from what Mr. Justice Black has written, I join his opinion because I thoroughly agree with the application of the principle to the circumstances of this case....

... A constitutional democracy like ours is perhaps the most difficult of man's social arrangements to manage successfully.... The Founders of this Nation ... acted on the conviction that the experience of man sheds a good deal of light on his nature. It sheds a good deal of light not merely on the need for effective power, if a society is to be at once cohesive and civilized, but also on the need for limitations on the power of governors over the governed.

To that end they rested the structure of our central government on the system of checks and balances. For them the doctrine of separation of powers was not mere theory; it was a felt necessity.... The experience through which the world has passed in our own day has made vivid the realization that the Framers of our Constitution were not inexperienced doctrinaires.... The accretion of dangerous power does not come in a day. It does come, however slowly, from the generative force of unchecked disregard of the restrictions that fence in even the most disinterested assertion of authority....

The pole-star for constitutional adjudications is John Marshall's greatest judicial utterance that "it is a *constitution* we are expounding." *McCulloch v. Maryland*, 4 Wheat. 316 (1819). That requires both a spacious view in applying an instrument of government "made for an undefined and expanding future," and as narrow a delimitation of the constitutional issues as the circumstances permit. Not the least characteristic of great statesmanship which the Framers manifested was the extent to which they did not attempt to bind the future. It is no less incumbent upon this Court to avoid putting fetters upon the future by needless pronouncements today.

Marshall's admonition ... is especially relevant when the Court is required to give legal sanctions to an underlying principle of the Constitution—that of separation of powers....

The issue before us can be met, and therefore should be, without attempting to define the President's powers comprehensively... The judiciary may, as this case proves, have to intervene in determining where authority lies as between the democratic forces in our scheme of government. But in doing so we should be wary and humble....

... Congress has frequently—at least 16 times since 1916—specifically provided for executive seizure of production, transportation, communications, or storage facilities. In every case it has qualified this grant of power with limitations and safeguards. This body of enactments ... demonstrates that Congress deemed seizure so drastic a power as to require that it be carefully circumscribed whenever the President was vested with this extraordinary authority....

Congress in 1947 was again called upon to consider whether governmental seizure should be used to avoid serious industrial shutdowns. Congress decided against conferring such power generally and in advance, without special congressional enactment to meet each particular need.... [Proponents] as well as the opponents of the bill which became the Labor Management Relations Act of 1947[*] clearly understood that as a result of that legislation the only recourse for preventing a shutdown in any basic industry, after failure of mediation, was Congress.

---

\* [Ed. Note: This was the formal title of the Taft-Hartley Act mentioned earlier in the opinion.]

... On a balance of considerations Congress chose not to lodge this power in the President. Congress made a conscious choice of policy in a field full of perplexity and peculiarly within legislative responsibility for choice....

It cannot be contended that the President would have had power to issue this order had Congress explicitly negated such authority in formal legislation....

... But it is now claimed that the President has seizure power by virtue of the Defense Production Act of 1950 and its Amendments. And the claim is based on the occurrence of new events — Korea and the need for stabilization.... Absence of authority in the President to deal with a crisis does not imply want of power in the Government. Conversely the fact that power exists in the Government does not vest it in the President. The need for new legislation does not enact it. Nor does it repeal or amend existing law....

It is one thing to draw an intention of Congress from general language and to say that Congress would have explicitly written what is inferred, where Congress has not addressed itself to a specific situation. It is quite impossible, however, when Congress did specifically address itself to a problem, as Congress did to that of seizure, to find secreted in the interstices of legislation the very grant of power which Congress consciously withheld. To find authority so explicitly withheld is not merely to disregard in a particular instance the clear will of Congress. It is to disrespect the whole legislative process and the constitutional division of authority between President and Congress....

Apart from his vast share of responsibility for the conduct of our foreign relations, the embracing function of the President is that "he shall take Care that the Laws be faithfully executed...." The nature of that authority has for me been comprehensively indicated by Mr. Justice Holmes. "The duty of the President to see that the laws be executed is a duty that does not go beyond the laws or require him to achieve more than Congress sees fit to leave within his power." The powers of the President are not as particularized as are those of Congress. But unenumerated powers do not mean undefined powers....

... Deeply embedded traditional ways of conducting government cannot supplant the Constitution or legislation, but they give meaning to the words of a text or supply them. It is an inadmissibly narrow conception of American constitutional law to confine it to the words of the Constitution and to disregard the gloss which life has written upon them. In short, a systematic, unbroken, executive practice, long pursued to the knowledge of the Congress and never before questioned, engaged in by Presidents who have also sworn to uphold the Constitution, making as it were such exercise of power part of the structure of our government, may be treated as a gloss on "executive Power" vested in the President....

... In his eleven seizures of industrial facilities, President Wilson acted, or at least purported to act, under authority granted by Congress. Thus his seizures cannot be adduced as interpretations by a President of his own powers in the absence of statute.

Down to the World War II period, then, the record is barren of instances comparable to the one before us. Of twelve seizures by President Roosevelt prior to the enactment of the War Labor Disputes Act in June, 1943, three were sanctioned by existing law, and six others were effected after Congress, on December 8, 1941, had declared the existence of a state of war. In this case, reliance on the powers that flow from declared war has been commendably disclaimed by the Solicitor General. Thus the list of executive assertions of the power of seizure in circumstances comparable to the present reduces to three in the six-month period from June to December of 1941.... [These] three isolated instances do not ... come to us sanctioned by long-continued acquiescence of Congress giving decisive weight to a construction by the Executive of its powers....

MR. JUSTICE JACKSON, concurring in the judgment and opinion of the court....

... Just what our forefathers did envision, or would have envisioned had they fore-seen modern conditions, must be divined from materials almost as enigmatic as the dreams Joseph was called upon to interpret for Pharaoh. A century and a half of par-tisan debate and scholarly speculation yields no net result but only supplies more or less apt quotations from respected sources on each side of any question. They largely cancel each other. And court decisions are indecisive because of the judicial practice of dealing with the largest questions in the most narrow way.

The actual art of governing under our Constitution does not and cannot conform to judicial definitions of the power of any of its branches based on isolated clauses or even single Articles torn from context. While the Constitution diffuses power the better to secure liberty, it also contemplates that practice will integrate the dispersed powers into a workable government. It enjoins upon its branches separateness but interdependence, autonomy but reciprocity. Presidential powers are not fixed but fluctuate, depending upon their disjunction or conjunction with those of Congress....

1. When the President acts pursuant to an express or implied authorization of Congress, his authority is at its maximum, for it includes all that he possesses in his own right plus all that Congress can delegate. In these circumstances, and in these only, may he be said (for what it may be worth) to personify the federal sovereignty.... A seizure executed by the President pursuant to an Act of Congress would be supported by the strongest of presumptions and the widest latitude of judicial interpretation, and the burden of persuasion would rest heavily upon any who might attack it.

2. When the President acts in absence of either a congressional grant or denial of authority, he can only rely upon his own independent powers, but there is a zone of twilight in which he and Congress may have concurrent authority, or in which its distribution is uncertain. Therefore, congressional inertia, indifference or quiescence may sometimes, at least as a practical matter, enable, if not invite, measures on in-dependent presidential responsibility. In this area, any actual test of power is likely to depend on the imperatives of events and contemporary imponderables rather than on abstract theories of law.

3. When the President takes measures incompatible with the expressed or implied will of Congress, his power is at its lowest ebb, for then he can rely only upon his own constitutional powers minus any constitutional powers of Congress over the

matter. Courts can sustain exclusive presidential control in such a case only by disabling the Congress from acting upon the subject. Presidential claim to a power at once so conclusive and preclusive must be scrutinized with caution, for what is at stake is the equilibrium established by our constitutional system.

Into which of these classifications does this executive seizure of the steel industry fit? It … is conceded that no congressional authorization exists for this seizure....

Can it then be defended under flexible tests available to the second category? It seems clearly eliminated from that class because Congress has not left seizure of private property an open field but has covered it by three statutory policies inconsistent with this seizure....

This leaves the current seizure to be justified only by the severe tests under the third grouping, where it can be supported only by any remainder of executive power after subtraction of such powers as Congress may have over the subject. In short, we can sustain the President only by holding that seizure of such strike-bound industries is within his domain and beyond control by Congress....

The Solicitor General seeks the power of seizure in three clauses of the Executive Article, the first reading, "The executive Power shall be vested in a President of the United States of America.".... I cannot accept the view that this clause is a grant in bulk of all conceivable executive power but regard it as an allocation to the presidential office of the generic powers thereafter stated.

The clause on which the Government next relies is that "The President shall be Commander in Chief of the Army and Navy of the United States." … [The] argument tendered at our bar [is] that the President having, on his own responsibility, sent American troops abroad derives from that act "affirmative power" to seize the means of producing a supply of steel for them....

… Nothing in our Constitution is plainer than that declaration of a war is entrusted only to Congress. Of course, a state of war may in fact exist without a formal declaration. But no doctrine that the Court could promulgate would seem to me more sinister and alarming than that a President whose conduct of foreign affairs is so largely controlled, and often even is unknown, can vastly enlarge his mastery over the internal affairs of the country by his own commitment of the Nation's armed forces to some foreign venture....

The third clause in which the Solicitor General finds seizure powers is that "he shall take Care that the Laws be faithfully executed...." That authority must be matched against words of the Fifth Amendment that "No person shall be deprived of life, liberty or property, without due process of law...." One gives a governmental authority that reaches so far as there is law, the other gives a private right that authority shall go no farther. These signify about all there is of the principle that ours is a government of laws, not men, and that we submit ourselves to rulers only if under rules.

The Solicitor General lastly grounds support of the seizure upon nebulous, inherent powers never expressly granted but said to have accrued to the office from the customs and claims of preceding administrations. The plea is for a resulting power to deal with a crisis or an emergency according to the necessities of the case, the unarticulated assumption being that necessity knows no law.

Loose and irresponsible use of adjectives colors all nonlegal and much legal discussion of presidential powers. "Inherent" powers, "implied" powers, "incidental" powers, "plenary" powers, "war" powers and "emergency" powers are used, often interchangeably and without fixed or ascertainable meanings.

The vagueness and generality of the clauses that set forth presidential powers afford a plausible basis for pressures within and without an administration for presidential action beyond that supported by those whose responsibility it is to defend his actions in court. The claim of inherent and unrestricted presidential powers has long been a persuasive dialectical weapon in political controversy.... [A] judge cannot accept self-serving press statements of the attorney for one of the interested parties as authority in answering a constitutional question, even if the advocate was himself. But prudence has counseled that actual reliance on such nebulous claims stop short of provoking a judicial test....

... Congress may and has granted extraordinary authorities which lie dormant in normal times but may be called into play by the Executive in war or upon proclamation of a national emergency.... The public may know the extent and limitations of the powers that can be asserted, and persons affected may be informed from the statute of their rights and duties.

In view of the ease, expedition and safety with which Congress can grant and has granted large emergency powers, certainly ample to embrace this crisis, I am quite unimpressed with the argument that we should affirm possession of them without statute. Such power either has no beginning or it has no end. If it exists, it need submit to no legal restraint. I am not alarmed that it would plunge us straightaway into dictatorship, but it is at least a step in that wrong direction....

Executive power has the advantage of concentration in a single head in whose choice the whole Nation has a part, making him the focus of public hopes and expectations. In drama, magnitude and finality his decisions so far overshadow any others that almost alone he fills the public eye and ear. No other personality in public life can begin to compete with him in access to the public mind through modern methods of communications. By his prestige as head of state and his influence upon public opinion he exerts a leverage upon those who are supposed to check and balance his power which often cancels their effectiveness.

Moreover, rise of the party system has made a significant extraconstitutional supplement to real executive power.... Party loyalties and interests, sometimes more binding than law, extend his effective control into branches of government other than his own and he often may win, as a political leader, what he cannot command under the Constitution.... I cannot be brought to believe that this country will suffer if the Court refuses further to aggrandize the presidential office, already so potent and so relatively immune from judicial review, at the expense of Congress.

But I have no illusion that any decision by this Court can keep power in the hands of Congress if it is not wise and timely in meeting its problems. A crisis that challenges the President equally, or perhaps primarily, challenges Congress.... We may say that power to legislate for emergencies belongs in the hands of Congress, but only Congress itself can prevent power from slipping through its fingers.

... With all its defects, delays and inconveniences, men have discovered no technique for long preserving free government except that the Executive be under the law, and that the law be made by parliamentary deliberations....

JUSTICE DOUGLAS, concurring. [omitted]

JUSTICE CLARK, concurring in the judgment. [omitted]

CHIEF JUSTICE VINSON, with whom MR. JUSTICE REED and MR. JUSTICE MINTON join, dissenting.

The President of the United States directed the Secretary of Commerce to take temporary possession of the Nation's steel mills during the existing emergency because "a work stoppage would immediately jeopardize and imperil our national defense and the defense of those joined with us in resisting aggression, and would add to the continuing danger of our soldiers, sailors and airmen engaged in combat in the field." ...

... Because we cannot agree that affirmance is proper on any ground, and because of the transcending importance of the questions presented not only in this critical litigation but also to the powers the President and of future Presidents to act in time of crisis, we are compelled to register this dissent.

I

... The Defense Production Act was extended in 1951, a Senate Committee noting that in the dislocation caused by the programs for purchase of military equipment "lies the seed of an economic disaster that might well destroy the military might we are straining to build." ... Even before Korea, steel production at levels above theoretical 100% capacity was not capable of supplying civilian needs alone. Since Korea, the tremendous military demand for steel has far exceeded the increases in productive capacity. This Committee emphasized that the shortage of steel, even with the mills operating at full capacity, coupled with increased civilian purchasing power, presented grave danger of disastrous inflation....

II

... Under this view, the President is left powerless at the very moment when the need for action may be most pressing and when no one, other than he, is immediately capable of action.... [He] is left powerless because a power not expressly given to Congress is nevertheless found to rest exclusively with Congress....

The whole of the "executive Power" is vested in the President. Before entering office, the President swears that he "will faithfully execute the Office of President of the United States, and will to the best of [his] Ability, preserve, protect and defend the Constitution of the United States." Art. II, § 1.... [The] Presidency was deliberately fashioned as an office of power and independence. Of course, the Framers created no autocrat capable of arrogating any power unto himself at any time. But neither did they create an automaton impotent to exercise the powers of Government at a time when the survival of the Republic itself may be at stake.

... Marshall admonished, that the Constitution is "intended to endure for ages to come, and, consequently, to be adapted to the various *crises* of human affairs," and that "its means are adequate to its ends." Cases do arise presenting questions which could not have been foreseen by the Framers. In such cases, the Constitution has been treated as a living document adaptable to new situations....

### III

A review of executive action demonstrates that our Presidents have on many occasions exhibited the leadership contemplated by the Framers when they made the President Commander in Chief, and imposed upon him the trust to "take Care that the Laws be faithfully executed." With or without explicit statutory authorization, Presidents have at such times dealt with national emergencies by acting promptly and resolutely to enforce legislative programs, at least to save those programs until Congress could act....

... The fact that temporary executive seizures of industrial plants to meet an emergency have not been directly tested in this Court furnishes not the slightest suggestion that such actions have been illegal. Rather, the fact that Congress and the courts have consistently recognized and given their support to such executive action indicates that such a power of seizure has been accepted throughout our history....

### VI

... Faced with the duty of executing the defense programs which Congress had enacted and the disastrous effects that any stoppage in steel production would have on those programs, the President acted to preserve those programs by seizing the steel mills. There is no question that the possession was other than temporary in character and subject to congressional direction—either approving, disapproving or regulating the manner in which the mills were to be administered and returned to the owners. The President immediately informed Congress of his action and clearly stated his intention to abide by the legislative will.... [In] this case the President acted in full conformity with his duties under the Constitution. Accordingly, we would reverse the order of the District Court.

## Note: Formalism and Functionalism in Separation of Powers Analysis

1. *Youngstown* reflects the basic tension between what are known as the formalist and functionalist approaches to separation of powers. "Formalism" refers to a mode of analysis that stresses clear divisions between the branches based on literal applications of constitutional text and *a priori* definitions of the functions each branch is assigned. In *Youngstown*, this approach is exemplified by Justice Black's approach, which stresses an abstract description of what constitutes "legislation," which he then

compares to the President's steel seizure order. Once Justice Black decided that the order met the definition of legislation, he had no difficulty concluding that the President was not authorized to issue it, since "the President's power to see that the laws are faithfully executed refutes the idea that he is to be a lawmaker."

By contrast, a functional approach is one that responds to the idea that the branches share powers, thus rendering it impossible to draw bright-line distinctions. Functionalist analysis focuses instead on how the issue in question affects the relationship between the branches, for example, by asking whether a particular government action threatens to weaken another branch to an unacceptable extent. Justice Jackson's concurrence in *Youngstown* exemplifies the functionalist approach, by focusing not on the *a priori* description of the seizure order as legislation or law enforcement, but rather on the degree to which Congress and the President were in conflict over the order's basic policy, and the extent to which the order could be supported as an exercise of the President's core powers. You've already seen the justices debate the merits of formalist and functionalist analysis in Chapter 1, most explicitly in *Schor v. Commodities Futures Trading Commission* (1986) and *Plaut v. Spendthrift Farm* (1994), but also in some of the standing cases.

2. Formalism and functionalism both have obvious appeal and obvious drawbacks, all of which are evident in *Youngstown*. Formalism has the benefit of drawing clear lines between branches, and reflects a methodology that promises clear results. By contrast, functionalism, as exemplified in Justice Jackson's analysis, employs an often-complex, context-specific analysis that does not yield predictable results. Indeed, Justice Jackson's famous description of a "zone of twilight" that exists when Congress has not spoken about a policy the President is attempting to implement reflects his recognition that his analysis does not yield predictable, clear, results.

But formalism has its drawbacks, as well. In particular, it often reaches clear results only at the cost of misdescribing empirical reality. In *Youngstown*, for example, Justice Black's description of legislation arguably covers much action taken by administrative agencies, for example, when they enact regulations. Later cases, most notably *INS v. Chadha*, 462 U.S. 919 (1983) (excerpted later in this chapter), attempt to grapple with this reality. In general, however, a criticism of formalism is that it ignores the realities of the system created by the Framers—in particular, the fact that in our system the branches share powers, at least to some degree. By contrast, functionalism, as expressed by Justice Jackson in *Youngstown*, accurately reflects these complexities. However, as explained above, it does so at the cost of providing a predictable legal standard.

The benefits and drawbacks of these two approaches are well-known. As you will see in the materials that follow, the Court has vacillated between these two approaches. At times this had made its separation of powers jurisprudence appear incoherent.

# B. Presidential Immunity from Judicial Process

Perhaps the most fundamental protection each branch enjoys from the other is protection from legal prosecution, or, more generally, from coercive judicial processes arising out of their official duties. Of course, Congress may impeach the President or any federal judge. (It may also "expel" one of its members, Art. I, §5, cl. 2.) Beyond such draconian remedies, the Speech and Debate Clause protects members of Congress from being "questioned in any other Place" but Congress itself. Judges enjoy life tenure (subject to impeachment).

Of course, it is one thing to impeach a judge or expel a member of Congress; as multi-member bodies, the federal judiciary or Congress continues to function even when one member is removed. But attacks on the President raise the specter of attacks on the Presidency itself, given the fact that Article II vests "the executive power" in one person—the President. To what extent does the President have a constitutional privilege to avoid judicial investigations or prosecutions?

### Note: Presidential Immunities Up to United States v. Nixon

1. Nowhere in the text of the Constitution is there any reference to executive privilege. In the Framers' debates, delegates cited concern about unchecked executive power as support for provisions requiring presidential cooperation and coordination with Congress (for example, by requiring Senate approval of the President's appointments), and establishing impeachment as a means of restraining presidential action. For example, James Wilson told the Pennsylvania Ratification Convention:

> The Executive power is better to be trusted when it has no screen. Sir, we have a responsibility in the person for our President; he cannot act improperly, and hide either his negligence or inattention; he cannot roll upon any other person the weight of his criminality.... Add to all this, that officer is placed high, and is possessed of power far from being contemptible, yet not a *single privilege* is annexed to his character.

2. In the trial of Aaron Burr, the Vice President during Jefferson's first term who was charged with treason, the issue of executive privilege was squarely before Chief Justice Marshall, sitting (as Supreme Court justices did in the past) as a lower court judge. Burr was the target of great hostility by Jefferson, who barely won the presidential race against Burr for a second term. During the trial, in response to President Jefferson's refusal to release a letter from a confidante and aide to Burr, Chief Justice John Marshall, sitting as trial judge in that case, countered that the President can be subpoenaed, examined as a witness, and required to produce papers. He reasoned that the President's circumstances were distinguishable from the prerogatives of a monarch. Consequently, the immunity from the legal process enjoyed by the King did not extend to the President. *United States v. Burr*, 25 F. Cas. 30 (C.C. Va. 1807). However, Justice Marshall also emphasized the special deference to be accorded requests by the President to be excused from producing documents or offering testimony:

> Although subject to the general rules which apply to others, [he] may have sufficient motives for declining to produce a particular paper, and those motives may be such as to restrain the court from enforcing its production.... The occasion for demanding it ought, in such a case, be very strong, and to be fully shown to the court before its production could be insisted on.

3. A few other cases preceding the Watergate controversy had directly addressed other aspects of the President's amenability to the judicial process in controversies not involving Congress. For example, in a lawsuit aimed at enjoining President Andrew Johnson from implementing certain Reconstruction laws, the question arose whether a President could be compelled to act or was exempt from judicial process. *Mississippi v. Johnson*, 71 U.S. (4 Wall.) 475 (1866). Chief Justice Chase, for a unanimous Court, ruled that in enforcing the Reconstruction Acts, the President would be exercising duties that were "purely executive and political," and thus outside the jurisdiction of the Court to enforce. Chief Justice Chase emphasized the confrontation among the three branches such judicial enforcement would impose: obeying the Court's injunction could subject the President to impeachment for failure to enforce the laws. If the President sought protection from the Court, the Court and the Senate would be in conflict. Chief Justice Chase observed: "The Congress is the legislative department of the government; the President is the executive department. Neither can be restrained in its action by the judicial department; though the acts of both, when performed, are, in proper cases, subject to its cognizance." In *Youngstown*, the issue of presidential immunity from a judicial proceeding was circumvented by the litigants who sued the Secretary of Commerce, Henry Sawyer.

4. In *United States v. Nixon*, excerpted below, the Court rejected the President's claim to absolute immunity from judicial process, in favor of a qualified privilege that would be balanced against the countervailing interest in disclosure. Following indictments alleging violation of federal laws by White House staff and political supporters of the President, the special prosecutor appointed to investigate these matters obtained a subpoena directing the President to produce tape recordings, papers, and other materials relating to the pending trial. The material concerned conversations with aides and advisors. President Nixon, who was not indicted but was named by the grand jury as an unindicted co-conspirator, claimed executive privilege in a motion to quash the subpoena. The district court, treating the requested material as presumptively privileged, ruled that the Special Prosecutor had made a sufficient showing to rebut the presumption and issued an order for in-chambers ("*in camera*") examination of the subpoenaed material. The court stayed its order pending appellate review, and the President sought review by the court of appeals. The Special Prosecutor immediately filed a petition for a writ of *certiorari* before judgment, and the President filed a cross petition for the writ. The Court granted both petitions "because of the public importance of the issues presented and the need for their prompt resolution."

## United States v. Nixon

### 418 U.S. 683 (1974)

Mr. Chief Justice Burger delivered the opinion of the Court.

This litigation presents for review the denial of a motion, filed in the District Court on behalf of the President of the United States, in the case of *United States v. Mitchell*, to quash a third-party subpoena *duces tecum* issued by the United States District Court for the District of Columbia, pursuant to Fed. Rule Crim. Proc. 17(c). The subpoena directed the President to produce certain tape recordings and documents relating to his conversations with aides and advisers. The court rejected the President's claims of absolute executive privilege, of lack of jurisdiction, and of failure to satisfy the requirements of Rule 17(c). The President appealed to the Court of Appeals. We granted both the United States' petition for certiorari before judgment and also the President's cross-petition for certiorari before judgment....

On March 1, 1974, a grand jury of the United States District Court for the District of Columbia returned an indictment charging seven named individuals with various offenses, including conspiracy to defraud the United States and to obstruct justice. Although he was not designated as such in the indictment, the grand jury named the President, among others, as an unindicted co-conspirator. On April 18, 1974, upon motion of the Special Prosecutor, a subpoena *duces tecum* was issued pursuant to Rule 17(c) to the President.... This subpoena required the production, in advance of the September 9 trial date, of certain tapes, memoranda, papers, transcripts or other writings relating to certain precisely identified meetings between the President and others. The Special Prosecutor was able to fix the time, place, and persons present at these discussions because the White House daily logs and appointment records had been delivered to him. On April 30, the President publicly released edited transcripts of 43 conversations; portions of 20 conversations subject to subpoena in the present case were included. On May 1, 1974, the President's counsel filed a "special appearance" and a motion to quash the subpoena under Rule 17(c). This motion was accompanied by a formal claim of privilege....

On May 20, 1974, the District Court denied the motion ... The District Court held that the judiciary, not the President, was the final arbiter of a claim of executive privilege. The court concluded that, under the circumstances of this case, the presumptive privilege was overcome by the Special Prosecutor's prima facie "demonstration of need sufficiently compelling to warrant judicial examination in chambers...." ...

IV

THE CLAIM OF PRIVILEGE

A

... [We] turn to the claim that the subpoena should be quashed because it demands "confidential conversations between a President and his close advisors that it would be inconsistent with the public interest to produce." The first contention is a broad claim that the separation of powers doctrine precludes judicial review of a President's claim of privilege. The second contention is that if he does not prevail on the claim of absolute privilege, the court should hold as a matter of constitutional law that the privilege prevails over the subpoena *duces tecum*.

In the performance of assigned constitutional duties each branch of the Government must initially interpret the Constitution, and the interpretation of its powers by any branch is due great respect from the others. The President's counsel, as we have noted, reads the Constitution as providing an absolute privilege of confidentiality for all

Presidential communications. Many decisions of this Court, however, have unequivocally reaffirmed the holding of *Marbury v. Madison* (1803) [*Supra.* Chapter 1], that "it is emphatically the province and duty of the judicial department to say what the law is."

No holding of the Court has defined the scope of judicial power specifically relating to the enforcement of a subpoena for confidential Presidential communications for use in a criminal prosecution, but other exercises of power by the Executive Branch and the Legislative Branch have been found invalid as in conflict with the Constitution. *Powell v. McCormack*, 395 U.S. 486 (1969) [Note *supra.* Chapter 1]; *Youngstown, Sheet & Tube Co. v. Sawyer* (1952) [*Supra.* this chapter]. In a series of cases, the Court interpreted the explicit immunity conferred by express provisions of the Constitution on Members of the House and Senate by the Speech or Debate Clause. Since this Court has consistently exercised the power to construe and delineate claims arising under express powers, it must follow that the Court has authority to interpret claims with respect to powers alleged to derive from enumerated powers.

Our system of government "requires that federal courts on occasion interpret the Constitution in a manner at variance with the construction given the document by another branch." *Powell v. McCormack, supra.* And in *Baker v. Carr* (1962) [*Supra.* Chapter 1], the Court stated:

> Deciding whether a matter has in any measure been committed by the Constitution to another branch of government, or whether the action of that branch exceeds whatever authority has been committed, is itself a delicate exercise in constitutional interpretation, and is a responsibility of this Court as ultimate interpreter of the Constitution.

Notwithstanding the deference each branch must accord the others, the "judicial Power of the United States" vested in the federal courts by Art. III, § 1, of the Constitution can no more be shared with the Executive Branch than the Chief Executive, for example, can share with the Judiciary the veto power, or the Congress share with the Judiciary the power to override a Presidential veto. Any other conclusion would be contrary to the basic concept of separation of powers and the checks and balances that flow from the scheme of a tripartite government. *The Federalist* No. 47. We therefore reaffirm that it is the province and duty of this Court "to say what the law is" with respect to the claim of privilege presented in this case.

B

In support of his claim of absolute privilege, the President's counsel urges two grounds, one of which is common to all governments and one of which is peculiar to our system of separation of powers. The first ground is the valid need for protection of communications between high Government officials and those who advise and assist them in the performance of their manifold duties; the importance of this confidentiality is too plain to require further discussion. Human experience teaches that those who expect public dissemination of their remarks may well temper candor with a concern for appearances and for their own interests to the detriment of the deci-

(1)

sionmaking process. Whatever the nature of the privilege of confidentiality of Presidential communications in the exercise of Art. II powers, the privilege can be said to derive from the supremacy of each branch within its own assigned area of constitutional duties. Certain powers and privileges flow from the nature of enumerated powers; the protection of the confidentiality of Presidential communications has similar constitutional underpinnings.

The second ground asserted by the President's counsel in support of the claim of absolute privilege rests on the doctrine of separation of powers. Here it is argued that the independence of the Executive Branch within its own sphere, *Humphrey's Executor v. United States*, 295 U.S. 602 (1935); *Kilbourn v. Thompson*, 103 U.S. 168 (1881), insulates a President from a judicial subpoena in an ongoing criminal prosecution, and thereby protects confidential Presidential communications.

However, neither the doctrine of separation of powers, nor the need for confidentiality of high-level communications, without more, can sustain an absolute, unqualified Presidential privilege of immunity from judicial process under all circumstances. The President's need for complete candor and objectivity from advisers calls for great deference from the courts. However, when the privilege depends solely on the broad, undifferentiated claim of public interest in the confidentiality of such conversations, a confrontation with other values arises. Absent a claim of need to protect military, diplomatic, or sensitive national security secrets, we find it difficult to accept the argument that even the very important interest in confidentiality of Presidential communications is significantly diminished by production of such material for *in camera* inspection with all the protection that a district court will be obliged to provide.

The impediment that an absolute, unqualified privilege would place in the way of the primary constitutional duty of the Judicial Branch to do justice in criminal prosecutions would plainly conflict with the function of the courts under Art. III. In designing the structure of our Government and dividing and allocating the sovereign power among three co-equal branches, the Framers of the Constitution sought to provide a comprehensive system, but the separate powers were not intended to operate with absolute independence.

> "While the Constitution diffuses power the better to secure liberty, it also contemplates that practice will integrate the dispersed powers into a workable government. It enjoins upon its branches separateness but interdependence, autonomy but reciprocity." *Youngstown Sheet & Tube Co. v. Sawyer* (Jackson, J., concurring).

To read the Art. II powers of the President as providing an absolute privilege as against a subpoena essential to enforcement of criminal statutes on no more than a generalized claim of the public interest in confidentiality of nonmilitary and nondiplomatic discussions would upset the constitutional balance of "a workable government" and gravely impair the role of the courts under Art. III.

## C

Since we conclude that the legitimate needs of the judicial process may outweigh Presidential privilege, it is necessary to resolve those competing interests in a manner that preserves the essential functions of each branch. The right and indeed the duty to resolve that question does not free the Judiciary from according high respect to the representations made on behalf of the President. *United States v. Burr*, 25 F. Cas. 187 (D. Va. 1807).

The expectation of a President to the confidentiality of his conversations and correspondence, like the claim of confidentiality of judicial deliberations, for example, has all the values to which we accord deference for the privacy of all citizens and, added to those values, is the necessity for protection of the public interest in candid, objective, and even blunt or harsh opinions in Presidential decisionmaking. A President and those who assist him must be free to explore alternatives in the process of shaping policies and making decisions and to do so in a way many would be unwilling to express except privately. These are the considerations justifying a presumptive privilege for Presidential communications. The privilege is fundamental to the operation of Government and inextricably rooted in the separation of powers under the Constitution. In *Nixon v. Sirica*, 487 F.2d 700 (D.C. Cir. 1973), the Court of Appeals held that such Presidential communications are "presumptively privileged," and this position is accepted by both parties in the present litigation. We agree with Mr. Chief Justice Marshall's observation, therefore, that "in no case of this kind would a court be required to proceed against the president as against an ordinary individual." *United States v. Burr.*

But this presumptive privilege must be considered in light of our historic commitment to the rule of law. This is nowhere more profoundly manifest than in our view that "the twofold aim [of criminal justice] is that guilt shall not escape or innocence suffer." *Berger v. United States*, 295 U.S. 78 (1935). We have elected to employ an adversary system of criminal justice in which the parties contest all issues before a court of law. The need to develop all relevant facts in the adversary system is both fundamental and comprehensive. The ends of criminal justice would be defeated if judgments were to be founded on a partial or speculative presentation of the facts. The very integrity of the judicial system and public confidence in the system depend on full disclosure of all the facts, within the framework of the rules of evidence. To ensure that justice is done, it is imperative to the function of courts that compulsory process be available for the production of evidence needed either by the prosecution or by the defense.

Only recently the Court restated the ancient proposition of law, albeit in the context of a grand jury inquiry rather than a trial,

> "that 'the public ... has a right to every man's evidence,' except for those persons protected by a constitutional, common-law, or statutory privilege, *United States v. Bryan*, 339 U.S. 323 (1950)."

The privileges referred to by the Court are designed to protect weighty and legitimate competing interests. Thus, the Fifth Amendment to the Constitution provides that no man "shall be compelled in any criminal case to be a witness against himself." And, generally, an attorney or a priest may not be required to disclose what has been revealed in professional confidence. These and other interests are recognized in law by privileges against forced disclosure, established in the Constitution, by statute, or at common law ... [but are not] expansively construed, for they are in derogation of the search for truth.

In this case the President challenges a subpoena served on him as a third party requiring the production of materials for use in a criminal prosecution; he does so on the claim that he has a privilege against disclosure of confidential communications. He does not place his claim of privilege on the ground they are military or diplomatic secrets. As to these areas of Art. II duties the courts have traditionally shown the utmost deference to Presidential responsibilities.... No case of the Court, however, has extended this high degree of deference to a President's generalized interest in confidentiality....

The right to the production of all evidence at a criminal trial similarly has constitutional dimensions. The Sixth Amendment explicitly confers upon every defendant in a criminal trial the right "to be confronted with the witnesses against him" and "to have compulsory process for obtaining witnesses in his favor." Moreover, the Fifth Amendment also guarantees that no person shall be deprived of liberty without due process of law. It is the manifest duty of the courts to vindicate those guarantees, and to accomplish that it is essential that all relevant and admissible evidence be produced.

In this case we must weigh the importance of the general privilege of confidentiality of Presidential communications in performance of the President's responsibilities against the inroads of such a privilege on the fair administration of criminal justice. The interest in preserving confidentiality is weighty indeed and entitled to great respect. However, we cannot conclude that advisers will be moved to temper the candor of their remarks by the infrequent occasions of disclosure because of the possibility that such conversations will be called for in the context of a criminal prosecution.

On the other hand, the allowance of the privilege to withhold evidence that is demonstrably relevant in a criminal trial would cut deeply into the guarantee of due process of law and gravely impair the basic function of the courts. A President's acknowledged need for confidentiality in the communications of his office is general in nature, whereas the constitutional need for production of relevant evidence in a criminal proceeding is specific and central to the fair adjudication of a particular criminal case in the administration of justice. Without access to specific facts a criminal prosecution may be totally frustrated. The President's broad interest in confidentiality of communications will not be vitiated by disclosure of a limited number of conversations preliminarily shown to have some bearing on the pending criminal cases.

We conclude that when the ground for asserting privilege as to subpoenaed materials sought for use in a criminal trial is based only on the generalized interest in confidentiality, it cannot prevail over the fundamental demands of due process of law in the fair administration of criminal justice. The generalized assertion of privilege must yield to the demonstrated, specific need for evidence in a pending criminal trial.

## D

… If a President concludes that compliance with a subpoena would be injurious to the public interest he may properly, as was done here, invoke a claim of privilege on the return of the subpoena. Upon receiving a claim of privilege from the Chief Executive, it became the further duty of the District Court to treat the subpoenaed material as presumptively privileged and to require the Special Prosecutor to demonstrate that the Presidential material was "essential to the justice of the [pending criminal] case." *United States v. Burr*. Here the District Court treated the material as presumptively privileged, proceeded to find that the Special Prosecutor had made a sufficient showing to rebut the presumption, and ordered an *in camera* examination of the subpoenaed material. On the basis of our examination of the record we are unable to conclude that the District Court erred in ordering the inspection. Accordingly we affirm the order of the District Court that subpoenaed materials be transmitted to that court. We now turn to the important question of the District Court's responsibilities in conducting the *in camera* examination of Presidential materials or communications delivered under the compulsion of the subpoena *duces tecum*.

## E

… "The guard, furnished to [the President] to protect him from being harassed by vexatious and unnecessary subpoenas, is to be looked for in the conduct of a district court after those subpoenas have issued; not in any circumstance which is to precede their being issued." *United States v. Burr*. Statements that meet the test of admissibility and relevance must be isolated; all other material must be excised. At this stage the District Court is not limited to representations of the Special Prosecutor as to the evidence sought by the subpoena; the material will be available to the District Court. It is elementary that *in camera* inspection of evidence is always a procedure calling for scrupulous protection against any release or publication of material not found by the court, at that stage, probably admissible in evidence and relevant to the issues of the trial for which it is sought. That being true of an ordinary situation, it is obvious that the District Court has a very heavy responsibility to see to it that Presidential conversations, which are either not relevant or not admissible, are accorded that high degree of respect due the President of the United States. Mr. Chief Justice Marshall, sitting as a trial judge in the *Burr* case, was extraordinarily careful to point out that

> in no case of this kind would a court be required to proceed against the president as against an ordinary individual.

Marshall's statement cannot be read to mean in any sense that a President is above the law, but relates to the singularly unique role under Art. II of a President's communications and activities, related to the performance of duties under that Article. Moreover, a President's communications and activities encompass a vastly wider range of sensitive material than would be true of any "ordinary individual." It is therefore necessary in the public interest to afford Presidential confidentiality the greatest protection consistent with the fair administration of justice. The need for confidentiality even as to idle conversations with associates in which casual reference might be made concerning political leaders within the country or foreign statesmen is too obvious to call for further treatment. We have no doubt that the District Judge will at all times accord to Presidential records that high degree of deference suggested in *United States v. Burr*, and will discharge his responsibility to see to it that until released to the Special Prosecutor no in camera material is revealed to anyone. This burden applies with even greater force to excised material; once the decision is made to excise, the material is restored to its privileged status and should be returned under seal to its lawful custodian.

Since this matter came before the Court during the pendency of a criminal prosecution, and on representations that time is of the essence, the mandate shall issue forthwith.

Mr. Justice Rehnquist took no part in the consideration or decision of these cases.

### Note: The Reach of the Presidential Immunity between Nixon *and* Clinton v. Jones

1. Three other cases involving the Nixon Administration bear on the reach of executive privilege. In *Nixon v. Administrator of General Services*, 433 U.S. 425 (1977), the former President challenged the constitutionality of a federal statute, the Presidential Recordings and Materials Preservation Act. The Act directed the Administrator of the General Services Administration to take custody of the presidential papers of former President Nixon, promulgate regulations for their orderly processing and screening by archivists, return personal papers, and determine the conditions for public access of the materials retained. The Court rejected the former President's contention that the regulation of the disposition of those materials violated the separation of powers. Justice Brennan, writing for the Court, stated:

> ... [In] determining whether the act disrupts the proper balance between the coordinate branches, the proper inquiry focuses on the extent to which it prevents the Executive Branch from accomplishing its constitutionally assigned functions.... Only where the potential for disruption is present must we then determine whether the impact is justified by an overriding need to promote objectives within the constitutional authority of Congress.

Because the Act gave the Executive Branch control of the papers, the Court rejected the claim that it caused undue disruption of executive functions.

The Court also rejected the former President's claims that presidential privilege shielded the papers from archival scrutiny and that the Act violated presidential privilege. It recognized that the presidential privilege was available to incumbents; however, it concluded that the lack of support for Nixon's claim from both President Ford (who had signed the Act) and President Carter "detracts from the weight of [Nixon's] contentions that the Act intrudes into the executive function and the needs of the Executive Branch." Observing that the scope of the privilege extended under the Act corresponded to that recognized in *United States v. Nixon*, and that the Act included a screening process that was unlikely to impair confidentiality, the Court concluded that the limited intrusion was justified in light of the substantial public interest in the "American people's ability to reconstruct and come to terms with their history [and] the desire to restore public confidence in our political processes by preserving materials as a source for facilitating a full airing of the events leading to appellant's resignation." Balanced against the presidential claims of privilege were these public interests, as well as Congress's interest in having the materials available because of "Congress' need to understand how those political processes had in fact operated in order to gauge the necessity for remedial legislation." Several Justices wrote concurring opinions. Chief Justice Burger, the author of *United States v. Nixon*, dissented, contending that the Act violated the Court's doctrine of presidential privilege. Justice Rehnquist, who had recused himself in *United States v. Nixon* due to his work in the Nixon Administration, also dissented.

2. In *Nixon v. Fitzgerald*, 457 U.S. 731 (1982), a case arising out of an alleged retaliatory discharge of an Air Force employee, the Court, through Justice Powell's opinion for five Justices, concluded that "a former President of the United States is entitled to absolute immunity from damages liability predicated on his official acts. We consider this immunity a functionally mandated incident of the President's unique office, rooted in the constitutional tradition of separation of powers and supported by our history." Justice Powell added, "we think it appropriate to recognize absolute Presidential immunity from damages liability for acts within the 'outer perimeter' of his official responsibility." In response to Justice White's claim, for four dissenters, that the presidential office is thereby "clothed with sovereign immunity, placing it above the law," the majority emphasized "other incentives to avoid misconduct;" among them the constitutional remedy of impeachment, as well as "constant scrutiny by the press," as well as "a desire to earn re-election, ... and a President's traditional concern for his historical stature."

3. On the same day, in *Harlow v. Fitzgerald*, 457 U.S. 800 (1982), the Court concluded that except in exceptional circumstances where the need for a derivative claim to Presidential immunity arises because of the function they are performing, executive officials, including senior aides and advisers to the President, are merely entitled to qualified immunity. Writing for eight Justices, Justice Powell explained: "A derivative claim to a Presidential immunity would be strongest in such central Presidential domains as foreign policy and national security, in which the president could not discharge his singularly vital mandate without delegating functions nearly as sensitive as his own." Chief Justice Burger dissented.

## Clinton v. Jones

### 520 U.S. 681 (1997)

JUSTICE STEVENS delivered the opinion of the Court.

This case raises a constitutional and a prudential question concerning the Office of the President of the United States. Respondent, a private citizen, seeks to recover damages from the current occupant of that office based on actions allegedly taken before his term began. The President submits that in all but the most exceptional cases the Constitution requires federal courts to defer such litigation until his term ends and that, in any event, respect for the office warrants such a stay. Despite the force of the arguments supporting the President's submissions, we conclude that they must be rejected.

I

Petitioner, William Jefferson Clinton, was elected to the Presidency in 1992, and reelected in 1996. His term of office expires on January 20, 2001. In 1991 he was the Governor of the State of Arkansas. Respondent, Paula Corbin Jones, is a resident of California. In 1991 she lived in Arkansas, and was an employee of the Arkansas Industrial Development Commission.

On May 6, 1994, she commenced this action in the United States District Court for the Eastern District of Arkansas by filing a complaint naming petitioner and Danny Ferguson, a former Arkansas State Police officer, as defendants. The complaint alleges two federal claims, and two state-law claims over which the federal court has jurisdiction because of the diverse citizenship of the parties. As the case comes to us, we are required to assume the truth of the detailed—but as yet untested—factual allegations in the complaint.

Those allegations principally describe events that are said to have occurred on the afternoon of May 8, 1991, during an official conference held at the Excelsior Hotel in Little Rock, Arkansas. The Governor delivered a speech at the conference; respondent—working as a state employee—staffed the registration desk. She alleges that Ferguson persuaded her to leave her desk and to visit the Governor in a business suite at the hotel, where he made "abhorrent" sexual advances that she vehemently rejected. She further claims that her superiors at work subsequently dealt with her in a hostile and rude manner, and changed her duties to punish her for rejecting those advances. Finally, she alleges that after petitioner was elected President, Ferguson defamed her by making a statement to a reporter that implied she had accepted petitioner's alleged overtures, and that various persons authorized to speak for the President publicly branded her a liar by denying that the incident had occurred....

IV

Petitioner's principal submission—that "in all but the most exceptional cases," the Constitution affords the President temporary immunity from civil damages litigation arising out of events that occurred before he took office—cannot be sustained on the basis of precedent....

The principal rationale for affording certain public servants immunity from suits for money damages arising out of their official acts is inapplicable to unofficial conduct. In cases involving prosecutors, legislators, and judges we have repeatedly explained that the immunity serves the public interest in enabling such officials to perform their designated functions effectively without fear that a particular decision may give rise to personal liability.... That rationale provided the principal basis for our holding that a former President of the United States was "entitled to absolute immunity from damages liability predicated on his official acts," *Nixon v. Fitzgerald* (1982) [Note *supra.* this chapter]. Our central concern was to avoid rendering the President "unduly cautious in the discharge of his official duties."

This reasoning provides no support for an immunity for *unofficial* conduct. As we explained in *Fitzgerald*, "the sphere of protected action must be related closely to the immunity's justifying purposes." Because of the President's broad responsibilities, we recognized in that case an immunity from damages claims arising out of official acts extending to the "outer perimeter of his authority." But we have never suggested that the President, or any other official, has an immunity that extends beyond the scope of any action taken in an official capacity.

Moreover, when defining the scope of an immunity for acts clearly taken *within* an official capacity, we have applied a functional approach. "Frequently our decisions have held that an official's absolute immunity should extend only to acts in performance of particular functions of his office." ... As our opinions have made clear, immunities are grounded in "the nature of the function performed, not the identity of the actor who performed it."

Petitioner's effort to construct an immunity from suit for unofficial acts grounded purely in the identity of his office is unsupported by precedent....

## VI

Petitioner's strongest argument supporting his immunity claim is based on the text and structure of the Constitution. He does not contend that the occupant of the Office of the President is "above the law," in the sense that his conduct is entirely immune from judicial scrutiny. The President argues merely for a postponement of the judicial proceedings that will determine whether he violated any law. His argument is grounded in the character of the office that was created by Article II of the Constitution, and relies on separation-of-powers principles that have structured our constitutional arrangement since the founding.

As a starting premise, petitioner contends that he occupies a unique office with powers and responsibilities so vast and important that the public interest demands that he devote his undivided time and attention to his public duties. He submits that—given the nature of the office—the doctrine of separation of powers places limits on the authority of the Federal Judiciary to interfere with the Executive Branch that would be transgressed by allowing this action to proceed.

We have no dispute with the initial premise of the argument. Former Presidents, from George Washington to George Bush, have consistently endorsed petitioner's characterization of the office....

It does not follow, however, that separation of powers principles would be violated by allowing this action to proceed....

Rather than arguing that the decision of the case will produce either an aggrandizement of judicial power or a narrowing of executive power, petitioner contends that—as a byproduct of an otherwise traditional exercise of judicial power—burdens will be placed on the President that will hamper the performance of his official duties. We have recognized that "even when a branch does not arrogate power to itself ... the separation-of-powers doctrine requires that a branch not impair another in the performance of its constitutional duties." As a factual matter, Petitioner contends that this particular case—as well as the potential additional litigation that an affirmance of the Court of Appeals judgment might spawn—may impose an unacceptable burden on the President's time and energy, and thereby impair the effective performance of his office.

Petitioner's predictive judgment finds little support in either history or the relatively narrow compass of the issues raised in this particular case. As we have already noted, in the more than 200-year history of the Republic, only three sitting Presidents have been subjected to suits for their private actions. If the past is any indicator, it seems unlikely that a deluge of such litigation will ever engulf the Presidency. As for the case at hand, if properly managed by the District Court, it appears to us highly unlikely to occupy any substantial amount of petitioner's time.

Of greater significance, petitioner errs by presuming that interactions between the Judicial Branch and the Executive, even quite burdensome interactions, necessarily rise to the level of constitutionally forbidden impairment of the Executive's ability to perform its constitutionally mandated functions. "Our ... system imposes upon the Branches a degree of overlapping responsibility, a duty of interdependence as well as independence the absence of which would preclude the establishment of a Nation capable of governing itself effectively." As Madison explained, separation of powers does not mean that the branches "ought to have no *partial agency* in, or no *controul* over the acts of each other." The fact that a federal court's exercise of its traditional Article III jurisdiction may significantly burden the time and attention of the Chief Executive is not sufficient to establish a violation of the Constitution. Two long-settled propositions, first announced by Chief Justice Marshall, support that conclusion.

First, we have long held that when the President takes official action, the Court has the authority to determine whether he has acted within the law. Perhaps the most dramatic example of such a case is our holding that President Truman exceeded his constitutional authority when he issued an order directing the Secretary of Commerce to take possession of and operate most of the Nation's steel mills in order to avert a national catastrophe. *Youngstown Sheet and Tube v. Sawyer* (1952) [*Supra.* this chapter] ...

Second, it is also settled that the President is subject to judicial process in appropriate circumstances....

The reasons for rejecting such a categorical rule apply as well to a rule that would require a stay "in all but the most exceptional cases." Indeed, if the Framers of the Constitution had thought it necessary to protect the President from the burdens of private litigation, we think it far more likely that they would have adopted a categorical rule than a rule that required the President to litigate the question whether a specific case belonged in the "exceptional case" subcategory. In all events, the question whether a specific case should receive exceptional treatment is more appropriately the subject of the exercise of judicial discretion than an interpretation of the Constitution. Accordingly, we turn to the question whether the District Court's decision to stay the trial until after petitioner leaves office was an abuse of discretion.

## VII

... The decision to postpone the trial was, furthermore, premature. The proponent of a stay bears the burden of establishing its need. In this case, at the stage at which the District Court made its ruling, there was no way to assess whether a stay of trial after the completion of discovery would be warranted. Other than the fact that a trial may consume some of the President's time and attention, there is nothing in the record to enable a judge to assess the potential harm that may ensue from scheduling the trial promptly after discovery is concluded. We think the District Court may have given undue weight to the concern that a trial might generate unrelated civil actions that could conceivably hamper the President in conducting the duties of his office. If and when that should occur, the court's discretion would permit it to manage those actions in such fashion (including deferral of trial) that interference with the President's duties would not occur. But no such impingement upon the President's conduct of his office was shown here....

JUSTICE BREYER, concurring in the judgment.

I agree with the majority that the Constitution does not automatically grant the President an immunity from civil lawsuits based upon his private conduct. Nor does the "doctrine of separation of powers ... require federal courts to stay" virtually "all private actions against the President until he leaves office." Rather, as the Court of Appeals stated, the President cannot simply rest upon the claim that a private civil lawsuit for damages will "interfere with the constitutionally assigned duties of the Executive Branch ... without detailing any specific responsibilities or explaining how or the degree to which they are affected by the suit." To obtain a postponement the President must "bear the burden of establishing its need."

In my view, however, once the President sets forth and explains a conflict between judicial proceeding and public duties, the matter changes. At that point, the Constitution permits a judge to schedule a trial in an ordinary civil damages action (where postponement normally is possible without overwhelming damage to a plaintiff) only within the constraints of a constitutional principle—a principle that forbids a federal judge in such a case to interfere with the President's discharge of his public duties. I have no doubt that the Constitution contains such a principle applicable to civil suits, based upon Article II's vesting of the entire "executive Power" in a single individual, implemented through the Constitution's structural separation of powers, and revealed both by history and case precedent.

I recognize that this case does not require us now to apply the principle specifically, thereby delineating its contours; nor need we now decide whether lower courts are to apply it directly or categorically through the use of presumptions or rules of administration. Yet I fear that to disregard it now may appear to deny it. I also fear that the majority's description of the relevant precedents de-emphasizes the extent to which they support a principle of the President's independent authority to control his own time and energy....

# C. Congress, the President, and the Administrative State

As the Introduction to this casebook stated (and as Part II of this book will examine in detail), today the federal government is understood to possess vast regulatory power over nearly every aspect of American economic and social life. Within the federal government, the size of this power, and the complexity of modern regulatory issues, has led to the creation of an equally vast administrative apparatus, usually (but not always) controlled by the President. The growth of what has been called "the administrative state" has resulted in continuous legal controversy. This part of Chapter 2 considers the main points of that controversy. To what extent can Congress legislate broadly-worded statutes that effectively grant administrative agencies power to make federal regulatory policy? To what extent can Congress retain for itself a hand in reviewing the policy those agencies make? To what extent can Congress limit the President's power to control the officials who lead that bureaucracy? The following materials take up these questions, in that order.

## 1. Limits on Congressional Authority to Delegate Legislative Power

### Note: The Evolution of the Non-Delegation Doctrine

1. The non-delegation doctrine grows out of a straightforward constitutional textual command, though that command presupposes some deep theory about the legitimacy of the American constitutional system. Article I begins with the following sentence: "All legislative powers herein granted shall be vested in a Congress of the United States, which shall consist of a Senate and House of Representatives." Because "We the people" vested this power in Congress, this sentence has been understood to mean that Congress may not delegate that power to another institution (or re-delegate it, since the people delegated as an original matter). But this view is not unanimous, as made clear in Justice Stevens' concurring opinion in *Whitman v. American Trucking*, below.

2. The conclusion that Article I forbids Congress from delegating its legislative powers does not by itself provide an easily-applicable legal standard for answering the constitutional questions that arise when Congress authorizes administrative agencies to act. Throughout the Nineteenth and early Twentieth centuries, the Supreme Court offered a number of verbal formulas to describe when congressional delegation of power to administrative agencies violated the grant of "all [federal] legislative powers" to Congress. In *The Brig Aurora*, 11 U.S. (7 Cranch) 382 (1813), the Court upheld, without providing a legal standard, a law authorizing the President to determine that

Great Britain and France had ceased interfering with American shipping, after which determination a congressionally-mandated trade embargo would be deemed lifted. In *Field v. Clark*, 143 U.S. 649 (1892), the Court relied on *The Brig Aurora* to uphold Congress's grant of power to the President to impose import tariffs when he found the "fact" that other nations imposed "unequal and unreasonable tariffs" on American exports. In *United States v. Grimaud*, 220 U.S. 506 (1911), the Court upheld a statute granting the Secretary of Agriculture the authority to "make provision for the protection … of the public forests." The Court described this latter statute as simply giving the Secretary the "power to fill in the details" of the statute.

The evolution of the Court's formal jurisprudence culminated with the standard enunciated by the Court in *J.W. Hampton, Jr. & Co. v. United States*, 276 U.S. 394 (1928), which stated that Congress was required to "lay down by legislative act an intelligible principle to which the person or body authorized to [act] is directed to conform." In *J.W. Hampton* itself the Court upheld a delegation to the President to impose tariffs on imported goods that were adequate to equalize the costs of production of the good in the United States and "the principal competing country."

3. The "intelligible principle" standard is the one used by courts today to test statutes against non-delegation claims. Nevertheless, it is sufficiently vague that its meaning can only be discerned by examining key cases. At the same time, the laxity of the standard—and of the non-delegation doctrine in general—is best revealed by the fact that the non-delegation doctrine has been invoked to strike down a law only twice.

In *A.L.A Schechter Poultry Corp. v. United States*, 295 U.S. 495 (1935), the Court struck down the National Industrial Recovery Act (NIRA), one of the early cornerstones of Franklin Roosevelt's New Deal. The NIRA was an exceptionally broad statute. It sought to attain a series of very broad goals, including "to provide for the general welfare by promoting the organization of industry for the purpose of cooperative action among trade groups, to induce and maintain united action of labor and management under adequate governmental sanctions and supervision," and "otherwise to rehabilitate industry and to conserve natural resources." It sought to achieve these goals by having the President approve "codes of fair competition," which were essentially codes by which competitors in a business agreed to limit their competitive behavior in order to avoid the ruinous competition that had reduced prices during the Depression. There were few limits on the content of these codes.

A unanimous Court struck down the statute. It noted that the statute included no limits on the content of a code except that the process of developing it had to be open to all members of that industry, and it could not promote monopolies. Chief Justice Hughes, writing for seven Justices, noted that the goal of "promoting fair competition" did not have the definite legal meaning that stamping out "unfair competition" did. Moreover, the NIRA's stated goals were so general, and internally inconsistent, that they also furnished no limitation on the President's discretion.

A few months before *Schechter*, the Court struck down the petroleum code promulgated under the NIRA in *Panama Refining v. Ryan*, 293 U.S. 388 (1935). Eight justices held that a section of the NIRA dealing with petroleum failed to provide sufficiently precise standards under which the President was authorized to prohibit the shipment of oil in interstate commerce that was produced in excess of state-law production quotas. Citing the NIRA's broad and conflicting goals partially set forth above, the Court held that the statute "declares no policy as to the transportation of the excess [oil] production. So far as this section is concerned, it gives to the President an unlimited authority to determine the policy and to lay down the prohibition, or not lay it down, as he may see fit." Justice Cardozo dissented.

4. After 1935, the Court never struck down a statute on non-delegation grounds. In subsequent years, the Court upheld broad delegations, such as that in the Federal Communications Act, which authorized the Federal Communications Commission to regulate broadcast services "in the public interest," *National Broadcasting Co. v. United States*, 319 U.S. 190 (1943), and that in the Public Utility Holding Company Act, which provided that the Securities and Exchange Commission shall act so as to ensure that the corporate structure of any public utility holding company does not "unduly or unnecessarily complicate the structure" or "unfairly or inequitably distribute voting power among security holders." *American Power & Light Co. v. SEC*, 329 U.S. 90 (1946). The following case reflects the leniency of the non-delegation doctrine.

## Yakus v. United States

### 321 U.S. 414 (1944)

Opinion of the Court by CHIEF JUSTICE STONE, announced by MR. JUSTICE ROBERTS.

The [question] for our decision [is] whether the Emergency Price Control Act of January 30, 1942 ... involves an unconstitutional delegation to the Price Administrator of the legislative power of Congress to control prices....

Petitioners in both of these cases were tried and convicted by the District Court for Massachusetts upon several counts of indictments charging violation of §§ 4(a) and 205(b) of the Act by the willful sale of wholesale cuts of beef at prices above the maximum prices prescribed by [federal price control regulations promulgated under the statute]....

I.

The Emergency Price Control Act provides for the establishment of the Office of Price Administration under the direction of a Price Administrator appointed by the President, and sets up a comprehensive scheme for the promulgation by the Administrator of regulations or orders fixing such maximum prices of commodities and rents as will effectuate the purposes of the Act and conform to the standards which it prescribes. The Act was adopted as a temporary wartime measure, and provides in § 1(b) for its termination on June 30, 1943, unless sooner terminated by Presidential proclamation or concurrent resolution of Congress. By the amendatory Act of October 2, 1942, it was extended to June 30, 1944.

Section 1(a) declares that the Act is "in the interest of the national defense and security and necessary to the effective prosecution of the present war," and that its purposes are:

> to stabilize prices and to prevent speculative, unwarranted, and abnormal increases in prices and rents; to eliminate and prevent profiteering, hoarding, manipulation, speculation, and other disruptive practices resulting from abnormal market conditions or scarcities caused by or contributing to the national emergency; to assure that defense appropriations are not dissipated by excessive prices; to protect persons with relatively fixed and limited incomes, consumers, wage earners, investors, and persons dependent on life insurance, annuities, and pensions, from undue impairment of their standard of living; to prevent hardships to persons engaged in business, ... and to the Federal, State, and local governments, which would result from abnormal increases in prices; to assist in securing adequate production of commodities and facilities; to prevent a post emergency collapse of values....

The standards which are to guide the Administrator's exercise of his authority to fix prices, so far as now relevant, are prescribed by § 2(a) and by § 1 of the amendatory Act of October 2, 1942, and Executive Order 9250. By § 2(a) the Administrator is authorized, after consultation with representative members of the industry so far as practicable, to promulgate regulations fixing prices of commodities which "in his judgment will be generally fair and equitable and will effectuate the purposes of this Act" when, in his judgment, their prices "have risen or threaten to rise to an extent or in a manner inconsistent with the purposes of this Act."

The section also directs that

> So far as practicable, in establishing any maximum price, the Administrator shall ascertain and give due consideration to the prices prevailing between October 1 and October 15, 1941 (or if, in the case of any commodity, there are no prevailing prices between such dates, or the prevailing prices between such dates are not generally representative because of abnormal or seasonal market conditions or other cause, then to the prices prevailing during the nearest two-week period in which, in the judgment of the Administrator, the prices for such commodity are generally representative) ... and shall make adjustments for such relevant factors as he may determine and deem to be of general applicability, including.... Speculative fluctuations, general increases or decreases in costs of production, distribution, and transportation, and general increases or decreases in profits earned by sellers of the commodity or commodities, during and subsequent to the year ended October 1, 1941.

By the Act of October 2, 1942, the President is directed to stabilize prices, wages and salaries "so far as practicable" on the basis of the levels which existed on September 15, 1942, except as otherwise provided in the Act. By Title I, § 4 of Executive Order No. 9250, he has directed "all departments and agencies of the Government" "to stabilize the cost of living in accordance with the Act of October 2, 1942." ...

That Congress has constitutional authority to prescribe commodity prices as a war emergency measure, and that the Act was adopted by Congress in the exercise of that power, are not questioned here, and need not now be considered....

Congress enacted the Emergency Price Control Act in pursuance of a defined policy and required that the prices fixed by the Administrator should further that policy and conform to standards prescribed by the Act. The boundaries of the field of the Administrator's permissible action are marked by the statute. It directs that the prices fixed shall effectuate the declared policy of the Act to stabilize commodity prices so as to prevent wartime inflation and its enumerated disruptive causes and effects. In addition the prices established must be fair and equitable, and in fixing them the Administrator is directed to give due consideration, so far as practicable, to prevailing prices during the designated base period, with prescribed administrative adjustments to compensate for enumerated disturbing factors affecting prices. In short the purposes of the Act specified in § 1 denote the objective to be sought by the Administrator in fixing prices — the prevention of inflation and its enumerated consequences. The standards set out in § 2 define the boundaries within which prices having that purpose must be fixed. It is enough to satisfy the statutory requirements that the Administrator finds that the prices fixed will tend to achieve that objective and will conform to those standards, and that the courts in an appropriate proceeding can see that substantial basis for those findings is not wanting.

The Act is thus an exercise by Congress of its legislative power. In it Congress has stated the legislative objective, has prescribed the method of achieving that objective — maximum price fixing —, and has laid down standards to guide the administrative determination of both the occasions for the exercise of the price-fixing power, and the particular prices to be established.

The Act is unlike the National Industrial Recovery Act considered in *Schechter Poultry Corp. v. United States* (1935) [Note *supra.* this chapter], which proclaimed in the broadest terms its purpose "to rehabilitate industry and to conserve natural resources." It prescribed no method of attaining that end save by the establishment of codes of fair competition, the nature of whose permissible provisions was left undefined. It provided no standards to which those codes were to conform. The function of formulating the codes was delegated, not to a public official responsible to Congress or the Executive, but to private individuals engaged in the industries to be regulated.

The Constitution as a continuously operative charter of government does not demand the impossible or the impracticable. It does not require that Congress find for itself every fact upon which it desires to base legislative action or that it make for itself detailed determinations which it has declared to be prerequisite to the application of the legislative policy to particular facts and circumstances impossible for Congress itself properly to investigate. The essentials of the legislative function are the determination of the legislative policy and its formulation and promulgation as a defined and binding rule of conduct — here the rule, with penal sanctions, that prices shall not be greater than those fixed by maximum price regulations which conform to standards and will tend to further the policy which Congress has established. These essentials are preserved when Congress has specified the basic conditions of fact upon whose existence or occurrence, ascertained from relevant data by a designated administrative agency, it directs that its statutory command shall be effective. It is no objection that the determination of facts and the inferences to be drawn from them in the light of the statutory standards and declaration of policy call for the exercise of judgment, and for the formulation of subsidiary administrative policy within the prescribed statutory framework.

Nor does the doctrine of separation of powers deny to Congress power to direct that an administrative officer properly designated for that purpose have ample latitude within which he is to ascertain the conditions which Congress has made prerequisite to the operation of its legislative command. Acting within its constitutional power to fix prices it is for Congress to say whether the data on the basis of which prices are to be fixed are to be confined within a narrow or a broad range. In either case the only concern of courts is to ascertain whether the will of Congress has been obeyed. This depends not upon the breadth of the definition of the facts or conditions which the administrative officer is to find but upon the determination whether the definition sufficiently marks the field within which the Administrator is to act so that it may be known whether he has kept within it in compliance with the legislative will.

As we have said: "The Constitution has never been regarded as denying to the Congress the necessary resources of flexibility and practicality ... to perform its function"... Only if we could say that there is an absence of standards for guidance of the Administrator's action, so that it would be impossible in a proper proceeding to ascertain whether the will of Congress has been obeyed, would we be justified in overriding its choice of means for effecting its declared purpose of preventing inflation.

The standards prescribed by the present Act, with the aid of the "statement of the considerations" required to be made by the Administrator, are sufficiently definite and precise to enable Congress, the courts and the public to ascertain whether the Administrator, in fixing the designated prices, has conformed to those standards. Hence we are unable to find in them an unauthorized delegation of legislative power....

## Note: The Non-Delegation Doctrine in the Modern Era

1. By the 1970's it was generally thought that the non-delegation doctrine was a dead letter. However, during that decade the doctrine made a reappearance of sorts. In *National Cable Television Association v. United States*, 415 U.S. 336 (1974), the Court gave a narrow construction to a statute authorizing administrative agencies to collect a "fee" reflecting the government's cost of providing regulatory services, in order to avoid the non-delegation problem that would arise if Congress were held to have granted agencies the power to tax. Several years later, in two cases interpreting the Occupational and Safety and Health Act, Justice Rehnquist (in the

latter case joined by Chief Justice Burger) concluded that the statute violated the non-delegation doctrine because it failed to make the difficult policy decisions balancing workers' health and costs. *See Industrial Union Dept, AFL-CIO v. American Petroleum Institute*, 448 U.S. 607 (1980); *American Textile Mfrs. Inst. v. Donovan*, 452 U.S. 490 (1981).

2. The *American Petroleum* and *American Textile* cases cited in the item above reflect a difficult issue that has arisen with many modern statutes that seek to safeguard health and safety. Often such statutes are written to impose an absolute or near-absolute mandate on the agency to protect the public health. Modern science, however, has revealed that such absolute protection is often not possible, or possible only if the agency asserts such broad power that the statute arguably violates the non-delegation doctrine. The next case—the most recent in which the Court seriously confronted a non-delegation claim—considers such a situation in the context of the Clean Air Act, a paradigmatic "health and safety" statute.

## Whitman v. American Trucking Ass'ns
### 531 U.S. 457 (2001)

Justice SCALIA delivered the opinion of the Court.

These cases present the following questions: (1) Whether § 109(b)(1) of the Clean Air Act (CAA) delegates legislative power to the Administrator of the Environmental Protection Agency (EPA). (2) Whether the Administrator may consider the costs of implementation in setting national ambient air quality standards (NAAQS) under § 109(b)(1). (3) Whether the Court of Appeals had jurisdiction to review the EPA's interpretation of Part D of Title I of the CAA.... (4) If so, whether the EPA's interpretation of that part was permissible.

I

Section 109(a) of the CAA ... requires the Administrator of the EPA to promulgate NAAQS for each air pollutant for which "air quality criteria" have been issued under § 108. Once a NAAQS has been promulgated, the Administrator must review the standard (and the criteria on which it is based) "at five-year intervals" and make "such revisions ... as may be appropriate." CAA § 109(d)(1). These cases arose when, on July 18, 1997, the Administrator revised the NAAQS for particulate matter and ozone. American Trucking Associations, Inc., and its co-respondents ... challenged the new standards in the Court of Appeals for the District of Columbia Circuit....

The District of Columbia Circuit accepted some of the challenges and rejected others. It agreed ... that § 109(b)(1) delegated legislative power to the Administrator in contravention of the United States Constitution, Art. I, § 1, because it found that the EPA had interpreted the statute to provide no "intelligible principle" to guide the agency's exercise of authority. The court thought, however, that the EPA could perhaps avoid the unconstitutional delegation by adopting a restrictive construction of § 109(b)(1), so instead of declaring the section unconstitutional the court remanded the NAAQS to the agency.... We granted certiorari....

## II

In *Lead Industries Assn., Inc. v. EPA*, 647 F.2d 1130 (C.A.D.C. 1980), the District of Columbia Circuit held that "economic considerations [may] play no part in the promulgation of ambient air quality standards under Section 109" of the CAA. In the present cases, the court adhered to that holding, as it had done on many other occasions. Respondents argue that these decisions are incorrect. We disagree; and since the first step in assessing whether a statute delegates legislative power is to determine what authority the statute confers, we address that issue of interpretation first and reach respondents' constitutional arguments in Part III, *infra*.

[The Court considered, and ultimately validated, the Court of Appeals' interpretation of the statute precluding a role for economic considerations in the promulgation of ambient air quality standards.]

## III

Section 109(b)(1) of the CAA instructs the EPA to set "ambient air quality standards the attainment and maintenance of which in the judgment of the Administrator ... and allowing an adequate margin of safety, are requisite to protect the public health." The Court of Appeals held that this section as interpreted by the Administrator did not provide an "intelligible principle" to guide the EPA's exercise of authority in setting NAAQS. "[The] EPA," it said, "lacked any determinate criteria for drawing lines. It has failed to state intelligibly how much is too much." The court hence found that the EPA's interpretation (but not the statute itself) violated the nondelegation doctrine. We disagree.

In a delegation challenge, the constitutional question is whether the statute has delegated legislative power to the agency. Article I, § 1, of the Constitution vests "all legislative Powers herein granted ... in a Congress of the United States." This text permits no delegation of those powers, and so we repeatedly have said that when Congress confers decisionmaking authority upon agencies *Congress* must "lay down by legislative act an intelligible principle to which the person or body authorized to [act] is directed to conform." *J.W. Hampton, Jr., & Co. v. United States* (1928) [Note *supra.* this chapter]. We have never suggested that an agency can cure an unlawful delegation of legislative power by adopting in its discretion a limiting construction of the statute.... The idea that an agency can cure an unconstitutionally standardless delegation of power by declining to exercise some of that power seems to us internally contradictory. The very choice of which portion of the power to exercise—that is to say, the prescription of the standard that Congress had omitted—would *itself* be an exercise of the forbidden legislative authority. Whether the statute delegates legislative power is a question for the courts, and an agency's voluntary self-denial has no bearing upon the answer.

We agree with the Solicitor General that the text of § 109(b)(1) of the CAA at a minimum requires that "for a discrete set of pollutants and based on published air quality criteria that reflect the latest scientific knowledge, [the] EPA must establish uniform national standards at a level that is requisite to protect public health from the adverse effects of the pollutant in the ambient air." Tr. of Oral Arg., p. 5. Requisite, in turn, "means sufficient, but not more than necessary." *Id.*, at 7. These limits on the EPA's discretion are strikingly similar to the ones we approved in *Touby v. United States*, 500 U.S. 160 (1991), which permitted the Attorney General to designate a drug as a controlled substance for purposes of criminal drug enforcement if doing so was "necessary to avoid an imminent hazard to the public safety." They also resemble the Occupational Safety and Health Act of 1970 provision requiring the agency to "set the standard which most adequately assures, to the extent feasible, on the basis of the best available evidence, that no employee will suffer any impairment of health" — which the Court upheld in *Industrial Union Dept., AFL-CIO v. American Petroleum Institute*, 448 U.S. 607 (1980) [Note *supra.* this chapter], and which even then-Justice REHNQUIST, who alone in that case thought the statute violated the non-delegation doctrine, would have upheld if, like the statute here, it did not permit economic costs to be considered.

The scope of discretion § 109(b)(1) allows is in fact well within the outer limits of our nondelegation precedents. In the history of the Court we have found the requisite "intelligible principle" lacking in only two statutes, one of which provided literally no guidance for the exercise of discretion, and the other of which conferred authority to regulate the entire economy on the basis of no more precise a standard than stimulating the economy by assuring "fair competition." See *Panama Refining Co. v. Ryan* (1935); *A.L.A. Schechter Poultry Corp. v. United States* (1935) [Both note *supra.* this chapter]. We have, on the other hand, upheld the validity of § 11(b)(2) of the Public Utility Holding Company Act of 1935, which gave the Securities and Exchange Commission authority to modify the structure of holding company systems so as to ensure that they are not "unduly or unnecessarily complicated" and do not "unfairly or inequitably distribute voting power among security holders." *American Power & Light Co. v. SEC* (1946) [Note *supra.* this chapter]. We have approved the wartime conferral of agency power to fix the prices of commodities at a level that "will be generally fair and equitable and will effectuate the [in some respects conflicting] purposes of the Act." *Yakus v. United States* (1944) [*Supra.* this chapter]. And we have found an "intelligible principle" in various statutes authorizing regulation in the "public interest." See, e.g., *National Broadcasting Co. v. United States* (1943) (Federal Communications Commission's power to regulate airwaves) [Note *supra.* this chapter]; *New York Central Securities Corp. v. United States*, 287 U.S. 12 (1932) (Interstate Commerce Commission's power to approve railroad consolidations). In short, we have "almost never felt qualified to second-guess Congress regarding the permissible degree of policy judgment that can be left to those executing or applying the law." *Mistretta v. United States*, 488 U.S. 361 (1989) (SCALIA, J., dissenting).

It is true enough that the degree of agency discretion that is acceptable varies according to the scope of the power congressionally conferred. While Congress need not provide any direction to the EPA regarding the manner in which it is to define "country elevators," which are to be exempt from new-stationary-source regulations governing grain elevators, see 42 U.S.C. § 7411(i), it must provide substantial guidance on setting air standards that affect the entire national economy. But even in sweeping regulatory schemes we have never demanded, as the Court of Appeals did here, that statutes provide a "determinate criterion" for saying "how much [of the regulated harm] is too much." In *Touby*, for example, we did not require the statute to decree how "imminent" was too imminent, or how "necessary" was necessary enough, or even — most relevant here — how "hazardous" was too hazardous. Similarly, the statute at issue in *Lichter* authorized agencies to recoup "excess profits" paid under wartime Government contracts, yet we did not insist that Congress specify how much profit was too much. It is therefore not conclusive for delegation purposes that, as respondents argue, ozone and particulate matter are "nonthreshold" pollutants that inflict a continuum of adverse health effects at any airborne concentration greater than zero, and hence require the EPA to make judgments of degree. "A certain degree of discretion, and thus of lawmaking, inheres in most executive or judicial action." Section 109(b)(1) of the CAA, which to repeat we interpret as requiring the EPA to set air quality standards at the level that is "requisite" — that is, not lower or higher than is necessary — to protect the public health with an adequate margin of safety, fits comfortably within the scope of discretion permitted by our precedent.

We therefore reverse the judgment of the Court of Appeals remanding for reinterpretation that would avoid a supposed delegation of legislative power. It will remain for the Court of Appeals — on the remand that we direct for other reasons — to dispose of any other preserved challenge to the NAAQS....

Justice THOMAS, concurring.

I agree with the majority that § 109's directive to the agency is no less an "intelligible principle" than a host of other directives that we have approved. I also agree that the Court of Appeals' remand to the agency to make its own corrective interpretation does not accord with our understanding of the delegation issue. I write separately, however, to express my concern that there may nevertheless be a genuine constitutional problem with § 109, a problem which the parties did not address.

The parties ... who briefed the constitutional issue wrangled over constitutional doctrine with barely a nod to the text of the Constitution. Although this Court since 1928 has treated the "intelligible principle" requirement as the only constitutional limit on congressional grants of power to administrative agencies, see *J.W. Hampton*, the Constitution does not speak of "intelligible principles." Rather, it speaks in much simpler terms: "*All* legislative Powers herein granted shall be vested in a Congress." U.S. Const., Art. 1, § 1 (emphasis added). I am not convinced that the intelligible principle doctrine serves to prevent all cessions of legislative power. I believe that there are cases in which the principle is intelligible and yet the significance of the delegated decision is simply too great for the decision to be called anything other than "legislative."

As it is, none of the parties to these cases has examined the text of the Constitution or asked us to reconsider our precedents on cessions of legislative power. On a future day, however, I would be willing to address the question whether our delegation jurisprudence has strayed too far from our Founders' understanding of separation of powers.

Justice STEVENS, with whom Justice SOUTER joins, concurring in part and concurring in the judgment.

Section 109(b)(1) delegates to the Administrator of the Environmental Protection Agency (EPA) the authority to promulgate national ambient air quality standards (NAAQS). In Part III of its opinion, the Court convincingly explains why the Court of Appeals erred when it concluded that § 109 effected "an unconstitutional delegation of legislative power." I wholeheartedly endorse the Court's result and endorse its explanation of its reasons, albeit with the following caveat.

The Court has two choices. We could choose to articulate our ultimate disposition of this issue by frankly acknowledging that the power delegated to the EPA is "legislative" but nevertheless conclude that the delegation is constitutional because adequately limited by the terms of the authorizing statute. Alternatively, we could pretend, as the Court does, that the authority delegated to the EPA is somehow not "legislative power." Despite the fact that there is language in our opinions that supports the Court's articulation of our holding,[1] I am persuaded that it would be both wiser and more faithful to what we have actually done in delegation cases to admit that agency rulemaking authority is "legislative power."[2]

The proper characterization of governmental power should generally depend on the nature of the power, not on the identity of the person exercising it. See Black's Law Dictionary 899 (6th ed.1990) (defining "legislation" as, inter alia, "formulation of rules for the future"); 1 K. Davis & R. Pierce, *Administrative Law Treatise* § 2.3 (1994) ("If legislative power means the power to make rules of conduct that bind everyone based on resolution of major policy issues, scores of agencies exercise legislative power routinely by promulgating what are candidly called 'legislative rules'"). If the NAAQS that the EPA promulgated had been prescribed by Congress, everyone would agree that those rules would be the product of an exercise of "legislative power." The same characterization is appropriate when an agency exercises rulemaking authority pursuant to a permissible delegation from Congress.

My view is not only more faithful to normal English usage, but is also fully consistent with the text of the Constitution. In Article I, the Framers vested "All legislative Powers" in the Congress, Art. I, § 1, just as in Article II they vested the "executive Power" in the President, Art. II, § 1. Those provisions do not purport to limit the authority of either recipient of power to delegate authority to others. See *Bowsher v.*

---

1. See, e.g., *Touby*; *United States v. Shreveport Grain & Elevator Co.*, 287 U.S. 77 (1932); *J.W. Hampton*; *Field v. Clark*, 143 U.S. 649 (1892) [Note *supra.* this chapter].

2. See *Mistretta* ("Our jurisprudence has been driven by a practical understanding that in our increasingly complex society ... Congress simply cannot do its job absent an ability to delegate power ..."). See also *Loving* ("[The nondelegation] principle does not mean ... that only Congress can make a rule of prospective force"); 1 K. Davis & R. Pierce, Administrative Law Treatise § 2.6, p. 66 (3d ed. 1994) ("Except for two 1935 cases, the Court has never enforced its frequently announced prohibition on congressional delegation of legislative power").

*Synar*, 478 U.S. 714 (1986) (STEVENS, J., concurring in judgment) ("Despite the statement in Article I of the Constitution that 'All legislative powers herein granted shall be vested in a Congress of the United States,' it is far from novel to acknowledge that independent agencies do indeed exercise legislative powers"); *INS v. Chadha*, 462 U.S. 919 (1983) (White, J., dissenting) ("Legislative power can be exercised by independent agencies and Executive departments ..."); 1 Davis & Pierce, Administrative Law Treatise § 2.6 ("The Court was probably mistaken from the outset in interpreting Article I's grant of power to Congress as an implicit limit on Congress' authority to delegate legislative power"). Surely the authority granted to members of the Cabinet and federal law enforcement agents is properly characterized as "Executive" even though not exercised by the President.

It seems clear that an executive agency's exercise of rulemaking authority pursuant to a valid delegation from Congress is "legislative." As long as the delegation provides a sufficiently intelligible principle, there is nothing inherently unconstitutional about it. Accordingly, while I ... agree with almost everything said in Part III, I would hold that when Congress enacted § 109, it effected a constitutional delegation of legislative power to the EPA.

Justice BREYER, concurring in part and concurring in the judgment. [omitted]

## 2. Congressional Control over Delegated Power

With the virtual disappearance of the non-delegation doctrine as a meaningful limit on Congress's authority to delegate away its legislative powers, one might have thought that the Court would look more approvingly at congressional attempts to retain supervisory authority over an agency receiving such power. One such measure, which had its origins in the 1930s, when Congress began delegating exceptionally broad power to agencies during the New Deal, was the legislative veto. In the following case, the Court struck down this then-common feature of the modern administrative state.

### Immigration and Naturalization Service v. Chadha
#### 462 U.S. 919 (1983)

CHIEF JUSTICE BURGER delivered the opinion of the Court.

We granted certiorari in ... a challenge to the constitutionality of the provision in § 244(c)(2) of the Immigration and Nationality Act, authorizing one House of Congress, by resolution, to invalidate the decision of the Executive Branch, pursuant to authority delegated by Congress to the Attorney General of the United States, to allow a particular deportable alien to remain in the United States.

I

[Pursuant to § 244(c)(1), a judge for the Immigration and Naturalization Service suspended a deportation order against Chadha, whose visa had expired. This order was suspended based upon a recommendation of the Attorney General. The Attorney General, as required by § 244(c)(1), found that Chadha had resided in the United

States for a minimum of seven years, possessed good moral character, and would experience "extreme hardship" if deported.]

The June 25, 1974, order of the Immigration Judge suspending Chadha's deportation remained outstanding as a valid order for a year and a half. For reasons not disclosed by the record, Congress did not exercise the veto authority reserved to it under § 244(c)(2) until the first session of the 94th Congress. This was the final session in which Congress, pursuant to § 244(c)(2), could act to veto the Attorney General's determination that Chadha should not be deported. The session ended on December 19, 1975. Absent Congressional action, Chadha's deportation proceedings would have been canceled after this date and his status adjusted to that of a permanent resident alien.

On December 12, 1975, Representative Eilberg, Chairman of the Judiciary Subcommittee on Immigration, Citizenship, and International Law, introduced a resolution opposing "the granting of permanent residence in the United States to [six] aliens," including Chadha. The resolution was referred to the House Committee on the Judiciary. On December 16, 1975, the resolution was discharged from further consideration by the House Committee on the Judiciary and submitted to the House of Representatives for a vote. The resolution had not been printed and was not made available to other Members of the House prior to or at the time it was voted on. So far as the record before us shows, the House consideration of the resolution was based on Representative Eilberg's statement from the floor that

> It was the feeling of the committee, after reviewing 340 cases, that the aliens contained in the resolution [Chadha and five others] did not meet these statutory requirements, particularly as it relates to hardship; and it is the opinion of the committee that their deportation should not be suspended.

The resolution was passed without debate or recorded vote. Since the House action was pursuant to § 244(c)(2), the resolution was not treated as an Article I legislative act; it was not submitted to the Senate or presented to the President for his action.

After the House veto of the Attorney General's decision to allow Chadha to remain in the United States, the Immigration Judge reopened the deportation proceedings to implement the House order deporting Chadha. Chadha moved to terminate the proceedings on the ground that § 244(c)(2) is unconstitutional. The Immigration Judge held that he had no authority to rule on the constitutional validity of § 244(c)(2). On November 8, 1976, Chadha was ordered deported pursuant to the House action.

Chadha appealed the deportation order to the Board of Immigration Appeals again contending that § 244(c)(2) is unconstitutional. The Board held that it had "no power to declare unconstitutional an act of Congress" and Chadha's appeal was dismissed.

Pursuant to § 106(a) of the Act, 8 U.S.C. § 1105a(a), Chadha filed a petition for review of the deportation order in the United States Court of Appeals for the Ninth Circuit....

After full briefing and oral argument, the Court of Appeals held that the House was without constitutional authority to order Chadha's deportation.... The essence of its holding was that § 244(c)(2) violates the constitutional doctrine of separation of powers....

III

A

... The fact that a given law or procedure is efficient, convenient, and useful in facilitating functions of government, standing alone, will not save it if it is contrary to the Constitution. Convenience and efficiency are not the primary objectives—or the hallmarks—of democratic government and our inquiry is sharpened rather than blunted by the fact that congressional veto provisions are appearing with increasing frequency in statutes which delegate authority to executive and independent agencies....

Explicit and unambiguous provisions of the Constitution prescribe and define the respective functions of the Congress and of the Executive in the legislative process. Since the precise terms of those familiar provisions are critical to the resolution of this case, we set them out verbatim. Article I provides:

> All legislative Powers herein granted shall be vested in a Congress of the United States, which shall consist of a Senate *and* a House of Representatives. Art. I, § 1 (emphasis added).

> Every Bill which shall have passed the House of Representatives *and* the Senate, *shall*, before it becomes a Law, be presented to the President of the United States.... Art. I, § 7, cl. 2 (emphasis added).

> *Every* Order, Resolution, or Vote to which the Concurrence of the Senate and House of Representatives may be necessary (except on a question of Adjournment) *shall be* presented to the President of the United States; and before the Same shall take Effect, *shall be* approved by him, or being disapproved by him, *shall be* repassed by two thirds of the Senate and House of Representatives, according to the Rules and Limitations prescribed in the Case of a Bill. Art. I, § 7, cl. 3 (emphasis added).

These provisions of Art. I are integral parts of the constitutional design for the separation of powers. We have recently noted that "the principle of separation of powers was not simply an abstract generalization in the minds of the Framers: it was woven into the documents that they drafted in Philadelphia in the summer of 1787." ...

B

*The Presentment Clauses*

The records of the Constitutional Convention reveal that the requirement that all legislation be presented to the President before becoming law was uniformly accepted by the Framers. Presentment to the President and the Presidential veto were considered so imperative that the draftsmen took special pains to assure that these requirements could not be circumvented. During the final debate on Art. I, § 7, cl. 2, James Madison expressed concern that it might easily be evaded by the simple expedient of calling a proposed law a "resolution" or "vote" rather than a "bill." As a consequence, Art. I, §7, cl. 3 was added.

The decision to provide the President with a limited and qualified power to nullify proposed legislation by veto was based on the profound conviction of the Framers that the powers conferred on Congress were the powers to be most carefully circumscribed. It is beyond doubt that lawmaking was a power to be shared by both Houses and the President. In *The Federalist* No. 73, Hamilton focused on the President's role in making laws:

> If even no propensity had ever discovered itself in the legislative body to invade the rights of the Executive, the rules of just reasoning and theoretic propriety would of themselves teach us that the one ought not to be left to the mercy of the other, but ought to possess a constitutional and effectual power of self-defense.

The President's role in the lawmaking process also reflects the Framers' careful efforts to check whatever propensity a particular Congress might have to enact oppressive, improvident, or ill-considered measures. The President's veto role in the legislative process was described later during public debate on ratification:

> It establishes a salutary check upon the legislative body, calculated to guard the community against the effects of faction, precipitancy, or of any impulse unfriendly to the public good, which may happen to influence a majority of that body.... The primary inducement to conferring the power in question upon the Executive, is to enable him to defend himself; the secondary one is to increase the chances in favor of the community against the passing of bad laws, through haste, inadvertence, or design. *The Federalist* No. 73 (A. Hamilton)....

The Court also has observed that the Presentment Clauses serve the important purpose of assuring that a "national" perspective is grafted on the legislative process:

> The President is a representative of the people just as the members of the Senate and of the House are, and it may be, at some times, on some subjects, that the President elected by all the people is rather more representative of them all than are the members of either body of the Legislature whose constituencies are local and not countrywide.... *Myers v. United States*, 272 U.S. 52, 123 (1926).

## C

### *Bicameralism*

The bicameral requirement of Art. I, §§1, 7 was of scarcely less concern to the Framers than was the Presidential veto and indeed the two concepts are interdependent. By providing that no law could take effect without the concurrence of the prescribed majority of the Members of both Houses, the Framers reemphasized their belief, already remarked upon in connection with the Presentment Clauses, that legislation should not be enacted unless it has been carefully and fully considered by the Nation's elected officials. In the Constitutional Convention debates on the need for a bicameral legislature, James Wilson, later to become a Justice of this Court, commented:

> Despotism comes on mankind in different shapes. Sometimes in an Executive, sometimes in a military, one. Is there danger of a Legislative despotism? Theory & practice both proclaim it. If the Legislative authority be not restrained, there can be neither liberty nor stability; and it can only be restrained by dividing it within itself, into distinct and independent branches. In a single house there is no check, but the inadequate one, of the virtue & good sense of those who compose it. 1 M. Farrand, *The Records of the Federal Convention of 1787* (1911).

Hamilton argued that a Congress comprised of a single House was antithetical to the very purposes of the Constitution. Were the Nation to adopt a Constitution providing for only one legislative organ, he warned:

> We shall finally accumulate, in a single body, all the most important prerogatives of sovereignty, and thus entail upon our posterity one of the most execrable forms of government that human infatuation ever contrived. Thus we should create in reality that very tyranny which the adversaries of the new Constitution either are, or affect to be, solicitous to avert. *The Federalist* No. 22.

This view was rooted in a general skepticism regarding the fallibility of human nature later commented on by Joseph Story:

> Public bodies, like private persons, are occasionally under the dominion of strong passions and excitements; impatient, irritable, and impetuous.... If [a legislature] feels no check but its own will, it rarely has the firmness to insist upon holding a question long enough under its own view, to see and mark it in all its bearings and relations to society. J. Story, *Commentaries on the Constitution of the United States* (3d ed. 1858).

These observations are consistent with what many of the Framers expressed, none more cogently than Madison in pointing up the need to divide and disperse power in order to protect liberty:

> In republican government, the legislative authority necessarily predominates. The remedy for this inconveniency is to divide the legislature into different branches; and to render them, by different modes of election and different principles of action, as little connected with each other as the nature of their common functions and their common dependence on the society will admit. *The Federalist* No. 51.

However familiar, it is useful to recall that apart from their fear that special interests could be favored at the expense of public needs, the Framers were also concerned, although not of one mind, over the apprehensions of the smaller states. Those states feared a commonality of interest among the larger states would work to their disadvantage; representatives of the larger states, on the other hand, were skeptical of a legislature that could pass laws favoring a minority of the people. *See* 1 M. Farrand, *supra*. It need hardly be repeated here that the Great Compromise, under which one House was viewed as representing the people and the other the states, allayed the fears of both the large and small states.

We see therefore that the Framers were acutely conscious that the bicameral requirement and the Presentment Clauses would serve essential constitutional functions. The President's participation in the legislative process was to protect the Executive Branch from Congress and to protect the whole people from improvident laws. The division of the Congress into two distinctive bodies assures that the legislative power would be exercised only after opportunity for full study and debate in separate settings. The President's unilateral veto power, in turn, was limited by the power of two-thirds of both Houses of Congress to overrule a veto thereby precluding final arbitrary action of one person. It emerges clearly that the prescription for legislative action in Art. I, §§ 1, 7 represents the Framers' decision that the legislative power of the Federal Government be exercised in accord with a single, finely wrought and exhaustively considered, procedure.

## IV

The Constitution sought to divide the delegated powers of the new Federal Government into three defined categories, Legislative, Executive, and Judicial, to assure, as nearly as possible, that each branch of government would confine itself to its assigned responsibility. The hydraulic pressure inherent within each of the separate Branches to exceed the outer limits of its power, even to accomplish desirable objectives, must be resisted.

Although not "hermetically" sealed from one another, the powers delegated to the three Branches are functionally identifiable. When any Branch acts, it is presumptively exercising the power the Constitution has delegated to it. When the Executive acts, it presumptively acts in an executive or administrative capacity as defined in Art. II. And when, as here, one House of Congress purports to act, it is presumptively acting within its assigned sphere.

Beginning with this presumption, we must nevertheless establish that the challenged action under § 244(c)(2) is of the kind to which the procedural requirements of Art. I, § 7 apply. Not every action taken by either House is subject to the bicameralism and presentment requirements of Art I. Whether actions taken by either House are, in law and fact, an exercise of legislative power depends not on their form but upon "whether they contain matter which is properly to be regarded as legislative in its character and effect."

Examination of the action taken here by one House pursuant to § 244(c)(2) reveals that it was essentially legislative in purpose and effect. In purporting to exercise power defined in Art. I, § 8, cl. 4, to "establish an uniform Rule of Naturalization," the House took action that had the purpose and effect of altering the legal rights, duties and relations of persons, including the Attorney General, Executive Branch officials and Chadha, all outside the Legislative Branch. Section 244(c)(2) purports to authorize one House of Congress to require the Attorney General to deport an individual alien whose deportation otherwise would be cancelled under § 244. The one-House veto operated in these cases to overrule the Attorney General and mandate Chadha's deportation; absent the House action, Chadha would remain in the United States. Congress has *acted* and its action has altered Chadha's status.

The legislative character of the one-House veto in these cases is confirmed by the character of the congressional action it supplants. Neither the House of Representatives nor the Senate contends that, absent the veto provision in § 244(c)(2), either of them, or both of them acting together, could effectively require the Attorney General to deport an alien once the Attorney General, in the exercise of legislatively delegated authority,[16] had determined the alien should remain in the United States. Without the challenged provision in § 244(c)(2), this could have been achieved, if at all, only by legislation requiring deportation. Similarly, a veto by one House of Congress under § 244(c)(2) cannot be justified as an attempt at amending the standards set out in § 244(a)(1), or as a repeal of § 244 as applied to Chadha. Amendment and repeal of statutes, no less than enactment, must conform with Art. I....

Finally, we see that when the Framers intended to authorize either House of Congress to act alone and outside of its prescribed bicameral legislative role, they narrowly and precisely defined the procedure for such action. There are four provisions in the

---

16. Congress protests that affirming the Court of Appeals in these cases will sanction "lawmaking by the Attorney General.... Why is the Attorney General exempt from submitting his proposed changes in the law to the full bicameral process?" Brief of the United States House of Representatives 40. To be sure, some administrative agency action—rule making, for example—may resemble "lawmaking." See 5 U.S.C. § 551(4), which defines an agency's "rule" as "the whole or part of an agency statement of general or particular applicability and future effect designed to implement, interpret, or prescribe *law or policy....*" This Court has referred to agency activity as being "quasi-legislative" in character. *Humphrey's Executor v. United States*, 295 U.S. 602 (1935). Clearly, however, "in the framework of our Constitution, the President's power to see that the laws are faithfully executed refutes the idea that he is to be a lawmaker." *Youngstown Sheet & Tube Co. v. Sawyer* (1952) [*Supra.* this chapter]. When the Attorney General performs his duties pursuant to § 244, he does not exercise "legislative" power. The bicameral process is not necessary as a check on the Executive's administration of the laws because his administrative activity cannot reach beyond the limits of the statute that created it—a statute duly enacted pursuant to Art. I, §§ 1, 7. The constitutionality of the Attorney General's execution of the authority delegated to him by § 244 involves only a question of delegation doctrine. The courts, when a case or controversy arises, can always "ascertain whether the will of Congress has been obeyed," *Yakus v. United States* (1944) [*Supra.* this chapter], and can enforce adherence to statutory standards. See *Youngstown.* It is clear, therefore, that the Attorney General acts in his presumptively Art. II capacity when he administers the Immigration and Nationality Act. Executive action under legislatively delegated authority that might resemble "legislative" action in some respects is not subject to the approval of both Houses of Congress and the President for the reason that the Constitution does not so require. That kind of Executive action is always subject to check by the terms of the legislation that authorized it; and if that authority is exceeded it is open to judicial review as well as the power of Congress to modify or revoke the authority entirely. A one-House veto is clearly legislative in both character and effect and is not so checked; the need for the check provided by Art. I, §§ 1, 7 is therefore clear. Congress' authority to delegate portions of its power to administrative agencies provides no support for the argument that Congress can constitutionally control administration of the laws by way of a Congressional veto.

Constitution, explicit and unambiguous, by which one House may act alone with the unreviewable force of law, not subject to the President's veto:

(a) The House of Representatives alone was given the power to initiate impeachments. Art. I, § 2, cl. 5;

(b) The Senate alone was given the power to conduct trials following impeachment on charges initiated by the House and to convict following trial. Art. I, § 3, cl. 6;

(c) The Senate alone was given final unreviewable power to approve or to disapprove Presidential appointments. Art. II, § 2, cl. 2;

(d) The Senate alone was given unreviewable power to ratify treaties negotiated by the President. Art. II, § 2, cl. 2.

Clearly, when the Draftsmen sought to confer special powers on one House, independent of the other House, or of the President, they did so in explicit, unambiguous terms. These carefully defined exceptions from presentment and bicameralism underscore the difference between the legislative functions of Congress and other unilateral but important and binding one-House acts provided for in the Constitution. These exceptions are narrow, explicit, and separately justified; none of them authorize the action challenged here. On the contrary, they provide further support for the conclusion that Congressional authority is not to be implied and for the conclusion that the veto provided for in § 244(c)(2) is not authorized by the constitutional design of the powers of the Legislative Branch.

Since it is clear that the action by the House under § 244(c)(2) was not within any of the express constitutional exceptions authorizing one House to act alone, and equally clear that it was an exercise of legislative power, that action was subject to the standards prescribed in Art. I. The bicameral requirement, the Presentment Clauses, the President's veto, and Congress' power to override a veto were intended to erect enduring checks on each Branch and to protect the people from the improvident exercise of power by mandating certain prescribed steps. To preserve those checks, and maintain the separation of powers, the carefully defined limits on the power of each Branch must not be eroded. To accomplish what has been attempted by one House of Congress in this case requires action in conformity with the express procedures of the Constitution's prescription for legislative action: passage by a majority of both Houses and presentment to the President.

The veto authorized by § 244(c)(2) doubtless has been in many respects a convenient shortcut; the "sharing" with the Executive by Congress of its authority over aliens in this manner is, on its face, an appealing compromise. In purely practical terms, it is obviously easier for action to be taken by one House without submission to the President; but it is crystal clear from the records of the Convention, contemporaneous writings and debates, that the Framers ranked other values higher than efficiency.... There is unmistakable expression of a determination that legislation by the national Congress be a step-by-step, deliberate and deliberative process.

The choices we discern as having been made in the Constitutional Convention impose burdens on governmental processes that often seem clumsy, inefficient, even

Jl. bryde

unworkable, but those hard choices were consciously made by men who had lived under a form of government that permitted arbitrary governmental acts to go unchecked.... With all the obvious flaws of delay, untidiness, and potential for abuse, we have not yet found a better way to preserve freedom than by making the exercise of power subject to the carefully crafted restraints spelled out in the Constitution.

## V

We hold that the Congressional veto provision in § 244(c)(2) is severable from the Act and that it is unconstitutional....

JUSTICE POWELL, concurring in the judgment.

The Court's decision, based on the Presentment Clauses, Art. I, § 7, cls. 2 and 3, apparently will invalidate every use of the legislative veto. The breadth of this holding gives one pause. Congress has included the veto in literally hundreds of statutes, dating back to the 1930s. Congress clearly views this procedure as essential to controlling the delegation of power to administrative agencies. One reasonably may disagree with Congress' assessment of the veto's utility, but the respect due its judgment as a coordinate branch of Government cautions that our holding should be no more extensive than necessary to decide this case. In my view, the case may be decided on a narrower ground. When Congress finds that a particular person does not satisfy the statutory criteria for permanent residence in this country it has assumed a judicial function in violation of the principle of separation of powers. Accordingly, I concur only in the judgment....

## II

... The impropriety of the House's assumption of this function is confirmed by the fact that its action raises the very danger the Framers sought to avoid—the exercise of unchecked power. In deciding whether Chadha deserves to be deported, Congress is not subject to any internal constraints that prevent it from arbitrarily depriving him of the right to remain in this country. Unlike the judiciary or an administrative agency, Congress is not bound by established substantive rules. Nor is it subject to the procedural safeguards, such as the right to counsel and a hearing before an impartial tribunal, that are present when a court or an agency adjudicates individual rights. The only effective constraint on Congress' power is political, but Congress is most accountable politically when it prescribes rules of general applicability. When it decides rights of specific persons, those rights are subject to "the tyranny of a shifting majority."

Chief Justice Marshall observed: "It is the peculiar province of the legislature to prescribe general rules for the government of society; the application of those rules ... would seem to be the duty of other departments." In my view, when Congress undertook to apply its rules to Chadha, it exceeded the scope of its constitutionally prescribed authority. I would not reach the broader question whether legislative vetoes are invalid under the Presentment Clauses.

JUSTICE WHITE, dissenting.

Today the Court not only invalidates § 244(c)(2) of the Immigration and Nationality Act, but also sounds the death knell for nearly 200 other statutory provisions in which

Congress has reserved a "legislative veto." For this reason, the Court's decision is of surpassing importance. And it is for this reason that the Court would have been well advised to decide the cases, if possible, on the narrower grounds of separation of powers, leaving for full consideration the constitutionality of other congressional review statutes operating on such varied matters as war powers and agency rulemaking, some of which concern the independent regulatory agencies.

The prominence of the legislative veto mechanism in our contemporary political system and its importance to Congress can hardly be overstated. It has become a central means by which Congress secures the accountability of executive and independent agencies. Without the legislative veto, Congress is faced with a Hobson's choice: either to refrain from delegating the necessary authority, leaving itself with a hopeless task of writing laws with the requisite specificity to cover endless special circumstances across the entire policy landscape, or in the alternative, to abdicate its law-making function to the Executive Branch and independent agencies....

## I

The legislative veto developed initially in response to the problems of reorganizing the sprawling Government structure created in response to the Depression....

The history of the legislative veto also makes clear that it has not been a sword with which Congress has struck out to aggrandize itself at the expense of the other branches—the concerns of Madison and Hamilton. Rather, the veto has been a means of defense, a reservation of ultimate authority necessary if Congress is to fulfill its designated role under Art. I as the Nation's lawmaker. While the President has often objected to particular legislative vetoes, generally those left in the hands of congressional Committees, the Executive has more often agreed to legislative review as the price for a broad delegation of authority. To be sure, the President may have preferred unrestricted power, but that could be precisely why Congress thought it essential to retain a check on the exercise of delegated authority.

## II

... If the legislative veto were as plainly unconstitutional as the Court strives to suggest, its broad ruling today would be more comprehensible. But, the constitutionality of the legislative veto is anything but clear-cut. The issue divides scholars, courts, Attorneys General, and the two other branches of the National Government. If the veto devices so flagrantly disregarded the requirements of Art. I as the Court today suggests, I find it incomprehensible that Congress, whose Members are bound by oath to uphold the Constitution, would have placed these mechanisms in nearly 200 separate laws over a period of 50 years.

... The Constitution does not directly authorize or prohibit the legislative veto. Thus, our task should be to determine whether the legislative veto is consistent with the purposes of Art. I and the principles of separation of powers which are reflected in that Article and throughout the Constitution. We should not find the lack of a specific constitutional authorization for the legislative veto surprising, and I would not infer disapproval of the mechanism from its absence. From the summer of 1787 to the present the Government of the United States has become an endeavor far beyond the contemplation of the Framers. Only within the last half century has the complexity and size of the Federal Government's responsibilities grown so greatly that the Congress must rely on the legislative veto as the most effective if not the only means to insure its role as the Nation's lawmakers. But the wisdom of the Framers was to anticipate that the Nation would grow and new problems of governance would require different solutions. Accordingly, our Federal Government was intentionally chartered with the flexibility to respond to contemporary needs without losing sight of fundamental democratic principles....

### III

... The power to exercise a legislative veto is not the power to write new law without bicameral approval or Presidential consideration. The veto must be authorized by statute and may only negative what an Executive department or independent agency has proposed. On its face, the legislative veto no more allows one House of Congress to make law than does the Presidential veto confer such power upon the President....

### B

... If Congress may delegate lawmaking power to independent and executive agencies, it is most difficult to understand Art. I as prohibiting Congress from also reserving a check on legislative power for itself. Absent the veto, the agencies receiving delegations of legislative or quasi-legislative power may issue regulations having the force of law without bicameral approval and without the President's signature. It is thus not apparent why the reservation of a veto over the exercise of that legislative power must be subject to a more exacting test. In both cases, it is enough that the initial statutory authorizations comply with the Art. I requirements....

### C

\* \* \*

### 2

The central concern of the presentment and bicameralism requirements of Art. I is that when a departure from the legal status quo is undertaken, it is done with the approval of the President and both Houses of Congress — or, in the event of a Presidential veto, a two-thirds majority in both Houses. This interest is fully satisfied by the operation of §244(c)(2). The President's approval is found in the Attorney General's action in recommending to Congress that the deportation order for a given alien be suspended. The House and the Senate indicate their approval of the Executive's action by not passing a resolution of disapproval within the statutory period. Thus, a change in the legal status quo — the deportability of the alien — is consummated only with the approval of each of the three relevant actors. The disagreement of any one of the three maintains the alien's pre-existing status: the Executive may choose not to recommend suspension; the House and Senate may each veto the recommendation. The effect on the rights and obligations of the affected individuals and upon the legislative system is precisely the same as if a private bill were introduced but failed to receive the necessary approval.... [Section] 244(c)(2) fully effectuates the purposes of the bicameralism and presentment requirements....

V

I regret that I am in disagreement with my colleagues on the fundamental questions that these cases present. But even more I regret the destructive scope of the Court's holding. It reflects a profoundly different conception of the Constitution than that held by the courts which sanctioned the modern administrative state. Today's decision strikes down in one fell swoop provisions in more laws enacted by Congress than the Court has cumulatively invalidated in its history.... I must dissent.

## Note: Continued Legislative Oversight over the Bureaucracy

1. *Chadha* should not be understood as immunizing the bureaucracy from any congressional influence short of a new statute revoking the initial grant of authority to the agency. Rather, a number of means remain by which Congress can exercise influence. Agencies still depend on Congress for their funding, which is usually heavily influenced by the relevant House and Senate committees that oversee the areas of that particular agency's responsibility. Moreover, agency heads requiring Senate confirmation must appear before the relevant committee, which provides an opportunity to extract commitments from the nominee. Perhaps most importantly, legislators and their staffs remain in regular contact with agency personnel, and continually communicate and negotiate about the agency's activities. In light of these avenues for influence, an agency that ignored ongoing congressional disapproval of its conduct would soon find itself with a powerful adversary.

2. In 1996 Congress enacted the Congressional Review Act (CRA). The CRA requires agencies to submit important regulatory actions to Congress, and gives Congress sixty days to enact a joint resolution disapproving of that action. The President may veto the resolution, in which case it is returned for a possible override vote by two-thirds of Congress. In short, the CRA largely mimics the standard law-making process by which Congress can always overturn an agency action. However, the CRA eliminated some procedural hurdles (such as the threat of Senate filibusters) that internal congressional rules impose on normal legislation. Since 1996 the CRA has been used very sparingly.

## Note: The Non-Delegation Doctrine and the Legislative Veto

1. To what extent is the Court being inconsistent in its approach to the non-delegation doctrine and the legislative veto? Justice White, dissenting in *Chadha*, argued that by 1983 the legislative veto had become a key means for Congress to retain administrative accountability in the face of very broad congressional delegations of power to administrative agencies. Of course, as he noted, Congress could ensure such accountability simply by writing more detailed statutes. But, he argued, that approach would likely be futile, given the complexity of most regulatory issues today. If the Court is going to recognize that futility, and thus allow Congress broad latitude to

delegate, then why should it restrict Congress when it attempts to provide for continued congressional oversight over agencies' use of that delegated power?

One answer may simply be that the legislative process is precisely delineated in Article I. Given that legislative vetoes closely resemble statutes in their practical effect, the ultimate explanation for *Chadha* may simply be that Article I clearly, if only implicitly, prohibits legislative vetoes. In that case, the combination of a (somewhat) clear prohibition on legislative vetoes with only a vague prohibition on congressional delegation of quasi-legislative power results in the seeming oddity of Congress enjoying a great deal of latitude to delegate power, but possessing only limited means to oversee how that power is exercised.

2. Justice White argued in *Chadha* that, even if the legislative veto did not satisfy the technical details of Article I's lawmaking process, it satisfied them in principle. (See Part III-C-2 of his opinion for that analysis.) His analysis is yet another example of the functional approach to separation of powers—an approach that seeks to determine whether the challenged practice satisfies the underlying goals of the separation of powers, rather than adhering to precise categorizations of each branch's powers.

3. Justice Powell concurred only in the result in *Chadha*. He argued that the legislative veto in that particular case amounted to Congress acting as an adjudicator. (Recall that the legislative veto in that case reversed the Attorney General's decision to allow particular individuals to remain in the country.) Justice Powell noted that, unlike courts, Congress is not required to follow any particular procedure when it conducts its business, and is not required to give affected persons a right to be heard. Thus, he concluded, Congress was not well-suited to performing functions that appeared in substance to be adjudicative. His concern with Congress possessing the power to single out individuals for burdens found echoes, twelve years later, in Justice Breyer's concurring opinion in *Plaut v. Spendthrift Farm*, excerpted in Chapter 1. Justice Powell's (and Justice Breyer's) analysis can be understood as yet another variant on functional analysis of the separation of powers.

## 3. Executive Control over the Bureaucracy

*Chadha*'s shift away from a functional and deferential approach to congressional judgment about institutional arrangements was subsequently tested when the Court considered whether Congress had the authority to limit executive control of officers. The Court has decided several cases challenging the statutory allocation of authority over administrative officers. The Court has vacillated in these cases between functionalist considerations of efficiency and workability and formalist arguments that Article II contemplates significant presidential control over high-ranking administrative officials. The next two cases consider a fundamental question about executive authority over the bureaucracy: to what degree does the Constitution's grant of "the Executive Power" in the President require that he possess the power to fire important executive branch officials for failure to adhere to his enforcement priorities? The note that follows those two cases considers other aspects of the problem of executive control over the bureaucracy.

## Morrison v. Olson

### 487 U.S. 654 (1988)

CHIEF JUSTICE REHNQUIST delivered the opinion of the Court.

This case presents us with a challenge to the independent counsel provisions of the Ethics in Government Act of 1978. We hold today that these provisions of the Act do not violate the Appointments Clause of the Constitution, Art. II, § 2, cl. 2, or the limitations of Article III, nor do they impermissibly interfere with the President's authority under Article II in violation of the constitutional principle of separation of powers.

### I

Briefly stated, Title VI of the Ethics in Government Act allows for the appointment of an "independent counsel" to investigate and, if appropriate, prosecute certain high-ranking Government officials for violations of federal criminal laws. The Act requires the Attorney General, upon receipt of information that he determines is "sufficient to constitute grounds to investigate whether any person [covered by the Act] may have violated any Federal criminal law," to conduct a preliminary investigation of the matter. When the Attorney General has completed this investigation, or 90 days has elapsed, he is required to report to a special court (the Special Division) created by the Act "for the purpose of appointing independent counsels."[3] If the Attorney General determines that "there are no reasonable grounds to believe that further investigation is warranted," then he must notify the Special Division of this result. In such a case, "the division of the court shall have no power to appoint an independent counsel." § 592(b)(1). If, however, the Attorney General has determined that there are "reasonable grounds to believe that further investigation or prosecution is warranted," then he "shall apply to the division of the court for the appointment of an independent counsel." The Attorney General's application to the court "shall contain sufficient information to assist the [court] in selecting an independent counsel and in defining that independent counsel's prosecutorial jurisdiction." § 592(d). Upon receiving this application, the Special Division "shall appoint an appropriate independent counsel and shall define that independent counsel's prosecutorial jurisdiction." § 593(b).

With respect to all matters within the independent counsel's jurisdiction, the Act grants the counsel "full power and independent authority to exercise all investigative and prosecutorial functions and powers of the Department of Justice, the Attorney General, and any other officer or employee of the Department of Justice." § 594(a). The functions of the independent counsel include conducting grand jury proceedings and other investigations, participating in civil and criminal court proceedings and litigation, and appealing any decision in any case in which the counsel participates in an official capacity. §§ 594(a)(1)–(3). Under § 594(a)(9), the counsel's powers in-

---

3. The Special Division is a division of the United States Court of Appeals for the District of Columbia Circuit....

clude "initiating and conducting prosecutions in any court of competent jurisdiction, framing and signing indictments, filing informations, and handling all aspects of any case, in the name of the United States." The counsel may appoint employees, §594(c), may request and obtain assistance from the Department of Justice, §594(d), and may accept referral of matters from the Attorney General if the matter falls within the counsel's jurisdiction as defined by the Special Division, §594(e).... An independent counsel has "full authority to dismiss matters within [his or her] prosecutorial jurisdiction without conducting an investigation or at any subsequent time before prosecution, if to do so would be consistent" with Department of Justice policy. §594(g).

Two statutory provisions govern the length of an independent counsel's tenure in office. The first defines the procedure for removing an independent counsel. Section 596(a)(1) provides:

> An independent counsel appointed under this chapter may be removed from office, other than by impeachment and conviction, only by the personal action of the Attorney General and only for good cause, physical disability, mental incapacity, or any other condition that substantially impairs the performance of such independent counsel's duties.

If an independent counsel is removed pursuant to this section, the Attorney General is required to submit a report to both the Special Division and the Judiciary Committees of the Senate and the House "specifying the facts found and the ultimate grounds for such removal." §596(a)(2). Under the current version of the Act, an independent counsel can obtain judicial review of the Attorney General's action by filing a civil action in the United States District Court for the District of Columbia. Members of the Special Division "may not hear or determine any such civil action or any appeal of a decision in any such civil action." The reviewing court is authorized to grant reinstatement or "other appropriate relief." §596(a)(3).

The other provision governing the tenure of the independent counsel defines the procedures for "terminating" the counsel's office. Under §596(b)(1), the office of an independent counsel terminates when he or she notifies the Attorney General that he or she has completed or substantially completed any investigations or prosecutions undertaken pursuant to the Act. In addition, the Special Division, acting either on its own or on the suggestion of the Attorney General, may terminate the office of an independent counsel at any time if it finds that "the investigation of all matters within the prosecutorial jurisdiction of such independent counsel ... have been completed or so substantially completed that it would be appropriate for the Department of Justice to complete such investigations and prosecutions." §596(b)(2).

Finally, the Act provides for congressional oversight of the activities of independent counsel. An independent counsel may from time to time send Congress statements or reports on his or her activities. §595(a)(2). The "appropriate committees of the Congress" are given oversight jurisdiction in regard to the official conduct of an independent counsel, and the counsel is required by the Act to cooperate with Congress in the exercise of this jurisdiction. §595(a)(1). The counsel is required to inform

Prop.   Con.

the House of Representatives of "substantial and credible information which [the counsel] receives ... that may constitute grounds for an impeachment." § 595(c). In addition, the Act gives certain congressional committee members the power to "request in writing that the Attorney General apply for the appointment of an independent counsel." § 592(g)(1). The Attorney General is required to respond to this request within a specified time but is not required to accede to the request. § 592(g)(2).

[At issue in *Morrison* was the appointment of an independent counsel to investigate an official in the Department of Justice Office of Legal Counsel. The head of that office was the focus of an investigation into allegations that he gave misleading testimony to a Congressional committee.]

### III

The Appointments Clause of Article II reads as follows:

> [The President] shall nominate, and by and with the Advice and Consent of the Senate, shall appoint Ambassadors, other public Ministers and Consuls, Judges of the Supreme Court, and all other Officers of the United States, whose Appointments are not herein otherwise provided for, and which shall be established by Law: but the Congress may by Law vest the Appointment of such inferior Officers, as they think proper, in the President alone, in the Courts of Law, or in the Heads of Departments. U.S. Const., Art. II, § 2, cl. 2.

Inferior v. Principal officers

The parties do not dispute that "the Constitution for purposes of appointment ... divides all its officers into two classes." As we stated in *Buckley v. Valeo*, 424 U.S. 1 (1976): "Principal officers are selected by the President with the advice and consent of the Senate. Inferior officers Congress may allow to be appointed by the President alone, by the heads of departments, or by the Judiciary." The initial question is, accordingly, whether appellant is an "inferior" or a "principal" officer. If she is the latter, as the Court of Appeals concluded, then the Act is in violation of the Appointments Clause.

The line between "inferior" and "principal" officers is one that is far from clear, and the Framers provided little guidance into where it should be drawn. We need not attempt here to decide exactly where the line falls between the two types of officers, because in our view appellant clearly falls on the "inferior officer" side of that line. Several factors lead to this conclusion.

First, appellant is subject to removal by a higher Executive Branch official.... Second, appellant is empowered by the Act to perform only certain, limited duties....

Third, appellant's office is limited in jurisdiction. Not only is the Act itself restricted in applicability to certain federal officials suspected of certain serious federal crimes, but an independent counsel can only act within the scope of the jurisdiction that has been granted by the Special Division pursuant to a request by the Attorney General. Finally, appellant's office is limited in tenure. There is concededly no time limit on the appointment of a particular counsel. Nonetheless, the office of independent counsel is "temporary" in the sense that an independent counsel is appointed essentially to accomplish a single task, and when that task is over the office is terminated, either by the counsel herself or by action of the Special Division. . . .

This does not, however, end our inquiry under the Appointments Clause. Appellees argue that even if appellant is an "inferior" officer, the Clause does not empower Congress to place the power to appoint such an officer outside the Executive Branch. They contend that the Clause does not contemplate congressional authorization of "interbranch appointments," in which an officer of one branch is appointed by officers of another branch. The relevant language of the Appointments Clause . . . admits of no limitation on interbranch appointments. Indeed, the [language] seems clearly to give Congress significant discretion to determine whether it is "proper" to vest the appointment of, for example, executive officials in the "courts of Law." . . .

We also note that the history of the Clause provides no support for appellees' position. . . . [There] was little or no debate on the question whether the [Appointment] Clause empowers Congress to provide for interbranch appointments, and there is nothing to suggest that the Framers intended to prevent Congress from having that power.

We do not mean to say that Congress' power to provide for interbranch appointments of "inferior officers" is unlimited. In addition to separation-of-powers concerns, which would arise if such provisions for appointment had the potential to impair the constitutional functions assigned to one of the branches, . . . Congress' decision to vest the appointment power in the courts would be improper if there was some "incongruity" between the functions normally performed by the courts and the performance of their duty to appoint. In this case, however, we do not think it impermissible for Congress to vest the power to appoint independent counsel in a specially created federal court. We thus disagree with the Court of Appeals' conclusion that there is an inherent incongruity about a court having the power to appoint prosecutorial officers. We have recognized that courts may appoint private attorneys to act as prosecutor for judicial contempt judgments. . . . Congress, of course was concerned when it created the office of independent counsel with the conflicts of interest that could arise in situations when the Executive Branch is called upon to investigate its own high-ranking officers. If it were to remove the appointing authority from the Executive Branch, the most logical place to put it was in the Judicial Branch. In the light of the Act's provision making the judges of the Special Division ineligible to participate in any matters relating to an independent counsel they have appointed, we do not think that appointment of the independent counsel by the court runs afoul of the constitutional limitation on "incongruous" interbranch appointments.

IV

Appellees next contend that the powers vested in the Special Division by the Act conflict with Article III of the Constitution. . . .

The Act . . . vests in the Special Division various powers and duties in relation to the independent counsel that, because they do not involve appointing the counsel or defining his or her jurisdiction, cannot be said to derive from the Division's Appointments Clause authority....

Leaving aside for the moment the Division's power to terminate an independent counsel, we do not think that Article III absolutely prevents Congress from vesting ... miscellaneous powers in the Special Division pursuant to the Act. As we observed above, one purpose of the broad prohibition upon the courts' exercise of "executive or administrative duties of a nonjudicial nature," is to maintain the separation between the Judiciary and the other branches of the Federal Government by ensuring that judges do not encroach upon executive or legislative authority or undertake tasks that are more properly accomplished by those branches. In this case, the miscellaneous powers described above do not impermissibly trespass upon the authority of the Executive Branch. Some of these allegedly "supervisory" powers conferred on the court are passive: the Division merely "receives" reports from the counsel or the Attorney General, it is not entitled to act on them or to specifically approve or disapprove of their contents. Other provisions of the Act do require the court to exercise some judgment and discretion, but the powers granted by these provisions are themselves essentially ministerial. The Act simply does not give the Division the power to "supervise" the independent counsel in the exercise of his or her investigative or prosecutorial authority. [And, the functions that the Special Division is empowered to perform are not inherently "Executive"; indeed, they are directly analogous to functions that federal judges perform in other contexts) such as deciding whether to allow disclosure of matters occurring before a grand jury, see Fed. Rule Crim. Proc. 6(e), deciding to extend a grand jury investigation, Rule 6(g), or awarding attorney's fees, *see, e.g.,* 42 U.S.C. §1988.

We are more doubtful about the Special Division's power to terminate the office of the independent counsel pursuant to §596(b)(2). As appellees suggest, the power to terminate, especially when exercised by the Division on its own motion, is "administrative" to the extent that it requires the Special Division to monitor the progress of proceedings of the independent counsel and come to a decision as to whether the counsel's job is "completed." §596(b)(2). It also is not a power that could be considered typically "judicial," as it has few analogues among the court's more traditional powers. Nonetheless, we do not, as did the Court of Appeals, view this provision as a significant judicial encroachment upon executive power or upon the prosecutorial discretion of the independent counsel.

*Court. Avoidance*

We think that the Court of Appeals overstated the matter when it described the power to terminate as a "broadsword and ... rapier" that enables the court to "control the pace and depth of the independent counsel's activities." The provision has not been tested in practice, and we do not mean to say that an adventurous special court could not reasonably construe the provision as did the Court of Appeals; but it is the duty of federal courts to construe a statute in order to save it from constitutional infirmities, and to that end we think a narrow construction is appropriate here. The termination provisions of the Act do not give the Special Division anything approaching the power to *remove* the counsel while an investigation or court proceeding is still underway—this power is vested solely in the Attorney General. As we see it, "termination" may occur only when the duties of the counsel are truly "completed" or "so substantially completed" that there remains no need for any continuing action by the independent counsel. It is basically a device for removing from the public payroll an independent counsel who has served his or her purpose, but is unwilling to acknowledge the fact. So construed, the Special Division's power to terminate does not pose a sufficient threat of judicial intrusion into matters that are more properly within the Executive's authority to require that the Act be invalidated as inconsistent with Article III....

## V

We now turn to consider whether the Act is invalid under the constitutional principle of separation of powers. Two related issues must be addressed: The first is whether the provision of the Act restricting the Attorney General's power to remove the independent counsel to only those instances in which he can show "good cause," taken by itself, impermissibly interferes with the President's exercise of his constitutionally appointed functions. The second is whether, taken as a whole, the Act violates the separation of powers by reducing the President's ability to control the prosecutorial powers wielded by the independent counsel.

## A

Two Terms ago we had occasion to consider whether it was consistent with the separation of powers for Congress to pass a statute that authorized a Government official who is removable only by Congress to participate in what we found to be "executive powers." *Bowsher v. Synar*, 478 U.S. 714 (1986). We held in *Bowsher* that "Congress cannot reserve for itself the power of removal of an officer charged with the execution of the laws except by impeachment." A primary antecedent for this ruling was our 1926 decision in *Myers v. United States*, 272 U.S. 52 (1926). *Myers* had considered the propriety of a federal statute by which certain postmasters of the United States could be removed by the President only "by and with the advice and consent of the Senate." There too, Congress' attempt to involve itself in the removal of an executive official was found to be sufficient grounds to render the statute invalid. As we observed in *Bowsher*, the essence of the decision in *Myers* was the judgment that the Constitution prevents Congress from "drawing to itself ... the power to remove or the right to participate in the exercise of that power. To do this would be to go beyond the words and implications of the [Appointments Clause] and to infringe the constitutional principle of the separation of governmental powers."

Unlike both *Bowsher* and *Myers*, this case does not involve an attempt by Congress itself to gain a role in the removal of executive officials other than its established powers of impeachment and conviction. The Act instead puts the removal power squarely in the hands of the Executive Branch; an independent counsel may be removed from office, "only by the personal action of the Attorney General, and only for good cause." §596(a)(1). There is no requirement of congressional approval of the Attorney General's removal decision, though the decision is subject to judicial review. §596(a)(3). In our view, the removal provisions of the Act make this case more analogous to *Humphrey's Executor v. United States*, 295 U.S. 602 (1935), and *Wiener v. United States*, 357 U.S. 349 (1958), than to *Myers* or *Bowsher*.

In *Humphrey's Executor*, the issue was whether a statute restricting the President's power to remove the Commissioners of the Federal Trade Commission (FTC) only for "inefficiency, neglect of duty, or malfeasance in office" was consistent with the Constitution. We stated that whether Congress can "condition the [President's power of removal] by fixing a definite term and precluding a removal except for cause, will depend upon the character of the office." Contrary to the implication of some dicta in *Myers*, the President's power to remove Government officials simply was not "all-inclusive in respect of civil officers with the exception of the judiciary provided for by the Constitution." At least in regard to "quasi-legislative" and "quasi-judicial" agencies such as the FTC, "the authority of Congress, in creating [such] agencies, to require them to act in discharge of their duties independently of executive control ... includes, as an appropriate incident, power to fix the period during which they shall continue in office, and to forbid their removal except for cause in the meantime." In *Humphrey's Executor*, we found it "plain" that the Constitution did not give the President "illimitable power of removal" over the officers of independent agencies....

Appellees contend that *Humphrey's Executor* and *Wiener* are distinguishable from this case because they did not involve officials who performed a "core executive function." They argue that our decision in *Humphrey's Executor* rests on a distinction between "purely executive" officials and officials who exercise "quasi-legislative" and "quasi-judicial" powers. In their view, when a "purely executive" official is involved, the governing precedent is *Myers*, not *Humphrey's Executor*. And, under *Myers*, the President must have absolute discretion to discharge "purely" executive officials at will. *See Myers.*

We undoubtedly did rely on the terms "quasi-legislative" and "quasi-judicial" to distinguish the officials involved in *Humphrey's Executor* and *Wiener* from those in *Myers*, but our present considered view is that the determination of whether the Constitution allows Congress to impose a "good cause"-type restriction on the President's power to remove an official cannot be made to turn on whether or not that official is classified as "purely executive." The analysis contained in our removal cases is designed not to define rigid categories of those officials who may or may not be removed at will by the President, but to ensure that Congress does not interfere with the President's exercise of the "executive power" and his constitutionally appointed duty to "take care that the laws be faithfully executed" under Article II.... [The] characterization of the agencies in *Humphrey's Executor* and *Wiener* as "quasi-legislative" or "quasi-judicial" in large part reflected our judgment that it was not essential to the President's proper execution of his Article II powers that these agencies be headed up by individuals who were removable at will. We do not mean to suggest that an analysis of the functions served by the officials at issue is irrelevant. But the real question is whether the removal restrictions are of such a nature that they impede the President's ability to perform his constitutional duty, and the functions of the officials in question must be analyzed in that light.

Considering for the moment the "good cause" removal provision in isolation from the other parts of the Act at issue in this case, we cannot say that the imposition of a "good cause" standard for removal by itself unduly trammels on executive authority. There is no real dispute that the functions performed by the independent counsel are "executive" in the sense that they are law enforcement functions that typically have been undertaken by officials within the Executive Branch. As we noted above, however, the independent counsel is an inferior officer under the Appointments Clause, with limited jurisdiction and tenure and lacking policymaking or significant administrative authority. Although the counsel exercises no small amount of discretion and judgment in deciding how to carry out his or her duties under the Act, we simply do not see how the President's need to control the exercise of that discretion is so central to the functioning of the Executive Branch as to require as a matter of constitutional law that the counsel be terminable at will by the President.

Nor do we think that the "good cause" removal provision at issue here impermissibly burdens the President's power to control or supervise the independent counsel, as an executive official, in the execution of his or her duties under the Act. This is not a case in which the power to remove an executive official has been completely stripped from the President, thus providing no means for the President to ensure the "faithful execution" of the laws. Rather, because the independent counsel may be terminated for "good cause," the Executive, through the Attorney General, retains ample authority to assure that the counsel is competently performing his or her statutory responsibilities in a manner that comports with the provisions of the Act....

## B

The final question to be addressed is whether the Act, taken as a whole, violates the principle of separation of powers by unduly interfering with the role of the Executive Branch. Time and again we have reaffirmed the importance in our constitutional scheme of the separation of governmental powers into the three coordinate branches.... We observe first that this case does not involve an attempt by Congress to increase its own powers at the expense of the Executive Branch. Unlike some of our previous cases, most recently *Bowsher v. Synar*, this case simply does not pose a "danger of congressional usurpation of Executive Branch functions." Indeed, with the exception of the power of impeachment—which applies to all officers of the United States—Congress retained for itself no powers of control or supervision over an independent counsel. The Act does empower certain Members of Congress to request the Attorney General to apply for the appointment of an independent counsel, but the Attorney General has no duty to comply with the request, although he must respond within a certain time limit. Other than that, Congress' role under the Act is limited to receiving reports or other information and oversight of the independent counsel's activities, § 595(a), functions that we have recognized generally as being incidental to the legislative function of Congress.

Similarly, we do not think that the Act works any *judicial* usurpation of properly executive functions. As should be apparent from our discussion of the Appointments Clause above, the power to appoint inferior officers such as independent counsel is not in itself an "executive" function in the constitutional sense, at least when Congress has exercised its power to vest the appointment of an inferior office in the "courts of Law." We note nonetheless that under the Act the Special Division has no power to appoint an independent counsel *sua sponte*; it may only do so upon the specific request of the Attorney General, and the courts are specifically prevented from reviewing the Attorney General's decision not to seek appointment, § 592(f). In addition, once the court has appointed a counsel and defined his or her jurisdiction, it has no power to supervise or control the activities of the counsel....

Finally, we do not think that the Act "impermissibly undermines" the powers of the Executive Branch, or "disrupts the proper balance between the coordinate branches [by] preventing the Executive Branch from accomplishing its constitutionally assigned functions." It is undeniable that the Act reduces the amount of control or supervision that the Attorney General and, through him, the President exercises over the investigation and prosecution of a certain class of alleged criminal activity. The Attorney General is not allowed to appoint the individual of his choice; he does not determine the counsel's jurisdiction; and his power to remove a counsel is limited. Nonetheless, the Act does give the Attorney General several means of supervising or controlling the prosecutorial powers that may be wielded by an independent counsel. Most importantly, the Attorney General retains the power to remove the counsel for "good cause," a power that we have already concluded provides the Executive with substantial ability to ensure that the laws are "faithfully executed" by an independent counsel....

JUSTICE KENNEDY took no part in the consideration or decision of this case.

JUSTICE SCALIA, dissenting.

It is the proud boast of our democracy that we have "a government of laws and not of men." ...

That is what this suit is about. Power. The allocation of power among Congress, the President, and the courts in such fashion as to preserve the equilibrium the Constitution sought to establish—so that "a gradual concentration of the several powers in the same department," *Federalist* No. 51, p. 321 (J. Madison), can effectively be resisted. Frequently an issue of this sort will come before the Court clad, so to speak, in sheep's clothing: the potential of the asserted principle to effect important change in the equilibrium of power is not immediately evident, and must be discerned by a careful and perceptive analysis. But this wolf comes as a wolf....

I

... [By] the application of this statute in the present case, Congress has effectively compelled a criminal investigation of a high-level appointee of the President in connection with his actions arising out of a bitter power dispute between the President and the Legislative Branch. Mr. Olson may or may not be guilty of a crime; we do not know. But we do know that the investigation of him has been commenced, not ... because the President or his authorized subordinates believe ... that an investigation is likely to unearth a violation worth prosecuting; but only because the Attorney General cannot affirm, as Congress demands, that there are *no reasonable grounds to believe* that further investigation is warranted. The decisions regarding the scope of that further investigation, its duration, and, finally, whether or not prosecution should ensue, are likewise beyond the control of the President and his subordinates.

## II

If to describe this case is not to decide it, the concept of a government of separate and coordinate powers no longer has meaning. The Court devotes most of its attention to such relatively technical details as the Appointments Clause and the removal power, addressing briefly and only at the end of its opinion the separation of powers.... I think that has it backwards. Our opinions are full of the recognition that it is the principle of separation of powers, and the inseparable corollary that each department's "defense must ... be made commensurate to the danger of attack," *The Federalist* No. 51 (J. Madison), which gives comprehensible content to the Appointments Clause, and determines the appropriate scope of the removal power. Thus, while I will subsequently discuss why our appointments and removal jurisprudence does not support today's holding, I begin with a consideration of the fountainhead of that jurisprudence, the separation and equilibration of powers.

[A premise that underlies this deliberation is that] where the issue pertains to separation of powers, and the political branches are (as here) in disagreement, neither can be presumed correct.... As one of the interested and coordinate parties to the underlying constitutional dispute, Congress, no more than the President, is entitled to the benefit of the doubt.

To repeat, Article II, § 1, cl. 1, of the Constitution provides:

"The executive Power shall be vested in a President of the United States."

As I described at the outset of this opinion, this does not mean *some* of the executive power, but *all* of the executive power....

As for ... whether the statute before us deprives the President of exclusive control over that quintessentially executive activity: The Court does not, and could not possibly, assert that it does not. That is indeed the whole object of the statute. Instead, the Court points out that the President, through his Attorney General, has at least *some* control. That concession is alone enough to invalidate the statute, but I cannot refrain from pointing out that the Court greatly exaggerates the extent of that "some" Presidential control. "Most important" among these controls, the Court asserts, is the Attorney General's "power to remove the counsel for 'good cause.'" This is somewhat like referring to shackles as an effective means of locomotion....

Moving on to the presumably "less important" controls that the President retains, the Court notes that no independent counsel may be appointed without a specific request from the Attorney General. As I have discussed above, the condition that renders such a request mandatory (inability to find "no reasonable grounds to believe" that further investigation is warranted) is so insubstantial that the Attorney General's discretion is severely confined. And once the referral is made, it is for the Special Division to determine the scope and duration of the investigation. And in any event, the limited power over referral is irrelevant to the question whether, *once appointed*, the independent counsel exercises executive power free from the President's control. Finally, the Court points out that the Act directs the independent counsel to abide by general Justice Department policy, except when not "possible." The exception alone shows this to be an empty promise. Even without that, however, one would be hard put to come up with many investigative or prosecutorial "policies" (other than those imposed by the Constitution or by Congress through law) that are absolute.... The balancing of various legal, practical, and political considerations, none of which is absolute, is the very essence of prosecutorial discretion. To take this away is to remove the core of the prosecutorial function, and not merely "some" Presidential control.

As I have said, however, it is ultimately irrelevant *how much* the statute reduces Presidential control. The case is over when the Court acknowledges, as it must, that "it is undeniable that the Act reduces the amount of control or supervision that the Attorney General and, through him, the President exercises over the investigation and prosecution of a certain class of alleged criminal activity." It effects a revolution in our constitutional jurisprudence for the Court, once it has determined that (1) purely executive functions are at issue here, and (2) those functions have been given to a person whose actions are not fully within the supervision and control of the President, nonetheless to proceed further to sit in judgment of whether "the President's need to control the exercise of [the independent counsel's] discretion is so *central* to the functioning of the Executive Branch" as to require complete control, ... whether the conferral of his powers upon someone else "*sufficiently* deprives the President of control over the independent counsel to interfere impermissibly with [his] constitutional obligation to ensure the faithful execution of the laws," ... and whether "the Act gives the Executive Branch *sufficient* control over the independent counsel to ensure that the President is able to perform his constitutionally assigned duties." It is not for us to determine, and we have never presumed to determine, how much of the purely executive powers of government must be within the full control of the President. The Constitution prescribes that they *all* are....

Is it unthinkable that the President should have such exclusive power, even when alleged crimes by him or his close associates are at issue? No more so than that Congress should have the exclusive power of legislation, even when what is at issue is its own exemption from the burdens of certain laws. *See* Civil Rights Act of 1964, Title VII, 42 U.S.C. § 2000e et seq. (prohibiting "employers," not defined to include the United States, from discriminating on the basis of race, color, religion, sex, or national origin). No more so than that this Court should have the exclusive power to pronounce the final decision on justiciable cases and controversies, even those pertaining to the constitutionality of a statute reducing the salaries of the Justices. A system of separate and coordinate powers necessarily involves an acceptance of exclusive power that can theoretically be abused.... While the separation of powers may prevent us from righting every wrong, it does so in order to ensure that we do not lose liberty....

The Court has, nonetheless, replaced the clear constitutional prescription that the executive power belongs to the President with a "balancing test." What are the standards to determine how the balance is to be struck, that is, how much removal of Presidential power is too much? ... The most amazing feature of the Court's opinion is that it does not even purport to give an answer. It simply *announces*, with no analysis, that the ability to control the decision whether to investigate and prosecute the President's closest advisers, and indeed the President himself, is not "so central to the functioning of the Executive Branch" as to be constitutionally required to be within the President's control. Apparently that is so because we say it is so. Having abandoned as the basis for our decisionmaking the text of Article II that "the executive Power" must be vested in the President, the Court does not even attempt to craft a *substitute* criterion — a "justiciable standard," *see, e.g., Baker v. Carr* (1962) [*Supra.* Chapter 1]....

# Free Enterprise Fund v. Public Company Accounting Oversight Board

### 561 U.S. 477 (2010)

Chief Justice ROBERTS delivered the opinion of the Court.

Our Constitution divided the "powers of the new Federal Government into three defined categories, Legislative, Executive, and Judicial." *INS v. Chadha* (1983) [*Supra.* this chapter]. Article II vests "the executive Power ... in a President of the United States of America," who must "take Care that the Laws be faithfully executed." In light of "the impossibility that one man should be able to perform all the great business of the State," the Constitution provides for executive officers to "assist the supreme Magistrate in discharging the duties of his trust."

Since 1789, the Constitution has been understood to empower the President to keep these officers accountable — by removing them from office, if necessary. See generally *Myers v. United States*, 272 U.S. 52 (1926). This Court has determined, however, that this authority is not without limit. In *Humphrey's Executor v. United States*, 295 U.S. 602 (1935), we held that Congress can, under certain circumstances, create independent agencies run by principal officers appointed by the President, whom the President may not remove at will but only for good cause. Likewise, in *United States v. Perkins*, 116 U.S. 483 (1886), and *Morrison v. Olson* (1988) [*Supra.* this chapter], the Court sustained similar restrictions on the power of principal executive officers — themselves responsible to the President — to remove their own inferiors. The parties do not ask us to reexamine any of these precedents, and we do not do so.

We are asked, however, to consider a new situation not yet encountered by the Court. The question is whether these separate layers of protection may be combined. May the President be restricted in his ability to remove a principal officer, who is in turn restricted in his ability to remove an inferior officer, even though that inferior officer determines the policy and enforces the laws of the United States?

We hold that such multilevel protection from removal is contrary to Article II's vesting of the executive power in the President. The President cannot "take Care that the Laws be faithfully executed" if he cannot oversee the faithfulness of the officers who execute them. Here the President cannot remove an officer who enjoys more than one level of good-cause protection, even if the President determines that the officer is neglecting his duties or discharging them improperly. That judgment is instead committed to another officer, who may or may not agree with the President's determination, and whom the President cannot remove simply because that officer disagrees with him. This contravenes the President's "constitutional obligation to ensure the faithful execution of the laws."

## I

## A

After a series of celebrated accounting debacles, Congress enacted the Sarbanes-Oxley Act of 2002 (or Act). Among other measures, the Act introduced tighter regulation of the accounting industry under a new Public Company Accounting Oversight Board. The Board is composed of five members, appointed to staggered 5-year terms by the Securities and Exchange Commission. It was modeled on private self-regulatory organizations in the securities industry—such as the New York Stock Exchange— that investigate and discipline their own members subject to Commission oversight....

Unlike the self-regulatory organizations, however, the Board is a Government-created, Government-appointed entity, with expansive powers to govern an entire industry.... The Board is charged with enforcing the Sarbanes-Oxley Act, the securities laws, the Commission's rules, its own rules, and professional accounting standards. To this end, the Board may regulate every detail of an accounting firm's practice....

The Act places the Board under the SEC's oversight, particularly with respect to the issuance of rules or the imposition of sanctions (both of which are subject to Commission approval and alteration). But the individual members of the Board ... are substantially insulated from the Commission's control. The Commission cannot remove Board members at will, but only "for good cause shown," "in accordance with" certain procedures....

Removal of a Board member requires a formal Commission order and is subject to judicial review.... The parties agree that the Commissioners cannot themselves be removed by the President except under the *Humphrey's Executor* standard of "inefficiency, neglect of duty, or malfeasance in office," and we decide the case with that understanding.

## B

Beckstead and Watts, LLP, is a Nevada accounting firm registered with the Board. The Board inspected the firm, released a report critical of its auditing procedures, and began a formal investigation. Beckstead and Watts and the Free Enterprise Fund, a nonprofit organization of which the firm is a member, then sued the Board and its members, seeking (among other things) a declaratory judgment that the Board is unconstitutional and an injunction preventing the Board from exercising its powers.

Before the District Court, petitioners argued that the Sarbanes-Oxley Act contravened the separation of powers by conferring wide-ranging executive power on Board members without subjecting them to Presidential control. Petitioners also challenged the Act under the Appointments Clause, which requires "Officers of the United States" to be appointed by the President with the Senate's advice and consent. The Clause provides an exception for "inferior Officers," whose appointment Congress may choose to vest "in the President alone, in the Courts of Law, or in the Heads of Departments." Because the Board is appointed by the SEC, petitioners argued that (1) Board members are not "inferior Officers" who may be appointed by "Heads of Departments"; (2) even if they are, the Commission is not a "Department"; and (3) even if it is, the several Commissioners (as opposed to the Chairman) are not its "Head." ... Both sides moved for summary judgment; the District Court determined that it had jurisdiction and granted summary judgment to respondents.

A divided Court of Appeals affirmed.... We granted certiorari....

## III

We hold that the dual for-cause limitations on the removal of Board members contravene the Constitution's separation of powers.

### A

The Constitution provides that "the executive Power shall be vested in a President of the United States of America." As Madison stated on the floor of the First Congress, "if any power whatsoever is in its nature Executive, it is the power of appointing, overseeing, and controlling those who execute the laws."

The removal of executive officers was discussed extensively in Congress when the first executive departments were created. The view that "prevailed, as most consonant to the text of the Constitution" and "to the requisite responsibility and harmony in the Executive Department," was that the executive power included a power to oversee executive officers through removal; because that traditional executive power was not "expressly taken away, it remained with the President." "This Decision of 1789 provides contemporaneous and weighty evidence of the Constitution's meaning since many of the Members of the First Congress had taken part in framing that instrument." And it soon became the "settled and well understood construction of the Constitution."

The landmark case of *Myers v. United States* reaffirmed the principle that Article II confers on the President "the general administrative control of those executing the laws." It is *his* responsibility to take care that the laws be faithfully executed. The buck stops with the President, in Harry Truman's famous phrase. As we explained in *Myers*, the President therefore must have some "power of removing those for whom he can not continue to be responsible."

Nearly a decade later in *Humphrey's Executor*, this Court held that *Myers* did not prevent Congress from conferring good-cause tenure on the principal officers of certain independent agencies. That case concerned the members of the Federal Trade Commission, who held 7-year terms and could not be removed by the President except for "'inefficiency, neglect of duty, or malfeasance in office.'" The Court distinguished *Myers* on the ground that *Myers* concerned "an officer [who] is merely one of the units in the executive department and, hence, inherently subject to the exclusive and illimitable power of removal by the Chief Executive, whose subordinate and aid he is." By contrast, the Court characterized the FTC as "quasi-legislative and quasi-judicial" rather than "purely executive," and held that Congress could require it "to act ... independently of executive control." Because "one who holds his office only during the pleasure of another, cannot be depended upon to maintain an attitude of independence against the latter's will," the Court held that Congress had power to "fix the period during which [the Commissioners] shall continue in office, and to forbid their removal except for cause in the meantime."

*Humphrey's Executor* did not address the removal of inferior officers, whose appointment Congress may vest in heads of departments. If Congress does so, it is ordinarily the department head, rather than the President, who enjoys the power of removal. This Court has upheld for-cause limitations on that power as well....

We ... considered the status of inferior officers in *Morrison*. That case concerned the Ethics in Government Act, which provided for an independent counsel to investigate allegations of crime by high executive officers. The counsel was appointed by a special court, wielded the full powers of a prosecutor, and was removable by the Attorney General only "for good cause." We recognized that the independent counsel was undoubtedly an executive officer, rather than "quasi-legislative" or "quasi-judicial," but we stated as "our present considered view" that Congress had power to impose good-cause restrictions on her removal. The Court noted that the statute "gave the Attorney General," an officer directly responsible to the President and "through [whom]" the President could act, "several means of supervising or controlling" the independent counsel—"most importantly ... the power to remove the counsel for good cause." Under those circumstances, the Court sustained the statute. *Morrison* did not, however, address the consequences of more than one level of good-cause tenure—leaving the issue ... "a question of first impression" in this Court.

## B

As explained, we have previously upheld limited restrictions on the President's removal power. In those cases, however, only one level of protected tenure separated the President from an officer exercising executive power. It was the President—or a subordinate he could remove at will—who decided whether the officer's conduct merited removal under the good-cause standard.

The Act before us does something quite different. It not only protects Board members from removal except for good cause, but withdraws from the President any decision on whether that good cause exists. That decision is vested instead in other tenured officers—the Commissioners—none of whom is subject to the President's direct control. The result is a Board that is not accountable to the President, and a President who is not responsible for the Board.

The added layer of tenure protection makes a difference. Without a layer of insulation between the Commission and the Board, the Commission could remove a Board member at any time, and therefore would be fully responsible for what the Board does. The President could then hold the Commission to account for its supervision of the Board, to the same extent that he may hold the Commission to account for everything else it does.

A second level of tenure protection changes the nature of the President's review. Now the Commission cannot remove a Board member at will. The President therefore cannot hold the Commission fully accountable for the Board's conduct, to the same extent that he may hold the Commission accountable for everything else that it does. The Commissioners are not responsible for the Board's actions. They are only responsible for their own determination of whether the Act's rigorous good-cause standard is met. And even if the President disagrees with their determination, he is powerless to intervene—unless that determination is so unreasonable as to constitute "inefficiency, neglect of duty, or malfeasance in office."

This novel structure does not merely add to the Board's independence, but transforms it. Neither the President, nor anyone directly responsible to him, nor even an officer whose conduct he may review only for good cause, has full control over the Board. The President is stripped of the power our precedents have preserved, and his ability to execute the laws—by holding his subordinates accountable for their conduct—is impaired.

That arrangement is contrary to Article II's vesting of the executive power in the President. Without the ability to oversee the Board, or to attribute the Board's failings to those whom he *can* oversee, the President is no longer the judge of the Board's conduct.... He can neither ensure that the laws are faithfully executed, nor be held responsible for a Board member's breach of faith. This violates the basic principle that the President "cannot delegate ultimate responsibility or the active obligation to supervise that goes with it," because Article II "makes a single President responsible for the actions of the Executive Branch." ...

The diffusion of power carries with it a diffusion of accountability. The people do not vote for the "Officers of the United States." They instead look to the President to guide the "assistants or deputies ... subject to his superintendence." *The Federalist* No. 72 (A. Hamilton). Without a clear and effective chain of command, the public cannot "determine on whom the blame or the punishment of a pernicious measure, or series of pernicious measures ought really to fall." That is why the Framers sought to ensure that "those who are employed in the execution of the law will be in their proper situation, and the chain of dependence be preserved; the lowest officers, the middle grade, and the highest, will depend, as they ought, on the President, and the President on the community." *1 Annals of Cong.,* at 499 (J. Madison).

By granting the Board executive power without the Executive's oversight, this Act subverts the President's ability to ensure that the laws are faithfully executed—as well as the public's ability to pass judgment on his efforts. The Act's restrictions are incompatible with the Constitution's separation of powers.

C

Respondents and the dissent resist this conclusion, portraying the Board as "the kind of practical accommodation between the Legislature and the Executive that should be permitted in a 'workable government.'" *Metropolitan Washington Airports Authority v. Citizens for Abatement of Aircraft Noise, Inc.,* 501 U.S. 252 (1991) (quoting

*Youngstown Sheet & Tube Co. v. Sawyer* (1952) (Jackson, J., concurring) [*Supra.* this chapter])....

No one doubts Congress's power to create a vast and varied federal bureaucracy. But where, in all this, is the role for oversight by an elected President? ...

... The growth of the Executive Branch, which now wields vast power and touches almost every aspect of daily life, heightens the concern that it may slip from the Executive's control, and thus from that of the people. This concern is largely absent from the dissent's paean to the administrative state....

The Framers created a structure in which "a dependence on the people" would be the "primary control on the government." *The Federalist* No. 51 (J. Madison). That dependence is maintained, not just by "parchment barriers," *id.*, No. 48 (same), but by letting "ambition ... counteract ambition," giving each branch "the necessary constitutional means, and personal motives, to resist encroachments of the others," *id.*, No. 51. A key "constitutional means" vested in the President—perhaps *the* key means—was "the power of appointing, overseeing, and controlling those who execute the laws." And while a government of "opposite and rival interests" may sometimes inhibit the smooth functioning of administration, *The Federalist* No. 51, "the Framers recognized that, in the long term, structural protections against abuse of power were critical to preserving liberty."

Calls to abandon those protections in light of "the era's perceived necessity" are not unusual. Nor is the argument from bureaucratic expertise limited only to the field of accounting. The failures of accounting regulation may be a "pressing national problem," but "a judiciary that licensed extraconstitutional government with each issue of comparable gravity would, in the long run, be far worse." ...

*Arg. for formalism 7 functionalism*

D

The United States concedes that some constraints on the removal of inferior executive officers might violate the Constitution. It contends, however, that the removal restrictions at issue here do not....

[Respondents] portray the Act's limitations on removal as irrelevant, because—as the Court of Appeals held—the Commission wields "at-will removal power over Board *functions* if not Board members." The Commission's general "oversight and enforcement authority over the Board," is said to "blunt the constitutional impact of for-cause removal," and to leave the President no worse off than "if Congress had lodged the Board's functions in the SEC's own staff."

Broad power over Board functions is not equivalent to the power to remove Board members. The Commission may, for example, approve the Board's budget, issue binding regulations, relieve the Board of authority, amend Board sanctions, or enforce Board rules on its own. But altering the budget or powers of an agency as a whole is a problematic way to control an inferior officer. The Commission cannot wield a free hand to supervise individual members if it must destroy the Board in order to fix it....

Finally, respondents suggest that our conclusion is contradicted by the past practice of Congress. But the Sarbanes-Oxley Act is highly unusual in committing substantial executive authority to officers protected by two layers of for-cause removal—including at one level a sharply circumscribed definition of what constitutes "good cause," and rigorous procedures that must be followed prior to removal.....

The dissent here suggests that other such positions might exist, and complains that we do not resolve their status in this opinion. The dissent itself, however, stresses the very size and variety of the Federal Government, and those features discourage general pronouncements on matters neither briefed nor argued here. In any event, the dissent fails to support its premonitions of doom; none of the positions it identifies are similarly situated to the Board....

V

Petitioners raise ... challenges to the Board under the Appointments Clause. None has merit.

]Petitioners] argue that Board members are principal officers requiring Presidential appointment with the Senate's advice and consent. We held in *Edmond v. United States*, 520 U.S. 651 (1997), that "whether one is an 'inferior' officer depends on whether he has a superior," and that "'inferior officers' are officers whose work is directed and supervised at some level" by other officers appointed by the President with the Senate's consent. In particular, we noted that "the power to remove officers" at will and without cause "is a powerful tool for control" of an inferior. As explained above, the statutory restrictions on the Commission's power to remove Board members are unconstitutional and void. Given that the Commission is properly viewed, under the Constitution, as possessing the power to remove Board members at will, and given the Commission's other oversight authority, we have no hesitation in concluding that under *Edmond* the Board members are inferior officers whose appointment Congress may permissibly vest in a "Head of Department." ...

Justice BREYER, with whom Justice STEVENS, Justice GINSBURG, and Justice SOTOMAYOR join, dissenting....

I

A

The legal question before us arises at the intersection of two general constitutional principles. On the one hand, Congress has broad power to enact statutes "necessary and proper" to the exercise of its specifically enumerated constitutional authority. As Chief Justice Marshall wrote for the Court nearly 200 years ago, the Necessary and Proper Clause reflects the Framers' efforts to create a Constitution that would "endure for ages to come." *McCulloch v. Maryland* 17 U.S. 316 (1819).... Thus the Necessary and Proper Clause affords Congress broad authority to "create" governmental "offices" and to structure those offices "as it chooses." And Congress has drawn on that power over the past century to create numerous federal agencies in response to "various crises of human affairs" as they have arisen. *McCulloch*.

On the other hand, the opening sections of Articles I, II, and III of the Constitution separately and respectively vest "all legislative Powers" in Congress, the "executive Power" in the President, and the "judicial Power" in the Supreme Court (and such "inferior Courts as Congress may from time to time ordain and establish"). In doing so, these provisions imply a structural separation-of-powers principle. And that principle, along with the instruction in Article II, §3 that the President "shall take Care that the Laws be faithfully executed," limits Congress' power to structure the Federal Government. See, e.g., *INS v. Chadha*; *Freytag*; *Northern Pipeline Constr. Co. v. Marathon Pipe Line Co.*, 458 U.S. 50 (1982); *Commodity Futures Trading Comm'n v. Schor* (1986) [*Supra*. Chapter 1]. Indeed, this Court has held that the separation-of-powers principle guarantees the President the authority to dismiss certain Executive Branch officials at will. *Myers*.

But neither of these two principles is absolute in its application to removal cases. The Necessary and Proper Clause does not grant Congress power to free *all* Executive Branch officials from dismissal at the will of the President. Nor does the separation-of-powers principle grant the President an absolute authority to remove any and all Executive Branch officials at will. Rather, depending on, say, the nature of the office, its function, or its subject matter, Congress sometimes may, consistent with the Constitution, limit the President's authority to remove an officer from his post. *See Humphrey's Executor*, overruling in part *Myers*; *Morrison*. And we must here decide whether the circumstances surrounding the statute at issue justify such a limitation.

In answering the question presented, we cannot look to more specific constitutional text, such as the text of the Appointments Clause or the Presentment Clause, upon which the Court has relied in other separation-of-powers cases. *See, e.g., Chadha*. That is because, with the exception of the general "vesting" and "take care" language, the Constitution is completely "silent with respect to the power of removal from office."

Nor does history offer significant help. The President's power to remove Executive Branch officers "was not discussed in the Constitutional Convention." The First Congress enacted federal statutes that limited the President's ability to *oversee* Executive Branch officials, including the Comptroller of the United States, federal district attorneys (precursors to today's United States Attorneys), and, to a lesser extent, the Secretary of the Treasury. But those statutes did not directly limit the President's authority to *remove* any of those officials—"a subject" that was "much disputed" during "the early history of this government," "and upon which a great diversity of opinion was entertained." Scholars, like Members of this Court, have continued to disagree, not only about the inferences that should be drawn from the inconclusive historical record, but also about the nature of the original disagreement.

Nor does this Court's precedent fully answer the question presented. At least it does not clearly invalidate the provision in dispute. See Part II-C, *infra*. In *Myers*, the Court invalidated—for the first and only time—a congressional statute on the ground that it unduly limited the President's authority to remove an Executive Branch official. But soon thereafter the Court expressly disapproved most of *Myers'* broad reasoning. *See Humphrey's Executor*, overruling in part *Myers*. Moreover, the Court has since said that "the essence of the decision in *Myers* was the judgment that the Constitution prevents Congress from '*drawing to itself* ... the power to remove or the right to participate in the exercise of that power.'" *Morrison*. And that feature of the statute—a feature that would *aggrandize* the power of Congress—is not present here. Congress has not granted itself any role in removing the members of the Accounting Board. *Cf. Freytag* ("separation-of-powers jurisprudence generally focuses on the danger of one branch's *aggrandizing its power* at the expense of another branch" (emphasis added)); *Schor* (same); *Bowsher v. Synar*, 478 U.S. 714 (1986) (same). Compare *Myers* (striking down statute where Congress granted *itself* removal authority over Executive Branch official), with *Humphrey's Executor* (upholding statute where such aggrandizing was absent); *Morrison* (same).

In short, the question presented lies at the intersection of two sets of conflicting, broadly framed constitutional principles. And no text, no history, perhaps no precedent provides any clear answer.

B

When previously deciding this kind of nontextual question, the Court has emphasized the importance of examining how a particular provision, taken in context, is likely to function.... The Court repeated this injunction in *Schor* and again in *Morrison*. *See Schor* (stating that the Court must look "beyond form to the substance of what Congress has done"); *Morrison* ("The analysis contained in our removal cases is designed *not to define rigid categories* of those officials who may or may not be removed at will by the President," but rather asks whether, given the "functions of the officials in question," a removal provision "interferes with the President's exercise of the 'executive power'" (emphasis added)). The Court has thereby written into law Justice Jackson's wise perception that "the Constitution ... contemplates that practice will integrate the dispersed powers into a *workable government*." *Youngstown* (opinion concurring in judgment). See also *ibid.* ("The actual art of governing under our Constitution does not and cannot conform to judicial definitions of the power of any of its branches based on isolated clauses or even single Articles torn from context").

It is not surprising that the Court in these circumstances has looked to function and context, and not to bright-line rules. For one thing, that approach embodies the intent of the Framers. As Chief Justice Marshall long ago observed, our Constitution is fashioned so as to allow the three coordinate branches, including this Court, to exercise practical judgment in response to changing conditions and "exigencies," which at the time of the founding could be seen only "dimly," and perhaps not at all. *McCulloch*.

For another, a functional approach permits Congress and the President the flexibility needed to adapt statutory law to changing circumstances. That is why the "powers conferred upon the Federal Government by the Constitution were phrased in language broad enough to allow for the expansion of the Federal Government's role" over time....

The functional approach required by our precedents recognizes this administrative complexity and, more importantly, recognizes the various ways presidential power operates within this context—and the various ways in which a removal provision might affect that power. As human beings have known ever since Ulysses tied himself to the mast so as safely to hear the Sirens' song, sometimes it is necessary to disable oneself in order to achieve a broader objective.... If the President seeks to regulate through impartial adjudication, then insulation of the adjudicator from removal at will can help him achieve that goal. And to free a technical decisionmaker from the fear of removal without cause can similarly help create legitimacy with respect to that official's regulatory actions by helping to insulate his technical decisions from non-technical political pressure.

Neither is power always susceptible to the equations of elementary arithmetic. A rule that takes power from a President's friends and allies may weaken him. But a rule that takes power from the President's opponents may strengthen him. And what if the rule takes power from a functionally *neutral* independent authority? In that case, it is difficult to predict how the President's power is affected in the abstract.

These practical reasons not only support our precedents' determination that cases such as this should examine the specific functions and context at issue; they also indicate that judges should hesitate before second-guessing a "for cause" decision made by the other branches....

There is no indication that the two comparatively more expert branches were divided in their support for the "for cause" provision at issue here....

Thus, here, as in similar cases, we should decide the constitutional question in light of the provision's practical functioning in context. And our decision should take account of the Judiciary's comparative lack of institutional expertise.

II

A

To what extent then is the Act's "for cause" provision likely, as a practical matter, to limit the President's exercise of executive authority? In practical terms no "for cause" provision can, in isolation, define the full measure of executive power. This is because a legislative decision to place ultimate administrative authority in, say, the Secretary of Agriculture rather than the President, the way in which the statute defines the scope of the power the relevant administrator can exercise, the decision as to who controls the agency's budget requests and funding, the relationships between one agency or department and another, as well as more purely political factors (including Congress' ability to assert influence) are more likely to affect the President's power to get something done. That is why President Truman complained that "the powers of the President amount to" bringing "people in and trying to persuade them to do what they ought to do without persuasion." And that is why scholars have written that the President "is neither dominant nor powerless" in his relationships with many Government entities, "whether denominated executive or independent." ...

Indeed, notwithstanding the majority's assertion that the removal authority is "*the* key" mechanism by which the President oversees inferior officers in the independent agencies, it appears that no President has ever actually sought to exercise that power by testing the scope of a "for cause" provision.

But even if we put all these other matters to the side, we should still conclude that the "for cause" restriction before us will not restrict presidential power significantly. For one thing, the restriction directly limits, not the President's power, but the power of an already independent agency. The Court seems to have forgotten that fact when it identifies its central constitutional problem: According to the Court, the President "is powerless to intervene" if he has determined that the Board members' "conduct merits removal" because "that decision is vested instead in other tenured officers— the Commissioners—none of whom is subject to the President's direct control." But so long as the President is *legitimately* foreclosed from removing the *Commissioners* except for cause (as the majority assumes), nullifying the Commission's power to re-move Board members only for cause will not resolve the problem the Court has iden-tified: The President will *still* be "powerless to intervene" by removing the Board members if the Commission reasonably decides not to do so.

In other words, the Court fails to show why *two* layers of "for cause" protection— Layer One insulating the Commissioners from the President, and Layer Two insulating the Board from the Commissioners—impose any more serious limitation upon the *President's* powers than *one* layer....

But once we leave the realm of hypothetical logic and view the removal provision at issue in the context of the entire Act, its lack of practical effect becomes readily apparent. That is because the statute provides the Commission with full authority and virtually comprehensive control over all of the Board's functions....

B

At the same time, Congress and the President had good reason for enacting the challenged "for cause" provision. First and foremost, the Board adjudicates cases. This Court has long recognized the appropriateness of using "for cause" provisions to protect the personal independence of those who even only sometimes engage in adjudicatory functions. Indeed, as early as 1789 James Madison stated that "there may be strong reasons why an" executive "officer" such as the Comptroller of the United States "should not hold his office at the pleasure of the Executive branch" if one of his "principal duties" "partakes strongly of the judicial character." ...

Moreover, in addition to their adjudicative functions, the Accounting Board mem-bers supervise, and are themselves, technical professional experts. This Court has recognized that the "difficulties involved in the preparation of" sound auditing reports require the application of "scientific accounting principles." And this Court has rec-ognized the constitutional legitimacy of a justification that rests agency independence upon the need for technical expertise....

In sum, Congress and the President could reasonably have thought it prudent to insulate the adjudicative Board members from fear of purely politically based removal. And in a world in which we count on the Federal Government to regulate matters as complex as, say, nuclear-power production, the Court's assertion that we should simply learn to get by "without being" regulated "by experts" is, at best, unrealistic— at worst, dangerously so.

## C

Where a "for cause" provision is so unlikely to restrict presidential power and so likely to further a legitimate institutional need, precedent strongly supports its constitutionality. First, in considering a related issue in *Nixon v. Administrator of General Services*, 433 U.S. 425 (1977) [Note *supra.* this chapter], the Court made clear that when "determining whether the Act disrupts the proper balance between the coordinate branches, the proper inquiry focuses on the extent to which it prevents the Executive Branch from accomplishing its constitutionally assigned functions." The Court said the same in *Morrison*, where it upheld a restriction on the President's removal power. ("The real question is whether the removal restrictions are of such a nature that they impede the President's ability to perform his constitutional duty, and the functions of the officials in question must be analyzed in that light"). Here, the removal restriction may somewhat diminish the *Commission's* ability to control the Board, but it will have little, if any, negative effect in respect to the President's ability to control the Board, let alone to coordinate the Executive Branch. See Part II-A, *supra.* Indeed, given *Morrison*, where the Court upheld a restriction that significantly interfered with the President's important historic power to control criminal prosecutions, a "purely executive" function, the constitutionality of the present restriction would seem to follow *a fortiori*.

Second, as previously pointed out, this Court has repeatedly upheld "for cause" provisions where they restrict the President's power to remove an officer with adjudicatory responsibilities. And we have also upheld such restrictions when they relate to officials with technical responsibilities that warrant a degree of special independence. E.g., *Humphrey's Executor*. The Accounting Board's functions involve both kinds of responsibility....

Third, consider how several cases fit together in a way that logically compels a holding of constitutionality here. In *United States v. Perkins*, 116 U.S. 483 (1886) ... the Court upheld a removal restriction limiting the authority of the Secretary of the Navy to remove a "cadet-engineer," whom the Court explicitly defined as an "inferior officer." The Court said,

> We have no doubt that when Congress, by law, vests the appointment of inferior officers in the heads of Departments *it may limit and restrict the power of removal as it deems best for the public interest*. The constitutional authority in Congress to thus vest the appointment implies authority to limit, restrict, and regulate the removal by such laws as Congress may enact in relation to the officers so appointed (emphasis added).

In *Humphrey's Executor*, the Court held that Congress may constitutionally limit the President's authority to remove certain principal officers, including heads of departments. And the Court has consistently recognized the validity of that holding....

Fourth, the Court has said that "our separation-of-powers jurisprudence generally focuses on the danger of one branch's *aggrandizing its power* at the expense of another branch." *Freytag*; accord, *Schor*; *Morrison*.... Congress here has "drawn" no power to itself to remove the Board members. It has instead sought to *limit* its own power, by, for example, providing the Accounting Board with a revenue stream independent of the congressional appropriations process. And this case thereby falls outside the ambit of the Court's most serious constitutional concern.

In sum, the Court's prior cases impose functional criteria that are readily met here. Once one goes beyond the Court's elementary arithmetical logic (i.e., "one plus one is greater than one") our precedent virtually dictates a holding that the challenged "for cause" provision is constitutional.

### D

We should ask one further question. Even if the "for cause" provision before us does not itself significantly interfere with the President's authority or aggrandize Congress' power, is it nonetheless necessary to adopt a bright-line rule forbidding the provision lest, through a series of such provisions, each itself upheld as reasonable, Congress might undercut the President's central constitutional role? The answer to this question is that no such need has been shown. Moreover, insofar as the Court seeks to create such a rule, it fails. And in failing it threatens a harm that is far more serious than any imaginable harm this "for cause" provision might bring about....

[I] ... see no way to avoid sweeping hundreds, perhaps thousands of high level government officials within the scope of the Court's holding, putting their job security and their administrative actions and decisions constitutionally at risk. To make even a conservative estimate, one would have to begin by listing federal departments, offices, bureaus and other agencies whose heads are by statute removable only "for cause." I have found 48 such agencies, which I have listed in Appendix A, *infra*. Then it would be necessary to identify the senior officials in those agencies (just below the top) who themselves are removable only "for cause." I have identified 573 such high-ranking officials, whom I have listed in Appendix B, *infra*....

The potential list of those whom today's decision affects is yet larger. As Justice SCALIA has observed, administrative law judges (ALJs) "are all executive officers." And ALJs are each removable "only for good cause established and determined by the Merit Systems Protection Board." But the members of the Merit Systems Protection Board are themselves protected from removal by the President absent good cause.

My research reflects that the Federal Government relies on 1,584 ALJs to adjudicate administrative matters in over 25 agencies.... Does every losing party before an ALJ now have grounds to appeal on the basis that the decision entered against him is unconstitutional? *Cf. ante* ("Our holding also does not address" this question)....

### III

... In my view the Court's decision is wrong—very wrong. As Parts II-A, II-B, and II-C of this opinion make clear, if the Court were to look to the proper functional and contextual considerations, it would find the Accounting Board provision constitutional. As Part II-D shows, insofar as the Court instead tries to create a bright-line rule, it fails to do so. Its rule of decision is both imprecise and overly broad. In light of the present imprecision, it must either narrow its rule arbitrarily, leaving it to apply virtually alone to the Accounting Board, or it will have to leave in place a broader rule of decision applicable to many other "inferior officers" as well. In doing the latter, it will undermine the President's authority. And it will create an obstacle, indeed pose a serious threat, to the proper functioning of that workable Government that the Constitution seeks to create—in provisions this Court is sworn to uphold.

With respect I dissent.

[The appendices to Justice Breyer's opinion are deleted.]

### Note: Congressional "Aggrandizement," "Incongruous" Appointments, and Other Aspects of Executive Control over the Bureaucracy

1. *Morrison* finds a close parallel to a case you read in Chapter 1, *Commodities Futures Trading Corp. v. Schor*, 478 U.S. 833 (1986). Both *Morrison* and *Schor* consider whether Congress can move out of another branch (the Presidency in *Morrison*, and the Article III judiciary in *Schor*) some part of the core power enjoyed by that other branch. In both cases, the Court refused to rest its decision on the fact that a core power belonging to the affected branch was being taken away, preferring instead to employ a balancing test that asked how much of that power was being taken away, and for what purpose. The parallel reaches even into the dissents: both Justice Brennan in *Schor* and Justice Scalia in *Morrison* attacked the majority's functional approach, and called for more formalist analysis in which the deprivation of a branch's core power (in *Schor*, to adjudicate private rights, and in *Morrison*, to prosecute legal violations) was necessarily unconstitutional.

Indeed, one can also draw a parallel between the cases that came *after Schor* and *Morrison*: respectively, *Stern v. Marshall* and *Free Enterprise Fund*. In both of those latter cases the Court distinguished the earlier cases, which had relied on functional tests examining the degree to which the challenged law impaired the core functioning of the affected branch, in favor of an analysis that turned on bright-line rules—in *Stern*, the private nature of the right the non-Article III court was authorized to adjudicate, and in *Free Enterprise Fund*, the double insulation of the Accounting Board from presidential removal authority. It may not be a coincidence that *Schor* and *Morrison* were decided within a few years of each other (in 1986 and 1989, respectively), as were *Stern* and *Free Enterprise Fund* (2011 and 2010, respectively).

2. *Morrison* and *Free Enterprise Fund* are not the only important modern statements on presidential control over the federal bureaucracy. Important facets of the problem are reflected in other cases.

In *Bowsher v. Synar*, 478 U.S. 714 (1986), the Court, on a 7–2 vote, struck down parts of a federal deficit reduction statute. Under the law, the Comptroller General was given the power to resolve conflicts between the Office of Management and Budget (a White House office) and the Congressional Budget Office regarding budget cuts. The Act also authorized the Comptroller General to make necessary cuts in the budget if these agencies could not reach an agreement to balance the budget. After concluding that the powers the law gave the Comptroller General were "executive" in nature,

Chief Justice Burger, writing for five Justices, reasoned that Congress' reservation of the power to remove the Comptroller General by joint resolution demonstrated that it "retained control over the execution of the Act and therefore unconstitutionally intruded in the executive function." Justice Stevens and Marshall concurred in the judgment, while Justices White and Blackmun each dissented separately.

As you saw in *Morrison*, *Bowsher* has been cited for the proposition that congressional "aggrandizement" of its own power is a principal evil to be guarded against in separation of powers cases. (See Parts V-A and V-B of the *Morrison* opinion for those citations.) Note again the similarity to the analysis in *Schor*. In *Schor*, just as in *Morrison* and *Bowsher*, the Court considered the extent to which Congress was acting for legitimate motives or inappropriate ones (for example, as in *Bowsher*, to aggrandize its own power). The Court has recognized this principle in other cases, as well. For example, in *Mistretta v. United States*, 488 U.S. 361 (1989), the Court concluded that "the Framers built into the tripartite Federal Government ... a self-executing safeguard against the encroachment of one branch at the expense of another."

3. *Morrison* reflects another theme in modern separation of powers law: the question whether Congress has housed in a given branch duties or functions that are inappropriate for it—or, as *Morrison* put it, "incongruous." In *Morrison*, the Court rejected the argument that it was "incongruous" for a "Special Division" of Article III judges to have the power to appoint a Special Prosecutor, noting, among other things, that the Special Division judges appointing the prosecutor would be ineligible to decide cases involving that official. In *Mistretta*, quoted in the previous item, the question was whether it was unconstitutional for Congress to locate within the judiciary a commission comprised of judges and non-judges tasked with creating guidelines for the sentencing of federal criminals. Eight Justices (Justice Scalia dissenting) rejected the argument. Justice Blackmun, writing for the Court, cited Justice Jackson's analysis in *Youngstown* and observed that "we have recognized the constitutionality of a 'twilight area' in which the activities of the separate Branches merge.... That judicial rule-making [such as the creation of sentencing guidelines] falls within this twilight area is no longer an issue for dispute."

4. *Morrison* reaffirmed the constitutionality of so-called "independent agencies," administrative agencies whose heads are statutorily immunized from presidential removal-at-will power. Such agencies, including the Federal Reserve Board, the Securities and Exchange Commission and the Federal Communications Commission, play exceptionally important roles in the federal government. Justice Scalia has described these agencies as constituting a "headless fourth branch" of government, independent from direct control by Congress, the President or the courts. *Freytag v. Commissioner of Internal Revenue*, 501 U.S. 868 (1991) (Scalia, J., concurring in part and concurring in the judgment).

5. As with congressional control after the demise of the legislative veto, *Morrison's* affirmance of congressional power to immunize at least some important executive personnel from presidential removal-at-will power does not affect the more informal means by which Presidents can seek to influence agency heads. "Officers of the United States" are still appointed by the President; to the extent the head of an independent

agency wants to be reappointed at the end of her term, she presumably must pursue policies agreeable to the President. The President also submits and defends budget requests made by such agencies. Finally, the informal power of the President, noted in Justice Jackson's *Youngstown* concurrence, gives him significant informal influence over how the agency conducts its business.

### Note: The Separation of Powers in Domestic Affairs

Throughout the materials you've seen thus far in Chapter 2 you've seen the Court vacillate between what we have roughly described as formalist and functional approaches to the separation of powers. (Indeed, you also saw this vacillation in several cases from Chapter 1.) What do you think explains this inconsistency? Would the Constitution and the Nation be better served by a more consistent approach, or is a level of inconsistency inevitable in a process that seeks both to divide power and to ensure that the branches work together to govern effectively?

When you read the federalism materials in Part II of this book you will encounter a somewhat analogous problem. To be sure, there are major differences between the structure of separated powers at the federal level and our federal-state system; most notably, the three federal branches are understood to be co-equal, while the states are distinctly and explicitly subordinate to the federal government. Nevertheless, both systems feature government entities that must work together but that also have claims to sovereignty and independence. As you'll see, the compromises and inconsistencies that mark the Court's separation of powers doctrine appear as well in the Court's federalism jurisprudence.

# D. Foreign Affairs and the War Power

So far, this chapter has focused on congressional and presidential prerogatives over domestic policy. (Recall that even in *Youngstown* the Court rejected the Truman Administration's argument that the war power justified its seizure of the steel mills, even though the seizure was designed to ensure continued production of war materiel.) Is the analysis different when the nation acts abroad?

## 1. Foreign Affairs

### Note: United States v. Curtiss-Wright Export Corp. *and the Expansiveness of Inherent Executive Power in Foreign Affairs*

1. The *Youngstown* case centered on a presidential action aimed at resolving a domestic labor dispute, albeit one with foreign policy implications. In controversies centering more explicitly on foreign affairs, the limits on executive action set forth in Justice Black's opinion in *Youngstown* have given way to judicial acknowledgment of the President's need for broad latitude and discretion, given his national leadership in foreign affairs. This discretion has roots in the concept of the "executive power"

granted by Article II, and in the President's duty to take care that the laws are faithfully executed.

2. In *United States v. Curtiss-Wright Export Corp.*, 299 U.S. 304 (1936), the Supreme Court upheld a presidential embargo on arms sales to Paraguay and Bolivia, proclaimed pursuant to a joint resolution of Congress. The arms sellers who were indicted for violating the ban asserted that the joint resolution unconstitutionally delegated legislative power to the President. In rejecting the non-delegation challenge, the Court recognized that the federal government possessed very expansive foreign affairs powers. To Justice Sutherland, such power, though unenumerated, flowed from the fact of sovereignty. Having acknowledged expansive power in the federal government, Justice Sutherland then located the authority to exercise that power in the Executive Branch. Quoting Chief Justice Marshall's speech in the House of Representatives on March 7, 1800 (when he was a Congressman), Justice Sutherland stated that "'the President is the sole organ of the nation in external relations, and its sole representative with foreign nations.'"

In 2015, the Court cast doubt on some of *Curtiss-Wright*'s expansive statements about presidential power in foreign affairs. *See Zivotofsky v. Kerry*, 135 S.Ct. 2076 (2015). *Zivotofsky* is presented in a note following the next excerpted case.

3. Since *Curtiss-Wright* (and — at least so far — despite *Zivotofsky*), the idea has persisted that presidential authority is more expansive in foreign affairs than in domestic issues. Thus, courts have been more deferential to claims of independent executive power undertaken in foreign affairs contexts, emphasizing the need for leadership, confidentiality and external sovereignty.

The hostage crisis and conflict with Iran during 1979–1981 provided a context for considering the constitutional role of the President in foreign affairs. After the seizure of American embassy personnel as hostages in Tehran on November 14, 1979, President Carter blocked the removal or transfer of all Iranian property and interests in property under United States jurisdiction. The goal was to preserve a set of assets that could be used to settle claims through a process that would constitute a part of the ultimate resolution of the crisis. The Treasury Department implemented regulations which essentially froze all Iranian assets.

Subsequently, on January 19, 1981, Iran released the American hostages pursuant to an agreement worked out by the President. The plaintiffs in *Dames & Moore v. Regan* challenged the constitutional and legal authority of the President's actions in effectuating the agreement which led to the hostages' release — in particular, his actions in nullifying the attachments on Iranian assets, transferring those assets to the international claims tribunal the agreement established, and suspending legal claims pending in American courts against Iranian entities with the expectation that those claims would be raised in the new tribunal. In reading the response of the Court, consider whether Justice Rehnquist's opinion is faithful to *Youngstown*.

# Dames & Moore v. Regan

## 453 U.S. 654 (1981)

JUSTICE REHNQUIST delivered the opinion of the Court.

The questions presented by this case touch fundamentally upon the matter in which our Republic is to be governed.... We have had the benefit of commentators such as John Jay, Alexander Hamilton, and James Madison writing in The Federalist Papers at the Nation's very inception, the benefit of astute foreign observers of our system such as Alexis de Tocqueville and James Bryce writing during the first century of the Nation's existence, and the benefit of many other treatises as well as more than 400 volumes of reports of decisions of this Court. As these writings reveal it is doubtless both futile and perhaps dangerous to find any epigrammatical explanation of how this country has been governed. Indeed, as Justice Jackson noted, "a judge ... may be surprised at the poverty of really useful and unambiguous authority applicable to concrete problems of executive power as they actually present themselves." *Youngstown Sheet & Tube Co. v. Sawyer* (1952) (Jackson, J., concurring) [*Supra.* this chapter].

Our decision today will not dramatically alter this situation, for the Framers "did not make the judiciary the overseer of our government." We are confined to a resolution of the dispute presented to us. That dispute involves various Executive Orders and regulations by which the President nullified attachments and liens on Iranian assets in the United States, directed that these assets be transferred to Iran, and suspended claims against Iran that may be presented to an International Claims Tribunal. This action was taken in an effort to comply with an Executive Agreement between the United States and Iran. We granted certiorari before judgment in this case, and set an expedited briefing and argument schedule, because lower courts had reached conflicting conclusions on the validity of the President's actions and, as the Solicitor General informed us, unless the Government acted by July 19, 1981, Iran could consider the United States to be in breach of the Executive Agreement....

### III

[The Court concluded that the President's actions in nullifying the attachments imposed on Iranian assets and ordering their transfer to the international claims tribunal established by the hostage agreement were supported by the International Economic Emergency Powers Act (IEEPA)] ... Because the President's action in nullifying the attachments and ordering the transfer of the assets was taken pursuant to specific congressional authorization, it is "supported by the strongest of presumptions and the widest latitude of judicial interpretation, and the burden of persuasion would rest heavily upon any who might attack it." *Youngstown* (Jackson, J., concurring). Under the circumstances of this case, we cannot say that petitioner has sustained that heavy burden. A contrary ruling would mean that the Federal Government as a whole lacked the power exercised by the President, and that we are not prepared to say.

## IV

Although we have concluded that the IEEPA constitutes specific congressional authorization to the President to nullify the attachments and order the transfer of Iranian assets, there remains the question of the President's authority to suspend claims pending in American courts. Such claims have, of course, an existence apart from the attachments which accompanied them. In terminating these claims ... the President purported to act under authority of both the IEEPA and 22 U.S.C. §1732, the so-called "Hostage Act".

We conclude that although the IEEPA authorized the nullification of the attachments, it cannot be read to authorize the suspension of the claims.... [The Court also concluded that the Hostage Act did not constitute "specific authorization to the President to suspend claims in American courts." ...

Concluding that neither the IEEPA nor the Hostage Act constitutes specific authorization of the President's action suspending claims, however, is not to say that these statutory provisions are entirely irrelevant to the question of the validity of the President's action. We think both statutes highly relevant in the looser sense of indicating congressional acceptance of a broad scope for executive action in circumstances such as those presented in this case. [The] IEEPA delegates broad authority to the President to act in times of national emergency with respect to property of a foreign country. The Hostage Act similarly indicates congressional willingness that the President have broad discretion when responding to the hostile acts of foreign sovereigns....

Although we have declined to conclude that the IEEPA or the Hostage Act directly authorizes the President's suspension of claims for the reasons noted, we cannot ignore the general tenor of Congress' legislation in this area in trying to determine whether the President is acting alone or at least with the acceptance of Congress. As we have noted, Congress cannot anticipate and legislate with regard to every possible action the President may find it necessary to take or every possible situation in which he might act. Such failure of Congress specifically to delegate authority does not, "especially ... in the areas of foreign policy and national security," imply "congressional disapproval" of action taken by the Executive. On the contrary, the enactment of legislation closely related to the question of the President's authority in a particular case which evinces legislative intent to accord the President broad discretion may be considered to "invite" "measures on independent presidential responsibility," *Youngstown* (Jackson, J., concurring). At least this is so where there is no contrary indication of legislative intent and when, as here, there is a history of congressional acquiescence in conduct of the sort engaged in by the President....

... Crucial to our decision today is the conclusion that Congress has implicitly approved the practice of claim settlement by executive agreement. This is best demonstrated by Congress' enactment of the International Claims Settlement Act of 1949. The Act had two purposes: (1) to allocate to United States nationals funds received in the course of an executive claims settlement with Yugoslavia, and (2) to provide a procedure whereby funds resulting from future settlements could be distributed.

To achieve these ends Congress created the International Claims Commission, now the Foreign Claims Settlement Commission, and gave it jurisdiction to make final and binding decisions with respect to claims by United States nationals against settlement funds. By creating a procedure to implement future settlement agreements, Congress placed its stamp of approval on such agreements. Indeed, the legislative history of the Act observed that the United States was seeking settlements with countries ... and that the bill contemplated settlements of a similar nature in the future.

Over the years Congress has frequently amended the International Claims Settlement Act to provide for particular problems arising out of settlement agreements, thus demonstrating Congress' continuing acceptance of the President's claim settlement authority.... As with legislation involving other executive agreements, Congress did not question the fact of the settlement or the power of the President to have concluded it.... Congress recently amended the International Claims Settlement Act to facilitate the settlement of claims against Vietnam.... Finally, the legislative history of the IEEPA further reveals that Congress has accepted the authority of the Executive to enter into settlement agreements. Though the IEEPA was enacted to provide for some limitation on the President's emergency powers, Congress stressed that "nothing in this act is intended ... to interfere with the authority of the President to [block assets], or to impede the settlement of claims of U.S. citizens against foreign countries."

In addition to congressional acquiescence in the President's power to settle claims, prior cases of this Court have also recognized that the President does have some measure of power to enter into executive agreements without obtaining the advice and consent of the Senate. In *United States v. Pink*, 315 U.S. 203 (1942), for example, the Court upheld the validity of the Litvinov Assignment, which was part of an Executive Agreement whereby the Soviet Union assigned to the United States amounts owed to it by American nationals so that outstanding claims of other American nationals could be paid. The Court explained that the resolution of such claims was integrally connected with normalizing United States' relations with a foreign state:

> Power to remove such obstacles to full recognition as settlement of claims of our nationals ... certainly is a modest implied power of the President.... No such obstacle can be placed in the way of rehabilitation of relations between this country and another nation, unless the historic conception of the powers and responsibilities ... is to be drastically revised....

In light of all of the foregoing—the inferences to be drawn from the character of the legislation Congress has enacted in the area, such as the IEEPA and the Hostage Act, and from the history of acquiescence in executive claims settlement—we conclude that the President was authorized to suspend pending claims pursuant to Executive Order No. 12294. As Justice Frankfurter pointed out in *Youngstown*, "a systematic, unbroken, executive practice, long pursued to the knowledge of the Congress and never before questioned ... may be treated as a gloss on 'Executive Power' vested in the President by § 1 of Art. II." Past practice does not, by itself, create power, but "long-continued practice, known to and acquiesced in by Congress, would raise a presumption that the [action] had been [taken] in pursuance of its consent...." Such practice is present here and such a presumption is also appropriate. In light of the fact that Congress may be considered to have consented to the President's action in suspending claims, we cannot say that action exceeded the President's powers.

Our conclusion is buttressed by the fact that the means chosen by the President to settle the claims of American nationals provided an alternative forum, the Claims Tribunal, which is capable of providing meaningful relief.... Moreover, it is important to remember that we have already held that the President has the *statutory* authority to nullify attachments and to transfer the assets out of the country. The President's power to do so does not depend on his provision of a forum whereby claimants can recover on those claims. The fact that the President has provided such a forum here means that the claimants are receiving something in return for the suspension of their claims, namely, access to an international tribunal before which they may well recover something on their claims. Because there does appear to be a real "settlement" here, this case is more easily analogized to the more traditional claim settlement cases of the past.

Just as importantly, Congress has not disapproved of the action taken here. Though Congress has held hearings on the Iranian Agreement itself, Congress has not enacted legislation, or even passed a resolution, indicating its displeasure with the Agreement. Quite the contrary, the relevant Senate Committee has stated that the establishment of the Tribunal is "of vital importance to the United States." ...

Finally, we re-emphasize the narrowness of our decision. We do not decide that the President possesses plenary power to settle claims, even as against foreign governmental entities.... But where, as here, the settlement of claims has been determined to be a necessary incident to the resolution of a major foreign policy dispute between our country and another, and where, as here, we can conclude that Congress acquiesced in the President's action, we are not prepared to say that the President lacks the power to settle such claims....

### Note: Foreign Affairs, Diplomatic Recognition, and a (Rare) Category Three Win for the Presidency

1. *Dames & Moore* dealt with a situation the Court described as one in which Congress had authorized the presidential decision challenged by the plaintiff, and thus, one that fell under Justice Jackson's first *Youngstown* category, where presidential authority was at its height. As a result, a unanimous Court upheld the challenged action. In 2015 the Court faced the opposite situation: one where all parties agreed that Congress *opposed* the President's action, thus placing it in Justice Jackson's third category. Nevertheless, the Court upheld the President's decision.

2. *Zivotofsky v. Kerry*, 135 S.Ct. 2076 (2015), involved a struggle between Congress and the President over American policy toward the Middle East, and in particular the status of Jerusalem. In 2002 Congress enacted a law, a provision of which allowed any American citizen born in Jerusalem to request that his passport list his place of birth as "Israel." Such a statement conflicted with longstanding American policy taking the position that the final status of Jerusalem had to be settled by diplomatic nego-

tiations. The President signed the law, but stated his position that the Jerusalem provision, if construed as mandatory rather than advisory, would unconstitutionally intrude on the President's authority to speak for the nation on foreign affairs, and in particular his authority to "determine the terms on which recognition is given to foreign states."

When an American citizen living in Jerusalem gave birth to a son, his parents requested that his passport state Israel as his place of birth. When embassy officials refused, his parents sued on his behalf. The lower court ruled for the government, concluding that the provision was unconstitutional.

3. Five justices agreed, with an additional justice agreeing in part. Writing for the five-Justice majority, Justice Kennedy began by acknowledging that Justice Jackson's three-category approach in *Youngstown* governed the case. He also noted the government's concession that this case fell into Justice Jackson's third category, thus requiring that "the President's ... claim ... be scrutinized with caution," and that "he may rely solely on powers the Constitution grants to him alone."

Applying that framework, Justice Kennedy concluded that the President did have the sole power to recognize foreign sovereignty. He grounded this conclusion in Article II's Reception Clause, which gives the President the power to "receive Ambassadors and other public Ministers." He also relied on the President's powers to negotiate treaties and nominate American ambassadors: even though Congress had roles in, respectively, ratifying treaties and approving ambassadorial appointments, he noted that those duties were not triggered until the President acted. He also noted that "recognition is a topic on which the Nation must speak ... with one voice." He relied on historical practice, which he conceded was not "all on one side," but which, he concluded, "on balance ... provides strong support for the conclusion that the recognition power is the President's alone."

Justice Kennedy acknowledged that Congress had powers — for example, over immigration, war-making and foreign commerce — that also touched on foreign relations generally and recognition in particular. Thus, he concluded, "Congress' powers, and its central role in making laws, give it substantial authority regarding many of the policy determinations that precede and follow the act of recognition itself."

Justice Kennedy also considered the government's reliance on the expansive language in *United States v. Curtiss-Wright*, 299 U.S. 304 (1935) (Note *supra.* this chapter) regarding presidential power in foreign affairs. Quoting the language provided in this book's note on that case — in particular, Justice Sutherland's statement that "the President is the sole organ of the nation in its external relations" — Justice Kennedy observed that "this description of the President's exclusive power was not necessary to the holding in *Curtiss-Wright*." He also noted that "whether the realm is foreign or domestic, it is still the Legislative Branch, not the Executive Branch, that makes the law."

4. Justice Breyer joined the majority opinion and wrote a short concurrence on an unrelated issue. Justice Thomas concurred in the main part of the Court's holding. But he declined to join the majority opinion, instead writing separately to sketch out

a much broader vision of presidential power in foreign affairs. He relied heavily on Article II's Vesting Clause ("the executive Power shall be vested in a President of the United States") to argue for an approach in which *all* executive powers were vested in the President. For Justice Thomas, those powers included all powers related to foreign affairs except for those Article I provided to Congress. He concluded that the challenged passport statute in this case "implicated the President's residual foreign affairs power." He recognized that Congress's Article I powers authorized some regulation of passports, but he concluded that none of those powers, nor Article I's Necessary and Proper Clause, justified the Jerusalem law.

5. Chief Justice Roberts and Justice Scalia both authored dissenting opinions. The Chief Justice, joined by Justice Alito, began by describing the Court's decision as "a first: Never before has this Court accepted a President's direct defiance of an Act of Congress in the field of foreign affairs." Just as Justice Kennedy's majority opinion had, the Chief Justice's dissent located this case as falling within Justice Jackson's third *Youngstown* category, where, he said, "the President's power reaches 'its lowest ebb.'" (quoting Justice Jackson). He questioned the majority's reliance on the Recognition Clause, observing that that clause "appears alongside the *duties* imposed on the President by Article II, Section 3, not the *powers* granted to him by Article II, Section 2" (emphasis in original). He also questioned the relevance of the President's powers to make treaties and appoint ambassadors, noting that Congress shared in those duties. Additionally, he questioned whether this case, involving notations on passports, really implicated American recognition of Israeli sovereignty over Jerusalem. Just like the majority, however, Chief Justice Roberts questioned the government's reliance on *Curtiss-Wright*. Like the majority, he noted that *Curtiss-Wright* involved a situation where Congress had delegated authority to the President, rather than, as here, explicitly disagreeing with his approach to a foreign policy issue.

Justice Scalia's dissent was joined by the Chief Justice and Justice Alito. Like Chief Justice Roberts, Justice Scalia doubted that formal recognition of a foreign government's sovereignty was in fact implicated by the passport statute. He argued that the statute was supportable by Congress's Article I power to make laws "Necessary and Proper" to carry into effect its authority to legislate on naturalization issues. He concluded by observing that the Framers sought to prevent tyranny by giving "each political department its own powers, and with that the freedom to contradict the other's policies," and that such dispersal of powers extended into the realm of foreign affairs.

Justice Scalia also took issue with Justice Thomas's understanding of executive power, concluding that it reflected "a presidency more reminiscent of George III than George Washington." In response, Justice Thomas argued that Justice Scalia "offered no competing interpretation of either the Article II Vesting Clause or the Necessary and Proper Clause. And his decision about the Constitution's resolution of conflict among the branches could itself be criticized as creating a supreme legislative body more reminiscent of the Parliament in England than the Congress in America."

## 2. The War Power

### a. General Concepts

### Note: The War Power in Theory, History, and Practice

1. As a textual matter, the War Power is divided between the President and Congress. Article II gives the President the status of "Commander in Chief of the Army and Navy of the United States, and of the Militia of the several States, when called into the actual Service of the United States." More generally, Article II begins by vesting "the executive power" in the President. As exemplified by President Truman's arguments in *Youngstown*, Presidents have relied on these powers when taking a wide variety of actions relevant to hostilities involving U.S. military forces. While the Commander-in-Chief power speaks for itself as a source of presidential war-fighting authority, it has been argued that, in addition, the grant to the President of "the executive power" implies the power to act with the speed and decisiveness inherently necessary to prosecuting wars successfully.

For its part, Article I vests in Congress a variety of powers relevant to war-fighting. Article I, Section 8 gives Congress the power "To declare War, grant Letters of Marque and Reprisal, and make Rules concerning Captures on Land and Water"; "To raise and support Armies"; "To provide and maintain a Navy"; "To make Rules for the Government and Regulation of the land and naval Forces"; "To provide for organizing, arming and disciplining the Militia"; and "To define and punish Piracies and Felonies committed on the high Seas, and Offences against the Law of Nations." In addition, Article II requires that two-thirds of the Senate "concur" in treaties made by the President. More generally, Article I's grant of power to Congress to tax and spend provides it the power of the purse that has often been its most effective tool in influencing the nation's war policies. For example, actual and threatened cut-offs of appropriations for the Vietnam War dogged President Nixon in the early 1970's.

One obvious power Congress possesses, which presumably the Framers intended as a major limit on presidential war-fighting power, is the power to declare war. In the modern era, however, the practice of formally declaring war has fallen into desuetude worldwide. The United States, for example, has not formally declared war since its declarations of war against the Axis Powers in World War II, despite the fact that since then it has fought major conflicts in Korea, Vietnam, Iraq (twice) and Afghanistan, in addition to a large number of smaller uses of hostile force, from Grenada and Panama in the 1980s to Bosnia and Somalia in the 1990s, to armed conflict with the self-proclaimed "Islamic State" in more recent years.

2. In claiming powers on war-related matters, each political branch can assert only incomplete explicit authority, suggesting once again that the Framers intended mutuality and coordination. Thus, the President, who is Commander-in-Chief, who has been seen as the principal instrument of government in foreign affairs, and who has the duty to see that the laws be faithfully executed, can assert authority to commit troops to battle in order to repel attacks, but lacks power to declare war. Congress, on the

other hand, possesses not only the power to declare war, but also the power to raise taxes, raise armies and provide for the common defense and general welfare, but its authorizations ultimately depend upon the leadership of the Commander-in-Chief.

3. The controversy over the proper division of war-making authority between Congress and the President is notable for the lack of judicial involvement. In the vast majority of cases, issues involving alleged separation of powers violations with regard to war-making authority have been resolved by the political branches, with federal courts relying on justiciability doctrines — most frequently, the political question doctrine — to avoid hearing those cases. Thus, the story of the War Power has largely been one of the political branches struggling to reach accommodation, without any authoritative judicial interpretation of the scope of Congress's and the President's powers.

4. Since World War II Presidents have often relied on the practice of other Presidents throughout history committing armed forces to action without a formal declaration of war, and indeed without consulting with Congress or obtaining its authorization. During the Vietnam conflict, a State Department memorandum cited 125 instances in which Presidents had committed U.S. armed forces to hostile action. In many cases the intervention could be regarded as action taken short of prosecuting a war, such as protecting United States nationals in foreign territory and "neutral" action which could be undertaken pursuant to the executive power. Office of the Legal Advisor, U.S. Dept. of State, "The Legality of the United States Participation in the Defense of Vietnam," reprinted in 75 *Yale L. J.* 1085 (1966). In others, Congress ratified the actions of the President or itself issued a declaration of war.

One of the very few cases where a legal challenge to presidential war-making reached the Supreme Court occurred during the Civil War. President Lincoln linked his role as Commander-in-Chief to his duty to execute laws and to preserve peace to authorize his blockade of southern ports in retaliation for the Confederate Army's firing on Fort Sumter. The Supreme Court in *The Prize Cases* stated that although Congress alone has the power to initiate or declare a national or foreign war,

> if a war be made by invasion of a foreign nation, the President is ... bound to resist force by force. He does not initiate the war, but is bound to accept the challenge without waiting for any special legislative authority. And whether the hostile party be a foreign invader, or states organized in rebellion, it is none the less a war, although declaration of it be '*unilateral*.' 67 U.S. 635 (1862).

### Note: The War Powers Resolution

As noted earlier, in the modern era formal declarations of war have faded in significance. No other conflict in that era more dramatically framed the war powers issue in a world without formal declarations of war than the conflict in Southeast Asia. President Johnson relied upon his role as Commander-in-Chief, congressional ratification of the Southeast Asia Treaty and the United Nations Charter, and a 1964 resolution by Congress — the Gulf of Tonkin Resolution — to justify a military involvement which lasted more than a decade and resulted in the commitment of a half million troops, a hundred billion dollars and fifty thousand American combat deaths.

Disillusionment with the Vietnam conflict, and a sense that the President had misled Congress about the need for war, and later, the prospects for victory, led Congress in 1973 to enact the War Powers Resolution, enacted over President Nixon's veto. The Resolution aimed to reassert a congressional role in the decision to commit American forces to combat and in ongoing decisions to continue the conflict.

## War Powers Resolution
### 50 U.S.C. §§ 1541–48

… Sec. 2. (a) It is the purpose of this [joint resolution] to fulfill the intent of the framers of the Constitution of the United States and insure that the collective judgment of both the Congress and the President will apply to the introduction of United States Armed Forces into hostilities, or into situations where imminent involvement in hostilities is clearly indicated by the circumstances, and to the continued use of such forces in hostilities or in such situations.

(b) Under article I, section 8, of the Constitution, it is specifically provided that the Congress shall have the power to make all laws necessary and proper for carrying into execution, not only its own powers but also other powers vested by the Constitution in the Government of the United States, or in any department or officer thereof.

(c) The constitutional powers of the President as Commander-in-Chief to introduce United States Armed Forces into hostilities, or into situations where imminent involvement in hostilities is clearly indicated by the circumstances, are exercised only pursuant to (1) a declaration of war, (2) specific statutory authorization, or (3) a national emergency created by attack upon the United States, its territories or possessions, or its armed forces.

### Consultation  - least used

Sec. 3. The President in every possible instance shall consult with Congress before introducing United States Armed Forces into hostilities or into situations where imminent involvement in hostilities is clearly indicated by the circumstances, and after every such introduction shall consult regularly with the Congress until United States Armed Forces are no longer engaged in hostilities or have been removed from such situations.

### Reporting

Sec. 4. (a) In the absence of a declaration of war, in any case in which United States Armed Forces are introduced—

(1) into hostilities or into situations where imminent involvement in hostilities is clearly indicated by the circumstances;

(2) into the territory, airspace or waters of a foreign nation, while equipped for combat, except for deployments which relate solely to supply, replacement, repair, or training of such forces; or

(3) in numbers which substantially enlarge United States Armed Forces equipped for combat already located in a foreign nation; the President shall submit within 48 hours to the Speaker of the House of Representatives and to the President pro tempore of the Senate a report, in writing, setting forth—

(A) the circumstance necessitating the introduction of United States Armed Forces;

(B) the constitutional and legislative authority under which such introduction took place; and

(C) the estimated scope and duration of the hostilities or involvement.

(b) The President shall provide other such information as the Congress may request in the fulfillment of its constitutional responsibilities with respect to committing the Nation to war and to the use of United States Armed Forces abroad.

(c) Whenever United States Armed Forces are introduced into hostilities or into any situation described in subsection (a) of this section, the President shall, so long as such armed forces continue to be engaged in such hostilities or situation, report to the Congress periodically on the status of such hostilities or situation as well as on the scope and duration of such hostilities or situation, but in no event shall he report to the Congress less often than once every six months.

Sec. 5.... (b) Within sixty calendar days after a report is submitted or is required to be submitted pursuant to section 4(a)(1), whichever is earlier, the President shall terminate any use of United States Armed Forces with respect to which such report was submitted (or required to be submitted), unless the Congress (1) has declared war or has enacted a specific authorization for such use of United States Armed Forces, (2) has extended by law such sixty-day period, or (3) is physically unable to meet as a result of an armed attack upon the United States. Such sixty-day period shall be extended for not more than an additional thirty days if the President determines and certifies to the Congress in writing that unavoidable military necessity respecting the safety of United States Armed Forces requires the continued use of such armed forces in the course of bringing about a prompt removal of such forces.

(c) Notwithstanding subsection (b), at any time that United States Armed Forces are engaged in hostilities outside the territory of the United States, its possessions and territories without a declaration of war or specific statutory authorization, such forces shall be removed by the President if the Congress so directs by concurrent resolution....

Interpretation of Joint Resolution

Sec. 8. (a) Authority to introduce United States Armed Forces into hostilities or into situations wherein involvement in hostilities is clearly indicated by the circumstances shall not be inferred—

(1) from any provision of law (whether or not in effect before [the date of the enactment of this joint resolution]), including any provision contained in any appro-

priations Act, unless such provision specifically authorizes the introduction of United States Armed Forces into hostilities or into such situation and states that it is intended to constitute specific statutory authorization within the meaning of this joint resolution; or

(2) from any treaty heretofore or hereafter ratified unless such treaty is implemented by legislation specifically authorizing the introduction of United States Armed Forces into hostilities or into such situation ... within the meaning of this [joint resolution].

(b) Nothing in this [joint resolution] —

(1) is intended to alter the constitutional authority of the Congress or of the President, or the provisions of existing treaties; or

(2) shall be construed as granting any authority to the President with respect to the introduction of United States Armed Forces into hostilities by the circumstances which authority he would not have had in the absence of this [joint resolution]....

## Note: The War Powers Resolution in Practice

An important issue raised by the War Powers Resolution is whether Congress can mandate a role for itself in the decisions to initiate and continue prosecuting a war. Notably, no President has formally invoked the War Powers Resolution, although Presidents have consulted with Congress about deployment of troops. Among many examples, in 1979, President Carter notified Congress of the attempt to rescue American hostages in Iran only after the fact, in 1983, President Reagan similarly notified Congress of the invasion of Grenada only after the troops had landed, and in 1999, President Clinton commenced a bombing campaign against Serbia without consulting Congress. In 1989, President Bush notified congressional leaders a few hours before the commencement of the invasion of Panama; however, he did not consult with Congress, as provided for in the Resolution. The Resolution's reporting provisions have been essentially ignored by Presidents. Even a President who shares the view that war-making requires the coordinated participation of Congress and the President is likely to be concerned about preserving the President's discretion to act in a crisis.

The impact — or non-impact — of the War Powers Resolution is illustrated by the sequence of statements made by Congress and the President in the run-up to the first Iraq war of 1991. As you read President Bush's statement upon signing the resolution authorizing the war, consider the reasons he may have had for seeking congressional authorization.

## Authorization for Use of Military Force against Iraq Resolution
Pub. L. 102-1, 105 Stat. 3
January 14, 1991

Joint Resolution to authorize the use of United States Armed Forces
pursuant to United Nations Security Council Resolution 678.

Whereas the Government of Iraq without provocation invaded and occupied the
territory of Kuwait on August 2, 1990;

Whereas both the House of Representatives ... and the Senate ... have condemned
Iraq's invasion of Kuwait and declared their support for international action to reverse
Iraq's aggression;

Whereas, Iraq's conventional, chemical, biological, and nuclear weapons and bal-
listic missile programs and its demonstrated willingness to use weapons of mass destruction pose a grave threat to world peace;

Whereas the international community has demanded that Iraq withdraw unconditionally and immediately from Kuwait and that Kuwait's independence and legitimate
government be restored;

Whereas the United Nations Security Council repeatedly affirmed the inherent
right of individual or collective self-defense in response to the armed attack by Iraq
against Kuwait in accordance with Article 51 of the United Nations Charter;

Whereas, in the absence of full compliance by Iraq with its resolutions, the United
Nations Security Council in Resolution 678 has authorized member states of the
United Nations to use all necessary means, after January 15, 1991, to uphold and
implement all relevant Security Council resolutions and to restore international peace
and security in the area; and

Whereas Iraq has persisted in its illegal occupation of, and brutal aggression against
Kuwait: Now, therefore, be it

*Resolved by the Senate and House of Representatives of the United States of America
in Congress assembled,*

### Sec. 1. Short Title

This joint resolution may be cited as the "Authorization for Use of Military Force
Against Iraq Resolution".

### Sec. 2. Authorization for Use of United States Armed Forces

(a) Authorization. — The President is authorized, subject to subsection (b), to use
United States Armed Forces pursuant to United Nations Security Council Resolution
678 (1990) in order to achieve implementation of Security Council Resolutions 660,
661, 662, 664, 665, 666, 667, 669, 670, 674, and 677.

(b) Requirement for Determination That Use of Military Force Is Necessary. —
Before exercising the authority granted in subsection (a), the President shall make
available to the Speaker of the House of Representatives and the President pro tempore
of the Senate his determination that—

(1) the United States has used all appropriate diplomatic and other peaceful means to obtain compliance by Iraq with the United Nations Security Council resolutions cited in subsection (a); and

(2) that those efforts have not been and would not be successful in obtaining such compliance.

(c) War Powers Resolution Requirements.—

(1) SPECIFIC STATUTORY AUTHORIZATION.—Consistent with section 8(a)(1) of the War Powers Resolution, the Congress declares that this section is intended to constitute specific statutory authorization within the meaning of section 5(b) of the War Powers Resolution.

(2) Applicability of Other Requirements.—Nothing in this resolution supersedes any requirement of the War Powers Resolution.

### Sec. 3. Reports to Congress

At least once every 60 days, the President shall submit to the Congress a summary on the status of efforts to obtain compliance by Iraq with the resolutions adopted by the United Nations Security Council in response to Iraq's aggression.

Approved January 14, 1991

## Statement by President George Bush upon Signing H. J. Res. 77

27 Weekly Compilation of Presidential Documents 48
(January 21, 1991)
January 14, 1991

Today I am signing H. J. Res. 77, the "Authorization for Use of Military Force Against Iraq Resolution." By passing H. J. Res. 77, the Congress of the United States has expressed its approval of the use of U.S. Armed Forces consistent with U.N. Security Council Resolution 678. I asked the Congress to support implementation of the U.N. Security Council Resolution 678 because such action would send the clearest possible message to Saddam Hussein that he must withdraw from Kuwait without condition or delay. I am grateful to those of both political parties who joined in the expression of resolve embodied in this resolution. To all, I emphasize again my conviction that this resolution provides the best hope for peace.

The debate on H. J. Res. 77 reflects the profound strength of our constitutional democracy. In coming to grips with the issues at stake in the Gulf, both Houses of Congress acted in the finest traditions of our country. This resolution provides unmistakable support for the international community's determination that Iraq's ongoing aggression against, and occupation of, Kuwait shall not stand. As I made clear to congressional leaders at the outset, my request for congressional support did not, and my signing this resolution does not, constitute any change in the long-standing positions of the executive branch on either the President's constitutional authority to use the Armed Forces to defend vital U.S. interests or the constitutionality of the War Powers Resolution. I am pleased, however, that differences on these issues between the President and many in the Congress have not prevented us from uniting in a common objective. I have had the benefit of extensive and meaningful consultations with the Congress throughout this crisis, and I shall continue to consult closely with the Congress in the days ahead.

George Bush

The White House,

January 14, 1991.

### b. Presidential Authority and the War On Terror

The attacks of September 11, 2001 ushered in a new era of American military activity in the world. Much of this activity—in particular aimed at terrorists and terrorism—takes the form of an unconventional war that is not waged against conventional national armies on normal battlefields. With no one target or centralized enemy apparatus, this war has the potential to be of indefinite duration with no clearly observable milestones that would mark its obvious end. Yet at the same time, the September 11 attacks illustrate the high stakes involved. In such a situation, the risks posed by executive branch overreaching stand against the risks terrorists pose to the nation.

The Court's resolution of these issues has taken the form of sharply divided opinions that construed both the language in statutes authorizing military action and detainee detention, and the constitutional authority of Congress and the President pursuant to their shared powers to wage war and protect national security.

## Authorization for Use of Military Force
### Pub. L. 107-40, 115 Stat. 224

### Sept. 18, 2001

Joint Resolution To authorize the use of United States Armed Forces against those responsible for the recent attacks launched against the United States.

Whereas, on September 11, 2001, acts of treacherous violence were committed against the United States and its citizens; and

Whereas, such acts render it both necessary and appropriate that the United States exercise its rights to self-defense and to protect United States citizens both at home and abroad; and

Whereas, in light of the threat to the national security and foreign policy of the United States posed by these grave acts of violence; and

Whereas, such acts continue to pose an unusual and extraordinary threat to the national security and foreign policy of the United States; and

Whereas, the President has authority under the Constitution to take action to deter and prevent acts of international terrorism against the United States: Now, therefore, be it

*Resolved by the Senate and House of Representatives of the United States of America in Congress assembled,*

SECTION 1. SHORT TITLE.

This joint resolution may be cited as the "Authorization for Use of Military Force".

SECTION 2. AUTHORIZATION FOR USE OF UNITED STATES ARMED FORCES.

(a) IN GENERAL.—That the President is authorized to use all necessary and appropriate force against those nations, organizations, or persons he determines planned, authorized, committed, or aided the terrorist attacks that occurred on September 11, 2001, or harbored such organizations or persons, in order to prevent any future acts of international terrorism against the United States by such nations, organizations or persons.

(b) War Powers Resolution Requirements—

(1) SPECIFIC STATUTORY AUTHORIZATION.—Consistent with section 8(a)(1) of the War Powers Resolution, the Congress declares that this section is intended to constitute specific statutory authorization within the meaning of section 5(b) of the War Powers Resolution.

(2) APPLICABILITY OF OTHER REQUIREMENTS.—Nothing in this resolution supercedes any requirement of the War Powers Resolution.

Approved September 18, 2001.

## Hamdi v. Rumsfeld

### 542 U.S. 507 (2004)

JUSTICE O'CONNOR announced the judgment of the Court and delivered an opinion, in which THE CHIEF JUSTICE, JUSTICE KENNEDY, and JUSTICE BREYER join.

[At issue in *Hamdi* was the legality of the government's detention, without judicial review, of an American citizen captured on the battlefield in Afghanistan and alleged to be an enemy combatant. Hamdi, after being captured, brought a writ of habeas corpus, alleging that he was not an enemy combatant. The government claimed that the congressional Authorization for Use of Military Force (AUMF) authorized such detentions.]

The Government maintains that no explicit congressional authorization is required, because the Executive possesses plenary authority to detain pursuant to Article II of the Constitution. We do not reach the question whether Article II provides such authority, however, because we agree with the Government's alternative position, that Congress has in fact authorized Hamdi's detention, through the AUMF.

Our analysis on that point, set forth below, substantially overlaps with our analysis of Hamdi's principal argument for the illegality of his detention. He posits that his detention is forbidden by 18 U.S.C. §4001(a). Section 4001(a) states that "no citizen shall be imprisoned or otherwise detained by the United States except pursuant to an Act of Congress." ... Congress was particularly concerned about the possibility that the Act could be used to reprise the Japanese-American internment camps of

World War II.... For the reasons that follow, we conclude that the AUMF is explicit congressional authorization for the detention of individuals in the narrow category [of enemy combatants in Afghanistan] and that the AUMF satisfied §4001(a)'s requirement that a detention be "pursuant to an Act of Congress"....

The AUMF authorizes the President to use "all necessary and appropriate force" against "nations, organizations, or persons" associated with the September 11, 2001, terrorist attacks. There can be no doubt that individuals who fought against the United States in Afghanistan as part of the Taliban, an organization known to have supported the al Qaeda terrorist network responsible for those attacks, are individuals Congress sought to target in passing the AUMF. We conclude that detention of individuals falling into the limited category we are considering, for the duration of the particular conflict in which they were captured, is so fundamental and accepted an incident to war as to be an exercise of the "necessary and appropriate force" Congress has authorized the President to use.

The capture and detention of lawful combatants and the capture, detention, and trial of unlawful combatants, by "universal agreement and practice," are "important incidents of war." *Ex parte Qurin*, 317 U.S. 1 (1942)....

There is no bar to this Nation's holding one of its own citizens as an enemy combatant. In *Quirin*, one of the detainees, Haupt, alleged that he was a naturalized United States citizen. We held that "citizens who associate themselves with the military arm of the enemy government, and with its aid, guidance and direction enter this country bent on hostile acts, are enemy belligerents within the meaning of ... the law of war." ...

In light of these principles, it is of no moment that the AUMF does not use specific language of detention. Because detention to prevent a combatant's return to the battlefield is a fundamental incident of waging war, in permitting the use of "necessary and appropriate force," Congress has clearly and unmistakably authorized detention in the narrow circumstances considered here.

Hamdi objects, nevertheless, that Congress has not authorized the *indefinite* detention to which he is now subject. The Government responds that "the detention of enemy combatants during World War II was just as 'indefinite' while that war was being fought." We take Hamdi's objection to be not to the lack of certainty regarding the date on which the conflict will end, but to the substantial prospect of perpetual detention. We recognize that the national security underpinnings of the "war on terror," although crucially important, are broad and malleable. As the Government concedes, "given its unconventional nature, the current conflict is unlikely to end with a formal cease-fire agreement." The prospect Hamdi raises is therefore not farfetched. If the Government does not consider this unconventional war won for two generations, and if it maintains during that time that Hamdi might, if released, rejoin forces fighting against the United States, then the position it has taken throughout the litigation of this case suggests that Hamdi's detention could last for the rest of his life.

It is a clearly established principle of the law of war that detention may last no longer than active hostilities. See Article 118 of the Geneva Convention (III) Relative to the Treatment of Prisoners of War, Aug. 12, 1949. Hamdi contends that the AUMF does not authorize indefinite or perpetual detention. Certainly, we agree that indefinite detention for the purpose of interrogation is not authorized. Further, we understand Congress' grant of authority for the use of "necessary and appropriate force" to include the authority to detain for the duration of the relevant conflict, and our understanding is based on longstanding law-of-war principles. If the practical circumstances of a given conflict are entirely unlike those of the conflicts that informed the development of the law of war, that understanding may unravel. But that is not the situation we face as of this date. Active combat operations against Taliban fighters apparently are ongoing in Afghanistan. The United States may detain, for the duration of these hostilities, individuals legitimately determined to be Taliban combatants who "engaged in an armed conflict against the United States." If the record establishes that United States troops are still involved in active combat in Afghanistan, those detentions are part of the exercise of "necessary and appropriate force," and therefore are authorized by the AUMF....

[The plurality then concluded that, despite the AUMF's authorization for Hamdi's detention, due process required that he be given some opportunity to contest the determination that he was an enemy combatant.]

JUSTICE SOUTER, with whom JUSTICE GINSBURG joins, concurring in part, dissenting in part, and concurring in the judgment....

## II

... The fact that Congress intended to guard against a repetition of the World War II internments when it repealed the 1950 statute and gave us § 4001(a) provides a powerful reason to think that § 4001(a) was meant to require clear congressional authorization before any citizen can be placed in a cell. It is not merely that the legislative history shows that § 4001(a) was thought necessary in anticipation of times just like the present, in which the safety of the country is threatened. To appreciate what is most significant, one must only recall that the internments of the 1940's were accomplished by Executive action. Although an Act of Congress ratified and confirmed an Executive order authorizing the military to exclude individuals from defined areas and to accommodate those it might remove, the statute said nothing whatever about the detention of those who might be removed; internment camps were creatures of the Executive, and confinement in them rested on assertion of Executive authority. When, therefore, Congress repealed the 1950 Act and adopted § 4001(a) ... it intended to preclude reliance on vague congressional authority ... as authority for detention or imprisonment at the discretion of the Executive.... In requiring that any Executive detention be "pursuant to an Act of Congress," then, Congress necessarily meant to require a congressional enactment that clearly authorized detention or imprisonment.

Second, when Congress passed § 4001(a) it was acting in light of an interpretive regime that subjected enactments limiting liberty in wartime to the requirement of a clear statement and it presumably intended § 4001(a) to be read accordingly....

Finally, even if history had spared us the cautionary example of the internments in World War II ... there would be a compelling reason to read § 4001(a) to demand manifest authority to detain before detention is authorized. The defining character of American constitutional government is its constant tension between security and liberty, serving both by partial helpings of each. In a government of separated powers, deciding finally on what is a reasonable degree of guaranteed liberty whether in peace or war (or some condition in between) is not well entrusted to the Executive Branch of Government, whose particular responsibility is to maintain security. For reasons of inescapable human nature, the branch of the Government asked to counter a serious threat is not the branch on which to rest the Nation's entire reliance in striking the balance between the will to win and the cost in liberty on the way to victory; the responsibility for security will naturally amplify the claim that security legitimately raises. A reasonable balance is more likely to be reached on the judgment of a different branch, just as Madison said in remarking that "the constant aim is to divide and arrange the several offices in such a manner as that each may be a check on the other — that the private interest of every individual may be a sentinel over the public rights." *The Federalist* No. 51. Hence the need for an assessment by Congress before citizens are subject to lockup, and likewise the need for a clearly expressed congressional resolution of the competing claims.

### III

Under this principle of reading § 4001(a) robustly to require a clear statement of authorization to detain, none of the Government's arguments suffices to justify Hamdi's detention.

### A

First, there is the argument that § 4001(a) does not even apply to wartime military detentions, a position resting on the placement of § 4001(a) in Title 18 of the United States Code, the gathering of federal criminal law. The text of the statute does not, however, so limit its reach, and the legislative history of the provision shows its placement in Title 18 was not meant to render the statute more restricted than its terms....

### B

Next, there is the Government's claim, accepted by the plurality, that the terms of the Force Resolution are adequate to authorize detention of an enemy combatant under the circumstances described, a claim the Government fails to support sufficiently to satisfy § 4001(a) as read to require a clear statement of authority to detain. Since the Force Resolution was adopted one week after the attacks of September 11, 2001, it naturally speaks with some generality, but its focus is clear, and that is on the use of military power. It is fairly read to authorize the use of armies and weapons, whether against other armies or individual terrorists. But ... it never so much as uses the word detention, and there is no reason to think Congress might have perceived any need to augment Executive power to deal with dangerous citizens within the United States, given the well-stocked statutory arsenal of defined criminal offenses covering the gamut of actions that a citizen sympathetic to terrorists might commit....

## C

Even so, there is one argument for treating the Force Resolution as sufficiently clear to authorize detention of a citizen consistently with § 4001(a). Assuming the argument to be sound, however, the Government is in no position to claim its advantage.

Because the Force Resolution authorizes the use of military force in acts of war by the United States, the argument goes, it is reasonably clear that the military and its Commander in Chief are authorized to deal with enemy belligerents according to the treaties and customs known collectively as the laws of war.... Thus, the Government here repeatedly argues that Hamdi's detention amounts to nothing more than customary detention of a captive taken on the field of battle: if the usages of war are fairly authorized by the Force Resolution, Hamdi's detention is authorized for purposes of § 4001(a).

There is no need, however, to address the merits of such an argument in all possible circumstances. For now it is enough to recognize that the Government's stated legal position in its campaign against the Taliban (among whom Hamdi was allegedly captured) is apparently at odds with its claim here to be acting in accordance with customary law of war and hence to be within the terms of the Force Resolution in its detention of Hamdi....

By holding him incommunicado ... the Government obviously has not been treating him as a prisoner of war, and in fact the Government claims that no Taliban detainee is entitled to prisoner of war status. This treatment appears to be a violation of the Geneva Convention provision that even in cases of doubt, captives are entitled to be treated as prisoners of war "until such time as their status has been determined by a competent tribunal." ...

Whether, or to what degree, the Government is in fact violating the Geneva Convention and is thus acting outside the customary usages of war are not matters I can resolve at this point. What I can say, though, is that the Government has not made out its claim that in detaining Hamdi in the manner described, it is acting in accord with the laws of war authorized to be applied against citizens by the Force Resolution. I conclude accordingly that the Government has failed to support the position that the Force Resolution authorizes the described detention of Hamdi for purposes of § 4001(a).

It is worth adding a further reason for requiring the Government to bear the burden of clearly justifying its claim to be exercising recognized war powers before declaring § 4001(a) satisfied. Thirty-eight days after adopting the Force Resolution, Congress passed the ... USA PATRIOT ACT; that Act authorized the detention of alien terrorists for no more than seven days in the absence of criminal charges or deportation proceedings. It is very difficult to believe that the same Congress that carefully circumscribed Executive power over alien terrorists on home soil would not have meant to require the Government to justify clearly its detention of an American citizen held on home soil incommunicado....

[In order to allow for a majority holding in the case, Justice Souter then agreed that due process would require that Hamdi receive a hearing on his claim that he was not an enemy combatant.]

JUSTICE SCALIA, with whom JUSTICE STEVENS joins, dissenting.

[Justice Scalia did not reach the statutory issue. He argued that before an American citizen could be detained as an enemy combatant, either he would have to be convicted of treason or Congress would have to suspend the writ of habeas corpus. As neither was done in this case, he would have ordered Hamdi's release.]

JUSTICE THOMAS, dissenting.

The Executive Branch, acting pursuant to the powers vested in the President by the Constitution and with explicit congressional approval, has determined that Yaser Hamdi is an enemy combatant and should be detained. This detention falls squarely within the Federal Government's war powers, and we lack the expertise and capacity to second-guess that decision. As such, petitioners' habeas challenge should fail, and there is no reason to remand the case....

## I

... The Founders intended that the President have primary responsibility—along with the necessary power—to protect the national security and to conduct the Nation's foreign relations. They did so principally because the structural advantages of a unitary Executive are essential in these domains. "Energy in the executive is a leading character in the definition of good government. It is essential to the protection of the community against foreign attacks." *The Federalist* No. 70 (A. Hamilton). The principle "ingredient" for "energy in the executive" is "unity." *Ibid.* This is because "decision, activity, secrecy, and dispatch will generally characterise the proceedings of one man, in a much more eminent degree, than the proceedings of any greater number." *Ibid.*...

The Court has acknowledged that the President has the authority to "employ [the Nation's Armed Forces] in the manner he may deem most effectual to harass and conquer and subdue the enemy." *Fleming v. Page*, 9 How. 603 (1850). With respect to foreign affairs as well, the Court has recognized the President's independent authority and need to be free from interference. See, e.g., *United States v. Curtiss-Wright Export Corp.*, 299 U.S. 304 (1936) [Note *supra.* this chapter].

Congress, to be sure, has a substantial and essential role in both foreign affairs and national security. But it is crucial to recognize that *judicial* interference in these domains destroys the purpose of vesting primary responsibility in a unitary Executive. I cannot improve on Justice Jackson's words, speaking for the Court:

The President, both as Commander-in-Chief and as the Nation's organ for foreign affairs, has available intelligence services whose reports are not and ought not to be published to the world. It would be intolerable that courts, without the relevant information, should review and perhaps nullify actions of the Executive taken on information properly held secret. Nor can courts sit *in camera* in order to be taken into executive confidences. But even if courts could require full disclosure, the very nature of executive decisions as to foreign policy is political, not judicial. Such decisions are wholly confided by our Constitution to the political departments of the government, Executive and Legislative. They are delicate, complex, and involve large elements of prophecy. They are and should be undertaken only by those directly responsible to the people whose welfare they advance or imperil. They are decisions of a kind for which the Judiciary has neither aptitude, facilities nor responsibility and which has long been held to belong in the domain of political power not subject to judicial intrusion or inquiry. *Chicago & Southern Air Lines, Inc. v. Waterman S.S. Corp.*, 333 U.S. 103 (1948).

Several points, made forcefully by Justice Jackson, are worth emphasizing. First, with respect to certain decisions relating to national security and foreign affairs, the courts simply lack the relevant information and expertise to second-guess determinations made by the President based on information properly withheld. Second, even if the courts could compel the Executive to produce the necessary information, such decisions are simply not amenable to judicial determination because "they are delicate, complex, and involve large elements of prophecy." *Ibid.* Third, the Court in *Chicago & Southern Air Lines* and elsewhere has correctly recognized the primacy of the political branches in the foreign-affairs and national-security contexts.

For these institutional reasons and because "Congress cannot anticipate and legislate with regard to every possible action the President may find it necessary to take or every possible situation in which he might act," it should come as no surprise that "such failure of Congress ... does not, especially ... in the areas of foreign policy and national security, imply 'congressional disapproval' of action taken by the Executive." *Dames & Moore v. Regan* (1981) [*Supra.* this chapter]. Rather, in these domains, the fact that Congress has provided the President with broad authorities does not imply— and the Judicial Branch should not infer— that Congress intended to deprive him of particular powers not specifically enumerated. See *Dames & Moore.* As far as the courts are concerned, "the enactment of legislation closely related to the question of the President's authority in a particular case which evinces legislative intent to accord the President broad discretion may be considered to 'invite' 'measures on independent presidential responsibility.'" *Ibid.* (quoting *Youngstown Sheet & Tube v. Sawyer* (1952) (Jackson, J., concurring) [*Supra.* this chapter]).

Finally, and again for the same reasons, where "the President acts pursuant to an express or implied authorization from Congress, he exercises not only his powers but also those delegated by Congress, [and] in such a case the executive action 'would be supported by the strongest of presumptions and the widest latitude of judicial interpretation, and the burden of persuasion would rest heavily upon any who might attack it.'" *Dames & Moore* (quoting *Youngstown* (Jackson, J., concurring))....

I acknowledge that the question whether Hamdi's executive detention is lawful is a question properly resolved by the Judicial Branch, though the question comes to the Court with the strongest presumptions in favor of the Government.... But the question whether Hamdi is actually an enemy combatant is "of a kind for which the Judiciary has neither aptitude, facilities nor responsibility and which has long been held to belong in the domain of political power not subject to judicial intrusion or inquiry." *Chicago & Southern Air Lines.* That is, although it is appropriate for the Court to determine the judicial question whether the President has the asserted authority, we lack the information and expertise to question whether Hamdi is actually an enemy combatant, a question the resolution of which is committed to other branches....

## II

... Although the President very well may have inherent authority to detain those arrayed against our troops, I agree with the plurality that we need not decide that question because Congress has authorized the President to do so....

## III

I agree with the plurality that the Federal Government has power to detain those that the Executive Branch determines to be enemy combatants. But I do not think that the plurality has adequately explained the breadth of the President's authority to detain enemy combatants, an authority that includes making virtually conclusive factual findings. In my view, the structural considerations discussed above, as recognized in our precedent, demonstrate that we lack the capacity and responsibility to second-guess this determination....

In this context, due process requires nothing more than a good-faith executive determination. To be clear: The Court has held [in *Moyer v. Peabody*, 212 U.S. 78 (1909)] that an Executive, acting pursuant to statutory and constitutional authority, may, consistent with the Due Process Clause, unilaterally decide to detain an individual if the Executive deems this necessary for the public safety *even if he is mistaken. Moyer* is not an exceptional case....

The Government's asserted authority to detain an individual that the President has determined to be an enemy combatant, at least while hostilities continue, comports with the Due Process Clause.... [The] Executive's decision that a detention is necessary to protect the public need not and should not be subjected to judicial second-guessing. Indeed, at least in the context of enemy-combatant determinations, this would defeat the unity, secrecy, and dispatch that the Founders believed to be so important to the warmaking function....

Accordingly, I conclude that the Government's detention of Hamdi as an enemy combatant does not violate the Constitution. By detaining Hamdi, the President, in the prosecution of a war and authorized by Congress, has acted well within his authority. Hamdi thereby received all the process to which he was due under the circumstances ...

## *Note: The Detainee Cases after* Hamdi

1. In the years after *Hamdi*, the Court continued to wrestle with difficult questions arising out of the roles of the judiciary and the political branches in the conduct of the ongoing war against terrorism. These questions largely concerned the extent to which the judiciary would review both executive branch determinations that detainees were in fact unlawful combatants, and the process by which the executive branch made those determinations.

2. In *Rasul v. Bush*, 542 U.S. 466 (2004), the Court held that federal courts had jurisdiction to hear habeas corpus petitions from non-American citizen detainees

held at Guantanamo Bay, Cuba. Writing for a majority of five Justices, Justice Stevens wrote that federal courts' habeas jurisdiction extended to aliens held in territory "over which the United States exercises plenary and exclusive jurisdiction," even if, as at Guantanamo (which is formally Cuban territory occupied by the United States under a lease), the United States did not exercise "ultimate sovereignty." Justice Kennedy concurred in the judgment. Justice Scalia dissented for three Justices.

3. In 2006 the Court, in a 5–3 vote (Chief Justice Roberts not participating), struck down the use of military commissions to try suspected al-Qaeda terrorists held at Guantanamo Bay. *Hamdan v. Rumsfeld*, 548 U.S. 557 (2006). Justice Stevens, again writing for the majority, began by concluding that the Detainee Treatment Act of 2005, which responded to *Rasul* by purporting to strip federal courts of jurisdiction to hear habeas petitions from Guantanamo detainees, did not apply to petitions pending when the statute was enacted. He then noted that longstanding statutes limited the jurisdiction of military commissions to situations provided for by statute or by the international law of war.

The Court considered the government's argument that the Uniform Code of Military Justice (UCMJ), the 2001 resolution authorizing the use of military force in Afghanistan (AUMF), and the Detainee Treatment Act of 2005 (DTA) authorized the use of commissions in situations like this. It rejected the argument:

> Together, the UCMJ, the AUMF and the DTA at most acknowledge a general Presidential authority to convene military commissions in circumstances where justified under the "Constitution and laws," including the law of war. Absent a more specific congressional authorization, the task of this Court is … to decide whether Hamdan's military commission is so justified.

Turning to that question, the Court held that the military commission's procedures violated the UCMJ, which set forth procedures that, under federal law, had to be used by military commissions "insofar as practicable." The Court also held that the international law of war did not authorize the commission, as it violated the Geneva Conventions' provisions on the procedures for the trying of crimes under the law of war.

Concurring, Justice Kennedy, writing for four of the five justices in the majority, relied on Justice Jackson's *Youngstown* analysis. He concluded that the history of congressional regulation of military commissions, and the conflict between congressionally-imposed limits and the President's proposed actions, placed this case in Jackson's third category—where there was a conflict between congressional policy and executive action, and thus, where the President's powers were at their weakest. He also noted (as did Justice Breyer, who also wrote a concurring opinion for four Justices) that nothing prevented the President from asking Congress for the authority he wished to constitute military commissions with different procedures.

Justice Scalia, joined by Justices Thomas and Alito, would have held that Congress had stripped the federal courts of jurisdiction to hear this type of case. Justice Thomas, joined by Justice Scalia, would have held that the congressional act authorizing the use of military force against Afghanistan authorized the creation of these military commissions. According to Justice Thomas, this conclusion was consistent with *Youngstown*, as interpreted in *Dames & Moore v. Regan*, given the importance of according the President broad power in foreign affairs. Chief Justice Roberts did not participate, as he had voted (in the government's favor) when the case was before the appellate court.

4. In *Boumediene v. Bush*, 553 U.S. 723 (2008) the Court confronted the question it avoided in *Hamdan*. After *Hamdan*, Congress enacted the Military Commissions Act of 2006, which denied federal court jurisdiction over detainees' habeas claims pending as of the date of the statute. However, the statute did not purport to "suspend" the right of habeas corpus, as the Constitution gives Congress the power to do. Given both the statute's unambiguous withdrawal of jurisdiction over pending habeas claims and its failure explicitly to suspend the right of habeas corpus, the Court in *Boumediene* was confronted with the question it avoided in *Hamdan*: whether such a denial of habeas jurisdiction, and its replacement with the military commissions established in the Detainee Treatment Act, were adequate substitutes for the habeas right.

5. In *Boumediene*, a five-justice majority held that the privilege to seek a writ of habeas corpus extended beyond the boundaries of the United States, and included persons held by federal authorities abroad (for example, at Guantanamo Bay). While the Court recognized that "the practical obstacles inherent in resolving the prisoner's entitlement to the writ" were relevant to such a prisoner's right to seek the writ, it concluded that Guantanamo Bay, which the United States has leased from Cuba since the early 20th century, was "in every practical sense not abroad," but rather "within the constant jurisdiction of the United States." Given that holding, it considered whether the procedures Congress had established for Guantanamo detainees to assert their innocence were adequate to satisfy the requirements of habeas review. It found those procedures to be inadequate. Toward the end of his opinion for the Court, Justice Kennedy wrote the following:

In considering both the procedural and substantive standards used to impose detention to prevent acts of terrorism, proper deference must be accorded to the political branches. *See United States v. Curtiss-Wright Export Corp.*, 299 U.S. 304 (1936) [Note *supra.* this chapter]. Unlike the President and some designated Members of Congress, neither the Members of this Court nor most federal judges begin the day with briefings that may describe new and serious threats to our Nation and its people. The law must accord the Executive substantial authority to apprehend and detain those who pose a real danger to our security.

Officials charged with daily operational responsibility for our security may consider a judicial discourse on the history of the Habeas Corpus Act of 1679 and like matters to be far removed from the Nation's present, urgent concerns. Established legal doctrine, however, must be consulted for its teaching. Remote in time it may be; irrelevant to the present it is not. Security depends upon a sophisticated intelligence apparatus and the ability of our Armed Forces to act and to interdict. There are further considerations, however. Security subsists, too, in fidelity to freedom's first principles. Chief among these are freedom from arbitrary and unlawful restraint and the personal liberty that is secured by adherence to the separation of powers. It is from these principles that the judicial authority to consider petitions for habeas corpus relief derives.

Our opinion does not undermine the Executive's powers as Commander in Chief. On the contrary, the exercise of those powers is vindicated, not eroded, when confirmed by the Judicial Branch. Within the Constitution's separation-of-powers structure, few exercises of judicial power are as legitimate or as necessary as the responsibility to hear challenges to the authority of the Executive to imprison a person. Some of these petitioners have been in custody for six years with no definitive judicial determination as to the legality of their detention. Their access to the writ is a necessity to determine the lawfulness of their status, even if, in the end, they do not obtain the relief they seek.

Because our Nation's past military conflicts have been of limited duration, it has been possible to leave the outer boundaries of war powers undefined. If, as some fear, terrorism continues to pose dangerous threats to us for years to come, the Court might not have this luxury. This result is not inevitable, however. The political branches, consistent with their independent obligations to interpret and uphold the Constitution, can engage in a genuine debate about how best to preserve constitutional values while protecting the Nation from terrorism.

It bears repeating that our opinion does not address the content of the law that governs petitioners' detention. That is a matter yet to be determined. We hold that petitioners may invoke the fundamental procedural protections of habeas corpus. The laws and Constitution are designed to survive, and remain in force, in extraordinary times. Liberty and security can be reconciled; and in our system they are reconciled within the framework of the law. The Framers decided that habeas corpus, a right of first importance, must be a part of that framework, a part of that law.

Justice Souter, joined by Justices Ginsburg and Breyer, joined the majority opinion but concurred separately. Chief Justice Roberts, joined by Justices Scalia, Thomas, and Alito, dissented. He argued that, regardless of whether the detainees enjoyed the privilege to seek a habeas writ, the procedures Congress put in place were an adequate substitute for a standard habeas proceeding.

Justice Scalia wrote an additional dissenting opinion, joined by the same justices who joined Chief Justice Roberts' dissent. He argued that the writ did not run to non-citizen combatants captured and held abroad. He reminded the majority that, two years earlier in *Hamdan*, four members of the *Boumediene* majority had stated that "'nothing prevents the President from returning to Congress to seek the authority [for trial by military commission] he believes necessary.'" After quoting from that concurring opinion in *Hamdan*, Justice Scalia concluded, "Turns out they were just kidding." He ended that part of his dissent with the following critique:

What competence does the Court have to second-guess the judgment of Congress and the President on such a point? None whatever. But the Court blunders in nonetheless. Henceforth, as today's opinion makes unnervingly clear, how to handle enemy prisoners in this war will ultimately lie with the branch that knows least about the national security concerns that the subject entails.

### c. The War Power in a World of Small Wars

As noted in this chapter's earlier discussion of the War Powers Resolution, military conflict after World War II has evolved, seemingly decisively, away from formal declarations of war. After the end of the Cold War in 1989, American involvement in military conflict has, with the notable exceptions of the Afghanistan war and the two Iraq wars, taken the form of short-term, limited objective missions, often justified on humanitarian grounds. Such conflicts pose difficult questions about the war power. Assuming that courts will continue refraining from judging the legality of such interventions, the respective roles of the President and Congress in initiating and ending these engagements will likely be determined by those branches themselves.

The following memo was written by the White House Office of Legal Counsel (OLC), an important White House office that provides legal advice to the President. The memo, written to consider the legality of American involvement in the Libyan Revolution of 2011, is a representative statement of White House views on the scope of the President's power to initiate American involvement in military conflict short of a formally-declared war. Consider the memo's arguments. What do they say about the role of Congress and the President in determining for themselves the constitutional questions surrounding the use of American military force? Consider in particular the memo's suggestion that the President has the authority to determine when a military engagement is so serious, or so likely to produce significant American casualties, that congressional authorization is required. Recall from Chapter 1 President Jackson's statement in his Bank veto message that the political branches enjoyed the power to determine whether a bank was "necessary and proper" to carry out powers the Constitution gave the federal government. How similar is that statement to this memo's suggestion?

## Authority to Use Military Force in Libya
### April 1, 2011

MEMORANDUM OPINION FOR THE ATTORNEY GENERAL

This memorandum memorializes advice this Office provided to you, prior to the commencement of recent United States military operations in Libya, regarding the President's legal authority to conduct such operations. For the reasons explained below, we concluded that the President had the constitutional authority to direct the use of force in Libya because he could reasonably determine that such use of force was in the national interest. We also advised that prior congressional approval was not constitutionally required to use military force in the limited operations under consideration.

I.

In mid-February 2011, amid widespread popular demonstrations seeking governmental reform in the neighboring countries of Tunisia and Egypt, as well as elsewhere in the Middle East and North Africa, protests began in Libya against the autocratic government of Colonel Muammar Qadhafi, who has ruled Libya since taking power in a 1969 coup. Qadhafi moved swiftly in an attempt to end the protests using military force....

On February 26, 2011, the United Nations Security Council ("UNSC") unanimously adopted Resolution 1970, which "expressed grave concern at the situation in the Libyan Arab Jamahiriya," "condemned the violence and use of force against civilians," and "deplored the gross and systematic violation of human rights" in Libya.... The resolution did not, however, authorize members of the United Nations to use military force in Libya....

By March 17, 2011, Qadhafi's forces were preparing to retake the city of Benghazi. Pledging that his forces would begin an assault on the city that night and show "no mercy and no pity" to those who would not give up resistance, Qadhafi stated in a radio address: "We will come house by house, room by room. It's over. The issue has been decided." ...

Later the same day, the UNSC addressed the situation in Libya again by adopting, by a vote of 10−0 (with five members abstaining), Resolution 1973, which imposed a no-fly zone and authorized the use of military force to protect civilians....

Despite a statement from Libya's Foreign Minister that Libya would honor the requested ceasefire, the Libyan government continued to conduct offensive operations, including attacks on civilians and civilian-populated areas. In response, on March 19, 2011, the United States, with the support of a number of its coalition partners, launched airstrikes against Libyan targets to enforce Resolution 1973. Consistent with the reporting provisions of the War Powers Resolution, President Obama provided a report to Congress less than forty-eight hours later, on March 21, 2011....

Before the initiation of military operations in Libya, White House and other executive branch officials conducted multiple meetings and briefings on Libya with members of Congress and testified on the Administration's policy at congressional hearings....

II.

The President explained in his March 21, 2011 report to Congress that the use of military force in Libya serves important U.S. interests in preventing instability in the Middle East and preserving the credibility and effectiveness of the United Nations Security Council. The President also stated that he intended the anticipated United States military operations in Libya to be limited in nature, scope, and duration. The goal of action by the United States was to "set the stage" for further action by coalition partners in implementing UNSC Resolution 1973, particularly through destruction of Libyan military assets that could either threaten coalition aircraft policing the UNSC-declared no-fly zone or engage in attacks on civilians and civilian-populated areas. In addition, no U.S. ground forces would be deployed, except possibly for any search and rescue missions, and the risk of substantial casualties for U.S. forces would be low. As we advised you prior to the commencement of military operations, we believe that, under these circumstances, the President had constitutional authority, as Commander in Chief and Chief Executive and pursuant to his foreign affairs powers, to direct such limited military operations abroad, even without prior specific congressional approval.

A.

... The Constitution, to be sure, divides authority over the military between the President and Congress, assigning to Congress the authority to "declare War," "raise and support Armies," and "provide and maintain a Navy," as well as general authority over the appropriations on which any military operation necessarily depends. U.S. Const. art. I, §8, cl. 1, 11–14. Yet, under "the historical gloss on the 'executive Power' vested in Article II of the Constitution," the President bears the "'vast share of responsibility for the conduct of our foreign relations,'" *Am. Ins. Ass'n v. Garamendi*, 539 U.S. 396 (2003) (quoting *Youngstown Sheet & Tube Co. v. Sawyer* (1952) (Frankfurter, J., concurring) [*Supra*. this chapter]), and accordingly holds "independent authority 'in the areas of foreign policy and national security.'" *Id.*; see also, e.g., *id.* (Jackson, J., concurring) (noting President's constitutional power to "act in external affairs without congressional authority"). Moreover, the President as Commander in Chief "superintends the military," *Loving v. United States*, 517 U.S. 748 (1996), and "is authorized to direct the movements of the naval and military forces placed by law at his command." *Fleming v. Page*, 50 U.S. 603 (1850); see also *Placing of United States Armed Forces Under United Nations Operational or Tactical Control*, 20 Op. O.L.C. 182 (1996).[*] The President also holds "the implicit advantage ... over the legislature under our constitutional scheme in situations calling for immediate action," given that imminent national security threats and rapidly evolving military and diplomatic circumstances may require a swift response by the United States without the opportunity for congressional deliberation and action. *Presidential Power to Use the Armed Forces Abroad Without Statutory Authorization*, 4A Op. O.L.C. 185 (1980) ("*Presidential Power*"). Accordingly, as Attorney General (later Justice) Robert Jackson observed over half a century ago, "the President's authority has long been recognized as extending to the dispatch of armed forces outside of the United States, either on missions of goodwill or rescue, or for the purpose of protecting American lives or property or American interests." *Training of British Flying Students in the United States*, 40 Op. Att'y Gen. 58 (1941).

This understanding of the President's constitutional authority reflects not only the express assignment of powers and responsibilities to the President and Congress in the Constitution, but also, as noted, the "historical gloss" placed on the Constitution by two centuries of practice. *Garamendi*. "Our history," this Office observed in 1980, "is replete with instances of presidential uses of military force abroad in the absence of prior congressional approval." *Presidential Power*. Since then, instances of such presidential initiative have only multiplied, with Presidents ordering, to give just a few examples, bombing in Libya (1986), an intervention in Panama (1989), troop deployments to Somalia (1992), Bosnia (1995), and Haiti (twice, 1994 and 2004),

---

\* [Ed Note: This citation is to a previous OLC opinion.]

air patrols and airstrikes in Bosnia (1993–1995), and a bombing campaign in Yugoslavia (1999), without specific prior authorizing legislation. This historical practice is an important indication of constitutional meaning, because it reflects the two political branches' practical understanding, developed since the founding of the Republic, of their respective roles and responsibilities with respect to national defense, and because "matters intimately related to foreign policy and national security are rarely proper subjects for judicial intervention." *Haig v. Agee*, 453 U.S. 280 (1981). In this context, the "pattern of executive conduct, made under claim of right, extended over many decades and engaged in by Presidents of both parties, 'evidences the existence of broad constitutional power.'" *Deployment of United States Armed Forces into Haiti*, 18 Op. O.L.C. at 173 (1994) ("*Haiti Deployment*") (quoting *Presidential Power*); see also *Proposed Deployment of United States Armed Forces into Bosnia*, 19 Op. O.L.C. 327 (1995) ("*Proposed Bosnia Deployment*") (noting that "the scope and limits" of Congress's power to declare war "are not well defined by constitutional text, case law, or statute," but the relationship between that power and the President's authority as Commander in Chief and Chief Executive has been instead "clarified by 200 years of practice").

Indeed, Congress itself has implicitly recognized this presidential authority. The War Powers Resolution ("WPR"), a statute Congress described as intended "to fulfill the intent of the framers of the Constitution of the United States," provides that, in the absence of a declaration of war, the President must report to Congress within 48 hours of taking certain actions, including introduction of U.S. forces "into hostilities or into situations where imminent involvement in hostilities is clearly indicated by the circumstances." The Resolution further provides that the President generally must terminate such use of force within 60 days (or 90 days for military necessity) unless Congress extends this deadline, declares war, or "enacts a specific authorization." As this Office has explained, although the WPR does not itself provide affirmative statutory authority for military operations, the Resolution's "structure ... recognizes and presupposes the existence of unilateral presidential authority to deploy armed forces" into hostilities or circumstances presenting an imminent risk of hostilities. *Haiti Deployment*. That structure—requiring a report within 48 hours after the start of hostilities and their termination within 60 days after that—"makes sense only if the President may introduce troops into hostilities or potential hostilities without prior authorization by the Congress." *Haiti Deployment*.

We have acknowledged one possible constitutionally-based limit on this presidential authority to employ military force in defense of important national interests—a planned military engagement that constitutes a "war" within the meaning of the Declaration of War Clause may require prior congressional authorization. See *Proposed Bosnia Deployment*. But the historical practice of presidential military action without congressional approval precludes any suggestion that Congress's authority to declare war covers every military engagement, however limited, that the President initiates. In our view, determining whether a particular planned engagement constitutes a "war" for constitutional purposes instead requires a fact-specific assessment of the "anticipated nature, scope, and duration" of the planned military operations. *Haiti Deployment*. This standard generally will be satisfied only by prolonged and substantial military engagements, typically involving exposure of U.S. military personnel to significant risk over a substantial period. Again, Congress's own key enactment on the subject reflects this understanding. By allowing United States involvement in hostilities to continue for 60 or 90 days, Congress signaled in the WPR that it considers congressional authorization most critical for "major, prolonged conflicts such as the wars in Vietnam and Korea," not more limited engagements. *Id....*

B.

Under the framework of these precedents, the President's legal authority to direct military force in Libya turns on two questions: first, whether United States operations in Libya would serve sufficiently important national interests to permit the President's action as Commander in Chief and Chief Executive and pursuant to his authority to conduct U.S. foreign relations; and second, whether the military operations that the President anticipated ordering would be sufficiently extensive in "nature, scope, and duration" to constitute a "war" requiring prior specific congressional approval under the Declaration of War Clause....

In our view, the combination of at least two national interests that the President reasonably determined were at stake here—preserving regional stability and supporting the UNSC's credibility and effectiveness—provided a sufficient basis for the President's exercise of his constitutional authority to order the use of military force. First, the United States has a strong national security and foreign policy interest in security and stability in the Middle East that was threatened by Qadhafi's actions in Libya....

The second important national interest implicated here, which reinforces the first, is the longstanding U.S. commitment to maintaining the credibility of the United Nations Security Council and the effectiveness of its actions to promote international peace and security....

We conclude, therefore, that the use of military force in Libya was supported by sufficiently important national interests to fall within the President's constitutional power. At the same time, turning to the second element of the analysis, we do not believe that anticipated United States operations in Libya amounted to a "war" in the constitutional sense necessitating congressional approval under the Declaration of War Clause. This inquiry, as noted, is highly fact-specific and turns on no single factor. See *Proposed Bosnia Deployment*. Here, considering all the relevant circumstances, we believe applicable historical precedents demonstrate that the limited military operations the President anticipated directing were not a "war" for constitutional purposes.

As in the case of the no-fly zone patrols and periodic airstrikes in Bosnia before the deployment of ground troops in 1995 and the NATO bombing campaign in connection with the Kosovo conflict in 1999—two military campaigns initiated without a prior declaration of war or other specific congressional authorization—President

Obama determined that the use of force in Libya by the United States would be limited to airstrikes and associated support missions; the President made clear that "the United States is not going to deploy ground troops in Libya." *Obama March 18, 2011 Remarks.* The planned operations thus avoided the difficulties of withdrawal and risks of escalation that may attend commitment of ground forces—two factors that this Office has identified as "arguably" indicating "a greater need for approval [from Congress] at the outset," to avoid creating a situation in which "Congress may be confronted with circumstances in which the exercise of its power to declare war is effectively foreclosed." ... Considering the historical practice of even intensive military action—such as the 17-day-long 1995 campaign of NATO airstrikes in Bosnia and some two months of bombing in Yugoslavia in 1999—without specific prior congressional approval, as well as the limited means, objectives, and intended duration of the anticipated operations in Libya, we do not think the "anticipated nature, scope, and duration" of the use of force by the United States in Libya rose to the level of a "war" in the constitutional sense, requiring the President to seek a declaration of war or other prior authorization from Congress.

Accordingly, we conclude that President Obama could rely on his constitutional power to safeguard the national interest by directing the anticipated military operations in Libya—which were limited in their nature, scope, and duration—without prior congressional authorization.

/s/

CAROLINE D. KRASS

Principal Deputy Assistant Attorney General

## *Note: The Foreign Affairs and War Power*

The foreign affairs and war powers provide especially difficult issues for separation of powers analysis. Not only are the relevant powers (*e.g.*, to declare war and to command the armed forces) explicitly divvied up between Congress and the President, but the background context for these powers has changed. Most notably, the decline of formal declarations of war, and the rise of small-scale, rapidly-unfolding conflicts have challenged Congress's traditional power to make the momentous decision whether to take the nation into armed hostilities. Moreover, vastly improved communications and mass media have given the President much more effective latitude to conduct foreign relations and to be perceived by the rest of the world as the spokesperson for the United States.

These developments present major challenges for constitutional law doctrine. While the Court will likely continue to stay out of clashes over the war power, disputes of the sorts in *Dames & Moore*, *Hamdi*, and *Zivotofsky* will continue to demand judicial responses. In deciding such cases, the Court may well continue to rely on the functional approach expressed in Justice Jackson's *Youngstown* opinion, rather than on a more formalistic analysis that cannot yield easy answers from the express words or underlying structures of Article I or Article II.

To the extent courts stay out of these issues, the political branches themselves will resolve them. Consider the constitutional analysis in the Libya memo. To what extent does it purport to interpret the Constitution, and to what extent does it "merely" purport to apply settled constitutional doctrine? The book's introduction to this memo invited you to compare the memo with President Jackson's message to Congress accompanying his veto of the bill reauthorizing the Bank of the United States. Now that you've read the memo, to what extent are these two executive branch statements analogous? What do they suggest about the scope of *Marbury*'s statement that "It is emphatically the province and duty of the judicial department to say what the law is"?

# Part II

# The Division of Federal and State Regulatory Power

## Introduction

Today the federal government possesses vast power to regulate nearly every aspect of Americans' lives. For modern Americans it is commonplace to encounter federal regulation of activities ranging from how we transact business to how we affect the environment, to the conditions under which we work and purchase and use consumer goods, to name but a few. But the constitutional foundation for this federal power is, at least in theory, surprisingly limited, and enmeshed in a complex federal structure. The federal government shares sovereign power with the states. Article I of the Constitution begins by vesting in Congress "All legislative Powers herein granted," and Section 8 then enumerates the subject-areas on which Congress may legislate. One of those powers, "to regulate Commerce among the several States," has become the source of much modern federal regulation of business and other commercial activity. Section 8 concludes by granting Congress a seemingly-broad power to enact "all Laws which shall be necessary and proper for carrying into Execution" both those enumerated powers and any other powers the rest of the Constitution grants to the national government. On the other hand, the Tenth Amendment, enacted by the first Congress, states that "The powers not delegated to the United States by the Constitution, nor prohibited by it to the States, are reserved to the States respectively, or to the people."

These textual provisions make it clear that the federal and state governments are mandated to share regulatory authority. But the exact delineation of that authority, and courts' role in demarcating the federal-state boundary, are highly contested matters. This Part of the book examines those matters. It begins, in Chapter 3, by considering the more abstract foundations for federal power, in particular, by asking what powers are necessary for the federal government to have in order for it to function as a sovereign government. Chapter 4 then examines the general scope of federal regulatory power, starting with the scope of Congress's power to enact laws "necessary and proper for carrying into Execution" its enumerated powers. It then examines what we will sometimes shorthand as "the commerce power" — that is, the power to regulate "Commerce among the several States."

Chapter 5 then considers state regulatory power. Chapter 5 focuses on three concepts: first, the limits that are imposed on that power by the negative implications of the commerce power (a concept known as "the dormant commerce clause"); second, Article IV's mandate that "The Citizens of each State shall be entitled to all Privileges and Immunities of Citizens in the several States"; and, finally, the concept that a state law must give way to a federal law that displaces, or "pre-empts," that state law. (While "preemption" doctrine is technically a matter of statutory interpretation, focusing on whether the federal law in question really does "preempt" a particular state law, it is studied in Constitutional Law because of its grounding in Article VI's provision that federal law is "the supreme Law of the Land," and because those statutory interpretation decisions are heavily freighted with constitutional concerns.)

Chapter 6 concludes this Part of the book by focusing on federal government regulation, not of individual citizens, but of state governments themselves. It considers the extent to which the Constitution allows such regulation if otherwise constitutionally valid (for example, as regulation of interstate commerce in which states are participants), and, conversely, the extent to which states' constitutionally-protected sovereignty is unconstitutionally impaired by federal regulation. In this sense, you should see this last chapter as circling back to the materials Part II starts with in Chapter 3: if those introductory materials consider the extent to which the *federal* government has the power to enact laws to ensure *its* sovereignty free from state interference, these concluding materials consider the extent to which *states* enjoy freedom from federal regulation in order to guarantee *their* sovereignty.

# Chapter 3

# Federal Law, Federal Institutions, and Federal Supremacy

As the Introduction implied, a fundamental question the Constitution's drafters faced was how, in Justice Kennedy's words, to "split the atom of sovereignty"—that is, how to create a system in which sovereign state governments co-existed with a federal government that, while possessing only enumerated powers, was nevertheless fully sovereign in enacting and enforcing those laws. At least two facts complicated this challenge even further. First, the Constitution as eventually drafted and enacted did not purport to hermetically separate the federal and state governments; it was decided—indeed, it was likely inevitable—that interdependence was called for. Second, Article VI's provision that federal law was "the supreme Law of the Land" necessarily meant that, ultimately, federal law enjoys a decisive advantage in any collision with state law or state government institutions. As demonstrated by the following three cases, two from the near-framing period and one from the modern era, the Court has faced difficult questions in ensuring the ultimate supremacy of federal law and federal institutions, consistent with respect for the sovereignty of state governments and the people of each state.

## Martin v. Hunter's Lessee

### 14 U.S. 304 (1816)

[This case arose out of a land ownership dispute in Virginia, in which one party (Martin) claimed the property by inheritance from a British subject, while the other (Hunter) claimed ownership through an act of the state legislature confiscating the land. Martin argued that a federal treaty with the United Kingdom restored the property rights of British subjects. The state court rejected the argument, but, on appeal, the U.S. Supreme Court disagreed, ruled in Martin's favor, and ordered the state court to rule in Martin's favor. In so ruling, the Supreme Court relied on Section 25 of the Judiciary Act of 1789 (a different section of the same statute at issue in *Marbury v. Madison*), which authorized the Court to hear cases appealed from state courts where the state court had ruled against a claim based on federal law (in this case, the treaty).

The Virginia courts refused to comply with the Supreme Court's order, concluding that a federal court—even the U.S. Supreme Court—did not have the power to reverse the state court's decision. This opinion followed.]

JUSTICE STORY delivered the opinion of the Court.

This is a writ of error from the court of appeals of Virginia, founded upon the refusal of that court to obey the mandate of this court, requiring the judgment rendered in this very cause, at February term, 1813, to be carried into due execution. The following is the judgment of the [state] court of appeals rendered on the mandate: 'The court is unanimously of opinion, that the appellate power of the supreme court of the United States does not extend to this court, under a sound construction of the constitution of the United States; that so much of the 25th section of the act of congress to establish the judicial courts of the United States, as extends the appellate jurisdiction of the supreme court to this court, is not in pursuance of the constitution of the United States; that the writ of error, in this cause, was improvidently allowed under the authority of that act; that the proceedings thereon in the supreme court were, *coram non judice*, in relation to this court, and that obedience to its mandate be declined by the court.'...

Before proceeding to the principal questions, it may not be unfit to dispose of some preliminary considerations which have grown out of the arguments at the bar.

The constitution of the United States was ordained and established, not by the states in their sovereign capacities, but emphatically, as the preamble of the constitution declares, by "the people of the United States." There can be no doubt that it was competent to the people to invest the general government with all the powers which they might deem proper and necessary; to extend or restrain these powers according to their own good pleasure, and to give them a paramount and supreme authority. As little doubt can there be, that the people had a right to prohibit to the states the exercise of any powers which were, in their judgment, incompatible with the objects of the general compact; to make the powers of the state governments, in given cases, subordinate to those of the nation, or to reserve to themselves those sovereign authorities which they might not choose to delegate to either. The constitution was not, therefore, necessarily carved out of existing state sovereignties, nor a surrender of powers already existing in state institutions, for the powers of the states depend upon their own constitutions; and the people of every state had the right to modify and restrain them, according to their own views of policy or principle. On the other hand, it is perfectly clear that the sovereign powers vested in the state governments, by their respective constitutions, remained unaltered and unimpaired, except so far as they were granted to the government of the United States....

The third article of the constitution is that which must principally attract our attention. The 1st. section declares, 'the judicial power of the United States shall be vested in one supreme court, and in such other inferior courts as the congress may, from time to time, ordain and establish.' The 2d section declares, that 'the judicial power shall extend to all cases in law or equity, arising under this constitution, the laws of the United States, and the treaties made, or which shall be made, under their authority; to all cases affecting ambassadors, other public ministers and consuls; to all cases of admiralty and maritime jurisdiction; to controversies to which the United States shall be a party; to controversies between two or more states; between a state and citizens of another state; between citizens of different states; between citizens of the same state, claiming lands under the grants of different states; and between a state or the citizens thereof, and foreign states, citizens, or subjects.' It then proceeds to declare, that 'in all cases affecting ambassadors, other public ministers and consuls, and those in which a state shall be a party, the supreme court shall have *original jurisdiction*. In all the other cases before mentioned the supreme court shall have *appellate jurisdiction*, both as to law and fact, with such exceptions, and under such regulations, as the congress shall make.'

Such is the language of the article creating and defining the judicial power of the United States. It is the voice of the whole American people solemnly declared, in establishing one great department of that government which was, in many respects, national, and in all, supreme. It is a part of the very same instrument which was to act not merely upon individuals, but upon states; and to deprive them altogether of the exercise of some powers of sovereignty, and to restrain and regulate them in the exercise of others....

As, then, by the terms of the constitution ... as to this court [appellate jurisdiction] may be exercised in all other cases than those of which it has original cognizance, what is there to restrain its exercise over state tribunals in the enumerated cases? The appellate power is not limited by the terms of the third article to any particular courts. The words are, 'the judicial power (which includes appellate power) shall extend *to all cases*,' &c., and 'in all other cases before mentioned the supreme court shall have appellate jurisdiction. [It is the *case*, then, and not *the court*,] that gives the jurisdiction. —> *Rule* If the judicial power extends to the case, it will be in vain to search in the letter of the constitution for any qualification as to the tribunal where it depends. It is incumbent, then, upon those who assert such a qualification to show its existence by necessary implication. If the text be clear and distinct, no restriction upon its plain and obvious import ought to be admitted, unless the inference be irresistible....

It must, therefore, be conceded that the constitution not only contemplated, but meant to provide for cases within the scope of the judicial power of the United States, which might yet depend before state tribunals. It was foreseen that in the exercise of their ordinary jurisdiction, state courts would incidentally take cognizance of cases arising under the constitution, the laws, and treaties of the United States. Yet to all these cases the judicial power, by the very terms of the constitution, is to extend. It cannot extend by original jurisdiction if that was already rightfully and exclusively attached in the state courts, which (as has been already shown) may occur; it must, therefore, extend by appellate jurisdiction, or not at all. It would seem to follow that the appellate power of the United States must, in such cases, extend to state tribunals; and if in such cases, there is no reason why it should not equally attach upon all others within the purview of the constitution.

It has been argued that such an appellate jurisdiction over state courts is inconsistent with the genius of our governments, and the spirit of the constitution. That the latter was never designed to act upon state sovereignties, but only upon the people, and that if the power exists, it will materially impair the sovereignty of the states, and the independence of their courts. We cannot yield to the force of this reasoning; it assumes principles which we cannot admit, and draws conclusions to which we do not yield our assent.

It is a mistake that the constitution was not designed to operate upon states, in their corporate capacities. It is crowded with provisions which restrain or annul the sovereignty of the states in some of the highest branches of their prerogatives. The tenth section of the first article contains a long list of disabilities and prohibitions imposed upon the states. Surely, when such essential portions of state sovereignty are taken away, or prohibited to be exercised, it cannot be correctly asserted that the constitution does not act upon the states. The language of the constitution is also imperative upon the states as to the performance of many duties. It is imperative upon the state legislatures to make laws prescribing the time, places, and manner of holding elections for senators and representatives, and for electors of president and vice-president. And in these, as well as some other cases, congress have a right to revise, amend, or supercede the laws which may be passed by state legislatures. When, therefore, the states are stripped of some of the highest attributes of sovereignty, and the same are given to the United States; when the legislatures of the states are, in some respects, under the control of congress, and in every case are, under the constitution, bound by the paramount authority of the United States; it is certainly difficult to support the argument that the appellate power over the decisions of state courts is contrary to the genius of our institutions....

*Uniformity Arg.*

It is further argued, that no great public mischief can result from a construction which shall limit the appellate power of the United States to cases in their own courts: first, because state judges are bound by an oath to support the constitution of the United States, and must be presumed to be men of learning and integrity; and, secondly, because congress must have an unquestionable right to remove all cases within the scope of the judicial power from the state courts to the courts of the United States, at any time before final judgment, though not after final judgment. As to the first reason—admitting that the judges of the state courts are, and always will be, of as much learning, integrity, and wisdom, as those of the courts of the United States, (which we very cheerfully admit,) it does not aid the argument. It is manifest that the constitution has proceeded upon a theory of its own, and given or withheld powers according to the judgment of the American people, by whom it was adopted. We can only construe its powers, and cannot inquire into the policy or principles which induced the grant of them....

This is not all. A motive of another kind, perfectly compatible with the most sincere respect for state tribunals, might induce the grant of appellate power over their decisions. That motive is the importance, and even necessity of *uniformity* of decisions throughout the whole United States, upon all subjects within the purview of the constitution. Judges of equal learning and integrity, in different states, might differently interpret a statute, or a treaty of the United States, or even the constitution itself: If there were no revising authority to control these jarring and discordant judgments, and harmonize them into uniformity, the laws, the treaties, and the constitution of the United States would be different in different states, and might, perhaps, never have precisely the same construction, obligation, or efficacy, in any two states. The public mischiefs that would attend such a state of things would be truly deplorable; and it cannot be believed that they could have escaped the enlightened convention which formed the constitution. What, indeed, might then have been only prophecy, has now become fact; and the appellate jurisdiction must continue to be the only adequate remedy for such evils....

On the whole, the court are of the opinion, that the appellate power of the United States does extend to cases pending in the state courts; and that the 25th section of the judiciary act, which authorizes the exercise of this jurisdiction in the specified cases, by a writ of error, is supported by the letter and spirit of the constitution. We find no clause in that instrument which limits this power; and we dare not interpose a limitation where the people have not been disposed to create one....

JOHNSON, J. [The concurring opinion of Justice Johnson is omitted.]

# McCulloch v. Maryland *Biggie*

### 17 U.S. (4 Wheat.) 316 (1819)

[The State of Maryland imposed a tax on the operations of all banks not chartered by the Maryland Legislature. The Bank of the United States, an institution established by Congress, refused to pay the tax. Maryland argued, first, that Congress exceeded its powers when it established the Bank, and, second, in the alternative, that if Congress did have the power to establish the Bank, Maryland had the right to tax its operations. The Court's discussion of the first question is presented in the next chapter.]

MARSHALL, Ch. J., delivered the opinion of the court.

The first question made in the cause is—has congress power to incorporate a bank? ...

It being the opinion of the court, that the act incorporating the bank is constitutional; and that the power of establishing a branch in the state of Maryland might be properly exercised by the bank itself, we proceed to inquire—

2. Whether the state of Maryland may, without violating the constitution, tax that branch? That the power of taxation is one of vital importance; that it is retained by the states; that it is not abridged by the grant of a similar power to the government of the Union; that it is to be concurrently exercised by the two governments—are truths which have never been denied. But such is the paramount character of the constitution, that its capacity to withdraw any subject from the action of even this power, is admitted. The states are expressly forbidden to lay any duties on imports or exports, except what may be absolutely necessary for executing their inspection laws. If the obligation of this prohibition must be conceded—if it may restrain a state from the exercise of its taxing power on imports and exports—the same paramount character would seem to restrain, as it certainly may restrain, a state from such other exercise of this power, as is in its nature incompatible with, and repugnant

to, the constitutional laws of the Union. A law, absolutely repugnant to another, as entirely repeals that other as if express terms of repeal were used.

On this ground, the counsel for the bank place its claim to be exempted from the power of a state to tax its operations. There is no express provision for the case, but the claim has been sustained on a principle which so entirely pervades the constitution, is so intermixed with the materials which compose it, so interwoven with its web, so blended with its texture, as to be incapable of being separated from it, without rending it into shreds. This great principle is, that the constitution and the laws made in pursuance thereof are supreme; that they control the constitution and laws of the respective states, and cannot be controlled by them. From this, which may be almost termed an axiom, other propositions are deduced as corollaries, on the truth or error of which, and on their application to this case, the cause has been supposed to depend. These are, 1st. That a power to create implies a power to preserve: 2d. That a power to destroy, if wielded by a different hand, is hostile to, and incompatible with these powers to create and to preserve: 3d. That where this repugnancy exists, that authority which is supreme must control, not yield to that over which it is supreme....

The power of congress to create, and of course, to continue, the bank, was the subject of the preceding part of this opinion; and is no longer to be considered as questionable. That the power of taxing it by the states may be exercised so as to destroy it, is too obvious to be denied. But taxation is said to be an absolute power, which acknowledges no other limits than those expressly prescribed in the constitution, and like sovereign power of every other description, is trusted to the discretion of those who use it. But the very terms of this argument admit, that the sovereignty of the state, in the article of taxation itself, is subordinate to, and may be controlled by the constitution of the United States. How far it has been controlled by that instrument, must be a question of construction. In making this construction, no principle, not declared, can be admissible, which would defeat the legitimate operations of a supreme government. It is of the very essence of supremacy, to remove all obstacles to its action within its own sphere, and so to modify every power vested in subordinate governments, as to exempt its own operations from their own influence. This effect need not be stated in terms. It is so involved in the declaration of supremacy, so necessarily implied in it, that the expression of it could not make it more certain. We must, therefore, keep it in view, while construing the constitution.

The argument on the part of the state of Maryland, is, not that the states may directly resist a law of congress, but that they may exercise their acknowledged powers upon it, and that the constitution leaves them this right, in the confidence that they will not abuse it. Before we proceed to examine this argument, and to subject it to test of the constitution, we must be permitted to bestow a few considerations on the nature and extent of this original right of taxation, which is acknowledged to remain with the states. It is admitted, that the power of taxing the people and their property, is essential to the very existence of government, and may be legitimately exercised on the objects to which it is applicable, to the utmost extent to which the government may choose to carry it. The only security against the abuse of this power, is found in the structure of the government itself. In imposing a tax, the legislature acts upon its constituents. This is, in general, a sufficient security against erroneous and oppressive taxation.

The people of a state, therefore, give to their government a right of taxing themselves and their property, and as the exigencies of government cannot be limited, they prescribe no limits to the exercise of this right, resting confidently on the interest of the legislator, and on the influence of the constituent over their representative, to guard them against its abuse. But the means employed by the government of the Union have no such security, nor is the right of a state to tax them sustained by the same theory. Those means are not given by the people of a particular state, not given by the constituents of the legislature, which claim the right to tax them, but by the people of all the states. They are given by all, for the benefit of all — and upon theory, should be subjected to that government only which belongs to all....

The sovereignty of a state extends to everything which exists by its own authority, or is introduced by its permission; but does it extend to those means which are employed by congress to carry into execution powers conferred on that body by the people of the United States? We think it demonstrable, that it does not. Those powers are not given by the people of a single state. They are given by the people of the United States, to a government whose laws, made in pursuance of the constitution, are declared to be supreme. Consequently, the people of a single state cannot confer a sovereignty which will extend over them....

But, waiving this theory for the present, let us resume the inquiry, whether this power can be exercised by the respective states, consistently with a fair construction of the constitution? That the power to tax involves the power to destroy; that the power to destroy may defeat and render useless the power to create; that there is a plain repugnance in conferring on one government a power to control the constitutional measures of another, which other, with respect to those very measures, is declared to be supreme over that which exerts the control, are propositions not to be denied. But all inconsistencies are to be reconciled by the magic of the word CONFIDENCE. Taxation, it is said, does not necessarily and unavoidably destroy. To carry it to the excess of destruction, would be an abuse, to presume which, would banish that confidence which is essential to all government. But is this a case of confidence? Would the people of any one state trust those of another with a power to control the most insignificant operations of their state government? We know they would not. Why, then, should we suppose, that the people of any one state should be willing to trust those of another with a power to control the operations of a government to which they have confided their most important and most valuable interests? In the legislature of the Union alone, are all represented. The legislature of the Union alone, therefore, can be trusted by the people with the power of controlling measures which concern all, in the confidence that it will not be abused. This, then, is not a case of confidence, and we must consider it is as it really is....

If we apply the principle for which the state of Maryland contends, to the constitution, generally, we shall find it capable of changing totally the character of that instrument. We shall find it capable of arresting all the measures of the government, and of prostrating it at the foot of the states. The American people have declared their constitution and the laws made in pursuance thereof, to be supreme; but this principle would transfer the supremacy, in fact, to the states. If the states may tax one instrument, employed by the government in the execution of its powers, they may tax any and every other instrument. They may tax the mail; they may tax the mint; they may tax patent-rights; they may tax the papers of the custom-house; they may tax judicial process; they may tax all the means employed by the government, to an excess which would defeat all the ends of government. This was not intended by the American people. They did not design to make their government dependent on the states. . . .

It has also been insisted, that, as the power of taxation in the general and state governments is acknowledged to be concurrent, every argument which would sustain the right of the general government to tax banks chartered by the states, will equally sustain the right of the states to tax banks chartered by the general government. But the two cases are not on the same reason. The people of all the states have created the general government, and have conferred upon it the general power of taxation. The people of all the states, and the states themselves, are represented in congress, and, by their representatives, exercise this power. When they tax the chartered institutions of the states, they tax their constituents; and these taxes must be uniform. But when a state taxes the operations of the government of the United States, it acts upon institutions created, not by their own constituents, but by people over whom they claim no control. It acts upon the measures of a government created by others as well as themselves, for the benefit of others in common with themselves. The difference is that which always exists, and always must exist, between the action of the whole on a part, and the action of a part on the whole — between the laws of a government declared to be supreme, and those of a government which, when in opposition to those laws, is not supreme. . . .

The court has bestowed on this subject its most deliberate consideration. The result is a conviction that the states have no power, by taxation or otherwise, to retard, impede, burden, or in any manner control, the operations of the constitutional laws enacted by congress to carry into execution the powers vested in the general government. This is, we think, the unavoidable consequence of that supremacy which the constitution has declared. We are unanimously of opinion, that the law passed by the legislature of Maryland, imposing a tax on the Bank of the United States, is unconstitutional and void.

This opinion does not deprive the states of any resources which they originally possessed. It does not extend to a tax paid by the real property of the bank, in common with the other real property within the state, nor to a tax imposed on the interest which the citizens of Maryland may hold in this institution, in common with other property of the same description throughout the state. But this is a tax on the operations of the bank, and is, consequently, a tax on the operation of an instrument employed by the government of the Union to carry its powers into execution. Such a tax must be unconstitutional....

# U.S. Term Limits, Inc. v. Thornton
## 514 U.S. 779 (1995)

Justice STEVENS delivered the opinion of the Court.

The Constitution sets forth qualifications for membership in the Congress of the United States. Article I, § 2, cl. 2, which applies to the House of Representatives, provides:

> No Person shall be a Representative who shall not have attained to the Age of twenty five Years, and been seven Years a Citizen of the United States, and who shall not, when elected, be an Inhabitant of that State in which he shall be chosen.

Article I, § 3, cl. 3, which applies to the Senate, similarly provides:

> No Person shall be a Senator who shall not have attained to the Age of thirty Years, and been nine Years a Citizen of the United States, and who shall not, when elected, be an Inhabitant of that State for which he shall be chosen.

Today's cases present a challenge to an amendment to the Arkansas State Constitution that prohibits the name of an otherwise-eligible candidate for Congress from appearing on the general election ballot if that candidate has already served three terms in the House of Representatives or two terms in the Senate. The Arkansas Supreme Court held that the amendment violates the Federal Constitution. We agree with that holding.... Allowing individual States to adopt their own qualifications for congressional service would be inconsistent with the Framers' vision of a uniform National Legislature representing the people of the United States. If the qualifications set forth in the text of the Constitution are to be changed, that text must be amended.

I

At the general election on November 3, 1992, the voters of Arkansas adopted Amendment 73 to their State Constitution. Proposed as a "Term Limitation Amendment," its preamble stated:

> The people of Arkansas find and declare that elected officials who remain in office too long become preoccupied with reelection and ignore their duties as representatives of the people. Entrenched incumbency has reduced voter participation and has led to an electoral system that is less free, less competitive, and less representative than the system established by the Founding Fathers. Therefore, the people of Arkansas, exercising their reserved powers, herein limit the terms of elected officials.

The limitations in Amendment 73 apply to three categories of elected officials. Section 1 provides that no elected official in the executive branch of the state government may serve more than two 4-year terms. Section 2 applies to the legislative branch of the state government; it provides that no member of the Arkansas House of Representatives may serve more than three 2-year terms and no member of the Arkansas Senate may serve more than two 4-year terms. Section 3, the provision at issue in these cases, applies to the Arkansas Congressional Delegation. It provides:

> (a) Any person having been elected to three or more terms as a member of the United States House of Representatives from Arkansas shall not be certified as a candidate and shall not be eligible to have his/her name placed on the ballot for election to the United States House of Representatives from Arkansas.

> (b) Any person having been elected to two or more terms as a member of the United States Senate from Arkansas shall not be certified as a candidate and shall not be eligible to have his/her name placed on the ballot for election to the United States Senate from Arkansas....

## II

... Twenty-six years ago, in *Powell v. McCormack,* 395 U.S. 486 (1969) [Note *supra.* Chapter 1], we reviewed the history and text of the Qualifications Clauses in a case involving an attempted exclusion of a duly elected Member of Congress. The principal issue was whether the power granted to each House in Art. I, § 5, cl. 1, to judge the "Qualifications of its own Members" includes the power to impose qualifications other than those set forth in the text of the Constitution. In an opinion by Chief Justice Warren for eight Members of the Court, we held that it does not....

## III

Our reaffirmation of *Powell* does not necessarily resolve the specific questions presented in these cases. For petitioners argue that whatever the constitutionality of additional qualifications for membership imposed by Congress, the historical and textual materials discussed in *Powell* do not support the conclusion that the Constitution prohibits additional qualifications imposed by States. In the absence of such a constitutional prohibition, petitioners argue, the Tenth Amendment and the principle of reserved powers require that States be allowed to add such qualifications....

Petitioners argue that the Constitution contains no express prohibition against state-added qualifications, and that Amendment 73 is therefore an appropriate exercise of a State's reserved power to place additional restrictions on the choices that its own voters may make. We disagree for two independent reasons. First, we conclude that the power to add qualifications is not within the "original powers" of the States, and thus is not reserved to the States by the Tenth Amendment. Second, even if States possessed some original power in this area, we conclude that the Framers intended the Constitution to be the exclusive source of qualifications for Members of Congress, and that the Framers thereby "divested" States of any power to add qualifications.

The "plan of the convention" as illuminated by the historical materials, our opinions, and the text of the Tenth Amendment draws a basic distinction between the powers of the newly created Federal Government and the powers retained by the pre-existing sovereign States. As Chief Justice Marshall explained, "it was neither necessary nor proper to define the powers retained by the States. These powers proceed, not from the people of America, but from the people of the several States; and remain, after the adoption of the constitution, what they were before, except so far as they may be abridged by that instrument." *Sturges.*

This classic statement by the Chief Justice endorsed Hamilton's reasoning in *The Federalist* No. 32 that the plan of the Constitutional Convention did not contemplate "an entire consolidation of the States into one complete national sovereignty," but only a partial consolidation in which "the State governments would clearly retain all the rights of sovereignty which they before had, and which were not, by that act, *exclusively* delegated to the United States." The text of the Tenth Amendment unambiguously confirms this principle:

> The powers not delegated to the United States by the Constitution, nor prohibited by it to the States, are reserved to the States respectively, or to the people.

As we have frequently noted, "the States unquestionably do retain a significant measure of sovereign authority. They do so, however, *only to the extent that the Constitution has not divested them of their original powers* and transferred those powers to the Federal Government." *Garcia v. San Antonio Metropolitan Transit Authority,* 469 U.S. 528 (1985) (emphasis added).

### Source of the Power

Contrary to petitioners' assertions, the power to add qualifications is not part of the original powers of sovereignty that the Tenth Amendment reserved to the States. Petitioners' Tenth Amendment argument misconceives the nature of the right at issue because that Amendment could only "reserve" that which existed before. As Justice Story recognized, "the states can exercise no powers whatsoever, which exclusively spring out of the existence of the national government, which the constitution does not delegate to them.... No state can say, that it has reserved, what it never possessed." 1 Story, *Commentaries on the Constitution of the United States* § 627 (3d ed. 1858).

Justice Story's position thus echoes that of Chief Justice Marshall in *McCulloch v. Maryland* (1824) [*Supra.* this chapter]. In *McCulloch,* the Court rejected the argument that the Constitution's silence on the subject of state power to tax corporations chartered by Congress implies that the States have "reserved" power to tax such federal instrumentalities. As Chief Justice Marshall pointed out, an "original right to tax" such federal entities "never existed, and the question whether it has been surrendered, cannot arise." ...

With respect to setting qualifications for service in Congress, no such right existed before the Constitution was ratified. The contrary argument overlooks the revolutionary character of the Government that the Framers conceived. Prior to the adoption of the Constitution, the States had joined together under the Articles of Confederation. In that system, "the States retained most of their sovereignty, like independent nations bound together only by treaties." After the Constitutional Convention convened, the

Framers were presented with, and eventually adopted a variation of, "a plan not merely to amend the Articles of Confederation but to create an entirely new National Government with a National Executive, National Judiciary, and a National Legislature." In adopting that plan, the Framers envisioned a uniform national system, rejecting the notion that the Nation was a collection of States, and instead creating a direct link between the National Government and the people of the United States. In that National Government, representatives owe primary allegiance not to the people of a State, but to the people of the Nation....

In short, as the Framers recognized, electing representatives to the National Legislature was a new right, arising from the Constitution itself. The Tenth Amendment thus provides no basis for concluding that the States possess reserved power to add qualifications to those that are fixed in the Constitution. Instead, any state power to set the qualifications for membership in Congress must derive not from the reserved powers of state sovereignty, but rather from the delegated powers of national sovereignty. In the absence of any constitutional delegation to the States of power to add qualifications to those enumerated in the Constitution, such a power does not exist....

### The Convention and Ratification Debates

... The provisions in the Constitution governing federal elections confirm the Framers' intent that States lack power to add qualifications. The Framers feared that the diverse interests of the States would undermine the National Legislature, and thus they adopted provisions intended to minimize the possibility of state interference with federal elections. For example, to prevent discrimination against federal electors, the Framers required in Art. I, §2, cl. 1, that the qualifications for federal electors be the same as those for state electors. As Madison noted, allowing States to differentiate between the qualifications for state and federal electors "would have rendered too dependent on the State governments that branch of the federal government which ought to be dependent on the people alone." *The Federalist* No. 52. Similarly, in Art. I, §4, cl. 1, though giving the States the freedom to regulate the "Times, Places and Manner of holding Elections," the Framers created a safeguard against state abuse by giving Congress the power to "by Law make or alter such Regulations." The Convention debates make clear that the Framers' overriding concern was the potential for States' abuse of the power to set the "Times, Places and Manner" of elections....

We find further evidence of the Framers' intent in Art. I, §5, cl. 1, which provides: "Each House shall be the Judge of the Elections, Returns and Qualifications of its own Members." That Art. I, §5, vests a federal tribunal with ultimate authority to judge a Member's qualifications is fully consistent with the understanding that those qualifications are fixed in the Federal Constitution, but not with the understanding that they can be altered by the States. If the States had the right to prescribe additional qualifications — such as property, educational, or professional qualifications — for their own representatives, state law would provide the standard for judging a Member's eligibility. As we concluded in *Murdock v. Memphis*, 87 U.S. 590 (1875), federal questions are generally answered finally by federal tribunals because rights which depend on federal law "should be the same everywhere" and "their construction should be uniform." The judging of questions concerning rights which depend on state law is not, however, normally assigned to federal tribunals. The Constitution's provision for each House to be the judge of its own qualifications thus provides further evidence that the Framers believed that the primary source of those qualifications would be federal law....

### Democratic Principles

Our conclusion that States lack the power to impose qualifications vindicates the same "fundamental principle of our representative democracy" that we recognized in *Powell*, namely, that "the people should choose whom they please to govern them." ...

Finally, state-imposed restrictions, unlike the congressionally imposed restrictions at issue in *Powell*, violate a third idea central to this basic principle: that the right to choose representatives belongs not to the States, but to the people. From the start, the Framers recognized that the "great and radical vice" of the Articles of Confederation was "the principle of LEGISLATION for STATES or GOVERNMENTS, in their COR-PORATE or COLLECTIVE CAPACITIES, and as contradistinguished from the IN-DIVIDUALS of whom they consist." *The Federalist* No. 15 (Hamilton). Thus the Framers, in perhaps their most important contribution, conceived of a Federal Government directly responsible to the people, possessed of direct power over the people, and chosen directly, not by States, but by the people. The Framers implemented this ideal most clearly in the provision, extant from the beginning of the Republic, that calls for the Members of the House of Representatives to be "chosen every second Year by the People of the several States." Art. I, §2, cl. 1. Following the adoption of the Seventeenth Amendment in 1913, this ideal was extended to elections for the Senate. The Congress of the United States, therefore, is not a confederation of nations in which separate sovereigns are represented by appointed delegates, but is instead a body composed of representatives of the people. As Chief Justice John Marshall observed: "The government of the Union, then, ... is, emphatically, and truly, a government of the people. In form and in substance it emanates from them. Its powers are granted by them, and are to be exercised directly on them, and for their benefit." *McCulloch*....

Permitting individual States to formulate diverse qualifications for their representatives would result in a patchwork of state qualifications, undermining the uniformity and the national character that the Framers envisioned and sought to ensure. Cf. *McCulloch* ("Those means are not given by the people of a particular State, not given by the constituents of the legislature, ... but by the people of all the States. They are given by all, for the benefit of all—and upon theory, should be subjected to that government only which belongs to all"). Such a patchwork would also sever the direct link that the Framers found so critical between the National Government and the people of the United States....

V

The merits of term limits, or "rotation," have been the subject of debate since the formation of our Constitution ... We are, however, firmly convinced that allowing the several States to adopt term limits for congressional service would effect a fundamental change in the constitutional framework. Any such change must come not by legislation adopted either by Congress or by an individual State, but rather ... through the amendment procedures set forth in Article V. The Framers decided that the qualifications for service in the Congress of the United States be fixed in the Constitution and be uniform throughout the Nation. That decision reflects the Framers' understanding that Members of Congress are chosen by separate constituencies, but that they become, when elected, servants of the people of the United States. They are not merely delegates appointed by separate, sovereign States; they occupy offices that are integral and essential components of a single National Government. In the absence of a properly passed constitutional amendment, allowing individual States to craft their own qualifications for Congress would thus erode the structure envisioned by the Framers, a structure that was designed, in the words of the Preamble to our Constitution, to form a "more perfect Union." ...

Justice KENNEDY, concurring.

I join the opinion of the Court.

The majority and dissenting opinions demonstrate the intricacy of the question whether or not the Qualifications Clauses are exclusive. In my view, however, it is well settled that the whole people of the United States asserted their political identity and unity of purpose when they created the federal system. The dissent's course of reasoning suggesting otherwise might be construed to disparage the republican character of the National Government, and it seems appropriate to add these few remarks to explain why that course of argumentation runs counter to fundamental principles of federalism.

Federalism was our Nation's own discovery. The Framers split the atom of sovereignty. It was the genius of their idea that our citizens would have two political capacities, one state and one federal, each protected from incursion by the other. The resulting Constitution created a legal system unprecedented in form and design, establishing two orders of government, each with its own direct relationship, its own privity, its own set of mutual rights and obligations to the people who sustain it and are governed by it. It is appropriate to recall these origins, which instruct us as to the nature of the two different governments created and confirmed by the Constitution.

A distinctive character of the National Government, the mark of its legitimacy, is that it owes its existence to the act of the whole people who created it. It must be remembered that the National Government, too, is republican in essence and in theory....

In one sense it is true that "the people of each State retained their separate political identities," for the Constitution takes care both to preserve the States and to make use of their identities and structures at various points in organizing the federal union. It does not at all follow from this that the sole political identity of an American is with the State of his or her residence. It denies the dual character of the Federal Government which is its very foundation to assert that the people of the United States do not have a political identity as well, one independent of, though consistent with, their identity as citizens of the State of their residence. It must be recognized that "for all the great purposes for which the Federal government was formed, we are one people, with one common country."

It might be objected that because the States ratified the Constitution, the people can delegate power only through the States or by acting in their capacities as citizens of particular States. But in *McCulloch v. Maryland,* the Court set forth its authoritative rejection of this idea:

> The Convention which framed the constitution was indeed elected by the State legislatures. But the instrument ... was submitted to the people.... It is true, they assembled in their several States—and where else should they have assembled? No political dreamer was ever wild enough to think of breaking down the lines which separate the States, and of compounding the American people into one common mass. Of consequence, when they act, they act in their States. But the measures they adopt do not, on that account, cease to be the measures of the people themselves, or become the measures of the State governments.

The political identity of the entire people of the Union is reinforced by the proposition, which I take to be beyond dispute, that, though limited as to its objects, the National Government is, and must be, controlled by the people without collateral interference by the States. *McCulloch* affirmed this proposition as well, when the Court rejected the suggestion that States could interfere with federal powers. "This was not intended by the American people. They did not design to make their government dependent on the States." That the States may not invade the sphere of federal sovereignty is as incontestable, in my view, as the corollary proposition that the Federal Government must be held within the boundaries of its own power when it intrudes upon matters reserved to the States.

Of course, because the Framers recognized that state power and identity were essential parts of the federal balance, see *The Federalist* No. 39, the Constitution is solicitous of the prerogatives of the States, even in an otherwise sovereign federal province. The Constitution uses state boundaries to fix the size of congressional delegations, Art. I, §2, cl. 3, ensures that each State shall have at least one representative, *ibid.,* grants States certain powers over the times, places, and manner of federal elections (subject to congressional revision), Art. I, §4, cl. 1, requires that when the President is elected by the House of Representatives, the delegations from each State have one vote, Art. II, §1, cl. 3, and Amdt. 12, and allows States to appoint electors for the President, Art. II, §1, cl. 2. Nothing in the Constitution or *The Federalist Papers,* however, supports the idea of state interference with the most basic relation between the National Government and its citizens, the selection of legislative representatives....

Not the least of the incongruities in the position advanced by Arkansas is the proposition, necessary to its case, that it can burden the rights of resident voters in federal elections by reason of the manner in which they earlier had exercised it. If the majority of the voters had been successful in selecting a candidate, they would be penalized from exercising that same right in the future. Quite apart from any First Amendment concerns, neither the law nor federal theory allows a State to burden the exercise of federal rights in this manner. Indeed, as one of the "rights of the citizens of this great country, protected by implied guarantees of its Constitution," the Court identified the right "to come to the seat of government ... to share its offices, to engage in administering its functions." This observation serves to illustrate the extent of the State's attempted interference with the federal right to vote (and the derivative right to serve if elected by majority vote) in a congressional election, rights that do not derive from the state power in the first instance but that belong to the voter in his or her capacity as a citizen of the United States....

Justice THOMAS, with whom THE CHIEF JUSTICE, Justice O'CONNOR, and Justice SCALIA join, dissenting.

It is ironic that the Court bases today's decision on the right of the people to "choose whom they please to govern them." Under our Constitution, there is only one State whose people have the right to "choose whom they please" to represent Arkansas in Congress. The Court holds, however, that neither the elected legislature of that State nor the people themselves (acting by ballot initiative) may prescribe any qualifications for those representatives. The majority therefore defends the right of the people of Arkansas to "choose whom they please to govern them" by invalidating a provision that won nearly 60% of the votes cast in a direct election and that carried every congressional district in the State.

I dissent. Nothing in the Constitution deprives the people of each State of the power to prescribe eligibility requirements for the candidates who seek to represent them in Congress. The Constitution is simply silent on this question. And where the Constitution is silent, it raises no bar to action by the States or the people.

## I

Because the majority fundamentally misunderstands the notion of "reserved" powers, I start with some first principles....

## A

Our system of government rests on one overriding principle: All power stems from the consent of the people. To phrase the principle in this way, however, is to be imprecise about something important to the notion of "reserved" powers. The ultimate source of the Constitution's authority is the consent of the people of each individual State, not the consent of the undifferentiated people of the Nation as a whole.

The ratification procedure erected by Article VII makes this point clear. The Constitution took effect once it had been ratified by the people gathered in convention in nine different States. But the Constitution went into effect only "between the States so ratifying the same," Art. VII; it did not bind the people of North Carolina until they had accepted it. In Madison's words, the popular consent upon which the Constitution's authority rests was "given by the people, not as individuals composing one entire nation, but as composing the distinct and independent States to which they respectively belong." *The Federalist* No. 39.

When they adopted the Federal Constitution, of course, the people of each State surrendered some of their authority to the United States (and hence to entities accountable to the people of other States as well as to themselves). They affirmatively deprived their States of certain powers, see, *e.g.,* Art. I, § 10, and they affirmatively conferred certain powers upon the Federal Government, see, *e.g.,* Art. I, § 8. Because the people of the several States are the only true source of power, however, the Federal Government enjoys no authority beyond what the Constitution confers: The Federal Government's powers are limited and enumerated....

In each State, the remainder of the people's powers — "the powers not delegated to the United States by the Constitution, nor prohibited by it to the States," Amdt. 10 — are either delegated to the state government or retained by the people. The Federal Constitution does not specify which of these two possibilities obtains; it is up to the various state constitutions to declare which powers the people of each State have delegated to their state government. As far as the Federal Constitution is concerned, then, the States can exercise all powers that the Constitution does not withhold from them. The Federal Government and the States thus face different default rules: Where the Constitution is silent about the exercise of a particular power — that is, where the Constitution does not speak either expressly or by necessary implication — the Federal Government lacks that power and the States enjoy it.

These basic principles are enshrined in the Tenth Amendment, which declares that all powers neither delegated to the Federal Government nor prohibited to the States "are reserved to the States respectively, or to the people." With this careful last phrase, the Amendment avoids taking any position on the division of power between the state governments and the people of the States: It is up to the people of each State to determine which "reserved" powers their state government may exercise. But the Amendment does make clear that powers reside at the state level except where the Constitution removes them from that level. All powers that the Constitution neither delegates to the Federal Government nor prohibits to the States are controlled by the people of each State ...

### B

The majority disagrees that it bears this burden. But its arguments are unpersuasive....

### 2

... Again citing Story, the majority suggests that it would be inconsistent with the notion of "national sovereignty" for the States or the people of the States to have any reserved powers over the selection of Members of Congress. The majority apparently reaches this conclusion in two steps. First, it asserts that because Congress as a whole is an institution of the National Government, the individual Members of Congress "owe primary allegiance not to the people of a State, but to the people of the Nation." Second, it concludes that because each Member of Congress has a nationwide constituency once he takes office, it would be inconsistent with the Framers' scheme to let a single State prescribe qualifications for him.

Political scientists can debate about who commands the "primary allegiance" of Members of Congress once they reach Washington. From the framing to the present, however, the *selection* of the Representatives and Senators from each State has been left entirely to the people of that State or to their state legislature. The very name "congress" suggests a coming together of representatives from distinct entities. In keeping with the complexity of our federal system, once the representatives chosen by the people of each State assemble in Congress, they form a national body and are beyond the control of the individual States until the next election. But the selection of representatives in Congress is indisputably an act of the people of each State, not some abstract people of the Nation as a whole....

In short, while the majority is correct that the Framers expected the selection process to create a "direct link" between Members of the House of Representatives and the people, the link was between the Representatives from each State and the people of that State; the people of Georgia have no say over whom the people of Massachusetts select to represent them in Congress. This arrangement must baffle the majority, whose understanding of Congress would surely fit more comfortably within a system of nationwide elections. But the fact remains that when it comes to the selection of Members of Congress, the people of each State have retained their independent political identity. As a result, there is absolutely nothing strange about the notion that the people of the States or their state legislatures possess "reserved" powers in this area....

## Note: History and Logic in the Federal Sovereignty Cases

1. The excerpts from the majority and dissenting opinions in *Term Limits* exclude extensive discussions of historical sources, including the views of the Framers and early national practice. The full opinions are worth a look in order to get a sense of how detailed the Justices' historical analysis can get when they are confronted with a difficult question to which the text fails to provide a clear answer.

2. Is there a unifying principle that runs through the decisions in these cases? At one level it is easy to describe these cases as standing for the proposition that the federal government must control how its decisions are implemented and how, more generally, it conducts its business. Thus, one might say, *Martin* stands for the proposition that Congress has the authority, via its power over federal court jurisdiction, to give the Supreme Court the ultimate word on the meaning of federal law, *McCulloch* stands for the proposition that Congress has the authority to create institutions (such as the Bank) that can operate free of state interference, and *U.S. Term Limits* stands for the proposition that the Constitution is itself the ultimate—indeed, the exclusive—source of qualifications for members of the national legislature. But that's not fully accurate. After all, *Martin* contemplates state courts deciding federal law issues in the first instance and *McCulloch* seems to have allowed the State of Maryland to impose some types of taxes on the Bank (see the last paragraph of the excerpt). Finally, as Justice Thomas notes in his *U.S. Term Limits* dissent, it is undeniable that, in some basic way, members of Congress represent the people of a particular state, and are electorally accountable only to those people. The fact of the matter is, federal operations often take the form of joint operations with states. To be sure, when push comes to shove legitimate federal interests trump state interests. What should the

implications be of that ultimate federal supremacy, given that states do retain some measure of sovereignty? In his *U.S. Term Limits* concurrence, Justice Kennedy remarked that the framers "split the atom of sovereignty." As you read the materials in this part of the book, consider the degree to which the framers' experiment in atomic fission succeeded.

# Chapter 4

# Congress's Regulatory Powers

## A. Federal Power under the Necessary and Proper Clause

Article I, Section 8, provides Congress with power to legislate on a wide variety of topics, although these materials focus primarily on its power to regulate interstate commerce. But in addition to these specific grants of power, Section 8 ends by giving Congress the power to "make all Laws which shall be necessary and proper for carrying into Execution the foregoing Powers, and all other Powers vested by this Constitution in the Government of the United States, or in any Department of Officer thereof." The "Necessary and Proper" Clause raises the possibility of federal regulatory power vastly broader than even that suggested by the enumerated grants of authority in the rest of Article I. The scope of that power was tested early in the nation's history, in *McCulloch*, part of which was excerpted in the previous Chapter, and the rest of which is excerpted immediately below. The scope of the clause has remained a matter of constitutional concern, as reflected in the second case this section discusses, *United States v. Comstock*, as well as in the 2012 case considering the constitutionality of the Affordable Care Act, *National Federation of Independent Business v. Sebelius. McCulloch* reflects a broad understanding of the Necessary and Proper Clause, a reading that remains the law today, even if *Comstock* and *National Federation* introduce notes of complexity into the analysis.

### McCulloch v. Maryland

#### 17 U.S. (4 Wheat.) 316 (1819)

[The Bank of the United States refused to pay a tax levied by Maryland against any bank that the state had not chartered. The state, in an action to collect from the Bank, asserted, among other arguments, that Congress lacked the power to charter the Bank.]

Mr. Chief Justice Marshall delivered the opinion of the Court.

In the case now to be determined, the defendant, a sovereign state, denies the obligation of a law enacted by the legislature of the Union, and the plaintiff ... contests the validity of an act which has been passed by the legislature of that state. The constitution of our country, in its most interesting and vital parts, is to be considered; the conflicting powers of the government of the Union and of its members, as marked in that constitution, are to be discussed; and an opinion given, which may essentially influence the great operations of the government. No tribunal can approach such a question without a deep sense of its importance, and of the awful responsibility involved in its decision. But it must be decided peacefully, or remain a source of hostile legislation, perhaps, of hostility of a still more serious nature; and if it is to be so decided, by this tribunal alone can the decision be made. On the Supreme Court of the United States has the constitution of our country devolved this important duty.

The first question made in the cause is, has congress power to incorporate a bank? …

The power now contested was exercised by the first Congress elected under the present constitution. The bill for incorporating the Bank of the United States did not steal upon an unsuspecting legislature, and pass unobserved. Its principle was completely understood, and was opposed with equal zeal and ability. After being resisted, first, in the fair and open field of debate, and afterwards, in the executive cabinet, with as much persevering talent as any measure has ever experienced, and being supported by arguments which convinced minds as pure and as intelligent as this country can boast, it became a law. The original act was permitted to expire; but a short experience of the embarrassments to which the refusal to revive it exposed the government, convinced those who were most prejudiced against the measure of its necessity, and induced the passage of the present law. It would require no ordinary share of intrepidity, to assert that a measure adopted under these circumstances, was a bold and plain usurpation, to which the constitution gave no countenance.

These observations belong to the cause; but they are not made under the impression, that, were the question entirely new, the law would be found irreconcilable with the constitution.

In discussing this question, the counsel for the State of Maryland have deemed it of some importance, in the construction of the constitution, to consider that instrument, not as emanating from the people, but as the act of sovereign and independent states. The powers of the general government, it has been said, are delegated by the states, who alone are truly sovereign; and must be exercised in subordination to the states, who alone possess supreme dominion.

It would be difficult to sustain this proposition. The convention which framed the constitution was indeed elected by the State legislatures. But the instrument, when it came from their hands, was a mere proposal, without obligation, or pretensions to it. It was reported to the then existing congress of the United States, with a request that it might "be submitted to a convention of delegates, chosen in each State by the people thereof, under the recommendation of its legislature, for their assent and ratification." This mode of proceeding was adopted; and by the Convention, by Congress, and by the State Legislatures, the instrument was submitted to the people. They acted upon it in the only manner in which they can act safely, effectively and wisely, on such a subject, by assembling in Convention. It is true, they assembled in their several States—and where else should they have assembled? No political dreamer was ever wild enough to think of breaking down the lines which separate the States, and of compounding the American people into one common mass. Of consequence, when they act, they act in their States. But the measures they adopt do not, on that account, cease to be the measures of the people themselves, or become the measures of the State governments.

From these Conventions, the constitution derives its whole authority. The government proceeds directly from the people; is "ordained and established," in the name of the people; and is declared to be ordained, "in order to form a more perfect union, establish justice, insure domestic tranquility, and secure the blessings of liberty to themselves and to their posterity." The assent of the States, in their sovereign capacity, is implied, in calling a Convention, and thus submitting that instrument to the people. But the people were at perfect liberty to accept or reject it; and their act was final. It required not the affirmance, and could not be negatived, by the State governments. The constitution, when thus adopted, was of complete obligation, and bound the State sovereignties.

It has been said, that the people had already surrendered all their powers to the State sovereignties, and had nothing more to give. But, surely, the question whether they may resume and modify the powers granted to government, does not remain to be settled in this country. Much more might the legitimacy of the general government be doubted, had it been created by the States. The powers delegated to the state sovereignties were to be exercised by themselves, not by a distinct and independent sovereignty, created by themselves. To the formation of a league, such as was the confederation, the State sovereignties were certainly competent. But when, "in order to form a more perfect union," it was deemed necessary to change this alliance into an effective government, possessing great and sovereign powers, and acting directly on the people, the necessity of referring it to the people, and of deriving its powers directly from them, was felt and acknowledged by all.

The government of the Union, then (whatever may be the influence of this fact on the case), is, emphatically and truly, a government of the people. In form, and in substance, it emanates from them. Its powers are granted by them, and are to be exercised directly on them, and for their benefit.

This government is acknowledged by all, to be one of enumerated powers. The principle, that it can exercise only the powers granted to it, would seem too apparent, to have required to be enforced by all those arguments, which its enlightened friends, while it was depending before the people, found it necessary to urge; that principle is now universally admitted. But the question respecting the extent of the powers actually granted, is perpetually arising, and will probably continue to arise, so long as our system shall exist.

In discussing these questions, the conflicting powers of the general and State governments must be brought into view, and the supremacy of their respective laws, when they are in opposition, must be settled.

If any one proposition could command the universal assent of mankind, we might expect it would be this—that the government of the Union, though limited in its powers, is supreme within its sphere of action. This would seem to result, necessarily, from its nature. It is the government of all; its powers are delegated by all; it represents all, and acts for all. Though any one State may be willing to control its operations, no State is willing to allow others to control them. The nation, on those subjects on which it can act, must necessarily bind its component parts. But this question is not left to mere reason: the people have, in express terms, decided it, by saying, "this constitution, and the laws of the United States, which shall be made in pursuance thereof," "shall be the supreme law of the land," and by requiring that the members of the State legislatures, and the officers of the executive and judicial departments of the States, shall take the oath of fidelity to it.

The government of the United States, then, though limited in its powers, is supreme; and its laws, when made in pursuance of the constitution, form the supreme law of the land, "anything in the constitution or laws of any State to the contrary notwithstanding."

Among the enumerated powers, we do not find that of establishing a bank or creating a corporation. But there is no phrase in the instrument which, like the articles of confederation, excludes incidental or implied powers; and which requires that everything granted shall be expressly and minutely described. Even the 10th amendment, which was framed for the purpose of quieting the excessive jealousies which had been excited, omits the word "expressly," and declares only, that the powers "not delegated to the United States, nor prohibited to the States, are reserved to the States or to the people;" thus leaving the question, whether the particular power which may become the subject of contest, has been delegated to the one government, or prohibited to the other, to depend on a fair construction of the whole instrument. The men who drew and adopted this amendment had experienced the embarrassments resulting from the insertion of this word in the articles of confederation, and probably omitted it, to avoid those embarrassments. A constitution, to contain an accurate detail of all the subdivisions of which its great powers will admit, and of all the means by which they may be carried into execution, would partake of the prolixity of a legal code, and could scarcely be embraced by the human mind. It would, probably, never be understood by the public. Its nature, therefore, requires, that only its great outlines should be marked, its important objects designated, and the minor ingredients which compose those objects, be deduced from the nature of the objects themselves. That this idea was entertained by the framers of the American constitution, is not only to be inferred from the nature of the instrument, but from the language. Why else were some of the limitations, found in the 9th section of the 1st article, introduced? It is also, in some degree, warranted, by their having omitted to use any restrictive term which might prevent its receiving a fair and just interpretation. In considering this question, then, we must never forget that it is a constitution we are expounding.

Although, among the enumerated powers of government, we do not find the word "bank" or "incorporation," we find the great powers, to lay and collect taxes; to borrow money; to regulate commerce; to declare and conduct a war; and to raise and support armies and navies. The sword and the purse, all the external relations, and no inconsiderable portion of the industry of the nation, are intrusted to its government.

It can never be pretended, that these vast powers draw after them others of inferior importance, merely because they are inferior. Such an idea can never be advanced. But it may with great reason be contended, that a government, intrusted with such ample powers, on the due execution of which the happiness and prosperity of the nation so vitally depends, must also be intrusted with ample means for their execution. The power being given, it is the interest of the nation to facilitate its execution. It can never be their interest, and cannot be presumed to have been their intention, to clog and embarrass its execution, by withholding the most appropriate means....

The government which has a right to do an act, and has imposed on it, the duty of performing that act, must, according to the *dicta*tes of reason, be allowed to select the means; and those who contend that it may not select any appropriate means, that one particular mode of effecting the object is excepted, take upon themselves the burden of establishing that exception....

[The] constitution of the United States has not left the right of Congress to employ the necessary means, for the execution of the powers conferred on the government, to general reasoning. To its enumeration of powers is added, that of making "all laws which shall be necessary and proper, for carrying into execution the foregoing powers, and all other powers vested by this constitution, in the government of the United States, or in any department thereof." ...

[The] argument on which most reliance is placed, is drawn from that peculiar language of this clause. Congress is not empowered by it to make all laws, which may have relation to the powers conferred on the government, but such only as may be "necessary and proper" for carrying them into execution. The word "necessary" is considered as controlling the whole sentence, and as limiting the right to pass laws for the execution of the granted powers, to such as are indispensable, and without which the power would be nugatory. That it excludes the choice of means, and leaves to congress, in each case, that only which is most direct and simple.

Is it true, that this is the sense in which the word "necessary" is always used? Does it always import an absolute physical necessity, so strong, that one thing to which another may be termed necessary, cannot exist without that other? We think it does not. If reference be had to its use, in the common affairs of the world, or in approved authors, we find that it frequently imports no more than that one thing is convenient, or useful, or essential to another. To employ the means necessary to an end, is generally understood as employing any means calculated to produce the end, and not as being confined to those single means, without which the end would be entirely unattainable. Such is the character of human language, that no word conveys to the mind, in all situations, one single definite idea; and nothing is more common than to use words in a figurative sense. Almost all compositions contain words, which, taken in their rigorous sense, would convey a meaning different from that which is obviously intended. It is essential to just construction, that many words which import something excessive, should be understood in a more mitigated sense—in that sense which common usage justifies. The word "necessary" is of this description. It has not a fixed character, peculiar to itself. It admits of all degrees of comparison; and is often connected with other words, which increase or diminish the impression the mind receives of the urgency it imports. A thing may be necessary, very necessary, absolutely or indispensably necessary. To no mind would the same idea be conveyed by these several phrases. The comment on the word is well illustrated by the passage cited at the bar, from the 10th section of the 1st article of the constitution. It is, we think, impossible to compare the sentence which prohibits a State from laying "imposts, or duties on imports or exports, except what may be absolutely necessary for executing its inspection laws," with that which authorizes congress "to make all laws which shall be necessary and proper for carrying into execution" the powers of the general government, without feeling a conviction, that the convention understood itself to change materially the meaning of the word "necessary," by prefixing the word "absolutely." This word, then, like others, is used in various senses; and, in its construction, the subject, the context, the intention of the person using them, are all to be taken into view.

Let this be done in the case under consideration. The subject is the execution of those great powers on which the welfare of a nation essentially depends. It must have been the intention of those who gave these powers, to insure, as far as human prudence could insure, their beneficial execution. This could not be done, by confiding the choice of means to such narrow limits as not to leave it in the power of Congress to adopt any which might be appropriate, and which were conducive to the end. This provision is made in a constitution, intended to endure for ages to come, and consequently, to be adapted to the various crises of human affairs. To have prescribed the means by which government should, in all future time, execute its powers, would have been to change, entirely, the character of the instrument, and give it the properties of a legal code. It would have been an unwise attempt to provide, by immutable rules, for exigencies which, if foreseen at all, must have been seen dimly, and which can be best provided for as they occur. To have declared, that the best means shall not be used, but those alone, without which the power given would be nugatory, would have been to deprive the legislature of the capacity to avail itself of experience, to exercise its reason, and to accommodate its legislation to circumstances. If we apply this principle of construction to any of the powers of the government, we shall find it so pernicious in its operation that we shall be compelled to discard it. The powers vested in congress may certainly be carried into execution, without prescribing an oath of office. The power to exact this security for the faithful performance of duty, is not given, nor is it indispensably necessary. . . .

Take, for example, the power "to establish post-offices and post-roads." This power is executed, by the single act of making the establishment. But, from this has been inferred the power and duty of carrying the mail along the post-road, from one post-office to another. And from this implied power, has again been inferred the right to punish those who steal letters from the post-office, or rob the mail. It may be said, with some plausibility, that the right to carry the mail, and to punish those who rob it, is not indispensably necessary to the establishment of a post-office and post-road. This right is indeed essential to the beneficial exercise of the power, but not indispensably necessary to its existence. So, of the punishment of the crimes of stealing or falsifying a record or process of a Court of the United States, or of perjury in such Court. To punish these offences, is certainly conducive to the due administration of justice. But courts may exist, and may decide the causes brought before them, though such crimes escape punishment....

In ascertaining the sense in which the word "necessary" is used in this clause of the constitution, we may derive some aid from that with which it is associated. Congress shall have power "to make all laws which shall be necessary and proper to carry into execution" the powers of the government. If the word "necessary" was used in that strict and rigorous sense for which the counsel for the State of Maryland contend, it would be an extraordinary departure from the usual course of the human mind, as exhibited in composition, to add a word, the only possible effect of which is, to qualify that strict and rigorous meaning; to present to the mind the idea of some choice of means of legislation, not strained and compressed within the narrow limits for which gentlemen contend.

But the argument which most conclusively demonstrates the error of the construction contended for by the counsel for the State of Maryland, is founded on the intention of the Convention, as manifested in the whole clause. To waste time and argument in proving that, without it, Congress might carry its powers into execution, would be not much less idle, than to hold a lighted taper to the sun. As little can it be required to prove, that in the absence of this clause, Congress would have some choice of means. That it might employ those which, in its judgment, would most advantageously effect the object to be accomplished. That any means adapted to the end, any means which tended directly to the execution of the constitutional powers of the government, were in themselves constitutional. This clause, as construed by the State of Maryland, would abridge, and almost annihilate, this useful and necessary right of the legislature to select its means. That this could not be intended, is, we should think, had it not been already controverted, too apparent for controversy. We think so for the following reasons:

1st. The clause is placed among the powers of Congress, not among the limitations on those powers.

2nd. Its terms purport to enlarge, not to diminish the powers vested in the government. It purports to be an additional power, not a restriction on those already granted. No reason has been, or can be assigned, for thus concealing an intention to narrow the discretion of the national legislature, under words which purport to enlarge it. The framers of the constitution wished its adoption, and well knew that it would be endangered by its strength, not by its weakness. Had they been capable of using language which would convey to the eye one idea, and, after deep reflection, impress on the mind, another, they would rather have disguised the grant of power, than its limitation. If, then, their intention had been, by this clause, to restrain the free use of means which might otherwise have been implied, that intention would have been inserted in another place, and would have been expressed in terms resembling these. "In carrying into execution the foregoing powers, and all others," &c., "no laws shall be passed but such as are necessary and proper." Had the intention been to make this clause restrictive, it would unquestionably have been so in form as well as in effect.

The result of the most careful and attentive consideration bestowed upon this clause is, that if it does not enlarge, it cannot be construed to restrain the powers of congress, or to impair the right of the legislature to exercise its best judgment in the selection of measures to carry into execution the constitutional powers of the government. If no other motive for its insertion can be suggested, a sufficient one is found in the desire to remove all doubts respecting the right to legislate on that vast mass of incidental powers which must be involved in the constitution, if that instrument be not a splendid bauble.

We admit, as all must admit, that the powers of the government are limited, and that its limits are not to be transcended. But we think the sound construction of the constitution must allow to the national legislature that discretion, with respect to the means by which the powers it confers are to be carried into execution, which will enable that body to perform the high duties assigned to it, in the manner most beneficial to the people. Let the end be legitimate, let it be within the scope of the constitution, and all means which are appropriate, which are plainly adapted to that end, which are not prohibited, but consist with the letter and spirit of the constitution, are constitutional....

... Should congress, in the execution of its powers, adopt measures which are prohibited by the constitution; or should congress, under the pretext of executing its powers, pass laws for the accomplishment of objects not intrusted to the government; it would become the painful duty of this tribunal, should a case requiring such a decision come before it, to say, that such an act was not the law of the land. But where the law is not prohibited, and is really calculated to effect any of the objects intrusted to the government, to undertake here to inquire into the decree of its necessity, would be to pass the line which circumscribes the judicial department, and to tread on legislative ground. This court disclaims all pretensions to such a power.

After this declaration, it can scarcely be necessary to say, that the existence of State banks can have no possible influence on the question. No trace is to be found in the constitution, of an intention to create a dependence of the government of the Union on those of the States, for the execution of the great powers assigned to it. Its means are adequate to its ends; and on those means alone was it expected to rely for the accomplishment of its ends. To impose on it the necessity of resorting to means which it cannot control, which another government may furnish or withhold, would render its course precarious, the result of its measures uncertain, and create a dependence on other governments, which might disappoint its most important designs, and is incompatible with the language of the constitution. But were it otherwise, the choice of means implies a right to choose a national bank in preference to State banks, and Congress alone can make the election.

After the most deliberate consideration, it is the unanimous and decided opinion of this Court, that the act to incorporate the Bank of the United States is a law made in pursuance of the constitution, and is a part of the supreme law of the land....

It being the opinion of the court, that the act incorporating the bank is constitutional; and that the power of establishing a branch in the state of Maryland might be properly exercised by the bank itself, we proceed to inquire—

2. Whether the State of Maryland may, without violating the constitution, tax that branch? [This part of the opinion is excerpted in the previous chapter.]

## Note: Modern Applications of the Necessary and Proper Clause

1. As you will see later in this chapter, from the late 1930s to the 1990s, the Court allowed Congress exceptionally broad latitude to use its Article I powers, including its power under the Commerce and Necessary and Proper Clauses. Starting in the early 1990s, however, the Court began reining in federal regulatory power. The Court's new skepticism of congressional power required the Court in *United States v. Comstock*, 560 U.S. 126 (2010), to engage in a complex analysis when it analyzed whether a federal statute dealing with confinement of sexually dangerous federal inmates beyond their release date was appropriate legislation under the Necessary and Proper Clause. It also led the Court to hold that that clause did not justify a crucial part of the Affordable Care Act, enacted in 2010.

2. The decision in *Comstock* upheld a statute authorizing the Department of Justice to detain mentally ill, sexually dangerous federal prisoners beyond their release dates. By a 7–2 vote, the Court upheld the law. Writing for five justices, Justice Breyer concluded that five factors authorized the law as necessary and proper to enumerated federal powers. First, he noted that the Necessary and Proper Clause "grants Congress broad authority to enact federal legislation," subject to judicial review only to determine "whether the statute constitutes a means that is rationally related to the implementation of a constitutionally enumerated power." Second, he concluded that the challenged statute constituted only a "modest addition" to the existing federal scheme regulating prison mental-health issues. Third, he concluded that Congress acted reasonably in extending that federal scheme. Fourth, he noted that the statute accounted for state interests, for example, by requiring that the home state of the prisoner be notified of the federal intention to hold the inmate, and that under the law the Attorney General must "encourage those States to assume custody of the individual." Finally, he concluded that the links between the statute and the enumerated Article I power were "not too attenuated."

3. Justices Kennedy and Alito each concurred separately in the result, but not in Justice Breyer's reasoning. Justice Kennedy expressed concern, among other things, with the majority's use of the so-called "rational basis" standard, which he suggested was inappropriately deferential. (In this context, the "rational basis" standard requires simply that government have a "rational basis" for concluding that the challenged action is necessary or proper to the accomplishment of one of the more specific regulatory powers Article I provides Congress.) Nevertheless, he agreed that the federal government, having acted to incarcerate an inmate for a long period far from his home, had a duty to act to ensure that his impending release did not endanger the state of his incarceration. Justice Alito wrote separately to explain his agreement with

the dissent that the Necessary and Proper Clause empowered Congress "to enact only those laws that carry into Execution one or more of the federal powers enumerated in the Constitution." But he concluded that, just as the federal government had the power to re-capture escaped federal prisoners, it also had the power to commit prisoners "who would otherwise escape civil commitment as a result of federal imprisonment."

4. Justice Thomas, joined in relevant part by Justice Scalia, dissented. He argued that the Necessary and Proper Clause only gave Congress the power to enact a law directly authorized by a specific Article I power. He concluded that there was no specific enumerated power that served as an adequate predicate for the challenged federal law; thus, he would have struck the law down.

5. In 2010 Congress enacted the Affordable Care Act, vastly reorganizing the insurance market in the United States. One of the law's key provisions was a requirement that most Americans obtain health insurance. In 2012, a five justice majority concluded that the so-called "individual mandate" exceeded Congress's powers under the Commerce Clause and the Necessary and Proper Clause. Because the Court's analysis of the Necessary and Proper Clause requires an understanding of the Court's Commerce Clause jurisprudence, discussion of this issue is postponed until the latter part of the following section, which traces the evolution of the Court's Commerce Clause jurisprudence.

## B. Federal Power to Regulate Interstate Commerce

Article I, Section 8 explicitly gives Congress the power to regulate commerce "among" the several states. The decision to vest this power in the federal government was not taken lightly. Leaders of the framing generation understood the lack of a central authority over interstate commerce to be a major failing of the government established by the Articles of Confederation. Under that regime, the states used their powers to protect their own economies at the expense of their neighbors, and it was generally thought that the resulting regulatory conflicts harmed the new nation's domestic economy and standing abroad. As the 1780s wore on, many began to call for a convention to amend the Articles. This convention, which convened in 1786, was supposed to propose amendments giving the national government increased power over commerce. But the delegates quickly realized that more drastic change was needed and called for a second convention to make more sweeping changes. This second convention, which ultimately became known as the Constitutional Convention, produced our present Constitution.

Under the Constitution, Congress was specifically given the power "to regulate commerce with foreign nations, and among the several states, and with the Indian Tribes." The "Interstate Commerce power" has become an immensely important tool for Congress, allowing it to enact a wide variety of regulations, including environmental laws, securities laws, and health and safety laws.

As you will see, after early statements suggesting that the Interstate Commerce power was quite broad, the Supreme Court in the late nineteenth and early twentieth centuries embraced a more limited reading of the power. Beginning in 1937 the Court again read the Interstate Commerce power quite broadly, leading many observers to wonder whether there was anything Congress could *not* regulate under that grant of authority. In 1995 the Court answered that question, striking down, for the first time since 1937, a federal law for exceeding congressional regulatory power. Since then the Court's jurisprudence has reflected a divided Court, making the modern scope of the power unclear, if still generally broad.

The historical nature of the book's presentation of this material is not for purely academic purposes. Understanding the modern law of the Interstate Commerce power requires a student to understand what came before. As you will see, current doctrine includes aspects of all the major historical periods reflected in the reading.

## 1. Seminal Principles and Early Doctrinal Development

### Gibbons v. Ogden

#### 22 U.S. (9 Wheat.) 1 (1824)

[The New York Legislature enacted a statute giving Robert Livingston and Robert Fulton the exclusive right to operate steamboats in New York waters. The license was enforced by strict penalties. Thereafter, Livingston and Fulton granted Aaron Ogden a license to operate a ferry between New York City and various points in New Jersey.

Under an act of Congress, Thomas Gibbons obtained a license to navigate steamboats in the same waters. When Gibbons began operating two competing steamboats, Ogden sought and obtained an injunction prohibiting the steamboats from operating in the State of New York. When the injunction was affirmed by the New York courts, Gibbons appealed to the U.S. Supreme Court.]

Mr. Chief Justice Marshall delivered the opinion of the Court....

The appellant contends that this decree is erroneous, because the laws which purport to give the exclusive privilege it sustains, are repugnant to ... that clause in the constitution which authorizes Congress to regulate commerce.... The words are, "Congress shall have power to regulate commerce with foreign nations, and among the several States, and with the Indian tribes." ...

If commerce does not include navigation, the government of the Union has no direct power over that subject, and can make no law prescribing what shall constitute American vessels, or requiring that they shall be navigated by American seamen. Yet this power has been exercised from the commencement of the government, has been exercised with the consent of all, and has been understood by all to be a commercial regulation. All America understands, and has uniformly understood, the word "commerce," to comprehend navigation....

The word used in the constitution, then, comprehends, and has been always understood to comprehend, navigation within its meaning; and a power to regulate navigation, is as expressly granted, as if that term had been added to the word "commerce."

To what commerce does this power extend? The constitution informs us, to commerce "with foreign nations, and among the several States, and with the Indian tribes." ...

The subject to which the power is next applied, is to commerce "among the several States." The word "among" means intermingled with. A thing which is among others, is intermingled with them. Commerce among the States, cannot stop at the external boundary line of each State, but may be introduced into the interior.

It is not intended to say that these words comprehend that commerce, which is completely internal, which is carried on between man and man in a State, or between different parts of the same State, and which does not extend to or affect other States. Such a power would be inconvenient, and is certainly unnecessary.

Comprehensive as the word "among" is, it may very properly be restricted to that commerce which concerns more States than one. The phrase is not one which would probably have been selected to indicate the completely interior traffic of a State, because it is not an apt phrase for that purpose; and the enumeration of the particular classes of commerce, to which the power was to be extended, would not have been made, had the intention been to extend the power to every description. The enumeration presupposes something not enumerated; and that something, if we regard the language or the subject of the sentence, must be the exclusively internal commerce of a State. The genius and character of the whole government seem to be, that its action is to be applied to all the external concerns of the nation, and to those internal concerns which affect the States generally; but not to those which are completely within a particular State, which do not affect other States, and with which it is not necessary to interfere, for the purpose of executing some of the general powers of the government. The completely internal commerce of a State, then, may be considered as reserved for the State itself.

But, in regulating commerce with foreign nations, the power of Congress does not stop at the jurisdictional lines of the several States. It would be a very useless power, if it could not pass those lines. The commerce of the United States with foreign nations, is that of the whole United States. Every district has a right to participate in it. The deep streams which penetrate our country in every direction, pass through the interior of almost every State in the Union, and furnish the means of exercising this right. If Congress has the power to regulate it, that power must be exercised whenever the subject exists. If it exists within the States, if a foreign voyage may commence or terminate at a port within a State, then the power of Congress may be exercised within a State.

This principle is, if possible, still more clear, when applied to commerce "among the several States." They either join each other, in which case they are separated by a mathematical line, or they are remote from each other, in which case other States lie between them. What is commerce "among" them; and how is it to be conducted? Can a trading expedition between two adjoining States, commence and terminate outside of each? And if the trading intercourse be between two States remote from each other, must it not commence in one, terminate in the other, and probably pass through a third? Commerce among the States must, of necessity, be commerce with the States. In the regulation of trade with the Indian tribes, the action of the law, especially when the constitution was made, was chiefly within a State. The power of Congress, then, whatever it may be, must be exercised within the territorial jurisdiction of the several States. The sense of the nation on this subject, is unequivocally manifested by the provisions made in the laws for transporting goods, by land, between Baltimore and Providence, between New York and Philadelphia, and between Philadelphia and Baltimore.

We are now arrived at the inquiry—What is this power?

It is the power to regulate; that is, to prescribe the rule by which commerce is to be governed. This power, like all others vested in Congress, is complete in itself, may be exercised to its utmost extent, and acknowledges no limitations, other than are prescribed in the constitution. These are expressed in plain terms, and do not affect the questions which arise in this case, or which have been discussed at the bar. If, as has always been understood, the sovereignty of Congress, though limited to specified objects, is plenary as to those objects, the power over commerce with foreign nations, and among the several States, is vested in Congress as absolutely as it would be in a single government, having in its constitution the same restrictions on the exercise of the power as are found in the constitution of the United States. The wisdom and the discretion of Congress, their identity with the people, and the influence which their constituents possess at elections, are, in this, as in many other instances, as that, for example, of declaring war, the sole restraints on which they have relied, to secure them from its abuse. They are the restraints on which the people must often rely solely, in all representative governments.

The power of Congress, then, comprehends navigation, within the limits of every State in the Union; so far as that navigation may be, in any manner, connected with "commerce with foreign nations, or among the several States, or with the Indian tribes." It may, of consequence, pass the jurisdictional line of New York, and act upon the very waters to which the prohibition now under consideration applies.

But it has been urged with great earnestness, that, although the power of Congress to regulate commerce with foreign nations, and among the several States, be co-extensive with the subject itself, and have no other limits than are prescribed in the constitution, yet the States may severally exercise the same power, within their respective jurisdictions. In support of this argument, it is said, that they possessed it as an inseparable attribute of sovereignty, before the formation of the constitution, and still retain it, except so far as they have surrendered it by that instrument; that this principle results from the nature of the government, and is secured by the tenth amendment; that an affirmative grant of power is not exclusive, unless in its own nature it be such that the continued exercise of it by the former possessor is inconsistent with the grant, and that this is not of that description....

The grant of the power to lay and collect taxes is, like the power to regulate commerce, made in general terms, and has never been understood to interfere with the exercise of the same power by the State; and hence has been drawn an argument which has been applied to the question under consideration. But the two grants are not, it is conceived, similar in their terms or their nature. Although many of the powers formerly exercised by the States, are transferred to the government of the Union, yet the State governments remain, and constitute a most important part of our system. The power of taxation is indispensable to their existence, and is a power which, in its own nature, is capable of residing in, and being exercised by, different authorities at the same time....

But the inspection laws are said to be regulations of commerce, and are certainly recognized in the constitution, as being passed in the exercise of a power remaining with the States.

That inspection laws may have a remote and considerable influence on commerce, will not be denied; but that a power to regulate commerce is the source from which the right to pass them is derived, cannot be admitted. The object of inspection laws, is to improve the quality of articles produced by the labour of a country; to fit them for exportation; or, it may be, for domestic use. They act upon the subject before it becomes an article of foreign commerce, or of commerce among the States, and prepare it for that purpose. They form a portion of that immense mass of legislation, which embraces every thing within the territory of a State, not surrendered to the general government: all which can be most advantageously exercised by the States themselves. Inspection laws, quarantine laws, health laws of every description, as well as laws for regulating the internal commerce of a State, and those which respect turnpike roads, ferries, &c., are component parts of this mass.

No direct general power over these objects is granted to Congress; and, consequently, they remain subject to State legislation. If the legislative power of the Union can reach them, it must be for national purposes; it must be where the power is expressly given for a special purpose, or is clearly incidental to some power which is expressly given....

It has been contended by the counsel for the appellant, that, as the word "to regulate" implies in its nature, full power over the thing to be regulated, it excludes, necessarily, the action of all others that would perform the same operation on the same thing. That regulation is designed for the entire result, applying to those parts which remain as they were, as well as to those which are altered. It produces a uniform whole, which is as much disturbed and deranged by changing what the regulating power designs to leave untouched, as that on which it has operated.

There is great force in this argument, and the Court is not satisfied that it has been refuted....

Since, however, in exercising the power of regulating their own purely internal affairs ... the States may sometimes enact laws, the validity of which depends on their interfering with, and being contrary to, an act of Congress passed in pursuance of the constitution, the Court will enter upon the inquiry, whether the laws of New-York, as expounded by the highest tribunal of that State, have, in their application to this case, come into collision with an act of Congress, and deprived a citizen of a right to which that act entitles him. Should this collision exist, it will be immaterial whether those laws were passed in virtue of a concurrent power 'to regulate commerce with foreign nations and among the several States,' or, in virtue of a power to regulate their domestic trade and police. In one case and the other, the acts of New-York must yield to the law of Congress; and the decision sustaining the privilege they confer, against a right given by a law of the Union, must be erroneous....

[The] framers of our constitution foresaw [the possibility that state and federal laws may conflict], and provided for it, by declaring the supremacy not only of itself, but of the laws made in pursuance of it.... The appropriate application of that part of the clause which confers the same supremacy on laws and treaties, is to such acts of the State Legislatures as do not transcend their powers, but, though enacted in the execution of acknowledged State powers, interfere with, or are contrary to the laws of Congress, made in pursuance of the constitution, or some treaty made under the authority of the United States. In every such case, the act of Congress, or the treaty, is supreme; and the law of the State, though enacted in the exercise of powers not controverted, must yield to it....

[The federal coasting license statute] demonstrates the opinion of Congress, that steam boats may be enrolled and licensed, in common with vessels using sails. They are, of course, entitled to the same privileges, and can no more be restrained from navigating waters, and entering ports which are free to such vessels, than if they were wafted on their voyage by the winds, instead of being propelled by the agency of fire. The one element may be as legitimately used as the other, for every commercial purpose authorized by the laws of the Union; and the act of a State inhibiting the use of either to any vessel having a license under the act of Congress, comes, we think, in direct collision with that act.

As this decides the cause, it is unnecessary to enter in an examination of that part of the constitution which empowers Congress to promote the progress of science and the useful arts....

### Note: State Laws and the Development of Commerce Clause Doctrine in the Nineteenth Century

For most of the nineteenth century, questions about the scope of the Interstate Commerce power were largely posed in the context, not of federal laws, but state laws. This may seem counter-intuitive, since the Commerce Clause is a grant of power to Congress. But remember that in *Gibbons* Chief Justice Marshall speculated that the Constitution vested this power exclusively in Congress, to the exclusion of the states. Thus, the way was open for parties seeking to invalidate a state law to argue that the law was an invalid attempt by the state to exercise the interstate commerce power that was exclusively vested in Congress. (In the modern era, such arguments come under the doctrinal heading of the "dormant Commerce Clause"; you will consider that doctrine in Chapter 5. In the nineteenth century these doctrines were not as cleanly divided.)

This type of argument provided most of the opportunities for the Supreme Court to pass on the scope of the Interstate Commerce power in the nineteenth century. Congress, while not completely passive during this time, did not regulate economic and commercial matters as frequently and comprehensively as it does today. Instead, most economic and commercial regulation emanated from states. The combination of *Gibbons'* suggestion of exclusive federal power and the fact that states were the primary regulators of the nineteenth century marketplace meant that the scope of the Interstate Commerce power was fleshed out in decisions reviewing state laws that were alleged to be unconstitutional attempts by states to regulate interstate commerce.

An influential example of the Court's response to such laws is set forth in *Kidd v. Pearson*, 128 U.S. 1 (1888). In *Kidd*, an Iowa manufacturer of liquor destined solely for export out of the state challenged a state law that severely restricted the manufacture of liquor. He alleged that, as applied to him (an exporter), the Iowa law effectively regulated interstate commerce in liquor and thus was unconstitutional.

The Court upheld the Iowa law. In an influential passage that was frequently cited in later cases considering challenges to *federal* legislation, the Court concluded that the regulation of manufacturing did not constitute a regulation of interstate commerce:

> No distinction is more popular to the common mind, or more clearly expressed in economic and political literature, than that between manufactures and commerce. Manufacture is transformation—the fashioning of raw materials into a change of form for use. The functions of commerce are different. The buying and selling and the transportation incidental thereto constitute commerce; and the regulation of commerce in the constitutional sense embraces the regulation at least of such transportation. The legal definition of the term, as given by this court in *County of Mobile v. Kimball*, 102 U.S. 691 (1880), is as follows: 'Commerce with foreign countries and among the states, strictly considered, consists in intercourse and traffic, including in these terms navigation and the transportation and transit of persons and property, as well as the purchase, sale, and exchange of commodities.' If it be held that the term includes the regulation of all such manufactures as are intended to be the subject of commercial transactions in the future, it is impossible to deny that it would also include all productive industries that contemplate the same thing. The result would be that congress would be invested, to the exclusion of the states, with the power to regulate, not only manufacture, but also agriculture, horticulture, stock-raising, domestic fisheries, mining—in short, every branch of human industry. For is there one of them that does not contemplate, more or less clearly, an interstate or foreign market? Does not the wheat-grower of the northwest, and the cotton-planter of the south, plant, cultivate, and harvest his crop with an eye on the prices at Liverpool, New York, and Chicago? The power being vested in congress and denied to the states, it would follow as an inevitable result that the duty would devolve on congress to regulate all of these delicate, multiform, and vital interests—interests which in their nature are, and must be, local in all the details of their successful management....
>
> ... It is true that, notwithstanding [the Iowa law's] purposes and ends are restricted to the jurisdictional limits of the state of Iowa, and apply to transactions wholly internal and between its own citizens, its effects may reach

beyond the state, by lessening the amount of intoxicating liquors exported. But it does not follow that, because the products of a domestic manufacture may ultimately become the subjects of interstate commerce, at the pleasure of the manufacturer, the legislation of the state respecting such manufacture is an attempted exercise of the power to regulate commerce exclusively conferred upon congress.

As you will see, the concerns expressed in *Kidd* would find their way into the Court's evaluation of *federal* legislation, once Congress began using its Interstate Commerce power in earnest.

## 2. Increased Federal Regulation — and Judicial Resistance

When the Constitution was ratified, the United States was a largely agrarian society. By the end of the nineteenth century, the economy was in a period of dramatic transition. Industrialization produced profound changes in the American economy. Developments in transportation (the railroad), communication (the telegraph and then telephone) and industrial organization (the modern large corporation) created conditions in which people and goods began moving across state lines in unprecedented numbers. This movement meant that many commercial problems which had formerly been local in nature were increasingly becoming national problems. As a result, Congress began to assume a more active regulatory role. In 1887 it enacted the Interstate Commerce Act, regulating railroads. In 1890 it enacted the Sherman Antitrust Act. More federal regulatory laws followed.

Congress's more aggressive posture forced the Court to confront difficult questions regarding the scope of Congress's power. It did so in several cases decided early in this period. In considering those questions, older doctrine concerning both federal and state regulatory power, as explained in the previous Note, played an important role. Some of the foundational cases considering this new federal regulation dealt with application of the Sherman Act. The following two cases reflect the difficulties the Court had in reaching stable results consistent with precedent.

### United States v. E.C. Knight Co.
#### 156 U.S. 1 (1895)

Mr. Chief Justice FULLER ... delivered the opinion of the court.

By the purchase of the stock of the four Philadelphia refineries with shares of its own stock the American Sugar Refining Company acquired nearly complete control of the manufacture of refined sugar within the United States. The bill [of indictment] charged that the contracts under which these purchases were made constituted combinations in restraint of trade, and that in entering into them the defendants combined and conspired to restrain the trade and commerce in refined sugar among the several states and with foreign nations, contrary to the [Sherman Antitrust Act, which prohibits "every ... combination ... or conspiracy of trade and commerce among the several states"]....

The fundamental question is whether, conceding that the existence of a monopoly in manufacture is established by the evidence, that monopoly can be directly suppressed under the act of congress in the mode attempted by this bill.

It cannot be denied that the power of a state to protect the lives, health, and property of its citizens, and to preserve good order and the public morals, 'the power to govern men and things within the limits of its dominion,' is a power originally and always belonging to the states, not surrendered by them to the general government, nor directly restrained by the constitution of the United States, and essentially exclusive. The relief of the citizens of each state from the burden of monopoly and the evils resulting from the restraint of trade among such citizens was left with the states to deal with.... On the other hand, the power of congress to regulate commerce among the several states is also exclusive. The constitution does not provide that interstate commerce shall be free, but, by the grant of this exclusive power to regulate it, it was left free, except as congress might impose restraints. Therefore it has been determined that the failure of congress to exercise this exclusive power in any case is an expression of its will that the subject shall be free from restrictions or impositions upon it by the several states.... 'Commerce undoubtedly is traffic,' said Chief Justice Marshall, 'but it is something more; it is intercourse. It describes the commercial intercourse between nations and parts of nations in all its branches, and is regulated by prescribing rules for carrying on that intercourse.' That which belongs to commerce is within the jurisdiction of the United States, but that which does not belong to commerce is within the jurisdiction of the police power of the state. *Gibbons v. Ogden* (1824) [*Supra.* this chapter].

The argument is that the power to control the manufacture of refined sugar is a monopoly over a necessary of life, to the enjoyment of which by a large part of the population of the United States interstate commerce is indispensable, and that, therefore, the general government, in the exercise of the power to regulate commerce, may repress such monopoly directly.... But this argument cannot be confined to necessaries of life merely, and must include all articles of general consumption. Doubtless the power to control the manufacture of a given thing involves, in a certain sense, the control of its disposition, but this is a secondary, and not the primary, sense; and, although the exercise of that power may result in bringing the operation of commerce into play, it does not control it, and affects it only incidentally and indirectly. Commerce succeeds to manufacture, and is not a part of it. The power to regulate commerce is the power to prescribe the rule by which commerce shall be governed, and is a power independent of the power to suppress monopoly. But it may operate in repression of monopoly whenever that comes within the rules by which commerce is governed, or whenever the transaction is itself a monopoly of commerce.

It is vital that the independence of the commercial power and of the police power, and the delimitation between them, however sometimes perplexing, should always be recognized and observed, for, while the one furnishes the strongest bond of union, the other is essential to the preservation of the autonomy of the states as required by our dual form of government; and acknowledged evils, however grave and urgent they may appear to be, had better be borne, than the risk be run, in the effort to suppress them, of more serious consequences by resort to expedients of even doubtful constitutionality.

It will be perceived how far-reaching the proposition is that the power of dealing with a monopoly directly may be exercised by the general government whenever interstate or international commerce may be ultimately affected. The regulation of commerce applies to the subjects of commerce, and not to matters of internal police. Contracts to buy, sell, or exchange goods to be transported among the several states, the transportation and its instrumentalities, and articles bought, sold, or exchanged for the purposes of such transit among the states, or put in the way of transit, may be regulated; but this is because they form part of interstate trade or commerce. The fact that an article is manufactured for export to another state does not of itself make it an article of interstate commerce, and the intent of the manufacturer does not determine the time when the article or product passes from the control of the state and belongs to commerce....

[In] *Kidd v. Pearson*, 128 U.S. 1 (1888) [Note *supra.* this chapter], where the question was discussed whether the right of a state to enact a statute prohibiting within its limits the manufacture of intoxicating liquors, except for certain purposes, could be overthrown by the fact that the manufacturer intended to export the liquors when made, it was held that the intent of the manufacturer did not determine the time when the article or product passed from the control of the state and belonged to commerce, and that, therefore, the statute, in omitting to except from its operation the manufacture of intoxicating liquors within the limits of the state for export, did not constitute an unauthorized interference with the right of congress to regulate commerce. And Mr. Justice Lamar remarked: 'No distinction is more popular to the common mind, or more clearly expressed in economic and political literature, than that between manufacture and commerce. Manufacture is transformation—the fashioning of raw materials into a change of form for use. The functions of commerce are different. The buying and selling, and the transportation incidental thereto, constitute commerce; and the regulation of commerce in the constitutional sense embraces the regulation at least of such transportation. * * * If it be held that the term includes the regulation of all such manufactures as are intended to be the subject of commercial transactions in the future, it is impossible to deny that it would also include all productive industries that contemplate the same thing. The result would be that congress would be invested, to the exclusion of the states, with the power to regulate, not only manufactures, but also agriculture, horticulture, stock-raising, domestic fisheries, mining; in short, every branch of human industry. For is there one of them that does not contemplate, more or less clearly, an interstate or foreign market? Does not the wheat grower of the Northwest, and the cotton planter of the South, plant, cultivate, and harvest his crop with an eye on the prices at Liverpool, New York, and Chicago? The power being vested in congress and denied to the states, it would follow as an inevitable result that the duty would devolve on congress to regulate all of these delicate, multiform, and vital interests—interests which in their nature are, and must be, local in all the details of their successful management. * * * The demands of such supervision would require, not uniform legislation generally applicable throughout the United States, but a swarm of statutes only locally applicable, and utterly inconsistent. Any movement towards the establishment of rules of production in this vast country, with its many different climates and opportunities, would only be at the sacrifice of the peculiar advantages of a large part of the localities in it, if not of every one of them. On the other hand, any movement towards the local, detailed, and incongruous legislation required by such interpretation would be about the widest possible departure from the declared object of the clause in question. Nor this alone. Even in the exercise of the power contended for, congress would be confined to the regulation, not of certain branches of industry, however numerous, but to those instances in each and every branch where the producer contemplated an interstate market. These instances would be almost infinite, as we have seen; but still there would always remain the possibility, and often it would be the case, that the producer contemplated a domestic market. In that case the supervisory power must be executed by the state; and the interminable trouble would be presented that whether the one power or the other should exercise the authority in question would be determined, not by any general or intelligible rule, but by the secret and changeable intention of the producer in each and every act of production. A situation more paralyzing to the state governments, and more provocative of conflicts between the general government and the states, and less likely to have been what the framers of the constitution intended, it would be difficult to imagine.'

In *Gibbons v. Ogden* ... and other cases often cited, the state laws, which were held inoperative, were instances of direct interference with, or regulations of, interstate or international commerce; yet in *Kidd v. Pearson* the refusal of a state to allow articles to be manufactured within her borders, even for export, was held not to directly affect external commerce; and state legislation which, in a great variety of ways, affected interstate commerce and persons engaged in it, has been frequently sustained because the interference was not direct.

Contracts, combinations, or conspiracies to control domestic enterprise in manufacture, agriculture, mining, production in all its forms, or to raise or lower prices or wages, might unquestionably tend to restrain external as well as domestic trade, but the restraint would be an indirect result, however inevitable, and whatever its extent, and such result would not necessarily determine the object of the contract, combination, or conspiracy....

... Slight reflection will show that, if the national power extends to all contracts and combinations in manufacture, agriculture, mining, and other productive industries, whose ultimate result may affect external commerce, comparatively little of business operations and affairs would be left for state control.

... Aside from the provisions applicable where congress might exercise municipal power, what the [Sherman Act] struck at was combinations, contracts, and conspiracies to monopolize trade and commerce among the several states or with foreign nations; but the contracts and acts of the defendants related exclusively to the acquisition of the Philadelphia refineries and the business of sugar refining in Pennsylvania, and bore no direct relation to commerce between the states or with foreign nations. The object was manifestly private gain in the manufacture of the commodity, but not through the control of interstate or foreign commerce....

Mr. Justice Harlan, dissenting.

... The court holds it to be vital in our system of government to recognize and give effect to both the commercial power of the nation and the police powers of the states, to the end that the Union be strengthened, and the autonomy of the states preserved. In this view I entirely concur.... But it is equally true that the preservation of the just authority of the general government is essential as well to the safety of the states as to the attainment of the important ends for which that government was ordained by the people of the United States; and the destruction of that authority would be fatal to the peace and well-being of the American people. The constitution, which enumerates the powers committed to the nation for objects of interest to the people of all the states, should not, therefore, be subjected to an interpretation so rigid, technical, and narrow that those objects cannot be accomplished. Learned counsel in *Gibbons v. Ogden*, having suggested that the constitution should be strictly construed, this court, speaking by Chief Justice Marshall, said ... 'What do gentlemen mean ... by a strict construction? ... If they contend for that narrow construction which ... would deny to the government those powers which the words of the grant, as usually understood, import, and which are consistent with the general views and objects of the instrument; for that narrow construction, which would cripple the government, and render it unequal to the objects for which it is declared to be instituted, and to which the powers given, as fairly understood, render it competent; then we cannot perceive the propriety of this strict construction, nor adopt it as the rule by which the constitution is to be expounded.' ...

What is commerce among the states? The decisions of this court fully answer the question. 'Commerce, undoubtedly, is traffic, but it is something more; it is intercourse.' It does not embrace the completely interior traffic of the respective states — that which is 'carried on between man and man in a state, or between different parts of the same state, and which does not extend to or affect other states' — but it does embrace 'every species of commercial intercourse' between the United States and foreign nations and among the states, and therefore it includes such traffic or trade, buying, selling, and interchange of commodities, as directly affects or necessarily involves the interests of the people of the United States. 'Commerce, as the word is used in the constitution, is a unit,' and 'cannot stop at the external boundary line of each state, but may be introduced into the interior.' 'The genius and character of the whole government seem to be that its action is to be applied to all the external concerns of the nation, and to those internal concerns which affect the states generally.'

These principles were announced in *Gibbons v. Ogden*, and have often been approved. It is the settled doctrine of this court that interstate commerce embraces something more than the mere physical transportation of articles of property, and the vehicles or vessels by which such transportation is effected.... In *Ferry Co. v. Pennsylvania*, 114 U.S. 196 (1885), the language of the court was: 'Commerce among the states consists of intercourse and traffic between their citizens, and includes the transportation of persons and property, and the navigation of public waters for that purpose, as well as the purchase, sale, and exchange of commodities. The power to regulate that commerce, as well as commerce with foreign nations, vested in congress, is the power to prescribe the rules by which it shall be governed—that is, the conditions upon which it shall be conducted; to determine when it shall be free, and when subject to duties or other exactions.' In *Kidd v. Pearson*, it was said that 'the buying and selling and the transportation *incidental thereto* constitute commerce.' Interstate commerce does not, therefore, consist in transportation simply. It includes the purchase and sale of articles that are intended to be transported from one state to another—every species of commercial intercourse among the states and with foreign nations.

In the light of these principles, determining as well the scope of the power to regulate commerce among the states as the nature of such commerce, we are to inquire whether the [Sherman Act] is repugnant to the constitution....

[There] is a trade among the several states which is distinct from that carried on within the territorial limits of a state. The regulation and control of the former are committed by the national constitution to congress.... Under the power with which it is invested, congress may remove unlawful obstructions, of whatever kind, to the free course of trade among the states.... Any combination, therefore, that disturbs or unreasonably obstructs freedom in buying and selling articles manufactured to be sold to persons in other states, or to be carried to other states ... affects, not incidentally, but directly, the people of all the states; and the remedy for such an evil is found only in the exercise of powers confided to a government which, this court has said, was the government of all, exercising powers delegated by all, representing all, acting for all. *McCulloch v. Maryland*, (1819) [*Supra.* this chapter]....

In *Kidd v. Pearson* we recognized, as had been done in previous cases, the distinction between the mere transportation of articles of interstate commerce and the purchasing and selling that precede transportation. It is said that manufacture precedes commerce, and is not a part of it. But it is equally true that when manufacture ends, that which has been manufactured becomes a subject of commerce; that buying and selling succeed manufacture, come into existence after the process of manufacture is completed, precede transportation, and are as much commercial intercourse, where articles are bought to be carried from one state to another, as is the manual transportation of such articles after they have been so purchased. The distinction was recognized by this court in *Gibbons v. Ogden*, where the principal question was whether commerce included navigation. Both the court and counsel recognized buying and selling or barter as included in commerce. Chief Justice Marshall said that the mind can scarcely conceive a system for regulating commerce, which was 'confined to prescribing rules for the conduct of individuals in the actual employment of buying and selling, or of barter.'...

## Swift & Co. v. United States

### 196 U.S. 375 (1905)

[Justice HOLMES delivered the opinion of the Court.]

[The federal government brought an action against major meat processors, alleging that they had violated the Sherman Antitrust Act by colluding through various means, including coordinated buying and selling of livestock at major slaughterhouses in order to manipulate prices.]

... Although the combination alleged embraces restraint and monopoly of trade within a single state, its effect upon commerce among the states is not accidental, secondary, remote, or merely probable. On the allegations of the bill the latter commerce no less, perhaps even more, than commerce within a single state, is an object of attack. Moreover, it is a direct object; it is that for the sake of which the several specific acts and courses of conduct are done and adopted. Therefore the case is not like *United States v. E. C. Knight Co.* (1895) [*Supra.* this chapter], where the subject-matter of the combination was manufacture, and the direct object monopoly of manufacture within a state. However likely monopoly of commerce among the states in the article manufactured was to follow from the agreement, it was not a necessary consequence nor a primary end. Here the subject-matter is sales, and the very point of the combination is to restrain and monopolize commerce among the states in respect to such sales. The two cases are near to each other, as sooner or later always must happen where lines are to be drawn, but the line between them is distinct.

So, again, the line is distinct between this case and *Hopkins v. United States*, 171 U.S. 578 (1898). All that was decided there was that the local business of commission merchants was not commerce among the states, even if what the brokers were employed to sell was an object of such commerce. The brokers were not like the defendants before us, themselves the buyers and sellers. They only furnished certain facilities for the sales. Therefore, there again the effects of the combination of brokers upon the commerce was only indirect, and not within the act. Whether the case would have been different if the combination had resulted in exorbitant charges was left open. In *Anderson v. United States*, 171 U.S. 604 (1898), the defendants were buyers and sellers at the stock yards, but their agreement was merely not to employ brokers, or to recognize yard-traders, who were not members of their association. Any yard-trader could become a member of the association on complying with the conditions, and there was said to be no feature of monopoly in the case. It was held that the combination did not directly regulate commerce between the states, and, being formed with a different intent, was not within the act....

For the foregoing reasons we are of opinion that the carrying out of the scheme alleged, by the means set forth, properly may be enjoined, and that the bill cannot be dismissed....

### *Note: Commerce Clause Analysis Up to 1937*

The cases excerpted above largely set the tone for the Court's treatment of Commerce Clause issues until 1937. After these early cases the Court added several doctrinal developments that complemented its general attempt to separate out the legitimate spheres for federal and state regulatory power.

1. When the activity being regulated was interstate commerce itself, the Court was generally supportive of federal regulation. For example, in *The Shreveport Rate Cases* (*Houston, East & West Texas Railway Co. v. United States*), 234 U.S. 342 (1914), the Court upheld an order of the Interstate Commerce Commission (ICC) setting rates for rail freight for trips wholly inside of Texas. The ICC justified this regulation of intrastate rail traffic on the ground that those intrastate rates (set by state authorities) unfairly undercut interstate traffic between Texas and Louisiana, which were governed by (higher) rates set by the ICC.

In a 7–2 opinion the Court upheld the ICC regulation. Writing for the Court, Chief Justice Hughes wrote as follows:

> Interstate trade was not left to be destroyed or impeded by the rivalries of local government.... [The] authority of Congress is at all times adequate ... to protect the national interest by securing the freedom of interstate commercial intercourse from local control. *Gibbons v. Ogden* (1824) [*Supra.* this chapter]....
>
> Its authority.... necessarily embraces the right to control [the operations of interstate carriers] in all matters having such a close and substantial relation to interstate traffic that the control is essential or appropriate to the security of that traffic ... and to the maintenance of conditions under which interstate commerce may be conducted upon fair terms and without molestation or hinderance....
>
> This is not to say that Congress possesses the authority to regulate the internal commerce of a state, as such, but that it does possess the power to foster and protect interstate commerce, and to take all measures necessary or appropriate to that end, although intrastate transactions of interstate carriers may thereby be controlled.

2. Other cases reflect a narrower reading of federal power, even to regulate interstate commerce itself. In *Hammer v. Dagenhart*, 247 U.S. 251 (1918), the Court considered a federal law banning the interstate shipment of items made with child labor. Even though the statute was on its face a regulation of interstate commerce (rather than, say, a regulation of manufacturing), the Court, in a 5–4 decision, concluded that the statute was an unconstitutional attempt to regulate manufacturing by "closing the channels of interstate commerce to manufacturing" in states that did not meet Congress's standards for child labor.

Thus, in *Hammer* the Court struck down an explicit regulation of interstate commerce because "its natural and reasonable effect" would be to regulate the internal affairs of a state. Justice Holmes wrote the dissent, which began as follows: "The single question in this case is whether Congress has power to prohibit the shipment in interstate or foreign commerce of any product [manufactured in violation of Congress's child labor standards]." He continued, "if an act is within the powers specifically conferred upon Congress, it seems to me that it is not made any less constitutional because of the indirect effects that it may have, however obvious it may be that it will have those effects, and that we are not at liberty upon such grounds to hold it void."

3. After the stock market crash in 1929 the nation entered the Great Depression, which in turn helped spur the election of Franklin D. Roosevelt in 1932. Roosevelt gained ratification of most of his "New Deal" program, which involved unprecedented federal involvement in the national economy. Congress enacted new federal regulation of, among other things, securities markets, the agricultural sector and the energy business. Much (though not all) of this legislation was struck down by the Supreme Court, often on Commerce Clause grounds. A notable example is *Carter v. Carter Coal Co.*, 298 U.S. 238 (1936), which struck down the Bituminous Coal Conservation Act of 1935. Among other things, the statute regulated the price of coal (to prevent market disruptions and price collapses caused by over-competition) and the working conditions in coal mines (to prevent strikes that, given the importance of coal as an energy source, would threaten the economy).

By a 5–4 vote, the Court struck these provisions down. Justice Sutherland wrote the opinion for the five justices in the majority. Quoting extensively from *Kidd v. Pearson* and *United States v. E.C. Knight*, he repeated the distinction between manufacturing and commerce, identifying the former as a matter purely for state regulation. He also distinguished *Swift & Co. v. United States*, describing that case as one where the regulated activity "constituted direct interferences with the 'flow' of commerce among the states." He continued, "It was nowhere suggested [in *Swift*] that the interstate commerce power extended to the growth or production of the things which, after production, entered the flow."

Justice Sutherland then considered whether coal prices and working conditions in the mines directly affected interstate commerce. He wrote as follows:

> The word 'direct' implies that the activity or condition invoked or blamed shall operate proximately—not mediately, remotely, or collaterally—to produce the effect. It connotes the absence of an efficient intervening agency or condition. And the extent of the effect bears no logical relation to its character. The distinction between a direct and an indirect effect turns, not upon the magnitude of either the cause or the effect, but entirely upon the manner in which the effect has been brought about. If the production by one man of a single ton of coal intended for interstate sale and shipment, and actually so sold and shipped, affects interstate commerce indirectly, the effect does not become direct by multiplying the tonnage, or increasing the number of men employed, or adding to the expense or complexities of the business, or by all combined. It is quite true that rules of law are sometimes qualified by considerations of degree, as the government argues. But the matter of degree has no bearing upon the question here, since that question is not—What is

the extent of the local activity or condition, or the extent of the effect produced upon interstate commerce? but—What is the relation between the activity or condition and the effect?

4. Decisions such as those in *Carter Coal*, as well as decisions striking down economic reform legislation on other constitutional grounds, provoked a great deal of public criticism. Politicians and others accused the Court of standing in the way of economic and social legislation that was needed to save the country from the Depression. This criticism was not limited to the Court's Commerce Clause jurisprudence. As you'll see in Chapter 7 (and as Justice Souter alludes to in his dissent in *United States v. Lopez*, excerpted later in this chapter), at the same time the Court was seen as obstructing *federal* regulation by a strict interpretation of the Interstate Commerce Clause it was also seen as obstructing both *state and federal* regulation by a similarly strict interpretation of the so-called "right to contract" that the Court located in the Due Process Clauses of the Fifth and Fourteenth Amendments.

After his overwhelming reelection in 1936, President Roosevelt went on the attack. Roosevelt's vehicle was the now infamous "Court Packing Plan," which would have altered the Court's membership (and, presumably, its decisions) by adding additional members to the Court. The plan provided that, when a judge or justice of any federal court reached the age of seventy without availing himself of the opportunity to retire on a pension, a new member could be appointed by the President then in office. The appointment would be made in the manner prescribed by the Constitution: nomination by the President with confirmation by the Senate. At the time, six justices were age 70 or older. If the plan had passed, the Court's membership would have expanded to 15 members, giving Roosevelt a majority of members sympathetic to his positions.

The Court Packing Plan died in Congress. Many questioned the wisdom and constitutionality of the plan, believing that it would upset the balance of powers between the three branches. The debate was effectively mooted when the Court began upholding economic legislation. On May 29, 1937, the Court upheld a minimum wage regulation against a due process "right to contract" challenge. *West Coast Hotel v. Parrish*, 300 U.S. 379 (1937) (*infra.* Chapter 7). On April 12, the Court decided the following case, which presaged a similar change of heart on the question of congressional power under the Commerce Clause.

## 3. The Evolution of Expanded Federal Power

### NLRB v. Jones & Laughlin Steel Corp.

301 U.S. 1 (1937)

Mr. Chief Justice HUGHES delivered the opinion of the Court.

In a proceeding under the National Labor Relations Act of 1935 the National Labor Relations Board found that the respondent, Jones & Laughlin Steel Corporation, had violated the act by engaging in unfair labor practices affecting commerce.... The unfair labor practices charged were that the corporation was discriminating against members of the union with regard to hire and tenure of employment, and was coercing and intimidating its employees in order to interfere with their self-organization....

The National Labor Relations Board, sustaining the charge, ordered the corporation to cease and desist from such discrimination and coercion.... As the corporation failed to comply, the Board petitioned the Circuit Court of Appeals to enforce the order. The court denied the petition holding that the order lay beyond the range of federal power. We granted certiorari.

The scheme of the National Labor Relations Act ... may be briefly stated. The first section sets forth findings with respect to the injury to commerce resulting from the denial by employers of the right of employees to organize and from the refusal of employers to accept the procedure of collective bargaining. There follows a declaration that it is the policy of the United States to eliminate these causes of obstruction to the free flow of commerce. The Act then defines the terms it uses, including the terms "commerce" and "affecting commerce." ...

The facts as to the nature and scope of the business of the Jones & Laughlin Steel Corporation ... are not in dispute. The Labor Board has found: The corporation ... is engaged in the business of manufacturing iron and steel in plants situated in Pittsburgh and nearby Aliquippa, Pa. It manufactures and distributes a widely diversified line of steel and pig iron, being the fourth largest producer of steel in the United States. With its subsidiaries—nineteen in number—it is a completely integrated enterprise, owning and operating ore, coal and limestone properties, lake and river transportation facilities and terminal railroads located at its manufacturing plants. It owns or controls mines in Michigan and Minnesota. It operates four ore steamships on the Great Lakes, used in the transportation of ore to its factories. It owns coal mines in Pennsylvania.... It owns limestone properties in various places in Pennsylvania and West Virginia. It owns the Monongahela connecting railroad which connects the plants of the Pittsburgh works and forms an interconnection with the Pennsylvania, New York Central and Baltimore & Ohio Railroad systems.... Much of its product is shipped to its warehouses in Chicago, Detroit, Cincinnati and Memphis, to the last two places by means of its own barges and transportation equipment.... It has sales offices in twenty cities in the United States and a wholly-owned subsidiary which is devoted exclusively to distributing its product in Canada. Approximately 75 per cent. of its product is shipped out of Pennsylvania.

Summarizing these operations, the Labor Board concluded that the works in Pittsburgh and Aliquippa 'might be likened to the heart of a self-contained, highly integrated body. They draw in the raw materials from Michigan, Minnesota, West Virginia, Pennsylvania in part through arteries and by means controlled by the respondent; they transform the materials and then pump them out to all parts of the nation through the vast mechanism which the respondent has elaborated.' ...

Respondent points to evidence that the Aliquippa plant, in which the discharged men were employed, contains complete facilities for the production of finished and semifinished iron and steel products from raw materials.... Respondent's operations ...

result in substantially changing the character, utility and value of the materials wrought upon, which is apparent from the nature and extent of the processes to which they are subjected and which respondent fully describes. Respondent also directs attention to the fact that the iron ore which is procured from mines in Minnesota and Michigan and transported to respondent's plant is stored in stock piles for future use, the amount of ore in storage varying with the season but usually being enough to maintain operations from nine to ten months; that the coal ... is there, like ore, stored for future use, approximately two to three months' supply of coal being always on hand; and that the limestone ... is also stored in amounts usually adequate to run the blast furnaces for a few weeks....

*First. The Scope of the Act.* — The act is challenged in its entirety as an attempt to regulate all industry, thus invading the reserved powers of the States over their local concerns.... The argument seeks support in the broad words of the preamble ... and in the sweep of the provisions of the act....

If this conception of terms, intent and consequent inseparability were sound, the act would necessarily fall by reason of the limitation upon the federal power which inheres in the constitutional grant, as well as because of the explicit reservation of the Tenth Amendment. The authority of the federal government may not be pushed to such an extreme as to destroy the distinction, which the commerce clause itself establishes, between commerce 'among the several States' and the internal concerns of a state. That distinction between what is national and what is local in the activities of commerce is vital to the maintenance of our federal system....

We think it clear that the National Labor Relations Act may be construed so as to operate within the sphere of constitutional authority.... The critical words of this provision, prescribing the limits of the Board's authority in dealing with the labor practices, are "affecting commerce." The Act specifically defines the 'commerce' to which it refers (section 2(6)):

"The term 'commerce' means trade, traffic, commerce, transportation, or communication among the several States...."

"The term 'affecting commerce' means in commerce, or burdening or obstructing commerce or the free flow of commerce, or having led or tending to lead to a labor dispute burdening or obstructing commerce or the free flow of commerce."

This definition is one of exclusion as well as inclusion.... Its terms do not impose collective bargaining upon all industry regardless of effects upon interstate or foreign commerce. It purports to reach only what may be deemed to burden or obstruct that commerce and, thus qualified, it must be construed as contemplating the exercise of control within constitutional bounds. It is a familiar principle that acts which directly burden or obstruct interstate or foreign commerce, or its free flow, are within the reach of the congressional power. Acts having that effect are not rendered immune because they grow out of labor disputes. It is the effect upon commerce, not the source of the injury, which is the criterion. We are thus to inquire whether in the instant case the constitutional boundary has been passed....

Third. The application of the Act to Employees Engaged in Production.—The Principle Involved.—Respondent says that, whatever may be said of employees engaged in interstate commerce, the industrial relations and activities in the manufacturing department of respondent's enterprise are not subject to federal regulation. The argument rests upon the proposition that manufacturing in itself is not commerce. *Kidd v. Pearson*, 128 U.S. 1 (1888) (Note *supra.* this chapter]; *Carter v. Carter Coal Co.*, 298 U.S. 238 (1936) [Both notes *supra.* this chapter].

The government distinguishes these cases. The various parts of respondent's enterprise are described as interdependent and as thus involving "a great movement of iron ore, coal and limestone along well-defined paths to the steel mills, thence through them, and thence in the form of steel products into the consuming centers of the country—a definite and well-understood course of business." It is urged that these activities constitute a "stream" or "flow" of commerce, of which the Aliquippa manufacturing plant is the focal point, and that industrial strife at that point would cripple the entire movement....

Respondent contends that the instant case presents material distinctions. Respondent says that the Aliquippa plant is extensive in size.... The finished products which emerge "are to a large extent manufactured without reference to pre-existing orders and contracts and are entirely different from the raw materials which enter at the other end." Hence respondent argues that, "If importation and exportation in interstate commerce do not singly transfer purely local activities into the field of congressional regulation, it should follow that their combination would not alter the local situation."

We do not find it necessary to determine whether these features of defendant's business dispose of the asserted analogy to the "stream of commerce" cases. The instances in which that metaphor has been used are but particular, and not exclusive, illustrations of the protective power which the government invokes in support of the present act. The congressional authority to protect interstate commerce from burdens and obstructions is not limited to transactions which can be deemed to be an essential part of a "flow" of interstate or foreign commerce. Burdens and obstructions may be due to injurious action springing from other sources. The fundamental principle is that the power to regulate commerce is the power to enact "all appropriate legislation" for its "protection or advancement"; to adopt measures "to promote its growth and insure its safety"; "to foster, protect, control, and restrain." ... Although activities may be intrastate in character when separately considered, if they have such a close and substantial relation to interstate commerce that their control is essential or appropriate to protect that commerce from burdens and obstructions, Congress cannot be denied the power to exercise that control. Undoubtedly the scope of this power must be considered in the light of our dual system of government and may not be extended so as to embrace effects upon interstate commerce so indirect and remote that to embrace them, in view of our complex society, would effectually obliterate the distinction between what is national and what is local and create a completely centralized government. The question is necessarily one of degree....

It is thus apparent that the fact that the employees here concerned were engaged in production is not determinative....

Fourth. Effects of the Unfair Labor Practice in Respondent's Enterprise. — Giving full weight to respondent's contention with respect to a break in the complete continuity of the "stream of commerce" by reason of respondent's manufacturing operations, the fact remains that the stoppage of those operations by industrial strife would have a most serious effect upon interstate commerce. In view of respondent's far-flung activities, it is idle to say that the effect would be indirect or remote. It is obvious that it would be immediate and might be catastrophic. We are asked to shut our eyes to the plainest facts of our national life and to deal with the question of direct and indirect effects in an intellectual vacuum. Because there may be but indirect and remote effects upon interstate commerce in connection with a host of local enterprises throughout the country, it does not follow that other industrial activities do not have such a close and intimate relation to interstate commerce as to make the presence of industrial strife a matter of the most urgent national concern. When industries organize themselves on a national scale, making their relation to interstate commerce the dominant factor in their activities, how can it be maintained that their industrial labor relations constitute a forbidden field into which Congress may not enter when it is necessary to protect interstate commerce from the paralyzing consequences of industrial war? We have often said that interstate commerce itself is a practical conception. It is equally true that interferences with that commerce must be appraised by a judgment that does not ignore actual experience....

Reversed and remanded.

Mr. Justice McREYNOLDS delivered the following dissenting opinion.

Mr. Justice VAN DEVANTER, Mr. Justice SUTHERLAND, Mr. Justice BUTLER and I are unable to agree with the decisions just announced....

The Court, as we think, departs from well-established principles followed in ... *Carter v. Carter Coal Co*....

## VII.

... The argument in support of the Board affirms: "Thus the validity of any specific application of the preventive measures of this Act depends upon whether industrial strife resulting from the practices in the particular enterprise under consideration would be of the character which Federal power could control if it occurred. If strife in that enterprise could be controlled, certainly it could be prevented."

Manifestly that view of congressional power would extend it into almost every field of human industry. With striking lucidity, fifty years ago, *Kidd v. Pearson* declared: "If it be held that the term (commerce with foreign nations and among the several states) includes the regulation of all such manufactures as are intended to be the subject of commercial transactions in the future, it is impossible to deny that it would also include all productive industries that contemplate the same thing. The result would be that congress would be invested, to the exclusion of the states, with the power to regulate, not only manufacture, but also agriculture, horticulture, stock-raising, domestic fisheries, mining,—in short, every branch of human industry." This doctrine found full approval in *United States v. E. C. Knight Co.*, (1895) [*Supra.* this chapter] ... *Carter v. Carter Coal Co....*

Any effect on interstate commerce by the discharge of employees shown here would be indirect and remote in the highest degree, as consideration of the facts will show. In [one of the cases before the Court] ten men out of ten thousand were discharged; in the other cases only a few. The immediate effect in the factory may be to create discontent among all those employed and a strike may follow, which, in turn, may result in reducing production, which ultimately may reduce the volume of goods moving in interstate commerce. By this chain of indirect and progressively remote events we finally reach the evil with which it is said the legislation under consideration undertakes to deal. A more remote and indirect interference with interstate commerce or a more definite invasion of the powers reserved to the states is difficult, if not impossible, to imagine....

It is gravely stated that experience teaches that if an employer discourages membership in "any organization of any kind" "in which employees participate, and which exists for the purpose in whole or in part of dealing with employers concerning grievances, labor disputes, wages, rates of pay, hours of employment or conditions of work," discontent may follow and this in turn may lead to a strike, and as the outcome of the strike there may be a block in the stream of interstate commerce. Therefore Congress may inhibit the discharge! Whatever effect any cause of discontent may ultimately have upon commerce is far too indirect to justify congressional regulation. Almost anything—marriage, birth, death—may in some fashion affect commerce....

## *Note: The Aftermath of* Jones & Laughlin

1. *Jones & Laughlin* was decided on April 12, 1937. As noted before the *Jones & Laughlin* excerpt, two weeks earlier, on March 29, the Court in *West Coast Hotel v. Parrish*, 300 U.S. 379 (1937), upheld a minimum wage law for women against a challenge that it violated employers' and employees' due process rights to contract. (*West Coast Hotel* appears in Chapter 7 of this book.) Chief Justice Charles Evans Hughes wrote both of these opinions. Both of them were 5–4; Justice Owen Roberts, who had often voted to strike down economic legislation on due process and Commerce Clause grounds, provided the decisive vote in both cases. The combination of these two decisions is generally thought to have blunted whatever momentum existed for President Roosevelt's "Court Packing" plan. A modified version of Roosevelt's plan continued to work its way through Congress, but was voted down. One commentator referred to Justice Roberts' supposed change in position as "the switch in time that saved nine."

2. Despite its importance, *Jones & Laughlin* was a cautious opinion. Most notably, it relied heavily on the fact that, as described in the opinion, the employer was a massive, vertically-integrated corporation that operated across state lines, mining coal and ore from its own fields, transporting it across state lines on its own railroad and

shipping lines, using it and other materials to fabricate the steel, and shipping the steel to its warehouses and sales centers across the nation. Note also that Chief Justice Hughes' opinion continued to refer to the Tenth Amendment and acknowledge the need to distinguish local from interstate activity; he also utilized the same direct/indirect effects language as the earlier cases.

3. The next step in the evolution of the doctrine was to apply the implications of *Jones & Laughlin* to a small business. In *National Labor Relations Board v. Fainblatt*, 306 U.S. 601 (1939), the Court upheld the National Labor Relations Board's jurisdiction over a small clothing company that did contract work for a large apparel manufacturer:

> Nor do we think it important, as respondents seem to argue, that the volume of the commerce here involved, though substantial, was relatively small as compared with that in the cases arising under the National Labor Relations Act which have hitherto engaged our attention. The power of Congress to regulate interstate commerce is plenary and extends to all such commerce be it great or small. The exercise of Congressional power under the Sherman [Antitrust] Act, the Clayton [Antitrust] Act, the Federal Trade Commission Act, or the National Motor Vehicle Theft Act, has never been thought to be constitutionally restricted because in any particular case the volume of the commerce affected may be small.

Chief Justice Stone wrote for seven justices (including two who had joined the Court since *Jones & Laughlin*). Justice McReynolds, joined by Justice Butler, dissented, as they had in *Jones & Laughlin*. They quoted, among other cases, *Kidd*, *E.C. Knight* and *Carter Coal* as support for the manufacturing/commerce distinction and to argue that upholding federal power in this case would effectively divest the states of authority over their domestic affairs.

4. By 1941 all the *Jones & Laughlin* dissenters had left the Court. As precedents such as *Jones & Laughlin* and *Fainblatt* began to accumulate, the way was open for the Court to begin formally dismantling the doctrine that it had been edging away from since 1937.

## United States v. Darby
### 312 U.S. 100 (1941)

Mr. Justice STONE delivered the opinion of the Court.

The two principal questions raised by the record in this case are, first, whether Congress has constitutional power to prohibit the shipment in interstate commerce of lumber manufactured by employees whose wages are less than a prescribed minimum or whose weekly hours of labor at that wage are greater than a prescribed maximum, and, second, whether it has power to prohibit the employment of workmen in the production of goods "for interstate commerce" at other than prescribed wages and hours. A subsidiary question is whether in connection with such prohibitions Congress can require the employer subject to them to keep records showing the hours worked each day and week by each of his employees including those engaged "in the production and manufacture of goods to wit, lumber, for 'interstate commerce.'" ...

The Fair Labor Standards Act set up a comprehensive legislative scheme for preventing the shipment in interstate commerce of certain products and commodities produced in the United States under labor conditions as respects wages and hours which fail to conform to standards set up by the Act. Its purpose, as we judicially know from the declaration of policy in § 2(a) of the Act, and the reports of Congressional committees proposing the legislation, is to exclude from interstate commerce goods produced for the commerce and to prevent their production for interstate commerce, under conditions detrimental to the maintenance of the minimum standards of living necessary for health and general well-being; and to prevent the use of interstate commerce as the means of competition in the distribution of goods so produced, and as the means of spreading and perpetuating such substandard labor conditions among the workers of the several states....

... Section 15(a)(1) makes unlawful the shipment in interstate commerce of any goods "in the production of which any employee was employed in violation of section 6(206) or section 7(207)", which provide, among other things, that during the first year of operation of the Act a minimum wage of 25 cents per hour shall be paid to employees "engaged in (interstate) commerce or in the production of goods for (interstate) commerce," and that the maximum hours of employment for employees "engaged in commerce or in the production of goods for commerce" without increased compensation for overtime, shall be forty-four hours a week.

Section 15(a)(2) makes it unlawful to violate ... the minimum wage and maximum hour requirements just mentioned for employees engaged in production of goods for commerce. Section 15(a)(5) ... requires [an employer] to keep such records of the persons employed by him and of their wages and hours of employment as the administrator shall prescribe by regulation or order.

The indictment charges that appellee is engaged, in the state of Georgia, in the business of acquiring raw materials, which he manufactures into finished lumber with the intent, when manufactured, to ship it in interstate commerce to customers outside the state, and that he does in fact so ship a large part of the lumber so produced. [The indictment charged the manufacturer with violating the provisions noted above.]....

While manufacture is not of itself interstate commerce, the shipment of manufactured goods interstate is such commerce and the prohibition of such shipment by Congress is indubitably a regulation of the commerce. The power to regulate commerce is the power "to prescribe the rule by which commerce is to be governed". *Gibbons v. Ogden* (1824) [*Supra.* this chapter]. It extends not only to those regulations which aid, foster and protect the commerce, but embraces those which prohibit it. *Lottery Case (Champion v. Ames)*, 188 U.S. 321 (1903)....

The power of Congress over interstate commerce "is complete in itself, may be exercised to its utmost extent, and acknowledges no limitations, other than are prescribed by the constitution." *Gibbons v. Ogden.* That power can neither be enlarged nor diminished by the exercise or non-exercise of state power. Congress, following its own conception of public policy concerning the restrictions which may appropriately be imposed on interstate commerce, is free to exclude from the commerce articles whose use in the states for which they are destined it may conceive to be injurious to the public health, morals or welfare, even though the state has not sought to regulate their use.

Such regulation is not a forbidden invasion of state power merely because either its motive or its consequence is to restrict the use of articles of commerce within the states of destination and is not prohibited unless by other Constitutional provisions. It is no objection to the assertion of the power to regulate interstate commerce that its exercise is attended by the same incidents which attend the exercise of the police power of the states.

The motive and purpose of the present regulation are plainly to make effective the Congressional conception of public policy that interstate commerce should not be made the instrument of competition in the distribution of goods produced under substandard labor conditions, which competition is injurious to the commerce and to the states from and to which the commerce flows. The motive and purpose of a regulation of interstate commerce are matters for the legislative judgment upon the exercise of which the Constitution places no restriction and over which the courts are given no control. *Sonzinsky v. United States,* 300 U.S. 506 (1937)....

In the more than a century which has elapsed since the decision of *Gibbons v. Ogden,* these principles of constitutional interpretation have been so long and repeatedly recognized by this Court as applicable to the Commerce Clause, that there would be little occasion for repeating them now were it not for the decision of this Court twenty-two years ago in *Hammer v. Dagenhart,* 247 U.S. 251 (1918) [Note *supra.* this chapter]. In that case it was held by a bare majority of the Court over the powerful and now classic dissent of Mr. Justice Holmes ... that Congress was without power to exclude the products of child labor from interstate commerce. The reasoning and conclusion of the Court's opinion there cannot be reconciled with the conclusion which we have reached, that the power of Congress under the Commerce Clause is plenary to exclude any article from interstate commerce subject only to the specific prohibitions of the Constitution.

*Hammer v. Dagenhart* has not been followed. The distinction on which the decision was rested that Congressional power to prohibit interstate commerce is limited to articles which in themselves have some harmful or deleterious property—a distinction which was novel when made and unsupported by any provision of the Constitution— has long since been abandoned. The thesis of the opinion that the motive of the prohibition or its effect to control in some measure the use or production within the states of the article thus excluded from the commerce can operate to deprive the regulation of its constitutional authority has long since ceased to have force. And finally we have declared "The authority of the Federal Government over interstate commerce does not differ in extent or character from that retained by the states over intrastate commerce".

The conclusion is inescapable that *Hammer v. Dagenhart*, was a departure from the principles which have prevailed in the interpretation of the commerce clause both before and since the decision and that such vitality, as a precedent, as it then had has long since been exhausted. It should be and now is overruled.

*Validity of the wage and hour requirements.* Section 15(a)(2) and §§ 6 and 7 require employers to conform to the wage and hour provisions with respect to all employees engaged in the production of goods for interstate commerce. As appellee's employees are not alleged to be "engaged in interstate commerce" the validity of the prohibition turns on the question whether the employment, under other than the prescribed labor standards, of employees engaged in the production of goods for interstate commerce is so related to the commerce and so affects it as to be within the reach of the power of Congress to regulate it....

... The power of Congress over interstate commerce is not confined to the regulation of commerce among the states. It extends to those activities intrastate which so affect interstate commerce or the exercise of the power of Congress over it as to make regulation of them appropriate means to the attainment of a legitimate end, the exercise of the granted power of Congress to regulate interstate commerce. See *McCulloch v. Maryland*, (1819) [*Supra.* Chapter 3 and this chapter].

While this Court has many times found state regulation of interstate commerce, when uniformity of its regulation is of national concern, to be incompatible with the Commerce Clause even though Congress has not legislated on the subject, the Court has never implied such restraint on state control over matters intrastate not deemed to be regulations of interstate commerce or its instrumentalities even though they affect the commerce. In the absence of Congressional legislation on the subject state laws which are not regulations of the commerce itself or its instrumentalities are not forbidden even though they affect interstate commerce. *Kidd v. Pearson*, 128 U.S. 1 (1888) [Note *supra.* this chapter].

But it does not follow that Congress may not by appropriate legislation regulate intrastate activities where they have a substantial effect on interstate commerce. A recent example is the National Labor Relations Act, for the regulation of employer and employee relations in industries in which strikes, induced by unfair labor practices named in the Act, tend to disturb or obstruct interstate commerce. See *National Labor Relations Board v. Jones & Laughlin Steel Corp.* (1937) [*Supra.* this chapter]; *National Labor Relations Board v. Fainblatt*, 306 U.S. 601 (1939) [Note *supra.* this chapter]. But long before the adoption of the National Labor Relations Act, this Court had many times held that the power of Congress to regulate interstate commerce extends to the regulation through legislative action of activities intrastate which have a substantial effect on the commerce or the exercise of the Congressional power over it.[3] ...

Congress, having by the present Act adopted the policy of excluding from interstate commerce all goods produced for the commerce which do not conform to the specified

---

3. ... It may regulate the activities of a local grain exchange shown to have an injurious effect on interstate commerce. *Chicago Board of Trade v. Olsen*, 262 U.S. 1 (1923). It may regulate intrastate

labor standards, it may choose the means reasonably adapted to the attainment of the permitted end, even though they involve control of intrastate activities. Such legislation has often been sustained with respect to powers, other than the commerce power granted to the national government, when the means chosen, although not themselves within the granted power, were nevertheless deemed appropriate aids to the accomplishment of some purpose within an admitted power of the national government. A familiar like exercise of power is the regulation of intrastate transactions which are so commingled with or related to interstate commerce that all must be regulated if the interstate commerce is to be effectively controlled. *Shreveport Case [Houston, E. & W. Texas R. Co. v. United States]*, 234 U.S. 342 (1914) [Note *supra.* this chapter]....

We think also that § 15(a)(2), now under consideration, is sustainable independently of § 15(a)(1), which prohibits shipment or transportation of the proscribed goods. As we have said the evils aimed at by the Act are the spread of substandard labor conditions through the use of the facilities of interstate commerce for competition by the goods so produced with those produced under the prescribed or better labor conditions; and the consequent dislocation of the commerce itself caused by the impairment or destruction of local businesses by competition made effective through interstate commerce. The Act is thus directed at the suppression of a method or kind of competition in interstate commerce which it has in effect condemned as "unfair"....

The Sherman Act and the National Labor Relations Act are familiar examples of the exertion of the commerce power to prohibit or control activities wholly intrastate because of their effect on interstate commerce. See as to the Sherman Act, *Swift & Co. v. United States* (1905) [*Supra.* this chapter]. As to the National Labor Relations Act, see *National Labor Relations Board v. Fainblatt,* and cases cited.

The means adopted by § 15(a)(2) for the protection of interstate commerce by the suppression of the production of the condemned goods for interstate commerce is so related to the commerce and so affects it as to be within the reach of the commerce power. Congress, to attain its objective in the suppression of nationwide competition in interstate commerce by goods produced under substandard labor conditions, has made no distinction as to the volume or amount of shipments in the commerce or of production for commerce by any particular shipper or producer. It recognized that in present day industry, competition by a small part may affect the whole and that the total effect of the competition of many small producers may be great. See H. Rept. No. 2182, 75th Cong. 1st Sess., p. 7. The legislation aimed at a whole embraces all its parts. Cf. *Fainblatt.*

So far as *Carter v. Carter Coal Co.*, 298 U.S. 238 (1936) [Note *supra.* this chapter], is inconsistent with this conclusion, its doctrine is limited in principle by the decisions under the Sherman Act and the National Labor Relations Act, which we have cited and which we follow.

---

rates of interstate carriers where the effect of the rates is to burden interstate commerce. *Houston, E. & W. Texas R. Co. v. United States*, 234 U.S. 342 (1914) [Note *supra.* this chapter]....

Our conclusion is unaffected by the Tenth Amendment which provides: "The powers not delegated to the United States by the Constitution, nor prohibited by it to the States, are reserved to the States respectively, or to the people." The amendment states but a truism that all is retained which has not been surrendered. There is nothing in the history of its adoption to suggest that it was more than declaratory of the relationship between the national and state governments as it had been established by the Constitution before the amendment or that its purpose was other than to allay fears that the new national government might seek to exercise powers not granted, and that the states might not be able to exercise fully their reserved powers.

From the beginning and for many years the amendment has been construed as not depriving the national government of authority to resort to all means for the exercise of a granted power which are appropriate and plainly adapted to the permitted end. *Martin v. Hunter's Lessee*, (1816) [*Supra.* Chapter 3]; *McCulloch v. Maryland*. Whatever doubts may have arisen of the soundness of that conclusion they have been put at rest by the decisions under the Sherman Act and the National Labor Relations Act which we have cited.

*Validity of the requirement of records of wages and hours.* These requirements are incidental to those for the prescribed wages and hours, and hence validity of the former turns on validity of the latter. Since, as we have held, Congress may require production for interstate Commerce to conform to those conditions, it may require the employer, as a means of enforcing the valid law, to keep a record showing whether he has in fact complied with it. The requirement for records even of the intrastate transaction is an appropriate means to the legitimate end....

## Wickard v. Filburn

### 317 U.S. 111 (1942)

Mr. Justice JACKSON delivered the opinion of the Court.

The appellee ... sought a declaratory judgment that the wheat marketing quota provisions of the [Agricultural Adjustment] Act as amended and applicable to him were unconstitutional because not sustainable under the Commerce Clause....

The appellee for many years past has owned and operated a small farm in Montgomery County, Ohio.... It has been his practice to raise a small acreage of winter wheat, sown in the Fall and harvested in the following July; to sell a portion of the crop; to feed part to poultry and livestock on the farm, some of which is sold; to use some in making flour for home consumption; and to keep the rest for the following seeding. The intended disposition of the crop here involved has not been expressly stated.

In July of 1940, pursuant to the Agricultural Adjustment Act of 1938 ... there were established for the appellee's 1941 crop a wheat acreage allotment of 11.1 acres and a normal yield of 20.1 bushels of wheat an acre.... He sowed, however, 23 acres, and harvested from his 11.9 acres of excess acreage 239 bushels, which under the terms of the Act as amended on May 26, 1941, constituted farm marketing excess, subject to a penalty of 49 cents a bushel, or $117.11 in all. The appellee has not paid the penalty and he has not postponed or avoided it by storing the excess under regulations of the Secretary of Agriculture, or by delivering it up to the Secretary. The Committee, therefore, refused him a marketing card, which was, under the terms of Regulations promulgated by the Secretary, necessary to protect a buyer from liability to the penalty and upon its protecting lien.

The general scheme of the Agricultural Adjustment Act of 1938 as related to wheat is to control the volume moving in interstate and foreign commerce in order to avoid surpluses and shortages and the consequent abnormally low or high wheat prices and obstructions to commerce. Within prescribed limits and by prescribed standards the Secretary of Agriculture is directed to ascertain and proclaim each year a national acreage allotment for the next crop of wheat, which is then apportioned to the states and their counties, and is eventually broken up into allotments for individual farms....

## II.

It is urged that under the Commerce Clause of the Constitution Congress does not possess the power it has in this instance sought to exercise. The question would merit little consideration since our decision in *United States v. Darby* [*Supra.* this chapter], sustaining the federal power to regulate production of goods for commerce except for the fact that this Act extends federal regulation to production not intended in any part for commerce but wholly for consumption on the farm.... Hence, marketing quotas not only embrace all that may be sold without penalty but also what may be consumed on the premises....

Appellee says that this is a regulation of production and consumption of wheat. Such activities are, he urges, beyond the reach of Congressional power under the Commerce Clause, since they are local in character, and their effects upon interstate commerce are at most "indirect." In answer the Government argues that the statute regulates neither production nor consumption, but only marketing; and, in the alternative, that if the Act does go beyond the regulation of marketing it is sustainable as a "necessary and proper"[15] implementation of the power of Congress over interstate commerce.

The Government's concern lest the Act be held to be a regulation of production or consumption rather than of marketing is attributable to a few *dicta* and decisions of this Court which might be understood to lay it down that activities such as "production," "manufacturing," and "mining" are strictly "local" and, except in special circumstances which are not present here, cannot be regulated under the commerce power because their effects upon interstate commerce are, as matter of law, only "indirect." Even today, when this power has been held to have great latitude, there is no decision of this Court that such activities may be regulated where no part of the product is intended for interstate commerce or intermingled with the subjects thereof. We believe that a review of the course of decision under the Commerce Clause will make plain, however, that questions of the power of Congress are not to be decided

---

15. Constitution, Article I, § 8, cl. 18.

by reference to any formula which would give controlling force to nomenclature such as "production" and "indirect" and foreclose consideration of the actual effects of the activity in question upon interstate commerce.

At the beginning Chief Justice Marshall described the Federal commerce power with a breadth never yet exceeded. *Gibbons v. Ogden* (1824) [*Supra.* this chapter]. He made emphatic the embracing and penetrating nature of this power by warning that effective restraints on its exercise must proceed from political rather than from judicial processes.

For nearly a century, however, decisions of this Court under the Commerce Clause dealt rarely with questions of what Congress might do in the exercise of its granted power under the Clause and almost entirely with the permissibility of state activity which it was claimed discriminated against or burdened interstate commerce. During this period there was perhaps little occasion for the affirmative exercise of the commerce power, and the influence of the Clause on American life and law was a negative one, resulting almost wholly from its operation as a restraint upon the powers of the states. In discussion and decision the point of reference instead of being what was "necessary and proper" to the exercise by Congress of its granted power, was often some concept of sovereignty thought to be implicit in the status of statehood. Certain activities such as "production," "manufacturing," and "mining" were occasionally said to be within the province of state governments and beyond the power of Congress under the Commerce Clause.[17]

It was not until 1887 with the enactment of the Interstate Commerce Act that the interstate commerce power began to exert positive influence in American law and life. This first important federal resort to the commerce power was followed in 1890 by the Sherman Anti-Trust Act and, thereafter, mainly after 1903, by many others. These statutes ushered in new phases of adjudication, which required the Court to approach the interpretation of the Commerce Clause in the light of an actual exercise by Congress of its power thereunder.

When it first dealt with this new legislation, the Court adhered to its earlier pronouncements, and allowed but little scope to the power of Congress. *United States v. E. C. Knight Co.* (1895) [*Supra.* this chapter]....

Even while important opinions in this line of restrictive authority were being written, however, other cases called forth broader interpretations of the Commerce Clause destined to supersede the earlier ones, and to bring about a return to the principles first enunciated by Chief Justice Marshall in *Gibbons v. Ogden.*

Not long after the decision of *United States v. E. C. Knight Co.*, Mr. Justice Holmes, in sustaining the exercise of national power over intrastate activity, stated for the Court that "commerce among the states is not a technical legal conception, but a practical one, drawn from the course of business." *Swift & Co. v. United States* (1905) [*Supra.* this chapter]. It was soon demonstrated that the effects of many kinds of intrastate activity upon interstate commerce were such as to make them a proper subject

---

17. *Veazie v. Moor,* 14 How. 568 (1852); *Kidd v. Pearson,* 128 U.S. 1 (1888) [Note *supra.* this chapter].

of federal regulation. In some cases sustaining the exercise of federal power over intrastate matters the term "direct" was used for the purpose of stating, rather than of reaching, a result; in others it was treated as synonymous with "substantial" or "material;" and in others it was not used at all. Of late its use has been abandoned in cases dealing with questions of federal power under the Commerce Clause.

In the *Shreveport Rate Cases (Houston, E. & W.T.R. Co. v. United States)*, 234 U.S. 342 (1914) [Note *supra.* this chapter], the Court held that railroad rates of an admittedly intrastate character and fixed by authority of the state might, nevertheless, be revised by the Federal Government because of the economic effects which they had upon interstate commerce. The opinion of Mr. Justice Hughes found federal intervention constitutionally authorized because of "matters having such a close and substantial relation to interstate traffic that the control is essential or appropriate to the security of that traffic, to the efficiency of the interstate service, and to the maintenance of the conditions under which interstate commerce may be conducted upon fair terms and without molestation or hindrance."

The Court's recognition of the relevance of the economic effects in the application of the Commerce Clause exemplified by this statement has made the mechanical application of legal formulas no longer feasible. Once an economic measure of the reach of the power granted to Congress in the Commerce Clause is accepted, questions of federal power cannot be decided simply by finding the activity in question to be "production" nor can consideration of its economic effects be foreclosed by calling them "indirect." The present Chief Justice has said in summary of the present state of the law: "The commerce power is not confined in its exercise to the regulation of commerce among the states. It extends to those activities intrastate which so affect interstate commerce, or the exertion of the power of Congress over it, as to make regulation of them appropriate means to the attainment of a legitimate end, the effective execution of the granted power to regulate interstate commerce. * * * The power of Congress over interstate commerce is plenary and complete in itself, may be exercised to its utmost extent, and acknowledges no limitations other than are prescribed in the Constitution. * * * It follows that no form of state activity can constitutionally thwart the regulatory power granted by the commerce clause to Congress. Hence the reach of that power extends to those intrastate activities which in a substantial way interfere with or obstruct the exercise of the granted power." *United States v. Wrightwood Dairy Co.*, 315 U.S. 110 (1942).

Whether the subject of the regulation in question was "production," "consumption," or "marketing" is, therefore, not material for purposes of deciding the question of federal power before us.... [Even] if appellee's activity be local and though it may not be regarded as commerce, it may still, whatever its nature, be reached by Congress if it exerts a substantial economic effect on interstate commerce and this irrespective of whether such effect is what might at some earlier time have been defined as "direct" or "indirect." ...

The wheat industry has been a problem industry for some years.... The decline in the export trade has left a large surplus in production.... In the absence of regulation the price of wheat in the United States would be much affected by world conditions. During 1941, producers who cooperated with the Agricultural Adjustment program received an average price on the farm of about $1.16 a bushel, as compared with the world market price of 40 cents a bushel....

The effect of consumption of homegrown wheat on interstate commerce is due to the fact that it constitutes the most variable factor in the disappearance of the wheat crop. Consumption on the farm where grown appears to vary in an amount greater than 20 per cent of average production. The total amount of wheat consumed as food varies but relatively little, and use as seed is relatively constant.

The maintenance by government regulation of a price for wheat undoubtedly can be accomplished as effectively by sustaining or increasing the demand as by limiting the supply. The effect of the statute before us is to restrict the amount which may be produced for market and the extent as well to which one may forestall resort to the market by producing to meet his own needs. That appellee's own contribution to the demand for wheat may be trivial by itself is not enough to remove him from the scope of federal regulation where, as here, his contribution, taken together with that of many others similarly situated, is far from trivial. *National Labor Relations Board v. Fainblatt*, 306 U.S. 601 (1939) [Note *supra.* this chapter]; *United States v. Darby*.

It is well established by decisions of this Court that the power to regulate commerce includes the power to regulate the prices at which commodities in that commerce are dealt in and practices affecting such prices. One of the primary purposes of the Act in question was to increase the market price of wheat and to that end to limit the volume thereof that could affect the market. It can hardly be denied that a factor of such volume and variability as home-consumed wheat would have a substantial influence on price and market conditions. This may arise because being in marketable condition such wheat overhangs the market and if induced by rising prices tends to flow into the market and check price increases. But if we assume that it is never marketed, it supplies a need of the man who grew it which would otherwise be reflected by purchases in the open market. Home-grown wheat in this sense competes with wheat in commerce. The stimulation of commerce is a use of the regulatory function quite as definitely as prohibitions or restrictions thereon. This record leaves us in no doubt that Congress may properly have considered that wheat consumed on the farm where grown if wholly outside the scheme of regulation would have a substantial effect in defeating and obstructing its purpose to stimulate trade therein at increased prices.

It is said, however, that this Act, forcing some farmers into the market to buy what they could provide for themselves, is an unfair promotion of the markets and prices of specializing wheat growers.... The conflicts of economic interest between the regulated and those who advantage by it are wisely left under our system to resolution by the Congress under its more flexible and responsible legislative process.[29] Such

---

29. Cf. *McCulloch v. Maryland* (1819) [*Supra.* Chapters 3 & 4]; *Gibbons v. Ogden*.

conflicts rarely lend themselves to judicial determination. And with the wisdom, workability, or fairness, of the plan of regulation we have nothing to do....

## Note: The Commerce Clause at Its Height

1. *Darby* and *Wickard* ushered in a period in which the Interstate Commerce power was generally thought to be nearly limitless. In the half-century following *Wickard* the federal government expanded the scope and depth of its regulation far beyond the reforms of the New Deal that had provoked the Court's resistance in the 1930s. During this latter period, however, the Court, applying its new, more generous Commerce Clause doctrine, was far more supportive.

2. *Civil Rights.* The Civil Rights Act of 1964 was a far-reaching law that brought the power of the federal government to oppose race and sex discrimination. While some policy-makers sought to ground the statute in Congress's power to enforce the Fourteenth Amendment, ultimately, the government chose to defend its constitutionality primarily under the Commerce Clause. The law's guarantees against employment discrimination were clearly constitutional, given the Court's approval of the National Labor Relations Act in *Jones & Laughlin* and *Fainblatt*. But Title II of the law prohibited discrimination in public accommodations, such as hotels, restaurants and theaters, and thus was not directly supported by earlier precedent.

In two important cases from 1964 the Court upheld Title II with sweeping language. In *Heart of Atlanta Motel v. United States*, 379 U.S. 241 (1964), the Court unanimously upheld application of Title II to a motel that refused to lodge African-Americans. After beginning with an extensive quotation from *Gibbons*, Justice Clark noted that movement of persons constitutes part of the "intercourse" that defined "commerce" for Chief Justice Marshall. He noted the evidence Congress had accumulated that racial discrimination in lodging had severely impeded the interstate movement of African-Americans, as they were often unable to secure reasonable lodgings. In response to the argument that the motel at issue was a local operation, he quoted *Darby*'s statement that "The power of Congress over interstate commerce ... extends to those activities intrastate which so affect interstate commerce ... as to make regulation of them appropriate means to the attainment of a legitimate end, the exercise of the granted power of Congress to regulate interstate commerce." He also stated that the fact "that Congress was legislating against moral wrongs ... rendered its enactments no less valid" given "the overwhelming evidence of the disruptive effect that racial discrimination has had on commercial intercourse."

*Heart of Atlanta* was litigated on the factual stipulation that the motel "is readily accessible to interstate highways" and "solicits patronage from outside the [state] through various national advertising media," and that "approximately 75% of its registered guests are from outside the State." In the companion case, *Katzenbach v. McClung*, 379 U.S. 294 (1964), the Court considered whether the Commerce Clause authorized application of Title II to a more local entity, Ollie's Barbecue. The Court described Ollie's as "a family-owned restaurant in Birmingham, Alabama ... with a seating capacity of 220.... [located] on a state highway 11 blocks from an interstate one and a somewhat greater distance from railroad and bus stations." It also noted that "in the 12 months preceding passage of [the Civil Rights Act], the restaurant purchased approximately $150,000 worth of food, $69,683 ... of which was meat it bought from a local supplier who had procured it from outside the state." Thus, as the Court phrased it, "the sole question ... narrows down to whether Title II, as applied to a restaurant annually receiving about $70,000 worth of food which has moved in commerce, is a valid exercise of the power of Congress."

Again, the Court unanimously upheld application of Title II. Speaking again through Justice Clark, the Court noted evidence in the legislative record indicating that African-Americans spent less on restaurants and theaters in areas where discrimination was practiced. In turn, such reduced spending depressed demand for goods and services, which ultimately impaired the interstate market. The Court also noted evidence that that discrimination in restaurants "had a direct and highly restrictive effect upon interstate travel by Negroes." Based on this evidence, the Court held that there was "ample basis for the conclusion that established restaurants in [discriminatory] areas sold less interstate goods because of the discrimination, that business in general suffered and that many new businesses refrained from establishing there because of it." In response to the argument that the amount of food Ollie's bought from out-of-state was insignificant in light of the larger interstate food market, the Court cited *Wickard* for the proposition that such individual insignificance "is not enough to remove [the regulated party] from the scope of federal regulation where ... his contribution, taken together with that of many others similarly situated, is far from trivial." As noted in item 5 of this Note, Justice Black wrote a separate concurrence.

3. *Crime.* In *Perez v. United States*, 402 U.S. 146 (1971), the Court upheld a federal law prohibiting "loan-sharking" activity (the making of loans to marginal credit risks on extortionate terms, accompanied by violence or threats of violence for non-repayment). Writing for eight Justices, Justice Douglas concluded that Congress had before it evidence detailing how loan-sharking affected interstate commerce because of its role in supporting organized crime. As set forth below, in item 5 of this Note, Justice Stewart dissented.

4. *Land Use.* In *Hodel v. Virginia Surface Mining and Reclamation Association*, 452 U.S. 264 (1981), the Court unanimously rejected a facial Commerce Clause-based challenge to a federal law regulating how surface coal miners must restore land used for surface coal mining. Writing for eight Justices, Justice Marshall deferred to "Congress's express findings ... about the effects of coal mining on interstate commerce." The Court quoted those findings that "many surface mining operations ... adversely affect commerce ... by ... destroying ... land..., polluting the water, ... [and] damaging the property of citizens." The Court continued, again quoting Congress's findings:

> Moreover, the Act responds to a congressional finding that nationwide 'surface mining ... standards are essential in order to insure that competition in interstate commerce among sellers of coal produced in different States will not be used to undermine the ability of the several States to improve and maintain adequate standards on coal mining operations within their borders.'

The Court observed that "in *United Sates v. Darby* the Court used a similar rationale." Quoting from *Darby*, it continued:

> The [*Darby*] Court explained that the statute implemented Congress' view that 'interstate commerce should not be made the instrument of competition in the distribution of goods produced under substandard labor conditions, which competition is injurious to the commerce and to the states from and to which the commerce flows.' The same rationale applies here....

5. *Caveats—and a dissent.* Not every Justice during this period accepted this expansion of federal power unconditionally. Concurring in both *Heart of Atlanta* and *McClung*, Justice Black wrote "I recognize that every remote, possible, speculative effect on commerce should not be accepted as an adequate constitutional ground to uproot ... all our traditional distinctions between what is purely local ... and what affects the national interest.... I recognize too that some isolated and remote lunchroom which sells only to local people and buys almost all its supplies in the locality may possibly be beyond the reach of the power of Congress to regulate commerce...." But he then said that "we do not consider the effect on interstate commerce of only one isolated, individual, local event, without regard to the fact that this single local event when added to many others of a similar nature may impose a burden on interstate commerce...."

Justice Stewart dissented in *Perez*. He stated that to uphold the loan-sharking law the Court, at the very least, would have to find a rational basis for a congressional conclusion "that loan sharking is an activity with interstate attributes that distinguish it in some substantial respect from other local crime." He continued: "[It] is not enough to say that loan sharking is a national problem, for all crime is a national problem. It is not enough to say that some loan sharking has interstate characteristics, for any crime may have an interstate setting. And the circumstance that loan sharking has an adverse impact on interstate business is not a distinguishing attribute, for interstate business suffers from almost all criminal activity...."

Finally, Justice Rehnquist concurred only in the judgment in *Hodel*. He recognized that the Commerce power is "broad indeed." But after quoting from cases including *Jones & Laughlin*, he offered the following caveat:

> [It] would be a mistake to conclude that Congress' power to regulate pursuant to the Commerce Clause is unlimited. Some activities may be so private or local in nature that they simply may not be in commerce. Nor is it sufficient that the person or activity reached have some nexus with interstate commerce. Our cases have consistently held that the regulated activity must have a *substantial* effect on interstate commerce.

Justice Rehnquist concurred only in the judgment because he expressed concern that the majority opinion at times seemed to state the relevant test as asking only whether there was an effect — not a *substantial* effect — on interstate commerce. (As you will see, he had a chance to settle the law (in favor of his preferred reading) in the next case.)

6. *The Exception.* During this period of otherwise extraordinarily broad congressional power, the Court did attempt to limit the Commerce Power in one area: when Congress used its power to regulate state governments when their activities affected interstate commerce (*e.g.*, when state governments acted as employers). The cases appear later in Part II, in Chapter 6.

7. Taken together, the cases described above suggested nearly boundless congressional power under the Commerce Clause. The "rational basis" gloss on the "substantial effects" test allowed courts to uphold essentially any regulation, since the integrated nature of the national economy by the mid-20th century meant that a rational basis could be found for concluding that any activity, in the aggregate, had a substantial effect on interstate commerce.

Still, the unease expressed by individual Justices shows that a limitless view of the Commerce Power never achieved complete acceptance. With the advent of new Justices in the 1980s and 1990s these individual strands came together to form the basis of a new (if narrow) majority.

## 4. A More Limited Commerce Power

In 1995, the Supreme Court did what many commentators considered unthinkable: it struck down a federal statute on Commerce Clause grounds for the first time in more than half a century.

### United States v. Lopez
#### 514 U.S. 549 (1995)

Chief Justice Rehnquist delivered the opinion of the Court.

In the Gun-Free School Zones Act of 1990, Congress made it a federal offense "for any individual knowingly to possess a firearm at a place that the individual knows, or has reasonable cause to believe, is a school zone." 18 U.S.C. § 922(q)(1)(A). The Act neither regulates a commercial activity nor contains a requirement that the possession be connected in any way to interstate commerce. We hold that the Act exceeds the authority of Congress "to regulate Commerce ... among the several States...."

On March 10, 1992, respondent, who was then a 12th-grade student, arrived at Edison High School in San Antonio, Texas, carrying a concealed .38 caliber handgun and five bullets. Acting upon an anonymous tip, school authorities confronted respondent, who admitted that he was carrying the weapon. He was arrested and charged ... with violating the Gun-Free School Zones Act of 1990....

The District Court ... concluded that § 922(q) "is a constitutional exercise of Congress' well-defined power to regulate activities in and affecting commerce, and the 'business' of elementary, middle and high schools ... affects interstate commerce." ... On appeal, respondent challenged his conviction based on his claim that § 922(q) exceeded Congress' power to legislate under the Commerce Clause. The Court of Appeals for the Fifth Circuit agreed and reversed respondent's conviction. It held that, in light of what it characterized as insufficient congressional findings and legislative history, "section 922(q), in the full reach of its terms, is invalid as beyond the power of Congress under the Commerce Clause." Because of the importance of the issue, we granted certiorari, and we now affirm.

We start with first principles. The Constitution creates a Federal Government of enumerated powers. As James Madison wrote, "the powers delegated by the proposed Constitution to the federal government are few and defined. Those which are to remain in the State governments are numerous and indefinite." *The Federalist* No. 45....

The Constitution delegates to Congress the power "to regulate Commerce with foreign Nations, and among the several States, and with the Indian Tribes." The Court, through Chief Justice Marshall, first defined the nature of Congress' commerce power in *Gibbons v. Ogden* (1824) [*Supra.* this chapter] ...

For nearly a century thereafter, the Court's Commerce Clause decisions dealt but rarely with the extent of Congress' power, and almost entirely with the Commerce Clause as a limit on state legislation that discriminated against interstate commerce. See, e.g., *Kidd v. Pearson*, 128 U.S. 1 (1888) [Note *supra.* this chapter] (upholding a state prohibition on the manufacture of intoxicating liquor because the commerce power "does not comprehend the purely internal domestic commerce of a State which is carried on between man and man within a State or between different parts of the same State") ...

In 1887, Congress enacted the Interstate Commerce Act, and in 1890, Congress enacted the Sherman Antitrust Act. These laws ushered in a new era of federal regulation under the commerce power. When cases involving these laws first reached this Court, we imported from our negative Commerce Clause cases the approach that Congress could not regulate activities such as "production," "manufacturing," and "mining." See, e.g., *United States v. E.C. Knight Co.* (1895) [*Supra.* this chapter] ("Commerce succeeds to manufacture, and is not part of it"); *Carter v. Carter Coal Co.*, 298 U.S. 238 (1936) [Note *supra.* this chapter] ("Mining brings the subject matter of commerce into existence. Commerce disposes of it"). Simultaneously, however, the Court held that, where the interstate and intrastate aspects of commerce were so mingled together that full regulation of interstate commerce required incidental regulation of intrastate commerce, the Commerce Clause authorized such regulation. See, e.g., *Shreveport Rate Cases*, 234 U.S. 342 (1914) [Note *supra.* this chapter].

In *A.L.A. Schechter Poultry Corp. v. United States*, 295 U.S. 495 (1935), the Court struck down regulations that fixed the hours and wages of individuals employed by an intrastate business because the activity being regulated related to interstate commerce only indirectly. In doing so, the Court characterized the distinction between direct and indirect effects of intrastate transactions upon interstate commerce as "a fundamental one, essential to the maintenance of our constitutional system." ... The justification for this formal distinction was rooted in the fear that otherwise "there would be virtually no limit to the federal power and for all practical purposes we should have a completely centralized government."

Two years later, in the watershed case of *NLRB v. Jones & Laughlin Steel Corp.* (1937) [*Supra.* this chapter], the Court upheld the National Labor Relations Act against a Commerce Clause challenge, and in the process, departed from the distinction between "direct" and "indirect" effects on interstate commerce. *Id.* ("The question [of the scope of Congress' power] is necessarily one of degree"). The Court held that intrastate activities that "have such a close and substantial relation to interstate commerce that their control is essential or appropriate to protect that commerce from burdens and obstructions" are within Congress' power to regulate.

In *United States v. Darby* (1941) [*Supra.* this chapter], the Court upheld the Fair Labor Standards Act, stating:

> The power of Congress over interstate commerce is not confined to the regulation of commerce among the states. It extends to those activities intrastate which so affect interstate commerce or the exercise of the power of Congress over it as to make regulation of them appropriate means to the attainment of a legitimate end, the exercise of the granted power of Congress to regulate interstate commerce.

In *Wickard v. Filburn* (1942) [*Supra.* this chapter], the Court upheld the application of amendments to the Agricultural Adjustment Act of 1938 to the production and consumption of homegrown wheat. The *Wickard* Court explicitly rejected earlier distinctions between direct and indirect effects on interstate commerce, stating:

> Even if appellee's activity be local and though it may not be regarded as commerce, it may still, whatever its nature, be reached by Congress if it exerts a substantial economic effect on interstate commerce, and this irrespective of whether such effect is what might at some earlier time have been defined as 'direct' or 'indirect.'

The *Wickard* Court emphasized that although Filburn's own contribution to the demand for wheat may have been trivial by itself, that was not "enough to remove him from the scope of federal regulation where, as here, his contribution, taken together with that of many others similarly situated, is far from trivial."

*Jones & Laughlin Steel*, *Darby*, and *Wickard* ushered in an era of Commerce Clause jurisprudence that greatly expanded the previously defined authority of Congress under that Clause. In part, this was a recognition of the great changes that had occurred in the way business was carried on in this country. Enterprises that had once been local or at most regional in nature had become national in scope. But the doctrinal change also reflected a view that earlier Commerce Clause cases artificially had constrained the authority of Congress to regulate interstate commerce.

But even these modern-era precedents which have expanded congressional power under the Commerce Clause confirm that this power is subject to outer limits. In *Jones & Laughlin Steel*, the Court warned that the scope of the interstate commerce power "must be considered in the light of our dual system of government and may not be extended so as to embrace effects upon interstate commerce so indirect and remote that to embrace them, in view of our complex society, would effectually obliterate the distinction between what is national and what is local and create a completely centralized government." Since that time, the Court has heeded that warning and undertaken to decide whether a rational basis existed for concluding that a regulated activity sufficiently affected interstate commerce. See, e.g., *Hodel v. Virginia Surface Mining & Reclamation Assn., Inc.*, 452 U.S. 264 (1981); *Perez v. United States*, 402 U.S. 146 (1971); *Katzenbach v. McClung*, 379 U.S. 294 (1964); *Heart of Atlanta Motel, Inc. v. United States*, 379 U.S. 241 (1964) [All note *supra.* this chapter].[2] ...

Consistent with this structure, we have identified three broad categories of activity that Congress may regulate under its commerce power. First, Congress may regulate the use of the channels of interstate commerce. Second, Congress is empowered to regulate and protect the instrumentalities of interstate commerce, or persons or things in interstate commerce, even though the threat may come only from intrastate activities. Finally, Congress' commerce authority includes the power to regulate those activities having a substantial relation to interstate commerce, *i.e.*, those activities that substantially affect interstate commerce.

Within this final category, admittedly, our case law has not been clear whether an activity must "affect" or "substantially affect" interstate commerce in order to be within Congress' power to regulate it under the Commerce Clause. We conclude, consistent with the great weight of our case law, that the proper test requires an analysis of whether the regulated activity "substantially affects" interstate commerce.

We now turn to consider the power of Congress, in the light of this framework, to enact § 922(q). The first two categories of authority may be quickly disposed of: § 922(q) is not a regulation of the use of the channels of interstate commerce, nor is it an attempt to prohibit the interstate transportation of a commodity through the channels of commerce; nor can § 922(q) be justified as a regulation by which Congress has sought to protect an instrumentality of interstate commerce or a thing in interstate commerce. Thus, if § 922(q) is to be sustained, it must be under the third category as a regulation of an activity that substantially affects interstate commerce.

First, we have upheld a wide variety of congressional Acts regulating intrastate economic activity where we have concluded that the activity substantially affected interstate commerce. Examples include the regulation of intrastate coal mining, *Hodel*, intrastate extortionate credit transactions, *Perez*, restaurants utilizing substantial interstate supplies, *McClung*, and hotels catering to interstate guests, *Heart of Atlanta Motel*, and production and consumption of home-grown wheat, *Wickard*. These examples are by no means exhaustive, but the pattern is clear. Where economic activity substantially affects interstate commerce, legislation regulating that activity will be sustained.

---

2. See also *Hodel* ("Simply because Congress may conclude that a particular activity substantially affects interstate commerce does not necessarily make it so") (REHNQUIST, J., concurring in judgment); *Heart of Atlanta Motel* ("Whether particular operations affect interstate commerce sufficiently to come under the constitutional power of Congress to regulate them is ultimately a judicial rather than a legislative question, and can be settled finally only by this Court") (Black, J., concurring).

Even *Wickard*, which is perhaps the most far reaching example of Commerce Clause authority over intrastate activity, involved economic activity in a way that the possession of a gun in a school zone does not....

Section 922(q) is a criminal statute that by its terms has nothing to do with "commerce" or any sort of economic enterprise, however broadly one might define those terms.[3] Section 922(q) is not an essential part of a larger regulation of economic activity, in which the regulatory scheme could be undercut unless the intrastate activity were regulated. It cannot, therefore, be sustained under our cases upholding regulations of activities that arise out of or are connected with a commercial transaction, which viewed in the aggregate, substantially affects interstate commerce.

Second, § 922(q) contains no jurisdictional element which would ensure, through case-by-case inquiry, that the firearm possession in question affects interstate commerce....

Although as part of our independent evaluation of constitutionality under the Commerce Clause we of course consider legislative findings, and indeed even congressional committee findings, regarding effect on interstate commerce, the Government concedes that "neither the statute nor its legislative history contains express congressional findings regarding the effects upon interstate commerce of gun possession in a school zone." We agree with the Government that Congress normally is not required to make formal findings as to the substantial burdens that an activity has on interstate commerce. *See Katzenbach v. McClung.* But to the extent that congressional findings would enable us to evaluate the legislative judgment that the activity in question substantially affected interstate commerce, even though no such substantial effect was visible to the naked eye, they are lacking here.[4] ...

The Government's essential contention, *in fine*, is that we may determine here that § 922(q) is valid because possession of a firearm in a local school zone does indeed substantially affect interstate commerce. The Government argues that possession of a firearm in a school zone may result in violent crime and that violent crime can be

---

3. Under our federal system, the "'States possess primary authority for defining and enforcing the criminal law.'" When Congress criminalizes conduct already denounced as criminal by the States, it effects a "change in the sensitive relation between federal and state criminal jurisdiction." The Government acknowledges that § 922(q) "displaces state policy choices in ... that its prohibitions apply even in States that have chosen not to outlaw the conduct in question." Brief for United States 29, n. 18; see also Statement of President George Bush on Signing the Crime Control Act of 1990, 26 Weekly Comp. of Pres. Doc. 1944, 1945 (Nov. 29, 1990) ("Most egregiously, section [922(q)] inappropriately overrides legitimate State firearms laws with a new and unnecessary Federal law. The policies reflected in these provisions could legitimately be adopted by the States, but they should not be imposed upon the States by the Congress").

4. We note that on September 13, 1994, President Clinton signed into law the Violent Crime Control and Law Enforcement Act of 1994. Section 320904 of that Act amends § 922(q) to include congressional findings regarding the effects of firearm possession in and around schools upon interstate and foreign commerce. The Government does not rely upon these subsequent findings as a substitute for the absence of findings in the first instance. Tr. of Oral Arg. 25 ("We're not relying on them in the strict sense of the word, but we think that at a very minimum they indicate that reasons can be identified for why Congress wanted to regulate this particular activity").

expected to affect the functioning of the national economy in two ways. First, the costs of violent crime are substantial, and, through the mechanism of insurance, those costs are spread throughout the population. Second, violent crime reduces the willingness of individuals to travel to areas within the country that are perceived to be unsafe. *Cf. Heart of Atlanta Motel.* The Government also argues that the presence of guns in schools poses a substantial threat to the educational process by threatening the learning environment. A handicapped educational process, in turn, will result in a less productive citizenry. That, in turn, would have an adverse effect on the Nation's economic well-being. As a result, the Government argues that Congress could rationally have concluded that § 922(q) substantially affects interstate commerce.

We pause to consider the implications of the Government's arguments. The Government admits, under its "costs of crime" reasoning, that Congress could regulate not only all violent crime, but all activities that might lead to violent crime, regardless of how tenuously they relate to interstate commerce. Similarly, under the Government's "national productivity" reasoning, Congress could regulate any activity that it found was related to the economic productivity of individual citizens: family law (including marriage, divorce, and child custody), for example. Under the theories that the Government presents in support of § 922(q), it is difficult to perceive any limitation on federal power, even in areas such as criminal law enforcement or education where States historically have been sovereign. Thus, if we were to accept the Government's arguments, we are hard-pressed to posit any activity by an individual that Congress is without power to regulate....

[A] determination whether an intrastate activity is commercial or noncommercial may in some cases result in legal uncertainty. But, so long as Congress' authority is limited to those powers enumerated in the Constitution, and so long as those enumerated powers are interpreted as having judicially enforceable outer limits, congressional legislation under the Commerce Clause always will engender "legal uncertainty." ... The Constitution mandates this uncertainty by withholding from Congress a plenary police power that would authorize enactment of every type of legislation. *See* U.S. Const., Art. I, § 8. Congress has operated within this framework of legal uncertainty ever since this Court determined that it was the judiciary's duty "to say what the law is." *Marbury v. Madison* (1803) [*Supra.* Chapter 1]. Any possible benefit from eliminating this "legal uncertainty" would be at the expense of the Constitution's system of enumerated powers....

... The possession of a gun in a local school zone is in no sense an economic activity that might, through repetition elsewhere, substantially affect any sort of interstate commerce. Respondent was a local student at a local school; there is no indication that he had recently moved in interstate commerce, and there is no requirement that his possession of the firearm have any concrete tie to interstate commerce.

To uphold the Government's contentions here, we would have to pile inference upon inference in a manner that would bid fair to convert congressional authority under the Commerce Clause to a general police power of the sort retained by the States. Admittedly, some of our prior cases have taken long steps down that road, giving great deference to congressional action. The broad language in these opinions has suggested the possibility of additional expansion, but we decline here to proceed any further....

JUSTICE KENNEDY, with whom JUSTICE O'CONNOR joins, concurring.

The history of the judicial struggle to interpret the Commerce Clause during the transition from the economic system the Founders knew to the single, national market still emergent in our own era counsels great restraint before the Court determines that the Clause is insufficient to support an exercise of the national power. That history gives me some pause about today's decision, but I join the Court's opinion with these observations on what I conceive to be its necessary though limited holding.

Chief Justice Marshall announced that the national authority reaches "that commerce which concerns more States than one" and that the commerce power "is complete in itself, may be exercised to its utmost extent, and acknowledges no limitations, other than are prescribed in the constitution." *Gibbons v. Ogden.* His statements can be understood now as an early and authoritative recognition that the Commerce Clause grants Congress extensive power and ample discretion to determine its appropriate exercise. The progression of our Commerce Clause cases from *Gibbons* to the present was not marked, however, by a coherent or consistent course of interpretation; for neither the course of technological advance nor the foundational principles for the jurisprudence itself were self-evident to the courts that sought to resolve contemporary disputes by enduring principles.

Furthermore, for almost a century after the adoption of the Constitution, the Court's Commerce Clause decisions did not concern the authority of Congress to legislate. Rather, the Court faced the related but quite distinct question of the authority of the States to regulate matters that would be within the commerce power had Congress chosen to act. The simple fact was that in the early years of the Republic, Congress seldom perceived the necessity to exercise its power in circumstances where its authority would be called into question. The Court's initial task, therefore, was to elaborate the theories that would permit the States to act where Congress had not done so. Not the least part of the problem was the unresolved question whether the congressional power was exclusive, a question reserved by Chief Justice Marshall in *Gibbons.*

At the midpoint of the 19th century, the Court embraced the principle that the States and the National Government both have authority to regulate certain matters absent the congressional determination to displace local law or the necessity for the Court to invalidate local law because of the dormant national power. *Cooley v. Board of Wardens of Port of Philadelphia, ex rel. Soc. for Relief of Distressed Pilots,* 12 How. 299 (1852). But the utility of that solution was not at once apparent, and difficulties of application persisted.

One approach the Court used to inquire into the lawfulness of state authority was to draw content-based or subject-matter distinctions, thus defining by semantic or formalistic categories those activities that were commerce and those that were not.

For instance, in deciding that a State could prohibit the in-state manufacture of liquor intended for out-of-state shipment, it distinguished between manufacture and commerce. "No distinction is more popular to the common mind, or more clearly expressed in economic and political literature, than that between manufacture and commerce. Manufacture is transformation — the fashioning of raw materials into a change of form for use. The functions of commerce are different." *Kidd v. Pearson.* Though that approach likely would not have survived even if confined to the question of a State's authority to enact legislation, it was not at all propitious when applied to the quite different question of what subjects were within the reach of the national power when Congress chose to exercise it.

This became evident when the Court began to confront federal economic regulation enacted in response to the rapid industrial development in the late 19th century. Thus, it relied upon the manufacture-commerce dichotomy in *United States v. E.C. Knight Co.*, where a manufacturers' combination controlling some 98% of the Nation's domestic sugar refining capacity was held to be outside the reach of the Sherman Act. Conspiracies to control manufacture, agriculture, mining, production, wages, or prices, the Court explained, had too "indirect" an effect on interstate commerce. And in *Adair v. United States*, 208 U.S. 161 (1908), the Court rejected the view that the commerce power might extend to activities that, although local in the sense of having originated within a single State, nevertheless had a practical effect on interstate commercial activity....

The history of our Commerce Clause decisions contains at least two lessons of relevance to this case. The first, as stated at the outset, is the imprecision of content-based boundaries used without more to define the limits of the Commerce Clause. The second, related to the first but of even greater consequence, is that the Court as an institution and the legal system as a whole have an immense stake in the stability of our Commerce Clause jurisprudence as it has evolved to this point. *Stare decisis* operates with great force in counseling us not to call in question the essential principles now in place respecting the congressional power to regulate transactions of a commercial nature. That fundamental restraint on our power forecloses us from reverting to an understanding of commerce that would serve only an 18th-century economy, dependent then upon production and trading practices that had changed but little over the preceding centuries; it also mandates against returning to the time when congressional authority to regulate undoubted commercial activities was limited by a judicial determination that those matters had an insufficient connection to an interstate system. Congress can regulate in the commercial sphere on the assumption that we have a single market and a unified purpose to build a stable national economy....

The statute before us upsets the federal balance to a degree that renders it an unconstitutional assertion of the commerce power, and our intervention is required. As THE CHIEF JUSTICE explains, unlike the earlier cases to come before the Court here neither the actors nor their conduct have a commercial character, and neither the purposes nor the design of the statute have an evident commercial nexus. The statute makes the simple possession of a gun within 1,000 feet of the grounds of the school a criminal offense. In a sense any conduct in this interdependent world of ours has an ultimate commercial origin or consequence, but we have not yet said the commerce power may reach so far. If Congress attempts that extension, then at the least we must inquire whether the exercise of national power seeks to intrude upon an area of traditional state concern.

An interference of these dimensions occurs here, for it is well established that education is a traditional concern of the States. The proximity to schools, including of course schools owned and operated by the States or their subdivisions, is the very premise for making the conduct criminal. In these circumstances, we have a particular duty to insure that the federal-state balance is not destroyed.

While it is doubtful that any State, or indeed any reasonable person, would argue that it is wise policy to allow students to carry guns on school premises, considerable disagreement exists about how best to accomplish that goal. In this circumstance, the theory and utility of our federalism are revealed, for the States may perform their role as laboratories for experimentation to devise various solutions where the best solution is far from clear....

The statute now before us forecloses the States from experimenting and exercising their own judgment in an area to which States lay claim by right of history and expertise, and it does so by regulating an activity beyond the realm of commerce in the ordinary and usual sense of that term....

JUSTICE THOMAS, concurring.

[I] write separately to observe that our case law has drifted far from the original understanding of the Commerce Clause. In a future case, we ought to temper our Commerce Clause jurisprudence in a manner that both makes sense of our more recent case law and is more faithful to the original understanding of that Clause....

In an appropriate case, I believe that we must ... reconsider our "substantial effects" test with an eye toward constructing a standard that reflects the text and history of the Commerce Clause without totally rejecting our more recent Commerce Clause jurisprudence....

I

At the time the original Constitution was ratified, "commerce" consisted of selling, buying, and bartering, as well as transporting for these purposes.... In fact, when Federalists and Anti-Federalists discussed the Commerce Clause during the ratification period, they often used trade (in its selling/bartering sense) and commerce interchangeably.

As one would expect, the term "commerce" was used in contradistinction to productive activities such as manufacturing and agriculture....

Interjecting a modern sense of commerce into the Constitution generates significant textual and structural problems. For example, one cannot replace "commerce" with a different type of enterprise, such as manufacturing. When a manufacturer produces a car, assembly cannot take place "with a foreign nation" or "with the Indian Tribes."

Parts may come from different States or other nations and hence may have been in the flow of commerce at one time, but manufacturing takes place at a discrete site. Agriculture and manufacturing involve the production of goods; commerce encompasses traffic in such articles....

The Constitution not only uses the word "commerce" in a narrower sense than our case law might suggest, it also does not support the proposition that Congress has authority over all activities that "substantially affect" interstate commerce. The Commerce Clause does not state that Congress may "regulate matters that substantially affect commerce with foreign Nations, and among the several States, and with the Indian Tribes." In contrast, the Constitution itself temporarily prohibited amendments that would "affect" Congress' lack of authority to prohibit or restrict the slave trade or to enact unproportioned direct taxation. U.S. Const., Art. V. Clearly, the Framers could have drafted a Constitution that contained a "substantially affects interstate commerce" clause had that been their objective....

[Much] if not all of Art. I, §8 (including portions of the Commerce Clause itself) would be surplusage if Congress had been given authority over matters that substantially affect interstate commerce. An interpretation of cl. 3 that makes the rest of §8 superfluous simply cannot be correct. Yet this Court's Commerce Clause jurisprudence has endorsed just such an interpretation: the power we have accorded Congress has swallowed Art. I, §8....

Our construction of the scope of congressional authority has the additional problem of coming close to turning the Tenth Amendment on its head....

## II

The exchanges during the ratification campaign reveal the relatively limited reach of the Commerce Clause and of federal power generally. The Founding Fathers confirmed that most areas of life (even many matters that would have substantial effects on commerce) would remain outside the reach of the Federal Government. Such affairs would continue to be under the exclusive control of the States....

The comments of Hamilton and others about federal power reflected the well-known truth that the new Government would have only the limited and enumerated powers found in the Constitution. Agriculture and manufacture, since they were not surrendered to the Federal Government, were state concerns. Even before the passage of the Tenth Amendment, it was apparent that Congress would possess only those powers "herein granted" by the rest of the Constitution. U.S. Const., Art. I, §1.

Where the Constitution was meant to grant federal authority over an activity substantially affecting interstate commerce, the Constitution contains an enumerated power over that particular activity....

In short, the Founding Fathers were well aware of what [Justice Breyer's] dissent calls "economic ... realities." Even though the boundary between commerce and other matters may ignore "economic reality" and thus seem arbitrary or artificial to some, we must nevertheless respect a constitutional line that does not grant Congress power over all that substantially affects interstate commerce.

## III

\* \* \*

### A

… From an early moment, the Court rejected the notion that Congress can regulate everything that affects interstate commerce. That the internal commerce of the States and the numerous state inspection, quarantine, and health laws had substantial effects on interstate commerce cannot be doubted. Nevertheless, they were not "surrendered to the general government." …

### B

I am aware of no cases prior to the New Deal that characterized the power flowing from the Commerce Clause as sweepingly as does our substantial effects test. My review of the case law indicates that the substantial effects test is but an innovation of the 20th century.…

As recently as 1936, the Court continued to insist that the Commerce Clause did not reach the wholly internal business of the States. *See Carter Coal.* The Federal Government simply could not reach such subjects regardless of their effects on interstate commerce.

These cases all establish a simple point: from the time of the ratification of the Constitution to the mid-1930's, it was widely understood that the Constitution granted Congress only limited powers, notwithstanding the Commerce Clause. Moreover, there was no question that activities wholly separated from business, such as gun possession, were beyond the reach of the commerce power. If anything, the "wrong turn" was the Court's dramatic departure in the 1930's from a century and a half of precedent.

## IV

The substantial effects test suffers from the further flaw that it appears to grant Congress a police power over the Nation. When asked at oral argument if there were any limits to the Commerce Clause, the Government was at a loss for words. Likewise, the principal dissent insists that there are limits, but it cannot muster even one example. Indeed, the dissent implicitly concedes that its reading has no limits when it criticizes the Court for "threatening legal uncertainty in an area of law that … seemed reasonably well settled." The one advantage of the dissent's standard is certainty: it is certain that under its analysis everything may be regulated under the guise of the Commerce Clause.

The substantial effects test suffers from this flaw, in part, because of its "aggregation principle." …

## V

This extended discussion of the original understanding and our first century and a half of case law does not necessarily require a wholesale abandonment of our more recent opinions. It simply reveals that our substantial effects test is far removed from both the Constitution and from our early case law and that the Court's opinion should not be viewed as "radical" or another "wrong turn" that must be corrected in the future. The analysis also suggests that we ought to temper our Commerce Clause jurisprudence.

Unless the dissenting Justices are willing to repudiate our long-held understanding of the limited nature of federal power, I would think that they too must be willing to reconsider the substantial effects test in a future case. If we wish to be true to a Constitution that does not cede a police power to the Federal Government, our Commerce Clause's boundaries simply cannot be "defined" as being "commensurate with the national needs" or self-consciously intended to let the Federal Government "defend itself against economic forces that Congress decrees inimical or destructive of the national economy." Such a formulation of federal power is no test at all: it is a blank check.

At an appropriate juncture, I think we must modify our Commerce Clause jurisprudence. Today, it is easy enough to say that the Clause certainly does not empower Congress to ban gun possession within 1,000 feet of a school.

JUSTICE STEVENS, dissenting.

The welfare of our future "Commerce with foreign Nations, and among the several States," U.S. Const., Art. I, §8, cl. 3, is vitally dependent on the character of the education of our children....

Guns are both articles of commerce and articles that can be used to restrain commerce. Their possession is the consequence, either directly or indirectly, of commercial activity. In my judgment, Congress' power to regulate commerce in firearms includes the power to prohibit possession of guns at any location because of their potentially harmful use; it necessarily follows that Congress may also prohibit their possession in particular markets. The market for the possession of handguns by school-age children is, distressingly, substantial. Whether or not the national interest in eliminating that market would have justified federal legislation in 1789, it surely does today.

JUSTICE SOUTER, dissenting....

I

... [The] period from the turn of the century to 1937 is better noted for a series of cases applying highly formalistic notions of "commerce" to invalidate federal social and economic legislation, see *e.g.*, *Carter Coal*; *Hammer v. Dagenhart*, 247 U.S. 251 (1918) [Note *supra.* this chapter].

These restrictive views of commerce subject to congressional power complemented the Court's activism in limiting the enforceable scope of state economic regulation. It is most familiar history that during this same period the Court routinely invalidated state social and economic legislation under an expansive conception of Fourteenth Amendment substantive due process. The fulcrums of judicial review in these cases were the notions of liberty and property characteristic of laissez-faire economics, whereas the Commerce Clause cases turned on what was ostensibly a structural limit of federal power, but under each conception of judicial review the Court's character for the first third of the century showed itself in exacting judicial scrutiny of a legislature's choice of economic ends and of the legislative means selected to reach them.

It was not merely coincidental, then, that sea changes in the Court's conceptions of its authority under the Due Process and Commerce Clauses occurred virtually together, in 1937.... In the years following these decisions, deference to legislative policy judgments on commercial regulation became the powerful theme under both the Due Process and Commerce Clauses, and in due course that deference became articulate in the standard of rationality review....

## II

There is today, however, a backward glance at both the old pitfalls, as the Court treats deference under the rationality rule as subject to gradation according to the commercial or noncommercial nature of the immediate subject of the challenged regulation. The distinction between what is patently commercial and what is not looks much like the old distinction between what directly affects commerce and what touches it only indirectly. And the act of calibrating the level of deference by drawing a line between what is patently commercial and what is less purely so will probably resemble the process of deciding how much interference with contractual freedom was fatal. Thus, it seems fair to ask whether the step taken by the Court today does anything but portend a return to the untenable jurisprudence from which the Court extricated itself almost 60 years ago. The answer is not reassuring. To be sure, the occasion for today's decision reflects the century's end, not its beginning. But if it seems anomalous that the Congress of the United States has taken to regulating school yards, the act in question is still probably no more remarkable than state regulation of bake shops 90 years ago [in *Lochner v. New York*, 198 U.S. 45 (1905)]. In any event, there is no reason to hope that the Court's qualification of rational basis review will be any more successful than the efforts at substantive economic review made by our predecessors as the century began. Taking the Court's opinion on its own terms, JUSTICE BREYER has explained both the hopeless porosity of "commercial" character as a ground of Commerce Clause distinction in America's highly connected economy, and the inconsistency of this categorization with our rational basis precedents from the last 50 years.

Further glosses on rationality review, moreover, may be in the offing. Although this case turns on commercial character, the Court gestures toward two other considerations that it might sometime entertain in applying rational basis scrutiny (apart from a statutory obligation to supply independent proof of a jurisdictional element): does the congressional statute deal with subjects of traditional state regulation, and does the statute contain explicit factual findings supporting the otherwise implicit determination that the regulated activity substantially affects interstate commerce? Once again, any appeal these considerations may have depends on ignoring the painful lesson learned in 1937, for neither of the Court's suggestions would square with rational basis scrutiny....

## III

Because JUSTICE BREYER's opinion demonstrates beyond any doubt that the Act in question passes the rationality review that the Court continues to espouse, today's decision may be seen as only a misstep, its reasoning and its suggestions not quite in gear with the prevailing standard, but hardly an epochal case. I would not argue otherwise, but I would raise a caveat. Not every epochal case has come in epochal trappings. *Jones & Laughlin* did not reject the direct-indirect standard in so many words; it just said the relation of the regulated subject matter to commerce was direct enough. But we know what happened.

I respectfully dissent.

JUSTICE BREYER, with whom JUSTICE STEVENS, JUSTICE SOUTER, and JUSTICE GINSBURG join, dissenting....

## II

... [We] must ask whether Congress could have had a rational basis for finding a significant (or substantial) connection between gun-related school violence and interstate commerce.... As long as one views the commerce connection, not as a "technical legal conception," but as "a practical one," the answer to this question must be yes. Numerous reports and studies—generated both inside and outside government—make clear that Congress could reasonably have found the empirical connection that its law, implicitly or explicitly, asserts.

For one thing, reports, hearings, and other readily available literature make clear that the problem of guns in and around schools is widespread and extremely serious. These materials report, for example, that four percent of American high school students (and six percent of inner-city high school students) carry a gun to school at least occasionally, that 12 percent of urban high school students have had guns fired at them; that 20 percent of those students have been threatened with guns; and that, in any 6-month period, several hundred thousand schoolchildren are victims of violent crimes in or near their schools. And, they report that this widespread violence in schools throughout the Nation significantly interferes with the quality of education in those schools. Based on reports such as these, Congress obviously could have thought that guns and learning are mutually exclusive. And, Congress could therefore have found a substantial educational problem—teachers unable to teach, students unable to learn—and concluded that guns near schools contribute substantially to the size and scope of that problem.

Having found that guns in schools significantly undermine the quality of education in our Nation's classrooms, Congress could also have found, given the effect of education upon interstate and foreign commerce, that gun-related violence in and around schools is a commercial, as well as a human, problem. Education, although far more than a matter of economics, has long been inextricably intertwined with the Nation's economy.... Scholars estimate that nearly a quarter of America's economic growth in the early years of this century is traceable directly to increased schooling; that investment in "human capital" (through spending on education) exceeded investment in "physical capital" by a ratio of almost two to one; and that the economic returns to this investment in education exceeded the returns to conventional capital investment.

In recent years the link between secondary education and business has strengthened, becoming both more direct and more important. Scholars on the subject report that technological changes and innovations in management techniques have altered the nature of the workplace so that more jobs now demand greater educational skills....

Increasing global competition also has made primary and secondary education economically more important.... Congress has said, when writing other statutes, that "functionally or technologically illiterate" Americans in the work force "erode" our economic "standing in the international marketplace," and that "our Nation is ... paying the price of scientific and technological illiteracy, with our productivity declining, our industrial base ailing, and our global competitiveness dwindling."

Finally, there is evidence that, today more than ever, many firms base their location decisions upon the presence, or absence, of a work force with a basic education....

The economic links I have just sketched seem fairly obvious. Why then is it not equally obvious, in light of those links, that a widespread, serious, and substantial physical threat to teaching and learning also substantially threatens the commerce to which that teaching and learning is inextricably tied? That is to say, guns in the hands of six percent of inner-city high school students and gun-related violence throughout a city's schools must threaten the trade and commerce that those schools support. The only question, then, is whether the latter threat is (to use the majority's terminology) "substantial." The evidence of (1) the *extent* of the gun-related violence problem, (2) the *extent* of the resulting negative effect on classroom learning, and (3) the *extent* of the consequent negative commercial effects, when taken together, indicate a threat to trade and commerce that is "substantial." At the very least, Congress could rationally have concluded that the links are "substantial." ...

To hold this statute constitutional is not to "obliterate" the "distinction between what is national and what is local," *ante*; nor is it to hold that the Commerce Clause permits the Federal Government to "regulate any activity that it found was related to the economic productivity of individual citizens," to regulate "marriage, divorce, and child custody," or to regulate any and all aspects of education. First, this statute is aimed at curbing a particularly acute threat to the educational process—the possession (and use) of life-threatening firearms in, or near, the classroom.... Second, the immediacy of the connection between education and the national economic well-being is documented by scholars and accepted by society at large in a way and to a degree that may not hold true for other social institutions. It must surely be the rare case, then, that a statute strikes at conduct that (when considered in the abstract) seems so removed from commerce, but which (practically speaking) has so significant an impact upon commerce.

In sum, a holding that the particular statute before us falls within the commerce power would not expand the scope of that Clause. Rather, it simply would apply pre-existing law to changing economic circumstances. It would recognize that, in today's economic world, gun-related violence near the classroom makes a significant difference to our economic, as well as our social, well-being....

### III

The majority's holding—that §922 falls outside the scope of the Commerce Clause—creates three serious legal problems. First, the majority's holding runs contrary to modern Supreme Court cases that have upheld congressional actions despite connections to interstate or foreign commerce that are less significant than the effect of school violence....

The second legal problem the Court creates comes from its apparent belief that it can reconcile its holding with earlier cases by making a critical distinction between "commercial" and noncommercial "transactions."... As a general matter, this approach fails to heed this Court's earlier warning not to turn "questions of the power of Congress" upon "formula[s]" that would give

> "controlling force to nomenclature such as 'production' and 'indirect' and foreclose consideration of the actual effects of the activity in question upon interstate commerce." *Wickard*....

More importantly, if a distinction between commercial and noncommercial activities is to be made, this is not the case in which to make it.... Schools that teach reading, writing, mathematics, and related basic skills serve both social and commercial purposes, and one cannot easily separate the one from the other. American industry itself has been, and is again, involved in teaching. When, and to what extent, does its involvement make education commercial? Does the number of vocational classes that train students directly for jobs make a difference? Does it matter if the school is public or private, nonprofit or profit-seeking? Does it matter if a city or State adopts a voucher plan that pays private firms to run a school? ...

Regardless, if there is a principled distinction that could work both here and in future cases, Congress (even in the absence of vocational classes, industry involvement, and private management) could rationally conclude that schools fall on the commercial side of the line....

The third legal problem created by the Court's holding is that it threatens legal uncertainty in an area of law that, until this case, seemed reasonably well settled. Congress has enacted many statutes (more than 100 sections of the United States Code), including criminal statutes (at least 25 sections), that use the words "affecting commerce" to define their scope, and other statutes that contain no jurisdictional language at all. Do these, or similar, statutes regulate noncommercial activities? If so, would that alter the meaning of "affecting commerce" in a jurisdictional element? More importantly, in the absence of a jurisdictional element, are the courts nevertheless to take *Wickard* (and later similar cases) as inapplicable, and to judge the effect of a single noncommercial activity on interstate commerce without considering similar instances of the forbidden conduct? However these questions are eventually resolved, the legal uncertainty now created will restrict Congress' ability to enact criminal laws aimed at criminal behavior that, considered problem by problem rather than instance by instance, seriously threatens the economic, as well as social, well-being of Americans....

## Note: The Congressional Response to Lopez

*Lopez* notes that a statute that does not regulate economic activity may nevertheless be a valid Commerce Clause regulation if it includes a "jurisdictional element" — that is, a statutory requirement that the item being regulated has traveled in interstate commerce. A year after *Lopez*, Congress amended 18 U.S.C. § 922(q) to include a jurisdictional element. As amended, the section reads as follows (italics added):

> It shall be unlawful for any individual knowingly to possess a firearm *that has moved in or that otherwise affects interstate or foreign commerce* at a place that the individual knows, or has reasonable cause to believe, is a school zone.

The requirement that the firearm have "moved in ... or otherwise affects interstate or foreign commerce" requires proof, on a case-by-case basis, that the particular firearm at issue moved in or affected interstate commerce. To what degree does this requirement limit the statute's scope, as compared with the version of the statute struck down in *Lopez*?

## Note: United States v. Morrison *and the Role of Congressional Fact Finding*

*Lopez* held open the possibility that the Court would uphold a federal statute with only tenuous links to interstate commerce if Congress found facts establishing the link between the regulated activity and interstate commerce. This raised at least the possibility that Congress could avoid having its handiwork struck down if it supplied fact findings to accompany any such statutes. In *United States v. Morrison*, 529 U.S. 598 (2000), the Court confronted the question of the legal significance of such findings to the Court's Commerce Clause analysis.

*Morrison* concerned a provision of the Violence Against Women Act (VAWA) that provided victims of gender-motivated violence with a federal law cause of action against their attackers. The government defended VAWA's constitutionality by pointing to Congress's fact findings tending to show that gender-motivated violence affected interstate commerce by, among other things, raising insurance costs and deterring interstate migration to areas where such violence was prevalent.

The Court did not find the fact findings relevant to the constitutional analysis. Writing for a five-Justice majority, Chief Justice Rehnquist wrote:

> In these cases, Congress' findings are substantially weakened by the fact that they rely so heavily on a method of reasoning that we have already rejected as unworkable if we are to maintain the Constitution's enumeration of powers. Congress found that gender-motivated violence affects interstate commerce

'by deterring potential victims from traveling interstate, from engaging in employment in interstate business, and from transacting with business, and in places involved in interstate commerce; … by diminishing national productivity, increasing medical and other costs, and decreasing the supply of and the demand for interstate products.' H.R. Conf. Rep. No. 103-711.

Given these findings and petitioners' arguments, the concern that we expressed in *Lopez* that Congress might use the Commerce Clause to completely obliterate the Constitution's distinction between national and local authority seems well founded. The reasoning that petitioners advance seeks to follow the but-for causal chain from the initial occurrence of violent crime (the suppression of which has always been the prime object of the States' police power) to every attenuated effect upon interstate commerce. If accepted, petitioners' reasoning would allow Congress to regulate any crime as long as the nationwide, aggregated impact of that crime has substantial effects on employment, production, transit, or consumption. Indeed, if Congress may regulate gender-motivated violence, it would be able to regulate murder or any other type of violence since gender-motivated violence, as a subset of all violent crime, is certain to have lesser economic impacts than the larger class of which it is a part.

Writing for the Court, Chief Justice Rehnquist thus "rejected the argument that Congress may regulate noneconomic, violent criminal conduct based solely on that conduct's aggregate effect on interstate commerce."

## Gonzales v. Raich

### 545 U.S. 1 (2005)

JUSTICE STEVENS delivered the opinion of the Court.

California is one of at least nine States that authorize the use of marijuana for medicinal purposes. The question presented in this case is whether the power vested in Congress by Article I, §8, of the Constitution "to make all Laws which shall be necessary and proper for carrying into Execution" its authority to "regulate Commerce with foreign Nations, and among the several States" includes the power to prohibit the local cultivation and use of marijuana in compliance with California law.…

### I

[This case involved two seriously-ill Californians who sought to ingest marijuana in order to alleviate serious pain. The marijuana was prescribed by physicians pursuant to California law allowing medical uses of marijuana. One of the plaintiffs cultivated her own marijuana; the other relied on two cultivators who provided it free of charge.] …

### III

Respondents in this case do not dispute that passage of the [Controlled Substances Act], as part of the Comprehensive Drug Abuse Prevention and Control Act, was well within Congress' commerce power.… Rather, respondents' challenge is actually quite limited; they argue that the CSA's categorical prohibition of the manufacture and possession of marijuana as applied to the intrastate manufacture and possession of marijuana for medical purposes pursuant to California law exceeds Congress' authority under the Commerce Clause....

Our case law firmly establishes Congress' power to regulate purely local activities that are part of an economic "class of activities" that have a substantial effect on interstate commerce. *Wickard v. Filburn* (1942) [*Supra.* this chapter]. As we stated in *Wickard,* "even if appellee's activity be local and though it may not be regarded as commerce, it may still, whatever its nature, be reached by Congress if it exerts a substantial economic effect on interstate commerce." We have never required Congress to legislate with scientific exactitude. When Congress decides that the "total incidence" of a practice poses a threat to a national market, it may regulate the entire class. In this vein, we have reiterated that when "a general regulatory statute bears a substantial relation to commerce, the *de minimis* character of individual instances arising under that statute is of no consequence." ...

The similarities between this case and *Wickard* are striking. Like the farmer in *Wickard,* respondents are cultivating, for home consumption, a fungible commodity for which there is an established, albeit illegal, interstate market. Just as the Agricultural Adjustment Act was designed "to control the volume [of wheat] moving in interstate and foreign commerce in order to avoid surpluses ..." and consequently control the market price, a primary purpose of the CSA is to control the supply and demand of controlled substances in both lawful and unlawful drug markets. In *Wickard* we had no difficulty concluding that Congress had a rational basis for believing that, when viewed in the aggregate, leaving home-consumed wheat outside the regulatory scheme would have a substantial influence on price and market conditions. Here too, Congress had a rational basis for concluding that leaving home-consumed marijuana outside federal control would similarly affect price and market conditions.

More concretely, one concern prompting inclusion of wheat grown for home consumption in the 1938 Act was that rising market prices could draw such wheat into the interstate market, resulting in lower market prices. The parallel concern making it appropriate to include marijuana grown for home consumption in the CSA is the likelihood that the high demand in the interstate market will draw such marijuana into that market. While the diversion of homegrown wheat tended to frustrate the federal interest in stabilizing prices by regulating the volume of commercial transactions in the interstate market, the diversion of homegrown marijuana tends to frustrate the federal interest in eliminating commercial transactions in the interstate market in their entirety. In both cases, the regulation is squarely within Congress' commerce power because production of the commodity meant for home consumption, be it wheat or marijuana, has a substantial effect on supply and demand in the national market for that commodity.

Nonetheless, respondents suggest that *Wickard* differs from this case in three respects: (1) the Agricultural Adjustment Act, unlike the CSA, exempted small farming operations; (2) *Wickard* involved a "quintessential economic activity" — a commercial farm — whereas respondents do not sell marijuana; and (3) the *Wickard* record made it clear that the aggregate production of wheat for use on farms had a significant impact on market prices. Those differences, though factually accurate, do not diminish the precedential force of this Court's reasoning.

The fact that Filburn's own impact on the market was "trivial by itself" was not a sufficient reason for removing him from the scope of federal regulation. That the Secretary of Agriculture elected to exempt even smaller farms from regulation does not speak to his power to regulate all those whose aggregated production was significant, nor did that fact play any role in the Court's analysis. Moreover, even though Filburn was indeed a commercial farmer, the activity he was engaged in—the cultivation of wheat for home consumption—was not treated by the Court as part of his commercial farming operation. And while it is true that the record in the *Wickard* case itself established the causal connection between the production for local use and the national market, we have before us findings by Congress to the same effect....

In assessing the scope of Congress' authority under the Commerce Clause, we stress that the task before us is a modest one. We need not determine whether respondents' activities, taken in the aggregate, substantially affect interstate commerce in fact, but only whether a "rational basis" exists for so concluding. *United States Lopez* (1995) [*Supra.* this chapter]. Given the enforcement difficulties that attend distinguishing between marijuana cultivated locally and marijuana grown elsewhere, and concerns about diversion into illicit channels, we have no difficulty concluding that Congress had a rational basis for believing that failure to regulate the intrastate manufacture and possession of marijuana would leave a gaping hole in the CSA. Thus, as in *Wickard* when it enacted comprehensive legislation to regulate the interstate market in a fungible commodity, Congress was acting well within its authority to "make all Laws which shall be necessary and proper" to "regulate Commerce ... among the several States." ...

### IV

To support their contrary submission, respondents rely heavily on two of our more recent Commerce Clause cases. In their myopic focus, they overlook the larger context of modern-era Commerce Clause jurisprudence preserved by those cases. Moreover ... they read those cases far too broadly.

Those two cases, of course, are *Lopez* and *United States v. Morrison*, 529 U.S. 598 (2000) [Note *supra.* this chapter]. As an initial matter, the statutory challenges at issue in those cases were markedly different from the challenge respondents pursue in the case at hand. Here, respondents ask us to excise individual applications of a concededly valid statutory scheme. In contrast, in both *Lopez* and *Morrison* the parties asserted that a particular statute or provision fell outside Congress' commerce power in its entirety. This distinction is pivotal for we have often reiterated that "where the class of activities is regulated and that class is within the reach of federal power, the courts have no power to excise, as trivial, individual instances of the class."

At issue in *Lopez* was the validity of the Gun-Free School Zones Act of 1990, which was a brief, single-subject statute making it a crime for an individual to possess a gun in a school zone. The Act did not regulate any economic activity and did not contain any requirement that the possession of a gun have any connection to past interstate activity or a pre*dict*able impact on future commercial activity. Distinguishing our earlier cases holding that comprehensive regulatory statutes may be validly applied to local conduct that does not, when viewed in isolation, have a significant impact on interstate commerce, we held the statute invalid. We explained:

> Section 922(q) is a criminal statute that by its terms has nothing to do with 'commerce' or any sort of economic enterprise, however broadly one might define those terms. Section 922(q) is not an essential part of a larger regulation of economic activity, in which the regulatory scheme could be undercut unless the intrastate activity were regulated. It cannot, therefore, be sustained under our cases upholding regulations of activities that arise out of or are connected with a commercial transaction, which viewed in the aggregate, substantially affects interstate commerce.

The statutory scheme that the Government is defending in this litigation is at the opposite end of the regulatory spectrum. As explained above, the CSA, enacted in 1970 as part of the Comprehensive Drug Abuse Prevention and Control Act, was a lengthy and detailed statute creating a comprehensive framework for regulating the production, distribution, and possession of five classes of "controlled substances." ...

While the statute provided for the periodic updating of the five schedules, Congress itself made the initial classifications. It identified 42 opiates, 22 opium derivatives, and 17 hallucinogenic substances as Schedule I drugs. Marijuana was listed as the 10th item in the third subcategory. That classification, unlike the discrete prohibition established by the Gun-Free School Zones Act of 1990, was merely one of many "essential parts of a larger regulation of economic activity, in which the regulatory scheme could be undercut unless the intrastate activity were regulated." *Lopez*. Our opinion in *Lopez* casts no doubt on the validity of such a program.

Nor does this Court's holding in *Morrison*. The Violence Against Women Act of 1994 created a federal civil remedy for the victims of gender-motivated crimes of violence. The remedy was enforceable in both state and federal courts, and generally depended on proof of the violation of a state law. Despite congressional findings that such crimes had an adverse impact on interstate commerce, we held the statute unconstitutional because, like the statute in *Lopez*, it did not regulate economic activity. We concluded that "the noneconomic, criminal nature of the conduct at issue was central to our decision" in *Lopez*, and that our prior cases had identified a clear pattern of analysis: "Where economic activity substantially affects interstate commerce, legislation regulating that activity will be sustained."

Unlike those at issue in *Lopez* and *Morrison*, the activities regulated by the CSA are quintessentially economic. "Economics" refers to "the production, distribution, and consumption of commodities." *Webster's Third New International Dictionary* (1966). The CSA is a statute that regulates the production, distribution, and consumption of commodities for which there is an established, and lucrative, interstate market. Prohibiting the intrastate possession or manufacture of an article of commerce is a rational (and commonly utilized) means of regulating commerce in that product....

The Court of Appeals was able to conclude otherwise only by isolating a "separate and distinct" class of activities that it held to be beyond the reach of federal power, defined as "the intrastate, noncommercial cultivation, possession and use of marijuana for personal medical purposes on the advice of a physician and in accordance with state law." ... The differences between the members of a class so defined and the principal traffickers in Schedule I substances might be sufficient to justify a policy decision exempting the narrower class from the coverage of the CSA. The question, however, is whether Congress' contrary policy judgment, *i.e.*, its decision to include this narrower "class of activities" within the larger regulatory scheme, was constitutionally deficient. We have no difficulty concluding that Congress acted rationally in determining that none of the characteristics making up the purported class, whether viewed individually or in the aggregate, compelled an exemption from the CSA; rather, the subdivided class of activities defined by the Court of Appeals was an essential part of the larger regulatory scheme.

First, the fact that marijuana is used "for personal medical purposes on the advice of a physician" cannot itself serve as a distinguishing factor. The CSA designates marijuana as contraband for *any* purpose; in fact, by characterizing marijuana as a Schedule I drug, Congress expressly found that the drug has no acceptable medical uses....

Nor can it serve as an "objective marker" or "objective factor" to arbitrarily narrow the relevant class as the dissenters suggest. More fundamentally, if, as the principal dissent contends, the personal cultivation, possession, and use of marijuana for medicinal purposes is beyond the "outer limits" of Congress' Commerce Clause authority, it must also be true that such personal use of marijuana (or any other homegrown drug) for recreational purposes is also beyond those "outer limits" whether or not a State elects to authorize or even regulate such use....

Second, limiting the activity to marijuana possession and cultivation "in accordance with state law" cannot serve to place respondents' activities beyond congressional reach. The Supremacy Clause unambiguously provides that if there is any conflict between federal and state law, federal law shall prevail....

Respondents acknowledge this proposition, but nonetheless contend that their activities were not "an essential part of a larger regulatory scheme" because they had been "isolated by the State of California, and [are] policed by the State of California," and thus remain "entirely separated from the market." The dissenters fall prey to similar reasoning. The notion that California law has surgically excised a discrete activity that is hermetically sealed off from the larger interstate marijuana market is a dubious proposition, and, more importantly, one that Congress could have rationally rejected....

The exemption for cultivation by patients and caregivers can only increase the supply of marijuana in the California market. The likelihood that all such production will promptly terminate when patients recover or will precisely match the patients' medical needs during their convalescence seems remote; whereas the danger that excesses will satisfy some of the admittedly enormous demand for recreational use seems obvious....

So, from the "separate and distinct" class of activities identified by the Court of Appeals (and adopted by the dissenters), we are left with "the intrastate, noncommercial cultivation, possession and use of marijuana." Thus the case for the exemption comes down to the claim that a locally cultivated product that is used domestically rather than sold on the open market is not subject to federal regulation. Given the findings in the CSA and the undisputed magnitude of the commercial market for marijuana, our decisions in *Wickard v. Fillburn* and the later cases endorsing its reasoning foreclose that claim....

JUSTICE SCALIA, concurring in the judgment.

I agree with the Court's holding that the Controlled Substances Act (CSA) may validly be applied to respondents' cultivation, distribution, and possession of marijuana for personal, medicinal use. I write separately because my understanding of the doctrinal foundation on which that holding rests is, if not inconsistent with that of the Court, at least more nuanced.

Since *Perez v. United States*, 402 U.S. 146 (1971) [Note *supra.* this chapter], our cases have mechanically recited that the Commerce Clause permits congressional regulation of three categories: (1) the channels of interstate commerce; (2) the instrumentalities of interstate commerce, and persons or things in interstate commerce; and (3) activities that "substantially affect" interstate commerce. The first two categories are self-evident, since they are the ingredients of interstate commerce itself. The third category, however, is different in kind, and its recitation without explanation is misleading and incomplete.

It is *misleading* because, unlike the channels, instrumentalities, and agents of interstate commerce, activities that substantially affect interstate commerce are not themselves part of interstate commerce, and thus the power to regulate them cannot come from the Commerce Clause alone. Rather ... Congress's regulatory authority over intrastate activities that are not themselves part of interstate commerce (including activities that have a substantial effect on interstate commerce) derives from the Necessary and Proper Clause. And the category of "activities that substantially affect interstate commerce" is *incomplete* because the authority to enact laws necessary and proper for the regulation of interstate commerce is not limited to laws governing intrastate activities that substantially affect interstate commerce. Where necessary to make a regulation of interstate commerce effective, Congress may regulate even those intrastate activities that do not themselves substantially affect interstate commerce.

I

Our cases show that the regulation of intrastate activities may be necessary to and proper for the regulation of interstate commerce in two general circumstances. Most directly, the commerce power permits Congress not only to devise rules for the governance of commerce between States but also to facilitate interstate commerce by eliminating potential obstructions, and to restrict it by eliminating potential stimulants. . . .

*Lopez* and *Morrison* recognized the expansive scope of Congress's authority in this regard: "The pattern is clear. Where economic activity substantially affects interstate commerce, legislation regulating that activity will be sustained."

This principle is not without limitation. In *Lopez* and *Morrison*, the Court — conscious of the potential of the "substantially affects" test to "obliterate the distinction between what is national and what is local," — rejected the argument that Congress may regulate *noneconomic* activity based solely on the effect that it may have on interstate commerce through a remote chain of inferences. "If we were to accept [such] arguments," the Court reasoned in *Lopez* "we are hard pressed to posit any activity by an individual that Congress is without power to regulate." Thus, although Congress's authority to regulate intrastate activity that substantially affects interstate commerce is broad, it does not permit the Court to "pile inference upon inference" in order to establish that noneconomic activity has a substantial effect on interstate commerce.

As we implicitly acknowledged in *Lopez*, however, Congress's authority to enact laws necessary and proper for the regulation of interstate commerce is not limited to laws directed against economic activities that have a substantial effect on interstate commerce. Though the conduct in *Lopez* was not economic, the Court nevertheless recognized that it could be regulated as "an essential part of a larger regulation of economic activity, in which the regulatory scheme could be undercut unless the intrastate activity were regulated." . . .

Although this power "to make . . . regulation effective" commonly overlaps with the authority to regulate economic activities that substantially affect interstate commerce, and may in some cases have been confused with that authority, the two are distinct. The regulation of an intrastate activity may be essential to a comprehensive regulation of interstate commerce even though the intrastate activity does not itself "substantially affect" interstate commerce. Moreover, as the passage from *Lopez* quoted above suggests, Congress may regulate even noneconomic local activity if that regulation is a necessary part of a more general regulation of interstate commerce. The relevant question is simply whether the means chosen are "reasonably adapted" to the attainment of a legitimate end under the commerce power. . . .

## II

Today's principal dissent objects that, by permitting Congress to regulate activities necessary to effective interstate regulation, the Court reduces *Lopez* and *Morrison* to "little more than a drafting guide." I think that criticism unjustified. Unlike the power to regulate activities that have a substantial effect on interstate commerce, the power to enact laws enabling effective regulation of interstate commerce can only be exercised in conjunction with congressional regulation of an interstate market, and it extends only to those measures necessary to make the interstate regulation effective. As *Lopez* itself states, and the Court affirms today, Congress may regulate noneconomic intrastate activities only where the failure to do so "could ... undercut" its regulation of interstate commerce. This is not a power that threatens to obliterate the line between "what is truly national and what is truly local." ...

### III

The application of these principles to the case before us is straightforward. In the CSA, Congress has undertaken to extinguish the interstate market in Schedule I controlled substances, including marijuana. The Commerce Clause unquestionably permits this.... To effectuate its objective, Congress has prohibited almost all intrastate activities related to Schedule I substances—both economic activities (manufacture, distribution, possession with the intent to distribute) and noneconomic activities (simple possession). That simple possession is a noneconomic activity is immaterial to whether it can be prohibited as a necessary part of a larger regulation. Rather, Congress's authority to enact all of these prohibitions of intrastate controlled-substance activities depends only upon whether they are appropriate means of achieving the legitimate end of eradicating Schedule I substances from interstate commerce.

By this measure, I think the regulation must be sustained. Not only is it impossible to distinguish "controlled substances manufactured and distributed intrastate" from "controlled substances manufactured and distributed interstate," but it hardly makes sense to speak in such terms. Drugs like marijuana are fungible commodities. As the Court explains, marijuana that is grown at home and possessed for personal use is never more than an instant from the interstate market—and this is so whether or not the possession is for medicinal use or lawful use under the laws of a particular State. Congress need not accept on faith that state law will be effective in maintaining a strict division between a lawful market for "medical" marijuana and the more general marijuana market....

JUSTICE O'CONNOR, with whom THE CHIEF JUSTICE and JUSTICE THOMAS join as to all but Part III, dissenting.

We enforce the "outer limits" of Congress' Commerce Clause authority not for their own sake, but to protect historic spheres of state sovereignty from excessive federal encroachment and thereby to maintain the distribution of power fundamental to our federalist system of government. One of federalism's chief virtues, of course, is that it promotes innovation by allowing for the possibility that "a single courageous State may, if its citizens choose, serve as a laboratory; and try novel social and economic experiments without risk to the rest of the country."

This case exemplifies the role of States as laboratories....

### II

#### A

... The Court's principal means of distinguishing *Lopez* from this case is to observe that the Gun-Free School Zones Act of 1990 was a "brief, single-subject statute," whereas the CSA is "a lengthy and detailed statute creating a comprehensive framework for regulating the production, distribution, and possession of five classes of 'controlled substances.'" Thus, according to the Court, it was possible in *Lopez* to evaluate in isolation the constitutionality of criminalizing local activity (there gun possession in school zones), whereas the local activity that the CSA targets (in this case cultivation and possession of marijuana for personal medicinal use) cannot be separated from the general drug control scheme of which it is a part.

Today's decision allows Congress to regulate intrastate activity without check, so long as there is some implication by legislative design that regulating intrastate activity is essential (and the Court appears to equate "essential" with "necessary") to the interstate regulatory scheme. Seizing upon our language in *Lopez* that the statute prohibiting gun possession in school zones was "not an essential part of a larger regulation of economic activity, in which the regulatory scheme could be undercut unless the intrastate activity were regulated," the Court appears to reason that the placement of local activity in a comprehensive scheme confirms that it is essential to that scheme. If the Court is right, then *Lopez* stands for nothing more than a drafting guide: Congress should have described the relevant crime as "transfer or possession of a firearm anywhere in the nation"—thus including commercial and noncommercial activity, and clearly encompassing some activity with assuredly substantial effect on interstate commerce....

The hard work for courts, then, is to identify objective markers for confining the analysis in Commerce Clause cases.... A number of objective markers are available to confine the scope of constitutional review here. Both federal and state legislation—including the CSA itself, the California Compassionate Use Act, and other state medical marijuana legislation—recognize that medical and nonmedical (*i.e.*, recreational) uses of drugs are realistically distinct and can be segregated, and regulate them differently. Respondents challenge only the application of the CSA to medicinal use of marijuana. Moreover, because fundamental structural concerns about dual sovereignty animate our Commerce Clause cases, it is relevant that this case involves the interplay of federal and state regulation in areas of criminal law and social policy, where "States lay claim by right of history and expertise." California, like other States, has drawn on its reserved powers to distinguish the regulation of medicinal marijuana. To ascertain whether Congress' encroachment is constitutionally justified in this case, then, I would focus here on the personal cultivation, possession, and use of marijuana for medicinal purposes.

B

Having thus defined the relevant conduct, we must determine whether, under our precedents, the conduct is economic and, in the aggregate, substantially affects interstate commerce. Even if intrastate cultivation and possession of marijuana for one's own medicinal use can properly be characterized as economic, and I question whether it can, it has not been shown that such activity substantially affects interstate commerce. Similarly, it is neither self-evident nor demonstrated that regulating such activity is necessary to the interstate drug control scheme.

The Court's definition of economic activity is breathtaking. It defines as economic any activity involving the production, distribution, and consumption of commodities.... The Court uses a dictionary definition of economics to skirt the real problem of drawing a meaningful line between "what is national and what is local." It will not do to say that Congress may regulate noncommercial activity simply because it may have an effect on the demand for commercial goods, or because the noncommercial endeavor can, in some sense, substitute for commercial activity. Most commercial goods or services have some sort of privately producible analogue. Home care substitutes for daycare. Charades games substitute for movie tickets. Backyard or windowsill gardening substitutes for going to the supermarket. To draw the line wherever private activity affects the demand for market goods is to draw no line at all, and to declare everything economic. We have already rejected the result that would follow—a federal police power. *Lopez.*

In *Lopez* and *Morrison* we suggested that economic activity usually relates directly to commercial activity. The homegrown cultivation and personal possession and use of marijuana for medicinal purposes has no apparent commercial character....

The Court suggests that *Wickard*, which we have identified as "perhaps the most far reaching example of Commerce Clause authority over intrastate activity," established federal regulatory power over any home consumption of a commodity for which a national market exists. I disagree. *Wickard* involved a challenge to the Agricultural Adjustment Act of 1938 (AAA), which directed the Secretary of Agriculture to set national quotas on wheat production, and penalties for excess production. The AAA itself confirmed that Congress made an explicit choice not to reach—and thus the Court could not possibly have approved of federal control over—small-scale, noncommercial wheat farming. In contrast to the CSA's limitless assertion of power, Congress provided an exemption within the AAA for small producers. When Filburn planted the wheat at issue in *Wickard* the statute exempted plantings less than 200 bushels (about six tons), and when he harvested his wheat it exempted plantings less than six acres. *Wickard*, then, did not extend Commerce Clause authority to something as modest as the home cook's herb garden. This is not to say that Congress may never regulate small quantities of commodities possessed or produced for personal use, or to deny that it sometimes needs to enact a zero tolerance regime for such commodities. It is merely to say that *Wickard* did not hold or imply that small-scale production of commodities is always economic, and automatically within Congress' reach.

Even assuming that economic activity is at issue in this case, the Government has made no showing in fact that the possession and use of homegrown marijuana for medical purposes, in California or elsewhere, has a substantial effect on interstate commerce. Similarly, the Government has not shown that regulating such activity is necessary to an interstate regulatory scheme. Whatever the specific theory of "substantial effects" at issue (*i.e.,* whether the activity substantially affects interstate commerce, whether its regulation is necessary to an interstate regulatory scheme, or both), a concern for dual sovereignty requires that Congress' excursion into the traditional domain of States be justified....

There is simply no evidence that homegrown medicinal marijuana users constitute, in the aggregate, a sizable enough class to have a discernable, let alone substantial, impact on the national illicit drug market—or otherwise to threaten the CSA regime. Explicit evidence is helpful when substantial effect is not "visible to the naked eye." And here, in part because common sense suggests that medical marijuana users may be limited in number and that California's Compassionate Use Act and similar state legislation may well isolate activities relating to medicinal marijuana from the illicit market, the effect of those activities on interstate drug traffic is not self-evidently substantial....

The Court recognizes that "the record in the *Wickard* case itself established the causal connection between the production for local use and the national market" and argues that "we have before us findings by Congress *to the same effect.*" The Court refers to a series of declarations in the introduction to the CSA saying that (1) local distribution and possession of controlled substances causes "swelling" in interstate traffic; (2) local production and distribution cannot be distinguished from interstate production and distribution; (3) federal control over intrastate incidents "is essential to effective control" over interstate drug trafficking. These bare declarations cannot be compared to the record before the Court in *Wickard*.

They amount to nothing more than a legislative insistence that the regulation of controlled substances must be absolute. They are asserted without any supporting evidence—descriptive, statistical, or otherwise. "Simply because Congress may conclude a particular activity substantially affects interstate commerce does not necessarily make it so." *Hodel v. Virginia Surface Mining and Reclamation Association*, 452 U.S. 264 (1981) (Rehnquist, J., concurring in the judgment) [Note *supra.* this chapter] ...

### III

We would do well to recall how James Madison, the father of the Constitution, described our system of joint sovereignty to the people of New York: "The powers delegated by the proposed constitution to the federal government are few and defined. Those which are to remain in the State governments are numerous and indefinite.... The powers reserved to the several States will extend to all the objects which, in the ordinary course of affairs, concern the lives, liberties, and properties of the people, and the internal order, improvement, and prosperity of the State." *The Federalist* No. 45.

Relying on Congress' abstract assertions, the Court has endorsed making it a federal crime to grow small amounts of marijuana in one's own home for one's own medicinal use. This overreaching stifles an express choice by some States, concerned for the lives and liberties of their people, to regulate medical marijuana differently. If I were a California citizen, I would not have voted for the medical marijuana ballot initiative; if I were a California legislator I would not have supported the Compassionate Use Act. But whatever the wisdom of California's experiment with medical marijuana, the federalism principles that have driven our Commerce Clause cases require that room for experiment be protected in this case. For these reasons I dissent.

JUSTICE THOMAS, dissenting.

Respondents Diane Monson and Angel Raich use marijuana that has never been bought or sold, that has never crossed state lines, and that has had no demonstrable effect on the national market for marijuana. If Congress can regulate this under the Commerce Clause, then it can regulate virtually anything — and the Federal Government is no longer one of limited and enumerated powers.

## I

\* \* \*

### A

As I explained at length in *Lopez*, the Commerce Clause empowers Congress to regulate the buying and selling of goods and services trafficked across state lines. The Clause's text, structure, and history all indicate that, at the time of the founding, the term "'commerce' consisted of selling, buying, and bartering, as well as transporting for these purposes." Commerce, or trade, stood in contrast to productive activities like manufacturing and agriculture. Throughout founding-era dictionaries, Madison's notes from the Constitutional Convention, *the Federalist Papers*, and the ratification debates, the term "commerce" is consistently used to mean trade or exchange — not all economic or gainful activity that has some attenuated connection to trade or exchange. The term "commerce" commonly meant trade or exchange (and shipping for these purposes) not simply to those involved in the drafting and ratification processes, but also to the general public....

On this traditional understanding of "commerce," the Controlled Substances Act (CSA), regulates a great deal of marijuana trafficking that is interstate and commercial in character. The CSA does not, however, criminalize only the interstate buying and selling of marijuana. Instead, it bans the entire market — intrastate or interstate, noncommercial or commercial — for marijuana. Respondents are correct that the CSA exceeds Congress' commerce power as applied to their conduct, which is purely intrastate and noncommercial.

### B

More difficult, however, is whether the CSA is a valid exercise of Congress' power to enact laws that are "necessary and proper for carrying into Execution" its power to regulate interstate commerce. The Necessary and Proper Clause is not a warrant to Congress to enact any law that bears some conceivable connection to the exercise of an enumerated power. Nor is it, however, a command to Congress to enact only laws that are absolutely indispensable to the exercise of an enumerated power....

### 1

... The Government contends that banning Monson and Raich's intrastate drug activity is "necessary and proper for carrying into Execution" its regulation of interstate drug trafficking. However, in order to be "necessary," the intrastate ban must be more than "a reasonable means of effectuating the regulation of interstate commerce." It must be "plainly adapted" to regulating interstate marijuana trafficking — in other words, there must be an "obvious, simple, and direct relation" between the intrastate ban and the regulation of interstate commerce....

California's Compassionate Use Act sets respondents' conduct apart from other intrastate producers and users of marijuana. The Act channels marijuana use to "seriously ill Californians," and prohibits "the diversion of marijuana for nonmedical purposes." California strictly controls the cultivation and possession of marijuana for medical purposes....

These controls belie the Government's assertion that placing medical marijuana outside the CSA's reach "would prevent effective enforcement of the interstate ban on drug trafficking." ...

But even assuming that States' controls allow some seepage of medical marijuana into the illicit drug market, there is a multibillion-dollar interstate market for marijuana. It is difficult to see how this vast market could be affected by diverted medical cannabis, let alone in a way that makes regulating intrastate medical marijuana obviously essential to controlling the interstate drug market.

To be sure, Congress declared that state policy would disrupt federal law enforcement.... But as JUSTICE O'CONNOR points out, Congress presented no evidence in support of its conclusions, which are not so much findings of fact as assertions of power. Congress cannot define the scope of its own power merely by declaring the necessity of its enactments....

2

Even assuming the CSA's ban on locally cultivated and consumed marijuana is "necessary," that does not mean it is also "proper." The means selected by Congress to regulate interstate commerce cannot be "prohibited" by, or inconsistent with the "letter and spirit" of, the Constitution.

In *Lopez* I argued that allowing Congress to regulate intrastate, noncommercial activity under the Commerce Clause would confer on Congress a general "police power" over the Nation.... If the Federal Government can regulate growing a half-dozen cannabis plants for personal consumption (not because it is interstate commerce, but because it is inextricably bound up with interstate commerce), then Congress' Article I powers—as expanded by the Necessary and Proper Clause—have no meaningful limits....

II

* * *

A

The majority holds that Congress may regulate intrastate cultivation and possession of medical marijuana under the Commerce Clause, because such conduct arguably has a substantial effect on interstate commerce. The majority's decision is further proof that the "substantial effects" test is a "rootless and malleable standard" at odds with the constitutional design.

The majority's treatment of the substantial effects test is rootless, because it is not tethered to either the Commerce Clause or the Necessary and Proper Clause. Under the Commerce Clause, Congress may regulate interstate commerce, not activities that substantially affect interstate commerce, any more than Congress may regulate activities that do not fall within, but that affect, the subjects of its other Article I powers. Whatever additional latitude the Necessary and Proper Clause affords, the question is whether Congress' legislation is essential to the regulation of interstate commerce itself—not whether the legislation extends only to economic activities that substantially affect interstate commerce.

The majority's treatment of the substantial effects test is malleable, because the majority expands the relevant conduct. By defining the class at a high level of generality (as the intrastate manufacture and possession of marijuana), the majority overlooks that individuals authorized by state law to manufacture and possess medical marijuana exert no demonstrable effect on the interstate drug market....

The substantial effects test is easily manipulated for another reason. This Court has never held that Congress can regulate noneconomic activity that substantially affects interstate commerce. To evade even that modest restriction on federal power, the majority defines economic activity in the broadest possible terms as the "the production, distribution, and consumption of commodities." This carves out a vast swath of activities that are subject to federal regulation. If the majority is to be taken seriously, the Federal Government may now regulate quilting bees, clothes drives, and potluck suppers throughout the 50 States. This makes a mockery of Madison's assurance to the people of New York that the "powers delegated" to the Federal Government are "few and defined," while those of the States are "numerous and indefinite." *The Federalist* No. 45.

### *Note:* National Federation of Independent Business v. Sebelius *and the Constitutionality of the Affordable Care Act under the Commerce Clause*

1. In 2010 Congress enacted a wide-ranging health care law known as the Affordable Care Act (ACA). Despite its complexity, for constitutional law purposes the relevant provisions can be narrowed to two. First, the law broadened eligibility under the federal Medicaid program, a program under which the federal government transfers money to participating states for use in providing health coverage for poor persons. The ACA broadened the class of persons who would be eligible for Medicaid. Because Medicaid is a program administered jointly by the federal government and the states, the ACA's expansion of Medicaid took the form of increased monetary grants to states. State participation in that expansion was voluntary, as was their participation in Medicaid more generally. However, the ACA sought to ensure maximum state participation by conditioning *all* of a state's federal Medicaid funds on its agreement to that expansion. This aspect of the challenge to the ACA was thus decided as a matter of Congress's Article I power to spend money "for the ... general Welfare." The Court's resolution of the Spending Clause issue is discussed in Chapter 6.

2. The second relevant feature of the ACA was a requirement that essentially all Americans obtain health insurance or pay a penalty, known as a "shared responsibility payment." The so-called "individual mandate" to buy insurance arose from the following reasoning. One of Congress's concerns in the ACA was with insurance companies' refusal to insure persons with pre-existing medical conditions. However, a simple requirement that insurers not refuse insurance to such persons was understood to be unworkable, as it would lead to a situation where persons waited until they became sick, and only then sought to purchase insurance. It was thought that that dynamic would severely harm insurance markets, as insurers would have to charge higher rates to compensate for the increased payouts they would have to make, which would in turn cause more healthy people to forego insurance until they got sick, which would in turn lead to a "death spiral" of constantly rising rates as healthy people exited the insurance market. In order to prevent this problem, Congress decided to require most Americans to obtain insurance, and to subject them to the "shared responsibility payment" if they failed to do so. The government defended the "individual mandate" primarily as regulation of the interstate commerce in insurance, but also as a tax on the decision not to buy insurance.

3. In *National Federation of Independent Business v. Sebelius*, 132 S.Ct. 2566 (2012), the Court offered a fragmented answer to the question of the independent mandate's constitutionality. Five justices (Chief Justice Roberts, and Justices Scalia, Kennedy, Thomas, and Alito) held that the mandate exceeded Congress's power to regulate interstate commerce, while four justices (Breyer, Ginsburg, Sotomayor and Kagan) would have upheld it on that ground. However, Chief Justice Roberts agreed with those four dissenters that the "shared responsibility payment" was a valid tax on the decision not to buy insurance; thus, by a 5–4 vote, the Court upheld the payment requirement (and thus the mandate itself) as a taxing measure. Like their analysis of the Medicaid expansion issue, the justices' analysis of the tax issue is presented in Chapter 6, which examines the taxing and spending powers together. This note considers their analysis of the individual mandate as a valid regulation of interstate commerce or as a "necessary and proper" regulation to effectuate such regulation.

4. Writing only for himself, Chief Justice Roberts concluded that the individual mandate exceeded Congress's powers under both the Commerce Clause and the Necessary and Proper Clause. His fundamental argument was that the individual mandate did not regulate interstate commerce, because "it … compels individuals to *become* active in commerce by purchasing a product, on the ground that their failure to do so affects interstate commerce." He conceded that persons' failure to act in certain ways "can readily have a substantial effect on interstate commerce." However, he expressed concern that that logic would give Congress the power to compel citizens to do anything that would have similar commercial effects. "That," he said, "is not the country the Framers of our Constitution envisioned.… The Framers gave Congress the power to *regulate* commerce, not to *compel* it, and for over 200 years both our decisions and Congress's actions have reflected this understanding."

With regard to the Necessary and Proper Clause, Chief Justice Roberts argued that earlier cases upholding laws under that Clause "involved exercises of authority derivative of, and in service to, a granted power." He contrasted the individual mandate, which, he said, "vests Congress with the extraordinary ability to create the necessary predicate to the exercise of an enumerated power." He concluded that such a power was "in no way an authority that is 'narrow in scope,'" *United States v. Comstock*, 560 U.S. 126 (2010) [Note *supra* this chapter], or 'incidental' to the exercise of the commerce power, *McCulloch v. Maryland* (1819) [*Supra.* Chapters 3 & 4]."

5. The four justices who agreed with Chief Justice Roberts' conclusion spoke through Justice Scalia. Like the Chief Justice, Justice Scalia worried that upholding the individual mandate as a regulation of interstate commerce would erase all limits on federal power. He rejected the argument that the mandate simply regulates how people interact with the health-care market, and thus regulates activities that, in the aggregate, have a substantial effect on that market. He argued that the mandate aimed "principally" at "the young people" who don't buy insurance and thus who, in his view, "are quite simply not participants in that market."

Turning to the Necessary and Proper Clause, Justice Scalia argued that the lesson of the Court's recent federalism cases was that "the Necessary and Proper Clause is not *carte blanche* for doing whatever will help achieve the ends Congress seeks by regulation of commerce." He further argued that "the scope of the Necessary and Proper Clause is exceeded [among other situations] when the congressional action violates ... the background principle of enumerated (and hence limited) power." He distinguished *Raich* on the ground that, unlike the individual mandate, the federal drug law challenged in that case "did not represent the expansion of the federal power to direct into a broad new field." By contrast, he concluded, the ACA did represent such an expansion into a "broad new field," which he described as "the mandating of economic activity."

Justice Thomas joined Justice Scalia's dissent, but also wrote a separate dissent of his own. He reiterated his dissatisfaction with the "substantial effects test," which, he argued, "has encouraged the Federal Government to persist in its view that the Commerce Clause has virtually no limits."

6. Writing for the four dissenters on the Commerce Clause issue, Justice Ginsburg argued that, "beyond dispute, Congress had a rational basis for concluding that the uninsured, as a class, substantially affect interstate commerce." She criticized the regulation/compulsion distinction as unsupported by precedent and factually wrong in this case, given the high likelihood that a particular American would use health care within several years and Congress's inability to separate those who will need emergency care today and those who would not need it for years to come. She concluded that the Court's precedents instructed that Congress had the authority to cast a wide regulatory net in order to ensure that it regulated the former group. In response to the concern that a decision to uphold the mandate would erase any limits on federal regulatory power, she argued that the health-care market was unique, given the high likelihood of near-universal use, and cited *Gibbons* for the proposition that the democratic process was the most important check on Congress's use of the commerce power.

With regard to the Necessary and Proper Clause, Justice Ginsburg argued that the justices in the majority had not shown how the individual mandate was a more far-reaching regulation that others the Court had upheld.

## Note: The Current State of the Commerce Clause

1. After *Lopez* and *Morrison*, many scholars and commentators believed that the Court might be on the verge of significantly restricting the scope of the Commerce power. Since then, however, the Court has vacillated: it upheld the federal marijuana possession law in *Raich*, but then concluded that the Affordable Care Act's "individual mandate" exceeded Congress's power under the Commerce Clause. As a result, the Court's Commerce Clause jurisprudence remains marked by uncertainty.

2. Consider that jurisprudence. How sensible was it for the Court in *Lopez* to draw a line at federal regulation of economic activity, but then to define "economic" as broadly as it did in *Raich*? What about the line in *National Federation* (the Affordable Care Act case) between, on the one hand, regulating preexisting commerce and, on the other, mandating (and then regulating) such commerce?

What accounts for the Court drawing these lines? One obvious answer is that the enumerated nature of Congress's Article I powers presupposes something not enumerated—in other words, that *some* activity *has to be* beyond congressional power. Does that answer convince you? If it does, are you convinced by the lines the Court has drawn to identify those activities that are beyond congressional power? Recall Justice O'Connor's complaint in *Raich* that the Court's distinguishing of *Lopez* essentially provides "a drafting guide" for Congress to evade serious judicial scrutiny of its Commerce Clause authority. How easy is it for Congress to evade those lines?

3. As you will see later in this book, Congress has other ways to ensure that particular regulations are imposed. Most notably, it can use its spending power to induce states to adopt regulations that Congress could not directly mandate itself under the Commerce Clause. Before 2012, the modern Court had not imposed serious limits on Congress's spending power, thus creating a situation in which formal limits on the Commerce Clause were sometimes thought to mean little, given Congress's *de facto* ability to impose those same regulations via the Spending Clause. But in 2012, the Court struck down a spending provision in the Affordable Care Act, thus tightening up that loophole. This story is told in Chapter 6.

# Chapter 5

# Residual State Powers — and Their Limits

## A. The Commerce Clause as a Limitation on State Regulatory Power

Do the states also have the power to regulate commerce? Many cases involving state power involve "dormant" power situations—situations in which the federal government has the power to regulate a subject, but has not done so (or has done so incompletely). In these situations, does the Commerce Clause contain negative, or "dormant," implications for state power which preclude states from regulating? In other words, is the federal commerce power "exclusive" such that the states are precluded from regulating an area within federal authority even in the absence of federal regulation? Or do the states have "concurrent" jurisdiction so that they are also free to regulate?

The Constitution's text provides little guidance on these issues. Article I, §8, explicitly gives Congress the power to regulate commerce "among" the several states, but the Constitution does not say whether the states can also regulate commerce. That issue was left to the courts. Today, it is generally accepted that the Commerce Clause, by its own force, restricts state regulatory power. In other words, even if Congress has not used its Commerce Clause power to legislate on a topic, a state law may still be struck down for violating what has been called the "negative" or "dormant" force of the Interstate Commerce power. (Hence the term "dormant Commerce Clause.") But this does not mean that states are disabled from regulating in ways that affect interstate commerce. Indeed, the Court early on recognized that regulatory powers generally understood to remain vested in the states could have such effects—think of speed limits on highways (which may slow down interstate commerce) or tort law (which may impede interstate commerce by raising the cost of doing business in a particular state).

The difficulty of determining when such local regulation intrudes on Congress's power over interstate commerce has bedeviled the Court for most of the nation's existence. Today, the general rule is that the question turns largely on whether the local law discriminates against interstate commerce or, conversely, is generally applicable to local and interstate commerce. If the state law discriminates, a court will subject it to "strict scrutiny." This means the court will ask whether there was any other less in-

337

terstate commerce-restrictive way of achieving the state's legitimate policy goals; if such a less restrictive alternative exists, the statute will be struck down. By contrast, if the statute regulates local and interstate commerce evenhandedly, a court will ask only whether the local benefits are clearly outweighed by the burdens the statute places on interstate commerce. This test generally results in the state law being upheld.

# 1. Early Analysis and the Evolution of the Modern Rule

## Note: The Court's Early Analysis

1. Several early Supreme Court decisions discussed whether the federal government's authority over commerce was exclusive or concurrent. In *Gibbons v. Ogden* (1824) (*Supra.* Chapter 4), Chief Justice Marshall described the argument that Congress enjoys exclusive power to regulate interstate commerce as one having "great force." However, in *Wilson v. The Black Bird Creek Marsh Co.*, 27 U.S. (2 Pet.) 245 (1829), the Court, again speaking through Chief Justice Marshall, upheld the validity of a Delaware law authorizing a corporation to dam up a tidal creek even though it had the effect of destroying navigation. He offered no analysis except to refer to "all the circumstances of the case," which included the observation that the state law at issue dealt with "those small navigable creeks into which the tide flows, and which abound throughout the lower country of the Middle and Southern states." He also noted that "the value of the property on [the creek's banks] must be enhanced by excluding the water from the marsh, and the health of the inhabitants probably improved." He also observed that "measures calculated to produce [improved property value and health], provided they do not come into collision with the powers of the general government, are undoubtedly within those measures which are reserved to the States."

2. Chief Justice Marshall's hesitation at embracing a broad view of the Commerce Clause's exclusivity was reflected in later cases as well. In *Cooley v. Board of Wardens*, 53 U.S. 299 (1852), the Court considered the constitutionality of a 1789 federal statute that gave the states the power to enact local laws governing the use of pilots to guide ships into ports. The law was attacked as an attempt by Congress to delegate to the states its authority to regulate interstate commerce, which was alleged to be beyond the power of states. Justice Curtis, writing for a majority of the Court, upheld the law, but wrote a carefully limited opinion:

> Either absolutely to affirm, or deny that the nature of [the Commerce] power requires exclusive legislation by Congress, is to lose sight of the nature of the subjects of this power, and to assert concerning all of them, what is really applicable but to a part. Whatever subjects of this power are in their nature national, or admit only of one uniform system, or plan of regulation, may justly be said to be of such a nature as to require exclusive legislation by Congress. That this cannot be affirmed of laws for the regulation of pilots and pilotage is plain. The act of 1789 contains a clear and authoritative declaration by the first Congress, that the nature of this subject is such, that until Congress should find it necessary to exert its power, it should be left to the legislation

of the states; that it is local and not national; that it is likely to be the best provided for, not by one system, or plan of regulations, but by as many as the legislative discretion of the several states should deem applicable to the local peculiarities of the ports within their limits. . . .

It is the opinion of a majority of the court that the mere grant to Congress of the power to regulate commerce, did not deprive the states of power to regulate pilots, and that although Congress has legislated on this subject, its legislation manifests an intention, with a single exception, not to regulate this subject, but to leave its regulation to the several states. To these precise questions, which are all we are called on to decide, this opinion must be understood to be confined. It does not extend to the question what other subjects, under the commercial power, are within the exclusive control of Congress, or may be regulated by the states in the absence of all congressional legislation; nor to the general question how far any regulation of a subject by Congress, may be deemed to operate as an exclusion of all legislation by the states upon the same subject. . . .

Justice Daniel concurred only in the judgment. He argued that the power to enact pilotage laws was an inherent state power. Justice McLean dissented, arguing that the effect of the majority opinion was to transfer to states Congress's power to regulate interstate commerce.

## 2. The Evolution of the Modern Rule

Starting in the 1930s the Court began moving toward what ultimately became the modern rule for the Dormant Commerce Clause. The following cases illustrate that evolution.

### a. Heightened Scrutiny for Discriminatory Laws

### Baldwin v. G.A.F. Seelig, Inc.

294 U.S. 511 (1935)

Mr. Justice Cardozo delivered the opinion of the Court. . . .

The New York Milk Control Act, with the aid of regulations made thereunder, has set up a system of minimum prices to be paid by dealers to producers. . . . From the farms of New York the inhabitants of the so-called Metropolitan Milk District, comprising the City of New York and certain neighboring communities, derive about 70 per cent. of the milk requisite for their use. To keep the system unimpaired by competition from afar, the Act has a provision whereby the protective [minimum] prices are extended to that part of the supply (about 30 per cent.) which comes from other states. The substance of the provision is that, so far as such a prohibition is permitted by the Constitution, there shall be no sale within the state of milk bought outside unless the price paid to the producers was one that would be lawful upon a like transaction within the state. . . .

Seelig buys its milk from the [Seelig Creamery Corporation] in Vermont at prices lower than the minimum payable to producers in New York. The Commissioner of Farms and Markets refuses to license the transaction of its business unless it signs an agreement to conform to the New York statute and regulations in the sale of the imported product. This the applicant declines to do....

New York has no power to project its legislation into Vermont by regulating the price to be paid in that state for milk acquired there. So much is not disputed. New York is equally without power to prohibit the introduction within her territory of milk of wholesome quality acquired in Vermont, whether at high prices or at low ones. This again is not disputed. Accepting those postulates, New York asserts her power to outlaw milk so introduced by prohibiting its sale thereafter if the price that has been paid for it to the farmers of Vermont is less than would be owing in like circumstances to farmers in New York. (The importer in that view may keep his milk or drink it, but sell it he may not.)*

Such a power, if exerted, will set a barrier to traffic between one state and another as effective as if customs duties, equal to the price differential, had been laid upon the thing transported.... Nice distinctions have been made at times between direct and indirect burdens. They are irrelevant when the avowed purpose of the obstruction, as well as its necessary tendency, is to suppress or mitigate the consequences of competition between the states. Such an obstruction is direct by the very terms of the hypothesis. We are reminded in the opinion below that a chief occasion of the commerce clauses was "the mutual jealousies and aggressions of the States, taking form in customs barriers and other economic retaliation." If New York, in order to promote the economic welfare of her farmers, may guard them against competition with the cheaper prices of Vermont, the door has been opened to rivalries and reprisals that were meant to be averted by subjecting commerce between the states to the power of the nation.

The argument is pressed upon us, however, that the end to be served by the Milk Control Act is something more than the economic welfare of the farmers or of any other class or classes. The end to be served is the maintenance of a regular and adequate supply of pure and wholesome milk; the supply being put in jeopardy when the farmers of the state are unable to earn a living income. Price security, we are told, is only a special form of sanitary security; the economic motive is secondary and subordinate; the state intervenes to make its inhabitants healthy, and not to make them rich. On that assumption we are asked to say that intervention will be upheld as a valid exercise by the state of its internal police power, though there is an incidental obstruction to commerce between one state and another. This would be to eat up the rule under the guise of an exception. Economic welfare is always related to health, for there can be no health if men are starving. Let such an exception be admitted, and all that a state will have to do in times of stress and strain is to say that its farmers and merchants and workmen must be protected against competition from without, lest they go upon the poor relief lists or perish altogether. To give entrance to that excuse would be to invite a speedy end of our national solidarity. The Constitution was framed under the dominion of a political philosophy less parochial in range. It was framed upon the theory that the peoples of the several states must sink or swim together, and that in the long run prosperity and salvation are in union and not division....

... [One] state in its dealings with another may not place itself in a position of economic isolation. Formulas and catchwords are subordinate to this overmastering requirement. Neither the power to tax nor the police power may be used by the state of destination with the aim and effect of establishing an economic barrier against competition with the products of another state or the labor of its residents. Restrictions so contrived are an unreasonable clog upon the mobility of commerce. They set up what is equivalent to a rampart of customs duties designed to neutralize advantages belonging to the place of origin. They are thus hostile in conception as well as burdensome in result....

## Dean Milk Co. v. Madison

### 340 U.S. 349 (1951)

Mr. Justice Clark delivered the opinion of the Court.

This appeal challenges the constitutional validity of two sections of an ordinance of the City of Madison, Wisconsin, regulating the sale of milk and milk products within the municipality's jurisdiction. One section in issue makes it unlawful to sell any milk as pasteurized unless it has been processed and bottled at an approved pasteurization plant within a radius of five miles from the central square of Madison. Another section, which prohibits the sale of milk, or the importation, receipt or storage of milk for sale, in Madison unless from a source of supply possessing a permit issued after inspection by Madison officials, is attacked insofar as it expressly relieves municipal authorities from any duty to inspect farms located beyond twenty-five miles from the center of the city.

Appellant is an Illinois corporation engaged in distributing milk and milk products in Illinois and Wisconsin. It contended below, as it does here, that both the five-mile limit on pasteurization plants and the twenty-five-mile limit on sources of milk violate the Commerce Clause and the Fourteenth Amendment to the Federal Constitution....

The City of Madison is the county seat of Dane County. Within the county are some 5,600 dairy farms with total raw milk production in excess of 600,000,000 pounds annually and more than ten times the requirements of Madison. Aside from the milk supplied to Madison, fluid milk produced in the county moves in large quantities to Chicago and more distant consuming areas, and the remainder is used in making cheese, butter and other products. At the time of trial the Madison milkshed was not of "Grade A" quality by the standards recommended by the United States Public Health Service, and no milk labeled "Grade A" was distributed in Madison.

The area defined by the ordinance with respect to milk sources encompasses practically all of Dane County and includes some 500 farms which supply milk for Madison. Within the five-mile area for pasteurization are plants of five processors, only three of which are engaged in the general wholesale and retail trade in Madison. Inspection of these farms and plants is scheduled once every thirty days and is performed by two municipal inspectors, one of whom is full-time. The courts below found that the ordinance in question promotes convenient, economical and efficient plant inspection.

Appellant purchases and gathers milk from approximately 950 farms in northern Illinois and southern Wisconsin, none being within twenty-five miles of Madison. Its pasteurization plants are located at Chemung and Huntley, Illinois, about 65 and 85 miles respectively from Madison. Appellant was denied a license to sell its products within Madison solely because its pasteurization plants were more than five miles away.

It is conceded that the milk which appellant seeks to sell in Madison is supplied from farms and processed in plants licensed and inspected by public health authorities of Chicago, and is labeled "Grade A" under the Chicago ordinance which adopts the rating standards recommended by the United States Public Health Service. Both the Chicago and Madison ordinances, though not the sections of the latter here in issue, are largely patterned after the Model Milk Ordinance of the Public Health Service. However, Madison contends and we assume that in some particulars its ordinance is more rigorous than that of Chicago.

Upon these facts we find it necessary to determine only the issue raised under the Commerce Clause, for we agree with appellant that the ordinance imposes an undue burden on interstate commerce.

This is not an instance in which an enactment falls because of federal legislation which, as a proper exercise of paramount national power over commerce, excludes measures which might otherwise be within the police power of the states. There is no pertinent national regulation by the Congress....

Nor can there be objection to the avowed purpose of this enactment. We assume that difficulties in sanitary regulation of milk and milk products originating in remote areas may present a situation in which "upon a consideration of all the relevant facts and circumstances it appears that the matter is one which may appropriately be regulated in the interest of the safety, health and well-being of local communities...." We also assume that since Congress has not spoken to the contrary, the subject matter of the ordinance lies within the sphere of state regulation even though interstate commerce may be affected.

But this regulation, like the provision invalidated in *Baldwin v. G.A.F. Seelig, Inc.* (1935) [*Supra.* this chapter], in practical effect excludes from distribution in Madison wholesome milk produced and pasteurized in Illinois. "The importer ... may keep his milk or drink it, but sell it he may not." *Baldwin.* In thus erecting an economic barrier protecting a major local industry against competition from without the State, Madison plainly discriminates against interstate commerce. This it cannot do, even in the exercise of its unquestioned power to protect the health and safety of its people, if reasonable nondiscriminatory alternatives, adequate to conserve legitimate local interests, are available. A different view, that the ordinance is valid simply because it professes to be a health measure, would mean that the Commerce Clause of itself imposes no limitations on state action other than those laid down by the Due Process

Clause, save for the rare instance where a state artlessly discloses an avowed purpose to discriminate against interstate goods. Our issue then is whether the discrimination inherent in the Madison ordinance can be justified in view of the character of the local interests and the available methods of protecting them.

It appears that reasonable and adequate alternatives are available. If the City of Madison prefers to rely upon its own officials for inspection of distant milk sources, such inspection is readily open to it without hardship for it could charge the actual and reasonable cost of such inspection to the importing producers and processors. Moreover, appellee Health Commissioner of Madison testified that as proponent of the local milk ordinance he had submitted the provisions here in controversy and an alternative proposal based on § 11 of the Model Milk Ordinance recommended by the United States Public Health Service. The model provision imposes no geographical limitation on location of milk sources and processing plants but excludes from the municipality milk not produced and pasteurized conformably to standards as high as those enforced by the receiving city. In implementing such an ordinance, the importing city obtains milk ratings based on uniform standards and established by health authorities in the jurisdiction where production and processing occur. The receiving city may determine the extent of enforcement of sanitary standards in the exporting area by verifying the accuracy of safety ratings of specific plants or of the milkshed in the distant jurisdiction through the United States Public Health Service, which routinely and on request spot checks the local ratings. The Commissioner testified that Madison consumers "would be safeguarded adequately" under either proposal and that he had expressed no preference. The milk sanitarian of the Wisconsin State Board of Health testified that the State Health Department recommends the adoption of a provision based on the Model Ordinance. Both officials agreed that a local health officer would be justified in relying upon the evaluation by the Public Health Service of enforcement conditions in remote producing areas.

To permit Madison to adopt a regulation not essential for the protection of local health interests and placing a discriminatory burden on interstate commerce would invite a multiplication of preferential trade areas destructive of the very purpose of the Commerce Clause. Under the circumstances here presented, the regulation must yield to the principle that "one state in its dealings with another may not place itself in a position of economic isolation." *Baldwin v. G.A.F. Seelig, Inc.*

For these reasons we conclude that the judgment below sustaining the five-mile provision as to pasteurization must be reversed....

Mr. Justice Black, with whom Mr. Justice Douglas and Mr. Justice Minton concur, dissenting....

... [Both] state courts below found that § 7.21 represents a good-faith attempt to safeguard public health by making adequate sanitation inspection possible. While we are not bound by these findings, I do not understand the Court to overturn them. Therefore, the fact that § 7.21, like all health regulations, imposes some burden on trade, does not mean that it "discriminates" against interstate commerce.

This health regulation should not be invalidated merely because the Court believes that alternative milk-inspection methods might insure the cleanliness and healthfulness of Dean's Illinois milk.... No case is cited, and I have found none, in which a bona fide health law was struck down on the ground that some other method of safeguarding health would be as good as, or better than, the one the Court was called on to review. In my view, to use this ground now elevates the right to traffic in commerce for profit above the power of the people to guard the purity of their daily diet of milk....

One of the Court's proposals is that Madison require milk processors to pay reasonable inspection fees at the milk supply "sources." Experience shows, however, that the fee method gives rise to prolonged litigation over the calculation and collection of the charges....

The Court's second proposal is that Madison adopt § 11 of the "Model Milk Ordinance." The state courts made no findings as to the relative merits of this inspection ordinance and the one chosen by Madison. The evidence indicates to me that enforcement of the Madison law would assure a more healthful quality of milk than that which is entitled to use the label of "Grade A" under the Model Ordinance. Indeed, the United States Board of Public Health, which drafted the Model Ordinance, suggests that the provisions are "minimum" standards only....

Furthermore, the Model Ordinance would force the Madison health authorities to rely on "spot checks" by the United States Public Health Service to determine whether Chicago enforced its milk regulations. The evidence shows that these "spot checks" are based on random inspection of farms and pasteurization plants: the United States Public Health Service rates the ten thousand or more dairy farms in the Chicago milkshed by a sampling of no more than two hundred farms. The same sampling technique is employed to inspect pasteurization plants. There was evidence that neither the farms supplying Dean with milk nor Dean's pasteurization plants were necessarily inspected in the last "spot check" of the Chicago milkshed made two years before the present case was tried.

From what this record shows, and from what it fails to show, I do not think that either of the alternatives suggested by the Court would assure the people of Madison as pure a supply of milk as they receive under their own ordinance....

### b. Balancing Local Benefits and Interstate Burdens

In a series of cases the Court considered the legitimate local benefits of a law (such as enhanced highway safety) against the burdens that law imposed on interstate commerce. In the following two cases, consider the varying degrees of deference the Court gave to the legislature's judgment that the law accomplished a legitimate goal. What explains the Court's different approaches in these cases?

# South Carolina State Highway Department v. Barnwell Bros.

## 303 U.S. 177 (1938)

MR. JUSTICE STONE delivered the opinion of the Court.

Act No. 259 of the General Assembly of South Carolina, of April 28, 1933, prohibits use on the state highways of motor trucks and "semi-trailer motor trucks" whose width exceeds 90 inches, and whose weight including load exceeds 20,000 pounds.... The principal question for decision is whether these prohibitions impose an unconstitutional burden upon interstate commerce....

[Congress] has not undertaken to regulate the weight and size of motor vehicles in interstate motor traffic and has left undisturbed whatever authority in that regard the states have retained under the Constitution.

While the constitutional grant to Congress of power to regulate interstate commerce has been held to operate of its own force to curtail state power in some measure,[2] it did not forestall all state action affecting interstate commerce. Ever since *Wilson v. Black Bird Creek Marsh Co.*, 27 U.S. 245 (1829) [Note *supra.* this chapter] and *Cooley v. Board of Wardens*, it has been recognized that there are matters of local concern, the regulation of which unavoidably involves some regulation of interstate commerce but which, because of their local character and their number and diversity, may never be fully dealt with by Congress. Notwithstanding the commerce clause, such regulation in the absence of Congressional action has for the most part been left to the states by the decisions of this Court, subject to the other applicable constitutional restraints....

[The] present case affords no occasion for saying that the bare possession of power by Congress to regulate the interstate traffic forces the states to conform to standards which Congress might, but has not adopted, or curtails their power to take measures to insure the safety and conservation of their highways which may be applied to like traffic moving intrastate. Few subjects of state regulation are so peculiarly of local concern as is the use of state highways. There are few, local regulation of which is so inseparable from a substantial effect on interstate commerce. Unlike the railroads, local highways are built, owned, and maintained by the state or its municipal subdivisions. The state has a primary and immediate concern in their safe and economical administration. The present regulations, or any others of like purpose, if they are to accomplish their end, must be applied alike to interstate and intrastate traffic both moving in large volume over the highways. The fact that they affect alike shippers in

---

2. State regulations affecting interstate commerce, whose purpose or effect is to gain for those within the state an advantage at the expense of those without, or to burden those out of the state without any corresponding advantage to those within, have been thought to impinge upon the constitutional prohibition even though Congress has not acted. Underlying the stated rule has been the thought, often expressed in judicial opinion, that when the regulation is of such a character that its burden falls principally upon those without the state, legislative action is not likely to be subjected to those political restraints which are normally exerted on legislation where it affects adversely some interests within the state. See *Cooley v. Port Wardens*, 53 U.S. 299 (1852) [Note *supra.* this chapter].

interstate and intrastate commerce in large number within as well as without the state is a safeguard against their abuse. . . .

. . . [A state] may not, under the guise of regulation, discriminate against interstate commerce. But, "in the absence of national legislation especially covering the subject of interstate commerce, the state may rightly prescribe uniform regulations adapted to promote safety upon its highways and the conservation of their use, applicable alike to vehicles moving in interstate commerce and those of its own citizens."... This Court has often sustained the exercise of that power, although it has burdened or impeded interstate commerce. It has upheld weight limitations lower than those presently imposed, applied alike to motor traffic moving interstate and intrastate. Restrictions favoring passenger traffic over the carriage of interstate merchandise by truck have been similarly sustained, as has the exaction of a reasonable fee for the use of the highways.

In each of these cases regulation involves a burden on interstate commerce. But so long as the state action does not discriminate, the burden is one the Constitution permits because it is an inseparable incident of the exercise of a legislative authority, which, under the Constitution, has been left to the states.

Congress, in the exercise of its plenary power to regulate interstate commerce, may determine whether the burdens imposed on it by state regulation, otherwise permissible, are too great, and may, by legislation designed to secure uniformity or in other respects to protect the national interest in the commerce, curtail to some extent the state's regulatory power. But that is a legislative, not a judicial, function, to be performed in the light of the congressional judgment of what is appropriate regulation of interstate commerce, and the extent to which, in that field, state power and local interests should be required to yield to the national authority and interest. In the absence of such legislation the judicial function, under the commerce clause, as well as the Fourteenth Amendment, stops with the inquiry whether the state Legislature in adopting regulations such as the present has acted within its province, and whether the means of regulation chosen are reasonably adapted to the end sought.

Here the first inquiry has already been resolved by our decisions that a state may impose nondiscriminatory restrictions with respect to the character of motor vehicles moving in interstate commerce as a safety measure and as a means of securing the economical use of its highways. In resolving the second, courts do not sit as Legislatures, either state or national. They cannot act as Congress does when, after weighing all the conflicting interests, state and national, it determines when and how much the state regulatory power shall yield to the larger interests of a national commerce. And in reviewing a state highway regulation where Congress has not acted, a court is not called upon, as are state Legislatures, to determine what, in its judgment, is the most suitable restriction to be applied of those that are possible, or to choose that one which in its opinion is best adapted to all the diverse interests affected. When the action of a Legislature is within the scope of its power, fairly debatable questions as to its reasonableness, wisdom, and propriety are not for the determination of courts, but for the legislative body, on which rests the duty and responsibility of decision. This is equally the case when the legislative power is one which may legitimately place an incidental burden on interstate commerce. It is not any the less a legislative power committed to the states because it affects interstate commerce, and courts are not any the more entitled, because interstate commerce is affected, to substitute their own for the legislative judgment.

Since the adoption of one weight or width regulation, rather than another, is a legislative, not a judicial, choice, its constitutionality is not to be determined by weighing in the judicial scales the merits of the legislative choice and rejecting it if the weight of evidence presented in court appears to favor a different standard. Being a legislative judgment it is presumed to be supported by facts known to the Legislature unless facts judicially known or proved preclude that possibility. Hence, in reviewing the present determination, we examine the record, not to see whether the findings of the court below are supported by evidence, but to ascertain upon the whole record whether it is possible to say that the legislative choice is without rational basis. Not only does the record fail to exclude that possibility but it shows affirmatively that there is adequate support for the legislative judgment....

Mr. Justice Cardozo and Mr. Justice Reed took no part in the consideration or decision of this case.

## Southern Pacific Co. v. Arizona
### 325 U.S. 761 (1945)

Mr. Chief Justice Stone delivered the opinion of the Court.

The Arizona Train Limit Law of May 16, 1912 makes it unlawful for any person or corporation to operate within the state a railroad train of more than fourteen passenger or seventy freight cars....

For a hundred years it has been accepted constitutional doctrine that the commerce clause, without the aid of Congressional legislation, thus affords some protection from state legislation inimical to the national commerce, and that in such cases, where Congress has not acted, this Court, and not the state legislature, is under the commerce clause the final arbiter of the competing demands of state and national interests....

[There] has thus been left to the states wide scope for the regulation of matters of local state concern, even though it in some measure affects the commerce, provided it does not materially restrict the free flow of commerce across state lines, or interfere with it in matters with respect to which uniformity of regulation is of predominant national concern.

Hence the matters for ultimate determination here are the nature and extent of the burden which the state regulation of interstate trains, adopted as a safety measure, imposes on interstate commerce, and whether the relative weights of the state and national interests involved are such as to make inapplicable the rule, generally observed, that the free flow of interstate commerce and its freedom from local restraints in matters requiring uniformity of regulation are interests safeguarded by the commerce clause from state interference....

The findings show that the operation of long trains, that is trains of more than fourteen passenger and more than seventy freight cars, is standard practice over the main lines of the railroads of the United States, and that, if the length of trains is to be regulated at all, national uniformity in the regulation adopted, such as only Congress can prescribe, is practically indispensable to the operation of an efficient and economical national railway system. On many railroads passenger trains of more than fourteen cars and freight trains of more than seventy cars are operated, and on some systems freight trains are run ranging from one hundred and twenty-five to one hundred and sixty cars in length. Outside of Arizona, where the length of trains is not restricted, appellant runs a substantial proportion of long trains. In 1939 on its comparable route for through traffic through Utah and Nevada from 66 to 85% of its freight trains were over 70 cars in length and over 43% of its passenger trains included more than fourteen passenger cars.

In Arizona, approximately 93% of the freight traffic and 95% of the passenger traffic is interstate. Because of the Train Limit Law appellant is required to haul over 30% more trains in Arizona than would otherwise have been necessary....

The unchallenged findings leave no doubt that the Arizona Train Limit Law imposes a serious burden on the interstate commerce conducted by appellant. It materially impedes the movement of appellant's interstate trains through that state and interposes a substantial obstruction to the national policy proclaimed by Congress, to promote adequate, economical and efficient railway transportation service. Enforcement of the law in Arizona, while train lengths remain unregulated or are regulated by varying standards in other states, must inevitably result in an impairment of uniformity of efficient railroad operation because the railroads are subjected to regulation which is not uniform in its application. Compliance with a state statute limiting train lengths requires interstate trains of a length lawful in other states to be broken up and reconstituted as they enter each state according as it may impose varying limitations upon train lengths. The alternative is for the carrier to conform to the lowest train limit restriction of any of the states through which its trains pass, whose laws thus control the carriers' operations both within and without the regulating state....

At present the seventy freight car laws are enforced only in Arizona and Oklahoma, with a fourteen car passenger car limit in Arizona. The record here shows that the enforcement of the Arizona statute results in freight trains being broken up and reformed at the California border and in New Mexico, some distance from the Arizona line. Frequently it is not feasible to operate a newly assembled train from the New Mexico yard nearest to Arizona, with the result that the Arizona limitation governs the flow of traffic as far east as El Paso, Texas. For similar reasons the Arizona law often controls the length of passenger trains all the way from Los Angeles to El Paso.

If one state may regulate train lengths, so may all the others, and they need not prescribe the same maximum limitation. The practical effect of such regulation is to control train operations beyond the boundaries of the state exacting it because of the necessity of breaking up and reassembling long trains at the nearest terminal points before entering and after leaving the regulating state. The serious impediment to the free flow of commerce by the local regulation of train lengths and the practical necessity that such regulation, if any, must be prescribed by a single body having a nation-wide authority are apparent.

The trial court found that the Arizona law had no reasonable relation to safety, and made train operation more dangerous. Examination of the evidence and the detailed findings makes it clear that this conclusion was rested on facts found which indicate that such increased danger of accident and personal injury as may result from the greater length of trains is more than offset by the increase in the number of accidents resulting from the larger number of trains when train lengths are reduced. In considering the effect of the statute as a safety measure, therefore, the factor of controlling significance for present purposes is not whether there is basis for the conclusion of the Arizona Supreme Court that the increase in length of trains beyond the statutory maximum has an adverse effect upon safety of operation. The decisive question is whether in the circumstances the total effect of the law as a safety measure in reducing accidents and casualties is so slight or problematical as not to outweigh the national interest in keeping interstate commerce free from interferences which seriously impede it and subject it to local regulation which does not have a uniform effect on the interstate train journey which it interrupts.

The principal source of danger of accident from increased length of trains is the resulting increase of "slack action" of the train. Slack action is the amount of free movement of one car before it transmits its motion to an adjoining coupled car. This free movement results from the fact that in railroad practice cars are loosely coupled, and the coupling is often combined with a shock-absorbing device, a "draft gear," which, under stress, substantially increases the free movement as the train is started or stopped. Loose coupling is necessary to enable the train to proceed freely around curves and is an aid in starting heavy trains, since the application of the locomotive power to the train operates on each car in the train successively, and the power is thus utilized to start only one car at a time....

We think, as the trial court found, that the Arizona Train Limit Law, viewed as a safety measure, affords at most slight and dubious advantage, if any, over unregulated train lengths, because it results in an increase in the number of trains and train operations and the consequent increase in train accidents of a character generally more severe than those due to slack action. Its undoubted effect on the commerce is the regulation, without securing uniformity, of the length of trains operated in interstate commerce, which lack is itself a primary cause of preventing the free flow of commerce by delaying it and by substantially increasing its cost and impairing its efficiency. In these respects the case differs from those where a state, by regulatory measures affecting the commerce, has removed or reduced safety hazards without substantial interference with the interstate movement of trains....

Here we conclude that the state does go too far. Its regulation of train lengths, admittedly obstructive to interstate train operation, and having a seriously adverse effect on transportation efficiency and economy, passes beyond what is plainly essential for safety since it does not appear that it will lessen rather than increase the danger of accident. Its attempted regulation of the operation of interstate trains cannot establish nation-wide control such as is essential to the maintenance of an efficient transportation system, which Congress alone can prescribe. The state interest cannot be preserved at the expense of the national interest by an enactment which regulates interstate train lengths without securing such control, which is a matter of national concern. To this the interest of the state here asserted is subordinate....

MR. JUSTICE BLACK, dissenting....

Before the state trial court finally determined that the dangers found by the legislature in 1912 no longer existed, it heard evidence over a period of 51/2 months which appears in about 3000 pages of the printed record before us. It then adopted findings of fact submitted to it by the railroad, which cover 148 printed pages, and conclusions of law which cover 5 pages.... This new pattern of trial procedure makes it necessary for a judge to hear all the evidence offered as to why a legislature passed a law and to make findings of fact as to the validity of those reasons. If under today's ruling a court does make findings, as to a danger contrary to the findings of the legislature, and the evidence heard "lends support" to those findings, a court can then invalidate the law. In this respect, the Arizona County Court acted, and this Court today is acting, as a "super-legislature."

Even if this method of invalidating legislative acts is a correct one, I still think that the "findings" of the state court do not authorize today's decision. That court did not find that there is no unusual danger from slack movements in long trains. It did decide on disputed evidence that the long train "slack movement" dangers were more than offset by prospective dangers as a result of running a larger number of short trains, since many people might be hurt at grade crossings. There was undoubtedly some evidence before the state court from which it could have reached such a conclusion. There was undoubtedly as much evidence before it which would have justified a different conclusion.

Under those circumstances, the determination of whether it is in the interest of society for the length of trains to be governmentally regulated is a matter of public policy. Someone must fix that policy—either the Congress, or the state, or the courts. A century and a half of constitutional history and government admonishes this Court to leave that choice to the elected legislative representatives of the people themselves, where it properly belongs both on democratic principles and the requirements of efficient government....

There have been many sharp divisions of this Court concerning its authority, in the absence of congressional enactment, to invalidate state laws as violating the Commerce Clause. That discussion need not be renewed here, because even the broadest exponents of judicial power in this field have not heretofore expressed doubt as to a state's power, absent a paramount congressional declaration, to regulate interstate trains in the interest of safety....

When we finally get down to the gist of what the Court today actually decides, it is this: Even though more railroad employees will be injured by "slack action" movements on long trains than on short trains, there must be no regulation of this danger in the absence of "uniform regulations." That means that no one can legislate against this danger except the Congress; and even though the Congress is perfectly content to leave the matter to the different state legislatures, this Court, on the ground of "lack of uniformity," will require it to make an express avowal of that fact before it will permit a state to guard against that admitted danger....

Mr. Justice Douglas, dissenting.

... My view has been that the courts should intervene only where the state legislation discriminated against interstate commerce or was out of harmony with laws which Congress had enacted....

## Note: Interstate Traffic and the Evolution of the Dormant Commerce Clause

1. *Barnwell* and *Southern Pacific* reflect very different approaches to the Dormant Commerce Clause. What explains these differences? Is it the difference between the fragmented highway system that existed in 1938 and the integrated rail network that existed in 1945? Or is there something about the Arizona law that made the Court especially suspicious?

2. *Bibb v. Navajo Freight Lines, Inc.*, 359 U.S. 520 (1959), involved an Illinois statute requiring the use of "contour" rear fender mudguards on trucks and trailers operated in Illinois. Illinois' contour mudflap differed from the conventional or "straight" mudflap permitted in 45 States and required in Arkansas. In enacting the law, the Illinois legislature relied on evidence that contour flaps promote safety by preventing trucks from throwing debris onto the windshields of passing and following vehicles. The district court struck the law down, finding that it was "conclusively shown that the contour mud flap possesses no advantages over the conventional or straight mud flap," and that "there is rather convincing testimony that use of the contour flap creates hazards previously unknown to those using the highways."

The Court unanimously struck down the law. Writing for seven Justices, Justice Douglas wrote the following:

> ... If we had here only a question whether the cost of adjusting an interstate operation to these new local safety regulations prescribed by Illinois unduly burden interstate commerce, we would have to sustain the law under the authority of ... *South Carolina v. Barnwell Brothers* (1938) [*Supra.* this chapter].... The same result would obtain if we had to resolve the much discussed issues of safety presented in this case.

> This case presents a different issue. The equipment in ... *Barnwell* ... could pass muster in any State.... We were not faced there with the question whether one State could prescribe standards for interstate carriers that would conflict with the standards of another State, making it necessary, say, for an interstate carrier to shift its cargo to differently designed vehicles once another state

line was reached. We had a related problem in *Southern P. Co. v. Arizona* (1945) [*Supra.* this chapter]....

It was ... found [by the district court] that the Illinois statute seriously interferes with the "interline" operations of motor carriers—that is to say, with the interchanging of trailers between an originating carrier and another carrier when the latter serves an area not served by the former ... [If] an interchanged trailer [of a carrier that did not itself operate in Illinois] were hauled to or through Illinois, the statute would require that it contain contour guards. Since carriers which operate in and through Illinois cannot compel the originating carriers to equip their trailers with contour guards, they may be forced to cease interlining with those who do not meet the Illinois requirements....

This is one of those cases—few in number—where local safety measures that are nondiscriminatory place an unconstitutional burden on interstate commerce. This conclusion is especially underlined by the deleterious effect which the Illinois law will have on the "interline" operation of interstate motor carriers. The conflict between the Arkansas regulation and the Illinois regulation also suggests that this regulation of mudguards is not one of those matters "admitting of diversity of treatment, according to the special requirements of local conditions," to use the words of Chief Justice Hughes in *Sproles v. Binford*, 286 U.S. 374 (1932). A State which insists on a design out of line with the requirements of almost all the other States may sometimes place a great burden of delay and inconvenience on those interstate motor carriers entering or crossing its territory. Such a new safety device—out of line with the requirements of the other States—may be so compelling that the innovating State need not be the one to give way. But the present showing—balanced against the clear burden on commerce—is far too inconclusive to make this mudguard meet that test.

... The state legislatures plainly have great leeway in providing safety regulations for all vehicles—interstate as well as local.... Yet the heavy burden which the Illinois mudguard law places on the interstate movement of trucks and trailers seems to us to pass the permissible limits even for safety regulations.

Justice Harlan, joined by Justice Stewart, concurred on largely the same grounds.

## 3. Modern Applications

The above cases, along with others, provided the foundation for the modern law of the Dormant Commerce Clause. The Court recently provided a summary of the basic rules:

A discriminatory law is "virtually *per se* invalid," and will survive only if it "advances a legitimate local purpose that cannot be adequately served by reasonable nondiscriminatory alternatives." Absent discrimination for the forbidden purpose, however, the law "will be upheld unless the burden imposed on [interstate] commerce is clearly excessive in relation to the putative local benefits." *Pike v. Bruce Church, Inc.*, 397 U.S. 137 (1970). State laws frequently survive this *Pike* scrutiny, though not always, as in *Pike* itself.

*Department of Revenue of Kentucky v. Davis*, 553 U.S. 328 (2008).

The following case illustrates the Court's application of these concepts.

## C.A. Carbone, Inc. v. City of Clarkstown, N.Y.
### 511 U.S. 383 (1994)

JUSTICE KENNEDY delivered the opinion of the Court.

As solid waste output continues apace and landfill capacity becomes more costly and scarce, state and local governments are expending significant resources to develop trash control systems that are efficient, lawful, and protective of the environment....

We consider a so-called flow control ordinance, which requires all solid waste to be processed at a designated transfer station before leaving the municipality. The avowed purpose of the ordinance is to retain the processing fees charged at the transfer station to amortize the cost of the facility. Because it attains this goal by depriving competitors, including out-of-state firms, of access to a local market, we hold that the flow control ordinance violates the Commerce Clause.

... In August 1989, Clarkstown entered into a consent decree with the New York State Department of Environmental Conservation. The town agreed to close its landfill ... and build a new solid waste transfer station on the same site. The station would receive bulk solid waste and separate recyclable from nonrecyclable items. Recyclable waste would be baled for shipment to a recycling facility; nonrecyclable waste, to a suitable landfill or incinerator.

The cost of building the transfer station was estimated at $1.4 million. A local private contractor agreed to construct the facility and operate it for five years, after which the town would buy it for $1. During those five years, the town guaranteed a minimum waste flow of 120,000 tons per year, for which the contractor could charge the hauler a so-called tipping fee of $81 per ton. If the station received less than 120,000 tons in a year, the town promised to make up the tipping fee deficit. The object of this arrangement was to amortize the cost of the transfer station: The town would finance its new facility with the income generated by the tipping fees.

The problem, of course, was how to meet the yearly guarantee. This difficulty was compounded by the fact that the tipping fee of $81 per ton exceeded the disposal cost of unsorted solid waste on the private market. The solution the town adopted was the flow control ordinance here in question, Local Laws 1990, No. 9 of the Town of Clarkstown. The ordinance requires all nonhazardous solid waste within the town to be deposited at the Route 303 transfer station. Noncompliance is punishable by as much as a $1,000 fine and up to 15 days in jail.

The petitioners in this case are C & A Carbone, Inc., a company engaged in the processing of solid waste.... Carbone operates a recycling center in Clarkstown, where it receives bulk solid waste, sorts and bales it, and then ships it to other processing facilities—much as occurs at the town's new transfer station. While the flow control ordinance permits recyclers like Carbone to continue receiving solid waste, it requires them to bring the nonrecyclable residue from that waste to the [new] station. It thus forbids Carbone to ship the nonrecyclable waste itself, and it requires Carbone to pay a tipping fee on trash that Carbone has already sorted.

[Upon discovering that Carbone was transporting nonrecyclable waste it had processed to out-of-town dumps,] the town of Clarkstown sued Carbone in New York Supreme Court, Rockland County, seeking an injunction requiring Carbone to ship all nonrecyclable waste to the [new] transfer station. Carbone responded by suing in United States District Court to enjoin the flow control ordinance. On July 11, the federal court granted Carbone's injunction, finding a sufficient likelihood that the ordinance violated the Commerce Clause of the United States Constitution.

Four days later, the New York court granted summary judgment to respondent. The court declared the flow control ordinance constitutional and enjoined Carbone to comply with it. The federal court then dissolved its injunction.

The Appellate Division affirmed.... We granted certiorari, and now reverse.

At the outset we confirm that the flow control ordinance does regulate interstate commerce, despite the town's position to the contrary. The town says that its ordinance reaches only waste within its jurisdiction and is in practical effect a quarantine: It prevents garbage from entering the stream of interstate commerce until it is made safe. This reasoning is premised, however, on an outdated and mistaken concept of what constitutes interstate commerce.

While the immediate effect of the ordinance is to direct local transport of solid waste to a designated site within the local jurisdiction, its economic effects are interstate in reach. The Carbone facility in Clarkstown receives and processes waste from places other than Clarkstown, including from out of State. By requiring Carbone to send the nonrecyclable portion of this waste to the Route 303 transfer station at an additional cost, the flow control ordinance drives up the cost for out-of-state interests to dispose of their solid waste. Furthermore, even as to waste originant in Clarkstown, the ordinance prevents everyone except the favored local operator from performing the initial processing step. The ordinance thus deprives out-of-state businesses of access to a local market. These economic effects are more than enough to bring the Clarkstown ordinance within the purview of the Commerce Clause. It is well settled that actions are within the domain of the Commerce Clause if they burden interstate commerce or impede its free flow. *NLRB v. Jones & Laughlin Steel Corp.* (1937) [*Supra.* Chapter 4].

The real question is whether the flow control ordinance is valid despite its undoubted effect on interstate commerce. For this inquiry, our case law yields two lines of analysis: first, whether the ordinance discriminates against interstate commerce, and second, whether the ordinance imposes a burden on interstate commerce that is "clearly excessive in relation to the putative local benefits," *Pike v. Bruce Church, Inc.*, 397 U.S. 137 (1970) [Note *supra.* this chapter]. As we find that the ordinance discriminates against interstate commerce, we need not resort to the *Pike* test.

The central rationale for the rule against discrimination is to prohibit state or municipal laws whose object is local economic protectionism, laws that would excite those jealousies and retaliatory measures the Constitution was designed to prevent. See *The Federalist* No. 22 (A. Hamilton); Madison, Vices of the Political System of the United States, in 2 Writings of James Madison 362–363. We have interpreted the Commerce Clause to invalidate local laws that impose commercial barriers or discriminate against an article of commerce by reason of its origin or destination out of State. See, e.g., *Philadelphia v. New Jersey*, 437 U.S. 617 (1978), (striking down New Jersey statute that prohibited the import of solid waste); *Hughes v. Oklahoma*, 441 U.S. 322 (1979) (striking down Oklahoma law that prohibited the export of natural minnows).

Clarkstown protests that its ordinance does not discriminate because it does not differentiate solid waste on the basis of its geographic origin. All solid waste, regardless of origin, must be processed at the designated transfer station before it leaves the town. Unlike the statute in *Philadelphia*, says the town, the ordinance erects no barrier to the import or export of any solid waste but requires only that the waste be channeled through the designated facility.

Our initial discussion of the effects of the ordinance on interstate commerce goes far toward refuting the town's contention that there is no discrimination in its regulatory scheme. The town's own arguments go the rest of the way. As the town itself points out, what makes garbage a profitable business is not its own worth but the fact that its possessor must pay to get rid of it. In other words, the article of commerce is not so much the solid waste itself, but rather the service of processing and disposing of it.

With respect to this stream of commerce, the flow control ordinance discriminates, for it allows only the favored operator to process waste that is within the limits of the town. The ordinance is no less discriminatory because in-state or in-town processors are also covered by the prohibition. In *Dean Milk Co. v. Madison* (1951) [*Supra.* this chapter], we struck down a city ordinance that required all milk sold in the city to be pasteurized within five miles of the city lines. We found it "immaterial that Wisconsin milk from outside the Madison area is subjected to the same proscription as that moving in interstate commerce."

In this light, the flow control ordinance is just one more instance of local processing requirements that we long have held invalid. See *Minnesota v. Barber*, 136 U.S. 313 (1890) (striking down a Minnesota statute that required any meat sold within the State, whether originating within or without the State, to be examined by an inspector within the State); *Foster-Fountain Packing Co. v. Haydel*, 278 U.S. 1 (1928) (striking down a Louisiana statute that forbade shrimp to be exported unless the heads and hulls had first been removed within the State); *Johnson v. Haydel*, 278 U.S. 16 (1928) (striking down analogous Louisiana statute for oysters); *Toomer v. Witsell*, 334 U.S. 385 (1948) (striking down South Carolina statute that required shrimp fishermen to unload, pack, and stamp their catch before shipping it to another State); *Pike* (striking down Arizona statute that required all Arizona-grown cantaloupes to be packaged within the State prior to export); *South-Central Timber Development, Inc. v. Wunnicke*, 467 U.S. 82 (1984) (striking down an Alaska regulation that required all Alaska timber to be processed within the State prior to export). The essential vice in laws of this sort is that they bar the import of the processing service. Out-of-state meat inspectors, or shrimp hullers, or milk pasteurizers, are deprived of access to local demand for their services. Put another way, the offending local laws hoard a local resource—be it meat, shrimp, or milk—for the benefit of local businesses that treat it.

The flow control ordinance has the same design and effect. It hoards solid waste, and the demand to get rid of it, for the benefit of the preferred processing facility. The only conceivable distinction from the cases cited above is that the flow control ordinance favors a single local proprietor. But this difference just makes the protectionist effect of the ordinance more acute. In *Dean Milk*, the local processing requirement at least permitted pasteurizers within five miles of the city to compete. An out-of-state pasteurizer who wanted access to that market might have built a pasteurizing facility within the radius. The flow control ordinance at issue here squelches competition in the waste-processing service altogether, leaving no room for investment from outside.

Discrimination against interstate commerce in favor of local business or investment is *per se* invalid, save in a narrow class of cases in which the municipality can demonstrate, under rigorous scrutiny, that it has no other means to advance a legitimate local interest. *Maine v. Taylor*, 477 U.S. 131 (1986) (upholding Maine's ban on the import of baitfish because Maine had no other way to prevent the spread of parasites and the adulteration of its native fish species). A number of *amici* contend that the flow control ordinance fits into this narrow class. They suggest that as landfill space diminishes and environmental cleanup costs escalate, measures like flow control become necessary to ensure the safe handling and proper treatment of solid waste.

The teaching of our cases is that these arguments must be rejected absent the clearest showing that the unobstructed flow of interstate commerce itself is unable to solve the local problem. The Commerce Clause presumes a national market free from local legislation that discriminates in favor of local interests. Here Clarkstown has any number of nondiscriminatory alternatives for addressing the health and environmental problems alleged to justify the ordinance in question. The most obvious would be uniform safety regulations enacted without the object to discriminate. These regulations would ensure that competitors like Carbone do not underprice the market by cutting corners on environmental safety.

Nor may Clarkstown justify the flow control ordinance as a way to steer solid waste away from out-of-town disposal sites that it might deem harmful to the environment. To do so would extend the town's police power beyond its jurisdictional bounds. States and localities may not attach restrictions to exports or imports in order to control commerce in other States. *Baldwin v. G.A.F. Seelig, Inc.* (1935) [*Supra.* this chapter] (striking down New York law that prohibited the sale of milk unless the price paid to the original milk producer equaled the minimum required by New York).

The flow control ordinance does serve a central purpose that a nonprotectionist regulation would not: It ensures that the town-sponsored facility will be profitable, so that the local contractor can build it and Clarkstown can buy it back at nominal cost in five years. In other words, as the most candid of *amici* and even Clarkstown admit, the flow control ordinance is a financing measure. By itself, of course, revenue generation is not a local interest that can justify discrimination against interstate commerce. Otherwise States could impose discriminatory taxes against solid waste originating outside the State.

Clarkstown maintains that special financing is necessary to ensure the long-term survival of the designated facility. If so, the town may subsidize the facility through general taxes or municipal bonds. *New Energy Co. of Ind. v. Limbach*, 486 U.S. 269 (1988). But having elected to use the open market to earn revenues for its project, the town may not employ discriminatory regulation to give that project an advantage over rival businesses from out of State....

State and local governments may not use their regulatory power to favor local enterprise by prohibiting patronage of out-of-state competitors or their facilities. We reverse the judgment and remand the case for proceedings not inconsistent with this decision.

Justice O'CONNOR, concurring in the judgment.

... I agree with the majority's ultimate conclusion that the ordinance violates the dormant Commerce Clause. In my view, however, the town's ordinance is unconstitutional not because of facial or effective discrimination against interstate commerce, but rather because it imposes an excessive burden on interstate commerce....

I

The scope of the dormant Commerce Clause is a judicial creation. On its face, the Clause provides only that "the Congress shall have Power ... To regulate Commerce ... among the several States...." This Court long ago concluded, however, that the Clause not only empowers Congress to regulate interstate commerce, but also imposes limitations on the States in the absence of congressional action:

> This principle that our economic unit is the Nation, which alone has the gamut of powers necessary to control of the economy, including the vital power of erecting customs barriers against foreign competition, has as its corollary that the states are not separable economic units.... What is ultimate is the principle that one state in its dealings with another may not place itself in a position of economic isolation. *H.P. Hood & Sons, Inc. v. Du Mond*, 336 U.S. 525 (1949).

Our decisions therefore hold that the dormant Commerce Clause forbids States and their subdivisions to regulate interstate commerce.

We have generally distinguished between two types of impermissible regulations. A facially nondiscriminatory regulation supported by a legitimate state interest which incidentally burdens interstate commerce is constitutional unless the burden on interstate trade is clearly excessive in relation to the local benefits. See *Pike*. Where, however, a regulation "affirmatively" or "clearly" discriminates against interstate commerce on its face or in practical effect, it violates the Constitution unless the discrimination is demonstrably justified by a valid factor unrelated to protectionism. See *Maine v. Taylor*. Of course, there is no clear line separating these categories. "In either situation the critical consideration is the overall effect of the statute on both local and interstate activity."

Local Law 9 prohibits anyone except the town-authorized transfer station operator from processing discarded waste and shipping it out of town. In effect, the town has given a waste processing monopoly to the transfer station. The majority concludes that this processing monopoly facially discriminates against interstate commerce. In support of this conclusion, the majority cites previous decisions of this Court striking down regulatory enactments requiring that a particular economic activity be performed within the jurisdiction. See, e.g., *Dean Milk* (unconstitutional for city to require milk to be pasteurized within five miles of the city); *Barber* (unconstitutional for State to require meat sold within the State to be examined by state inspector); *Foster-Fountain Packing Co.* (unconstitutional for State to require that shrimp heads and hulls must be removed before shrimp can be removed from the State); *South-Central Timber Development* (unconstitutional for State to require all timber to be processed within the State prior to export).

Local Law 9, however, lacks an important feature common to the regulations at issue in these cases—namely, discrimination on the basis of geographic origin. In each of the cited cases, the challenged enactment gave a competitive advantage to local business as a group vis-à-vis their out-of-state or nonlocal competitors as a group. In effect, the regulating jurisdiction—be it a State (*Pike*), a county (*Fort Gratiot Sanitary Landfill, Inc. v. Michigan Dept. of Natural Resources*, 504 U.S. 353 (1992)), or a city (*Dean Milk*)—drew a line around itself and treated those inside the line more favorably than those outside the line. Thus, in *Pike*, the Court held that an Arizona law requiring that Arizona cantaloupes be packaged in Arizona before being shipped out of state facially discriminated against interstate commerce: The benefits of the discriminatory scheme benefited the Arizona packaging industry, at the expense of its competition in California. Similarly, in *Dean Milk*, on which the majority heavily relies, the city of Madison drew a line around its perimeter and required that all milk sold in the city be pasteurized only by dairies located inside the line. This type of geographic distinction, which confers an economic advantage on local interests in general, is common to all the local processing cases cited by the majority. And the Court has, I believe, correctly concluded that these arrangements are protectionist either in purpose or practical effect, and thus amount to virtually *per se* discrimination.

In my view, the majority fails to come to terms with a significant distinction between the laws in the local processing cases discussed above and Local Law 9. Unlike the regulations we have previously struck down, Local Law 9 does not give more favorable treatment to local interests as a group as compared to out-of-state or out-of-town economic interests. Rather, the garbage sorting monopoly is achieved at the expense of all competitors, be they local or nonlocal. That the ordinance does not discriminate on the basis of geographic origin is vividly illustrated by the identity of the plaintiffs in this very action: Petitioners are local recyclers, physically located in Clarkstown, that desire to process waste themselves, and thus bypass the town's designated transfer facility. Because in-town processors—like petitioners—and out-of-town processors are treated equally, I cannot agree that Local Law 9 "discriminates" against interstate commerce. Rather, Local Law 9 "discriminates" evenhandedly against all potential participants in the waste processing business, while benefiting only the chosen operator of the transfer facility.

I believe this distinction has more doctrinal significance than the majority acknowledges. In considering state health and safety regulations such as Local Law 9, we have consistently recognized that the fact that interests within the regulating jurisdiction are equally affected by the challenged enactment counsels against a finding of discrimination. And for good reason. The existence of substantial in-state interests harmed by a regulation is "a powerful safeguard" against legislative discrimination. The Court generally defers to health and safety regulations because "their burden usually falls on local economic interests as well as other States' economic interests, thus insuring that a State's own political processes will serve as a check against unduly burdensome regulations." Thus, while there is no bright line separating those enactments which are virtually *per se* invalid and those which are not, the fact that in-town competitors of the transfer facility are equally burdened by Local Law 9 leads me to conclude that Local Law 9 does not discriminate against interstate commerce.

II

That the ordinance does not discriminate against interstate commerce does not, however, end the Commerce Clause inquiry. Even a nondiscriminatory regulation may nonetheless impose an excessive burden on interstate trade when considered in relation to the local benefits conferred. Indeed, we have long recognized that "a burden imposed by a State upon interstate commerce is not to be sustained simply because the statute imposing it applies alike to … the people of the State enacting such statute." Moreover, "the extent of the burden that will be tolerated will of course depend on the nature of the local interest involved, and on whether it could be promoted as well with a lesser impact on interstate activities." *Pike.* Judged against these standards, Local Law 9 fails.

The local interest in proper disposal of waste is obviously significant. But this interest could be achieved by simply requiring that all waste disposed of in the town be properly processed somewhere. For example, the town could ensure proper processing by setting specific standards with which all town processors must comply.

In fact, however, the town's purpose is narrower than merely ensuring proper disposal. Local Law 9 is intended to ensure the financial viability of the transfer facility. I agree with the majority that this purpose can be achieved by other means that would have a less dramatic impact on the flow of goods. For example, the town could finance the project by imposing taxes, by issuing municipal bonds, or even by lowering its price for processing to a level competitive with other waste processing facilities. But by requiring that all waste be processed at the town's facility, the ordinance "squelches competition in the waste-processing service altogether, leaving no room for investment from outside." *Ante* (majority opinion).

In addition, "the practical effect of [Local Law 9] must be evaluated not only by considering the consequences of the statute itself, but also by considering how the challenged statute may interact with the legitimate regulatory regimes of the other States and what effect would arise if not one, but many or every, [jurisdiction] adopted similar legislation." *Wyoming v. Oklahoma*, 502 U.S 437 (1992). This is not a hypothetical inquiry. Over 20 states have enacted statutes authorizing local governments to adopt flow control laws. If the localities in these States impose the type of restriction on the movement of waste that Clarkstown has adopted, the free movement of solid waste in the stream of commerce will be severely impaired. Indeed, pervasive flow control would result in the type of balkanization the Clause is primarily intended to prevent.

Given that many jurisdictions are contemplating or enacting flow control, the potential for conflicts is high. For example, in the State of New Jersey, just south of Clarkstown, local waste may be removed from the State for the sorting of recyclables "as long as the residual solid waste is returned to New Jersey." Brief for New Jersey as Amicus Curiae 5. Under Local Law 9, however, if petitioners bring waste from New Jersey for recycling at their Clarkstown operation, the residual waste may not be returned to New Jersey, but must be transported to Clarkstown's transfer facility. As a consequence, operations like petitioners' cannot comply with the requirements of both jurisdictions. Nondiscriminatory state or local laws which actually conflict with the enactments of other States are constitutionally infirm if they burden interstate commerce. See *Bibb v. Navajo Freight Lines, Inc.*, 359 U.S. 520 (1959) [Note *supra.* this chapter] (unconstitutional for Illinois to require truck mudguards when that requirement conflicts with the requirements of other States); *Southern Pacific Co. v. Arizona* (1945) [*Supra.* this chapter] (same). The increasing number of flow control regimes virtually ensures some inconsistency between jurisdictions, with the effect of eliminating the movement of waste between jurisdictions. I therefore conclude that the burden Local Law 9 imposes on interstate commerce is excessive in relation to Clarkstown's interest in ensuring a fixed supply of waste to supply its project.

### III

Although this Court can—and often does—enforce the dormant aspect of the Commerce Clause, the Clause is primarily a grant of congressional authority to regulate commerce among the States. Amicus National Association of Bond Lawyers (NABL) argues that the flow control ordinance in this case has been authorized by Congress. Given the residual nature of our authority under the Clause, and because the argument that Congress has in fact authorized flow control is substantial, I think it appropriate to address it directly.

Congress must be "unmistakably clear" before we will conclude that it intended to permit state regulation which would otherwise violate the dormant Commerce Clause. *South-Central Timber*. The State or locality has the burden of demonstrating this intent.

Amicus NABL argues that Subchapter IV of the Resource Conservation and Recovery Act of 1976 (RCRA), 42 U.S.C. § 6941 et seq., and its amendments, remove the constitutional constraints on local implementation of flow control. RCRA is a sweeping statute intended to regulate solid waste from cradle to grave....

Under RCRA, States are to submit solid waste management plans that "prohibit the establishment of new open dumps within the State," and ensure that solid waste will be "utilized for resource recovery or ... disposed of in sanitary landfills ... or otherwise disposed of in an environmentally sound manner." § 6943(a)(2). The plans must also ensure that state and local governments not be "prohibited under State or local law from negotiating and entering into long-term contracts for the supply of solid waste to resource recovery facilities [or] from entering into long-term contracts for the operation of such facilities." § 6943(a)(5).

Amicus also points to a statement in a House Report addressing § 6943(a)(5), a statement evincing some concern with flow control:

> This prohibition [on state or local laws prohibiting long-term contracts] is not to be construed to affect state planning *which may require all discarded materials to be transported to a particular location.*... H.R.Rep. No. 94-1491 (1976) (emphasis added).

Finally, in the Solid Waste Disposal Act Amendments of 1980, Congress authorized the Environmental Protection Agency (EPA) to "provide technical assistance to States [and local governments] to assist in the removal or modification of legal, institutional, and economic impediments which have the effect of impeding the development of systems and facilities [for resource recovery]." § 6948(d)(3). Among the obstacles to effective resource recovery are "impediments to institutional arrangements necessary to undertake projects ... *including the creation of special districts, authorities, or corporations where necessary having the power to secure the supply of waste of a project.*" § 6948(d)(3)(C) (emphasis added).

I agree with amicus NABL that these references indicate that Congress expected local governments to implement some form of flow control. Nonetheless, they neither individually nor cumulatively rise to the level of the "explicit" authorization required by our dormant Commerce Clause decisions. First, the primary focus of the references is on legal impediments imposed as a result of state—not federal—law.... And while the House Report seems to contemplate that municipalities may require waste to be brought to a particular location, this stronger language is not reflected in the text of the statute. Cf. *United States v. Nordic Village, Inc.*, 503 U.S. 30, 37 (1992) (for waiver of sovereign immunity, "if clarity does not exist [in the text], it cannot be supplied by a committee report"). In short, these isolated references do not satisfy our requirement of an explicit statutory authorization.

It is within Congress' power to authorize local imposition of flow control. Should Congress revisit this area, and enact legislation providing a clear indication that it intends States and localities to implement flow control, we will, of course, defer to that legislative judgment. Until then, however, Local Law 9 cannot survive constitutional scrutiny. Accordingly, I concur in the judgment of the Court.

Justice SOUTER, with whom THE CHIEF JUSTICE and Justice BLACKMUN join, dissenting.

… Previous cases have held that the "negative" or "dormant" aspect of the Commerce Clause renders state or local legislation unconstitutional when it discriminates against out-of-state or out-of-town businesses such as those that pasteurize milk, hull shrimp, or mill lumber, and the majority relies on these cases because of what they have in common with this one: out-of-state processors are excluded from the local market (here, from the market for trash processing services). What the majority ignores, however, are the differences between our local processing cases and this one: the exclusion worked by Clarkstown's Local Law 9 bestows no benefit on a class of local private actors, but instead directly aids the government in satisfying a traditional governmental responsibility. The law does not differentiate between all local and all out-of-town providers of a service, but instead between the one entity responsible for ensuring that the job gets done and all other enterprises, regardless of their location. The ordinance thus falls outside that class of tariff or protectionist measures that the Commerce Clause has traditionally been thought to bar States from enacting against each other, and when the majority subsumes the ordinance within the class of laws this Court has struck down as facially discriminatory (and so avails itself of our "virtually *per se* rule" against such statutes), the majority is in fact greatly extending the Clause's dormant reach.

There are, however, good and sufficient reasons against expanding the Commerce Clause's inherent capacity to trump exercises of state authority such as the ordinance at issue here. There is no indication in the record that any out-of-state trash processor has been harmed, or that the interstate movement or disposition of trash will be affected one whit. To the degree Local Law 9 affects the market for trash processing services, it does so only by subjecting Clarkstown residents and businesses to burdens far different from the burdens of local favoritism that dormant Commerce Clause jurisprudence seeks to root out. The town has found a way to finance a public improvement, not by transferring its cost to out-of-state economic interests, but by spreading it among the local generators of trash, an equitable result with tendencies that should not disturb the Commerce Clause and should not be disturbed by us.

## I

… Carbone's complaint is one that any Clarkstown trash generator could have made: the town has created a monopoly on trash processing services, and residents are no longer free to provide these services for themselves or to contract for them with others at a mutually agreeable price.

## II

We are not called upon to judge the ultimate wisdom of creating this local monopoly, but we are asked to say whether Clarkstown's monopoly violates the Commerce Clause, as long read by this Court to limit the power of state and local governments to discriminate against interstate commerce.…

A

The majority argues that resolution of the issue before us is controlled by a line of cases in which we have struck down state or local laws that discriminate against out-of-state or out-of-town providers of processing services. With perhaps one exception,[2] the laws invalidated in those cases were patently discriminatory, differentiating by their very terms between in-state and out-of-state (or local and nonlocal) processors. One ordinance, for example, forbad selling pasteurized milk "unless the same shall have been pasteurized and bottled ... within a radius of five miles from the central portion of the City of Madison...." *Dean Milk.* The other laws expressly discriminated against commerce crossing state lines, placing these local processing cases squarely within the larger class of cases in which this Court has invalidated facially discriminatory legislation.

As the majority recognizes, Local Law 9 shares two features with these local processing cases. It regulates a processing service available in interstate commerce, *i.e.*, the sorting and baling of solid waste for disposal. And it does so in a fashion that excludes out-of-town trash processors by its very terms. These parallels between Local Law 9 and the statutes previously invalidated confer initial plausibility on the majority's classification of this case with those earlier ones on processing, and they even bring this one within the most general language of some of the earlier cases, abhorring the tendency of such statutes "to impose an artificial rigidity on the economic pattern of the industry," *Toomer v. Witsell*, 334 U.S. 385 (1948).

B

There are, however, both analytical and practical differences between this and the earlier processing cases, differences the majority underestimates or overlooks but which, if given their due, should prevent this case from being decided the same way. First, the terms of Clarkstown's ordinance favor a single processor, not the class of all such businesses located in Clarkstown. Second, the one proprietor so favored is essentially an agent of the municipal government, which (unlike Carbone or other private trash processors) must ensure the removal of waste according to acceptable standards of public health. Any discrimination worked by Local Law 9 thus fails to produce the sort of entrepreneurial favoritism we have previously defined and condemned as protectionist.

1

The outstanding feature of the statutes or ordinances reviewed in the local processing cases is their distinction between two classes of private economic actors according to location, favoring shrimp hullers within Louisiana, milk pasteurizers

---

2. The arguable exception is *Pike*, where the Court invalidated an administrative order issued pursuant to a facially neutral statute. While the order discriminated on its face, prohibiting the interstate shipment of respondent's cantaloupes unless they were first packaged locally, the statute it sought to enforce merely required that Arizona-grown cantaloupes advertise their State of origin on each package. In Part III, I discuss the line of cases in which we have struck down statutes that, although lacking explicit geographical sorting mechanisms, are discriminatory in practical effect.

within five miles of the center of Madison, and so on. See *Foster-Fountain Packing Co.*; *Dean Milk*. Since nothing in these local processing laws prevented a proliferation of local businesses within the State or town, the out-of-town processors were not excluded as part and parcel of a general exclusion of private firms from the market, but as a result of discrimination among such firms according to geography alone. It was because of that discrimination in favor of local businesses, preferred at the expense of their out-of-town or out-of-state competitors, that the Court struck down those local processing laws as classic examples of the economic protectionism the dormant Commerce Clause jurisprudence aims to prevent....

The majority recognizes, but discounts, this difference between laws favoring all local actors and this law favoring a single municipal one. According to the majority, "this difference just makes the protectionist effect of the ordinance more acute" because outside investors cannot even build competing facilities within Clarkstown. But of course Clarkstown investors face the same prohibition, which is to say that Local Law 9's exclusion of outside capital is part of a broader exclusion of private capital, not a discrimination against out-of-state investors as such. Thus, while these differences may underscore the ordinance's anticompetitive effect, they substantially mitigate any protectionist effect, for subjecting out-of-town investors and facilities to the same constraints as local ones is not economic protectionism.

2

Nor is the monopolist created by Local Law 9 just another private company successfully enlisting local government to protect the jobs and profits of local citizens. While our previous local processing cases have barred discrimination in markets served by private companies, Clarkstown's transfer station is essentially a municipal facility, built and operated under a contract with the municipality and soon to revert entirely to municipal ownership. This, of course, is no mere coincidence, since the facility performs a municipal function that tradition as well as state and federal law recognize as the domain of local government....

The majority ignores this distinction between public and private enterprise, equating Local Law 9's "hoarding" of solid waste for the municipal transfer station with the design and effect of ordinances that restrict access to local markets for the benefit of local private firms. But private businesses, whether local or out of State, first serve the private interests of their owners, and there is therefore only rarely a reason other than economic protectionism for favoring local businesses over their out-of-town competitors. The local government itself occupies a very different market position, however, being the one entity that enters the market to serve the public interest of local citizens quite apart from private interest in private gain. Reasons other than economic protectionism are accordingly more likely to explain the design and effect of an ordinance that favors a public facility. The facility as constructed might, for example, be one that private economic actors, left to their own devices, would not have built, but which the locality needs in order to abate (or guarantee against creating) a public nuisance.... An ordinance that favors a municipal facility, in any event, is one that favors the public sector, and if "we continue to recognize that the States occupy a special and specific position in our constitutional system and that the scope of Congress' authority under the Commerce Clause must reflect that position," *Garcia v. San Antonio Metropolitan Transit Authority*, 469 U.S. 528 (1985), then surely this Court's dormant Commerce Clause jurisprudence must itself see that favoring state-sponsored facilities differs from discriminating among private economic actors, and is much less likely to be protectionist.

3

Having established that Local Law 9 does not serve the competitive class identified in previous local processing cases and that Clarkstown differs correspondingly from other local processors, we must ask whether these differences justify a standard of dormant Commerce Clause review that differs from the virtually fatal scrutiny imposed in those earlier cases. I believe they do.

The justification for subjecting the local processing laws and the broader class of clearly discriminatory commercial regulation to near-fatal scrutiny is the virtual certainty that such laws, at least in their discriminatory aspect, serve no legitimate, non-protectionist purpose. Whether we find "the evil of protectionism" in the clear import of specific statutory provisions or in the legislature's ultimate purpose, the discriminatory scheme is almost always designed either to favor local industry, as such, or to achieve some other goal while exporting a disproportionate share of the burden of attaining it, which is merely a subtler form of local favoritism.

On the other hand, in a market served by a municipal facility, a law that favors that single facility over all others is a law that favors the public sector over all private-sector processors, whether local or out of State. Because the favor does not go to local private competitors of out-of-state firms, out-of-state governments will at the least lack a motive to favor their own firms in order to equalize the positions of private competitors. While a preference in favor of the government may incidentally function as local favoritism as well, a more particularized enquiry is necessary before a court can say whether such a law does in fact smack too strongly of economic protectionism. If Local Law 9 is to be struck down, in other words, it must be under that test most readily identified with *Pike*.

III

We have said that when legislation that does not facially discriminate "comes into conflict with the Commerce Clause's overriding requirement of a national 'common market,' we are confronted with the task of effecting an accommodation of the competing national and local interests." Although this analysis of competing interests has sometimes been called a "balancing test," it is not so much an open-ended weighing of an ordinance's pros and cons, as an assessment of whether an ordinance discriminates in practice or otherwise unjustifiably operates to isolate a State's economy from the national common market. If a statute or local ordinance serves a legitimate local interest and does not patently discriminate, "it will be upheld unless the burden imposed on [interstate] commerce is clearly excessive in relation to the putative local benefits." *Pike*. The analysis is similar to, but softer around the edges than, the test we employ in cases of overt discrimination. "The question becomes one of degree," and its answer depends on the nature of the burden on interstate commerce, the nature of the local interest, and the availability of alternative methods for advancing the local interest without hindering the national one.

The primary burden Carbone attributes to flow control ordinances such as Local Law 9 is that they "prevent trash from being sent to the most cost-effective disposal facilities, and insulate the designated facility from all price competition." In this case, customers must pay $11 per ton more for dumping trash at the Clarkstown transfer station than they would pay at Carbone's facility, although this dollar figure presumably overstates the burden by disguising some differences between the two....

Fortunately, the dollar cost of the burden need not be pinpointed, its nature being more significant than its economic extent. When we look to its nature, it should be clear that the monopolistic character of Local Law 9's effects is not itself suspicious for purposes of the Commerce Clause. Although the right to compete is a hallmark of the American economy ... the bar to monopolies (or, rather, the authority to dismember and penalize them) arises from a statutory, not a constitutional, mandate.... The dormant Commerce Clause does not "protect the particular structure or methods of operation in any ... market." The only right to compete that it protects is the right to compete on terms independent of one's location.

While the monopolistic nature of the burden may be disregarded, any geographically discriminatory elements must be assessed with care. We have already observed that there is no geographically based selection among private firms, and it is clear from the face of the ordinance that nothing hinges on the source of trash that enters Clarkstown or upon the destination of the processed waste that leaves the transfer station. There is, to be sure, an incidental local economic benefit, for the need to process Clarkstown's trash in Clarkstown will create local jobs. But this local boon is mitigated by another feature of the ordinance, in that it finances whatever benefits it confers on the town from the pockets of the very citizens who passed it into law. On the reasonable assumption that no one can avoid producing some trash, every resident of Clarkstown must bear a portion of the burden Local Law 9 imposes to support the municipal monopoly, an uncharacteristic feature of statutes claimed to violate the Commerce Clause.

By way of contrast, most of the local processing statutes we have previously invalidated imposed requirements that made local goods more expensive as they headed into the national market, so that out-of-state economies bore the bulk of any burden.... Courts step in through the dormant Commerce Clause to prevent such exports because legislative action imposing a burden " 'principally upon those without the state ... is not likely to be subjected to those political restraints which are normally exerted on legislation where it affects adversely some interests within the state.' " *South-Central Timber* (quoting *South Carolina Highway Dept. v. Barnwell Brothers, Inc.* (1938) [*Supra.* this chapter]). Here, in contrast, every voter in Clarkstown pays to fund the benefits of flow control, however high the tipping fee is set. Since, indeed, the mandate to use the town facility will only make a difference when the tipping fee raises the cost of using the facility above what the market would otherwise set, the Clarkstown voters are funding their benefit by assessing themselves and paying an economic penalty. Any whiff of economic protectionism is far from obvious.

An examination of the record confirms skepticism that enforcement of the ordinance portends a Commerce Clause violation, for it shows that the burden falls entirely on Clarkstown residents. If the record contained evidence that Clarkstown's ordinance burdened out-of-town providers of garbage sorting and baling services, rather than just the local business that is a party in this case, that fact might be significant. But petitioners have presented no evidence that there are transfer stations outside Clarkstown capable of handling the town's business, and the record is devoid of evidence that such enterprises have lost business as a result of this ordinance. Similarly, if the record supported an inference that above-market pricing at the Clarkstown transfer station caused less trash to flow to out-of-state landfills and incinerators, that, too, might have constitutional significance. There is, however, no evidence of any disruption in the flow of trash from curbsides in Clarkstown to landfills in Florida and Ohio. Here we can confidently say that the only business lost as a result of this ordinance is business lost in Clarkstown, as customers who had used Carbone's facility drift away in response to any higher fees Carbone may have to institute to afford its share of city services; but business lost in Clarkstown as a result of a Clarkstown ordinance is not a burden that offends the Constitution.

This skepticism that protectionism is afoot here is confirmed again when we examine the governmental interests apparently served by the local law. As mentioned already, the State and its municipalities need prompt, sanitary trash processing, which is imperative whether or not the private market sees fit to serve this need at an affordable price and to continue doing so dependably into the future. The state and local governments also have a substantial interest in the flow-control feature to minimize the risk of financing this service, for ... there is no question that a "put or pay" contract of the type Clarkstown signed will be a significant inducement to accept municipal responsibility to guarantee efficiency and sanitation in trash processing. Waste disposal with minimal environmental damage requires serious capital investment.... Protection of the public fisc is a legitimate local benefit directly advanced by the ordinance and quite unlike the generalized advantage to local businesses that we have condemned as protectionist in the past....

There is, in short, no evidence that Local Law 9 causes discrimination against out-of-town processors, because there is no evidence in the record that such processors have lost business as a result of it. Instead, we know only that the ordinance causes the local residents who adopted it to pay more for trash disposal services. But local burdens are not the focus of the dormant Commerce Clause, and this imposition is in any event readily justified by the ordinance's legitimate benefits in reliable and sanitary trash processing....

The Commerce Clause was not passed to save the citizens of Clarkstown from themselves. It should not be wielded to prevent them from attacking their local garbage problems with an ordinance that does not discriminate between local and out-of-town participants in the private market for trash disposal services and that is not protectionist in its purpose or effect. Local Law 9 conveys a privilege on the municipal government alone, the only market participant that bears responsibility for ensuring that adequate trash processing services continue to be available to Clarkstown residents. Because the Court's decision today is neither compelled by our local processing cases nor consistent with this Court's reason for inferring a dormant or negative aspect to the Commerce Clause in the first place, I respectfully dissent.

## Note: Identifying Discrimination

1. As *Carbone* and the earlier cases make clear, a determination that a state law is or is not discriminatory is critical to the law's fate in a dormant commerce clause challenge. This fact makes the discrimination determination a crucial part of the doctrinal analysis. Sometimes, as for example with the Madison ordinance in *Dean Milk*, it is obvious that the law is discriminatory. Other times, as with the Clarkstown ordinance in *Carbone*, the matter is not as clear. This note provides two additional illustrative examples of how the Court makes the discrimination determination.

2. *Hunt v. Washington State Apple Advertising Commission*, 432 U.S. 333 (1977), involved a North Carolina law that required that apples imported into the state display on their containers only the applicable federal apple quality grade. The effect of the law was to require that apples imported from Washington, a major apple producing state, not display the Washington state-based grades. Those state-based grades were more elaborate and stringent than the federal grades.

The Court struck down the North Carolina law by an 8–0 vote (Justice Rehnquist not participating). Writing for the Court, Chief Justice Burger noted that the law forced Washington apple producers to alter their marketing by removing the state-based grades from their crates. He also concluded that the law had the effect of leveling the marketplace to the detriment of the (superior) Washington products, by removing the guarantees of superior quality the Washington apples would otherwise feature. The Chief Justice wrote: "Such 'downgrading' offers the North Carolina apple industry the very sort of protection against competing out-of-state products that the Commerce Clause was designed to prohibit."

The Court also cited statements suggesting that the North Carolina legislature intended this discriminatory effect. Chief Justice Burger then wrote: "However, we need not ascribe an economic protection motive to the North Carolina Legislature to resolve this case; we conclude that the challenged statute cannot stand insofar as it prohibits the display of Washington State grades even if enacted for the declared purpose of protecting consumers from deception and fraud in the marketplace."

Based on this analysis, the Court struck the law down, rejecting the argument that the law furthered the state's asserted legitimate interest in preventing confusion caused by a proliferation of grading mechanisms. Among other things, it noted that the law operated at the wholesale, rather than the retail level, and thus reduced confusion only at the marketing stage where knowledge of the Washington grading system was likely quite high and thus the potential for confusion minimal. It also suggested that any confusion could have been allayed by simply requiring all apple containers to contain *at least* the federal grade, so as to provide a minimum level of comparability between apples from different states.

3. The very next year the Court split on the meaning of *Hunt*. *Exxon v. Governor of Maryland*, 437 U.S. 117 (1978), involved a Maryland law that prohibited oil producers and refiners from operating retail gas stations in the state. The law was claimed to have been motivated by reports that major refiners, such as Exxon and Shell, had favored their own gas stations during previous periods of shortage. The burden of the law fell almost exclusively on out-of-state firms, who were forced to exit the retail gasoline market in Maryland, to the benefit of smaller in-state retailers who did not themselves refine oil and thus were not affected by the law.

On a 7–1 vote (Justice Powell not participating), the Court upheld the law against a refiner's dormant Commerce Clause challenge. Writing for the Court, Justice Stevens began by noting that there were several out-of-state gasoline marketers who were not affected by the law, and who could continue competing with in-state retailers. He then found that there was no dormant Commerce Clause violation because the law did not disrupt the interstate market in gasoline. He noted that interstate shipments of gasoline continued as they had before, but simply through a different market structure. He concluded that "the absence of any of these factors fully distinguishes this case from those in which a State has been found to have discriminated against interstate commerce [citing *Dean Milk v. Madison* and *Hunt*]."

He continued that the dormant Commerce Clause "protects the interstate market, not particular interstate firms, from prohibitive or burdensome regulations." Thus, he rejected the plaintiff's argument that "the Commerce Clause protects the particular structure or methods of operation in a retail market."

Justice Blackmun dissented. He noted that "the effect [of the law] is to exclude a class of predominantly out-of-state gasoline retailers while providing protection from competition to a class of nonintegrated retailers that is overwhelmingly composed of local businessmen." He wrote: "Of the class of stations statutorily insulated from the competition of the out-of-state integrated firms, ... more than 99% were operated by local business interests. Of the class of enterprises excluded entirely from participation in the retail gasoline market, 95% were out-of-state firms, operating 98% of the stations in the class." He challenged the majority's reliance on *Hunt*, arguing that the *Hunt* Court "declared the [North Carolina apple] provision unconstitutional because it discriminated against a single segment of out-of-state marketers of apples, namely the Washington State growers who employed the superior [state] grading system." He continued: "In this regard, the Maryland divestiture provisions are identical to, not distinguishable from, the North Carolina statute in *Hunt*. Here, the discrimination has been imposed against a segment of the out-of-state retailers of gasoline, namely, those who also refine or produce petroleum."

### *Note: More on Discrimination and Strict Scrutiny*

1. In addition to setting forth the basic rules applied in *Carbone*, the Court has confronted a number of particular fact patterns forcing the Court to decide either the constitutionality of a concededly discriminatory statute, or whether a statute does in fact discriminate.

2. Are discriminatory statutes always unconstitutional? The Court sometimes says (as it said in *Carbone*) that discriminatory laws are subject to a "virtually *per se* rule of invalidity." However, in *Maine v. Taylor*, 477 U.S. 131 (1986), referred to in *Carbone*, the Court upheld a Maine statute banning the importation of live baitfish. The statute clearly discriminated against interstate commerce, by imposing an embargo against imports of such products, and thus was subject to the Court's highest scrutiny. The Court held that the statute satisfied that strict scrutiny, because the state identified a legitimate local purpose (protection of Maine's "unique and ecologically fragile" fisheries) which could not be protected by a less commerce-burdening method. The Court relied heavily on the trial court's factual finding that sampling methods (by which a percentage of a load of baitfish would be tested for dangerous parasites) were not reliable means of determining whether the entire shipment was disease-free. The Court also rejected arguments that other means existed by which Maine fisheries could be infected with disease-carrying fish (for example, they could simply swim in from New Hampshire waters), saying in effect that the possibility that a discriminatory statute would not be completely effective was not by itself a sufficient reason for striking it down.

3. Can a state justify a discriminatory statute on the ground that it is seeking to force other states to adopt more open trade policies? In *Great Atlantic & Pacific Tea Co. v. Cottrell*, 424 U.S. 366 (1976), the Court considered a Mississippi law that prohibited the sale of out-of-state milk and milk products in Mississippi unless the exporting state accepted on a reciprocal basis Grade A milk and milk products produced and processed in Mississippi. A Louisiana milk producer, who was denied entry to the Mississippi market because Louisiana did not give Mississippi milk reciprocity, challenged the Mississippi law. The Louisiana milk met Mississippi's health standards. In an opinion written by Justice Brennan, the Court struck down the Mississippi law:

> The ... appellee's argument that the reciprocity requirement promotes trade between the States draws upon Mississippi's allegations that Louisiana is itself violating the Commerce Clause by refusing to admit milk produced in Mississippi.... Hence, the reciprocity agreement, it is argued, is a legitimate means by which Mississippi may seek to gain access to Louisiana markets for its own producers as a condition to allowing Louisiana milk to be sold in Mississippi. We cannot agree.

> To the extent, if any, that Louisiana is unconstitutionally burdening the flow of milk in interstate commerce by erecting and enforcing economic trade barriers to protect its own producers from competition under the guise of health regulations, the Commerce Clause itself creates the necessary reciprocity: Mississippi and its producers may pursue their constitutional remedy

by suit in state or federal court challenging Louisiana's actions as violative of the Commerce Clause.

4. Subsidies — grants of cash assistance to local firms to help them be more competitive as compared with out-of-state competitors — are an everyday part of state government business. Are subsidies subject to Dormant Commerce Clause scrutiny? In *New Energy Co. of Indiana v. Limbach*, 486 U.S. 269 (1986), the Court, speaking through Justice Scalia, said "no":

> [The] Commerce Clause does not prohibit all state action designed to give its residents an advantage in the marketplace, but only action of that description *in connection with the State's regulation of interstate commerce.* Direct subsidization of domestic industry does not ordinarily run afoul of that prohibition; discriminatory taxation of out-of-state manufacturers does.

## Note: The State as a Market Participant and Provider of Government Services

1. Beyond the doctrinal rules set forth above, the Court has identified two special situations where the normal rules of the dormant Commerce Clause do not apply: when the state acts as a "market participant" and when it provides public services. In 2008 the Court explained both of these exceptions:

> [An] exception [to standard Dormant Commerce Clause doctrine] covers States that go beyond regulation and themselves "participate in the market" so as to "exercise the right to favor [their] own citizens over others." *Hughes v. Alexandria Scrap*, 426 U.S. 794 (1976). This "market-participant" exception reflects a "basic distinction ... between States as market participants and States as market regulators," *Reeves v. Stake*, 447 U.S. 429 (1980), "there [being] no indication of a constitutional plan to limit the ability of the States themselves to operate freely in the free market." Thus, in *Alexandria Scrap*, we found that a state law authorizing state payments to processors of automobile hulks validly burdened out-of-state processors with more onerous documentation requirements than their in-state counterparts. Likewise, *Reeves* accepted South Dakota's policy of giving in-state customers first dibs on cement produced by a state-owned plant, and *White v. Mass. Council of Construction Employers*, 460 U.S. 204 (1983), held that a Boston executive order requiring half the workers on city-financed construction projects to be city residents passed muster.
>
> Our most recent look at the reach of the dormant Commerce Clause came just last Term, in a case decided independently of the market participation precedents. *United Haulers Ass'n, Inc. v. Oneida-Herkimer Solid Waste Management Authority*, 550 U.S. 330 (2007), upheld a "flow control" ordinance requiring trash haulers to deliver solid waste to a processing plant owned and operated by a public authority in New York State. We found "compelling reasons" for "treating [the ordinance] differently from laws favoring particular private businesses over their competitors." State and local governments that

provide public goods and services on their own, unlike private businesses, are "vested with the responsibility of protecting the health, safety, and welfare of [their] citizens," and laws favoring such States and their subdivisions may "be directed toward any number of legitimate goals unrelated to protectionism." That was true in *United Haulers*, where the ordinance addressed waste disposal, "both typically and traditionally a local government function." And if more had been needed to show that New York's object was consequently different from forbidden protectionism, we pointed out that "the most palpable harm imposed by the ordinances—more expensive trash removal—[was] likely to fall upon the very people who voted for the laws," rather than out-of-state interests. Being concerned that a "contrary approach ... would lead to unprecedented and unbounded interference by the courts with state and local government," we held that the ordinance did "not discriminate against interstate commerce for purposes of the dormant Commerce Clause."

*Department of Revenue of Kentucky v. Davis*, 553 U.S. 328 (2008).

2. In *South-Central Timber Development, Inc., v. Wunnicke*, 467 U.S. 82 (1984), the Court recognized a limitation to the market-participant exception. *Wunnicke* struck down an Alaska law requiring purchasers of state-owned timber to process the timber in the state before exporting it. While the initial limitation on who the state sells to might be protected by the market-participant exception, Justice White, writing for a plurality of four Justices (out of eight participating in the case), wrote: "The limit of the market-participant doctrine must be that it allows a State to impose burdens on commerce within the market in which it is a participant, but allows it to go no further. The State may not impose conditions, whether by statute, regulation, or contract, that have a substantial regulatory effect outside of that particular market." Justice Powell, joined by Chief Justice Burger, would have remanded the case to determine if the initial limitation on the sale unconstitutionally burdened interstate commerce. Then-Justice Rehnquist, joined by Justice O'Connor, dissented.

3. In *United Haulers Ass'n, Inc. v. Oneida-Herkimer Solid Waste Management Authority*, 550 U.S. 330 (2007), cited in the excerpt in item 1 of this Note, the Court relied on the second limitation discussed in the above excerpt from *Davis* to uphold a "flow control" waste disposal ordinance very similar to the one struck down in *Carbone*, except for the fact that in *United Haulers* the favored waste-treatment facility was government-owned. Writing for five Justices, Chief Justice Roberts held that this difference was significant enough to warrant the conclusion that the ordinance, unlike the one in *Carbone*, was not discriminatory. He noted that any "discrimination" in favor of the government-owned treatment facility was not discrimination of the sort condemned by the Dormant Commerce Clause, since government has the responsibility for ensuring the health and safety of its citizens. He wrote, "Given these differences, it does not make sense to regard laws favoring local government and laws favoring private industry with equal skepticism."

# 4. The Limits of the Doctrine—and Critiques

## *Note: The Limits of Political Process Theory*

Political process theory—the theory that the existence of political interests inside the state that are harmed by a state law mitigates concern that the statute is an inappropriate attempt to favor insiders at the expense of outsiders—has been a recurring theme in dormant Commerce Clause doctrine at least since *Barnwell Brothers*. Both Justice O'Connor and Justice Souter cited it in *Carbone*. The Court also relied on it in *West Lynn Creamery v. Healy*, 512 U.S. 186 (1994). But in *West Lynn* the Court encountered a problem with this theory.

*West Lynn* considered a challenge to a Massachusetts dairy statute, which assessed a fee on all milk sold by dealers in Massachusetts, whether imported or domestic. The proceeds from the fee went into a dedicated fund which funded a subsidy to Massachusetts farmers. The state argued that since both the non-discriminatory tax and the subsidy were constitutional, their combination had to be constitutional as well. The Court rejected the theory, relying on political process analysis:

> [Respondent] errs in assuming that the constitutionality of the pricing order follows logically from the constitutionality of its component parts. By conjoining a tax and a subsidy, Massachusetts has created a program more dangerous to interstate commerce than either part alone. Nondiscriminatory measures, like the evenhanded tax at issue here, are generally upheld, in spite of any adverse effects on interstate commerce, in part because "the existence of major in-state interests adversely affected … is a powerful safeguard against legislative abuse." *Minnesota v. Clover Leaf Creamery Co.*, 449 U.S. 456 (1981); *see also South Carolina State Highway Dept. v. Barnwell Bros., Inc.* (1938) [*Supra.* this chapter]. However, when a nondiscriminatory tax is coupled with a subsidy to one of the groups hurt by the tax, a state's political processes can no longer be relied upon to prevent legislative abuse, because one of the in-state interests which would otherwise lobby against the tax has been mollified by the subsidy. So, in this case, one would ordinarily have expected at least three groups to lobby against the order premium, which, as a tax, raises the price (and hence lowers demand) for milk: dairy farmers, milk dealers, and consumers. But because the tax was coupled with a subsidy, one of the most powerful of these groups, Massachusetts dairy farmers, instead of exerting their influence against the tax, were in fact its primary supporters.

But what about consumers? Under the Massachusetts law, in-state consumers would pay more for milk. Wouldn't that fact prove "the existence of major in-state interest adversely affected" by the statute? In a footnote, the Court disagreed:

> As the Governor's Special Commission Relative to the Establishment of a Dairy Stabilization Fund realized, consumers would be unlikely to organize effectively to oppose the pricing order. The commission's report remarked, "the estimated two cent increase per quart of milk would not be noticed by the consuming public," because the price of milk varies so often and for so

many reasons that consumers would be unlikely to feel the price increases or to attribute them to the pricing order.

The Court then responded to a related argument:

> Respondent also argues that "the operation of the Order disproves any claim of protectionism," because "only in-state consumers feel the effect of any retail price increase ... [and] the dealers themselves ... have a substantial in-state presence." This argument, if accepted, would undermine almost every discriminatory tax case. State taxes are ordinarily paid by in-state businesses and consumers, yet if they discriminate against out-of-state products, they are unconstitutional.... The cost of a tariff is also borne primarily by local consumers, yet a tariff is the paradigmatic Commerce Clause violation.

Dissenting, Chief Justice Rehnquist, joined by Justice Blackmun, signaled disagreement with the political process approach:

> The Court [strikes the law down] because of its view that the method of imposing the tax and subsidy distorts the State's political process: The dairy farmers, who would otherwise lobby against the tax, have been mollified by the subsidy. But as the Court itself points out, there are still at least two strong interest groups opposed to the milk order—consumers and milk dealers.... Analysis of interest group participation in the political process may serve many useful purposes, but serving as a basis for interpreting the dormant Commerce Clause is not one of them.

### Note: Critiques of Benefit-Burden "Balancing" and the Dormant Commerce Clause Generally

1. Another aspect of dormant commerce clause analysis was critiqued in *Bendix Autolite Corp. v. Midwesco Enterprises*, 486 U.S. 888 (1988). *Bendix* considered a dormant Commerce Clause challenge to an Ohio law that tolled a statute of limitations for lawsuits against corporations that were not "present" in the state. For a foreign corporation to be "present," it had to appoint an agent for service of process, which operated as consent to the jurisdiction of Ohio state courts.

The Court struck the statute down. Writing for seven Justices, Justice Kennedy concluded that the statute could be analyzed either as one that discriminated against out-of-staters, or as an even-handed statute that failed benefit-burden balancing. He took the latter course:

> The burden the tolling statute places on interstate commerce is significant. Midwesco has no corporate office in Ohio, is not registered to do business there, and has not appointed an agent for service of process in the State. To gain the protection of the limitations period, Midwesco would have had to appoint a resident agent for service of process in Ohio and subject itself to the general jurisdiction of the Ohio courts. This jurisdiction would extend to any suit against Midwesco, whether or not the transaction in question had any connection with Ohio. The designation of an agent subjects the foreign

corporation to the general jurisdiction of the Ohio courts in matters to which Ohio's tenuous relation would not otherwise extend. The Ohio statutory scheme thus forces a foreign corporation to choose between exposure to the general jurisdiction of Ohio courts or forfeiture of the limitations defense, remaining subject to suit in Ohio in perpetuity. Requiring a foreign corporation to appoint an agent for service in all cases and to defend itself with reference to all transactions, including those in which it did not have the minimum contacts necessary for supporting personal jurisdiction, is a significant burden....

The ability to execute service of process on foreign corporations and entities is an important factor to consider in assessing the local interest in subjecting out-of-state entities to requirements more onerous than those imposed on domestic parties. It is true that serving foreign corporate defendants may be more arduous than serving domestic corporations or foreign corporations with a designated agent for service, and we have held for equal protection purposes that a State rationally may make adjustments for this difference by curtailing limitations protection for absent foreign corporations. Nevertheless, state interests that are legitimate for equal protection or due process purposes may be insufficient to withstand Commerce Clause scrutiny.

In the particular case before us, the Ohio tolling statute must fall under the Commerce Clause. Ohio cannot justify its statute as a means of protecting its residents from corporations who become liable for acts done within the State but later withdraw from the jurisdiction, for it is conceded by all parties that the Ohio long-arm statute would have permitted service on Midwesco throughout the period of limitations. The Ohio statute of limitations is tolled only for those foreign corporations that do not subject themselves to the general jurisdiction of Ohio courts. In this manner the Ohio statute imposes a greater burden on out-of-state companies than it does on Ohio companies, subjecting the activities of foreign and domestic corporations to inconsistent regulations....

Justice Scalia concurred in the judgment, but on the theory that the Ohio statute discriminated against out-of-state corporations. He attacked the Court's balancing analysis, and, indeed, the entire concept of balancing in dormant Commerce Clause doctrine:

Having evaluated the interests on both sides as roughly as [it does], the Court then proceeds to judge which is more important. This process is ordinarily called "balancing," *Pike v. Bruce Church, Inc.*, 397 U.S. 137 (1970) [Note *supra.* this chapter], but the scale analogy is not really appropriate, since the interests on both sides are incommensurate. It is more like judging whether a particular line is longer than a particular rock is heavy. All I am really persuaded of by the Court's opinion is that the burdens the Court labels "significant" are more determinative of its decision than the benefits it labels "important." Were it not for the brief implication that there is here a discrimination unjustified by any state interest, I suggest an opinion could as persuasively have been written coming out the opposite way. We sometimes make similar "balancing" judgments in determining how far the needs of the State can intrude upon the liberties of the individual, but that is of the essence of the courts' function as the nonpolitical branch. Weighing the governmental interests of a State against the needs of interstate commerce is, by contrast, a task squarely within the responsibility of Congress, *see* U.S. Const., Art. I, § 8, cl. 3, and "ill suited to the judicial function."

I would therefore abandon the "balancing" approach to these negative Commerce Clause cases, first explicitly adopted 18 years ago in *Pike v. Bruce Church, Inc.*, and leave essentially legislative judgments to the Congress. Issues already decided I would leave untouched, but would adopt for the future an analysis more appropriate to our role and our abilities. This does no damage to the interests protected by the doctrine of *stare decisis*. Since the outcome of any particular still-undecided issue under the current methodology is in my view not pre*dict*able—except within the broad range that would in any event come out the same way under the test I would apply—no expectations can possibly be upset. To the contrary, the ultimate objective of the rule of *stare decisis* will be furthered. Because the outcome of the test I would apply is considerably more clear, confident expectations will more readily be able to be entertained.

In my view, a state statute is invalid under the Commerce Clause if, and only if, it accords discriminatory treatment to interstate commerce in a respect not required to achieve a lawful state purpose....

Chief Justice Rehnquist dissented, finding that the Ohio statute did not discriminate and that there was no other reason to strike down the Ohio law.

2. Justice Scalia's skepticism about the dormant Commerce Clause has been amplified by Justice Thomas. In 1997 Justice Thomas launched another, even broader attack on the dormant Commerce Clause, in his dissent in *Camps Newfound/ Owatonna, Inc. v. Town of Harrison, Me.*, 520 U.S. 564 (1997). In a part of his opinion joined by Chief Justice Rehnquist and Justice Scalia, he wrote the following:

The negative Commerce Clause has no basis in the text of the Constitution, makes little sense, and has proved virtually unworkable in application. See, e.g., *Bendix* (SCALIA, J., concurring in judgment).... [I] think it worth revisiting the underlying justifications for our involvement in the negative aspects of the Commerce Clause, and the compelling arguments demonstrating why those justifications are illusory.

To cover its exercise of judicial power in an area for which there is no textual basis, the Court has historically offered two different theories in support of its negative Commerce Clause jurisprudence. The first theory posited was that the Commerce Clause itself constituted an exclusive grant of power to Congress. *See, e.g., Passenger Cases*, 7 How. 283 (1849).[5] The "exclusivity"

---

5. See also *Cooley v. Board of Wardens*, 12 How. 299 (1852) [Note *supra.* this chapter] (adopting a partial-exclusivity rationale for dormant Commerce Clause cases).

rationale was likely wrong from the outset, however. See, e.g., *The Federalist* No. 32 (A. Hamilton) ("Notwithstanding the affirmative grants of general authorities, there has been the most pointed care in those cases where it was deemed improper that the like authorities should reside in the states, to insert negative clauses prohibiting the exercise of them by the states").[6] ... And, in any event, the Court has long since "repudiated" the notion that the Commerce Clause operates as an exclusive grant of power to Congress, and thereby forecloses state action respecting interstate commerce. *Freeman v. Hewit*, 329 U.S. 249 (1946) (Rutledge, J., concurring); *see also, e.g., Southern Pacific Co. v. Arizona ex rel. Sullivan* (1945) [*Supra.* this chapter] ("Ever since *Willson v. Black-Bird Creek Marsh Co.*, 2 Pet. 245 (1829), and *Cooley v. Board of Wardens*, 53 U.S. 299 (1852) [Both note *supra.* this chapter], it has been recognized that, in the absence of conflicting legislation by Congress, there is a residuum of power in the state to make laws governing matters of local concern which nevertheless in some measure affect interstate commerce or even, to some extent, regulate it.").

Indeed, the Court's early view that the Commerce Clause, on its own, prohibited state impediments to interstate commerce such that "Congress cannot re-grant, or in any manner reconvey to the states that power," *Cooley*, quickly proved untenable. And, as this Court's definition of the scope of congressional authority under the positive Commerce Clause has expanded, the exclusivity rationale has moved from untenable to absurd.

The second theory offered to justify creation of a negative Commerce Clause is that Congress, by its silence, pre-empts state legislation. *See Robbins v. Shelby County Taxing Dist.*, 120 U.S. 489 (1887) (asserting that congressional silence evidences congressional intent that there be no state regulation of commerce). In other words, we presumed that congressional "inaction" was "equivalent to a declaration that inter-State commerce shall be free and untrammelled." *Welton v. Missouri*, 91 U.S. 275 (1876). To the extent that the "pre-emption-by-silence" rationale ever made sense, it, too, has long since been rejected by this Court in virtually every analogous area of the law....

In sum, neither of the Court's proffered theoretical justifications—exclusivity or pre-emption-by-silence—currently supports our negative Commerce Clause jurisprudence, if either ever did....

Moreover, our negative Commerce Clause jurisprudence has taken us well beyond the invalidation of obviously discriminatory taxes on interstate commerce. We have used the Clause to make policy-laden judgments that we are

---

6. See also F. Frankfurter, *The Commerce Clause Under Marshall, Taney and Waite* (noting that Chief Justice Marshall's discussion of the "exclusiveness" doctrine in *Gibbons v. Ogden* (1824) [*Supra.* this chapter], "was logically irrelevant to [his] holding," and adding: "It was an audacious doctrine, which, one may be sure, would hardly have been publicly avowed in support of the adoption of the Constitution. Indeed, *The Federalist* in effect denied it, by assuring that only express prohibitions in the Constitution limited the taxing power of the states" (citing *The Federalist* No. 32)).

ill equipped and arguably unauthorized to make. In so doing, we have developed multifactor tests in order to assess the perceived "effect" any particular state tax or regulation has on interstate commerce. And in an unabashedly legislative manner, we have balanced that "effect" against the perceived interests of the taxing or regulating State, as the very description of our "general rule" indicates:

> "Where the statute regulates even-handedly to effectuate a legitimate local public interest, and its effects on interstate commerce are only incidental, it will be upheld unless the burden imposed on such commerce is clearly excessive in relation to the putative local benefits. If a legitimate local purpose is found, then the question becomes one of degree. And the extent of the burden that will be tolerated will of course depend on the nature of the local interest involved, and on whether it could be promoted as well with a lesser impact on interstate activities." *Pike.*

Any test that requires us to assess (1) whether a particular statute serves a "legitimate" local public interest; (2) whether the effects of the statute on interstate commerce are merely "incidental" or "clearly excessive in relation to the putative benefits"; (3) the "nature" of the local interest; and (4) whether there are alternative means of furthering the local interest that have a "lesser impact" on interstate commerce, and even then makes the question "one of degree," surely invites us, if not compels us, to function more as legislators than as judges. *See Bendix* (SCALIA, J., concurring in judgment) (urging abandonment of the *Pike* balancing test so as to "leave essentially legislative judgments to the Congress").

### *Note: Evaluating the Dormant Commerce Clause*

1. As the previous note made clear, the principle underlying the dormant Commerce Clause is controversial, with regard not just to how best to apply it, but whether it should exist at all. Now that you've considered that principle, how it is applied, and various justices' critiques, what do you think?

One fundamental critique of the dormant Commerce Clause is that it is unnecessary. Congress can always legislate to restrict, prohibit, or (conversely) allow the types of state regulation that are subject to scrutiny under the dormant Commerce Clause. (Recall that Justice O'Connor's opinion in *Carbone* considers the possibility that Congress had done just that in the field of municipal waste regulation.) Some judges and commentators have thus argued that the Court should leave to Congress the determination whether a particular state law should be allowed to survive or whether it should be preempted by federal law. At the very least, some judges say, the fact that Congress has this power should give the Court pause before it scrutinizes *evenhanded* state regulations to determine if the burdens they impose on interstate commerce are outweighed by the local benefits they bestow. Justice Thomas argued in his *Camps Newfound* dissent that such weighing is a quintessentially legislative function, ill-suited to courts. As indicated by the number of justices who joined his opinion, this critique of the Court's dormant Commerce Clause jurisprudence represents more than one justice's idiosyncratic view.

On the other hand, remember early cases such as *Baldwin v. G.A.F. Seelig* and *Dean Milk v. Madison.* Those cases appear to directly violate the principle that states may not impose barriers to trade from other states. This principle is fundamental: recall that a primary reason for the Constitutional Convention in 1787 was to create a system in which states would *not* be allowed to balkanize the national economy. As trouble-prone as the dormant Commerce Clause might be, it does appear to reflect a basic commitment the framers intended to write into the Constitution. But again, Congress can always vindicate this principle by preempting state laws it believes violate it. Does the Court have a legitimate role in this task as well?

2. What one thinks about the dormant Commerce Clause as an idea may turn on how one evaluates the Court's work in applying it. How persuaded are you by the decisions you've read in this part of the chapter? Recall *Southern Pacific* and *Bibb v. Navajo Freight,* two of the earlier cases in this sequence: what do you make of the Court's second guessing of, respectively, the Arizona legislature's decision about the relative safety of fewer-but-longer trains versus more-but-shorter trains, and the Illinois legislature's analogous decision about the safety of contour versus standard mudflaps? What about *Carbone*? Are you satisfied that the Court accurately described the Clarkstown ordinance as discriminatory? What about *Hunt* and *Exxon,* the note cases where the Court reached different conclusions on the discrimination question, despite Justice Blackmun's *Exxon* dissent arguing that the cases were analogous?

More generally, what do you think of the political process analysis sketched out in *South Carolina v. Barnwell Brothers*? At first blush, such analysis appears to be an attractive way to analyze dormant Commerce Clause issues. Did the Court in *Carbone* truly understand *Barnwell,* or did Justices O'Connor and Souter (both of whom concluded that the Clarkstown ordinance was not discriminatory) get the better of that argument? What about *West Lynn Creamery* (the note case involving the combination of an evenhanded tax and a subsidy)? Did the Court effectively apply political process analysis in that case?

Note that political process analysis is not limited to the dormant Commerce Clause. As you'll see in Chapter 12, similar analysis has been applied in equal protection doctrine. Indeed, that branch of political process analysis grew from a case that, just like *Barnwell Brothers,* was decided in 1938—and by the same justice. Chapter 12 will tell that story.

## B. Interstate Privileges and Immunities

Article IV, § 2, contains the Interstate Privileges and Immunities Clause: "The Citizens of each State shall be entitled to all Privileges and Immunities of Citizens in the several States." Art. IV, § 2, cl. 1. (Note that the Constitution includes a similarly-worded clause, in the 14th Amendment, which will be presented in Chapter 7.) The clause appearing in Article IV was designed to ensure that states would not discriminate against the citizens of other states because of their citizenship in those states. In an early case, *Paul v. Virginia*, 75 U.S. 168 (1868), the Court held that the Clause applies only to natural persons; thus, corporations do not enjoy the benefits of the Clause.

Today, application of the Clause entails a two-step analysis. First, a court asks whether a state has discriminated against out-of-staters with regard to "'privileges' and 'immunities' bearing upon the vitality of the Nation as a single entity." *Baldwin v. Fish and Game Comm'n of Montana*, 436 U.S. 371 (1978). Such rights are usually thought to include constitutional rights and the right to earn a livelihood. If the state has discriminated with regard to such rights, a court then asks whether the state has a good reason for the discrimination, and whether the discrimination closely fits the asserted justification. In *Supreme Court of New Hampshire v. Piper*, excepted below, the Court stated as follows: "The Clause does not preclude discrimination against nonresidents where (i) there is a substantial reason for the difference in treatment; and (ii) the discrimination practiced against nonresidents bears a substantial relationship to the State's objective."

As suggested by the test expressed in *Piper*, the Privileges and Immunities Clause does not require states to treat citizens of other states in exactly the same way that they treat their own citizens. States can treat the citizens of other states differently in some instances, either when the interest at issue is not considered sufficiently important, or when the state has sufficiently important reasons for the differential treatment. A question that often arises in these cases is the extent to which a state's sovereign existence justifies treating its non-citizens differently from its own citizens. In the next case, the Court considered the implications of our federal system in applying the Clause's general requirement of non-discrimination.

## Supreme Court of New Hampshire v. Piper
### 470 U.S. 274 (1985)

Justice POWELL delivered the opinion of the Court.

The Rules of the Supreme Court of New Hampshire limit bar admission to state residents. We here consider whether this restriction violates the Privileges and Immunities Clause of the United States Constitution, Art. IV, § 2.

### I
### A

Kathryn Piper lives in Lower Waterford, Vermont, about 400 yards from the New Hampshire border. In 1979, she applied to take the February 1980 New Hampshire bar examination. Piper submitted with her application a statement of intent to become a New Hampshire resident. Following an investigation, the Board of Bar Examiners found that Piper was of good moral character and met the other requirements for admission. She was allowed to take, and passed, the examination. Piper was informed by the Board that she would have to establish a home address in New Hampshire prior to being sworn in.

On May 7, 1980, Piper requested from the Clerk of the New Hampshire Supreme Court a dispensation from the residency requirement. Although she had a "possible job" with a lawyer in Littleton, New Hampshire, Piper stated that becoming a resident of New Hampshire would be inconvenient. Her house in Vermont was secured by a mortgage with a favorable interest rate, and she and her husband recently had become parents. According to Piper, these "problems peculiar to [her] situation ... warranted that an exception be made."

On May 13, 1980, the Clerk informed Piper that her request had been denied. She then formally petitioned the New Hampshire Supreme Court for permission to become a member of the bar. She asserted that she was well qualified and that her "situation [was] sufficiently unique that the granting of an exception ... [would] not result in the setting of any undesired precedent." The Supreme Court denied Piper's formal request on December 31, 1980.

B

On March 22, 1982, Piper filed this action in the United States District Court for the District of New Hampshire. She named as defendants the State Supreme Court, its five Justices, and its Clerk. She alleged that Rule 42 of the New Hampshire Supreme Court, that excludes nonresidents from the bar, violates the Privileges and Immunities Clause of Art. IV, §2, of the United States Constitution.

On May 17, 1982, the District Court granted Piper's motion for summary judgment. The court first stated that the opportunity to practice law is a "fundamental" right within the meaning of *Baldwin v. Montana Fish & Game Comm'n*, 436 U.S. 371 (1978). It then found that Piper had been denied this right in the absence of a "substantial reason," and that Rule 42 was not "closely tailored" to achieve its intended goals. The court therefore concluded that New Hampshire's residency requirement violated the Privileges and Immunities Clause.

An evenly divided Court of Appeals for the First Circuit, sitting en banc, affirmed the judgment in favor of Piper ... The Supreme Court of New Hampshire filed a timely notice of appeal, and we noted probable jurisdiction. We now affirm the judgment of the court below.

II

A

Article IV, §2, of the Constitution provides that the "Citizens of each State shall be entitled to all Privileges and Immunities of Citizens in the several States."[6] This Clause was intended to "fuse into one Nation a collection of independent, sovereign States." *Toomer v. Witsell*, 334 U.S. 385 (1948). Recognizing this purpose, we have held that it is "only with respect to those 'privileges' and 'immunities' bearing on the vitality of the Nation as a single entity" that a State must accord residents and non-residents equal treatment. *Baldwin*. In *Baldwin*, for example, we concluded that a

---

6. Under this Clause, the terms "citizen" and "resident" are used interchangeably. See *Austin v. New Hampshire*, 420 U.S. 656 (1975).

State may charge a nonresident more than it charges a resident for the same elk-hunting license. Because elk hunting is "recreation" rather than a "means of a livelihood," we found that the right to a hunting license was not "fundamental" to the promotion of interstate harmony.

Derived, like the Commerce Clause, from the fourth of the Articles of Confederation,[7] the Privileges and Immunities Clause was intended to create a national economic union.[8] It is therefore not surprising that this Court repeatedly has found that "one of the privileges which the Clause guarantees to citizens of State A is that of doing business in State B on terms of substantial equality with the citizens of that State." *Toomer.* In *Ward v. Maryland*, 12 Wall. 418 (1871), the Court invalidated a statute under which nonresidents were required to pay $300 per year for a license to trade in goods not manufactured in Maryland, while resident traders paid a fee varying from $12 to $150. Similarly, in *Toomer*, the Court held that nonresident fishermen could not be required to pay a license fee of $2,500 for each shrimp boat owned when residents were charged only $25 per boat. Finally, in *Hicklin v. Orbeck*, 437 U.S. 518 (1978), we found violative of the Privileges and Immunities Clause a statute containing a resident hiring preference for all employment related to the development of the State's oil and gas resources.

There is nothing in *Ward*, *Toomer*, or *Hicklin* suggesting that the practice of law should not be viewed as a "privilege" under Art. IV, § 2.[10] Like the occupations considered in our earlier cases, the practice of law is important to the national economy. As the Court noted in *Goldfarb v. Virginia State Bar*, 421 U.S. 773 (1975), the "activities of lawyers play an important part in commercial intercourse."

The lawyer's role in the national economy is not the only reason that the opportunity to practice law should be considered a "fundamental right." We believe that the legal profession has a noncommercial role and duty that reinforce the view that the practice of law falls within the ambit of the Privileges and Immunities Clause. Out-of-state lawyers may—and often do—represent persons who raise unpopular

---

7. Article IV of the Articles of Confederation provided:

The better to secure and perpetuate mutual friendship and intercourse among the people of the different States in this Union, the free inhabitants of each of these States ... shall be entitled to all privileges and immunities of free citizens in the several States; and the people of each State shall have free ingress and regress to and from any other State, and shall enjoy therein all the privileges of trade and commerce, subject to the same duties, impositions and restrictions as the inhabitants thereof....

Charles Pinckney, who drafted the Privileges and Immunities Clause, stated that it was "formed exactly upon the principles of the 4th article of the present Confederation." 3 M. Farrand, Records of the Federal Convention of 1787 (1911).

8. This Court has recognized the "mutually reinforcing relationship" between the Commerce Clause and the Privileges and Immunities Clause. *Hicklin v. Orbeck*, 437 U.S. 518 (1978).

10. In *Corfield v. Coryell*, 6 F.Cas. 546 (No. 3,230) (CCED Pa.1825), Justice Bushrod Washington, sitting as Circuit Justice, stated that the "fundamental rights" protected by the Clause included:

"The right of a citizen of one state to pass through, or to reside in any other state, for purposes of trade, agriculture, professional pursuits, or otherwise; to claim the benefit of the writ of habeas corpus; to institute and maintain actions of any kind in the courts of the state; to take, hold and dispose of property, either real or personal...." ...

federal claims. In some cases, representation by nonresident counsel may be the only means available for the vindication of federal rights. The lawyer who champions unpopular causes surely is as important to the "maintenance or well-being of the Union," *Baldwin*, as was the shrimp fisherman in *Toomer*, or the pipeline worker in *Hicklin*.

### B

Appellant asserts that the Privileges and Immunities Clause should be held inapplicable to the practice of law because a lawyer's activities are "bound up with the exercise of judicial power and the administration of justice." Its contention is based on the premise that the lawyer is an "officer of the court," who "exercises state power on a daily basis." Appellant concludes that if the State cannot exclude nonresidents from the bar, its ability to function as a sovereign political body will be threatened.[13]

Lawyers do enjoy a "broad monopoly ... to do things other citizens may not lawfully do." *In re Griffiths*, 413 U.S. 717 (1973). We do not believe, however, that the practice of law involves an "exercise of state power" justifying New Hampshire's residency requirement. In *In re Griffiths*, we held that the State could not exclude an alien from the bar on the ground that a lawyer is an "officer of the Court who ... is entrusted with the exercise of actual governmental power." We concluded that a lawyer is not an "officer" within the ordinary meaning of that word. He "makes his own decisions, follows his own best judgment, collects his own fees and runs his own business." Moreover, we held that the state powers entrusted to lawyers do not "involve matters of state policy or acts of such unique responsibility as to entrust them only to citizens."

Because, under *Griffiths*, a lawyer is not an "officer" of the State in any political sense, there is no reason for New Hampshire to exclude from its bar nonresidents. We therefore conclude that the right to practice law is protected by the Privileges and Immunities Clause.

### III

The conclusion that Rule 42 deprives nonresidents of a protected privilege does not end our inquiry. The Court has stated that "like many other constitutional provisions, the privileges and immunities clause is not an absolute." *Toomer*. The Clause does not preclude discrimination against nonresidents where (i) there is a substantial reason for the difference in treatment; and (ii) the discrimination practiced against nonresidents bears a substantial relationship to the State's objective. *Ibid*. In deciding whether the discrimination bears a close or substantial relationship to the State's objective, the Court has considered the availability of less restrictive means.[17]

---

13. We recognize that without certain residency requirements the State "would cease to be the separate political community that history and the constitutional text make plain was contemplated." Simson, "Discrimination Against Nonresidents and the Privileges and Immunities Clause of Article IV," 128 *U. Pa. L. Rev.* 379 (1979). A State may restrict to its residents, for example, both the right to vote, see *Dunn v. Blumstein*, 405 U.S. 330 (1972), and the right to hold state elective office. *Baldwin*.

17. In *Toomer*, for example, the Court noted that the State could eliminate the danger of excessive trawling through less restrictive means: restricting the type of equipment used in its fisheries, graduating license fees according to the size of the boats, or charging nonresidents a differential to compensate for the added enforcement burden they imposed.

The Supreme Court of New Hampshire offers several justifications for its refusal to admit nonresidents to the bar. It asserts that nonresident members would be less likely (i) to become, and remain, familiar with local rules and procedures; (ii) to behave ethically; (iii) to be available for court proceedings; and (iv) to do pro bono and other volunteer work in the State.[18] We find that none of these reasons meets the test of "substantiality," and that the means chosen do not bear the necessary relationship to the State's objectives.

There is no evidence to support appellant's claim that nonresidents might be less likely to keep abreast of local rules and procedures. Nor may we assume that a nonresident lawyer—any more than a resident—would disserve his clients by failing to familiarize himself with the rules. As a practical matter, we think that unless a lawyer has, or anticipates, a considerable practice in the New Hampshire courts, he would be unlikely to take the bar examination and pay the annual dues of $125.[19]

We also find the appellant's second justification to be without merit, for there is no reason to believe that a nonresident lawyer will conduct his practice in a dishonest manner. The nonresident lawyer's professional duty and interest in his reputation should provide the same incentive to maintain high ethical standards as they do for resident lawyers.... Furthermore, a nonresident lawyer may be disciplined for unethical conduct. The Supreme Court of New Hampshire has the authority to discipline all members of the bar, regardless of where they reside. See N.H.Sup.Ct. Rule 37.

There is more merit to the appellant's assertion that a nonresident member of the bar at times would be unavailable for court proceedings.... Even the most conscientious lawyer residing in a distant State may find himself unable to appear in court for an unscheduled hearing or proceeding. Nevertheless, we do not believe that this type of problem justifies the exclusion of nonresidents from the state bar. One may assume that a high percentage of nonresident lawyers willing to take the state bar examination and pay the annual dues will reside in places reasonably convenient to New Hampshire. Furthermore, in those cases where the nonresident counsel will be unavailable on short notice, the State can protect its interests through less restrictive means. The trial court, by rule or as an exercise of discretion, may require any lawyer

---

18. A former president of the American Bar Association has suggested another possible reason for the rule: "Many of the states that have erected fences against out-of-state lawyers have done so primarily to protect their own lawyers from professional competition." Smith, "Time for a National Practice of Law Act," 64 *A.B.A. J.* 557 (1978). This reason is not "substantial." The Privileges and Immunities Clause was designed primarily to prevent such economic protectionism.

19. Because it is markedly overinclusive, the residency requirement does not bear a substantial relationship to the State's objective. A less restrictive alternative would be to require mandatory attendance at periodic seminars on state practice. There already is a rule requiring all new admittees to complete a "practical skills course" within one year of their admission. N.H.Sup.Ct.Rule 42(7).

New Hampshire's "simple residency" requirement is underinclusive as well, because it permits lawyers who move away from the State to retain their membership in the bar. There is no reason to believe that a former resident would maintain a more active practice in the New Hampshire courts than would a nonresident lawyer who had never lived in the State.

who resides at a great distance to retain a local attorney who will be available for unscheduled meetings and hearings.

The final reason advanced by appellant is that nonresident members of the state bar would be disinclined to do their share of pro bono and volunteer work. Perhaps this is true to a limited extent, particularly where the member resides in a distant location. We think it is reasonable to believe, however, that most lawyers who become members of a state bar will endeavor to perform their share of these services. This sort of participation, of course, would serve the professional interest of a lawyer who practices in the State. Furthermore, a nonresident bar member, like the resident member, could be required to represent indigents and perhaps to participate in formal legal-aid work.

In summary, appellant neither advances a "substantial reason" for its discrimination against nonresident applicants to the bar,[23] nor demonstrates that the discrimination practiced bears a close relationship to its proffered objectives.

### IV

We conclude that New Hampshire's bar residency requirement violates the Privileges and Immunities Clause of Art. IV, §2, of the United States Constitution. The nonresident's interest in practicing law is a "privilege" protected by the Clause. Although the lawyer is "an officer of the court," he does not hold a position that can be entrusted only to a "full-fledged member of the political community." A State may discriminate against nonresidents only where its reasons are "substantial," and the difference in treatment bears a close or substantial relation to those reasons. No such showing has been made in this case. Accordingly, we affirm the judgment of the Court of Appeals.

Justice WHITE, concurring in the result.

Appellee Piper lives only 400 yards from the New Hampshire border. She has passed the New Hampshire bar examination and intends to practice law in New Hampshire. Indeed, insofar as this record reveals, the only law office she will maintain is in New Hampshire. But because she will commute from Vermont rather than reside in New Hampshire, she will not be allowed to practice in the latter State.

I have no doubt that the New Hampshire residency requirement is invalid as applied to appellee Piper. Except for the fact that she will commute from Vermont, she would be indistinguishable from other New Hampshire lawyers.... Hence, I conclude that the Privileges and Immunities Clause forbids her exclusion from the New Hampshire Bar.

---

23. Justice REHNQUIST suggests another "substantial reason" for the residency requirement: the State's "interest in maximizing the number of resident lawyers, so as to increase the quality of the pool from which its lawmakers can be drawn." Only 8 of the 424 members of New Hampshire's bicameral legislature are lawyers. Moreover, New Hampshire, unlike many other States, does not prohibit nonlawyers from serving on its Supreme Court or its intermediate appellate court. Therefore, it is not surprising that the dissent's justification for the residency requirement was not raised by appellant or addressed by the courts below.

The foregoing is enough to dispose of this case. I do not, and the Court itself need not, reach out to decide the facial validity of the New Hampshire residency requirement....

Justice REHNQUIST, dissenting.

Today the Court holds that New Hampshire cannot decide that a New Hampshire lawyer should live in New Hampshire. This may not be surprising to those who view law as just another form of business frequently practiced across state lines by interchangeable actors; the Privileges and Immunities Clause of Art. IV, § 2, has long been held to apply to States' attempts to discriminate against nonresidents who seek to ply their trade interstate. The decision will be surprising to many, however, because it so clearly disregards the fact that the practice of law is—almost by definition—fundamentally different from those other occupations that are practiced across state lines without significant deviation from State to State. The fact that each State is free, in a large number of areas, to establish independently of the other States its own laws for the governance of its citizens, is a fundamental precept of our Constitution that, I submit, is of equal stature with the need for the States to form a cohesive union. What is at issue here is New Hampshire's right to decide that those people who in many ways will intimately deal with New Hampshire's self-governance should reside within that State.

The Court's opinion states that the Privileges and Immunities Clause of Art. IV, § 2, "was intended to 'fuse into one Nation a collection of independent, sovereign States.'" *Ante* (quoting *Toomer*). To this end, we are told, the Clause has been construed to protect the fundamental "privilege" of citizens of one State to do business in another State on terms substantially equal with that State's citizens. This privilege must be protected to effectuate the Clause's purpose to "create a national economic union." And for the Court, the practice of law is no different from those occupations considered in earlier Privileges and Immunities Clause cases, because "the practice of law is important to the national economy." After concluding that the Clause applies to lawyers, the Court goes on to reject the many reasons the Supreme Court of New Hampshire advances for limiting the State's lawyers to those who reside in state. The Court either labels these reasons insubstantial, or it advances, with the assurance of an inveterate second-guesser, a "less restrictive means" for the State to attack the perceived problem.

The Framers of our Constitution undoubtedly wished to ensure that the newly created Union did not revert to its component parts because of interstate jealousies and insular tendencies, and it seems clear that the Art. IV Privileges and Immunities Clause was one result of these concerns. But the Framers also created a system of federalism that deliberately allowed for the independent operation of many sovereign States, each with their own laws created by their own legislators and judges. The assumption from the beginning was that the various States' laws need not, and would not, be the same; the lawmakers of each State might endorse different philosophies and would have to respond to differing interests of their constituents, based on various factors that were of inherently local character. Any student of our Nation's history is well aware of the differing interests of the various States that were represented at Philadelphia; despite the tremendous improvements in transportation and communication that have served to create a more homogeneous country the differences among the various States have hardly disappeared.

It is but a small step from these facts to the recognition that a State has a very strong interest in seeing that its legislators and its judges come from among the constituency of state residents, so that they better understand the local interests to which they will have to respond. The Court does not contest this point; it recognizes that a State may require its lawmakers to be residents without running afoul of the Privileges and Immunities Clause of Art. IV, §2. See ante, n. 13.

Unlike the Court, I would take the next step, and recognize that the State also has a very "substantial" interest in seeing that its lawyers also are members of that constituency. I begin with two important principles that the Court seems to have forgotten: first, that in reviewing state statutes under this Clause "States should have considerable leeway in analyzing local evils and prescribing appropriate cures," *United Building & Construction Trades Council v. Mayor & Council of Camden*, 465 U.S. 208 (1984) (citing *Toomer*), and second, that regulation of the practice of law generally has been "left exclusively to the States...." *Leis v. Flynt*, 439 U.S. 438 (1979) (per curiam). My belief that the practice of law differs from other trades and businesses for Art. IV, §2, purposes is not based on some notion that law is for some reason a superior profession. The reason that the practice of law should be treated differently is that law is one occupation that does not readily translate across state lines.[1] Certain aspects of legal practice are distinctly and intentionally nonnational; in this regard one might view this country's legal system as the antithesis of the norms embodied in the Art. IV Privileges and Immunities Clause. Put simply, the State has a substantial interest in creating its own set of laws responsive to its own local interests, and it is reasonable for a State to decide that those people who have been trained to analyze law and policy are better equipped to write those state laws and adjudicate cases arising under them. The State therefore may decide that it has an interest in maximizing the number of resident lawyers, so as to increase the quality of the pool from which its lawmakers can be drawn.[2] A residency law such as the one at issue is the obvious way to accomplish these goals. Since at any given time within a State there is only enough legal work to support a certain number of lawyers, each out-of-state lawyer who is allowed to practice necessarily takes legal work that could support an in-state lawyer, who would otherwise be available to perform various functions that a State has an interest in promoting.

---

1. I do not mean to suggest that the practice of law, unlike other occupations, is not a "fundamental" interest subject to the two-step analysis outlined by the Court. It makes little difference to me which prong of the Court's analysis is implicated, although the thrust of my position is that there are significant state interests justifying this type of interstate discrimination....

2. The Court attempts to rebut this argument with statistics indicating the number of presently practicing lawyers in the New Hampshire Legislature. *Ante*, n. 23. While I am not convinced of the usefulness of these statistics, I note in any event that the Court neglects to point out that only 6 of the 124 judges presently sitting in New Hampshire courts are nonlawyers, and that only 12 of the 89 Supreme Court Justices in the State's history have been nonlawyers.

Nor does the State's interest end with enlarging the pool of qualified lawmakers. A State similarly might determine that because lawyers play an important role in the formulation of state policy through their adversary representation, they should be intimately conversant with the local concerns that should inform such policies. And the State likewise might conclude that those citizens trained in the law are likely to bring their useful expertise to other important functions that benefit from such expertise and are of interest to state governments—such as trusteeships, or directorships of corporations or charitable organizations, or school board positions, or merely the role of the interested citizen at a town meeting. Thus, although the Court suggests that state bars can require out-of-state members to "represent indigents and perhaps to participate in formal legal-aid work," the Court ignores a host of other important functions that a State could find would likely be performed only by in-state bar members. States may find a substantial interest in members of their bar being residents, and this insular interest—as with the opposing interest in interstate harmony represented by Art. IV, §2—itself has its genesis in the language and structure of the Constitution.[4]

It is no answer to these arguments that many lawyers simply will not perform these functions, or that out-of-state lawyers can perform them equally well, or that the State can devise less restrictive alternatives for accomplishing these goals. Conclusory second-guessing of difficult legislative decisions, such as the Court resorts to today, is not an attractive way for federal courts to engage in judicial review. Thus, whatever the reality of how much New Hampshire can expect to gain from having the members of its bar reside within that State, the point is that New Hampshire is entitled to believe and hope that its lawyers will provide the various unique services mentioned above, just as it is entitled to believe that the residency requirement is the appropriate way to that end. As noted, some of these services can only be provided by lawyers who also are residents. With respect to the other services, the State can reasonably find that lawyers who reside in state are more likely to undertake them.

In addition, I find the Court's "less restrictive means" analysis both ill-advised and potentially unmanageable. Initially I would note ... that such an analysis, when carried too far, will ultimately lead to striking down almost any statute on the ground that the Court could think of another "less restrictive" way to write it. This approach to judicial review, far more than the usual application of a standard of review, tends to place courts in the position of second-guessing legislators on legislative matters. Surely this is not a consequence to be desired.

In any event, I find the less-restrictive-means analysis, which is borrowed from our First Amendment jurisprudence, to be out of place in the context of the Art. IV

---

4. I do not find the analysis of *In re Griffiths* to be controlling here. *Griffiths* dealt with an Equal Protection Clause challenge to a state bar admission rule that excluded aliens. In the course of striking down that restriction this Court held that lawyers should not be considered "officers of the court" in the sense that they actually wield state powers. Whatever the merits of that conclusion, my point here is different; whether or not lawyers actually wield state powers, the State nevertheless has a substantial interest in having resident lawyers. In *Griffiths* the alien lawyers were state residents....

Privileges and Immunities Clause. *Toomer* and *Hicklin* indicate that the means employed by the State should bear a "substantial" or "close relation" to the State's objectives, and they speak in terms of whether the State's approach is "tailored" to its stated goal. This approach perhaps has a place: to the extent that an obvious way to accomplish the State's proffered goal is apparent, the fact that the State did not follow that path may indicate that the State had another, less legitimate goal in mind. But I believe the challenge of a "less restrictive means" should be overcome if merely a legitimate reason exists for not pursuing that path. And in any event courts should not play the game that the Court has played here—independently scrutinizing each asserted state interest to see if it could devise a better way than the State to accomplish that goal. Here the appellee primarily argues that if the State really was concerned about out-of-state lawyers it would not allow those who leave the State after joining the bar to remain members. The answer to this argument was well stated by the dissenting judges in the Court of Appeals for the First Circuit: "The Supreme Court of New Hampshire might have concluded that not many New Hampshire lawyers will both pull up stakes and continue to practice in the state. And it might further believe that the bureaucracy required to keep track of such comings and goings would not be worth the trouble...."

There is yet another interest asserted by the State that I believe would justify a decision to limit membership in the state bar to state residents. The State argues that out-of-state bar members pose a problem in situations where counsel must be available on short notice to represent clients on unscheduled matters. The Court brushes this argument aside, speculating that "a high percentage of nonresident lawyers willing to take the state bar examination and pay the annual dues will reside in places reasonably convenient to New Hampshire," and suggesting that in any event the trial court could alleviate this problem by requiring the lawyer to retain local counsel. Assuming that the latter suggestion does not itself constitute unlawful discrimination under the Court's test, there nevertheless may be good reasons why a State or a trial court would rather not get into structuring attorney-client relationships by requiring the retention of local counsel for emergency matters. The situation would have to be explained to the client, and the allocation of responsibility between resident and nonresident counsel could cause as many problems as the Court's suggestion might cure.

... Thus, I think that New Hampshire had more than enough "substantial reasons" to conclude that its lawyers should also be its residents. I would hold that the Rule of the New Hampshire Supreme Court does not violate the Privileges and Immunities Clause of Art. IV.

# C. Federal Pre-Emption of State Law

## Note: Introduction to Pre-Emption Doctrine

Even if a state law does not violate the Dormant Commerce Clause or the Privileges and Immunities Clause, it may still be rendered null if Congress enacts a valid federal law that has the effect of superseding, or "pre-empting," the state law. In *Gibbons v. Ogden*, for example, once the Court decided that the federal coasting license was valid, that law pre-empted the state-granted monopoly over the steamboat route that the holder of the federal license wished to service. The pre-emptive effect exerted by federal law flows from the Supremacy Clause of Article VI, Section 2, which states, in relevant part, that "This Constitution, and the Laws of the United States which shall be made in pursuance thereof ... shall be the supreme Law of the Land ... any Thing in the Constitution or Laws of any State to the Contrary notwithstanding."

Pre-emption is a matter of courts determining whether Congress intended to displace the state law in question. However, making such determinations—like answering any statutory interpretation question—is often quite difficult. In addition to the general complexity of interpreting often complex and unclear federal statutes, pre-emption analysis raises an additional difficulty: in areas where states have traditionally regulated, courts sometimes enforce a "presumption against pre-emption"—that is, they interpret the federal statute against a background assumption that Congress does not intend to displace the states' historic regulatory powers.

## Gade v. National Solid Wastes Management Association
### 505 U.S. 88 (1992)

Justice O'Connor delivered the opinion of the Court with respect to Parts I, III and IV, and an opinion with respect to Part II in which The Chief Justice, Justice White and Justice Scalia join.

In 1988, the Illinois General Assembly enacted the Hazardous Waste Crane and Hoisting Equipment Operators Licensing Act, and the Hazardous Waste Laborers Licensing Act (together, licensing acts). The stated purpose of the licensing acts is both "to promote job safety" and "to protect life, limb and property." In this case, we consider whether these "dual impact" statutes, which protect both workers and the general public, are pre-empted by the federal Occupational Safety and Health Act of 1970 (OSH Act), and the standards promulgated thereunder by the Occupational Safety and Health Administration (OSHA).

I

The OSH Act authorizes the Secretary of Labor to promulgate federal occupational safety and health standards. In the Superfund Amendments and Reauthorization Act of 1986 (SARA), Congress directed the Secretary of Labor to "promulgate standards for the health and safety protection of employees engaged in hazardous waste operations" pursuant to her authority under the OSH Act.

In response to this congressional directive, OSHA ... promulgated regulations on "Hazardous Waste Operations and Emergency Response," including detailed regulations on worker training requirements ...

In 1988, while OSHA's interim hazardous waste regulations were in effect, the State of Illinois enacted the licensing acts at issue here. The laws are designated as acts "in relation to environmental protection," and their stated aim is to protect both employees and the general public by licensing hazardous waste equipment operators and laborers working at certain facilities....

The respondent in this case, National Solid Wastes Management Association (Association), is a national trade association of businesses that remove, transport, dispose, and handle waste material, including hazardous waste....

Shortly before the state licensing acts were due to go into effect, the Association brought a declaratory judgment action in United States District Court.... The Association sought to enjoin [the Illinois Environmental Protection Agency] from enforcing the Illinois licensing acts, claiming that the acts were pre-empted by the OSH Act and OSHA regulations ... The District Court held that state laws that attempt to regulate workplace safety and health are not pre-empted by the OSH Act when the laws have a "legitimate and substantial purpose apart from promoting job safety." ...

On appeal, the United States Court of Appeals for the Seventh Circuit affirmed in part and reversed in part ... We granted certiorari to resolve a conflict between the decision below and decisions in which other Courts of Appeals have found the OSH Act to have a much narrower pre-emptive effect on "dual impact" state regulations.

## II

Before addressing the scope of the OSH Act's pre-emption of dual impact state regulations, we consider petitioner's threshold argument, drawn from Judge Easterbrook's separate opinion below, that the Act does not pre-empt nonconflicting state regulations at all. "The question whether a certain state action is pre-empted by federal law is one of congressional intent. 'The purpose of Congress is the ultimate touchstone.'" ...

In the OSH Act, Congress endeavored "to assure so far as possible every working man and woman in the Nation safe and healthful working conditions." To that end, Congress authorized the Secretary of Labor to set mandatory occupational safety and health standards applicable to all businesses affecting interstate commerce, and thereby brought the Federal Government into a field that traditionally had been occupied by the States. Federal regulation of the workplace was not intended to be all encompassing, however. First, Congress expressly saved two areas from federal pre-emption. Section 4(b)(4) of the OSH Act states that the Act does not "supersede or in any manner affect any workmen's compensation law or ... enlarge or diminish or affect in any other manner the common law or statutory rights, duties, or liabilities of employers and employees under any law with respect to injuries, diseases, or death of employees arising out of, or in the course of, employment." Section 18(a) provides that the Act does not "prevent any State agency or court from asserting jurisdiction under State law over any occupational safety or health issue with respect to which no [federal] standard is in effect."

Congress not only reserved certain areas to state regulation, but it also, in § 18(b) of the Act, gave the States the option of pre-empting federal regulation entirely. That section provides:

Submission of State plan for development and enforcement of State standards to preempt applicable Federal standards.

Any State which, at any time, desires to assume responsibility for development and enforcement therein of occupational safety and health standards relating to any occupational safety or health issue with respect to which a Federal standard has been promulgated [by the Secretary under the OSH Act] shall submit a State plan for the development of such standards and their enforcement.

About half the States have received the Secretary's approval for their own state plans as described in this provision. Illinois is not among them.

In the decision below, the Court of Appeals held that § 18(b) "unquestionably" pre-empts any state law or regulation that establishes an occupational health and safety standard on an issue for which OSHA has already promulgated a standard, unless the State has obtained the Secretary's approval for its own plan. Every other federal and state court confronted with an OSH Act pre-emption challenge has reached the same conclusion, and so do we.

Pre-emption may be either expressed or implied, and "is compelled whether Congress' command is explicitly stated in the statute's language or implicitly contained in its structure and purpose." Absent explicit pre-emptive language, we have recognized at least two types of implied pre-emption: field pre-emption, where the scheme of federal regulation is "so pervasive as to make reasonable the inference that Congress left no room for the States to supplement it," and conflict pre-emption, where "compliance with both federal and state regulations is a physical impossibility," or where state law "stands as an obstacle to the accomplishment and execution of the full purposes and objectives of Congress."

Our ultimate task in any pre-emption case is to determine whether state regulation is consistent with the structure and purpose of the statute as a whole. Looking to "the provisions of the whole law, and to its object and policy," we hold that nonapproved state regulation of occupational safety and health issues for which a federal standard is in effect is impliedly pre-empted as in conflict with the full purposes and objectives of the OSH Act. The design of the statute persuades us that Congress intended to subject employers and employees to only one set of regulations, be it federal or state, and that the only way a State may regulate an OSHA regulated occupational safety and health issue is pursuant to an approved state plan that displaces the federal standards.

The principal indication that Congress intended to pre-empt state law is § 18(b)'s statement that a State "shall" submit a plan if it wishes to "assume responsibility" for "development and enforcement ... of occupational safety and health standards relating to any occupational safety or health issue with respect to which a Federal standard has been promulgated." The unavoidable implication of this provision is that a State may not enforce its own occupational safety and health standards without obtaining the Secretary's approval, and petitioner concedes that § 18(b) would require an approved plan if Illinois wanted to "assume responsibility" for the regulation of occupational safety and health within the State. Petitioner contends, however, that an approved plan is necessary only if the State wishes completely to replace the federal regulations, not merely to supplement them. She argues that the correct interpretation of § 18(b) is that posited by Judge Easterbrook below: *i.e.*, a State may either "oust" the federal standard by submitting a state plan to the Secretary for approval or "add to" the federal standard without seeking the Secretary's approval.

Petitioner's interpretation of § 18(b) might be plausible were we to interpret that provision in isolation, but it simply is not tenable in light of the OSH Act's surrounding provisions.... The OSH Act as a whole evidences Congress' intent to avoid subjecting workers and employers to duplicative regulation; a State may develop an occupational safety and health program tailored to its own needs, but only if it is willing completely to displace the applicable federal regulations.

Cutting against petitioner's interpretation of § 18(b) is the language of § 18(a), which saves from pre-emption any state law regulating an occupational safety and health issue with respect to which no federal standard is in effect. Although this is a saving clause, not a pre-emption clause, the natural implication of this provision is that state laws regulating the same issue as federal laws are not saved, even if they merely supplement the federal standard. Moreover, if petitioner's reading of § 18(b) were correct, and if a State were free to enact nonconflicting safety and health regulations, then § 18(a) would be superfluous: There is no possibility of conflict where there is no federal regulation. Because "it is our duty 'to give effect, if possible, to every clause and word of a statute,'" we conclude that § 18(a)'s preservation of state authority in the absence of a federal standard presupposes a background pre-emption of all state occupational safety and health standards whenever a federal standard governing the same issue is in effect.

Our understanding of the implications of § 18(b) is likewise bolstered by § 18(c) of the Act, which sets forth the conditions that must be satisfied before the Secretary can approve a plan submitted by a State under subsection (b). State standards that affect interstate commerce will be approved only if they "are required by compelling local conditions" and "do not unduly burden interstate commerce." If a State could supplement federal regulations without undergoing the § 18(b) approval process, then the protections that § 18(c) offers to interstate commerce would easily be undercut. It would make little sense to impose such a condition on state programs intended to supplant federal regulation and not those that merely supplement it: The burden on interstate commerce remains the same.

Section 18(f) also confirms our view that States are not permitted to assume an enforcement role without the Secretary's approval, unless no federal standard is in effect. That provision gives the Secretary the authority to withdraw her approval of a state plan. Once approval is withdrawn, the plan "ceases to be in effect" and the State is permitted to assert jurisdiction under its occupational health and safety law only for those cases "commenced before the withdrawal of the plan." Under petitioner's reading of § 18(b), § 18(f) should permit the continued exercise of state jurisdiction over purely "supplemental" and nonconflicting standards. Instead, § 18(f) assumes that the State loses the power to enforce all of its occupational safety and health standards once approval is withdrawn....

Looking at the provisions of § 18 as a whole, we conclude that the OSH Act precludes any state regulation of an occupational safety or health issue with respect to which a federal standard has been established, unless a state plan has been submitted and approved pursuant to § 18(b). Our review of the Act persuades us that Congress sought to promote occupational safety and health while at the same time avoiding duplicative, and possibly counterproductive, regulation. It thus established a system of uniform federal occupational health and safety standards, but gave States the option of pre-empting federal regulations by developing their own occupational safety and health programs. In addition, Congress offered the States substantial federal grant moneys to assist them in developing their own programs. To allow a State selectively to "supplement" certain federal regulations with ostensibly nonconflicting standards would be inconsistent with this federal scheme of establishing uniform federal standards, on the one hand, and encouraging States to assume full responsibility for development and enforcement of their own OSH programs, on the other.

We cannot accept petitioner's argument that the OSH Act does not pre-empt nonconflicting state laws because those laws, like the Act, are designed to promote worker safety. In determining whether state law "stands as an obstacle" to the full implementation of a federal law "it is not enough to say that the ultimate goal of both federal and state law" is the same. "A state law also is pre-empted if it interferes with the methods by which the federal statute was designed to reach that goal." ...

### III

Petitioner next argues that, even if Congress intended to pre-empt all nonapproved state occupational safety and health regulations whenever a federal standard is in effect, the OSH Act's pre-emptive effect should not be extended to state laws that address public safety as well as occupational safety concerns. As we explained in Part II, we understand § 18(b) to mean that the OSH Act pre-empts all state "occupational safety and health standards relating to any occupational safety or health issue with respect to which a Federal standard has been promulgated." We now consider whether a dual impact law can be an "occupational safety and health standard" subject to pre-emption under the Act....

Although "part of the pre-empted field is defined by reference to the purpose of the state law in question ... another part of the field is defined by the state law's actual effect." In assessing the impact of a state law on the federal scheme, we have refused to rely solely on the legislature's professed purpose and have looked as well to the effects of the law. As we explained over two decades ago:

> We can no longer adhere to the aberrational doctrine ... that state law may frustrate the operation of federal law as long as the state legislature in passing its law had some purpose in mind other than one of frustration. Apart from the fact that it is at odds with the approach taken in nearly all our Supremacy Clause cases, such a doctrine would enable state legislatures to nullify nearly

all unwanted federal legislation by simply publishing a legislative committee report articulating some state interest or policy—other than frustration of the federal objective—that would be tangentially furthered by the proposed state law.... Any state legislation which frustrates the full effectiveness of federal law is rendered invalid by the Supremacy Clause. *Perez v. Campbell*, 402 U.S. 637 (1971).

Our precedents leave no doubt that a dual impact state regulation cannot avoid OSH Act pre-emption simply because the regulation serves several objectives rather than one. As the Court of Appeals observed, "it would defeat the purpose of section 18 if a state could enact measures stricter than OSHA's and largely accomplished through regulation of worker health and safety simply by asserting a non-occupational purpose for the legislation." Whatever the purpose or purposes of the state law, pre-emption analysis cannot ignore the effect of the challenged state action on the pre-empted field. The key question is thus at what point the state regulation sufficiently interferes with federal regulation that it should be deemed pre-empted under the Act.

... In the decision below, the Court of Appeals [held] that, in the absence of the approval of the Secretary, the OSH Act pre-empts all state law that "constitutes, in a direct, clear and substantial way, regulation of worker health and safety." We agree that this is the appropriate standard for determining OSH Act pre-emption. On the other hand, state laws of general applicability (such as laws regarding traffic safety or fire safety) that do not conflict with OSHA standards and that regulate the conduct of workers and nonworkers alike would generally not be pre-empted. Although some laws of general applicability may have a "direct and substantial" effect on worker safety, they cannot fairly be characterized as "occupational" standards, because they regulate workers simply as members of the general public. In this case, we agree with the court below that a law directed at workplace safety is not saved from pre-emption simply because the State can demonstrate some additional effect outside of the workplace.

In sum, a state law requirement that directly, substantially, and specifically regulates occupational safety and health is an occupational safety and health standard within the meaning of the Act. That such a law may also have a nonoccupational impact does not render it any less of an occupational standard for purposes of pre-emption analysis. If the State wishes to enact a dual impact law that regulates an occupational safety or health issue for which a federal standard is in effect, § 18 of the Act requires that the State submit a plan for the approval of the Secretary....

JUSTICE KENNEDY, concurring in part and concurring in the judgment.

Though I concur in the Court's judgment and with the ultimate conclusion that the state law is pre-empted, I would find express pre-emption from the terms of the federal statute. I cannot agree that we should denominate this case as one of implied pre-emption. The contrary view of the plurality is based on an undue expansion of our implied pre-emption jurisprudence which, in my view, is neither wise nor necessary.

... The plurality would hold today that state occupational safety and health standards regulating an issue on which a federal standard exists conflict with Congress' purpose to "subject employers and employees to only one set of regulations." This is not an application of our pre-emption standards, it is but a conclusory statement of pre-emption, as it assumes that Congress intended exclusive federal jurisdiction. I do not see how such a mode of analysis advances our consideration of the case.

Our decisions establish that a high threshold must be met if a state law is to be pre-empted for conflicting with the purposes of a federal Act. Any conflict must be "irreconcilable.... The existence of a hypothetical or potential conflict is insufficient to warrant the pre-emption of the state statute." *Rice v. Norman Williams Co.*, 458 U.S. 654 (1982). In my view, this type of pre-emption should be limited to state laws which impose prohibitions or obligations which are in direct contradiction to Congress' primary objectives, as conveyed with clarity in the federal legislation.

I do not believe that supplementary state regulation of an occupational safety and health issue can be said to create the sort of actual conflict required by our decisions. The purpose of state supplementary regulation, like the federal standards promulgated by the Occupational Safety and Health Administration (OSHA), is to protect worker safety and health. Any potential tension between a scheme of federal regulation of the workplace and a concurrent, supplementary state scheme would not, in my view, rise to the level of "actual conflict" described in our pre-emption cases. Absent the express provisions of § 18 of the Occupational Safety and Health Act of 1970 (OSH Act), I would not say that state supplementary regulation conflicts with the purposes of the OSH Act, or that it "interferes with the methods by which the federal statute was designed to reach [its] goal."

The plurality's broad view of actual conflict pre-emption is contrary to two basic principles of our pre-emption jurisprudence. First, we begin "with the assumption that the historic police powers of the States [are] not to be superseded ... unless that was the clear and manifest purpose of Congress." Second, "the purpose of Congress is the ultimate touchstone" in all pre-emption cases. A free wheeling judicial inquiry into whether a state statute is in tension with federal objectives would undercut the principle that it is Congress rather than the courts that pre-empts state law.

Nonetheless, I agree with the Court that "the OSH Act pre-empts all state 'occupational safety and health standards relating to any occupational safety or health issue with respect to which a Federal standard has been promulgated.' " I believe, however, that this result is mandated by the express terms of § 18(b) of the OSH Act. It follows from this that the pre-emptive scope of the Act is also limited to the language of the statute. When the existence of pre-emption is evident from the statutory text, our inquiry must begin and end with the statutory framework itself.

A finding of express pre-emption in this case is not contrary to our longstanding rule that we will not infer pre-emption of the States' historic police powers absent a clear statement of intent by Congress. Though most statutes creating express pre-emption contain an explicit statement to that effect, a statement admittedly lacking in § 18(b), we have never required any particular magic words in our express pre-emption cases. Our task in all pre-emption cases is to enforce the "clear and manifest purpose of Congress." We have held, in express pre-emption cases, that Congress' intent must be divined from the language, structure, and purposes of the statute as a whole. The language of the OSH statute sets forth a scheme in light of which the provisions of § 18 must be interpreted, and from which the express pre-emption that displaces state law follows.

As the plurality's analysis amply demonstrates, Congress has addressed the issue of pre-emption in the OSH Act. The dissent's position that the Act does not pre-empt supplementary state regulation becomes most implausible when the language of § 18(b) is considered in conjunction with the other provisions of § 18. Section 18(b) provides as follows:

> Any State which ... desires to assume responsibility for development and enforcement therein of occupational safety and health standards relating to any occupational safety or health issue with respect to which a Federal standard has been promulgated ... shall submit a State plan....

The statute is clear: When a State desires to assume responsibility for an occupational safety and health issue already addressed by the Federal Government, it must submit a state plan. The most reasonable inference from this language is that when a State does not submit and secure approval of a state plan, it may not enforce occupational safety and health standards in that area....

The necessary implication of finding express pre-emption in this case is that the pre-emptive scope of the OSH Act is defined by the language of § 18(b). Because this provision requires federal approval of state occupational safety and health standards alone, only state laws fitting within that description are pre-empted. For that reason I agree with the Court that state laws of general applicability are not pre-empted.... I therefore join all but Part II of the Court's opinion, and concur in the judgment of the Court.

Justice Souter, with who Justice Blackmun, Justice Stevens, and Justice Thomas join, dissenting.

... In light of our rule that federal pre-emption of state law is only to be found in a clear congressional purpose to supplant exercises of the States' traditional police powers, the text of the Act fails to support the Court's conclusion.

I

Our cases recognize federal pre-emption of state law in three variants: express pre-emption, field pre-emption, and conflict pre-emption. Express pre-emption requires "explicit pre-emptive language." Field pre-emption is wrought by a manifestation of congressional intent to occupy an entire field such that even without a federal rule on some particular matter within the field, state regulation on that matter is pre-empted, leaving it untouched by either state or federal law. Finally, there is conflict pre-emption in either of two senses. The first is found when compliance with both state and federal law is impossible, the second when a state law "stands as an obstacle to the accomplishment and execution of the full purposes and objectives of Congress."

The plurality today finds pre-emption of this last sort, discerning a conflict between any state legislation on a given issue as to which a federal standard is in effect, and a congressional purpose "to subject employers and employees to only one set of regulations." Thus, under the plurality's reading, any regulation on an issue as to which a federal standard has been promulgated has been pre-empted. As one commentator has observed, this kind of purpose conflict pre-emption, which occurs when state law is held to "undermine a congressional decision in favor of national uniformity of standards," presents "a situation similar in practical effect to that of federal occupation of a field." ... I find the language of the statute insufficient to demonstrate an intent to pre-empt state law in this way.

II

... "Where, as here, the field which Congress is said to have pre-empted has been traditionally occupied by the States, we start with the assumption that the historic police powers of the States were not to be superseded by the Federal Act unless that was the clear and manifest purpose of Congress." This assumption provides assurance that the federal state balance will not be disturbed unintentionally by Congress or unnecessarily by the courts.... Subject to this principle, the enquiry into the possibly pre-emptive effect of federal legislation is an exercise of statutory construction. If the statute's terms can be read sensibly not to have a pre-emptive effect, the presumption controls and no pre-emption may be inferred.

III

At first blush, respondent's strongest argument might seem to rest on § 18(a) of the Act, the full text of which is this:

> (a) Assertion of State standards in absence of applicable Federal standards
>
> Nothing in this chapter shall prevent any State agency or court from asserting jurisdiction under State law over any occupational safety or health issue with respect to which no standard is in effect under section 655 of this title.

That is to say, where there is no federal standard in effect, there is no pre-emption. The plurality reasons that there must be pre-emption, however, when there is a federal standard in effect, else § 18(a) would be rendered superfluous because "there is no possibility of conflict where there is no federal regulation."

The plurality errs doubly. First, its premise is incorrect. In the sense in which the plurality uses the term, there is the possibility of "conflict" even absent federal regulation since the mere enactment of a federal law like the Act may amount to an occupation of an entire field, preventing state regulation. Second, the necessary implication of § 18(a) is not that every federal regulation pre-empts all state law on the issue in question, but only that some federal regulations may pre-empt some state law. The plurality ignores the possibility that the provision simply rules out field pre-emption and is otherwise entirely compatible with the possibility that pre-emption will occur only when actual conflict between a federal regulation and a state rule renders compliance with both impossible. Indeed, if Congress had meant to say that any state rule should be pre-empted if it deals with an issue as to which there is a federal regulation in effect, the text of subsection (a) would have been a very inept way of trying to make the point. It was not, however, an inept way to make the different point that Congress intended no field pre-emption of the sphere of health and safety subject to regulation, but not necessarily regulated, under the Act. Unlike the case where field pre-emption occurs, the provision tells us, absence of a federal standard leaves a State free to do as it will on the issue. Beyond this, subsection (a) does not necessarily mean anything, and the provision is perfectly consistent with the conclusion that as long as compliance with both a federal standard and a state regulation is not physically impossible, each standard shall be enforceable. If, indeed, the presumption against pre-emption means anything, §18(a) must be read in just this way.

Respondent also relies on §18(b):

> (b) Submission of State plan for development and enforcement of State standards to preempt applicable Federal standards

> Any State which, at any time, desires to assume responsibility for development and enforcement therein of occupational safety and health standards relating to any occupational safety or health issue with respect to which a Federal standard has been promulgated under section 655 of this title shall submit a State plan for the development of such standards and their enforcement.

Respondent argues that the necessary implication of this provision is clear: the only way that a state rule on a particular occupational safety and health issue may be enforced once a federal standard on the issue is also in place is by incorporating the state rule in a plan approved by the Secretary.

As both the plurality and Justice KENNEDY acknowledge, however, that is not the necessary implication of §18(b). The subsection simply does not say that unless a plan is approved, state law on an issue is pre-empted by the promulgation of a federal standard. In fact it tugs the other way, and in actually providing a mechanism for a State to "assume responsibility" for an issue with respect to which a federal standard has been promulgated (that is, to pre-empt federal law), §18(b) is far from pre-emptive of anything adopted by the States. Its heading, enacted as part of the statute and properly considered under our canons of construction for whatever light it may shed, speaks expressly of the "development and enforcement of State standards to preempt applicable Federal standards." The provision does not in any way provide that absent such state pre-emption of federal rules, the State may not even supplement the federal standards with consistent regulations of its own. Once again, nothing in the provision's language speaks one way or the other to the question whether promulgation of a federal standard pre-empts state regulation, or whether, in the absence of a plan, consistent federal and state regulations may coexist. The provision thus makes perfect sense on the assumption that a dual regulatory scheme is permissible but subject to state pre-emption if the State wishes to shoulder enough of the federal mandate to gain approval of a plan.

Nor does the provision setting out conditions for the Secretary's approval of a plan indicate that a state regulation on an issue federally addressed is never enforceable unless incorporated in a plan so approved. Subsection (c)(2) requires the Secretary to approve a plan when in her judgment, among other things, it will not "unduly burden interstate commerce." Respondent argues, and the plurality concludes, that if state regulations were not pre-empted, this provision would somehow suggest that States acting independently could enforce regulations that did burden interstate commerce unduly. But this simply does not follow. The subsection puts a limit on the Secretary's authority to approve a plan that burdens interstate commerce, thus capping the discretion that might otherwise have been read into the congressional delegation of authority to the Secretary to approve state plans. From this restriction applying only to the Secretary's federal authority it is clearly a non sequitur to conclude that pre-emption must have been intended to avoid the equally objectionable undue burden that independent state regulation might otherwise impose. Quite the contrary; the dormant Commerce Clause can take care of that, without any need to assume pre-emption....

## IV

In sum, our rule is that the traditional police powers of the State survive unless Congress has made a purpose to pre-empt them clear. The Act does not, in so many words, pre-empt all state regulation of issues on which federal standards have been promulgated, and respondent's contention at oral argument that reading subsections (a), (b), and (h) could leave no other "logical" conclusion but one of pre-emption is wrong. Each provision can be read consistently with the others without any implication of pre-emptive intent. They are in fact just as consistent with a purpose and objective to permit overlapping state and federal regulation as with one to guarantee that employers and employees would be subjected to only one regulatory regime. Restriction to one such regime by precluding supplemental state regulation might or might not be desirable. But in the absence of any clear expression of congressional intent to pre-empt, I can only conclude that, as long as compliance with federally promulgated standards does not render obedience to Illinois' regulations impossible, the enforcement of the state law is not prohibited by the Supremacy Clause. I respectfully dissent.

## *Note: Pre-Emption Analysis*

1. *Gade* illustrates several aspects of preemption doctrine: textual analysis as part of the inquiry into express preemption, inquiry into statutory purpose as part of the inquiry into whether a state law frustrates Congress's objectives, and the presumption against preemption. The relationship between these concepts is sometimes contested. For example, note Justice Kennedy's concern about the plurality's reliance on federal objective frustration as the ground for finding the state law preempted. Why does he prefer grounding his analysis on express preemption rather than this type of implied preemption?

2. Another tension between the various types of preemption is the scope of the presumption against preemption. In *Cipollone v. Ligget Group*, 505 U.S. 504 (1992), the Court considered a cigarette manufacturer's claim that the federal law man-

dating health warnings on cigarette packages preempted state common-law tort claims against it based on a variety of tort theories. In the course of deciding those claims, the Court applied the presumption against preemption to the manufacturer's claim that the federal law expressly preempted state law. Justice Scalia, joined by Justice Thomas, protested the application of the presumption against preemption to claims of express preemption. He wrote: "The proper rule of construction for express pre-emption provisions is, it seems to me, the one that is customary for statutory provisions in general: Their language should be given its ordinary meaning." Sixteen years later, in *Altria Group v. Good*, 555 U.S. 70 (2008), the Court considered similar claims, and engaged in a similar analysis. This time, however, the number of justices expressing opposition to the use of the presumption against preemption in express preemption cases grew to four: in addition to Justices Scalia and Thomas, Chief Justice Roberts and Justice Alito also joined an opinion (by Justice Thomas) criticizing the use of the presumption against preemption in express preemption cases.

Recall how intricately Justice Souter analyzed the statutory text in *Gade*, in the service of demonstrating that the federal law lacked an unmistakably clear intent to preempt. Given how important to a result it might be if the Court employs (or, conversely, disregards) the presumption against preemption, the current dispute about when that presumption applies has important implications for preemption analysis.

3. One important, but difficult, area not implicated in *Gade* is field preemption. The plurality in *Gade* described field preemption as a situation "where the scheme of federal regulation is so pervasive as to make reasonable the inference that Congress left no room for the States to supplement it." An illustration of field preemption is *City of Burbank v. Lockheed Air Terminal*, 411 U.S. 624 (1973). *City of Burbank* involved a preemption challenge to a city's noise ordinance, which restricted the times at which commercial aircraft could land and take off from an airport. In holding the city ordinance preempted as it applied to such aircraft, a five-Justice majority, speaking through Justice Douglas, wrote the following:

> It is the pervasive nature of the scheme of federal regulation of aircraft noise that leads us to conclude that there is pre-emption. As Mr. Justice Jackson stated, concurring in *Northwest Airlines, Inc. v. Minnesota*, 322 U.S. 292 (1944):
>
>> 'Federal control [over aviation] is intensive and exclusive. Planes do not wander about in the sky like vagrant clouds. They move only by federal permission, subject to federal inspection, in the hands of federally certified personnel and under an intricate system of federal commands. The moment a ship taxis onto a runway it is caught up in an elaborate and detailed system of controls.' . . .
>
> Our prior cases on pre-emption are not precise guidelines in the present controversy, for each case turns on the peculiarities and special features of the federal regulatory scheme in question. Control of noise is of course deep-seated in the police power of the States. Yet the pervasive control vested in

EPA and in FAA under [federal aviation law] seems to us to leave no room for local curfews or other local controls....

Writing for four dissenters, Justice Rehnquist concluded that the federal statutes the majority relied on did not feature "the clear intent to preclude local regulations, that our prior decisions require."

# Chapter 6

# Federal Regulation of the States

Even if a federal law is an otherwise-valid use of Congress's Article I powers, federalism principles may nevertheless limit the law's effect on states. The Tenth Amendment, which provides in part that "The powers not delegated to the United States by the Constitution ... are reserved to the States," has been read as a limitation on Congress's Article I power to regulate state governments. For example, between 1976 and 1985 otherwise valid federal laws (such as minimum wage laws) could not be applied to states if they impaired states' ability to provide "traditional government functions." *See National League of Cities v. Usery*, 426 U.S. 833 (1976), *overruled by Garcia v. San Antonio Metro. Transit Authority*, 469 U.S. 528 (1985). Because *Garcia* overruled *National League of Cities*, this restriction on federal power no longer exists. However, the Court has erected other Tenth Amendment-based limits on federal regulation of state governments. Most notably, it has interpreted that Amendment to prohibit Congress from "commandeering" the legislative and law-enforcement apparatus of state government. Thus, it has struck down federal legislation requiring state legislatures and law-enforcers, respectively, to consider particular legislative issues or to enforce federal laws.

The Eleventh Amendment also limits Congress's Article I powers. The Eleventh Amendment states that "The Judicial power of the United States shall not be construed to extend to any suit in law or equity, commenced or prosecuted against one of the United States by Citizens of another State, or by Citizens or Subjects of any Foreign State." The Court has interpreted the Eleventh Amendment to mean that Congress lacks authority under several important Article I powers to make states liable for retrospective relief (such as damages) in private-party suits alleging a violation of the federal law. Most notably, in *Seminole Tribe v. Florida*, 517 U.S. 44 (1996), the Court overruled an earlier decision holding that the Interstate Commerce Clause authorized Congress to make states liable for such relief. However, ten years later the Court held that Congress's Article I power to enact bankruptcy laws did authorize laws that made states liable for a type of retrospective relief typical in bankruptcy proceedings. *Central Va. Comm. College v. Katz*, 546 U.S. 356 (2006). Congress can also abrogate state sovereign immunity when it legislates pursuant to its power to enforce the Fourteenth Amendment. The scope of this "enforcement" power is examined later in this book, after you have been presented with the substantive law of the Fourteenth Amendment.

Despite this limitation, the Court allows private parties to sue states to allege violation of federal law, as long as the plaintiff requests only prospective relief, such as an injunction. Such claims, known as "*Ex parte Young*" claims (after the case in which this theory was announced), require that the plaintiff sue the state official, not the state itself, for prospective relief for a violation of federal (not state) law, and only when the prospective relief requested did not impact the state's sovereign interests. Moreover, the federal law cannot feature a detailed remedial scheme which could be read as a congressional intent to preclude the type of relief typically available in a *Young* claim.

These decisions were based on the Eleventh Amendment. In *Alden v. Maine*, 527 U.S. 706 (1999), the Court applied these rules to private-party suits against non-consenting states in the state's own court. Since the Eleventh Amendment does not apply to state court suits, the Court grounded this extension of these sovereign immunity principles in the Tenth Amendment.

# A. Regulation of the States as Economic Actors
## *Note: From* Wirtz *to* Garcia

Over the last forty years the Court has vacillated when considering whether the federal nature of our system imposes limits on Congress's ability to regulate states in their capacity as economic actors (*e.g.*, employers or other participants in commerce).

1. In 1968, in *Maryland v. Wirtz*, 392 U.S. 183 (1968), the Court rejected a state's argument that extension of federal labor laws to state-run hospitals unconstitutionally infringed on state sovereignty. The seven-Justice majority stated that "the Federal Government, when acting within a delegated power, may override countervailing state interests whether these be described as 'governmental' or 'proprietary' in character," and that "valid general regulations of commerce do not cease to be regulations of commerce because a State is involved." It thus concluded: "If a State is engaging in economic activities that are validly regulated by the Federal Government when engaged in by private persons, the State too may be forced to conform its activities to federal regulation."

Justice Douglas, joined by Justice Stewart, dissented. He argued that the federal regulation of states in that case constituted "such a serious invasion of state sovereignty protected by the Tenth Amendment that it [was] not ... consistent with our constitutional federalism." He concluded that "the Court must draw the constitutional line between the State as government and the State as trader," and that "in this case the State as a sovereign power is being seriously tampered with, potentially crippled."

2. In 1976 the Court reached a different conclusion. In *National League of Cities v. Usery*, 426 U.S. 833 (1976), a sharply divided Court overruled *Wirtz* and struck down a federal law that expanded application of federal minimum wage and maximum hour provisions to the states. Writing for the five-Justice majority, Justice Rehnquist noted that the expanded application of federal labor law to the states not only presented the states with increased costs for performing "traditional governmental functions," but "displaced state policies regarding the manner in which they will structure delivery of those governmental services." He continued:

> Our examination of the effect of the 1974 amendments, as sought to be extended to the States and their political subdivisions, satisfies us that both the

minimum wage and the maximum hour provisions will impermissibly interfere with the integral governmental functions of these bodies. Their application [will] significantly alter or displace the States' abilities to structure employer-employee relationships in such areas as fire prevention, police protection, sanitation, public health, and parks and recreation. These activities are typical of those performed by state and local governments in discharging their dual functions of administering the public law and furnishing public services. Indeed, it is functions such as these which governments are created to provide, services such as these which the States have traditionally afforded their citizens. If Congress may withdraw from the States the authority to make those fundamental employment decisions upon which their systems for performance of these functions must rest, we think there would be little left of the States' "separate and independent existence." Thus, [the] dispositive factor is that Congress has attempted to exercise its Commerce Clause authority to prescribe minimum wages and maximum hours to be paid by the States in their capacities as sovereign governments. In so doing, Congress has sought to wield its power in a fashion that would impair the States' "ability to function effectively in a federal system." This exercise of congressional authority does not comport with the federal system of government embodied in the Constitution. We hold that insofar as the challenged amendments operate to directly displace the States' freedom to structure integral operations in areas of traditional governmental functions, they are not within the authority granted Congress by Art. I, §8, cl. 3.

Justice Blackmun joined the majority, but explained that he was "not untroubled by certain possible implications of the Court's opinion." He explained his own reading of the majority opinion:

I may misinterpret the Court's opinion, but it seems to me that it adopts a balancing approach, and does not outlaw federal power in areas such as environmental protection, where the federal interest is demonstrably greater and where state facility compliance with imposed federal standards would be essential.

Justice Brennan dissented for three Justices. He began by quoting *Gibbons v. Ogden*'s statement that "The wisdom and the discretion of Congress, their identity with the people, and the influence which their constituents possess at elections, are … the sole restraints on which they have relied, to secure them from its abuse. They are the restraints on which the people must often rely solely, in all representative governments." In response to the majority's location of federalism-based limits on the Commerce Power in the Tenth Amendment, he quoted the language from *United States v. Darby* describing the Tenth Amendment as reflecting "but a truism that all is retained which has not been surrendered" and merely "declaratory of the relationship between the national and state governments as it had been established by the Constitution before the amendment." Arguing against a judicial role in policing this aspect of the federal-state balance, Justice Brennan cited the Constitution's political structure as a safeguard for state interests:

Judicial restraint in this area merely recognizes that the political branches of our Government are structured to protect the interests of the States, as well as the Nation as a whole, and that the States are fully able to protect their own interests in the premises. Congress is constituted of representatives in both the Senate and House Elected from the States. *The Federalist* No. 45; *The Federalist* No. 46. Decisions upon the extent of federal intervention under the Commerce Clause into the affairs of the States are in that sense decisions of the States themselves.

Justice Stevens dissented separately.

3. The debate in *National League of Cities* was reprised nine years later, in *Garcia v. San Antonio Metropolitan Transit Authority*, 469 U.S. 528 (1985). *Garcia* raised the same issue as *National League of Cities*. The Court split just as it had before (with Justice O'Connor voting as her predecessor, Justice Stewart, had), except that Justice Blackmun switched sides, and became the fifth vote to overrule *National League of Cities* and uphold application of federal minimum wage and maximum working hour law to the states.

Writing for the five-Justice majority, Justice Blackmun began by observing that in the previous nine years lower courts had experienced a great deal of difficulty determining when a government function was "traditional" and thus came within the *National League of Cities* rule. He then observed that a historical approach to that question— one that was often used by lower courts—was unfaithful to the federal ideal that states should be free to experiment and take on new (and hence, non-traditional) functions.

Turning to the broader question about the constitutional status of state sovereignty, Justice Blackmun rejected "freestanding conceptions of state sovereignty" as inconsistent with the Constitution's general lack of explicit guarantees of particular state prerogatives. He recognized that "the States unquestionably do retain a significant measure of sovereign authority," but he said that "they do so ... only to the extent that the Constitution has not divested them of their original powers and transferred those powers to the Federal Government." Instead of substantive regulatory areas allocated to states, Justice Blackmun, like Justice Brennan in his *National League of Cities* dissent, found those limits "in the structure of the Federal Government itself," in particular, the state-by-state presidential election system, and the representation of the states in the Senate. He recognized that the Seventeenth Amendment made the Senate elected by the *people* of each state, rather than by the state government. Nevertheless, he concluded that "the fundamental limitation that the constitutional scheme imposes on the Commerce Clause to protect the "States as States" is one of process rather than one of result." He also noted that states had done well in the political process, obtaining exemptions from a number of federal laws and obtaining financial and other benefits from the federal government.

Justices Powell, O'Connor and then-Justice Rehnquist all wrote separate dissents. Their common theme was a commitment to a judicially-enforced federalism that protected state sovereignty in substantively demarcated areas. Justice Powell criticized the majority's process-based federalism, observing that members of the Senate are not chosen by state governments themselves. Defending *National League of Cities*, he noted Justice Blackmun's concurrence that described that opinion as enshrining a balancing test, rather than rigidly isolating from federal regulation "traditional government functions." He also described the functions immunized in *National League of Cities* as those "that epitomize the concerns of local, democratic, self-government." Applying these principles, he would have struck down application of federal labor wage and hour law to municipal mass transit services, such as the one at issue in *Garcia*.

Justice O'Connor stressed that, while the Commerce Clause was broad, concerns about state autonomy appropriately enter into judicial determinations whether Congress used appropriate means to regulate interstate commerce. She argued that "This principle requires the Court to enforce affirmative limits on federal regulation of the States to complement the judicially crafted expansion of the interstate commerce power." She argued that "the proper resolution" of these competing tendencies "lies in weighing state autonomy as a factor in the balance when interpreting the means by which Congress can exercise its authority on the States as States."

Justice Rehnquist's short dissent closed with the prediction that the dissenting views "will … in time again command the support of a majority of this Court." Justice O'Connor's dissent closed with a similar prediction.

# B. The Prohibition on "Commandeering"

## Note: The Precursors to the Anti-Commandeering Doctrine

Closely related to the question answered in the *Wirtz* line of cases is the question whether Congress has the power to direct how states perform sovereign functions. In *Hodel v. Virginia Surface Mining and Reclamation Authority*, 452 U.S. 264 (1981) (Note *supra.* Chapter 4), the Court considered a federal surface mining law that prescribed federal standards for mine operators, but allowed states to substitute their own regulations as long as the federal government concluded that the state program met certain standards. The Court unanimously upheld the law. In addition to holding that the statute came within Congress's powers under the Commerce Clause (a part of the case discussed in Chapter 4), the Court also concluded that the law did not violate the Tenth Amendment's guarantee of state sovereignty by displacing states' ability to regulate. Writing for eight Justices, Justice Marshall wrote that "the States are not compelled to enforce [the law's] standards, to expend any state funds, or to participate in the federal regulatory program in any manner whatsoever.… Thus, there can be no suggestion that the Act commandeers the legislative processes of the States by directly compelling them to enact and enforce a federal regulatory program."

The Court was more divided the next year in *Federal Energy Regulatory Commission v. Mississippi*, 456 U.S. 742 (1982) ("*FERC*"). In *FERC* the Court considered the Public Utility Regulatory Policies Act (PURPA), a federal energy law that, among other things, required state public utility commissions to consider using certain standards to govern rate-setting for electric utilities, and prescribed the procedures the commissions had to use when engaging in that consideration. The Court upheld these provisions. Justice Blackmun wrote, for five Justices:

> In a sense ... this case is only one step beyond *Hodel*. There, the Federal Government could have pre-empted all surface mining regulations; instead, it allowed the States to enter the field if they promulgated regulations consistent with federal standards. In this Court's view, this raised no Tenth Amendment problem....

> Similarly here, Congress could have pre-empted the field ... ; PURPA should not be invalid simply because, out of deference to state authority, Congress adopted a less intrusive scheme and allowed the States to continue regulating in the area on the condition that they *consider* the suggested federal standards.

Justice O'Connor, writing for three Justices, dissented. She argued that PURPA violated the federalism principles of *National League of Cities* (which had not yet been overruled). She wrote: "State legislative and administrative bodies are not field offices of the national bureaucracy. Nor are they think tanks to which Congress may assign problems for extended study." She also attacked Justice Blackmun's pre-emption argument:

> When Congress pre-empts a field, it precludes only state legislation that conflicts with the national approach. The States usually retain the power to complement congressional legislation, either by regulating details unsupervised by Congress or by imposing requirements that go beyond the national threshold. Most importantly, after Congress pre-empts a field, the States may simply devote their resources elsewhere.... PURPA, however, drains the inventive energy of state governmental bodies by requiring them to weigh its detailed standards, enter written findings, and defend their determinations in state court.... The States might well prefer that Congress simply impose the standards described in PURPA; this, at least, would leave them free to exercise their power in other areas.

> Federal pre-emption is less intrusive than PURPA's approach for a second reason. Local citizens hold their utility commissions accountable for the choices they make.... Congressional compulsion of state agencies, unlike pre-emption, blurs the lines of political accountability and leaves citizens feeling that their representatives are no longer responsive to local needs.

Justice Powell dissented only with regard to PURPA's imposition of procedural requirements governing how state agencies consider the federally-specified ratemaking standards.

Recall from the prior section of this chapter that in 1985, *Garcia* overruled *National League of Cities* and allowed Congress to regulate states when their conduct affected interstate commerce. Given *Garcia* and *FERC*, it was unclear whether any federalism-based principle limited congressional power to compel state governments to act in their capacity as sovereigns. The Court provided an answer in 1992.

# New York v. United States

## 505 U.S. 144 (1992)

These cases implicate one of our Nation's newest problems of public policy and perhaps our oldest question of constitutional law. The public policy issue involves the disposal of radioactive waste: In these cases, we address the constitutionality of three provisions of the Low-Level Radioactive Waste Policy Amendments Act of 1985. The constitutional question is as old as the Constitution: It consists of discerning the proper division of authority between the Federal Government and the States. We conclude that while Congress has substantial power under the Constitution to encourage the States to provide for the disposal of the radioactive waste generated within their borders, the Constitution does not confer upon Congress the ability simply to compel the States to do so. We therefore find that only two of the Act's three provisions at issue are consistent with the Constitution's allocation of power to the Federal Government.

I

We live in a world full of low level radioactive waste.... The waste must be isolated from humans for long periods of time, often for hundreds of years.... [By the late 1970s the several states that had waste disposal facilities for low-level radioactive waste had begun to shut them down, leading to fear that soon no sites would be available.] ...

Faced with the possibility that the Nation would be left with no disposal sites for low level radioactive waste, Congress responded by enacting the Low-Level Radioactive Waste Policy Act. Relying largely on a report submitted by the National Governors' Association, Congress declared a federal policy of holding each State "responsible for providing for the availability of capacity either within or outside the State for the disposal of low-level radioactive waste generated within its borders," and found that such waste could be disposed of "most safely and efficiently ... on a regional basis." The 1980 Act authorized States to enter into regional compacts that, once ratified by Congress, would have the authority beginning in 1986 to restrict the use of their disposal facilities to waste generated within member States. The 1980 Act included no penalties for States that failed to participate in this plan.

By 1985, only three approved regional compacts had operational disposal facilities; not surprisingly, these were the compacts formed around South Carolina, Nevada, and Washington, the three sited States [i.e., the three states with existing disposal facilities]. The following year, the 1980 Act would have given these three compacts the ability to exclude waste from nonmembers, and the remaining 31 States would have had no assured outlet for their low level radioactive waste. With this prospect looming, Congress once again took up the issue of waste disposal. The result was the legislation challenged here, the Low-Level Radioactive Waste Policy Amendments Act of 1985.

... In broad outline, the [1985] Act embodies a compromise among the sited and unsited States. The sited States agreed to extend for seven years the period in which they would accept low level radioactive waste from other States. In exchange, the unsited States agreed to end their reliance on the sited States by 1992....

The Act provides three types of incentives to encourage the States to comply with their statutory obligation to provide for the disposal of waste generated within their borders.

1. *Monetary incentives.* [Under these provisions of the statute a portion of the surcharges collected by the sited states were to be held by the federal government and paid out to states that met a series of milestones for providing for disposal of their own waste.] ... Each State that has not met the [final] deadline must either take title to the waste generated within its borders or forfeit to the waste generators the incentive payments it has received.

2. *Access incentives.* [Under these provisions of the statute states with waste disposal sites can charge progressively higher fees to process waste from states that have not met those milestones. Eventually the states with such sites are authorized to deny access to waste from non-complying states.]

3. *The take title provision.* The third type of incentive is the most severe. The Act provides:

> "If a State (or, where applicable, a compact region) in which low-level radioactive waste is generated is unable to provide for the disposal of all such waste generated within such State or compact region by January 1, 1996, each State in which such waste is generated, upon the request of the generator or owner of the waste, shall take title to the waste, be obligated to take possession of the waste, and shall be liable for all damages directly or indirectly incurred by such generator or owner as a consequence of the failure of the State to take possession of the waste as soon after January 1, 1996, as the generator or owner notifies the State that the waste is available for shipment."....

Petitioners—the State of New York and the two counties—filed this suit against the United States in 1990. They sought a declaratory judgment that the Act is inconsistent with the Tenth and Eleventh Amendments to the Constitution, with the Due Process Clause of the Fifth Amendment, and with the Guarantee Clause of Article IV of the Constitution.... The District Court dismissed the complaint. The Court of Appeals affirmed. Petitioners have abandoned their due process and Eleventh Amendment claims on their way up the appellate ladder; as the cases stand before us, petitioners claim only that the Act is inconsistent with the Tenth Amendment and the Guarantee Clause.

## II

### A

In 1788, in the course of explaining to the citizens of New York why the recently drafted Constitution provided for federal courts, Alexander Hamilton observed: "The erection of a new government, whatever care or wisdom may distinguish the work, cannot fail to originate questions of intricacy and nicety; and these may, in a particular manner, be expected to flow from the establishment of a constitution founded upon the total or partial incorporation of a number of distinct sovereignties." *The Federalist* No. 82. Hamilton's prediction has proved quite accurate. While no one disputes the proposition that "[t]he Constitution created a Federal Government of limited powers," and while the Tenth Amendment makes explicit that "the powers not delegated to the United States by the Constitution, nor prohibited by it to the States, are reserved to the States respectively, or to the people"; the task of ascertaining the constitutional line between federal and state power has given rise to many of the Court's most difficult and celebrated cases. At least as far back as *Martin v. Hunter's Lessee*, 1 Wheat. 304 (1816), the Court has resolved questions "of great importance and delicacy" in determining whether particular sovereign powers have been granted by the Constitution to the Federal Government or have been retained by the States.

These questions can be viewed in either of two ways. In some cases the Court has inquired whether an Act of Congress is authorized by one of the powers delegated to Congress in Article I of the Constitution. See, e.g., *Perez v. United States*, 402 U.S. 146 (1971) [Note *supra.* Chapter 4]; *McCulloch v. Maryland* (1819) [*Supra.* Chapters 3 & 4]. In other cases the Court has sought to determine whether an Act of Congress invades the province of state sovereignty reserved by the Tenth Amendment. See, e.g., *Garcia v. San Antonio Metropolitan Transit Authority*, 469 U.S. 528 (1985) [Note *supra.* this chapter]; *Lane County v. Oregon*, 7 Wall. 71 (1869). In a case like these, involving the division of authority between federal and state governments, the two inquiries are mirror images of each other. If a power is delegated to Congress in the Constitution, the Tenth Amendment expressly disclaims any reservation of that power to the States; if a power is an attribute of state sovereignty reserved by the Tenth Amendment, it is necessarily a power the Constitution has not conferred on Congress....

It is in this sense that the Tenth Amendment "states but a truism that all is retained which has not been surrendered." *United States v. Darby* (1941) [*Supra.* Chapter 4].... This has been the Court's consistent understanding: "The States unquestionably do retain a significant measure of sovereign authority ... to the extent that the Constitution has not divested them of their original powers and transferred those powers to the Federal Government." *Garcia.*

Congress exercises its conferred powers subject to the limitations contained in the Constitution. Thus, for example, under the Commerce Clause Congress may regulate publishers engaged in interstate commerce, but Congress is constrained in the exercise of that power by the First Amendment. The Tenth Amendment likewise restrains the power of Congress, but this limit is not derived from the text of the Tenth Amendment itself, which, as we have discussed, is essentially a tautology. Instead, the Tenth Amendment confirms that the power of the Federal Government is subject to limits that may, in a given instance, reserve power to the States. The Tenth Amendment thus directs us to determine, as in this case, whether an incident of state sovereignty is protected by a limitation on an Article I power....

This framework has been sufficiently flexible over the past two centuries to allow for enormous changes in the nature of government. The Federal Government undertakes activities today that would have been unimaginable to the Framers in two senses; first, because the Framers would not have conceived that *any* government would conduct such activities; and second, because the Framers would not have believed that the *Federal Government*, rather than the States, would assume such responsibilities. Yet the powers conferred upon the *Federal* Government by the Constitution were phrased in language broad enough to allow for the expansion of the Federal Government's role. Among the provisions of the Constitution that have been particularly important in this regard, three concern us here.

First, the Constitution allocates to Congress the power "to regulate Commerce ... among the several States." Art. I, § 8, cl. 3. Interstate commerce was an established feature of life in the late 18th century. The volume of interstate commerce and the range of commonly accepted objects of government regulation have, however, expanded considerably in the last 200 years, and the regulatory authority of Congress has expanded along with them. As interstate commerce has become ubiquitous, activities once considered purely local have come to have effects on the national economy, and have accordingly come within the scope of Congress' commerce power. See, e.g., *Katzenbach v. McClung*, 379 U.S. 294 (1964) [Note *supra.* Chapter 4]; *Wickard v. Filburn* (1942) [*Supra.* Chapter 4].

Second, the Constitution authorizes Congress "to pay the Debts and provide for the ... general Welfare of the United States." Art. I, § 8, cl. 1. As conventional notions of the proper objects of government spending have changed over the years, so has the ability of Congress to "fix the terms on which it shall disburse federal money to the States." Compare, e.g., *United States v. Butler*, 297 U.S. 1 (1936) (spending power does not authorize Congress to subsidize farmers), with *South Dakota v. Dole*, 483 U.S. 203 (1987) (spending power permits Congress to condition highway funds on States' adoption of minimum drinking age).[*] While the spending power is "subject to several general restrictions articulated in our cases," *id.*, these restrictions have not been so severe as to prevent the regulatory authority of Congress from generally keeping up with the growth of the federal budget.

The Court's broad construction of Congress' power under the Commerce and Spending Clauses has of course been guided, as it has with respect to Congress' power generally, by the Constitution's Necessary and Proper Clause, which authorizes Congress "to make all Laws which shall be necessary and proper for carrying into Execution the foregoing Powers." U.S. Const., Art. I, § 8, cl. 18. See, e.g., *McCulloch*.

Finally, the Constitution provides that "the Laws of the United States ... shall be the supreme Law of the Land ... any Thing in the Constitution or Laws of any State to the Contrary notwithstanding." U.S. Const., Art. VI, cl. 2. As the Federal Government's willingness to exercise power within the confines of the Constitution has grown, the authority of the States has correspondingly diminished to the extent that federal and state policies have conflicted. We have observed that the Supremacy Clause gives the Federal Government "a decided advantage in the delicate balance" the Constitution strikes between state and federal power.

The actual scope of the Federal Government's authority with respect to the States has changed over the years, therefore, but the constitutional structure underlying

---

\* [Ed. Note: Congress's power under Article I's Spending Clause is presented later in this chapter.]

and limiting that authority has not. In the end, just as a cup may be half empty or half full, it makes no difference whether one views the question at issue in these cases as one of ascertaining the limits of the power delegated to the Federal Government under the affirmative provisions of the Constitution or one of discerning the core of sovereignty retained by the States under the Tenth Amendment. Either way, we must determine whether any of the three challenged provisions of the Low-Level Radioactive Waste Policy Amendments Act of 1985 oversteps the boundary between federal and state authority.

*Challenge is not to Congress's power; challenge to means*

B

Petitioners do not contend that Congress lacks the power to regulate the disposal of low level radioactive waste.... Regulation of the ... interstate market in waste disposal is ... well within Congress' authority under the Commerce Clause. Petitioners likewise do not dispute that under the Supremacy Clause Congress could, if it wished, pre-empt state radioactive waste regulation. Petitioners contend only that the Tenth Amendment limits the power of Congress to regulate in the way it has chosen. Rather than addressing the problem of waste disposal by directly regulating the generators and disposers of waste, petitioners argue, Congress has impermissibly directed the States to regulate in this field.

Most of our recent cases interpreting the Tenth Amendment have concerned the authority of Congress to subject state governments to generally applicable laws. The Court's jurisprudence in this area has traveled an unsteady path. See *Maryland v. Wirtz*, 392 U.S. 183 (1968) (state schools and hospitals are subject to Fair Labor Standards Act); *National League of Cities v. Usery*, 426 U.S. 833 (1976) (overruling *Wirtz*) (state employers are not subject to Fair Labor Standards Act); *Garcia* (overruling *National League of Cities*) (state employers are once again subject to Fair Labor Standards Act) [All note *supra.* this chapter]. This litigation presents no occasion to apply or revisit the holdings of any of these cases, as this is not a case in which Congress has subjected a State to the same legislation applicable to private parties. Cf. *FERC v. Mississippi*, 456 U.S. 742 (1982) [Note *supra.* this chapter].

*key distinction*

This litigation instead concerns the circumstances under which Congress may use the States as implements of regulation; that is, whether Congress may direct or otherwise motivate the States to regulate in a particular field or a particular way. Our cases have established a few principles that guide our resolution of the issue.

1

As an initial matter, Congress may not simply "commandeer the legislative processes of the States by directly compelling them to enact and enforce a federal regulatory program." *Hodel v. Virginia Surface Mining & Reclamation Assn., Inc.*, 452 U.S. 264 (1981) [Notes *supra.* Chapter 4 and this chapter]. In *Hodel*, the Court upheld the Surface Mining Control and Reclamation Act of 1977 precisely because it did not "commandeer" the States into regulating mining. The Court found that "the States are not compelled to enforce the steep-slope standards, to expend any state funds, or to participate in the federal regulatory program in any manner whatsoever. If a

State does not wish to submit a proposed permanent program that complies with the Act and implementing regulations, the full regulatory burden will be borne by the Federal Government."

The Court reached the same conclusion the following year in *FERC v. Mississippi*. . . . We observed that "this Court never has sanctioned explicitly a federal command to the States to promulgate and enforce laws and regulations." As in *Hodel*, the Court upheld the statute at issue because it did not view the statute as such a command. . . .

These statements in *FERC* and *Hodel* were not innovations. While Congress has substantial powers to govern the Nation directly, including in areas of intimate concern to the States, the Constitution has never been understood to confer upon Congress the ability to require the States to govern according to Congress' instructions. The Court has been explicit about this distinction. "Both the States and the United States existed before the Constitution. The people, through that instrument, established a more perfect union by substituting a national government, acting, with ample power, *directly upon the citizens*, instead of the Confederate government, which acted with powers, greatly restricted, only upon the States." *Lane County*. . . .

Indeed, the question whether the Constitution should permit Congress to employ state governments as regulatory agencies was a topic of lively debate among the Framers. Under the Articles of Confederation, Congress lacked the authority in most respects to govern the people directly. . . .

The inadequacy of this governmental structure was responsible in part for the Constitutional Convention. Alexander Hamilton observed: "The great and radical vice in the construction of the existing Confederation is in the principle of LEGISLATION for STATES or GOVERNMENTS, in their CORPORATE or COLLECTIVE CAPACITIES, and as contradistinguished from the INDIVIDUALS of whom they consist." *The Federalist* No. 15. As Hamilton saw it, "we must resolve to incorporate into our plan those ingredients which may be considered as forming the characteristic difference between a league and a government; we must extend the authority of the Union to the persons of the citizens—the only proper objects of government." The new National Government "must carry its agency to the persons of the citizens. It must stand in need of no intermediate legislations. . . . The government of the Union, like that of each State, must be able to address itself immediately to the hopes and fears of individuals." *Id.*, No. 16.

The Convention generated a great number of proposals for the structure of the new Government, but two quickly took center stage. Under the Virginia Plan, as first introduced by Edmund Randolph, Congress would exercise legislative authority directly upon individuals, without employing the States as intermediaries. Under the New Jersey Plan, as first introduced by William Paterson, Congress would continue to require the approval of the States before legislating, as it had under the Articles of Confederation. . . . One frequently expressed objection to the New Jersey Plan was that it might require the Federal Government to coerce the States into implementing legislation. . . . Madison echoed this view: "The practicability of making laws, with coercive sanctions, for the States as political bodies, had been exploded on all hands."....

In the end, the Convention opted for a Constitution in which Congress would exercise its legislative authority directly over individuals rather than over States; for a variety of reasons, it rejected the New Jersey Plan in favor of the Virginia Plan. This choice was made clear to the subsequent state ratifying conventions....

In providing for a stronger central government, therefore, the Framers explicitly chose a Constitution that confers upon Congress the power to regulate individuals, not States. As we have seen, the Court has consistently respected this choice. We have always understood that even where Congress has the authority under the Constitution to pass laws requiring or prohibiting certain acts, it lacks the power directly to compel the States to require or prohibit those acts. E.g., *FERC*; *Hodel*; *Lane County*. The allocation of power contained in the Commerce Clause, for example, authorizes Congress to regulate interstate commerce directly; it does not authorize Congress to regulate state governments' regulation of interstate commerce.

2

This is not to say that Congress lacks the ability to encourage a State to regulate in a particular way, or that Congress may not hold out incentives to the States as a method of influencing a State's policy choices. Our cases have identified a variety of methods, short of outright coercion, by which Congress may urge a State to adopt a legislative program consistent with federal interests. Two of these methods are of particular relevance here.

First, under Congress' spending power, "Congress may attach conditions on the receipt of federal funds." *Dole*. Such conditions must (among other requirements) bear some relationship to the purpose of the federal spending; otherwise, of course, the spending power could render academic the Constitution's other grants and limits of federal authority. Where the recipient of federal funds is a State, as is not unusual today, the conditions attached to the funds by Congress may influence a State's legislative choices. *Dole* was one such case: The Court found no constitutional flaw in a federal statute directing the Secretary of Transportation to withhold federal highway funds from States failing to adopt Congress' choice of a minimum drinking age. Similar examples abound.

Second, where Congress has the authority to regulate private activity under the Commerce Clause, we have recognized Congress' power to offer States the choice of regulating that activity according to federal standards or having state law pre-empted by federal regulation. *Hodel*. See also *FERC*. This arrangement, which has been termed "a program of cooperative federalism," *Hodel*, is replicated in numerous federal statutory schemes. These include ... the Occupational Safety and Health Act of 1970, *see Gade v. National Solid Wastes Management Assn.* (1992) [*Supra.* Chapter 5] ...

By either of these methods, as by any other permissible method of encouraging a State to conform to federal policy choices, the residents of the State retain the ultimate decision as to whether or not the State will comply. If a State's citizens view federal policy as sufficiently contrary to local interests, they may elect to decline a federal grant. If state residents would prefer their government to devote its attention and resources to problems other than those deemed important by Congress, they may choose to have the Federal Government rather than the State bear the expense of a federally mandated regulatory program, and they may continue to supplement that program to the extent state law is not pre-empted. Where Congress encourages state regulation rather than compelling it, state governments remain responsive to the local electorate's preferences; state officials remain accountable to the people.

By contrast, where the Federal Government compels States to regulate, the accountability of both state and federal officials is diminished. If the citizens of New York, for example, do not consider that making provision for the disposal of radioactive waste is in their best interest, they may elect state officials who share their view. That view can always be pre-empted under the Supremacy Clause if it is contrary to the national view, but in such a case it is the Federal Government that makes the decision in full view of the public, and it will be federal officials that suffer the consequences if the decision turns out to be detrimental or unpopular. But where the Federal Government directs the States to regulate, it may be state officials who will bear the brunt of public disapproval, while the federal officials who devised the regulatory program may remain insulated from the electoral ramifications of their decision. Accountability is thus diminished when, due to federal coercion, elected state officials cannot regulate in accordance with the views of the local electorate in matters not pre-empted by federal regulation.

With these principles in mind, we turn to the three challenged provisions of the Low-Level Radioactive Waste Policy Amendments Act of 1985.

### III

\* \* \*

### A

The first set of incentives works in three steps. First, Congress has authorized States with disposal sites to impose a surcharge on radioactive waste received from other States. Second, the Secretary of Energy collects a portion of this surcharge and places the money in an escrow account. Third, States achieving a series of milestones receive portions of this fund.

The first of these steps is an unexceptionable exercise of Congress' power to authorize the States to burden interstate commerce. While the Commerce Clause has long been understood to limit the States' ability to discriminate against interstate commerce, that limit may be lifted, as it has been here, by an expression of the "unambiguous intent" of Congress....

The second step, the Secretary's collection of a percentage of the surcharge, is no more than a federal tax on interstate commerce, which petitioners do not claim to be an invalid exercise of either Congress' commerce or taxing power.

The third step is a conditional exercise of Congress' authority under the Spending Clause: Congress has placed conditions—the achievement of the milestones—on the receipt of federal funds. Petitioners do not contend that Congress has exceeded its authority in any of the four respects our cases have identified. See generally *Dole*. The expenditure is for the general welfare; the States are required to use the money they receive for the purpose of assuring the safe disposal of radioactive waste. The conditions imposed are unambiguous; the Act informs the States exactly what they must do and by when they must do it in order to obtain a share of the escrow account. The conditions imposed are reasonably related to the purpose of the expenditure; both the conditions and the payments embody Congress' efforts to address the pressing problem of radioactive waste disposal. Finally, petitioners do not claim that the conditions imposed by the Act violate any independent constitutional prohibition....

The Act's first set of incentives, in which Congress has conditioned grants to the States upon the States' attainment of a series of milestones, is thus well within the authority of Congress under the Commerce and Spending Clauses. Because the first set of incentives is supported by affirmative constitutional grants of power to Congress, it is not inconsistent with the Tenth Amendment.

### B

In the second set of incentives, Congress has authorized States and regional compacts with disposal sites gradually to increase the cost of access to the sites, and then to deny access altogether, to radioactive waste generated in States that do not meet federal deadlines. As a simple regulation, this provision would be within the power of Congress to authorize the States to discriminate against interstate commerce. Where federal regulation of private activity is within the scope of the Commerce Clause, we have recognized the ability of Congress to offer States the choice of regulating that activity according to federal standards or having state law pre-empted by federal regulation. See *Hodel*; *FERC*.

This is the choice presented to nonsited States by the Act's second set of incentives: States may either regulate the disposal of radioactive waste according to federal standards by attaining local or regional self-sufficiency, or their residents who produce radioactive waste will be subject to federal regulation authorizing sited States and regions to deny access to their disposal sites.... A State whose citizens do not wish it to attain the Act's milestones may devote its attention and its resources to issues its citizens deem more worthy; the choice remains at all times with the residents of the State, not with Congress.... Nor must the State abandon the field if it does not accede to federal direction; the State may continue to regulate the generation and disposal of radioactive waste in any manner its citizens see fit.

The Act's second set of incentives thus represents a conditional exercise of Congress' commerce power, along the lines of those we have held to be within Congress' authority. As a result, the second set of incentives does not intrude on the sovereignty reserved to the States by the Tenth Amendment.

### C

The take title provision is of a different character. This third so-called "incentive" offers States, as an alternative to regulating pursuant to Congress' direction, the option of taking title to and possession of the low level radioactive waste generated within their borders and becoming liable for all damages waste generators suffer as a result of the States' failure to do so promptly. In this provision, Congress has crossed the line distinguishing encouragement from coercion....

The take title provision offers state governments a "choice" of either accepting ownership of waste or regulating according to the instructions of Congress. Respondents do not claim that the Constitution would authorize Congress to impose either option as a freestanding requirement. On one hand, the Constitution would not permit Congress simply to transfer radioactive waste from generators to state governments. Such a forced transfer, standing alone, would in principle be no different than a congressionally compelled subsidy from state governments to radioactive waste producers. The same is true of the provision requiring the States to become liable for the generators' damages.... Either type of federal action would "commandeer" state governments into the service of federal regulatory purposes, and would for this reason be inconsistent with the Constitution's division of authority between federal and state governments. On the other hand, the second alternative held out to state governments—regulating pursuant to Congress' direction—would, standing alone, present a simple command to state governments to implement legislation enacted by Congress. As we have seen, the Constitution does not empower Congress to subject state governments to this type of instruction.

Because an instruction to state governments to take title to waste, standing alone, would be beyond the authority of Congress, and because a direct order to regulate, standing alone, would also be beyond the authority of Congress, it follows that Congress lacks the power to offer the States a choice between the two. Unlike the first two sets of incentives, the take title incentive does not represent the conditional exercise of any congressional power enumerated in the Constitution. In this provision, Congress has not held out the threat of exercising its spending power or its commerce power; it has instead held out the threat, should the States not regulate according to one federal instruction, of simply forcing the States to submit to another federal instruction. A choice between two unconstitutionally coercive regulatory techniques is no choice at all. Either way, "the Act commandeers the legislative processes of the States by directly compelling them to enact and enforce a federal regulatory program," *Hodel*, an outcome that has never been understood to lie within the authority conferred upon Congress by the Constitution....

The take title provision appears to be unique. No other federal statute has been cited which offers a state government no option other than that of implementing legislation enacted by Congress. Whether one views the take title provision as lying outside Congress' enumerated powers, or as infringing upon the core of state sovereignty reserved by the Tenth Amendment, the provision is inconsistent with the federal structure of our Government established by the Constitution.

IV

Respondents raise a number of objections to this understanding of the limits of Congress' power.

## A

The United States proposes three alternative views of the constitutional line separating state and federal authority. While each view concedes that Congress generally may not compel state governments to regulate pursuant to federal direction, each purports to find a limited domain in which such coercion is permitted by the Constitution.

First, the United States argues that the Constitution's prohibition of congressional directives to state governments can be overcome where the federal interest is sufficiently important to justify state submission. This argument contains a kernel of truth: In determining whether the Tenth Amendment limits the ability of Congress to subject state governments to generally applicable laws, the Court has in some cases stated that it will evaluate the strength of federal interests in light of the degree to which such laws would prevent the State from functioning as a sovereign; that is, the extent to which such generally applicable laws would impede a state government's responsibility to represent and be accountable to the citizens of the State. See, e.g., *National League of Cities*. The Court has more recently departed from this approach. See, e.g., *Garcia*. But whether or not a particularly strong federal interest enables Congress to bring state governments within the orbit of generally applicable federal regulation, no Member of the Court has ever suggested that such a federal interest would enable Congress to command a state government to enact state regulation. No matter how powerful the federal interest involved, the Constitution simply does not give Congress the authority to require the States to regulate....

Second, the United States argues that the Constitution does, in some circumstances, permit federal directives to state governments. Various cases are cited for this proposition, but none support it. Some of these cases discuss the well established power of Congress to pass laws enforceable in state courts. See *Testa v. Katt*, 330 U.S. 386 (1947); see also *Second Employers' Liability Cases, N.H. & H.R. Co.*, 223 U.S. 1 (1912). These cases involve no more than an application of the Supremacy Clause's provision that federal law "shall be the supreme Law of the Land," enforceable in every State. More to the point, all involve congressional regulation of individuals, not congressional requirements that States regulate. Federal statutes enforceable in state courts do, in a sense, direct state judges to enforce them, but this sort of federal "direction" of state judges is mandated by the text of the Supremacy Clause. No comparable constitutional provision authorizes Congress to command state legislatures to legislate.

Additional cases cited by the United States discuss the power of federal courts to order state officials to comply with federal law. See *Puerto Rico v. Branstad*, 483 U.S. 219 (1987); see also *Cooper v. Aaron*, 358 U.S. 1 (1958) [Note *supra*. Chapter 1]; *Brown v. Board of Education*, 349 U.S. 294 (1955); *Ex parte Young*, 209 U.S. 123 (1908). Again, however, the text of the Constitution plainly confers this authority on the federal courts, the "judicial Power" of which "shall extend to all Cases, in Law and Equity, arising under this Constitution, [and] the Laws of the United States ... ; [and] to Controversies between two or more States; [and] between a State and Citizens of another State." U.S. Const., Art. III, § 2. The Constitution contains no analogous grant of authority to Congress. Moreover, the Supremacy Clause makes federal law paramount over the contrary positions of state officials; the power of federal courts to enforce federal law thus presupposes some authority to order state officials to comply.

In sum, the cases relied upon by the United States hold only that federal law is enforceable in state courts and that federal courts may in proper circumstances order state officials to comply with federal law, propositions that by no means imply any authority on the part of Congress to mandate state regulation.

Third, the United States, supported by ... *amici*, argues that the Constitution envisions a role for Congress as an arbiter of interstate disputes. The United States observes that federal courts, and this Court in particular, have frequently resolved conflicts among States.... The United States suggests that if the Court may resolve such interstate disputes, Congress can surely do the same under the Commerce Clause. The [*amici*] support this argument with a series of quotations from *The Federalist* and other contemporaneous documents, which the compacts contend demonstrate that the Framers established a strong National Legislature for the purpose of resolving trade disputes among the States.

While the Framers no doubt endowed Congress with the power to regulate interstate commerce in order to avoid further instances of the interstate trade disputes that were common under the Articles of Confederation, the Framers did *not* intend that Congress should exercise that power through the mechanism of mandating state regulation. The Constitution established Congress as "a superintending authority over the reciprocal trade" among the States, *The Federalist* No. 42, by empowering Congress to regulate that trade directly, not by authorizing Congress to issue trade-related orders to state governments. As Madison and Hamilton explained, "a sovereignty over sovereigns, a government over governments, a legislation for communities, as contradistinguished from individuals, as it is a solecism in theory, so in practice it is subversive of the order and ends of civil polity." *Id.*, No. 20.

### B

The sited state respondents focus their attention on the process by which the Act was formulated. They correctly observe that public officials representing the State of New York lent their support to the Act's enactment.... Respondents note that the Act embodies a bargain among the sited and unsited States, a compromise to which New York was a willing participant and from which New York has reaped much benefit. Respondents then pose what appears at first to be a troubling question: How can a federal statute be found an unconstitutional infringement of state sovereignty when state officials consented to the statute's enactment?

The answer follows from an understanding of the fundamental purpose served by our Government's federal structure. The Constitution does not protect the sovereignty of States for the benefit of the States or state governments as abstract political entities, or even for the benefit of the public officials governing the States. To the contrary, the Constitution divides authority between federal and state governments for the protection of individuals. State sovereignty is not just an end in itself: "Rather, federalism secures to citizens the liberties that derive from the diffusion of sovereign power." *Coleman v. Thompson*, 501 U.S. 722 (1991) (BLACKMUN, J., dissenting). "Just as the separation and independence of the coordinate branches of the Federal Government serves to prevent the accumulation of excessive power in any one branch, a healthy balance of power between the States and the Federal Government will reduce the risk of tyranny and abuse from either front."

Where Congress exceeds its authority relative to the States, therefore, the departure from the constitutional plan cannot be ratified by the "consent" of state officials. An analogy to the separation of powers among the branches of the Federal Government clarifies this point. The Constitution's division of power among the three branches is violated where one branch invades the territory of another, whether or not the encroached-upon branch approves the encroachment.... In *INS v. Chadha* (1983) [*Supra*. Chapter 2], we held that the legislative veto violated the constitutional requirement that legislation be presented to the President, despite Presidents' approval of hundreds of statutes containing a legislative veto provision. The constitutional authority of Congress cannot be expanded by the "consent" of the governmental unit whose domain is thereby narrowed, whether that unit is the Executive Branch or the States.

State officials thus cannot consent to the enlargement of the powers of Congress beyond those enumerated in the Constitution. Indeed, the facts of these cases raise the possibility that powerful incentives might lead both federal and state officials to view departures from the federal structure to be in their personal interests. Most citizens recognize the need for radioactive waste disposal sites, but few want sites near their homes. As a result, while it would be well within the authority of either federal or state officials to choose where the disposal sites will be, it is likely to be in the political interest of each individual official to avoid being held accountable to the voters for the choice of location. If a federal official is faced with the alternatives of choosing a location or directing the States to do it, the official may well prefer the latter, as a means of shifting responsibility for the eventual decision. If a state official is faced with the same set of alternatives—choosing a location or having Congress direct the choice of a location—the state official may also prefer the latter, as it may permit the avoidance of personal responsibility. The interests of public officials thus may not coincide with the Constitution's intergovernmental allocation of authority. Where state officials purport to submit to the direction of Congress in this manner, federalism is hardly being advanced....

## V

Petitioners also contend that the Act is inconsistent with the Constitution's Guarantee Clause, which directs the United States to "guarantee to every State in this Union a Republican Form of Government." U.S. Const., Art. IV, §4. Because we have found the take title provision of the Act irreconcilable with the powers delegated to Congress by the Constitution and hence with the Tenth Amendment's reservation to the States of those powers not delegated to the Federal Government, we need only address the applicability of the Guarantee Clause to the Act's other two challenged provisions.

We approach the issue with some trepidation, because the Guarantee Clause has been an infrequent basis for litigation throughout our history. In most of the cases in which the Court has been asked to apply the Clause, the Court has found the claims presented to be non-justiciable under the "political question" doctrine. See, e.g., *Baker v. Carr*, (1962) [*Supra.* Chapter 1] (challenge to apportionment of state legislative districts)....

More recently, the Court has suggested that perhaps not all claims under the Guarantee Clause present nonjusticiable political questions.... We need not resolve this difficult question today. Even if we assume that petitioners' claim is justiciable, neither the monetary incentives provided by the Act nor the possibility that a State's waste producers may find themselves excluded from the disposal sites of another State can reasonably be said to deny any State a republican form of government.... The twin threats imposed by the first two challenged provisions of the Act—that New York may miss out on a share of federal spending or that those generating radioactive waste within New York may lose out-of-state disposal outlets—do not pose any realistic risk of altering the form or the method of functioning of New York's government. Thus even indulging the assumption that the Guarantee Clause provides a basis upon which a State or its subdivisions may sue to enjoin the enforcement of a federal statute, petitioners have not made out such a claim in these cases....

## VII

Some truths are so basic that, like the air around us, they are easily overlooked. Much of the Constitution is concerned with setting forth the form of our government, and the courts have traditionally invalidated measures deviating from that form. The result may appear "formalistic" in a given case to partisans of the measure at issue, because such measures are typically the product of the era's perceived necessity. But the Constitution protects us from our own best intentions: It divides power among sovereigns and among branches of government precisely so that we may resist the temptation to concentrate power in one location as an expedient solution to the crisis of the day. The shortage of disposal sites for radioactive waste is a pressing national problem, but a judiciary that licensed extraconstitutional government with each issue of comparable gravity would, in the long run, be far worse.

States are not mere political subdivisions of the United States. State governments are neither regional offices nor administrative agencies of the Federal Government. The positions occupied by state officials appear nowhere on the Federal Government's most detailed organizational chart. The Constitution instead "leaves to the several States a residuary and inviolable sovereignty," *The Federalist* No. 39, reserved explicitly to the States by the Tenth Amendment.

Whatever the outer limits of that sovereignty may be, one thing is clear: The Federal Government may not compel the States to enact or administer a federal regulatory program. The Constitution permits both the Federal Government and the States to enact legislation regarding the disposal of low level radioactive waste. The Constitution enables the Federal Government to pre-empt state regulation contrary to federal interests, and it permits the Federal Government to hold out incentives to the States as a means of encouraging them to adopt suggested regulatory schemes. It does not, however, authorize Congress simply to direct the States to provide for the disposal of the radioactive waste generated within their borders. While there may be many constitutional methods of achieving regional self-sufficiency in radioactive waste disposal, the method Congress has chosen is not one of them. The judgment of the Court of Appeals is accordingly affirmed in part and reversed in part.

Justice WHITE, with whom Justice BLACKMUN and Justice STEVENS join, concurring in part and dissenting in part....

III

The Court announces that it has no occasion to revisit such decisions as ... *Garcia* and *National League of Cities* because "this is not a case in which Congress has subjected a State to the same legislation applicable to private parties." Although this statement sends the welcome signal that the Court does not intend to cut a wide swath through our recent Tenth Amendment precedents, it nevertheless is unpersuasive. I have several difficulties with the Court's analysis in this respect: It builds its rule around an insupportable and illogical distinction in the types of alleged incursions on state sovereignty; it derives its rule from cases that do not support its analysis; it fails to apply the appropriate tests from the cases on which it purports to base its rule; and it omits any discussion of the most recent and pertinent test for determining the take title provision's constitutionality.

The Court's distinction between a federal statute's regulation of States and private parties for general purposes, as opposed to a regulation solely on the activities of States, is unsupported by our recent Tenth Amendment cases. In no case has the Court rested its holding on such a distinction. Moreover, the Court makes no effort to explain why this purported distinction should affect the analysis of Congress' power under general principles of federalism and the Tenth Amendment. The distinction, facilely thrown out, is not based on any defensible theory. Certainly one would be hard-pressed to read the spirited exchanges between the Court and dissenting Justices in *National League of Cities* and in *Garcia* as having been based on the distinction now drawn by the Court. An incursion on state sovereignty hardly seems more constitutionally acceptable if the federal statute that "commands" specific action also applies to private parties. The alleged diminution in state authority over its own affairs is not any less because the federal mandate restricts the activities of private parties.

Even were such a distinction to be logically sound, the Court's "anticommandeering" principle cannot persuasively be read as springing from the two cases cited for the proposition, *Hodel* and *FERC*. The Court purports to draw support for its rule against Congress "commandeering" state legislative processes from a solitary statement in dictum in *Hodel*. See *ante*: "As an initial matter, Congress may not simply 'commandeer the legislative processes of the States by directly compelling them to enact and enforce a federal regulatory program'" (quoting *Hodel*). That statement was not necessary to the decision in *Hodel* … ; the language about "commandeering" States was classic *dicta*.…

The Court also claims support for its rule from our decision in *FERC*, and quotes a passage from that case in which we stated that "'this Court never has sanctioned explicitly a federal command to the States to promulgate and enforce laws and regulations.'" *Ante*, (quoting *FERC*). In so reciting, the Court extracts from the relevant passage in a manner that subtly alters the Court's meaning. In full, the passage reads: "While this Court never has sanctioned explicitly a federal command to the States to promulgate and enforce laws and regulations, there are instances where the Court has upheld federal statutory structures that in effect directed state decisionmakers to take or to refrain from taking certain actions." *Ibid*. The phrase highlighted by the Court merely means that we have not had the occasion to address whether Congress may "command" the States to enact a certain law.…

Rather than seek guidance from *FERC* and *Hodel*, therefore, the more appropriate analysis should flow from *Garcia*, even if these cases do not involve a congressional law generally applicable to both States and private parties. In *Garcia*, we stated the proper inquiry: "We are convinced that the fundamental limitation that the constitutional scheme imposes on the Commerce Clause to protect the 'States as States' is one of process rather than one of result.… Where it addresses this aspect of respondents' argument, the Court tacitly concedes that a failing of the political process cannot be shown in these cases because it refuses to rebut the unassailable arguments that the States were well able to look after themselves in the legislative process that culminated in the 1985 Act's passage.… The Court rejects this process-based argument by resorting to generalities and platitudes about the purpose of federalism being to protect individual rights.

Ultimately, I suppose, the entire structure of our federal constitutional government can be traced to an interest in establishing checks and balances to prevent the exercise of tyranny against individuals. But these fears seem extremely far distant to me in a situation such as this. We face a crisis of national proportions in the disposal of low-level radioactive waste, and Congress has acceded to the wishes of the States by permitting local decisionmaking rather than imposing a solution from Washington. New York itself participated and supported passage of this legislation at both the gubernatorial and federal representative levels, and then enacted state laws specifically to comply with the deadlines and timetables agreed upon by the States in the 1985 Act. For me, the Court's civics lecture has a decidedly hollow ring at a time when action, rather than rhetoric, is needed to solve a national problem.[3]

---

3. With selective quotations from the era in which the Constitution was adopted, the majority attempts to bolster its holding that the take title provision is tantamount to federal "commandeering" of the States. In view of the many Tenth Amendment cases decided over the past two decades in which resort to the kind of historical analysis generated in the majority opinion was not deemed necessary, I do not read the majority's many invocations of history to be anything other than elaborate window dressing. Certainly nowhere does the majority announce that its rule is compelled by an understanding

IV

Though I disagree with the Court's conclusion that the take title provision is unconstitutional, I do not read its opinion to preclude Congress from adopting a similar measure through its powers under the Spending or Commerce Clauses....

V

The ultimate irony of the decision today is that in its formalistically rigid obeisance to "federalism," the Court gives Congress fewer incentives to defer to the wishes of state officials in achieving local solutions to local problems.... By invalidating the measure designed to ensure compliance for recalcitrant States, such as New York, the Court upsets the delicate compromise achieved among the States and forces Congress to erect several additional formalistic hurdles to clear before achieving exactly the same objective. Because the Court's justifications for undertaking this step are unpersuasive to me, I respectfully dissent.

Justice STEVENS, concurring in part and dissenting in part. [omitted]

### Note: The Scope—and Limits—of the "Anti-Commandeering" Doctrine

1. The inevitable question after *New York* was whether the anti-commandeering principle applied to other parts of state government. In *Printz v. United States*, 521 U.S. 898 (1997), the Court, by a 5–4 vote, applied the principle to state law enforcement. *Printz* concerned a federal gun control law that required state law enforcement authorities to conduct background checks on prospective gun buyers until a federal background check program was established. The Court, speaking through Justice Scalia, struck it down, largely on the authority of *New York*. The Court also concluded that prior practice militated against the law, since early Congresses did not attempt

---

of what the Framers may have thought about statutes of the type at issue here. Moreover, I would observe that, while its quotations add a certain flavor to the opinion, the majority's historical analysis has a distinctly wooden quality. One would not know from reading the majority's account, for instance, that the nature of federal-state relations changed fundamentally after the Civil War. That conflict produced in its wake a tremendous expansion in the scope of the Federal Government's law-making authority, so much so that the persons who helped to found the Republic would scarcely have recognized the many added roles the National Government assumed for itself. Moreover, the majority fails to mention the New Deal era, in which the Court recognized the enormous growth in Congress' power under the Commerce Clause. While I believe we should not be blind to history, neither should we read it so selectively as to restrict the proper scope of Congress' powers under Article I, especially when the history not mentioned by the majority fully supports a more expansive understanding of the legislature's authority than may have existed in the late 18th century.

Given the scanty textual support for the majority's position, it would be far more sensible to defer to a coordinate branch of government in its decision to devise a solution to a national problem of this kind. Certainly in other contexts, principles of federalism have not insulated States from mandates by the National Government. The Court has upheld congressional statutes that impose clear directives on state officials, including those enacted pursuant to the Extradition Clause, *see, e.g., Puerto Rico v. Branstad*, 483 U.S. 219 (1987), the post-Civil War Amendments, *see, e.g., South Carolina v. Katzenbach*, 383 U.S. 301 (1966), as well as congressional statutes that require state courts to hear certain actions, *see, e.g., Testa v. Katt*, 330 U.S. 386 (1947).

to mandate that state law enforcement officers enforce federal law. Justice Scalia also noted the separation of powers problem inherent in congressional delegation of federal law enforcement power to someone other than a federal executive branch official.

Justice Stevens dissented for four Justices. He argued that the historical materials, including the actions of the early Congresses, suggested that Congress did in fact enjoy the power to require state officials to enforce federal law. He repeated *Garcia*'s argument that the structure of the national government was the states' main protection against domination from the central government. He also argued that the majority's result effectively meant *more* federal intrusion on states, since the federal government would now have to send its own law enforcement officers into the field to enforce laws such as the gun buyer background check requirement. Finally, he questioned whether the decision could be reconciled with *Testa v. Katt*, 330 U.S. 386 (1947). *Testa* is discussed in the last item of this note.

Justice Souter, who joined the majority in *New York*, also wrote a separate dissent to explain his view that *The Federalist Papers*, notably Number 27, reflected a founding era understanding that the federal government did have the power to order state personnel to enforce federal law. Justice Breyer also wrote a separate dissent to observe that the experience of other federal systems was useful in answering questions about our own.

2. The anti-commandeering principle reached a limit in *Reno v. Condon*, 528 U.S. 141 (2000). In *Condon* the Court upheld the Driver's Privacy Protection Act of 1994, which regulated state sales of information it gathered as part of its process of providing drivers' licenses. Writing for a unanimous Court, Chief Justice Rehnquist concluded that the statute was valid under the Commerce Clause because it regulated states as owners of databases, not as sovereigns. The Court noted the state's argument that the statute was unconstitutional because it regulated states exclusively, rather than through a "generally applicable law" that applies to individuals as well as the states. The Court did not address that argument, because it concluded that the statute regulated both states and private entities that re-sell the data purchased from state motor vehicle departments.

3. Taken together, *New York* and *Printz* prohibit Congress from "commandeering," respectively, the legislative and executive branches of state government. What about the judicial branch? In *Testa v. Katt*, 330 U.S. 386 (1947), the Court unanimously held that Congress could require state courts to hear federal law causes of action. Justice Black's opinion for all nine Justices quoted from an earlier case, *Second Employers' Liability Cases (Mondou v. NY, NH & H. RR Co.)*, 223 U.S. 1 (1912):

> 'The suggestion that the act of Congress is not in harmony with the policy of the State, and therefore that the courts of the State are free to decline jurisdiction, is quite inadmissible, because it presupposes what in legal contemplation does not exist. When Congress ... adopted [the statute at issue], it spoke for all the people and all the States, and thereby established a policy for all. That policy is as much the policy of Connecticut as if the act had em-

anated from its own legislature, and should be respected accordingly in the courts of the State.' *Testa* (*quoting Mondou*).

In both *New York* and *Printz*, the majority distinguished *Testa* on the ground that *Testa* was simply an application of the Supremacy Clause, which authorized federal "commandeering" of state courts. Dissenting in *Printz*, Justice Stevens argued for a broader reading of *Testa*:

> Finally, the majority provides an incomplete explanation of our decision in *Testa*, and demeans its importance. In that case the Court unanimously held that state courts of appropriate jurisdiction must occupy themselves adjudicating claims brought by private litigants under the federal Emergency Price Control Act of 1942, regardless of how otherwise crowded their dockets might be with state-law matters. That is a much greater imposition on state sovereignty than the Court's characterization of the case as merely holding that 'state courts cannot refuse to apply federal law.' That characterization describes only the narrower duty to apply federal law in cases that the state courts have consented to entertain.

> The language drawn from the Supremacy Clause upon which the majority relies ("the Judges in every State shall be bound [by federal law], any Thing in the Constitution or Laws of any state to the Contrary notwithstanding"), expressly embraces that narrower conflict of laws principle. Art. VI, cl. 2. But the Supremacy Clause means far more. As *Testa* held, because the 'Laws of the United States ... [are] the supreme Law of the Land,' state courts of appropriate jurisdiction must hear federal claims whenever a federal statute, such as the Emergency Price Control Act, requires them to do so.

> Hence, the Court's textual argument is quite misguided. The majority focuses on the Clause's specific attention to the point that 'Judges in every State shall be bound.' *Ibid.* That language commands state judges to 'apply federal law' in cases that they entertain, but it is not the source of their duty to accept jurisdiction of federal claims that they would prefer to ignore. Our opinions in *Testa*, and earlier the *Second Employers' Liability Cases*, rested generally on the language of the Supremacy Clause, without any specific focus on the reference to judges.

4. Is there anything special about state courts that allows them to be "commandeered," consistent with the holdings in *New York* and *Printz*? Indeed, as a general matter does commandeering present a special problem for governmental accountability? After all, the Court recognizes that Congress can completely displace states' regulatory choices by pre-empting state law. Does the Court presume a level of sophistication in voters, who are presumed to be able to excuse inaction by state officials in cases of pre-emption, but unable to excuse undesirable state *action* when that action is mandated by a federal law commandeering those officials?

5. In *New York* the Court states that it is not reopening the question answered by *Garcia* about Congress's power to regulate states as part of a program of general eco-

nomic regulation (*e.g.*, regulating states by requiring them, like all other employers, to pay a minimum wage). How clear is the line between such regulation and the commandeering *New York* rejects? Doesn't requiring a state to pay the federal minimum wage require the state to decide how to pay that wage, or otherwise how to provide government services consistent with that mandate? If so, doesn't the minimum wage law intrude on states' legislative agendas in the same manner as that condemned by the commandeering doctrine? In *Condon* the Court locates the sale of driver's license information on the *Garcia*, rather than the *New York*, side of the line. How persuasive is the Court on that point?

# C. Constitutional Limits on Judicial Remedies against States

The Eleventh Amendment to the Constitution, and the concept of sovereign immunity it embodies, has been one of the most troublesome areas for the Supreme Court. In its entirety, the Amendment reads: "The Judicial power of the United States shall not be construed to extend to any suit in law or equity, commenced or prosecuted against one of the United States by Citizens of another State, or by Citizens or Subjects of any Foreign State." The Amendment was adopted in response to the Supreme Court's decision in *Chisholm v. Georgia*, 2 U.S. (2 Dall.) 219 (1793), where the Supreme Court took original jurisdiction over a suit brought by South Carolina residents against the State of Georgia, seeking to collect on a debt. This assertion of jurisdiction created great apprehension in the states, which feared that the Court would provide a favorable forum for creditors seeking to collect on states' debts incurred during the Revolution. As a result the Eleventh Amendment was enacted and ratified.

Beyond these basic facts, however, there has been little agreement on the scope of the Amendment. For example, in *Hans v. Louisiana*, 134 U.S. 1 (1890), the Court interpreted the Amendment as prohibiting not just suits between a state and "Citizens of another State" (as the Amendment literally reads), but also suits between a state and one of its own citizens.

The materials that follow will focus on another issue that is more structural, and thus more intractable, than the issue in *Hans*: namely, how can states' sovereign immunity from suit in federal court be squared with the Constitution's bestowal of individual rights as against the states? In other words, how can individuals enjoy, as a matter of federal law, rights against the states, consistent with a rule that states cannot be sued in federal court when states allegedly violate those rights? The Court has offered several responses. The following materials consider the two most important ones. First, the Court has developed a theory known as the "*Young* doctrine" (after *Ex parte Young*, 209 U.S. 123 (1908)), suggesting that in certain circumstances a lawsuit against a state official does not violate the Eleventh Amendment's state sovereignty rule. Second, the Court has considered whether particular constitutional provisions impliedly waive states' sovereign immunity, with the result that, when Congress legislates pursuant to those provisions, it has the power to abrogate that immunity and make states liable for remedies from which they would otherwise be immune. The materials that follow consider these two responses. The materials end with *Alden v. Maine*, 527 U.S. 706 (1999), where the Court considered whether Congress may abrogate state sovereign immunity in lawsuits brought in the state's own courts. *Alden* thus does not implicate the Eleventh Amendment, which speaks to the *federal* judicial power. However, in that case the Court imported much Eleventh Amendment doctrine into its analysis, which it grounded on general principles of federalism and the Tenth Amendment.

## 1. The *Young* Doctrine

### Edelman v. Jordan

415 U.S. 651 (1974)

MR. JUSTICE REHNQUIST delivered the opinion of the Court.

Respondent John Jordan filed a complaint in the United States District Court for the Northern District of Illinois, individually and as a representative of a class, seeking declaratory and injunctive relief against two former directors of the Illinois Department of Public Aid, the director of the Cook County Department of Public Aid, and the comptroller of Cook County. Respondent alleged that these state officials were administering the federal-state programs of Aid to the Aged, Blind, or Disabled (AABD) in a manner inconsistent with various federal regulations and with the Fourteenth Amendment to the Constitution....

In its judgment of March 15, 1972, the District Court declared § 4004 of the manual of [state welfare regulations] to be invalid insofar as it was inconsistent with ... federal regulations ... and granted a permanent injunction requiring compliance with the federal time limits for processing and paying AABD applicants. The District Court, in paragraph 5 of its judgment, also ordered the state officials to "release and remit AABD benefits wrongfully withheld to all applicants for AABD in the State of Illinois who applied between July 1, 1968 (the date of the federal regulations) and April 16, 1971 (the date of the preliminary injunction issued by the District Court) and were determined eligible...."

On appeal to the United States Court of Appeals for the Seventh Circuit, the Illinois officials contended, *inter alia*, that the Eleventh Amendment barred the award of retroactive benefits, that the judgment of inconsistency between the federal regulations and the provisions of the Illinois Categorical Assistance Manual could be given prospective effect only.... The Court of Appeals rejected these contentions and affirmed the judgment of the District Court.... Because we believe the Court of Appeals erred in its disposition of the Eleventh Amendment claim, we reverse that portion of the Court of Appeals decision which affirmed the District Court's order that retroactive benefits be paid by the Illinois state officials.

The historical basis of the Eleventh Amendment has been oft stated, and it represents one of the more dramatic examples of this Court's effort to derive meaning from the document given to the Nation by the Framers nearly 200 years ago....

The issue was squarely presented to the Court in a suit brought at the August 1792 Term by two citizens of South Carolina, executors of a British creditor, against the State of Georgia. After a year's postponement for preparation on the part of the State of Georgia, the Court, after argument, rendered in February 1793, its short-lived decision in *Chisholm v. Georgia*, 2 Dall. 419 (1793) [Note *supra.* this chapter]. The decision in that case, that a State was liable to suit by a citizen of another State or of a foreign country, literally shocked the Nation. Sentiment for passage of a constitutional amendment to override the decision rapidly gained momentum, and five years after *Chisholm* the Eleventh Amendment was officially announced by President John Adams. Unchanged since then, the Amendment provides:

> "The judicial power of the United States shall not be construed to extend to any suit in law or equity, commenced or prosecuted against one of the United States by Citizens of another State, or by Citizens or Subjects of any Foreign State."

While the Amendment by its terms does not bar suits against a State by its own citizens, this Court has consistently held that an unconsenting State is immune from suits brought in federal courts by her own citizens as well as by citizens of another State. *Hans v. Louisiana*, 134 U.S. 1 (1890) [Note *supra.* this chapter]. It is also well established that even though a State is not named a party to the action, the suit may nonetheless be barred by the Eleventh Amendment. *In Ford Motor Co. v. Department of Treasury*, 323 U.S. 459 (1945), the Court said:

> When the action is in essence one for the recovery of money from the state, the state is the real, substantial party in interest and is entitled to invoke its sovereign immunity from suit even though individual officials are nominal defendants.

Thus the rule has evolved that a suit by private parties seeking to impose a liability which must be paid from public funds in the state treasury is barred by the Eleventh Amendment.

The Court of Appeals in this case, while recognizing that the *Hans* line of cases permitted the State to raise the Eleventh Amendment as a defense to suit by its own citizens, nevertheless concluded that the Amendment did not bar the award of retroactive payments of the statutory benefits found to have been wrongfully withheld. The Court of Appeals held that the above-cited cases, when read in light of this Court's landmark decision in *Ex parte Young*, 209 U.S. 123 (1908) [Note *supra.* this chapter], do not preclude the grant of such a monetary award in the nature of equitable restitution.

Petitioner concedes that *Ex parte Young* is no bar to that part of the District Court's judgment that prospectively enjoined petitioner's predecessors from failing to process applications within the time limits established by the federal regulations. Petitioner argues, however, that *Ex parte Young* does not extend so far as to permit a suit which seeks the award of an accrued monetary liability which must be met from the general revenues of a State, absent consent or waiver by the State of its Eleventh Amendment immunity, and that therefore the award of retroactive benefits by the District Court was improper.

*Ex parte Young* was a watershed case in which this Court held that the Eleventh Amendment did not bar an action in the federal courts seeking to enjoin the Attorney General of Minnesota from enforcing a statute claimed to violate the Fourteenth Amendment of the United States Constitution. This holding has permitted the Civil War Amendments to the Constitution to serve as a sword, rather than merely as a shield, for those whom they were designed to protect. But the relief awarded in *Ex parte Young* was prospective only; the Attorney General of Minnesota was enjoined to conform his future conduct of that office to the requirement of the Fourteenth Amendment. Such relief is analogous to that awarded by the District Court in the prospective portion of its order under review in this case.

But the retroactive position of the District Court's order here, which requires the payment of a very substantial amount of money which that court held should have been paid, but was not, stands on quite a different footing. These funds will obviously not be paid out of the pocket of petitioner Edelman. Addressing himself to a similar situation in *Rothstein v. Wyman*, 467 F.2d 226 (2d Cir. 1972), Judge McGowan observed for the court:

> It is not pretended that these payments are to come from the personal resources of these appellants. Appellees expressly contemplate that they will, rather, involve substantial expenditures from the public funds of the state....

> It is one thing to tell the Commissioner of Social Services that he must comply with the federal standards for the future if the state is to have the benefit of federal funds in the programs he administers. It is quite another thing to order the Commissioner to use state funds to make reparation for the past. The latter would appear to us to fall afoul of the Eleventh Amendment if that basic constitutional provision is to be conceived of as having any present force....

We agree with Judge McGowan's observations. The funds to satisfy the award in this case must inevitably come from the general revenues of the State of Illinois, and thus the award resembles far more closely the monetary award against the State itself, *Ford Motor Co. v. Department of Treasury*, than it does the prospective injunctive relief awarded in *Ex parte Young*.

The Court of Appeals, in upholding the award in this case, held that it was permissible because it was in the form of "equitable restitution" instead of damages, and therefore capable of being tailored in such a way as to minimize disruptions of the state program of categorical assistance. But we must judge the award actually made in this case, and not one which might have been differently tailored in a different case, and we must judge it in the context of the important constitutional principle embodied in the Eleventh Amendment.[11]

We do not read *Ex parte Young* or subsequent holdings of this Court to indicate that any form of relief may be awarded against a state officer, no matter how closely it may in practice resemble a money judgment payable out of the state treasury, so long as the relief may be labeled "equitable" in nature. The Court's opinion in *Ex parte Young* hewed to no such line.…

As in most areas of the law, the difference between the type of relief barred by the Eleventh Amendment and that permitted under *Ex parte Young* will not in many instances be that between day and night. The injunction issued in *Ex parte Young* was not totally without effect on the State's revenues, since the state law which the Attorney General was enjoined from enforcing provided substantial monetary penalties against railroads which did not conform to its provisions. Later cases from this Court have authorized equitable relief which has probably had greater impact on state treasuries than did that awarded in *Ex parte Young*.… But the fiscal consequences to state treasuries in these cases were the necessary result of compliance with decrees which by their terms were prospective in nature. State officials, in order to shape their official conduct to the mandate of the Court's decrees, would more likely have to spend money from the state treasury than if they had been left free to pursue their previous course of conduct. Such an ancillary effect on the state treasury is a permissible and often an inevitable consequence of the principle announced in *Ex parte Young*.

But that portion of the District Court's decree which petitioner challenges on Eleventh Amendment grounds goes much further than any of the cases cited. It requires payment of state funds, not as a necessary consequence of compliance in the future with a substantive federal-question determination, but as a form of compensation to those whose applications were processed on the slower time schedule at a time when petitioner was under no court-imposed obligation to conform to a different standard. While the Court of Appeals described this retroactive award of monetary relief as a form of "equitable restitution," it is in practical effect indistinguishable in many aspects from an award of damages against the State. It will to a virtual certainty be paid from state funds, and not from the pockets of the individual state officials

---

11. It may be true, as stated by our Brother DOUGLAS in dissent, that 'most welfare decisions by federal courts have a financial impact on the States.' But we cannot agree that such a financial impact is the same where a federal court applies *Ex parte Young* to grant prospective declaratory and injunctive relief, as opposed to an order of retroactive payments as was made in the instant case. It is not necessarily true that 'whether the decree is prospective only or requires payments for the weeks or months wrongfully skipped over by the state officials, the nature of the impact on the state treasury is precisely the same.' This argument neglects the fact that where the State has a definable allocation to be used in the payment of public aid benefits, and pursues a certain course of action such as the processing of applications within certain time periods as did Illinois here, the subsequent ordering by a federal court of retroactive payments to correct delays in such processing will invariably mean there is less money available for payments for the continuing obligations of the public aid system.…

who were the defendants in the action. It is measured in terms of a monetary loss resulting from a past breach of a legal duty on the part of the defendant state officials....

Respondent urges that since the various Illinois officials sued in the District Court failed to raise the Eleventh Amendment as a defense to the relief sought by respondent, petitioner is therefore barred from raising the Eleventh Amendment defense in the Court of Appeals or in this Court. The Court of Appeals apparently felt the defense was properly presented, and dealt with it on the merits. We approve of this resolution, since it has been well settled since the decision in *Ford Motor Co. v. Department of Treasury, supra,* that the Eleventh Amendment defense sufficiently partakes of the nature of a jurisdictional bar so that it need not be raised in the trial court:

> [The Attorney General of Indiana] appealed in the federal District Court and the Circuit Court of Appeals and defended the suit on the merits. The objection to petitioner's suit as a violation of the Eleventh Amendment was first made and argued by Indiana in this Court. This was in time, however. The Eleventh Amendment declares a policy and sets forth an explicit limitation on federal judicial power of such compelling force that this Court will consider the issue arising under this Amendment in this case even though urged for the first time in this Court.

For the foregoing reasons we decide that the Court of Appeals was wrong in holding that the Eleventh Amendment did not constitute a bar to that portion of the District Court decree which ordered retroactive payment of benefits found to have been wrongfully withheld. The judgment of the Court of Appeals is therefore reversed and the cause remanded for further proceedings consistent with this opinion.

MR. JUSTICE DOUGLAS, dissenting....

In *Ex parte Young,* a suit by stockholders of a railroad was brought in a federal court against state officials to enjoin the imposition of confiscatory rates on the railroad in violation of the Fourteenth Amendment. The Eleventh Amendment was interposed as a defense. The Court rejected the defense, saying that state officials with authority to enforce state laws "who threaten and are about to commence proceedings, either of a civil or criminal nature, to enforce against parties affected an unconstitutional act, violating the Federal Constitution, may be enjoined by a Federal court of equity from such action." The Court went on to say that a state official seeking to enforce in the name of a State an unconstitutional act "comes into conflict with the superior authority of that Constitution, and he is in that case stripped of his official or representative character and is subjected in his person to the consequence of his individual conduct. The state has no power to impart to him any immunity from responsibility to the supreme authority of the United States."

As the complaint in the instant case alleges violations by officials of Illinois of the Equal Protection Clause of the Fourteenth Amendment, it seems that the case is governed by *Ex parte Young* so far as injunctive relief is concerned. The main thrust of the argument is that the instant case asks for relief which if granted would affect the treasury of the State.

Most welfare decisions by federal courts have a financial impact on the States.... The welfare cases coming here have involved ultimately the financial responsibility of the State to beneficiaries claiming they were deprived of federal rights.... *Rosado v. Wyman*, 397 U.S. 397 (1970), held that under this state-federal cooperative program a State could not reduce its standard of need in conflict with the federal standard. It is true that *Rosado* did not involve retroactive payments as are involved here. But the distinction is not relevant or material because the result in every welfare case coming here is to increase or reduce the financial responsibility of the participating State. In no case when the responsibility of the State is increased to meet the lawful demand of the beneficiary, is there any levy on state funds. Whether the decree is prospective only or requires payments for the weeks or months wrongfully skipped over by the state officials, the nature of the impact on the state treasury is precisely the same....

What is asked by the instant case is minor compared to the relief granted in *Griffin v. School Board*, 377 U.S. 218 (1964). In that case we authorized entry of an order putting an end to a segregated school system. We held, *inter alia*, that "the District Court may, if necessary to prevent further racial discrimination, require the Supervisors to exercise the power that is theirs to levy taxes to raise funds adequate to reopen, operate, and maintain without racial discrimination a public school system in Prince Edward County like that operated in other counties in Virginia." ...

Yet petitioner asserts that money damages may not be awarded against state offenses, as such a judgment will expend itself on the state treasury. But we are unable to say that Illinois on entering the federal-state welfare program waived its immunity to suit for injunctions but did not waive its immunity for compensatory awards which remedy its willful defaults of obligations undertaken when it joined the cooperative venture.

It is said however, that the Eleventh Amendment is concerned, not with immunity of States from suit, but with the jurisdiction of the federal courts to entertain the suit. The Eleventh Amendment does not speak of "jurisdiction"; it withholds the "judicial power" of federal courts "to any suit in law or equity ... against one of the United States...." If that "judicial power," or "jurisdiction" if one prefers that concept, may not be exercised even in "any suit in ... equity" then *Ex parte Young* should be overruled. But there is none eager to take the step. Where a State has consented to join a federal-state cooperative project, it is realistic to conclude that the State has agreed to assume its obligations under that legislation. There is nothing in the Eleventh Amendment to suggest a difference between suits at law and suits in equity, for it treats the two without distinction. If common sense has any role to play in constitutional adjudication, once there is a waiver of immunity it must be true that it is complete so far as effective operation of the state-federal joint welfare program is concerned....

MR. JUSTICE BRENNAN, dissenting.

This suit is brought by Illinois citizens against Illinois officials. In that circumstance, Illinois may not invoke the Eleventh Amendment, since that Amendment bars only federal court suits against States by citizens of other States. Rather, the question is whether Illinois may avail itself of the nonconstitutional but ancient doctrine of sovereign immunity as a bar to respondent's claim for retroactive AABD payments. In my view Illinois may not assert sovereign immunity for the reason I expressed in dissent in *Employees v. Department of Public Health and Welfare*, 411 U.S. 279 (1973): the States surrendered that immunity in Hamilton's words, "in the plan of the Convention," that formed the Union, at least insofar as the States granted Congress specifically enumerated powers. Congressional authority to enact the Social Security Act ... is to be found in Art. I, § 8, cl. 1, one of the enumerated powers granted Congress by the States in the Constitution. I remain of the opinion that "because of its surrender, no immunity exists that can be the subject of a congressional declaration or a voluntary waiver," and thus have no occasion to inquire whether or not Congress authorized an action for AABD retroactive benefits, or whether or not Illinois voluntarily waived the immunity by its continued participation in the program against the background of precedents which sustained judgments ordering retroactive payments.

MR. JUSTICE MARSHALL, with whom MR. JUSTICE BRENNAN joins, dissenting. [omitted]

## Pennhurst State School & Hospital v. Halderman
### 465 U.S. 89 (1984)

JUSTICE POWELL delivered the opinion of the Court.

This case presents the question whether a federal court may award injunctive relief against state officials on the basis of state law.

I

This litigation, here for the second time, concerns the conditions of care at petitioner Pennhurst State School and Hospital, a Pennsylvania institution for the care of the mentally retarded....

[Respondents'] amended complaint charged that conditions at Pennhurst violated the class members' rights under the Eighth and Fourteenth Amendments; § 504 of the Rehabilitation Act of 1973; the Developmentally Disabled Assistance and Bill of Rights Act, 42 U.S.C. §§ 6001–6081; and the Pennsylvania Mental Health and Mental Retardation Act of 1966 (the "MH/MR Act"). Both damages and injunctive relief were sought.

In 1977, following a lengthy trial, the District Court rendered its decision.... [The] court's findings were undisputed: "Conditions at Pennhurst are not only dangerous, with the residents often physically abused or drugged by staff members, but also inadequate for the 'habilitation' of the retarded." ... The District Court held that these conditions violated each resident's right to "minimally adequate habilitation" under the Due Process Clause and the MH/MR Act, "freedom from harm" under the Eighth and Fourteenth Amendments, and "nondiscriminatory habilitation" under the Equal Protection Clause and § 504 of the Rehabilitation Act. After concluding that the large size of Pennhurst prevented it from providing the necessary habilitation in the least restrictive environment, the court ordered "that immediate steps be taken to remove the retarded residents from Pennhurst." Petitioners were ordered "to provide suitable community living arrangements" for the class members, ... and the court appointed a Special Master "with the power and duty to plan, organize, direct, supervise and monitor the implementation of this and any further Orders of the Court."

The Court of Appeals for the Third Circuit affirmed most of the District Court's judgment.... This Court reversed the judgment of the Court of Appeals, finding that 42 U.S.C. § 6010 did not create any substantive rights. We remanded the case to the Court of Appeals to determine if the remedial order could be supported on the basis of state law, the Constitution, or § 504 of the Rehabilitation Act. We also remanded for consideration of whether any relief was available under other provisions of the Developmentally Disabled Assistance and Bill of Rights Act....

On remand the Court of Appeals affirmed its prior judgment in its entirety. It determined that in a recent decision the Supreme Court of Pennsylvania had "spoken definitively" in holding that the [state law] MH/MR Act required the State to adopt the "least restrictive environment" approach for the care of the mentally retarded. The Court of Appeals concluded that this state statute fully supported its prior judgment, and therefore did not reach the remaining issues of federal law. It also rejected petitioners' argument that the Eleventh Amendment barred a federal court from considering this pendent state-law claim. The court noted that the Amendment did not bar a federal court from granting prospective injunctive relief against state officials on the basis of federal claims, and concluded that the same result obtained with respect to a pendent state-law claim....

We granted certiorari, and now reverse and remand.

## II

Petitioners raise three challenges to the judgment of the Court of Appeals: (i) the Eleventh Amendment prohibited the District Court from ordering state officials to conform their conduct to state law; (ii) the doctrine of comity prohibited the District Court from issuing its injunctive relief; and (iii) the District Court abused its discretion in appointing two masters to supervise the decisions of state officials in implementing state law. We need not reach the latter two issues, for we find the Eleventh Amendment challenge dispositive.

## A

Article III, § 2 of the Constitution provides that the federal judicial power extends, *inter alia*, to controversies "between a State and Citizens of another State." Relying on this language, this Court in 1793 assumed original jurisdiction over a suit brought by a citizen of South Carolina against the State of Georgia. *Chisholm v. Georgia*, 2 U.S. 419 (1793) [Note *supra.* this chapter]. The decision "created such a shock of surprise that the Eleventh Amendment was at once proposed and adopted." The Amendment provides:

> The Judicial power of the United States shall not be construed to extend to any suit in law or equity, commenced or prosecuted against one of the United States by Citizens of another State, or by Citizens or Subjects of any Foreign State.

The Amendment's language overruled the particular result in *Chisholm*, but this Court has recognized that its greater significance lies in its affirmation that the fundamental principle of sovereign immunity limits the grant of judicial authority in Art. III. Thus, in *Hans v. Louisiana*, 134 U.S. 1 (1890) [Note *supra.* this chapter], the Court held that, despite the limited terms of the Eleventh Amendment, a federal court could not entertain a suit brought by a citizen against his own State. After reviewing the constitutional debates concerning the scope of Art. III, the Court determined that federal jurisdiction over suits against unconsenting States "was not contemplated by the Constitution when establishing the judicial power of the United States." In short, the principle of sovereign immunity is a constitutional limitation on the federal judicial power established in Art. III:

> That a State may not be sued without its consent is a fundamental rule of jurisprudence having so important a bearing upon the construction of the Constitution of the United States that it has become established by repeated decisions of this court that the entire judicial power granted by the Constitution does not embrace authority to entertain a suit brought by private parties against a State without consent given: not one brought by citizens of another State, or by citizens or subjects of a foreign State, because of the Eleventh Amendment; and not even one brought by its own citizens, because of the fundamental rule of which the Amendment is but an exemplification. *Ex parte New York*, 256 U.S. 490 (1921).[8]

A sovereign's immunity may be waived, and the Court consistently has held that a State may consent to suit against it in federal court. We have insisted, however, that the State's consent be unequivocally expressed. See, e.g., *Edelman v. Jordan* (1974) [*Supra.* this chapter]. Similarly, although Congress has power with respect to the rights protected by the Fourteenth Amendment to abrogate the Eleventh Amendment immunity, see *Fitzpatrick v. Bitker*, 427 U.S. 445 (1976), we have required an unequivocal expression of congressional intent to "overturn the constitutionally guaranteed immunity of the several States." Our reluctance to infer that a State's immunity from suit in the federal courts has been negated stems from recognition of the vital role of the doctrine of sovereign immunity in our federal system.... Accordingly, in

---

8. The limitation deprives federal courts of any jurisdiction to entertain such claims, and thus may be raised at any point in a proceeding. "The Eleventh Amendment declares a policy and sets forth an explicit limitation on federal judicial power of such compelling force that this Court will consider the issue arising under this Amendment ... even though urged for the first time in this Court." *Ford Motor Co. v. Department of Treasury*, 323 U.S. 459 (1945).

deciding this case we must be guided by "the principles of federalism that inform Eleventh Amendment doctrine."

## B

This Court's decisions thus establish that "an unconsenting State is immune from suits brought in federal courts by her own citizens as well as by citizens of another state." There may be a question, however, whether a particular suit in fact is a suit against a State. It is clear, of course, that in the absence of consent a suit in which the State or one of its agencies or departments is named as the defendant is proscribed by the Eleventh Amendment. This jurisdictional bar applies regardless of the nature of the relief sought.

When the suit is brought only against state officials, a question arises as to whether that suit is a suit against the State itself. Although prior decisions of this Court have not been entirely consistent on this issue, certain principles are well established. The Eleventh Amendment bars a suit against state officials when "the state is the real, substantial party in interest." Thus, "the general rule is that relief sought nominally against an officer is in fact against the sovereign if the decree would operate against the latter." And, as when the State itself is named as the defendant, a suit against state officials that is in fact a suit against a State is barred regardless of whether it seeks damages or injunctive relief.

The Court has recognized an important exception to this general rule: a suit challenging the constitutionality of a state official's action is not one against the State. This was the holding in *Ex parte Young*, in which a federal court enjoined the Attorney General of the State of Minnesota from bringing suit to enforce a state statute that allegedly violated the Fourteenth Amendment. This Court held that the Eleventh Amendment did not prohibit issuance of this injunction. The theory of the case was that an unconstitutional enactment is "void" and therefore does not "impart to [the officer] any immunity from responsibility to the supreme authority of the United States." Since the State could not authorize the action, the officer was "stripped of his official or representative character and [was] subjected to the consequences of his official conduct."

While the rule permitting suits alleging conduct contrary to "the supreme authority of the United States" has survived, the theory of *Young* has not been provided an expansive interpretation. Thus, in *Edelman v. Jordan*, the Court emphasized that the Eleventh Amendment bars some forms of injunctive relief against state officials for violation of federal law. In particular, *Edelman* held that when a plaintiff sues a state official alleging a violation of federal law, the federal court may award an injunction that governs the official's future conduct, but not one that awards retroactive monetary relief. Under the theory of *Young*, such a suit would not be one against the State since the federal-law allegation would strip the state officer of his official authority. Nevertheless, retroactive relief was barred by the Eleventh Amendment.

## III

With these principles in mind, we now turn to the question whether the claim that petitioners violated state law in carrying out their official duties at Pennhurst is one against the State and therefore barred by the Eleventh Amendment. Respondents advance two principal arguments in support of the judgment below. First, they contend that under the doctrine of *Edelman v. Jordan*, the suit is not against the State because the courts below ordered only prospective injunctive relief. Second, they assert that the state-law claim properly was decided under the doctrine of pendent jurisdiction. Respondents rely on decisions of this Court awarding relief against state officials on the basis of a pendent state-law claim.

### A

We first address the contention that respondents' state-law claim is not barred by the Eleventh Amendment because it seeks only prospective relief as defined in *Edelman v. Jordan*. The Court of Appeals held that if the judgment below rested on federal law, it could be entered against petitioner state officials under the doctrine established in *Edelman* and *Young* even though the prospective financial burden was substantial and ongoing. The court assumed, and respondents assert, that this reasoning applies as well when the official acts in violation of state law. This argument misconstrues the basis of the doctrine established in *Young* and *Edelman*.

As discussed above, the injunction in *Young* was justified, notwithstanding the obvious impact on the State itself, on the view that sovereign immunity does not apply because an official who acts unconstitutionally is "stripped of his official or representative character." This rationale, of course, created the "well-recognized irony" that an official's unconstitutional conduct constitutes state action under the Fourteenth Amendment but not the Eleventh Amendment. Nonetheless, the *Young* doctrine has been accepted as necessary to permit the federal courts to vindicate federal rights and hold state officials responsible to "the supreme authority of the United States." As JUSTICE BRENNAN has observed, "*Ex parte Young* was the culmination of efforts by this Court to harmonize the principles of the Eleventh Amendment with the effective supremacy of rights and powers secured elsewhere in the Constitution." Our decisions repeatedly have emphasized that the *Young* doctrine rests on the need to promote the vindication of federal rights.

The Court also has recognized, however, that the need to promote the supremacy of federal law must be accommodated to the constitutional immunity of the States. This is the significance of *Edelman v. Jordan*. We recognized that the prospective relief authorized by *Young* "has permitted the Civil War Amendments to the Constitution to serve as a sword, rather than merely a shield, for those whom they were designed to protect." But we declined to extend the fiction of *Young* to encompass retroactive relief, for to do so would effectively eliminate the constitutional immunity of the States. Accordingly, we concluded that although the difference between permissible and impermissible relief "will not in many instances be that between day and night," an award of retroactive relief necessarily "falls afoul of the Eleventh Amendment if that basic constitutional provision is to be conceived of as having any present force." In sum, *Edelman's* distinction between prospective and retroactive relief fulfills the underlying purpose of *Ex parte Young* while at the same time preserving to an important degree the constitutional immunity of the States.

This need to reconcile competing interests is wholly absent, however, when a plaintiff alleges that a state official has violated state law. In such a case the entire basis for the doctrine of *Young* and *Edelman* disappears. A federal court's grant of relief against state officials on the basis of state law, whether prospective or retroactive, does not vindicate the supreme authority of federal law. On the contrary, it is difficult to think of a greater intrusion on state sovereignty than when a federal court instructs state officials on how to conform their conduct to state law. Such a result conflicts directly with the principles of federalism that underlie the Eleventh Amendment. We conclude that *Young* and *Edelman* are inapplicable in a suit against state officials on the basis of state law.

B

The contrary view of JUSTICE STEVENS' dissent rests on fiction, is wrong on the law, and, most important, would emasculate the Eleventh Amendment. Under his view, an allegation that official conduct is contrary to a state statute would suffice to override the State's protection under that Amendment. The theory is that such conduct is contrary to the official's "instructions," and thus *ultra vires* his authority. Accordingly, official action based on a reasonable interpretation of any statute might, if the interpretation turned out to be erroneous, provide the basis for injunctive relief against the actors in their official capacities. In this case, where officials of a major state department, clearly acting within the scope of their authority, were found not to have improved conditions in a state institution adequately under state law, the dissent's result would be that the State itself has forfeited its constitutionally provided immunity.

The theory is out of touch with reality. The dissent's underlying view that the named defendants here were acting beyond and contrary to their authority cannot be reconciled with reality — or with the record. The District Court in this case held that the individual defendants "acted in the utmost good faith ... *within the sphere of their official responsibilities.*" ... The named defendants had nothing to gain personally from their conduct.... As a result, all the relief ordered by the courts below was institutional and official in character. To the extent there was a violation of state law in this case, it is a case of the State itself not fulfilling its legislative promises....

[While] there is language in the early cases that advances the authority-stripping theory advocated by the dissent, this theory had never been pressed as far as JUSTICE STEVENS would do in this case. And when the expansive approach of the dissent was advanced, this Court plainly and explicitly rejected it. In *Larson v. Domestic & Foreign Commerce Corp.*, 337 U.S. 682 (1949), the Court was faced with the argument that an allegation that a government official committed a tort sufficed to distinguish the official from the sovereign. Therefore, the argument went, a suit for an injunction to remedy the injury would not be against the sovereign. The Court rejected the argument, noting that it would make the doctrine of sovereign immunity superfluous. A plaintiff would need only to "claim an invasion of his legal rights" in order to override sovereign immunity. In the Court's view, the argument "confused the doctrine of sovereign immunity with the requirement that a plaintiff state a cause of action." The dissent's theory suffers a like confusion. Under the dissent's view, a plaintiff would need only to claim a denial of rights protected or provided by statute in order to override sovereign immunity. Except in rare cases it would make the constitutional doctrine of sovereign immunity a nullity....

... Under the dissent's view of the *ultra vires* doctrine, the Eleventh Amendment would have force only in the rare case in which a plaintiff foolishly attempts to sue the State in its own name, or where he cannot produce some state statute that has been violated to his asserted injury. Thus, the *ultra vires* doctrine, a narrow and questionable exception, would swallow the general rule that a suit is against the State if the relief will run against it. That result gives the dissent no pause presumably because of its view that the Eleventh Amendment and sovereign immunity "undoubtedly run counter to modern democratic notions of the moral responsibility of the State." This argument has not been adopted by this Court. Moreover, the argument substantially misses the point with respect to Eleventh Amendment sovereign immunity. As JUSTICE MARSHALL has observed, the Eleventh Amendment's restriction on the federal judicial power is based in large part on "the problems of federalism inherent in making one sovereign appear against its will in the courts of the other." *Employees v. Missouri Public Health Dept.*, 411 U.S. 279 (1973) (MARSHALL, J., concurring in the result). The dissent totally rejects the Eleventh Amendment's basis in federalism....

D

Respondents urge that application of the Eleventh Amendment to pendent state-law claims will have a disruptive effect on litigation against state officials. They argue that the "considerations of judicial economy, convenience, and fairness to litigants" that underlie pendent jurisdiction, counsel against a result that may cause litigants to split causes of action between state and federal courts. They also contend that the policy of avoiding unnecessary constitutional decisions will be contravened if plaintiffs choose to forgo their state-law claims and sue only in federal court or, alternatively, that the policy of *Ex parte Young* will be hindered if plaintiffs choose to forgo their right to a federal forum and bring all of their claims in state court.

It may be that applying the Eleventh Amendment to pendent claims results in federal claims being brought in state court, or in bifurcation of claims. That is not uncommon in this area. Under *Edelman v. Jordan*, a suit against state officials for retroactive monetary relief, whether based on federal or state law, must be brought in state court. Challenges to the validity of state tax systems under 42 U.S.C. § 1983 also must be brought in state court. Under the abstention doctrine, unclear issues of state law commonly are split off and referred to the state courts.

In any case, the answer to respondents' assertions is that such considerations of policy cannot override the constitutional limitation on the authority of the federal judiciary to adjudicate suits against a State. That a litigant's choice of forum is reduced "has long been understood to be a part of the tension inherent in our system of federalism." ...

... The judgment of the Court of Appeals is reversed, and the case remanded for further proceedings consistent with this opinion....

JUSTICE BRENNAN, dissenting. [omitted]

JUSTICE STEVENS, with whom JUSTICE BRENNAN, JUSTICE MARSHALL, and JUSTICE BLACKMUN join, dissenting....

### III

On its face, the Eleventh Amendment applies only to suits against a State brought by citizens of other States and foreign nations. This textual limitation upon the scope of the states' immunity from suit in federal court was set aside in *Hans v. Louisiana*. *Hans* was a suit against the State of Louisiana, brought by a citizen of Louisiana seeking to recover interest on the state's bonds. The Court stated that some of the arguments favoring sovereign immunity for the States made during the process of the Amendment's ratification had become a part of the judicial scheme created by the Constitution. As a result, the Court concluded that the Constitution prohibited a suit by a citizen against his or her own state. When called upon to elaborate in *Monaco v. Mississippi*, 292 U.S. 313 (1934), the Court explained that the Eleventh Amendment did more than simply prohibit suits brought by citizens of one State against another State. Rather, it exemplified the broader and more ancient doctrine of sovereign immunity, which operates to bar a suit brought by a citizen against his own State without its consent.

The Court has subsequently adhered to this interpretation.... Thus, under our cases it is the doctrine of sovereign immunity, rather than the text of the Amendment itself, which is critical to the analysis of any Eleventh Amendment problem.

The doctrine of sovereign immunity developed in England, where it was thought that the King could not be sued. However, common law courts, in applying the doctrine, traditionally distinguished between the King and his agents, on the theory that the King would never authorize unlawful conduct, and that therefore the unlawful acts of the King's officers ought not to be treated as acts of the sovereign.... In the 19th century this view was taken by the court to be so well settled as to not require the citation of authority.

It was only natural, then, that this Court, in applying the principles of sovereign immunity, recognized the distinction between a suit against a State and one against its officer. For example, while the Court did inquire as to whether a suit was "in essence" against the sovereign, it soon became settled law that the Eleventh Amendment did not bar suits against state officials in their official capacities challenging unconstitutional conduct. This rule was reconciled with sovereign immunity principles by use of the traditional rule that an action against an agent of the sovereign who had acted unlawfully was not considered to be against the sovereign. When an official acts pursuant to an unconstitutional statute, the Court reasoned, the absence of valid authority leaves the official *ultra vires* his authority, and thus a private actor stripped of his status as a representative of the sovereign....

The majority states that the holding of *Ex parte Young* is limited to cases in which relief is provided on the basis of federal law, and that it rests entirely on the need to protect the supremacy of federal law. That position overlooks the foundation of the rule of *Young* [and other] predecessors.

The *Young* Court distinguished between the State and its attorney general because the latter, in violating the Constitution, had engaged in conduct the sovereign could not authorize. The pivotal consideration was not that the conduct violated federal law, since nothing in the jurisprudence of the Eleventh Amendment permits a suit against a sovereign merely because federal law is at issue....

The pivotal consideration in *Young* was that it was not conduct of the sovereign that was at issue.[29] The rule that unlawful acts of an officer should not be attributed to the sovereign has deep roots in the history of sovereign immunity and makes *Young* reconcilable with the principles of sovereign immunity found in the Eleventh Amendment, rather than merely an unprincipled accommodation between federal and state interests that ignores the principles contained in the Eleventh Amendment.

This rule plainly applies to conduct of state officers in violation of state law.... Since a state officer's conduct in violation of state law is certainly no less illegal than his violation of federal law, in either case the official, by committing an illegal act, is "stripped of his official or representative character." ...

... In the final analysis the distinction between the State and its officers, realistic or not, is one firmly embedded in the doctrine of sovereign immunity. It is that doctrine and not any theory of federal supremacy which the Framers placed in the Eleventh Amendment and which this Court therefore has a duty to respect.

It follows that the basis for the *Young* rule is present when the officer sued has violated the law of the sovereign; in all such cases the conduct is of a type that would not be permitted by the sovereign and hence is not attributable to the sovereign under traditional sovereign immunity principles.... The majority's position that the Eleventh Amendment does not permit federal courts to enjoin conduct that the sovereign State itself seeks to prohibit thus is inconsistent with both the doctrine of sovereign immunity and the underlying respect for the integrity of State policy which the Eleventh Amendment protects. The issuance of injunctive relief which enforces state laws and policies, if anything, enhances federal courts' respect for the sovereign prerogatives of the States. The majority's approach, which requires federal courts to ignore questions of state law and to rest their decisions on federal bases, will create more rather than less friction between the States and the federal judiciary.

Moreover, the majority's rule has nothing to do with the basic reason the Eleventh Amendment was added to the Constitution. There is general agreement that the

---

29. The distinction between the sovereign and its agents not only explains why the rationale of *Ex parte Young* and its predecessors is consistent with established sovereign immunity doctrine, but it also explains the critical difference between actions for injunctive relief and actions for damages recognized in *Edelman v. Jordan*. Since the damages remedy sought in that case would have required payment by the State, it could not be said that the action ran only against the agents of the State. Therefore, while the agents' unlawful conduct was considered *ultra vires* vires and hence could be enjoined, a remedy which did run against the sovereign and not merely its agent could not fit within the *ultra vires* vires doctrine and hence was impermissible. If damages are not sought from the State and the relief will run only against the state official, damages are a permissible remedy under the Eleventh Amendment.

Amendment was passed because the States were fearful that federal courts would force them to pay their Revolutionary War debts, leading to their financial ruin. Entertaining a suit for injunctive relief based on state law implicates none of the concerns of the Framers. Since only injunctive relief is sought there is no threat to the state treasury of the type that concerned the Framers, and if the State wishes to avoid the federal injunction, it can easily do so simply by changing its law. The possibility of States left helpless in the face of disruptive federal decrees which led to the passage of the Eleventh Amendment simply is not presented by this case. Indeed, the Framers no doubt would have preferred federal courts to base their decisions on state law, which the State is then free to reexamine, rather than forcing courts to decide cases on federal grounds, leaving the litigation beyond state control....

In sum, a century and a half of this Court's Eleventh Amendment jurisprudence has established the following. A suit alleging that the official had acted within his authority but in a manner contrary to state statutes was not barred because the Eleventh Amendment prohibits suits against States; it does not bar suits against state officials for actions not permitted by the State under its own law. The sovereign could not and would not authorize its officers to violate its own law; hence an action against a state officer seeking redress for conduct not permitted by state law is a suit against the officer, not the sovereign. *Ex parte Young* concluded in as explicit a fashion as possible that unconstitutional action by state officials is not action by the State even if it purports to be authorized by state law, *because the federal Constitution strikes down the state law shield....* These precedents make clear that there is no foundation for the contention that the majority embraces—that *Ex parte Young* authorizes injunctive relief against state officials only on the basis of federal law. To the contrary, *Young* is as clear as a bell: the Eleventh Amendment does not apply where there is no state-law shield. That simple principle should control this case....

V

One basic fact underlies this case: far from immunizing petitioners' conduct, the State of Pennsylvania prohibited it. Respondents do not complain about the conduct of the State of Pennsylvania—it is Pennsylvania's commands which they seek to enforce. Respondents seek only to have Pennhurst run the way Pennsylvania envisioned that it be run. Until today, the Court understood that the Eleventh Amendment does not shield the conduct of state officers which has been prohibited by their sovereign....

## *Note: Further Limitations on* Young *Relief*

1. Later in this section there appears an excerpt from *Seminole Tribe of Florida v. Florida*, 517 U.S. 44 (1996). *Seminole Tribe* is mainly known for its holding (qualified in a later case) that Congress cannot use its Article I powers to abrogate state sovereign immunity. However, after so holding, the five-Justice majority in that case also considered whether the Native Tribe-plaintiff could maintain its suit on the theory of *Ex parte Young*. (Despite the title of the case, a *Young* suit was at least theoretically possible because the Tribe named the Governor of Florida as one of the defendants.)

*Seminole Tribe* involved the Indian Gaming Regulatory Act (IGRA), a federal statute designed to facilitate resolution of disputes between Native tribes and the states in which their reservations are located, arising out of a tribe's wish to conduct gaming operations. The IGRA authorized tribes to sue in federal court when they believed that the state was not negotiating in good faith. In turn, the statute set forth a sequential set of remedies that the judge could order against the state: for example, among other remedies the judge could order the two sides to reach an agreement within 60 days, and, failing such an agreement, could order the two sides to submit their compromise proposals to a mediator, who would choose between them.

2. As set forth in the excerpt from this case presented later in this section, the Court first concluded that the Indian Commerce Clause, the Article I authority supporting the IGRA, did not authorize Congress's abrogation of state sovereign immunity. The tribe then argued that its suit could be allowed as a *Young*-type suit against the Governor. The Court, speaking through Chief Justice Rehnquist, rejected that argument. Referring to the statute's provisions of a particular set of remedies the trial judge could order, the Chief Justice observed that the IGRA contained "a carefully crafted and intricate remedial scheme." He interpreted that scheme as reflecting a congressional intent to limit the types of remedies available against state defendants in these types of lawsuits. Therefore, Congress's provision of that remedial scheme operated as implicit congressional disallowance of a *Young* suit, which might feature other remedies, such as a simple injunction against the Governor.

But what about the fact that the Court had earlier concluded that the statute's abrogation of state sovereign immunity was invalid? If the IGRA's authorization of lawsuits against states was unconstitutional, how could that same authorization nevertheless serve to defeat the availability of a *Young* claim? Chief Justice Rehnquist wrote the following response:

> Here, of course, we have found that Congress does not have authority under the Constitution to make the State suable in federal court under [the IGRA]. Nevertheless, the fact that Congress chose to impose upon the State a liability that is significantly more limited than would be the liability imposed upon the state officer under *Ex parte Young* strongly suggests that Congress had no wish to create the latter under [the IGRA]. Nor are we free to rewrite the statutory scheme in order to approximate what we think Congress might have wanted had it known that [the IGRA's authorization of lawsuits] was beyond its authority.

Justice Souter, writing for four dissenters, disagreed with the Court's analysis on both the abrogation and *Young* issues. Addressing the *Young* issue, he argued that the Court's analysis would lead to "revolutionary" consequences. Among other points, he observed that habeas corpus petitions—which are brought against the warden of the prison where the prisoner is incarcerated—are based on *Young*, yet he noted that Congress has prescribed a number of procedural and remedial limitations on those suits. Justice Souter argued that the IGRA's limits on the relief a court could provide should be analogized to those statutory limits on the habeas remedy, with the result that in both cases Congress should be seen as modifying the remedies otherwise available under *Young*, rather than simply expressing an intent to preclude *Young* suits entirely.

3. In *Idaho v. Coeur d'Alene Tribe*, 521 U.S. 261 (1997), the Court erected yet another limit on *Young* relief. *Coeur d'Alene* again featured a lawsuit by a Native tribe against a state, this time for violating a federal treaty that the tribe alleged gave it control over the land that lay under rivers and lakes found on its reservation. As in *Seminole Tribe*, the tribe sued both the state and, relevant for our purposes, state officials on a *Young* theory.

Five justices rejected the *Young*-based suit against those officials. Writing the lead opinion for only himself and Chief Justice Rehnquist, Justice Kennedy argued that *Young* properly applied only when either "there is no state forum to vindicate federal interests, thereby placing upon Article III courts the special obligation to ensure the supremacy of federal statutory and constitutional law," or "when the case calls for the interpretation of federal law." But, according to Justice Kennedy, even when one of these situations was present it was still appropriate to consider "the real affront to a State of allowing a suit to proceed." He described this case as "unusual in that the Tribe's suit is the functional equivalent of a quiet title action, which implicates special sovereignty interests." In his view, that factor justified denying *Young* relief, and requiring the tribe to litigate its claim in the state's own courts, which he said "are open to hear and determine the case."

Justice O'Connor, joined by Justices Scalia and Thomas, concurred in the result, but not in Justice Kennedy's reasoning. She rejected what she described as Justice Kennedy's requirement of a "case-by-case analysis of a number of concerns" when deciding whether a *Young* suit was appropriate, describing that approach as a "vague balancing test" that "unnecessarily recharacterized and narrowed much of our *Young* jurisprudence." Nevertheless, she agreed that the tribe's suit could not go forward in federal court, as the tribe's claim to control over the disputed lands was effectively a suit against the state, and not a state official as *Young* requires.

Justice Souter, writing for himself and Justices Stevens, Ginsburg, and Breyer, dissented. He characterized the tribe's suit as "falling squarely within the *Young* doctrine." In response to the claim that the suit was the "functional equivalent" of a quiet title suit against the state, he argued that the relief in *Young* itself—a federal court order prohibiting the state Attorney General from enforcing a state law regulating railroad rates—was indistinguishable from the relief the tribe sought in terms of its impact on the state's sovereign interests.

## *Note: The Meaning of* Ex parte Young

Running through the justices' debates in the preceding cases is a fundamental disagreement about the foundation for *Ex parte Young*. The justices calling for a limited role for *Young*-based suits often imply (or, as in *Pennhurst*, state explicitly) that *Young* was simply a practical accommodation of the competing imperatives of state sovereign immunity and the need to ensure that litigants are able to vindicate federal rights against state government violators of those rights. By contrast, the justices calling for a broader role for *Young* often argue that the *Young* "stripping" idea is a principled legal theory, which justifies a broad variety of suits as long as those suits are brought against state officials rather than the state itself. Which argument makes more sense to you?

Regardless of the merits of this debate, the cases discussed above demonstrate that a majority of the Court is uneasy with a broad reading of *Young*. To be sure, that majority is a slim one: *Pennhurst*, *Seminole Tribe*, and *Coeur d'Alene* were all 5–4 decisions. The law in this area is likely to remain unsettled, and to be influenced by future appointments to the Court.

## 2. State "Waiver" of Sovereign Immunity

Another way in which states can be sued in federal court, despite the Eleventh Amendment, is when a state consents to such a suit. Explicit consent presents an easy case: if the point of the Amendment is simply to protect the dignity of states as sovereignties in their own right, it surely does that dignity no harm when a state consents to be sued in federal court. A harder case is presented when a plaintiff argues that the state *implicitly* consented to such a lawsuit. The following cases illustrate the idea of implicit waiver, and the Court's disagreement about where it can be found.

### Fitzpatrick v. Bitzer
427 U.S. 445 (1976)

MR. JUSTICE REHNQUIST delivered the opinion of the Court.

In the 1972 Amendments to Title VII of the Civil Rights Act of 1964, Congress, acting under § 5 of the Fourteenth Amendment, authorized federal courts to award money damages in favor of a private individual against a state government found to have subjected that person to employment discrimination on the basis of "race, color, religion, sex, or national origin." The principal question presented by these cases is whether, as against the shield of sovereign immunity afforded the State by the Eleventh Amendment, Congress has the power to authorize Federal courts to enter such an award against the State as a means of enforcing the substantive guarantees of the Fourteenth Amendment. The Court of Appeals for the Second Circuit held that the effect of our decision in *Edelman v. Jordan* (1974) [*Supra.* this chapter] was to foreclose Congress' power. We granted certiorari to resolve this important constitutional question. We reverse.

I

Petitioners ... sued in the United States District Court for the District of Connecticut on behalf of all present and retired male employees of the State of Connecticut. Their amended complaint asserted, *inter alia*, that certain provisions in the State's statutory retirement benefit plan discriminated against them because of their sex, and therefore contravened Title VII of the 1964 Act. Title VII, which originally did not include state and local governments, had in the interim been amended to bring the States within its purview.

The District Court held that the Connecticut State Employees Retirement Act violated Title VII's prohibition against sex-based employment discrimination. It entered prospective injunctive relief in petitioners' favor against respondent state officials. Petitioners also sought an award of retroactive retirement benefits as compensation for losses caused by the State's discrimination, as well as "a reasonable attorney's fee as part of the costs." But the District Court held that both would constitute recovery of money damages from the State's treasury, and were therefore precluded by the Eleventh Amendment and by this Court's decision in *Edelman v. Jordan*.

On petitioners' appeal, the Court of Appeals affirmed in part and reversed in part.... The petition filed here by the state employees contends that Congress does possess the constitutional power under § 5 of the Fourteenth Amendment to authorize their Title VII damages action against the State. The state officials' cross-petition argues that under *Edelman* the Eleventh Amendment bars any award of attorneys' fees here because it would be paid out of the state treasury.

II

In *Edelman* this Court held that monetary relief awarded by the District Court to welfare plaintiffs, by reason of wrongful denial of benefits which had occurred previous to the entry of the District Court's determination of their wrongfulness, violated the Eleventh Amendment. Such an award was found to be indistinguishable from a monetary award against the State itself which had been prohibited in *Ford Motor Co. v. Department of Treasury*, 323 U.S. 459 (1945). It was therefore controlled by that case rather than by *Ex parte Young*, which permitted suits against state officials to obtain prospective relief against violations of the Fourteenth Amendment.

*Edelman* went on to hold that the plaintiffs in that case could not avail themselves of the doctrine of waiver ... because the necessary predicate for that doctrine was congressional intent to abrogate the immunity conferred by the Eleventh Amendment. We concluded that none of the statutes relied upon by plaintiffs in *Edelman* contained any authorization by Congress to join a State as defendant.... Our analysis begins where *Edelman* ended, for in this Title VII case the "threshold fact of congressional authorization" to sue the State as employer is clearly present.... [Here], the Eleventh Amendment defense is asserted in the context of legislation passed pursuant to Congress' authority under § 5 of the Fourteenth Amendment.

As ratified by the States after the Civil War, that Amendment quite clearly contemplates limitations on their authority. In relevant part, it provides:

> Section 1.... No State shall make or enforce any law which shall abridge the privileges or immunities of citizens of the United States; nor shall any State deprive any person of life, liberty, or property, without due process of law; nor deny to any person within its jurisdiction the equal protection of the laws....

Section 5. The Congress shall have power to enforce by appropriate legislation, the provisions of this article.

The substantive provisions are by express terms directed at the States. Impressed upon them by those provisions are duties with respect to their treatment of private individuals. Standing behind the imperatives is Congress' power to "enforce" them "by appropriate legislation." ...

... [We] think that the Eleventh Amendment, and the principle of state sovereignty which it embodies, see *Hans v. Louisiana*, 134 U.S. 1 (1890) [Note *supra.* this chapter], are necessarily limited by the enforcement provisions of § 5 of the Fourteenth Amendment. In that section Congress is expressly granted authority to enforce "by appropriate legislation" the substantive provisions of the Fourteenth Amendment, which themselves embody significant limitations on state authority. When Congress acts pursuant to § 5, not only is it exercising legislative authority that is plenary within the terms of the constitutional grant, it is exercising that authority under one section of a constitutional Amendment whose other sections by their own terms embody limitations on state authority. We think that Congress may, in determining what is "appropriate legislation" for the purpose of enforcing the provisions of the Fourteenth Amendment, provide for private suits against States or state officials which are constitutionally impermissible in other contexts....

BRENNAN, J., concurring in the judgment. [omitted]

STEVENS, J., concurring in the judgment. [omitted]

## *Note:* Pennsylvania v. Union Gas *and Congress's Article I Authority to Abrogate State Sovereign Immunity*

1. In *Pennsylvania v. Union Gas*, 491 U.S. 1 (1989), the Court considered whether Congress's Article I powers, including its power to regulate interstate commerce, authorized it to abrogate state sovereign immunity, as *Fitzpatrick* had decided with regard to Congress's powers to enforce the Fourteenth Amendment. By a 5–4 vote, the Court held that it did. However, the Court majority was splintered.

> Writing for a plurality of four Justices, Justice Brennan analogized Congress's Article I powers—and in particular its power over interstate commerce—to its Fourteenth Amendment enforcement power. He argued that both powers represented a diminution of state power in favor of congressional power. He noted that both the Fourteenth Amendment and the Interstate Commerce Clause granted power to Congress at the expense of the states: the former by prohibiting states from violating civil rights and granting Congress the power to enforce that prohibition, and the latter by granting to Congress an exclusive power to regulate interstate commerce. (*Gibbons v. Ogden*, excerpted in Chapter 4, suggested the exclusivity of federal power; Chapter 5 explained how this power developed under the dormant Commerce Clause doctrine.) While the Fourteenth Amendment accomplished this power shift in two steps (with Section 1 prohibiting states from violating due process

and equal protection rights, and Section 5 granting Congress the power to enforce those prohibitions) and the Interstate Commerce Clause did so only in one (the Article I, Section 8 grant of the commerce power to Congress), Justice Brennan argued that this distinction was irrelevant.

2. Justice Scalia, writing for four dissenters, took issue with Justice Brennan's analysis. He distinguished *Fitzpatrick* on the ground that the Fourteenth Amendment came after the Eleventh, and thus was best understood as a limitation on the Eleventh Amendment's sovereign immunity rule.

For his part, Justice Brennan attempted to turn Justice Scalia's chronological argument against him. Justice Brennan noted that the text of the Eleventh Amendment does not refer to a state's immunity from lawsuits against citizens of its own state; rather, it speaks to immunity from suits "by Citizens of another State." He noted that *Hans v. Louisiana*, 134 U.S. 1 (1890) (Note *supra.* this chapter) held that the Eleventh Amendment codified the pre-existing doctrine of sovereign immunity that had always existed. Thus, Justice Brennan concluded, Justice Scalia had his chronology backward. According to Justice Brennan, what came first was the pre-existing doctrine of sovereign immunity, which in turn was limited by Article I's grant of enumerated legislative powers to Congress. Thus, he concluded, Justice Scalia's chronological argument actually cut in favor of the majority's result.

3. Justice White provided the crucial fifth vote for interpreting the Commerce Clause as authorizing Congress to abrogate state sovereign immunity. But he concurred separately, and explicitly distanced himself from the plurality's reasoning. His entire statement on the Eleventh Amendment issue is as follows: "I agree with the conclusion reached by Justice Brennan ... that Congress has the authority under Article I to abrogate the Eleventh Amendment immunity of the States, although I do not agree with much of his reasoning." Thus, the result of *Union Gas* was in favor of congressional power, although a majority of the Court was on record as disagreeing with at least "much" of the reasoning in Justice Brennan's opinion. This disarray opened the door for the Court's reconsideration of *Union Gas*, seven years later.

## Seminole Tribe of Florida v. Florida

### 517 U.S. 44 (1996)

CHIEF JUSTICE REHNQUIST delivered the opinion of the Court.

The Indian Gaming Regulatory Act provides that an Indian tribe may conduct certain gaming activities only in conformance with a valid compact between the tribe and the State in which the gaming activities are located. The Act, passed by Congress under the Indian Commerce Clause, U.S. Const., Art. I, §8, cl. 3, imposes upon the States a duty to negotiate in good faith with an Indian tribe toward the formation of a compact, §2710(d)(3)(A), and authorizes a tribe to bring suit in federal court against a State in order to compel performance of that duty, §2710(d)(7). We hold that notwithstanding Congress' clear intent to abrogate the States' sovereign immunity, the Indian Commerce Clause does not grant Congress that power, and therefore

§ 2710(d)(7) cannot grant jurisdiction over a State that does not consent to be sued. We further hold that the doctrine of *Ex parte Young*, 209 U.S. 123 (1908), may not be used to enforce § 2710(d)(3) against a state official.

I

Congress passed the Indian Gaming Regulatory Act in 1988 in order to provide a statutory basis for the operation and regulation of gaming by Indian tribes. The Act divides gaming on Indian lands into three classes—I, II, and III—and provides a different regulatory scheme for each class. Class III gaming—the type with which we are here concerned—[is] lawful only where it is: ... (3) "conducted in conformance with a Tribal-State compact entered into by the Indian tribe and the State under paragraph (3) that is in effect." § 2710(d)(1).

The "paragraph (3)" to which the last prerequisite of § 2710(d)(1) refers is § 2710(d)(3), which describes the permissible scope of a Tribal-State compact.... § 2710(d)(3) describes the process by which a State and an Indian tribe begin negotiations toward a Tribal-State compact:

(A) Any Indian tribe having jurisdiction over the Indian lands upon which a class III gaming activity is being conducted, or is to be conducted, shall request the State in which such lands are located to enter into negotiations for the purpose of entering into a Tribal-State compact governing the conduct of gaming activities. Upon receiving such a request, the State shall negotiate with the Indian tribe in good faith to enter into such a compact.

The State's obligation to "negotiate with the Indian tribe in good faith," is made judicially enforceable by §§ 2710(d)(7)(A)(i) and (B)(i):

(A) The United States district courts shall have jurisdiction over—

(i) any cause of action initiated by an Indian tribe arising from the failure of a State to enter into negotiations with the Indian tribe for the purpose of entering into a Tribal-State compact under paragraph (3) or to conduct such negotiations in good faith....

(B)(i) An Indian tribe may initiate a cause of action described in subparagraph (A)(i) only after the close of the 180-day period beginning on the date on which the Indian tribe requested the State to enter into negotiations under paragraph (3)(A).

Sections 2710(d)(7)(B)(ii)–(vii) describe an elaborate remedial scheme designed to ensure the formation of a Tribal-State compact. A tribe that brings an action under § 2710(d)(7)(A)(i) must show that no Tribal-State compact has been entered and that the State failed to respond in good faith to the tribe's request to negotiate; at that point, the burden then shifts to the State to prove that it did in fact negotiate in good faith. § 2710(d)(7)(B)(ii). If the district court concludes that the State has failed to negotiate in good faith toward the formation of a Tribal-State compact, then it "shall order the State and Indian tribe to conclude such a compact within a 60-day period." § 2710(d)(7)(B)(iii). If no compact has been concluded 60 days after the court's order, then "the Indian tribe and the State shall each submit to a mediator appointed by the court a proposed compact that represents their last best offer for a compact." § 2710(d)(7)(B)(iv). The mediator chooses from between the two proposed compacts the one "which best comports with the terms of [the Act] ..." and submits it to the State and the Indian tribe, § 2710(d)(7)(B)(v). If the State consents to the proposed compact within 60 days of its submission by the mediator, then the proposed compact is "treated as a Tribal-State compact entered into under paragraph (3)." § 2710(d)(7)(B)(vi). If, however, the State does not consent within that 60-day period, then the Act provides that the mediator "shall notify the Secretary [of the Interior]" and that the Secretary "shall prescribe ... procedures ... under which class III gaming may be conducted on the Indian lands over which the Indian tribe has jurisdiction." § 2710(d)(7)(B)(vii).

In September 1991, the Seminole Tribe of Indians, petitioner, sued the State of Florida and its Governor, Lawton Chiles, respondents. Invoking jurisdiction under 25 U.S.C. § 2710(d)(7)(A), as well as 28 U.S.C. §§ 1331 and 1362, petitioner alleged that respondents had "refused to enter into any negotiation for inclusion of [certain gaming activities] in a tribal-state compact," thereby violating the "requirement of good faith negotiation" contained in § 2710(d)(3). Respondents moved to dismiss the complaint, arguing that the suit violated the State's sovereign immunity from suit in federal court. The District Court denied respondents' motion and the respondents took an interlocutory appeal of that decision.

The Court of Appeals for the Eleventh Circuit reversed the decision of the District Court, holding that the Eleventh Amendment barred petitioner's suit against respondents. The court agreed with the District Court that Congress in § 2710(d)(7) intended to abrogate the States' sovereign immunity, and also agreed that the Act had been passed pursuant to Congress' power under the Indian Commerce Clause, U.S. Const., Art. I, § 8, cl. 3. The court disagreed with the District Court, however, that the Indian Commerce Clause grants Congress the power to abrogate a State's Eleventh Amendment immunity from suit, and concluded therefore that it had no jurisdiction over petitioner's suit against Florida. The court further held that *Ex parte Young*, 209 U.S. 123 (1908) [Note *supra.* this chapter], does not permit an Indian tribe to force good faith negotiations by suing the Governor of a State. Finding that it lacked subject-matter jurisdiction, the Eleventh Circuit remanded to the District Court with directions to dismiss petitioner's suit.

Petitioner sought our review of the Eleventh Circuit's decision, and we granted certiorari in order to consider two questions: (1) Does the Eleventh Amendment prevent Congress from authorizing suits by Indian tribes against States for prospective injunctive relief to enforce legislation enacted pursuant to the Indian Commerce Clause?; and (2) Does the doctrine of *Ex parte Young* permit suits against a State's governor for prospective injunctive relief to enforce the good faith bargaining requirement of the Act? We answer the first question in the affirmative, the second in the negative, and we therefore affirm the Eleventh Circuit's dismissal of petitioner's suit....

The Eleventh Amendment provides:

> The Judicial power of the United States shall not be construed to extend to any suit in law or equity, commenced or prosecuted against one of the United States by Citizens of another State, or by Citizens or Subjects of any Foreign State.

Although the text of the Amendment would appear to restrict only the Article III diversity jurisdiction of the federal courts, "we have understood the Eleventh Amendment to stand not so much for what it says, but for the presupposition ... which it confirms." That presupposition, first observed over a century ago in *Hans v. Louisiana*, 134 U.S. 1 (1890), has two parts: first, that each State is a sovereign entity in our federal system; and second, that "'it is inherent in the nature of sovereignty not to be amenable to the suit of an individual without its consent.'" ...

Here, petitioner has sued the State of Florida and it is undisputed that Florida has not consented to the suit. Petitioner nevertheless contends that its suit is not barred by state sovereign immunity. First, it argues that Congress through the Act abrogated the States' sovereign immunity. Alternatively, petitioner maintains that its suit against the Governor may go forward under *Ex parte Young*. We consider each of those arguments in turn.

## II

... In order to determine whether Congress has abrogated the States' sovereign immunity, we ask two questions: first, whether Congress has "unequivocally expressed its intent to abrogate the immunity," and second, whether Congress has acted "pursuant to a valid exercise of power."

### A

... Here, we agree with the parties [and] the Eleventh Circuit ... that Congress has in §2710(d)(7) provided an "unmistakably clear" statement of its intent to abrogate....

### B

Having concluded that Congress clearly intended to abrogate the States' sovereign immunity through §2710(d)(7), we turn now to consider whether the Act was passed "pursuant to a valid exercise of power." ...

[Our] inquiry into whether Congress has the power to abrogate unilaterally the States' immunity from suit is narrowly focused on one question: Was the Act in question passed pursuant to a constitutional provision granting Congress the power to abrogate? Previously, in conducting that inquiry, we have found authority to abrogate under only two provisions of the Constitution. In *Fitzpatrick v. Bitzer* (1976) [*Supra*. this chapter], we recognized that the Fourteenth Amendment, by expanding federal power at the expense of state autonomy, had fundamentally altered the balance of state and federal power struck by the Constitution.... We noted that §1 of the Fourteenth Amendment contained prohibitions expressly directed at the States and that §5 of the Amendment expressly provided that "The Congress shall have the power to enforce, by appropriate legislation, the provisions of this article." We held that through the

Fourteenth Amendment, federal power extended to intrude upon the province of the Eleventh Amendment and therefore that §5 of the Fourteenth Amendment allowed Congress to abrogate the immunity from suit guaranteed by that Amendment.

In only one other case has congressional abrogation of the States' Eleventh Amendment immunity been upheld. In *Pennsylvania v. Union Gas Co.*, 491 U.S. 1 (1989) [Note *supra.* this chapter], a plurality of the Court found that the Interstate Commerce Clause, Art. I, §8, cl. 3, granted Congress the power to abrogate state sovereign immunity, stating that the power to regulate interstate commerce would be "incomplete without the authority to render States liable in damages." Justice White added the fifth vote necessary to the result in that case, but wrote separately in order to express that he "[did] not agree with much of [the plurality's] reasoning."

In arguing that Congress through the Act abrogated the States' sovereign immunity, petitioner does not challenge the Eleventh Circuit's conclusion that the Act was passed pursuant to neither the Fourteenth Amendment nor the Interstate Commerce Clause. Instead, accepting the lower court's conclusion that the Act was passed pursuant to Congress' power under the Indian Commerce Clause, petitioner now asks us to consider whether that clause grants Congress the power to abrogate the States' sovereign immunity....

Following the rationale of the *Union Gas* plurality, our inquiry is limited to determining whether the Indian Commerce Clause, like the Interstate Commerce Clause, is a grant of authority to the Federal Government at the expense of the States. The answer to that question is obvious. If anything, the Indian Commerce Clause accomplishes a greater transfer of power from the States to the Federal Government than does the Interstate Commerce Clause.... Under the rationale of *Union Gas*, if the States' partial cession of authority over a particular area includes cession of the immunity from suit, then their virtually total cession of authority over a different area must also include cession of the immunity from suit....

... [Respondents contend] that if we find the rationale of the *Union Gas* plurality to extend to the Indian Commerce Clause, then "*Union Gas* should be reconsidered and overruled." Generally, the principle of *stare decisis*, and the interests that it serves, *viz.*, "the evenhanded, pre*dicta*ble, and consistent development of legal principles..., reliance on judicial decisions, and ... the actual and perceived integrity of the judicial process," ... counsel strongly against reconsideration of our precedent. Nevertheless, we always have treated *stare decisis* as a "principle of policy." ... "When governing decisions are unworkable or are badly reasoned, 'this Court has never felt constrained to follow precedent.' Our willingness to reconsider our earlier decisions has been "particularly true in constitutional cases, because in such cases correction through legislative action is practically impossible."

The Court in *Union Gas* reached a result without an expressed rationale agreed upon by a majority of the Court.... Since it was issued, *Union Gas* has created confusion among the lower courts that have sought to understand and apply the deeply fractured decision.

The plurality's rationale also deviated sharply from our established federalism jurisprudence and essentially eviscerated our decision in *Hans*....

Never before the decision in *Union Gas* had we suggested that the bounds of Article III could be expanded by Congress operating pursuant to any constitutional provision other than the Fourteenth Amendment. Indeed, it had seemed fundamental that Congress could not expand the jurisdiction of the federal courts beyond the bounds of Article III. *Marbury v. Madison* (1803) [*Supra.* Chapter 1]. The plurality's citation of prior decisions for support was based upon what we believe to be a misreading of precedent. The plurality claimed support for its decision from a case holding the unremarkable, and completely unrelated, proposition that the States may waive their sovereign immunity....

The plurality's extended reliance upon our decision in *Fitzpatrick v. Bitzer*, that Congress could under the Fourteenth Amendment abrogate the States' sovereign immunity was also, we believe, misplaced. *Fitzpatrick* was based upon a rationale wholly inapplicable to the Interstate Commerce Clause, *viz.*, that the Fourteenth Amendment, adopted well after the adoption of the Eleventh Amendment and the ratification of the Constitution, operated to alter the pre-existing balance between state and federal power achieved by Article III and the Eleventh Amendment. As the dissent in *Union Gas* made clear, *Fitzpatrick* cannot be read to justify "limitation of the principle embodied in the Eleventh Amendment through appeal to antecedent provisions of the Constitution."

In the five years since it was decided, *Union Gas* has proven to be a solitary departure from established law. Reconsidering the decision in *Union Gas*, we conclude that none of the policies underlying *stare decisis* require our continuing adherence to its holding.... We feel bound to conclude that *Union Gas* was wrongly decided and that it should be, and now is, overruled.

... For over a century, we have grounded our decisions in the oft-repeated understanding of state sovereign immunity as an essential part of the Eleventh Amendment. In *Principality of Monaco v. Mississippi*, 292 U.S. 313 (1934), the Court held that the Eleventh Amendment barred a suit brought against a State by a foreign state. Chief Justice Hughes wrote for a unanimous Court:

> ... Manifestly, we cannot rest with a mere literal application of the words of § 2 of Article III, or assume that the letter of the Eleventh Amendment exhausts the restrictions upon suits against non-consenting States. Behind the words of the constitutional provisions are postulates which limit and control. There is the essential postulate that the controversies, as contemplated, shall be found to be of a justiciable character. There is also the postulate that States of the Union, still possessing attributes of sovereignty, shall be immune from suits, without their consent, save where there has been a 'surrender of this immunity in the plan of the convention.' ...

... [The Amendment's] text dealt in terms only with the problem presented by the decision in *Chisholm v. Georgia* (1793), 2 U.S. 419 [Note *supra.* this chapter]; in light of the fact that the federal courts did not have federal question jurisdiction at the time the Amendment was passed (and would not have it until 1875), it seems unlikely that much thought was given to the prospect of federal question jurisdiction over the States....

In overruling *Union Gas* today, we reconfirm that the background principle of state sovereign immunity embodied in the Eleventh Amendment is not so ephemeral as to dissipate when the subject of the suit is an area, like the regulation of Indian commerce, that is under the exclusive control of the Federal Government. Even when the Constitution vests in Congress complete law-making authority over a particular area, the Eleventh Amendment prevents congressional authorization of suits by private parties against unconsenting States. The Eleventh Amendment restricts the judicial power under Article III, and Article I cannot be used to circumvent the constitutional limitations placed upon federal jurisdiction. Petitioner's suit against the State of Florida must be dismissed for a lack of jurisdiction.

## III

[The Court then considered, and rejected, the tribe's claim that its lawsuit could be heard under the *Young* theory. This part of the Court's opinion is discussed in the previous subsection.]

JUSTICE STEVENS, dissenting. [omitted]

JUSTICE SOUTER, with whom JUSTICE GINSBURG and JUSTICE BREYER join, dissenting.

In holding the State of Florida immune to suit under the Indian Gaming Regulatory Act, the Court today holds for the first time since the founding of the Republic that Congress has no authority to subject a State to the jurisdiction of a federal court at the behest of an individual asserting a federal right. Although the Court invokes the Eleventh Amendment as authority for this proposition, the only sense in which that amendment might be claimed as pertinent here was tolerantly phrased by JUSTICE STEVENS in his concurring opinion in *Pennsylvania v. Union Gas*. There, he explained how it has come about that we have two Eleventh Amendments, the one ratified in 1795, the other (so-called) invented by the Court nearly a century later in *Hans v. Louisiana*. JUSTICE STEVENS saw in that second Eleventh Amendment no bar to the exercise of congressional authority under the Commerce Clause in providing for suits on a federal question by individuals against a State, and I can only say that after my own canvass of the matter I believe he was entirely correct in that view, for reasons given below. His position, of course, was also the holding in *Union Gas*, which the Court now overrules and repudiates.

The fault I find with the majority today is not in its decision to reexamine *Union Gas*, for the Court in that case produced no majority for a single rationale supporting congressional authority. Instead, I part company from the Court because I am convinced that its decision is fundamentally mistaken, and for that reason I respectfully dissent.

## I

It is useful to separate three questions: (1) whether the States enjoyed sovereign immunity if sued in their own courts in the period prior to ratification of the National

Constitution; (2) if so, whether after ratification the States were entitled to claim some such immunity when sued in a federal court exercising jurisdiction either because the suit was between a State and a non-state litigant who was not its citizen, or because the issue in the case raised a federal question; and (3) whether any state sovereign immunity recognized in federal court may be abrogated by Congress.

The answer to the first question is not clear, although some of the Framers assumed that States did enjoy immunity in their own courts. The second question was not debated at the time of ratification, except as to citizen-state diversity jurisdiction; there was no unanimity, but in due course the Court in *Chisholm v. Georgia*, answered that a state defendant enjoyed no such immunity. As to federal question jurisdiction, state sovereign immunity seems not to have been debated prior to ratification, the silence probably showing a general understanding at the time that the States would have no immunity in such cases.

The adoption of the Eleventh Amendment soon changed the result in *Chisholm*, not by mentioning sovereign immunity, but by eliminating citizen-state diversity jurisdiction over cases with state defendants. I will explain why the Eleventh Amendment did not affect federal question jurisdiction, a notion that needs to be understood for the light it casts on the soundness of *Hans's* holding that States did enjoy sovereign immunity in federal question suits. The *Hans* Court erroneously assumed that a State could plead sovereign immunity against a noncitizen suing under federal question jurisdiction, and for that reason held that a State must enjoy the same protection in a suit by one of its citizens. The error of *Hans's* reasoning is underscored by its clear inconsistency with the Founders' hostility to the implicit reception of common-law doctrine as federal law, and with the Founders' conception of sovereign power as divided between the States and the National Government for the sake of very practical objectives.

The Court's answer today to the third question is likewise at odds with the Founders' view that common law, when it was received into the new American legal systems, was always subject to legislative amendment. In ignoring the reasons for this pervasive understanding at the time of the ratification, and in holding that a nontextual common-law rule limits a clear grant of congressional power under Article I, the Court follows a course that has brought it to grief before in our history, and promises to do so again.

Beyond this third question that elicits today's holding, there is one further issue. To reach the Court's result, it must not only hold the *Hans* doctrine to be outside the reach of Congress, but must also displace the doctrine of *Ex parte Young*, that an officer of the government may be ordered prospectively to follow federal law, in cases in which the government may not itself be sued directly. None of its reasons for displacing *Young's* jurisdictional doctrine withstand scrutiny....

[Because] the plaintiffs in today's case are citizens of the State that they are suing, the Eleventh Amendment simply does not apply to them. We must therefore look elsewhere for the source of that immunity by which the Court says their suit is barred from a federal court.

## II

The obvious place to look elsewhere, of course, is *Hans v. Louisiana*.... The parties in *Hans* raised, and the Court in that case answered, only what I have called the second question, that is, whether the Constitution, without more, permits a State to plead sovereign immunity to bar the exercise of federal question jurisdiction. Although the Court invoked a principle of sovereign immunity to cure what it took to be the Eleventh Amendment's anomaly of barring only those state suits brought by noncitizen plaintiffs, the *Hans* Court had no occasion to consider whether Congress could abrogate that background immunity by statute. Indeed (except in the special circumstance of Congress's power to enforce the Civil War Amendments), this question never came before our Court until *Union Gas*, and any intimations of an answer in prior cases were mere *dicta*....

## A

The Louisiana plaintiff in *Hans* held bonds issued by that State, which, like virtually all of the Southern States, had issued them in substantial amounts during the Reconstruction era to finance public improvements aimed at stimulating industrial development. As Reconstruction governments collapsed, however, the post-Reconstruction regimes sought to repudiate these debts, and the *Hans* litigation arose out of Louisiana's attempt to renege on its bond obligations.

Hans sued the State in federal court, asserting that the State's default amounted to an impairment of the obligation of its contracts in violation of the Contract Clause. This Court affirmed the dismissal of the suit, despite the fact that the case fell within the federal court's "arising under," or federal question, jurisdiction. Justice Bradley's opinion did not purport to hold that the terms either of Article III or of the Eleventh Amendment barred the suit, but that the ancient doctrine of sovereign immunity that had inspired adoption of the Eleventh Amendment applied to cases beyond the Amendment's scope and otherwise within the federal question jurisdiction.... The Court elected, ... to recognize [this immunity] ... despite the want of any textual manifestation, because of what the Court described as the anomaly that would have resulted otherwise: the Eleventh Amendment (according to the Court) would have barred a federal question suit by a noncitizen, but the State would have been subject to federal jurisdiction at its own citizen's behest....

*Hans* thus addressed the issue implicated (though not directly raised) in the pre-ratification debate about the Citizen-State Diversity Clauses and implicitly settled by *Chisholm*: whether state sovereign immunity was cognizable by federal courts on the exercise of federal question jurisdiction. According to *Hans*, and contrary to *Chisholm*, it was. But that is all that *Hans* held. Because no federal legislation purporting to pierce state immunity was at issue, it cannot fairly be said that *Hans* held state sovereign immunity to have attained some constitutional status immunizing it from abrogation....

## B

The majority does not dispute the point that *Hans* ... had no occasion to decide whether Congress could abrogate a State's immunity from federal question suits.

The Court insists, however, that the negative answer to that question that it finds in *Hans* and subsequent opinions is not "mere *obiter dicta*, but rather … the well-established rationale upon which the Court based the results of its earlier decisions." …

The "rationale" which the majority seeks to invoke is, I think, more nearly stated in its quotation from *Principality of Monaco v. Mississippi*. There, the Court said that "we cannot rest with a mere literal application of the words of § 2 of Article III, or assume that the letter of the Eleventh Amendment exhausts the restrictions upon suits against non-consenting States." …

The majority, however, would read the "rationale" of *Hans* and its line of subsequent cases as answering the further question whether the "postulate" of sovereign immunity that "limits and controls" the exercise of Article III jurisdiction, is constitutional in stature and therefore unalterable by Congress. It is true that there are statements in the cases that point toward just this conclusion. These statements, however, are *dicta* in the classic sense, that is, sheer speculation about what would happen in cases not before the court. But this is not the only weakness of these statements, which are counterbalanced by many other opinions that have … suggested that the *Hans* immunity is not of constitutional stature. …

The most damning evidence for the Court's theory that *Hans* rests on a broad rationale of immunity unalterable by Congress, however, is the Court's proven tendency to disregard the post-*Hans dicta* in cases where that *dicta* would have mattered. If it is indeed true that "private suits against States [are] not permitted under Article III (by virtue of the understanding represented by the Eleventh Amendment)," … then it is hard to see how a State's sovereign immunity may be waived any more than it may be abrogated by Congress. After all, consent of a party is in all other instances wholly insufficient to create subject-matter jurisdiction where it would not otherwise exist. Likewise, the Court's broad theory of immunity runs doubly afoul of the appellate jurisdiction problem that I noted earlier.… If "the whole sum of the judicial power granted by the Constitution to the United States does not embrace the authority to entertain a suit brought by a citizen against his own State without its consent," and if consent to suit in state court is not sufficient to show consent in federal court, then Article III would hardly permit this Court to exercise appellate jurisdiction over issues of federal law arising in lawsuits brought against the States in their own courts. We have, however, quite rightly ignored any post-*Hans dicta* in that sort of case and exercised the jurisdiction that the plain text of Article III provides.…

IV

[Justice Souter then argued that the tribe's suit could be heard under the *Young* theory. This part of his opinion is discussed in a note in the previous subsection.]

V

Absent the application of *Ex parte Young*, I would, of course, follow *Union Gas* in recognizing congressional power under Article I to abrogate *Hans* immunity. Since the reasons for this position, as explained in Parts II–III, *supra*, tend to unsettle *Hans* as well as support *Union Gas*, I should add a word about my reasons for continuing to accept *Hans*'s holding as a matter of *stare decisis*.

The *Hans* doctrine was erroneous, but it has not previously proven to be unworkable or to conflict with later doctrine or to suffer from the effects of facts developed since its decision (apart from those indicating its original errors). I would therefore treat *Hans* as it has always been treated in fact until today, as a doctrine of federal common law. For, as so understood, it has formed one of the strands of the federal relationship for over a century now, and the stability of that relationship is itself a value that *stare decisis* aims to respect.

In being ready to hold that the relationship may still be altered, not by the Court but by Congress, I would tread the course laid out elsewhere in our cases. The Court has repeatedly stated its assumption that insofar as the relative positions of States and Nation may be affected consistently with the Tenth Amendment, they would not be modified without deliberately expressed intent. The plain statement rule, which "assures that the legislature has in fact faced, and intended to bring into issue, the critical matters involved in the judicial decision," is particularly appropriate in light of our primary reliance on "the effectiveness of the federal political process in preserving the States' interests." *Garcia v. San Antonio Metropolitan Transit Authority*, 469 U.S. 528 (1985). Hence, we have required such a plain statement when Congress pre-empts the historic powers of the States, imposes a condition on the grant of federal moneys, or seeks to regulate a State's ability to determine the qualifications of its own officials....

When judging legislation passed under unmistakable Article I powers, no further restriction could be required.... It is hard to contend that this rule has set the bar too low, for (except in *Union Gas*) we have never found the requirement to be met outside the context of laws passed under § 5 of the Fourteenth Amendment. The exception I would recognize today proves the rule, moreover, because the federal abrogation of state immunity comes as part of a regulatory scheme which is itself designed to invest the States with regulatory powers that Congress need not extend to them. This fact suggests to me that the political safeguards of federalism are working, that a plain statement rule is an adequate check on congressional overreaching, and that today's abandonment of that approach is wholly unwarranted.

... Because neither text, precedent, nor history supports the majority's abdication of our responsibility to exercise the jurisdiction entrusted to us in Article III, I would reverse the judgment of the Court of Appeals.

## Note: Article I Power to Abrogate State Sovereign Immunity After Seminole Tribe

While *Seminole Tribe* considered congressional power under the Indian Commerce Clause, not the far more significant *Interstate* Commerce Clause, it was generally understood that the result in that case prohibited Congress from using its Interstate Commerce power to abrogate state sovereign immunity. This understanding was explicitly confirmed in *Florida Prepaid Postsecondary Education Expense Board v. College*

*Savings Bank*, 527 U.S. 627 (1999), where Chief Justice Rehnquist, again speaking for the same five-Justice majority as in *Seminole Tribe*, wrote that "*Seminole Tribe* makes clear that Congress may not abrogate state sovereign immunity pursuant to its Article I powers." *Florida Prepaid* considered whether Congress could use, among other powers, its power under the Interstate Commerce Clause and the Patent Clause to abrogate state sovereign immunity when states violated private parties' patents. The language quoted above led the Court to conclude that the answer to that question was "no."

However, ten years after *Seminole Tribe*, the Court made an exception to its seeming blanket rule against construing Congress's Article I authority to allow Congress to abrogate state sovereign immunity. In *Central Virginia Community College v. Katz*, 546 U.S. 356 (2006), the Court allowed a federal bankruptcy trustee to sue a state agency-creditor to recover a debtor's alleged fraudulent transfer of funds before the debtor filed for bankruptcy. The five-Justice majority was composed of the four *Seminole Tribe* dissenters, and Justice O'Connor, who joined the majorities in *Seminole Tribe* and *Florida Prepaid*. Writing for this group, Justice Stevens stressed the unique features of Congress's Article I bankruptcy power. He argued that the Framers felt a special need to provide for a uniform bankruptcy law, to avoid the problem of debtors being discharged from their debts in one state but still subject to creditors' claims in other states. He also noted that bankruptcy cases such as this one were technically "*in rem*," that is, against the assets themselves rather than against a party, which mitigated the sovereign immunity concern. He also noted that an early federal bankruptcy statute authorized federal courts to order state jailers to release debtors arrested despite having their debts discharged by another state's court. Justice Stevens interpreted this early statute as evidence that the generation that enacted the Eleventh Amendment was not concerned about intrusions on state sovereign immunity in the bankruptcy area.

Writing for the four dissenting Justices, Justice Thomas argued that the Court's decision was inconsistent with *Seminole Tribe*. He disagreed with Justice Stevens' reading of history, and he disputed the logic of the idea that the Framers' desire for a uniform bankruptcy law implied an acceptance of federal power to abrogate state sovereign immunity.

## 3. The Tenth Amendment as the Source of State Sovereign Immunity

Up to now in this section of the chapter, state sovereign immunity has been described as based on the Eleventh Amendment. Indeed, the opinions above all refer to the Eleventh Amendment as if it was the unquestioned source of the immunity at issue. In 1999, however, the Court held that the states enjoy in their own courts the same type of immunity the Eleventh Amendment established in federal courts. The Court explained that this state court immunity derives from the general implications of our federal system, as expressed in the Tenth Amendment.

# Alden v. Maine

## 527 U.S. 706 (1999)

Justice Kennedy delivered the opinion of the Court.

In 1992, petitioners, a group of probation officers, filed suit against their employer, the State of Maine, in the United States District Court for the District of Maine. The officers alleged the State had violated the overtime provisions of the Fair Labor Standards Act of 1938, and sought compensation and liquidated damages. While the suit was pending, this Court decided *Seminole Tribe of Fla. v. Florida* (1996) [*Supra.* this chapter], which made it clear that Congress lacks power under Article I to abrogate the States' sovereign immunity from suits commenced or prosecuted in the federal courts. Upon consideration of *Seminole Tribe*, the District Court dismissed petitioners' action, and the Court of Appeals affirmed. Petitioners then filed the same action in state court. The state trial court dismissed the suit on the basis of sovereign immunity, and the Maine Supreme Judicial Court affirmed....

We hold that the powers delegated to Congress under Article I of the United States Constitution do not include the power to subject nonconsenting States to private suits for damages in state courts. We decide as well that the State of Maine has not consented to suits for overtime pay and liquidated damages under the FLSA. On these premises we affirm the judgment sustaining dismissal of the suit.

## I

The Eleventh Amendment makes explicit reference to the States' immunity from suits "commenced or prosecuted against one of the United States by Citizens of another State, or by Citizens or Subjects of any Foreign State." We have, as a result, sometimes referred to the States' immunity from suit as "Eleventh Amendment immunity." The phrase is convenient shorthand but something of a misnomer, for the sovereign immunity of the States neither derives from nor is limited by the terms of the Eleventh Amendment. Rather, as the Constitution's structure, and its history, and the authoritative interpretations by this Court make clear, the States' immunity from suit is a fundamental aspect of the sovereignty which the States enjoyed before the ratification of the Constitution, and which they retain today (either literally or by virtue of their admission into the Union upon an equal footing with the other States) except as altered by the plan of the Convention or certain constitutional Amendments.

## A

Although the Constitution establishes a National Government with broad, often plenary authority over matters within its recognized competence, the founding document "specifically recognizes the States as sovereign entities." *Seminole Tribe*. Various textual provisions of the Constitution assume the States' continued existence and active participation in the fundamental processes of governance. *See Printz v. United States*, 521 U.S. 898 (1997) [Note *supra.* this chapter].... Any doubt regarding the constitutional role of the States as sovereign entities is removed by the Tenth Amendment, which, like the other provisions of the Bill of Rights, was enacted to allay lingering concerns about the extent of the national power. The Amendment confirms the promise implicit in the original document: "The powers not delegated to the United States by the Constitution, nor prohibited by it to the States, are reserved to the States respectively, or to the people."

The federal system established by our Constitution preserves the sovereign status of the States in two ways. First, it reserves to them a substantial portion of the Nation's primary sovereignty, together with the dignity and essential attributes inhering in that status. The States "form distinct and independent portions of the supremacy, no more subject, within their respective spheres, to the general authority than the general authority is subject to them, within its own sphere." *The Federalist* No. 39 (J. Madison).

Second, even as to matters within the competence of the National Government, the constitutional design secures the founding generation's rejection of "the concept of a central government that would act upon and through the States" in favor of "a system in which the State and Federal Governments would exercise concurrent authority over the people—who were, in Hamilton's words, 'the only proper objects of government.'" *Printz*. In this the founders achieved a deliberate departure from the Articles of Confederation: Experience under the Articles had "exploded on all hands" the "practicality of making laws, with coercive sanctions, for the States as political bodies."

The States thus retain "a residuary and inviolable sovereignty." *The Federalist* No. 39. They are not relegated to the role of mere provinces or political corporations, but retain the dignity, though not the full authority, of sovereignty.

B

The generation that designed and adopted our federal system considered immunity from private suits central to sovereign dignity. When the Constitution was ratified, it was well established in English law that the Crown could not be sued without consent in its own courts....

Although the American people had rejected other aspects of English political theory, the doctrine that a sovereign could not be sued without its consent was universal in the States when the Constitution was drafted and ratified....

Despite the persuasive assurances of the Constitution's leading advocates and the expressed understanding of the only state conventions to address the issue in explicit terms, this Court held, just five years after the Constitution was adopted, that Article III authorized a private citizen of another State to sue the State of Georgia without its consent. *Chisholm v. Georgia*, 2 U.S. 419 (1793) (Note *supra.* this chapter]....

C

The Court has been consistent in interpreting the adoption of the Eleventh Amendment as conclusive evidence "that the decision in *Chisholm* was contrary to the well-understood meaning of the Constitution." ... In accordance with this understanding, we have recognized a "presumption that no anomalous and unheard-of proceedings or suits were intended to be raised up by the Constitution — anomalous and unheard of when the constitution was adopted." As a consequence, we have looked to "history and experience, and the established order of things," rather than "adhering to the mere letter" of the Eleventh Amendment, in determining the scope of the States' constitutional immunity from suit.

Following this approach, the Court has upheld States' assertions of sovereign immunity in various contexts falling outside the literal text of the Eleventh Amendment. In *Hans v. Louisiana*, 134 U.S. 1 (1890) [Note *supra*. this chapter], the Court held that sovereign immunity barred a citizen from suing his own State under the federal-question head of jurisdiction.... Later decisions rejected similar requests to conform the principle of sovereign immunity to the strict language of the Eleventh Amendment....

## II

In this case we must determine whether Congress has the power, under Article I, to subject nonconsenting States to private suits in their own courts. As the foregoing discussion makes clear, the fact that the Eleventh Amendment by its terms limits only "the Judicial power of the United States" does not resolve the question....

While the constitutional principle of sovereign immunity does pose a bar to federal jurisdiction over suits against nonconsenting States, this is not the only structural basis of sovereign immunity implicit in the constitutional design. Rather, "there is also the postulate that States of the Union, still possessing attributes of sovereignty, shall be immune from suits, without their consent, save where there has been 'a surrender of this immunity in the plan of the convention.'" This separate and distinct structural principle is not directly related to the scope of the judicial power established by Article III, but inheres in the system of federalism established by the Constitution. In exercising its Article I powers Congress may subject the States to private suits in their own courts only if there is "compelling evidence" that the States were required to surrender this power to Congress pursuant to the constitutional design.

## A

Petitioners contend the text of the Constitution and our recent sovereign immunity decisions establish that the States were required to relinquish this portion of their sovereignty. We turn first to these sources.

## 1

Article I, § 8 grants Congress broad power to enact legislation in several enumerated areas of national concern. The Supremacy Clause, furthermore, provides:

> This Constitution, and the Laws of the United States which shall be made in Pursuance thereof..., shall be the supreme Law of the Land; and the Judges in every State shall be bound thereby, any Thing in the Constitution or Laws of any state to the Contrary notwithstanding. U.S. Const., Art. VI.

It is contended that, by virtue of these provisions, where Congress enacts legislation subjecting the States to suit, the legislation by necessity overrides the sovereign immunity of the States.

As is evident from its text, however, the Supremacy Clause enshrines as "the supreme Law of the Land" only those federal Acts that accord with the constitutional design. *See Printz*. Appeal to the Supremacy Clause alone merely raises the question whether a law is a valid exercise of the national power.

The Constitution, by delegating to Congress the power to establish the supreme law of the land when acting within its enumerated powers, does not foreclose a State from asserting immunity to claims arising under federal law merely because that law derives not from the State itself but from the national power. A contrary view could not be reconciled with *Hans v. Louisiana*, which sustained Louisiana's immunity in a private suit arising under the Constitution itself.... We reject any contention that substantive federal law by its own force necessarily overrides the sovereign immunity of the States. When a State asserts its immunity to suit, the question is not the primacy of federal law but the implementation of the law in a manner consistent with the constitutional sovereignty of the States.

*Interesting / Rejection*

(Nor can we conclude that the specific Article I powers delegated to Congress necessarily include, by virtue of the Necessary and Proper Clause or otherwise, the incidental authority to subject the States to private suits as a means of achieving objectives otherwise within the scope of the enumerated powers) Although some of our decisions had endorsed this contention, *see Parden v. Terminal R. Co. of Ala. Docks Dept.*, 377 U.S. 184 (1964); *Pennsylvania v. Union Gas Co.*, 491 U.S. 1 (1989) (plurality opinion) [Note *supra.* this chapter], they have since been overruled....

The cases we have cited, of course, came at last to the conclusion that neither the Supremacy Clause nor the enumerated powers of Congress confer authority to abrogate the States' immunity from suit in federal court. The logic of the decisions, however, does not turn on the forum in which the suits were prosecuted but extends to state-court suits as well....

B

Whether Congress has authority under Article I to abrogate a State's immunity from suit in its own courts is ... a question of first impression. In determining whether there is "compelling evidence" that this derogation of the States' sovereignty is "inherent in the constitutional compact," we continue our discussion of history, practice, precedent, and the structure of the Constitution.

1

We look first to evidence of the original understanding of the Constitution. Petitioners contend that because the ratification debates and the events surrounding the adoption of the Eleventh Amendment focused on the States' immunity from suit in federal courts, the historical record gives no instruction as to the founding generation's intent to preserve the States' immunity from suit in their own courts.

We believe, however, that the founders' silence is best explained by the simple fact that no one, not even the Constitution's most ardent opponents, suggested the document might strip the States of the immunity. In light of the overriding concern regarding the States' war-time debts, together with the well known creativity, foresight, and vivid imagination of the Constitution's opponents, the silence is most instructive. It suggests the sovereign's right to assert immunity from suit in its own courts was a principle so well established that no one conceived it would be altered by the new Constitution....

2

Our historical analysis is supported by early congressional practice, which provides "contemporaneous and weighty evidence of the Constitution's meaning." *Printz*. Although early Congresses enacted various statutes authorizing federal suits in state court, we have discovered no instance in which they purported to authorize suits against nonconsenting States in these fora. The "numerousness of these statutes [authorizing suit in state court], contrasted with the utter lack of statutes" subjecting States to suit, "suggests an assumed absence of such power." *Printz*. It thus appears early Congresses did not believe they had the power to authorize private suits against the States in their own courts....

4

Our final consideration is whether a congressional power to subject nonconsenting States to private suits in their own courts is consistent with the structure of the Constitution. We look both to the essential principles of federalism and to the special role of the state courts in the constitutional design.

Although the Constitution grants broad powers to Congress, our federalism requires that Congress treat the States in a manner consistent with their status as residuary sovereigns and joint participants in the governance of the Nation. *See, e.g., United States v. Lopez* (1995) [*Supra*. Chapter 4]; *Printz*. The founding generation thought it "neither becoming nor convenient that the several States of the Union, invested with that large residuum of sovereignty which had not been delegated to the United States, should be summoned as defendants to answer the complaints of private persons." The principle of sovereign immunity preserved by constitutional design "thus accords the States the respect owed them as members of the federation."

Petitioners contend that immunity from suit in federal court suffices to preserve the dignity of the States. Private suits against nonconsenting States, however, present "the indignity of subjecting a State to the coercive process of judicial tribunals at the instance of private parties," regardless of the forum. Not only must a State defend or default but also it must face the prospect of being thrust, by federal fiat and against its will, into the disfavored status of a debtor, subject to the power of private citizens to levy on its treasury or perhaps even government buildings or property which the State administers on the public's behalf.

In some ways, of course, a congressional power to authorize private suits against nonconsenting States in their own courts would be even more offensive to state sovereignty than a power to authorize the suits in a federal forum. Although the immunity of one sovereign in the courts of another has often depended in part on comity or agreement, the immunity of a sovereign in its own courts has always been understood to be within the sole control of the sovereign itself. A power to press a State's own courts into federal service to coerce the other branches of the State, furthermore, is the power first to turn the State against itself and ultimately to commandeer the entire political machinery of the State against its will and at the behest of individuals. *Cf. Coeur d'Alene Tribe*, 521 U.S. 261 (1997) [Note *supra.* this chapter]. Such plenary federal control of state governmental processes denigrates the separate sovereignty of the States.

It is unquestioned that the Federal Government retains its own immunity from suit not only in state tribunals but also in its own courts. In light of our constitutional system recognizing the essential sovereignty of the States, we are reluctant to conclude that the States are not entitled to a reciprocal privilege.

Underlying constitutional form are considerations of great substance. Private suits against nonconsenting States — especially suits for money damages — may threaten the financial integrity of the States.... A congressional power to strip the States of their immunity from private suits in their own courts would pose more subtle risks as well. "The principle of immunity from litigation assures the states and the nation from unanticipated intervention in the processes of government." When the States' immunity from private suits is disregarded, "the course of their public policy and the administration of their public affairs" may become "subject to and controlled by the mandates of judicial tribunals without their consent, and in favor of individual interests." While the States have relinquished their immunity from suit in some special contexts — at least as a practical matter — this surrender carries with it substantial costs to the autonomy, the decisionmaking ability, and the sovereign capacity of the States.

A general federal power to authorize private suits for money damages would place unwarranted strain on the States' ability to govern in accordance with the will of their citizens. Today, as at the time of the founding, the allocation of scarce resources among competing needs and interests lies at the heart of the political process. While the judgment creditor of the State may have a legitimate claim for compensation, other important needs and worthwhile ends compete for access to the public fisc. Since all cannot be satisfied in full, it is inevitable that difficult decisions involving the most sensitive and political of judgments must be made. If the principle of representative government is to be preserved to the States, the balance between competing interests must be reached after deliberation by the political process established by the citizens of the State, not by judicial decree mandated by the Federal Government and invoked by the private citizen. "It needs no argument to show that the political power cannot be thus ousted of its jurisdiction and the judiciary set in its place."

By "splitting the atom of sovereignty," the Founders established "two orders of government, each with its own direct relationship, its own privity, its own set of mutual rights and obligations to the people who sustain it and are governed by it." "The Constitution thus contemplates that a State's government will represent and remain accountable to its own citizens." *Printz.* When the Federal Government asserts authority over a State's most fundamental political processes, it strikes at the heart of the political accountability so essential to our liberty and republican form of government....

Congress cannot abrogate the States' sovereign immunity in federal court; were the rule to be different here, the National Government would wield greater power in the state courts than in its own judicial instrumentalities.

The resulting anomaly cannot be explained by reference to the special role of the state courts in the constitutional design. Although Congress may not require the legislative or executive branches of the States to enact or administer federal regulatory programs, *see Printz*, it may require state courts of "adequate and appropriate" jurisdiction, *Testa v. Katt*, 330 U.S. 386 (1947) [Note *supra*. this chapter], "to enforce federal prescriptions, insofar as those prescriptions relate to matters appropriate for the judicial power." It would be an unprecedented step, however, to infer from the fact that Congress may declare federal law binding and enforceable in state courts the further principle that Congress' authority to pursue federal objectives through the state judiciaries exceeds not only its power to press other branches of the State into its service but even its control over the federal courts themselves. The conclusion would imply that Congress may in some cases act only through instrumentalities of the States. Yet, as Chief Justice Marshall explained: "No trace is to be found in the constitution of an intention to create a dependence of the government of the Union on those of the States, for the execution of the great powers assigned to it. Its means are adequate to its ends; and on those means alone was it expected to rely for the accomplishment of its ends." *McCulloch v. Maryland* (1819) [*Supra*. Chapters 3 & 4]....

In light of history, practice, precedent, and the structure of the Constitution, we hold that the States retain immunity from private suit in their own courts, an immunity beyond the congressional power to abrogate by Article I legislation.

### III

The constitutional privilege of a State to assert its sovereign immunity in its own courts does not confer upon the State a concomitant right to disregard the Constitution or valid federal law. The States and their officers are bound by obligations imposed by the Constitution and by federal statutes that comport with the constitutional design. We are unwilling to assume the States will refuse to honor the Constitution or obey the binding laws of the United States. The good faith of the States thus provides an important assurance that "this Constitution, and the Laws of the United States which shall be made in Pursuance thereof ... shall be the supreme Law of the Land." U.S. Const., Art. VI.

Sovereign immunity, moreover, does not bar all judicial review of state compliance with the Constitution and valid federal law. Rather, certain limits are implicit in the constitutional principle of state sovereign immunity.

The first of these limits is that sovereign immunity bars suits only in the absence of consent....

The States have consented, moreover, to some suits pursuant to the plan of the Convention or to subsequent constitutional amendments. In ratifying the Constitution, the States consented to suits brought by other States or by the Federal Government.... We have held also that in adopting the Fourteenth Amendment, the people required the States to surrender a portion of the sovereignty that had been preserved to them by the original Constitution, so that Congress may authorize private suits against nonconsenting States pursuant to its § 5 enforcement power. *Fitzpatrick v. Bitzer* (1976) [*Supra.* this chapter]....

The second important limit to the principle of sovereign immunity is that it bars suits against States but not lesser entities. The immunity does not extend to suits prosecuted against a municipal corporation or other governmental entity which is not an arm of the State. Nor does sovereign immunity bar all suits against state officers. Some suits against state officers are barred by the rule that sovereign immunity is not limited to suits which name the State as a party if the suits are, in fact, against the State. The rule, however, does not bar certain actions against state officers for injunctive or declaratory relief. *Compare Ex parte Young*, 209 U.S. 123 (1908) [Note *supra.* this chapter] with *Coeur d'Alene Tribe of Idaho, Seminole Tribe*, and *Edelman v. Jordan* (1974) [*Supra.* this chapter]....

The principle of sovereign immunity as reflected in our jurisprudence strikes the proper balance between the supremacy of federal law and the separate sovereignty of the States. *See Pennhurst State School* and *Hospital v. Halderman* [*Supra.* this chapter]. Established rules provide ample means to correct ongoing violations of law and to vindicate the interests which animate the Supremacy Clause. That we have, during the first 210 years of our constitutional history, found it unnecessary to decide the question presented here suggests a federal power to subject nonconsenting States to private suits in their own courts is unnecessary to uphold the Constitution and valid federal statutes as the supreme law.

### IV

The sole remaining question is whether Maine has waived its immunity. The State of Maine "regards the immunity from suit as one of the highest attributes inherent in the nature of sovereignty," *Cushing v. Cohen*, 420 A.2d 919 (Me.1981).... The State, we conclude, has not consented to suit.

### V

This case at one level concerns the formal structure of federalism, but in a Constitution as resilient as ours form mirrors substance. Congress has vast power but not all power. When Congress legislates in matters affecting the States, it may not treat these sovereign entities as mere prefectures or corporations. Congress must accord States the esteem due to them as joint participants in a federal system, one beginning with the premise of sovereignty in both the central Government and the separate States. Congress has ample means to ensure compliance with valid federal laws, but it must respect the sovereignty of the States....

Justice SOUTER, with whom Justice STEVENS, Justice GINSBURG, and Justice BREYER join, dissenting.

In *Seminole Tribe of Fla. v. Florida*, a majority of this Court invoked the Eleventh Amendment to declare that the federal judicial power under Article III of the Constitution does not reach a private action against a State, even on a federal question....

Today's issue arises naturally in the aftermath of the decision in *Seminole Tribe*. The Court holds that the Constitution bars an individual suit against a State to enforce a federal statutory right under the Fair Labor Standards Act of 1938 (FLSA), when brought in the State's courts over its objection. In thus complementing its earlier decision, the Court of course confronts the fact that the state forum renders the Eleventh Amendment beside the point, and it has responded by discerning a simpler and more straightforward theory of state sovereign immunity than it found in *Seminole Tribe*: a State's sovereign immunity from all individual suits is a "fundamental aspect" of state sovereignty "confirmed" by the Tenth Amendment. As a consequence, *Seminole Tribe*'s contorted reliance on the Eleventh Amendment and its background was presumably unnecessary; the Tenth would have done the work with an economy that the majority in *Seminole Tribe* would have welcomed. Indeed, if the Court's current reasoning is correct, the Eleventh Amendment itself was unnecessary. Whatever Article III may originally have said about the federal judicial power, the embarrassment to the State of Georgia occasioned by attempts in federal court to enforce the State's war debt could easily have been avoided if only the Court that decided *Chisholm v. Georgia* had understood a State's inherent, Tenth Amendment right to be free of any judicial power, whether the court be state or federal, and whether the cause of action arise under state or federal law.

The sequence of the Court's positions prompts a suspicion of error, and skepticism is confirmed by scrutiny of the Court's efforts to justify its holding. There is no evidence that the Tenth Amendment constitutionalized a concept of sovereign immunity as inherent in the notion of statehood, and no evidence that any concept of inherent sovereign immunity was understood historically to apply when the sovereign sued was not the font of the law. Nor does the Court fare any better with its subsidiary lines of reasoning, that the state-court action is barred by the scheme of American federalism, a result supposedly confirmed by a history largely devoid of precursors to the action considered here. The Court's federalism ignores the accepted authority of Congress to bind States under the FLSA and to provide for enforcement of federal rights in state court. The Court's history simply disparages the capacity of the Constitution to order relationships in a Republic that has changed since the founding.

On each point the Court has raised it is mistaken, and I respectfully dissent from its judgment.

I

The Court rests its decision principally on the claim that immunity from suit was "a fundamental aspect of the sovereignty which the States enjoyed before the ratification of the Constitution," an aspect which the Court understands to have survived the ratification of the Constitution in 1788 and to have been "confirmed" and given constitutional status by the adoption of the Tenth Amendment in 1791. If the Court truly means by "sovereign immunity" what that term meant at common law, its argument would be insupportable. While sovereign immunity entered many new state legal systems as a part of the common law selectively received from England, it was not understood to be indefeasible or to have been given any such status by the new

National Constitution, which did not mention it. See *Seminole Tribe* (SOUTER, J., dissenting). Had the question been posed, state sovereign immunity could not have been thought to shield a State from suit under federal law on a subject committed to national jurisdiction by Article I of the Constitution. Congress exercising its conceded Article I power may unquestionably abrogate such immunity. I set out this position at length in my dissent in *Seminole Tribe* and will not repeat it here.

The Court does not, however, offer today's holding as a mere corollary to its reasoning in *Seminole Tribe,* substituting the Tenth Amendment for the Eleventh as the occasion demands, and it is fair to read its references to a "fundamental aspect" of state sovereignty as referring not to a prerogative inherited from the Crown, but to a conception necessarily implied by statehood itself. The conception is thus not one of common law so much as of natural law, a universally applicable proposition discoverable by reason. This, I take it, is the sense in which the Court so emphatically relies on Alexander Hamilton's reference in *The Federalist* No. 81 to the States' sovereign immunity from suit as an "inherent" right, a characterization that does not require, but is at least open to, a natural law reading.

I understand the Court to rely on the Hamiltonian formulation with the object of suggesting that its conception of sovereign immunity as a "fundamental aspect" of sovereignty was a substantially popular, if not the dominant, view in the periods of Revolution and Confederation.... The Court's principal rationale for today's result, then, turns on history: was the natural law conception of sovereign immunity as inherent in any notion of an independent State widely held in the United States in the period preceding the ratification of 1788 (or the adoption of the Tenth Amendment in 1791)?

The answer is certainly no. There is almost no evidence that the generation of the Framers thought sovereign immunity was fundamental in the sense of being unalterable. Whether one looks at the period before the framing, to the ratification controversies, or to the early republican era, the evidence is the same. Some Framers thought sovereign immunity was an obsolete royal prerogative inapplicable in a republic; some thought sovereign immunity was a common law power defeasible, like other common law rights, by statute; and perhaps a few thought, in keeping with a natural law view distinct from the common law conception, that immunity was inherent in a sovereign because the body that made a law could not logically be bound by it. Natural law thinking on the part of a doubtful few will not, however, support the Court's position.

[Justice Souter then provided a long discussion of English, colonial, and framing-era constitutional theory.]

### C

At the Constitutional Convention, the notion of sovereign immunity, whether as natural law or as common law, was not an immediate subject of debate, and the sovereignty of a State in its own courts seems not to have been mentioned. This comes as no surprise, for although the Constitution required state courts to apply federal law, the Framers did not consider the possibility that federal law might bind States, say, in their relations with their employees. In the subsequent ratification debates, however, the issue of jurisdiction over a State did emerge in the question whether States might be sued on their debts in federal court, and on this point, too, a variety of views emerged and the diversity of sovereign immunity conceptions displayed itself....

## II

The Court's rationale for today's holding based on a conception of sovereign immunity as somehow fundamental to sovereignty or inherent in statehood fails for the lack of any substantial support for such a conception in the thinking of the founding era. The Court cannot be counted out yet, however, for it has a second line of argument looking not to a clause-based reception of the natural law conception or even to its recognition as a "background principle," but to a structural basis in the Constitution's creation of a federal system. Immunity, the Court says, "inheres in the system of federalism established by the Constitution," its "contours [being] determined by the Founders' understanding, not by the principles or limitations derived from natural law." Again, "we look both to the essential principles of federalism and to the special role of the state courts in the constitutional design." That is, the Court believes that the federal constitutional structure itself necessitates recognition of some degree of state autonomy broad enough to include sovereign immunity from suit in a State's own courts, regardless of the federal source of the claim asserted against the State. If one were to read the Court's federal structure rationale in isolation from the preceding portions of the opinion, it would appear that the Court's position on state sovereign immunity might have been rested entirely on federalism alone. If it had been, however, I would still be in dissent, for the Court's argument that state-court sovereign immunity on federal questions is inherent in the very concept of federal structure is demonstrably mistaken.

## A

The National Constitution formally and finally repudiated the received political wisdom that a system of multiple sovereignties constituted the "great solecism of an *imperium in imperio.*" Once "the atom of sovereignty" had been split, *U.S. Term Limits, Inc. v. Thornton* (1995) (KENNEDY, J., concurring) [*Supra.* Chapter 3], the general scheme of delegated sovereignty as between the two component governments of the federal system was clear, and was succinctly stated by Chief Justice Marshall: "In America, the powers of sovereignty are divided between the government of the Union, and those of the States. They are each sovereign, with respect to the objects committed to it, and neither sovereign with respect to the objects committed to the other." *McCulloch.*

Hence the flaw in the Court's appeal to federalism. The State of Maine is not sovereign with respect to the national objectives of the Fair Labor Standards Act. It is not the authority that promulgated the FLSA, on which the right of action in this case depends. That authority is the United States acting through the Congress, whose legislative power under Article I of the Constitution to extend FLSA coverage to state employees has already been decided, see *Garcia v. San Antonio Metropolitan Transit Authority*, 469 U.S. 528 (1985) [Note *supra*. this chapter], and is not contested here....

### B

It is symptomatic of the weakness of the structural notion proffered by the Court that it seeks to buttress the argument by relying on " 'the dignity and respect afforded a State, which the immunity is designed to protect,' " (quoting *Idaho v. Coeur d'Alene Tribe of Idaho*), and by invoking the many demands on a State's fisc. Apparently beguiled by Gilded Era language describing private suits against States as "neither becoming nor convenient," the Court calls "immunity from private suits central to sovereign dignity," and assumes that this "dignity" is a quality easily translated from the person of the King to the participatory abstraction of a republican State. The thoroughly anomalous character of this appeal to dignity is obvious from a reading of Blackstone's description of royal dignity, which he sets out as a premise of his discussion of sovereignty:

> First, then, of the royal dignity. Under every monarchical establishment, it is necessary to distinguish the prince from his subjects.... The law therefore ascribes to the king ... certain attributes of a great and transcendent nature; by which the people are led to consider him in the light of a superior being, and to pay him that awful respect, which may enable him with greater ease to carry on the business of government. This is what I understand by the royal dignity, the several branches of which we will now proceed to examine.
> 1 Blackstone, *Commentaries* *241.

It would be hard to imagine anything more inimical to the republican conception, which rests on the understanding of its citizens precisely that the government is not above them, but of them, its actions being governed by law just like their own. Whatever justification there may be for an American government's immunity from private suit, it is not dignity.

It is equally puzzling to hear the Court say that "federal power to authorize private suits for money damages would place unwarranted strain on the States' ability to govern in accordance with the will of their citizens." So long as the citizens' will, expressed through state legislation, does not violate valid federal law, the strain will not be felt; and to the extent that state action does violate federal law, the will of the citizens of the United States already trumps that of the citizens of the State: the strain then is not only expected, but necessarily intended.

Least of all does the Court persuade by observing that "other important needs" than that of the "judgment creditor" compete for public money. The "judgment creditor" in question is not a dunning bill collector, but a citizen whose federal rights have been violated, and a constitutional structure that stints on enforcing federal rights out of an abundance of delicacy toward the States has substituted politesse in place of respect for the rule of law.

### III

If neither theory nor structure can supply the basis for the Court's conceptions of sovereign immunity and federalism, then perhaps history might. The Court apparently believes that because state courts have not historically entertained Commerce Clause based federal-law claims against the States, such an innovation carries a presumption of unconstitutionality. At the outset, it has to be noted that this approach assumes a more cohesive record than history affords.... But even if the record were less unkempt, the problem with arguing from historical practice in this case is that past practice, even if unbroken, provides no basis for demanding preservation when the conditions on which the practice depended have changed in a constitutionally relevant way.

It was at one time, though perhaps not from the framing, believed that "Congress' authority to regulate the States under the Commerce Clause" was limited by "certain underlying elements of political sovereignty ... deemed essential to the States' separate and independent existence." *Garcia*. On this belief, the preordained balance between state and federal sovereignty was understood to trump the terms of Article I and preclude Congress from subjecting States to federal law on certain subjects.... As a consequence it was rare, if not unknown, for state courts to confront the situation in which federal law enacted under the Commerce Clause provided the authority for a private right of action against a State in state court. The question of state immunity from a Commerce Clause based federal-law suit in state court thus tended not to arise for the simple reason that Acts of Congress authorizing such suits did not exist.

Today, however, in light of *Garcia* ... the law is settled that federal legislation enacted under the Commerce Clause may bind the States without having to satisfy a test of undue incursion into state sovereignty.... Because the commerce power is no longer thought to be circumscribed, the dearth of prior private federal claims entertained against the States in state courts does not tell us anything, and reflects nothing but an earlier and less expansive application of the commerce power.

Least of all is it to the point for the Court to suggest that because the Framers would be surprised to find States subjected to a federal-law suit in their own courts under the commerce power, the suit must be prohibited by the Constitution. The Framers' intentions and expectations count so far as they point to the meaning of the Constitution's text or the fair implications of its structure, but they do not hover over the instrument to veto any application of its principles to a world that the Framers could not have anticipated.

If the Framers would be surprised to see States subjected to suit in their own courts under the commerce power, they would be astonished by the reach of Congress under the Commerce Clause generally. The proliferation of Government, State and Federal, would amaze the Framers, and the administrative state with its reams of regulations would leave them rubbing their eyes. But the Framers' surprise at, say, the FLSA, or the Federal Communications Commission, or the Federal Reserve Board is no threat to the constitutionality of any one of them, for a very fundamental reason:

> When we are dealing with words that also are a constituent act, like the Constitution of the United States, we must realize that they have called into life a being the development of which could not have been foreseen completely by the most gifted of its begetters. It was enough for them to realize or to

hope that they had created an organism; it has taken a century and has cost their successors much sweat and blood to prove that they created a nation. The case before us must be considered in the light of our whole experience and not merely in that of what was said a hundred years ago. *Missouri v. Holland*, 252 U.S. 416 (1920) (Holmes, J.).

" 'We must never forget,' said Mr. Chief Justice Marshall in *McCulloch*, 'that it is a Constitution we are expounding.' Since then this Court has repeatedly sustained the exercise of power by Congress, under various clauses of that instrument, over objects of which the Fathers could not have dreamed." *Olmstead v. United States*, 277 U.S. 438 (1928) (Brandeis, J., dissenting).

## IV
### A

If today's decision occasions regret at its anomalous versions of history and federal theory, it is the more regrettable in being the second time the Court has suddenly changed the course of prior decision in order to limit the exercise of authority over a subject now concededly within the Article I jurisdiction of the Congress. [Justice Souter discussed the Court's shifting line of cases, beginning with *Maryland v. Wirtz*, 392 U.S. 183 (1968) (Note *supra.* this chapter) and ending in *Garcia*, about the applicability of the FLSA to state employers.] … The Court in *Seminole Tribe* created a significant impediment to the [FLSA's] practical application by rendering its damages provisions unenforceable against the States by private suit in federal court. Today's decision blocking private actions in state courts makes the barrier to individual enforcement a total one.

### B

The Court might respond … that the United States may bring suit in federal court against a State for damages under the FLSA … but unless Congress plans a significant expansion of the National Government's litigating forces to provide a lawyer whenever private litigation is barred by today's decision and *Seminole Tribe,* the allusion to enforcement of private rights by the National Government is probably not much more than whimsy.…

So there is much irony in the Court's profession that it grounds its opinion on a deeply rooted historical tradition of sovereign immunity, when the Court abandons a principle nearly as inveterate, and much closer to the hearts of the Framers: that where there is a right, there must be a remedy.… When Chief Justice Marshall asked about Marbury: "If he has a right, and that right has been violated, do the laws of his country afford him a remedy?," *Marbury* [Supra. *Chapter 1], the question was rhetorical, and the answer clear:*

> The very essence of civil liberty certainly consists in the right of every individual to claim the protection of the laws, whenever he receives an injury. One of the first duties of government is to afford that protection. In Great Britain the king himself is sued in the respectful form of a petition, and he never fails to comply with the judgment of his court.

Yet today the Court has no qualms about saying frankly that the federal right to damages afforded by Congress under the FLSA cannot create a concomitant private remedy. The right was "made for the benefit of" petitioners; they have been "hindered by another of that benefit"; but despite what has long been understood as the "necessary consequence of law," they have no action. It will not do for the Court to respond that a remedy was never available where the right in question was against the sovereign. A State is not the sovereign when a federal claim is pressed against it, and even the English sovereign opened itself to recovery and, unlike Maine, provided the remedy to complement the right. To the Americans of the founding generation it would have been clear (as it was to Chief Justice Marshall) that if the King would do right, the democratically chosen Government of the United States could do no less....

## Note: The Scope of State Sovereignty

1. The materials on direct federal regulation of the states and state sovereign immunity combine to create a picture of American federalism in which states are sovereign in some important ways, but not others. Thus, after *Garcia* Congress can regulate states as economic actors, but after *New York* and *Printz* it cannot "commandeer," respectively, state legislative or law enforcement processes. After the sovereign immunity cases, individual beneficiaries of federal regulation (*e.g.*, employees of state governments covered by federal wage and hour laws) can vindicate their federal rights against states who violate them, but only by seeking certain types of relief, or only when Congress legislates pursuant to certain grants of power. The tensions inherent in these rules reflect the Court's concern for both the supremacy of federal law and the continued existence of the states as entities that remain sovereign within their appropriate realms. In this sense, these materials dovetail with the problem raised in Chapter 3. Chapter 3 asked what powers the federal government needs in order to be fully sovereign and superior to the states. The materials you have just finished ask what freedoms *states* need *from* federal power in order to remain meaningfully sovereign, consistent with the ultimate superiority of the federal government.

2. What do you make of the Court's attempt to square state sovereignty and federal supremacy? As you've seen, the Court's jurisprudence requires the drawing of lines that may seem to you somewhat arbitrary. For example, doesn't regulating states as employers (allowed under *Garcia*) arguably "commandeer" state legislatures (prohibited under *New York*) when that regulation requires states to deliberate on how best to structure government employment so as to comply with federal law? Does *Reno v. Condon* (the note case dealing with driver's license information sales) demonstrate the impossibility of drawing this distinction with any precision?

Similarly, doesn't the availability of prospective relief under *Ex parte Young* seriously threaten states' treasuries, if such relief takes the form of wide-ranging injunctions? Such injunctions can be quite broad—for example, they can require the state to revamp its prison system, desegregate its schools, or, as in *Edelman*, change its formula for calculating welfare benefits. Justice Rehnquist probably understated the point when he wrote in *Edelman* that "the difference between the type of relief barred by the

Eleventh Amendment and that permitted under *Ex parte Young* will not in many instances be that between day and night." Is there really any practical difference at all?

3. In light of these puzzles, how persuaded are you that the Court's jurisprudence in this area makes any sense? Would it be sufficient for the Court to adopt *Garcia* across the board, and conclude that the national political process presents the states with their most effective protection in our federal system? How would you respond to the objection that reliance on that process might have been appropriate when State legislatures had the power to name their Senators, but not after the Seventeenth Amendment (ratified in 1913) made the Senate elected by the *people* of each state? Does the federal-state balance need judicial policing? If so, what principles would you suggest to guide that effort?

# D. The Taxing and Spending Power as an Alternative to Regulation

In addition to regulatory powers, Article I also gives Congress "Power To lay and collect Taxes, … to pay the Debts and provide for the common Defense and general Welfare of the United States." Art. I, § 8, cl. 1. The "Taxing and Spending" power gives Congress exceptional authority to shape policy in every area of American life. These powers are construed broadly. However, federalism concerns have led the Court to impose restrictions when Congress uses those powers to interact with states. This book does not treat the complex topic of intergovernmental tax immunity—but recall the excerpt from *McCulloch v. Maryland* (1819) in Chapter 3, which rejected Maryland's attempt to impose a direct tax on the operations of the Bank of the United States. This book does, however, consider federalism-based limits on the Spending Clause—in particular, the limits on Congress's ability to grant money to states but only on the condition that the state take particular regulatory actions.

## 1. The General Scope of the Power

The taxing and spending power appears at the start of Article I, Section 8, the section that enumerates Congress's powers, such as the power to regulate interstate commerce and establish a patent system. A question raised early in the Constitution's history, but not decided until 1936, was whether the taxing and spending power had to be exercised in furtherance of one or more of those regulatory grants, or whether it was a freestanding power limited only by the requirement that the taxing or spending be in pursuit of the general welfare. In *United States v. Butler*, 297 U.S. 1 (1936), the Court embraced the latter, broader conception:

> Since the foundation of the nation, sharp differences of opinion have persisted as to the true interpretation of the phrase ["to provide for the general welfare"]. Madison asserted it amounted to no more than a reference to the other powers enumerated in the subsequent clauses of the same section; that,

as the United States is a government of limited and enumerated powers, the grant of power to tax and spend for the general national welfare must be confined to the enumerated legislative fields committed to the Congress. In this view the phrase is mere tautology, for taxation and appropriation are or may be necessary incidents of the exercise of any of the enumerated legislative powers. Hamilton, on the other hand, maintained the clause confers a power separate and distinct from those later enumerated, is not restricted in meaning by the grant of them, and Congress consequently has a substantive power to tax and to appropriate, limited only by the requirement that it shall be exercised to provide for the general welfare of the United States. Each contention has had the support of those whose views are entitled to weight. This court has noticed the question, but has never found it necessary to decide which is the true construction. Mr. Justice Story, in his *Commentaries on the Constitution*, espouses the Hamiltonian position. We shall not review the writings of public men and commentators or discuss the legislative practice. Study of all these leads us to conclude that the reading advocated by Mr. Justice Story is the correct one. While, therefore, the power to tax is not unlimited, its confines are set in the clause which confers it, and not in those of section 8 which bestow and define the legislative powers of the Congress. It results that the power of Congress to authorize expenditure of public moneys for public purposes is not limited by the direct grants of legislative power found in the Constitution.

Despite this broad reading of the spending power, *Butler* nevertheless struck down the spending at issue, on the ground that the spending program (an agricultural price support program) was actually a covert attempt to regulate agriculture rather than a bona fide taxing and spending program. This limitation on the otherwise broad congressional taxing and spending power was an artifact of the Court's pre-1937 jurisprudence. The following case suggested that the Court would no longer examine whether a tax or an appropriation was really a covert attempt to regulate. Note, however, that the *Butler* principle reappeared in different form 50 years later in Justice O'Connor's dissent in *South Dakota v. Dole*, excerpted in the next sub-section. And note also the Court's 2012 decision in the Affordable Care Act case, where the Court split sharply on whether the payment at issue could be upheld as a tax.

## Sonzinsky v. United States

### 300 U.S. 506 (1937)

Mr. Justice Stone delivered the opinion of the Court.

The question for decision is whether section 2 of the National Firearms Act of June 26, 1934, which imposes a $200 annual license tax on dealers in firearms, is a constitutional exercise of the legislative power of Congress....

Section 2 of the National Firearms Act requires every dealer in firearms ... to pay a special excise tax of $200 a year. Importers or manufacturers are taxed $500 a year.

Section 3 imposes a tax of $200 on each transfer of a firearm, payable by the transferor.... The term "firearm" is defined by section 1 as meaning a shotgun or a rifle having a barrel less than eighteen inches in length, or any other weapon, except a pistol or revolver, from which a shot is discharged by an explosive, if capable of being concealed on the person, or a machine gun, and includes a muffler or silencer for any firearm....

In the exercise of its constitutional power to lay taxes, Congress may select the subjects of taxation, choosing some and omitting others. Petitioner ... insists that the present levy is not a true tax, but a penalty imposed for the purpose of suppressing traffic in a certain noxious type of firearms, the local regulation of which is reserved to the states because not granted to the national government. To establish its penal and prohibitive character, he relies on the amounts of the tax imposed by section 2 on dealers, manufacturers, and importers, and of the tax imposed by section 3 on each transfer of a "firearm," payable by the transferor. The cumulative effect on the distribution of a limited class of firearms, of relatively small value, by the successive imposition of different taxes, one on the business of the importer or manufacturer, another on that of the dealer, and a third on the transfer to a buyer, is said to be prohibitive in effect and to disclose unmistakably the legislative purpose to regulate rather than to tax.

The case is not one where the statute contains regulatory provisions related to a purported tax in such a way as has enabled this Court to say in other cases that the latter is a penalty resorted to as a means of enforcing the regulations.... On its face it is only a taxing measure, and we are asked to say that the tax, by virtue of its deterrent effect on the activities taxed, operates as a regulation which is beyond the congressional power.

Every tax is in some measure regulatory. To some extent it interposes an economic impediment to the activity taxed as compared with others not taxed. But a tax is not any the less a tax because it has a regulatory effect ... and it has long been established that an Act of Congress which on its face purports to be an exercise of the taxing power is not any the less so because the tax is burdensome or tends to restrict or suppress the thing taxed.

Inquiry into the hidden motives which may move Congress to exercise a power constitutionally conferred upon it is beyond the competency of courts. They will not undertake, by collateral inquiry as to the measure of the regulatory effect of a tax, to ascribe to Congress an attempt, under the guise of taxation, to exercise another power denied by the Federal Constitution.

Here the annual tax of $200 is productive of some revenue.[1] We are not free to speculate as to the motives which moved Congress to impose it, or as to the extent to which it may operate to restrict the activities taxed. As it is not attended by an of-

---

1. The $200 tax was paid by 27 dealers in 1934, and by 22 dealers in 1935. Annual Report of the Commissioner of Internal Revenue, Fiscal Year Ended June 30, 1935, pp. 129–131; Id., Fiscal Year Ended June 30, 1936, pp. 139–141.

fensive regulation, and since it operates as a tax, it is within the national taxing power....

### *Note:* National Federation of Independent Business v. Sebelius *and the Taxing Power*

1. As noted in Chapter 4, in 2012 the Court held that the so-called "individual mandate" of the 2010 Affordable Care Act (ACA) was not a valid regulation of interstate commerce, nor was it regulation "necessary and proper" to implement the commerce power. However, one of the members of that 5-Justice majority, Chief Justice Roberts, joined with the four dissenters on the Commerce Clause/Necessary and Proper Clause issues to hold that the individual mandate *was* valid as a taxing measure, given that the ACA imposed a "shared responsibility payment," payable to the Internal Revenue Service, when a taxpayer failed to obtain insurance as contemplated by the individual mandate.

2. Writing for that five-justice majority, the Chief Justice concluded that the Court's taxing power cases had employed a "functional" approach marked by three criteria: the burdensomeness of the purported tax, the existence of a knowledge, or "scienter," requirement as a predicate to liability under the purported tax, and the process by which the purported tax was enforced. Applying those criteria, he wrote as follows:

> The same ["functional"] analysis here suggests that the shared responsibility payment may for constitutional purposes be considered a tax, not a penalty: First, for most Americans the amount due will be far less than the price of insurance, and, by statute, it can never be more. It may often be a reasonable financial decision to make the payment rather than purchase insurance, unlike the "prohibitory" financial punishment in [an earlier case where a purported tax was struck down as an invalid attempt at regulation.] Second, the individual mandate contains no scienter requirement. Third, the payment is collected solely by the IRS through the normal means of taxation — except that the Service is not allowed to use those means most suggestive of a punitive sanction, such as criminal prosecution....

> None of this is to say that the payment is not intended to affect individual conduct. Although the payment will raise considerable revenue, it is plainly designed to expand health insurance coverage. But taxes that seek to influence conduct are nothing new.... Today, federal and state taxes can compose more than half the retail price of cigarettes, not just to raise more money, but to encourage people to quit smoking. And we have upheld such obviously regulatory measures as taxes on selling marijuana and sawed-off shotguns. See *United States v. Sanchez*, 340 U.S. 42 (1950); *Sonzinsky v. United States* (1937) [*Supra.* this chapter]. Indeed, "every tax is in some measure regulatory. To some extent it interposes an economic impediment to the activity taxed as compared with others not taxed." *Sonzinsky.* That § 5000A [the individual mandate] seeks to shape decisions about whether to buy health insurance does not mean that it cannot be a valid exercise of the taxing power....

The joint dissenters argue that we cannot uphold § 5000A as a tax because Congress did not "frame" it as such. In effect, they contend that even if the Constitution permits Congress to do exactly what we interpret this statute to do, the law must be struck down because Congress used the wrong labels.... Our precedent demonstrates that Congress had the power to impose the exaction in § 5000A under the taxing power, and that § 5000A need not be read to do more than impose a tax. That is sufficient to sustain it. The "question of the constitutionality of action taken by Congress does not depend on recitals of the power which it undertakes to exercise."

Nevertheless, the Chief Justice signaled his willingness to police the line between taxation and regulation:

... Congress's ability to use its taxing power to influence conduct is not without limits. A few of our cases policed these limits aggressively, invalidating punitive exactions obviously designed to regulate behavior otherwise regarded at the time as beyond federal authority. See, e.g., *United States v. Butler*, 297 U.S. 1 (1936) [Note *supra.* this chapter]. More often and more recently we have declined to closely examine the regulatory motive or effect of revenue-raising measures. We have nonetheless maintained that "there comes a time in the extension of the penalizing features of the so-called tax when it loses its character as such and becomes a mere penalty with the characteristics of regulation and punishment."

We have already explained that the shared responsibility payment's practical characteristics pass muster as a tax under our narrowest interpretations of the taxing power. Because the tax at hand is within even those strict limits, we need not here decide the precise point at which an exaction becomes so punitive that the taxing power does not authorize it....

3. Justices Scalia, Kennedy, Thomas, and Alito dissented on the taxing power issue. Writing for them, Justice Scalia argued that the government could not argue that the "shared responsibility payment" was a valid regulation, but that, in the alternative, it was a tax. He concluded that "there is simply no way, without doing violence to the fair meaning of the words used, to escape what Congress enacted: a mandate that individuals maintain minimum essential coverage, enforced by a penalty." He disagreed with the majority about the relevance of the payment's collection by the IRS, or the lack of a scienter requirement; as he observed with regard to the last point, "The presence of such a requirement suggests a penalty—though one can imagine a tax imposed only on willful action; but the absence of such a requirement does not suggest a tax. Penalties for absolute-liability offenses are commonplace."

## 2. The Spending Power as a Means of Influencing State Government Conduct

Despite the modern Court's broad reading of the taxing and spending power in general, special rules grounded in federalism concerns apply when Congress grants money to states, on the condition that the recipient state act in a certain way. While the *Dole* case excerpted below suggested that the Court would review such conditions deferentially, its decision in another aspect of the Affordable Care Act case suggested its willingness to police Congress's conditional spending power more carefully.

## South Dakota v. Dole

### 483 U.S. 203 (1987)

CHIEF JUSTICE REHNQUIST delivered the opinion of the Court.

Petitioner South Dakota permits persons 19 years of age or older to purchase beer containing up to 3.2% alcohol. In 1984 Congress enacted 23 U.S.C. § 158, which directs the Secretary of Transportation to withhold a percentage of federal highway funds otherwise allocable from States "in which the purchase or public possession ... of any alcoholic beverage by a person who is less than twenty-one years of age is lawful." The State sued in United States District Court seeking a declaratory judgment that § 158 violates the constitutional limitations on congressional exercise of the spending power and violates the Twenty-first Amendment to the United States Constitution. The District Court rejected the State's claims, and the Court of Appeals for the Eighth Circuit affirmed....

The Constitution empowers Congress to "lay and collect Taxes, Duties, Imposts, and Excises, to pay the Debts and provide for the common Defence and general Welfare of the United States." Incident to this power, Congress may attach conditions on the receipt of federal funds, and has repeatedly employed the power "to further broad policy objectives by conditioning receipt of federal moneys upon compliance by the recipient with federal statutory and administrative directives." The breadth of this power was made clear in *United States v. Butler*, 297 U.S. 1 (1936) [Note *supra.* this chapter], where the Court, resolving a longstanding debate over the scope of the Spending Clause, determined that "the power of Congress to authorize expenditure of public moneys for public purposes is not limited by the direct grants of legislative power found in the Constitution." Thus, objectives not thought to be within Article I's "enumerated legislative fields" ... may nevertheless be attained through the use of the spending power and the conditional grant of federal funds.

The spending power is of course not unlimited ... but is instead subject to several general restrictions articulated in our cases. The first of these limitations is derived from the language of the Constitution itself: the exercise of the spending power must be in pursuit of "the general welfare." In considering whether a particular expenditure is intended to serve general public purposes, courts should defer substantially to the judgment of Congress.[2] Second, we have required that if Congress desires to condition the States' receipt of federal funds, it "must do so unambiguously..., enabling the States

---

2. The level of deference to the congressional decision is such that the Court has more recently questioned whether "general welfare" is a judicially enforceable restriction at all.

to exercise their choice knowingly, cognizant of the consequences of their participation." Third, our cases have suggested (without significant elaboration) that conditions on federal grants might be illegitimate if they are unrelated "to the federal interest in particular national projects or programs." Finally, we have noted that other constitutional provisions may provide an independent bar to the conditional grant of federal funds.

... We can readily conclude that the provision is designed to serve the general welfare, especially in light of the fact that "the concept of welfare or the opposite is shaped by Congress...." Congress found that the differing drinking ages in the States created particular incentives for young persons to combine their desire to drink with their ability to drive, and that this interstate problem required a national solution. The means it chose to address this dangerous situation were reasonably calculated to advance the general welfare. The conditions upon which States receive the funds, moreover, could not be more clearly stated by Congress. And the State itself, rather than challenging the germaneness of the condition to federal purposes, admits that it "has never contended that the congressional action was ... unrelated to a national concern in the absence of the Twenty-first Amendment." Indeed, the condition imposed by Congress is directly related to one of the main purposes for which highway funds are expended—safe interstate travel....[3] This goal of the interstate highway system had been frustrated by varying drinking ages among the States. A Presidential commission appointed to study alcohol-related accidents and fatalities on the Nation's highways concluded that the lack of uniformity in the States' drinking ages created "an incentive to drink and drive" because "young persons commute to border States where the drinking age is lower." By enacting § 158, Congress conditioned the receipt of federal funds in a way reasonably calculated to address this particular impediment to a purpose for which the funds are expended.

The remaining question about the validity of § 158—and the basic point of disagreement between the parties—is whether the Twenty-first Amendment constitutes an "independent constitutional bar" to the conditional grant of federal funds. Petitioner, relying on its view that the Twenty-first Amendment prohibits direct regulation of drinking ages by Congress, asserts that "Congress may not use the spending power to regulate that which it is prohibited from regulating directly under the Twenty-first Amendment." But our cases show that this "independent constitutional bar" limitation on the spending power is not of the kind petitioner suggests. *United States v. Butler* ... for example, established that the constitutional limitations on Congress when exercising its spending power are less exacting than those on its authority to regulate directly....

---

3. Our cases have not required that we define the outer bounds of the "germaneness" or "relatedness" limitation on the imposition of conditions under the spending power. *Amici* urge that we take this occasion to establish that a condition on federal funds is legitimate only if it relates directly to the purpose of the expenditure to which it is attached. See Brief for National Conference of State Legislatures et al. as *Amici Curiae*. Because petitioner has not sought such a restriction, see Tr. of Oral Arg. 19–21, and because we find any such limitation on conditional federal grants satisfied in this case in any event, we do not address whether conditions less directly related to the particular purpose of the expenditure might be outside the bounds of the spending power.

These cases establish that the "independent constitutional bar" limitation on the spending power is not, as petitioner suggests, a prohibition on the indirect achievement of objectives which Congress is not empowered to achieve directly. Instead, we think that the language in our earlier opinions stands for the unexceptionable proposition that the power may not be used to induce the States to engage in activities that would themselves be unconstitutional. Thus, for example, a grant of federal funds conditioned on invidiously discriminatory state action or the infliction of cruel and unusual punishment would be an illegitimate exercise of the Congress' broad spending power. But no such claim can be or is made here. Were South Dakota to succumb to the blandishments offered by Congress and raise its drinking age to 21, the State's action in so doing would not violate the constitutional rights of anyone.

Our decisions have recognized that in some circumstances the financial inducement offered by Congress might be so coercive as to pass the point at which "pressure turns into compulsion." Here, however, Congress has directed only that a State desiring to establish a minimum drinking age lower than 21 lose a relatively small percentage of certain federal highway funds. Petitioner contends that the coercive nature of this program is evident from the degree of success it has achieved. We cannot conclude, however, that a conditional grant of federal money of this sort is unconstitutional simply by reason of its success in achieving the congressional objective....

Here Congress has offered relatively mild encouragement to the States to enact higher minimum drinking ages than they would otherwise choose. But the enactment of such laws remains the prerogative of the States not merely in theory but in fact. Even if Congress might lack the power to impose a national minimum drinking age directly, we conclude that encouragement to state action found in § 158 is a valid use of the spending power. Accordingly, the judgment of the Court of Appeals is Affirmed.

Justice Brennan, dissenting. [omitted]

Justice O'Connor, dissenting....

My disagreement with the Court is relatively narrow on the spending power issue: it is a disagreement about the application of a principle rather than a disagreement on the principle itself.... In my view, establishment of a minimum drinking age of 21 is not sufficiently related to interstate highway construction to justify so conditioning funds appropriated for that purpose.

In support of its contrary conclusion, the Court relies on a supposed concession by counsel for South Dakota that the State "has never contended that the congressional action was ... unrelated to a national concern in the absence of the Twenty-first Amendment." ...

Aside from these "concessions" by counsel, the Court asserts the reasonableness of the relationship between the supposed purpose of the expenditure — "safe interstate travel" — and the drinking age condition. The Court reasons that Congress wishes that the roads it builds may be used safely, that drunken drivers threaten highway safety, and that young people are more likely to drive while under the influence of alcohol under existing law than would be the case if there were a uniform national drinking age of 21. It hardly needs saying, however, that if the purpose of § 158 is to deter drunken driving, it is far too over- and under-inclusive. It is over-inclusive because it stops teenagers from drinking even when they are not about to drive on interstate highways. It is under-inclusive because teenagers pose only a small part of the drunken driving problem in this Nation.

When Congress appropriates money to build a highway, it is entitled to insist that the highway be a safe one. But it is not entitled to insist as a condition of the use of highway funds that the State impose or change regulations in other areas of the State's social and economic life because of an attenuated or tangential relationship to highway use or safety. Indeed, if the rule were otherwise, the Congress could effectively regulate almost any area of a State's social, political, or economic life on the theory that use of the interstate transportation system is somehow enhanced. If, for example, the United States were to condition highway moneys upon moving the state capital, I suppose it might argue that interstate transportation is facilitated by locating local governments in places easily accessible to interstate highways—or, conversely, that highways might become overburdened if they had to carry traffic to and from the state capital. In my mind, such a relationship is hardly more attenuated than the one which the Court finds supports § 158.

There is a clear place at which the Court can draw the line between permissible and impermissible conditions on federal grants. It is the line identified in the Brief for the National Conference of State Legislatures et al. as *Amici Curiae*:

> Congress has the power to *spend* for the general welfare, it has the power to *legislate* only for delegated purposes.... The appropriate inquiry, then, is whether the spending requirement or prohibition is a condition on a grant or whether it is regulation. The difference turns on whether the requirement specifies in some way how the money should be spent, so that Congress' intent in making the grant will be effectuated. Congress has no power under the Spending Clause to impose requirements on a grant that go beyond specifying how the money should be spent. A requirement that is not such a specification is not a condition, but a regulation, which is valid only if it falls within one of Congress' delegated regulatory powers.

This approach harks back to *United States v. Butler....* The *Butler* Court saw the Agricultural Adjustment Act for what it was—an exercise of regulatory, not spending, power. The error in *Butler* was not the Court's conclusion that the Act was essentially regulatory, but rather its crabbed view of the extent of Congress' regulatory power under the Commerce Clause. The Agricultural Adjustment Act was regulatory but it was regulation that today would likely be considered within Congress' commerce power. *See, e.g., Katzenbach v. McClung*, 379 U.S. 294 (1964) [Note *supra*. Chapter 4]; *Wickard v. Filburn* (1942) [*Supra*. Chapter 4].

While *Butler*'s authority is questionable insofar as it assumes that Congress has no regulatory power over farm production, its discussion of the spending power and its description of both the power's breadth and its limitations remain sound. The Court's decision in *Butler* also properly recognizes the gravity of the task of appropriately limiting the spending power. If the spending power is to be limited only by Congress' notion of the general welfare, the reality, given the vast financial resources of the Federal Government, is that the Spending Clause gives "power to the Congress to tear down the barriers, to invade the states' jurisdiction, and to become a parliament of the whole people, subject to no restrictions save such as are self-imposed." *Butler*. This, of course, as *Butler* held, was not the Framers' plan and it is not the meaning of the Spending Clause....

Of the other possible sources of congressional authority for regulating the sale of liquor only the commerce power comes to mind. But in my view, the regulation of the age of the purchasers of liquor, just as the regulation of the price at which liquor may be sold, falls squarely within the scope of those powers reserved to the States by the Twenty-first Amendment.... Accordingly, Congress simply lacks power under the Commerce Clause to displace state regulation of this kind....

## *Note:* National Federation of Independent Business v. Sebelius *and the Medicaid Expansion*

*National Federation* has been discussed earlier in Part II, both with regard to its analysis of the taxing and commerce/necessary-and-proper groundings for the individual mandate. Another part of *National Federation* concerned the law's expansion of Medicaid. Medicaid is a program cooperatively run by the federal government and participating states. (All fifty states participate in the program in some way.) The Affordable Care Act (ACA) expanded eligibility for Medicaid, and offered additional funds to states who chose to take part in that expansion. However, the statute conditioned a state's receipt of *all* of its federal Medicaid funding on the state's agreement to participate in the expansion. Thus, while a state could choose to decline to participate in that expansion, if it did it would lose all of its federal funding for the Medicaid plan more generally.

In *National Federation* a seven-justice majority struck down that condition as unduly coercive of states. Writing for himself and Justices Breyer and Kagan, Chief Justice Roberts distinguished the spending condition upheld in *South Dakota v. Dole*, which *Dole* described as a "relative mild encouragement" to the state to adopt the desired federal policy, from the analogous condition in the ACA, which Chief Justice Roberts described as "a gun to the head." As support for that distinction, he relied heavily on the large size of states' Medicaid expenditures (which he described as accounting for over 20% of a state's average budget) and the large proportion of that funding that came from the federal government (which he described as ranging from 50–83%). He also argued that the ACA's Medicaid expansion was so different from what Medicaid had been before, that it was a new program. Thus, he concluded, Congress was conditioning its funding of one state program on its acceptance of a different one. He therefore disagreed with the dissent's claim that in the ACA Congress simply threatened states with loss of their Medicaid funding if they did not fully participate in that (same) program.

Justice Scalia wrote for the same group of justices (himself, Kennedy, Thomas, and Alito) who had joined his opinion rejecting the constitutionality of the individual mandate. On the Spending Clause issue, he agreed with the Chief Justice about the magnitude of the impact on the states of losing their existing federal Medicaid funding if they declined to participate in the expanded program. He also stated that Congress's failure to provide a backup plan for poor citizens of states that lost their Medicaid funding suggested that Congress itself understood that states would not have a realistic choice to reject participation in the expanded program.

Justice Ginsburg, writing for herself and Justice Sotomayor, dissented. She argued that the ACA simply expanded the existing Medicaid program, which had always put states on notice that the terms of participation might be changed. She also took issue with his coercion analysis, arguing that such analysis involves subjective political judgments which courts could not competently make.

The voting in *National Federation* raised the possibility that the entire Medicaid expansion, and not just the condition the ACA imposed on state participation in that expansion, might be invalid. However, the Chief Justice's opinion for three justices and Justice Ginsburg's dissent for two justices created a majority for a decision that invalidated the condition, but left the expansion in place, as an offer that states could accept or reject without any conditions. Justice Scalia's dissent would have struck the entire expansion down, since, in his view, retaining the expansion but dropping the condition would create an entirely new regulatory scheme.

## Note: Distinguishing Inducement from "a Gun to the Head"

The quoted phrase in the title of this note comes from Chief Justice Roberts' Spending Clause analysis in *National Federation* where he described the Affordable Care Act's threat to states of losing their full Medicaid funding as "a gun to the head," effectively coercing them to accept the statute's expansion of the Medicaid program. As you might intuitively understand from real life, distinguishing inducement from coercion is a tricky business. We all know that when a robber tells a victim, "your money or your life," he's not really offering a choice. But once we get past that example, how easy is it to tell one from the other? Is the coercion question even susceptible to standard legal analysis?

The Spending Clause analysis in *National Federation* may well have important implications for the future. Congress often uses conditional spending grants in order to "induce" states to take actions Congress does not have the power to mandate directly. For example, Congress provides enormous amounts of federal funding to states for their education and local crime-fighting efforts. Since direct federal regulation of those areas under the Commerce Clause appears to be on shaky constitutional ground after *United States v. Lopez* and *United States v. Morrison*, the spending power is likely the most effective way for Congress to work its will on those issues. Perhaps even more than its Commerce Clause analysis, *National Federation*'s cutback on the Spending Clause may well end up as that case's most lasting legacy.

# Part III

# Substantive Rights under the Due Process Clause

## Introduction

Parts III, IV, and V of this book consider the most consequential addition to the Constitution since the Bill of Rights—the Fourteenth Amendment. By providing individuals a catalog of rights as against their own states, that Amendment radically changed the structure of the federal system. With the enactment of the Amendment, the federal government—and federal courts in particular—would henceforth maintain a deep interest in how states related to their own citizens. Part III of this book considers the most important substantive rights the Fourteenth Amendment grants— Section 1's grant of the right to be free of state government actions that "deprive any person of life, liberty, or property, without due process of law." Part IV considers Section 1's grant of the right to be free of state actions which "deny to any person within its jurisdiction the equal protection of the laws." Part V considers two issues that apply to these rights more generally: Congress's power, under Section 5 of the Amendment, to "enforce" those rights, and the limitation imposed by the fact that these rights apply only to "state action."

Part III is organized partially chronologically, as the Court's focus in due process cases has shifted over time. Chapter 7 considers the rise and fall of the Court's concern with the so-called "right to contract"—that is, the right, normally expressed as one of the "liberties" the Clause protects without explicitly enumerating, to buy and sell in the marketplace free of unreasonable government interference. Chapter 8 charts the Court's evolving concern with non-economic rights. It focuses on both the process by which the Court included within, or "incorporated," most Bill of Rights provisions as liberties protected by the Fourteenth Amendment. It also considers the rise of non-economic liberties beyond those provided in the Bill of Rights. This latter branch of due process analysis eventually flowered into the Court's modern "substantive due process" jurisprudence, most notably its protection for the rights to abortion, family structure, sexual autonomy, and, in 2015, marriage rights for same-sex couples. Chapter 9 considers the Court's abortion rights jurisprudence. Chapter 10 concludes by examining the differing methodologies the modern Court has used to identify and protect other unenumerated, non-economic liberties.

## *Note: A False Start*

1. Despite the foundational nature of the Fourteenth Amendment, much of the impetus for its enactment and ratification grew out of doubts about the breadth of the previous amendment, the Thirteenth Amendment. Ratified in 1865, the Thirteenth Amendment prohibited slavery, and gave Congress the power to enforce that prohibition. The following year, Congress enacted The Civil Rights Act of 1866. That law gave to all Americans, among other rights, "the same right ... to make or enforce contracts ... [and] to full and equal benefit of all laws and proceedings for the security of person and property" "as white citizens." While the statute was enacted over President Johnson's veto, key congresspersons nevertheless expressed concern about whether the Thirteenth Amendment provided Congress with authority to enact it. Work soon started on what became the Fourteenth Amendment (and, indeed, the Civil Rights Act was re-enacted after that latter amendment was ratified).

2. When reading Section 1's grant of individual rights, one might be struck by the seeming straightforwardness of the structure. After starting by granting birthright citizenship (and thus overruling *Dred Scott v. Sandford*, 60 U.S. 393 (1857), which denied American citizenship to African-Americans), Section 1 then requires that states would not "abridge the privileges or immunities of citizens of the United States," deprive persons of "life, liberty, or property, without due process of law," or "deny to any person within its jurisdiction the equal protection of the laws." One might think that these latter three provisions fit neatly together: the Privileges or Immunities Clause prevents states from abridging a set of important substantive rights, the Due Process Clause ensures procedural fairness anytime a state seeks to deprive someone of an important interest ("life, liberty, or property"), and the Equal Protection Clause constitutes a general mandate of equal government treatment. Regardless of whether this understanding reflects the drafters' original intentions, an early Supreme Court decision, discussed in the rest of this Note, made it difficult for it to reach full flower.

3. The first case construing the Fourteenth Amendment concerned, not the rights of freed slaves, or of African-Americans more generally, but instead the rights of butchers in New Orleans. The Louisiana state government created a corporation for the purpose of enjoying a monopoly on slaughter-house services in the city. Slaughterhouses were, as one can imagine, a major health concern in the nineteenth century, given their practices of disposing of offal and other by-products of the slaughtering process into rivers and other waterways where they could endanger the public health. The state defended its decision to create The Crescent City Stock Landing and Slaughter House Corporation as just such a health measure. The statute at least ostensibly guar-

anteed that all butchers in New Orleans would have equal access to the corporation's slaughtering and dressing facilities.

Nevertheless, butchers in New Orleans sued, alleging that the statute violated the Fourteenth Amendment, by depriving them of the privilege or immunity of engaging in a lawful occupation (butchering). There was reason to think the butchers had a strong argument: in an important early case construing *Article IV*'s similarly-phrased Privileges and Immunities Clause, a Supreme Court justice deciding a circuit court case had given an expansive definition of "privileges" and "immunities" to include "the right to acquire and possess property of every kind, and to pursue and obtain happiness and safety, subject, nevertheless, to such restraints as the government may prescribe for the general good of the whole."

The Court nevertheless rejected the butchers' argument in *The Slaughter-House Cases*, 83 U.S. 36 (1873). In the part of the opinion most important for our purposes, Justice Miller, writing for the Court, provided a narrow definition of the terms "privileges" and "immunities" as the Fourteenth Amendment used those terms. He observed that the Amendment protected "the privileges or immunities *of citizens of the United States*" (emphasis added). He also observed that the Citizenship Clause of that Amendment provided for both national and state citizenship. Thus, he concluded, the Privileges or Immunities Clause simply protected a set of rights that inhered in national citizenship—literally, the "privileges" and "immunities" that attach to national citizenship—which did not include the right to pursue a trade. While he declined to provide an exhaustive catalog of the rights the clause *did* protect, he did say that they included the rights:

> to come to the seat of government to assert any claim he may have upon that government, to transact any business he may have with it, to seek its protection, to share its offices, to engage in administering its functions. He has the right of free access to its seaports, through which all operations of foreign commerce are conducted, to the subtreasuries, land offices, and courts of justice in the several States....

> Another privilege of a citizen of the United States is to demand the care and protection of the Federal government over his life, liberty, and property when on the high seas or within the jurisdiction of a foreign government. Of this there can be no doubt, nor that the right depends upon his character as a citizen of the United States. The right to peaceably assemble and petition for redress of grievances, the privilege of the writ of *habeas corpus*, are rights of the citizen guaranteed by the Federal Constitution. The right to use the navigable waters of the United States, however they may penetrate the territory of the several States, all rights secured to our citizens by treaties with foreign nations, are dependent upon citizenship of the United States, and not citizenship of a State. One of these privileges is conferred by the very article under consideration. It is that a citizen of the United States can, of his own volition, become a citizen of any State of the Union by a *bona fide* residence

therein, with the same rights as other citizens of that State. To these may be added the rights secured by the thirteenth and fifteenth [Amendments].

4. Justices Bradley, Swaine, and Field dissented. Most importantly for our purposes, Justice Field took a broad view of the rights the Privileges or Immunities Clause protected, to include the right to pursue a lawful occupation under reasonable and equal regulation—a right he argued was violated by the creation of a slaughterhouse monopoly that had no necessary connection to the health justifications for regulating the butchering trade. He pointed to the Civil Rights Act of 1866's protection of an equal right to hold property and engage in contracts as evidence that Congress understood the Fourteenth Amendment to reach such rights. Finally, he argued that the majority's more limited catalog of rights rendered the Clause superfluous; according to Justice Field, the foundation for these rights in federal citizenship meant that states had always been prohibited from interfering with them.

5. The result in *Slaughter-House* made it essentially impossible to rely on the Privileges and Immunities Clause once the Court became interested in finding substantive rights protections in the Fourteenth Amendment. While calls to overrule *Slaughter-House* have continued since 1873, the Court has avoided that issue by relying on the Due Process Clause as a source of fundamental rights, as set forth in the rest of Part III.

# Chapter 7

# The Rise and Fall of
# Economic Due Process

## Munn v. Illinois

### 94 U.S. 113 (1877)

MR. CHIEF JUSTICE WAITE delivered the opinion of the court.

The question to be determined in this case is whether the general assembly of Illinois can, under the limitations upon the legislative power of the States imposed by the Constitution of the United States, fix by law the maximum of charges for the storage of grain in warehouses at Chicago and other places in the State having not less than one hundred thousand inhabitants, 'in which grain is stored in bulk, and in which the grain of different owners is mixed together, or in which grain is stored in such a manner that the identity of different lots or parcels cannot be accurately preserved.'

It is claimed that such a law is repugnant—

1. To that part of sect. 8, art. 1, of the Constitution of the United States which confers upon Congress the power 'to regulate commerce with foreign nations and among the several States;'

2. To that part of sect. 9 of the same article which provides that 'no preference shall be given by any regulation of commerce or revenue to the ports of one State over those of another;' and

3. To that part of amendment 14 which ordains that no State shall 'deprive any person of life, liberty, or property, without due process of law, nor deny to any person within its jurisdiction the equal protection of the laws.'

We will consider the last of these objections first.

Every statute is presumed to be constitutional. The courts ought not to declare one to be unconstitutional, unless it is clearly so. If there is doubt, the expressed will of the legislature should be sustained.

The Constitution contains no definition of the word 'deprive,' as used in the Fourteenth Amendment. To determine its signification, therefore, it is necessary to ascertain the effect which usage has given it, when employed in the same or a like connection.

While this provision of the amendment is new in the Constitution of the United States, as a limitation upon the powers of the States, it is old as a principle of civilized government. It is found in Magna Charta, and, in substance if not in form, in nearly or quite all the constitutions that have been from time to time adopted by the several States of the Union. By the Fifth Amendment, it was introduced into the Constitution of the United States as a limitation upon the powers of the national government, and by the Fourteenth, as a guaranty against any encroachment upon an acknowledged right of citizenship by the legislatures of the States....

When one becomes a member of society, he necessarily parts with some rights or privileges which, as an individual not affected by his relations to others, he might retain. 'A body politic,' as aptly defined in the preamble of the Constitution of Massachusetts, 'is a social compact by which the whole people covenants with each citizen, and each citizen with the whole people, that all shall be governed by certain laws for the common good.' This does not confer power upon the whole people to control rights which are purely and exclusively private, but it does authorize the establishment of laws requiring each citizen to so conduct himself, and so use his own property, as not unnecessarily to injure another. This is the very essence of government, and has found expression in the maxim *sic utere tuo ut alienum non laedas*.[*] From this source come the police powers, which, as was said by Mr. Chief Justice Taney in the *License Cases*, 5 How. 504 (1847), 'are nothing more or less than the powers of government inherent in every sovereignty, ... that is to say, ... the power to govern men and things.' Under these powers the government regulates the conduct of its citizens one towards another, and the manner in which each shall use his own property, when such regulation becomes necessary for the public good. In their exercise it has been customary in England from time immemorial, and in this country from its first colonization, to regulate ferries, common carriers, hackmen, bakers, millers, wharfingers, innkeepers, &c., and in so doing to fix a maximum of charge to be made for services rendered, accommodations furnished, and articles sold....

From this it is apparent that, down to the time of the adoption of the Fourteenth Amendment, it was not supposed that statutes regulating the use, or even the price of the use, of private property necessarily deprived an owner of his property without due process of law. Under some circumstances they may, but not under all. The amendment does not change the law in this particular: it simply prevents the States from doing that which will operate as such a deprivation.

This brings us to inquire as to the principles upon which this power of regulation rests, in order that we may determine what is within and what without its operative effect. Looking, then, to the common law, from whence came the right which the Constitution protects, we find that when private property is 'affected with a public interest, it ceases to be *juris privati* only.'... When, therefore, one devotes his property to a use in which the public has an interest, he, in effect, grants to the public an interest in that use, and must submit to be controlled by the public for the common good, to the extent of the interest he has thus created. He may withdraw his grant

---

\* [Ed. Note: This Latin phrase means, roughly, "use your land so as not to injure others."]

by discontinuing the use; but, so long as he maintains the use, he must submit to the control.

Thus, as to ferries, Lord Hale says, in his treatise *De Jure Maris*, the king has 'a right of franchise or privilege, that no man may set up a common ferry for all passengers, without a prescription time out of mind, or a charter from the king.' ... So if one owns the soil and landing-places on both banks of a stream, he cannot use them for the purposes of a public ferry, except upon such terms and conditions as the body politic may from time to time impose; and this because the common good requires that all public ways shall be under the control of the public authorities. This privilege or prerogative of the king, who in this connection only represents and gives another name to the body politic, is not primarily for his profit, but for the protection of the people and the promotion of the general welfare....

From the same source comes the power to regulate the charges of common carriers, which was done in England as long ago as the third year of the reign of William and Mary, and continued until within a comparatively recent period.... Common carriers exercise a sort of public office, and have duties to perform in which the public is interested. Their business is, therefore, 'affected with a public interest,' within the meaning of the doctrine which Lord Hale has so forcibly stated.

But we need not go further. Enough has already been said to show that, when private property is devoted to a public use, it is subject to public regulation. It remains only to ascertain whether the warehouses of these plaintiffs in error, and the business which is carried on there, come within the operation of this principle.

For this purpose we accept as true the statements of fact contained in the elaborate brief of one of the counsel of the plaintiffs in error. From these it appears that 'the great producing region of the West and North-west sends its grain by water and rail to Chicago, where the greater part of it is shipped by vessel for transportation to the seaboard by the Great Lakes, and some of it is forwarded by railway to the Eastern ports.... Vessels, to some extent, are loaded in the Chicago harbor, and sailed through the St. Lawrence directly to Europe.... The quantity [of grain] received in Chicago has made it the greatest grain market in the world. This business has created a demand for means by which the immense quantity of grain can be handled or stored, and these have been found in grain warehouses, which are commonly called elevators....

In this connection it must also be borne in mind that, although in 1874 there were in Chicago fourteen warehouses adapted to this particular business, and owned by about thirty persons, nine business firms controlled them, and that the prices charged and received for storage were such 'as have been from year to year agreed upon and established by the different elevators or warehouses in the city of Chicago, and which rates have been annually published in one or more newspapers printed in said city.... 'Thus it is apparent that all the elevating facilities through which these vast productions 'of seven or eight great States of the West' must pass on the way 'to four or five of the States on the seashore' may be a 'virtual' monopoly.

Under such circumstances it is difficult to see why, if the common carrier, or the miller, or the ferryman, or the innkeeper, or the wharfinger, or the baker, or the cartman, or the hackney-coachman, pursues a public employment and exercises 'a sort of public office,' these plaintiffs in error do not. They stand, to use again the language of their counsel, in the very 'gateway of commerce,' and take toll from all who pass. Their business most certainly 'tends to a common charge, and is become a thing of public interest and use.' Every bushel of grain for its passage 'pays a toll, which is a common charge,' and, therefore, according to Lord Hale, every such warehouseman 'ought to be under public regulation, viz., that he ... take but reasonable toll.' Certainly, if any business can be clothed 'with a public interest, and cease to be *juris privati* only,' this has been. It may not be made so by the operation of the Constitution of Illinois or this statute, but it is by the facts.

We also are not permitted to overlook the fact that, for some reason, the people of Illinois, when they revised their Constitution in 1870, saw fit to make it the duty of the general assembly to pass laws 'for the protection of producers, shippers, and receivers of grain and produce' .... This indicates very clearly that during the twenty years in which this peculiar business had been assuming its present 'immense proportions,' something had occurred which led the whole body of the people to suppose that remedies such as are usually employed to prevent abuses by virtual monopolies might not be inappropriate here. For our purposes we must assume that, if a state of facts could exist that would justify such legislation, it actually did exist when the statute now under consideration was passed. For us the question is one of power, not of expediency. If no state of circumstances could exist to justify such a statute, then we may declare this one void, because is excess of the legislative power of the State. But if it could, we must presume it did. Of the propriety of legislative interference within the scope of legislative power, the legislature is the exclusive judge.

Neither is it a matter of any moment that no precedent can be found for a statute precisely like this. It is conceded that the business is one of recent origin, that its growth has been rapid, and that it is already of great importance. And it must also be conceded that it is a business in which the whole public has a direct and positive interest. It presents, therefore, a case for the application of a long-known and well-established principle in social science, and this statute simply extends the law so as to meet this new development of commercial progress. There is no attempt to compel these owners to grant the public an interest in their property, but to declare their obligations, if they use it in this particular manner....

It is insisted, however, that the owner of property is entitled to a reasonable compensation for its use, even though it be clothed with a public interest, and that what is reasonable is a judicial and not a legislative question.

As has already been shown, the practice has been otherwise. In countries where the common law prevails, it has been customary from time immemorial for the legislature to declare what shall be a reasonable compensation under such circumstances, or, perhaps more properly speaking, to fix a maximum beyond which any charge made would be unreasonable....

But a mere common-law regulation of trade or business may be changed by statute. A person has no property, no vested interest, in any rule of the common law. That is only one of the forms of municipal law, and is no more sacred than any other. Rights of property which have been created by the common law cannot be taken away without due process; but the law itself, as a rule of conduct, may be changed at the will, or even at the whim, of the legislature, unless prevented by constitutional limitations. Indeed, the great office of statutes is to remedy defects in the common law as they are developed, and to adapt it to the changes of time and circumstances. To limit the rate of charge for services rendered in a public employment, or for the use of property in which the public has an interest, is only changing a regulation which existed before. It establishes no new principle in the law, but only gives a new effect to an old one....

We conclude, therefore, that the statute in question is not repugnant to the Constitution of the United States, and that there is no error in the judgment....

MR. JUSTICE FIELD and MR. JUSTICE STRONG dissented.

MR. JUSTICE FIELD.

I am compelled to dissent from the decision of the court in this case, and from the reasons upon which that decision is founded. The principle upon which the opinion of the majority proceeds is, in my judgment, subversive of the rights of private property, heretofore believed to be protected by constitutional guaranties against legislative interference, and is in conflict with the authorities cited in its support....

The power of the State over the property of the citizen under the constitutional guaranty is well defined. The State may take his property for public uses, upon just compensation being made therefor. It may take a portion of his property by way of taxation for the support of the government. It may control the use and possession of his property, so far as may be necessary for the protection of the rights of others, and to secure to them the equal use and enjoyment of their property. The doctrine that each one must so use his own as not to injure his neighbor—*sic utere tuo ut alienum non laedas*—is the rule by which every member or society must possess and enjoy his property; and all legislation essential to secure this common and equal enjoyment is a legitimate exercise of State authority....

It is true that the legislation which secures to all protection in their rights, and the equal use and enjoyment of their property, embraces an almost infinite variety of subjects. Whatever affects the peace, good order, morals, and health of the community, comes within its scope; and every one must use and enjoy his property subject to the restrictions which such legislation imposes. What is termed the police power of the State ... can only interfere with the conduct of individuals in their intercourse with each other, and in the use of their property, so far as may be required to secure these objects. The compensation which the owners of property, not having any special rights or privileges from the government in connection with it, may demand for its use, or for their own services in union with it, forms no element of consideration in prescribing regulations for that purpose. If one construct a building in a city, the

State, or the municipality exercising a delegated power from the State, may require its walls to be of sufficient thickness for the uses intended; it may forbid the employment of inflammable materials in its construction, so as not to endanger the safety of his neighbors; if designed as a theatre, church, or public hall, it may prescribe ample means of egress, so as to afford facility for escape in case of accident; it may forbid the storage in it of powder, nitro-glycerine, or other explosive material; it may require its occupants daily to remove decayed vegetable and animal matter, which would otherwise accumulate and engender disease; it may exclude from it all occupations and business calculated to disturb the neighborhood or infect the air. Indeed, there is no end of regulations with respect to the use of property which may not be legitimately prescribed, having for their object the peace, good order, safety, and health of the community, thus securing to all the equal enjoyment of their property; but in establishing these regulations it is evident that compensation to the owner for the use of his property, or for his services in union with it, is not a matter of any importance: whether it be one sum or another does not affect the regulation, either in respect to its utility or mode of enforcement. One may go, in like manner, through the whole round of regulations authorized by legislation, State or municipal, under what is termed the police power, and in no instance will he find that the compensation of the owner for the use of his property has any influence in establishing them. It is only where some right or privilege is conferred by the government or municipality upon the owner, which he can use in connection with his property, or by means of which the use of his property is rendered more valuable to him, or he thereby enjoys an advantage over others, that the compensation to be received by him becomes a legitimate matter of regulation. Submission to the regulation of compensation in such cases is an implied condition of the grant, and the State, in exercising its power of prescribing the compensation, only determines the conditions upon which its concession shall be enjoyed. When the privilege ends, the power of regulation ceases....

There is nothing in the character of the business of the defendants as warehousemen which called for the interference complained of in this case. Their buildings are not nuisances; their occupation of receiving and storing grain infringes upon no rights of others, disturbs no neighborhood, infects not the air, and in no respect prevents others from using and enjoying their property as to them may seem best. The legislation in question is nothing less than a bold assertion of absolute power by the State to control at its discretion the property and business of the citizen, and fix the compensation he shall receive. The will of the legislature is made the condition upon which the owner shall receive the fruits of his property and the just reward of his labor, industry, and enterprise. 'That government,' says [former Supreme Court Justice Joseph] Story, 'can scarcely be deemed to be free where the rights of property are left solely dependent upon the will of a legislative body without any restraint. The fundamental maxims of a free government seem to require that the rights of personal liberty and private property should be held sacred.' The decision of the court in this case gives unrestrained license to legislative will....

MR. JUSTICE STRONG.

When the judgment in this case was announced by direction of a majority of the court, it was well known by all my brethren that I did not concur in it. It had been my purpose to prepare a dissenting opinion, but I found no time for the preparation, and I was reluctant to dissent in such a case without stating my reasons. Mr. Justice Field has now stated them as fully as I can, and I concur in what he has said.

## Note: Munn, *The Police Power, and Businesses "Affected with a Public Interest"*

What is it about the grain elevators in Chicago that rendered them susceptible to rate regulation by the state? If the answer is that that industry is a "business affected with a public interest," what brings it within that category? Because it is important? In a part of his dissent not excerpted above, Justice Field wrote, "The public is interested in the manufacture of cotton, woollen, and silken fabrics, in the construction of machinery, in the printing and publication of books and periodicals, and in the making of utensils of every variety, useful and ornamental; indeed, there is hardly an enterprise or business engaging the attention and labor of any considerable portion of the community, in which the public has not an interest in the sense in which that term is used by the court in its opinion...." If the category of businesses "affected with a public interest" does not extend as far as Justice Field believes the Court's logic suggests, then what is the stopping point? Does the majority suggest any such point?

Consider also *who* gets to decide which businesses are "affected" in this way. Toward the end of its opinion the Court suggests that the people of the state largely get to decide this question, with only deferential judicial review. If that's true, then why did the Court engage in such a detailed examination of how grain elevators in 1870s Chicago resembled ferries and other "affected" businesses in earlier centuries? As you will see, the "who decides" question—and more generally, the question of how much deference legislatures merit when they regulate otherwise-private economic relationships—became a crucial one for the Court's economic rights jurisprudence.

## Note: *"The Police Power," "Class Legislation," and the Rise of "Liberty of Contract"*

1. *Munn* did not explicitly speak of a liberty of contract, even one that could be constitutionally infringed under certain circumstances. Rather, its focus on businesses "affected with a public interest" reflects a slightly different conception of the permissible scope of government regulation of the marketplace—one that focuses on the scope of governmental power rather than the extent of individual rights.

2. During the late nineteenth century—that is, during the period when the Supreme Court first considered the limits the Fourteenth Amendment placed on state regulatory activity—a central organizing concept of American constitutional law was the idea of "the police power." *Munn* quoted from an earlier, pre-Civil War opinion defining the police power as "nothing more or less than the powers of government inherent in every sovereignty, ... that is to say, ... the power to govern men and

things." In other words, the police power was simply the power states had to regulate for the health, safety, and prosperity of society. (And, to be completely clear, the "police" power extended far beyond what we think of today as traditional law enforcement activities.)

The idea that governments traditionally had the power to regulate for these purposes, and that the Fourteenth Amendment did not deprive states of that power, held powerful sway during this period. Today we are accustomed to thinking of constitutional rights as "trumps." In other words, we are accustomed to thinking of such rights as requiring government to provide especially powerful justifications for actions that impair such rights. For example, as you'll see later in Part III, today, claims that a law has impaired "a fundamental right" require government to prove that that impairment is "narrowly tailored" to achieve a "compelling" government interest.

Nineteenth century judicial doctrine had a different focus. For lawyers and judges of that era, the question was not so much whether the plaintiff had stated a rights claim that triggered a requirement of unusually stringent governmental justification for the challenged law, but rather, whether the challenged law was within the proper scope of governmental power — *i.e.*, whether it was a proper police regulation. These two approaches may seem like essentially the same thing. But they require a different analysis. In *Munn*, for example, the Court never considered whether the plaintiffs' asserted right was fundamental. Instead, the Court simply considered whether the state's regulation of the rates the plaintiffs could charge for grain storage was appropriate regulation for the public good — that is, whether it was an appropriate use of the police power.

3. One type of regulation that was *not* considered appropriate police regulation was regulation that constituted what nineteenth century lawyers and judges called "class legislation." The concept of "class legislation" had been present in state court jurisprudence before the Civil War. Essentially, the idea was that all legislation had to serve the interest of the general public, rather than the narrow interests of a particular "class." This idea in turn had deep roots: in American history it could be found in the writings of James Madison, in which he expressed concern that self-interested "factions" would legislate for their own selfish goals, even at the expense of the public interest. (Madison's most famous expression of this idea was in Federalist Paper Number 10.) Antebellum state courts sometimes found this prohibition in their state constitutions' clauses, based on the similar provision in Magna Carta (the Thirteenth Century English document announcing basic rights), that liberty and property could not be denied "except by the law of the land." Sometimes those state constitutional provisions substituted "due process of law" for "law of the land." Other times state courts found the class legislation prohibition to be implied in the very idea of republican government.

4. In the decades following its enactment, the Fourteenth Amendment was often seen as an embodiment of this same prohibition on class legislation. Thus, federal courts during this era would scrutinize economic regulation to ensure that it did not constitute merely a self-interested giveaway to a favored group, but instead promoted the interests of society as a whole. Under this test, even legislation that burdened particular groups might nevertheless be valid, if those burdens were necessary for

the achievement of some public benefit. Notably, even Justice Field, who dissented in *Munn* and the *Slaughter-House Cases*, recognized government's ability to regulate particular types of conduct when necessary for the public good. He wrote the following in an 1884 opinion upholding a San Francisco ordinance regulating laundry facilities to ensure their cleanliness and fire safety:

> Special burdens are often necessary for general benefits, — for supplying water, preventing fires, lighting districts, cleaning streets, opening parks, and many other objects. Regulations for these purposes may press with more or less weight upon one than upon another, but they are designed, not to impose unequal or unnecessary restrictions upon any one, but to promote, with as little individual inconvenience as possible, the general good. Though, in many respects, necessarily special in their character, they do not furnish just ground of complaint if they operate alike upon all persons and property under the same circumstances and conditions. Class legislation, discriminating against some and favoring others, is prohibited; but legislation which, in carrying out a public purpose, is limited in its application, if within the sphere of its operation it affects alike all persons similarly situated, is not [prohibited by] the [Fourteenth] amendment. *Barbier v. Connolly*, 113 U.S. 27 (1884).

5. Ultimately, concern about proper police power regulation evolved into a recognition of a liberty, protected by the Due Process Clause, to contract for goods and labor services as one wished. Scholars disagree on when this transition occurred. In *Allgeyer v. Louisiana*, 165 U.S. 578 (1897), the Court spoke of the "right to contract" as part of the "liberty" protected by the Due Process Clause. In language that would become important later, Justice Peckham (also the author of the *Lochner* opinion which follows) wrote the following:

> The 'liberty' mentioned in [the Due Process Clause of the Fourteenth Amendment] means not only the right of the citizen to be free from the mere physical restraint of his person, as by incarceration, but the term is deemed to embrace the right of the citizen to be free in the enjoyment of all his faculties, to be free to use them in all lawful ways, to live and work where he will, to earn his livelihood by any lawful calling, to pursue any livelihood or avocation, and for that purpose to enter into all contracts which may be proper, necessary and essential to his carrying out to a successful conclusion the purposes above mentioned.

By the early part of the twentieth century, both class legislation and liberty of contract were part of the Court's vocabulary when considering economic regulation.

## Lochner v. New York

### 198 U.S. 45 (1905)

MR. JUSTICE PECKHAM ... delivered the opinion of the court:

The indictment, it will be seen, charges that the plaintiff in error violated the one hundred and tenth section of article 8, chapter 415, of the Laws of 1897, known as the labor law of the state of New York, in that he wrongfully and unlawfully required and permitted an employee working for him to work more than sixty hours in one week.... The mandate of the statute ... is the substantial equivalent of an enactment that 'no employee shall contract or agree to work,' more than ten hours per day [or more than sixty hours per week]; and, as there is no provision for special emergencies the statute is mandatory in all cases.... The employee may desire to earn the extra money, which would arise from his working more than the prescribed time, but this statute forbids the employer from permitting the employee to earn it.

The statute necessarily interferes with the right of contract between the employer and employees, concerning the number of hours in which the latter may labor in the bakery of the employer. The general right to make a contract in relation to his business is part of the liberty of the individual protected by the Fourteenth Amendment of the Federal Constitution. *Allgeyer v. Louisiana*, 165 U.S. 578 (1897) [Note *supra.* this chapter]. Under that provision no State can deprive any person of life, liberty or property without due process of law. The right to purchase or to sell labor is part of the liberty protected by this amendment, unless there are circumstances which exclude the right. There are, however, certain powers, existing in the sovereignty of each State in the Union, somewhat vaguely termed police powers, the exact description and limitation of which have not been attempted by the courts. Those powers, broadly stated and without, at present, any attempt at a more specific limitation, relate to the safety, health, morals, and general welfare of the public. Both property and liberty are held on such reasonable conditions as may be imposed by the governing power of the State in the exercise of those powers, and with such conditions the Fourteenth Amendment was not designed to interfere.

The State, therefore, has power to prevent the individual from making certain kinds of contracts, and in regard to them the Federal Constitution offers no protection. If the contract be one which the State, in the legitimate exercise of its police power, has the right to prohibit, it is not prevented from prohibiting it by the Fourteenth Amendment.... Therefore, when the State, by its legislature, in the assumed exercise of its police powers, has passed an act which seriously limits the right to labor or the right of contract in regard to their means of livelihood between persons who are *sui juris* (both employer and employee), it becomes of great importance to determine which shall prevail—the right of the individual to labor for such time as he may choose, or the right of the State to prevent the individual from laboring or from entering into any contract to labor, beyond a certain time prescribed by the State.

This court has recognized the existence and upheld the exercise of the police powers of the States in many cases which might fairly be considered as border ones, and it has, in the course of its determination of questions regarding the asserted invalidity of such statutes, on the ground of their violation of the rights secured by the Federal Constitution, been guided by rules of a very liberal nature, the application of which has resulted, in numerous instances, in upholding the validity of state statutes thus assailed. Among the later cases where the state law has been upheld by this court is that of *Holden v. Hardy*, 169 U.S. 366 (1898). A provision in the act of the legislature of Utah was there under consideration, the act limiting the employment of workmen in all underground mines or workings, to eight hours per day, 'except in cases of emergency, where life or property is in imminent danger.'... It was held that the kind of employment, mining, smelting, etc., and the character of the employees in such kinds of labor, were such as to make it reasonable and proper for the State to interfere to prevent the employees from being constrained by the rules laid down by the proprietors in regard to labor....

It will be observed that, even with regard to that class of labor, the Utah statute provided for cases of emergency wherein the provisions of the statute would not apply. The statute now before this court has no emergency clause in it, and, if the statute is valid, there are no circumstances and no emergencies under which the slightest violation of the provisions of the act would be innocent. There is nothing in *Holden v. Hardy* which covers the case now before us.... *Knoxville Iron Co. v. Harbison*, 183 U.S. 13 (1901), is equally far from an authority for this legislation. The employees in that case were held to be at a disadvantage with the employer in matters of wages, they being miners and coal workers, and the act simply provided for the cashing of coal orders when presented by the miner to the employer....

It must, of course, be conceded that there is a limit to the valid exercise of the police power by the state. There is no dispute concerning this general proposition. Otherwise the Fourteenth Amendment would have no efficacy and the legislatures of the States would have unbounded power, and it would be enough to say that any piece of legislation was enacted to conserve the morals, the health or the safety of the people; such legislation would be valid, no matter how absolutely without foundation the claim might be.... In every case that comes before this court, therefore, where legislation of this character is concerned and where the protection of the Federal Constitution is sought, the question necessarily arises: Is this a fair, reasonable, and appropriate exercise of the police power of the State, or is it an unreasonable, unnecessary and arbitrary interference with the right of the individual to his personal liberty or to enter into those contracts in relation to labor which may seem to him appropriate or necessary for the support of himself and his family? Of course the liberty of contract relating to labor includes both parties to it. The one has as much right to purchase as the other to sell labor.

This is not a question of substituting the judgment of the court for that of the legislature. If the act be within the power of the State it is valid, although the judgment of the court might be totally opposed to the enactment of such a law. But the question would still remain. Is it within the police power of the State? and that question must be answered by the court.

The question whether this act is valid as a labor law, pure and simple, may be dismissed in a few words. There is no reasonable ground for interfering with the liberty of person or the right of free contract, by determining the hours of labor, in the occupation of a baker. There is no contention that bakers as a class are not equal in intelligence and capacity to men in other trades or manual occupations, or that they are not able to assert their rights and care for themselves without the protecting arm of the State, interfering with their independence of judgment and of action. They are in no sense wards of the State. Viewed in the light of a purely labor law, with no reference whatever to the question of health, we think that a law like the one before us involves neither the safety, the morals nor the welfare of the public, and that the interest of the public is not in the slightest degree affected by such an act. The law must be upheld, if at all, as a law pertaining to the health of the individual engaged in the occupation of a baker. It does not affect any other portion of the public than those who are engaged in that occupation. Clean and wholesome bread does not depend upon whether the baker works but ten hours per day or only sixty hours a week. The limitation of the hours of labor does not come within the police power on that ground....

We think that there can be no fair doubt that the trade of a baker, in and of itself, is not an unhealthy one to that degree which would authorize the legislature to interfere with the right to labor, and with the right of free contract on the part of the individual, either as employer or employee. In looking through statistics regarding all trades and occupations, it may be true that the trade of a baker does not appear to be as healthy as some other trades, and is also vastly more healthy than still others.... Some occupations are more healthy than others, but we think there are none which might not come under the power of the legislature to supervise and control the hours of working therein, if the mere fact that the occupation is not absolutely and perfectly healthy is to confer that right upon the legislative department of the Government.... It is unfortunately true that labor, even in any department, may possibly carry with it the seeds of unhealthiness. But are we all, on that account, at the mercy of legislative majorities? A printer, a tinsmith, a locksmith, a carpenter, a cabinetmaker, a dry goods clerk, a bank's, a lawyer's, or a physician's clerk, or a clerk in almost any kind of business, would all come under the power of the legislature, on this assumption. No trade, no occupation, no mode of earning one's living, could escape this all-pervading power, and the acts of the legislature in limiting the hours of labor in all employments would be valid, although such limitation might seriously cripple the ability of the laborer to support himself and his family. In our large cities there are many buildings into which the sun penetrates for but a short time in each day, and these buildings are occupied by people carrying on the business of bankers, brokers, lawyers, real estate, and many other kinds of business, aided by many clerks, messengers, and other employees. Upon the assumption of the validity of this act under review, it is not possible to say that an act, prohibiting lawyers' or bank clerks, or others, from contracting to labor for their employers more than eight hours a day would be invalid....

It is also urged, pursuing the same line of argument, that it is to the interest of the state that its population should be strong and robust, and therefore any legislation which may be said to tend to make people healthy must be valid as health laws, enacted under the police power. If this be a valid argument and a justification for this kind of legislation, it follows that the protection of the Federal Constitution from undue interference with liberty of person and freedom of contract is visionary, wherever the law is sought to be justified as a valid exercise of the police power. Scarcely any law but might find shelter under such assumptions, and conduct, properly so called, as well as contract, would come under the restrictive sway of the legislature. Not only the hours of employees, but the hours of employers, could be regulated, and doctors, lawyers, scientists, all professional men, as well as athletes and artisans, could be forbidden to fatigue their brains and bodies by prolonged hours of exercise, lest the fighting strength of the State be impaired. We mention these extreme cases because the contention is extreme. We do not believe in the soundness of the views which uphold this law. On the contrary, we think that such a law as this, although passed in the assumed exercise of the police power, and as relating to the public health, or the health of the employees named, is not within that power, and is invalid....

This interference on the part of the legislatures of the several States with the ordinary trades and occupations of the people seems to be on the increase.... It is impossible for us to shut our eyes to the fact that many of the laws of this character, while passed under what is claimed to be the police power for the purpose of protecting the public health or welfare, are, in reality, passed from other motives. We are justified in saying so when, from the character of the law and the subject upon which it legislates, it is apparent that the public health or welfare bears but the most remote relation to the law....

It is manifest to us that the limitation of the hours of labor as provided for in this section of the statute under which the indictment was found, and the plaintiff in error convicted, has no such direct relation to and no such substantial effect upon the health of the employee, as to justify us in regarding the section as really a health law. It seems to us that the real object and purpose were simply to regulate the hours of labor between the master and his employees (all being men, *sui juris*), in a private business, not dangerous in any degree to morals or in any real and substantial degree, to the health of the employees. Under such circumstances the freedom of master and employee to contract with each other in relation to their employment, and in defining the same, cannot be prohibited or interfered with, without violating the Federal Constitution....

Mr. Justice HARLAN (with whom Mr. Justice WHITE and Mr. Justice DAY concurred) dissenting:

... I take it to be firmly established that what is called the liberty of contract may, within certain limits, be subjected to regulations designed and calculated to promote the general welfare or to guard the public health, the public morals or the public safety. 'The liberty secured by the Constitution of the United States to every person within its jurisdiction does not import,' this court has recently said, 'an absolute right in each person to be, at all times and in all circumstances, wholly freed from restraint. There are manifold restraints to which every person is necessarily subject for the common good.' *Jacobson v. Massachusetts.*

Granting then that there is a liberty of contract which cannot be violated even under the sanction of direct legislative enactment, but assuming, as according to settled law we may assume, that such liberty of contract is subject to such regulations as the State may reasonably prescribe for the common good and the well-being of society, what are the conditions under which the judiciary may declare such regulations to be in excess of legislative authority and void? Upon this point there is no room for dispute, for, the rule is universal that a legislative enactment, Federal or state, is never to be disregarded or held invalid unless it be, beyond question, plainly and palpably in excess of legislative power.... If there be doubt as to the validity of the statute, that doubt must therefore be resolved in favor of its validity, and the courts must keep their hands off, leaving the legislature to meet the responsibility for unwise legislation. If the end which the legislature seeks to accomplish be one to which its power extends, and if the means employed to that end, although not the wisest or best, are yet not plainly and palpably unauthorized by law, then the court cannot interfere. In other words, when the validity of a statute is questioned, the burden of proof, so to speak, is upon those who assert it to be unconstitutional. *McCulloch*.

Let these principles be applied to the present case.... It is plain that this statute was enacted in order to protect the physical well-being of those who work in bakery and confectionery establishments. It may be that the statute had its origin, in part, in the belief that employers and employees in such establishments were not upon an equal footing, and that the necessities of the latter often compelled them to submit to such exactions as unduly taxed their strength. Be this as it may, the statute must be taken as expressing the belief of the people of New York that, as a general rule, and in the case of the average man, labor in excess of sixty hours during a week in such establishments may endanger the health of those who thus labor. Whether or not this be wise legislation it is not the province of the court to inquire. Under our systems of government the courts are not concerned with the wisdom or policy of legislation. So that in determining the question of power to interfere with liberty of contract, the court may inquire whether the means devised by the State are germane to an end which may be lawfully accomplished and have a real or substantial relation to the protection of health, as involved in the daily work of the persons, male and female, engaged in bakery and confectionery establishments. But when this inquiry is entered upon I find it impossible, in view of common experience, to say that there is here no real or substantial relation between the means employed by the State and the end sought to be accomplished by its legislation. Nor can I say that the statute has no appropriate or direct connection with that protection to health which each State owes to her citizens; or that it is not promotive of the health of the employees in question; or that the regulation prescribed by the State is utterly unreasonable and extravagant or wholly arbitrary. Still less can I say that the statute is, beyond question, a plain, palpable invasion of rights secured by the fundamental law. Therefore I submit that this court will transcend its functions if it assumes to annul the statute of New York. It must be remembered that this statute does not apply to all kinds of business. It applies only to work in bakery and confectionery establishments, in which, as all know, the air constantly breathed by workmen is not as pure and healthful as that to be found in some other establishments or out of doors.

Professor Hirt in his treatise on the 'Diseases of the Workers' has said: 'The labor of the bakers is among the hardest and most laborious imaginable, because it has to be performed under conditions injurious to the health of those engaged in it. It is hard, very hard work, not only because it requires a great deal of physical exertion in an overheated workshop and during unreasonably long hours, but more so because of the erratic demands of the public, compelling the baker to perform the greater part of his work at night, thus depriving him of an opportunity to enjoy the necessary rest and sleep, a fact which is highly injurious to his health.'...

In the Eighteenth Annual Report by the New York Bureau of Statistics of Labor it is stated that among the occupations involving exposure to conditions that interfere with nutrition is that of a baker. In that Report it is also stated that, 'from a social point of view, production will be increased by any change in industrial organization which diminishes the number of idlers, paupers, and criminals. Shorter hours of work, by allowing higher standards of comfort and purer family life, promise to enhance the industrial efficiency of the wage-working class, — improved health, longer life, more content and greater intelligence and inventiveness.'

Statistics show that the average daily working time among workingmen in different countries is, in Australia, eight hours; in Great Britain, nine; in the United States, nine and three-quarters; in Denmark, nine and three-quarters; in Norway, ten; Sweden, France, and Switzerland, ten and one-half; Germany, ten and one-quarter; Belgium, Italy, and Austria, eleven; and in Russia, twelve hours.

We judicially know that the question of the number of hours during which a workman should continuously labor has been, for a long period, and is yet, a subject of serious consideration among civilized peoples, and by those having special knowledge of the laws of health.... But the statute before us ... may be said to occupy a middle ground in respect of the hours of labor. What is the true ground for the state to take between legitimate protection, by legislation, of the public health and liberty of contract is not a question easily solved, nor one in respect of which there is or can be absolute certainty....

I do not stop to consider whether any particular view of this economic question presents the sounder theory. What the precise facts are it may be difficult to say. It is enough for the determination of this case, and it is enough for this court to know, that the question is one about which there is room for debate and for an honest difference of opinion....

Mr. Justice HOLMES dissenting:

I regret sincerely that I am unable to agree with the judgment in this case, and that I think it my duty to express my dissent.

This case is decided upon an economic theory which a large part of the country does not entertain. If it were a question whether I agreed with that theory, I should desire to study it further and long before making up my mind. But I do not conceive that to be my duty, because I strongly believe that my agreement or disagreement has nothing to do with the right of a majority to embody their opinions in law. It is settled by various decisions of this court that state constitutions and state laws may regulate life in many ways which we as legislators might think as injudicious or if you like as tyrannical as this, and which equally with this interfere with the liberty to contract. Sunday laws and usury laws are ancient examples. A more modern one is the prohibition of lotteries. The liberty of the citizen to do as he likes so long as he does not interfere with the liberty of others to do the same, which has been a shibboleth for some well-known writers, is interfered with by school laws, by the Post Office, by every state or municipal institution which takes his money for purposes thought desirable, whether he likes it or not. The Fourteenth Amendment does not enact Mr. Herbert Spencer's *Social Statics*. The other day we sustained the Massachusetts vaccination law. *Jacobson v. Massachusetts*, 197 U.S. 11 (1905).... The decision sustaining an eight hour law for miners is still recent. *Holden v. Hardy*. Some of these laws embody convictions or prejudices which judges are likely to share. Some may not. But a constitution is not intended to embody a particular economic theory, whether of paternalism and the organic relation of the citizen to the State or of *laissez faire*. It is made for people of fundamentally differing views, and the accident of our finding certain opinions natural and familiar or novel and even shocking ought not to conclude our judgment upon the question whether statutes embodying them conflict with the Constitution of the United States.

... I think that the word liberty in the Fourteenth Amendment, is perverted when it is held to prevent the natural outcome of a dominant opinion, unless it can be said that a rational and fair man necessarily would admit that the statute proposed would infringe fundamental principles as they have been understood by the traditions of our people and our law. It does not need research to show that no such sweeping condemnation can be passed upon the statute before us. A reasonable man might think it a proper measure on the score of health. Men whom I certainly could not pronounce unreasonable would uphold it as a first instalment of a general regulation of the hours of work. Whether in the latter aspect it would be open to the charge of inequality I think it unnecessary to discuss.

### Note: "The Lochner Era"

1. While *Lochner* was not the first case to use liberty of contract reasoning to strike down legislation regulating market transactions, it eventually became the symbol of the era, from the end of the nineteenth century to 1937, when the Court gave careful scrutiny to such laws and often struck them down on due process grounds. As reflected in *Lochner* itself, this judicial scrutiny sought to ensure that infringements on the liberty to contract were justified by legitimate public purposes, such as the public health or the protection of workers that suffered from unusual disparities in bargaining power.

Despite claims to the contrary, the Court in this era did not unfailingly strike down laws that regulated the market. Indeed, the Court appeared to overrule *Lochner* itself after only twelve years, when in *Bunting v. Oregon*, 243 U.S. 426 (1917), it upheld a maximum working hours law for factory workers. Recall also that *Lochner* itself referred to cases such as *Holden v. Hardy*, which upheld labor regulation when the Court appeared convinced that it served some unusual need. More generally, scholars have argued that "the *Lochner* era" is best understood as several sub-eras, where different personnel on the Court led the Court to oscillate between more and less accommodating review of regulatory legislation.

2. One of the more interesting economic regulatory issues that reached the Court during this period was the question of differential regulation for male and female workers. In *Muller v. Oregon*, 208 U.S. 412 (1908), the Court unanimously upheld a law that established maximum working hours for women employed in certain workplaces. The Court noted a variety of factors, from women's asserted disadvantage in "the struggle for subsistence" due to their "physical structure and the performance of maternal functions," to the history of women's lack of access to education. Fifteen years later, however, in *Adkins v. Children's Hospital*, 261 U.S. 525 (1923), the Court by a 5–3 vote (Justice Brandeis not participating) struck down a District of Columbia minimum wage law for women. The majority in that case cited the "revolutionary" changes in women's social status since *Muller*, and stated that, aside from women's asserted inequality with regard to physical strength, differences relating to "the ancient inequality of the sexes ... have come almost, if not quite, to the vanishing point." In 1937, in a major step in the Court's repudiation of *Lochner*-era jurisprudence, the Court overruled *Adkins* and upheld a minimum wage law aimed at women. *West Coast Hotel v. Parrish*, 300 U.S. 379 (1937) (excerpted later in this chapter).

3. *Lochner*-era scrutiny of economic regulation inevitably embroiled the Court in reviewing the policy wisdom underlying such legislation. As a reaction to such scrutiny, pioneering lawyers such as Louis Brandeis (who eventually served on the Court) began including detailed economic and social analysis in their legal briefs. "Brandeis briefs" became known as briefs that sought to convince the Court of the need for or wisdom of such laws. For example, in *Muller v. Oregon*, Brandeis submitted a 113-page brief that presented in great detail medical and social science evidence about the ill effects, on women, their families, and society at large, from their overwork.

4. In 1929 the stock market crashed; by 1931 the nation was in a serious economic depression. At the federal level, the election of Franklin Roosevelt ushered in an era of unprecedented federal regulation of the economy, designed to help the economy recover. States also stepped up their own regulation, for example, by legislating minimum prices for commodities in order to ensure at least minimal incomes for farmers. As Chapter 4 of this book illustrated, federal legislation during the New Deal era was often challenged as exceeding Congress's power to regulate interstate commerce. But both federal and state legislation was also subject to challenge as violating the right to contract. Those challenges put pressure on the "affected with a public interest" approach associated with *Munn*.

## Nebbia v. New York
### 291 U.S. 502 (1934)

Mr. Justice ROBERTS delivered the opinion of the Court.

The Legislature of New York established, by Chapter 158 of the Laws of 1933, a Milk Control Board with power, among other things, to 'fix minimum and maximum

... retail prices to be charged by ... stores to consumers for consumption off the premises where sold.' The Board fixed nine cents as the price to be charged by a store for a quart of milk. Nebbia, the proprietor of a grocery store in Rochester, sold two quarts and a 5-cent loaf of bread for 18 cents; and was convicted for violating the board's order. At his trial he asserted the statute and order contravene the equal protection clause and the due process clause of the Fourteenth Amendment, and renewed the contention in successive appeals to the county court and Court of Appeals. Both overruled his claim and affirmed the conviction.

The question for decision is whether the Federal Constitution prohibits a state from so fixing the selling price of milk. We first inquire as to the occasion for the legislation and its history.

During 1932 the prices received by farmers for milk were much below the cost of production.... The situation of the families of dairy producers had become desperate and called for state aid similar to that afforded the unemployed, if conditions should not improve.

On March 10, 1932, the senate and assembly resolved, 'That a joint Legislative committee is hereby created ... to investigate the causes of the decline of the price of milk to producers and the resultant effect of the low prices upon the dairy industry and the future supply of milk to the cities of the State; to investigate the cost of distribution of milk and its relation to prices paid to milk producers, to the end that the consumer may be assured of an adequate supply of milk at a reasonable price, both to producer and consumer.' The committee organized May 6, 1932, and its activities lasted nearly a year. It held 13 public hearings at which 254 witnesses testified and 2,350 typewritten pages of testimony were taken.... The conscientious effort and thoroughness exhibited by the report lend weight to the committee's conclusions.

In part those conclusions are:

Milk is an essential item of diet. It cannot long be stored....

The production and distribution of milk is a paramount industry of the state, and largely affects the health and prosperity of its people....

In addition to the general price decline, other causes for the low price of milk include: a periodic increase in the number of cows and in milk production; the prevalence of unfair and destructive trade practices in the distribution of milk, leading to a demoralization of prices in the metropolitan area and other markets; and the failure of transportation and distribution charges to be reduced in proportion to the reduction in retail prices for milk and cream.

The fluid milk industry is affected by factors of instability peculiar to itself which call for special methods of control....

The Legislature adopted Chapter 158 as a method of correcting the evils, which the report of the committee showed could not be expected to right themselves through the ordinary play of the forces of supply and demand, owing to the peculiar and uncontrollable factors affecting the industry....

*First.* The appellant urges that the order of the Milk Control Board denies him the equal protection of the laws. [The Court rejected the equal protection argument.]

*Second.* The more serious question is whether, in the light of the conditions disclosed, the enforcement of section 312(e) denied the appellant the due process secured to him by the Fourteenth Amendment....

Under our form of government the use of property and the making of contracts are normally matters of private and not of public concern. The general rule is that both shall be free of governmental interference. But neither property rights[8] nor contract rights[9] are absolute; for government cannot exist if the citizen may at will use his property to the detriment of his fellows, or exercise his freedom of contract to work them harm. Equally fundamental with the private right is that of the public to regulate it in the common interest....

Thus has this court from the early days affirmed that the power to promote the general welfare is inherent in government.... These correlative rights, that of the citizen to exercise exclusive dominion over property and freely to contract about his affairs, and that of the state to regulate the use of property and the conduct of business, are always in collision. No exercise of the private right can be imagined which will not in some respect, however slight, affect the public; no exercise of the legislative prerogative to regulate the conduct of the citizen which will not to some extent abridge his liberty or affect his property. But subject only to constitutional restraint the private right must yield to the public need.

The Fifth Amendment, in the field of federal activity, and the Fourteenth, as respects state action, do not prohibit governmental regulation for the public welfare. They merely condition the exertion of the admitted power, by securing that the end shall be accomplished by methods consistent with due process. And the guaranty of due process, as has often been held, demands only that the law shall not be unreasonable, arbitrary or capricious, and that the means selected shall have a real and substantial relation to the object sought to be attained. It results that a regulation valid for one sort of business, or in given circumstances, may be invalid for another sort, or for the same business under other circumstances, because the reasonableness of each regulation depends upon the relevant facts.

... The court has repeatedly sustained curtailment of enjoyment of private property, in the public interest. The owner's rights may be subordinated to the needs of other private owners whose pursuits are vital to the paramount interests of the community. The state may control the use of property in various ways; may prohibit advertising bill boards except of a prescribed size and location, or their use for certain kinds of advertising; may in certain circumstances authorize encroachments by party walls in cities; may fix the height of buildings, the character of materials, and methods of construction, the adjoining area which must be left open, and may exclude from residential sections offensive trades, industries and structures likely injuriously to affect

---

8. *Munn v. Illinois* (1877) [*Supra.* this chapter].
9. *Allgeyer v. Louisiana*, 165 U.S. 578 (1897) [Note *supra.* this chapter].

the public health or safety; or may establish zones within which certain types of buildings or businesses are permitted and others excluded....

But we are told that because the law essays to control prices it denies due process. Notwithstanding the admitted power to correct existing economic ills by appropriate regulation of business, even though an indirect result may be a restriction of the freedom of contract or a modification of charges for services or the price of commodities, the appellant urges that direct fixation of prices is a type of regulation absolutely forbidden. His position is that the Fourteenth Amendment requires us to hold the challenged statute void for this reason alone. The argument runs that the public control of rates or prices is *per se* unreasonable and unconstitutional, save as applied to businesses affected with a public interest; that a business so affected is one in which property is devoted to an enterprise of a sort which the public itself might appropriately undertake, or one whose owner relies on a public grant or franchise for the right to conduct the business, or in which he is bound to serve all who apply; in short, such as is commonly called a public utility; or a business in its nature a monopoly. The milk industry, it is said, possesses none of these characteristics, and, therefore, not being affected with a public interest, its charges may not be controlled by the state. Upon the soundness of this contention the appellant's case against the statute depends.

We may as well say at once that the dairy industry is not, in the accepted sense of the phrase, a public utility. We think the appellant is also right in asserting that there is in this case no suggestion of any monopoly or monopolistic practice. It goes without saying that those engaged in the business are in no way dependent upon public grants or franchises for the privilege of conducting their activities. But if, as must be conceded, the industry is subject to regulation in the public interest, what constitutional principle bars the state from correcting existing maladjustments by legislation touching prices? We think there is no such principle. The due process clause makes no mention of sales or of prices any more than it speaks of business or contracts or buildings or other incidents of property. The thought seems nevertheless to have persisted that there is something peculiarly sacrosanct about the price one may charge for what he makes or sells, and that, however able to regulate other elements of manufacture or trade, with incidental effect upon price, the state is incapable of directly controlling the price itself. This view was negatived many years ago. *Munn v. Illinois.* The appellant's claim is, however, that this court, in there sustaining a statutory prescription of charges for storage by the proprietors of a grain elevator, limited permissible legislation of that type to businesses affected with a public interest, and he says no business is so affected except it have one or more of the characteristics he enumerates. But this is a misconception. Munn and Scott [the operators of the grain elevators in *Munn*] held no franchise from the state. They owned the property upon which their elevator was situated and conducted their business as private citizens. No doubt they felt at liberty to deal with whom they pleased and on such terms as they might deem just to themselves. Their enterprise could not fairly be called a monopoly, although it was referred to in the decision as a 'virtual monopoly.' This meant only that their elevator was strategically situated and that a large portion of the public found it highly inconvenient to deal with others. This court concluded the circumstances justified the legislation as an exercise of the governmental right to control the business in the public interest; that is, as an exercise of the police power....

It is clear that there is no closed class or category of businesses affected with a public interest, and the function of courts in the application of the Fifth and Fourteenth Amendments is to determine in each case whether circumstances vindicate the challenged regulation as a reasonable exertion of governmental authority or condemn it as arbitrary or discriminatory. The phrase 'affected with a public interest' can, in the nature of things, mean no more than that an industry, for adequate reason, is subject to control for the public good....

So far as the requirement of due process is concerned, and in the absence of other constitutional restriction, a state is free to adopt whatever economic policy may reasonably be deemed to promote public welfare, and to enforce that policy by legislation adapted to its purpose. The courts are without authority either to declare such policy, or, when it is declared by the legislature, to override it. If the laws passed are seen to have a reasonable relation to a proper legislative purpose, and are neither arbitrary nor discriminatory, the requirements of due process are satisfied....

Tested by these considerations we find no basis in the due process clause of the Fourteenth Amendment for condemning the provisions of the Agriculture and Markets Law here drawn into question.

Separate opinion of Mr. Justice McREYNOLDS....

The Fourteenth Amendment wholly disempowered the several States to 'deprive any person of life, liberty, or property, without due process of law.' The assurance of each of these things is the same. If now liberty or property may be struck down because of difficult circumstances, we must expect that hereafter every right must yield to the voice of an impatient majority when stirred by distressful exigency.... Constitutional guaranties are not to be 'thrust to and fro and carried about with every wind of doctrine.' They were intended to be immutable so long as within our charter. Rights shielded yesterday should remain indefeasible today and tomorrow. Certain fundamentals have been set beyond experimentation; the Constitution has released them from control by the State. Again and again this Court has so declared....

If validity of the enactment depends upon emergency, then to sustain this conviction we must be able to affirm that an adequate one has been shown by competent evidence of essential facts.... If she relied upon the existence of emergency, the burden was upon the State to establish it by competent evidence. None was presented at the trial. If necessary for appellant to show absence of the asserted conditions, the little grocer was helpless from the beginning—the practical difficulties were too great for the average man....

It is argued that the report of the Legislative Committee ... disclosed the essential facts. May one be convicted of crime upon such findings? Are federal rights subject to extinction by reports of committees? Heretofore, they have not been.

Apparently the legislature acted upon this report.... We have no basis for determining whether the findings of the committee or Legislature are correct or otherwise....

Is the milk business so affected with public interest that the Legislature may prescribe prices for sales by stores? This Court has approved the contrary view; has emphatically declared that a State lacks power to fix prices in similar private businesses....

Regulation to prevent recognized evils in business has long been upheld as permissible legislative action. But fixation of the price at which "A," engaged in an ordinary business, may sell, in order to enable "B," a producer, to improve his condition, has not been regarded as within legislative power. This is not regulation, but management, control, dictation — it amounts to the deprivation of the fundamental right which one has to conduct his own affairs honestly and along customary lines. The argument advanced here would support general prescription of prices for farm products, groceries, shoes, clothing, all the necessities of modern civilization, as well as labor, when some legislature finds and declares such action advisable and for the public good. This Court has declared that a State may not by legislative fiat convert a private business into a public utility. And if it be now ruled that one dedicates his property to public use whenever he embarks on an enterprise which the Legislature may think it desirable to bring under control, this is but to declare that rights guaranteed by the Constitution exist only so long as supposed public interest does not require their extinction. To adopt such a view, of course, would put an end to liberty under the Constitution.

*Munn* has been much discussed in the opinions referred to above. And always the conclusion was that nothing there sustains the notion that the ordinary business of dealing in commodities is charged with a public interest and subject to legislative control.... The painstaking effort there to point out that certain businesses like ferries, mills, [etc.], were subject to legislative control at common law and then to show that warehousing at Chicago occupied like relation to the public would have been pointless if 'affected with a public interest' only means that the public has serious concern about the perpetuity and success of the undertaking. That is true of almost all ordinary business affairs. Nothing in the opinion lends support, directly or otherwise to the notion that in times of peace a legislature may fix the price of ordinary commodities — grain, meat, milk, cotton, [etc.].

Of the assailed statute the Court of Appeals says ... 'With the wisdom of the legislation we have naught to do. It may be vain to hope by laws to oppose the general course of trade.' ... But plainly, I think, this Court must have regard to the wisdom of the enactment. At least, we must inquire concerning its purpose and decide whether the means proposed have reasonable relation to something within legislative power — whether the end is legitimate, and the means appropriate. If a statute to prevent conflagrations, should require householders to pour oil on their roofs as a means of curbing the spread of fire when discovered in the neighborhood, we could hardly uphold it. Here, we find direct interference with guaranteed rights defended upon the ground that the purpose was to promote the public welfare by increasing milk prices at the farm. Unless we can affirm that the end proposed is proper and the means adopted have reasonable relation to it, this action is unjustifiable....

The judgment of the court below should be reversed.

Mr. Justice VAN DEVANTER, Mr. Justice SUTHERLAND, and Mr. Justice BUTLER authorize me to say that they concur in this opinion.

## *Note: From* Nebbia *to* West Coast Hotel

1. *Nebbia* is a crucial opinion in the evolution of the Court's thinking about due process-based limits on government regulation of the economy. Its broad statements about government power to determine which businesses are "affected with a public interest" such that they become appropriate targets for government regulation appeared to sound the death knell for serious judicial scrutiny of such regulation. Moreover, while *Nebbia* considered — and upheld — the regulation of *prices*, it is not a great conceptual stretch to apply *Nebbia*'s deferential attitude to government regulation to cases involving regulation of *wages* (which, after all, are essentially the "price" of labor).

Nevertheless, two years after *Nebbia*, in *Morehead v. New York ex rel. Tipaldo*, 298 U.S. 587 (1936), the Court, by a 5–4 vote, struck down New York's minimum wage law, relying heavily on *Adkins* (Note *supra.* this chapter), the 1923 case striking down the District of Columbia's women's minimum wage law. *Tipaldo*, along with other post-*Nebbia* cases that struck down federal New Deal legislation on Due Process, Commerce Clause, and other grounds, reinforced the impression that the Court remained committed to resisting economic reform legislation at both the federal and state level. Thus, *Tipaldo* helped trigger the Court-packing plan President Roosevelt announced after his overwhelming re-election victory in 1936. (The Court-packing plan was discussed in Chapter 4.)

2. The vote in *Tipaldo* mirrored the vote in *Nebbia*, except that Justice Roberts, the author of *Nebbia*, changed sides and voted to strike down the New York law. On the surface, it appears that Roberts simply was not willing to acknowledge and apply the logical implications of his own opinion in *Nebbia*. On that reading, his final switch, in the *Parrish* case excerpted below, stands as the dramatic final act of the Court-packing crisis, with Roberts voting in *Parrish* to uphold Washington State's minimum wage law for women in order to defuse the crisis. Indeed, a saying quickly gained currency that Roberts' vote in *West Coast Hotel* was "the switch in time that saved nine" — that is, a Court of nine justices. Subsequent scholarship, however, has suggested that Roberts' vote in *Tipaldo* reflected a combination of concerns, including the failure of the state's attorney in *Tipaldo* to argue that *Adkins* should be overruled.

# West Coast Hotel Co. v. Parrish

## 300 U.S. 379 (1937)

Mr. Chief Justice HUGHES delivered the opinion of the Court.

This case presents the question of the constitutional validity of the minimum wage law of the State of Washington.

The Act, entitled 'Minimum Wages for Women,' authorizes the fixing of minimum wages for women and minors....

The appellant conducts a hotel. The appellee Elsie Parrish was employed as a chambermaid and (with her husband) brought this suit to recover the difference between the wages paid her and the minimum wage fixed pursuant to the state law. The minimum wage was $14.50 per week of 48 hours. The appellant challenged the act as repugnant to the due process clause of the Fourteenth Amendment of the Constitution of the United States....

The appellant relies upon the decision of this Court in *Adkins v. Children's Hospital*, 261 U.S. 525 (1923) [Note *supra.* this chapter], which held invalid the District of Columbia Minimum Wage Act, which was attacked under the due process clause of the Fifth Amendment.... The recent case of *Morehead v. New York ex rel. Tipaldo*, 298 U.S. 587 (1936) [Note *supra.* this chapter], came here on certiorari to the New York court, which had held the New York minimum wage act for women to be invalid. A minority of this Court thought that the New York statute was distinguishable in a material feature from that involved in the *Adkins* case and that for that and other reasons the New York statute should be sustained. But the Court of Appeals of New York had said that it found no material difference between the two statutes.... That view led to the affirmance by this Court of the judgment in the *Morehead* case, as the Court considered that the only question before it was whether the *Adkins* case was distinguishable and that reconsideration of that decision had not been sought....

We think that the question which was not deemed to be open in the *Morehead* case is open and is necessarily presented here. The Supreme Court of Washington ... has decided that the statute is a reasonable exercise of the police power of the State.... The state court has refused to regard the decision in the *Adkins* case as determinative and has pointed to our decisions both before and since that case as justifying its position. We are of the opinion that this ruling of the state court demands on our part a re-examination of the *Adkins* case....

The principle which must control our decision is not in doubt. The constitutional provision invoked is the due process clause of the Fourteenth Amendment governing the States, as the due process clause invoked in the *Adkins* case governed Congress. In each case the violation alleged by those attacking minimum wage regulation for women is deprivation of freedom of contract. What is this freedom? The Constitution does not speak of freedom of contract. It speaks of liberty and prohibits the deprivation of liberty without due process of law. In prohibiting that deprivation the Constitution does not recognize an absolute and uncontrollable liberty. Liberty in each of its phases has its history and connotation. But the liberty safeguarded is liberty in a social organization which requires the protection of law against the evils which menace the health, safety, morals and welfare of the people. Liberty under the Constitution is thus necessarily subject to the restraints of due process, and regulation which is reasonable in relation to its subject and is adopted in the interests of the community is due process....

This power under the Constitution to restrict freedom of contract has had many illustrations. That it may be exercised in the public interest with respect to contracts between employer and employee is undeniable. Thus statutes have been sustained limiting employment in underground mines and smelters to eight hours a day (*Holden v. Hardy*, 169 U.S. 366 (1898) [Note *supra.* this chapter]); in requiring redemption in cash of store orders or other evidences of indebtedness issued in the payment of wages (*Knoxville Iron Co. v. Harbison*, 183 U.S. 13 (1901)); in forbidding the payment of seamen's wages in advance; in making it unlawful to contract to pay miners employed at quantity rates upon the basis of screened coal instead of the weight of the coal as originally produced in the mine; in prohibiting contracts limiting liability for injuries to employees; in limiting hours of work of employees in manufacturing establishments (*Bunting v. Oregon*, 243 U.S. 426 (1917) [Note *supra.* this chapter]); and in maintaining workmen's compensation laws. In dealing with the relation of employer and employed, the legislature has necessarily a wide field of discretion in order that there may be suitable protection of health and safety, and that peace and good order may be promoted through regulations designed to insure wholesome conditions of work and freedom from oppression.

The point that has been strongly stressed that adult employees should be deemed competent to make their own contracts was decisively met nearly forty years ago in *Holden v. Hardy*, 169 U.S. 366 (1898) [Note *supra.* this chapter] where we pointed out the inequality in the footing of the parties. We said:

> The legislature has also recognized the fact, which the experience of legislators in many states has corroborated, that the proprietors of these establishments and their operatives do not stand upon an equality, and that their interests are, to a certain extent, conflicting. The former naturally desire to obtain as much labor as possible from their employees, while the latter are often induced by the fear of discharge to conform to regulations which their judgment, fairly exercised, would pronounce to be detrimental to their health or strength. In other words, the proprietors lay down the rules, and the laborers are practically constrained to obey them. In such cases self-interest is often an unsafe guide, and the legislature may properly interpose its authority.

And we added that the fact 'that both parties are of full age and competent to contract does not necessarily deprive the State of the power to interfere where the parties do not stand upon an equality, or where the public health demands that one party to the contract shall be protected against himself.' 'The State still retains an interest in his welfare, however reckless he may be. The whole is no greater than the sum of all the parts, and when the individual health, safety and welfare are sacrificed or neglected, the State must suffer.'

It is manifest that this established principle is peculiarly applicable in relation to the employment of women in whose protection the state has a special interest. That phase of the subject received elaborate consideration in *Muller v. Oregon*, 208 U.S. 412 (1908) [Note *supra.* this chapter], where the constitutional authority of the State to limit the working hours of women was sustained. We emphasized the consideration that 'woman's physical structure and the performance of maternal functions place her at a disadvantage in the struggle for subsistence' and that her physical well being 'becomes an object of public interest and care in order to preserve the strength and vigor of the race.' ... We said that 'though limitations upon personal and contractual rights may be removed by legislation, there is that in her disposition and habits of life which will operate against a full assertion of those rights. She will still be where some legislation to protect her seems necessary to secure a real equality of right.' ...

This array of precedents and the principles they applied were thought by the dissenting Justices in the *Adkins* case to demand that the minimum wage statute be sustained.... 

The minimum wage to be paid under the Washington statute is fixed after full consideration by representatives of employers, employees, and the public.... The statement of Mr. Justice Holmes in the *Adkins* case is pertinent: 'This statute does not compel anybody to pay anything. It simply forbids employment at rates below those fixed as the minimum requirement of health and right living. It is safe to assume that women will not be employed at even the lowest wages allowed unless they earn them, or unless the employer's business can sustain the burden. In short the law in its character and operation is like hundreds of so-called police laws that have been up-held.' ...

We think that the views thus expressed are sound and that the decision in the *Adkins* case was a departure from the true application of the principles governing the regulation by the State of the relation of employer and employed. Those principles have been reinforced by our subsequent decisions. Thus, in ... *Nebbia v. New York* (1934) [*Supra.* this chapter], dealing with the New York statute providing for minimum prices for milk, the general subject of the regulation of the use of private property and of the making of private contracts received an exhaustive examination and we again declared that if such laws 'have a reasonable relation to a proper legislative purpose, and are neither arbitrary nor discriminatory, the requirements of due process are satisfied'; that 'with the wisdom of the policy adopted, with the adequacy or practicability of the law enacted to forward it, the courts are both incompetent and unauthorized to deal'; that 'times without number we have said that the legislature is primarily the judge of the necessity of such an enactment, that every possible presumption is in favor of its validity, and that though the court may hold views inconsistent with the wisdom of the law, it may not be annulled unless palpably in excess of legislative power.'

With full recognition of the earnestness and vigor which characterize the prevailing opinion in the *Adkins* case, we find it impossible to reconcile that ruling with these well-considered declarations. What can be closer to the public interest than the health of women and their protection from unscrupulous and overreaching employers? And if the protection of women is a legitimate end of the exercise of state power, how can it be said that the requirement of the payment of a minimum wage fairly fixed in order to meet the very necessities of existence is not an admissible means to that end? The legislature of the State was clearly entitled to consider the situation of women in employment, the fact that they are in the class receiving the least pay, that their bargaining power is relatively weak, and that they are the ready victims of those who would take advantage of their necessitous circumstances....

There is an additional and compelling consideration which recent economic experience has brought into a strong light. The exploitation of a class of workers who are in an unequal position with respect to bargaining power and are thus relatively defenseless against the denial of a living wage is not only detrimental to their health and well being but casts a direct burden for their support upon the community.... We may take judicial notice of the unparalleled demands for relief which arose during the recent period of depression and still continue to an alarming extent despite the degree of economic recovery which has been achieved.... While in the instant case no factual brief has been presented, there is no reason to doubt that the State of Washington has encountered the same social problem that is present elsewhere. The community is not bound to provide what is in effect a subsidy for unconscionable employers. The community may direct its law-making power to correct the abuse which springs from their selfish disregard of the public interest. The argument that the legislation in question constitutes an arbitrary discrimination, because it does not extend to men, is unavailing. This Court has frequently held that the legislative authority, acting within its proper field, is not bound to extend its regulation to all cases which it might possibly reach. The legislature 'is free to recognize degrees of harm and it may confine its restrictions to those classes of cases where the need is deemed to be clearest.' If 'the law presumably hits the evil where it is most felt, it is not to be overthrown because there are other instances to which it might have been applied.'...

Our conclusion is that the case of *Adkins v. Children's Hospital* should be, and it is, overruled. The judgment of the Supreme Court of the state of Washington is affirmed.

Mr. Justice SUTHERLAND.

Mr. Justice VAN DEVANTER, Mr. Justice McREYNOLDS, Mr. Justice BUTLER, and I think the judgment of the court below should be reversed....

It is urged that the question involved should now receive fresh consideration, among other reasons, because of 'the economic conditions which have supervened'; but the meaning of the Constitution does not change with the ebb and flow of economic events. We frequently are told in more general words that the Constitution must be construed in the light of the present. If by that it is meant that the Constitution is made up of living words that apply to every new condition which they include, the statement is quite true. But to say, if that be intended, that the words of the Constitution mean today what they did not mean when written—that is, that they do not apply to a situation now to which they would have applied then—is to rob that instrument of the essential element which continues it in force as the people have made it until they, and not their official agents, have made it otherwise....

If the Constitution, intelligently and reasonably construed..., stands in the way of desirable legislation, the blame must rest upon that instrument, and not upon the court for enforcing it according to its terms. The remedy in that situation—and the only true remedy—is to amend the Constitution....

Coming, then, to a consideration of the Washington statute, it first is to be observed that it is in every substantial respect identical with the statute involved in the *Adkins* case. Such vices as existed in the latter are present in the former. And if the *Adkins* case was properly decided, as we who join in this opinion think it was, it necessarily follows that the Washington statute is invalid....

We ... pointed out [in *Adkins*] that minimum wage-legislation such as that here involved does not deal with any business charged with a public interest, or with public work, or with a temporary emergency, or with the character, methods, or periods of wage payments, or with hours of labor, or with the protection of persons under legal disability, or with the prevention of fraud. It is, simply and exclusively, a law fixing wages for adult women who are legally as capable of contracting for themselves as men, and cannot be sustained unless upon principles apart from those involved in cases already decided by the court....

The Washington statute, like the one for the District of Columbia [in *Adkins*], fixes minimum wages for adult women. Adult men and their employers are left free to bargain as they please; and it is a significant and an important fact that all state statutes to which our attention has been called are of like character. The common-law rules restricting the power of women to make contracts have, under our system, long since practically disappeared. Women today stand upon a legal and political equality with men. There is no longer any reason why they should be put in different classes in respect of their legal right to make contracts; nor should they be denied, in effect, the right to compete with men for work paying lower wages which men may be willing to accept. And it is an arbitrary exercise of the legislative power to do so....

## Note: Economic Due Process after 1937

After *West Coast Hotel* the four dissenters in that case began to leave the Court; by 1941, death or resignation had removed all of them. Their replacements—all Roosevelt appointees—continued *West Coast Hotel*'s highly deferential approach to government infringements on contractual liberty. In *Railway Express Agency v. New York*, 336 U.S. 106 (1949), the Court unanimously rejected a due process challenge to a law restricting the ability of truck owners to rent out the sides of their trucks for advertising, with Justice Douglas writing that "We do not sit to weigh evidence on the due process issue in order to determine whether the regulation is sound or appropriate; nor is it our function to pass judgment on its wisdom." In *Williamson v. Lee Optical*, 348 U.S. 483 (1955), the Court similarly had no difficulty rejecting a due process challenge to an Oklahoma law limiting the ability of opticians to fit eyeglasses without a prescription from an optometrist or ophthalmologist. Again writing for the Court, Justice Douglas wrote that "The day is gone when this Court uses the Due Process Clause of the Fourteenth Amendment to strike down state laws, regulatory of business and industrial conditions, because they may be unwise, improvident, or out of harmony with a particular school of thought. We emphasize again what Chief Justice Waite said in *Munn v. Illinois* (1877) [*Supra*. this chapter], 'For protection against abuses by legislatures the people must resort to the polls, not to the courts.'"

## Ferguson v. Skrupa
### 372 U.S. 726 (1963)

Mr. Justice BLACK delivered the opinion of the Court.

In this case … we are asked to review the judgment of a three-judge District Court enjoining, as being in violation of the Due Process Clause of the Fourteenth Amendment, a Kansas statute making it a misdemeanor for any person to engage 'in the business of debt adjusting' except as an incident to 'the lawful practice of law in this state.' The statute defines 'debt adjusting' as 'the making of a contract, express, or implied with a particular debtor whereby the debtor agrees to pay a certain amount of money periodically to the person engaged in the debt adjusting business who shall for a consideration distribute the same among certain specified creditors in accordance with a plan agreed upon.'

The complaint, filed by appellee Skrupa doing business as 'Credit Advisors,' alleged that Skrupa was engaged in the business of 'debt adjusting' as defined by the statute, that his business was a 'useful and desirable' one, that his business activities were not 'inherently immoral or dangerous' or in any way contrary to the public welfare, and that therefore the business could not be 'absolutely prohibited' by Kansas. The three-judge court heard evidence by Skrupa tending to show the usefulness and desirability of his business and evidence by the state officials tending to show that 'debt adjusting' lends itself to grave abuses against distressed debtors, particularly in the lower income brackets, and that these abuses are of such gravity that a number of States have strictly regulated 'debt adjusting' or prohibited it altogether. The court … concluded, one judge dissenting, that the Act was prohibitory, not regulatory, but that even if construed in part as regulatory it was an unreasonable regulation of a 'lawful business,' which the court held amounted to a violation of the Due Process Clause of the Fourteenth Amendment. The court accordingly enjoined enforcement of the statute.

The only case discussed by the court below as support for its invalidation of the statute was *Commonwealth v. Stone*, 155 A.2d 453 (1959), in which the Superior Court of Pennsylvania struck down a statute almost identical to the Kansas act involved here. In *Stone* the Pennsylvania court held that the State could regulate, but could not prohibit, a 'legitimate' business. Finding debt adjusting, called 'budget planning' in the Pennsylvania statute, not to be 'against the public interest' and concluding that it could 'see no justification for such interference' with this business, the Pennsylvania court ruled that State's statute to be unconstitutional. In doing so, the Pennsylvania court relied heavily on *Adams v. Tanner*, 244 U.S. 590 (1917), which held that the Due Process Clause forbids a State to prohibit a business which is 'useful' and not 'inherently immoral or dangerous to public welfare.'

Both the District Court in the present case and the Pennsylvania court in *Stone* adopted the philosophy of *Adams v. Tanner*, and cases like it, that it is the province of courts to draw on their own views as to the morality, legitimacy, and usefulness of a particular business in order to decide whether a statute bears too heavily upon that business and by so doing violates due process. Under the system of government created by our Constitution, it is up to legislatures, not courts, to decide on the wisdom and utility of legislation. There was a time when the Due Process Clause was used by this Court to strike down laws which were thought unreasonable, that is, unwise or incompatible with some particular economic or social philosophy. In this manner the Due Process Clause was used, for example, to nullify laws prescribing maximum hours for work in bakeries, *Lochner v. New York* (1905) [*Supra.* this chapter], outlawing 'yellow dog' contracts, *Coppage v. Kansas*, 236 U.S. 1 (1915), setting minimum wages for women, *Adkins v. Children's Hospital*, 261 U.S. 525 (1923) [Note *supra.* this chapter], and fixing the weight of loaves of bread, *Jay Burns Baking Co. v. Bryan*, 264 U.S. 504 (1924)....

The doctrine that prevailed in *Lochner, Coppage, Adkins, Burns*, and like cases — that due process authorizes courts to hold laws unconstitutional when they believe the legislature has acted unwisely — has long since been discarded. We have returned to the original constitutional proposition that courts do not substitute their social and economic beliefs for the judgment of legislative bodies, who are elected to pass laws.... It is now settled that States 'have power to legislate against what are found to be injurious practices in their internal commercial and business affairs, so long as their laws do not run afoul of some specific federal constitutional prohibition, or of some valid federal law.'...

Mr. Justice HARLAN concurs in the judgment on the ground that this state measure bears a rational relation to a constitutionally permissible objective.

# Chapter 8

# The Development of
# Non-Economic Liberties

Since at least the early part of the twentieth century, the Court has understood the liberty entitled to substantive protection by the Due Process Clause to include more than just economic rights. Broadly considered, the Court has pursued two lines of thinking with regard to the content of those non-economic liberty rights. First, it has considered whether that liberty includes unenumerated rights—liberties that are nowhere explicitly mentioned in the Constitution. Second, it has considered whether that liberty includes some, or all, of the Bill of Rights—that is, it has considered whether the Fourteenth Amendment Due Process Clause "incorporated" all or part of the Bill of Rights. This chapter examines these two issues. The remaining two chapters in Part III consider modern variants on the Court's search for non-economic rights in the Due Process Clause.

## A. Unenumerated Rights to Liberty
### Meyer v. Nebraska
262 U.S. 390 (1923)

Mr. Justice McREYNOLDS delivered the opinion of the Court.

Plaintiff in error was tried and convicted in the District Court for Hamilton County, Nebraska, under an information which charged that on May 25, 1920, while an instructor in Zion Parochial School he unlawfully taught the subject of reading in the German language to Raymond Parpart, a child of 10 years, who had not attained and successfully passed the eighth grade. The information is based upon 'An act relating to the teaching of foreign languages in the State of Nebraska,' … which follows:

'Section 1. No person, individually or as a teacher, shall, in any private, denominational, parochial or public school, teach any subject to any person in any language than the English language.

'Sec. 2. Languages, other than the English language, may be taught as languages only after a pupil shall have attained and successfully passed the eighth grade as evidenced by a certificate of graduation issued by the county superintendent of the county in which the child resides.

'Sec. 3. Any person who violates any of the provisions of this act shall be deemed guilty of a misdemeanor and upon conviction, shall be subject to a fine of not less than twenty-five dollars ($25), nor more than one hundred dollars ($100), or be confined in the county jail for any period not exceeding thirty days for each offense.

'Sec. 4. Whereas, an emergency exists, this act shall be in force from and after its passage and approval.'

The Supreme Court of the State affirmed the judgment of conviction.... The following excerpts from the opinion sufficiently indicate the reasons advanced to support the conclusion:

'The salutary purpose of the statute is clear. The legislature had seen the baneful effects of permitting foreigners, who had taken residence in this country, to rear and educate their children in the language of their native land. The result of that condition was found to be inimical to our own safety. To allow the children of foreigners, who had emigrated here, to be taught from early childhood the language of the country of their parents was to rear them with that language as their mother tongue. It was to educate them so that they must always think in that language, and, as a consequence, naturally inculcate in them the ideas and sentiments foreign to the best interests of this country. The statute, therefore, was intended not only to require that the education of all children be conducted in the English language, but that, until they had grown into that language and until it had become a part of them, they should not in the schools be taught any other language. The obvious purpose of this statute was that the English language should be and become the mother tongue of all children reared in this state. The enactment of such a statute comes reasonably within the police power of the state....

The problem for our determination is whether the statute as construed and applied unreasonably infringes the liberty guaranteed to the plaintiff in error by the Fourteenth Amendment:

'No State shall ... deprive any person of life, liberty, or property, without due process of law.'

While this court has not attempted to define with exactness the liberty thus guaranteed, the term has received much consideration and some of the included things have been definitely stated. Without doubt, it denotes not merely freedom from bodily restraint but also the right of the individual to contract, to engage in any of the common occupations of life, to acquire useful knowledge, to marry, establish a home and bring up children, to worship God according to the dictates of his own conscience, and generally to enjoy those privileges long recognized at common law as essential to the orderly pursuit of happiness by free men. *Slaughter-House Cases*, 83 U.S. 36 (1873) [Note *supra*. Introduction this part]; *Allegeyer v. Louisiana*, 165 U.S. 578 (1897) [Note *supra*. Chapter 7]; *Lochner v. New York* (1905) [*Supra*. Chapter 7]; *Adkins v. Children's Hospital*, 261 U.S. 525 (1923) [Note *supra*. Chapter 7]. The established doctrine is that this liberty may not be interfered with, under the guise of protecting the public interest, by legislative action which is arbitrary or without reasonable relation to some purpose within the competency of the State to effect. Determination by the legislature of what constitutes proper exercise of police power is not final or conclusive but is subject to supervision by the courts.

The American people have always regarded education and acquisition of knowledge as matters of supreme importance which should be diligently promoted.... Practically, education of the young is only possible in schools conducted by especially qualified persons who devote themselves thereto. The calling always has been regarded as useful and honorable, essential, indeed, to the public welfare. Mere knowledge of the German language cannot reasonably be regarded as harmful.... Plaintiff in error taught this language in school as part of his occupation. His right thus to teach and the right of parents to engage him so to instruct their children, we think, are within the liberty of the Amendment....

It is said the purpose of the legislation was to promote civic development by inhibiting training and education of the immature in foreign tongues and ideals before they could learn English and acquire American ideals, and 'that the English language should be and become the mother tongue of all children reared in this State.' It is also affirmed that the foreign born population is very large, that certain communities commonly use foreign words, follow foreign leaders, move in a foreign atmosphere, and that the children are thereby hindered from becoming citizens of the most useful type and the public safety is imperiled.

That the State may do much, go very far, indeed, in order to improve the quality of its citizens, physically, mentally and morally, is clear; but the individual has certain fundamental rights which must be respected. The protection of the Constitution extends to all, to those who speak other languages as well as to those born with English on the tongue. Perhaps it would be highly advantageous if all had ready understanding of our ordinary speech, but this cannot be coerced by methods which conflict with the Constitution—a desirable end cannot be promoted by prohibited means.

For the welfare of his Ideal Commonwealth, Plato suggested a law which should provide:

> That the wives of our guardians are to be common, and their children are to be common, and no parent is to know his own child, nor any child his parent. ... The proper officers will take the offspring of the good parents to the pen or fold, and there they will deposit them with certain nurses who dwell in a separate quarter; but the offspring of the inferior, or of the better when they chance to be deformed, will be put away in some mysterious, unknown place, as they should be.

In order to submerge the individual and develop ideal citizens, Sparta assembled the males at seven into barracks and intrusted their subsequent education and training to official guardians. Although such measures have been deliberately approved by men of great genius their ideas touching the relation between individual and State were wholly different from those upon which our institutions rest; and it hardly will be affirmed that any legislature could impose such restrictions upon the people of a state without doing violence to both letter and spirit of the Constitution....

Mr. Justice HOLMES and Mr. Justice SUTHERLAND, dissent.

## Note: From Parenting to Procreation

1. In the two decades after *Meyer*, the Court continued to encounter arguments that the "liberty" protected by the Due Process Clause included various rights related to children and child-rearing. Two years after *Meyer*, in *Pierce v. Society of Sisters*, 268 U.S. 510 (1925), the Court relied on *Meyer* to strike down an Oregon law that required most parents to send their children to public school. Justice McReynolds, the author of *Meyer*, wrote the following:

> As often heretofore pointed out, rights guaranteed by the Constitution may not be abridged by legislation which has no reasonable relation to some purpose within the competency of the state. The fundamental theory of liberty upon which all governments in this Union repose excludes any general power of the state to standardize its children by forcing them to accept instruction from public teachers only. The child is not the mere creature of the state; those who nurture him and direct his destiny have the right, coupled with the high duty, to recognize and prepare him for additional obligations.

Two years later, the Court relied on *Meyer* and *Pierce* to strike down a federal territorial law restricting foreign language schools in Hawaii. *Farrington v. Tokushige*, 273 U.S. 284 (1927).

2. To be sure, parental rights—or, rather, rights to be a parent—were not always vindicated. Most notoriously, in *Buck v. Bell*, 274 U.S. 200 (1927), eight justices upheld a Virginia statute requiring the sterilization of what the Court called "mental defectives" housed in state mental institutions, as applied to Carrie Buck, a patient in one of those institutions. After noting the procedures the statute afforded to a person who was targeted for sterilization, Justice Holmes, writing for the Court, wrote the following:

> In view of the general declarations of the Legislature and the specific findings of the Court [relating to Carrie Buck] obviously we cannot say as matter of law that the grounds do not exist, and if they exist they justify the result. We have seen more than once that the public welfare may call upon the best citizens for their lives. It would be strange if it could not call upon those who already sap the strength of the State for these lesser sacrifices, often not felt to be such by those concerned, in order to prevent our being swamped with incompetence. It is better for all the world, if instead of waiting to execute degenerate offspring for crime, or to let them starve for their imbecility, society can prevent those who are manifestly unfit from continuing their kind. The principle that sustains compulsory vaccination is broad enough to cover cutting the Fallopian tubes. *Jacobson v. Massachusetts*, 197 U.S. 11 (1905)

[upholding a compulsory vaccination law]. Three generations of imbeciles are enough.

Justice Butler dissented without opinion.

3. The last case of this type before the modern era also involved forced sterilizations. In *Skinner v. Oklahoma*, 316 U.S. 545 (1942), the Court struck down an Oklahoma law authorizing the state to sterilize certain categories of repeat offender criminals. Writing for the majority, Justice Douglas noted, but refused to pass on, the plaintiff's due process claims. Instead, he concluded that the statute violated equal protection, because certain criminal offenses (which he intimated were white-collar crimes) did not make the inmate liable to forced sterilization. But his discussion of equal protection noted that the Court was dealing with "legislation which involves one of the basic civil rights of man. Marriage and procreation are fundamental to the very existence and survival of the race." Chief Justice Stone concurred on the ground that the criminal targeted for sterilization had a due process right to a hearing at which he could attempt to show that his crimes were not of the variety that (at the time) were thought to be inheritable. Justice Jackson agreed with both of these approaches. But he wrote separately to express a more substantive concern about the constitutionality of such laws: "There are limits to the extent to which a legislatively represented majority may conduct biological experiments at the expense of the dignity and personality and natural powers of a minority—even those who have been guilty of what the majority define as crimes." He did not decide that issue, given his agreement with the less sweeping justifications for striking the law down offered by his colleagues.

4. With the demise of *Lochner*-type judicial review of economic regulation in 1937, a question remained about the viability of the *Meyer* line of cases, given its reliance on *Lochner*'s conception of liberty. As set forth in the previous item in this note, *Skinner*, the first major post-1937 case raising this question, largely avoided the issue by focusing on equal protection and *procedural* due process. But Justice Jackson's speculation that the Oklahoma law may have been substantively invalid, regardless of the inequality it created or the inadequate procedures it provided, suggests that even in the immediate post-1937 period the Court had not fully abandoned the idea that the Due Process Clause protects unenumerated rights.

# B. Incorporation of the Bill of Rights

## Note: The Early History of Incorporation

1. In 1833, the Supreme Court decided that the Bill of Rights did not bind the states. *Barron v. Baltimore*, 32 U.S. 243 (1833). Writing for the Court in one of his last major opinions, Chief Justice Marshall wrote that the question of the Bill of Rights' applicability to the states was "of great importance, but of not much difficulty," in light of the evidence that the Bill of Rights was intended to restrict the potential tyrannical power of the new federal government. Nevertheless, as the crisis over slavery grew, concerns arose that state governments could not be trusted to protect

the fundamental rights of their citizens. Southern states in particular repressed anti-slavery speech, and forbade the teaching of literacy to slaves, even by ministers who thereby hoped to teach slaves to read the Bible. By the end of the Civil War, many northerners had come to believe that it was necessary to institute federal protection for fundamental rights.

2. The *Slaughter-House Cases*, 83 U.S. 36 (1873) (Note *supra*. this chapter) slowed the momentum toward recognizing that the Fourteenth Amendment had effectively imposed some or all of the liberties of the Bill of Rights on the states. However, by the end of the Nineteenth Century the rise of liberty of contract ideas made it possible to conceive of other liberties that might come within the Fourteenth Amendment's protection.

The process by which Bill of Rights provisions were deemed applicable to the states proceeded slowly. In 1897 the Court held that the Fourteenth Amendment's Due Process Clause prohibited states from taking property without just compensation, parallel to the Fifth Amendment's analogous prohibition on the federal government. *Chicago, Burlington & Quincy RR v. City of Chicago*, 166 U.S. 226 (1897). In 1908, it rejected the argument that the Clause prohibited state judges from instructing jurors that they could draw negative inferences from a criminal defendant's failure to testify (thus violating the Fifth Amendment); nevertheless, it suggested that some Bill of Rights provisions might apply to states. However, it cautioned that, if some of those provisions did restrict state conduct, this was not because of their status as Bill of Rights provisions *per se*, but rather, because such rights "are of such a nature that they are included in the conception of due process of law." *Twining v. New Jersey*, 211 U.S. 78 (1908).

3. This process of "selective incorporation" became the Court's settled approach for deciding which Bill of Rights provisions applied against the states. However, that approach elicited criticism that it involved justices in making incorporation decisions based on their personal views about the importance of a given Bill of Rights provision. This criticism is most closely identified with Justice Hugo Black, as expressed most forcefully in his dissent in *Adamson v. California*, excerpted below. This approach also raised the question of whether, when incorporated, the given Bill of Rights provision applied exactly as its textually-explicit version did against the federal government. The most prominent critique of so called "jot-for-jot" incorporation was the second Justice Harlan. Finally, the debate over incorporation — whether the Fourteenth Amendment required total, exact incorporation of the Bill of Rights, or whether instead it required an exercise of judicial judgment — inevitably raised the question of whether the Due Process Clause provided substantive protection to *other* rights. As illustrated in the previous section, during the *Lochner* era the Court had no difficulty finding due process to include liberties beyond those provided in the Bill of Rights. After the Court repudiated the *Lochner* approach in 1937, the question remained whether its more free-form approach to non-economic due process "liberty" remained, or whether the Court would limit itself to protecting some or all of the substantive rights in the Bill of Rights, but nothing more.

# Palko v. Connecticut

302 U.S. 319 (1937)

Mr. Justice CARDOZO delivered the opinion of the Court.

A statute of Connecticut permitting appeals in criminal cases to be taken by the state is challenged by appellant as an infringement of the Fourteenth Amendment of the Constitution of the United States. Whether the challenge should be upheld is now to be determined.

Appellant was indicted in Fairfield County, Connecticut, for the crime of murder in the first degree. A jury found him guilty of murder in the second degree, and he was sentenced to confinement in the state prison for life. Thereafter the State of Connecticut, with the permission of the judge presiding at the trial, gave notice of appeal to the Supreme Court of Errors.... Upon such appeal, the Supreme Court of Errors reversed the judgment and ordered a new trial. It found that there had been error of law to the prejudice of the state (1) in excluding testimony as to a confession by defendant; (2) in excluding testimony upon cross-examination of defendant to impeach his credibility; and (3) in the instructions to the jury as to the difference between first and second degree murder.

Pursuant to the mandate of the Supreme Court of Errors, defendant was brought to trial again. Before a jury was impaneled and also at later stages of the case, he made the objection that the effect of the new trial was to place him twice in jeopardy for the same offense, and in so doing to violate the Fourteenth Amendment of the Constitution of the United States. Upon the overruling of the objection the trial proceeded. The jury returned a verdict of murder in the first degree, and the court sentenced the defendant to the punishment of death. The Supreme Court of Errors affirmed the judgment of conviction ...

... The execution of the sentence will not deprive appellant of his life without the process of law assured to him by the Fourteenth Amendment of the Federal Constitution.

The argument for appellant is that whatever is forbidden by the Fifth Amendment is forbidden by the Fourteenth also. The Fifth Amendment, which is not directed to the states, but solely to the federal government, creates immunity from double jeopardy. No person shall be 'subject for the same offense to be twice put in jeopardy of life or limb.' The Fourteenth Amendment ordains, 'nor shall any State deprive any person of life, liberty, or property, without due process of law.' To retry a defendant, though under one indictment and only one, subjects him, it is said, to double jeopardy in violation of the Fifth Amendment, if the prosecution is one on behalf of the United States. From this the consequence is said to follow that there is a denial of life or liberty without due process of law, if the prosecution is one on behalf of the People of a State....

We have said that in appellant's view the Fourteenth Amendment is to be taken as embodying the prohibitions of the Fifth. His thesis is even broader. Whatever would be a violation of the original bill of rights (Amendments 1 to 8) if done by the federal government is now equally unlawful by force of the Fourteenth Amendment if done by a state. There is no such general rule.

The Fifth Amendment provides, among other things, that no person shall be held to answer for a capital or otherwise infamous crime unless on presentment or indictment of a grand jury. This court has held that, in prosecutions by a state, presentment or indictment by a grand jury may give way to informations at the instance of a public officer. The Fifth Amendment provides also that no person shall be compelled in any criminal case to be a witness against himself. This court has said that, in prosecutions by a state, the exemption will fail if the state elects to end it. The Sixth Amendment calls for a jury trial in criminal cases and the Seventh for a jury trial in civil cases at common law where the value in controversy shall exceed $20. This court has ruled that consistently with those amendments trial by jury may be modified by a state or abolished altogether....

On the other hand, the due process clause of the Fourteenth Amendment may make it unlawful for a state to abridge by its statutes the freedom of speech which the First Amendment safeguards against encroachment by the Congress or the like freedom of the press, or the free exercise of religion, or the right of peaceable assembly, without which speech would be unduly trammeled, or the right of one accused of crime to the benefit of counsel. In these and other situations immunities that are valid as against the federal government by force of the specific pledges of particular amendments have been found to be implicit in the concept of ordered liberty, and thus, through the Fourteenth Amendment, become valid as against the states.

The line of division may seem to be wavering and broken if there is a hasty catalogue of the cases on the one side and the other. Reflection and analysis will induce a different view. There emerges the perception of a rationalizing principle which gives to discrete instances a proper order and coherence. The right to trial by jury and the immunity from prosecution except as the result of an indictment may have value and importance. Even so, they are not of the very essence of a scheme of ordered liberty. To abolish them is not to violate a 'principle of justice so rooted in the traditions and conscience of our people as to be ranked as fundamental.' *Snyder v. Massachusetts*, 291 U.S. 97 (1934). Few would be so narrow or provincial as to maintain that a fair and enlightened system of justice would be impossible without them. What is true of jury trials and indictments is true also, as the cases show, of the immunity from compulsory self-incrimination. This too might be lost, and justice still be done. Indeed, today as in the past there are students of our penal system who look upon the immunity as a mischief rather than a benefit, and who would limit its scope, or destroy it altogether.... The exclusion of these immunities and privileges from the privileges and immunities protected against the action of the states has not been arbitrary or casual. It has been dictated by a study and appreciation of the meaning, the essential implications, of liberty itself.

We reach a different plane of social and moral values when we pass to the privileges and immunities that have been taken over from the earlier articles of the federal bill of rights and brought within the Fourteenth Amendment by a process of absorption.

These in their origin were effective against the federal government alone. If the Fourteenth Amendment has absorbed them, the process of absorption has had its source in the belief that neither liberty nor justice would exist if they were sacrificed. This is true, for illustration, of freedom of thought, and speech. Of that freedom one may say that it is the matrix, the indispensable condition, of nearly every other form of freedom. With rare aberrations a pervasive recognition of that truth can be traced in our history, political and legal....

Our survey of the cases serves, we think, to justify the statement that the dividing line between them, if not unfaltering throughout its course, has been true for the most part to a unifying principle. On which side of the line the case made out by the appellant has appropriate location must be the next inquiry and the final one. Is that kind of double jeopardy to which the statute has subjected him a hardship so acute and shocking that our polity will not endure it? Does it violate those 'fundamental principles of liberty and justice which lie at the base of all our civil and political institutions'? The answer surely must be 'no.' What the answer would have to be if the state were permitted after a trial free from error to try the accused over again or to bring another case against him, we have no occasion to consider. We deal with the statute before us and no other. The state is not attempting to wear the accused out by a multitude of cases with accumulated trials. It asks no more than this, that the case against him shall go on until there shall be a trial free from the corrosion of substantial legal error. This is not cruelty at all, nor even vexation in any immoderate degree. If the trial had been infected with error adverse to the accused, there might have been review at his instance, and as often as necessary to purge the vicious taint. A reciprocal privilege, subject at all times to the discretion of the presiding judge, has now been granted to the state. There is here no seismic innovation. The edifice of justice stands, its symmetry, to many, greater than before.... The judgment is affirmed.

Mr. Justice BUTLER dissents.

## Adamson v. California
### 332 U.S. 46 (1947)

Mr. Justice REED delivered the opinion of the Court.

The appellant, Adamson, a citizen of the United States, was convicted, without recommendation for mercy, by a jury in a Superior Court of the State of California of murder in the first degree. After considering the same objections to the conviction that are pressed here, the sentence of death was affirmed by the Supreme Court of the state. Review of that judgment by this Court was sought and allowed.... The provisions of California law which were challenged in the state proceedings as invalid under the Fourteenth Amendment to the Federal Constitution ... permit the failure of a defendant to explain or to deny evidence against him to be commented upon by court and by counsel and to be considered by court and jury....

In the first place, appellant urges that the provision of the Fifth Amendment that no person 'shall be compelled in any criminal case to be a witness against himself' is a fundamental national privilege or immunity protected against state abridgment by the Fourteenth Amendment or a privilege or immunity secured, through the Fourteenth Amendment, against deprivation by state action because it is a personal right, enumerated in the federal Bill of Rights.

Secondly, appellant relies upon the due process of law clause of the Fourteenth Amendment to invalidate the provisions of the California law ... (a) because comment on failure to testify is permitted, (b) because appellant was forced to forego testimony in person because of danger of disclosure of his past convictions through cross-examination and (c) because the presumption of innocence was infringed by the shifting of the burden of proof to appellant in permitting comment on his failure to testify.

We shall assume, but without any intention thereby of ruling upon the issue, that state permission by law to the court, counsel and jury to comment upon and consider the failure of defendant 'to explain or to deny by his testimony any evidence or facts in the case against him' would infringe defendant's privilege against self-incrimination under the Fifth Amendment if this were a trial in a court of the United States under a similar law. Such an assumption does not determine appellant's rights under the Fourteenth Amendment. It is settled law that the clause of the Fifth Amendment, protecting a person against being compelled to be a witness against himself, is not made effective by the Fourteenth Amendment as a protection against state action on the ground that freedom from testimonial compulsion is a right of national citizenship, or because it is a personal privilege or immunity secured by the Federal Constitution as one of the rights of man that are listed in the Bill of Rights.

The reasoning that leads to those conclusions starts with the unquestioned premise that the Bill of Rights, when adopted, was for the protection of the individual against the federal government and its provisions were inapplicable to similar actions done by the states. *Barron v. Baltimore*, 32 U.S. 243 (1833) [Note *supra.* this chapter]. With the adoption of the Fourteenth Amendment, it was suggested that the dual citizenship recognized by its first sentence secured for citizens federal protection for their elemental privileges and immunities of state citizenship. The *Slaughter-House Cases*, 83 U.S. 36 [Note *supra.* Introduction this part] decided, contrary to the suggestion, that these rights, as privileges and immunities of state citizenship, remained under the sole protection of the state governments....

Appellant secondly contends that if the privilege against self-incrimination is not a right protected by the privileges and immunities clause of the Fourteenth Amendment against state action, this privilege, to its full scope under the Fifth Amendment, inheres in the right to a fair trial.... Therefore, appellant argues, the due process clause of the Fourteenth Amendment protects his privilege against self-incrimination. The due process clause of the Fourteenth Amendment, however, does not draw all the rights of the federal Bill of Rights under its protection. That contention was made and rejected in *Palko.*...

Specifically, the due process clause does not protect, by virtue of its mere existence, the accused's freedom from giving testimony by compulsion in state trials that is secured to him against federal interference by the Fifth Amendment. *Twining v. New Jersey*, 211 U.S. 78 (1908) [Note *supra.* this chapter]

Mr. Justice FRANKFURTER (concurring).

Less than ten years ago, Mr. Justice Cardozo announced as settled constitutional law that while the Fifth Amendment, 'which is not directed to the states, but solely to the federal government,' provides that no person shall be compelled in any criminal case to be a witness against himself, the process of law assured by the Fourteenth Amendment does not require such immunity from self-crimination: 'in prosecutions by a state, the exemption will fail if the state elects to end it.' *Palko.*... The matter no longer called for discussion; a reference to *Twining*, decided years before the *Palko* case, sufficed....

For historical reasons a limited immunity from the common duty to testify was written into the Federal Bill of Rights, and I am prepared to agree that, as part of that immunity, comment on the failure of an accused to take the witness stand is forbidden in federal prosecutions.... But to suggest that such a limitation can be drawn out of 'due process' in its protection of ultimate decency in a civilized society is to suggest that the Due Process Clause fastened fetters of unreason upon the States....

Between the incorporation of the Fourteenth Amendment into the Constitution and the beginning of the present membership of the Court—a period of seventy years—the scope of that Amendment was passed upon by forty-three judges. Of all these judges, only one, who may respectfully be called an eccentric exception, ever indicated the belief that the Fourteenth Amendment was a shorthand summary of the first eight Amendments theretofore limiting only the Federal Government, and that due process incorporated those eight Amendments as restrictions upon the powers of the States. Among these judges were not only those who would have to be included among the greatest in the history of the Court, but—it is especially relevant to note—they included those whose services in the cause of human rights and the spirit of freedom are the most conspicuous in our history. It is not invidious to single out Miller, Davis, Bradley, Waite, Matthews, Gray, Fuller, Holmes, Brandeis, Stone and Cardozo (to speak only of the dead) as judges who were alert in safeguarding and promoting the interests of liberty and human dignity through law. But they were also judges mindful of the relation of our federal system to a progressively democratic society and therefore duly regardful of the scope of authority that was left to the States even after the Civil War. And so they did not find that the Fourteenth Amendment, concerned as it was with matters fundamental to the pursuit of justice, fastened upon the States procedural arrangements which, in the language of Mr. Justice Cardozo, only those who are 'narrow or provincial' would deem essential to 'a fair and enlightened system of justice.' *Palko.* To suggest that it is inconsistent with a truly free society to begin prosecutions without an indictment, to try petty civil cases without the paraphernalia of a common law jury, to take into consideration that one who has full opportunity to make a defense remains silent is, in de Tocqueville's phrase, to confound the familiar with the necessary.

The short answer to the suggestion that the provision of the Fourteenth Amendment, which ordains 'nor shall any State deprive any person of life, liberty, or property, without due process of law,' was a way of saying that every State must thereafter initiate prosecutions through indictment by a grand jury, must have a trial by a jury of twelve in criminal cases, and must have trial by such a jury in common law suits where the amount in controversy exceeds twenty dollars, is that it is a strange way of saying it. It would be extraordinarily strange for a Constitution to convey such specific commands in such a roundabout and inexplicit way.... Those reading the English language with the meaning which it ordinarily conveys, those conversant with the political and legal history of the concept of due process, those sensitive to the relations of the States to the central government as well as the relation of some of the provisions of the Bill of Rights to the process of justice, would hardly recognize the Fourteenth Amendment as a cover for the various explicit provisions of the first eight Amendments. Some of these are enduring reflections of experience with human nature, while some express the restricted views of Eighteenth-Century England regarding the best methods for the ascertainment of facts. The notion that the Fourteenth Amendment was a covert way of imposing upon the States all the rules which it seemed important to Eighteenth Century statesmen to write into the Federal Amendments, was rejected by judges who were themselves witnesses of the process by which the Fourteenth Amendment became part of the Constitution....

Indeed, the suggestion that the Fourteenth Amendment incorporates the first eight Amendments as such is not unambiguously urged. Even the boldest innovator would shrink from suggesting to more than half the States that they may no longer initiate prosecutions without indictment by grand jury, or that thereafter all the States of the Union must furnish a jury of 12 for every case involving a claim above $20. There is suggested merely a selective incorporation of the first eight Amendments into the Fourteenth Amendment. Some are in and some are out, but we are left in the dark as to which are in and which are out. Nor are we given the calculus for determining which go in and which stay out. If the basis of selection is merely that those provisions of the first eight Amendments are incorporated which commend themselves to individual justices as indispensable to the dignity and happiness of a free man, we are thrown back to a merely subjective test.... In the history of thought 'natural law' has a much longer and much better founded meaning and justification than such subjective selection of the first eight Amendments for incorporation into the Fourteenth. If all that is meant is that due process contains within itself certain minimal standards which are 'of the very essence of a scheme of ordered liberty,' *Palko*, putting upon this Court the duty of applying these standards from time to time, then we have merely arrived at the insight which our predecessors long ago expressed....

It may not be amiss to restate the pervasive function of the Fourteenth Amendment in exacting from the States observance of basic liberties. The Amendment neither comprehends the specific provisions by which the founders deemed it appropriate to restrict the federal government nor is it confined to them. The Due Process Clause of the Fourteenth Amendment has an independent potency, precisely as does the Due Process Clause of the Fifth Amendment in relation to the Federal Government....

A construction which gives to due process no independent function but turns it into a summary of the specific provisions of the Bill of Rights would, as has been noted, tear up by the roots much of the fabric of law in the several States, and would deprive the States of opportunity for reforms in legal process designed for extending the area of freedom. It would assume that no other abuses would reveal themselves in the course of time than those which had become manifest in 1791. Such a view not only disregards the historic meaning of 'due process.' It leads inevitably to a warped construction of specific provisions of the Bill of Rights to bring within their scope conduct clearly condemned by due process but not easily fitting into the pigeon-holes of the specific provisions. It seems pretty late in the day to suggest that a phrase so laden with historic meaning should be given an improvised content consisting of some but not all of the provisions of the first eight Amendments, selected on an undefined basis, with improvisation of content for the provisions so selected.

And so, when, as in a case like the present, a conviction in a State court is here for review under a claim that a right protected by the Due Process Clause of the Fourteenth Amendment has been denied, the issue is not whether an infraction of one of the specific provisions of the first eight Amendments is disclosed by the record. The relevant question is whether the criminal proceedings which resulted in conviction deprived the accused of the due process of law to which the United States Constitution entitled him. Judicial review of that guaranty of the Fourteenth Amendment inescapably imposes upon this Court an exercise of judgment upon the whole course of the proceedings in order to ascertain whether they offend those canons of decency and fairness which express the notions of justice of English-speaking peoples even toward those charged with the most heinous offenses. These standards of justice are not authoritatively formulated anywhere as though they were prescriptions in a pharmacopoeia. But neither does the application of the Due Process Clause imply that judges are wholly at large. The judicial judgment in applying the Due Process Clause must move within the limits of accepted notions of justice and is not to be based upon the idiosyncrasies of a merely personal judgment. The fact that judges among themselves may differ whether in a particular case a trial offends accepted notions of justice is not disproof that general rather than idiosyncratic standards are applied. An important safeguard against such merely individual judgment is an alert deference to the judgment of the State court under review.

Mr. Justice BLACK, dissenting....

This decision reasserts a constitutional theory spelled out in *Twining* that this Court is endowed by the Constitution with boundless power under 'natural law' periodically to expand and contract constitutional standards to conform to the Court's conception of what at a particular time constitutes 'civilized decency' and 'fundamental principles of liberty and justice.' Invoking this *Twining* rule, the Court concludes that although comment upon testimony in a federal court would violate the Fifth Amendment, identical comment in a state court does not violate today's fashion in civilized decency and fundamentals and is therefore not prohibited by the Federal Constitution as amended....

My study of the historical events that culminated in the Fourteenth Amendment, and the expressions of those who sponsored and favored, as well as those who opposed its submission and passage, persuades me that one of the chief objects that the provisions of the Amendment's first section, separately, and as a whole, were intended to accomplish was to make the Bill of Rights, applicable to the states. With full knowledge of the import of the *Barron* decision, the framers and backers of the Fourteenth Amendment proclaimed its purpose to be to overturn the constitutional rule that case had announced. This historical purpose has never received full consideration or exposition in any opinion of this Court interpreting the Amendment....

For this reason, I am attaching to this dissent an appendix which contains a resume, by no means complete, of the Amendment's history. In my judgment that history conclusively demonstrates that the language of the first section of the Fourteenth Amendment, taken as a whole, was thought by those responsible for its submission to the people, and by those who opposed its submission, sufficiently explicit to guarantee that thereafter no state could deprive its citizens of the privileges and protections of the Bill of Rights. Whether this Court ever will, or whether it now should, in the light of past decisions, give full effect to what the Amendment was intended to accomplish is not necessarily essential to a decision here. However that may be, our prior decisions, including *Twining*, do not prevent our carrying out that purpose, at least to the extent of making applicable to the states, not a mere part, as the Court has, but the full protection of the Fifth Amendment's provision against compelling evidence from an accused to convict him of crime. And I further contend that the 'natural law' formula which the Court uses to reach its conclusion in this case should be abandoned as an incongruous excrescence on our Constitution. I believe that formula to be itself a violation of our Constitution, in that it subtly conveys to courts, at the expense of legislatures, ultimate power over public policies in fields where no specific provision of the Constitution limits legislative power....

I cannot consider the Bill of Rights to be an outworn 18th Century 'strait jacket' as the *Twining* opinion did. Its provisions may be thought outdated abstractions by some. And it is true that they were designed to meet ancient evils. But they are the same kind of human evils that have emerged from century to century wherever excessive power is sought by the few at the expense of the many. In my judgment the people of no nation can lose their liberty so long as a Bill of Rights like ours survives and its basic purposes are conscientiously interpreted, enforced and respected so as to afford continuous protection against old, as well as new, devices and practices which might thwart those purposes. I fear to see the consequences of the Court's practice of substituting its own concepts of decency and fundamental justice for the language of the Bill of Rights as its point of departure in interpreting and enforcing that Bill of Rights. If the choice must be between the selective process of the *Palko* decision applying some of the Bill of Rights to the States, or the *Twining* rule applying none of them, I would choose the *Palko* selective process. But rather than accept either of these choices. I would follow what I believe was the original purpose of the Fourteenth Amendment—to extend to all the people of the nation the complete protection of the Bill of Rights. To hold that this Court can determine what, if any, provisions of the Bill of Rights will be enforced, and if so to what degree, is to frustrate the great design of a written Constitution....

Mr. Justice DOUGLAS joins in this opinion.

APPENDIX to Justice Black's opinion. [omitted]

Mr. Justice MURPHY, with whom Mr. Justice RUTLEDGE concurs, dissenting.

While in substantial agreement with the views of Mr. Justice BLACK, I have one reservation and one addition to make.

I agree that the specific guarantees of the Bill of Rights should be carried over intact into the first section of the Fourteenth Amendment. But I am not prepared to say that the latter is entirely and necessarily limited by the Bill of Rights. Occasions may arise where a proceeding falls so far short of conforming to fundamental standards of procedure as to warrant constitutional condemnation in terms of a lack of due process despite the absence of a specific provision in the Bill of Rights....

## Note: Incorporated Right or Unenumerated Liberty?

The debate between Justice Frankfurter and Justice Black about the content of due process liberty took a perhaps unusual turn in *Rochin v. California*, 342 U.S. 165 (1952). *Rochin* involved a police raid on a suspected drug dealer's home. When the police entered Rochin's home, Rochin swallowed pills that were on his nightstand. The police took Rochin into custody, drove him to a hospital, and had a doctor pump his stomach out to retrieve the pills.

The Supreme Court unanimously reversed Rochin's conviction, which was based on a trial that featured the introduction of the pills into evidence. Writing for seven justices, Justice Frankfurter cited *Palko*'s "so rooted in the traditions and conscience of our people as to be ranked as fundamental" and "implicit in the concept of ordered liberty" language, and found that the police conduct violated the Due Process Clause, because it "shocked the conscience." Concurring, Justice Black insisted that the police conduct amounted to forced self-incrimination, which, by violating the Fifth Amendment, necessarily violated the Fourteenth Amendment as well, given his view that the Fourteenth Amendment's Due Process Clause incorporated all of the Bill of Rights, but had no other substantive content.

## Note: The Current State of Incorporation

1. Despite the inhospitable tenor of cases such as *Palko* and *Adamson*, during the Warren Court (1954–1969) the Court incorporated almost all of the criminal procedure provisions of the Bill of Rights. When combined with the decisions of earlier courts, by 2015 the only Bill of Rights provisions that have not been incorporated are the Third Amendment right against quartering of soldiers, the Fifth Amendment right to a grand jury indictment in criminal cases, the Seventh Amend-

ment right to jury trials in civil cases, and the Eighth Amendment right against excessive fines.

2. The Warren Court's incorporation campaign encountered at least some resistance on the question of how precisely the incorporated right had to track the textual right provided in the Bill of Rights itself. Most notably, Justice Harlan waged a largely solitary campaign against what he called "jot-for-jot" incorporation. Despite occasional statements of sympathy from subsequent justices (and occasional supporting statements from earlier justices), the Court has essentially always insisted that the two versions of a given right have the precise same meaning.

3. To date the Bill of Rights provision most recently incorporated was the Second Amendment right to keep and bear arms. *McDonald v. City of Chicago*, 561 U.S. 742 (2010). The Court concluded that the proper test for incorporation was whether the given provision was "fundamental to our nation's particular scheme of ordered liberty and system of justice." However, one of the five justices in the majority, Justice Thomas, rejected the Due Process Clause as the source of that incorporation, in favor of the Fourteenth Amendment's Privileges or Immunities Clause.

### Note: Justice Harlan's Dissent in Poe v. Ullman *and the* State of Due Process Liberty on the Eve of Griswold

1. By the early 1960s, it was clear that the *Lochner*-era due process right to contract was moribund. However, it was also clear that, at the very least, the Due Process Clause incorporated several (and, at that time, a growing number) of Bill of Rights provisions. The real question was becoming whether due process provided substantive protection to liberties *beyond* the Bill of Rights. As noted earlier in this chapter, that question arose in the context of incorporation itself, where several justices took the view that Bill of Rights provisions were incorporated because the Fourteenth Amendment's Due Process Clause had an independent meaning that included some of the Bill of Rights—a view that at least offered the possibility that due process also included rights that did not appear in the Bill of Rights. But the question also arose because precedents such as *Meyer* and *Pierce* at least potentially survived the repudiation of the *Lochner*-era economic rights cases on which they had been based.

2. This question came to a head when the Court confronted Connecticut's law severely restricting access to contraceptives. In *Griswold v. Connecticut*, 381 U.S. 479 (1965), the Court ultimately reached the merits of that question, concluding that the Constitution protected the right of a married couple to possess contraceptives. As you'll see in the next chapter, *Griswold* did not rely on the Due Process Clause, but rather on a complex argument about the "penumbras" of textually-explicit Bill of Rights provisions, which the majority concluded implied the existence of a "right to privacy."

3. *Griswold*, however, was not the Court's first encounter with the Connecticut law. In 1961, the Court decided that a challenge to that law was non-justiciable because there was no realistic probability that it would be enforced. *Poe v. Ullman*, 367 U.S. 497 (1961). Justice Harlan dissented from that conclusion, and, reaching the merits, would have struck down the Connecticut law as an unconstitutional deprivation of

the "liberty" protected by the Due Process Clause. In explaining his approach to substantive due process, Justice Harlan wrote the following language, which was to become highly influential as the Court began again to expand the protections of substantive due process.

It is but a truism to say that [the Due Process Clauses of the Fifth and Fourteenth Amendments are] not self-explanatory. As to the Fourteenth, which is involved here, the history of the Amendment also sheds little light on the meaning of the provision. It is important to note, however, that two views of the Amendment have not been accepted by this Court as delineating its scope. One view, which was ably and insistently argued in response to what were felt to be abuses by this Court of its reviewing power, sought to limit the provision to a guarantee of procedural fairness. The other view which has been rejected would have it that the Fourteenth Amendment, whether by way of the Privileges and Immunities Clause or the Due Process Clause, applied against the States only and precisely those restraints which had prior to the Amendment been applicable merely to federal action. However, "due process" in the consistent view of this Court has ever been a broader concept than the first view and more flexible than the second.

Were due process merely a procedural safeguard it would fail to reach those situations where the deprivation of life, liberty or property was accomplished by legislation which by operating in the future could, given even the fairest possible procedure in application to individuals, nevertheless destroy the enjoyment of all three. Thus the guaranties of due process, though having their roots in Magna Carta's *per legem terrae*[*] and considered as procedural safeguards "against executive usurpation and tyranny," have in this country "become bulwarks also against arbitrary legislation."

However it is not the particular enumeration of rights in the first eight Amendments which spells out the reach of Fourteenth Amendment due process, but rather, as was suggested in another context long before the adoption of that Amendment, those concepts which are considered to embrace those rights "which are ... fundamental; which belong ... to the citizens of all free governments," for "the purposes [of securing] which men enter into society." Again and again this Court has resisted the notion that the Fourteenth Amendment is no more than a shorthand reference to what is explicitly set out elsewhere in the Bill of Rights. *Palko v. State of Connecticut* (1937) [*Supra.* this chapter]....

Due process has not been reduced to any formula; its content cannot be determined by reference to any code. The best that can be said is that through the course of this Court's decisions it has represented the balance which our Nation, built upon postulates of respect for the liberty of the individual, has struck between that liberty and the demands of organized society. If the sup-

---

* [Ed. Note: This Latin phrase is roughly translated as "by the law of the land."]

plying of content to this Constitutional concept has of necessity been a rational process, it certainly has not been one where judges have felt free to roam where unguided speculation might take them. The balance of which I speak is the balance struck by this country, having regard to what history teaches are the traditions from which it developed as well as the traditions from which it broke. That tradition is a living thing. A decision of this Court which radically departs from it could not long survive, while a decision which builds on what has survived is likely to be sound. No formula could serve as a substitute, in this area, for judgment and restraint.

It is this outlook which has led the Court continuingly to perceive distinctions in the imperative character of Constitutional provisions, since that character must be discerned from a particular provision's larger context. And inasmuch as this context is one not of words, but of history and purposes, the full scope of the liberty guaranteed by the Due Process Clause cannot be found in or limited by the precise terms of the specific guarantees elsewhere provided in the Constitution. This "liberty" is not a series of isolated points pricked out in terms of the taking of property; the freedom of speech, press, and religion; the right to keep and bear arms; the freedom from unreasonable searches and seizures; and so on. It is a rational continuum which, broadly speaking, includes a freedom from all substantial arbitrary impositions and purposeless restraints, *Allgeyer v. Louisiana* (1897), 165 U.S. 578 [Note *supra.* Chapter 7]; *Holden v. Hardy*, 169 U.S. 3566 (1898) [Note *supra.* Chapter 7]; *Nebbia v. New York* (1934) [*Supra.* Chapter 7]; *Skinner v. Oklahoma*, 316 U.S. 535 (1942) (concurring opinion) [Note *supra.* this chapter], and which also recognizes, what a reasonable and sensitive judgment must, that certain interests require particularly careful scrutiny of the state needs asserted to justify their abridgment.

# Chapter 9

# The Right to an Abortion

## A. The Foundations

### Griswold v. Connecticut

381 U.S. 479 (1965)

Mr. Justice DOUGLAS delivered the opinion of the Court.

Appellant Griswold is Executive Director of the Planned Parenthood League of Connecticut. Appellant Buxton is a licensed physician and a professor at the Yale Medical School who served as Medical Director for the League at its Center in New Haven....

They gave information, instruction, and medical advice to married persons as to the means of preventing conception. They examined the wife and prescribed the best contraceptive device or material for her use. Fees were usually charged, although some couples were serviced free.

The statutes whose constitutionality is involved in this appeal are §§ 53-32 and 54-196 of the General Statutes of Connecticut. The former provides:

> Any person who uses any drug, medicinal article or instrument for the purpose of preventing conception shall be fined not less than fifty dollars or imprisoned not less than sixty days nor more than one year or be both fined and imprisoned.

Section 54-196 provides:

> Any person who assists, abets, counsels, causes, hires or commands another to commit any offense may be prosecuted and punished as if he were the principal offender.

The appellants were found guilty as accessories and fined $100 each, against the claim that the accessory statute as so applied violated the Fourteenth Amendment. The Appellate Division of the Circuit Court affirmed. The Supreme Court of Errors affirmed that judgment. We noted probable jurisdiction....

Coming to the merits, we are met with a wide range of questions that implicate the Due Process Clause of the Fourteenth Amendment. Overtones of some arguments suggest that *Lochner v. State of New York* (1905) [*Supra.* Chapter 7], should be our guide. But we decline that invitation as we did in *West Coast Hotel Co. v. Parrish* [*Supra.* Chapter 7]. We do not sit as a super-legislature to determine the wisdom, need, and propriety of laws that touch economic problems, business affairs, or social conditions. This law, however, operates directly on an intimate relation of husband and wife and their physician's role in one aspect of that relation.

The association of people is not mentioned in the Constitution nor in the Bill of Rights. The right to educate a child in a school of the parents' choice whether public or private or parochial—is also not mentioned. Nor is the right to study any particular subject or any foreign language. Yet the First Amendment has been construed to include certain of those rights....

In *NAACP v. State of Alabama*, 357 U.S. 449 (1958), we protected the 'freedom to associate and privacy in one's associations,' noting that freedom of association was a peripheral First Amendment right.... In like context, we have protected forms of 'association' that are not political in the customary sense but pertain to the social, legal, and economic benefit of the members....

The foregoing cases suggest that specific guarantees in the Bill of Rights have penumbras, formed by emanations from those guarantees that help give them life and substance. Various guarantees create zones of privacy. The right of association contained in the penumbra of the First Amendment is one, as we have seen. The Third Amendment in its prohibition against the quartering of soldiers 'in any house' in time of peace without the consent of the owner is another facet of that privacy. The Fourth Amendment explicitly affirms the 'right of the people to be secure in their persons, houses, papers, and effects, against unreasonable searches and seizures.' The Fifth Amendment in its Self-Incrimination Clause enables the citizen to create a zone of privacy which government may not force him to surrender to his detriment. The Ninth Amendment provides: 'The enumeration in the Constitution, of certain rights, shall not be construed to deny or disparage others retained by the people.'...

The present case, then, concerns a relationship lying within the zone of privacy created by several fundamental constitutional guarantees. And it concerns a law which, in forbidding the use of contraceptives rather than regulating their manufacture or sale, seeks to achieve its goals by means having a maximum destructive impact upon that relationship. Such a law cannot stand in light of the familiar principle, so often applied by this Court, that a 'governmental purpose to control or prevent activities constitutionally subject to state regulation may not be achieved by means which sweep unnecessarily broadly and thereby invade the area of protected freedoms.' Would we allow the police to search the sacred precincts of marital bedrooms for telltale signs of the use of contraceptives? The very idea is repulsive to the notions of privacy surrounding the marriage relationship.

We deal with a right of privacy older than the Bill of Rights—older than our political parties, older than our school system. Marriage is a coming together for better or for worse, hopefully enduring, and intimate to the degree of being sacred. It is an association that promotes a way of life, not causes; a harmony in living, not political faiths; a bilateral loyalty, not commercial or social projects. Yet it is an association for as noble a purpose as any involved in our prior decisions.

Mr. Justice GOLDBERG, whom THE CHIEF JUSTICE and Mr. Justice BRENNAN join, concurring.

I agree with the Court that Connecticut's birth-control law unconstitutionally intrudes upon the right of marital privacy, and I join in its opinion and judgment. Although I have not accepted the view that 'due process' as used in the Fourteenth Amendment incorporates all of the first eight Amendments ... I do agree that the concept of liberty protects those personal rights that are fundamental, and is not confined to the specific terms of the Bill of Rights. My conclusion that the concept of liberty is not so restricted and that it embraces the right of marital privacy though that right is not mentioned explicitly in the Constitution is supported both by numerous decisions of this Court, referred to in the Court's opinion, and by the language and history of the Ninth Amendment. In reaching the conclusion that the right of marital privacy is protected, as being within the protected penumbra of specific guarantees of the Bill of Rights, the Court refers to the Ninth Amendment. I add these words to emphasize the relevance of that Amendment to the Court's holding....

A dissenting opinion suggests that my interpretation of the Ninth Amendment somehow 'broadens the powers of this Court.' With all due respect, I believe that it misses the import of what I am saying. I do not take the position of my Brother BLACK in his dissent in *Adamson v. California* (1947) [*Supra.* Chapter 8], that the entire Bill of Rights is incorporated in the Fourteenth Amendment, and I do not mean to imply that the Ninth Amendment is applied against the States by the Fourteenth. Nor do I mean to state that the Ninth Amendment constitutes an independent source of rights protected from infringement by either the States or the Federal Government. Rather, the Ninth Amendment shows a belief of the Constitution's authors that fundamental rights exist that are not expressly enumerated in the first eight amendments and an intent that the list of rights included there not be deemed exhaustive. As any student of this Court's opinions knows, this Court has held, often unanimously, that the Fifth and Fourteenth Amendments protect certain fundamental personal liberties from abridgment by the Federal Government or the States. The Ninth Amendment simply shows the intent of the Constitution's authors that other fundamental personal rights should not be denied such protection or disparaged in any other way simply because they are not specifically listed in the first eight constitutional amendments. I do not see how this broadens the authority of the Court; rather it serves to support what this Court has been doing in protecting fundamental rights.

Nor am I turning somersaults with history in arguing that the Ninth Amendment is relevant in a case dealing with a *State's* infringement of a fundamental right. While the Ninth Amendment—and indeed the entire Bill of Rights—originally concerned restrictions upon *federal* power, the subsequently enacted Fourteenth Amendment prohibits the States as well from abridging fundamental personal liberties. And, the Ninth Amendment, in indicating that not all such liberties are specifically mentioned in the first eight amendments, is surely relevant in showing the existence of other fundamental personal rights, now protected from state, as well as federal, infringement. In sum, the Ninth Amendment simply lends strong support to the view that the 'liberty' protected by the Fifth And Fourteenth Amendments from infringement by the Federal Government or the States is not restricted to rights specifically mentioned in the first eight amendments.

In determining which rights are fundamental, judges are not left at large to decide cases in light of their personal and private notions. Rather, they must look to the 'traditions and [collective] conscience of our people' to determine whether a principle is 'so rooted [there] ... as to be ranked as fundamental.' The inquiry is whether a right involved 'is of such a character that it cannot be denied without violating those 'fundamental principles of liberty and justice which lie at the base of all our civil and political institutions' ...' *Powell v. Alabama*, 287 U.S. 45 (1932). 'Liberty' also 'gains content from the emanations of ... specific [constitutional] guarantees' and 'from experience with the requirements of a free society.' *Poe v. Ullman*, 367 U.S. 497 (1961) (dissenting opinion of Mr. Justice Douglas) [Note *supra*. Chapter 8]....

I agree fully with the Court that, applying these tests, the right of privacy is a fundamental personal right, emanating 'from the totality of the constitutional scheme under which we live.'...

Mr. Justice HARLAN, concurring in the judgment.

I fully agree with the judgment of reversal, but find myself unable to join the Court's opinion. The reason is that it seems to me to evince an approach to this case very much like that taken by my Brothers BLACK and STEWART in dissent, namely: the Due Process Clause of the Fourteenth Amendment does not touch this Connecticut statute unless the enactment is found to violate some right assured by the letter or penumbra of the Bill of Rights.

In other words, what I find implicit in the Court's opinion is that the 'incorporation' doctrine may be used to *restrict* the reach of Fourteenth Amendment Due Process. For me this is just as unacceptable constitutional doctrine as is the use of the 'incorporation' approach to *impose* upon the States all the requirements of the Bill of Rights as found in the provisions of the first eight amendments and in the decisions of this Court interpreting them.

In my view, the proper constitutional inquiry in this case is whether this Connecticut statute infringes the Due Process Clause of the Fourteenth Amendment because the enactment violates basic values 'implicit in the concept of ordered liberty,' *Palko v. Connecticut* [*Supra*. Chapter 8]. For reasons stated at length in my dissenting opinion in *Poe v. Ullman*, I believe that it does. While the relevant inquiry may be aided by resort to one or more of the provisions of the Bill of Rights, it is not dependent on them or any of their radiations. The Due Process Clause of the Fourteenth Amendment stands, in my opinion, on its own bottom....

A further observation seems in order respecting the justification of my Brothers BLACK and STEWART for their 'incorporation' approach to this case. Their approach does not rest on historical reasons, which are ... wholly lacking, but on the thesis that by limiting the content of the Due Process Clause of the Fourteenth Amendment to the protection of rights which can be found elsewhere in the Constitution, in this instance in the Bill of Rights, judges will thus be confined to 'interpretation' of specific constitutional provisions, and will thereby be restrained from introducing their own notions of constitutional right and wrong into the 'vague contours of the Due Process Clause.' *Rochin v. California*, 342 U.S. 165 (1952) [Note *supra*. Chapter 8].

While I could not more heartily agree that judicial 'self restraint' is an indispensable ingredient of sound constitutional adjudication, I do submit that the formula suggested for achieving it is more hollow than real. 'Specific' provisions of the Constitution, no less than 'due process,' lend themselves as readily to 'personal' interpretations by judges whose constitutional outlook is simply to keep the Constitution in supposed 'tune with the times.'...

Judicial self-restraint will not, I suggest, be brought about in the 'due process' area by the historically unfounded incorporation formula long advanced by my Brother BLACK, and now in part espoused by my Brother STEWART. It will be achieved in this area, as in other constitutional areas, only by continual insistence upon respect for the teachings of history, solid recognition of the basic values that underlie our society, and wise appreciation of the great roles that the doctrines of federalism and separation of powers have played in establishing and preserving American freedoms....

Mr. Justice WHITE, concurring in the judgment.

In my view this Connecticut law as applied to married couples deprives them of 'liberty' without due process of law, as that concept is used in the Fourteenth Amendment. I therefore concur in the judgment of the Court reversing these convictions under Connecticut's aiding and abetting statute.

It would be unduly repetitious, and belaboring the obvious, to expound on the impact of this statute on the liberty guaranteed by the Fourteenth Amendment against arbitrary or capricious denials or on the nature of this liberty. Suffice it to say that this is not the first time this Court has had occasion to articulate that the liberty entitled to protection under the Fourteenth Amendment includes the right 'to marry, establish a home and bring up children,' *Meyer v. State of Nebraska* (1923) [*Supra*. Chapter 8], and 'the liberty ... to direct the upbringing and education of children,' *Pierce v. Society of Sisters*, 268 U.S. 510 (1925) [Note *supra*. Chapter 8], and that these are among 'the basic civil rights of man.' *Skinner v. State of Oklahoma*, 316 U.S. 535 (1942) [Note *supra*. this chapter]. These decisions affirm that there is a 'realm of family life which the state cannot enter' without substantial justification. Surely the right invoked in this case, to be free of regulation of the intimacies of the marriage relationship, 'comes to this Court with a momentum for respect lacking when appeal is made to liberties which derive merely from shifting economic arrangements.'

The Connecticut anti-contraceptive statute deals rather substantially with this relationship.... An examination of the justification offered, however, cannot be avoided by saying that the Connecticut anti-use statute invades a protected area of privacy and association or that it demeans the marriage relationship. The nature of the right invaded is pertinent, to be sure, for statutes regulating sensitive areas of liberty do, under the cases of this Court, require 'strict scrutiny,' *Skinner*, and 'must be viewed in the light of less drastic means for achieving the same basic purpose.' 'Where there is a significant encroachment upon personal liberty, the State may prevail only upon showing a subordinating interest which is compelling.' But such statutes, if reasonably necessary for the effectuation of a legitimate and substantial state interest, and not arbitrary or capricious in application, are not invalid under the Due Process Clause.

As I read the opinions of the Connecticut courts and the argument of Connecticut in this Court, the State claims but one justification for its anti-use statute.... [The] statute is said to serve the State's policy against all forms of promiscuous or illicit sexual relationships, be they premarital or extramarital, concededly a permissible and legitimate legislative goal.

Without taking issue with the premise that the fear of conception operates as a deterrent to such relationships in addition to the criminal proscriptions Connecticut has against such conduct, I wholly fail to see how the ban on the use of contraceptives by married couples in any way reinforces the State's ban on illicit sexual relationships.... I find nothing in this record justifying the sweeping scope of this statute, with its telling effect on the freedoms of married persons, and therefore conclude that it deprives such persons of liberty without due process of law.

Mr. Justice BLACK, with whom Mr. Justice STEWART joins, dissenting....

The Court talks about a constitutional 'right of privacy' as though there is some constitutional provision or provisions forbidding any law ever to be passed which might abridge the 'privacy' of individuals. But there is not. There are, of course, guarantees in certain specific constitutional provisions which are designed in part to protect privacy at certain times and places with respect to certain activities. Such, for example, is the Fourth Amendment's guarantee against 'unreasonable searches and seizures.' But I think it belittles that Amendment to talk about it as though it protects nothing but 'privacy.' To treat it that way is to give it a niggardly interpretation, not the kind of liberal reading I think any Bill of Rights provision should be given. The average man would very likely not have his feelings soothed any more by having his property seized openly than by having it seized privately and by stealth. He simply wants his property left alone. And a person can be just as much, if not more, irritated, annoyed and injured by an unceremonious public arrest by a policeman as he is by a seizure in the privacy of his office or home....

.... Brothers HARLAN and WHITE would invalidate [the law] by reliance on the Due Process Clause of the Fourteenth Amendment, but Brother GOLDBERG, while agreeing with Brother HARLAN, relies also on the Ninth Amendment. I have no doubt that the Connecticut law could be applied in such a way as to abridge freedom of speech and press and therefore violate the First and Fourteenth Amendments. My disagreement with the Court's opinion holding that there is such a violation here is a narrow one, relating to the application of the First Amendment to the facts and circumstances of this particular case. But my disagreement with Brothers HARLAN, WHITE and GOLDBERG is more basic. I think that, if properly construed, neither the Due Process Clause, nor the Ninth Amendment, nor both together, could under any circumstances be a proper basis for invalidating the Connecticut law.... [On] analysis [both arguments] turn out to be the same thing — merely using different words to claim for this Court and the federal judiciary power to invalidate any legislative act which the judges find irrational, unreasonable or offensive....

Of the cases on which my Brothers WHITE and GOLDBERG rely so heavily, undoubtedly the reasoning of two of them supports their result here — as would that of a number of others which they do not bother to name, e.g., *Lochner*; and *Adkins v. Children's Hospital*, 261 U.S. 525 (1923) [Note *supra*. Chapter 7]. The two they do cite and quote from, *Meyer* and *Pierce*, were both decided in opinions by Mr. Justice McReynolds which elaborated the same natural law due process philosophy found in *Lochner*, one of the cases on which he relied in *Meyer*, along with such other long-discredited decisions as, e.g., *Adkins*.... Without expressing an opinion as to whether either of those cases reached a correct result in light of our later decisions applying the First Amendment to the States through the Fourteenth, I merely point out that the reasoning stated in *Meyer* and *Pierce* was the same natural law due process philosophy which many later opinions repudiated, and which I cannot accept....

Mr. Justice STEWART, whom Mr. Justice BLACK joins, dissenting.

Since 1879 Connecticut has had on its books a law which forbids the use of contraceptives by anyone. I think this is an uncommonly silly law. As a practical matter, the law is obviously unenforceable, except in the oblique context of the present case. As a philosophical matter, I believe the use of contraceptives in the relationship of marriage should be left to personal and private choice, based upon each individual's moral, ethical, and religious beliefs. As a matter of social policy, I think professional counsel about methods of birth control should be available to all, so that each individual's choice can be meaningfully made. But we are not asked in this case to say whether we think this law is unwise, or even asinine. We are asked to hold that it violates the United States Constitution. And that I cannot do.

In the course of its opinion the Court refers to no less than six Amendments to the Constitution: the First, the Third, the Fourth, the Fifth, the Ninth, and the Fourteenth. But the Court does not say which of these Amendments, if any, it thinks is infringed by this Connecticut law.

We *are* told that the Due Process Clause of the Fourteenth Amendment is not, as such, the 'guide' in this case. With that much I agree....

As to the First, Third, Fourth, and Fifth Amendments, I can find nothing in any of them to invalidate this Connecticut law, even assuming that all those Amendments are fully applicable against the States....

The Court also quotes the Ninth Amendment, and my Brother GOLDBERG's concurring opinion relies heavily upon it. But to say that the Ninth Amendment has anything to do with this case is to turn somersaults with history. The Ninth Amendment, like its companion the Tenth, which this Court held 'states but a truism that all is retained which has not been surrendered,' *United States v. Darby* (1941) [*Supra*. Chapter 4], was framed by James Madison and adopted by the States simply to make clear that the adoption of the Bill of Rights did not alter the plan that the *Federal* Government was to be a government of express and limited powers, and that all rights and powers not delegated to it were retained by the people and the individual States. Until today no member of this Court has ever suggested that the Ninth Amendment meant anything else, and the idea that a federal court could ever use the Ninth Amendment to annul a law passed by the elected representatives of the people of the State of Connecticut would have caused James Madison no little wonder. . . .

## *Note:* Eisenstadt v. Baird

1. *Griswold* focused heavily on the rights of a married couple to use contraceptives. Seven years later, in *Eisenstadt v. Baird*, 405 U.S. 438 (1972), the Court confronted the question whether *Griswold*'s limitation to married couples could survive.

2. In *Eisenstadt*, William Baird gave a university lecture on contraception, during which he exhibited contraceptives, and after which he gave a contraceptive to an attendee. He was convicted of violating a Massachusetts law that limited the distribution of contraceptives to unmarried persons except as prescribed by a doctor or pharmacist for medical reasons.

The Court struck the law down as failing equal protection review, by distinguishing between married and unmarried persons. Writing for four justices on a seven-justice Court (Justices Powell and Rehnquist had not yet taken their seats), Justice Brennan discounted the state's justifications for distinguishing between married and unmarried persons. In particular, he questioned whether the law was a rational way of furthering any interest the state had in discouraging non-marital sex, given the severity of the penalty for contraceptive distribution in comparison with the light penalty the state imposed for non-marital sex, and the fact that married persons could still obtain contraception even if the goal was to facilitate risk-free extra-marital sex.

3. The most important part of Justice Brennan's opinion, though, simply questioned whether unmarried persons had a lesser right to contraceptives than married persons. He wrote: "It is true that in *Griswold* the right of privacy in question inhered in the marital relationship. Yet the marital couple is not an independent entity with a mind and heart of its own, but an association of two individuals each with a separate intellectual and emotional makeup. If the right of privacy means anything, it is the right of the *individual*, married or single, to be free from unwarranted governmental intrusion into matters so fundamentally affecting a person as the decision whether to bear or beget a child" (emphasis in original).

4. Justice Douglas joined the majority opinion but wrote separately to note his belief that Baird had a First Amendment right to discuss contraceptives by handing them out at the lecture. Justice White, joined by Justice Blackmun, concurred in the result, noting ambiguity in the record as to the marital status of the person who received the contraceptive. Chief Justice Burger dissented, arguing that the state had an interest in controlling the channels through which potentially dangerous medical devices were distributed.

5. *Eisenstadt*, by focusing on individuals' rights (rather than the rights of married couples), laid the groundwork for the Court's consideration of whether a woman had a right to terminate a pregnancy. Indeed, *Roe v. Wade*, excepted below, was argued only a month after the argument in *Eisenstadt*. However, it appears that dissatisfaction with the original proposed majority opinion (striking down the Texas abortion law for vagueness), along with the fact that two new members of the Court (Justices Powell and Rehnquist) had not taken their seats in time for participating in the decision, led the Court to put the case over for reargument in the next term.

# B. *Roe* and Its Aftermath

## Roe v. Wade

### 410 U.S. 113 (1973)

Mr. Justice Blackmun delivered the opinion of the Court....

We forthwith acknowledge our awareness of the sensitive and emotional nature of the abortion controversy, of the vigorous opposing views, even among physicians, and of the deep and seemingly absolute convictions that the subject inspires. One's philosophy, one's experiences, one's exposure to the raw edges of human existence, one's religious training, one's attitudes toward life and family and their values, and the moral standards one establishes and seeks to observe, are all likely to influence and to color one's thinking and conclusions about abortion.

In addition, population growth, pollution, poverty, and racial overtones tend to complicate and not to simplify the problem.

Our task, of course, is to resolve the issue by constitutional measurement, free of emotion and of predilection. We seek earnestly to do this, and, because we do, we have inquired into, and in this opinion place some emphasis upon, medical and medical-legal history and what that history reveals about man's attitudes toward the abortion procedure over the centuries. We bear in mind, too, Mr. Justice Holmes' admonition in his now-vindicated dissent in *Lochner v. New York* (1905) [*Supra.* Chapter 7]:

> [The Constitution] is made for people of fundamentally differing views, and the accident of our finding certain opinions natural and familiar or novel and even shocking ought not to conclude our judgment upon the question whether statutes embodying them conflict with the Constitution of the United States....

V

The principal thrust of appellant's attack on the Texas statutes is that they improperly invade a right, said to be possessed by the pregnant woman, to choose to terminate her pregnancy. Appellant would discover this right in the concept of personal "liberty" embodied in the Fourteenth Amendment's Due Process Clause; or in personal, marital, familial, and sexual privacy said to be protected by the Bill of

Rights or its penumbras, *see Griswold v. Connecticut* ((1965) [*Supra.* this chapter]; *Eisenstadt v. Baird*, 405 U.S. 438 (1972) [Note *supra.* this chapter], or among those rights reserved to the people by the Ninth Amendment, *Griswold* (Goldberg, J., concurring). Before addressing this claim, we feel it desirable briefly to survey, in several aspects, the history of abortion, for such insight as that history may afford us, and then to examine the state purposes and interests behind the criminal abortion laws.

## VI

It perhaps is not generally appreciated that the restrictive criminal abortion laws in effect in a majority of States today are of relatively recent vintage. Those laws, generally proscribing abortion or its attempt at any time during pregnancy except when necessary to preserve the pregnant woman's life, are not of ancient or even of common-law origin. Instead, they derive from statutory changes effected, for the most part, in the latter half of the 19th century. [Justice Blackmun then provided a detailed examination of attitudes toward abortion, from ancient times to the modern day.]

## VII

It has been argued occasionally that these laws were the product of a Victorian social concern to discourage illicit sexual conduct. Texas, however, does not advance this justification in the present case, and it appears that no court or commentator has taken the argument seriously....

A second reason is concerned with abortion as a medical procedure. When most criminal abortion laws were first enacted, the procedure was a hazardous one for the woman.... Modern medical techniques have altered this situation. Appellants and various *amici* refer to medical data indicating that abortion in early pregnancy, that is, prior to the end of the first trimester, although not without its risk, is now relatively safe. Mortality rates for women undergoing early abortions, where the procedure is legal, appear to be as low as or lower than the rates for normal childbirth. Consequently, any interest of the State in protecting the woman from an inherently hazardous procedure, except when it would be equally dangerous for her to forgo it, has largely disappeared. Of course, important state interests in the areas of health and medical standards do remain.... Moreover, the risk to the woman increases as her pregnancy continues. Thus, the State retains a definite interest in protecting the woman's own health and safety when an abortion is proposed at a late stage of pregnancy.

The third reason is the State's interest — some phrase it in terms of duty — in protecting prenatal life.... Logically, of course, a legitimate state interest in this area need not stand or fall on acceptance of the belief that life begins at conception or at some other point prior to life birth. In assessing the State's interest, recognition may be given to the less rigid claim that as long as at least *potential* life is involved, the State may assert interests beyond the protection of the pregnant woman alone....

It is with these interests, and the weight to be attached to them, that this case is concerned.

## VIII

The Constitution does not explicitly mention any right of privacy. In a line of decisions, however, going back perhaps as far as *Union Pacific R. Co. v. Botsford*, 141 U.S. 250 (1891), the Court has recognized that a right of personal privacy, or a guarantee of certain areas or zones of privacy, does exist under the Constitution. In varying contexts, the Court or individual Justices have, indeed, found at least the roots of that right in the First Amendment; in the Fourth and Fifth Amendments; in the penumbras of the Bill of Rights; in the Ninth Amendment; or in the concept of liberty guaranteed by the first section of the Fourteenth Amendment. These decisions make it clear that only personal rights that can be deemed "fundamental" or "implicit in the concept of ordered liberty," are included in this guarantee of personal privacy. They also make it clear that the right has some extension to activities relating to marriage, procreation, *Skinner v. Oklahoma*, 316 U.S. 535 (1942) [Note *supra.* Chapter 8]; contraception, *Eisenstadt*; family relationships, *Prince v. Massachusetts*, 321 U.S. 158 (1944); and child rearing and education, *Pierce v. Society of Sisters*, 268 U.S. 510 (1925) [Note *supra.* Chapter 8]; *Meyer* (1923) [*Supra.* Chapter 8].

This right of privacy, whether it be founded in the Fourteenth Amendment's concept of personal liberty and restrictions upon state action, as we feel it is, or, as the District Court determined, in the Ninth Amendment's reservation of rights to the people, is broad enough to encompass a woman's decision whether or not to terminate her pregnancy. The detriment that the State would impose upon the pregnant woman by denying this choice altogether is apparent. Specific and direct harm medically diagnosable even in early pregnancy may be involved. Maternity, or additional offspring, may force upon the woman a distressful life and future. Psychological harm may be imminent. Mental and physical health may be taxed by child care. There is also the distress, for all concerned, associated with the unwanted child, and there is the problem of bringing a child into a family already unable, psychologically and otherwise, to care for it. In other cases, as in this one, the additional difficulties and continuing stigma of unwed motherhood may be involved. All these are factors the woman and her responsible physician necessarily will consider in consultation.

On the basis of elements such as these, appellant and some *amici* argue that the woman's right is absolute and that she is entitled to terminate her pregnancy at whatever time, in whatever way, and for whatever reason she alone chooses. With this we do not agree. Appellant's arguments that Texas either has no valid interest at all in regulating the abortion decision, or no interest strong enough to support any limitation upon the woman's sole determination, are unpersuasive. The Court's decisions recognizing a right of privacy also acknowledge that some state regulation in areas protected by that right is appropriate.... [A] State may properly assert important interests in safeguarding health, in maintaining medical standards, and in protecting potential life. At some point in pregnancy, these respective interests become sufficiently compelling to sustain regulation of the factors that govern the abortion decision. The privacy right involved, therefore, cannot be said to be absolute. In fact, it is not clear to us that the claim asserted by some *amici* that one has an unlimited right to do with one's body as one pleases bears a close relationship to the right of privacy previously articulated in the Court's decisions. The Court has refused to recognize an unlimited right of this kind in the past. *Jacobson v. Massachusetts*, 197 U.S. 11 (1905) (vaccination); *Buck v. Bell*, 274 U.S. 200 (1927) [Note *supra*. Chapter 8] (sterilization).

We, therefore, conclude that the right of personal privacy includes the abortion decision, but that this right is not unqualified and must be considered against important state interests in regulation....

\* \* \*

A. The appellee and certain *amici* argue that the fetus is a "person" within the language and meaning of the Fourteenth Amendment.... If this suggestion of personhood is established, the appellant's case, of course, collapses, for the fetus' right to life would then be guaranteed specifically by the Amendment....

The Constitution does not define "person" in so many words. Section 1 of the Fourteenth Amendment contains three references to "person." The first, in defining "citizens," speaks of "persons born or naturalized in the United States." The word also appears both in the Due Process Clause and in the Equal Protection Clause. "Person" is used in other places in the Constitution.... But in nearly all these instances, the use of the word is such that it has application only postnatally. None indicates, with any assurance, that it has any possible pre-natal application.

All this, together with our observation that throughout the major portion of the 19th century prevailing legal abortion practices were far freer than they are today, persuades us that the word "person," as used in the Fourteenth Amendment, does not include the unborn....

B. The pregnant woman cannot be isolated in her privacy. She carries an embryo and, later, a fetus, if one accepts the medical definitions of the developing young in the human uterus. The situation therefore is inherently different from marital intimacy, or bedroom possession of obscene material, or marriage, or procreation, or education.... As we have intimated above, it is reasonable and appropriate for a State to decide that at some point in time another interest, that of health of the mother or that of potential human life, becomes significantly involved. The woman's privacy is no longer sole and any right of privacy she possesses must be measured accordingly....

### X

In view of all this, we do not agree that, by adopting one theory of life, Texas may override the rights of the pregnant woman that are at stake. We repeat, however, that the State does have an important and legitimate interest in preserving and protecting the health of the pregnant woman, whether she be a resident of the State or a nonresident who seeks medical consultation and treatment there, and that it has still *another* important and legitimate interest in protecting the potentiality of human life. These interests are separate and distinct. Each grows in substantiality as the woman approaches term and, at a point during pregnancy, each becomes 'compelling.'

With respect to the State's important and legitimate interest in the health of the mother, the 'compelling' point, in the light of present medical knowledge, is at approximately the end of the first trimester. This is so because of the now-established medical fact ... that until the end of the first trimester mortality in abortion may be less than mortality in normal childbirth. It follows that, from and after this point, a State may regulate the abortion procedure to the extent that the regulation reasonably relates to the preservation and protection of maternal health. Examples of permissible state regulation in this area are requirements as to the qualifications of the person who is to perform the abortion; as to the licensure of that person; as to the facility in which the procedure is to be performed, that is, whether it must be a hospital or may be a clinic or some other place of less-than-hospital status; as to the licensing of the facility; and the like.

This means, on the other hand, that, for the period of pregnancy prior to this 'compelling' point, the attending physician, in consultation with his patient, is free to determine, without regulation by the State, that, in his medical judgment, the patient's pregnancy should be terminated. If that decision is reached, the judgment may be effectuated by an abortion free of interference by the State.

With respect to the State's important and legitimate interest in potential life, the 'compelling' point is at viability. This is so because the fetus then presumably has the capability of meaningful life outside the mother's womb. State regulation protective of fetal life after viability thus has both logical and biological justifications. If the State is interested in protecting fetal life after viability, it may go so far as to proscribe abortion during that period, except when it is necessary to preserve the life or health of the mother.

Measured against these standards, Art. 1196 of the Texas Penal Code, in restricting legal abortions to those 'procured or attempted by medical advice for the purpose of saving the life of the mother,' sweeps too broadly. The statute makes no distinction between abortions performed early in pregnancy and those performed later, and it limits to a single reason, 'saving' the mother's life, the legal justification for the procedure. The statute, therefore, cannot survive the constitutional attack made upon it here....

## XI

To summarize and to repeat:

A state criminal abortion statute of the current Texas type, that excepts from criminality only a *life-saving* procedure on behalf of the mother, without regard to pregnancy stage and without recognition of the other interests involved, is violative of the Due Process Clause of the Fourteenth Amendment.

(a) For the stage prior to approximately the end of the first trimester, the abortion decision and its effectuation must be left to the medical judgment of the pregnant woman's attending physician.

(b) For the stage subsequent to approximately the end of the first trimester, the State, in promoting its interest in the health of the mother, may, if it chooses, regulate the abortion procedure in ways that are reasonably related to maternal health.

(c) For the stage subsequent to viability, the State in promoting its interest in the potentiality of human life may, if it chooses, regulate, and even proscribe, abortion except where it is necessary, in appropriate medical judgment, for the preservation of the life or health of the mother....

This holding, we feel, is consistent with the relative weights of the respective interests involved, with the lessons and examples of medical and legal history, with the lenity of the common law, and with the demands of the profound problems of the present day. The decision leaves the State free to place increasing restrictions on abortion as the period of pregnancy lengthens, so long as those restrictions are tailored to the recognized state interests. The decision vindicates the right of the physician to administer medical treatment according to his professional judgment up to the points where important state interests provide compelling justifications for intervention. Up to those points, the abortion decision in all its aspects is inherently, and primarily, a medical decision, and basic responsibility for it must rest with the physician. If an individual practitioner abuses the privilege of exercising proper medical judgment, the usual remedies, judicial and intra-professional, are available....

Mr. Justice Stewart, concurring. [omitted]

Mr. Chief Justice Burger, concurring.

I agree that, under the Fourteenth Amendment to the Constitution, the abortion statutes of Georgia and Texas impermissibly limit the performance of abortion necessary to protect the health of pregnant women, using the term health in its broadest medical context. I am somewhat troubled that the Court has taken notice of various scientific and medical data in reaching its conclusion; however, I do not believe that the Court has exceeded the scope of judicial notice accepted in other contexts....

I do not read the Court's holdings today as having the sweeping consequences attributed to them by the dissenting Justices; the dissenting views discount the reality that the vast majority of physicians observe the standards of their profession, and act only on the basis of carefully deliberated medical judgments relating to life and health. Plainly, the Court today rejects any claim that the Constitution requires abortions on demand.

Mr. Justice Douglas, concurring. [omitted]

Mr. Justice Rehnquist, dissenting.

The Court's opinion brings to the decision of this troubling question both extensive historical fact and a wealth of legal scholarship. While the opinion thus commands my respect, I find myself nonetheless in fundamental disagreement with those parts of it that invalidate the Texas statute in question, and therefore dissent....

## II

... I have difficulty in concluding, as the Court does, that the right of 'privacy' is involved in this case.... A transaction resulting in an operation such as this is not 'private' in the ordinary usage of that word....

If the Court means by the term 'privacy' no more than that the claim of a person to be free from unwanted state regulation of consensual transactions may be a form of 'liberty' protected by the Fourteenth Amendment, there is no doubt that similar claims have been upheld in our earlier decisions on the basis of that liberty.... But that liberty is not guaranteed absolutely against deprivation, only against deprivation without due process of law. The test traditionally applied in the area of social and economic legislation is whether or not a law such as that challenged has a rational relation to a valid state objective. The Due Process Clause of the Fourteenth Amendment undoubtedly does place a limit, albeit a broad one, on legislative power to enact laws such as this. If the Texas statute were to prohibit an abortion even where the mother's life is in jeopardy, I have little doubt that such a statute would lack a rational relation to a valid state objective.... But the Court's sweeping invalidation of any restrictions on abortion during the first trimester is impossible to justify under that standard, and the conscious weighing of competing factors that the Court's opinion apparently substitutes for the established test is far more appropriate to a legislative judgment than to a judicial one....

While the Court's opinion quotes from the dissent of Mr. Justice Holmes in *Lochner*, the result it reaches is more closely attuned to the majority opinion of Mr. Justice Peckham in that case. As in *Lochner* and similar cases applying substantive due process standards to economic and social welfare legislation, the adoption of the compelling state interest standard will inevitably require this Court to examine the legislative policies and pass on the wisdom of these policies in the very process of deciding whether a particular state interest put forward may or may not be 'compelling.' The decision here to break pregnancy into three distinct terms and to outline the permissible restrictions the State may impose in each one, for example, partakes more of judicial legislation than it does of a determination of the intent of the drafters of the Fourteenth Amendment....

To reach its result, the Court necessarily has had to find within the Scope of the Fourteenth Amendment a right that was apparently completely unknown to the drafters of the Amendment.... By the time of the adoption of the Fourteenth Amendment in 1868, there were at least 36 laws enacted by state or territorial legislatures limiting abortion....

There apparently was no question concerning the validity of this provision or of any of the other state statutes when the Fourteenth Amendment was adopted. The only conclusion possible from this history is that the drafters did not intend to have the Fourteenth Amendment withdraw from the States the power to legislate with respect to this matter....

Mr. Justice White, with whom Mr. Justice Rehnquist joins, dissenting....

With all due respect, I dissent. I find nothing in the language or history of the Constitution to support the Court's judgments. The Court simply fashions and announces a new constitutional right for pregnant women and, with scarcely any reason or authority for its action, invests that right with sufficient substance to override most existing state abortion statutes. The upshot is that the people and the legislatures of the 50 States are constitutionally disentitled to weigh the relative importance of the continued existence and development of the fetus, on the one hand, against a spectrum of possible impacts on the mother, on the other hand. As an exercise of raw judicial power, the Court perhaps has authority to do what it does today; but in my view its judgment is an improvident and extravagant exercise of the power of judicial review that the Constitution extends to this Court.

The Court apparently values the convenience of the pregnant woman more than the continued existence and development of the life or potential life that she carries. Whether or not I might agree with that marshaling of values, I can in no event join the Court's judgment because I find no constitutional warrant for imposing such an order of priorities on the people and legislatures of the States. In a sensitive area such as this, involving as it does issues over which reasonable men may easily and heatedly differ, I cannot accept the Court's exercise of its clear power of choice by interposing a constitutional barrier to state efforts to protect human life and by investing women and doctors with the constitutionally protected right to exterminate it. This issue, for the most part, should be left with the people and to the political processes the people have devised to govern their affairs....

## Note: From Roe to Casey

1. After its decision in *Roe*, the Court considered the constitutionality of a series of state and federal statutes that restricted women's access to abortion services. Most notably, the Court generally invalidated state regulations that discouraged women from seeking an abortion or made the procedure more difficult or expensive to obtain. For example, the Court struck down regulations that required that second trimester abortions be performed in a hospital, that physicians inform women of particular medical risks of abortion, that physicians determine the viability of the fetus, and that a second physician be present during an abortion when viability is possible. The Court also struck down a requirement of spousal consent for married women seeking an abortion and parental consent for unmarried teenagers under age eighteen, unless the abortion was necessary to save the mother's life. During this period, however, the Court refused to require government to pay for the cost of abortions for poor women.

2. Starting in the late 1970s, abortion started becoming a highly partisan issue, as the two major political parties gravitated toward opposite views about abortion, and *Roe* in particular. In 1980 the Republican Party platform for the first time took a strong anti-abortion position, while the national Democratic Party began to line up in defense of abortion rights. The politicization of the abortion issue meant that abortion would become a major factor in the parties' positions about Supreme Court appointments.

3. Throughout the 1980s, personnel changes on the Court and the continued political pressure for more robust abortion regulation combined to move the Court toward increased tolerance for abortion restrictions. In 1989, in a decision upholding many of Missouri's abortion restrictions, a plurality attacked *Roe*'s trimester framework, weakened the standard of review, and appeared to invite the states to impose

greater restrictions on women's access to abortions. *Webster v. Reproductive Health Services*, 492 U.S. 490 (1989). When Justices David Souter and Clarence Thomas replaced, respectively, *Roe* defenders William Brennan and Thurgood Marshall, both abortion-rights foes and supporters believed the Court was poised to overrule *Roe*. These dynamics set the stage for the next case.

# C. The *Casey* Resolution (?)

## Planned Parenthood of South-Eastern Pennsylvania v. Casey

### 505 U.S. 833 (1992)

JUSTICE O'CONNOR, JUSTICE KENNEDY, and JUSTICE SOUTER announced the judgment of the Court and delivered the opinion of the Court with respect to Parts I, II, III, V-A, V-C, and VI, an opinion with respect to Part V-E, in which JUSTICE STEVENS joins, and an opinion with respect to Parts IV, V-B, and V-D.

I

Liberty finds no refuge in a jurisprudence of doubt. Yet 19 years after our holding that the Constitution protects a woman's right to terminate her pregnancy in its early stages, *Roe v. Wade* (1973) [*Supra.* this chapter], that definition of liberty is still questioned. Joining the respondents as *amicus curiae*, the United States, as it has done in five other cases in the last decade, again asks us to overrule *Roe*.

At issue in these cases are five provisions of the Pennsylvania Abortion Control Act of 1982 as amended in 1988 and 1989.... The Act requires that a woman seeking an abortion give her informed consent prior to the abortion procedure, and specifies that she be provided with certain information at least 24 hours before the abortion is performed. For a minor to obtain an abortion, the Act requires the informed consent of one of her parents, but provides for a judicial bypass option if the minor does not wish to or cannot obtain a parent's consent. Another provision of the Act requires that, unless certain exceptions apply, a married woman seeking an abortion must sign a statement indicating that she has notified her husband of her intended abortion. The Act exempts compliance with these three requirements in the event of a "medical emergency." ... In addition to the above provisions regulating the performance of abortions, the Act imposes certain reporting requirements on facilities that provide abortion services....

... [We] acknowledge that our decisions after *Roe* cast doubt upon the meaning and reach of its holding. Further, THE CHIEF JUSTICE admits that he would overrule the central holding of *Roe* and adopt the rational relationship test as the sole criterion of constitutionality. State and federal courts as well as legislatures throughout the Union must have guidance as they seek to address this subject in conformance with the Constitution. Given these premises, we find it imperative to review once more the principles that define the rights of the woman and the legitimate authority of the State respecting the termination of pregnancies by abortion procedures.

After considering the fundamental constitutional questions resolved by *Roe*, principles of institutional integrity, and the rule of *stare decisis*, we are led to conclude this: the essential holding of *Roe v. Wade* should be retained and once again reaffirmed.

It must be stated at the outset and with clarity that *Roe*'s essential holding, the holding we reaffirm, has three parts. First is a recognition of the right of the woman to choose to have an abortion before viability and to obtain it without undue interference from the State. Before viability, the State's interests are not strong enough to support a prohibition of abortion or the imposition of a substantial obstacle to the woman's effective right to elect the procedure. Second is a confirmation of the State's power to restrict abortions after fetal viability, if the law contains exceptions for pregnancies which endanger a woman's life or health. And third is the principle that the State has legitimate interests from the outset of the pregnancy in protecting the health of the woman and the life of the fetus that may become a child. These principles do not contradict one another; and we adhere to each.

## II

Constitutional protection of the woman's decision to terminate her pregnancy derives from the Due Process Clause of the Fourteenth Amendment.... Neither the Bill of Rights nor the specific practices of States at the time of the adoption of the Fourteenth Amendment marks the outer limits of the substantive sphere of liberty which the Fourteenth Amendment protects. As the second Justice Harlan recognized:

> "The full scope of the liberty guaranteed by the Due Process Clause cannot
> be found in or limited by the precise terms of the specific guarantees elsewhere
> provided in the Constitution.... It is a rational continuum which, broadly
> speaking, includes a freedom from all substantial arbitrary impositions and
> purposeless restraints, ... and which also recognizes, what a reasonable and
> sensitive judgment must, that certain interests require particularly careful
> scrutiny of the state needs asserted to justify their abridgment." *Poe v. Ullman*,
> 367 U.S. 497 (1961) (Harlan, J., dissenting from dismissal on jurisdictional
> grounds) [Note *supra.* Chapter 8].

... The inescapable fact is that adjudication of substantive due process claims may call upon the Court in interpreting the Constitution to exercise that same capacity which by tradition courts always have exercised: reasoned judgment. Its boundaries are not susceptible of expression as a simple rule. That does not mean we are free to invalidate state policy choices with which we disagree; yet neither does it permit us to shrink from the duties of our office....

Men and women of good conscience can disagree, and we suppose some always shall disagree, about the profound moral and spiritual implications of terminating a pregnancy, even in its earliest stage. Some of us as individuals find abortion offensive to our most basic principles of morality, but that cannot control our decision. Our obligation is to define the liberty of all, not to mandate our own moral code. The underlying constitutional issue is whether the State can resolve these philosophic questions in such a definitive way that a woman lacks all choice in the matter, except perhaps in those rare circumstances in which the pregnancy is itself a danger to her own life or health, or is the result of rape or incest....

Our law affords constitutional protection to personal decisions relating to marriage, procreation, contraception, family relationship, child rearing, and education.... These matters, involving the most intimate and personal choices a person may make in a lifetime, choices central to personal dignity and autonomy, are central to the liberty protected by the Fourteenth Amendment. At the heart of liberty is the right to define one's own concept of existence, of meaning, of the universe, and of the mystery of human life. Beliefs about these matters could not define the attributes of personhood were they formed under compulsion of the State.

These considerations begin our analysis of the woman's interest in terminating her pregnancy but cannot end it, for this reason: though the abortion decision may originate within the zone of conscience and belief, it is more than a philosophic exercise. Abortion is a unique act. It is an act fraught with consequences for others: for the woman who must live with the implications of her decision; for the persons who perform and assist in the procedure; for the spouse, family, and society which must confront the knowledge that these procedures exist, procedures some deem nothing short of an act of violence against innocent human life; and, depending on one's beliefs, for the life or potential life that is aborted. Though abortion is conduct, it does not follow that the State is entitled to proscribe it in all instances. That is because the liberty of the woman is at stake in a sense unique to the human condition and so unique to the law. The mother who carries a child to full term is subject to anxieties, to physical constraints, to pain that only she must bear. That these sacrifices have from the beginning of the human race been endured by woman with a pride that ennobles her in the eyes of others and give to the infant a bond of love cannot alone be grounds for the State to insist she make the sacrifice. Her suffering is too intimate and personal for the State to insist, without more, upon its own vision of the woman's role, however dominant that vision has been in the course of our history and our culture. The destiny of the woman must be shaped to a large extent on her own conception of her spiritual imperatives and her place in society....

While we appreciate the weight of the arguments made on behalf of the State in the case before us, arguments which in their ultimate formulation conclude that *Roe* should be overruled, the reservations any of us may have in reaffirming the central holding of *Roe* are outweighed by the explication of individual liberty we have given combined with the force of *stare decisis*. We turn now to that doctrine.

### III

### A

... [When] this Court reexamines a prior holding, its judgment is customarily informed by a series of prudential and pragmatic considerations designed to test the consistency of overruling a prior decision with the ideal of the rule of law, and to gauge the respective costs of reaffirming and overruling a prior case. Thus, for example, we may ask whether the rule has proven to be intolerable simply in defying practical workability; whether the rule is subject to a kind of reliance that would lend a special hardship to the consequences of overruling and add inequity to the cost of repudiation; whether related principles of law have so far developed as to have left the old rule no more than a remnant of abandoned doctrine; or whether facts have so changed, or come to be seen so differently, as to have robbed the old rule of significant application or justification....

### 1

Although *Roe* has engendered opposition, it has in no sense proven "unworkable," representing as it does a simple limitation beyond which a state law is unenforceable....

### 2

The inquiry into reliance counts the cost of a rule's repudiation as it would fall on those who have relied reasonably on the rule's continued application.... Abortion is customarily chosen as an unplanned response to the consequence of unplanned activity or to the failure of conventional birth control, and except on the assumption that no intercourse would have occurred but for *Roe*'s holding, such behavior may appear to justify no reliance claim.

To eliminate the issue of reliance that easily, however, ... would be simply to refuse to face the fact that for two decades of economic and social developments, people have organized intimate relationships and made choices that define their views of themselves and their places in society, in reliance on the availability of abortion in the event that contraception should fail. The ability of women to participate equally in the economic and social life of the Nation has been facilitated by their ability to control their reproductive lives....

### 3

No evolution of legal principle has left *Roe*'s doctrinal footings weaker than they were in 1973. No development of constitutional law since the case was decided has implicitly or explicitly left *Roe* behind as a mere survivor of obsolete constitutional thinking....

### 4

We have seen how time has overtaken some of *Roe*'s factual assumptions: advances in maternal health care allow for abortions safe to the mother later in pregnancy than was true in 1973, and advances in neonatal care have advanced viability to a point somewhat earlier. But these facts go only to the scheme of time limits on the realization of competing interests, and the divergences from the factual premises of 1973 have no bearing on the validity of *Roe*'s central holding, that viability marks the earliest point at which the State's interest in fetal life is constitutionally adequate to justify a legislative ban on nontherapeutic abortions....

### B

In a less significant case, *stare decisis* analysis could, and would, stop at the point we have reached. But the sustained and widespread debate *Roe* has provoked calls for some comparison between that case and others of comparable dimension that have responded to national controversies and taken on the impress of the controversies addressed. Only two such decisional lines from the past century present themselves for examination, and in each instance the result reached by the Court accorded with the principles we apply today.

The first example is that line of cases identified with *Lochner v. New York* (1905) [*Supra.* Chapter 7] ... The *Lochner* decisions were exemplified by *Adkins v. Children's Hospital of District of Columbia*, 261 U.S. 525 (1923) [Note *supra.* Chapter 7].... Fourteen years later, *West Coast Hotel Co. v. Parrish* (1937) [*Supra.* Chapter 7], signaled the demise of *Lochner* by overruling *Adkins.* In the meantime, the Depression had come and, with it, the lesson that seemed unmistakable to most people by 1937, that the interpretation of contractual freedom protected in *Adkins* rested on fundamentally false factual assumptions about the capacity of a relatively unregulated market to satisfy minimal levels of human welfare....

The second comparison that 20th century history invites is with the cases employing the separate-but-equal rule for applying the Fourteenth Amendment's equal protection guarantee. They began with *Plessy v. Ferguson*, 163 U.S. 537 (1896), holding that legislatively mandated racial segregation in public transportation works no denial of equal protection, rejecting the argument that racial separation enforced by the legal machinery of American society treats the black race as inferior....

The Court in *Brown v. Board of Education*, 347 U.S. 483 (1954), addressed these facts of life by observing that whatever may have been the understanding in *Plessy's* time of the power of segregation to stigmatize those who were segregated with a "badge of inferiority," it was clear by 1954 that legally sanctioned segregation had just such an effect, to the point that racially separate public educational facilities were deemed inherently unequal....

*West Coast Hotel* and *Brown* each rested on facts, or an understanding of facts, changed from those which furnished the claimed justifications for the earlier constitutional resolutions. Each case was comprehensible as the Court's response to facts that the country could understand, or had come to understand already, but which the Court of an earlier day, as its own declarations disclosed, had not been able to perceive. As the decisions were thus comprehensible they were also defensible, not merely as the victories of one doctrinal school over another by dint of numbers (victories though they were), but as applications of constitutional principle to facts as they had not been seen by the Court before. In constitutional adjudication as elsewhere in life, changed circumstances may impose new obligations, and the thoughtful part of the Nation could accept each decision to overrule a prior case as a response to the Court's constitutional duty.

Because the cases before us present no such occasion it could be seen as no such response....

## C

The examination of the conditions justifying the repudiation of *Adkins* by *West Coast Hotel* and *Plessy* by *Brown* is enough to suggest the terrible price that would have been paid if the Court had not overruled as it did. In the present cases, however, as our analysis to this point makes clear, the terrible price would be paid for overruling. Our analysis would not be complete, however, without explaining why overruling *Roe*'s central holding would not only reach an unjustifiable result under principles of *stare decisis*, but would seriously weaken the Court's capacity to exercise the judicial power and to function as the Supreme Court of a Nation dedicated to the rule of law. To understand why this would be so it is necessary to understand the source of this Court's authority, the conditions necessary for its preservation, and its relationship to the country's understanding of itself as a constitutional Republic.

The root of American governmental power is revealed most clearly in the instance of the power conferred by the Constitution upon the Judiciary of the United States and specifically upon this Court. As Americans of each succeeding generation are rightly told, the Court cannot buy support for its decisions by spending money and, except to a minor degree, it cannot independently coerce obedience to its decrees. The Court's power lies, rather, in its legitimacy, a product of substance and perception that shows itself in the people's acceptance of the Judiciary as fit to determine what the Nation's law means and to declare what it demands.

… The Court must take care to speak and act in ways that allow people to accept its decisions on the terms the Court claims for them, as grounded truly in principle, not as compromises with social and political pressures having, as such, no bearing on the principled choices that the Court is obliged to make. Thus, the Court's legitimacy depends on making legally principled decisions under circumstances in which their principled character is sufficiently plausible to be accepted by the Nation.

… Where, in the performance of its judicial duties, the Court decides a case in such a way as to resolve the sort of intensely divisive controversy reflected in *Roe* and those rare, comparable cases, its decision has a dimension that the resolution of the normal case does not carry. It is the dimension present whenever the Court's interpretation of the Constitution calls the contending sides of national controversy to end their national division by accepting a common mandate rooted in the Constitution.

The Court is not asked to do this very often, having thus addressed the Nation only twice in our lifetime, in the decisions of *Brown* and *Roe*. But when the Court does act in this way, its decision requires an equally rare precedential force to counter the inevitable efforts to overturn it and to thwart its implementation.… So to overrule under fire in the absence of the most compelling reason to reexamine a watershed decision would subvert the Court's legitimacy beyond any serious question.…

The Court's duty in the present case is clear. In 1973, it confronted the already-divisive issue of governmental power to limit personal choice to undergo abortion, for which it provided a new resolution based on the due process guaranteed by the Fourteenth Amendment. Whether or not a new social consensus is developing on that issue, its divisiveness is no less today than in 1973, and pressure to overrule the decision, like pressure to retain it, has grown only more intense. A decision to overrule *Roe*'s essential holding under the existing circumstances would address error, if error there was, at the cost of both profound and unnecessary damage to the Court's legitimacy, and to the Nation's commitment to the rule of law. It is therefore imperative to adhere to the essence of *Roe*'s original decision, and we do so today.

## IV

From what we have said so far it follows that it is a constitutional liberty of the woman to have some freedom to terminate her pregnancy. We conclude that the basic decision in *Roe* was based on a constitutional analysis which we cannot now repudiate. The woman's liberty is not so unlimited, however, that from the outset the State cannot show its concern for the life of the unborn, and at a later point in fetal development the State's interest in life has sufficient force so that the right of the woman to terminate the pregnancy can be restricted.

That brings us, of course, to the point where much criticism has been directed at *Roe*, a criticism that always inheres when the Court draws a specific rule from what in the Constitution is but a general standard. We conclude, however, that the urgent claims of the woman to retain the ultimate control over her destiny and her body, claims implicit in the meaning of liberty, require us to perform that function. Liberty must not be extinguished for want of a line that is clear. And it falls to us to give some real substance to the woman's liberty to determine whether to carry her pregnancy to full term.

We conclude the line should be drawn at viability, so that before that time the woman has a right to choose to terminate her pregnancy.... The woman's right to terminate her pregnancy before viability is the most central principle of *Roe v. Wade*. It is a rule of law and a component of liberty we cannot renounce.

On the other side of the equation is the interest of the State in the protection of potential life. The *Roe* Court recognized the State's "important and legitimate interest in protecting the potentiality of human life." The weight to be given this state interest, not the strength of the woman's interest, was the difficult question faced in *Roe*....

Yet it must be remembered that *Roe v. Wade* speaks with clarity in establishing not only the woman's liberty but also the State's "important and legitimate interest in potential life." That portion of the decision in *Roe* has been given too little acknowledgment and implementation by the Court in its subsequent cases.... In resolving this tension, we choose to rely upon *Roe*, as against the later cases....

We reject [*Roe*'s] trimester framework, which we do not consider to be part of the essential holding of *Roe*. Measures aimed at ensuring that a woman's choice contemplates the consequences for the fetus do not necessarily interfere with the right recognized in *Roe*, although those measures have been found to be inconsistent with the rigid trimester framework announced in that case.... The trimester framework suffers from these basic flaws: in its formulation it misconceives the nature of the pregnant woman's interest; and in practice it undervalues the State's interest in potential life, as recognized in *Roe*.

As our jurisprudence relating to all liberties save perhaps abortion has recognized, not every law which makes a right more difficult to exercise is, *ipso facto*, an infringement of that right.... The fact that a law which serves a valid purpose, one not designed to strike at the right itself, has the incidental effect of making it more difficult or more expensive to procure an abortion cannot be enough to invalidate it. Only where state regulation imposes an undue burden on a woman's ability to make this decision does the power of the State reach into the heart of the liberty protected by the Due Process Clause....

A finding of an undue burden is a shorthand for the conclusion that a state regulation has the purpose or effect of placing a substantial obstacle in the path of a woman seeking an abortion of a nonviable fetus. A statute with this purpose is invalid because the means chosen by the State to further the interest in potential life must be calculated to inform the woman's free choice, not hinder it. And a statute which, while furthering the interest in potential life or some other valid state interest, has the effect of placing a substantial obstacle in the path of a woman's choice cannot be considered a permissible means of serving its legitimate ends.... In our considered judgment, an undue burden is an unconstitutional burden....

Some guiding principles should emerge. What is at stake is the woman's right to make the ultimate decision, not a right to be insulated from all others in doing so. Regulations which do no more than create a structural mechanism by which the State, or the parent or guardian of a minor, may express profound respect for the life of the unborn are permitted, if they are not a substantial obstacle to the woman's exercise of the right to choose. Unless it has that effect on her right of choice, a state measure designed to persuade her to choose childbirth over abortion will be upheld if reasonably related to that goal. Regulations designed to foster the health of a woman seeking an abortion are valid if they do not constitute an undue burden.

… We give this summary:

(a) To protect the central right recognized by *Roe v. Wade* while at the same time accommodating the State's profound interest in potential life, we will employ the undue burden analysis as explained in this opinion. An undue burden exists, and therefore a provision of law is invalid, if its purpose or effect is to place a substantial obstacle in the path of a woman seeking an abortion before the fetus attains viability.

(b) We reject the rigid trimester framework of *Roe v. Wade*. To promote the State's profound interest in potential life, throughout pregnancy the State may take measures to ensure that the woman's choice is informed, and measures designed to advance this interest will not be invalidated as long as their purpose is to persuade the woman to choose childbirth over abortion. These measures must not be an undue burden on the right.

(c) As with any medical procedure, the State may enact regulations to further the health or safety of a woman seeking an abortion. Unnecessary health regulations that have the purpose or effect of presenting a substantial obstacle to a woman seeking an abortion impose an undue burden on the right.

(d) Our adoption of the undue burden analysis does not disturb the central holding of *Roe v. Wade*, and we reaffirm that holding. Regardless of whether exceptions are made for particular circumstances, a State may not prohibit any woman from making the ultimate decision to terminate her pregnancy before viability.

(e) We also reaffirm *Roe*'s holding that "subsequent to viability, the State in promoting its interest in the potentiality of human life may, if it chooses, regulate, and even proscribe, abortion except where it is necessary, in appropriate medical judgment, for the preservation of the life or health of the mother." ...

## V

[The joint opinion then construed the statute's allowance of abortions in a "medical emergency" to include several serious conditions the district court had found the statute to exclude. Based on that conclusion, the Court upheld the statute's "medical emergency" definition as not imposing an undue burden.]

## B

... Except in a medical emergency, the statute requires that at least 24 hours before performing an abortion a physician inform the woman of the nature of the procedure, the health risks of the abortion and of childbirth, and the "probable gestational age of the unborn child." The physician or a qualified nonphysician must inform the woman of the availability of printed materials published by the State describing the fetus and providing information about medical assistance for childbirth, information about child support from the father, and a list of agencies which provide adoption and other services as alternatives to abortion. An abortion may not be performed unless the woman certifies in writing that she has been informed of the availability of these printed materials and has been provided them if she chooses to view them.

... It cannot be questioned that psychological well-being is a facet of health. Nor can it be doubted that most women considering an abortion would deem the impact on the fetus relevant, if not dispositive, to the decision. In attempting to ensure that a woman apprehend the full consequences of her decision, the State furthers the legitimate purpose of reducing the risk that a woman may elect an abortion, only to discover later, with devastating psychological consequences, that her decision was not fully informed. If the information the State requires to be made available to the woman is truthful and not misleading, the requirement may be permissible.

We also see no reason why the State may not require doctors to inform a woman seeking an abortion of the availability of materials relating to the consequences to the fetus, even when those consequences have no direct relation to her health.... [Requiring] that the woman be informed of the availability of information relating to fetal development and the assistance available should she decide to carry the pregnancy to full term is a reasonable measure to ensure an informed choice.... This requirement cannot be considered a substantial obstacle to obtaining an abortion.... In theory, at least, the waiting period is a reasonable measure to implement the State's interest in protecting the life of the unborn, a measure that does not amount to an undue burden....

Whether the mandatory 24-hour waiting period is nonetheless invalid because in practice it is a substantial obstacle to a woman's choice to terminate her pregnancy is a closer question. The findings of fact by the District Court indicate that because of the distances many women must travel to reach an abortion provider, the practical effect will often be a delay of much more than a day because the waiting period requires that a woman seeking an abortion make at least two visits to the doctor.... These findings are troubling in some respects, but they do not demonstrate that the waiting period constitutes an undue burden....

We also disagree with the District Court's conclusion that the "particularly burdensome" effects of the waiting period on some women require its invalidation. A particular burden is not of necessity a substantial obstacle. Whether a burden falls on a particular group is a distinct inquiry from whether it is a substantial obstacle even as to the women in that group. And the District Court did not conclude that the waiting period is such an obstacle even for the women who are most burdened by it. Hence, on the record before us, and in the context of this facial challenge, we are not convinced that the 24-hour waiting period constitutes an undue burden....

## C

Section 3209 of Pennsylvania's abortion law provides, except in cases of medical emergency, that no physician shall perform an abortion on a married woman without receiving a signed statement from the woman that she has notified her spouse that she is about to undergo an abortion. The woman has the option of providing an alternative signed statement certifying that her husband is not the man who impregnated her; that her husband could not be located; that the pregnancy is the result of spousal sexual assault which she has reported; or that the woman believes that notifying her husband will cause him or someone else to inflict bodily injury upon her....

[The opinion presented the District Court's findings of fact and various studies documenting the prevalence of domestic violence.]

The spousal notification requirement is ... likely to prevent a significant number of women from obtaining an abortion. It does not merely make abortions a little more difficult or expensive to obtain; for many women, it will impose a substantial obstacle. We must not blind ourselves to the fact that the significant number of women who fear for their safety and the safety of their children are likely to be deterred from procuring an abortion as surely as if the Commonwealth had outlawed abortion in all cases....

[Parts V-D and V-E of the opinion concluded that the informed parental consent and recordkeeping and reporting requirements (except one pertaining to spousal notification) were constitutional.]

## VI

Our Constitution is a covenant running from the first generation of Americans to us and then to future generations. It is a coherent succession. Each generation must learn anew that the Constitution's written terms embody ideas and aspirations that must survive more ages than one. We accept our responsibility not to retreat from interpreting the full meaning of the covenant in light of all of our precedents. We invoke it once again to define the freedom guaranteed by the Constitution's own promise, the promise of liberty....

JUSTICE STEVENS, concurring in part and dissenting in part.

The portions of the Court's opinion that I have joined are more important than those with which I disagree....

## II

My disagreement with the joint opinion begins with its understanding of the trimester framework established in *Roe*. Contrary to the suggestion of the joint opinion, it is not a "contradiction" to recognize that the State may have a legitimate interest in potential human life and, at the same time, to conclude that that interest does not justify the regulation of abortion before viability (although other interests, such as maternal health, may). The fact that the State's interest is legitimate does not tell us when, if ever, that interest outweighs the pregnant woman's interest in personal liberty....

Weighing the State's interest in potential life and the woman's liberty interest, I agree with the joint opinion that the State may "express a preference for normal childbirth," that the State may take steps to ensure that a woman's choice "is thoughtful and informed," and that "States are free to enact laws to provide a reasonable framework for a woman to make a decision that has such profound and lasting meaning." Serious questions arise, however, when a State attempts to "persuade the woman to choose childbirth over abortion." Decisional autonomy must limit the State's power to inject into a woman's most personal deliberations its own views of what is best. The State may promote its preferences by funding childbirth, by creating and maintaining alternatives to abortion, and by espousing the virtues of family; but it must respect the individual's freedom to make such judgments....

... Those sections [of the state law which] require a physician or counselor to provide the woman with a range of materials clearly designed to persuade her to choose not to undergo the abortion [are unconstitutional]. While the Commonwealth is free ... to produce and disseminate such material, the Commonwealth may not inject such information into the woman's deliberations just as she is weighing such an important choice.

[Those sections of the law] which require the physician to inform a woman of the nature and risks of the abortion procedure and the medical risks of carrying to term, are neutral requirements comparable to those imposed in other medical procedures [and thus are constitutional]. Those sections indicate no effort by the Commonwealth to influence the woman's choice in any way. If anything, such requirements *enhance*, rather than skew, the woman's decisionmaking.

## III

The 24-hour waiting period ... raises even more serious concerns. Such a requirement arguably furthers the State's interests in two ways, neither of which is constitutionally permissible.

First, it may be argued that the 24-hour delay is justified by the mere fact that it is likely to reduce the number of abortions, thus furthering the Commonwealth's interest in potential life. But such an argument would justify any form of coercion that placed an obstacle in the woman's path. The Commonwealth cannot further its interests by simply wearing down the ability of the pregnant woman to exercise her constitutional right.

Second, it can more reasonably be argued that the 24-hour delay furthers the Commonwealth's interest in ensuring that the woman's decision is informed and thoughtful. But there is no evidence that the mandated delay benefits women or that it is necessary to enable the physician to convey any relevant information to the patient. The mandatory delay thus appears to rest on outmoded and unacceptable assumptions about the decisionmaking capacity of women....

In the alternative, the delay requirement may be premised on the belief that the decision to terminate a pregnancy is presumptively wrong. This premise is illegitimate. [Justice Stevens thus concluded that the waiting period was unconstitutional.] ...

JUSTICE BLACKMUN, concurring in part, concurring in the judgment in part, and dissenting in part.

I join parts I, II, III, V-A, V-C, and VI of the joint opinion of JUSTICES O'CONNOR, KENNEDY, and SOUTER.

Three years ago, in *Webster v. Reproductive Health Services*, 492 U.S. 490 (1989) [Note *supra.* this chapter], four Members of this Court appeared poised to "cast into darkness the hopes and visions of every woman in this country" who had come to believe that the Constitution guaranteed her the right to reproductive choice. All that remained between the promise of *Roe* and the darkness of the plurality was a single, flickering flame.... But now, just when so many expected the darkness to fall, the flame has grown bright.

I do not underestimate the significance of today's joint opinion. Yet I remain steadfast in my belief that the right to reproductive choice is entitled to the full protection afforded by this Court before *Webster*. And I fear for the darkness as four Justices anxiously await the single vote necessary to extinguish the light.

## I

Make no mistake, the joint opinion of JUSTICES O'CONNOR, KENNEDY, and SOUTER is an act of personal courage and constitutional principle. In contrast to previous decisions in which JUSTICES O'CONNOR and KENNEDY postponed reconsideration of *Roe v. Wade*, the authors of the joint opinion today join JUSTICE STEVENS and me in concluding that "the essential holding of *Roe* should be retained and once again reaffirmed." In brief, five Members of this Court today recognize that "the Constitution protects a woman's right to terminate her pregnancy in its early stages." ...

## II

Today, no less than yesterday, the Constitution and decisions of this Court require that a State's abortion restrictions be subjected to the strictest judicial scrutiny. Our precedents and the joint opinion's principles require us to subject all non-*de minimis* abortion regulations to strict scrutiny. Under this standard, the Pennsylvania statute's provisions requiring content-based counseling, a 24-hour delay, informed parental consent, and reporting of abortion-related information must be invalidated....

### A

The Court today reaffirms the long recognized rights of privacy and bodily integrity....

A State's restrictions on a woman's right to terminate her pregnancy also implicate constitutional guarantees of gender equality. State restrictions on abortion compel women to continue pregnancies they otherwise might terminate. By restricting the right to terminate pregnancies, the State conscripts women's bodies into its service, forcing women to continue their pregnancies, suffer the pains of childbirth, and in most instances, provide years of maternal care. The State does not compensate women for their services; instead, it assumes that they owe this duty as a matter of course. This assumption—that women can simply be forced to accept the "natural" status and incidents of motherhood—appears to rest upon a conception of women's role that has triggered the protection of the Equal Protection Clause. The joint opinion recognizes that these assumptions about women's place in society "are no longer consistent with our understanding of the family, the individual, or the Constitution." . . .

### III

At long last, THE CHIEF JUSTICE and those who have joined him admit it. Gone are the contentions that the issue need not be (or has not been) considered. There, on the first page, for all to see, is what was expected: "We believe that *Roe* was wrongly decided, and that it can and should be overruled consistently with our traditional approach to *stare decisis* in constitutional cases." If there is much reason to applaud the advances made by the joint opinion today, there is far more to fear from THE CHIEF JUSTICE's opinion.

THE CHIEF JUSTICE's criticism of *Roe* follows from his stunted conception of individual liberty. While recognizing that the Due Process Clause protects more than simple physical liberty, he then goes on to construe this Court's personal-liberty cases as establishing only a laundry list of particular rights, rather than a principled account of how these particular rights are grounded in a more general right of privacy. This constricted view is reinforced by THE CHIEF JUSTICE's exclusive reliance on tradition as a source of fundamental rights. . . .

Even more shocking than THE CHIEF JUSTICE's cramped notion of individual liberty is his complete omission of any discussion of the effects that compelled childbirth and motherhood have on women's lives. The only expression of concern with women's health is purely instrumental—for THE CHIEF JUSTICE, only women's *psychological* health is a concern, and only to the extent that he assumes that every woman who decides to have an abortion does so without serious consideration of the moral implications of their decision. In short, THE CHIEF JUSTICE's view of the State's compelling interest in maternal health has less to do with health than it does with compelling women to be maternal. . . .

### IV

In one sense, the Court's approach is worlds apart from that of THE CHIEF JUSTICE and JUSTICE SCALIA. And yet, in another sense, the distance between the two approaches is short—the distance is but a single vote.

I am 83 years old. I cannot remain on this Court forever, and when I do step down, the confirmation process for my successor well may focus on the issue before us today. That, I regret, may be exactly where the choice between the two worlds will be made.

CHIEF JUSTICE REHNQUIST, with whom JUSTICE WHITE, JUSTICE SCALIA, and JUSTICE THOMAS join, concurring in the judgment in part and dissenting in part.

The joint opinion, following its newly minted variation on *stare decisis*, retains the outer shell of *Roe v. Wade* but beats a wholesale retreat from the substance of that case. We believe that *Roe* was wrongly decided, and that it can and should be overruled consistently with our traditional approach to *stare decisis* in constitutional cases. We would adopt the approach of the plurality in *Webster v. Reproductive Health Services*, and uphold the challenged provisions of the Pennsylvania statute in their entirety.

I

… We agree with the Court of Appeals that our decision in *Roe* is not directly implicated by the Pennsylvania statute, which does not prohibit, but simply regulates abortion. But, as the Court of Appeals found, the state of our post-*Roe* decisional law dealing with the regulation of abortion is confusing and uncertain, indicating that a reexamination of that line of cases is in order. Unfortunately for those who must apply this Court's decisions, the reexamination undertaken today leaves the Court no less divided than beforehand. Although they reject the trimester framework that formed the underpinning of *Roe*, JUSTICES O'CONNOR, KENNEDY, and SOUTER adopt a revised undue burden standard to analyze the challenged regulations. We conclude, however, that such an outcome is an unjustified constitutional compromise, one which leaves the Court in a position to closely scrutinize all types of abortion regulations despite the fact that it lacks the power to do so under the Constitution….

In *Roe v. Wade*, the Court recognized a "guarantee of personal privacy" which "is broad enough to encompass a woman's decision whether or not to terminate her pregnancy." We are now of the view that, in terming this right fundamental, the Court in *Roe* read the earlier opinions upon which it based its decision much too broadly. Unlike marriage, procreation and contraception, abortion "involves the purposeful termination of potential life." The abortion decision must therefore "be recognized as *sui generis*, different in kind from the others that the Court has protected under the rubric of personal or family privacy and autonomy." One cannot ignore the fact that a woman is not isolated in her pregnancy, and that the decision to abort necessarily involves the destruction of a fetus.

Nor do the historical traditions of the American people support the view that the right to terminate one's pregnancy is "fundamental." The common law which we inherited from England made abortion after "quickening" an offense. At the time of the adoption of the Fourteenth Amendment, statutory prohibitions or restrictions on abortion were commonplace; in 1868, at least 28 of the then-37 States and 8 Territories had statutes banning or limiting abortion. By the turn of the century virtually every State had a law prohibiting or restricting abortion on its books. By the middle of the present century, a liberalization trend had set in. But 21 of the restrictive abortion laws in effect in 1868 were still in effect in 1973 when *Roe* was decided, and an overwhelming majority of the States prohibited abortion unless necessary to preserve the life or health of the mother. On this record, it can scarcely be said that any deeply rooted tradition of relatively unrestricted abortion in our history supported the classification of the right to abortion as "fundamental" under the Due Process Clause of the Fourteenth Amendment.

We think, therefore, both in view of this history and of our decided cases dealing with substantive liberty under the Due Process Clause, that the Court was mistaken in *Roe* when it classified a woman's decision to terminate her pregnancy as a "fundamental right" that could be abridged only in a manner which withstood "strict scrutiny." ...

## II

The joint opinion of JUSTICES O'CONNOR, KENNEDY, and SOUTER cannot bring itself to say that *Roe* was correct as an original matter, but the authors are of the view that "the immediate question is not the soundness of *Roe*'s resolution of the issue, but the precedential force that must be accorded to its holding." Instead of claiming that *Roe* was correct as a matter of original constitutional interpretation, the opinion therefore contains an elaborate discussion of *stare decisis*. This discussion of the principle of *stare decisis* appears to be almost entirely dicta, because the joint opinion does not apply that principle in dealing with *Roe*. *Roe* decided that a woman had a fundamental right to an abortion. The joint opinion rejects that view. *Roe* decided that abortion regulations were to be subjected to "strict scrutiny" and could be justified only in the light of "compelling state interest." The joint opinion rejects that view. *Roe* analyzed abortion regulation under a rigid trimester framework, a framework which has guided this Court's decisionmaking for 19 years. The joint opinion rejects that framework.

*Stare decisis* is defined in Black's Law Dictionary as meaning "to abide by, or adhere to, decided cases." Whatever the "central holding" of *Roe* that is left after the joint opinion finishes dissecting it is surely not the result of that principle. While purporting to adhere to precedent, the joint opinion instead revises it. *Roe* continues to exist, but only in the way a storefront on a western movie set exists: a mere facade to give the illusion of reality....

In our view, authentic principles of *stare decisis* do not require that any portion of the reasoning in *Roe* be kept intact.... The joint opinion discusses several *stare decisis* factors which, it asserts, point toward retaining a portion of *Roe*. Two of these factors are that the main "factual underpinning" of *Roe* has remained the same, and that its doctrinal foundation is no weaker now than it was in 1973. Of course, what might be called the basic facts which gave rise to *Roe* have remained the same — women become pregnant, there is a point somewhere, depending on medical technology, where a fetus becomes viable, and women give birth to children. But this is only to say that the same facts which gave rise to *Roe* will continue to give rise to similar cases. It is not a reason, in and of itself, why those cases must be decided in the same incorrect manner as was the first case to deal with the question. And surely there is no requirement, in considering whether to depart from *stare decisis* in a constitutional case, that a decision be more wrong now than it was at the time it was rendered. If that were true, the most outlandish constitutional decision could survive forever, based simply on the fact that it was no more outlandish later than it was when originally rendered....

The joint opinion also points to the reliance interests involved in this context in its effort to explain why precedent must be followed for precedent's sake.... But, as the joint opinion apparently agrees, any traditional notion of reliance is not applicable here.... The joint opinion thus turns to what can only be described as an unconventional—and unconvincing—notion of reliance, a view based on the surmise that the availability of abortion since *Roe* has led to "two decades of economic and social developments" that would be undercut if the error of *Roe* were recognized. The joint opinion's assertion of this fact is undeveloped and totally conclusory. In fact, one cannot be sure to what economic and social developments the opinion is referring. Surely it is dubious to suggest that women have reached their "places in society" in reliance upon *Roe,* rather than as a result of their determination to obtain higher education and compete with men in the job market, and of society's increasing recognition of their ability to fill positions that were previously thought to be reserved only for men....

In the end, having failed to put forth any evidence to prove any true reliance, the joint opinion's argument is based solely on generalized assertions about the national psyche, on a belief that the people of this country have grown accustomed to the *Roe* decision over the last 19 years and have "ordered their thinking and living around" it....

Apparently realizing that conventional *stare decisis* principles do not support its position, the joint opinion advances a belief that retaining a portion of *Roe* is necessary to protect the "legitimacy" of this Court.... The joint opinion agrees that the Court's stature would have been seriously damaged if in *Brown* and *West Coast Hotel* it had dug in its heels and refused to apply normal principles of *stare decisis* to the earlier decisions. But the opinion contends that the Court was entitled to overrule *Plessy* and *Lochner* in those cases, despite the existence of opposition to the original decisions, only because both the Nation and the Court had learned new lessons in the interim. This is at best a feebly supported, *post hoc* rationalization for those decisions....

The end result of the joint opinion's paeans of praise for legitimacy is the enunciation of a brand new standard for evaluating state regulation of a woman's right to abortion—the "undue burden" standard. As indicated above, *Roe v. Wade* adopted a "fundamental right" standard under which state regulations could survive only if they met the requirement of "strict scrutiny." While we disagree with that standard, it at least had a recognized basis in constitutional law at the time *Roe* was decided. The same cannot be said for the "undue burden" standard, which is created largely out of whole cloth by the authors of the joint opinion. It is a standard which even today does not command the support of a majority of this Court. And it will not, we believe, result in the sort of "simple limitation," easily applied, which the joint opinion anticipates. In sum, it is a standard which is not built to last....

The sum of the joint opinion's labors in the name of *stare-decisis* and "legitimacy" is this: *Roe v. Wade* stands as a sort of judicial Potemkin Village, which may be pointed out to passers by as a monument to importance of adhering to precedent. But behind the facade, an entirely new method of analysis, without any roots in constitutional law, is imported to decide the constitutionality of state laws regulating abortion. Neither *stare decisis* nor "legitimacy" are truly served by such an effort.

We have stated above our belief that the Constitution does not subject state abortion regulations to heightened scrutiny. Accordingly, we think that the correct analysis is that set forth by the plurality opinion in *Webster*. A woman's interest in having an abortion is a form of liberty protected by the Due Process Clause, but States may regulate abortion procedures in ways rationally related to a legitimate state interest.

### III

[Chief Justice Rehnquist argued that all of the challenged law's provisions satisfied the rational basis test, and thus should be upheld, thereby creating, along with the joint opinion, a majority for upholding the statute's waiting period, informed consent, parental notification, and record-keeping requirements.]

Justice Scalia, with whom The Chief Justice, Justice White, and Justice Thomas join, concurring in the judgement in part and dissenting in part.

My views on this matter are unchanged from those I set forth in my separate opinions in [earlier cases]. The States may, if they wish, permit abortion on demand, but the Constitution does not *require* them to do so. The permissibility of abortion, and the limitations upon it, are to be resolved like most important questions in our democracy: by citizens trying to persuade one another and then voting.... A State's choice between two positions on which reasonable people can disagree is constitutional even when (as is often the case) it intrudes upon a "liberty" in the absolute sense. Laws against bigamy, for example—with which entire societies of reasonable people disagree—intrude upon men and women's liberty to marry and live with one another. But bigamy happens not to be a liberty specially "protected" by the Constitution.

That is, quite simply, the issue in this case: not whether the power of a woman to abort her unborn child is a "liberty" in the absolute sense; or even whether it is a liberty of great importance to many women. Of course it is both. The issue is whether it is a liberty protected by the Constitution of the United States. I am sure it is not. I reach that conclusion not because of anything so exalted as my views concerning the "concept of existence, of meaning, of the universe, and of the mystery of human life." Rather, I reach it for the same reason I reach the conclusion that bigamy is not constitutionally protected—because of two simple facts: (1) the Constitution says absolutely nothing about it, and (2) the longstanding traditions of American society have permitted it to be legally proscribed....

Beyond that brief summary of the essence of my position, I will not swell the United States Reports with repetition of what I have said before; and applying the rational basis test, I would uphold the Pennsylvania statute in its entirety. I must, however, respond to a few of the more outrageous arguments in today's opinion, which it is beyond human nature to have unanswered. I shall discuss each of them under a quotation from the Court's opinion to which they pertain.

**"The inescapable fact is that adjudication of substantive due process claims may call upon the Court in interpreting the Constitution to exercise that same capacity which by tradition courts always have exercised: reasoned judgment."**

Assuming that the question before us is to be resolved at such a level of philosophical abstraction, in such isolation from the traditions of American society, as by simply applying "reasoned judgment," I do not see how that could possibly have produced the answer the Court arrived at in *Roe v. Wade*. Today's opinion describes the methodology of *Roe*, quite accurately, as weighing against the woman's interest the State's "'important and legitimate interest in protecting the potentiality of human life.'" But "reasoned judgment" does not begin by begging the question, as *Roe* and subsequent cases unquestionably did by assuming that what the State is protecting is the mere "potentiality of human life." The whole argument of abortion opponents is that what the Court calls the fetus and what others call the unborn child *is a human life*. Thus, whatever answer *Roe* came up with after conducting its "balancing" is bound to be wrong, unless it is correct that the human fetus is in some critical sense merely potentially human. There is of course no way to determine that as a legal matter; it is in fact a value judgment. Some societies have considered newborn children not yet human, or the incompetent elderly no longer so.

The authors of the joint opinion, of course, do not squarely contend that *Roe v. Wade* was a *correct* application of "reasoned judgment"; merely that it must be followed, because of *stare decisis*. But in their exhaustive discussion of all the factors that go into the determination of when *stare decisis* should be observed and when disregarded, they never mention "how wrong was the decision on its face?" Surely, if "the Court's power lies … in its legitimacy, a product of substance and perception," the "substance" part of the equation demands that plain error be acknowledged and eliminated. *Roe* was plainly wrong—even on the Court's methodology of "reasoned judgment," and even more so (of course) if the proper criteria of text and tradition are applied.

The emptiness of the "reasoned judgment" that produced *Roe* is displayed in plain view by the fact that, after more than 19 years of effort by some of the brightest (and most determined) legal minds in the country, after more than 10 cases upholding abortion rights in this Court, and after dozens upon dozens of *amicus* briefs submitted in this and other cases, the best the Court can do to explain how it is that the word "liberty" *must* be thought to include the right to destroy human fetuses is to rattle off a collection of adjectives that simply decorate a value judgment and conceal a political choice.... Those adjectives might be applied, for example, to homosexual sodomy, polygamy, adult incest, and suicide, all of which are equally "intimate" and "deeply personal" decisions involving "personal autonomy and bodily integrity," and all of which can constitutionally be proscribed because it is our unquestionable constitutional tradition that they are proscribable. It is not reasoned judgment that supports the Court's decision; only personal predilection....

**"Liberty finds no refuge in jurisprudence of doubt."**

One might have feared to encounter this august and sonorous phrase in an opinion defending the real *Roe v. Wade*, rather than the revised version fabricated today by the authors of the joint opinion. The shortcomings of *Roe* did not include lack of clarity: Virtually all regulation of abortion before the third trimester was invalid. But to come across this phrase in the joint opinion—which calls upon federal district judges to apply an "undue burden" standard as doubtful in application as it is unprincipled in origin—is really more than one should have to bear....

The joint opinion explains that a state regulation imposes an "undue burden" if it "has the purpose or effect of placing a substantial obstacle in the path of a woman seeking an abortion of a nonviable fetus." An obstacle is "substantial," we are told, if it is "calculated[,] [not] to inform the woman's free choice, [but to] hinder it." This latter statement cannot possibly mean what it says. *Any* regulation of abortion that is intended to advance what the joint opinion concedes is the State's "substantial" interest in protecting unborn life will be "calculated [to] hinder" a decision to have an abortion. It thus seems more accurate to say that the joint opinion would uphold abortion regulations only if they do not unduly hinder the woman's decision. That, of course, brings us right back to square one: Defining an "undue burden" as an "undue hindrance" (or a "substantial obstacle") hardly "clarifies" the test. Consciously or not, the joint opinion's verbal shell game will conceal raw judicial policy choices concerning what is "appropriate" abortion legislation....

Because the portion of the joint opinion adopting and describing the undue burden test provides no more useful guidance than the empty phrases discussed above, one must turn to the 23 pages applying that standard to the present facts for further guidance....

I do not, of course, have any objection to the notion that, in applying legal principles, one should rely only upon the facts that are contained in the record or that are properly subject to judicial notice. But what is remarkable about the joint opinion's fact-intensive analysis is that it does not result in any measurable clarification of the "undue burden" standard. Rather, the approach of the joint opinion is, for the most part, simply to highlight certain facts in the record that apparently strike the three Justices as particularly significant in establishing (or refuting) the existence of an undue burden; after describing these facts, the opinion then simply announces that the provision either does or does not impose a "substantial obstacle" or an "undue burden." We do not know whether the same conclusions could have been reached on a different record, or in what respects the record would have had to differ before an opposite conclusion would have been appropriate. The inherently standardless nature of this inquiry invites the district judge to give effect to his personal preferences about abortion....

To the extent I can discern *any* meaningful content in the "undue burden" standard as applied ... in the joint opinion, it appears to be that a State may not regulate abortion in such a way as to reduce significantly its incidence. Thus, despite flowery rhetoric about the State's "substantial" and "profound" interest in "potential human life," and criticism of *Roe* for undervaluing that interest, the joint opinion permits the State to pursue that interest only so long as it is not too successful.... Reason finds no refuge in this jurisprudence of confusion.

**"While we appreciate the weight of the arguments ... that *Roe* should be overruled, the reservations any of us may have in reaffirming the central holding of *Roe* are outweighed by the explication of individual liberty we have given combined with the force of *stare decisis*."**

The Court's reliance upon *stare decisis* can best be described as contrived. It insists upon the necessity of adhering not to all of *Roe*, but only to what it calls the "central holding." It seems to me that *stare decisis* ought to be applied even to the doctrine of *stare decisis*, and I confess never to have heard of this new, keep-what-you-want-and-throw-away-the-rest version. I wonder whether, as applied to *Marbury v. Madison*, for example, the new version of *stare decisis* would be satisfied if we allowed courts to review the constitutionality of only those statutes that (like the one in *Marbury*) pertain to the jurisdiction of the courts.

I am certainly not in a good position to dispute that the Court *has saved* the "central holding" of *Roe*, since to do that effectively I would have to know what the Court has saved, which in turn would require me to understand (as I do not) what the "undue burden" test means. I must confess, however, that I have always thought, and I think a lot of other people have always thought, that the arbitrary trimester framework, which the Court today discards, was quite as central to *Roe* as the arbitrary viability test, which the Court today retains. It seems particularly ungrateful to carve the trimester framework out of the core of *Roe*, since its very rigidity (in sharp contrast to the utter indeterminability of the "undue burden" test) is probably the only reason the Court is able to say, in urging *stare decisis*, that *Roe* "has in no sense proven unworkable." ...

**"Where, in the performance of its judicial duties, the Court decides a case in such a way as to resolve the sort of intensely divisive controversy reflected in *Roe*..., its decision has a dimension that the resolution of the normal case does not carry. It is the dimension present whenever the Court's interpretation of the Constitution calls the contending sides of a national controversy to end their national division by accepting a common mandate rooted in the Constitution."**

The Court's description of the place of *Roe* in the social history of the United States is unrecognizable. Not only did *Roe* not, as the Court suggests, *resolve* the deeply divisive issue of abortion; it did more than anything else to nourish it, by elevating it to the national level where it is infinitely more difficult to resolve. National politics were not plagued by abortion protests, national abortion lobbying, or abortion marches on Congress before *Roe v. Wade* was decided. Profound disagreement existed among our citizens over the issue—as it does over other issues, such as the death penalty—but that disagreement was being worked out at the state level. As with many other issues, the division of sentiment within each State was not as closely balanced as it was among the population of the Nation as a whole, meaning not only that more people would be satisfied with the results of state-by-state resolution, but also that those results would be more stable. Pre-*Roe* moreover, political compromise was possible.

*Roe*'s mandate for abortion on demand destroyed the compromises of the past, rendered compromise impossible for the future, and required the entire issue to be resolved uniformly, at the national level. At the same time, *Roe* created a vast new class of abortion consumers and abortion proponents by eliminating the moral opprobrium that had attached to the act. ("If the Constitution *guarantees* abortion, how can it be bad?"—not an accurate line of thought, but a natural one.) Many favor all of those developments, and it is not for me to say that they are wrong. But to portray *Roe* as the statesmanlike "settlement" of a divisive issue, a jurisprudential Peace of Westphalia that is worth preserving, is nothing less than Orwellian. *Roe* fanned into life an issue that has inflamed our national politics in general, and has obscured with its smoke the selection of Justices to this Court in particular, ever since. And by keeping us in the abortion-umpiring business, it is the perpetuation of that disruption, rather than of any *Pax Roeana*, that the Court's new majority decrees.

"[To] overrule under fire ... would subvert the Court's legitimacy....

"To all those who will be ... tested by following, the Court implicitly undertakes to remain steadfast....

"[The American people's] belief in themselves as ... a people [who aspire to live according to the rule of law] is not readily separable from their understanding of the Court invested with the authority to decide their constitutional cases and speak before all others for their constitutional ideals. If the Court's legitimacy should be undermined, then, so would the country be in its very ability to see itself through its constitutional ideals."

The Imperial Judiciary lives. It is instructive to compare this Nietzschean vision of us unelected, life-tenured judges—leading a Volk who will be "tested by following," and whose very "belief in themselves" is mystically bound up in their "understanding" of a Court that "speaks before all others for their constitutional ideals"—with the somewhat more modest role envisioned for these lawyers by the Founders.

> "The judiciary ... has ... no direction either of the strength or of the wealth of the society, and can take no active resolution whatever. It may truly be said to have neither Force nor Will but merely judgment...." *The Federalist* No. 78.

Or, again, to compare this ecstasy of a Supreme Court in which there is, especially on controversial matters, no shadow of change or hint of alteration ... with the more democratic views of a more humble man:

> "The candid citizen must confess that if the policy of the Government upon vital questions affecting the whole people is to be irrevocably fixed by decisions of the Supreme Court, ... the people will have ceased to be their own rulers,

having to that extent practically resigned their Government into the hands of that eminent tribunal." A. Lincoln, *First Inaugural Address* (Mar. 4, 1861)....

I cannot agree with, indeed I am appalled by, the Court's suggestion that the decision whether to stand by an erroneous constitutional decision must be strongly influenced—*against* overruling, no less—by the substantial and continuing public opposition the decision has generated. The Court's judgment that any other course would "subvert the Court's legitimacy" must be another consequence of reading the error-filled history book that described the deeply divided country brought together by *Roe*. In my history book, the Court was covered with dishonor and deprived of legitimacy by *Dred Scott v. Sanford*, 60 U.S. 393 (1857), an erroneous (and widely opposed) opinion that it did not abandon, rather than by *West Coast Hotel Co. v. Parrish*, which produced the famous "switch in time" from the Court's erroneous (and widely opposed) constitutional opposition to the social measures of the New Deal. (Both *Dred Scott* and one line of the cases resisting the New Deal rested upon the concept of "substantive due process" that the Court praises and employs today. Indeed, *Dred Scott* was "very possibly the first application of substantive due process in the Supreme Court, the original precedent for *Lochner v. New York* and *Roe v. Wade*." D. Currie, *The Constitution in the Supreme Court* (1985).)

But whether it would "subvert the Court's legitimacy" or not, the notion that we would decide a case differently from the way we otherwise would have in order to show that we can stand firm against public disapproval is frightening. It is a bad enough idea, even in the head of someone like me, who believes that the text of the Constitution, and our traditions, say what they say and there is no fiddling with them. But when it is in the mind of a Court that believes the Constitution has an evolving meaning; that the Ninth Amendment's reference to "other" rights is not a disclaimer, but a charter for action; and that the function of this Court is to "speak before all others for [the people's] constitutional ideals" unrestrained by meaningful text or tradition—then the notion that the Court must adhere to a decision for as long as the decision faces "great opposition" and the Court is "under fire" acquires a character of almost czarist arrogance. We are offended by these marchers who descend upon us, every year on the anniversary of *Roe*, to protest our saying that the Constitution requires what our society has never thought the Constitution requires. These people who refuse to be "tested by following" must be taught a lesson. We have no Cossacks, but at least we can stubbornly refuse to abandon an erroneous opinion that we might otherwise change—to show how little they intimidate us.

[Instead] of engaging in the hopeless task of predicting public perception—a job not for lawyers but for political campaign managers—the Justices should do what is *legally* right by asking two questions: (1) Was *Roe* correctly decided? (2) Has *Roe* succeeded in producing a settled body of law? If the answer to both questions is no, *Roe* should undoubtedly be overruled....

There is a poignant aspect to today's opinion. Its length, and what might be called its epic tone, suggest that its authors believe they are bringing to an end a troublesome era in the history of our Nation and of our Court....

There comes vividly to mind a portrait by Emanuel Leutze that hangs in the Harvard Law School: Roger Brooke Taney, painted in 1859, the 82d year of his life, the 24th of his Chief Justiceship, the second after his opinion in *Dred Scott*. He is all in black, sitting in a shadowed red armchair, left hand resting upon a pad of paper in his lap, right hand hanging limply, almost lifelessly, beside the inner arm of the chair. He sits facing the viewer and staring straight out. There seems to be on his face, and in his deep-set eyes, an expression of profound sadness and disillusionment. Perhaps he always looked that way, even when dwelling upon the happiest of thoughts. But those of us who know how the lustre of his great Chief Justiceship came to be eclipsed by *Dred Scott* cannot help believing that he had that case—its already apparent consequences for the Court, and its soon-to-be-played-out consequences for the Nation—burning on his mind. I expect that two years earlier he, too, had thought himself "calling the contending sides of national controversy to end their national division by accepting a common mandate rooted in the Constitution."

It is no more realistic for us in this litigation, than it was for him in that, to think that an issue of the sort they both involved—an issue involving life and death, freedom and subjugation—can be "speedily and finally settled" by the Supreme Court, as President James Buchanan in his inaugural address said the issue of slavery in the territories would be. Quite to the contrary, by foreclosing all democratic outlet for the deep passions this issue arouses, by banishing the issue from the political forum that gives all participants, even the losers, the satisfaction of a fair hearing and an honest fight, by continuing the imposition of a rigid national rule instead of allowing for regional differences, the Court merely prolongs and intensifies the anguish.

We should get out of this area, where we have no right to be, and where we do neither ourselves nor the country any good by remaining.

### Note: Post-Casey *Abortion Regulation*

1. The abortion wars did not end with *Casey*. Eventually, abortion-rights opponents shifted their focus away from a direct attack on *Roe*, and toward chipping away at the abortion right *Casey* recognized. By the end of the 1990s, they had focused on so-called "partial-birth" abortions—late-term abortions that involved some degree of extraction of the fetus prior to its destruction. Because these were late-term abortions, *Casey* generally allowed the prohibition of such procedures. However, *Casey* insisted that even late-term abortion restrictions contain exceptions for maternal life and health.

2. In *Stenberg v. Carhart*, 530 U.S. 914 (2000), a five-justice majority struck down a Nebraska law that sought to prohibit such abortions. Writing for the Court, Justice Breyer, citing the trial court's factual findings, held that the state had failed to prove that the banned procedure was never medically necessary for women's health. Given the uncertainty of that issue, the Court held that the Constitution required such a law to include a health exception. The Court also concluded that the statute was sufficiently vague that it might be understood to prohibit abortion methods for second-trimester, pre-viability abortions, and thus constituted an undue burden on a woman's

right to choose to have a pre-viability abortion. Justices O'Connor and Ginsburg joined the majority opinion and each wrote a separate concurrence, each emphasizing *Casey*'s requirement of a health exception.

The four dissenters (Chief Justice Rehnquist and Justices Scalia, Kennedy, and Thomas) all wrote separate dissents. Chief Justice Rehnquist stated his continued disagreement with *Casey*, but expressed his agreement with the other dissenters who claimed that, properly understood, *Casey* allowed the challenged Nebraska law. Justice Scalia dissented, both to criticize the result as both unwarranted in light of *Casey* and to criticize *Casey* itself and call for its overruling. Justice Kennedy, one of the authors of the joint opinion in *Casey*, also dissented, explaining his view that *Casey* did not divest the state of authority to regulate abortions in the interest of ensuring respect for the medical profession, which he argued was at risk from "partial-birth" abortion procedures. He also argued that there was no evidence that the banned procedure was in fact necessary for the health of women seeking an abortion. Justice Thomas wrote to express his agreement with Justice Scalia that *Casey* should be overruled and also that *Casey* did not mandate the strike-down of the Nebraska law.

3. In 2003, Congress entered the debate, enacting a law similar to Nebraska's, but with two important differences. First, the federal law defined the banned procedure more precisely. Second, it included several findings, including one stating that the banned procedures were never medically necessary. By the time the challenge to the law reached the Supreme Court, two justices had left the Court and been replaced: Chief Justice Rehnquist had died and been replaced by John Roberts, and Justice O'Connor had retired and been replaced by Samuel Alito.

4. The second of these changes proved decisive. In *Gonzalez v. Carhart*, 550 U.S. 124 (2007), a five-justice majority consisting of the *Stenberg* dissenters and Justice Alito upheld the federal law. (Chief Justice Roberts voted to uphold the law, just as his predecessor, Chief Justice Rehnquist, did in *Stenberg*.) Speaking through Justice Kennedy, the Court concluded that the federal law did not suffer from the vagueness of the Nebraska law struck down in *Stenberg*, with its attendant potential for un-constitutionally restricting pre-viability abortion rights. Second, it concluded that Congress's finding about the lack of a medical need for the banned procedure merited judicial deference; thus, there was no need for the law to contain an exception for women's health. Turning to the state's interest in enacting the law, the Court concluded that Congress had a right to be concerned about the larger social effects of allowing a procedure in which a doctor performed an abortion on a fetus that was partially delivered while still alive. Justice Kennedy also noted that Congress had a right to be concerned about the psychological effects such a procedure would have on the woman herself. The Court concluded by observing that, if a particular woman did in fact have a medical need for the banned procedure, she and her doctor could seek a judicial declaration that, as applied to her, the federal law was unconstitutional. Justice Thomas, joined by Justice Scalia, concurred, to again call for *Casey* to be overruled.

5. Justice Ginsburg dissented for four justices. She criticized the majority for adopting what she called "ancient notions about women's place in the family and under the Constitution," citing, among other cases, *Lochner*-era decisions relying on women's supposed frailty to uphold labor laws specifically benefitting women. She also noted that the federal law did not stop any abortions from occurring, but merely shifted the procedures to those that might be riskier for women. She also argued that lower courts considering the federal law had appropriately concluded that Congress's finding about the procedure's lack of medical necessity was incorrect.

# Chapter 10

# Modern Due Process Methodologies

### Note: Due Process Methodologies

The cases in this chapter cover a wide variety of subject-areas where plaintiffs have claimed a due process liberty right to be free of government regulation, ranging from family living arrangements to sexuality to assisted suicide. The point of this chapter is not simply, or even primarily, to provide you with the details of what the Court has said about each of these areas—although it does provide that information. Instead, it focuses on the methodologies the Court has used in the modern era to identify the right at issue, to determine how carefully the Court should scrutinize infringements of that right, and to examine whether the challenged law survives that scrutiny. As you read these cases, consider the strengths and weaknesses of each of the approaches you'll encounter.

With the exception of the note on *Bowers v. Hardwick*, these cases are presented chronologically. This presentation allows you to experience the unsteady evolution of the Court's thinking about these issues, and to examine how the Court has used its earlier precedents when deciding the due process claim in front of it.

### Moore v. City of East Cleveland
### 431 U.S. 494 (1977)

Mr. Justice POWELL announced the judgment of the Court, and delivered an opinion in which Mr. Justice BRENNAN, Mr. Justice MARSHALL, and Mr. Justice BLACKMUN joined.

East Cleveland's housing ordinance, like many throughout the country, limits occupancy of a dwelling unit to members of a single family. But the ordinance contains an unusual and complicated definitional section that recognizes as a "family" only a few categories of related individuals.[2] Because her family, living together in her home,

---

2. Section 1341.08 [of the City's Housing Code] provides:
   "'Family' means a number of individuals related to the nominal head of the household or to the spouse of the nominal head of the household living as a single housekeeping unit in a single dwelling unit, but limited to the following:
   "(a) Husband or wife of the nominal head of the household.
   "(b) Unmarried children of the nominal head of the household or of the spouse of the nominal head of the household, provided, however, that such unmarried children have no children residing with them.
   "(c) Father or mother of the nominal head of the household or of the spouse of the nominal

fits none of those categories, appellant stands convicted of a criminal offense. The question in this case is whether the ordinance violates the Due Process Clause of the Fourteenth Amendment.

Appellant, Mrs. Inez Moore, lives in her East Cleveland home together with her son, Dale Moore Sr., and her two grandsons, Dale, Jr., and John Moore, Jr. The two boys are first cousins rather than brothers; we are told that John came to live with his grandmother and with the elder and younger Dale Moores after his mother's death.

In early 1973, Mrs. Moore received a notice of violation from the city, stating that John was an "illegal occupant" and directing her to comply with the ordinance. When she failed to remove him from her home, the city filed a criminal charge. Mrs. Moore moved to dismiss, claiming that the ordinance was constitutionally invalid on its face. Her motion was overruled, and upon conviction she was sentenced to five days in jail and a $25 fine. The Ohio Court of Appeals affirmed after giving full consideration to her constitutional claims, and the Ohio Supreme Court denied review. We noted probable jurisdiction of her appeal.

The city argues that our decision in *Village of Belle Terre v. Boraas*, 416 U.S. 1 (1974), requires us to sustain the ordinance attacked here. Belle Terre, like East Cleveland, imposed limits on the types of groups that could occupy a single dwelling unit. Applying the constitutional standard announced in this Court's leading land-use case, *Euclid v. Ambler Realty Co.*, 272 U.S. 365 (1926), we sustained the Belle Terre ordinance on the ground that it bore a rational relationship to permissible state objectives.

But one overriding factor sets this case apart from *Belle Terre*. The ordinance there affected only unrelated individuals. It expressly allowed all who were related by "blood, adoption, or marriage" to live together, and in sustaining the ordinance we were careful to note that it promoted "family needs" and "family values." East Cleveland, in contrast, has chosen to regulate the occupancy of its housing by slicing deeply into the family itself. This is no mere incidental result of the ordinance. On its face it selects certain categories of relatives who may live together and declares that others may not. In particular, it makes a crime of a grandmother's choice to live with her grandson in circumstances like those presented here.

When a city undertakes such intrusive regulation of the family, neither *Belle Terre* nor *Euclid* governs; the usual judicial deference to the legislature is inappropriate. "This Court has long recognized that freedom of personal choice in matters of marriage and family life is one of the liberties protected by the Due Process Clause of the Fourteenth Amendment." A host of cases, tracing their lineage to *Meyer v. Nebraska*

---

head of the household.

"(d) Notwithstanding the provisions of subsection (b) hereof, a family may include not more than one dependent married or unmarried child of the nominal head of the household or of the spouse of the nominal head of the household and the spouse and dependent children of such dependent child. For the purpose of this subsection, a dependent person is one who has more than fifty percent of his total support furnished for him by the nominal head of the household and the spouse of the nominal head of the household.

"(e) A family may consist of one individual."

(1923) [*Supra.* Chapter 8], and *Pierce v. Society of Sisters*, 268 U.S. 510 (1925) [Note *supra.* Chapter 8], have consistently acknowledged a "private realm of family life which the state cannot enter." See, e.g., *Roe v. Wade* (1973) [*Supra.* this chapter]; *Poe v. Ullman*, 367 U.S. 497 (1961) (Harlan, J., dissenting) [Note *supra.* Chapter 8]; *Skinner v. Oklahoma*, 316 U.S. 535 (1942) [Note *supra.* Chapter 8] Of course, the family is not beyond regulation. But when the government intrudes on choices concerning family living arrangements, this Court must examine carefully the importance of the governmental interests advanced and the extent to which they are served by the challenged regulation. See *Poe* (Harlan, J., dissenting).

When thus examined, this ordinance cannot survive. The city seeks to justify it as a means of preventing overcrowding, minimizing traffic and parking congestion, and avoiding an undue financial burden on East Cleveland's school system. Although these are legitimate goals, the ordinance before us serves them marginally, at best. For example, the ordinance permits any family consisting only of husband, wife, and unmarried children to live together, even if the family contains a half dozen licensed drivers, each with his or her own car. At the same time it forbids an adult brother and sister to share a household, even if both faithfully use public transportation. The ordinance would permit a grandmother to live with a single dependent son and children, even if his school-age children number a dozen, yet it forces Mrs. Moore to find another dwelling for her grandson John, simply because of the presence of his uncle and cousin in the same household. We need not labor the point. Section 1341.08 has but a tenuous relation to alleviation of the conditions mentioned by the city.

## III.

The city would distinguish the cases based on *Meyer* and *Pierce*. It points out that none of them "gives grandmothers any fundamental rights with respect to grandsons," Brief for Appellee 18, and suggests that any constitutional right to live together as a family extends only to the nuclear family — essentially a couple and their dependent children.

To be sure, these cases did not expressly consider the family relationship presented here. They were immediately concerned with freedom of choice with respect to child-bearing, e.g., *Roe, Griswold v. Connecticut* (1965) [*Supra.* Chapter 9], or with the rights of parents to the custody and companionship of their own children, or with traditional parental authority in matters of child rearing and education. *Pierce, Meyer.* But unless we close our eyes to the basic reasons why certain rights associated with the family have been accorded shelter under the Fourteenth Amendment's Due Process Clause, we cannot avoid applying the force and rationale of these precedents to the family choice involved in this case.

Understanding those reasons requires careful attention to this Court's function under the Due Process Clause. Mr. Justice Harlan described it eloquently:

"Due process has not been reduced to any formula; its content cannot be determined by reference to any code. The best that can be said is that through the course of this Court's decisions it has represented the balance which our

Nation, built upon postulates of respect for the liberty of the individual, has struck between that liberty and the demands of organized society. If the supplying of content to this Constitutional concept has of necessity been a rational process, it certainly has not been one where judges have felt free to roam where unguided speculation might take them. The balance of which I speak is the balance struck by this country, having regard to what history teaches are the traditions from which it developed as well as the traditions from which it broke. That tradition is a living thing. A decision of this Court which radically departs from it could not long survive, while a decision which builds on what has survived is likely to be sound.[8] No formula could serve as a substitute, in this area, for judgment and restraint.

"... The full scope of the liberty guaranteed by the Due Process Clause cannot be found in or limited by the precise terms of the specific guarantees elsewhere provided in the Constitution. This 'liberty' is not a series of isolated points pricked out in terms of the taking of property; the freedom of speech, press, and religion; the right to keep and bear arms; the freedom from unreasonable searches and seizures; and so on. It is a rational continuum which, broadly speaking, includes a freedom from all substantial arbitrary impositions and purposeless restraints, ... and which also recognizes, what a reasonable and sensitive judgment must, that certain interests require particularly careful scrutiny of the state needs asserted to justify their abridgment." *Poe* (dissenting opinion).

Substantive due process has at times been a treacherous field for this Court. There *are* risks when the judicial branch gives enhanced protection to certain substantive liberties without the guidance of the more specific provisions of the Bill of Rights. As the history of the *Lochner* era demonstrates, there is reason for concern lest the only limits to such judicial intervention become the predilections of those who happen at the time to be Members of this Court. That history counsels caution and restraint. But it does not counsel abandonment, nor does it require what the city urges here: cutting off any protection of family rights at the first convenient, if arbitrary boundary the boundary of the nuclear family.

Appropriate limits on substantive due process come not from drawing arbitrary lines but rather from careful "respect for the teachings of history [and] solid recognition of the basic values that underlie our society".[10] *Griswold* (Harlan, J., concurring).

---

8. This explains why Meyer and Pierce have survived and enjoyed frequent reaffirmance, while other substantive due process cases of the same era have been repudiated including a number written, as were *Meyer* and *Pierce*, by Mr. Justice McReynolds. [Ed. note: This footnote appears in bracketed form in the *Moore* opinion.]

10. A similar restraint marks our approach to the questions whether an asserted substantive right is entitled to heightened solicitude under the Equal Protection Clause because it is "explicitly or implicitly guaranteed by the Constitution," and whether or to what extent a guarantee in the Bill of Rights should be "incorporated" in the Due Process Clause because it is "necessary to an Anglo-American regime of ordered liberty."

See generally *Lochner v. New York* (Holmes, J., dissenting) [*Supra*. Chapter 7]. Our decisions establish that the Constitution protects the sanctity of the family precisely because the institution of the family is deeply rooted in this Nation's history and tradition. It is through the family that we inculcate and pass down many of our most cherished values, moral and cultural.

Ours is by no means a tradition limited to respect for the bonds uniting the members of the nuclear family. The tradition of uncles, aunts, cousins, and especially grandparents sharing a household along with parents and children has roots equally venerable and equally deserving of constitutional recognition.[14] Over the years millions of our citizens have grown up in just such an environment, and most, surely, have profited from it. Even if conditions of modern society have brought about a decline in extended family households, they have not erased the accumulated wisdom of civilization, gained over the centuries and honored throughout our history, that supports a larger conception of the family. Out of choice, necessity, or a sense of family responsibility, it has been common for close relatives to draw together and participate in the duties and the satisfactions of a common home. Decisions concerning child rearing, which ... *Meyer, Pierce* and other cases have recognized as entitled to constitutional protection, long have been shared with grandparents or other relatives who occupy the same household indeed who may take on major responsibility for the rearing of the children. Especially in times of adversity, such as the death of a spouse or economic need, the broader family has tended to come together for mutual sustenance and to maintain or rebuild a secure home life....

Whether or not such a household is established because of personal tragedy, the choice of relatives in this degree of kinship to live together may not lightly be denied by the State. *Pierce* struck down an Oregon law requiring all children to attend the State's public schools, holding that the Constitution "excludes any general power of the State to standardize its children by forcing them to accept instruction from public teachers only." By the same token the Constitution prevents East Cleveland from standardizing its children—and its adults—by forcing all to live in certain narrowly defined family patterns.

Mr. Justice BRENNAN, with whom Mr. Justice MARSHALL joins, concurring.

I join the plurality's opinion. I agree that the Constitution is not powerless to prevent East Cleveland from prosecuting as a criminal and jailing a 63-year-old grandmother for refusing to expel from her home her now 10-year-old grandson who has lived with her and been brought up by her since his mother's death when he was less than a year old. I do not question that a municipality may constitutionally zone to

---

14. See generally B. Yorburg, The Changing Family (1973); Bronfenbrenner, The Calamitous Decline of the American Family, Washington Post, Jan. 2, 1977, p. C1. Recent census reports bear out the importance of family patterns other than the prototypical nuclear family. In 1970, 26.5% of all families contained one or more members over 18 years of age, other than the head of household and spouse. U.S. Department of Commerce, 1970 Census of Population, vol. 1, pt. 1, Table 208. In 1960 the comparable figure was 26.1%. U.S. Department of Commerce, 1960 Census of Population, vol. 1, pt. 1, Table 187. Earlier data are not available.

alleviate noise and traffic congestion and to prevent overcrowded and unsafe living conditions, in short to enact reasonable land-use restrictions in furtherance of the legitimate objectives East Cleveland claims for its ordinance. But the zoning power is not a license for local communities to enact senseless and arbitrary restrictions which cut deeply into private areas of protected family life. East Cleveland may not constitutionally define "family" as essentially confined to parents and the parents' own children. The plurality's opinion conclusively demonstrates that classifying family patterns in this eccentric way is not a rational means of achieving the ends East Cleveland claims for its ordinance, and further that the ordinance unconstitutionally abridges the "freedom of personal choice in matters of ... family life [that] is one of the liberties protected by the Due Process Clause of the Fourteenth Amendment." I write only to underscore the cultural myopia of the arbitrary boundary drawn by the East Cleveland ordinance in the light of the tradition of the American home that has been a feature of our society since our beginning as a Nation—the "tradition" in the plurality's words, "of uncles, aunts, cousins, and especially grandparents sharing a household along with parents and children...." The line drawn by this ordinance displays a depressing insensitivity toward the economic and emotional needs of a very large part of our society.

In today's America, the "nuclear family" is the pattern so often found in much of white suburbia. J. Vander Zanden, *Sociology: A Systematic Approach* 322 (3d ed. 1975). The Constitution cannot be interpreted, however, to tolerate the imposition by government upon the rest of us of white suburbia's preference in patterns of family living. The "extended family" that provided generations of early Americans with social services and economic and emotional support in times of hardship, and was the beachhead for successive waves of immigrants who populated our cities, remains not merely still a pervasive living pattern, but under the goad of brutal economic necessity, a prominent pattern—virtually a means of survival—for large numbers of the poor and deprived minorities of our society. For them compelled pooling of scant resources requires compelled sharing of a household.

The "extended" form is especially familiar among black families.... I do not wish to be understood as implying that East Cleveland's enforcement of its ordinance is motivated by a racially discriminatory purpose. The record of this case would not support that implication. But the prominence of other than nuclear families among ethnic and racial minority groups, including our black citizens, surely demonstrates that the "extended family" pattern remains a vital tenet of our society. It suffices that in prohibiting this pattern of family living as a means of achieving its objectives, appellee city has chosen a device that deeply intrudes into family associational rights that historically have been central, and today remain central, to a large proportion of our population....

Mr. Justice STEVENS, concurring in the judgment.

In my judgment the critical question presented by this case is whether East Cleveland's housing ordinance is a permissible restriction on appellant's right to use her own property as she sees fit....

There appears to be no precedent for an ordinance which excludes any of an owner's relatives from the group of persons who may occupy his residence on a permanent basis. Nor does there appear to be any justification for such a restriction on an owner's use of his property. The city has failed totally to explain the need for a rule which would allow a homeowner to have two grandchildren live with her if they are brothers, but not if they are cousins. Since this ordinance has not been shown to have any "substantial relation to the public health, safety, morals, or general welfare" of the city of East Cleveland, and since it cuts so deeply into a fundamental right normally associated with the ownership of residential property—that of an owner to decide who may reside on his or her property—it must fall under the limited standard of review of zoning decisions which this Court preserved in *Euclid* ... Under that standard, East Cleveland's unprecedented ordinance constitutes a taking of property without due process and without just compensation....

Mr. Chief Justice BURGER, dissenting. [omitted]

Mr. Justice STEWART, with whom Mr. Justice REHNQUIST joins, dissenting.

... In my view, the appellant's claim that the ordinance in question invades constitutionally protected rights of association and privacy is in large part answered by the *Belle Terre* decision. The argument was made there that a municipality could not zone its land exclusively for single-family occupancy because to do so would interfere with protected rights of privacy or association. We rejected this contention, and held that the ordinance at issue "involved no 'fundamental' right guaranteed by the Constitution, such as ... the right of association ... or any rights of privacy, cf. *Griswold*; *Eisenstadt v. Baird*, 405 U.S. 438 (1972) [Note *supra*. Chapter 9]....

To be sure, the ordinance involved in *Belle Terre* did not prevent blood relatives from occupying the same dwelling, and the Court's decision in that case does not, therefore, foreclose the appellant's arguments based specifically on the ties of kinship present in this case. Nonetheless, I would hold, for the reasons that follow, that the existence of those ties does not elevate either the appellant's claim of associational freedom or her claim of privacy to a level invoking constitutional protection.

To suggest that the biological fact of common ancestry necessarily gives related persons constitutional rights of association superior to those of unrelated persons is to misunderstand the nature of the associational freedoms that the Constitution has been understood to protect. Freedom of association has been constitutionally recognized because it is often indispensable to effectuation of explicit First Amendment guarantees....

The "association" in this case is not for any purpose relating to the promotion of speech, assembly, the press, or religion. And wherever the outer boundaries of constitutional protection of freedom of association may eventually turn out to be, they surely do not extend to those who assert no interest other than the gratification, convenience, and economy of sharing the same residence.

The appellant is considerably closer to the constitutional mark in asserting that the East Cleveland ordinance intrudes upon "the private realm of family life which the state cannot enter." Several decisions of the Court have identified specific aspects of what might broadly be termed "private family life" that are constitutionally protected against state interference. See, e.g., *Roe* (woman's right whether to terminate pregnancy); *Loving v. Virginia* (1967) (freedom to marry person of another race); *Griswold* (right to use contraceptives); *Pierce* (parents' right to send children to private schools); *Meyer* (parents' right to have children instructed in foreign language).

Although the appellant's desire to share a single-dwelling unit also involves "private family life" in a sense, that desire can hardly be equated with any of the interests protected in the cases just cited. The ordinance about which the appellant complains did not impede her choice to have or not to have children, and it did not dictate to her how her own children were to be nurtured and reared. The ordinance clearly does not prevent parents from living together or living with their unemancipated offspring.

But even though the Court's previous cases are not directly in point, the appellant contends that the importance of the "extended family" in American society requires us to hold that her decision to share her residence with her grandsons may not be interfered with by the State. This decision, like the decisions involved in bearing and raising children, is said to be an aspect of "family life" also entitled to substantive protection under the Constitution. Without pausing to inquire how far under this argument an "extended family" might extend, I cannot agree.[7] When the Court has found that the Fourteenth Amendment placed a substantive limitation on a State's power to regulate, it has been in those rare cases in which the personal interests at issue have been deemed " 'implicit in the concept of ordered liberty.' " See *Roe*, quoting *Palko v. Connecticut* (1937) [*Supra.* Chapter 8]. The interest that the appellant may have in permanently sharing a single kitchen and a suite of contiguous rooms with some of her relatives simply does not rise to that level. To equate this interest with the fundamental decisions to marry and to bear and raise children is to extend the limited substantive contours of the Due Process Clause beyond recognition....

Mr. Justice WHITE, dissenting....

I

The emphasis of the Due Process Clause is on "process." As Mr. Justice Harlan once observed, it has been "ably and insistently argued in response to what were felt to be abuses by this Court of its reviewing power," that the Due Process Clause should be limited "to a guarantee of procedural fairness." *Poe* (dissenting opinion). These arguments had seemed "persuasive" to Justices Brandeis and Holmes, *Whitney v. California*, 274 U.S. 357 (1927), but they recognized that the Due Process Clause, by virtue of case-to-case "judicial inclusion and exclusion," had been construed to pro-

---

7. The opinion of Mr. Justice POWELL and Mr. Justice BRENNAN's concurring opinion both emphasize the traditional importance of the extended family in American life. But I fail to understand why it follows that the residents of East Cleveland are constitutionally prevented from following what Mr. Justice BRENNAN calls the "pattern" of "white suburbia," even though that choice may reflect "cultural myopia." In point of fact, East Cleveland is a predominantly Negro community, with a Negro City Manager and City Commission.

scribe matters of substance, as well as inadequate procedures, and to protect from invasion by the States "all fundamental rights comprised within the term liberty."

Mr. Justice Black also recognized that the Fourteenth Amendment had substantive as well as procedural content. But believing that its reach should not extend beyond the specific provisions of the Bill of Rights, see *Adamson v. California* (1947) [*Supra.* Chapter 8] (dissenting opinion), he never embraced the idea that the Due Process Clause empowered the courts to strike down merely unreasonable or arbitrary legislation, nor did he accept Mr. Justice Harlan's consistent view. Writing at length in dissent in *Poe*, Mr. Justice Harlan stated the essence of his position as follows:

> This "liberty" is not a series of isolated points pricked out in terms of the taking of property; the freedom of speech, press, and religion, the right to keep and bear arms, the freedom from unreasonable searches and seizures; and so on. It is a rational continuum which, broadly speaking, includes a freedom from all substantial arbitrary impositions and purposeless restraints, and which also recognizes, what a reasonable and sensitive judgment must, that certain interests require particularly careful scrutiny of the state needs asserted to justify their abridgment.

This construction was far too open ended for Mr. Justice Black. For him, *Meyer* and *Pierce*, as substantive due process cases, were as suspect as *Lochner*. In his view, *Ferguson v. Skrupa* (1963) [*Supra.* Chapter 7], should have finally disposed of them all. But neither *Meyer* nor *Pierce* has been overruled, and recently there have been decisions of the same genre — *Roe v. Wade*; *Loving v. Virginia*; *Griswold v. Connecticut*; and *Eisenstadt v. Baird*. Not all of these decisions purport to rest on substantive due process grounds, compare *Roe* with *Eisenstadt*, but all represented substantial reinterpretations of the Constitution.

Although the Court regularly proceeds on the assumption that the Due Process Clause has more than a procedural dimension, we must always bear in mind that the substantive content of the Clause is suggested neither by its language nor by preconstitutional history; that content is nothing more than the accumulated product of judicial interpretation of the Fifth and Fourteenth Amendments. This is not to suggest, at this point, that any of these cases should be overruled, or that the process by which they were decided was illegitimate, or even unacceptable, but only to underline Mr. Justice Black's constant reminder to his colleagues that the Court has no license to invalidate legislation which it thinks merely arbitrary or unreasonable. And no one was more sensitive than Mr. Justice Harlan to any suggestion that his approach to the Due Process Clause would lead to judges "roaming at large in the constitutional field." *Griswold* (concurring opinion). No one proceeded with more caution than he did when the validity of state or federal legislation was challenged in the name of the Due Process Clause.

This is surely the preferred approach. That the Court has ample precedent for the creation of new constitutional rights should not lead it to repeat the process at will. The Judiciary, including this Court is the most vulnerable and comes nearest to illegitimacy when it deals with judge-made constitutional law having little or no cognizable roots in the language or even the design of the Constitution. Realizing that the present construction of the Due Process Clause represents a major judicial gloss on its terms, as well as on the anticipation of the Framers, and that much of the underpinning for the broad, substantive application of the Clause disappeared in the conflict between the Executive and the Judiciary in the 1930's and 1940's, the Court should be extremely reluctant to breathe still further substantive content into the Due Process Clause so as to strike down legislation adopted by a State or city to promote its welfare. Whenever the Judiciary does so, it unavoidably pre-empts for itself another part of the governance of the country without express constitutional authority.

## II

Accepting the cases as they are and the Due Process Clause as construed by them, however, I think it evident that the threshold question in any due process attack on legislation, whether the challenge is procedural or substantive, is whether there is a deprivation of life, liberty, or property. With respect to "liberty," the statement of Mr. Justice Harlan in *Poe*, quoted *supra.*, most accurately reflects the thrust of prior decisions—that the Due Process Clause is triggered by a variety of interests, some much more important than others. These interests have included a wide range of freedoms in the purely commercial area such as the freedom to contract and the right to set one's own prices and wages. *Meyer* took a characteristically broad view of "liberty":

> While this Court has not attempted to define with exactness the liberty thus guaranteed, the term has received much consideration and some of the included things have been definitely stated. Without doubt, it denotes not merely freedom from bodily restraint but also the right of the individual to contract, to engage in any of the common occupations of life, to acquire useful knowledge, to marry, establish a home and bring up children, to worship God according to the dictates of his own conscience, and generally to enjoy those privileges long recognized at common law as essential to the orderly pursuit of happiness by free men.

As I have said, *Meyer* has not been overruled nor its definition of liberty rejected. The results reached in some of the cases cited by *Meyer* have been discarded or undermined by later cases, but those cases did not cut back the definition of liberty espoused by earlier decisions. They disagreed only, but sharply, as to the protection that was "due" the particular liberty interests involved. See, for example, *West Coast Hotel v. Parrish* (1937) [*Supra.* Chapter 7].

Just a few years ago, we recognized that while "the range of interests protected by procedural due process is not infinite," ... the term "liberty" has been given broad meaning in our cases....

It would not be consistent with prior cases to restrict the liberties protected by the Due Process Clause to those fundamental interests "implicit in the concept of ordered liberty." *Palko*, from which this much-quoted phrase is taken, is not to the contrary. *Palko* was a criminal case, and the issue was thus not whether a protected liberty interest was at stake but what protective process was "due" that interest.... Nor do I think the broader view of "liberty" is inconsistent with or foreclosed by the dicta in *Roe*, [which] at most asserts that only fundamental liberties will be given *substantive* protection, and ... may be understood as merely identifying certain fundamental interests that the Court has deemed deserving of a heightened degree of protection under the Due Process Clause.

It seems to me that Mr. Justice Douglas was closest to the mark in *Poe*, when he said that the trouble with the holdings of the "old Court" was not in its definition of liberty but in its definition of the protections guaranteed to that liberty — "not in entertaining inquiries concerning the constitutionality of social legislation but in applying the standards that it did."

The term "liberty" is not, therefore, to be given a crabbed construction. I have no more difficulty than Mr. Justice POWELL apparently does in concluding that appellant in this case properly asserts a liberty interest within the meaning of the Due Process Clause. The question is not one of liberty *vel non*. Rather, there being no procedural issue at stake, the issue is whether the precise interest involved — the interest in having more than one set of grandchildren live in her home — is entitled to such substantive protection under the Due Process Clause that this ordinance must be held invalid.

### III

Looking at the doctrine of "substantive" due process as having to do with the possible invalidity of an official rule of conduct rather than of the procedures for enforcing that rule, I see the doctrine as taking several forms under the cases, each differing in the severity of review and the degree of protection offered to the individual. First, a court may merely assure itself that there is in fact a duly enacted law which proscribes the conduct sought to be prevented or sanctioned. In criminal cases, this approach is exemplified by the refusal of courts to enforce vague statutes that no reasonable person could understand as forbidding the challenged conduct. There is no such problem here.

Second is the general principle that "liberty may not be interfered with, under the guise of protecting the public interest, by legislative action which is arbitrary or without reasonable relation to some purpose within the competency of the State." This means-end test appears to require that any statute restrictive of liberty have an ascertainable purpose and represent a rational means to achieve that purpose, whatever the nature of the liberty interest involved. This approach was part of the substantive due process doctrine prevalent earlier in the century, and it made serious inroads on the presumption of constitutionality supposedly accorded to state and federal legislation. But with *Nebbia v. New York* (1934) [*Supra.* Chapter 7], and other cases of the 1930's and 1940's such as *West Coast Hotel*, the courts came to demand far less from and to accord far more deference to legislative judgments. This was particularly true with respect to legislation seeking to control or regulate the economic life of the State or Nation. Even so, "while the legislative judgment on economic and business matters is 'well-nigh conclusive'..., it is not beyond judicial inquiry." *Poe* (Douglas, J., dissenting). No case that I know of, including *Ferguson v. Skrupa*, has announced that there is some legislation with respect to which there no longer exists a means-ends test as a matter of substantive due process law. This is not surprising, for otherwise a protected liberty could be infringed by a law having no purpose or utility whatsoever. Of course, the current approach is to deal more gingerly with a state statute and to insist that the challenger bear the burden of demonstrating its unconstitutionality; and there is a broad category of cases in which substantive review is indeed mild and very similar to the original thought of *Munn v. Illinois* (1877) [*Supra.* Chapter 7], that "if a state of facts could exist that would justify such legislation," it passes its initial test.

There are various "liberties," however, which require that infringing legislation be given closer judicial scrutiny, not only with respect to existence of a purpose and the means employed, but also with respect to the importance of the purpose itself relative to the invaded interest. Some interests would appear almost impregnable to invasion, such as the freedoms of speech, press, and religion, and the freedom from cruel and unusual punishments. Other interests, for example, the right of association, the right to vote, and various claims sometimes referred to under the general rubric of the right to privacy, also weigh very heavily against state claims of authority to regulate. It is this category of interests which, as I understand it, Mr. Justice STEWART refers to as "'implicit in the concept of ordered liberty.'" Because he would confine the reach of substantive due process protection to interests such as these and because he would not classify in this category the asserted right to share a house with the relatives involved here, he rejects the due process claim.

Given his premise, he is surely correct. Under our cases, the Due Process Clause extends substantial protection to various phases of family life, but none requires that the claim made here be sustained. I cannot believe that the interest in residing with more than one set of grandchildren is one that calls for any kind of heightened protection under the Due Process Clause. To say that one has a personal right to live with all, rather than some, of one's grandchildren and that this right is implicit in ordered liberty is, as my Brother STEWART says, "to extend the limited substantive contours of the Due Process Clause beyond recognition." The present claim is hardly one of which it could be said that "neither liberty nor justice would exist if (it) were sacrificed." *Palko*.

Mr. Justice POWELL would apparently construe the Due Process Clause to protect from all but quite important state regulatory interests any right or privilege that in his estimate is deeply rooted in the country's traditions. For me, this suggests a far too expansive charter for this Court and a far less meaningful and less confining guiding principle than Mr. Justice STEWART would use for serious substantive due process review. What the deeply rooted traditions of the country are is arguable; which of them deserve the protection of the Due Process Clause is even more debatable. The suggested view would broaden enormously the horizons of the Clause; and, if the interest involved here is any measure of what the States would be forbidden to regulate, the courts would be substantively weighing and very likely invalidating a wide range of measures that Congress and state legislatures think appropriate to respond to a changing economic and social order.

Mrs. Moore's interest in having the offspring of more than one dependent son live with her qualifies as a liberty protected by the Due Process Clause; but, because of the nature of that particular interest, the demands of the Clause are satisfied once the Court is assured that the challenged proscription is the product of a duly enacted or promulgated statute, ordinance, or regulation and that it is not wholly lacking in purpose or utility....

# Michael H. v. Gerald D.
## 491 U.S. 110 (1989)

Justice SCALIA announced the judgment of the Court and delivered an opinion, in which THE CHIEF JUSTICE joins, and in all but footnote 6 of which Justice O'CONNOR and Justice KENNEDY join.

Under California law, a child born to a married woman living with her husband is presumed to be a child of the marriage. Cal.Evid.Code Ann. §621. The presumption of legitimacy may be rebutted only by the husband or wife, and then only in limited circumstances. *Ibid.* The instant appeal presents the claim that this presumption infringes upon the due process rights of a man who wishes to establish his paternity of a child born to the wife of another man, and the claim that it infringes upon the constitutional right of the child to maintain a relationship with her natural father.

I

The facts of this case are, we must hope, extraordinary. On May 9, 1976, in Las Vegas, Nevada, Carole D., an international model, and Gerald D., a top executive in a French oil company, were married. The couple established a home in Playa del Rey, California, in which they resided as husband and wife when one or the other was not out of the country on business. In the summer of 1978, Carole became involved in an adulterous affair with a neighbor, Michael H. In September 1980, she conceived a child, Victoria D., who was born on May 11, 1981. Gerald was listed as father on the birth certificate and has always held Victoria out to the world as his daughter. Soon after delivery of the child, however, Carole informed Michael that she believed he might be the father.

In the first three years of her life, Victoria remained always with Carole, but found herself within a variety of quasi-family units. In October 1981, Gerald moved to New York City to pursue his business interests, but Carole chose to remain in California. At the end of that month, Carole and Michael had blood tests of themselves and Victoria, which showed a 98.07% probability that Michael was Victoria's father. In January 1982, Carole visited Michael in St. Thomas, where his primary business interests were based. There Michael held Victoria out as his child. In March, however, Carole left Michael and returned to California, where she took up residence with yet another man, Scott K. Later that spring, and again in the summer, Carole and Victoria spent time with Gerald in New York City, as well as on vacation in Europe. In the fall, they returned to Scott in California.

In November 1982, rebuffed in his attempts to visit Victoria, Michael filed a filiation action in California Superior Court to establish his paternity and right to visitation. In March 1983, the court appointed an attorney and guardian ad litem to represent Victoria's interests. Victoria then filed a cross-complaint asserting that if she had more than one psychological or *de facto* father, she was entitled to maintain her filial relationship, with all of the attendant rights, duties, and obligations, with both. In May 1983, Carole filed a motion for summary judgment. During this period, from March through July 1983, Carole was again living with Gerald in New York. In August, however, she returned to California, became involved once again with Michael, and instructed her attorneys to remove the summary judgment motion from the calendar.

For the ensuing eight months, when Michael was not in St. Thomas he lived with Carole and Victoria in Carole's apartment in Los Angeles and held Victoria out as his daughter. In April 1984, Carole and Michael signed a stipulation that Michael was Victoria's natural father. Carole left Michael the next month, however, and instructed her attorneys not to file the stipulation. In June 1984, Carole reconciled with Gerald and joined him in New York, where they now live with Victoria and two other children since born into the marriage.

In May 1984, Michael and Victoria, through her guardian ad litem, sought visitation rights for Michael *pendente lite.* To assist in determining whether visitation would be in Victoria's best interests, the Superior Court appointed a psychologist to evaluate Victoria, Gerald, Michael, and Carole. The psychologist recommended that Carole retain sole custody, but that Michael be allowed continued contact with Victoria pursuant to a restricted visitation schedule. The court concurred and ordered that Michael be provided with limited visitation privileges *pendente lite.*

On October 19, 1984, Gerald, who had intervened in the action, moved for summary judgment on the ground that under Cal.Evid.Code §621 there were no triable issues of fact as to Victoria's paternity. This law provides that "the issue of a wife cohabiting with her husband, who is not impotent or sterile, is conclusively presumed to be a child of the marriage." Cal.Evid.Code Ann. §621(a). The presumption may be rebutted by blood tests, but only if a motion for such tests is made, within two years from the date of the child's birth, either by the husband or, if the natural father has filed an affidavit acknowledging paternity, by the wife.

On January 28, 1985, having found that affidavits submitted by Carole and Gerald sufficed to demonstrate that the two were cohabiting at conception and birth and that Gerald was neither sterile nor impotent, the Superior Court granted Gerald's motion for summary judgment, rejecting Michael's and Victoria's challenges to the constitutionality of §621....

On appeal, Michael asserted, *inter alia,* that the Superior Court's application of §621 had violated his procedural and substantive due process rights.... After submission of briefs and a hearing, the California Court of Appeal affirmed the judgment of the Superior Court and upheld the constitutionality of the statute....

The Court of Appeal denied Michael's and Victoria's petitions for rehearing, and, on July 30, 1987, the California Supreme Court denied discretionary review. On February 29, 1988, we noted probable jurisdiction of the present appeal. Before us, Michael and Victoria both raise equal protection and due process challenges. We do not reach Michael's equal protection claim, however, as it was neither raised nor passed upon below.

## II

The California statute that is the subject of this litigation is, in substance, more than a century old. California Code of Civ.Proc. § 1962(5), enacted in 1872, provided that "the issue of a wife cohabiting with her husband, who is not impotent, is indisputably presumed to be legitimate." ... In 1980, the legislature ... amended the statute to provide the husband an opportunity to introduce blood-test evidence in rebuttal of the presumption, and in 1981 amended it to provide the mother such an opportunity....

## III

... At the outset, it is necessary to clarify what [Michael] sought and what he was denied. California law, like nature itself, makes no provision for dual fatherhood. Michael was seeking to be declared *the* father of Victoria. The immediate benefit he evidently sought to obtain from that status was visitation rights. But if Michael were successful in being declared the father, other rights would follow — most importantly, the right to be considered as the parent who should have custody, a status which "embraces the sum of parental rights with respect to the rearing of a child"....

Michael raises two related challenges to the constitutionality of § 621. First, he asserts that requirements of procedural due process prevent the State from terminating his liberty interest in his relationship with his child without affording him an opportunity to demonstrate his paternity in an evidentiary hearing. We believe this claim derives from a fundamental misconception of the nature of the California statute. While § 621 is phrased in terms of a presumption, that rule of evidence is the implementation of a substantive rule of law. California declares it to be, except in limited circumstances, *irrelevant* for paternity purposes whether a child conceived during, and born into, an existing marriage was begotten by someone other than the husband and had a prior relationship with him.... We therefore reject Michael's procedural due process challenge and proceed to his substantive claim.

Michael contends as a matter of substantive due process that, because he has established a parental relationship with Victoria, protection of Gerald's and Carole's marital union is an insufficient state interest to support termination of that relationship. This argument is, of course, predicated on the assertion that Michael has a constitutionally protected liberty interest in his relationship with Victoria.

It is an established part of our constitutional jurisprudence that the term "liberty" in the Due Process Clause extends beyond freedom from physical restraint. See, *e.g., Pierce v. Society of Sisters*, 268 U.S. 510 (1925) [Note *supra.* Chapter 8]; *Meyer v. Ne-*

*braska* (1923) [*Supra.* Chapter 8]. Without that core textual meaning as a limitation, defining the scope of the Due Process Clause "has at times been a treacherous field for this Court," giving "reason for concern lest the only limits to ... judicial intervention become the predilections of those who happen at the time to be Members of this Court." *Moore v. East Cleveland* (1977) [*Supra.* this chapter]. The need for restraint has been cogently expressed by Justice WHITE:

> "That the Court has ample precedent for the creation of new constitutional rights should not lead it to repeat the process at will. The Judiciary, including this Court, is the most vulnerable and comes nearest to illegitimacy when it deals with judge-made constitutional law having little or no cognizable roots in the language or even the design of the Constitution. Realizing that the present construction of the Due Process Clause represents a major judicial gloss on its terms, as well as on the anticipation of the Framers..., the Court should be extremely reluctant to breathe still further substantive content into the Due Process Clause so as to strike down legislation adopted by a State or city to promote its welfare. Whenever the Judiciary does so, it unavoidably pre-empts for itself another part of the governance of the country without express constitutional authority." *Moore* (dissenting opinion).

In an attempt to limit and guide interpretation of the Clause, we have insisted not merely that the interest denominated as a "liberty" be "fundamental" (a concept that, in isolation, is hard to objectify), but also that it be an interest traditionally protected by our society. As we have put it, the Due Process Clause affords only those protections "so rooted in the traditions and conscience of our people as to be ranked as fundamental." *Snyder v. Massachusetts*, 291 U.S. 97 (1934) (Cardozo, J.). Our cases reflect "continual insistence upon respect for the teachings of history [and] solid recognition of the basic values that underlie our society...." *Griswold v. Connecticut* (1965) (Harlan, J., concurring in judgment) [*Supra.* Chapter 9].

This insistence that the asserted liberty interest be rooted in history and tradition is evident, as elsewhere, in our cases according constitutional protection to certain parental rights. Michael reads the landmark case of *Stanley v. Illinois*, 405 U.S. 645 (1972), and the subsequent cases of *Quilloin v. Walcott*, 434 U.S. 246 (1978), *Caban v. Mohammed*, 441 U.S. 380 (1979), and *Lehr v. Robertson*, 463 U.S. 248 (1983), as establishing that a liberty interest is created by biological fatherhood plus an established parental relationship—factors that exist in the present case as well. We think that distorts the rationale of those cases. As we view them, they rest not upon such isolated factors but upon the historic respect—indeed, sanctity would not be too strong a term—traditionally accorded to the relationships that develop within the unitary family. In *Stanley,* for example, we forbade the destruction of such a family when, upon the death of the mother, the State had sought to remove children from the custody of a father who had lived with and supported them and their mother for 18 years. As Justice Powell stated for the plurality in *Moore v. East Cleveland:* "Our decisions establish that the Constitution protects the sanctity of the family precisely because the institution of the family is deeply rooted in this Nation's history and tradition."

Thus, the legal issue in the present case reduces to whether the relationship between persons in the situation of Michael and Victoria has been treated as a protected family unit under the historic practices of our society, or whether on any other basis it has been accorded special protection. We think it impossible to find that it has. In fact, quite to the contrary, our traditions have protected the marital family (Gerald, Carole, and the child they acknowledge to be theirs) against the sort of claim Michael asserts.

The presumption of legitimacy was a fundamental principle of the common law. H. Nicholas, *Adulturine Bastardy* 1 (1836). Traditionally, that presumption could be rebutted only by proof that a husband was incapable of procreation or had had no access to his wife during the relevant period. *Id.* (citing Bracton, *De Legibus et Consuetudinibus Angliae* (1569)). As explained by Blackstone, nonaccess could only be proved "if the husband be out of the kingdom of England (or, as the law somewhat loosely phrases it, *extra quatuor maria* [beyond the four seas]) for above nine months...." 1 *Blackstone's Commentaries* 456 (J. Chitty ed. 1826). And, under the common law both in England and here, "neither husband nor wife [could] be a witness to prove access or nonaccess." J. Schouler, *Law of the Domestic Relations* § 225 (3d ed. 1882). The primary policy rationale underlying the common law's severe restrictions on rebuttal of the presumption appears to have been an aversion to declaring children illegitimate, thereby depriving them of rights of inheritance and succession, 2 J. Kent, *Commentaries on American Law* *175, and likely making them wards of the state. A secondary policy concern was the interest in promoting the "peace and tranquillity of States and families," a goal that is obviously impaired by facilitating suits against husband and wife asserting that their children are illegitimate. Even though, as bastardy laws became less harsh, "judges in both [England and the United States] gradually widened the acceptable range of evidence that could be offered by spouses, and placed restraints on the 'four seas rule'... [,] the law retained a strong bias against ruling the children of married women illegitimate."

We have found nothing in the older sources, nor in the older cases, addressing specifically the power of the natural father to assert parental rights over a child born into a woman's existing marriage with another man. Since it is Michael's burden to establish that such a power (at least where the natural father has established a relationship with the child) is so deeply embedded within our traditions as to be a fundamental right, the lack of evidence alone might defeat his case. But the evidence shows that even in modern times—when, as we have noted, the rigid protection of the marital family has in other respects been relaxed—the ability of a person in Michael's position to claim paternity has not been generally acknowledged. For example, a 1957 annotation on the subject: "Who may dispute presumption of legitimacy of child conceived or born during wedlock," 53 A.L.R.2d 572, shows three States (including California) with statutes limiting standing to the husband or wife and their descendants, one State (Louisiana) with a statute limiting it to the husband, two States (Florida and Texas) with judicial decisions limiting standing to the husband,

and two States (Illinois and New York) with judicial decisions denying standing even to the mother. Not a single decision is set forth specifically according standing to the natural father, and "express indications of the nonexistence of any ... limitation" upon standing were found only "in a few jurisdictions."

Moreover, even if it were clear that one in Michael's position generally possesses, and has generally always possessed, standing to challenge the marital child's legitimacy, that would still not establish Michael's case. As noted earlier, what is at issue here is not entitlement to a state pronouncement that Victoria was begotten by Michael. It is no conceivable denial of constitutional right for a State to decline to declare facts unless some legal consequence hinges upon the requested declaration. What Michael asserts here is a right to have himself declared the natural father *and thereby to obtain parental prerogatives.* What he must establish, therefore, is not that our society has traditionally allowed a natural father in his circumstances to establish paternity, but that it has traditionally accorded such a father parental rights, or at least has not traditionally denied them. Even if the law in all States had always been that the entire world could challenge the marital presumption and obtain a declaration as to who was the natural father, that would not advance Michael's claim. Thus, it is ultimately irrelevant, even for purposes of determining *current* social attitudes towards the alleged substantive right Michael asserts, that the present law in a number of States appears to allow the natural father—including the natural father who has not established a relationship with the child—the theoretical power to rebut the marital presumption. What counts is whether the States in fact award substantive parental rights to the natural father of a child conceived within, and born into, an extant marital union that wishes to embrace the child. We are not aware of a single case, old or new, that has done so. This is not the stuff of which fundamental rights qualifying as liberty interests are made.[6] ...

---

6. Justice BRENNAN criticizes our methodology in using historical traditions specifically relating to the rights of an adulterous natural father, rather than inquiring more generally "whether parenthood is an interest that historically has received our attention and protection." There seems to us no basis for the contention that this methodology is "novel." For example, in *Bowers v. Hardwick*, 478 U.S. 186 (1986), we noted that at the time the Fourteenth Amendment was ratified all but 5 of the 37 States had criminal sodomy laws, that all 50 of the States had such laws prior to 1961, and that 24 States and the District of Columbia continued to have them; and we concluded from that record, regarding that very specific aspect of sexual conduct, that "to claim that a right to engage in such conduct is 'deeply rooted in this Nation's history and tradition' or 'implicit in the concept of ordered liberty' is, at best, facetious." In *Roe v. Wade* (1973) [*Supra.* Chapter 9], we spent about a fifth of our opinion negating the proposition that there was a longstanding tradition of laws proscribing abortion.

We do not understand why, having rejected our focus upon the societal tradition regarding the natural father's rights vis-à-vis a child whose mother is married to another man, Justice BRENNAN would choose to focus instead upon "parenthood." Why should the relevant category not be even more general—perhaps "family relationships"; or "personal relationships"; or even "emotional attachments in general"? Though the dissent has no basis for the level of generality it would select, we do: We refer to the most specific level at which a relevant tradition protecting, or denying protection to, the asserted right can be identified. If, for example, there were no societal tradition, either way, regarding the rights of the natural father of a child adulterously conceived, we would have to consult,

We do not accept Justice BRENNAN's criticism that this result "squashes" the liberty that consists of "the freedom not to conform." It seems to us that reflects the erroneous view that there is only one side to this controversy—that one disposition can expand a "liberty" of sorts without contracting an equivalent "liberty" on the other side. Such a happy choice is rarely available. Here, to *provide* protection to an adulterous natural father is to *deny* protection to a marital father, and vice versa. If Michael has a "freedom not to conform" (whatever that means), Gerald must equivalently have a "freedom to conform." One of them will pay a price for asserting that "freedom"—Michael by being unable to act as father of the child he has adulterously begotten, or Gerald by being unable to preserve the integrity of the traditional family unit he and Victoria have established. Our disposition does not choose between these two "freedoms," but leaves that to the people of California. Justice BRENNAN's approach chooses one of them as the constitutional imperative, on no apparent basis except that the unconventional is to be preferred....

Justice O'CONNOR, with whom Justice KENNEDY joins, concurring in part.

I concur in all but footnote 6 of Justice SCALIA's opinion. This footnote sketches a mode of historical analysis to be used when identifying liberty interests protected by the Due Process Clause of the Fourteenth Amendment that may be somewhat inconsistent with our past decisions in this area. See *Griswold*; *Eisenstadt*. On occasion the Court has characterized relevant traditions protecting asserted rights at levels of generality that might not be "the most specific level" available. I would not foreclose the unanticipated by the prior imposition of a single mode of historical analysis. *Poe v. Ullman*, 367 U.S. 497 (1961) (Harlan, J., dissenting) [Note *supra*. Chapter 8].

---

and (if possible) reason from, the traditions regarding natural fathers in general. But there is such a more specific tradition, and it unqualifiedly denies protection to such a parent.

One would think that Justice BRENNAN would appreciate the value of consulting the most specific tradition available, since he acknowledges that "even if we can agree ... that 'family' and 'parenthood' are part of the good life, it is absurd to assume that we can agree on the content of those terms and destructive to pretend that we do." Because such general traditions provide such imprecise guidance, they permit judges to dictate rather than discern the society's views. The need, if arbitrary decisionmaking is to be avoided, to adopt the most specific tradition as the point of reference—or at least to announce, as Justice BRENNAN declines to do, some other criterion for selecting among the innumerable relevant traditions that could be consulted—is well enough exemplified by the fact that in the present case Justice BRENNAN's opinion and Justice O'CONNOR's opinion, which disapproves this footnote, both appeal to tradition, but on the basis of the tradition they select reach opposite results. Although assuredly having the virtue (if it be that) of leaving judges free to decide as they think best when the unanticipated occurs, a rule of law that binds neither by text nor by any particular, identifiable tradition is no rule of law at all.

Finally, we may note that this analysis is not inconsistent with the result in cases such as *Griswold v. Connecticut* (1965) [*Supra*. Chapter 9], or *Eisenstadt v. Baird*, 405 U.S. 438 (1972) [Note *supra*. Chapter 9]. None of those cases acknowledged a longstanding and still extant societal tradition withholding the very right pronounced to be the subject of a liberty interest and then rejected it. Justice BRENNAN must do so here. In this case, the existence of such a tradition, continuing to the present day, refutes any possible contention that the alleged right is "so rooted in the traditions and conscience of our people as to be ranked as fundamental," *Snyder v. Massachusetts*, or "implicit in the concept of ordered liberty," *Palko v. Connecticut* (1937) [*Supra*. Chapter 8].

Justice STEVENS, concurring in the judgment.

As I understand this case, it raises two different questions about the validity of California's statutory scheme. First, is Cal.Evid.Code Ann. §621 unconstitutional because it prevents Michael and Victoria from obtaining a judicial determination that he is her biological father—even if no legal rights would be affected by that determination? Second, does the California statute deny appellants a fair opportunity to prove that Victoria's best interests would be served by granting Michael visitation rights?

On the first issue I agree with Justice SCALIA that the Federal Constitution imposes no obligation upon a State to declare facts unless some legal consequence hinges upon the requested declaration....

On the second issue I do not agree with Justice SCALIA's analysis. He seems to reject the possibility that a natural father might ever have a constitutionally protected interest in his relationship with a child whose mother was married, to and cohabiting with, another man at the time of the child's conception and birth. I think cases like *Stanley v. Illinois,* 405 U.S. 645 (1972), and *Caban v. Mohammed* (1979), demonstrate that enduring "family" relationships may develop in unconventional settings. I therefore would not foreclose the possibility that a constitutionally protected relationship between a natural father and his child might exist in a case like this. Indeed, I am willing to assume for the purpose of deciding this case that Michael's relationship with Victoria is strong enough to give him a constitutional right to try to convince a trial judge that Victoria's best interest would be served by granting him visitation rights. I am satisfied, however, that the California statute, as applied in this case, gave him that opportunity....

Justice BRENNAN, with whom Justice MARSHALL and Justice BLACKMUN join, dissenting.

In a case that has yielded so many opinions as has this one, it is fruitful to begin by emphasizing the common ground shared by a majority of this Court. Five Members of the Court refuse to foreclose "the possibility that a natural father might ever have a constitutionally protected interest in his relationship with a child whose mother was married to, and cohabiting with, another man at the time of the child's conception and birth." *Ante* (STEVENS, J., concurring in judgment), see *infra*; *post* (WHITE, J., dissenting).... Four Members of the Court agree that Michael H. has a liberty interest in his relationship with Victoria, see *infra*; *post* (WHITE, J., dissenting), and one assumes for purposes of this case that he does, see *ante* (STEVENS, J., concurring in judgment).

In contrast, only one other Member of the Court fully endorses Justice SCALIA's view of the proper method of analyzing questions arising under the Due Process Clause. See *ante* (O'CONNOR, J., concurring in part). Nevertheless, because the plurality opinion's exclusively historical analysis portends a significant and unfortunate departure from our prior cases and from sound constitutional decisionmaking, I devote a substantial portion of my discussion to it.

I

Once we recognized that the "liberty" protected by the Due Process Clause of the Fourteenth Amendment encompasses more than freedom from bodily restraint, today's plurality opinion emphasizes, the concept was cut loose from one natural limitation on its meaning. This innovation paved the way, so the plurality hints, for judges to substitute their own preferences for those of elected officials. Dissatisfied with this supposedly unbridled and uncertain state of affairs, the plurality casts about for another limitation on the concept of liberty.

It finds this limitation in "tradition." Apparently oblivious to the fact that this concept can be as malleable and as elusive as "liberty" itself, the plurality pretends that tradition places a discernible border around the Constitution. The pretense is seductive; it would be comforting to believe that a search for "tradition" involves nothing more idiosyncratic or complicated than poring through dusty volumes on American history. Yet, as Justice WHITE observed in his dissent in *Moore*: "What the deeply rooted traditions of the country are is arguable." Indeed, wherever I would begin to look for an interest "deeply rooted in the country's traditions," one thing is certain: I would not stop (as does the plurality) at Bracton, or Blackstone, or Kent, or even the American Law Reports in conducting my search. Because reasonable people can disagree about the content of particular traditions, and because they can disagree even about which traditions are relevant to the definition of "liberty," the plurality has not found the objective boundary that it seeks.

Even if we could agree, moreover, on the content and significance of particular traditions, we still would be forced to identify the point at which a tradition becomes firm enough to be relevant to our definition of liberty and the moment at which it becomes too obsolete to be relevant any longer. The plurality supplies no objective means by which we might make these determinations. . . .

It is ironic that an approach so utterly dependent on tradition is so indifferent to our precedents. Citing barely a handful of this Court's numerous decisions defining the scope of the liberty protected by the Due Process Clause to support its reliance on tradition, the plurality acts as though English legal treatises and the American Law Reports always have provided the sole source for our constitutional principles. They have not. . . . On the contrary, "'liberty' and 'property' are broad and majestic terms. They are among the 'great [constitutional] concepts . . . purposely left to gather meaning from experience. . . . They relate to the whole domain of social and economic fact, and the statesmen who founded this Nation knew too well that only a stagnant society remains unchanged.'" *Board of Regents of State Colleges v. Roth*, 408 U.S. 564 (1972), quoting *National Ins. Co. v. Tidewater Co.*, 337 U.S. 582 (1949) (Frankfurter, J., dissenting).

It is not that tradition has been irrelevant to our prior decisions. Throughout our decisionmaking in this important area runs the theme that certain interests and practices—freedom from physical restraint, marriage, childbearing, childrearing, and others—form the core of our definition of "liberty." Our solicitude for these interests is partly the result of the fact that the Due Process Clause would seem an empty promise if it did not protect them, and partly the result of the historical and traditional importance of these interests in our society. In deciding cases arising under the Due Process Clause, therefore, we have considered whether the concrete limitation under consideration impermissibly impinges upon one of these more generalized interests.

Today's plurality, however, does not ask whether parenthood is an interest that historically has received our attention and protection; the answer to that question is too clear for dispute. Instead, the plurality asks whether the specific variety of parenthood under consideration—a natural father's relationship with a child whose mother is married to another man—has enjoyed such protection.

If we had looked to tradition with such specificity in past cases, many a decision would have reached a different result. Surely the use of contraceptives by unmarried couples, *Eisenstadt,* or even by married couples, *Griswold*; the freedom from corporal punishment in schools, *Ingraham v. Wright,* 430 U.S. 651 (1977); the freedom from an arbitrary transfer from a prison to a psychiatric institution, *Vitek v. Jones,* 445 U.S. 480 (1980); and even the right to raise one's natural but illegitimate children, *Stanley v. Illinois,* 405 U.S. 645 (1972), were not "interests traditionally protected by our society," at the time of their consideration by this Court. If we had asked, therefore, in *Eisenstadt, Griswold, Ingraham, Vitek,* or *Stanley* itself whether the specific interest under consideration had been traditionally protected, the answer would have been a resounding "no." That we did not ask this question in those cases highlights the novelty of the interpretive method that the plurality opinion employs today.

The plurality's interpretive method is more than novel; it is misguided. It ignores the good reasons for limiting the role of "tradition" in interpreting the Constitution's deliberately capacious language. In the plurality's constitutional universe, we may not take notice of the fact that the original reasons for the conclusive presumption of paternity are out of place in a world in which blood tests can prove virtually beyond a shadow of a doubt who sired a particular child and in which the fact of illegitimacy no longer plays the burdensome and stigmatizing role it once did. Nor, in the plurality's world, may we deny "tradition" its full scope by pointing out that the rationale for the conventional rule has changed over the years, as has the rationale for Cal.Evid.Code Ann. §621[1] instead, our task is simply to identify a rule denying the asserted interest and not to ask whether the basis for that rule—which is the true reflection of the values undergirding it—has changed too often or too recently to call the rule embodying that rationale a "tradition." Moreover, by describing the decisive question as whether Michael's and Victoria's interest is one that has been "traditionally *protected by* our society," (emphasis added), rather than one that society traditionally has thought important (with or without protecting it), and by suggesting that our sole function is to "*discern* the society's views," *ante* n. 6 (emphasis added), the plurality acts as if the only purpose of the Due Process Clause is to confirm the importance of interests already protected by a majority of the States. Transforming the protection afforded by the Due Process Clause into a redundancy mocks those who, with care and purpose, wrote the Fourteenth Amendment.

---

1. See *In re Marriage of Sharyne and Stephen B.*, 124 Cal.App.3d 524 (1981) (noting that California courts initially justified conclusive presumption of paternity on the ground that biological paternity was impossible to prove, but that the preservation of family integrity became the rule's paramount justification when paternity tests became reliable).

In construing the Fourteenth Amendment to offer shelter only to those interests specifically protected by historical practice, moreover, the plurality ignores the kind of society in which our Constitution exists. We are not an assimilative, homogeneous society, but a facilitative, pluralistic one, in which we must be willing to abide someone else's unfamiliar or even repellent practice because the same tolerant impulse protects our own idiosyncracies. Even if we can agree, therefore, that "family" and "parenthood" are part of the good life, it is absurd to assume that we can agree on the content of those terms and destructive to pretend that we do. In a community such as ours, "liberty" must include the freedom not to conform. The plurality today squashes this freedom by requiring specific approval from history before protecting anything in the name of liberty.

The document that the plurality construes today is unfamiliar to me. It is not the living charter that I have taken to be our Constitution; it is instead a stagnant, archaic, hidebound document steeped in the prejudices and superstitions of a time long past. *This* Constitution does not recognize that times change, does not see that sometimes a practice or rule outlives its foundations. I cannot accept an interpretive method that does such violence to the charter that I am bound by oath to uphold.

II

The plurality's reworking of our interpretive approach is all the more troubling because it is unnecessary. This is not a case in which we face a "new" kind of interest, one that requires us to consider for the first time whether the Constitution protects it. On the contrary, we confront an interest — that of a parent and child in their relationship with each other — that was among the first that this Court acknowledged in its cases defining the "liberty" protected by the Constitution, *see, e.g., Meyer; Skinner v. Oklahoma*, 316 U.S. 535 (1942) [Note *supra*. Chapter 8], and I think I am safe in saying that no one doubts the wisdom or validity of those decisions. Where the interest under consideration is a parent-child relationship, we need not ask, over and over again, whether that interest is one that society traditionally protects.

Thus, to describe the issue in this case as whether the relationship existing between Michael and Victoria "has been treated as a protected family unit under the historic practices of our society, or whether on any other basis it has been accorded special protection," is to reinvent the wheel. The better approach — indeed, the one commanded by our prior cases and by common sense — is to ask whether the specific parent-child relationship under consideration is close enough to the interests that we already have protected to be deemed an aspect of "liberty" as well. On the facts before us, therefore, the question is not what "level of generality" should be used to describe the relationship between Michael and Victoria, see *ante*, n. 6, but whether the relationship under consideration is sufficiently substantial to qualify as a liberty interest under our prior cases.

On four prior occasions, we have considered whether unwed fathers have a constitutionally protected interest in their relationships with their children. See *Stanley v. Illinois*, 405 U.S. 645 (1972); *Quilloin v. Walcott*, 434 U.S. 246 (1978); *Caban v. Mohammed*, 441 U.S. 380 (1979); and *Lehr v. Robertson*, 463 U.S. 248 (1983). Though different in factual and legal circumstances, these cases have produced a unifying theme: although an unwed father'sbiological link to his child does not, in and of itself, guarantee him a constitutional stake in his relationship with that child, such a link combined with a substantial parent-child relationship will do so. "When an unwed father demonstrates a full commitment to the responsibilities of parenthood by 'coming forward to participate in the rearing of his child,'... his interest in personal contact with his child acquires substantial protection under the Due Process Clause. At that point it may be said that he 'acts as a father toward his children.'" *Lehr*, quoting *Caban*. This commitment is why Mr. Stanley and Mr. Caban won; why Mr. Quilloin and Mr. Lehr lost; and why Michael H. should prevail today. Michael H. is almost certainly Victoria D.'s natural father, has lived with her as her father, has contributed to her support, and has from the beginning sought to strengthen and maintain his relationship with her....

IV

The atmosphere surrounding today's decision is one of make-believe. Beginning with the suggestion that the situation confronting us here does not repeat itself every day in every corner of the country, moving on to the claim that it is tradition alone that supplies the details of the liberty that the Constitution protects, and passing finally to the notion that the Court always has recognized a cramped vision of "the family," today's decision lets stand California's pronouncement that Michael—whom blood tests show to a 98 percent probability to be Victoria's father—is not Victoria's father. When and if the Court awakes to reality, it will find a world very different from the one it expects.

Justice WHITE, with whom Justice BRENNAN joins, dissenting ...

I

Like Justices BRENNAN, MARSHALL, BLACKMUN, and STEVENS, I do not agree with the plurality opinion's conclusion that a natural father can never "have a constitutionally protected interest in his relationship with a child whose mother was married to, and cohabiting with, another man at the time of the child's conception and birth." Prior cases here have recognized the liberty interest of a father in his re-lationship with his child. In none of these cases did we indicate that the father's rights were dependent on the marital status of the mother or biological father. The basic principle enunciated in the Court's unwed father cases is that an unwed father who has demonstrated a sufficient commitment to his paternity by way of personal, fi-nancial, or custodial responsibilities has a protected liberty interest in a relationship with his child....

In the case now before us, Michael H. is not a father unwilling to assume his re-sponsibilities as a parent. To the contrary, he is a father who has asserted his interests in raising and providing for his child since the very time of the child's birth. In contrast to the father in *Lehr,* Michael had begun to develop a relationship with his daughter. There is no dispute on this point.... *Lehr* was predicated on the absence of a substantial relationship between the man and the child and emphasized the "difference between the developed parent-child relationship that was implicated in *Stanley* and *Caban*, and the potential relationship involved in *Quilloin* and [*Lehr*]." "When an unwed father demonstrates a full commitment to the responsibilities of parenthood by 'coming forward to participate in the rearing of his child,' his interest in personal contact with his child acquires substantial protection under the Due Process Clause." *Lehr* [quoting *Caban*]. The facts in this case satisfy the *Lehr* criteria ... It is clear enough that Michael more than meets the mark in establishing the constitutionally protected liberty interest discussed in *Lehr* and recognized in *Stanley v. Illinois* and *Caban v. Mohammed*. He therefore has a liberty interest entitled to protection under the Due Process Clause of the Fourteenth Amendment....

## Washington v. Glucksberg
### 521 U.S. 702 (1997)

Chief Justice REHNQUIST delivered the opinion of the Court.

The question presented in this case is whether Washington's prohibition against "causing" or "aiding" a suicide offends the Fourteenth Amendment to the United States Constitution. We hold that it does not.

It has always been a crime to assist a suicide in the State of Washington.... Today, Washington law provides: "A person is guilty of promoting a suicide attempt when he knowingly causes or aids another person to attempt suicide." ... At the same time, Washington's Natural Death Act, enacted in 1979, states that the "withholding or withdrawal of life-sustaining treatment" at a patient's direction "shall not, for any purpose, constitute a suicide."

... Respondents Harold Glucksberg, M. D., Abigail Halperin, M. D., Thomas A. Preston, M. D., and Peter Shalit, M. D., are physicians who practice in Washington. These doctors occasionally treat terminally ill, suffering patients, and declare that they would assist these patients in ending their lives if not for Washington's assisted-suicide ban. In January 1994, respondents, along with three gravely ill, pseudonymous plaintiffs who have since died and Compassion in Dying, a nonprofit organization that counsels people considering physician-assisted suicide, sued in the United States District Court, seeking a declaration that [the state's assisted suicide ban] is, on its face, unconstitutional.

The plaintiffs asserted "the existence of a liberty interest protected by the Fourteenth Amendment which extends to a personal choice by a mentally competent, terminally ill adult to commit physician-assisted suicide." Relying primarily on *Planned Parenthood of Southeastern Pa. v. Casey* (1992) [*Supra.* Chapter 9], and *Cruzan v. Director, Mo. Dept. of Health*, 497 U.S. 261 (1990), the District Court agreed, and concluded that Washington's assisted-suicide ban is unconstitutional because it "places an undue burden on the exercise of [that] constitutionally protected liberty interest."

A panel of the Court of Appeals for the Ninth Circuit reversed.... The Ninth Circuit reheard the case en banc, reversed the panel's decision, and affirmed the District Court.... We granted certiorari, and now reverse.

I

We begin, as we do in all due process cases, by examining our Nation's history, legal traditions, and practices. See, *e.g.*, *Casey*; *Moore v. East Cleveland* (1977) (plurality opinion) [*Supra*. this chapter] (noting importance of "careful 'respect for the teachings of history'"). In almost every State—indeed, in almost every western democracy—it is a crime to assist a suicide. The States' assisted-suicide bans are not innovations. Rather, they are longstanding expressions of the States' commitment to the protection and preservation of all human life. Indeed, opposition to and condemnation of suicide—and, therefore, of assisting suicide—are consistent and enduring themes of our philosophical, legal, and cultural heritages. See generally New York State Task Force on Life and the Law, *When Death is Sought: Assisted Suicide and Euthanasia in the Medical Context* (1994) (hereinafter New York Task Force).

More specifically, for over 700 years, the Anglo-American common-law tradition has punished or otherwise disapproved of both suicide and assisting suicide. *Cruzan* (SCALIA, J., concurring). In the 13th century, Henry de Bracton, one of the first legal-treatise writers, observed that "just as a man may commit felony by slaying another so may he do so by slaying himself." 2 *Bracton on Laws and Customs of England*.... Centuries later, Sir William Blackstone, whose *Commentaries on the Laws of England* not only provided a definitive summary of the common law but was also a primary legal authority for 18th- and 19th-century American lawyers, referred to suicide as "self-murder" and "the pretended heroism, but real cowardice, of the Stoic philosophers, who destroyed themselves to avoid those ills which they had not the fortitude to endure...." 4 W. Blackstone, *Commentaries* *189. Blackstone emphasized that "the law has ... ranked [suicide] among the highest crimes," *ibid.*, although, anticipating later developments, he conceded that the harsh and shameful punishments imposed for suicide "border a little upon severity." *Id.*, at *190.

For the most part, the early American Colonies adopted the common-law approach.... Over time, however, the American Colonies abolished these harsh common-law penalties.... However, ... the movement away from the common law's harsh sanctions did not represent an acceptance of suicide; rather, ... this change reflected the growing consensus that it was unfair to punish the suicide's family for his wrongdoing. Nonetheless, although States moved away from Blackstone's treatment of suicide, courts continued to condemn it as a grave public wrong.

That suicide remained a grievous, though nonfelonious, wrong is confirmed by the fact that colonial and early state legislatures and courts did not retreat from prohibiting assisting suicide.... The earliest American statute explicitly to outlaw assisting suicide was enacted in New York in 1828, and many of the new States and Territories followed New York's example.... By the time the Fourteenth Amendment was ratified, it was a crime in most States to assist a suicide....

Though deeply rooted, the States' assisted-suicide bans have in recent years been reexamined and, generally, reaffirmed. Because of advances in medicine and technology, Americans today are increasingly likely to die in institutions, from chronic illnesses. Public concern and democratic action are therefore sharply focused on how best to protect dignity and independence at the end of life, with the result that there have been many significant changes in state laws and in the attitudes these laws reflect. Many States, for example, now permit "living wills," surrogate health-care decision-making, and the withdrawal or refusal of life-sustaining medical treatment. At the same time, however, voters and legislators continue for the most part to reaffirm their States' prohibitions on assisting suicide....

Attitudes toward suicide itself have changed since Bracton, but our laws have consistently condemned, and continue to prohibit, assisting suicide. Despite changes in medical technology and notwithstanding an increased emphasis on the importance of end-of-life decisionmaking, we have not retreated from this prohibition. Against this backdrop of history, tradition, and practice, we now turn to respondents' constitutional claim.

## II

The Due Process Clause guarantees more than fair process, and the "liberty" it protects includes more than the absence of physical restraint. The Clause also provides heightened protection against government interference with certain fundamental rights and liberty interests. In a long line of cases, we have held that, in addition to the specific freedoms protected by the Bill of Rights, the "liberty" specially protected by the Due Process Clause includes the rights to marry, *Loving v. Virginia,* 388 U.S. 1 (1967); to have children, *Skinner v. Oklahoma,* 316 U.S. 535 (1942) [Note *supra.* Chapter 8]; to direct the education and upbringing of one's children, *Meyer v. Nebraska* (1923) [*Supra.* Chapter 8]; *Pierce v. Society of Sisters,* 268 U.S. 510 (1925) [Note *supra.* Chapter 8]; to marital privacy, *Griswold v. Connecticut* (1965) [*Supra.* Chapter 9]; to use contraception, *ibid.; Eisenstadt v. Baird,* 405 U.S. 438(1972) [Note *supra.* Chapter 9]; to bodily integrity, *Rochin v. California,* 342 U.S. 165 (1952) [Note *supra.* Chapter 8], and to abortion, *Casey.* We have also assumed, and strongly suggested, that the Due Process Clause protects the traditional right to refuse unwanted lifesaving medical treatment. *Cruzan.*

But we "have always been reluctant to expand the concept of substantive due process because guideposts for responsible decisionmaking in this unchartered area are scarce and open-ended." By extending constitutional protection to an asserted right or liberty interest, we, to a great extent, place the matter outside the arena of public debate and legislative action. We must therefore "exercise the utmost care whenever we are asked to break new ground in this field," lest the liberty protected by the Due Process Clause be subtly transformed into the policy preferences of the Members of this Court, *Moore* (plurality opinion).

Our established method of substantive-due-process analysis has two primary features: First, we have regularly observed that the Due Process Clause specially protects those fundamental rights and liberties which are, objectively, "deeply rooted in this Nation's history and tradition," *Moore* (plurality opinion), and "implicit in the concept of ordered liberty," such that "neither liberty nor justice would exist if they were sacrificed," *Palko v. Connecticut* (1937) [*Supra.* Chapter 8]. Second, we have required in substantive-due-process cases a "careful description" of the asserted fundamental liberty interest. Our Nation's history, legal traditions, and practices thus provide the crucial "guideposts for responsible decisionmaking," that direct and restrain our exposition of the Due Process Clause. As we stated recently ... the Fourteenth Amendment "forbids the government to infringe ... 'fundamental' liberty interests *at all*, no matter what process is provided, unless the infringement is narrowly tailored to serve a compelling state interest."

Justice SOUTER, relying on Justice Harlan's dissenting opinion in *Poe v. Ullman*, 367 U.S. 497 (1961) [Note *supra*. Chapter 8], would largely abandon this restrained methodology, and instead ask "whether [Washington's] statute sets up one of those 'arbitrary impositions' or 'purposeless restraints' at odds with the Due Process Clause of the Fourteenth Amendment," *post* (quoting *Poe* (Harlan, J., dissenting)).[17] In our view, however, the development of this Court's substantive-due-process jurisprudence ... has been a process whereby the outlines of the "liberty" specially protected by the Fourteenth Amendment—never fully clarified, to be sure, and perhaps not capable of being fully clarified—have at least been carefully refined by concrete examples involving fundamental rights found to be deeply rooted in our legal tradition. This approach tends to rein in the subjective elements that are necessarily present in due-process judicial review. In addition, by establishing a threshold requirement—that a challenged state action implicate a fundamental right—before requiring more than a reasonable relation to a legitimate state interest to justify the action, it avoids the need for complex balancing of competing interests in every case.

Turning to the claim at issue here, the Court of Appeals stated that "properly analyzed, the first issue to be resolved is whether there is a liberty interest in determining the time and manner of one's death," or, in other words, "is there a right to die?" ... As noted above, we have a tradition of carefully formulating the interest at stake in substantive-due-process cases. For example, although *Cruzan* is often described as a "right to die" case, we were, in fact, more precise: We assumed that the Constitution granted competent persons a "constitutionally protected right to refuse lifesaving hydration and nutrition." The Washington statute at issue in this case prohibits "aiding another person to attempt suicide," and, thus, the question before us is whether the "liberty" specially protected by the Due Process Clause includes a right to commit suicide which itself includes a right to assistance in doing so.

---

17. In Justice SOUTER's opinion, Justice Harlan's *Poe* dissent supplies the "modern justification" for substantive-due-process review. But although Justice Harlan's opinion has often been cited in due process cases, we have never abandoned our fundamental-rights-based analytical method. Just four Terms ago, six of the Justices now sitting joined the Court's opinion in *Reno v. Flores,* 507 U.S. 292 (1993); *Poe* was not even cited. And in *Cruzan*, neither the Court's nor the concurring opinions relied on *Poe*; rather, we concluded that the right to refuse unwanted medical treatment was so rooted in our history, tradition, and practice as to require special protection under the Fourteenth Amendment. True, the Court relied on Justice Harlan's dissent in *Casey*, but, as *Flores* demonstrates, we did not in so doing jettison our established approach. Indeed, to read such a radical move into the Court's opinion in *Casey* would seem to fly in the face of that opinion's emphasis on *stare decisis*.

We now inquire whether this asserted right has any place in our Nation's traditions. Here, as discussed *supra*, we are confronted with a consistent and almost universal tradition that has long rejected the asserted right, and continues explicitly to reject it today, even for terminally ill, mentally competent adults. To hold for respondents, we would have to reverse centuries of legal doctrine and practice, and strike down the considered policy choice of almost every State.

Respondents contend, however, that the liberty interest they assert *is* consistent with this Court's substantive-due-process line of cases, if not with this Nation's history and practice. Pointing to *Casey* and *Cruzan*, respondents read our jurisprudence in this area as reflecting a general tradition of "self-sovereignty," and as teaching that the "liberty" protected by the Due Process Clause includes "basic and intimate exercises of personal autonomy." According to respondents, our liberty jurisprudence, and the broad, individualistic principles it reflects, protects the "liberty of competent, terminally ill adults to make end-of-life decisions free of undue government interference." The question presented in this case, however, is whether the protections of the Due Process Clause include a right to commit suicide with another's assistance. With this "careful description" of respondents' claim in mind, we turn to *Casey* and *Cruzan*.

In *Cruzan*, we considered whether Nancy Beth Cruzan, who had been severely injured in an automobile accident and was in a persistive vegetative state, "had a right under the United States Constitution which would require the hospital to withdraw life-sustaining treatment" at her parents' request. We began with the observation that "at common law, even the touching of one person by another without consent and without legal justification was a battery." We then discussed the related rule that "informed consent is generally required for medical treatment." After reviewing a long line of relevant state cases, we concluded that "the common-law doctrine of informed consent is viewed as generally encompassing the right of a competent individual to refuse medical treatment." Next, we reviewed our own cases on the subject, and stated that "the principle that a competent person has a constitutionally protected liberty interest in refusing unwanted medical treatment may be inferred from our prior decisions." Therefore, "for purposes of [that] case, we assumed that the United States Constitution would grant a competent person a constitutionally protected right to refuse lifesaving hydration and nutrition." We concluded that, notwithstanding this right, the Constitution permitted Missouri to require clear and convincing evidence of an incompetent patient's wishes concerning the withdrawal of life-sustaining treatment....

The right assumed in *Cruzan* ... was not simply deduced from abstract concepts of personal autonomy. Given the common-law rule that forced medication was a battery, and the long legal tradition protecting the decision to refuse unwanted medical treatment, our assumption was entirely consistent with this Nation's history and constitutional traditions. The decision to commit suicide with the assistance of another may be just as personal and profound as the decision to refuse unwanted medical treatment, but it has never enjoyed similar legal protection. Indeed, the two acts are widely and reasonably regarded as quite distinct....

Respondents also rely on *Casey*. There, the Court's opinion concluded that "the essential holding of *Roe v. Wade* (1973) [*Supra.* Chapter 9] should be retained and once again reaffirmed." ... In reaching this conclusion, the opinion discussed in some detail this Court's substantive-due-process tradition of interpreting the Due Process Clause to protect certain fundamental rights and "personal decisions relating to marriage, procreation, contraception, family relationships, child rearing, and education," and noted that many of those rights and liberties "involve the most intimate and personal choices a person may make in a lifetime."

The Court of Appeals, like the District Court, found *Casey* "highly instructive" and "almost prescriptive" for determining "what liberty interest may inhere in a terminally ill person's choice to commit suicide":

> Like the decision of whether or not to have an abortion, the decision how and when to die is one of 'the most intimate and personal choices a person may make in a lifetime,' a choice "central to personal dignity and autonomy."

Similarly, respondents emphasize the statement in *Casey* that:

> At the heart of liberty is the right to define one's own concept of existence, of meaning, of the universe, and of the mystery of human life. Beliefs about these matters could not define the attributes of personhood were they formed under compulsion of the State.

By choosing this language, the Court's opinion in *Casey* described, in a general way and in light of our prior cases, those personal activities and decisions that this Court has identified as so deeply rooted in our history and traditions, or so fundamental to our concept of constitutionally ordered liberty, that they are protected by the Fourteenth Amendment. The opinion moved from the recognition that liberty necessarily includes freedom of conscience and belief about ultimate considerations to the observation that "though the abortion decision may originate within the zone of conscience and belief, it is *more than a philosophic exercise.*" *Casey* (emphasis added). That many of the rights and liberties protected by the Due Process Clause sound in personal autonomy does not warrant the sweeping conclusion that any and all important, intimate, and personal decisions are so protected, and *Casey* did not suggest otherwise.

The history of the law's treatment of assisted suicide in this country has been and continues to be one of the rejection of nearly all efforts to permit it. That being the case, our decisions lead us to conclude that the asserted "right" to assistance in committing suicide is not a fundamental liberty interest protected by the Due Process Clause. The Constitution also requires, however, that Washington's assisted-suicide ban be rationally related to legitimate government interests. This requirement is unquestionably met here. As the court below recognized, Washington's assisted-suicide ban implicates a number of state interests.

First, Washington has an "unqualified interest in the preservation of human life." The State's prohibition on assisted suicide, like all homicide laws, both reflects and advances its commitment to this interest....

Relatedly, all admit that suicide is a serious public-health problem, especially among persons in otherwise vulnerable groups. The State has an interest in preventing suicide, and in studying, identifying, and treating its causes.

Those who attempt suicide — terminally ill or not — often suffer from depression or other mental disorders. Research indicates, however, that many people who request physician-assisted suicide withdraw that request if their depression and pain are treated. The New York Task Force, however, expressed its concern that, because depression is difficult to diagnose, physicians and medical professionals often fail to respond adequately to seriously ill patients' needs. Thus, legal physician-assisted suicide could make it more difficult for the State to protect depressed or mentally ill persons, or those who are suffering from untreated pain, from suicidal impulses.

The State also has an interest in protecting the integrity and ethics of the medical profession. In contrast to the Court of Appeals' conclusion that "the integrity of the medical profession would [not] be threatened in any way by [physician-assisted suicide]," the American Medical Association, like many other medical and physicians' groups, has concluded that "physician-assisted suicide is fundamentally incompatible with the physician's role as healer." ...

Next, the State has an interest in protecting vulnerable groups — including the poor, the elderly, and disabled persons — from abuse, neglect, and mistakes. The Court of Appeals dismissed the State's concern that disadvantaged persons might be pressured into physician-assisted suicide as "ludicrous on its face." We have recognized, however, the real risk of subtle coercion and undue influence in end-of-life situations.....

The State's interest here goes beyond protecting the vulnerable from coercion; it extends to protecting disabled and terminally ill people from prejudice, negative and inaccurate stereotypes, and "societal indifference." ...

Finally, the State may fear that permitting assisted suicide will start it down the path to voluntary and perhaps even involuntary euthanasia.....

We need not weigh exactly the relative strengths of these various interests. They are unquestionably important and legitimate, and Washington's ban on assisted suicide is at least reasonably related to their promotion and protection. We therefore hold that Wash. Rev. Code § 9A.36.060(1) does not violate the Fourteenth Amendment, either on its face or "as applied to competent, terminally ill adults who wish to hasten their deaths by obtaining medication prescribed by their doctors."

Throughout the Nation, Americans are engaged in an earnest and profound debate about the morality, legality, and practicality of physician-assisted suicide. Our holding permits this debate to continue, as it should in a democratic society. The decision of the en banc Court of Appeals is reversed, and the case is remanded for further proceedings consistent with this opinion.

Justice O'CONNOR, concurring.

Death will be different for each of us. For many, the last days will be spent in physical pain and perhaps the despair that accompanies physical deterioration and a loss of control of basic bodily and mental functions. Some will seek medication to alleviate that pain and other symptoms.

The Court frames the issue … as whether the Due Process Clause of the Constitution protects a "right to commit suicide which itself includes a right to assistance in doing so," and concludes that our Nation's history, legal traditions, and practices do not support the existence of such a right. I … agree that there is no generalized right to "commit suicide." But respondents urge us to address the narrower question whether a mentally competent person who is experiencing great suffering has a constitutionally cognizable interest in controlling the circumstances of his or her imminent death. I see no need to reach that question in the context of the facial challenges to the … laws at issue here.… I agree that the State's interests in protecting those who are not truly competent or facing imminent death, or those whose decisions to hasten death would not truly be voluntary, are sufficiently weighty to justify a prohibition against physician-assisted suicide.

Every one of us at some point may be affected by our own or a family member's terminal illness. There is no reason to think the democratic process will not strike the proper balance between the interests of terminally ill, mentally competent individuals who would seek to end their suffering and the State's interests in protecting those who might seek to end life mistakenly or under pressure. As the Court recognizes, States are presently undertaking extensive and serious evaluation of physician-assisted suicide and other related issues. In such circumstances, "the … challenging task of crafting appropriate procedures for safeguarding … liberty interests is entrusted to the 'laboratory' of the States … in the first instance." *Cruzan* (O'CONNOR, J., concurring).

In sum, there is no need to address the question whether suffering patients have a constitutionally cognizable interest in obtaining relief from the suffering that they may experience in the last days of their lives. There is no dispute that dying patients in Washington … can obtain palliative care, even when doing so would hasten their deaths. The difficulty in defining terminal illness and the risk that a dying patient's request for assistance in ending his or her life might not be truly voluntary justifies the prohibitions on assisted suicide we uphold here.

Justice STEVENS, concurring in the judgments.

The Court ends its opinion with the important observation that our holding today is fully consistent with a continuation of the vigorous debate about the "morality, legality, and practicality of physician-assisted suicide" in a democratic society. I write separately to make it clear that there is also room for further debate about the limits that the Constitution places on the power of the States to punish the practice.

I

… Today, the Court decides that Washington's statute prohibiting assisted suicide is not invalid "on its face," that is to say, in all or most cases in which it might be applied. That holding, however, does not foreclose the possibility that some applications of the statute might well be invalid.…

History and tradition provide ample support for refusing to recognize an open-ended constitutional right to commit suicide.... But just as our conclusion that capital punishment is not always unconstitutional did not preclude later decisions holding that it is sometimes impermissibly cruel, so is it equally clear that a decision upholding a general statutory prohibition of assisted suicide does not mean that every possible application of the statute would be valid. A State, like Washington, that has authorized the death penalty, and thereby has concluded that the sanctity of human life does not require that it always be preserved, must acknowledge that there are situations in which an interest in hastening death is legitimate. Indeed, not only is that interest sometimes legitimate, I am also convinced that there are times when it is entitled to constitutional protection.

## II

... While I agree with the Court that *Cruzan* does not decide the issue presented by these cases, *Cruzan* did give recognition, not just to vague, unbridled notions of autonomy, but to the more specific interest in making decisions about how to confront an imminent death. Although there is no absolute right to physician-assisted suicide, *Cruzan* makes it clear that some individuals who no longer have the option of deciding whether to live or to die because they are already on the threshold of death have a constitutionally protected interest that may outweigh the State's interest in preserving life at all costs. The liberty interest at stake in a case like this differs from, and is stronger than, both the common-law right to refuse medical treatment and the un-bridled interest in deciding whether to live or die. It is an interest in deciding how, rather than whether, a critical threshold shall be crossed....

Justice SOUTER, concurring in the judgment.

... The question is whether the [Washington] statute sets up one of those "arbitrary impositions" or "purposeless restraints" at odds with the Due Process Clause of the Fourteenth Amendment. *Poe* (Harlan, J., dissenting). I conclude that the statute's application to the doctors has not been shown to be unconstitutional, but I write separately to give my reasons for analyzing the substantive due process claims as I do, and for rejecting this one....

## II

When the physicians claim that the Washington law deprives them of a right falling within the scope of liberty that the Fourteenth Amendment guarantees against denial without due process of law, they are not claiming some sort of procedural defect in the process through which the statute has been enacted or is administered. Their claim, rather, is that the State has no substantively adequate justification for barring the assistance sought by the patient and sought to be offered by the physician. Thus, we are dealing with a claim to one of those rights sometimes described as rights of substantive due process and sometimes as unenumerated rights, in view of the breadth and indeterminacy of the "due process" serving as the claim's textual basis. The doctors accordingly arouse the skepticism of those who find the Due Process Clause an unduly vague or oxymoronic warrant for judicial review of substantive state law, just as they also invoke two centuries of American constitutional practice in recognizing unenumerated, substantive limits on governmental action. Although this practice has neither rested on any single textual basis nor expressed a consistent theory (or, before *Poe,* a much articulated one), a brief overview of its history is instructive on two counts. The persistence of substantive due process in our cases points to the legitimacy of the modern justification for such judicial review found in Justice Harlan's dissent in *Poe,*[4] on which I will dwell further on, while the acknowledged failures of some of these cases point with caution to the difficulty raised by the present claim.

Before the ratification of the Fourteenth Amendment, substantive constitutional review resting on a theory of unenumerated rights occurred largely in the state courts applying state constitutions that commonly contained either due process clauses like that of the Fifth Amendment (and later the Fourteenth) or the textual antecedents of such clauses, repeating Magna Carta's guarantee of "the law of the land."[5] On the basis of such clauses, or of general principles untethered to specific constitutional language, state courts evaluated the constitutionality of a wide range of statutes....

Even in this early period, however, this Court anticipated the developments that would presage both the Civil War and the ratification of the Fourteenth Amendment, by making it clear on several occasions that it too had no doubt of the judiciary's power to strike down legislation that conflicted with important but unenumerated principles of American government. In most such instances, after declaring its power to invalidate what it might find inconsistent with rights of liberty and property, the Court nevertheless went on to uphold the legislative Acts under review. But in *Fletcher v. Peck,* 6 Cranch 87, (1810), the Court went further. It struck down an Act of the Georgia Legislature that purported to rescind a sale of public land *ab initio* and reclaim title for the State.... The Court rested the invalidation on alternative sources of authority [including] "general principles which are common to our free institutions," by which Chief Justice Marshall meant that a simple deprivation of property by the State could not be an authentically "legislative" Act.

*Fletcher* was not, though, the most telling early example of such review. For its most salient instance in this Court before the adoption of the Fourteenth Amendment was, of course, the case that the Amendment would in due course overturn, *Dred Scott v. Sandford,* 60 U.S. 393 (1857). Unlike *Fletcher, Dred Scott* was textually based on a Due Process Clause (in the Fifth Amendment, applicable to the National Government), and it was in reliance on that Clause's protection of property that the Court invalidated the Missouri Compromise. This substantive protection of an owner's property in a slave taken to the territories was traced to the absence of any enumerated

---

4. The status of the Harlan dissent in *Poe* is shown by the Court's adoption of its result in *Griswold,* and by the Court's acknowledgment of its status and adoption of its reasoning in *Casey.* See also *Moore* (plurality opinion) (opinion for four Justices treating Justice Harlan's *Poe* dissent as a central explication of the methodology of judicial review under the Due Process Clause).

5. Coke indicates that prohibitions against deprivations without "due process of law" originated in an English statute that "rendred" Magna Carta's "law of the land" in such terms. See 2 E. Coke, *Institutes* (1797); see also E. Corwin, *Liberty Against Government* (1948).

power to affect that property granted to the Congress by Article I of the Constitution, the implication being that the Government had no legitimate interest that could support the earlier congressional compromise. The ensuing judgment of history needs no recounting here.

After the ratification of the Fourteenth Amendment, with its guarantee of due process protection against the States, interpretation of the words "liberty" and "property" as used in Due Process Clauses became a sustained enterprise, with the Court generally describing the due process criterion in converse terms of reasonableness or arbitrariness....

The theory became serious ... beginning with *Allgeyer v. Louisiana,* 165 U.S. 578 (1897) [Note *supra.* Chapter 7], where the Court invalidated a Louisiana statute for excessive interference with Fourteenth Amendment liberty to contract, and offered a substantive interpretation of "liberty," that in the aftermath of the so-called *Lochner* Era has been scaled back in some respects, but expanded in others, and never repudiated in principle. The Court said that Fourteenth Amendment liberty includes "the right of the citizen to be free in the enjoyment of all his faculties; to be free to use them in all lawful ways; to live and work where he will; to earn his livelihood by any lawful calling; to pursue any livelihood or avocation; and for that purpose to enter into all contracts which may be proper, necessary and essential to his carrying out to a successful conclusion the purposes above mentioned." "We do not intend to hold that in no such case can the State exercise its police power," the Court added, but "when and how far such power may be legitimately exercised with regard to these subjects must be left for determination to each case as it arises."

Although this principle was unobjectionable, what followed for a season was, in the realm of economic legislation, the echo of *Dred Scott. Allgeyer* was succeeded within a decade by *Lochner v. New York* (1905) [*Supra.* Chapter 7], and the era to which that case gave its name, famous now for striking down as arbitrary various sorts of economic regulations that post-New Deal courts have uniformly thought constitutionally sound....

Even before the deviant economic due process cases had been repudiated, however, the more durable precursors of modern substantive due process were reaffirming this Court's obligation to conduct arbitrariness review, beginning with *Meyer....* After *Meyer* and *Pierce,* two further opinions took the major steps that lead to the modern law. The first was not even in a due process case but one about equal protection, *Skinner,* where the Court emphasized the "fundamental" nature of individual choice about procreation and so foreshadowed not only the later prominence of procreation as a subject of liberty protection, but the corresponding standard of "strict scrutiny," in this Court's Fourteenth Amendment law. *Skinner,* that is, added decisions regarding procreation to the list of liberties recognized in *Meyer* and *Pierce* and loosely suggested, as a gloss on their standard of arbitrariness, a judicial obligation to scrutinize any impingement on such an important interest with heightened care. In so doing, it suggested a point that Justice Harlan would develop, that the kind and degree of justification that a sensitive judge would demand of a State would depend on the importance of the interest being asserted by the individual. *Poe.*

The second major opinion leading to the modern doctrine was Justice Harlan's *Poe* dissent just cited.... The dissent is important for three things that point to our responsibilities today. The first is Justice Harlan's respect for the tradition of substantive due process review itself, and his acknowledgment of the Judiciary's obligation to carry it on.... This enduring tradition of American constitutional practice is, in Justice Harlan's view, nothing more than what is required by the judicial authority and obligation to construe constitutional text and review legislation for conformity to that text. See *Marbury v. Madison* (1803) [*Supra.* Chapter 1]. Like many judges who preceded him and many who followed, he found it impossible to construe the text of due process without recognizing substantive, and not merely procedural, limitations. "Were due process merely a procedural safeguard it would fail to reach those situations where the deprivation of life, liberty or property was accomplished by legislation which by operating in the future could, given even the fairest possible procedure in application to individuals, nevertheless destroy the enjoyment of all three." *Poe.* The text of the Due Process Clause thus imposes nothing less than an obligation to give substantive content to the words "liberty" and "due process of law."

Following the first point of the *Poe* dissent, on the necessity to engage in the sort of examination we conduct today, the dissent's second and third implicitly address those cases, already noted, that are now condemned with virtual unanimity as disastrous mistakes of substantive due process review. The second of the dissent's lessons is a reminder that the business of such review is not the identification of extratextual absolutes but scrutiny of a legislative resolution (perhaps unconscious) of clashing principles, each quite possibly worthy in and of itself, but each to be weighed within the history of our values as a people. It is a comparison of the relative strengths of opposing claims that informs the judicial task, not a deduction from some first premise. Thus informed, judicial review still has no warrant to substitute one reasonable resolution of the contending positions for another, but authority to supplant the balance already struck between the contenders only when it falls outside the realm of the reasonable. Part III, below, deals with this second point, and also with the dissent's third, which takes the form of an object lesson in the explicit attention to detail that is no less essential to the intellectual discipline of substantive due process review than an understanding of the basic need to account for the two sides in the controversy and to respect legislation within the zone of reasonableness.

### III

My understanding of unenumerated rights in the wake of the *Poe* dissent and subsequent cases avoids the absolutist failing of many older cases without embracing the opposite pole of equating reasonableness with past practice described at a very specific level. That understanding begins with a concept of "ordered liberty," *Poe*, comprising a continuum of rights to be free from "arbitrary impositions and purposeless restraints."

> Due Process has not been reduced to any formula; its content cannot be determined by reference to any code. The best that can be said is that through the course of this Court's decisions it has represented the balance which our Nation, built upon postulates of respect for the liberty of the individual, has

> struck between that liberty and the demands of organized society. If the sup-
> plying of content to this Constitutional concept has of necessity been a ra-
> tional process, it certainly has not been one where judges have felt free to
> roam where unguided speculation might take them. The balance of which I
> speak is the balance struck by this country, having regard to what history
> teaches are the traditions from which it developed as well as the traditions
> from which it broke. That tradition is a living thing. A decision of this Court
> which radically departs from it could not long survive, while a decision which
> builds on what has survived is likely to be sound. No formula could serve as
> a substitute, in this area, for judgment and restraint.

See also *Moore* (plurality opinion of Powell, J.) ("Appropriate limits on substantive due process come not from drawing arbitrary lines but rather from careful 'respect for the teachings of history [and] solid recognition of the basic values that underlie our society'") (quoting *Griswold*) (Harlan, J., concurring)).

After the *Poe* dissent, as before it, this enforceable concept of liberty would bar statutory impositions even at relatively trivial levels when governmental restraints are undeniably irrational as unsupported by any imaginable rationale. Such instances are suitably rare. The claims of arbitrariness that mark almost all instances of un-enumerated substantive rights are those resting on "certain interests requiring par-ticularly careful scrutiny of the state needs asserted to justify their abridgment," that is, interests in liberty sufficiently important to be judged "fundamental." *Poe*. In the face of an interest this powerful a State may not rest on threshold rationality or a pre-sumption of constitutionality, but may prevail only on the ground of an interest suf-ficiently compelling to place within the realm of the reasonable a refusal to recognize the individual right asserted. *Poe* (Harlan, J., dissenting) (an "enactment involving ... a most fundamental aspect of 'liberty'... [is] subject to 'strict scrutiny'") (quoting *Skinner*).

This approach calls for a court to assess the relative "weights" or dignities of the contending interests, and to this extent the judicial method is familiar to the common law. Common-law method is subject, however, to two important constraints in the hands of a court engaged in substantive due process review. First, such a court is bound to confine the values that it recognizes to those truly deserving constitutional stature, either to those expressed in constitutional text, or those exemplified by "the traditions from which [the Nation] developed," or revealed by contrast with "the tra-ditions from which it broke." *Poe* (Harlan, J., dissenting). "We may not draw on our merely personal and private notions and disregard the limits ... derived from con-siderations that are fused in the whole nature of our judicial process ... [,] consid-erations deeply rooted in reason and in the compelling traditions of the legal profession." *Id.*

The second constraint, again, simply reflects the fact that constitutional review, not judicial lawmaking, is a court's business here.... It is no justification for judicial intervention merely to identify a reasonable resolution of contending values that differs from the terms of the legislation under review. It is only when the legislation's justifying principle, critically valued, is so far from being commensurate with the individual interest as to be arbitrarily or pointlessly applied that the statute must give way. Only if this standard points against the statute can the individual claimant be said to have a constitutional right.[10] ...

Although the *Poe* dissent disclaims the possibility of any general formula for due process analysis (beyond the basic analytic structure just described), Justice Harlan of course assumed that adjudication under the Due Process Clauses is like any other instance of judgment dependent on common-law method, being more or less persuasive according to the usual canons of critical discourse. When identifying and assessing the competing interests of liberty and authority, for example, the breadth of expression that a litigant or a judge selects in stating the competing principles will have much to do with the outcome and may be dispositive. As in any process of rational argumentation, we recognize that when a generally accepted principle is challenged, the broader the attack the less likely it is to succeed....

Just as results in substantive due process cases are tied to the selections of statements of the competing interests, the acceptability of the results is a function of the good reasons for the selections made. It is here that the value of common-law method becomes apparent, for the usual thinking of the common law is suspicious of the all-or-nothing analysis that tends to produce legal petrification instead of an evolving boundary between the domains of old principles. Common-law method tends to pay respect instead to detail, seeking to understand old principles afresh by new examples and new counterexamples. The "tradition is a living thing," *Poe* (Harlan, J., dissenting), albeit one that moves by moderate steps carefully taken. "The decision of an apparently novel claim must depend on grounds which follow closely on well-accepted principles and criteria. The new decision must take its place in relation to what went before and further [cut] a channel for what is to come." *Id.* (Harlan, J., dissenting). Exact analysis and characterization of any due process claim are critical to the method and to the result....

The same insistence on exactitude lies behind questions, in current terminology, about the proper level of generality at which to analyze claims and counterclaims, and the demand for fitness and proper tailoring of a restrictive statute is just another way of testing the legitimacy of the generality at which the government sets up its justification. We may therefore classify Justice Harlan's example of proper analysis in any of these ways: as applying concepts of normal critical reasoning, as pointing to

---

10. Our cases have used various terms to refer to fundamental liberty interests, see, *e.g., Poe* (Harlan, J., dissenting) ("'basic liberty'") (quoting *Skinner*); *Poe* (Harlan, J., dissenting) ("certain interests" must bring "particularly careful scrutiny"); *Casey* ("protected liberty"); *Cruzan* ("constitutionally protected liberty interest"), and at times we have also called such an interest a "right" even before balancing it against the government's interest, see, *e.g., Roe; Poe* ("rights 'which are ... *fundamental*'") (quoting *Corfield v. Coryell*, 4 Wash. C.C. 371 (C.C.E.D.Pa.1825)). Precision in terminology, however, favors reserving the label "right" for instances in which the individual's liberty interest actually trumps the government's countervailing interests; only then does the individual have anything legally enforceable as against the state's attempt at regulation.

the need to attend to the levels of generality at which countervailing interests are stated, or as examining the concrete application of principles for fitness with their own ostensible justifications. But whatever the categories in which we place the dissent's example, it stands in marked contrast to earlier cases whose reasoning was marked by comparatively less discrimination, and it points to the importance of evaluating the claims of the parties now before us with comparable detail. For here we are faced with an individual claim not to a right on the part of just anyone to help anyone else commit suicide under any circumstances, but to the right of a narrow class to help others also in a narrow class under a set of limited circumstances. And the claimants are met with the State's assertion, among others, that rights of such narrow scope cannot be recognized without jeopardy to individuals whom the State may concededly protect through its regulations.

## IV

### A

Respondents claim that a patient facing imminent death, who anticipates physical suffering and indignity, and is capable of responsible and voluntary choice, should have a right to a physician's assistance in providing counsel and drugs to be administered by the patient to end life promptly. They accordingly claim that a physician must have the corresponding right to provide such aid, contrary to the provisions of Wash. Rev.Code § 9A.36.060 (1994). I do not understand the argument to rest on any assumption that rights either to suicide or to assistance in committing it are historically based as such. Respondents, rather, acknowledge the prohibition of each historically, but rely on the fact that to a substantial extent the State has repudiated that history. The result of this, respondents say, is to open the door to claims of such a patient to be accorded one of the options open to those with different, traditionally cognizable claims to autonomy in deciding how their bodies and minds should be treated. They seek the option to obtain the services of a physician to give them the benefit of advice and medical help, which is said to enjoy a tradition so strong and so devoid of specifically countervailing state concern that denial of a physician's help in these circumstances is arbitrary when physicians are generally free to advise and aid those who exercise other rights to bodily autonomy....

### 2

The argument supporting respondents' position thus progresses through three steps of increasing forcefulness. First, it emphasizes the decriminalization of suicide. Reliance on this fact is sanctioned under the standard that looks not only to the tradition retained, but to society's occasional choices to reject traditions of the legal past. See *Poe*. While the common law prohibited both suicide and aiding a suicide, with the prohibition on aiding largely justified by the primary prohibition on self-inflicted death itself, the State's rejection of the traditional treatment of the one leaves the criminality of the other open to questioning that previously would not have been appropriate. The second step in the argument is to emphasize that the State's own act of decriminalization gives a freedom of choice much like the individual's option in recognized instances of bodily autonomy. One of these, abortion, is a legal right to choose in spite of the interest a State may legitimately invoke in discouraging the practice, just as suicide is now subject to choice, despite a state interest in discouraging it. The third step is to emphasize that respondents claim a right to assistance not on the basis of some broad principle that would be subject to exceptions if that continuing interest of the State's in discouraging suicide were to be recognized at all. Respondents base their claim on the traditional right to medical care and counsel, subject to the limiting conditions of informed, responsible choice when death is imminent, conditions that support a strong analogy to rights of care in other situations in which medical counsel and assistance have been available as a matter of course. There can be no stronger claim to a physician's assistance than at the time when death is imminent, a moral judgment implied by the State's own recognition of the legitimacy of medical procedures necessarily hastening the moment of impending death.

In my judgment, the importance of the individual interest here ... as within that class of "certain interests" demanding careful scrutiny of the State's contrary claim, see *Poe*, cannot be gainsaid. Whether that interest might in some circumstances, or at some time, be seen as "fundamental" to the degree entitled to prevail is not, however, a conclusion that I need draw here, for I am satisfied that the State's interests described in the following section are sufficiently serious to defeat the present claim that its law is arbitrary or purposeless.

### B

The State has put forward several interests to justify the Washington law as applied to physicians treating terminally ill patients, even those competent to make responsible choices: protecting life generally, discouraging suicide even if knowing and voluntary, and protecting terminally ill patients from involuntary suicide and euthanasia, both voluntary and nonvoluntary.

It is not necessary to discuss the exact strengths of the first two claims of justification in the present circumstances, for the third is dispositive for me. That third justification is different from the first two, for it addresses specific features of respondents' claim, and it opposes that claim not with a moral judgment contrary to respondents', but with a recognized state interest in the protection of nonresponsible individuals and those who do not stand in relation either to death or to their physicians as do the patients whom respondents describe.

[Justice Souter then acknowledged that the plaintiffs' claims were strengthened by the fact that they sought, not a broad right to assisted suicide, but a right to professional medical assistance in ending one's life when death was imminent, backed up by stringent regulatory safeguards. Nevertheless, he concluded that the conflicting evidence about the effectiveness of such regulations in the Netherlands, which had instituted government-regulated physician-assisted suicide, made Washington's rejection of that approach a reasonable decision.]

Justice GINSBURG, concurring in the judgments.

I concur ... substantially for the reasons stated by Justice O'CONNOR in her concurring opinion.

Justice BREYER, concurring in the judgments.

I believe that Justice O'CONNOR's views, which I share, have greater legal significance than the Court's opinion suggests. I join her separate opinion, except insofar as it joins the majority. And I concur in the judgments. I shall briefly explain how I differ from the Court.

... I do not agree ... with the Court's formulation of [the] claimed "liberty" interest. The Court describes it as a "right to commit suicide with another's assistance." But I would not reject the respondents' claim without considering a different formulation, for which our legal tradition may provide greater support. That formulation would use words roughly like a "right to die with dignity." But irrespective of the exact words used, at its core would lie personal control over the manner of death, professional medical assistance, and the avoidance of unnecessary and severe physical suffering—combined.

As Justice SOUTER points out, Justice Harlan's dissenting opinion in *Poe* offers some support for such a claim.

... The respondents here ... argue that one can find a "right to die with dignity" by examining the protection the law has provided for related, but not identical, interests relating to personal dignity, medical treatment, and freedom from state-inflicted pain.

I do not believe, however, that this Court need or now should decide whether or a not such a right is "fundamental." That is because, in my view, the avoidance of severe physical pain (connected with death) would have to constitute an essential part of any successful claim and because, as Justice O'CONNOR points out, the laws before us do not force a dying person to undergo that kind of pain. Rather, the laws of ... Washington do not prohibit doctors from providing patients with drugs sufficient to control pain despite the risk that those drugs themselves will kill....

This legal circumstance means that the ... laws before us do not infringe directly upon the (assumed) central interest (what I have called the core of the interest in dying with dignity) as, by way of contrast, the state anticontraceptive laws at issue in *Poe* did interfere with the central interest there at stake—by bringing the State's police powers to bear upon the marital bedroom.

Were the legal circumstances different—for example, were state law to prevent the provision of palliative care, including the administration of drugs as needed to avoid pain at the end of life—then the law's impact upon serious and otherwise unavoidable physical pain (accompanying death) would be more directly at issue. And as Justice O'CONNOR suggests, the Court might have to revisit its conclusions in these cases.

### Note: Due Process Analysis in **Moore, Michael H.,** *and* **Glucksberg**

1. The various opinions in the three preceding cases reflect the approaches to substantive due process analysis prominent in the last quarter of the Twentieth century. This note considers those approaches, and asks you to analyze and evaluate them.

2. Begin with Justice Powell's opinion in *Moore.* His opinion can be understood as reflecting one of the foundational approaches to modern due process analysis: the approach that first determines whether the interest at stake ranks as "fundamental,"

and then, second, applies heightened review (what has been come to be called "strict scrutiny") to the interests that can be so identified. What is it about Mrs. Moore's claim that led him to identify it as meriting such heightened scrutiny? How did Justice Stewart analyze her claim? What does Stewart's analysis—in particular, his evaluation of the two aspects of Mrs. Moore's associational rights claim—suggest about his view of the appropriate scope of substantive due process? What about Justice White: how did he decide whether that claim merited heightened scrutiny? Note that Justice White discussed both Justice Black's extreme skepticism about unenumerated substantive due process rights, and Justice Harlan's approach to such rights in his *Poe v. Ullman* dissent. How would you describe his evaluation of those two approaches?

3. Consider now *Michael H.* and, in particular, the conflict between Justices Scalia and Brennan over the level of generality appropriate to expressing and analyzing due process claims. Justice Scalia argued that his "narrow" approach to identifying the liberty interest at issue provides a level of objectivity to due process analysis. Do you agree, or do you agree with Justice Brennan's critique of that argument? If you agree with Justice Brennan's broader approach to identifying due process interests, can you articulate a principle governing the level of generality that would be appropriate in a given case?

Levels of generality aside, Justice Brennan protested that Justice Scalia's "plurality acts as if the only purpose of the Due Process Clause is to confirm the importance of interests already protected by a majority of the States." What did he mean by that? Do you agree with his critique? Is that limitation the price of grounding substantive due process on a principled legal analysis, rather than on the policy preferences of any particular justice?

4. The majority opinion in *Glucksberg* applied Justice Scalia's approach in *Michael H.*.(Indeed, Chief Justice Rehnquist, *Glucksberg*'s author, was the only justice to join Footnote 6 of Justice Scalia's opinion in *Michael H.*, which defended the "narrowest possible grounds" approach to identifying substantive due process interests.) By contrast, Justice Souter's opinion concurring in the judgment constituted a full defense and application of Justice Harlan's approach from Harlan's dissent in *Poe v. Ullman*.

Consider Justice Souter's opinion. How did his analysis differ from the purely historical-based approach in Chief Justice Rehnquist's dissent? What use did he make of the evolution of American society's (and thus American law's) attitude toward suicide? Note in particular that, in Part IV of his opinion, he identified the plaintiffs' claimed interest more narrowly than a generalized interest in assistance in committing suicide. How does his "narrow" approach differ from Justice Scalia's embrace of "narrowness" in identifying the interest at issue in *Michael H.*?

5. Which of the approaches illustrated in these three cases do you find most appealing? Why?

## *Note:* Bowers v. Hardwick

1. *Lawrence v. Texas*, 539 U.S. 558 (2003), excerpted below, struck down Texas's law criminalizing "deviant sexual intercourse"—defined as oral or anal sex—between

persons of the same sex. In striking down that law in 2003, the Court overruled a precedent from seventeen years before, *Bowers v. Hardwick*, 478 U.S. 186 (1986).

2. *Bowers* involved a claim by Michael Hardwick, a Georgia man who was arrested but not prosecuted for violating Georgia's law criminalizing "sodomy," whether it was performed by same-sex or opposite-sex couples, when a police officer entering Hardwick's apartment observed Hardwick having sex with another man. A heterosexual couple joined Hardwick as plaintiffs in the lawsuit, arguing that the law and Hardwick's arrested "chilled and deterred" them from engaging in the proscribed conduct; however, the lower courts held that they lacked standing because there was no realistic likelihood that they would be arrested for violating the law. Thus, the Supreme Court concluded that "the only claim properly before the Court ... is Hardwick's challenge to the Georgia statute as applied to consensual homosexual sodomy."

3. As thus framed, the Court, in a 5–4 vote, upheld the Georgia law. Writing for the majority, Justice White presented the issue as "whether the Federal Constitution confers a fundamental right upon homosexuals to engage in sodomy and hence invalidates the laws of the many States that still make such conduct illegal and have done so for a very long time." After citing the foundational due process cases presented above and in the previous two chapters, he distinguished them by stating that "none of the rights announced in those cases bears any resemblance to the claimed constitutional right of homosexuals to engage in acts of sodomy that is asserted in this case. No connection between family, marriage, or procreation on the one hand and homosexual activity on the other has been demonstrated, either by the Court of Appeals or by respondent." He then considered whether, "precedent aside," Hardwick had made out a claim that he had suffered a violation of a fundamental due process right. After canvassing the history of sodomy proscriptions that American jurisdictions had historically imposed and that remained in effect, he concluded that "against this background, to claim that a right to engage in such conduct is 'deeply rooted in this Nation's history and tradition' or 'implicit in the concept of ordered liberty' is, at best, facetious."

4. Chief Justice Burger joined the majority opinion but wrote a separate concurrence, emphasizing that "the proscriptions against sodomy have very 'ancient roots'" and that "condemnation of [homosexual conduct] is firmly rooted in Judeao-Christian moral and ethical standards."

5. Justice Powell also joined the majority and wrote a separate opinion to suggest that imprisonment of Hardwick for his conduct might violate the Eighth Amendment's prohibition on cruel and unusual punishments. (He observed that the Georgia law provided for a penalty of up to twenty years of imprisonment for a single violation.) As a fascinating sidelight, historians have suggested that Justice Powell originally voted to strike the Georgia law down, thus creating a (fleeting) majority for that result. *See* Joyce Murdoch & Deb Price, *Courting Justice* 339 (2001). After stepping down from the Court, Justice Powell stated publicly that he had come to believe that the dissent had the better argument.

6. Justice Blackmun dissented for himself, and Justices Brennan, Marshall, and Stevens. He emphasized both the importance of persons' freedom to engage in sexual

intimacy, and the importance of the home as a space the government had limited authority to enter. Justice Stevens also wrote a dissent, joined by Justices Brennan and Marshall, in which he concluded both that cases such as *Griswold* and *Eisenstadt* established a right of individuals to engage in non-procreative sex.

7. *Bowers* was heavily criticized, in ways that Justice Kennedy notes in his *Lawrence* opinion. But its immediate effect was to shift the attention of gay rights advocates away from federal constitutional due process claims. In the years after *Bowers*, advocates shifted to states, winning a number of state constitutional law decisions and legislative repeals of sodomy laws. In the federal system, *Bowers* led advocates to focus on equal protection rather than due process. At the Supreme Court, the first major victory from that approach was *Romer v. Evans*, 517 U.S. 620 (1996), which appears in Chapter 15 of this book. While you have not yet encountered the Court's equal protection jurisprudence, you should still consider how Justice Kennedy used ideas about equality in his due process analysis in *Lawrence*.

## Lawrence v. Texas

### 539 U.S. 558 (2003)

Justice KENNEDY delivered the opinion of the Court.

Liberty protects the person from unwarranted government intrusions into a dwelling or other private places. In our tradition the State is not omnipresent in the home. And there are other spheres of our lives and existence, outside the home, where the State should not be a dominant presence. Freedom extends beyond spatial bounds. Liberty presumes an autonomy of self that includes freedom of thought, belief, expression, and certain intimate conduct. The instant case involves liberty of the person both in its spatial and in its more transcendent dimensions.

I

The question before the Court is the validity of a Texas statute making it a crime for two persons of the same sex to engage in certain intimate sexual conduct.

In Houston, Texas, officers of the Harris County Police Department were dispatched to a private residence in response to a reported weapons disturbance. They entered an apartment where one of the petitioners, John Geddes Lawrence, resided. The right of the police to enter does not seem to have been questioned. The officers observed Lawrence and another man, Tyron Garner, engaging in a sexual act. The two petitioners were arrested, held in custody overnight, and charged and convicted before a Justice of the Peace.

The complaints described their crime as "deviate sexual intercourse, namely anal sex, with a member of the same sex (man)." The applicable state law is Tex. Penal Code Ann. § 21.06(a) (2003). It provides: "A person commits an offense if he engages in deviate sexual intercourse with another individual of the same sex." The statute defines "deviate sexual intercourse" as follows:

"(A) any contact between any part of the genitals of one person and the mouth or anus of another person; or

"(B) the penetration of the genitals or the anus of another person with an object."

The petitioners exercised their right to a trial *de novo* in Harris County Criminal Court. They challenged the statute as a violation of the Equal Protection Clause of the Fourteenth Amendment and of a like provision of the Texas Constitution. Those contentions were rejected. The petitioners, having entered a plea of *nolo contendere*, were each fined $200 and assessed court costs of $141.25.

The Court of Appeals for the Texas Fourteenth District considered the petitioners' federal constitutional arguments under both the Equal Protection and Due Process Clauses of the Fourteenth Amendment. After hearing the case en banc the court, in a divided opinion, rejected the constitutional arguments and affirmed the convictions. The majority opinion indicates that the Court of Appeals considered our decision in *Bowers v. Hardwick*, 478 U.S. 186 (1986) [Note *supra*. this chapter], to be controlling on the federal due process aspect of the case. *Bowers* then being authoritative, this was proper.

We granted certiorari, to consider three questions:

1. Whether petitioners' criminal convictions under the Texas 'Homosexual Conduct' law — which criminalizes sexual intimacy by same-sex couples, but not identical behavior by different-sex couples — violate the Fourteenth Amendment guarantee of equal protection of the laws.

2. Whether petitioners' criminal convictions for adult consensual sexual intimacy in the home violate their vital interests in liberty and privacy protected by the Due Process Clause of the Fourteenth Amendment.

3. Whether *Bowers v. Hardwick, supra.*, should be overruled.

The petitioners were adults at the time of the alleged offense. Their conduct was in private and consensual.

## II

We conclude the case should be resolved by determining whether the petitioners were free as adults to engage in the private conduct in the exercise of their liberty under the Due Process Clause of the Fourteenth Amendment to the Constitution. For this inquiry we deem it necessary to reconsider the Court's holding in *Bowers*.

There are broad statements of the substantive reach of liberty under the Due Process Clause in earlier cases, including *Pierce v. Society of Sisters*, 268 U.S. 510 (1925) [Note *supra*. Chapter 8], and *Meyer v. Nebraska* (1923) [*Supra*. Chapter 8; but the most pertinent beginning point is our decision in *Griswold v. Connecticut* (1965) [*Supra*. Chapter 9].

In *Griswold* the Court invalidated a state law prohibiting the use of drugs or devices of contraception and counseling or aiding and abetting the use of contraceptives. The Court described the protected interest as a right to privacy and placed emphasis on the marriage relation and the protected space of the marital bedroom.

After *Griswold* it was established that the right to make certain decisions regarding sexual conduct extends beyond the marital relationship. In *Eisenstadt v. Baird*, 405

U.S. 438 (1972) [Note *supra*. Chapter 9], the Court invalidated a law prohibiting the distribution of contraceptives to unmarried persons. The case was decided under the Equal Protection Clause, but with respect to unmarried persons, the Court went on to state the fundamental proposition that the law impaired the exercise of their personal rights. It quoted from the statement of the Court of Appeals finding the law to be in conflict with fundamental human rights, and it followed with this statement of its own:

> It is true that in *Griswold* the right of privacy in question inhered in the marital relationship.... If the right of privacy means anything, it is the right of the *individual*, married or single, to be free from unwarranted governmental intrusion into matters so fundamentally affecting a person as the decision whether to bear or beget a child.

The opinions in *Griswold* and *Eisenstadt* were part of the background for the decision in *Roe v. Wade* (1973) [*Supra*. Chapter 9].... Although the Court held the woman's rights were not absolute, her right to elect an abortion did have real and substantial protection as an exercise of her liberty under the Due Process Clause. The Court cited cases that protect spatial freedom and cases that go well beyond it. *Roe* recognized the right of a woman to make certain fundamental decisions affecting her destiny and confirmed once more that the protection of liberty under the Due Process Clause has a substantive dimension of fundamental significance in defining the rights of the person.

In *Carey v. Population Services Int'l*, 431 U.S. 678 (1977), the Court confronted a New York law forbidding sale or distribution of contraceptive devices to persons under 16 years of age. Although there was no single opinion for the Court, the law was invalidated. Both *Eisenstadt* and *Carey*, as well as the holding and rationale in *Roe*, confirmed that the reasoning of *Griswold* could not be confined to the protection of rights of married adults. This was the state of the law with respect to some of the most relevant cases when the Court considered *Bowers v. Hardwick*.

The facts in *Bowers* had some similarities to the instant case. A police officer, whose right to enter seems not to have been in question, observed Hardwick, in his own bedroom, engaging in intimate sexual conduct with another adult male. The conduct was in violation of a Georgia statute making it a criminal offense to engage in sodomy. One difference between the two cases is that the Georgia statute prohibited the conduct whether or not the participants were of the same sex, while the Texas statute, as we have seen, applies only to participants of the same sex.... The Court, in an opinion by Justice White, sustained the Georgia law. Chief Justice Burger and Justice Powell joined the opinion of the Court and filed separate, concurring opinions. Four Justices dissented.

The Court began its substantive discussion in *Bowers* as follows: "The issue presented is whether the Federal Constitution confers a fundamental right upon homosexuals to engage in sodomy and hence invalidates the laws of the many States that still make such conduct illegal and have done so for a very long time." That statement, we now conclude, discloses the Court's own failure to appreciate the extent of the liberty at stake. To say that the issue in *Bowers* was simply the right to engage in certain sexual conduct demeans the claim the individual put forward, just as it would demean a married couple were it to be said marriage is simply about the right to have sexual intercourse. The laws involved in *Bowers* and here are, to be sure, statutes that purport to do no more than prohibit a particular sexual act. Their penalties and purposes, though, have more far-reaching consequences, touching upon the most private human conduct, sexual behavior, and in the most private of places, the home. The statutes do seek to control a personal relationship that, whether or not entitled to formal recognition in the law, is within the liberty of persons to choose without being punished as criminals.

This, as a general rule, should counsel against attempts by the State, or a court, to define the meaning of the relationship or to set its boundaries absent injury to a person or abuse of an institution the law protects. It suffices for us to acknowledge that adults may choose to enter upon this relationship in the confines of their homes and their own private lives and still retain their dignity as free persons. When sexuality finds overt expression in intimate conduct with another person, the conduct can be but one element in a personal bond that is more enduring. The liberty protected by the Constitution allows homosexual persons the right to make this choice.

Having misapprehended the claim of liberty there presented to it, and thus stating the claim to be whether there is a fundamental right to engage in consensual sodomy, the *Bowers* Court said: "Proscriptions against that conduct have ancient roots." In academic writings, and in many of the scholarly *amicus* briefs filed to assist the Court in this case, there are fundamental criticisms of the historical premises relied upon by the majority and concurring opinions in *Bowers*. Brief for Cato Institute as Amicus Curiae 16–17; Brief for American Civil Liberties Union et al. as Amici Curiae 15–21; Brief for Professors of History et al. as Amici Curiae 3–10. We need not enter this debate in the attempt to reach a definitive historical judgment, but the following considerations counsel against adopting the definitive conclusions upon which *Bowers* placed such reliance.

At the outset it should be noted that there is no longstanding history in this country of laws directed at homosexual conduct as a distinct matter. Beginning in colonial times there were prohibitions of sodomy derived from the English criminal laws passed in the first instance by the Reformation Parliament of 1533. The English prohibition was understood to include relations between men and women as well as relations between men and men. Nineteenth-century commentators similarly read American sodomy, buggery, and crime-against-nature statutes as criminalizing certain relations between men and women and between men and men. The absence of legal prohibitions focusing on homosexual conduct may be explained in part by noting that according to some scholars the concept of the homosexual as a distinct category of person did not emerge until the late 19th century. See, e.g., J. D'Emilio & E. Freedman, *Intimate Matters: A History of Sexuality in America* (2d ed. 1997) ("The modern terms *homosexuality* and *heterosexuality* do not apply to an era that had not yet articulated these distinctions"). Thus early American sodomy laws were not directed at homosexuals as such but instead sought to prohibit nonprocreative sexual activity more generally. This does not suggest approval of homosexual conduct. It does tend to show that this particular form of conduct was not thought of as a separate category from like conduct between heterosexual persons.

Laws prohibiting sodomy do not seem to have been enforced against consenting adults acting in private.... In all events that infrequency makes it difficult to say that society approved of a rigorous and systematic punishment of the consensual acts committed in private and by adults. The longstanding criminal prohibition of homosexual sodomy upon which the *Bowers* decision placed such reliance is as consistent with a general condemnation of nonprocreative sex as it is with an established tradition of prosecuting acts because of their homosexual character....

It was not until the 1970's that any State singled out same-sex relations for criminal prosecution, and only nine States have done so. Post-*Bowers* even some of these States did not adhere to the policy of suppressing homosexual conduct. Over the course of the last decades, States with same-sex prohibitions have moved toward abolishing them.

In summary, the historical grounds relied upon in *Bowers* are more complex than the majority opinion and the concurring opinion by Chief Justice Burger indicate. Their historical premises are not without doubt and, at the very least, are overstated.

It must be acknowledged, of course, that the Court in *Bowers* was making the broader point that for centuries there have been powerful voices to condemn homosexual conduct as immoral. The condemnation has been shaped by religious beliefs, conceptions of right and acceptable behavior, and respect for the traditional family. For many persons these are not trivial concerns but profound and deep convictions accepted as ethical and moral principles to which they aspire and which thus determine the course of their lives. These considerations do not answer the question before us, however. The issue is whether the majority may use the power of the State to enforce these views on the whole society through operation of the criminal law. "Our obligation is to define the liberty of all, not to mandate our own moral code." *Planned Parenthood of Southeastern Pa. v. Casey* (1992) [*Supra.* Chapter 9].

Chief Justice Burger joined the opinion for the Court in *Bowers* and further explained his views as follows: "Decisions of individuals relating to homosexual conduct have been subject to state intervention throughout the history of Western civilization. Condemnation of those practices is firmly rooted in Judeao-Christian moral and ethical standards." As with Justice White's assumptions about history, scholarship casts some doubt on the sweeping nature of the statement by Chief Justice Burger as it pertains to private homosexual conduct between consenting adults. See, e.g., Eskridge, "*Hardwick* and Historiography," 1999 *U. Ill. L.Rev.* 631. In all events we think that our laws and traditions in the past half century are of most relevance here. These references show an emerging awareness that liberty gives substantial protection to adult persons in deciding how to conduct their private lives in matters pertaining to sex. "History and tradition are the starting point but not in all cases the ending point of the substantive due process inquiry." *County of Sacramento v. Lewis*, 523 U.S. 833 (1998) (KENNEDY, J., concurring).

This emerging recognition should have been apparent when *Bowers* was decided. In 1955 the American Law Institute promulgated the Model Penal Code and made clear that it did not recommend or provide for "criminal penalties for consensual sexual relations conducted in private." ... In 1961 Illinois changed its laws to conform to the Model Penal Code. Other States soon followed....

The sweeping references by Chief Justice Burger to the history of Western civilization and to Judeo-Christian moral and ethical standards did not take account of other authorities pointing in an opposite direction. A committee advising the British Parliament recommended in 1957 repeal of laws punishing homosexual conduct. Parliament enacted the substance of those recommendations 10 years later.

Of even more importance, almost five years before *Bowers* was decided the European Court of Human Rights considered a case with parallels to *Bowers* and to today's case. An adult male resident in Northern Ireland alleged he was a practicing homosexual who desired to engage in consensual homosexual conduct. The laws of Northern Ireland forbade him that right. He alleged that he had been questioned, his home had been searched, and he feared criminal prosecution. The court held that the laws proscribing the conduct were invalid under the European Convention on Human Rights. Authoritative in all countries that are members of the Council of Europe (21 nations then, 45 nations now), the decision is at odds with the premise in *Bowers* that the claim put forward was insubstantial in our Western civilization.

In our own constitutional system the deficiencies in *Bowers* became even more apparent in the years following its announcement. The 25 States with laws prohibiting the relevant conduct referenced in the *Bowers* decision are reduced now to 13, of which 4 enforce their laws only against homosexual conduct. In those States where sodomy is still proscribed, whether for same-sex or heterosexual conduct, there is a pattern of nonenforcement with respect to consenting adults acting in private. The State of Texas admitted in 1994 that as of that date it had not prosecuted anyone under those circumstances.

Two principal cases decided after *Bowers* cast its holding into even more doubt. In *Casey* the Court ... again confirmed that our laws and tradition afford constitutional protection to personal decisions relating to marriage, procreation, contraception, family relationships, child rearing, and education. In explaining the respect the Constitution demands for the autonomy of the person in making these choices, we stated as follows:

> These matters, involving the most intimate and personal choices a person may make in a lifetime, choices central to personal dignity and autonomy, are central to the liberty protected by the Fourteenth Amendment. At the heart of liberty is the right to define one's own concept of existence, of meaning, of the universe, and of the mystery of human life. Beliefs about these matters could not define the attributes of personhood were they formed under compulsion of the State.

Persons in a homosexual relationship may seek autonomy for these purposes, just as heterosexual persons do. The decision in *Bowers* would deny them this right.

The second post-*Bowers* case of principal relevance is *Romer v. Evans*, 517 U.S. 620 (1996). There the Court struck down class-based legislation directed at homosexuals as a violation of the Equal Protection Clause. *Romer* invalidated an amendment to Colorado's Constitution which named as a solitary class persons who were homosexuals, lesbians, or bisexual either by "orientation, conduct, practices or relationships," and deprived them of protection under state antidiscrimination laws. We concluded that the provision was "born of animosity toward the class of persons affected" and further that it had no rational relation to a legitimate governmental purpose.

As an alternative argument in this case, counsel for the petitioners and some *amici* contend that *Romer* provides the basis for declaring the Texas statute invalid under the Equal Protection Clause. That is a tenable argument, but we conclude the instant case requires us to address whether *Bowers* itself has continuing validity. Were we to hold the statute invalid under the Equal Protection Clause some might question whether a prohibition would be valid if drawn differently, say, to prohibit the conduct both between same-sex and different-sex participants.

Equality of treatment and the due process right to demand respect for conduct protected by the substantive guarantee of liberty are linked in important respects, and a decision on the latter point advances both interests. If protected conduct is made criminal and the law which does so remains unexamined for its substantive validity, its stigma might remain even if it were not enforceable as drawn for equal protection reasons. When homosexual conduct is made criminal by the law of the State, that declaration in and of itself is an invitation to subject homosexual persons to discrimination both in the public and in the private spheres. The central holding of *Bowers* has been brought in question by this case, and it should be addressed. Its continuance as precedent demeans the lives of homosexual persons.

The stigma this criminal statute imposes, moreover, is not trivial. The offense, to be sure, is but a class C misdemeanor, a minor offense in the Texas legal system. Still, it remains a criminal offense with all that imports for the dignity of the persons charged.... We are advised that if Texas convicted an adult for private, consensual homosexual conduct under the statute here in question the convicted person would come within the registration laws of at least four States were he or she to be subject to their jurisdiction.... Furthermore, the Texas criminal conviction carries with it the other collateral consequences always following a conviction, such as notations on job application forms, to mention but one example.

The foundations of *Bowers* have sustained serious erosion from our recent decisions in *Casey* and *Romer*. When our precedent has been thus weakened, criticism from other sources is of greater significance. In the United States criticism of *Bowers* has been substantial and continuing, disapproving of its reasoning in all respects, not just as to its historical assumptions....

To the extent *Bowers* relied on values we share with a wider civilization, it should be noted that the reasoning and holding in *Bowers* have been rejected elsewhere. The European Court of Human Rights has followed not *Bowers* but its own decision in *Dudgeon v. United Kingdom*, 45 Eur. Ct. H.R. (1981). Other nations, too, have taken action consistent with an affirmation of the protected right of homosexual adults to engage in intimate, consensual conduct. The right the petitioners seek in this case has been accepted as an integral part of human freedom in many other countries. There has been no showing that in this country the governmental interest in circumscribing personal choice is somehow more legitimate or urgent....

The rationale of *Bowers* does not withstand careful analysis. In his dissenting opinion in *Bowers* Justice STEVENS came to these conclusions:

> Our prior cases make two propositions abundantly clear. First, the fact that the governing majority in a State has traditionally viewed a particular practice as immoral is not a sufficient reason for upholding a law prohibiting the practice; neither history nor tradition could save a law prohibiting miscegenation from constitutional attack. Second, individual decisions by married persons, concerning the intimacies of their physical relationship, even when not intended to produce offspring, are a form of 'liberty' protected by the Due Process Clause of the Fourteenth Amendment. Moreover, this protection extends to intimate choices by unmarried as well as married persons.

Justice STEVENS' analysis, in our view, should have been controlling in *Bowers* and should control here.

*Bowers* was not correct when it was decided, and it is not correct today. It ought not to remain binding precedent. *Bowers v. Hardwick* should be and now is overruled.

The present case does not involve minors. It does not involve persons who might be injured or coerced or who are situated in relationships where consent might not easily be refused. It does not involve public conduct or prostitution. It does not involve whether the government must give formal recognition to any relationship that homosexual persons seek to enter. The case does involve two adults who, with full and mutual consent from each other, engaged in sexual practices common to a homosexual lifestyle. The petitioners are entitled to respect for their private lives. The State cannot demean their existence or control their destiny by making their private sexual conduct a crime. Their right to liberty under the Due Process Clause gives them the full right to engage in their conduct without intervention of the government. "It is a promise of the Constitution that there is a realm of personal liberty which the government may not enter." *Casey*. The Texas statute furthers no legitimate state interest which can justify its intrusion into the personal and private life of the individual.

Had those who drew and ratified the Due Process Clauses of the Fifth Amendment or the Fourteenth Amendment known the components of liberty in its manifold possibilities, they might have been more specific. They did not presume to have this insight. They knew times can blind us to certain truths and later generations can see that laws once thought necessary and proper in fact serve only to oppress. As the

Constitution endures, persons in every generation can invoke its principles in their own search for greater freedom.

The judgment of the Court of Appeals for the Texas Fourteenth District is reversed....

Justice O'CONNOR, concurring in the judgment.

The Court today overrules *Bowers.* I joined *Bowers,* and do not join the Court in overruling it. Nevertheless, I agree with the Court that Texas' statute banning same-sex sodomy is unconstitutional. Rather than relying on the substantive component of the Fourteenth Amendment's Due Process Clause, as the Court does, I base my conclusion on the Fourteenth Amendment's Equal Protection Clause. [Justice O'Connor's equal protection analysis is presented in Chapter 15 of this book.]

Justice SCALIA, with whom THE CHIEF JUSTICE and Justice THOMAS join, dissenting....

Most of ... today's opinion has no relevance to its actual holding—that the Texas statute "furthers no legitimate state interest which can justify" its application to petitioners under rational-basis review. Though there is discussion of "fundamental propositions," and "fundamental decisions," nowhere does the Court's opinion declare that homosexual sodomy is a "fundamental right" under the Due Process Clause; nor does it subject the Texas law to the standard of review that would be appropriate (strict scrutiny) if homosexual sodomy *were* a "fundamental right." Thus, while over-ruling the *outcome* of *Bowers,* the Court leaves strangely untouched its central legal conclusion: "Respondent would have us announce ... a fundamental right to engage in homosexual sodomy. This we are quite unwilling to do." Instead the Court simply describes petitioners' conduct as "an exercise of their liberty"—which it undoubtedly is—and proceeds to apply an unheard-of form of rational-basis review that will have far-reaching implications beyond this case....

II

... Texas Penal Code Ann. § 21.06(a) (2003) undoubtedly imposes constraints on liberty. So do laws prohibiting prostitution, recreational use of heroin, and, for that matter, working more than 60 hours per week in a bakery. But there is no right to "liberty" under the Due Process Clause, though today's opinion repeatedly makes that claim. The Fourteenth Amendment *expressly allows* States to deprive their citizens of "liberty," *so long as "due process of law" is provided....*

Our opinions applying the doctrine known as "substantive due process" hold that the Due Process Clause prohibits States from infringing *fundamental* liberty interests, unless the infringement is narrowly tailored to serve a compelling state interest. *Washington v. Glucksberg* (1997) [*Supra.* this chapter]. We have held repeatedly, in cases the Court today does not overrule, that *only* fundamental rights qualify for this so-called "heightened scrutiny" protection—that is, rights which are "deeply rooted in this Nation's history and tradition.[3] All other liberty interests may be abridged or ab-

---

3. The Court is quite right that "history and tradition are the starting point but not in all cases the ending point of the substantive due process inquiry." An asserted "fundamental liberty interest"

rogated pursuant to a validly enacted state law if that law is rationally related to a legitimate state interest....

III

The Court's description of "the state of the law" at the time of *Bowers* only confirms that *Bowers* was right. The Court points to *Griswold*. But that case *expressly disclaimed* any reliance on the doctrine of "substantive due process," and grounded the so-called "right to privacy" in penumbras of constitutional provisions *other than* the Due Process Clause. *Eisenstadt* likewise had nothing to do with "substantive due process"; it invalidated a Massachusetts law prohibiting the distribution of contraceptives to unmarried persons solely on the basis of the Equal Protection Clause. Of course *Eisenstadt* contains well-known dictum relating to the "right to privacy," but this referred to the right recognized in *Griswold*—a right penumbral to the *specific* guarantees in the Bill of Rights, and not a "substantive due process" right.

*Roe* recognized that the right to abort an unborn child was a "fundamental right" protected by the Due Process Clause. The *Roe* Court, however, made no attempt to establish that this right was "deeply rooted in this Nation's history and tradition"; instead, it based its conclusion that "the Fourteenth Amendment's concept of personal liberty ... is broad enough to encompass a woman's decision whether or not to terminate her pregnancy" on its own normative judgment that antiabortion laws were undesirable. We have since rejected *Roe*'s holding that regulations of abortion must be narrowly tailored to serve a compelling state interest, see *Casey*—and thus, by logical implication, *Roe*'s holding that the right to abort an unborn child is a "fundamental right."

After discussing the history of antisodomy laws, the Court proclaims that, "it should be noted that there is no longstanding history in this country of laws directed at homosexual conduct as a distinct matter." This observation in no way casts into doubt the "definitive [historical] conclusion," on which *Bowers* relied: that our Nation has a longstanding history of laws prohibiting *sodomy in general*—regardless of whether it was performed by same-sex or opposite-sex couples:

> It is obvious to us that neither of these formulations would extend a fundamental right to homosexuals to engage in acts of consensual sodomy. Proscriptions against that conduct have ancient roots. *Sodomy* was a criminal offense at common law and was forbidden by the laws of the original 13 States when they ratified the Bill of Rights. In 1868, when the Fourteenth Amendment was ratified, all but 5 of the 37 States in the Union had *criminal sodomy laws*. In fact, until 1961, all 50 States outlawed *sodomy*, and today, 24 States and the District of Columbia continue to provide criminal penalties

---

must not only be "deeply rooted in this Nation's history and tradition," *Glucksberg*, but it must *also* be "implicit in the concept of ordered liberty," so that "neither liberty nor justice would exist if [it] were sacrificed," *id*. Moreover, liberty interests unsupported by history and tradition, though not deserving of "heightened scrutiny," are *still* protected from state laws that are not rationally related to any legitimate state interest. As I proceed to discuss, it is this latter principle that the Court applies in the present case.

for *sodomy* performed in private and between consenting adults. Against this background, to claim that a right to engage in such conduct is 'deeply rooted in this Nation's history and tradition' or 'implicit in the concept of ordered liberty' is, at best, facetious.

It is (as *Bowers* recognized) entirely irrelevant whether the laws in our long national tradition criminalizing homosexual sodomy were "directed at homosexual conduct as a distinct matter." Whether homosexual sodomy was prohibited by a law targeted at same-sex sexual relations or by a more general law prohibiting both homosexual and heterosexual sodomy, the only relevant point is that it *was* criminalized—which suffices to establish that homosexual sodomy is not a right "deeply rooted in our Nation's history and tradition." The Court today agrees that homosexual sodomy was criminalized and thus does not dispute the facts on which *Bowers actually* relied.

Next the Court makes the claim, again unsupported by any citations, that "laws prohibiting sodomy do not seem to have been enforced against consenting adults acting in private." The key qualifier here is "acting in private"—since the Court admits that sodomy laws *were* enforced against consenting adults (although the Court contends that prosecutions were "infrequent").… Surely that lack of evidence would not sustain the proposition that consensual sodomy on private premises with the doors closed and windows covered was regarded as a "fundamental right," even though all other consensual sodomy was criminalized. There are 203 prosecutions for consensual, adult homosexual sodomy reported in the West Reporting system and official state reporters from the years 1880–1995.… *Bowers'* conclusion that homosexual sodomy is not a fundamental right "deeply rooted in this Nation's history and tradition" is utterly unassailable.

Realizing that fact, the Court instead says: "We think that our laws and traditions in the past half century are of most relevance here. These references show *an emerging awareness* that liberty gives substantial protection to adult persons in deciding how to conduct their private lives *in matters pertaining to sex*." Apart from the fact that such an "emerging awareness" does not establish a "fundamental right," the statement is factually false. States continue to prosecute all sorts of crimes by adults "in matters pertaining to sex": prostitution, adult incest, adultery, obscenity, and child pornography. Sodomy laws, too, have been enforced "in the past half century," in which there have been 134 reported cases involving prosecutions for consensual, adult, homosexual sodomy.…

In any event, an "emerging awareness" is by definition not "deeply rooted in this Nation's history and traditions," as we have said "fundamental right" status requires.…

IV

I turn now to the ground on which the Court squarely rests its holding: the contention that there is no rational basis for the law here under attack. This proposition is so out of accord with our jurisprudence—indeed, with the jurisprudence of any society we know—that it requires little discussion.

The Texas statute undeniably seeks to further the belief of its citizens that certain forms of sexual behavior are "immoral and unacceptable," *Bowers*—the same interest furthered by criminal laws against fornication, bigamy, adultery, adult incest, bestiality, and obscenity. *Bowers* held that this *was* a legitimate state interest. The Court today reaches the opposite conclusion.... The Court embraces instead Justice STEVENS' declaration in his *Bowers* dissent, that "'the fact that the governing majority in a State has traditionally viewed a particular practice as immoral is not a sufficient reason for upholding a law prohibiting the practice.'" This effectively decrees the end of all morals legislation. If, as the Court asserts, the promotion of majoritarian sexual morality is not even a *legitimate* state interest, none of the above-mentioned laws can survive rational-basis review....

*  *  *

Today's opinion is the product of a Court, which is the product of a law-profession culture, that has largely signed on to the so-called homosexual agenda, by which I mean the agenda promoted by some homosexual activists directed at eliminating the moral opprobrium that has traditionally attached to homosexual conduct. I noted in an earlier opinion the fact that the American Association of Law Schools (to which any reputable law school *must* seek to belong) excludes from membership any school that refuses to ban from its job-interview facilities a law firm (no matter how small) that does not wish to hire as a prospective partner a person who openly engages in homosexual conduct. See *Romer*.

One of the most revealing statements in today's opinion is the Court's grim warning that the criminalization of homosexual conduct is "an invitation to subject homosexual persons to discrimination both in the public and in the private spheres." It is clear from this that the Court has taken sides in the culture war, departing from its role of assuring, as neutral observer, that the democratic rules of engagement are observed. Many Americans do not want persons who openly engage in homosexual conduct as partners in their business, as scoutmasters for their children, as teachers in their children's schools, or as boarders in their home. They view this as protecting themselves and their families from a lifestyle that they believe to be immoral and destructive. The Court views it as "discrimination" which it is the function of our judgments to deter. So imbued is the Court with the law profession's anti-anti-homosexual culture, that it is seemingly unaware that the attitudes of that culture are not obviously "mainstream"; that in most States what the Court calls "discrimination" against those who engage in homosexual acts is perfectly legal; that proposals to ban such "discrimination" under Title VII have repeatedly been rejected by Congress; that in some cases such "discrimination" is *mandated* by federal statute, see 10 U.S.C. §654(b)(1) (mandating discharge from the Armed Forces of any service member who engages in or intends to engage in homosexual acts); and that in some cases such "discrimination" is a constitutional right, see *Boy Scouts of America v. Dale*, 530 U.S. 640 (2000).

Let me be clear that I have nothing against homosexuals, or any other group, promoting their agenda through normal democratic means. Social perceptions of sexual and other morality change over time, and every group has the right to persuade its fellow citizens that its view of such matters is the best. That homosexuals have achieved some success in that enterprise is attested to by the fact that Texas is one of the few remaining States that criminalize private, consensual homosexual acts. But persuading one's fellow citizens is one thing, and imposing one's views in absence of democratic majority will is something else. I would no more *require* a State to criminalize homosexual acts—or, for that matter, display any moral disapproval of them—than I would *forbid* it to do so. What Texas has chosen to do is well within the range of traditional democratic action, and its hand should not be stayed through the invention of a brand-new "constitutional right" by a Court that is impatient of democratic change. It is indeed true that "later generations can see that laws once thought necessary and proper in fact serve only to oppress;" and when that happens, later generations can repeal those laws. But it is the premise of our system that those judgments are to be made by the people, and not imposed by a governing caste that knows best.

One of the benefits of leaving regulation of this matter to the people rather than to the courts is that the people, unlike judges, need not carry things to their logical conclusion. The people may feel that their disapproval of homosexual conduct is strong enough to disallow homosexual marriage, but not strong enough to criminalize private homosexual acts—and may legislate accordingly. The Court today pretends that it possesses a similar freedom of action, so that we need not fear judicial imposition of homosexual marriage, as has recently occurred in Canada.... At the end of its opinion—after having laid waste the foundations of our rational-basis jurisprudence—the Court says that the present case "does not involve whether the government must give formal recognition to any relationship that homosexual persons seek to enter." Do not believe it. More illuminating than this bald, unreasoned disclaimer is the progression of thought displayed by an earlier passage in the Court's opinion, which notes the constitutional protections afforded to "personal decisions relating to *marriage*, procreation, contraception, family relationships, child rearing, and education," and then declares that "persons in a homosexual relationship may seek autonomy for these purposes, just as heterosexual persons do." Today's opinion dismantles the structure of constitutional law that has permitted a distinction to be made between heterosexual and homosexual unions, insofar as formal recognition in marriage is concerned. If moral disapproval of homosexual conduct is "no legitimate state interest" for purposes of proscribing that conduct, and if, as the Court coos (casting aside all pretense of neutrality), "when sexuality finds overt expression in intimate conduct with another person, the conduct can be but one element in a personal bond that is more enduring," what justification could there possibly be for denying the benefits of marriage to homosexual couples exercising "the liberty protected by the Constitution"? Surely not the encouragement of procreation, since the sterile and the elderly are allowed to marry. This case "does not involve" the issue of homosexual marriage only if one entertains the belief that principle and logic have nothing to do with the decisions of this Court. Many will hope that, as the Court comfortingly assures us, this is so.

The matters appropriate for this Court's resolution are only three: Texas's prohibition of sodomy neither infringes a "fundamental right" (which the Court does not dispute), nor is unsupported by a rational relation to what the Constitution considers a legitimate state interest, nor denies the equal protection of the laws. I dissent.

Justice THOMAS, dissenting.

I join Justice SCALIA's dissenting opinion. I write separately to note that the law before the Court today "is ... uncommonly silly." *Griswold* (Stewart, J., dissenting). If I were a member of the Texas Legislature, I would vote to repeal it. Punishing someone for expressing his sexual preference through noncommercial consensual conduct with another adult does not appear to be a worthy way to expend valuable law enforcement resources.

Notwithstanding this, I recognize that as a Member of this Court I am not empowered to help petitioners and others similarly situated. My duty, rather, is to "decide cases agreeably to the Constitution and laws of the United States." And, just like Justice Stewart, I "can find [neither in the Bill of Rights nor any other part of the Constitution a] general right of privacy," or as the Court terms it today, the "liberty of the person both in its spatial and more transcendent dimensions."

## *Note:* Lawrence *and Its Ambiguities*

1. Justice Kennedy's opinion in *Lawrence* raises a number of difficult issues about due process analysis. In many ways, his opinion marks a break with the older traditions reflected in cases such as *Moore*, *Michael H.*, and *Glucksberg*—a suggestion that is strengthened by Justice Kennedy's use of similar analysis in his follow-on gay rights opinion in *Obergefell v. Hodges*, excerpted after this note. *Lawrence's* possible novelty, and reinforcement in *Obergefell*, justifies giving his opinion a close look.

2. Consider (again) the level of generality problem that occupied a central role in *Michael H.*. In *Lawrence*, Justice Kennedy rejected *Bowers'* statement of the issue to be decided, describing it as "the Court's ... failure to appreciate the extent of the liberty at stake." Justice Kennedy thus seemingly cast his lot with Justice Brennan, who would have defined the interest at issue in *Michael H.* more broadly than did Justice Scalia. Indeed, recall that Justice Kennedy joined Justice O'Connor's opinion in *Michael H.*, which took pains to distance itself from Justice Scalia's view on the level of generality issue. But consider also the fact that Justice Kennedy joined Chief Justice Rehnquist's majority opinion in *Glucksberg*, which insisted on "a careful description of the asserted fundamental liberty interest." How did Justice Kennedy analyze the level of generality question in *Lawrence*? Keep this issue in mind when you read *Obergefell*; as you'll see, Justice Kennedy confronted this question again in his majority opinion in that case.

Despite his embrace of a broader methodology for identifying substantive due process interests, Justice Kennedy's *Lawrence* opinion nevertheless recognized a role for history in determining whether there existed a tradition criminalizing same-sex sexual conduct. Recall that the *Bowers* Court had identified such a tradition; by contrast, Justice Kennedy found *Bowers'* history to be faulty. What does this disagreement, and Justice Kennedy's seemingly-shifting views on the level of generality question, suggest about the objectivity of *Glucksberg's* and *Michael H.'s* approach to substantive due process? Does it mean that that approach's aspiration to objectivity failed? Or simply that substantive due process analysis is inevitably a difficult enterprise about which reasonable minds might differ? Is there a difference between these two suggestions?

3. Consider now Justice Kennedy's citation of the fact that, in the years after *Bowers*, nearly half the states that had sodomy laws on the books in 1986 had either repealed them or had them struck down by state courts on state law grounds. What role did that development play for Justice Kennedy? Did that evolution somehow make it easier, or more defensible, for the Court to act in *Lawrence* in a way that it was not willing to act in *Bowers*? *Should* such evolution matter? Why?

4. Finally, note that Justice Kennedy weaved equal protection considerations into his due process analysis. What role did those considerations play? Revisit this question after *Obergefell*, which, if anything, combined due process and equal protection analysis even more intricately. Revisit it again after you conclude the equal protection materials, at the end of Chapter 16. Note that Justice O'Connor concurred in *Lawrence*, relying explicitly and solely on equal protection grounds. Her opinion is excerpted in Chapter 15.

5. Justice Scalia, joined by Chief Justice Rehnquist and Justice Thomas, dissented in *Lawrence*. Early in his opinion he claimed that the majority, "while overruling the *outcome* of *Bowers*, ... leaves strangely untouched its central legal conclusion," which he identified as *Bowers'* refusal to find "a fundamental right to engage in homosexual sodomy." (Emphasis in original). Was he correct? Does that mean that *Lawrence* rested on a rational basis ground? Or did *Lawrence* somehow transcend the standard doctrinal template, in which infringements on fundamental due process interests trigger strict scrutiny while infringements on non-fundamental interests trigger only (highly deferential) rational basis review? If Justice Kennedy did transcend that template, what did he replace it with?

### *Note: The Path to* Obergefell *and Same-Sex Marriage*

1. In retrospect, *Lawrence* appeared at a turning point in the movement for same-sex marriage. As a legal matter, that movement had existed for decades; as you'll see in the next case, *Obergefell v. Hodges*, in 1972 the Court quickly disposed of a constitutional claim for same-sex marriage rights. *Baker v. Nelson*, 409 U.S. 510 (1972). After lying dormant as the LGBT community confronted the AIDS crisis in the 1980s, the movement for same-sex marriage rights accelerated in the 1990s. At first, progress was halting; as Justice Kennedy explained in *Obergefell*, early judicial victories were quickly undone by legislative action. But in the early years of the new century, gay rights advocates won victories that withstood legislative efforts at repeal. Most notably, in 2003 the highest court in Massachusetts held that denying same-sex couples the right to marry violated the state constitution. *Goodridge v. Department of Public Health*, 798 N.E.2d 941 (Mass. 2003). As you saw, both Justice Kennedy's majority opinion and Justice Scalia's dissent in *Lawrence* discussed the relevance of the Court's decision for same-sex marriage.

2. The decade after *Lawrence* witnessed constant legal and political skirmishing between the forces advocating for and against same-sex marriage. As was the case in the 1990's, one common manifestation of that conflict featured marriage rights advocates prevailing in court, only to have their victories repealed by legislative or

direct voter action. In one notable example, the California Supreme Court found in that state's constitution a right to same-sex marriage in May, 2008, which the voters of the state repealed that following November. This was not the universal pattern, however: some state courts during this period rejected marriage rights claims, while a small, but ultimately growing, number of legislatures provided for such marriages.

3. During this period, national gay-rights litigation organizations shied away from mounting federal constitutional challenges to marriage bans, on the theory that the doctrinal (and political) groundwork had not yet been laid for a federal constitutional challenge. In particular, same-sex marriage advocates feared that a premature challenge would lead to a defeat at the Supreme Court that would set the marriage rights movement back by many years. However, independent litigators occasionally mounted such challenges. The most notable was the case brought by Theodore Olson and Ted Boies (prominent Washington lawyers who had opposed each other in the *Bush v. Gore* litigation of 2000), challenging California's voter-enacted marriage ban. That challenge succeeded at the district court and the federal appellate court. When the state declined to defend the law at the Supreme Court, that Court held that the proponents of the successful ballot referendum revoking same-sex marriage rights lacked standing to step into the state's shoes and defend the law. *Hollingsworth v. Perry*, 570 U.S. ___ (2013). The effect of *Hollingsworth* was to reaffirm the district court's statewide injunction against California enforcing its same-sex marriage ban — and thus, *de facto*, to recognize same-sex marriage in California.

The first challenge to a same-sex marriage restriction that the Court decided on the merits (after *Baker v. Nelson*) was *United States v. Windsor*, 570 U.S. ___ (2013), decided on the same day as *Hollingsworth*. *Windsor* was a challenge to a *federal* law, Section 3 of the Defense of Marriage Act (DOMA). DOMA had been enacted in 1996, in response to litigation in Hawaii that had suggested that a same-sex marriage claim might succeed. Section 3 provided that the federal government did not recognize, for federal government purposes (*e.g.*, immigration and social security law), same-sex marriages, including those recognized by the state where the married couple lived. In *Windsor*, a five-justice majority, speaking through Justice Kennedy, concluded that Section 3 violated the equality principles implicit in the Fifth Amendment's Due Process Clause. *Windsor* is discussed in the equal protection materials in Chapter 15.

4. *Windsor* accelerated the trend among lower courts — both state and federal — toward vindicating same-sex marriage claims. At the same time, state legislatures slowly began enacting legislation providing those same rights. On the other hand, a number of states, responding to earlier judicial victories by same-sex marriage rights advocates, had adopted voter-enacted state constitutional amendments prohibiting same-sex marriage. It was at this point that the Supreme Court granted *cert.* in the cases that became known as *Obergefell*. In *Obergefell*, the federal Sixth Circuit court rejected same-sex marriage claims brought by a group of same-sex couples. In so doing, that court created a split among the federal circuit courts, which increased pressure on the Supreme Court to decide the issue conclusively.

# Obergefell v. Hodges

576 U.S. ___ (2015)

Justice KENNEDY delivered the opinion of the Court.

The Constitution promises liberty to all within its reach, a liberty that includes certain specific rights that allow persons, within a lawful realm, to define and express their identity. The petitioners in these cases seek to find that liberty by marrying someone of the same sex and having their marriages deemed lawful on the same terms and conditions as marriages between persons of the opposite sex.

## I

These cases come from Michigan, Kentucky, Ohio, and Tennessee, States that define marriage as a union between one man and one woman. The petitioners are 14 same-sex couples and two men whose same-sex partners are deceased. The respondents are state officials responsible for enforcing the laws in question. The petitioners claim the respondents violate the Fourteenth Amendment by denying them the right to marry or to have their marriages, lawfully performed in another State, given full recognition....

## II

Before addressing the principles and precedents that govern these cases, it is appropriate to note the history of the subject now before the Court.

### A

From their beginning to their most recent page, the annals of human history reveal the transcendent importance of marriage.... Rising from the most basic human needs, marriage is essential to our most profound hopes and aspirations.

The centrality of marriage to the human condition makes it unsurprising that the institution has existed for millennia and across civilizations.... That history is the beginning of these cases. The respondents say it should be the end as well. To them, it would demean a timeless institution if the concept and lawful status of marriage were extended to two persons of the same sex. Marriage, in their view, is by its nature a gender-differentiated union of man and woman. This view long has been held — and continues to be held — in good faith by reasonable and sincere people here and throughout the world.

The petitioners acknowledge this history but contend that these cases cannot end there. Were their intent to demean the revered idea and reality of marriage, the petitioners' claims would be of a different order. But that is neither their purpose nor their submission. To the contrary, it is the enduring importance of marriage that underlies the petitioners' contentions. This, they say, is their whole point. Far from seeking to devalue marriage, the petitioners seek it for themselves because of their respect — and need — for its privileges and responsibilities. And their immutable nature dictates that same-sex marriage is their only real path to this profound commitment.

Recounting the circumstances of three of these cases illustrates the urgency of the petitioners' cause from their perspective. Petitioner James Obergefell, a plaintiff in the Ohio case, met John Arthur over two decades ago. They fell in love and started a life together, establishing a lasting, committed relation. In 2011, however, Arthur was diagnosed with amyotrophic lateral sclerosis, or ALS. This debilitating disease is progressive, with no known cure. Two years ago, Obergefell and Arthur decided to commit to one another, resolving to marry before Arthur died. To fulfill their mutual promise, they traveled from Ohio to Maryland, where same-sex marriage was legal. It was difficult for Arthur to move, and so the couple were wed inside a medical transport plane as it remained on the tarmac in Baltimore. Three months later, Arthur died. Ohio law does not permit Obergefell to be listed as the surviving spouse on Arthur's death certificate. By statute, they must remain strangers even in death, a state-imposed separation Obergefell deems "hurtful for the rest of time." He brought suit to be shown as the surviving spouse on Arthur's death certificate.

April DeBoer and Jayne Rowse are co-plaintiffs in the case from Michigan. They celebrated a commitment ceremony to honor their permanent relation in 2007. They both work as nurses, DeBoer in a neonatal unit and Rowse in an emergency unit. In 2009, DeBoer and Rowse fostered and then adopted a baby boy. Later that same year, they welcomed another son into their family. The new baby, born prematurely and abandoned by his biological mother, required around-the-clock care. The next year, a baby girl with special needs joined their family. Michigan, however, permits only opposite-sex married couples or single individuals to adopt, so each child can have only one woman as his or her legal parent. If an emergency were to arise, schools and hospitals may treat the three children as if they had only one parent. And, were tragedy to befall either DeBoer or Rowse, the other would have no legal rights over the children she had not been permitted to adopt. This couple seeks relief from the continuing uncertainty their unmarried status creates in their lives.

Army Reserve Sergeant First Class Ijpe DeKoe and his partner Thomas Kostura, co-plaintiffs in the Tennessee case, fell in love. In 2011, DeKoe received orders to deploy to Afghanistan. Before leaving, he and Kostura married in New York. A week later, DeKoe began his deployment, which lasted for almost a year. When he returned, the two settled in Tennessee, where DeKoe works full-time for the Army Reserve. Their lawful marriage is stripped from them whenever they reside in Tennessee, returning and disappearing as they travel across state lines. DeKoe, who served this Nation to preserve the freedom the Constitution protects, must endure a substantial burden.

The cases now before the Court involve other petitioners as well, each with their own experiences. Their stories reveal that they seek not to denigrate marriage but rather to live their lives, or honor their spouses' memory, joined by its bond.

B

The ancient origins of marriage confirm its centrality, but it has not stood in isolation from developments in law and society. The history of marriage is one of both continuity and change. That institution—even as confined to opposite-sex relations—has evolved over time....

These new insights have strengthened, not weakened, the institution of marriage. Indeed, changed understandings of marriage are characteristic of a Nation where new dimensions of freedom become apparent to new generations, often through perspectives that begin in pleas or protests and then are considered in the political sphere and the judicial process.

This dynamic can be seen in the Nation's experiences with the rights of gays and lesbians. Until the mid-20th century, same-sex intimacy long had been condemned as immoral by the state itself in most Western nations, a belief often embodied in the criminal law. For this reason, among others, many persons did not deem homosexuals to have dignity in their own distinct identity. A truthful declaration by same-sex couples of what was in their hearts had to remain unspoken. Even when a greater awareness of the humanity and integrity of homosexual persons came in the period after World War II, the argument that gays and lesbians had a just claim to dignity was in conflict with both law and widespread social conventions. Same-sex intimacy remained a crime in many States. Gays and lesbians were prohibited from most government employment, barred from military service, excluded under immigration laws, targeted by police, and burdened in their rights to associate.

For much of the 20th century, moreover, homosexuality was treated as an illness.... Only in more recent years have psychiatrists and others recognized that sexual orientation is both a normal expression of human sexuality and immutable.

In the late 20th century, following substantial cultural and political developments, same-sex couples began to lead more open and public lives and to establish families. This development was followed by a quite extensive discussion of the issue in both governmental and private sectors and by a shift in public attitudes toward greater tolerance. As a result, questions about the rights of gays and lesbians soon reached the courts, where the issue could be discussed in the formal discourse of the law.

This Court first gave detailed consideration to the legal status of homosexuals in *Bowers v. Hardwick*, 478 U.S. 186 (1986) [Note *supra.* this chapter]. There it upheld the constitutionality of a Georgia law deemed to criminalize certain homosexual acts. Ten years later, in *Romer v. Evans*, 517 U.S. 620 (1996), the Court invalidated an amendment to Colorado's Constitution that sought to foreclose any branch or political subdivision of the State from protecting persons against discrimination based on sexual orientation. Then, in 2003, the Court overruled *Bowers*, holding that laws making same-sex intimacy a crime "demean the lives of homosexual persons." *Lawrence v. Texas* (2003) [*Supra.* this chapter].

Against this background, the legal question of same-sex marriage arose. In 1993, the Hawaii Supreme Court held Hawaii's law restricting marriage to opposite-sex couples constituted a classification on the basis of sex and was therefore subject to strict scrutiny under the Hawaii Constitution. Although this decision did not mandate that same-sex marriage be allowed, some States were concerned by its implications and reaffirmed in their laws that marriage is defined as a union between opposite-sex partners. So too in 1996, Congress passed the Defense of Marriage Act (DOMA), defining marriage for all federal-law purposes as "only a legal union between one man and one woman as husband and wife."

The new and widespread discussion of the subject led other States to a different conclusion. In 2003, the Supreme Judicial Court of Massachusetts held the State's Constitution guaranteed same-sex couples the right to marry. After that ruling, some additional States granted marriage rights to same-sex couples, either through judicial or legislative processes.... Two Terms ago, in *United States v. Windsor*, 570 U.S. ___ (2013), this Court invalidated DOMA to the extent it barred the Federal Government from treating same-sex marriages as valid even when they were lawful in the State where they were licensed. DOMA, the Court held, impermissibly disparaged those same-sex couples "who wanted to affirm their commitment to one another before their children, their family, their friends, and their community."

Numerous cases about same-sex marriage have reached the United States Courts of Appeals in recent years.... With the exception of the opinion here under review and one other, the Courts of Appeals have held that excluding same-sex couples from marriage violates the Constitution. There also have been many thoughtful District Court decisions addressing same-sex marriage—and most of them, too, have concluded same-sex couples must be allowed to marry. In addition the highest courts of many States have contributed to this ongoing dialogue in decisions interpreting their own State Constitutions....

### III

Under the Due Process Clause of the Fourteenth Amendment, no State shall "deprive any person of life, liberty, or property, without due process of law." The fundamental liberties protected by this Clause include most of the rights enumerated in the Bill of Rights. In addition these liberties extend to certain personal choices central to individual dignity and autonomy, including intimate choices that define personal identity and beliefs. See, e.g., *Eisenstadt v. Baird*, 405 U.S. 438 (1972) [Note *supra*. Chapter 9]; *Griswold v. Connecticut* (1965) [*Supra*. Chapter 9].

The identification and protection of fundamental rights is an enduring part of the judicial duty to interpret the Constitution. That responsibility, however, "has not been reduced to any formula." *Poe v. Ullman*, 367 U.S. 497 (1961) (Harlan, J., dissenting) [Note *supra*. Chapter 8]. Rather, it requires courts to exercise reasoned judgment in identifying interests of the person so fundamental that the State must accord them its respect. See *ibid*. That process is guided by many of the same considerations relevant to analysis of other constitutional provisions that set forth broad principles rather than specific requirements. History and tradition guide and discipline this inquiry but do not set its outer boundaries. See *Lawrence*. That method respects our history and learns from it without allowing the past alone to rule the present.

The nature of injustice is that we may not always see it in our own times. The generations that wrote and ratified the Bill of Rights and the Fourteenth Amendment did not presume to know the extent of freedom in all of its dimensions, and so they entrusted to future generations a charter protecting the right of all persons to enjoy liberty as we learn its meaning. When new insight reveals discord between the Constitution's central protections and a received legal stricture, a claim to liberty must be addressed.

Applying these established tenets, the Court has long held the right to marry is protected by the Constitution. In *Loving v. Virginia*, 388 U.S. 1 (1967), which invalidated bans on interracial unions, a unanimous Court held marriage is "one of the vital personal rights essential to the orderly pursuit of happiness by free men." The Court reaffirmed that holding in *Zablocki v. Redhail*, 434 U.S. 374 (1978), which held the right to marry was burdened by a law prohibiting fathers who were behind on child support from marrying. The Court again applied this principle in *Turner v. Safley*, 482 U.S. 784 (1987), which held the right to marry was abridged by regulations limiting the privilege of prison inmates to marry. Over time and in other contexts, the Court has reiterated that the right to marry is fundamental under the Due Process Clause.

It cannot be denied that this Court's cases describing the right to marry presumed a relationship involving opposite-sex partners. The Court, like many institutions, has made assumptions defined by the world and time of which it is a part. This was evident in *Baker v. Nelson*, 409 U.S. 810 (1972), a one-line summary decision issued in 1972, holding the exclusion of same-sex couples from marriage did not present a substantial federal question.

Still, there are other, more instructive precedents. This Court's cases have expressed constitutional principles of broader reach. In defining the right to marry these cases have identified essential attributes of that right based in history, tradition, and other constitutional liberties inherent in this intimate bond. See, e.g., *Lawrence; Turner; Zablocki; Loving; Griswold*. And in assessing whether the force and rationale of its cases apply to same-sex couples, the Court must respect the basic reasons why the right to marry has been long protected. See, e.g., *Eisenstadt; Poe* (Harlan, J., dissenting).

This analysis compels the conclusion that same-sex couples may exercise the right to marry. The four principles and traditions to be discussed demonstrate that the reasons marriage is fundamental under the Constitution apply with equal force to same-sex couples.

A first premise of the Court's relevant precedents is that the right to personal choice regarding marriage is inherent in the concept of individual autonomy.... Like choices concerning contraception, family relationships, procreation, and childrearing, all of which are protected by the Constitution, decisions concerning marriage are among the most intimate that an individual can make....

Choices about marriage shape an individual's destiny.... The nature of marriage is that, through its enduring bond, two persons together can find other freedoms, such as expression, intimacy, and spirituality. This is true for all persons, whatever their sexual orientation. See *Windsor*. There is dignity in the bond between two men or two women who seek to marry and in their autonomy to make such profound choices.

A second principle in this Court's jurisprudence is that the right to marry is fundamental because it supports a two-person union unlike any other in its importance to the committed individuals. This point was central to *Griswold*.... Suggesting that marriage is a right "older than the Bill of Rights," *Griswold* described marriage this way:

> Marriage is a coming together for better or for worse, hopefully enduring, and intimate to the degree of being sacred. It is an association that promotes a way of life, not causes; a harmony in living, not political faiths; a bilateral loyalty, not commercial or social projects. Yet it is an association for as noble a purpose as any involved in our prior decisions....

As this Court held in *Lawrence*, same-sex couples have the same right as opposite-sex couples to enjoy intimate association.... But while *Lawrence* confirmed a dimension of freedom that allows individuals to engage in intimate association without criminal liability, it does not follow that freedom stops there. Outlaw to outcast may be a step forward, but it does not achieve the full promise of liberty.

A third basis for protecting the right to marry is that it safeguards children and families and thus draws meaning from related rights of childrearing, procreation, and education. See *Pierce v. Society of Sisters*, 268 U.S. 510 (1925) [Note *supra.* Chapter 8]; *Meyer v. Nebraska* (1923) [*Supra.* Chapter 8]....

As all parties agree, many same-sex couples provide loving and nurturing homes to their children, whether biological or adopted. And hundreds of thousands of children are presently being raised by such couples. Most States have allowed gays and lesbians to adopt, either as individuals or as couples, and many adopted and foster children have same-sex parents. This provides powerful confirmation from the law itself that gays and lesbians can create loving, supportive families....

Fourth and finally, this Court's cases and the Nation's traditions make clear that marriage is a keystone of our social order.... This idea has been reiterated even as the institution has evolved in substantial ways over time, superseding rules related to parental consent, gender, and race once thought by many to be essential. Marriage remains a building block of our national community....

There is no difference between same- and opposite-sex couples with respect to this principle. Yet by virtue of their exclusion from that institution, same-sex couples are denied the constellation of benefits that the States have linked to marriage. This harm results in more than just material burdens. Same-sex couples are consigned to an instability many opposite-sex couples would deem intolerable in their own lives. As the State itself makes marriage all the more precious by the significance it attaches to it, exclusion from that status has the effect of teaching that gays and lesbians are unequal in important respects. It demeans gays and lesbians for the State to lock them out of a central institution of the Nation's society. Same-sex couples, too, may aspire to the transcendent purposes of marriage and seek fulfillment in its highest meaning.

The limitation of marriage to opposite-sex couples may long have seemed natural and just, but its inconsistency with the central meaning of the fundamental right to marry is now manifest. With that knowledge must come the recognition that laws excluding same-sex couples from the marriage right impose stigma and injury of the kind prohibited by our basic charter.

Objecting that this does not reflect an appropriate framing of the issue, the respondents refer to *Washington v. Glucksberg* (1997) [*Supra.* this chapter], which called for a "careful description" of fundamental rights. They assert the petitioners do not seek to exercise the right to marry but rather a new and nonexistent "right to same-sex marriage." *Glucksberg* did insist that liberty under the Due Process Clause must be defined in a most circumscribed manner, with central reference to specific historical practices. Yet while that approach may have been appropriate for the asserted right there involved (physician-assisted suicide), it is inconsistent with the approach this Court has used in discussing other fundamental rights, including marriage and intimacy. *Loving* did not ask about a "right to interracial marriage"; *Turner* did not ask about a "right of inmates to marry"; and *Zablocki* did not ask about a "right of fathers with unpaid child support duties to marry." Rather, each case inquired about the right to marry in its comprehensive sense, asking if there was a sufficient justification for excluding the relevant class from the right. See also *Glucksberg* (Souter, J., concurring in judgment); *id.* (BREYER, J., concurring in judgments).

That principle applies here. If rights were defined by who exercised them in the past, then received practices could serve as their own continued justification and new groups could not invoke rights once denied. This Court has rejected that approach, both with respect to the right to marry and the rights of gays and lesbians. See *Loving*; *Lawrence*.

The right to marry is fundamental as a matter of history and tradition, but rights come not from ancient sources alone. They rise, too, from a better informed understanding of how constitutional imperatives define a liberty that remains urgent in our own era. Many who deem same-sex marriage to be wrong reach that conclusion based on decent and honorable religious or philosophical premises, and neither they nor their beliefs are disparaged here. But when that sincere, personal opposition becomes enacted law and public policy, the necessary consequence is to put the imprimatur of the State itself on an exclusion that soon demeans or stigmatizes those whose own liberty is then denied. Under the Constitution, same-sex couples seek in marriage the same legal treatment as opposite-sex couples, and it would disparage their choices and diminish their personhood to deny them this right.

The right of same-sex couples to marry that is part of the liberty promised by the Fourteenth Amendment is derived, too, from that Amendment's guarantee of the equal protection of the laws. The Due Process Clause and the Equal Protection Clause are connected in a profound way, though they set forth independent principles. Rights implicit in liberty and rights secured by equal protection may rest on different precepts and are not always co-extensive, yet in some instances each may be instructive as to the meaning and reach of the other. In any particular case one Clause may be thought to capture the essence of the right in a more accurate and comprehensive way, even as the two Clauses may converge in the identification and definition of the right. This interrelation of the two principles furthers our understanding of what freedom is and must become.

The Court's cases touching upon the right to marry reflect this dynamic. In *Loving* the Court invalidated a prohibition on interracial marriage under both the Equal Protection Clause and the Due Process Clause. The Court first declared the prohibition invalid because of its unequal treatment of interracial couples. It stated: "There can be no doubt that restricting the freedom to marry solely because of racial classifications violates the central meaning of the Equal Protection Clause." With this link to equal protection the Court proceeded to hold the prohibition offended central precepts of liberty: "To deny this fundamental freedom on so unsupportable a basis as the racial classifications embodied in these statutes, classifications so directly subversive of the principle of equality at the heart of the Fourteenth Amendment, is surely to deprive all the State's citizens of liberty without due process of law." The reasons why marriage is a fundamental right became more clear and compelling from a full awareness and understanding of the hurt that resulted from laws barring interracial unions....

Other cases confirm this relation between liberty and equality.... In *Eisenstadt*, the Court invoked both principles to invalidate a prohibition on the distribution of contraceptives to unmarried persons but not married persons. And in *Skinner v. Oklahoma*, 316 U.S. 535 (1942) [Note *supra*. Chapter 8] the Court invalidated under both principles a law that allowed sterilization of habitual criminals.

In *Lawrence* the Court acknowledged the interlocking nature of these constitutional safeguards in the context of the legal treatment of gays and lesbians. Although *Lawrence* elaborated its holding under the Due Process Clause, it acknowledged, and sought to remedy, the continuing inequality that resulted from laws making intimacy in the lives of gays and lesbians a crime against the State. *Lawrence* therefore drew upon principles of liberty and equality to define and protect the rights of gays and lesbians, holding the State "cannot demean their existence or control their destiny by making their private sexual conduct a crime."

This dynamic also applies to same-sex marriage. It is now clear that the challenged laws burden the liberty of same-sex couples, and it must be further acknowledged that they abridge central precepts of equality. Here the marriage laws enforced by the respondents are in essence unequal: same-sex couples are denied all the benefits afforded to opposite-sex couples and are barred from exercising a fundamental right. Especially against a long history of disapproval of their relationships, this denial to same-sex couples of the right to marry works a grave and continuing harm. The imposition of this disability on gays and lesbians serves to disrespect and subordinate them. And the Equal Protection Clause, like the Due Process Clause, prohibits this unjustified infringement of the fundamental right to marry.

These considerations lead to the conclusion that the right to marry is a fundamental right inherent in the liberty of the person, and under the Due Process and Equal Protection Clauses of the Fourteenth Amendment couples of the same-sex may not be deprived of that right and that liberty. The Court now holds that same-sex couples may exercise the fundamental right to marry. No longer may this liberty be denied to them. *Baker v. Nelson* must be and now is overruled, and the State laws challenged by Petitioners in these cases are now held invalid to the extent they exclude same-sex couples from civil marriage on the same terms and conditions as opposite-sex couples.

IV

There may be an initial inclination in these cases to proceed with caution — to await further legislation, litigation, and debate. The respondents warn there has been insufficient democratic discourse before deciding an issue so basic as the definition of marriage....

Yet there has been far more deliberation than this argument acknowledges. There have been referenda, legislative debates, and grassroots campaigns, as well as countless studies, papers, books, and other popular and scholarly writings. There has been extensive litigation in state and federal courts.... As more than 100 *amici* make clear in their filings, many of the central institutions in American life — state and local governments, the military, large and small businesses, labor unions, religious organizations, law enforcement, civic groups, professional organizations, and universities — have devoted substantial attention to the question. This has led to an enhanced understanding of the issue — an understanding reflected in the arguments now presented for resolution as a matter of constitutional law.

Of course, the Constitution contemplates that democracy is the appropriate process for change, so long as that process does not abridge fundamental rights.... But ... when the rights of persons are violated, "the Constitution requires redress by the courts," notwithstanding the more general value of democratic decisionmaking. This holds true even when protecting individual rights affects issues of the utmost importance and sensitivity....

This is not the first time the Court has been asked to adopt a cautious approach to recognizing and protecting fundamental rights. In *Bowers*, a bare majority upheld a law criminalizing same-sex intimacy. That approach might have been viewed as a cautious endorsement of the democratic process, which had only just begun to consider the rights of gays and lesbians. Yet, in effect, *Bowers* upheld state action that denied gays and lesbians a fundamental right and caused them pain and humiliation.... Although *Bowers* was eventually repudiated in *Lawrence*, men and women were harmed in the interim, and the substantial effects of these injuries no doubt lingered long after *Bowers* was overruled. Dignitary wounds cannot always be healed with the stroke of a pen....

The respondents also argue allowing same-sex couples to wed will harm marriage as an institution by leading to fewer opposite-sex marriages. This may occur, the respondents contend, because licensing same-sex marriage severs the connection between natural procreation and marriage. That argument, however, rests on a counterintuitive view of opposite-sex couple's decisionmaking processes regarding marriage and parenthood. Decisions about whether to marry and raise children are based on many personal, romantic, and practical considerations; and it is unrealistic to conclude that an opposite-sex couple would choose not to marry simply because same-sex couples may do so. See *Kitchen v. Herbert*, 755 F.3d 1193 (C.A.10 2014) ("It is wholly illogical to believe that state recognition of the love and commitment between same-sex couples will alter the most intimate and personal decisions of opposite-sex couples")....

Finally, it must be emphasized that religions, and those who adhere to religious doctrines, may continue to advocate with utmost, sincere conviction that, by divine precepts, same-sex marriage should not be condoned. The First Amendment ensures that religious organizations and persons are given proper protection as they seek to teach the principles that are so fulfilling and so central to their lives and faiths, and to their own deep aspirations to continue the family structure they have long revered. The same is true of those who oppose same-sex marriage for other reasons. In turn, those who believe allowing same-sex marriage is proper or indeed essential, whether as a matter of religious conviction or secular belief, may engage those who disagree with their view in an open and searching debate. The Constitution, however, does not permit the State to bar same-sex couples from marriage on the same terms as accorded to couples of the opposite sex.

## V

... As counsel for the respondents acknowledged at argument, if States are required by the Constitution to issue marriage licenses to same-sex couples, the justifications for refusing to recognize those marriages performed elsewhere are undermined. The Court, in this decision, holds same-sex couples may exercise the fundamental right to marry in all States. It follows that the Court also must hold—and it now does hold—that there is no lawful basis for a State to refuse to recognize a lawful same-sex marriage performed in another State on the ground of its same-sex character.

\* \* \*

No union is more profound than marriage, for it embodies the highest ideals of love, fidelity, devotion, sacrifice, and family. In forming a marital union, two people become something greater than once they were. As some of the petitioners in these cases demonstrate, marriage embodies a love that may endure even past death. It would misunderstand these men and women to say they disrespect the idea of marriage. Their plea is that they do respect it, respect it so deeply that they seek to find its fulfillment for themselves. Their hope is not to be condemned to live in loneliness, excluded from one of civilization's oldest institutions. They ask for equal dignity in the eyes of the law. The Constitution grants them that right.

The judgment of the Court of Appeals for the Sixth Circuit is reversed.

Chief Justice ROBERTS, with whom Justice SCALIA and Justice THOMAS join, dissenting.

Petitioners make strong arguments rooted in social policy and considerations of fairness. They contend that same-sex couples should be allowed to affirm their love and commitment through marriage, just like opposite-sex couples. That position has undeniable appeal; over the past six years, voters and legislators in eleven States and the District of Columbia have revised their laws to allow marriage between two people of the same sex.

But this Court is not a legislature. Whether same-sex marriage is a good idea should be of no concern to us. Under the Constitution, judges have power to say what the law is, not what it should be. . . .

Today, however, the Court takes the extraordinary step of ordering every State to license and recognize same-sex marriage. Many people will rejoice at this decision, and I begrudge none their celebration. But for those who believe in a government of laws, not of men, the majority's approach is deeply disheartening. Supporters of same-sex marriage have achieved considerable success persuading their fellow citizens — through the democratic process — to adopt their view. That ends today. Five lawyers have closed the debate and enacted their own vision of marriage as a matter of constitutional law. Stealing this issue from the people will for many cast a cloud over same-sex marriage, making a dramatic social change that much more difficult to accept.

The majority's decision is an act of will, not legal judgment. The right it announces has no basis in the Constitution or this Court's precedent. The majority expressly disclaims judicial "caution" and omits even a pretense of humility, openly relying on its desire to remake society according to its own "new insight" into the "nature of injustice." As a result, the Court invalidates the marriage laws of more than half the States and orders the transformation of a social institution that has formed the basis of human society for millennia. . . .

It can be tempting for judges to confuse our own preferences with the requirements of the law. But as this Court has been reminded throughout our history, the Constitution "is made for people of fundamentally differing views." *Lochner v. New York* (1905) (Holmes, J., dissenting) [*Supra.* Chapter 7]. Accordingly, "courts are not concerned with the wisdom or policy of legislation." *Id.* (Harlan, J., dissenting). The majority today neglects that restrained conception of the judicial role. It seizes for itself a question the Constitution leaves to the people, at a time when the people are engaged in a vibrant debate on that question. And it answers that question based not on neutral principles of constitutional law, but on its own "understanding of what freedom is and must become." I have no choice but to dissent.

Understand well what this dissent is about: It is not about whether, in my judgment, the institution of marriage should be changed to include same-sex couples. It is instead about whether, in our democratic republic, that decision should rest with the people acting through their elected representatives, or with five lawyers who happen to hold commissions authorizing them to resolve legal disputes according to law. The Constitution leaves no doubt about the answer.

I

Petitioners and their *amici* base their arguments on the "right to marry" and the imperative of "marriage equality." There is no serious dispute that, under our precedents, the Constitution protects a right to marry and requires States to apply their marriage laws equally. The real question in these cases is what constitutes "marriage," or — more precisely — *who decides* what constitutes "marriage"?

The majority largely ignores these questions, relegating ages of human experience with marriage to a paragraph or two. Even if history and precedent are not "the end" of these cases, *ante*, I would not "sweep away what has so long been settled" without showing greater respect for all that preceded us.

### A

As the majority acknowledges, marriage "has existed for millennia and across civilizations." For all those millennia, across all those civilizations, "marriage" referred to only one relationship: the union of a man and a woman....

As the majority notes, some aspects of marriage have changed over time. Arranged marriages have largely given way to pairings based on romantic love. States have replaced coverture, the doctrine by which a married man and woman became a single legal entity, with laws that respect each participant's separate status. Racial restrictions on marriage, which "arose as an incident to slavery" to promote "White Supremacy," were repealed by many States and ultimately struck down by this Court. *Loving.*

The majority observes that these developments "were not mere superficial changes" in marriage, but rather "worked deep transformations in its structure." They did not, however, work any transformation in the core structure of marriage as the union between a man and a woman. If you had asked a person on the street how marriage was defined, no one would ever have said, "Marriage is the union of a man and a woman, where the woman is subject to coverture." The majority may be right that the "history of marriage is one of both continuity and change," but the core meaning of marriage has endured....

### II

... The majority purports to identify four "principles and traditions" in this Court's due process precedents that support a fundamental right for same-sex couples to marry. In reality, however, the majority's approach has no basis in principle or tradition, except for the unprincipled tradition of judicial policymaking that characterized discredited decisions such as *Lochner.* Stripped of its shiny rhetorical gloss, the majority's argument is that the Due Process Clause gives same-sex couples a fundamental right to marry because it will be good for them and for society. If I were a legislator, I would certainly consider that view as a matter of social policy. But as a judge, I find the majority's position indefensible as a matter of constitutional law.

### A

Petitioners' "fundamental right" claim falls into the most sensitive category of constitutional adjudication. Petitioners do not contend that their States' marriage laws violate an *enumerated* constitutional right, such as the freedom of speech protected by the First Amendment. There is, after all, no "Companionship and Understanding" or "Nobility and Dignity" Clause in the Constitution. See *ante.* They argue instead that the laws violate a right *implied* by the Fourteenth Amendment's requirement that "liberty" may not be deprived without "due process of law."

This Court has interpreted the Due Process Clause to include a "substantive" component that protects certain liberty interests against state deprivation "no matter what process is provided." The theory is that some liberties are "so rooted in the traditions and conscience of our people as to be ranked as fundamental," and therefore cannot be deprived without compelling justification.

Allowing unelected federal judges to select which unenumerated rights rank as "fundamental" — and to strike down state laws on the basis of that determination — raises obvious concerns about the judicial role. Our precedents have accordingly insisted that judges "exercise the utmost care" in identifying implied fundamental rights, "lest the liberty protected by the Due Process Clause be subtly transformed into the policy preferences of the Members of this Court." *Glucksberg*.

The need for restraint in administering the strong medicine of substantive due process is a lesson this Court has learned the hard way. The Court first applied substantive due process to strike down a statute in *Dred Scott v. Sanford*, 60 U.S. 393 (1857). There the Court invalidated the Missouri Compromise on the ground that legislation restricting the institution of slavery violated the implied rights of slaveholders. The Court relied on its own conception of liberty and property in doing so. It asserted that "an act of Congress which deprives a citizen of the United States of his liberty or property, merely because he came himself or brought his property into a particular Territory of the United States ... could hardly be dignified with the name of due process of law." In a dissent that has outlasted the majority opinion, Justice Curtis explained that when the "fixed rules which govern the interpretation of laws [are] abandoned, and the theoretical opinions of individuals are allowed to control" the Constitution's meaning, "we have no longer a Constitution; we are under the government of individual men, who for the time being have power to declare what the Constitution is, according to their own views of what it ought to mean."

*Dred Scott*'s holding was overruled on the battlefields of the Civil War and by constitutional amendment after Appomattox, but its approach to the Due Process Clause reappeared. In a series of early 20th-century cases, most prominently *Lochner*, this Court invalidated state statutes that presented "meddlesome interferences with the rights of the individual," and "undue interference with liberty of person and freedom of contract." In *Lochner* itself, the Court struck down a New York law setting maximum hours for bakery employees, because there was "in our judgment, no reasonable foundation for holding this to be necessary or appropriate as a health law."

The dissenting Justices in *Lochner* explained that the New York law could be viewed as a reasonable response to legislative concern about the health of bakery employees, an issue on which there was at least "room for debate and for an honest difference of opinion." *Id.* (opinion of Harlan, J.). The majority's contrary conclusion required adopting as constitutional law "an economic theory which a large part of the country does not entertain." As Justice Holmes memorably put it, "The Fourteenth Amendment does not enact Mr. Herbert Spencer's Social Statics," a leading work on the philosophy of Social Darwinism. The Constitution "is not intended to embody a particular economic theory.... It is made for people of fundamentally differing views, and the accident of our finding certain opinions natural and familiar or novel and even shocking ought not to conclude our judgment upon the question whether statutes embodying them conflict with the Constitution."

In the decades after *Lochner*, the Court struck down nearly 200 laws as violations of individual liberty, often over strong dissents contending that "[t]he criterion of constitutionality is not whether we believe the law to be for the public good." ...

Eventually, the Court recognized its error and vowed not to repeat it. "The doctrine that ... due process authorizes courts to hold laws unconstitutional when they believe the legislature has acted unwisely," we later explained, "has long since been discarded. We have returned to the original constitutional proposition that courts do not substitute their social and economic beliefs for the judgment of legislative bodies, who are elected to pass laws." *Ferguson v. Skrupa* (1963) [*Supra.* Chapter 7]. Thus, it has become an accepted rule that the Court will not hold laws unconstitutional simply because we find them "unwise, improvident, or out of harmony with a particular school of thought."

Rejecting *Lochner* does not require disavowing the doctrine of implied fundamental rights, and this Court has not done so. But to avoid repeating *Lochner*'s error of converting personal preferences into constitutional mandates, our modern substantive due process cases have stressed the need for "judicial self-restraint." Our precedents have required that implied fundamental rights be "objectively, deeply rooted in this Nation's history and tradition," and "implicit in the concept of ordered liberty, such that neither liberty nor justice would exist if they were sacrificed." *Glucksberg*....

Proper reliance on history and tradition of course requires looking beyond the individual law being challenged, so that every restriction on liberty does not supply its own constitutional justification. The Court is right about that. But given the few "guideposts for responsible decisionmaking in this unchartered area," "an approach grounded in history imposes limits on the judiciary that are more meaningful than any based on [an] abstract formula." Expanding a right suddenly and dramatically is likely to require tearing it up from its roots. Even a sincere profession of "discipline" in identifying fundamental rights does not provide a meaningful constraint on a judge, for "what he is really likely to be 'discovering,' whether or not he is fully aware of it, are his own values," The only way to ensure restraint in this delicate enterprise is "continual insistence upon respect for the teachings of history, solid recognition of the basic values that underlie our society, and wise appreciation of the great roles [of] the doctrines of federalism and separation of powers." *Griswold* (Harlan, J., concurring in judgment).

### B

The majority acknowledges none of this doctrinal background, and it is easy to see why: Its aggressive application of substantive due process breaks sharply with decades of precedent and returns the Court to the unprincipled approach of *Lochner*.

### 1

The majority's driving themes are that marriage is desirable and petitioners desire it.... When the majority turns to the law, it relies primarily on precedents discussing the fundamental "right to marry." *Turner*; *Zablocki*; see *Loving*. These cases do not hold, of course, that anyone who wants to get married has a constitutional right to do so. They instead require a State to justify barriers to marriage as that institution has always been understood....

None of the laws at issue in those cases purported to change the core definition of marriage as the union of a man and a woman.... In short, the "right to marry" cases stand for the important but limited proposition that particular restrictions on access to marriage *as traditionally defined* violate due process. These precedents say nothing at all about a right to make a State change its definition of marriage, which is the right petitioners actually seek here. Neither petitioners nor the majority cites a single case or other legal source providing any basis for such a constitutional right. None exists, and that is enough to foreclose their claim.

2

The majority suggests that "there are other, more instructive precedents" informing the right to marry. Although not entirely clear, this reference seems to correspond to a line of cases discussing an implied fundamental "right of privacy." *Griswold*. In the first of those cases, the Court invalidated a criminal law that banned the use of contraceptives. *Id.*... In the Court's view, such laws infringed the right to privacy in its most basic sense: the "right to be let alone."

The Court also invoked the right to privacy in *Lawrence*.... *Lawrence* relied on the position that criminal sodomy laws, like bans on contraceptives, invaded privacy by inviting "unwarranted government intrusions" that "touch upon the most private human conduct, sexual behavior ... in the most private of places, the home."

Neither *Lawrence* nor any other precedent in the privacy line of cases supports the right that petitioners assert here. Unlike criminal laws banning contraceptives and sodomy, the marriage laws at issue here involve no government intrusion. They create no crime and impose no punishment. Same-sex couples remain free to live together, to engage in intimate conduct, and to raise their families as they see fit.... At the same time, the laws in no way interfere with the "right to be let alone."

The majority also relies on Justice Harlan's influential dissenting opinion in *Poe*. But far from conferring the broad interpretive discretion that the majority discerns, Justice Harlan's opinion makes clear that courts implying fundamental rights are not "free to roam where unguided speculation might take them." They must instead have "regard to what history teaches" and exercise not only "judgment" but "restraint." Of particular relevance, Justice Harlan explained that "laws regarding marriage which provide both when the sexual powers may be used and the legal and societal context in which children are born and brought up ... form a pattern so deeply pressed into the substance of our social life that any Constitutional doctrine in this area must build upon that basis."

In sum, the privacy cases provide no support for the majority's position, because petitioners do not seek privacy. Quite the opposite, they seek public recognition of their relationships, along with corresponding government benefits. Our cases have consistently refused to allow litigants to convert the shield provided by constitutional liberties into a sword to demand positive entitlements from the State. Thus, although the right to privacy recognized by our precedents certainly plays a role in protecting the intimate conduct of same-sex couples, it provides no affirmative right to redefine marriage and no basis for striking down the laws at issue here.

### 3

Perhaps recognizing how little support it can derive from precedent, the majority goes out of its way to jettison the "careful" approach to implied fundamental rights taken by this Court in *Glucksberg*. It is revealing that the majority's position requires it to effectively overrule *Glucksberg*, the leading modern case setting the bounds of substantive due process. At least this part of the majority opinion has the virtue of candor. Nobody could rightly accuse the majority of taking a careful approach. Ultimately, only one precedent offers any support for the majority's methodology: *Lochner*....

To be fair, the majority does not suggest that its individual autonomy right is entirely unconstrained. The constraints it sets are precisely those that accord with its own "reasoned judgment," informed by its "new insight" into the "nature of injustice," which was invisible to all who came before but has become clear "as we learn [the] meaning" of liberty. The truth is that today's decision rests on nothing more than the majority's own conviction that same-sex couples should be allowed to marry because they want to, and that "it would disparage their choices and diminish their personhood to deny them this right." Whatever force that belief may have as a matter of moral philosophy, it has no more basis in the Constitution than did the naked policy preferences adopted in *Lochner*....

One immediate question invited by the majority's position is whether States may retain the definition of marriage as a union of two people. Although the majority randomly inserts the adjective "two" in various places, it offers no reason at all why the two-person element of the core definition of marriage may be preserved while the man-woman element may not. Indeed, from the standpoint of history and tradition, a leap from opposite-sex marriage to same-sex marriage is much greater than one from a two-person union to plural unions, which have deep roots in some cultures around the world. If the majority is willing to take the big leap, it is hard to see how it can say no to the shorter one....

I do not mean to equate marriage between same-sex couples with plural marriages in all respects. There may well be relevant differences that compel different legal analysis. But if there are, petitioners have not pointed to any. When asked about a plural marital union at oral argument, petitioners asserted that a State "doesn't have such an institution." But that is exactly the point: the States at issue here do not have an institution of same-sex marriage, either....

### III

In addition to their due process argument, petitioners contend that the Equal Protection Clause requires their States to license and recognize same-sex marriages. The majority does not seriously engage with this claim. Its discussion is, quite frankly, difficult to follow. The central point seems to be that there is a "synergy between" the

Equal Protection Clause and the Due Process Clause, and that some precedents relying on one Clause have also relied on the other. Absent from this portion of the opinion, however, is anything resembling our usual framework for deciding equal protection cases. It is casebook doctrine that the "modern Supreme Court's treatment of equal protection claims has used a means-ends methodology in which judges ask whether the classification the government is using is sufficiently related to the goals it is pursuing." The majority's approach today is different:

> Rights implicit in liberty and rights secured by equal protection may rest on different precepts and are not always co-extensive, yet in some instances each may be instructive as to the meaning and reach of the other. In any particular case one Clause may be thought to capture the essence of the right in a more accurate and comprehensive way, even as the two Clauses may converge in the identification and definition of the right.

The majority goes on to assert in conclusory fashion that the Equal Protection Clause provides an alternative basis for its holding. Yet the majority fails to provide even a single sentence explaining how the Equal Protection Clause supplies independent weight for its position.... In any event, the marriage laws at issue here do not violate the Equal Protection Clause, because distinguishing between opposite-sex and same-sex couples is rationally related to the States' "legitimate state interest" in "preserving the traditional institution of marriage." ...

## IV

The legitimacy of this Court ultimately rests "upon the respect accorded to its judgments." That respect flows from the perception—and reality—that we exercise humility and restraint in deciding cases according to the Constitution and law. The role of the Court envisioned by the majority today, however, is anything but humble or restrained. Over and over, the majority exalts the role of the judiciary in delivering social change. In the majority's telling, it is the courts, not the people, who are responsible for making "new dimensions of freedom ... apparent to new generations," for providing "formal discourse" on social issues, and for ensuring "neutral discussions, without scornful or disparaging commentary."

Nowhere is the majority's extravagant conception of judicial supremacy more evident than in its description—and dismissal—of the public debate regarding same-sex marriage. Yes, the majority concedes, on one side are thousands of years of human history in every society known to have populated the planet. But on the other side, there has been "extensive litigation," "many thoughtful District Court decisions," "countless studies, papers, books, and other popular and scholarly writings," and "more than 100" *amicus* briefs in these cases alone. *Ante.* What would be the point of allowing the democratic process to go on? It is high time for the Court to decide the meaning of marriage, based on five lawyers' "better informed understanding" of "a liberty that remains urgent in our own era." *Ante.* The answer is surely there in one of those *amicus* briefs or studies.

Those who founded our country would not recognize the majority's conception of the judicial role. They after all risked their lives and fortunes for the precious right to govern themselves. They would never have imagined yielding that right on a question of social policy to unaccountable and unelected judges....

... By deciding this question under the Constitution, the Court removes it from the realm of democratic decision. There will be consequences to shutting down the political process on an issue of such profound public significance. Closing debate tends to close minds. People denied a voice are less likely to accept the ruling of a court on an issue that does not seem to be the sort of thing courts usually decide. As a thoughtful commentator observed about another issue, "The political process was moving..., not swiftly enough for advocates of quick, complete change, but majoritarian institutions were listening and acting. Heavy-handed judicial intervention was difficult to justify and appears to have provoked, not resolved, conflict." Ginsburg, Some Thoughts on Autonomy and Equality in Relation to *Roe v. Wade*, 63 *N.C.L.Rev.* 375 (1985). Indeed, however heartened the proponents of same-sex marriage might be on this day, it is worth acknowledging what they have lost, and lost forever: the opportunity to win the true acceptance that comes from persuading their fellow citizens of the justice of their cause. And they lose this just when the winds of change were freshening at their backs....

*  *  *

If you are among the many Americans—of whatever sexual orientation—who favor expanding same-sex marriage, by all means celebrate today's decision. Celebrate the achievement of a desired goal. Celebrate the opportunity for a new expression of commitment to a partner. Celebrate the availability of new benefits. But do not celebrate the Constitution. It had nothing to do with it. I respectfully dissent.

Justice SCALIA, with whom Justice THOMAS joins, dissenting.

I join THE CHIEF JUSTICE's opinion in full. I write separately to call attention to this Court's threat to American democracy.

The substance of today's decree is not of immense personal importance to me.... It is of overwhelming importance, however, who it is that rules me. Today's decree says that my Ruler, and the Ruler of 320 million Americans coast-to-coast, is a majority of the nine lawyers on the Supreme Court. The opinion in these cases is the furthest extension in fact—and the furthest extension one can even imagine—of the Court's claimed power to create "liberties" that the Constitution and its Amendments neglect to mention. This practice of constitutional revision by an unelected committee of nine, always accompanied (as it is today) by extravagant praise of liberty, robs the People of the most important liberty they asserted in the Declaration of Independence and won in the Revolution of 1776: the freedom to govern themselves.

I

Until the courts put a stop to it, public debate over same-sex marriage displayed American democracy at its best. Individuals on both sides of the issue passionately, but respectfully, attempted to persuade their fellow citizens to accept their views. Americans considered the arguments and put the question to a vote. The electorates of 11

States, either directly or through their representatives, chose to expand the traditional definition of marriage. Many more decided not to. Win or lose, advocates for both sides continued pressing their cases, secure in the knowledge that an electoral loss can be negated by a later electoral win. That is exactly how our system of government is supposed to work.

The Constitution places some constraints on self-rule—constraints adopted *by the People themselves* when they ratified the Constitution and its Amendments.... These cases ask us to decide whether the Fourteenth Amendment contains a limitation that requires the States to license and recognize marriages between two people of the same sex. Does it remove *that* issue from the political process?

Of course not.... When the Fourteenth Amendment was ratified in 1868, every State limited marriage to one man and one woman, and no one doubted the constitutionality of doing so. That resolves these cases. When it comes to determining the meaning of a vague constitutional provision—such as "due process of law" or "equal protection of the laws"—it is unquestionable that the People who ratified that provision did not understand it to prohibit a practice that remained both universal and uncontroversial in the years after ratification. We have no basis for striking down a practice that is not expressly prohibited by the Fourteenth Amendment's text, and that bears the endorsement of a long tradition of open, widespread, and unchallenged use dating back to the Amendment's ratification. Since there is no doubt whatever that the People never decided to prohibit the limitation of marriage to opposite-sex couples, the public debate over same-sex marriage must be allowed to continue.

But the Court ends this debate, in an opinion lacking even a thin veneer of law. Buried beneath the mummeries and straining-to-be-memorable passages of the opinion is a candid and startling assertion: No matter *what* it was the People ratified, the Fourteenth Amendment protects those rights that the Judiciary, in its "reasoned judgment," thinks the Fourteenth Amendment ought to protect. That is so because "the generations that wrote and ratified the Bill of Rights and the Fourteenth Amendment did not presume to know the extent of freedom in all of its dimensions...." One would think that sentence would continue: "... and therefore they provided for a means by which the People could amend the Constitution," or perhaps " ... and therefore they left the creation of additional liberties, such as the freedom to marry someone of the same sex, to the People, through the never-ending process of legislation." But no. What logically follows, in the majority's judge-empowering estimation, is: "and so they entrusted to future generations a charter protecting the right of all persons to enjoy liberty as we learn its meaning." The "we," needless to say, is the nine of us....

This is a naked judicial claim to legislative—indeed, *super*-legislative—power; a claim fundamentally at odds with our system of government. Except as limited by a constitutional prohibition agreed to by the People, the States are free to adopt whatever laws they like, even those that offend the esteemed Justices' "reasoned judgment." A system of government that makes the People subordinate to a committee of nine unelected lawyers does not deserve to be called a democracy....

Justice THOMAS, with whom Justice SCALIA joins, dissenting.

The Court's decision today is at odds not only with the Constitution, but with the principles upon which our Nation was built. Since well before 1787, liberty has been understood as freedom from government action, not entitlement to government benefits. The Framers created our Constitution to preserve that understanding of liberty. Yet the majority invokes our Constitution in the name of a "liberty" that the Framers would not have recognized, to the detriment of the liberty they sought to protect. Along the way, it rejects the idea—captured in our Declaration of Independence— that human dignity is innate and suggests instead that it comes from the Government. This distortion of our Constitution not only ignores the text, it inverts the relationship between the individual and the state in our Republic. I cannot agree with it.

## I

The majority's decision today will require States to issue marriage licenses to same-sex couples and to recognize same-sex marriages entered in other States largely based on a constitutional provision guaranteeing "due process" before a person is deprived of his "life, liberty, or property." I have elsewhere explained the dangerous fiction of treating the Due Process Clause as a font of substantive rights. *McDonald v. Chicago*, 561 U.S. 742 (2010) (THOMAS, J., concurring in part and concurring in judgment) [Note *supra*. Chapter 8]. It distorts the constitutional text, which guarantees only whatever "process" is "due" before a person is deprived of life, liberty, and property. Worse, it invites judges to do exactly what the majority has done here—"roam at large in the constitutional field guided only by their personal views" as to the "fundamental rights" protected by that document....

## II

Even if the doctrine of substantive due process were somehow defensible—it is not—petitioners still would not have a claim. To invoke the protection of the Due Process Clause at all—whether under a theory of "substantive" or "procedural" due process—a party must first identify a deprivation of "life, liberty, or property." The majority claims these state laws deprive petitioners of "liberty," but the concept of "liberty" it conjures up bears no resemblance to any plausible meaning of that word as it is used in the Due Process Clauses.

## A
### 1

As used in the Due Process Clauses, "liberty" most likely refers to "the power of loco-motion, of changing situation, or removing one's person to whatsoever place one's own inclination may direct; without imprisonment or restraint, unless by due course of law." W. Blackstone, *Commentaries on the Laws of England* (1769). That definition is drawn from the historical roots of the Clauses and is consistent with our Constitution's text and structure.

Both of the Constitution's Due Process Clauses reach back to Magna Carta.... After Magna Carta became subject to renewed interest in the 17th century, William Blackstone referred to this provision as protecting the "absolute rights of every Englishman."

And he formulated those absolute rights as "the right of personal security," which included the right to life; "the right of personal liberty"; and "the right of private property." He defined "the right of personal liberty" as "the power of loco-motion, of changing situation, or removing one's person to whatsoever place one's own inclination may direct; without imprisonment or restraint, unless by due course of law."

The Framers drew heavily upon Blackstone's formulation, adopting provisions in early State Constitutions that replicated Magna Carta's language, but were modified to refer specifically to "life, liberty, or property." ... In enacting the Fifth Amendment's Due Process Clause, the Framers similarly chose to employ the "life, liberty, or property" formulation, though they otherwise deviated substantially from the States' use of Magna Carta's language in the Clause. When read in light of the history of that formulation, it is hard to see how the "liberty" protected by the Clause could be interpreted to include anything broader than freedom from physical restraint. That was the consistent usage of the time when "liberty" was paired with "life" and "property." And that usage avoids rendering superfluous those protections for "life" and "property."

If the Fifth Amendment uses "liberty" in this narrow sense, then the Fourteenth Amendment likely does as well....

2

Even assuming that the "liberty" in those Clauses encompasses something more than freedom from physical restraint, it would not include the types of rights claimed by the majority. In the American legal tradition, liberty has long been understood as individual freedom *from* governmental action, not as a right *to* a particular governmental entitlement....

B

Whether we define "liberty" as locomotion or freedom from governmental action more broadly, petitioners have in no way been deprived of it.

Petitioners cannot claim, under the most plausible definition of "liberty," that they have been imprisoned or physically restrained by the States for participating in same-sex relationships. To the contrary, they have been able to cohabitate and raise their children in peace. They have been able to hold civil marriage ceremonies in States that recognize same-sex marriages and private religious ceremonies in all States. They have been able to travel freely around the country, making their homes where they please. Far from being incarcerated or physically restrained, petitioners have been left alone to order their lives as they see fit....

Petitioners' misconception of liberty carries over into their discussion of our precedents identifying a right to marry, not one of which has expanded the concept of "liberty" beyond the concept of negative liberty. Those precedents all involved absolute prohibitions on private actions associated with marriage. *Loving v. Virginia*, for example, involved a couple who was criminally prosecuted for marrying in the District of Columbia and cohabiting in Virginia They were each sentenced to a year of imprisonment, suspended for a term of 25 years on the condition that they not reenter the Commonwealth together during that time. In a similar vein, *Zablocki v. Redhail* involved a man who was prohibited, on pain of criminal penalty, from "marrying in Wisconsin or elsewhere" because of his outstanding child-support obligations. And *Turner v. Safley* involved state inmates who were prohibited from entering marriages without the permission of the superintendent of the prison, permission that could not be granted absent compelling reasons. In *none* of those cases were individuals denied solely governmental recognition and benefits associated with marriage....

## IV

Perhaps recognizing that these cases do not actually involve liberty as it has been understood, the majority goes to great lengths to assert that its decision will advance the "dignity" of same-sex couples. The flaw in that reasoning, of course, is that the Constitution contains no "dignity" Clause, and even if it did, the government would be incapable of bestowing dignity.

Human dignity has long been understood in this country to be innate. When the Framers proclaimed in the Declaration of Independence that "all men are created equal" and "endowed by their Creator with certain unalienable Rights," they referred to a vision of mankind in which all humans are created in the image of God and therefore of inherent worth. That vision is the foundation upon which this Nation was built.

The corollary of that principle is that human dignity cannot be taken away by the government. Slaves did not lose their dignity (any more than they lost their humanity) because the government allowed them to be enslaved. Those held in internment camps did not lose their dignity because the government confined them. And those denied governmental benefits certainly do not lose their dignity because the government denies them those benefits. The government cannot bestow dignity, and it cannot take it away....

\* \* \*

Our Constitution—like the Declaration of Independence before it—was predicated on a simple truth: One's liberty, not to mention one's dignity, was something to be shielded from—not provided by—the State. Today's decision casts that truth aside. In its haste to reach a desired result, the majority misapplies a clause focused on "due process" to afford substantive rights, disregards the most plausible understanding of the "liberty" protected by that clause, and distorts the principles on which this Nation was founded. Its decision will have inestimable consequences for our Constitution and our society. I respectfully dissent.

Justice ALITO, with whom Justice SCALIA and Justice THOMAS join, dis - senting....

## I

The Constitution says nothing about a right to same-sex marriage, but the Court holds that the term "liberty" in the Due Process Clause of the Fourteenth Amendment encompasses this right. Our Nation was founded upon the principle that every person has the unalienable right to liberty, but liberty is a term of many meanings. For classical liberals, it may include economic rights now limited by government regulation. For social democrats, it may include the right to a variety of government benefits. For today's majority, it has a distinctively postmodern meaning.

To prevent five unelected Justices from imposing their personal vision of liberty upon the American people, the Court has held that "liberty" under the Due Process Clause should be understood to protect only those rights that are "deeply rooted in this Nation's history and tradition." *Glucksberg*. And it is beyond dispute that the right to same-sex marriage is not among those rights. See *Windsor* (ALITO, J., dissenting) Indeed:

> In this country, no State permitted same-sex marriage until the Massachusetts Supreme Judicial Court held in 2003 that limiting marriage to opposite-sex couples violated the State Constitution. Nor is the right to same-sex marriage deeply rooted in the traditions of other nations. No country allowed same-sex couples to marry until the Netherlands did so in 2000. *Id.*...

## II

Attempting to circumvent the problem presented by the newness of the right found in these cases, the majority claims that the issue is the right to equal treatment. Noting that marriage is a fundamental right, the majority argues that a State has no valid reason for denying that right to same-sex couples. This reasoning is dependent upon a particular understanding of the purpose of civil marriage. Although the Court expresses the point in loftier terms, its argument is that the fundamental purpose of marriage is to promote the well-being of those who choose to marry. Marriage provides emotional fulfillment and the promise of support in times of need. And by benefiting persons who choose to wed, marriage indirectly benefits society because persons who live in stable, fulfilling, and supportive relationships make better citizens. It is for these reasons, the argument goes, that States encourage and formalize marriage, confer special benefits on married persons, and also impose some special obligations. This understanding of the States' reasons for recognizing marriage enables the majority to argue that same-sex marriage serves the States' objectives in the same way as opposite-sex marriage.

This understanding of marriage, which focuses almost entirely on the happiness of persons who choose to marry, is shared by many people today, but it is not the traditional one. For millennia, marriage was inextricably linked to the one thing that only an opposite-sex couple can do: procreate....

While, for many, the attributes of marriage in 21st-century America have changed, those States that do not want to recognize same-sex marriage have not yet given up on the traditional understanding. They worry that by officially abandoning the older understanding, they may contribute to marriage's further decay. It is far beyond the outer reaches of this Court's authority to say that a State may not adhere to the understanding of marriage that has long prevailed, not just in this country and others with similar cultural roots, but also in a great variety of countries and cultures all around the globe....

### III

Today's decision usurps the constitutional right of the people to decide whether to keep or alter the traditional understanding of marriage. The decision will also have other important consequences.

It will be used to vilify Americans who are unwilling to assent to the new orthodoxy. In the course of its opinion, the majority compares traditional marriage laws to laws that denied equal treatment for African-Americans and women. The implications of this analogy will be exploited by those who are determined to stamp out every vestige of dissent....

The system of federalism established by our Constitution provides a way for people with different beliefs to live together in a single nation. If the issue of same-sex marriage had been left to the people of the States, it is likely that some States would recognize same-sex marriage and others would not. It is also possible that some States would tie recognition to protection for conscience rights. The majority today makes that impossible. By imposing its own views on the entire country, the majority facilitates the marginalization of the many Americans who have traditional ideas. Recalling the harsh treatment of gays and lesbians in the past, some may think that turnabout is fair play. But if that sentiment prevails, the Nation will experience bitter and lasting wounds.

Today's decision will also have a fundamental effect on this Court and its ability to uphold the rule of law. If a bare majority of Justices can invent a new right and impose that right on the rest of the country, the only real limit on what future majorities will be able to do is their own sense of what those with political power and cultural influence are willing to tolerate. Even enthusiastic supporters of same-sex marriage should worry about the scope of the power that today's majority claims.

Today's decision shows that decades of attempts to restrain this Court's abuse of its authority have failed. A lesson that some will take from today's decision is that preaching about the proper method of interpreting the Constitution or the virtues of judicial self-restraint and humility cannot compete with the temptation to achieve what is viewed as a noble end by any practicable means. I do not doubt that my colleagues in the majority sincerely see in the Constitution a vision of liberty that happens to coincide with their own. But this sincerity is cause for concern, not comfort. What it evidences is the deep and perhaps irremediable corruption of our legal culture's conception of constitutional interpretation.

Most Americans—understandably—will cheer or lament today's decision because of their views on the issue of same-sex marriage. But all Americans, whatever their thinking on that issue, should worry about what the majority's claim of power portends.

## Note: The State of Due Process Jurisprudence Today

1. *Obergefell* raises several ambiguities about substantive due process doctrine today. Consider first Justice Kennedy's discussion of *Glucksberg*. He acknowledges that *Glucks-*

*berg* called for a "careful description" of the asserted due process right. But he then claims that this approach is inconsistent with how previous courts had approached the task of defining the right at stake in due process cases involving "marriage and intimacy." Does that mean there is a "marriage and intimacy" exception to the *Glucksberg* approach? Why should that be? Or is the point simply (and more generally) that each and every due process right is *sui generis*, such that each such right has to be described consistent with an approach that is tailored to that particular topic?

2. Consider also how *Obergefell* uses equality analysis. In many ways the key part of the majority opinion is its argument that legal recognition of same-sex unions reflects the same principles and rests on the same justifications as recognition of opposite-sex unions. Later in the opinion Justice Kennedy explicitly invokes the Equal Protection Clause when he notes the history of demeaning governmental treatment of gays and lesbians. What role does this analysis play in the Court's argument? Was it necessary to rebut "slippery slope" claims (*e.g.*, "if we let same-sex couples marry, then what's to stop a polygamous trio, or some other similarly unconventional combination of persons, from seeking to marry?"). If so, why do you think Justice Kennedy grounded his analysis primarily on due process, rather than equal protection? Chapter 16 of the book will invite you to reconsider this question once you've been exposed to the Court's equal protection jurisprudence.

3. The cases in this chapter illustrate the variety of approaches the modern Court has taken when confronted with claims of an unenumerated substantive due process right. The introduction to this chapter invited you to consider those different approaches. What do you make of the wide variation in those approaches? Is that variation simply a matter of different justices' assumptions about substantive due process? Do the differences in factual contexts matter? If so, how? How would you describe the state of substantive due process today, after *Lawrence* and *Obergefell*?

4. At least since the *Lochner* era, substantive due process has been criticized as allowing justices to create individual rights based more on their own personal preferences rather than law. Defenders of due process have attempted to state and apply legal principles that allow them to rebut that critique. Now that you've seen the most prominent examples of substantive due process analysis, which side of that debate are you on?

# Part IV

# Constitutional Equality

The Fourteenth Amendment states, in part, that "No State shall ... deny to any person within its jurisdiction the equal protection of the laws." Unlike the guarantee against deprivation of life, liberty, or property without due process of law, there is no equivalent equal protection clause that applies to the federal government. However, as you will see, the Court has understood the Fifth Amendment's Due Process Clause, which *does* apply to the federal government, to include a requirement of equality that is understood to be equivalent to the Fourteenth Amendment's Equal Protection Clause.

As one might imagine from such a broadly worded command, the Equal Protection Clause is susceptible of many different meanings. Today, it has become understood as an all-encompassing guarantee of equality across the universe of government actions. But the breadth of that guarantee obscures crucial nuances. In particular, modern judicial doctrine has, at least until very recently, settled on an approach in which courts vary the scrutiny with which they review equal protection challenges according to the degree of inherent "suspectness" of the particular type of discrimination at issue.

This part of the book opens, in Chapter 11, by examining the Court's approach to equal protection up to 1937. As you will see, during this era the Court's main concern was not with the types of discrimination that dominates the Court's equal protection docket today. Sex discrimination was not a serious for the Court until much later. Race *was* a concern of the Court during this time. But as you'll see, the Court did not treat race as a special situation—what we now call a "suspect classification." Instead, during most of the pre-1937 period the Court viewed race discrimination through the same jurisprudential lens that it viewed other types of government classifications. Chapter 11 includes a note discussing the Court's race jurisprudence during this era. But a fuller discussion of the Court's treatment of race is deferred until Chapter 13.

Chapter 12 picks up the story in 1938, by discussing Footnote 4 of *United States v. Carolene Products*, 304 U.S. 144 (1938). Footnote 4 is the foundation for the post-1937 Court's focus on "suspect class" analysis. Chapter 12 examines Footnote 4, briefly considers the Court's reluctance to use suspect class analysis in cases of racial discrimination, and then considers how, by contrast, that analysis came to play a large role in the modern Court's expansion of its role in reviewing many other types of discrimination.

Chapter 13 rewinds the tape and considers race. Race, and racial equality, was unquestionably a central concern of those who drafted and enacted the Fourteenth Amendment. Thus, the Court has considered race discrimination cases throughout the approximately 150 years since the Amendment was enacted. To be sure, the Court's race jurisprudence has evolved considerably during that period; thus, Chapter 13 also takes a chronological approach, from the earliest cases arising under the Equal Protection Clause to the most recent.

With the basics of modern equal protection law thus established, Chapter 14 considers the requirement that equal protection plaintiffs must show that the government "intended" to discriminate on the claimed ground, *e.g.*, race.

Chapter 15 examines the contemporary Court's evolution away from a focus on "suspect classes." The shape of this modern jurisprudence is still not fully clear. But over the last several decades the Court has been moving away from a heavily reliance on suspect class analysis and toward a more granular, case-by-case approach to equal protection claims. Chapter 15 examines some of those cases.

Chapter 16 examines the so-called "fundamental rights strand" of equal protection. This doctrinal area considers rights that, while not fundamental for due process purposes, are nevertheless important enough that the Court requires their presumptive equal distribution, if government chooses to provide it at all.

This structure defers a consideration of race discrimination until the third chapter of the equal protection materials. That placement should not be taken as a suggestion that race is somehow an equal protection afterthought. To the contrary, race was a core concern of the Fourteenth Amendment's drafters. But how the Court has thought about race since 1868 has been influenced by more general jurisprudential trends in equal protection doctrine. Fully understanding how the Court has dealt with race requires that we understand those larger trends. Thus, Chapters 11 and 12 explain those trends, which Chapter 13 then applies to race. However, it's still important that we keep race in mind as we consider those trends. Thus, sprinkled throughout Chapters 11 and 12 are notes that explain the Court's approach to race under the approaches that those parts of the book are presenting at that point. Chapter 13 unites those doctrinal strands.

## Note: Equality Before Equal Protection

1. The inclusion of an equal protection provision in the Fourteenth Amendment did not come out of the blue. Rather, American political and legal thinkers had been concerned with equality, in one way or another, at least since the framing of the Constitution.

2. Before the Civil War an important strand of equality thinking took the form of a concern with so-called "class legislation." As the name implies, "class legislation" was understood as legislation that was designed simply to benefit (or harm) a particular favored (or disfavored) group, or "class," rather than legislation that sought to promote the more general public interest. This concern traced back to foundational American political thought, most notably *Federalist* Number 10, written by James Madison. In *Federalist* 10, Madison expressed concern about what he called "factions," or what we might today very roughly describe as "interest groups." Such factions, he said, sought political power simply as a tool for enriching their own group. As a response, Madison argued in favor of dividing up sovereign power (for example, between independent legislative, executive, and judicial branches) in order to make it harder for such groups to attain overwhelming political power. He also argued that a larger political entity, such as the proposed federal government, would be better-placed to resist factions, given the difficulty any such group might face in gaining majority control of an institution representing such a large and diverse population.

While the separated power structure of the federal government was designed in part to resist the influence of factions, no explicit federal constitutional provision spoke to the class legislation issue. Moreover, everyday regulation of social and economic relations was almost exclusively left to the states. These facts left state courts as the primary enforcers against class legislation. Sometimes they did this by interpreting broad terms in their state constitutions, such as equality provisions or provisions that prohibited deprivations of life, liberty, or property except "by the law of the land"—a term borrowed from Magna Carta, which eventually became phrased as "due process of law." (Justice Souter mentions this connection in footnote 5 of his separate opinion in *Washington v. Glucksberg*, excerpted in Chapter 10. It's also mentioned in the next note.) Other times they relied on unwritten principles of republican government which, in those courts' view, required government to regulate impartially, and only for the public good.

3. As noted above, the Congress that enacted the Fourteenth Amendment and sent it to the states for ratification was deeply concerned with ensuring the equal rights of newly-freed slaves, and African-Americans more generally. Indeed, as Part III of the book explained, much of the impetus for the drafting of Section 1 of that amendment came from a desire to ensure the constitutionality of the Civil Rights Act of 1866. Among other things, that statute gave all persons "the same right ... to make or enforce contracts ... [and] to full and equal benefit of all laws and proceedings for the security of person and property" "as white citizens." Congress had originally grounded that statute on its power to enforce the Thirteenth Amendment, which abolished slavery. But enough doubts existed about that constitutional foundation that work soon started on what became the Fourteenth Amendment.

Nevertheless, this focus on the rights of former slaves did not completely obviate Congress's broader goals in enacting the Fourteenth Amendment, Section 1 in particular, and the Equal Protection Clause specifically. Republican congressmen spoke of the mistreatment suffered by white unionists in the South and others, and argued that the proposed amendment would ensure broad equality. Indeed, to bring matters full circle, Jacob Howard, an influential Republican Senator and proponent of the Amendment, argued in a Senate speech that the Amendment "abolishes all class legislation in the States and does away with the injustice of subjecting one caste of persons to a code not applicable to another."

# Chapter 11

# Equal Protection and Social and Economic Regulation

## Note: Equality, Due Process, and the Police Power

1. Contemporary students of constitutional law often have a difficult time reading Fourteenth Amendment cases from the Nineteenth century because those cases rest on jurisprudential foundations very different from our own. Today, when we encounter a constitutional rights claim we understand the claimed right as a "trump" that, if successfully argued, outweighs any legitimate justification the state may have to regulate. But this was not always the way courts thought of rights. As explained in a note early in Chapter 7, throughout the Nineteenth century the jurisprudential picture was often reversed. During that period, a Fourteenth Amendment rights claim would be analyzed by considering whether the challenged state regulation was within the state's legitimate power to regulate for the health, safety, and morals of its citizens—whether, in the term of the era, the challenged regulation was within the state's "police power." If it was, then the rights claim was rejected. But if the challenged action exceeded the state's legitimate police power, then the claim succeeded.

2. This focus on the extent of government's legitimate power, rather than on the scope of an asserted right, helps explain one sometimes-confusing feature of this era: courts' failure to specify the particular right the plaintiff was claiming. As you'll see in the following case, the Court often simply cited "the Fourteenth Amendment" as the source of the plaintiff's claim, and then moved immediately to a consideration of whether the law was a valid police power regulation.

3. By the early decades of the Twentieth century, if not earlier, the Court was beginning to edge away from this focus solely on the police power, and toward a more clause-specific approach to constitutional rights claims. For example, Chief Justice (and former President) Taft wrote the following in a 1921 case, *Truax v. Corrigan*, 257 U.S. 312 (1921):

> This brings us to consider the effect in this case of that provision of the Fourteenth Amendment which forbids any state to deny to any person the equal protection of the laws. The clause is associated in the Amendment with the due process clause and it is customary to consider them together. It may be that they overlap, that a violation of one may involve at times the violation of the other, but the spheres of the protection they offer are not coterminous. The due process clause, brought down from Magna Charta, was found in

671

the early state constitutions, and later in the Fifth Amendment to the Federal Constitution as a limitation upon the executive, legislative and judicial powers of the Federal Government, while the equality clause does not appear in the Fifth Amendment and so does not apply to congressional legislation. The due process clause requires that every man shall have the protection of his day in court, and the benefit of the general law, a law which hears before it condemns, which proceeds not arbitrarily or capriciously but upon inquiry, and renders judgment only after trial, so that every citizen shall hold his life, liberty, property and immunities under the protection of the general rules which govern society. It, of course, tends to secure equality of law in the sense that it makes a required minimum of protection for every one's right of life, liberty, and property, which the Congress or the legislature may not withhold. Our whole system of law is predicated on the general, fundamental principle of equality of application of the law. 'All men are equal before the law,' 'This is a government of laws and not of men,' 'No man is above the law,' are all maxims showing the spirit in which legislatures, executives and courts are expected to make, execute and apply laws. But the framers and adopters of this Amendment were not content to depend on a mere minimum secured by the due process clause, or upon the spirit of equality which might not be insisted on by local public opinion. They therefore embodied that spirit in a specific guaranty.

The guaranty was aimed at undue favor and individual or class privilege, on the one hand, and at hostile discrimination or the oppression of inequality, on the other. It sought an equality of treatment of all persons, even though all enjoyed the protection of due process.

The following three cases, one from the height of the police power era, and two related cases from the very end of that era, highlight the differences in the Court's approach. The latter two cases—which involved the same statute, were decided the same day, but which reached different results—also suggest the difficulties this approach caused for the Court.

## Barbier v. Connolly
### 113 U.S. 27 (1884)

Field, J. [for the Court].

In this case we ... consider whether the fourth section of the ordinance of the city and county of San Francisco is in conflict with the Constitution or laws of the United States.... That fourth section, so far as it is involved in the case before the police judge, was simply a prohibition to carry on the washing and ironing of clothes in public laundries and wash-houses, within certain prescribed limits of the city and county, from ten o'clock at night until six o'clock on the morning of the following day.... The provision is purely a police regulation within the competency of any municipality possessed of the ordinary powers belonging to such bodies. And it would be an extraordinary usurpation of the authority of a municipality, if a federal tribunal should undertake to supervise such regulations. It may be a necessary measure of precaution in a city composed largely of wooden buildings like San Francisco, that occupations, in which fires are constantly required, should cease after certain hours at night until the following morning; and of the necessity of such regulations the municipal bodies are the exclusive judges; at least, any correction of their action in such matters can come only from State legislation or State tribunals. The same municipal authority which directs the cessation of labor must necessarily prescribe the limits within which it shall be enforced, as it does the limits in a city within which wooden buildings cannot be constructed. There is no invidious discrimination against any one within the prescribed limits by such regulations.... All persons engaged in the same business within it are treated alike; are subject to the same restrictions and are entitled to the same privileges under similar conditions.

The Fourteenth Amendment, in declaring that no State 'shall deprive any person of life, liberty, or property without due process of law, nor deny to any person within its jurisdiction the equal protection of the laws,' undoubtedly intended not only that there should be no arbitrary deprivation of life or liberty, or arbitrary spoliation of property, but that equal protection and security should be given to all under like circumstances in the enjoyment of their personal and civil rights; that all persons should be equally entitled to pursue their happiness and acquire and enjoy property; that they should have like access to the courts of the country for the protection of their persons and property, the prevention and redress of wrongs, and the enforcement of contracts; that no impediment should be interposed to the pursuits of any one except as applied to the same pursuits by others under like circumstances; that no greater burdens should be laid upon one than are laid upon others in the same calling and condition; and that in the administration of criminal justice no different or higher punishment should be imposed upon one than such as is prescribed to all for like offenses. But neither the amendment—broad and comprehensive as it is—nor any other amendment, was designed to interfere with the power of the State, sometimes termed its police power, to prescribe regulations to promote the health, peace, morals, education, and good order of the people, and to legislate so as to increase the industries of the State, develop its resources, and add to its wealth and prosperity. From the very necessities of society, legislation of a special character, having these objects in view, must often be had in certain districts, such as for draining marshes and irrigating arid plains. Special burdens are often necessary for general benefits—for supplying water, preventing fires, lighting districts, cleaning streets, opening parks, and many other objects. Regulations for these purposes may press with more or less weight upon one than upon another, but they are designed, not to impose unequal or unnecessary restrictions upon any one, but to promote, with as little individual inconvenience as possible, the general good. Though, in many respects, necessarily special in their character, they do not furnish just ground of complaint if they operate alike upon all persons and property under the same circumstances and conditions. Class legislation, discriminating against some and favoring others, is prohibited, but legislation which, in carrying out a public purpose, is limited in its application, if within the sphere of its operation it affects alike all persons similarly situated, is not within the amendment.

In the execution of admitted powers unnecessary proceedings are often required which are cumbersome, dilatory and expensive, yet, if no discrimination against any one be made and no substantial right be impaired by them, they are not obnoxious to any constitutional objection.... The case before us the provisions requiring certificates from the health officer and the Board of Fire Wardens may, in some instances, be unnecessary, and the changes to be made to meet the conditions prescribed may be burdensome, but, as we have said, this is a matter for the determination of the municipality in the execution of its police powers, and not a violation of any substantial right of the individual. Judgment affirmed.

## Borden's Farm Products Co., Inc. v. Ten Eyck
### 297 U.S. 251 (1936)

[This and the following case grew out of a New York milk marketing statute passed in response to the market instability during the Great Depression. The statute set a minimum price that milk wholesalers had to pay dairy farmers, and controlled the retail price of milk. The part of the statute at issue here provided that "off-brand" milk could be retailed at a price one cent per quart lower than the price at which "name brand" milk could be sold. Borden's, a name brand retailer, challenged the statute, lost at the lower courts, and appealed to the Supreme Court.]

Mr. Justice ROBERTS delivered the opinion of the Court.

The appellant's complaint is that the fixing of a differential of not to exceed one cent per quart on sales to stores, in favor of milk dealers not having a 'well advertised trade name,' by the Milk Control Law of April 10, 1933 ... was an invasion of rights guaranteed by the Fourteenth Amendment....

In this court the appellees sought to justify the differential by the assertion that the statute was temporary in character, intended to relieve a temporary economic situation, and meanwhile to prevent monopoly of the business by dealers having well advertised names. In support of this position it was said that prior to the adoption of the Milk Control Act of 1933 independent dealers, so-called, had purchased from producers at prices lower than those paid by appellant and other purveyors of well advertised brands, and in turn charged less to stores than the appellant and others in its class. By the Milk Control Act the independent dealers were compelled to purchase from the farmers on the same basis as the well-known dealers; and to deprive them of this advantage and in turn to compel them to charge the same price for their milk as the well advertised brands commanded would be to transfer all their customers to the owners of well known brands, and put them out of business....

The findings of the master establish that the dealers having a well advertised trade name, of which appellant is one, are in keen competition with each other and with the independent dealers, and have no monopoly, nor anything approaching a monopoly, of the sale of bottled milk to stores. The findings further demonstrate that the good will incident to appellant's well known trade name 'Borden's' has been built up largely by advertising, and there is no finding that the appellant's methods in that respect, or its trade practices, have been illegal.... It is plain from these facts that the allowance of the differential cannot be justified as a preventive of monopoly or as a deterrent of illegal combination or illegal trade practices, or as a recognition of differences in the service rendered.

We are brought to the remaining issue of fact to resolve which the case was remanded. Was there a differential during a substantial period prior to adoption of the act between the price charged to stores by dealers having well advertised trade-names and that charged by those lacking this advantage?

The master's findings upon the point, though the appellant excepted to them, were adopted by the court below. They are to the effect that from November, 1931, to April, 1933, and for several years prior thereto, the independent dealers sold their bottled milk to stores in New York City for resale to consumers at one or more cents per quart below the price at which the advertised dealers were selling their bottled milk to stores in that city; and during the same years the stores were selling the independents' bottled milk to consumers from one cent to two cents per quart below the price at which they were vending the bottled milk of the advertised dealers. The District Court made additional findings, supplementing those of the master, that independent dealers on occasions before November 1, 1931, and until April 1, 1933, tried to sell bottled milk to stores at the same price as that charged by the appellant and another advertised dealer, and in each case were compelled by loss of business to resume their earlier and lower price; and during the same period customers when offered the several brands at the same price would usually take a bottle of the well-advertised dealer's milk in preference to that of an independent dealer. These findings of the master and the court disclose the circumstances in the light of which the appellant's claim that it was denied the equal protection of the laws must be considered....

We hold that the fixing of the differential in favor of the sellers of milk not having a well advertised trade-name, in the situation exhibited by the findings, does not deny the appellant equal protection.

The argument is that the classification is arbitrary since the statute puts the appellant and other dealers who have well advertised trade-names in a single class solely by reason of the fact that their legitimate advertising has brought them good will. So, it is said, they are penalized for their business skill and acumen. The answer seems sufficiently obvious. In enforcing its policy of price fixing, — a temporary expedient to redress an injurious economic condition, — the legislature believed that a fixed minimum price by dealers to stores would not preserve the existing economic method of attaining equality of opportunity. That method was for the well-advertised dealers to rely on their advertising to obtain a given price, and for the independents to retain their share of the market, not by counter advertising but by a slight reduction of price. The one expedient the law did not purport to touch; the other by fixing the same minimum for all dealers it would effectually destroy. In these circumstances, it was competent to the lawmakers to attempt, during the limited term of the legislative experiment, to preserve the existing relationship of advantage established by the past trade practices of the two groups. So to do, we must assume, was within the legislative power under the state constitution. No prohibition of the expedient is found in the Federal Constitution, unless in the Fourteenth Amendment. We have held that article does not prevent the fixing of maximum and minimum prices for milk, in the circumstances existing in the state of New York in 1933.[3] We now hold that to provide that a differential of one cent maintained by the independent dealers shall continue does not deny their advertised competitors equal protection. There was a plain reason for the classification. It was not merely that appellant had established a good will; it was that there had resulted a balance between that advantage and the resulting disadvantage to the unadvertised dealer, a balance maintained by a price differential. To attempt the maintenance of that balance was to strive for equality of treatment, equality of burden, not to create inequality. To adapt the law to the existing trade practice was neither unreasonable nor arbitrary. The present case affords an excellent example of the difficulties and complexities which confront the legislator who essays to interfere in sweeping terms with the natural laws of trade or industry. The danger in such efforts always is that unintended dislocations will bring hardship to groups whose situation the broad rules fail to fit. Where, as here, there is recognition of an existing status and an attempt to equate the incidence of the statute in accordance with it, we find a compliance with, rather than a disregard of the constitutional guarantee of equal protection. The appellant cannot complain if, in fact, the discrimination embodied in the law is but a perpetuation of a classification created and existing by the action of the dealers. In the light of the facts found the legislature might reasonably have thought trade conditions existed justifying the fixing of a differential. Judicial inquiry does not concern itself with the accuracy of the legislative finding, but only with the question whether it so lacks any reasonable basis as to be arbitrary....

Mr. Justice McREYNOLDS, dissenting....

... Assuming that the general price fixing provisions of the Control Act are valid, do the provisions which permit other dealers to sell below the minimum price prescribed for appellant deprive it of the equal protection of the laws? The answer should be in the affirmative.

Rational classification, based on substantial differences, is within legislative power. An act which permits dealer A to sell at less than the price fixed for dealer B obviously denies equality; and in the absence of some adequate reason for different treatment, the enactment is invalid.

Here appellant differs from favored dealers only in that it possesses a well advertised brand, while they do not. And solely because of that fact, the Legislature undertook to handicap it and thus enable others profitably to share the trade. There is no question of unfair trade practices or monopoly.

---

3. *Nebbia v. New York* (1934) [*Supra.* chapter 7].

By fair advertisement and commendable service, appellant acquired the public's good will. The purpose is to deprive it of the right to benefit by this and thereby aid competitors to secure the business. This is grossly arbitrary and oppressive.

To support the legislation, it is said the Legislature believed that a fixed minimum price to stores would not preserve the existing economic method of attaining equality of opportunity. Apparently, this means that a dealer, who through merit has acquired a good reputation, can be deprived of the consequent benefit in order that another may trade successfully. Thus the statute destroys equality of opportunity—puts appellant at a disadvantage because of merit.

Merely because on a given date there were differences in prices under open competition, offers no rational reason for legislation abolishing competition and perpetuating such differences. The status existing under competitive conditions certainly is not preserved by destroying competition. Formerly, appellant had the right to adjust prices to meet trade exigencies and thus protect itself from loss of business. Now it must stand helpless while adversaries take possession of the field. It may suffer utter ruin solely because of good reputation, honestly acquired.

## Mayflower Farms, Inc. v. Ten Eyck

### 297 U.S. 266 (1936)

Mr. Justice ROBERTS delivered the opinion of the Court.

[This case dealt with the same milk price-support statute considered in the *Borden's* case above. This case considers the statute's provision that the one cent per-quart differential allowed non-brand name dealers applied only to such dealers who were in the milk business as of April 10, 1933. Appellant in this case was a milk dealer that began operations after that date, and thus was not allowed to sell at the lower price.]

... The question is whether the provision denying the benefit of the differential to all who embark in the business after April 10, 1933, works a discrimination which has no foundation in the circumstances of those engaging in the milk business in New York City, and is therefore so unreasonable as to deny appellant the equal protection of the laws in violation of the Fourteenth Amendment.

The record discloses no reason for the discrimination.... While the legislative history indicates that the differential provision was intended to preserve competitive conditions affecting the store trade in milk, it affords no clue to the genesis of the clause denying the benefit of the differential to those entering the business after April 10, 1933.

The Court of Appeals thought a possible reason for the time limitation might be that, without it, the companies having well-advertised names could, through subsidiaries, sell milk not bearing their names in competition with unadvertised dealers and thus drive some of the latter out of the field with consequent injury to the farmers who sell them milk.... The appellees do not attempt now to support the provision on this ground.

Another suggested reason for the discrimination is that the legislature believed an equal price basis for all dealers would cause most of the business of selling milk through stores to pass into the hands of the large and well known dealers; the differential provision was designed to prevent this result, and save existing businesses of the independent dealers, but was limited in its scope by the reason for it; the legislature did not wish to increase the lower price competition against well advertised dealers by permitting new independent dealers to go into the business, and so required persons or corporations desiring to make investments in the milk business after April 10, 1933, to attach themselves to the higher price group. This is but another way of saying the legislature determined that during the life of the law no person or corporation might enter the business of a milk dealer in New York City. The very reason for the differential was the belief that no one could successfully market an unadvertised brand on an even price basis with the seller of a well advertised brand. One coming fresh into the field would not possess such a brand and clearly could not meet the competition of those having an established trade name and good will, unless he were allowed the same differential as others in his class. By denying him this advantage the law effectually barred him from the business.

We are referred to a host of decisions to the effect that a regulatory law may be prospective in operation and may except from its sweep those presently engaged in the calling or activity to which it is directed.... The challenged provision is unlike such laws, since, on its face, it is not a regulation of a business or an activity in the interest of, or for the protection of, the public, but an attempt to give an economic advantage to those engaged in a given business at an arbitrary date as against all those who enter the industry after that date. The appellees do not intimate that the classification bears any relation to the public health or welfare generally; that the provision will discourage monopoly; or that it was aimed at any abuse, cognizable by law, in the milk business. In the absence of any such showing, we have no right to conjure up possible situations which might justify the discrimination. The classification is arbitrary and unreasonable and denies the appellant the equal protection of the law....

Mr. Justice CARDOZO, dissenting.

The judgment just announced is irreconcilable in principle with the judgment in Borden's case, announced a minute or so earlier.

A minimum price for fluid milk was fixed by law in April, 1933. At that time, 'independents' were underselling their competitors, the dealers in well-advertised brands, by approximately a cent a quart. There was reason to believe that unless that differential was preserved, they would be driven out of business. To give them an opportunity to survive, the lawmakers maintained the differential in the City of New York, the field of keenest competition. We have learned from the opinion in Borden's case that this might lawfully be done.

The problem was then forced upon the lawmakers, what were to be the privileges of independents who came upon the scene thereafter? Were they to have the benefit of a differential though they had not invested a dollar in the milk business at the passage of the act, or were they to take the chances of defeat by rivals stronger than themselves, as they would have to do in other callings? ... To concede the differential to newcomers might mean an indefinite extension of an artificial preference, thereby aggravating the handicap, the factitious barrier to expansion, for owners of established brands. There was danger that the preference would become so general as to occupy an unfair proportion of the field, the statutory norm being thus disrupted altogether. On the other hand, to refuse the differential might mean that newcomers would be deterred from putting capital and labor at the risk of such a business, and, even if they chose to do so, would wage a losing fight.

Hardships, great or little, were inevitable, whether the field of the differential was narrowed or enlarged. The legislature, and not the court, has been charged with the duty of determining their comparative extent. To some minds an expansion of the field might seem the course of wisdom and even that of duty; to others wisdom and duty might seem to point the other way. The judicial function is discharged when it appears from a survey of the scene that the lawmakers did not play the part of arbitrary despots in choosing as they did.... When a line or point has to be fixed, and 'there is no mathematical or logical way of fixing it precisely, the decision of the legislature must be accepted unless we can say that it is very wide of any reasonable mark.'... The judgment of the court commits us to a larger role. In declaring the equities of newcomers to be not inferior to those of others, the judgment makes a choice between competing considerations of policy and fairness, however emphatic its professions that it applies a rule of law.

For the situation was one to tax the wisdom of the wisest. At the very least it was a situation where thoughtful and honest men might see their duty differently. [The minimum-price statute] was an experiment, and a novel one, in that form of business enterprise. Relations between groups had grown up and crystallized under cover of the regime of unrestricted competition. They were threatened with disruption by a system of regulated prices which might crowd the little dealers out and leave the strong and the rich in possession of the field. If there was to be dislocation of the price structure by the action of the state, there was a duty, or so the lawmakers might believe, to spread the consequences among the groups with a minimum of change and hence a minimum of hardship. But the position of men in business at the beginning of the change was very different from those who might go into the business afterwards. Those already there would lose something more than an opportunity for a choice between one business and another. They would lose capital already ventured; they would lose experience already bought; they would suffer the pains incidental to the sudden and enforced abandonment of an accustomed way of life. A newcomer could not pretend that he was exposed to those afflictions. Then, too, the ephemeral character of the project counted heavily in favor of the older dealers, and little in favor of a newcomer, or rather, indeed, against him. The system of regulation had been set up as a temporary one, to tide producers over the rigors of the great depression. If independents already in the field could have their business saved from ruin, it might come back to them intact when the statute was no longer needed. Those who went into the system later would have to count the cost.

... It is juggling with words to say that all the independents make up a single 'class,' and by reason of that fact must be subjected to a single rule. Whether the class is divisible into subclasses is the very question to be answered. There may be division and subdivision unless separation can be found to be so void of rationality as to be the expression of a whim rather than an exercise of judgment. 'We have no right,' it is now said, 'to conjure up possible situations which might justify the discrimination.' The court has taught a different doctrine in its earlier decisions. 'A statutory discrimination will not be set aside as the denial of equal protection of the laws if any state of facts reasonably may be conceived to justify it.' On this occasion, happily, the facts are not obscure. Big dealers and little ones, newcomers in the trade and veterans, were clamorously asserting to the legislature their title to its favor. I have not seen the judicial scales so delicately poised and so accurately graduated as to balance and record the subtleties of all these rival equities, and make them ponderable and legible beyond a reasonable doubt.

To say that the statute is not void beyond a reasonable doubt is to say that it is valid.

Mr. Justice BRANDEIS and Mr. Justice STONE join in this opinion.

## Note: The Difficulties of Police Power/ Class Legislation Jurisprudence

*Barbier* is a typical statement of the police powers/class legislation approach to the Fourteenth Amendment in general, and equal protection in particular. It recognized broad government power to treat different persons or groups differently, but only if that differential treatment was imposed in order to promote some public good. But as one might imagine, it's not always easy to determine why government imposes such differential treatment. In the late Nineteenth century that difficulty only increased as America grew and industrialized, and as American society became more diverse and more complex. Justice Field wrote in *Barbier* that "From the very necessities of society, legislation of a special character ... must often be had." As the American economy and American society evolved, those "necessities" grew more numerous and more pressing. In turn, legislation responding to those "necessities" became more prevalent. More and more, courts were confronted with the task of distinguishing such appropriate legislation from purely private-regarding "class" legislation.

Taken together, *Borden's* and *Mayflower Farms* illustrate the difficulties inherent in the Court's performance of that task. The two provisions at issue in these cases were part of a comprehensive regulation of the milk industry in New York, which sought to prop up milk prices while ensuring both that all retailers, name-brand and off-brand, were treated fairly. As Justice Cardozo noted in his dissent in *Mayflower Farms*, the legislature's establishment of the name-brand/off-brand price differential (upheld in *Borden's*) created a new problem—who should enjoy the benefit of the allowance for lower off-brand prices?—that the provision struck down in *Mayflower Farms* attempted to address. To what extent does it make sense for the Court to split up its analysis of these two provisions and consider each in isolation from the other? One way to understand Justice Cardozo's sly remark at the start of his *Mayflower Farms* dissent is as a critique of the Court's piecemeal approach to the statute.

Another, deeper issue these cases raise is the question of deference. As reflected in the dueling opinions in both cases, it is not difficult to provide plausible alternative explanations demonstrating that these provisions were either reasonable or arbitrary. What this suggests is that, without a theory explaining *how carefully* the Court would perform the police power inquiry, the results were likely to be inconsistent and unpredictable. As you will see in the materials that follow, soon after 1936 the Court began applying a more deferential approach to most types of legislative classifications. Just as importantly, you'll also see that in 1938 the Court suggested a theory explaining *why* it would defer in most cases — and why in certain cases it would not.

## Note: Equal Protection and Race in the Class Legislation Era

1. By nearly any measure, the Court's treatment of race in the sixty-nine years between 1868 and 1937 was dismal. Within several years after the ratification of the Fourteenth Amendment the Court was giving narrow interpretations to efforts to enforce it. For example, following the example of *The Slaughter-House Cases*, 83 U.S. 36 (1873) (Note *supra*. Part III Introduction), in *United States v. Cruikshank*, 92 U.S. 542 (1875), the Court gave a narrow reading to the rights protected by the Fourteenth Amendment. On that ground it threw out a federal indictment charging a gang of white men with massacring a group of African-Americans at the culmination of a violent political struggle in Louisiana. The Court also struck down a federal law that sought to enforce the right to racial equality by requiring that all public accommodations (such as theaters) admit persons on a race-neutral basis, on the ground that the law did not regulate the conduct of states, which were the only institutions bound by the Fourteenth Amendment. *The Civil Rights Cases*, 109 U.S. 3 (1883). On the other hand, the Court upheld a federal law allowing African-Americans to remove to federal court cases where African-Americans were excluded from jury service. *Strauder v. West Virginia*, 100 U.S. 303 (1879). (Congress's power to enforce the Fourteenth Amendment is considered in Chapter 17.)

2. The most notable race case of this era, and the one that most closely reflected the then-prevailing police power-approach to the Fourteenth Amendment, was *Plessy v. Ferguson*, 163 U.S. 537 (1896). (*Plessy* is discussed more fully in Chapter 13.) The case considered a challenge to a Louisiana law requiring racial segregation in railway cars. In upholding the law, an eight-justice majority reasoned that the law was a reasonable police-power regulation. Employing the language of the police power era, Justice Brown wrote the following, after citing earlier cases upholding segregated facilities:

> It is ... suggested by the learned counsel for the plaintiff in error that the same argument that will justify the state legislature in requiring railways to provide separate accommodations for the two races will also authorize them to require separate cars to be provided for people whose hair is of a certain

color, or who are aliens, or who belong to certain nationalities, or to enact laws requiring colored people to walk upon one side of the street, and white people upon the other, or requiring white men's houses to be painted white, and colored men's black, or their vehicles or business signs to be of different colors, upon the theory that one side of the street is as good as the other, or that a house or vehicle of one color is as good as one of another color. The reply to all this is that every exercise of the police power must be reasonable, and extend only to such laws as are enacted in good faith for the promotion of the public good, and not for the annoyance or oppression of a particular class....

So far, then, as a conflict with the Fourteenth Amendment is concerned, the case reduces itself to the question whether the statute of Louisiana is a reasonable regulation, and with respect to this there must necessarily be a large discretion on the part of the legislature. In determining the question of reasonableness it is at liberty to act with reference to the established usages, customs and traditions of the people, and with a view to the promotion of their comfort, and the preservation of the public peace and good order. Gauged by this standard, we cannot say that a law which authorizes or even requires the separation of the two races in public conveyances is unreasonable....

*Plessy* was seen as establishing the constitutionality of legislation providing separate-but-equal facilities for blacks and whites, known as "Jim Crow" legislation. The fate of Jim Crow legislation is discussed in Chapter 13.

## Note: Equal Protection and the Revolution of 1937

Chapters 4 and 7 told the stories of, respectively, the Court's 1937 shift toward more deferential Commerce Clause review and its shift toward similarly deferential review of legislation alleged to violate the Due Process Clause right to contract. No similarly dramatic or explicit demarcation separates the Court's approach to equal protection before and after 1937. Nevertheless, the deference accorded regulatory legislation under the Commerce Clause and Due Process Clause after 1937 was mirrored in the Court's equal protection jurisprudence, as illustrated in the following case.

It is worth mentioning one caveat to the statement that equal protection doctrine lacks the dramatic turning point that marks these other doctrines. In 1938, the Court decided *United States v. Carolene Products Co.*, 304 U.S. 144 (1938), an otherwise-unremarkable case where a plaintiff unsuccessfully brought Commerce Clause and Due Process Clause objections to a federal statute regulating interstate sales of a type of food. In rejecting those claims the *Carolene Products* Court deferred heavily to Congress's determinations about the need for the challenged law and the impact of the regulated activity on interstate commerce. However, the author of *Carolene Products*, Justice Harlan Fiske Stone, included a footnote in the opinion that implied that in certain situations the Court would not be so deferential. While that footnote was not necessary to the Court's resolution of the case in front of it, in retrospect "Footnote

4" came to be understood as enormously significant for constitutional law in general, and equal protection law in particular. The story of *Carolene Products* and its famous footnote is told in the next chapter.

## Railway Express Agency v. People of State of New York
### 336 U.S. 106 (1949)

Mr. Justice DOUGLAS delivered the opinion of the Court.

Section 124 of the Traffic Regulations of the City of New York promulgated by the Police Commissioner provides:

> No person shall operate, or cause to be operated, in or upon any street an advertising vehicle; provided that nothing herein contained shall prevent the putting of business notices upon business delivery vehicles, so long as such vehicles are engaged in the usual business or regular work of the owner and not used merely or mainly for advertising.

Appellant is engaged in a nation-wide express business. It operates about 1,900 trucks in New York City and sells the space on the exterior sides of these trucks for advertising. That advertising is for the most part unconnected with its own business. It was convicted ... and fined....

The Court of Special Sessions concluded that advertising on vehicles using the streets of New York City constitutes a distraction to vehicle drivers and to pedestrians alike and therefore affects the safety of the public in the use of the streets. We do not sit to weigh evidence on the due process issue in order to determine whether the regulation is sound or appropriate; nor is it our function to pass judgment on its wisdom.... We would be trespassing on one of the most intensely local and specialized of all municipal problems if we held that this regulation had no relation to the traffic problem of New York City. It is the judgment of the local authorities that it does have such a relation. And nothing has been advanced which shows that to be palpably false.

The question of equal protection of the laws is pressed ... strenuously on us. It is pointed out that the regulation draws the line between advertisements of products sold by the owner of the truck and general advertisements. It is argued that unequal treatment on the basis of such a distinction is not justified by the aim and purpose of the regulation. It is said, for example, that one of appellant's trucks carrying the advertisement of a commercial house would not cause any greater distraction of pedestrians and vehicle drivers than if the commercial house carried the same advertisement on its own truck. Yet the regulation allows the latter to do what the former is forbidden from doing. It is therefore contended that the classification which the regulation makes has no relation to the traffic problem since a violation turns not on what kind of advertisements are carried on trucks but on whose trucks they are carried.

That, however, is a superficial way of analyzing the problem, even if we assume that it is premised on the correct construction of the regulation. The local authorities may well have concluded that those who advertised their own wares on their trucks do not present the same traffic problem in view of the nature or extent of the advertising which they use. It would take a degree of omniscience which we lack to say that such is not the case. If that judgment is correct, the advertising displays that are exempt have less incidence on traffic than those of appellants.

We cannot say that that judgment is not an allowable one. Yet if it is, the classification has relation to the purpose for which it is made and does not contain the kind of discrimination against which the Equal Protection Clause affords protection. It is by such practical considerations based on experience rather than by theoretical inconsistencies that the question of equal protection is to be answered.... And the fact that New York City sees fit to eliminate from traffic this kind of distraction but does not touch what may be even greater ones in a different category, such as the vivid displays on Times Square, is immaterial. It is no requirement of equal protection that all evils of the same genus be eradicated or none at all....

Mr. Justice JACKSON, concurring.

There are two clauses of the Fourteenth Amendment which this Court may invoke to invalidate ordinances by which municipal governments seek to solve their local problems. One says that no state shall 'deprive any person of life, liberty, or property, without due process of law'. The other declares that no state shall 'deny to any person within its jurisdiction the equal protection of the laws.'

My philosophy as to the relative readiness with which we should resort to these two clauses is almost diametrically opposed to the philosophy which prevails on this Court. While claims of denial of equal protection are frequently asserted, they are rarely sustained. But the Court frequently uses the due process clause to strike down measures taken by municipalities to deal with activities in their streets and public places which the local authorities consider to create hazards, annoyances or discomforts to their inhabitants. And I have frequently dissented when I thought local power was improperly denied....

The burden should rest heavily upon one who would persuade us to use the due process clause to strike down a substantive law or ordinance. Even its provident use against municipal regulations frequently disables all government—state, municipal and federal—from dealing with the conduct in question because the requirement of due process is also applicable to State and Federal Governments. Invalidation of a statute or an ordinance on due process grounds leaves ungoverned and ungovernable conduct which many people find objectionable.

Invocation of the equal protection clause, on the other hand, does not disable any governmental body from dealing with the subject at hand. It merely means that the prohibition or regulation must have a broader impact. I regard it as a salutary doctrine that cities, states and the Federal Government must exercise their powers so as not to discriminate between their inhabitants except upon some reasonable differentiation fairly related to the object of regulation. This equality is not merely abstract justice. The framers of the Constitution knew, and we should not forget today, that there is no more effective practical guaranty against arbitrary and unreasonable government than to require that the principles of law which officials would impose upon a minority must be imposed generally. Conversely, nothing opens the door to arbitrary action so effectively as to allow those officials to pick and choose only a few to whom they will apply legislation and thus to escape the political retribution that might be visited upon them if larger numbers were affected. Courts can take no better measure to assure that laws will be just than to require that laws be equal in operation....

The question in my mind comes to this. Where individuals contribute to an evil or danger in the same way and to the same degree, may those who do so for hire be prohibited, while those who do so for their own commercial ends but not for hire be allowed to continue? I think the answer has to be that the hireling may be put in a class by himself and may be dealt with differently than those who act on their own. But this is not merely because such a discrimination will enable the lawmaker to diminish the evil. That might be done by many classifications, which I should think wholly unsustainable. It is rather because there is a real difference between doing in self-interest and doing for hire, so that it is one thing to tolerate action from those who act on their own and it is another thing to permit the same action to be promoted for a price.

Certainly the presence of absence of hire has been the hook by which much highway regulations has been supported.... I think the judgment below must be affirmed.

## United States Railroad Retirement Board v. Fritz
### 449 U.S. 166 (1980)

Justice REHNQUIST delivered the opinion of the Court.

The United States District Court for the Southern District of Indiana held unconstitutional a section of the Railroad Retirement Act of 1974, and the United States Railroad Retirement Board has appealed to this Court....

The 1974 Act fundamentally restructured the railroad retirement system. The Act's predecessor statute, adopted in 1937, provided a system of retirement and disability benefits for persons who pursued careers in the railroad industry. Under that statute, a person who worked for both railroad and nonrailroad employers and who qualified for railroad retirement benefits and social security benefits received retirement benefits under both systems and an accompanying "windfall" benefit. The legislative history of the 1974 Act shows that the payment of windfall benefits threatened the railroad retirement system with bankruptcy by the year 1981. Congress therefore determined to place the system on a "sound financial basis" by eliminating future accruals of those benefits. Congress also enacted various transitional provisions, including a grandfather provision which expressly preserved windfall benefits for some classes of employees.

In restructuring the Railroad Retirement Act in 1974, Congress divided employees into various groups. *First*, those employees who lacked the requisite 10 years of railroad employment to qualify for railroad retirement benefits as of January 1, 1975, the changeover date, would have their retirement benefits computed under the new system and would not receive any windfall benefit. *Second*, those individuals already retired and already receiving dual benefits as of the changeover date would have their benefits computed under the old system and would continue to receive a windfall benefit. *Third*, those employees who had qualified for both railroad and social security benefits as of the changeover date, but who had not yet retired as of that date (and thus were not yet receiving dual benefits), were entitled to windfall benefits if they had (1) performed some railroad service in 1974 or (2) had a "current connection" with the railroad industry as of December 31, 1974, or (3) completed 25 years of railroad service as of December 31, 1974. *Fourth*, those employees who had qualified for railroad benefits as of the changeover date, but lacked a current connection with the railroad industry in 1974 and lacked 25 years of railroad employment, could obtain a lesser amount of windfall benefit if they had qualified for social security benefits as of the year (prior to 1975) they left railroad employment.... It was with these complicated comparisons that Congress wrestled in 1974.

Appellee and others filed this class action in the United States District Court for the Southern District of Indiana, seeking a declaratory judgment that 45 U.S.C. §231b(h) is unconstitutional under the Due Process Clause of the Fifth Amendment because it irrationally distinguishes between classes of annuitants.[8] ... Appellee contended below that it was irrational for Congress to have drawn a distinction between employees who had more than 10 years but less than 25 years of railroad employment simply on the basis of whether they had a "current connection" with the railroad industry as of the changeover date or as of the date of retirement.

The District Court agreed with appellee that a differentiation based solely on whether an employee was "active" in the railroad business as of 1974 was not "rationally related" to the congressional purposes of insuring the solvency of the railroad retirement system and protecting vested benefits. We disagree and reverse.

... This Court in earlier cases has not been altogether consistent in its pronouncements in [the equal protection] area. In *Lindsley v. Natural Carbonic Gas Co.*, 220 U.S. 61 (1911), the Court said that "when the classification in such a law is called in question, if any state of facts reasonably can be conceived that would sustain it, the existence of that state of facts at the time that the law was enacted must be assumed." On the other hand, only nine years later in *F.S. Royster Guano Co. v. Virginia*, 253 U.S. 412 (1920), the Court said that for a classification to be valid under the Equal Protection Clause of the Fourteenth Amendment it "must rest upon some ground of difference having a fair and substantial relation to the object of the legislation...."

In more recent years, however, the Court in cases involving social and economic benefits has consistently refused to invalidate on equal protection grounds legislation which it simply deemed unwise or unartfully drawn.

---

8. Although "the Fifth Amendment contains no equal protection clause, it does forbid discrimination that is 'so unjustifiable as to be violative of due process.'" Thus, if a federal statute is valid under the equal protection component of the Fifth Amendment, it is perforce valid under the Due Process Clause of that Amendment.

Thus in *Dandridge v. Williams*, 397 U.S. 471 (1970), the Court rejected a claim that Maryland welfare legislation violated the Equal Protection Clause of the Fourteenth Amendment. It said:

> In the area of economics and social welfare, a State does not violate the Equal Protection Clause merely because the classifications made by its laws are imperfect. If the classification has some 'reasonable basis,' it does not offend the Constitution simply because the classification 'is not made with mathematical nicety or because in practice it results in some inequality.' *Lindsley v. Natural Carbonic Gas Co.* 'The problems of government are practical ones and may justify, if they do not require, rough accommodations—illogical, it may be, and unscientific.'...

> ... [The rational-basis standard] is true to the principle that the Fourteenth Amendment gives the federal courts no power to impose upon the States their views of what constitutes wise economic or social policy....

Applying those principles to this case, the plain language of §231b(h) marks the beginning and end of our inquiry.[10] There Congress determined that some of those who in the past received full windfall benefits would not continue to do so. Because Congress could have eliminated windfall benefits for all classes of employees, it is not constitutionally impermissible for Congress to have drawn lines between groups of employees for the purpose of phasing out those benefits.

The only remaining question is whether Congress achieved its purpose in a patently arbitrary or irrational way. The classification here is not arbitrary, says appellant, because it is an attempt to protect the relative equities of employees and to provide benefits to career railroad employees. Congress fully protected, for example, the expectations of those employees who had already retired and those unretired employees who had 25 years of railroad employment. Conversely, Congress denied all windfall benefits to those employees who lacked 10 years of railroad employment. Congress additionally provided windfall benefits, in lesser amount, to those employees with

---

10. This opinion and Justice BRENNAN's dissent cite a number of equal protection cases including *Lindsley v. Natural Carbonic Gas Co.* (1911); *F.S. Royster Guano Co. v. Virginia*, (1920); *Morey v. Doud*, 354 U.S. 457 (1957); *Flemming v. Nestor*, (1960); *Massachusetts Board of Retirement v. Murgia*, 427 U.S. 307 (1976); *New Orleans v. Dukes*, 427 U.S. 297 (1976); *Johnson v. Robison*, 415 U.S. 361 (1974); *U.S. Dept. of Agriculture v. Moreno*, 413 U.S. 528 (1973); *U.S. Dept. of Agriculture v. Murry*, 413 U.S. 508 (1973); *Weinberger v. Wiesenfeld*, 420 U.S. 636 (1975); and *James v. Strange*, 407 U.S. 128 (1972). The most arrogant legal scholar would not claim that all of these cases applied a uniform or consistent test under equal protection principles. And realistically speaking, we can be no more certain that this opinion will remain undisturbed than were those who joined the opinion in *Lindsley*, *Royster Guano Co.*, or any of the other cases referred to in this opinion and in the dissenting opinion. But like our predecessors and our successors, we are obliged to apply the equal protection component of the Fifth Amendment as we believe the Constitution requires and in so doing we have no hesitation in asserting, contrary to the dissent, that where social or economic regulations are involved *Dandridge v. Williams*, and *Jefferson v. Hackney*, 406 U.S. 535 (1972), together with this case, state the proper application of the test. The comments in the dissenting opinion about the proper cases for which to look for the correct statement of the equal protection rational-basis standard, and about which cases limit earlier cases, are just that: comments in a dissenting opinion.

10 years' railroad employment who had qualified for social security benefits at the time they had left railroad employment, regardless of a current connection with the industry in 1974 or on their retirement date.

Thus, the only eligible former railroad employees denied full windfall benefits are those, like appellee, who had no statutory entitlement to dual benefits at the time they left the railroad industry, but thereafter became eligible for dual benefits when they subsequently qualified for social security benefits. Congress could properly conclude that persons who had actually acquired statutory entitlement to windfall benefits while still employed in the railroad industry had a greater equitable claim to those benefits than the members of appellee's class who were no longer in railroad employment when they became eligible for dual benefits. Furthermore, the "current connection" test is not a patently arbitrary means for determining which employees are "career railroaders," particularly since the test has been used by Congress elsewhere as an eligibility requirement for retirement benefits. Congress could assume that those who had a current connection with the railroad industry when the Act was passed in 1974, or who returned to the industry before their retirement, were more likely than those who had left the industry prior to 1974 and who never returned, to be among the class of persons who pursue careers in the railroad industry, the class for whom the Railroad Retirement Act was designed....

Where, as here, there are plausible reasons for Congress' action, our inquiry is at an end. It is, of course, "constitutionally irrelevant whether this reasoning in fact underlay the legislative decision," *Flemming v. Nestor*, because this Court has never insisted that a legislative body articulate its reasons for enacting a statute. This is particularly true where the legislature must necessarily engage in a process of line-drawing. The "task of classifying persons for ... benefits ... inevitably requires that some persons who have an almost equally strong claim to favored treatment be placed on different sides of the line," and the fact the line might have been drawn differently at some points is a matter for legislative, rather than judicial, consideration.

Finally, we disagree with the District Court's conclusion that Congress was unaware of what it accomplished or that it was misled by the groups that appeared before it. If this test were applied literally to every member of any legislature that ever voted on a law, there would be very few laws which would survive it. The language of the statute is clear, and we have historically assumed that Congress intended what it enacted. To be sure, appellee lost a political battle in which he had a strong interest, but this is neither the first nor the last time that such a result will occur in the legislative forum. What we have said is enough to dispose of the claims that Congress not only failed to accept appellee's argument as to restructuring *in toto*, but that such failure denied him equal protection of the laws guaranteed by the Fifth Amendment.[12] ...

---

12. As we have recently stated: "The Constitution presumes that, absent some reason to infer antipathy, even improvident decisions will eventually be rectified by the democratic process and that judicial intervention is generally unwarranted no matter how unwisely we may think a political branch has acted." *Vance v. Bradley*, 440 U.S. 93 (1979).

Justice STEVENS, concurring in the judgment.

In my opinion Justice BRENNAN's criticism of the Court's approach to this case merits a more thoughtful response than that contained in footnote 10, *ante*. Justice BRENNAN correctly points out that if the analysis of legislative purpose requires only a reading of the statutory language in a disputed provision, and if any "conceivable basis" for a discriminatory classification will repel a constitutional attack on the statute, judicial review will constitute a mere tautological recognition of the fact that Congress did what it intended to do. Justice BRENNAN is also correct in reminding us that even though the statute is an example of "social and economic legislation," the challenge here is mounted by individuals whose legitimate expectations of receiving a fixed retirement income are being frustrated by, in effect, a breach of a solemn commitment by their Government. When Congress deprives a small class of persons of vested rights that are protected—and, indeed, even enhanced—for others who are in a similar though not identical position, I believe the Constitution requires something more than merely a "conceivable" or a "plausible" explanation for the unequal treatment.

I do not, however, share Justice BRENNAN's conclusion that every statutory classification must further an objective that can be confidently identified as the "actual purpose" of the legislature. Actual purpose is sometimes unknown. Moreover, undue emphasis on actual motivation may result in identically worded statutes being held valid in one State and invalid in a neighboring State. I therefore believe that we must discover a correlation between the classification and either the actual purpose of the statute or a legitimate purpose that we may reasonably presume to have motivated an impartial legislature. If the adverse impact on the disfavored class is an apparent aim of the legislature, its impartiality would be suspect. If, however, the adverse impact may reasonably be viewed as an acceptable cost of achieving a larger goal, an impartial lawmaker could rationally decide that that cost should be incurred.

In this case we need not look beyond the actual purpose of the legislature. As is often true, this legislation is the product of multiple and somewhat inconsistent purposes that led to certain compromises. One purpose was to eliminate in the future the benefit that is described by the Court as a "windfall benefit" and by Justice BRENNAN as an "earned dual benefit." That aim was incident to the broader objective of protecting the solvency of the entire railroad retirement program. Two purposes that conflicted somewhat with this broad objective were the purposes of preserving those benefits that had already vested and of increasing the level of payments to beneficiaries whose rights were not otherwise to be changed. As Justice BRENNAN emphasizes, Congress originally intended to protect all vested benefits, but it ultimately sacrificed some benefits in the interest of achieving other objectives.

Given these conflicting purposes, I believe the decisive questions are (1) whether Congress can rationally reduce the vested benefits of some employees to improve the solvency of the entire program while simultaneously increasing the benefits of others; and (2) whether, in deciding which vested benefits to reduce, Congress may favor annuitants whose railroad service was more recent than that of disfavored annuitants who had an equal or greater quantum of employment.

My answer to both questions is in the affirmative. The congressional purpose to eliminate dual benefits is unquestionably legitimate; that legitimacy is not undermined by the adjustment in the level of remaining benefits in response to inflation in the economy. As for the second question, some hardship—in the form of frustrated long-term expectations—must inevitably result from any reduction in vested benefits. Arguably, therefore, Congress had a duty—and surely it had the right to decide—to eliminate no more vested benefits than necessary to achieve its fiscal purpose. Having made that decision, any distinction it chose within the class of vested beneficiaries would involve a difference of degree rather than a difference in entitlement. I am satisfied that a distinction based upon currency of railroad employment represents an impartial method of identifying that sort of difference. Because retirement plans frequently provide greater benefits for recent retirees than for those who retired years ago—and thus give a greater reward for recent service than for past service of equal duration—the basis for the statutory discrimination is supported by relevant precedent. It follows, in my judgment, that the timing of the employees' railroad service is a "reasonable basis" for the classification as that term is used in *Lindsley v. Natural Carbonic Gas Co.*, and *Dandridge v. Williams*, as well as a "ground of difference having a fair and substantial relation to the object of the legislation," as those words are used in *F.S. Royster Guano Co. v. Virginia*.

Accordingly, I concur in the judgment.

Justice BRENNAN, with whom Justice MARSHALL joins, dissenting.

Appellee Gerhard Fritz represents a class of retired former railroad employees who were statutorily entitled to Railroad Retirement and Social Security benefits, including an overlap herein called the "earned dual benefit," until enactment of the Railroad Retirement Act of 1974, which divested them of their entitlement to the earned dual benefit. The Act did not affect the entitlements of other railroad employees with equal service in railroad and nonrailroad jobs, who can be distinguished from appellee class only because they worked at least one day for, or retained a "current connection" with, a railroad in 1974.

The only question in this case is whether the equal protection component of the Fifth Amendment bars Congress from allocating pension benefits in this manner. The answer to this question turns in large part on the way in which the strictures of equal protection are conceived by this Court.... The parties agree that the legal standard applicable to this case is the "rational basis" test. The District Court applied this standard below ... The Court today purports to apply this standard, but in actuality fails to scrutinize the challenged classification in the manner established by our governing precedents. I suggest that the mode of analysis employed by the Court in this case virtually immunizes social and economic legislative classifications from judicial review.

I

A legislative classification may be upheld only if it bears a rational relationship to a legitimate state purpose.... Perhaps the clearest statement of this Court's present approach to "rational basis" scrutiny may be found in *Johnson v. Robison*, 415 U.S. 361 (1974). In considering the constitutionality of limitations on the availability of educational benefits under the Veterans' Readjustment Benefits Act of 1966, eight Members of this Court agreed that

> our analysis of the classification proceeds on the basis that, although an individual's right to equal protection of the laws does not deny ... the power to treat different classes of persons in different ways[;] ... [it denies] the power to legislate that different treatment be accorded to persons placed by a statute into different classes on the basis of criteria wholly unrelated to the objective of that statute. *A classification "must be reasonable, not arbitrary, and must rest upon some ground of difference having a fair and substantial relation to the object of the legislation, so that all persons similarly circumstanced shall be treated alike"* (emphasis added).

The enactments of Congress are entitled to a presumption of constitutionality, and the burden rests on those challenging a legislative classification to demonstrate that it does not bear the "fair and substantial relation to the object of the legislation" required under the Constitution.

Nonetheless, the rational-basis standard "is not a toothless one," and will not be satisfied by flimsy or implausible justifications for the legislative classification, proffered after the fact by Government attorneys.... When faced with a challenge to a legislative classification under the rational-basis test, the court should ask, first, what the purposes of the statute are, and, second, whether the classification is rationally related to achievement of those purposes.

## II

The purposes of the Railroad Retirement Act of 1974 are clear, because Congress has commendably stated them in the House and Senate Reports accompanying the Act. A section of the Reports is entitled "Principal Purpose of the Bill." It notes generally that "the bill provides for a complete restructuring of the Railroad Retirement Act of 1937, and will place it on a sound financial basis," and then states:

> "Persons who already have vested rights under both the Railroad Retirement and the Social Security systems will in the future be permitted to receive benefits computed under both systems just as is true under existing law." H.R.Rep.No.93-1345, pp. 1, 2 (1974); S.Rep.No.93-1163, pp. 1, 2 (1974).

Moreover, Congress explained that this purpose was based on considerations of fairness and the legitimate expectations of the retirees....

Thus, a "principal purpose" of the Railroad Retirement Act of 1974, as explicitly stated by Congress, was to preserve the vested earned benefits of retirees who had already qualified for them. The classification at issue here, which deprives some retirees of vested dual benefits that they had earned prior to 1974, directly conflicts with Congress' stated purpose. As such, the classification is not only rationally unrelated to the congressional purpose; it is inimical to it.

### III

The Court today avoids the conclusion that § 231b(h) must be invalidated by deviating in three ways from traditional rational-basis analysis. First, the Court adopts a tautological approach to statutory purpose, thereby avoiding the necessity for evaluating the relationship between the challenged classification and the legislative purpose. Second, it disregards the actual stated purpose of Congress in favor of a justification which was never suggested by any Representative or Senator, and which in fact conflicts with the stated congressional purpose. Third, it upholds the classification without any analysis of its rational relationship to the identified purpose.

### A

The Court states that "the plain language of § 231b(h) marks the beginning and end of our inquiry." ... This statement is strange indeed, for the "plain language" of the statute can tell us only what the classification is; it can tell us nothing about the purpose of the classification, let alone the relationship between the classification and that purpose. Since § 231b(h) deprives the members of appellee class of their vested earned dual benefits, the Court apparently assumes that Congress must have *intended* that result. But by presuming purpose from result, the Court reduces analysis to tautology. It may always be said that Congress intended to do what it in fact did. If that were the extent of our analysis, we would find every statute, no matter how arbitrary or irrational, perfectly tailored to achieve its purpose. But equal protection scrutiny under the rational-basis test requires the courts first to deduce the independent objectives of the statute, usually from statements of purpose and other evidence in the statute and legislative history, and second to analyze whether the challenged classification rationally furthers achievement of those objectives. The Court's tautological approach will not suffice.

### B

The Court analyzes the rationality of § 231b(h) in terms of a justification suggested by Government attorneys, but never adopted by Congress. The Court states that it is "'constitutionally irrelevant whether this reasoning in fact underlay the legislative decision,'" *ante* (quoting *Flemming v. Nestor*). In fact, however, equal protection analysis has evolved substantially on this question since *Flemming* was decided. Over the past 10 years, this Court has frequently recognized that the actual purposes of Congress, rather than the *post hoc* justifications offered by Government attorneys, must be the primary basis for analysis under the rational-basis test. In *Weinberger v. Wiesenfeld*, 420 U.S. 636 (1975), we said:

> "This Court need not in equal protection cases accept at face value assertions of legislative purposes, when an examination of the legislative scheme and its history demonstrates that the asserted purpose could not have been a goal of the legislation" (citing cases).

... From these cases and others it is clear that this Court will no longer sustain a challenged classification under the rational-basis test merely because Government attorneys can suggest a "conceivable basis" upon which it might be thought rational. The standard we have applied is properly deferential to the Legislative Branch: where Congress has articulated a legitimate governmental objective, and the challenged classification rationally furthers that objective, we must sustain the provision. In other cases, however, the courts must probe more deeply. Where Congress has expressly stated the purpose of a piece of legislation, but where the challenged classification is either irrelevant to or counter to that purpose, we must view any *post hoc* justifications proffered by Government attorneys with skepticism. A challenged classification may be sustained only if it is rationally related to achievement of an *actual* legitimate governmental purpose.

The Court argues that Congress chose to discriminate against appellee for reasons of equity, stating that "Congress could properly conclude that persons who had actually acquired statutory entitlement to windfall benefits while still employed in the railroad industry had a greater equitable claim to those benefits than the members of appellee's class who were no longer in railroad employment when they became eligible for dual benefits." ... This statement turns Congress' assessment of the equities on its head. As I have shown, Congress expressed the view that it would be inequitable to deprive any retirees of any portion of the benefits they had been promised and that they had earned under prior law. The Court is unable to cite even one statement in the legislative history by a Representative or Senator that makes the equitable judgment it imputes to Congress. In the entire legislative history of the Act, the only persons to state that the equities justified eliminating appellee's earned dual benefits were representatives of railroad management and labor, whose self-serving interest in bringing about this result destroys any basis for attaching weight to their statements.

The factual findings of the District Court concerning the development of § 231b(h), amply supported by the legislative history, are revealing on this point.... [Justice Brennan then gave a lengthy recounting of the legislative process leading to enactment of the law, which suggested that railway union officials and management attempted to mislead Congress about the effects of the bill they had helped draft on the status of retired railway workers.]

Most striking is the following colloquy between Representative Dingell and Mr. Dempsey [one of the management negotiators]:

Mr. DINGELL. Who is going to be adversely affected? Somebody has to get it in the neck on this. Who is going to be that lucky fellow?

Mr. DEMPSEY. Well, I don't think so really. I think this is the situation in which every one wins. Let me explain.

\* \* \*

"Mr. DINGELL. Mr. Dempsey, I see some sleight of hand here but I don't see how it is happening. I applaud it but I would like to understand it. My problem is that you are going to go to a realistic system that is going to cost less but pay more in benefits. Now if you have accomplished this, I suggest we should put you in charge of the social security system.

The Act was passed in the form drafted by the Joint Committee without any amendment relevant to this case.[9]

Of course, a misstatement or several misstatements by witnesses before Congress would not ordinarily lead us to conclude that Congress misapprehended what it was doing. In this instance, however, where complex legislation was drafted by outside parties and Congress relied on them to explain it, where the misstatements are frequent and unrebutted, and where no Member of Congress can be found to have stated the effect of the classification correctly, we are entitled to suspect that Congress may have been misled. As the District Court found: "At no time during the hearings did Congress even give a hint that it understood that the bill by its language eliminated an earned benefit of plaintiff's class."

Therefore, I do not think that this classification was rationally related to an *actual* governmental purpose.

## C

The third way in which the Court has deviated from the principles of rational-basis scrutiny is its failure to analyze whether the challenged classification is genuinely related to the purpose identified by the Court. Having suggested that "equitable considerations" underlay the challenged classification—in direct contradiction to Congress' evaluation of those considerations, and in the face of evidence that the classification was the product of private negotiation by interested parties, inadequately examined and understood by Congress—the Court proceeds to accept that suggestion without further analysis....

In my view, the following considerations are of greatest relevance to the equities of this case: (1) contribution to the system; (2) reasonable expectation and reliance; (3) need; and (4) character of service to the railroad industry. With respect to each of these considerations, I would conclude that the members of appellee class have as great an equitable claim to their earned dual benefits as do their more favored co-workers, who remain entitled to their earned dual benefits under §231b(h).... [Justice Brennan then analyzed each of these considerations.]

## IV

Equal protection rationality analysis does not empower the courts to second-guess the wisdom of legislative classifications. On this we are agreed, and have been for over 40 years. On the other hand, we are not powerless to probe beneath claims by

---

9. Congress' unfortunate tendency to pass Railroad Retirement legislation drafted by labor and management representatives without adequate scrutiny was criticized by the Commission on Railroad Retirement in its 1972 report:

"The historical record shows that past policy formulation has not always abided by the key criteria of equity and sound financing. Generally the major provisions of the system have been the product of negotiations between railway labor and the carriers in a bargaining process often reflecting conflicts or the exercise of power in an industry which directly affects the public welfare. The results of this bargaining process have, at times, been less than fully screened by the Federal Government before they were ratified by Congressional action and given Presidential approval." H.R.Doc.No.92-350.

Government attorneys concerning the means and ends of Congress. Otherwise, we would defer not to the considered judgment of Congress, but to the arguments of litigators. The instant case serves as an example of the unfortunate consequence of such misplaced deference. Because the Court is willing to accept a tautological analysis of congressional purpose, an assertion of "equitable" considerations contrary to the expressed judgment of Congress, and a classification patently unrelated to achievement of the identified purpose, it succeeds in effectuating neither equity nor congressional intent.

I respectfully dissent.

## Note: Continued Unease With Deferential Scrutiny?

1. The unease some justices felt in *Fritz* about truly toothless rational basis scrutiny has continued to simmer. No modern justice has explicitly called for searching judicial review of classifications legislatures draw when they regulate everyday economic transactions and social relationships. However, justices — and in one case, a unanimous Court — have at times called for more stringent review than that reflected in the majority opinion in *Fritz*.

2. In *Allegheny Pittsburgh Coal Co. v. Commission of Webster County*, 488 U.S. 336 (1989), the Court unanimously struck down a West Virginia county's practice of assessing property taxes based on the value the land had when it was last purchased. Writing for the Court, Chief Justice Rehnquist (the author of the majority opinion in *Fritz*) noted that that practice had the effect of taxing a given land parcel from eight to 35 times more than a comparable parcel, depending on when the two parcels were last sold. But more important for the Court was the fact that West Virginia law provided that land would be taxed at equal rates. Given that degree of inequality and the county's inability to cite any state legislative policy justifying it, the Court concluded that the county's particular valuation practice violated the Equal Protection Clause.

3. Three years later the Court split on the scope of *Allegheny Pittsburgh*'s rationale. In *Nordlinger v. Hahn*, 505 U.S. 1 (1992), the Court considered an equal protection challenge to Proposition 13, an initiative enacted by California voters that instituted an acquisition value-based scheme for property taxation. The plaintiff in *Nordlinger* was a recent homebuyer who faced property taxes that were five times greater than the taxes assessed on her neighbors in comparable homes but who had lived in those homes a longer time. She alleged that that disparity violated her equal protection rights.

By an 8–1 vote, the Court rejected the plaintiff's claim. Writing for seven of those justices, Justice Blackmun explained that Proposition 13's acquisition value-based assessment scheme might have rationally furthered several legitimate government interests. For example, he suggested that it might promote neighborhood stability by preventing long-time residents from facing the constantly-rising property taxes that might flow from a scheme that required regular reassessments of property value in a rising real estate market (which California was experiencing when Proposition 13 was enacted). He distinguished *Allegheny Pittsburgh* in part by noting that the county assessor's scheme in that case conflicted with a state law provision guaranteeing equal taxation of comparable properties. No such law existed in California; indeed, the very point of Proposition 13 was to protect longtime homeowners who would otherwise face rising taxes as their properties appreciated.

Two justices in *Nordlinger* questioned the majority's attempt to distinguish *Allegheny Pittsburgh*. Justice Stevens, the sole dissenter, argued that Proposition 13's basis in state law made it an even more serious equal protection violation than the county tax assessor's conduct in *Allegheny Pittsburgh*. In his view, the California law codified the inequality that in the earlier case resulted only from what he called the assessor's "mal-administration" of state property tax law.

Turning to the rational basis standard, Justice Stevens echoed his approach in *Fritz*, writing that

> A *legitimate* state interest must encompass the interests of members of the disadvantaged class and the community at large, as well as the direct interests of the members of the favored class. It must have a purpose or goal independent of the direct effect of the legislation and one that we may reasonably presume to have motivated an impartial legislature.

He also insisted that, even under the rational basis standard, a law would be unconstitutional if its underinclusiveness or inclusiveness is "so severe that it cannot be said that the legislative distinction rationally furthers the posited state interest."

Applying these principles, he found that while interests such as neighborhood preservation were legitimate, Proposition 13's broad scope—applying to all real estate in the state, including, for example, commercial property—was too overinclusive.

Justice Thomas agreed with the majority that Proposition 13 was constitutional. However, he also agreed with Justice Stevens that *Allegheny Pittsburgh* could not be distinguished. He called for that case to be overruled, as "a needlessly intrusive judicial infringement on the State's legislative powers."

4. The Court again disagreed on the stringency of rational basis review in 2012. *Armour v. City of Indianapolis*, 132 S.Ct. 2073 (2012), involved a challenge to the City of Indianapolis's decision to change the means by which sewer projects were funded. Originally, such projects were funded by tax assessments levied on the owners of property that would benefit from the sewer improvements. The City allowed owners to either pay the tax in one lump sum, or over time. After several years, the City changed its funding mechanism. It stopped assessing individual property owners for projects in their neighborhoods, and it stopped collecting such payments for pending projects. However, the City refused to refund the payments made by those property owners who had paid their assessments in full at the start of those projects. Those property owners sued, alleging that the City's refusal constituted a violation of equal protection.

By a 6–3 vote, the Court upheld the City's decision. Writing for the majority, Justice Breyer agreed with the City that its "administrative concerns" justified its action. He explained:

The City had decided to switch to the [new funding] system. After that change, to continue [old system-based] unpaid-debt collection could have proved complex and expensive. It would have meant maintaining an administrative system that for years to come would have had to collect debts arising out of 20-plus different construction projects built over the course of a decade, involving monthly payments as low as $25 per household, with the possible need to maintain credibility by tracking down defaulting debtors and bringing legal action.

He also noted that if the City had decided to refund only the plaintiffs, who had been assessed for one particular sewer project, then it would have faced a different unfairness complaint from property owners who had fully paid their assessments for other sewer projects. He concluded his argument about administrative ease by analogizing the City's forgive-but-don't-refund policy to amnesty programs for payment of bills such as back taxes and parking tickets. He described such programs as reflecting "a line well known to the law" — "distinguishing past payments from future obligations."

Dissenting for himself and Justices Scalia and Alito, Chief Justice Roberts wasn't convinced. He did not think that the administrative difficulties with issuing refunds presented a serious concern, noting that the City had accurate records on which property owners had paid what. He also noted that the plaintiffs were complaining about payments on a particular project that had just started when the City switched its funding mechanism, thus resulting in "dramatic" disparities between the plaintiffs, who had fully paid their obligations, and other property owners who had only just begun to make their installment payments. Finally, Chief Justice Roberts compared the case to *Allegheny Pittsburgh*, observing that, just like West Virginia law in that case, the Indiana law in *Armour* mandated equal treatment of all taxpayers paying for sewer projects.

Toward the end of his dissent, Chief Justice Roberts wrote the following:

Our precedents do not ask for much from government in this area — only "rough equality in tax treatment." *Allegheny Pittsburgh*. The Court reminds us that *Allegheny Pittsburgh* is a "rare case." It is and should be; we give great leeway to taxing authorities in this area, for good and sufficient reasons. But every generation or so a case comes along when this Court needs to say enough is enough, if the Equal Protection Clause is to retain any force in this context. *Allegheny Pittsburgh* was such a case; so is this one.

5. Concede for argument's sake that *Armour* presents the "rare case" when a court needs to say "enough is enough." What guidance could the Court provide to lower courts about what constitutes a failure to satisfy the rational basis standard?

# Chapter 12

# Suspect Classes and Suspect Class Analysis

## Note: "The Most Celebrated Footnote in Constitutional Law"

1. The quoted phrase in the title of this note comes from Justice Lewis Powell, describing footnote 4 of *United States v. Carolene Products Co.*, 304 U.S. 144, 152 n. 4 (1938). *See* Lewis Powell, "*Carolene Products* Revisited," 82 *Columbia L. Rev.* 1087 (1982). Indeed, footnote 4 has been the font of much of the modern Supreme Court's jurisprudence. This note explains the case and the footnote, as the foundation for this chapter's consideration of what has come to be known as the "suspect class" approach to equal protection.

2. *Carolene Products* itself was a relatively inconsequential decision. It involved Commerce Clause and Due Process Clause challenges brought by the Carolene Products Company to a federal statute prohibiting the interstate shipment of "filled milk" (a product that resembled milk but was, rather than pure milk, a combination of milk combined (or "filled") with other fats). By 1938, the Court had largely embraced legal principles that easily disposed of both the plaintiff's Commerce Clause and Due Process Clause right to contract claims. (For discussions of those doctrines, see, respectively, Chapters 4 and 7.) In applying the deferential judicial review that had been then-recently adopted in Commerce Clause and Due Process Clause cases, Justice Stone wrote that "regulatory legislation affecting ordinary commercial transactions is not to be pronounced unconstitutional unless in the light of the facts made known or generally assumed it is of such a character as to preclude the assumption that it rests upon some rational basis within the knowledge and experience of the legislators."

But Justice Stone added a footnote to that statement that eventually became more important than the text to which it was appended. That note—which became known as simply "Footnote 4"—is reproduced in its entirety here, with some deletion of cases he cited:

> There may be narrower scope for operation of the presumption of constitutionality when legislation appears on its face to be within a specific prohibition of the Constitution, such as those of the first ten amendments, which are deemed equally specific when held to be embraced within the Fourteenth.

> It is unnecessary to consider now whether legislation which restricts those political processes which can ordinarily be expected to bring about repeal of undesirable legislation, is to be subjected to more exacting judicial scrutiny

under the general prohibitions of the Fourteenth Amendment than are most other types of legislation. On restrictions upon the right to vote, see *Nixon v. Herndon*, 273 U.S. 536 (1927); on restraints upon the dissemination of information, see *Near v. Minnesota*, 283 U.S. 697 (1931); on interferences with political organizations, see *Stromberg v. California*, 283 U.S. 359 (1931); as to prohibition of peaceable assembly, see *De Jonge v. Oregon*, 299 U.S. 353 (1937).

Nor need we enquire whether similar considerations enter into the review of statutes directed at particular religious, *Pierce v. Society of Sisters*, 268 U.S. 510 (1925) [Note *supra*. Chapter 8], or national, *Meyer v. Nebraska* (1923) [*Supra*. Chapter 8], or racial minorities, *Nixon v. Herndon*; whether prejudice against discrete and insular minorities may be a special condition, which tends seriously to curtail the operation of those political processes ordinarily to be relied upon to protect minorities, and which may call for a correspondingly more searching judicial inquiry. Compare *McCulloch v. Maryland* (1819) [*Supra*. Chapters 3 & 4]; *South Carolina State Highway Department v. Barnwell Bros.* (1938) [*Supra*. Chapter 5], and cases cited.

Thus, Footnote 4 addressed itself to situations where the Court's willingness to presume the constitutionality of legislation would not necessarily apply. It identified three such situations: (1) where a statute appeared on its face to violate a Bill of Rights provision (in the case of state legislation, where a statute appeared to violate a provision that had been incorporated to apply against states via the Fourteenth Amendment); (2) where a law restricted "political processes which can ordinarily be expected to bring about repeal of undesirable legislation," such as laws restricting speech and voting rights; and (3) where a law discriminated on certain grounds (against racial or religious minorities) or, more generally, where "prejudice against discrete and insular minorities" somehow made the political process less effective in protecting minorities. Unless a law fell under one of these categories, the Court would defer to the legislature's judgments. Indeed, the sentence in the opinion to which Footnote was appended reads, in relevant part, as follows:

> [The] existence of facts supporting the legislative judgment is to be presumed, for regulatory legislation affecting ordinary commercial transactions is not to be pronounced unconstitutional unless in the light of the facts made known or generally assumed it is of such a character as to preclude the assumption that it rests upon some rational basis within the knowledge and experience of the legislators.

The principle announced in this sentence reflects the Court's decisive turn away from careful review of "regulatory legislation affecting ordinary commercial transactions" as part of the police power/class legislation approach to equal protection discussed in Chapter 11.

Note that none of the three situations Footnote 4 identified was implicated in *Carolene Products* itself. In that sense Footnote 4 was pure *dicta*, a fact suggested by Justice

Stone's ambiguous phrasing at the start of each paragraph ("There may be narrower scope …", "It is unnecessary to consider now …", and "Nor need we inquire …"). Indeed, it was *dicta* from only four justices: only seven justices participated in *Carolene Products*, and of those seven, one (Justice McReynolds) dissented, one (Justice Butler) concurred separately, and one (Justice Black) did not join the part of the opinion containing that footnote.

3. Nevertheless, soon after 1938 the justices began experimenting with the possibilities Footnote 4 offered for refocusing judicial review away from its then-recently abandoned focus on limiting federal Commerce Clause authority and enforcing the Due Process Clause right to contract. For example, in 1940, in *Minersville School District v. Gobitis*, 310 U.S. 586 (1940), the Court on an 8–1 vote rejected the First Amendment challenge of Jehovah's Witnesses schoolchildren to a school board rule requiring students to salute the flag and pledge allegiance. Writing for seven of those justices, Justice Frankfurter emphasized that the Witnesses were free to lobby the board for a religious exemption to the flag salute requirement. Dissenting, Justice Stone argued that the right to free religious exercise merited heightened protection as a specifically guaranteed constitutional right. He also cited Footnote 4 (which he had authored) when arguing that prejudice against small, disliked minorities such as the Witnesses justified heightened judicial protection. Thus, between them those two Justices used all three ideas from Footnote 4. (Three years later the Court reversed itself, overruling *Gobitis* and holding that the First Amendment protected students who objected to the forced flag salute and recitation of the pledge. *West Virginia State Board of Education v. Barnette*, 319 U.S. 624 (1943).)

4. As you will see in the next chapter (and as very briefly previewed in the next note), during the 1940s, '50s and '60s the Court made great strides toward using the Equal Protection Clause to promote racial equality. Perhaps surprisingly, however, Footnote 4 did not play an explicit role in that campaign, even though paragraph three specifically mentioned racial discrimination and even though Justice Stone was known to have been thinking about discrimination against African-Americans when he wrote the footnote.

Nevertheless, by the early 1970s the Court was starting to utilize the third paragraph of Footnote 4, and its focus on when discrimination somehow infected the political process. As that decade opened, equal protection doctrine could be stated quite simply. Except in two situations—(1) where a law unequally distributed a limited set of fundamental rights, and (2) where a law discriminated on the basis of race—equal protection scrutiny would be very deferential, as suggested by cases such as *Railway Express*, excerpted in Chapter 11. That would soon change, as the Court began experimenting with using insights derived from Footnote 4 to raise other types of discrimination to "suspect" status, justifying, in Footnote 4's words, "more searching judicial inquiry."

### *Note: Footnote 4 and Race*

1. One might think that racial discrimination would be a prime area for application of Footnote 4's analysis, in particular its concern about "prejudice against discrete and insular minorities" creating political dysfunction justfiying more intrusive judicial

review. Indeed, that last paragraph of Footnote 4 explicitly mentioned statutes "directed at ... racial minorities" as potentially meriting such scrutiny. And, in fact, the historical evidence suggests that Justice Stone was concerned about growing racial intolerance around the world, and, domestically, discrimination against African-Americans, when he wrote the footnote.

Nevertheless, in the years immediately following Footnote 4 the Court's approach to race issues remained ambivalent. Indeed, it took the Court over twenty years after 1938 before it began to adopt a decisive rule condemning all racial classifications as presumptively unconstitutional. And even when it did, the Court did not ground its conclusion on Footnote 4 political process analysis. The Court's progression toward this rule is examined in Chapter 13. This Note provides a very rudimentary preview of this issue.

2. In 1944 the Court decided a momentous race case, *Korematsu v. United States*, 323 U.S. 214 (1944). In *Korematsu* the Court, on a 6–3 vote, upheld the wartime internment of Japanese-Americans living on the West Coast, without individualized loyalty hearings. Writing for the six-Justice majority, Justice Black began his analysis as follows:

> It should be noted, to begin with, that all legal restrictions which curtail the civil rights of a single racial group are immediately suspect. That is not to say that all such restrictions are unconstitutional. It is to say that courts must subject them to the most rigid scrutiny. Pressing public necessity may sometimes justify the existence of such restrictions; racial antagonism never can.

Despite that language, the Court upheld the exclusion and internment order, reasoning that military exigencies in early 1942—in particular, the fear of an imminent Japanese invasion of the West Coast—made it reasonable for the military to feel that it needed to act quickly to remove potentially disloyal people from the area.

Justices Roberts, Murphy, and Jackson dissented. Most notably for our purposes, Justice Murphy used reasoning that echoed Footnote 4 (although not citing Footnote 4 itself) to argue that the order violated the plaintiff's equality rights under the Due Process Clause of the Fifth Amendment. After critiquing a variety of arguments made in favor of the reasonableness of the order's suspicion of Japanese-Americans as a group, he concluded that

> The main reasons relied upon by those responsible for the forced evacuation ... do not prove a reasonable relation between the group characteristics of Japanese Americans and the dangers of invasion, sabotage and espionage. The reasons appear, instead, to be largely an accumulation of much of the misinformation, half-truths and insinuations that for years have been directed against Japanese Americans by people with racial and economic prejudices—the same people who have been among the foremost advocates of the evacuation.

He also stated, in a footnote, that "Special interest groups were extremely active in applying pressure for mass evacuation," and quoted testimony from agricultural interests in California that reflected a dislike of Japanese-American competition and desire to exclude them. Echoing Footnote 4's concern about "discrete and insular" minorities, he also noted that "Individuals of Japanese ancestry are condemned because they are said to be 'a large, unassimilated, tightly knit racial group, bound to an enemy nation by strong ties of race, culture, custom and religion.'"

3. Despite the *Korematsu* majority's seeming strong condemnation of racial classifications, that case did not immediately establish their presumptive invalidity. For example, only one year later, in *Akins v. Texas*, 325 U.S. 398 (1945), the Court rejected a challenge to a Texas county's grand jury selection process, despite the commissioners' testimony that they refused to seat more than one African-American on any given grand jury. Two years later, in *Fay v. New York*, 332 U.S. 261 (1947), the Court rejected a challenge to New York's "blue ribbon" jury system, which established a special set of criteria for certain juries. While the challengers in *Fay* did not claim that those criteria discriminated on the basis of race, the Court, speaking through Justice Jackson, nevertheless observed that the rule against racial exclusion in jury selection derived primarily, and perhaps only, from legislation enforcing the Fourteenth Amendment, not from the Amendment itself.

The same ambivalence about any presumptive rule against racial classifications appeared in education cases. As the post-war Court moved toward dismantling separate-but-equal in public education, it never simply stated that race classifications, or racial exclusions, were necessarily constitutionally problematic. For example, in *Sweatt v. Painter*, 339 U.S. 629 (1950), where the Court held that a separate-but-equal law school for African-Americans did not provide equal protection, the Court simply disagreed that the new law school was truly "equal" to the flagship state law school, the University of Texas, to which the black plaintiff had applied but had been rejected due to his race.

The same focus on true "equality" underlay the Court's decision in *Brown v. Board of Education*, 347 U.S. 483 (1954). In *Brown*, the Court relied heavily on the importance of education to civic and economic opportunity, and concluded—controversially citing sociological evidence—that segregated education "generates a feeling of inferiority as to [black schoolchildren's] status in the community that may affect their hearts and minds in a way unlikely ever to be undone." *Brown* is presented in more detail in Chapter 13.

Soon after *Brown* the Court began striking down separate-but-equal laws across all areas of government action. But, as Chapter 13 examines, those cases also ignored Footnote 4's political-process reasoning. By the early 1960s, the Court was able to cite those post-*Brown* cases for the proposition that racial classifications were presumptively unconstitutional. But again, the Court never relied on political process reasoning.

4. The most recent part of the story about race and the Court concerns race-conscious government action designed to *benefit* racial minorities—so-called "affirmative action." As Chapter 13 explains, despite protests from some individual justices the Court never performed a serious political process analysis of whether such laws merited the same or lesser judicial scrutiny as the Jim Crow laws of a generation before.

5. Perhaps ironically, the analysis in Footnote 4's final paragraph found more enthusiastic judicial application in areas other than race. The remainder of this chapter considers the Court's attempt to translate Footnote 4's final paragraph into workable judicial doctrine in those other areas. Chapter 13 then examines in more detail the Court's approach to race.

# A. Sex Discrimination

In many ways, sex discrimination is the paradigmatic *Carolene Products*-style "suspect class." While other classifications—in particular, out-of-wedlock birth—had earlier been identified as potentially problematic, sex discrimination has been the subject of the most careful—and often the most controversial—suspect class analysis. Moreover, sex discrimination claims have continued to come to the Court, thus, allowing it opportunities to alter its approach in response to changing social realities and changing personnel.

### *Note: Sex Discrimination Jurisprudence before* Frontiero v. Richardson

1. Sex discrimination claims have been brought before the Court since the first years of the Fourteenth Amendment. Indeed, crusaders for women's equality were disappointed when the draft of the Fourteenth Amendment introduced the word "male" into the Constitution for the first time.

Early judicial decisions were equally disappointing. In *Bradwell v. Illinois*, 16 Wall. 130 (1873), the Court upheld Illinois's prohibition on women practicing law. Justice Bradley wrote a famous concurring opinion where he wrote the following:

> The civil law, as well as nature herself, has always recognized a wide difference in the respective spheres and destinies of man and woman. Man is, or should be, woman's protector and defender. The natural and proper timidity and delicacy which belongs to the female sex evidently unfits it for many of the occupations of civil life. The constitution of the family organization, which is founded in the divine ordinance, as well as in the nature of things, indicates the domestic sphere as that which properly belongs to the domain and functions of womanhood. The harmony, not to say identity, of interest and views which belong, or should belong, to the family institution is repugnant to the idea of a woman adopting a distinct and independent career from that of her husband....

> It is true that many women are unmarried and not affected by any of the duties, complications, and incapacities arising out of the married state, but these are exceptions to the general rule. The paramount destiny and mission of woman are to fulfil the noble and benign offices of wife and mother. This is the law of the Creator. And the rules of civil society must be adapted to the general constitution of things, and cannot be based upon exceptional cases.

2. Sex equality claims fared no better throughout much of the Twentieth century. Perhaps ironically, the only victories won by women before the 1970s occurred during the *Lochner* era, where at times the Court would strike down minimum wage and maximum working hours laws limited to women, in part on the ground that they arbitrarily singled out women for special treatment. *See, e.g., Adkins v. Children's Hospital*, 261 U.S. 525 (1923) (Note *supra.* Chapter 7). At other times, the Court upheld such laws, with the Court sometimes relying on what it viewed as women's particular vulnerabilities in the marketplace or the state's interest in ensuring that women remained healthy enough for motherhood. *See, e.g., Muller v. Oregon*, 208 U.S. 412 (1908) (Note *supra.* Chapter 7).

With the demise of the *Lochner* era, liberty of contract-based guarantees against such laws disappeared, and states became free to classify based on sex with only minimal judicial scrutiny. Thus, in *Goeseart v. Cleary*, 335 U.S. 464 (1948), the Court easily and unanimously rejected an equal protection challenge to a Michigan law prohibiting women from being bartenders unless they were the wife or daughter of the bar owner. The Court observed that "Michigan could, beyond question, forbid all women from working behind a bar," and thus concluded that the state could reasonably decide that allowing only the female relatives of the owner to work in the bar would minimize the "hazards" that might otherwise arise. Similarly, in *Hoyt v. Florida*, 368 U.S. 57 (1961), the Court upheld a state law allowing women to excuse themselves from jury service. As with *Goeseart*, the Court was again unanimous. Writing for six of the justices, Justice Harlan concluded that the state law was reasonable, since, despite "the enlightened emancipation of women," "woman is still regarded as the center of home and family life," thus justifying their right to excuse themselves from jury service "unless she herself determines that such service is consistent with her own special responsibilities."

3. The first modern victory for women's equality rights was in *Reed v. Reed*, 404 U.S. 71 (1971). In *Reed*, the Court struck down an Idaho law providing that, when selecting between equally-related relatives of a decedent, a man should be preferred over a woman as executor of the estate. Writing for a unanimous Court, Chief Justice Burger rejected the argument that the male preference was an appropriate tool for eliminating at least one form of contest when two persons petitioned to be named executor, describing it as "the very kind of arbitrary legislative choice forbidden by the Equal Protection Clause of the Fourteenth Amendment." Thus, *Reed* did not state that it was reviewing the Idaho law unusually carefully.

Consider how Justice Brennan used *Reed* in the next case, the first one where a justice argued for heightened scrutiny of sex classifications.

# Frontiero v. Richardson

## 411 U.S. 677 (1973)

Mr. Justice BRENNAN announced the judgment of the Court in an opinion in which Mr. Justice DOUGLAS, Mr. Justice WHITE, and Mr. Justice MARSHALL join.

The question before us concerns the right of a female member of the uniformed services to claim her spouse as a 'dependent' for the purposes of obtaining increased quarters allowances and medical and dental benefits ... on an equal footing with male members. Under these statutes, a serviceman may claim his wife as a 'dependent' without regard to whether she is in fact dependent upon him for any part of her support. A servicewoman, on the other hand, may not claim her husband as a 'dependent' under these programs unless he is in fact dependent upon her for over one-half of his support. Thus, the question for decision is whether this difference in treatment constitutes an unconstitutional discrimination against servicewomen in violation of the Due Process Clause of the Fifth Amendment....

## II

At the outset, appellants contend that classifications based upon sex, like classifications based upon race, alienage, and national origin, are inherently suspect and must therefore be subjected to close judicial scrutiny. We agree and, indeed, find at least implicit support for such an approach in our unanimous decision only last Term in *Reed v. Reed*, 404 U.S. 71 (1971) [Note *supra*. this chapter].

In *Reed*, the Court considered the constitutionality of an Idaho statute providing that, when two individuals are otherwise equally entitled to appointment as administrator of an estate, the male applicant must be preferred to the female....

The Court noted that the Idaho statute 'provides that different treatment be accorded to the applicants on the basis of their sex; it thus establishes a classification subject to scrutiny under the Equal Protection Clause.' Under 'traditional' equal protection analysis, a legislative classification must be sustained unless it is 'patently arbitrary' and bears no rational relationship to a legitimate governmental interest.

In an effort to meet this standard, appellee [in *Reed*] contended that the statutory scheme was a reasonable measure designed to reduce the workload on probate courts by eliminating one class of contests. Moreover, appellee argued that the mandatory preference for male applicants was in itself reasonable since 'men [are] as a rule more conversant with business affairs than ... women.'... And the Idaho Supreme Court, in upholding the constitutionality of this statute, suggested that the Idaho Legislature might reasonably have 'concluded that in general men are better qualified to act as an administrator than are women.'

Despite these contentions, however, the Court held the statutory preference for male applicants unconstitutional. In reaching this result, the Court implicitly rejected appellee's apparently rational explanation of the statutory scheme, and concluded that, by ignoring the individual qualifications of particular applicants, the challenged statute provided 'dissimilar treatment for men and women who are ... similarly situated.' The Court therefore held that, even though the State's interest in achieving administrative efficiency 'is not without some legitimacy,' 'to give a mandatory preference to members of either sex over members of the other, merely to accomplish the elimination of hearings on the merits, is to make the very kind of arbitrary legislative choice forbidden by the [Constitution]....' This departure from 'traditional' rational-basis analysis with respect to sex-based classifications is clearly justified.

There can be no doubt that our Nation has had a long and unfortunate history of sex discrimination. Traditionally, such discrimination was rationalized by an attitude of 'romantic paternalism' which, in practical effect, put women, not on a pedestal, but in a cage. Indeed, this paternalistic attitude became so firmly rooted in our national consciousness that, 100 years ago, a distinguished Member of this Court was able to proclaim:

> 'Man is, or should be, women's protector and defender. The natural and proper timidity and delicacy which belongs to the female sex evidently unfits it for many of the occupations of civil life. The constitution of the family organization, which is founded in the divine ordinance, as well as in the nature of things, indicates the domestic sphere as that which properly belongs to the domain and functions of womanhood. The harmony, not to say identity, of interests and views which belong, or should belong, to the family institution is repugnant to the idea of a woman adopting a distinct and independent career from that of her husband....
>
> '... The paramount destiny and mission of woman are to fulfil the noble and benign offices of wife and mother. This is the law of the Creator.' *Bradwell v. State of Illinois*, 83 U.S. 130 (1873) (Bradley, J., concurring) [Note *supra.* this chapter].

As a result of notions such as these, our statute books gradually became laden with gross, stereotyped distinctions between the sexes and, indeed, throughout much of the 19th century the position of women in our society was, in many respects, comparable to that of blacks under the pre-Civil War slave codes. Neither slaves nor women could hold office, serve on juries, or bring suit in their own names, and married women traditionally were denied the legal capacity to hold or convey property or to serve as legal guardians of their own children. And although blacks were guaranteed the right to vote in 1870, women were denied even that right—which is itself 'preservative of other basic civil and political rights'—until adoption of the Nineteenth Amendment half a century later.

It is true, of course, that the position of women in America has improved markedly in recent decades. Nevertheless, it can hardly be doubted that, in part because of the high visibility of the sex characteristic, women still face pervasive, although at times more subtle, discrimination in our educational institutions, in the job market and, perhaps most conspicuously, in the political arena.[17]

---

17. It is true, of course, that when viewed in the abstract, women do not constitute a small and powerless minority. Nevertheless, in part because of past discrimination, women are vastly under-

Moreover, since sex, like race and national origin, is an immutable characteristic determined solely by the accident of birth, the imposition of special disabilities upon the members of a particular sex because of their sex would seem to violate 'the basic concept of our system that legal burdens should bear some relationship to individual responsibility....' *Weber v. Aetna Casualty & Surety Co.*, 406 U.S. 164 (1972). And what differentiates sex from such non-suspect statuses as intelligence or physical disability, and aligns it with the recognized suspect criteria, is that the sex characteristic frequently bears no relation to ability to perform or contribute to society. As a result, statutory distinctions between the sexes often have the effect of invidiously relegating the entire class of females to inferior legal status without regard to the actual capabilities of its individual members.

We might also note that, over the past decade, Congress has itself manifested an increasing sensitivity to sex-based classifications. In Tit. VII of the Civil Rights Act of 1964, for example, Congress expressly declared that no employer, labor union, or other organization subject to the provisions of the Act shall discriminate against any individual on the basis of 'race, color, religion, *sex*, or national origin.' Similarly, the Equal Pay Act of 1963 provides that no employer covered by the Act 'shall discriminate ... between employees on the basis of *sex*.' And § 1 of the Equal Rights Amendment, passed by Congress on March 22, 1972, and submitted to the legislatures of the States for ratification, declares that 'equality of rights under the law shall not be denied or abridged by the United States or by any State on account of sex.' Thus, Congress itself has concluded that classifications based upon sex are inherently invidious, and this conclusion of a coequal branch of Government is not without significance to the question presently under consideration.

With these considerations in mind, we can only conclude that classifications based upon sex, like classifications based upon race, alienage, or national origin, are inherently suspect, and must therefore be subjected to strict judicial scrutiny. Applying the analysis mandated by that stricter standard of review, it is clear that the statutory scheme now before us is constitutionally invalid.

### III

... In essence, the Government maintains that, as an empirical matter, wives in our society frequently are dependent upon their husbands, while husbands rarely are dependent upon their wives. Thus, the Government argues that Congress might reasonably have concluded that it would be both cheaper and easier simply conclusively to presume that wives of male members are financially dependent upon their husbands, while burdening female members with the task of establishing dependency in fact.

The Government offers no concrete evidence, however, tending to support its view that such differential treatment in fact saves the Government any money. In order to

---

represented in this Nation's decisionmaking councils. There has never been a female President, nor a female member of this Court. Not a single woman presently sits in the United States Senate, and only 14 women hold seats in the House of Representatives. And, as appellants point out, this underrepresentation is present throughout all levels of our State and Federal Government.

satisfy the demands of strict judicial scrutiny, the Government must demonstrate, for example, that it is actually cheaper to grant increased benefits with respect to *all* male members, than it is to determine which male members are in fact entitled to such benefits and to grant increased benefits only to those members whose wives actually meet the dependency requirement. Here, however, there is substantial evidence that, if put to the test, many of the wives of male members would fail to qualify for benefits. And in light of the fact that the dependency determination with respect to the husbands of female members is presently made solely on the basis of affidavits, rather than through the more costly hearing process, the Government's explanation of the statutory scheme is, to say the least, questionable.

In any case, our prior decisions make clear that, although efficacious administration of governmental programs is not without some importance, 'the Constitution recognizes higher values than speed and efficiency.' And when we enter the realm of 'strict judicial scrutiny,' there can be no doubt that 'administrative convenience' is not a shibboleth, the mere recitation of which dictates constitutionality. On the contrary, any statutory scheme which draws a sharp line between the sexes, *solely* for the purpose of achieving administrative convenience, necessarily commands 'dissimilar treatment for men and women who are … similarly situated,' and therefore involves the 'very kind of arbitrary legislative choice forbidden by the [Constitution]….' *Reed.*…

Mr. Justice STEWART concurs in the judgment, agreeing that the statutes before us work an invidious discrimination in violation of the Constitution. *Reed.*

Mr. Justice REHNQUIST dissents for the reasons stated by Judge Rives in his opinion for the District Court.

Mr. Justice POWELL, with whom THE CHIEF JUSTICE and Mr. Justice BLACKMUN join, concurring in the judgment.

I agree that the challenged statutes constitute an unconstitutional discrimination against servicewomen in violation of the Due Process Clause of the Fifth Amendment, but I cannot join the opinion of Mr. Justice BRENNAN, which would hold that all classifications based upon sex, 'like classifications based upon race, alienage, and national origin,' are 'inherently suspect and must therefore be subjected to close judicial scrutiny.' It is unnecessary for the Court in this case to characterize sex as a suspect classification, with all of the far-reaching implications of such a holding. *Reed v. Reed*, which abundantly supports our decision today, did not add sex to the narrowly limited group of classifications which are inherently suspect. In my view, we can and should decide this case on the authority of *Reed* and reserve for the future any expansion of its rationale.

There is another, and I find compelling, reason for deferring a general categorizing of sex classifications as invoking the strictest test of judicial scrutiny. The Equal Rights Amendment, which if adopted will resolve the substance of this precise question, has been approved by the Congress and submitted for ratification by the States. If this Amendment is duly adopted, it will represent the will of the people accomplished in the manner prescribed by the Constitution. By acting prematurely and unnecessarily, as I view it, the Court has assumed a decisional responsibility at the very time when state legislatures, functioning within the traditional democractic process, are debating the proposed Amendment. It seems to me that this reaching out to pre-empt by judicial action a major political decision which is currently in process of resolution does not reflect appropriate respect for duly prescribed legislative processes.

There are times when this Court, under our system, cannot avoid a constitutional decision on issues which normally should be resolved by the elected representatives of the people. But democratic institutions are weakened, and confidence in the restraint of the Court is impaired, when we appear unnecessarily to decide sensitive issues of broad social and political importance at the very time they are under consideration within the prescribed constitutional processes.

### Note: Litigating Sex Equality from Reed to Craig

1. *Reed* and *Frontiero* inaugurated a decade in which the Court decided a steady stream of sex discrimination cases. Many of those cases were brought by the ACLU's Women Right's Project, headed during this period by Ruth Bader Ginsburg, who was eventually appointed as a federal appeals court judge and ultimately a Supreme Court justice. Even in cases she did not litigate she often participated as an amicus. Her arguments were often influential, both with the plaintiffs' lawyers and the Court.

2. In her brief in *Reed*, Ginsburg argued that sex discrimination should be considered a suspect classification. She employed reasoning that she would repeat (as an amicus) in *Frontiero*, which Justice Brennan repeated in his plurality opinion. In particular, she stressed the analogy between race and sex, and noted the lack of women in positions of political power. Her brief also explicitly addressed *Muller*, *Goeseart*, and *Hoyt*, describing them as the cases "invoked most frequently to justify second class status for women."

3. In the three years after *Frontiero*, the Court decided several sex discrimination cases, with mixed results. In *Kahn v. Shevin*, 416 U.S. 351 (1974), the Court upheld a Florida law that gave a tax break to (female) widows, but not (male) widowers. Justice Douglas's majority opinion explained that the state could legitimately compensate women for prior discrimination in employment. Justices White, Brennan, and Marshall dissented. In *Schlesinger v. Ballard*, 419 U.S. 498 (1975), the Court upheld a Navy policy allowing female officers a longer time than males to be promoted before being forced to retire. A five-justice majority, speaking through Justice Stewart, explained that the differential was constitutional in light of women's lesser ability to rise through the ranks given their limited opportunities for sea duty and combat. Justice Brennan, writing for the *Kahn* dissenters and Justice Douglas, questioned whether the differential had in fact been intended to account for this difference. Thus, he concluded that the law failed the strict scrutiny he had called for in *Frontiero*.

This period did include one victory for women, in a case that Ginsburg herself identified as one of the most important sex equality cases she litigated. *Weinberger v. Wiesenfeld*, 420 U.S. 636 (1975), involved a male widower's challenge to a Social Security statute that denied so-called "widows and orphans" benefits to the male spouse of a deceased female worker and the child of that worker. The plaintiff in that case was a widower and father who wished to stay at home to care for his infant child, but who was denied survivors' benefits because he was a male. De-emphasizing her previous argument for strict scrutiny, Ginsburg contended that the law was invalid because it reflected a stereotype that women were not breadwinners and men were not stay-at-home caregivers. Writing for five of the justices in the unanimous (eight-justice) opinion, Justice Brennan agreed, describing the law as reflecting an "archaic and overbroad generalization" that "cannot suffice to justify the denigration of the efforts of women who do work and whose earnings contribute significantly to their families' support."

4. How is a focus on "stereotyping" and "archaic and overbroad generalization" different from the strict scrutiny that Ginsburg sought, but failed (by one vote) to achieve in *Frontiero*? Consider that question as you read the following case, which established the modern rule, today described as "intermediate scrutiny," for sex classifications.

## Craig v. Boren

### 429 U.S. 190 (1976)

Mr. Justice BRENNAN delivered the opinion of the Court.

The interaction of two sections of an Oklahoma statute prohibits the sale of "non-intoxicating" 3.2% beer to males under the age of 21 and to females under the age of 18. The question to be decided is whether such a gender-based differential constitutes a denial to males 18–20 years of age of the equal protection of the laws in violation of the Fourteenth Amendment....

II

A

... Analysis may appropriately begin with the reminder that *Reed v. Reed*, 404 U.S. 71 (1971) [Note *supra.* this chapter] emphasized that statutory classifications that distinguish between males and females are "subject to scrutiny under the Equal Protection Clause." To withstand constitutional challenge, previous cases establish that classifications by gender must serve important governmental objectives and must be substantially related to achievement of those objectives. Thus, in *Reed*, the objectives of "reducing the workload on probate courts" and "avoiding intrafamily controversy" were deemed of insufficient importance to sustain use of an overt gender criterion in the appointment of administrators of intestate decedents' estates. Decisions following *Reed* similarly have rejected administrative ease and convenience as sufficiently important objectives to justify gender-based classifications. See, e.g., *Frontiero v. Richardson* (1973) [*Supra.* this chapter]. And only two Terms ago, *Stanton v. Stanton*, 421 U.S. 7 (1975), expressly stating that *Reed v. Reed* was "controlling," held that *Reed* required invalidation of a Utah differential age-of-majority statute, notwithstanding the statute's coincidence with and furtherance of the State's purpose of fostering "old notions" of role typing and preparing boys for their expected performance in the economic and political worlds.[6]

*Reed v. Reed* has also provided the underpinning for decisions that have invalidated statutes employing gender as an inaccurate proxy for other, more germane bases of classification. Hence, "archaic and overbroad" generalizations concerning the financial position of servicewomen, *Frontiero*, and working women, *Weinberger v. Wiesenfeld*, 420 U.S. 636 (1975) [Note *supra*. this chapter], could not justify use of a gender line in determining eligibility for certain governmental entitlements. Similarly, increasingly outdated misconceptions concerning the role of females in the home rather than in the "marketplace and world of ideas" were rejected as loose-fitting characterizations incapable of supporting state statutory schemes that were premised upon their accuracy. In light of the weak congruence between gender and the characteristic or trait that gender purported to represent, it was necessary that the legislatures choose either to realign their substantive laws in a gender-neutral fashion, or to adopt procedures for identifying those instances where the sex-centered generalization actually comported with fact.

In this case, too, "*Reed*, we feel is controlling...," *Stanton*. We turn then to the question whether, under *Reed*, the difference between males and females with respect to the purchase of 3.2% beer warrants the differential in age drawn by the Oklahoma statute. We conclude that it does not....

C

We accept for purposes of discussion the District Court's identification of the objective underlying [the laws] as the enhancement of traffic safety. Clearly, the protection of public health and safety represents an important function of state and local governments. However, appellees' statistics in our view cannot support the conclusion that the gender-based distinction closely serves to achieve that objective and therefore the distinction cannot under *Reed* withstand equal protection challenge.

The appellees introduced a variety of statistical surveys. First, an analysis of arrest statistics for 1973 demonstrated that 18–20-year-old male arrests for "driving under the influence" and "drunkenness" substantially exceeded female arrests for that same age period. Similarly, youths aged 17–21 were found to be overrepresented among those killed or injured in traffic accidents, with males again numerically exceeding females in this regard. Third, a random roadside survey in Oklahoma City revealed that young males were more inclined to drive and drink beer than were their female counterparts. Fourth, Federal Bureau of Investigation nationwide statistics exhibited

---

6. *Kahn v. Shevin*, 416 U.S. 351 (1974) and *Schlesinger v. Ballard*, 419 U.S. 498 (1975) [Both note *supra*. this chapter], upholding the use of gender-based classifications, rested upon the Court's perception of the laudatory purposes of those laws as remedying disadvantageous conditions suffered by women in economic and military life. Needless to say, in this case Oklahoma does not suggest that the age-sex differential was enacted to ensure the availability of 3.2% beer for women as compensation for previous deprivations

a notable increase in arrests for "driving under the influence." Finally, statistical evidence gathered in other jurisdictions, particularly Minnesota and Michigan, was offered to corroborate Oklahoma's experience by indicating the pervasiveness of youthful participation in motor vehicle accidents following the imbibing of alcohol. Conceding that "the case is not free from doubt," the District Court nonetheless concluded that this statistical showing substantiated "a rational basis for the legislative judgment underlying the challenged classification."

Even were this statistical evidence accepted as accurate, it nevertheless offers only a weak answer to the equal protection question presented here. The most focused and relevant of the statistical surveys, arrests of 18–20-year-olds for alcohol-related driving offenses, exemplifies the ultimate unpersuasiveness of this evidentiary record. Viewed in terms of the correlation between sex and the actual activity that Oklahoma seeks to regulate — driving while under the influence of alcohol — the statistics broadly establish that .18% of females and 2% of males in that age group were arrested for that offense. While such a disparity is not trivial in a statistical sense, it hardly can form the basis for employment of a gender line as a classifying device. Certainly if maleness is to serve as a proxy for drinking and driving, a correlation of 2% must be considered an unduly tenuous "fit." Indeed, prior cases have consistently rejected the use of sex as a decisionmaking factor even though the statutes in question certainly rested on far more predictive empirical relationships than this.

Moreover, the statistics exhibit a variety of other shortcomings that seriously impugn their value to equal protection analysis. Setting aside the obvious methodological problems,[14] the surveys do not adequately justify the salient features of Oklahoma's gender-based traffic-safety law. None purports to measure the use and dangerousness of 3.2% beer as opposed to alcohol generally, a detail that is of particular importance since, in light of its low alcohol level, Oklahoma apparently considers the 3.2% beverage to be "nonintoxicating." Moreover, many of the studies, while graphically documenting the unfortunate increase in driving while under the influence of alcohol, make no effort to relate their findings to age-sex differentials as involved here. Indeed, the only survey that explicitly centered its attention upon young drivers and their use of beer — albeit apparently not of the diluted 3.2% va-

---

14. The very social stereotypes that find reflection in age-differential laws are likely substantially to distort the accuracy of these comparative statistics. Hence "reckless" young men who drink and drive are transformed into arrest statistics, whereas their female counterparts are chivalrously escorted home. See, e.g., W. Reckless & B. Kay, *The Female Offender* (Report to Presidential Commission on Law Enforcement and Administration of Justice, 1967). Moreover, the Oklahoma surveys, gathered under a regime where the age-differential law in question has been in effect, are lacking in controls necessary for appraisal of the actual effectiveness of the male 3.2% beer prohibition. In this regard, the disproportionately high arrest statistics for young males — and, indeed, the growing alcohol-related arrest figures for all ages and sexes — simply may be taken to document the relative futility of controlling driving behavior by the 3.2% beer statute and like legislation, although we obviously have no means of estimating how many individuals, if any, actually were prevented from drinking by these laws.

riety—reached results that hardly can be viewed as impressive in justifying either a gender or age classification.

There is no reason to belabor this line of analysis. It is unrealistic to expect either members of the judiciary or state officials to be well versed in the rigors of experimental or statistical technique. But this merely illustrates that proving broad sociological propositions by statistics is a dubious business, and one that inevitably is in tension with the normative philosophy that underlies the Equal Protection Clause. Suffice to say that the showing offered by the appellees does not satisfy us that sex represents a legitimate, accurate proxy for the regulation of drinking and driving. In fact, when it is further recognized that Oklahoma's statute prohibits only the selling of 3.2% beer to young males and not their drinking the beverage once acquired (even after purchase by their 18–20-year-old female companions), the relationship between gender and traffic safety becomes far too tenuous to satisfy Reed's requirement that the gender-based difference be substantially related to achievement of the statutory objective.

We hold, therefore, that under *Reed*, Oklahoma's 3.2% beer statute invidiously discriminates against males 18–20 years of age....

Mr. Justice POWELL, concurring.

I join the opinion of the Court as I am in general agreement with it. I do have reservations as to some of the discussion concerning the appropriate standard for equal protection analysis and the relevance of the statistical evidence. Accordingly, I add this concurring statement.

With respect to the equal protection standard, I agree that *Reed* is the most relevant precedent. But I find it unnecessary, in deciding this case, to read that decision as broadly as some of the Court's language may imply. *Reed* and subsequent cases involving gender-based classifications make clear that the Court subjects such classifications to a more critical examination than is normally applied when "fundamental" constitutional rights and "suspect classes" are not present.*

I view this as a relatively easy case. No one questions the legitimacy or importance of the asserted governmental objective: the promotion of highway safety. The decision of the case turns on whether the state legislature, by the classification it has chosen, has adopted a means that bears a "'fair and substantial relation'" to this objective. *Reed*, quoting *Royster Guano Co. v. Virginia*, 253 U.S. 412 (1920).

---

* As is evident from our opinions, the Court has had difficulty in agreeing upon a standard of equal protection analysis that can be applied consistently to the wide variety of legislative classifications. There are valid reasons for dissatisfaction with the "two-tier" approach that has been prominent in the Court's decisions in the past decade. Although viewed by many as a result-oriented substitute for more critical analysis, that approach—with its narrowly limited "upper-tier"—now has substantial precedential support. As has been true of *Reed* and its progeny, our decision today will be viewed by some as a "middle-tier" approach. While I would not endorse that characterization and would not welcome a further subdividing of equal protection analysis, candor compels the recognition that the relatively deferential "rational basis" standard of review normally applied takes on a sharper focus when we address a gender-based classification. So much is clear from our recent cases....

It seems to me that the statistics offered by appellees and relied upon by the District Court do tend generally to support the view that young men drive more, possibly are inclined to drink more, and—for various reasons—are involved in more accidents than young women. Even so, I am not persuaded that these facts and the inferences fairly drawn from them justify this classification based on a three-year age differential between the sexes, and especially one that it so easily circumvented as to be virtually meaningless. Putting it differently, this gender-based classification does not bear a fair and substantial relation to the object of the legislation.

Mr. Justice STEVENS, concurring.

There is only one Equal Protection Clause. It requires every State to govern impartially. It does not direct the courts to apply one standard of review in some cases and a different standard in other cases. Whatever criticism may be leveled at a judicial opinion implying that there are at least three such standards applies with the same force to a double standard.

I am inclined to believe that what has become known as the two-tiered analysis of equal protection claims does not describe a completely logical method of deciding cases, but rather is a method the Court has employed to explain decisions that actually apply a single standard in a reasonably consistent fashion. I also suspect that a careful explanation of the reasons motivating particular decisions may contribute more to an identification of that standard than an attempt to articulate it in all-encompassing terms. It may therefore be appropriate for me to state the principal reasons which persuaded me to join the Court's opinion.

In this case, the classification is not as obnoxious as some the Court has condemned,[1] nor as inoffensive as some the Court has accepted. It is objectionable because it is based on an accident of birth,[2] because it is a mere remnant of the now almost universally rejected tradition of discriminating against males in this age bracket, and because, to the extent it reflects any physical difference between males and females, it is actually perverse.[4] The question then is whether the traffic safety justification put forward by the State is sufficient to make an otherwise offensive classification acceptable.

The classification is not totally irrational.... Nevertheless, there are several reasons why I regard the justification as unacceptable. It is difficult to believe that the statute was actually intended to cope with the problem of traffic safety, since it has only a minimal effect on access to a not very intoxicating beverage and does not prohibit

---

1. Men as a general class have not been the victims of the kind of historic, pervasive discrimination that has disadvantaged other groups.

2. "Since sex, like race and national origin, is an immutable characteristic determined solely by the accident of birth, the imposition of special disabilities upon the members of a particular sex because of their sex would seem to violate 'the basic concept of our system that legal burdens should bear some relationship to individual responsibility ...'" *Frontiero.*

4. Because males are generally heavier than females, they have a greater capacity to consume alcohol without impairing their driving ability than do females.

its consumption. Moreover, the empirical data submitted by the State accentuate the unfairness of treating all 18–20-year-old males as inferior to their female counterparts. The legislation imposes a restraint on 100% of the males in the class allegedly because about 2% of them have probably violated one or more laws relating to the consumption of alcoholic beverages. It is unlikely that this law will have a significant deterrent effect either on that 2% or on the law-abiding 98%. But even assuming some such slight benefit, it does not seem to me that an insult to all of the young men of the State can be justified by visiting the sins of the 2% on the 98%.

Mr. Justice BLACKMUN, concurring in part. [Justice Blackmun stated his agreement with the excerpted portions of Justice Brennan's opinion, which he joined.]

Mr. Justice STEWART, concurring in the judgment.

… The disparity created by these Oklahoma statutes amounts to total irrationality. For the statistics upon which the State now relies, whatever their other shortcomings, wholly fail to prove or even suggest that 3.2% beer is somehow more deleterious when it comes into the hands of a male aged 18–20 than of a female of like age. The disparate statutory treatment of the sexes here, without even a colorably valid justification or explanation, thus amounts to invidious discrimination. See *Reed*.

Mr. Chief Justice BURGER, dissenting.

I am in general agreement with Mr. Justice REHNQUIST's dissent, but even at the risk of compounding the obvious confusion created by those voting to reverse the District Court, I will add a few words.…

On the merits, we have only recently recognized that our duty is not "to create substantive constitutional rights in the name of guaranteeing equal protection of the laws." … Though today's decision does not go so far as to make gender-based classifications "suspect," it makes gender a disfavored classification. Without an independent constitutional basis supporting the right asserted or disfavoring the classification adopted, I can justify no substantive constitutional protection other than the normal … protection afforded by the Equal Protection Clause.

The means employed by the Oklahoma Legislature to achieve the objectives sought may not be agreeable to some judges, but since eight Members of the Court think the means not irrational, I see no basis for striking down the statute as violative of the Constitution simply because we find it unwise, unneeded, or possibly even a bit foolish.…

Mr. Justice REHNQUIST, dissenting.

The Court's disposition of this case is objectionable on two grounds. First is its conclusion that *men* challenging a gender-based statute which treats them less favorably than women may invoke a more stringent standard of judicial review than pertains to most other types of classifications. Second is the Court's enunciation of this standard, without citation to any source, as being that "classifications by gender must serve *important* governmental objectives and must be *substantially* related to achievement of those objectives." The only redeeming feature of the Court's opinion, to my mind, is that it apparently signals a retreat by those who joined the plurality opinion in *Frontiero* from their view that sex is a "suspect" classification for purposes of equal protection analysis. I think the Oklahoma statute challenged here need pass only the "rational basis" equal protection analysis expounded in cases such as *McGowan v. Maryland*, 366 U.S. 420 (1961), and *Williamson v. Lee Optical Co.*, 348 U.S. 483 (1955) [Note *supra.* Chapter 7], and I believe that it is constitutional under that analysis.

I

In *Frontiero*, the opinion for the plurality sets forth the reasons of four Justices for concluding that sex should be regarded as a suspect classification for purposes of equal protection analysis.... Subsequent to *Frontiero*, the Court has declined to hold that sex is a suspect class, and no such holding is imported by the Court's resolution of this case. However, the Court's application here of an elevated or "intermediate" level scrutiny, like that invoked in cases dealing with discrimination against females, raises the question of why the statute here should be treated any differently from countless legislative classifications unrelated to sex which have been upheld under a minimum rationality standard.

Most obviously unavailable to support any kind of special scrutiny in this case, is a history or pattern of past discrimination, such as was relied on by the plurality in *Frontiero* to support its invocation of strict scrutiny. There is no suggestion in the Court's opinion that males in this age group are in any way peculiarly disadvantaged, subject to systematic discriminatory treatment, or otherwise in need of special solicitude from the courts....

It is true that a number of our opinions contain broadly phrased dicta implying that the same test should be applied to all classifications based on sex, whether affecting females or males. E.g., *Frontiero*; *Reed*. However, before today, no decision of this Court has applied an elevated level of scrutiny to invalidate a statutory discrimination harmful to males, except where the statute impaired an important personal interest protected by the Constitution. There being no such interest here, and there being no plausible argument that this is a discrimination against females,[2] the Court's reliance on our previous sex-discrimination cases is ill-founded. It treats gender classification as a talisman which—without regard to the rights involved or the persons affected—calls into effect a heavier burden of judicial review.

The Court's conclusion that a law which treats males less favorably than females "must serve important governmental objectives and must be substantially related to

---

2. I am not unaware of the argument from time to time advanced, that all discriminations between the sexes ultimately redound to the detriment of females, because they tend to reinforce "old notions" restricting the roles and opportunities of women. As a general proposition applying equally to all sex categorizations, I believe that this argument was implicitly found to carry little weight in our decisions upholding gender-based differences. Seeing no assertion that it has special applicability to the situation at hand, I believe it can be dismissed as an insubstantial consideration.

achievement of those objectives" apparently comes out of thin air. The Equal Protection Clause contains no such language, and none of our previous cases adopt that standard. I would think we have had enough difficulty with the two standards of review which our cases have recognized—the norm of "rational basis," and the "compelling state interest" required where a "suspect classification" is involved—so as to counsel weightily against the insertion of still another "standard" between those two. How is this Court to divine what objectives are important? How is it to determine whether a particular law is "substantially" related to the achievement of such objective, rather than related in some other way to its achievement? Both of the phrases used are so diaphanous and elastic as to invite subjective judicial preferences or prejudices relating to particular types of legislation, masquerading as judgments whether such legislation is directed at "important" objectives or, whether the relationship to those objectives is "substantial" enough.

I would have thought that if this Court were to leave anything to decision by the popularly elected branches of the Government, where no constitutional claim other than that of equal protection is invoked, it would be the decision as to what governmental objectives to be achieved by law are "important," and which are not. As for the second part of the Court's new test, the Judicial Branch is probably in no worse position than the Legislative or Executive Branches to determine if there is *any* rational relationship between a classification and the purpose which it might be thought to serve. But the introduction of the adverb "substantially" requires courts to make subjective judgments as to operational effects, for which neither their expertise nor their access to data fits them. And even if we manage to avoid both confusion and the mirroring of our own preferences in the development of this new doctrine, the thousands of judges in other courts who must interpret the Equal Protection Clause may not be so fortunate.

## II

… Our decisions indicate that application of the Equal Protection Clause in a context not justifying an elevated level of scrutiny does not demand "mathematical nicety" or the elimination of all inequality. Those cases recognize that the practical problems of government may require rough accommodations of interests, and hold that such accommodations should be respected unless no reasonable basis can be found to support them. Whether the same ends might have been better or more precisely served by a different approach is no part of the judicial inquiry under the traditional minimum rationality approach.

The Court "accepts for purposes of discussion" the District Court's finding that the purpose of the provisions in question was traffic safety, and proceeds to examine the statistical evidence in the record in order to decide if "the gender-based distinction *closely* serves to achieve that objective." … I believe that a more traditional type of scrutiny is appropriate in this case, and I think that the Court would have done well here to heed its own warning that "it is unrealistic to expect … members of the judiciary … to be well versed in the rigors of experimental or statistical technique." …

The Court's criticism of the statistics relied on by the District Court conveys the impression that a legislature in enacting a new law is to be subjected to the judicial equivalent of a doctoral examination in statistics. Legislatures are not held to any rules of evidence such as those which may govern courts or other administrative bodies, and are entitled to draw factual conclusions on the basis of the determination of probable cause which an arrest by a police officer normally represents. In this situation, they could reasonably infer that the incidence of drunk driving is a good deal higher than the incidence of arrest....

Quite apart from these alleged methodological deficiencies in the statistical evidence, the Court appears to hold that that evidence, on its face, fails to support the distinction drawn in the statute. The Court notes that only 2% of males (as against .18% of females) in the age group were arrested for drunk driving, and that this very low figure establishes "an unduly tenuous fit" between maleness and drunk driving in the 18 to 20-year-old group. On this point the Court misconceives the nature of the equal protection inquiry.

The rationality of a statutory classification for equal protection purposes does not depend upon the statistical "fit" between the class and the trait sought to be singled out. It turns on whether there may be a sufficiently higher incidence of the trait within the included class than in the excluded class to justify different treatment. Therefore the present equal protection challenge to this gender-based discrimination poses only the question whether the incidence of drunk driving among young men is sufficiently greater than among young women to justify differential treatment. Notwithstanding the Court's critique of the statistical evidence, that evidence suggests clear differences between the drinking and driving habits of young men and women. Those differences are grounds enough for the State reasonably to conclude that young males pose by far the greater drunk-driving hazard, both in terms of sheer numbers and in terms of hazard on a per-driver basis. The gender-based difference in treatment in this case is therefore not irrational....

## *Note: The Equal Rights Amendment*

1. The Court's sex equality jurisprudence in the 1970s evolved against the backdrop of a political struggle over ratification of the proposed Equal Rights Amendment (ERA). The Amendment, which had been introduced in Congress frequently since the 1920s, was passed by Congress in 1972 and sent to the states for ratification. Its operative provision reads: "Equality of rights under the law shall not be denied or abridged by the United States or by any state on account of sex." The Amendment was politically popular, and a large number of states quickly ratified it. By the mid-1970s, however, progress stalled at 35 states, three short of the 38 required for ratification. Opponents successfully argued, among other things, that the amendment would require women to serve in combat, repeal whatever benefits women enjoyed in obtaining alimony and child custody in divorce proceedings, and require unisex bathrooms.

2. What should that political debate, and its result, have meant for the Court's sex equality jurisprudence? Recall that in *Frontiero,* Justice Powell, joined by Chief Justice

Burger and Justice Blackmun, argued that the Court should not elevate sex to suspect class status in light of the then-ongoing debate about the ERA (a debate that, when *Frontiero* was decided, showed every indication that ERA would easily be ratified). Was he correct? Note, however, that Justice Powell still voted to strike down the military's sex discrimination in *Frontiero*, on the authority of *Reed*. Does that mean that, regardless of the result of the ERA debate, sex discrimination would still be subject to *Reed*'s version of rational basis review? Why should sex discrimination have been of any concern to the Court, if the nation was in fact at that moment engaged in a debate about amending the Constitution to address that very topic?

3. Leave aside the question of what the Court should have done while the ERA debate was ongoing. By the early 1980s that debate was settled, with the ERA's defeat. Should the Court have altered its sex discrimination jurisprudence accordingly? Should the nation's rejection of the ERA have been interpreted as a *de facto* overruling, by the American people, of cases such as *Frontiero*, *Wiesenfeld*, and *Craig*? Regardless of your views on the matter, the Court's sex equality jurisprudence continued to evolve in the direction of heightened scrutiny of sex classification, as set forth in the next note and particularly the case that follows that note, *United States v. Virginia*.

### *Note: What Does Intermediate Scrutiny Mean?*

1. *Craig* has come to be understood as stating the proposition that sex classifications receive "intermediate scrutiny," which requires that any such classification be "substantially related" to "an important government interest." Dissenting in *Craig*, Justice Rehnquist objected that that those two components of the standard were "so diaphanous and elastic as to invite subjective judicial preferences or prejudices relating to particular types of legislation, masquerading as judgments whether such legislation is directed at 'important' objectives or, whether the relationship to those objectives is 'substantial' enough." Consider that critique in light of the following small sampling of post-*Craig* cases.

2. In *Rostker v. Goldberg*, 453 U.S. 57 (1981), the Court upheld a federal law requiring draft registration for young males, but not for young females, in a case that was litigated based on the assumption—unchallenged in that case—that only men were eligible for combat duty. Writing for a six-justice majority, Justice Rehnquist stressed the deference due Congress in the realm of military planning. Turning to the *Craig* standard, he described the government's interest "in raising and supporting armies" as "important." He also found the government to have satisfied *Craig*'s "substantial relationship" test. He concluded that the congressional debate about draft registration had been careful and thoughtful, and that Congress had not acted "unthinkingly or reflexively" in exempting women, given the understanding that a draft would likely focus on building up combat forces.

Justice White, joined by Justice Brennan, dissented, finding the majority's analysis "most unpersuasive." He argued that drafting women, even for non-combat positions, would free up men for combat duty, thus making women's exclusion from draft registration insufficiently related to the government's interest in fielding a combat force.

Justice Marshall also dissented. He argued that, under *Craig*, the burden was on the government to show that the registration system's sex classification was substantially related to the goal of building up combat forces. He concluded that the government had not met that burden, given the option of registering all young persons but only drafting men in case of a war, or reinstituting a peacetime draft of men and women if the all-volunteer Army proved inadequate.

3. In *Michael M. v. Superior Court*, 450 U.S. 464 (1981), the Court upheld yet another sex classification. *Michael M.* considered California's statutory rape law, which made males, but not females, criminally liable. On a 5–4 vote, the Court upheld the law. Writing for four Justices, Justice Rehnquist concluded that the law reflected a real difference between males and females, since females bore a disproportionate risk from sex given the possibility of pregnancy. Thus, he concluded that the state could legitimately seek to prevent teenage pregnancies by imposing a legal burden only on males who engage in underage sex.

In describing the relevant standard, Justice Rehnquist avoided using the term "intermediate scrutiny" or even stating its requirements. Instead, he noted that the Court did not apply strict scrutiny to sex classifications, and quoted Justice Powell's concurrence in *Craig* for the proposition that "the traditional minimum rationality test takes on a somewhat 'sharper focus' when gender-based classifications are challenged." Justice Stewart joined this opinion, but also concurred to stress his agreement with the idea that males and females were not similarly situated with regard to sexual activity. Justice Blackmun concurred in the judgment, concluding that the law satisfied the type of scrutiny performed in *Reed* and *Craig*.

Justice Brennan, joined by Justices White and Marshall, dissented. He questioned the effectiveness of California's sex-classified scheme in preventing teenage pregnancies. He also suggested that that lack of effectiveness may have flowed from the fact that the statute was originally not designed for that purpose, but instead was based on "outmoded sexual stereotypes" about the need to protect fragile girls from sexually rapacious boys. Justice Stevens also dissented. He accepted the plausibility of the idea that underage sexuality imposes special risks on females, but he questioned the rationality of a statute that responded to that special risk by exempting that class from liability for engaging in the risky conduct.

4. The last case in this short tour, *Mississippi University for Women v. Hogan*, 458 U.S. 718 (1982), is notable for its influence on later sex discrimination cases. *Hogan* dealt with a state university's exclusion of men from its nursing program. Writing for five Justices, Justice O'Connor, the first woman to sit on the Supreme Court, cited earlier cases to interpret *Craig*'s intermediate scrutiny standard to require an "exceedingly persuasive justification" for sex classifications. She also explained that the state's goals must be examined carefully to determine that they are free of "archaic and stereotypic notions" about men and women. Finally, she stated that examination of the statute's fit with the state's goals must show that the state acted based on "reasoned analysis rather than through the mechanical application of traditional, often inaccurate, assumptions about the proper roles of men and women."

Based on this analysis, the Court struck down the male exclusion. It rejected the state's argument that the preservation of a female-only nursing program compensated women for past discrimination, concluding that the policy perpetuated the stereotype of nursing as a women's profession. The Court also rejected the argument that the state wished to preserve an all-female educational environment, noting that men were allowed to attend class as auditors.

Chief Justice Burger, Justice Blackmun, and Justice Powell (joined by Justice Rehnquist) all wrote separate dissents. A common thread in those dissents was concern about the implications of the opinion for educational diversity, and, in particular, single-sex education. Justice Powell stated that he would have applied rational-basis scrutiny to the state policy, but that, in his view, the policy survived even the intermediate scrutiny applied by the majority.

5. Is there any consistency in these cases? If there is at least a doctrinal consistency, do the differing factual contexts (the military, sex crimes law, and higher education) mean that even application of a consistent standard will often yield differing results?

6. One thing you should *not* do when thinking about these cases is simply tally up the results (one win and two losses for the plaintiff) and on that basis conclude that women's equality claims tended to lose during this period. In fact, women won a number of equal protection cases at the Court during this era. *See, e.g., California v. Westcott*, 443 U.S. 76 (1979) (striking down a welfare law providing children with aid when the father was unemployed, but not providing similar aid when the mother was unemployed); *Orr v. Orr*, 440 U.S. 268 (1979) (striking down a state divorce law providing for alimony to be paid to wives but not to husbands). The result was a growing body of caselaw striking down sex classifications, which set the stage for the Court's more aggressive approach to sex discrimination in the following case.

## United States v. Virginia

### 518 U.S. 515 (1996)

Justice GINSBURG delivered the opinion of the Court.

Virginia's public institutions of higher learning include an incomparable military college, Virginia Military Institute (VMI). The United States maintains that the Constitution's equal protection guarantee precludes Virginia from reserving exclusively to men the unique educational opportunities VMI affords. We agree.

I

Founded in 1839, VMI is today the sole single-sex school among Virginia's 15 public institutions of higher learning. VMI's distinctive mission is to produce "citizen-soldiers," men prepared for leadership in civilian life and in military service. VMI pursues this mission through pervasive training of a kind not available anywhere else in Virginia. Assigning prime place to character development, VMI uses an "adversative method" modeled on English public schools and once characteristic of military instruction. VMI constantly endeavors to instill physical and mental discipline in its cadets and impart to them a strong moral code. The school's graduates leave VMI with heightened comprehension of their capacity to deal with duress and stress, and a large sense of accomplishment for completing the hazardous course.

VMI has notably succeeded in its mission to produce leaders; among its alumni are military generals, Members of Congress, and business executives. The school's alumni overwhelmingly perceive that their VMI training helped them to realize their personal goals....

Neither the goal of producing citizen-soldiers nor VMI's implementing methodology is inherently unsuitable to women. And the school's impressive record in producing leaders has made admission desirable to some women. Nevertheless, Virginia has elected to preserve exclusively for men the advantages and opportunities a VMI education affords.

## II
## A

From its establishment in 1839 as one of the Nation's first state military colleges, VMI has remained financially supported by Virginia and "subject to the control of the [Virginia] General Assembly." ... VMI today enrolls about 1,300 men as cadets. Its academic offerings in the liberal arts, sciences, and engineering are also available at other public colleges and universities in Virginia. But VMI's mission is special. It is the mission of the school

> to produce educated and honorable men, prepared for the varied work of civil life, imbued with love of learning, confident in the functions and attitudes of leadership, possessing a high sense of public service, advocates of the American democracy and free enterprise system, and ready as citizen-soldiers to defend their country in time of national peril.

... VMI's program "is directed at preparation for both military and civilian life"; "only about 15% of VMI cadets enter career military service."

VMI produces its "citizen-soldiers" through "an adversative, or doubting, model of education" which features "physical rigor, mental stress, absolute equality of treatment, absence of privacy, minute regulation of behavior, and indoctrination in desirable values." ... VMI cadets live in spartan barracks where surveillance is constant and privacy nonexistent; they wear uniforms, eat together in the mess hall, and regularly participate in drills....

VMI's "adversative model" is further characterized by a hierarchical "class system" of privileges and responsibilities, a "dyke system" for assigning a senior class mentor to each entering class "rat," and a stringently enforced "honor code," which prescribes that a cadet " 'does not lie, cheat, steal nor tolerate those who do.' "

VMI attracts some applicants because of its reputation as an extraordinarily challenging military school, and "because its alumni are exceptionally close to the school." "Women have no opportunity anywhere to gain the benefits of [the system of education at VMI]."

## B

In 1990, prompted by a complaint filed with the Attorney General by a female high-school student seeking admission to VMI, the United States sued the Commonwealth of Virginia and VMI, alleging that VMI's exclusively male admission policy violated the Equal Protection Clause of the Fourteenth Amendment....

In the two years preceding the lawsuit, the District Court noted, VMI had received inquiries from 347 women, but had responded to none of them. "Some women, at least," the court said, "would want to attend the school if they had the opportunity." The court further recognized that, with recruitment, VMI could "achieve at least 10% female enrollment"—"a sufficient 'critical mass' to provide the female cadets with a positive educational experience." And it was also established that "some women are capable of all of the individual activities required of VMI cadets." In addition, experts agreed that if VMI admitted women, "the VMI ROTC experience would become a better training program from the perspective of the armed forces, because it would provide training in dealing with a mixed-gender army." ...

## C

In response to the Fourth Circuit's ruling [against VMI] Virginia proposed a parallel program for women: Virginia Women's Institute for Leadership (VWIL). The 4-year, state-sponsored undergraduate program would be located at Mary Baldwin College, a private liberal arts school for women, and would be open, initially, to about 25 to 30 students. Although VWIL would share VMI's mission—to produce "citizen-soldiers"—the VWIL program would differ ... from VMI in academic offerings, methods of education, and financial resources.

The average combined SAT score of entrants at Mary Baldwin is about 100 points lower than the score for VMI freshmen. Mary Baldwin's faculty holds "significantly fewer Ph.D.'s than the faculty at VMI," and receives significantly lower salaries. While VMI offers degrees in liberal arts, the sciences, and engineering, Mary Baldwin, at the time of trial, offered only bachelor of arts degrees. A VWIL student seeking to earn an engineering degree could gain one, without public support, by attending Washington University in St. Louis, Missouri, for two years, paying the required private tuition.

Experts in educating women at the college level composed the Task Force charged with designing the VWIL program; Task Force members were drawn from Mary Baldwin's own faculty and staff. Training its attention on methods of instruction appropriate for "most women," the Task Force determined that a military model would be "wholly inappropriate" for VWIL. In lieu of VMI's adversative method, the VWIL Task Force favored "a cooperative method which reinforces self-esteem." In addition to the standard bachelor of arts program offered at Mary Baldwin, VWIL students would take courses in leadership, complete an off-campus leadership externship, participate in community service projects, and assist in arranging a speaker series.

Virginia represented that it will provide equal financial support for in-state VWIL students and VMI cadets and the VMI Foundation agreed to supply a $5.4625 million endowment for the VWIL program. Mary Baldwin's own endowment is about $19 million; VMI's is $131 million. Mary Baldwin will add $35 million to its endowment based on future commitments; VMI will add $220 million....

## D

The District Court [and Court of Appeals concluded that the remedial] plan met the requirements of the Equal Protection Clause....

## III

The cross-petitions in this case present two ultimate issues. First, does Virginia's exclusion of women from the educational opportunities provided by VMI — extraordinary opportunities for military training and civilian leadership development — deny to women "capable of all of the individual activities required of VMI cadets," the equal protection of the laws guaranteed by the Fourteenth Amendment? Second, if VMI's "unique" situation — as Virginia's sole single-sex public institution of higher education — offends the Constitution's equal protection principle, what is the remedial requirement?

## IV

We note, once again, the core instruction of this Court's pathmarking decisions in *J.E.B. v. Alabama ex rel. T.B.*, 511 U.S. 127 (1994), and *Mississippi Univ. for Women v. Hogan*, 458 U.S. 718 (1982) [Note *supra.* this chapter]: "Parties who seek to defend gender-based government action must demonstrate an exceedingly persuasive justification" for that action.

Today's skeptical scrutiny of official action denying rights or opportunities based on sex responds to volumes of history. As a plurality of this Court acknowledged a generation ago, "our Nation has had a long and unfortunate history of sex discrimination." *Frontiero v. Richardson* (1973) [*Supra.* this chapter]. Through a century plus three decades and more of that history, women did not count among voters composing "We the People"; not until 1920 did women gain a constitutional right to the franchise. And for a half century thereafter, it remained the prevailing doctrine that government, both federal and state, could withhold from women opportunities accorded men so long as any "basis in reason" could be conceived for the discrimination.

In 1971, for the first time in our Nation's history, this Court ruled in favor of a woman who complained that her State had denied her the equal protection of its laws. *Reed....* Without equating gender classifications, for all purposes, to classifications based on race or national origin, the Court, in post-*Reed* decisions, has carefully inspected official action that closes a door or denies opportunity to women (or to men). To summarize the Court's current directions for cases of official classification based on gender: Focusing on the differential treatment or denial of opportunity for which relief is sought, the reviewing court must determine whether the proffered justification is "exceedingly persuasive." The burden of justification is demanding and it rests entirely on the State. See *Mississippi Univ. for Women.* The State must show "at least that the [challenged] classification serves important governmental objectives and that the discriminatory means employed are substantially related to the achievement of those objectives." *Ibid.* The justification must be genuine, not hypothesized or invented post hoc in response to litigation. And it must not rely on overbroad generalizations about the different talents, capacities, or preferences of males and females. See *Weinberger v. Wiesenfeld*, 420 U.S. 636 (1975) [Note *supra.* this chapter].

The heightened review standard our precedent establishes does not make sex a proscribed classification. Supposed "inherent differences" are no longer accepted as a ground for race or national origin classifications. Physical differences between men and women, however, are enduring: "The two sexes are not fungible; a community made up exclusively of one [sex] is different from a community composed of both."

"Inherent differences" between men and women, we have come to appreciate, remain cause for celebration, but not for denigration of the members of either sex or for artificial constraints on an individual's opportunity. Sex classifications may be used to compensate women "for particular economic disabilities [they have] suffered" to "promote equal employment opportunity," to advance full development of the talent and capacities of our Nation's people. But such classifications may not be used, as they once were to create or perpetuate the legal, social, and economic inferiority of women.

Measuring the record in this case against the review standard just described, we conclude that Virginia has shown no "exceedingly persuasive justification" for excluding all women from the citizen-soldier training afforded by VMI. We therefore affirm the Fourth Circuit's initial judgment, which held that Virginia had violated the Fourteenth Amendment's Equal Protection Clause. Because the remedy proffered by Virginia—the Mary Baldwin VWIL program—does not cure the constitutional violation, i.e., it does not provide equal opportunity, we reverse the Fourth Circuit's final judgment in this case.

V

… Virginia challenges [the lower court's initial determination that the state had violated the Constitution] and asserts two justifications in defense of VMI's exclusion of women. First, the Commonwealth contends, "single-sex education provides important educational benefits," and the option of single-sex education contributes to "diversity in educational approaches." Second, the Commonwealth argues, "the unique VMI method of character development and leadership training," the school's adversative approach, would have to be modified were VMI to admit women. We consider these two justifications in turn.

A

Single-sex education affords pedagogical benefits to at least some students, Virginia emphasizes, and that reality is uncontested in this litigation. Similarly, it is not disputed that diversity among public educational institutions can serve the public good. But Virginia has not shown that VMI was established, or has been maintained, with a view to diversifying, by its categorical exclusion of women, educational opportunities within the Commonwealth. In cases of this genre, our precedent instructs that "benign" justifications proffered in defense of categorical exclusions will not be accepted automatically; a tenable justification must describe actual state purposes, not rationalizations for actions in fact differently grounded.

*Mississippi Univ. for Women* is immediately in point. There the State asserted, in justification of its exclusion of men from a nursing school, that it was engaging in "educational affirmative action" by "compensating for discrimination against women." Undertaking a "searching analysis," the Court found no close resemblance between "the alleged objective" and "the actual purpose underlying the discriminatory classification." Pursuing a similar inquiry here, we reach the same conclusion.

Neither recent nor distant history bears out Virginia's alleged pursuit of diversity through single-sex educational options. In 1839, when the Commonwealth established VMI, a range of educational opportunities for men and women was scarcely contemplated. Higher education at the time was considered dangerous for women.... VMI was not at all novel in this respect: In admitting no women, VMI followed the lead of the Commonwealth's flagship school, the University of Virginia, founded in 1819. "No struggle for the admission of women to a state university," a historian has recounted, "was longer drawn out, or developed more bitterness, than that at the University of Virginia." Despite this recognition, no new opportunities were instantly open to women.

Virginia eventually provided for several women's seminaries and colleges.... By the mid-1970's, all four [such] schools had become coeducational....

Virginia describes the current absence of public single-sex higher education for women as "an historical anomaly." But the historical record indicates action more deliberate than anomalous: First, protection of women against higher education; next, schools for women far from equal in resources and stature to schools for men; finally, conversion of the separate schools to coeducation. The state legislature, prior to the advent of this controversy, had repealed "all Virginia statutes requiring individual institutions to admit only men or women." And in 1990, an official commission, "legislatively established to chart the future goals of higher education in Virginia," reaffirmed the policy "of affording broad access" while maintaining "autonomy and diversity." Significantly, the Commission reported:

> Because colleges and universities provide opportunities for students to develop values and learn from role models, it is extremely important that they deal with faculty, staff, and students without regard to sex, race, or ethnic origin....

In sum, we find no persuasive evidence in this record that VMI's male-only admission policy "is in furtherance of a state policy of diversity." ...

### B

Virginia next argues that VMI's adversative method of training provides educational benefits that cannot be made available, unmodified, to women.... The District Court forecast from expert witness testimony, and the Court of appeals accepted, that coeducation would materially affect at least three aspects of VMI's program—physical training, the absence of privacy, and the adversative approach.... It is also undisputed, however, that "the VMI methodology could be used to educate women." ...

It may be assumed, for purposes of this decision, that most women would not choose VMI's adversative method.... Education, to be sure, is not a "one size fits all" business. The issue, however, is not whether "women—or men—should be forced to attend VMI"; rather, the question is whether the Commonwealth can constitutionally deny to women who have the will and capacity, the training and attendant opportunities that VMI uniquely affords.

The notion that admission of women would downgrade VMI's stature, destroy the adversative system and, with it, even the school, is a judgment hardly proved, a prediction hardly different from other "self-fulfilling prophec[ies]" once routinely used to deny rights or opportunities.... Women's successful entry into the federal military academies, and their participation in the Nation's military forces, indicate that Virginia's fears for the future of VMI may not be solidly grounded. The Commonwealth's justification for excluding all women from "citizen-soldier" training for which some are qualified, in any event, cannot rank as "exceedingly persuasive," as we have explained and applied that standard....

## VI

In the second phase of the litigation, Virginia presented its remedial plan—maintain VMI as a male-only college and create VWIL as a separate program for women. [Both lower courts approved of the plan as a remedy for VMI's discrimination.]

## A

A remedial decree, this Court has said, must closely fit the constitutional violation; it must be shaped to place persons unconstitutionally denied an opportunity or advantage in "the position they would have occupied in the absence of [discrimination]." The constitutional violation in this case is the categorical exclusion of women from an extraordinary educational opportunity afforded men. A proper remedy for an unconstitutional exclusion, we have explained, aims to "eliminate [so far as possible] the discriminatory effects of the past" and to "bar like discrimination in the future."

Virginia chose not to eliminate, but to leave untouched, VMI's exclusionary policy. For women only, however, Virginia proposed a separate program, different in kind from VMI and unequal in tangible and intangible facilities. Having violated the Constitution's equal protection requirement, Virginia was obliged to show that its remedial proposal "directly addressed and related to" the violation, *i.e.*, the equal protection denied to women ready, willing, and able to benefit from educational opportunities of the kind VMI offers. Virginia described VWIL as a "parallel program," and asserted that VWIL shares VMI's mission of producing "citizen-soldiers" and VMI's goals of providing "education, military training, mental and physical discipline, character ... and leadership development." ...

VWIL affords women no opportunity to experience the rigorous military training for which VMI is famed. Instead, the VWIL program "deemphasizes" military education, and uses a "cooperative method" of education "which reinforces self-esteem."

VWIL students participate in ROTC and a "largely ceremonial" Virginia Corps of Cadets, but Virginia deliberately did not make VWIL a military institute.... VWIL students receive their "leadership training" in seminars, externships, and speaker series, episodes and encounters lacking the "physical rigor, mental stress, ... minute regulation of behavior, and indoctrination in desirable values" made hallmarks of VMI's citizen-soldier training. Kept away from the pressures, hazards, and psychological bonding characteristic of VMI's adversative training, VWIL students will not know the "feeling of tremendous accomplishment" commonly experienced by VMI's successful cadets.

Virginia maintains that these methodological differences are "justified pedagogically," based on "important differences between men and women in learning and developmental needs," "psychological and sociological differences" Virginia describes as "real" and "not stereotypes." The Task Force charged with developing the leadership program for women, drawn from the staff and faculty at Mary Baldwin College, "determined that a military model and, especially VMI's adversative method, would be wholly inappropriate for educating and training *most women*" (emphasis added).

As earlier stated, generalizations about "the way women are," estimates of what is appropriate for *most women*, no longer justify denying opportunity to women whose talent and capacity place them outside the average description. Notably, Virginia never asserted that VMI's method of education suits most men. It is also revealing that Virginia accounted for its failure to make the VWIL experience "the entirely militaristic experience of VMI" on the ground that VWIL "is planned for women who do not necessarily expect to pursue military careers." By that reasoning, VMI's "entirely militaristic" program would be inappropriate for men in general or *as a group*, for "only about 15% of VMI cadets enter career military service."

In contrast to the generalizations about women on which Virginia rests, we note again these dispositive realities: VMI's "implementing methodology" is not "inherently unsuitable to women"; [and] "some women ... do well under [the] adversative model." ... It is on behalf of these women that the United States has instituted this suit, and it is for them that a remedy must be crafted....

B

In myriad respects other than military training, VWIL does not qualify as VMI's equal. VWIL's student body, faculty, course offerings, and facilities hardly match VMI's. Nor can the VWIL graduate anticipate the benefits associated with VMI's 157-year history, the school's prestige, and its influential alumni network....

Virginia, in sum, while maintaining VMI for men only, has failed to provide any "comparable single-gender women's institution." Instead, the Commonwealth has created a VWIL program fairly appraised as a "pale shadow" of VMI in terms of the range of curricular choices and faculty stature, funding, prestige, alumni support and influence.

Virginia's VWIL solution is reminiscent of the remedy Texas proposed 50 years ago, in response to a state trial court's 1946 ruling that, given the equal protection guarantee, African Americans could not be denied a legal education at a state facility. See *Sweatt v. Painter*, 339 U.S. 629 (1950). Reluctant to admit African Americans to its flagship University of Texas Law School, the State set up a separate school for Herman Sweatt and other black law students. As originally opened, the new school had no independent faculty or library, and it lacked accreditation....

More important than the tangible features, the Court emphasized, are "those qualities which are incapable of objective measurement but which make for greatness" in a school, including "reputation of the faculty, experience of the administration, position and influence of the alumni, standing in the community, traditions and prestige." Facing the marked differences reported in the *Sweatt* opinion, the Court unanimously ruled that Texas had not shown "substantial equality in the [separate] educational opportunities" the State offered. Accordingly, the Court held, the Equal Protection Clause required Texas to admit African Americans to the University of Texas Law School. In line with *Sweatt*, we rule here that Virginia has not shown substantial equality in the separate educational opportunities the Commonwealth supports at VWIL and VMI....

CHIEF JUSTICE REHNQUIST, concurring in the judgment.

The Court holds first that Virginia violates the Equal Protection Clause by maintaining the Virginia Military Institute's (VMI's) all-male admissions policy, and second that establishing the Virginia Women's Institute for Leadership (VWIL) program does not remedy that violation. While I agree with these conclusions, I disagree with the Court's analysis and so I write separately.

I

Two decades ago in *Craig v. Boren* (1976) [*Supra.* this chapter] we announced that "to withstand constitutional challenge, ... classifications by gender must serve important governmental objectives and must be substantially related to achievement of those objectives." We have adhered to that standard of scrutiny ever since. While the majority adheres to this test today, it also says that the Commonwealth must demonstrate an " 'exceedingly persuasive justification' " to support a gender-based classification. It is unfortunate that the Court thereby introduces an element of uncertainty respecting the appropriate test.

While terms like "important governmental objective" and "substantially related" are hardly models of precision, they have more content and specificity than does the phrase "exceedingly persuasive justification." That phrase is best confined, as it was first used, as an observation on the difficulty of meeting the applicable test, not as a formulation of the test itself. To avoid introducing potential confusion, I would have adhered more closely to our traditional, "firmly established," *Hogan*, standard that a gender-based classification "must bear a close and substantial relationship to important governmental objectives." ...

Before this Court, Virginia has sought to justify VMI's single-sex admissions policy primarily on the basis that diversity in education is desirable, and that while most of the public institutions of higher learning in the Commonwealth are coeducational, there should also be room for single-sex institutions. I agree with the Court that there is scant evidence in the record that this was the real reason that Virginia decided to maintain VMI as men only. But, unlike the majority, I would consider only evidence that postdates our decision in *Hogan*, and would draw no negative inferences from the Commonwealth's actions before that time....

... Had Virginia [after *Hogan*] made a genuine effort to devote comparable public resources to a facility for women, and followed through on such a plan, it might well have avoided an equal protection violation. I do not believe the Commonwealth was faced with the stark choice of either admitting women to VMI, on the one hand, or abandoning VMI and starting from scratch for both men and women, on the other....

II

The Court defines the constitutional violation in these cases as "the categorical exclusion of women from an extraordinary educational opportunity afforded to men." By defining the violation in this way, and by emphasizing that a remedy for a constitutional violation must place the victims of discrimination in "'the position they would have occupied in the absence of [discrimination],'" the Court necessarily implies that the only adequate remedy would be the admission of women to the all-male institution. As the foregoing discussion suggests, I would not define the violation in this way; it is not the "exclusion of women" that violates the Equal Protection Clause, but the maintenance of an all-men school without providing any — much less a comparable — institution for women.

Accordingly, the remedy should not necessarily require either the admission of women to VMI or the creation of a VMI clone for women. An adequate remedy in my opinion might be a demonstration by Virginia that its interest in educating men in a single-sex environment is matched by its interest in educating women in a single-sex institution.... It would be a sufficient remedy, I think, if the two institutions offered the same quality of education and were of the same overall caliber....

In the end, the women's institution Virginia proposes, VWIL, fails as a remedy, because it is distinctly inferior to the existing men's institution and will continue to be for the foreseeable future. VWIL simply is not, in any sense, the institution that VMI is.... I therefore ultimately agree with the Court that Virginia has not provided an adequate remedy.

JUSTICE SCALIA, dissenting.

Today the Court shuts down an institution that has served the people of the Commonwealth of Virginia with pride and distinction for over a century and a half. To achieve that desired result, it rejects (contrary to our established practice) the factual findings of two courts below, sweeps aside the precedents of this Court, and ignores the history of our people. As to facts: It explicitly rejects the finding that there exist "gender-based developmental differences" supporting Virginia's restriction of the "adversative" method to only a men's institution, and the finding that the all-male composition of the Virginia Military Institute (VMI) is essential to that institution's character. As to precedent: It drastically revises our established standards for reviewing sex-based classifications. And as to history: It counts for nothing the long tradition, enduring down to the present, of men's military colleges supported by both States and the Federal Government.

... The virtue of a democratic system with a First Amendment is that it readily enables the people, over time, to be persuaded that what they took for granted is not so, and to change their laws accordingly. That system is destroyed if the smug assurances of each age are removed from the democratic process and written into the Constitution. So to counterbalance the Court's criticism of our ancestors, let me say a word in their praise: They left us free to change. The same cannot be said of this most illiberal Court, which has embarked on a course of inscribing one after another of the current preferences of the society (and in some cases only the countermajoritarian preferences of the society's law-trained elite) into our Basic Law. Today it enshrines the notion that no substantial educational value is to be served by an all-men's military academy—so that the decision by the people of Virginia to maintain such an institution denies equal protection to women who cannot attend that institution but can attend others. Since it is entirely clear that the Constitution of the United States—the old one—takes no side in this educational debate, I dissent.

I

... I have no problem with a system of abstract tests such as rational-basis, intermediate, and strict scrutiny (though I think we can do better than applying strict scrutiny and intermediate scrutiny whenever we feel like it). Such formulas are essential to evaluating whether the new restrictions that a changing society constantly imposes upon private conduct comport with that "equal protection" our society has always accorded in the past. But in my view the function of this Court is *to preserve* our society's values regarding (among other things) equal protection, not to *revise* them.... For that reason it is my view that, whatever abstract tests we may choose to devise, they cannot supersede—and indeed ought to be crafted *so as to reflect*—those constant and unbroken national traditions that embody the people's understanding of ambiguous constitutional texts. More specifically, it is my view that "when a practice not expressly prohibited by the text of the Bill of Rights bears the endorsement of a long tradition of open, widespread, and unchallenged use that dates back to the beginning of the Republic, we have no proper basis for striking it down." The same applies, *mutatis mutandis*, to a practice asserted to be in violation of the post-Civil War Fourteenth Amendment.

The all-male constitution of VMI comes squarely within such a governing tradition. Founded by the Commonwealth of Virginia in 1839 and continuously maintained by it since, VMI has always admitted only men. And in that regard it has not been unusual. For almost all of VMI's more than a century and a half of existence, its single-sex status reflected the uniform practice for government-supported military colleges.... In other words, the tradition of having government-funded military schools for men is as well rooted in the traditions of this country as the tradition of sending only men into military combat. The people may decide to change the one tradition, like the other, through democratic processes; but the assertion that either tradition has been unconstitutional through the centuries is not law, but politics-smuggled-into-law....

## II

To reject the Court's disposition today, however, it is not necessary to accept my view that the Court's made-up tests cannot displace longstanding national traditions as the primary determinant of what the Constitution means. It is only necessary to apply honestly the test the Court has been applying to sex-based classifications for the past two decades. It is well settled, as JUSTICE O'CONNOR stated some time ago for a unanimous Court, that we evaluate a statutory classification based on sex under a standard that lies "between the extremes of rational basis review and strict scrutiny." We have denominated this standard "intermediate scrutiny" and under it have inquired whether the statutory classification is "substantially related to an important governmental objective." ...

Although the Court in two places recites the test as stated in *Hogan* ... the Court never answers the question presented in anything resembling that form. When it engages in analysis, the Court instead prefers the phrase "exceedingly persuasive justification" from *Hogan*. The Court's nine invocations of that phrase ... would be unobjectionable if the Court acknowledged that *whether* a "justification" is "exceedingly persuasive" must be assessed by asking "[whether] the classification serves important governmental objectives and [whether] the discriminatory means employed are substantially related to the achievement of those objectives." Instead, however, the Court proceeds to interpret "exceedingly persuasive justification" in a fashion that contradicts the reasoning of *Hogan* and our other precedents.

That is essential to the Court's result, which can only be achieved by establishing that intermediate scrutiny is not survived if there are *some* women interested in attending VMI, capable of undertaking its activities, and able to meet its physical demands....

Only the amorphous "exceedingly persuasive justification" phrase, and not the standard elaboration of intermediate scrutiny, can be made to yield this conclusion that VMI's single-sex composition is unconstitutional because there exist several women (or, one would have to conclude under the Court's reasoning, a single woman) willing and able to undertake VMI's program. Intermediate scrutiny has never required a least-restrictive-means analysis, but only a "substantial relation" between the classification and the state interests that it serves....

Not content to execute a de facto abandonment of the intermediate scrutiny that has been our standard for sex-based classifications for some two decades, the Court purports to reserve the question whether, even in principle, a higher standard (i.e., strict scrutiny) should apply ... and it describes our earlier cases as having done no more than decline to "equate gender classifications, *for all purposes*, to classifications based on race or national origin." ... The statements are irresponsible, insofar as they are calculated to destabilize current law....

The Court's intimations are particularly out of place because it is perfectly clear that, if the question of the applicable standard of review for sex-based classifications were to be regarded as an appropriate subject for reconsideration, the stronger argument would be not for elevating the standard to strict scrutiny, but for reducing it to rational-basis review. The latter certainly has a firmer foundation in our past jurisprudence: Whereas no majority of the Court has ever applied strict scrutiny in a case involving sex-based classifications, we routinely applied rational-basis review until the 1970's, see, e.g., *Hoyt v. Florida*, 368 U.S. 57 (1961); *Goesaert v. Cleary*, 335 U.S. 464 (1948) [Both notes *supra.* this chapter]. And of course normal, rational-basis review of sex-based classifications would be much more in accord with the genesis of heightened standards of judicial review, the famous footnote in *United States v. Carolene Products Co.*, 304 U.S. 144 (1938) [Note *supra.* this chapter], which said (intimatingly) that we did not have to inquire in the case at hand

> whether prejudice against discrete and insular minorities may be a special condition, which tends seriously to curtail the operation of those political processes ordinarily to be relied upon to protect minorities, and which may call for a correspondingly more searching judicial inquiry.

It is hard to consider women a "discrete and insular minority" unable to employ the "political processes ordinarily to be relied upon," when they constitute a majority of the electorate. And the suggestion that they are incapable of exerting that political power smacks of the same paternalism that the Court so roundly condemns. Moreover, a long list of legislation proves the proposition false. See, e.g., Equal Pay Act of 1963; Title VII of the Civil Rights Act of 1964; Title IX of the Education Amendments of 1972; Women's Business Ownership Act of 1988; Violence Against Women Act of 1994.

III

\* \* \*

A

It is beyond question that Virginia has an important state interest in providing effective college education for its citizens. That single-sex instruction is an approach substantially related to that interest should be evident enough from the long and continuing history in this country of men's and women's colleges. ...

But besides its single-sex constitution, VMI is different from other colleges in another way. It employs a "distinctive educational method," sometimes referred to as the "adversative, or doubting, model of education." ... Just as a State may wish to support junior colleges, vocational institutes, or a law school that emphasizes case practice instead of classroom study, so too a State's decision to maintain within its system one school that provides the adversative method is "substantially related" to its goal of good education. Moreover, it was uncontested that "if the state were to establish a women's VMI-type [i.e., adversative] program, the program would attract an insufficient number of participants to make the program work," and it was found by the District Court that if Virginia were to include women in VMI, the school "would eventually find it necessary to drop the adversative system altogether." Thus,

Virginia's options were an adversative method that excludes women or no adversative method at all....

... As a theoretical matter, Virginia's educational interest would have been *best* served (insofar as the two factors we have mentioned are concerned) by six different types of public colleges—an all-men's, an all-women's, and a coeducational college run in the "adversative method," and an all-men's, an all-women's, and a coeducational college run in the "traditional method." But as a practical matter, of course, Virginia's financial resources, like any State's, are not limitless, and the Commonwealth must select among the available options. Virginia thus has decided to fund, in addition to some 14 coeducational 4-year colleges, one college that is run as an all-male school on the adversative model: the Virginia Military Institute....

... In these circumstances, Virginia's election to fund one public all-male institution and one on the adversative model—and to concentrate its resources in a single entity that serves both these interests in diversity—is substantially related to the Commonwealth's important educational interests....

THOMAS, J., took no part in the consideration or decision of this case.

## *Note:* Virginia *and the "Exceedingly Persuasive Justification" Requirement*

1. *Virginia* was not the first case where the Court applied the "exceedingly persuasive justification" requirement. But its application in a highly controversial context—single-sex education—and its authorship by Justice Ginsburg, the leading sex equality litigator of the 1970's, makes it especially important.

Justice Ginsburg did not seem to reject the constitutionality of single-sex education as a general matter. But why did she then reject VMI's single-sex status? If the reason relates to Virginia's motives in making or keeping VMI all-male, does her approach therefore require courts to examine the subjective mindset of state educational authorities whenever they establish or maintain a single-sex institution?

2. Consider now the Court's rejection of VWIL as an all-female counterpart to VMI. At one level, it was easy for the Court to reject VWIL, at least if one assumes that the correctness of the Court's description of VWIL as simply not as good an institution as VMI. But what if it were? What do you think the result would have been if Virginia had funded VWIL to the same extent as VMI, but retained the two schools' different pedagogical characteristics (respectively, cooperative and adversative), and justified that distinction as based on conclusions about how most women and most men learn? What do you think the result *should* have been? What evidence would you have demanded of Virginia in order to uphold this distinction?

If you think that any sex distinction with regard to education is *per se* unconstitutional, then what do you make of Justice Ginsburg's statement that "Physical differences between men and women ... are enduring: The two sexes are not fungible; a community made up exclusively of one [sex] is different from a community composed of both." Is she really only talking about biology in the last phrase of that quotation?

## Note: "Real Differences" Redux?

1. After *Virginia* one might have thought that, for all practical purposes, sex classifications (except perhaps those that compensated women for past discrimination) would likely be reviewed with something akin to strict scrutiny. But in 2001 the Court returned again to an apparently more relaxed review of sex classifications, based in large part on the idea that the classification in question reflected a real difference between men and women.

2. At issue in *Nguyen v. INS*, 533 U.S. 53 (2001), was a federal law that made it easier for a foreign-born child of an American citizen mother to obtain citizenship than a foreign-born child of an American citizen father. By a 5–4 vote, the Court held that the different requirements for the child depending on the sex of his citizen parent did not violate equal protection. According to Justice Kennedy, the differential treatment was justified largely by the fact that a mother would necessarily know of the birth of the child, with the result that the mother would always have an opportunity to develop a relationship with the child that the father—who might not be present at the birth or even aware that he had fathered a child—would not. Justice Kennedy concluded that this difference justified the sex classification under the Court's intermediate scrutiny standard, including its insistence on an "exceedingly persuasive justification." Justice Scalia, joined by Justice Thomas, joined the majority, but wrote separately on a different point.

Justice O'Connor dissented for herself and Justices Souter, Breyer, and Ginsburg. She accused the majority of merely stating the applicable standard, but then failing to apply it with the rigor it demanded. She stated, "In all, the majority opinion represents far less than the rigorous application of heightened scrutiny that our precedents require."

3. Consider again the question asked immediately after the *Craig v. Boren* excerpt, and again after the note describing several post-*Craig* excerpts. Is intermediate scrutiny anything more than the justices' intuitions about when a sex classification appears reasonable?

# B. Legitimacy

Illegitimacy—the status of having been born to an unmarried couple—historically carried serious legal disabilities and burdens. Starting in the late 1960s, the Supreme Court began questioning the constitutionality of such laws.

## Note: The Court's Early Legitimacy Cases

1. The Court's first significant foray into legitimacy classifications occurred in 1968, when the Court struck down two Louisiana laws that limited the relationships illegitimate children had to their parents in the context of tort recoveries. First, in *Levy v. Louisiana*, 391 U.S. 68 (1968), the Court struck down a law that allowed only legitimate children to recover damages based on the wrongful death of their mother.

Writing for six Justices, Justice Douglas described the discrimination as "invidious," writing the following:

> Legitimacy or illegitimacy of birth has no relation to the nature of the wrong allegedly inflicted on the mother. These children, though illegitimate, were dependent on her; she cared for them and nurtured them; they were indeed hers in the biological and in the spiritual sense; in her death they suffered wrong in the sense that any dependent would.

Second, in *Glona v. American Guaranty & Liability Ins. Co.*, 391 U.S. 73 (1968), decided the same day as *Levy*, the Court struck down another Louisiana law, this one limiting the ability of a mother to recover in tort for the wrongful death of her illegitimate child. Again speaking through Justice Douglas, the Court acknowledged that the case differed from *Levy* in that the state could argue here that it was seeking to "deal with sin," and could do so selectively, rather than enacting "comprehensive or even consistent measures."

Nevertheless, the Court struck the law down, with the same majority as in *Levy* concluding that the law failed rational basis review. Justice Douglas wrote:

> It would, indeed, be farfetched to assume that women have illegitimate children so that they can be compensated in damages for their death. A law which creates an open season on illegitimates in the area of automobile accidents gives a windfall to tortfeasors. But it hardly has a causal connection with the 'sin,' which is, we are told, the historic reason for the creation of the disability.

He acknowledged that there might be proof issues if a woman came forward claiming to be the mother of a deceased person, and on that ground sought recovery for his death. But he said that in a case like the one before the Court, where the plaintiff was "plainly" the mother, the Equal Protection Clause prohibited the law from barring her recovery "merely because the child wrongfully killed, was born to her out of wedlock."

Justice Harlan, dissenting for himself and Justices Stewart and Black, described *Levy* and *Glona* as "constitutional curiosities," with the Court having reached its results "by brute force." He saw an "obvious" justification for the law:

> There is obvious justification for this decision. If it be conceded, as I assume it is, that the State has power to provide that people who choose to live together should go through the formalities of marriage and, in default, that people who bear children should acknowledge them, it is logical to enforce these requirements by declaring that the general class of rights that are dependent upon family relationships shall be accorded only when the formalities as well as the biology of those relationships are present. Moreover, and for many of the same reasons why a State is empowered to require formalities in the first place, a State may choose to simplify a particular proceeding by reliance on formal papers rather than a contest of proof. That suits for wrongful death, actions to determine the heirs of intestates, and the like, must as a constitutional matter deal with every claim of biological paternity or maternity on its merits is an exceedingly odd proposition.

2. *Weber v. Aetna Casualty and Surety Co.*, 406 U.S. 164 (1972), concerned a Louisiana law that placed illegitimate children at a lower priority for recovering under a parent's workmen's compensation claim. In *Weber* the parent died in a workplace accident. The state court judge awarded a workmen's compensation award to his children (some legitimate and some illegitimate), but the legitimate children had first claim on the funds. Their claims exhausted the amount available, and the illegitimate children were left with nothing.

By an 8–1 vote, the Court struck down the apportionment scheme. After rejecting the lower courts' attempt to distinguish *Levy*, the Court, speaking through Justice Powell, then said the following about the applicable standard of scrutiny:

> Having determined that *Levy* is the applicable precedent, we briefly reaffirm here the reasoning which produced that result. The tests to determine the validity of state statutes under the Equal Protection Clause have been variously expressed, but this Court requires, at a minimum, that a statutory classification bear some rational relationship to a legitimate state purpose. *Williamson v. Lee Optical Co.*, 348 U.S. 483 (1955) [Note *supra.* Chapter 7]. Though the latitude given state economic and social regulation is necessarily broad, when state statutory classifications approach sensitive and fundamental personal rights, this Court exercises a stricter scrutiny, *Brown v. Board of Education*, 347 U.S. 483 (1954). The essential inquiry in all the foregoing cases is, however, inevitably a dual one: What legitimate state interest does the classification promote? What fundamental personal rights might the classification endanger?

Turning to the issue in front of it, the Court did not question the legitimacy of the state's interest in protecting "legitimate family relationships." But it did question whether the law actually promoted that interest. Citing *Glona*'s doubt that a law depriving a mother of the right to recover for an illegitimate child's wrongful death would deter extra-marital sexual activity, Justice Powell said "Nor can it be thought here that persons will shun illicit relations because the offspring may not one day reap the benefits of workmen's compensation." He also acknowledged that illegitimate children might as a class be thought to be less dependent on their parents. However, he dismissed this idea as a justification for law like the one before the Court, which required that the child actually be dependent on the parent for whose death he sought recovery.

Justice Rehnquist dissented, repeating, in the context of this case, Justice Harlan's critique of *Levy* and *Glona* as "constitutional curiosities." He also criticized Justice Powell's formulation of the relevant questions, as focusing on policy judgments that were not property for the Court:

> The Court in today's opinion, recognizing that two different standards have been applied in equal protection cases, apparently formulates a hybrid standard which is the basis of decision here. The standard is a two-pronged one:

> 'What legitimate state interest does the classification promote? What fundamental personal rights might the classification endanger?'

Surely there could be no better nor more succinct guide to sound legislation than that suggested by these two questions. They are somewhat less useful, however, as guides to constitutional adjudication. How is this Court to determine whether or not a state interest is 'legitimate'? And how is the Court to know when it is dealing with a 'fundamental personal right'?

Justice Rehnquist would have applied traditional rational basis scrutiny to the law, and on that ground, would have upheld it.

## Mathews v. Lucas

### 427 U.S. 495 (1976)

Mr. Justice BLACKMUN delivered the opinion of the Court.

This case presents the issue of the constitutionality, under the Due Process Clause of the Fifth Amendment, of those provisions of the Social Security Act that condition the eligibility of certain illegitimate children for a surviving child's insurance benefits upon a showing that the deceased wage earner was the claimant child's parent and, at the time of his death, was living with the child or was contributing to his support.

### I

Robert Cuffee, now deceased, lived with Belmira Lucas during the years 1948 through 1966, but they were never married. Two children were born to them during these years: Ruby M. Lucas, in 1953, and Darin E. Lucas, in 1960. In 1966 Cuffee and Lucas separated. Cuffee died in Providence, R. I., his home, in 1968. He died without ever having acknowledged in writing his paternity of either Ruby or Darin, and it was never determined in any judicial proceeding during his lifetime that he was the father of either child. After Cuffee's death, Mrs. Lucas filed an application on behalf of Ruby and Darin for surviving children's benefits under §202(d)(1) of the Social Security Act, based upon Cuffee's earnings record.

### II

In operative terms, the Act provides that an unmarried son or daughter of an individual, who died fully or currently insured under the Act, may apply for and be entitled to a survivor's benefit, if the applicant is under 18 years of age at the time of application (or is a full-time student and under 22 years of age) and was dependent, within the meaning of the statute, at the time of the parent's death. A child is considered dependent for this purpose if the insured father was living with or contributing to the child's support at the time of death. Certain children, however, are relieved of the burden of such individualized proof of dependency. Unless the child has been adopted by some other individual, a child who is legitimate, or a child who would be entitled to inherit personal property from the insured parent's estate under the applicable state intestacy law, is considered to have been dependent at the time of the parent's death. Even lacking this relationship under state law, a child, unless adopted by some other individual, is entitled to a presumption of dependency if the decedent, before death, (a) had gone through a marriage ceremony with the other parent, resulting in a purported marriage between them which, but for a nonobvious legal defect, would have been valid, or (b) in writing had acknowledged the child to be his, or (c) had been decreed by a court to be the child's father, or (d) had been ordered by a court to support the child because the child was his.

An Examiner of the Social Security Administration, after hearings, determined that while Cuffee's paternity was established, the children had failed to demonstrate their dependency by proof that Cuffee either lived with them or was contributing to their support at the time of his death, or by any of the statutory presumptions of dependency, and thus that they were not entitled to survivorship benefits under the Act....

### III

The Secretary does not disagree that the Lucas children and others similarly circumstanced are treated differently, as a class, from those children—legitimate and illegitimate—who are relieved by statutory presumption of any requirement of proving actual dependency.... Statutory classifications, of course, are not *per se* unconstitutional; the matter depends upon the character of the discrimination and its relation to legitimate legislative aims. "The essential inquiry ... is ... inevitably a dual one: What legitimate [governmental] interest does the classification promote? What fundamental personal rights might the classification endanger?" *Weber v. Aetna Casualty & Surety Co.*, 406 U.S. 164 (1972) [Note *supra*. this chapter].

Although the District Court concluded that close judicial scrutiny of the statute's classifications was not necessary to its conclusion invalidating those classifications, it also concluded that legislation treating legitimate and illegitimate offspring differently is constitutionally suspect, and requires the judicial scrutiny traditionally devoted to cases involving discrimination along lines of race or national origin. Appellees echo this approach. We disagree.[11]

It is true, of course, that the legal status of illegitimacy, however defined, is, like race or national origin, a characteristic determined by causes not within the control of the illegitimate individual, and it bears no relation to the individual's ability to participate in and contribute to society. The Court recognized in *Weber* that visiting condemnation upon the child in order to express society's disapproval of the parents' liaisons

> is illogical and unjust. Moreover, imposing disabilities on the illegitimate child is contrary to the basic concept of our system that legal burdens should bear some relationship to individual responsibility or wrongdoing. Obviously, no child is responsible for his birth and penalizing the illegitimate child is an ineffectual—as well as an unjust—way of deterring the parent.

But where the law is arbitrary in such a way, we have had no difficulty in finding the discrimination impermissible on less demanding standards than those advocated

---

11. That the statutory classifications challenged here discriminate among illegitimate children does not mean, of course, that they are not also properly described as discriminating between legitimate and illegitimate children. In view of our conclusion regarding the applicable standard of judicial scrutiny, we need not consider how the classes of legitimate and illegitimate children would be constitutionally defined under appellees' approach.

here. *New Jersey Welfare Rights Org. v. Cahill*, 411 U.S. 619 (1973); *Richardson v. Davis*, 409 U.S. 1069 (1972); *Richardson v. Griffin*, 409 U.S. 1069 (1972); *Weber*; *Levy v. Louisiana*, 391 U.S. 73 (1968) [Note *supra.* this chapter]. And such irrationality in some classifications does not in itself demonstrate that other, possibly rational, distinctions made in part on the basis of legitimacy are inherently untenable. Moreover, while the law has long placed the illegitimate child in an inferior position relative to the legitimate in certain circumstances, particularly in regard to obligations of support or other aspects of family law, perhaps in part because the roots of the discrimination rest in the conduct of the parents rather than the child, and perhaps in part because illegitimacy does not carry an obvious badge, as race or sex do, this discrimination against illegitimates has never approached the severity or pervasiveness of the historic legal and political discrimination against women and Negroes. See *Frontiero v. Richardson* (1973) (plurality opinion) [*Supra.* this chapter].

We therefore adhere to our earlier view, see *Labine v. Vincent*, 401 U.S. 532 (1971), that the Act's discrimination between individuals on the basis of their legitimacy does not "command extraordinary protection from the majoritarian political process" which our most exacting scrutiny would entail. See *Weber*.

## IV

... [The] Secretary explains the design of the statutory scheme assailed here as a program to provide for all children of deceased insureds who can demonstrate their "need" in terms of dependency at the times of the insureds' deaths.... Taking this explanation at face value, we think it clear that conditioning entitlement upon dependency at the time of death is not impermissibly discriminatory in providing only for those children for whom the loss of the parent is an immediate source of the need.

But appellees contend that the actual design of the statute belies the Secretary's description, and that the statute was intended to provide support for insured decedents' children generally, if they had a "legitimate" claim to support, without regard to actual dependency at death; in any case, they assert, the statute's matrix of classifications bears no adequate relationship to actual dependency at death. Since such dependency does not justify the statute's discriminations, appellees argue, those classifications must fall.... These assertions are in effect one and the same. The basis for appellees' argument is the obvious fact that each of the presumptions of dependency renders the class of benefit-recipients incrementally overinclusive, in the sense that some children within each class of presumptive dependents are automatically entitled to benefits under the statute although they could not in fact prove their economic dependence upon insured wage earners at the time of death. We conclude that the statutory classifications are permissible, however, because they are reasonably related to the likelihood of dependency at death.

## A

Congress' purpose in adopting the statutory presumptions of dependency was obviously to serve administrative convenience. While Congress was unwilling to assume that every child of a deceased insured was dependent at the time of death, by presuming dependency on the basis of relatively readily documented facts, such as legitimate birth, or existence of a support order or paternity decree, which could be relied upon to indicate the likelihood of continued actual dependency, Congress was able to avoid the burden and expense of specific case-by-case determination in the large number of cases where dependency is objectively probable. Such presumptions in aid of administrative functions, though they may approximate, rather than precisely mirror, the results that case-by-case adjudication would show, are permissible under the Fifth Amendment, so long as that lack of precise equivalence does not exceed the bounds of substantiality tolerated by the applicable level of scrutiny.

In cases of strictest scrutiny, such approximations must be supported at least by a showing that the Government's dollar "lost" to overincluded benefit recipients is returned by a dollar "saved" in administrative expense avoided. *Frontiero* (plurality opinion). Under the standard of review appropriate here, however, the materiality of the relation between the statutory classifications and the likelihood of dependency they assertedly reflect need not be "scientifically substantiated." Nor, in any case, do we believe that Congress is required in this realm of less than strictest scrutiny to weigh the burdens of administrative inquiry solely in terms of dollars ultimately "spent," ignoring the relative amounts devoted to administrative rather than welfare uses. Finally, while the scrutiny by which their showing is to be judged is not a toothless one, *Frontiero* (Stewart, J., concurring in judgment, Powell, J., concurring in judgment); *Reed v. Reed*, 404 U.S. 71 (1971) [Note *supra.* this chapter], the burden remains upon the appellees to demonstrate the insubstantiality of that relation. See *Lindsley v. Natural Carbonic Gas Co.*, 220 U.S. 61 (1911).

B

Applying these principles, we think that the statutory classifications challenged here are justified as reasonable empirical judgments that are consistent with a design to qualify entitlement to benefits upon a child's dependency at the time of the parent's death....

It is, of course, not enough simply that any child of a deceased insured is eligible for benefits upon *some* showing of dependency. In *Frontiero*, we found it impermissible to qualify the entitlement to dependent's benefits of a married woman in the uniformed services upon an individualized showing of her husband's actual dependence upon her for more than half his income, when no such showing of actual dependency was required of a married man in the uniformed services to obtain dependent's benefits on account of his wife. The invalidity of that gender-based discrimination rested upon the "overbroad" assumption, *Schlesinger v. Ballard*, 419 U.S. 498 (1975) [Note *supra.* this chapter], underlying the discrimination "that male workers' earnings are vital to the support of their families, while the earnings of female wage earners do not significantly contribute to their families' support." *Weinberger v. Wiesenfeld*, 420 U.S. 636 (1975) [Note *supra.* this chapter]. Here, by contrast, the statute does not broadly discriminate between legitimates and illegitimates without more, but is carefully tuned to alternative considerations. The presumption of dependency is withheld only in the absence of any significant indication of the likelihood of actual dependency. Moreover, we cannot say that the factors that give rise to a presumption of dependency lack any substantial relation to the likelihood of actual dependency. Rather, we agree with the assessment of the three-judge court as it originally ruled in *Norton v. Weinberger*, 364 F.Supp. 1117 (Md.1973):

> It is clearly rational to presume the overwhelming number of legitimate children are actually dependent upon their parents for support. Likewise … the children of an invalid marriage … would typically live in the wage earner's home or be supported by him.… When an order of support is entered by a court, it is reasonable to assume compliance occurred. A paternity decree, while not necessarily ordering support, would almost as strongly suggest support was subsequently obtained. Conceding that a written acknowledgment lacks the imprimatur of a judicial proceeding, it too establishes the basis for a rational presumption. Men do not customarily affirm in writing their responsibility for an illegitimate child unless the child is theirs and a man who has acknowledged a child is more likely to provide it support than one who does not.

Similarly, we think, where state intestacy law provides that a child may take personal property from a father's estate, it may reasonably be thought that the child will more likely be dependent during the parent's life and at his death. For in its embodiment of the popular view within the jurisdiction of how a parent would have his property devolve among his children in the event of death, without specific directions, such legislation also reflects to some degree the popular conception within the jurisdiction of the felt parental obligation to such an "illegitimate" child in other circumstances, and thus something of the likelihood of actual parental support during, as well as after, life.

To be sure, none of these statutory criteria compels the extension of a presumption of dependency. But the constitutional question is not whether such a presumption is required, but whether it is permitted. Nor, in ratifying these statutory classifications, is our role to hypothesize independently on the desirability or feasibility of any possible alternative basis for presumption. These matters of practical judgment and empirical calculation are for Congress. Drawing upon its own practical experience, Congress has tailored statutory classifications in accord with its calculations of the likelihood of actual support suggested by a narrow set of objective and apparently reasonable indicators. Our role is simply to determine whether Congress' assumptions are so inconsistent or insubstantial as not to be reasonably supportive of its conclusions that individualized factual inquiry in order to isolate each non-dependent child in a given class of cases is unwarranted as an administrative exercise. In the end, the precise accuracy of Congress' calculations is not a matter of specialized judicial competence; and we have no basis to question their detail beyond the evident consistency and substantiality. We cannot say that these expectations are unfounded, or so indiscriminate as to render the statute's classifications baseless. We conclude, in short, that, in failing to extend any presumption of dependency to appellees and others like them, the Act does not impermissibly discriminate against them as compared with legitimate children or those illegitimate children who are statutorily deemed dependent.

Mr. Justice STEVENS, with whom Mr. Justice BRENNAN and Mr. Justice MARSHALL join, dissenting.

The reason why the United States Government should not add to the burdens that illegitimate children inevitably acquire at birth is radiantly clear: We are committed to the proposition that all persons are created equal. The Court's reason for approving discrimination against this class — "administrative convenience" — is ... insufficient because it unfairly evaluates the competing interests at stake....

II

The Court recognizes "that the legal status of illegitimacy, however defined, is, like race or national origin, a characteristic determined by causes not within the control of the illegitimate individual, and it bears no relation to the individual's ability to participate in and contribute to society." For that reason, as the Court also recognizes, "imposing disabilities on the illegitimate child is contrary to the basic concept of our system that legal burdens should bear some relationship to individual responsibility or wrongdoing." Thus the Court starts its analysis from the premise that the statutory classification is both "illogical and unjust." It seems rather plain to me that this premise demands a conclusion that the classification is invalid unless it is justified by a weightier governmental interest than merely "administrative convenience."

The Court has characterized the purpose of the statute as providing benefits not for those individuals who had a legitimate claim to support from the deceased wage earner but rather for those who were actually dependent on the wage earner at the time of his death. In this analysis, the provisions of the statute which allow certain classes — such as legitimate children — to receive benefits without showing actual dependency are no more than statutory presumptions in aid of administrative convenience. This is an appropriate reading of the statute.

The Court goes on, however, to hold that such presumptions in aid of "administrative convenience" are permissible so long as the lack of precise equivalence between the fact giving rise to the presumption and the fact presumed "does not exceed the bounds of substantiality tolerated by the applicable level of scrutiny." The opinion tells us very little, however, about the "applicable level of scrutiny." It is not "our most exacting scrutiny"; on the other hand, if the classification derives "possibly rational" support from another source, it is not "inherently untenable" simply because it rests in part on illegitimacy. I believe an admittedly illogical and unjust result should not be accepted without both a better explanation and also something more than a "possibly rational" basis.

The Court has repeatedly held that distinctions which disfavor illegitimates simply because they are illegitimate are invalid. *Weber.* However irrational it may be to burden innocent children because their parents did not marry, illegitimates are nonetheless a traditionally disfavored class in our society. Because of that tradition of disfavor the Court should be especially vigilant in examining any classification which involves illegitimacy. For a traditional classification is more likely to be used without pausing to consider its justification than is a newly created classification. Habit, rather than analysis, makes it seem acceptable and natural to distinguish between male and female, alien and citizen, legitimate and illegitimate; for too much of our history there was the same inertia in distinguishing between black and white. But that sort of stereotyped reaction may have no rational relationship—other than pure prejudicial discrimination[3]—to the stated purpose for which the classification is being made.

In this case, the "true" classification, according to the Court, is one between children dependent on their fathers and children who are not so dependent. All of the subsidiary classifications (which have the actual effect of allowing certain children to be eligible for benefits regardless of actual dependency) are supposedly justified by the increased convenience for the agency in not being required in every case to determine dependency. But do these classifications actually bear any substantial relationship to the fact of dependency?

In this statute, one or another of the criteria giving rise to a "presumption of dependency" exists to make almost all children of deceased wage earners eligible. If a child is legitimate, he qualifies. If the child is illegitimate only because of a nonobvious defect in his parents' marriage, he qualifies. If a court has declared his father to be in fact his father, or has issued an order of support against his father, or if the father has acknowledged the child in writing, he qualifies. Apart from any of these qualifications, if the child is lucky enough to live in a State which allows him to inherit from his intestate father on a par with other children, he also qualifies. And in none of these situations need he allege, much less prove, actual dependency. Indeed, if the contrary fact is undisputed, he is nevertheless qualified.

The Court today attempts, at some length, to explain that each of these factors is rationally and substantially related to the actual fact of dependency, adopting even

---

3. Such pure discrimination is most certainly not a "legitimate purpose" for our Federal Government, which should be especially sensitive to discrimination on grounds of birth. "Distinctions between citizens solely because of their ancestry are by their very nature odious to a free people whose institutions are founded upon the doctrine of equality." From its inception, the Federal Government has been directed to treat all its citizens as having been "created equal" in the eyes of the law. The Declaration of Independence states:

> "We hold these truths to be self-evident, that all men are created equal, that they are endowed by their Creator with certain unalienable Rights, that among these are Life, Liberty and the pursuit of Happiness."

And the rationale behind the prohibition against the grant of any title of nobility by the United States, see U.S.Const. Art. I, s 9, cl. 8, equally would prohibit the United States from attaching any badge of ignobility to a citizen at birth.

the somewhat tenuous rationalization of the District Court that "men do not customarily affirm in writing their responsibility for an illegitimate child unless the child is theirs and a man who has acknowledged a child is more likely to provide it support than one who does not," without also noting that a man who lives with a woman for 18 years, during which two children are born, who has always orally acknowledged that the children are his, and who has lived with the children a supported them, may never perceive a need to make a formal written acknowledgment of paternity. Even more tenuous is the asserted relationship between the status of the illegitimate under state intestacy law and actual dependency. The Court asserts that "in its embodiment of the popular view within the jurisdiction of how a parent would have his property devolve among his children in the event of death, without specific directions, such legislation also reflects to some degree the popular conception within the jurisdiction of the felt parental obligation to such an 'illegitimate' child in other circumstances, and thus something of the likelihood of actual parental support during, as well as after, life." That nebulous inference upon inference is treated as more acceptable evidence of actual dependency than proof of actual support for many years.

Whether the classification is expressed in terms of eligible classes or in terms of presumptions of dependency, the fact remains that legitimacy, written acknowledgments, or state law make eligible many children who are no more likely to be "dependent" than are the children in appellees'situation. Yet in the name of "administrative convenience" the Court allows these survivors' benefits to be allocated on grounds which have only the most tenuous connection to the supposedly controlling factor — the child's dependency on his father.

I am persuaded that the classification which is sustained today in the name of "administrative convenience" is more probably the product of a tradition of thinking of illegitimates as less deserving persons than legitimates. The sovereign should firmly reject that tradition. The fact that illegitimacy is not as apparent to the observer as sex or race does not make this governmental classification any less odious. It cannot be denied that it is a source of social opprobrium, even if wholly unmerited, or that it is a circumstance for which the individual has no responsibility whatsoever....

I respectfully dissent.

### Clark v. Jeter
486 U.S. 456 (1988)

Justice O'CONNOR delivered the opinion of the Court.

Under Pennsylvania law, an illegitimate child must prove paternity before seeking support from his or her father, and a suit to establish paternity ordinarily must be brought within six years of an illegitimate child's birth. By contrast, a legitimate child may seek support from his or her parents at any time. We granted certiorari to consider the constitutionality of this legislative scheme....

## II

... In considering whether state legislation violates the Equal Protection Clause of the Fourteenth Amendment, U.S. Const., Amdt. 14, § 1, we apply different levels of scrutiny to different types of classifications. At a minimum, a statutory classification must be rationally related to a legitimate governmental purpose. Classifications based on race or national origin, e.g., *Loving v. Virginia*, 388 U.S. 1 (1967), and classifications affecting fundamental rights, e.g., *Harper v. Virginia Bd. of Elections*, 383 U.S. 663 (1966), are given the most exacting scrutiny. Between these extremes of rational basis review and strict scrutiny lies a level of intermediate scrutiny, which generally has been applied to discriminatory classifications based on sex or illegitimacy. See, e.g., *Mississippi University for Women v. Hogan*, 458 U.S. 718 (1982) [Note *supra.* this chapter]; *Craig v. Boren* (1976) [*Supra.* this chapter]; *Mathews v. Lucas* (1976) [*Supra.* this chapter].

To withstand intermediate scrutiny, a statutory classification must be substantially related to an important governmental objective. Consequently we have invalidated classifications that burden illegitimate children for the sake of punishing the illicit relations of their parents, because "visiting this condemnation on the head of an infant is illogical and unjust." *Weber v. Aetna Casualty & Surety Co.*, 406 U.S. 164 (1972) [Note *supra.* this chapter]. Yet, in the seminal case concerning the child's right to support, this Court acknowledged that it might be appropriate to treat illegitimate children differently in the support context because of "lurking problems with respect to proof of paternity." *Gomez v. Perez*, 409 U.S. 535 (1973).

This Court has developed a particular framework for evaluating equal protection challenges to statutes of limitations that apply to suits to establish paternity, and thereby limit the ability of illegitimate children to obtain support.

> "First, the period for obtaining support ... must be sufficiently long in duration to present a reasonable opportunity for those with an interest in such children to assert claims on their behalf. Second, any time limitation placed on that opportunity must be substantially related to the State's interest in avoiding the litigation of stale or fraudulent claims." *Mills v. Habluetzel*, 456 U.S. 91 (1982).

... In light of this authority, we conclude that Pennsylvania's 6-year statute of limitations violates the Equal Protection Clause. Even six years does not necessarily provide a reasonable opportunity to assert a claim on behalf of an illegitimate child. "The unwillingness of the mother to file a paternity action on behalf of her child, which could stem from her relationship with the natural father or ... from the emotional strain of having an illegitimate child, or even from the desire to avoid community and family disapproval, may continue years after the child is born. The problem may be exacerbated if, as often happens, the mother herself is a minor." *Mills* (O'CONNOR, J., concurring). Not all of these difficulties are likely to abate in six years. A mother might realize only belatedly "a loss of income attributable to the need to care for the child." Furthermore, financial difficulties are likely to increase as the child matures and incurs expenses for clothing, school, and medical care. Thus it is questionable whether a State acts reasonably when it requires most paternity and support actions to be brought within six years of an illegitimate child's birth.

We do not rest our decision on this ground, however, for it is not entirely evident that six years would necessarily be an unreasonable limitations period for child support actions involving illegitimate children. We are, however, confident that the 6-year statute of limitations is not substantially related to Pennsylvania's interest in avoiding the litigation of stale or fraudulent claims. In a number of circumstances, Pennsylvania permits the issue of paternity to be litigated more than six years after the birth of an illegitimate child. The statute itself permits a suit to be brought more than six years after the child's birth if it is brought within two years of a support payment made by the father. And in other types of suits, Pennsylvania places no limits on when the issue of paternity may be litigated. For example, the intestacy statute, permits a child born out of wedlock to establish paternity as long as "there is clear and convincing evidence that the man was the father of the child." Likewise, no statute of limitations applies to a father's action to establish paternity. Recently, the Pennsylvania Legislature enacted a statute that tolls most other civil actions during a child's minority. In *Pickett v. Brown*, 462 U.S. 1 (1983) and *Mills*, similar tolling statutes cast doubt on the State's purported interest in avoiding the litigation of stale or fraudulent claims. Pennsylvania's tolling statute has the same implications here.

A more recent indication that Pennsylvania does not consider proof problems insurmountable is the enactment by the Pennsylvania Legislature in 1985 of an 18-year statute of limitations for paternity and support actions. To be sure the legislature did not act spontaneously, but rather under the threat of losing some federal funds. Nevertheless, the new statute is a tacit concession that proof problems are not overwhelming. The legislative history of the federal Child Support Enforcement Amendments explains why Congress thought such statutes of limitations are reasonable. Congress adverted to the problem of stale and fraudulent claims, but recognized that increasingly sophisticated tests for genetic markers permit the exclusion of over 99% of those who might be accused of paternity, regardless of the age of the child. This scientific evidence is available throughout the child's minority, and it is an additional reason to doubt that Pennsylvania had a substantial reason for limiting the time within which paternity and support actions could be brought.

We conclude that the Pennsylvania statute does not withstand heightened scrutiny under the Equal Protection Clause. We therefore find it unnecessary to reach Clark's due process claim. The judgment of the Superior Court is reversed, and the case is remanded for further proceedings not inconsistent with this opinion.

### *Note: The Suspectness of Illegitimacy*

1. How could the *Clark* Court cite *Lucas* for the proposition that legitimacy classifications merit intermediate scrutiny? Re-read the *Lucas* excerpt to see where it might have found support for that proposition.

2. What does intermediate scrutiny mean in the context of legitimacy? If both *Lucas* and *Clark* reflect such scrutiny, how would you describe it? How would you

compare it with the scrutiny that is accorded sex classifications? Can those two types of scrutiny be equated?

3. Finally, what is the justification for whatever level of heightened scrutiny the Court accords legitimacy justifications? Do the materials above present a full-blown, *Frontiero*-type case for heightened scrutiny of legitimacy classifications?

# C. Alienage

Alienage—the status of being a non-citizen—has generated a complex equal protection doctrine. As you read the following materials, consider the arguments for and against heightened scrutiny. How do they relate to the classic Footnote 4 statement about "prejudice" and political dysfunction?

## *Note: Early Alienage Cases*

1. In early cases challenging state laws that discriminated against non-citizens, the Court often held that a state could reserve for its own citizens the benefits of the state's resources, as against both non-U.S. citizens and citizens of other states. *See Truax v. Raich*, 239 U.S. 33, 39–40 (1915) (citing cases). However, in *Truax* itself the Court struck down an Arizona law limiting employers to a certain percentage of non-U.S. citizen employees. The Court distinguished the cases it cited on the ground that the Arizona law limited "the conduct of ordinary private enterprise."

The early cases' focus on preservation of resources for its own residents began to erode in *Takahashi v. Fish and Game Comm'n*, 334 U.S. 410 (1948). In that case the Court struck down California's denial of a commercial fishing license to a Japanese citizen alien, rejecting California's argument that it could reserve its natural resources for its own citizens.

2. *Graham v. Richardson*, 403 U.S. 365 (1971) was the first modern case considering state laws that discriminated based on citizenship status. *Graham* dealt with Arizona and Pennsylvania laws that imposed durational and other limits on non-U.S. citizens who wished to receive public assistance benefits. The Court unanimously struck those laws down. Writing for eight Justices, Justice Blackmun noted the states' reliance on the public-resource argument for withholding benefits. However, he observed that *Takahashi* had "cast doubt on the continuing validity" of that argument. He also stated, without elaboration, that "Aliens as a class are a prime example of a 'discrete and insular' minority (see *United States v. Carolene Products Co.*, 304 U.S. 144 (1938) [Note *supra.* this chapter]) for whom such heightened judicial solicitude is appropriate." Justice Harlan concurred in the result, but did not join the part of the Court's opinion raising these points.

3. Later cases expanded on *Graham*'s rationale for heightened scrutiny, while also cabining its scope. As you read the following materials, consider the debate, mostly between the Court and Justice Rehnquist, about whether heightened scrutiny for alienage is appropriate, and under what circumstances.

# Sugarman v. Dougall

413 U.S. 634 (1973)

Mr. Justice BLACKMUN delivered the opinion of the Court.

Section 53(1) of the New York Civil Service Law reads:

> Except as herein otherwise provided, no person shall be eligible for appointment for any position in the competitive class unless he is a citizen of the United States.

The four appellees, Patrick McL.Dougall, Esperanza Jorge, Teresa Vargas, and Sylvia Castro, are federally registered resident aliens. When, because of their alienage, they were discharged in 1971 from their competitive civil service positions with the city of New York, the appellees instituted this class action challenging the constitutionality of § 53....

## II

As is so often the case, it is important at the outset to define the precise and narrow issue that is here presented. The Court is faced only with the question whether New York's flat statutory prohibition against the employment of aliens in the competitive classified civil service is constitutionally valid. The Court is not asked to decide whether a particular alien, any more than a particular citizen, may be refused employment or discharged on an individual basis for whatever legitimate reason the State might possess.

Neither is the Court reviewing a legislative scheme that bars some or all aliens from closely defined and limited classes of public employment on a uniform and consistent basis. The New York scheme, instead, is indiscriminate....

## III

It is established, of course, that an alien is entitled to the shelter of the Equal Protection Clause. *Graham v. Richardson*, 403 U.S. 365 (1971); *Truax v. Raich*, 239 U.S. 33 (1915) [Both note *supra.* this chapter]. This protection extends, specifically, in the words of Mr. Justice Hughes, to aliens who 'work for a living in the common occupations of the community.' *Truax.*

A. Appellants argue, however, that § 53 does not violate the equal protection guarantee of the Fourteenth Amendment because the statute 'establishes a generic classification reflecting the special requirements of public employment in the career civil service.' The distinction drawn between the citizen and the alien, it is said, 'rests on the fundamental concept of identity between a government and the members, or citizens, of the state.' The civil servant 'participates directly in the formulation and execution of government policy,' and thus must be free of competing obligations to another power. The State's interest in having an employee of undivided loyalty is substantial, for obligations attendant upon foreign citizenship 'might impair the exercise of his judgment or jeopardize public confidence in his objectivity.'...

It is at once apparent, however, that appellants' asserted justification proves both too much and too little. As the above outline of the New York scheme reveals, the State's broad prohibition of the employment of aliens applies to many positions with respect to which the State's proffered justification has little, if any, relationship. At the same time, the prohibition has no application at all to positions that would seem naturally to fall within the State's asserted purpose. Our standard of review of statutes that treat aliens differently from citizens requires a greater degree of precision.

In *Graham*, we observed that aliens as a class 'are a prime example of a 'discrete and insular' minority (see *United States v. Carolene Products Co.*, 304 U.S. 144 (1938) [Note *supra*. this chapter]),' and that classifications based on alienage are 'subject to close judicial scrutiny.' And as long as a quarter century ago we held that the State's power 'to apply its laws exclusively to its alien inhabitants as a class is confined within narrow limits.' *Takahashi v. Fish Comm'n*, 334 U.S. 410 (1948) [Note *supra*. this chapter]. We therefore look to the substantiality of the State's interest in enforcing the statute in question, and to the narrowness of the limits within which the discrimination is confined.

Applying this standard to New York's purpose in confining civil servants in the competitive class to those persons who have no ties of citizenship elsewhere, § 53 does not withstand the necessary close scrutiny. We recognize a State's interest in establishing its own form of government, and in limiting participation in that government to those who are within 'the basic conception of a political community.' We recognize, too, the State's broad power to define its political community. But in seeking to achieve this substantial purpose, with discrimination against aliens, the means the State employs must be precisely drawn in light of the acknowledged purpose.

Section 53 is neither narrowly confined nor precise in its application. Its imposed ineligibility may apply to the 'sanitation man, class B,' to the typist, and to the office worker, as well as to the person who directly participates in the formulation and execution of important state policy. The citizenship restriction sweeps indiscriminately....

### IV

While we rule that § 53 is unconstitutional, we do not hold that, on the basis of an individualized determination, an alien may not be refused, or discharged from, public employment, even on the basis of noncitizenship, if the refusal to hire, or the discharge, rests on legitimate state interests that relate to qualifications for a particular position or to the characteristics of the employee. We hold only that a flat ban on the employment of aliens in positions that have little, if any, relation to a State's legitimate interest, cannot withstand scrutiny under the Fourteenth Amendment.

Neither do we hold that a State may not, in an appropriately defined class of positions, require citizenship as a qualification for office. Just as 'the Framers of the Constitution intended the States to keep for themselves, as provided in the Tenth Amendment, the power to regulate elections,' 'each State has the power to prescribe the qualifications of its officers and the manner in which they shall be chosen.' Such power inheres in the State by virtue of its obligation, already noted above, 'to preserve the basic conception of a political community.' And this power and responsibility of the State applies, not only to the qualifications of voters, but also to persons holding state elective or important nonelective executive, legislative, and judicial positions, for officers who participate directly in the formulation, execution, or review of broad public policy perform functions that go to the heart of representative government. There, as Judge Lumbard phrased it in his separate concurrence [in the lower court opinion in this case], is 'where citizenship bears some rational relationship to the special demands of the particular position.'

We have held, of course, that such state action, particularly with respect to voter qualifications, is not wholly immune from scrutiny under the Equal Protection Clause. But our scrutiny will not be so demanding where we deal with matters resting firmly within a State's constitutional prerogatives. This is no more than a recognition of a State's historical power to exclude aliens from participation in its democratic political institutions, and a recognition of a State's constitutional responsibility for the establishment and operation of its own government, as well as the qualifications of an appropriately designated class of public office holders. This Court has never held that aliens have a constitutional right to vote or to hold high public office under the Equal Protection Clause. Indeed, implicit in many of this Court's voting rights decisions is the notion that citizenship is a permissible criterion for limiting such rights. A restriction on the employment of noncitizens, narrowly confined, could have particular relevance to this important state responsibility, for alienage itself is a factor that reasonably could be employed in defining 'political community.' ...

Mr. Justice REHNQUIST, dissenting.[*]

The Court in these two cases holds that an alien is not really different from a citizen, and that any legislative classification on the basis of alienage is 'inherently suspect'. The Fourteenth Amendment, the Equal Protection Clause of which the Court interprets as invalidating the state legislation here involved, contains no language concerning 'inherently suspect classifications,' or, for that matter, merely 'suspect classifications.' The principal purpose of those who drafted and adopted the Amendment was to prohibit the States from invidiously discriminating by reason of race, *Slaughter-House Cases* (1873) [Note *supra.* Part III Introduction], and, because of this plainly manifested intent, classifications based on race have rightly been held 'suspect' under the Amendment. But there is no language used in the Amendment nor any historical evidence as to the intent of the Framers, which would suggest to the slightest degree that it was intended to render alienage a 'suspect' classification, that it was designed in any way to protect 'discrete and insular minorities' other than racial minorities, or that it would in any way justify the result reached by the Court in these two cases.

Two factual considerations deserve more emphasis than accorded by the Court's opinions. First, the records ... contain no indication that the aliens suffered any disability that precluded them, either as a group or individually, from applying for and being granted the status of naturalized citizens. [One of the] appellees [in *Sug-*

---

* [Ed note: Justice Rehnquist's dissent applies to both *Sugarman* and *In re: Griffiths*, 413 U.S. 717 (1973), decided the same day. *Griffiths* is discussed in the note appearing after this excerpt.]

*arman*], as far as the record discloses, took no steps to obtain citizenship or indicate any affirmative desire to become citizens. [In the facts of another case decided in *Sugarman*], appellant was eligible for naturalization but 'elected to remain a citizen of the Netherlands'.... The 'status' of these individuals was not, therefore, one with which they were forever encumbered; they could take steps to alter it when and if they chose.

Second, [one set of plaintiffs in *Sugarman*] sought to be employees of administrative agencies of the New York City government. Of the 20 members of the class represented by the named appellees, three were typists, one a 'senior clerk,' two 'human resources technicians,' three 'senior human resources technicians,' six 'human resource specialists,' three 'senior human resources specialists,' and two 'supervising human resource specialists.' The record does not reveal what functions are performed by these civil servants, although appellee Dougall apparently was the chief administrator of a program; the remaining appellees were all employees of the New York City Human Resources Administration, the governmental body with numerous employees which administers many types of social welfare programs, spending a great deal of money and dealing constantly with the public and other arms of the federal, state, and local governments.

I

The Court, by holding in these cases and in *Graham* that a citizen-alien classification is 'suspect' in the eyes of our Constitution, fails to mention, let alone rationalize, the fact that the Constitution itself recognizes a basic difference between citizens and aliens. That distinction is constitutionally important in no less than 11 instances in a political document noted for its brevity....

This Court has held time and again that legislative classifications on the basis of citizenship were subject to the rational-basis test of equal protection, and that the justifications then advanced for the legislation were rational. See *Ohio ex rel. Clarke v. Deckebach*, 274 U.S. 392 (1927); *Terrace v. Thompson*, 263 U.S. 197 (1923); *Porterfield v. Webb*, 263 U.S. 225 (1923); *Webb v. O'Brien*, 263 U.S. 313 (1923); *Frick v. Webb*, 263 U.S. 326 (1923); *Patsone v. Pennsylvania*, 232 U.S. 138 (1914); *Blythe v. Hinckley*, 180 U.S. 333 (1901); *Hauenstein v. Lynham*, 100 U.S. 483 (1880)....

To reject the methodological approach of these decisions, the Court now relies in part on the decisions in *Truax* and *Takahashi*. [Justice Rehnquist then argued that *Truax* itself stated that it was not overruling those earlier cases, and that the statute struck down in *Takahashi* had a severely disparate ethnic impact on Japanese-Americans.]

The third, and apparently paramount, 'decision' upon which the Court relied in *Graham*, and which is merely quoted in the instant decisions, is [Footnote 4] from *Carolene Products*....

On the 'authority' of this footnote, which only four Members of the Court in *Carolene Products* joined, the Court in *Graham* merely stated that 'classifications based on alienage ... are inherently suspect' because 'aliens as a class are a prime example of a 'discrete and insular' minority ... for whom such heightened judicial solicitude is appropriate.'

As Mr. Justice Frankfurter so aptly observed:

'A footnote hardly seems to be an appropriate way of announcing a new constitutional doctrine, and the *Carolene* footnote did not purport to announce any new doctrine....' *Kovacs v. Cooper*, 336 U.S. 77 (1949) (concurring opinion).

Even if that judicial approach were accepted, however, the Court is conspicuously silent as to why that 'doctrine' should apply to these cases.

The footnote itself did not refer to 'searching judicial inquiry' when a classification is based on alienage, perhaps because there was a long line of authority holding such classifications entirely consonant with the Fourteenth Amendment. The 'national' category mentioned involved legislative attempts to prohibit education in languages other than English, which attempts were held unconstitutional as a deprivation of 'liberty' within the meaning of the Fourteenth and Fifth Amendments. These cases do not mention a 'citizen-alien' distinction, nor do they support a reasoning that 'nationality' is the same as 'alienage.'

The mere recitation of the words 'insular and discrete minority' is hardly a *constitutional* reason for prohibiting state legislative classifications such as are involved here, and is not necessarily consistent with the theory propounded in that footnote. The approach taken in *Graham* and these cases appears to be that whenever the Court feels that a societal group is 'discrete and insular,' it has the constitutional mandate to prohibit legislation that somehow treats the group differently from some other group.

Our society, consisting of over 200 million individuals of multitudinous origins, customs, tongues, beliefs, and cultures is, to say the least, diverse. It would hardly take extraordinary ingenuity for a lawyer to find 'insular and discrete' minorities at every turn in the road. Yet, unless the Court can precisely define and constitutionally justify both the terms and analysis it uses, these decisions today stand for the proposition that the Court can choose a 'minority' it 'feels' deserves 'solicitude' and thereafter prohibit the States from classifying that 'minority' differently from the 'majority.' I cannot find, and the Court does not cite, any constitutional authority for such a 'ward of the Court' approach to equal protection.

The only other apparent rationale for the invocation of the 'suspect classification' approach in these cases is that alienage is a 'status,' and the Court does not feel it 'appropriate' to classify on that basis. This rationale would appear to be similar to that utilized in *Weber v. Aetna Casualty & Surety Co.*, 406 U.S. 164 (1972) [Note *supra*. this chapter], in which the Court cited, without discussion, *Graham*. But there is a marked difference between a status or condition such as illegitimacy, national origin, or race, which cannot be altered by an individual and the 'status' of the appellant in [these cases]. There is nothing in the record indicating that their status as aliens cannot be changed by their affirmative acts.

## II

In my view, the proper judicial inquiry is whether any rational justification exists for prohibiting aliens from employment in the competitive civil service [in *Sugarman*] and from admission to a state bar [in *Griffiths*]. [Justice Rehnquist found such a rational justification for both exclusions.]

## Note: The Political Function Exception

1. *Sugarman* acknowledged states' authority to discriminate based on alienage when legislating on matters affecting what it called a state's "democratic political institutions." Based on that exception, the Court noted in *Sugarman* that a state could exclude aliens from voting and office-holding. Three years later, in *Perkins v. Smith*, 426 U.S. 913 (1976), it also held, through a summary affirmance of the lower court opinion, that a state could exclude aliens from jury service. The Court has also relied on the exception to allow states to exclude aliens from being police officers, probation officers, and school teachers. *See Foley v. Connelie*, 435 U.S. 291 (1978) (police officers); *Cabell v. Chavez-Salido*, 454 U.S. 432 (1982) (probation officers); *Ambach v. Norwick*, 441 U.S. 68 (1979) (teachers). In such cases, the Court reviewed and upheld the classification under the rational basis standard.

2. Nevertheless, there are limits to the exception. In *In re Griffiths*, 413 U.S. 717 (1973), decided the same day as *Sugarman*, the Court applied strict scrutiny to a Connecticut law denying aliens the right to practice law. Writing for a seven-justice majority, Justice Powell acknowledged that lawyers were "officers of the court." Nevertheless, he refused to characterize them in ways that would justify more relaxed review of a state's exclusion of aliens from legal practice:

> "We note at the outset that this argument goes beyond the opinion of the Connecticut Supreme Court, which recognized that a lawyer is not an officer in the ordinary sense. This comports with the view of the Court expressed ... in *Cammer v. United States*, 350 U.S. 999 (1956):
>
> > 'It has been stated many times that lawyers are 'officers of the court.' One of the most frequently repeated statements to this effect appears in *Ex parte Garland*, 4 Wall. 333, 378 (1866). The Court pointed out there, however, that an attorney was not an 'officer' within the ordinary meaning of that term. Certainly nothing that was said in *Ex parte Garland* or in any other case decided by this Court places attorneys in the same category as marshals, bailiffs, court clerks or judges. Unlike these officials a lawyer is engaged in a private profession, important though it be to our system of justice. In general he makes his own decisions, follows his own best judgment, collects his own fees and runs his own business. The word 'officer' as it has always been applied to lawyers conveys quite a different meaning from the word 'officer' as applied to people serving as officers within the conventional meaning of that term.' *Cammer.*
>
> Lawyers do indeed occupy professional positions of responsibility and influence that impose on them duties correlative with their vital right of access to the courts. Moreover, by virtue of their professional aptitudes and natural interests, lawyers have been leaders in government throughout the history of our country. Yet, they are not officials of government by virtue of being

lawyers. Nor does the status of holding a license to practice law place one so close to the core of the political process as to make him a formulator of government policy.

Chief Justice Burger, joined by Justice Rehnquist, dissented in *Griffiths*. He relied heavily on the history of lawyers as persons who both enjoyed a legally-granted monopoly and on whom were placed ethical obligations not placed on members of the general public. Justice Rehnquist, in a dissenting opinion (excerpted above) that applied to both *Griffiths* and *Sugarman*, wrote the following about law practice exclusions:

> More important than [the power to "sign writs and subpoenas, take recognizances and administer oaths"] is the tremendous responsibility and trust that our society places in the hands of lawyers. The liberty and property of the client may depend upon the competence and fidelity of the representation afforded by the lawyer in any number of particular lawsuits. But by virtue of their office lawyers are also given, and have increasingly undertaken to exercise, authority to seek to alter some of the social relationships and institutions of our society by use of the judicial process. No doubt an alien even under today's decision may be required to be learned in the law and familiar with the language spoken in the courts of the particular State involved. But Connecticut's requirement of citizenship reflects its judgment that something more than technical skills are needed to be a lawyer under our system. I do not believe it is irrational for a State that makes that judgment to require that lawyers have an understanding of the American political and social experience, whether gained from growing up in this country, as in the case of a native-born citizen, or from the naturalization process, as in the case of a foreign-born citizen.

### Note: State Classification against Undocumented Immigrants

In the cases discussed above there was no question that the aliens claiming unconstitutional discrimination were residing in the nation legally. The implications of that assumption were tested in 1982, in *Plyler v. Doe*, 457 U.S. 202 (1982).

*Plyler* considered a Texas law that denied funds for the public education of children who were not "legally admitted" into the United States. By a 5–4 vote the Court struck the law down. Writing for the majority, Justice Brennan, in a footnote, explicitly rejected "the claim that 'illegal aliens' are a 'suspect class,'" noting that "entry into this class … is a product of voluntary action" and "a crime." Nevertheless, he described undocumented immigrants who were minors as "special members" of this class, citing an illegitimacy case, *Trimble v. Gordon*, 430 U.S. 762 (1977) for the proposition that children, unlike their parents, cannot control their own status. He reasoned:

> Of course, undocumented status is not irrelevant to any proper legislative goal. Nor is undocumented status an absolutely immutable characteristic since it is the product of conscious, indeed unlawful, action. But [the Texas

law] is directed against children, and imposes its discriminatory burden on the basis of a legal characteristic over which children can have little control. It is thus difficult to conceive of a rational justification for penalizing these children for their presence within the United States. Yet that appears to be precisely the effect of [the Texas law].

He continued:

> More is involved in these cases than the abstract question whether [the challenged law] discriminates against a suspect class, or whether education is a fundamental right. [That law] imposes a lifetime hardship on a discrete class of children not accountable for their disabling status. The stigma of illiteracy will mark them for the rest of their lives. By denying these children a basic education, we deny them the ability to live within the structure of our civic institutions, and foreclose any realistic possibility that they will contribute in even the smallest way to the progress of our Nation. In determining the rationality of [the law], we may appropriately take into account its costs to the Nation and to the innocent children who are its victims. In light of these countervailing costs, the discrimination contained in [that law] can hardly be considered rational unless it furthers some substantial goal of the State.

He concluded that the law failed to meet that standard, rejecting the state's arguments that it could deny these children an education as a cost-saving measure, because of the special burdens they impose, or because they were less likely to remain in and contribute to the state. Justices Marshall, Blackmun, and Powell all joined the majority opinion but each concurred separately.

Writing for himself and Justices White, Rehnquist, and O'Connor, Chief Justice Burger dissented. Among other points, he disputed the majority's analogy between the plaintiff-children in this case and illegitimate children, noting that the *Plyler* plaintiffs were not burdened because of their "status of birth." More generally, he also questioned the breadth of any rule according heightened scrutiny to discrimination based on circumstances that were unchangeable. He wrote: "The Equal Protection Clause protects against arbitrary and irrational classifications, and against invidious discrimination stemming from prejudice and hostility; it is not an all-encompassing 'equalizer' designed to eradicate every distinction for which persons are not 'responsible.'" He would have held that it was rational for the state to deny an education to children who had no legal right to be in the nation.

## Note: Federal Power to Discriminate against Aliens

1. The cases above all speak to *states'* power to classify against aliens. But ever since the foundational cases of the 1970's, the Court has recognized broad *federal* power to regulate the status of aliens within the nation's borders. In *Graham v. Richardson*, 403 U.S. 365 (1971), discussed in a previous note, one of the reasons for striking down state-law durational restrictions on aliens' receipt of public assistance was that those restrictions conflicted with federal immigration policy.

2. In later cases, the force of federal authority over immigration was interpreted to extend beyond prohibiting inconsistent state policies, to also include the power to draw the very types of classifications states themselves could not draw. In *Mathews v. Diaz*, 426 U.S. 67 (1976), the Court upheld a federal law limiting eligibility for Medicare benefits to aliens who were admitted for permanent residence and who had resided in the nation for five years. Justice Stevens wrote the following for a unanimous Court:

> In the exercise of its broad power over naturalization and immigration, Congress regularly makes rules that would be unacceptable if applied to citizens. The exclusion of aliens and the reservation of the power to deport have no permissible counterpart in the Federal Government's power to regulate the conduct of its own citizenry. The fact that an Act of Congress treats aliens differently from citizens does not in itself imply that such disparate treatment is "invidious."

> In particular, the fact that Congress has provided some welfare benefits for citizens does not require it to provide like benefits for all aliens. Neither the overnight visitor, the unfriendly agent of a hostile foreign power, the resident diplomat, nor the illegal entrant, can advance even a colorable constitutional claim to a share in the bounty that a conscientious sovereign makes available to its own citizens and Some of its guests. The decision to share that bounty with our guests may take into account the character of the relationship between the alien and this country: Congress may decide that as the alien's tie grows stronger, so does the strength of his claim to an equal share of that munificence....

> For reasons long recognized as valid, the responsibility for regulating the relationship between the United States and our alien visitors has been committed to the political branches of the Federal Government. Since decisions in these matters may implicate our relations with foreign powers, and since a wide variety of classifications must be defined in the light of changing political and economic circumstances, such decisions are frequently of a character more appropriate to either the Legislature or the Executive than to the Judiciary....

> The task of classifying persons for medical benefits, like the task of drawing lines for federal tax purposes, inevitably requires that some persons who have an almost equally strong claim to favored treatment be placed on different sides of the line; the differences between the eligible and the ineligible are differences in degree rather than differences in the character of their respective claims. When this kind of policy choice must be made, we are especially reluctant to question the exercise of congressional judgment. In this case, since appellees have not identified a principled basis for prescribing a different standard than the one selected by Congress, they have, in effect, merely invited us to substitute our judgment for that of Congress in deciding which aliens shall be eligible to participate in the supplementary insurance program on the same conditions as citizens. We decline the invitation.

# D. Unsuccessful Candidates for Heightened Scrutiny

Not every group that made a claim for heightened judicial review was successful, even during the period of the Court's most aggressive experimentation with suspect class analysis. The materials that follow trace the suspect class fate of two such groups—the poor and the elderly (or at least no longer young).

## Note: Wealth as a Suspect Class?

1. During the early period of the Court's experimentation with suspect class analysis justices had several occasions to consider the constitutional status of discrimination based on wealth. For a time it appeared that the Court might be on the verge of pronouncing wealth a suspect classification. Ultimately, however, it rejected that argument.

2. The Court's early consideration of this question arose mainly in the context of criminal procedure—in particular, state requirements that criminal defendants pay their own costs for obtaining the services and items requisite to accessing the criminal justice process. For example, in *Griffin v. Illinois*, 351 U.S. 12 (1956), the Court invalidated an Illinois requirement that defendants who wished to appeal their convictions pay the cost of obtaining a transcript of their trial, even though the state conceded that a transcript was sometimes indispensable to the filings required for such appeals. Writing for four justices, Justice Black explained that it was irrational for the state to use poverty as a justification for denying a defendant a fair trial. While he conceded that appellate review was different, in that a state was under no constitutional obligation to provide appeals of criminal convictions, he concluded that if a state did provide for such appeals, it was similarly irrational to deny access to them based on poverty. Justice Frankfurter wrote a separate concurrence that largely agreed with the plurality's analysis, and that described the discrimination at issue as "squalid." Justice Burton, joined by Justices Minton, Reed, and Harlan, dissented. Justice Harlan also wrote a separate dissent.

3. Ten years later, in *Harper v. Virginia State Board of Elections*, 383 U.S. 663 (1966), the Court struck down Virginia's "poll tax"—a requirement that anyone wishing to vote pay a certain amount. (Virginia required a payment of $1.50.) Writing for six justices, Justice Douglas wrote that "wealth, like race, creed, or color, is not germane to one's ability to participate intelligently in the electoral process," and that "lines drawn on the basis of wealth or property, like those of race, are traditionally disfavored." At the very end of his opinion, he wrote that "wealth or fee paying has, in our view, no relation to voting qualifications; the right to vote is too precious, too fundamental to be so burdened or conditioned." Justice Black dissented, as did Justice Harlan (who was joined by Justice Stewart). Neither dissent took issue with the majority's dislike of poll taxes, but both dissents argued that the Equal Protection Clause did not condemn this type of discrimination.

4. Four years after *Harper*, the Court shrunk back from *Harper*'s more expansive implications. In *Dandridge v. Williams*, 397 U.S. 471 (1970), the Court rejected an

equal protection challenge to a Maryland law capping the benefits families could receive under a joint federal-state welfare program. The effect of that law was to burden members of large families, who because of that cap did not receive the same per-person benefit as members of small families.

Writing for the six-justice majority, Justice Stewart characterized this law as "state regulation in the social and economic field," which thus merited only the most deferential level of judicial review. He recognized that the law dealt not with "state regulation of business or industry," but instead "the most basic economic needs of impoverished human beings." Nevertheless, he concluded that "we can find no basis for applying a different constitutional standard" than the one that applied to such "social and economic" regulation. Justice Harlan joined the majority but also wrote a separate concurrence.

Justice Douglas dissented on a statutory ground. Justice Marshall, joined by Justice Brennan, reached the constitutional issue, and would have found the law to violate the Equal Protection Clause. Stating a view that he would come to repeat over the course of his career on the Court, Justice Marshall argued that in equal protection cases "concentration must be placed upon the character of the classification in question, the relative importance to individuals in the class discriminated against of the governmental benefits that they do not receive, and the asserted state interests in support of the classification." In other words, in his view equal protection scrutiny should turn both on the "character of the classification" and the importance of the interest at stake. Noting the majority's recognition of the importance of these welfare benefits to "the basic economic needs of impoverished human beings," he argued that "it is the individual interests here at stake that ... most clearly distinguish this case from the 'business regulation' equal protection cases." Given the importance of the interest, he accorded more stringent review to Maryland's law, which he concluded classified unreasonably.

5. *Dandridge* did not conclusively decide the question of whether poverty was a suspect class; after all, as Justice Marshall observed, the classification in that case turned on family size, not wealth or poverty itself. Three years later, however, in *San Antonio Independent School District v. Rodriguez*, 411 U.S. 1 (1973), the Court squarely confronted that issue. *Rodriguez* involved an equal protection challenge to Texas's public school funding scheme, which relied heavily on local property taxes and which thus led to a situation in which districts with high value property were more easily able than property value-poor districts to fund their schools at high levels.

A five-justice majority rejected the challenge. Justice Powell's opinion for the Court began by characterizing the Court's opinions in cases such as *Griffin* as dealing with situations where the challenged wealth classification had the effect of completely denying poor persons access to the government service at issue — for example, in *Griffin* itself, the requirement that criminal appellants pay for a trial transcript resulted in the complete deprivation of their right to appeal their convictions.

Turning to the plaintiffs' discrimination claim, Justice Powell concluded that the evidence showed that the only systematic disadvantage the Texas system created was among residents who lived in property-rich and property-poor districts. (By contrast, he concluded, the Texas system did not systematically discriminate against poor *in-dividuals*, since at least in some circumstances poor individuals might live in school districts—such as those containing commercial or industrial property—that was in fact valued highly.) Given this understanding of the poverty that formed the basis of the discrimination claim, Justice Powell rejected that classification tool as inherently suspect: "The system of alleged discrimination and the class it defines have none of the traditional indicia of suspectness: the class is not saddled with such disabilities, or subjected to such a history of purposeful unequal treatment, or relegated to such a position of political powerlessness as to command extraordinary protection from the majoritarian political process." He then went on to consider whether education was a "fundamental right" for equal protection purposes, such that unequal distri-bution of education triggered heightened scrutiny regardless of the suspect class status of the plaintiff-group itself. He rejected that argument as well. This concept—the "fundamental rights strand of equal protection"—is considered in more detail later in Chapter 16.

Justice White, joined by Justices Douglas and Brennan, dissented. He argued that the Texas funding scheme was irrational because the cap state law imposed on the tax rates districts could impose made it impossible for property-poor districts to im-pose taxes that could generate funds equal to those property-rich districts could obtain through lower, legally-allowable, tax rates.

Justice Marshall, joined by Justice Douglas, also dissented. He reiterated his argu-ment from his dissent in *Dandridge* that equal protection cases should be judged ac-cording to both the character of the classification at issue and the importance of the right at stake. In this case, he argued that the importance of education helped justify more careful judicial scrutiny. (Justice Brennan wrote a short separate dissent to express his basic agreement with this part of Justice Marshall's analysis.)

Turning to the character of poverty classifications, Justice Marshall cited *Griffin* and *Harper*, among other cases, for the proposition that "discrimination on the basis of wealth may create a classification of a suspect character and thereby call for exacting judicial scrutiny." He explained his thinking about the status of wealth as a justification for discrimination:

> That wealth classifications alone have not necessarily been considered to bear the same high degree of suspectness as have classifications based on, for in-stance, race or alienage may be explainable on a number of grounds. The 'poor' may not be seen as politically powerless as certain discrete and insular minority groups. Personal poverty may entail much the same social stigma as historically attached to certain racial or ethnic groups. But personal poverty is not a permanent disability; its shackles may be escaped. Perhaps most im-portantly, though, personal wealth may not necessarily share the general ir-relevance as a basis for legislative action that race or nationality is recognized to have. While the 'poor' have frequently been a legally disadvantaged group, it cannot be ignored that social legislation must frequently take cognizance of the economic status of our citizens. Thus, we have generally gauged the

invidiousness of wealth classifications with an awareness of the importance of the interests being affected and the relevance of personal wealth to those interests. See *Harper.*

Nevertheless, he concluded that the wealth of the school district in which a child lived had no relationship to the child's interest in educational opportunity. Citing the Court's then-recent illegitimacy cases (*Weber* and *Levy*), he observed that discrimination on such grounds was problematic in that it "is no reflection of the individual's characteristics or his abilities," and is beyond the child's ability to control. He continued:

> The disability of the disadvantaged class in this case extends as well into the political processes upon which we ordinarily rely as adequate for the protection and promotion of all interests. Here legislative reallocation of the State's property wealth must be sought in the face of inevitable opposition from significantly advantaged districts that have a strong vested interest in the preservation of the status quo....

Finally, he suggested that Texas might bear some responsibility for the wealth discrimination. Unlike cases such as *Griffin*, where the plaintiff's indigency was caused by private conduct, here, he suggested, Texas had a greater hand in the wealth discrimination by establishing the school financing scheme, creating local school districts with certain geographical lines, and regulating land use in ways that made certain districts property-rich and others property-poor. For all these reasons, he concluded, "the invidious characteristics of the group wealth classification present in this case merely serve to emphasize the need for careful judicial scrutiny of the State's justifications for the resulting interdistrict discrimination."

## Massachusetts Board of Retirement v. Murgia

### 427 U.S. 307 (1976)

PER CURIAM

This case presents the question whether the provision of Mass.Gen.Laws Ann. c. 32, §26(3)(a) (1969), that a uniformed state police officer "shall be retired ... upon his attaining age fifty," denies appellee police officer equal protection of the laws in violation of the Fourteenth Amendment....

The primary function of the Uniformed Branch of the Massachusetts State Police is to protect persons and property and maintain law and order.... As the District Court observed, "service in this branch is, or can be, arduous." ... Thus, "even (appellee's) experts concede that there is a general relationship between advancing age and decreasing physical ability to respond to the demands of the job."

These considerations prompt the requirement that uniformed state officers pass a comprehensive physical examination biennially until age 40. After that, until mandatory retirement at age 50, uniformed officers must pass annually a more rigorous examination, including an electrocardiogram and tests for gastro-intestinal bleeding. Appellee Murgia had passed such an examination four months before he was retired, and there is no dispute that, when he retired, his excellent physical and mental health still rendered him capable of performing the duties of a uniformed officer.

The record includes the testimony of three physicians: that of the State Police Surgeon, who testified to the physiological and psychological demands involved in the performance of uniformed police functions; that of an associate professor of medicine, who testified generally to the relationship between aging and the ability to perform under stress; and that of a surgeon, who also testified to aging and the ability safely to perform police functions. The testimony clearly established that the risk of physical failure, particularly in the cardiovascular system, increases with age, and that the number of individuals in a given age group incapable of performing stress functions increases with the age of the group. The testimony also recognized that particular individuals over 50 could be capable of safely performing the functions of uniformed officers. The associate professor of medicine, who was a witness for the appellee, further testified that evaluating the risk of cardiovascular failure in a given individual would require a number of detailed studies....

I

... This Court's decisions give no support to the proposition that a right of governmental employment *per se* is fundamental....

Nor does the class of uniformed state police officers over 50 constitute a suspect class for purposes of equal protection analysis. *San Antonio School Dist. v. Rodriguez*, 411 U.S. 1 (1973) [Note *supra.* this chapter], observed that a suspect class is one "saddled with such disabilities, or subjected to such a history of purposeful unequal treatment, or relegated to such a position of political powerlessness as to command extraordinary protection from the majoritarian political process." While the treatment of the aged in this Nation has not been wholly free of discrimination, such persons, unlike, say, those who have been discriminated against on the basis of race or national origin, have not experienced a "history of purposeful unequal treatment" or been subjected to unique disabilities on the basis of stereotyped characteristics not truly indicative of their abilities. The class subject to the compulsory retirement feature of the Massachusetts statute consists of uniformed state police officers over the age of 50. It cannot be said to discriminate only against the elderly. Rather, it draws the line at a certain age in middle life. But even old age does not define a "discrete and insular" group, *United States v. Carolene Products Co.*, 304 U.S. 144 (1938) [Note *supra.* this chapter], in need of "extraordinary protection from the majoritarian political process." Instead, it marks a stage that each of us will reach if we live out our normal span. Even if the statute could be said to impose a penalty upon a class defined as the aged, it would not impose a distinction sufficiently akin to those classifications that we have found suspect to call for strict judicial scrutiny.

Under the circumstances, it is unnecessary to subject the State's resolution of competing interests in this case to the degree of critical examination that our cases under the Equal Protection Clause recently have characterized as "strict judicial scrutiny."

## II·

We turn then to examine this state classification under the rational-basis standard. This inquiry employs a relatively relaxed standard reflecting the Court's awareness that the drawing of lines that create distinctions is peculiarly a legislative task and an unavoidable one. Perfection in making the necessary classifications is neither possible nor necessary. Such action by a legislature is presumed to be valid.

In this case, the Massachusetts statute clearly meets the requirements of the Equal Protection Clause, for the State's classification rationally furthers the purpose identified by the State. Through mandatory retirement at age 50, the legislature seeks to protect the public by assuring physical preparedness of its uniformed police. Since physical ability generally declines with age, mandatory retirement at 50 serves to remove from police service those whose fitness for uniformed work presumptively has diminished with age. This clearly is rationally related to the State's objective. There is no indication that § 26(3)(a) has the effect of excluding from service so few officers who are in fact unqualified as to render age 50 a criterion wholly unrelated to the objective of the statute....

Mr. Justice STEVENS took no part in the consideration or decision of this case.

Mr. Justice MARSHALL, dissenting....

## I

Although there are signs that its grasp on the law is weakening, the rigid two-tier model still holds sway as the Court's articulated description of the equal protection test. Again, I must object to its perpetuation. The model's two fixed modes of analysis, strict scrutiny and mere rationality, simply do not describe the inquiry the Court has undertaken or should undertake in equal protection cases. Rather, the inquiry has been much more sophisticated and the Court should admit as much. It has focused upon the character of the classification in question, the relative importance to individuals in the class discriminated against of the governmental benefits that they do not receive, and the state interests asserted in support of the classification.

Although the Court outwardly adheres to the two-tier model, it has apparently lost interest in recognizing further "fundamental" rights and "suspect" classes. See *San Antonio School District v. Rodriguez* (rejecting education as a fundamental right); *Frontiero v. Richardson* (1973) [*Supra.* this chapter] (declining to treat women as a suspect class). In my view, this result is the natural consequence of the limitations of the Court's traditional equal protection analysis. If a statute invades a "fundamental" right or discriminates against a "suspect" class, it is subject to strict scrutiny. If a statute is subject to strict scrutiny, the statute always, or nearly always, is struck down. Quite obviously, the only critical decision is whether strict scrutiny should be invoked at all. It should be no surprise, then, that the Court is hesitant to expand the number of categories of rights and classes subject to strict scrutiny, when each expansion involves the invalidation of virtually every classification bearing upon a newly covered category.

But however understandable the Court's hesitancy to invoke strict scrutiny, all remaining legislation should not drop into the bottom tier, and be measured by the mere rationality test. For that test, too, when applied as articulated, leaves little doubt about the outcome; the challenged legislation is always upheld. It cannot be gainsaid that there remain rights, not now classified as "fundamental," that remain vital to the flourishing of a free society, and classes, not now classified as "suspect," that are unfairly burdened by invidious discrimination unrelated to the individual worth of their members. Whatever we call these rights and classes, we simply cannot forgo all judicial protection against discriminatory legislation bearing upon them, but for the rare instances when the legislative choice can be termed "wholly irrelevant" to the legislative goal....

## II

The danger of the Court's verbal adherence to the rigid two-tier test, despite its effective repudiation of that test in the cases, is demonstrated by its efforts here. There is simply no reason why a statute that tells able-bodied police officers, ready and willing to work, that they no longer have the right to earn a living in their chosen profession merely because they are 50 years old should be judged by the same minimal standards of rationality that we use to test economic legislation that discriminates against business interests. Yet, the Court today not only invokes the minimal level of scrutiny, it wrongly adheres to it. Analysis of the three factors I have identified above — the importance of the governmental benefits denied, the character of the class, and the asserted state interests — demonstrates the Court's error.

Whether "fundamental" or not, "the right of the individual ... to engage in any of the common occupations of life" has been repeatedly recognized by this Court as falling within the concept of liberty guaranteed by the Fourteenth Amendment....

While depriving any government employee of his job is a significant deprivation, it is particularly burdensome when the person deprived is an older citizen. Once terminated, the elderly cannot readily find alternative employment. The lack of work is not only economically damaging, but emotionally and physically draining. Deprived of his status in the community and of the opportunity for meaningful activity, fearful of becoming dependent on others for his support, and lonely in his new-found isolation, the involuntarily retired person is susceptible to physical and emotional ailments as a direct consequence of his enforced idleness. Ample clinical evidence supports the conclusion that mandatory retirement poses a direct threat to the health and life expectancy of the retired person, and these consequences of termination for age are not disputed by appellants....

Of course, the Court is quite right in suggesting that distinctions exist between the elderly and traditional suspect classes such as Negroes, and between the elderly and "quasi-suspect" classes such as women or illegitimates. The elderly are protected not only by certain anti-discrimination legislation, but by legislation that provides them with positive benefits not enjoyed by the public at large. Moreover, the elderly are not isolated in society, and discrimination against them is not pervasive but is centered primarily in employment. The advantage of a flexible equal protection standard, however, is that it can readily accommodate such variables. The elderly are undoubtedly discriminated against, and when legislation denies them an important benefit employment I conclude that to sustain the legislation appellants must show a reasonably substantial interest and a scheme reasonably closely tailored to achieving that interest. This inquiry, ultimately, is not markedly different from that undertaken by the Court in *Reed v. Reed*, 404 U.S. 71 (1971) [Note *supra.* this chapter].

Turning, then, to appellants' arguments, I agree that the purpose of the mandatory retirement law is legitimate, and indeed compelling, the Commonwealth has every reason to assure that its state police officers are of sufficient physical strength and health to perform their jobs. In my view, however, the means chosen, the forced retirement of officers at age 50, is so over-inclusive that it must fall.

All potential officers must pass a rigorous physical examination. Until age 40, this same examination must be passed every two years when the officer re-enlists and, after age 40, every year.... Thus, the only members of the state police still on the force at age 50 are those who have been determined repeatedly by the Commonwealth to be physically fit for the job. Yet, all of these physically fit officers are automatically terminated at age 50.... In these circumstances, I see no reason at all for automatically terminating those officers who reach the age of 50; indeed, that action seems the height of irrationality.

Accordingly, I conclude that the Commonwealth's mandatory retirement law cannot stand when measured against the significant deprivation the Commonwealth's action works upon the terminated employees. I would affirm the judgment of the District Court.

## *Note: The Court and Suspect Class Analysis*

1. The materials presented in this chapter reflect the most important instances of the Court's experimentation with suspect class analysis during the 1970's. (The sex and illegitimacy discrimination materials go beyond that decade, of course, to complete their respective stories.) How would you evaluate the success of the Court's efforts? Recall that Footnote 4 of *Carolene Products*, the ultimate foundation for suspect class analysis, arose out of an attempt by the Court to find a role for itself consistent with democratic governance. In particular, Footnote 4 sketched out a theory of judicial review that focused on reinforcing, not overruling, democracy, by giving careful scrutiny to laws that blocked self-government, such as voting and speech restrictions (the second paragraph of that footnote) and laws that reflected some sort of political process breakdown, as expressed in the third paragraph's observation that "prejudice against discrete and insular minorities may be a special condition, which tends seriously to curtail the operation of those political processes ordinarily to be relied upon to protect minorities." (The first paragraph of the footnote, by focusing on judicial protection of textually-specific Bill of Rights provisions, is not necessarily democracy reinforcing; nevertheless, the specificity of those rights provided, in the footnote's view, a warrant for counter-majoritarian judicial review.)

But leave aside the first paragraph, and even the second, and focus on the third paragraph of the footnote, which ultimately flowered into suspect class analysis. Does that analysis tell a convincing story about political process breakdown? Consider sex discrimination. Are women a "minority" that suffers from "prejudice"? If they were in 1973, are they today? Does the political system somehow not take account of their interests? If you think it doesn't, then how can you explain the litany of sex equality laws Justice Brennan was able to cite in *Frontiero* in 1973?

2. Does the analysis get even more complex (and perhaps less convincing) when the Court reaches an equivocal answer to its suspect class analysis? Recall the Court's conclusion in *Mathews v. Lucas* about illegitimate persons:

> While the law has long placed the illegitimate child in an inferior position relative to the legitimate in certain circumstances, particularly in regard to obligations of support or other aspects of family law, perhaps in part because the roots of the discrimination rest in the conduct of the parents rather than the child, and perhaps in part because illegitimacy does not carry an obvious badge, as race or sex do, this discrimination against illegitimates has never approached the severity or pervasiveness of the historic legal and political discrimination against women and Negroes.

What should the Court do when it finds that a group satisfies some, but not all, of the criteria for suspect class status, or satisfies them, but not fully? If your answer is that such a group should receive intermediate scrutiny, then recall Justice Rehnquist's complaint in *Craig v. Boren* about how "diaphanous and elastic" intermediate scrutiny is. Recall also how the Court actually has applied intermediate scrutiny in the sex and legitimacy cases. Do those applications represent anything more than an intuition about when a challenged classification is unreasonable?

3. Consider the argument that, whatever the difficulties in applying it, suspect class analysis aspires to be a value-neutral, process-based approach to judicial review that calls for heightened judicial scrutiny only when the Court suspects a dysfunctional political process. Was that potential ever realized? As early as *Frontiero* and the early legitimacy cases, the Court was remarking on the "irrelevance" of the particular trait at issue to the asserted government purpose. If suspect class analysis calls for stronger judicial intervention only when the Court suspects that the political process has broken down, then why is it even mentioning the relevance or irrelevance of the trait at issue?

4. If these problems weren't obvious when the Court embarked on its suspect class experimentation in the early 1970's, they had become clear by the end of the decade. Indeed, they had become so clear that by the middle of the next decade the Court began to back away from that approach. That story—of the Court's retreat from suspect class analysis, and its search for a replacement approach to equal protection—is told in Chapter 15. But before we reach that story, we need to rewind the historical tape and consider how race, and racial equality, relates to the Equal Protection Clause. Chapter 13 presents those materials. Chapter 14 picks up on a closely related point, but one that applies to equal protection law more generally: the so-called "discriminatory intent" requirement. With these crucial building blocks

of equal protection doctrine in place, Chapter 15 then considers the overall state of equal protection today. Finally, Chapter 16 concludes Part IV by examining the analytically distinct strand of equal protection that focuses on the unequal deprivation of fundamental rights.

# Chapter 13

# Race and the Constitution

## A. The Constitution and Slavery

### Note: The Constitution's Compromise with Slavery

1. Slavery had existed in the American colonies since the first decades of English settlement. Nevertheless, by 1787 the institution was declining throughout most of the nation, especially in the North but also in the South. Nevertheless, at the constitutional convention deep southern states, in particular South Carolina and Georgia, insisted on protecting it. It is generally thought that the framers, even those opposed to slavery, gave in to those demands as a price of obtaining those states' support for the new Constitution.

2. The Constitution itself accommodated slavery in several important ways. Perhaps most notoriously, a slave was counted as 3/5 of a person for purposes of apportioning congressional representatives—and hence, presidential electors. This provision inflated southern electoral strength far beyond the free white population of the region. Article IV provided for the recapture of escaped slaves, while the slave trade was protected for a period of twenty years. Indeed, the slave trade provision was one of only two provisions that was made unamendable.

3. The invention of the cotton gin by Eli Whitney in 1793 resurrected what had been a declining institution. The cotton gin allowed much more efficient harvesting of cotton, which made large cotton plantations economically viable, and thus increased the attractiveness of slave labor in cotton fields. The settlement of Alabama and Mississippi, and later of Louisiana, Texas, and other southern states, increased the scale of the agricultural economy based on slave labor, thus ending any realistic hope that slavery would simply become economically unviable as it had in northern states.

4. The increased importance of slavery to southern life eventually created a competition between north and south over the settlement of western lands. Northerners, even those who had no particularly egalitarian racial sentiments, feared the expansion of the slave system and the competition it posed to free white labor. Southerners feared that the creation of new free states in the Louisiana Purchase lands would eventually erode the political power of the slaveholding states, and put slavery itself in peril. Starting in 1820, Congress began crafting a series of compromises, whereby free states and slave states would be admitted in equal numbers, so as to maintain the free state/slave state balance in the Senate. Those compromises, such as the Mis-

souri Compromise of 1820, also attempted to delineate the geographic boundaries of slavery. For example, as noted in the *Dred Scott* case that follows this note, the Missouri Compromise itself prohibited slavery in the territories north of 36 degrees, 30 minutes latitude.

Despite such compromises, tensions remained. In particular, concerns arose about slaveholders' attempts to recapture runaway slaves who had escaped into free states. Congress enacted the first fugitive slave law in 1793. Those laws empowered slave-catchers to recapture runaway slaves in free states, and involved the federal government in assisting those efforts. The Supreme Court affirmed Congress's power to enact recapture legislation in *Prigg v. Pennsylvania*, 41 U.S. 539 (1842).

Over time, American politics became increasingly polarized over the slavery issue. To be sure, most northerners did not oppose slavery where it existed; nevertheless, many northerners opposed its expansion into the territories. Others opposed the intrusion of federal fugitive slave laws into the free states, believing those laws to reflect an intrusion of slavery itself into the free parts of the nation. Such opposition created a sharp conflict with southern interests, which consistently sought both to protect slavery and expand the territory open to it. By the 1850s, the nation's continued territorial expansion — with its annexation of Texas, Mexico's cession of vast lands after the Mexican War, and the settlement with Great Britain over the Oregon Territory — caused the slavery issue to become even more contentious. The opening of the Kansas and Nebraska territories to both pro- and anti-slavery settlers led to large-scale violence and political strife in those areas, as both sides competed to control those territories and thus, eventually, the states that would be formed from them.

It was against this backdrop that the Supreme Court considered *Dred Scott v. Sandford*.

## Dred Scott v. Sandford
### 60 U.S. (19 How.) 393 (1857)

This case was brought up, by writ of error, from the Circuit Court of the United States for the district of Missouri.

It was an action of trespass *vi et armis* instituted in the Circuit Court by Scott against Sandford.... The declaration of Scott contained three counts: one, that Sandford had assaulted the plaintiff; one, that he had assaulted Harriet Scott, his wife; and one, that he had assaulted Eliza Scott and Lizzie Scott, his children....

And the said John F. A. Sandford, in his own proper person, comes and says that this court ought not to have or take further cognizance of the action aforesaid, because he says the said cause of action ... accrued to the said Dred Scott out of the jurisdiction of the courts of the State of Missouri, for that, to wit: the said plaintiff, Dred Scott, is not a citizen of the State of Missouri, as alleged in his declaration, because he is a Negro of African descent; his ancestors were of pure African blood, and were brought into this country and sold as Negro slaves, and this the said Sandford is ready to verify. Wherefore, he prays judgment whether this court can or will take further cognizance of the action aforesaid....

In the year 1834, the plaintiff was a Negro slave belonging to Dr. Emerson, who was a surgeon in the army of the United States. In that year, 1834, said Dr. Emerson took the plaintiff from the State of Missouri to the military post at Rock Island, in the State of Illinois, and held him there as a slave until the month of April or May, 1836. At the time last mentioned, said Dr. Emerson removed the plaintiff from said military post at Rock Island to the military post at Fort Snelling, situated on the west bank of the Mississippi river, in the Territory known as Upper Louisiana, acquired by the United States from France, and situate north of the latitude of thirty-six degrees thirty minutes north, and north of the State of Missouri. Said Dr. Emerson held the plaintiff in slavery at said Fort Snelling, from said last-mentioned date until the year 1838.

In the year 1835, Harriet, who is named in the second count of the plaintiff's declaration, was the Negro slave of Major Taliaferre, who belonged to the army of the United States. In that year, 1835, said Major Taliaferre took said Harriet to said Fort Snelling, a military post, situated as hereinbefore stated, and kept her there as a slave until the year 1836, and then sold and delivered her as a slave at said Fort Snelling unto the said Dr. Emerson hereinbefore named. Said Dr. Emerson held said Harriet in slavery at said Fort Snelling until the year 1838.

In the year 1836, the plaintiff and said Harriet at said Fort Snelling, with the consent of said Dr. Emerson, who then claimed to be their master and owner, intermarried, and took each other for husband and wife. Eliza and Lizzie, named in the third count of the plaintiff's declaration, are the fruit of that marriage. Eliza is about fourteen years old, and was born on board the steamboat *Gipsey*, north of the north line of the State of Missouri, and upon the river Mississippi. Lizzie is about seven years old, and was born in the State of Missouri, at the military post called Jefferson Barracks.

In the year 1838, said Dr. Emerson removed the plaintiff and said Harriet and their said daughter Eliza, from said Fort Snelling to the State of Missouri, where they have ever since resided.

Before the commencement of this suit, said Dr. Emerson sold and conveyed the plaintiff, said Harriet, Eliza, and Lizzie, to the defendant, as slaves, and the defendant has ever since claimed to hold them and each of them as slaves.

At the times mentioned in the plaintiff's declaration, the defendant, claiming to be owner as aforesaid, laid his hands upon said plaintiff, Harriet, Eliza, and Lizzie, and imprisoned them, doing in this respect, however, no more than what he might lawfully do if they were of right his slaves at such times....

TANEY, CHIEF JUSTICE.

... We proceed to examine the case as presented by the pleadings.

The words "people of the United States" and "citizens" are synonymous terms, and mean the same thing. They both describe the political body who, according to our republican institutions, form the sovereignty, and who hold the power and conduct the Government through their representatives. They are what we familiarly call the "sovereign people," and every citizen is one of this people, and a constituent member of this sovereignty. The question before us is, whether the class of persons described in the plea in abatement compose a portion of this people, and are constituent members of this sovereignty? We think they are not, and that they are not included, and were not intended to be included, under the word "citizens" in the Constitution, and can therefore claim none of the rights and privileges which that instrument provides for and secures to citizens of the United States. On the contrary, they were at that time considered as a subordinate and inferior class of beings, who had been subjugated by the dominant race, and, whether emancipated or not, yet remained subject to their authority, and had no rights or privileges but such as those who held the power and the Government might choose to grant them.

It is not the province of the court to decide upon the justice or injustice, the policy or impolicy, of these laws. The decision of that question belonged to the political or law-making power; to those who formed the sovereignty and framed the Constitution. The duty of the court is, to interpret the instrument they have framed, with the best lights we can obtain on the subject, and to administer it as we find it, according to its true intent and meaning when it was adopted.

In discussing this question, we must not confound the rights of citizenship which a State may confer within its own limits, and the rights of citizenship as a member of the Union. It does not by any means follow, because he has all the rights and privileges of a citizen of a State, that he must be a citizen of the United States. He may have all of the rights and privileges of the citizen of a State, and yet not be entitled to the rights and privileges of a citizen in any other State. For, previous to the adoption of the constitution of the United States, every State had the undoubted right to confer on whomsoever it pleased, the character of citizen, and to endow him with all its rights. But this character of course was confined to the boundaries of the State, and gave him no rights or privileges in other States beyond those secured to him by the laws of nations and the comity of States. Nor have the several States surrendered the power of conferring these rights and privileges by adopting the Constitution of the United States. Each State may still confer them upon an alien, or any one it thinks proper, or upon any class or description of persons; yet he would not be a citizen in the sense in which that word is used in the Constitution of the United States, nor entitled to sue as such in one of its courts, nor to the privileges and immunities of a citizen in the other States. The rights which he would acquire would be restricted to the State which gave them....

The question then arises, whether the provisions of the Constitution, in relation to the personal rights and privileges to which the citizen of a State should be entitled, embraced the Negro African race, at that time in this country, or who might afterwards be imported, who had then or should afterwards be made free in any State; and to put it in the power of a single State to make him a citizen of the United States, and endow him with the full rights of citizenship in every other State without their consent? ...

It is true, every person, and every class and description of persons, who were at the time of the adoption of the Constitution recognized as citizens in the several States, became also citizens of this new political body; but none other; it was formed by them, and for them and their posterity, but for no one else. And the personal rights and privileges guaranteed to citizens of this new sovereignty were intended to embrace those only who were then members of the several State communities, or who should afterwards by birthright or otherwise become members, according to the provisions of the Constitution and the principles on which it was founded. It was the union of those who were at that time members of distinct and separate political communities into one political family, whose power, for certain specified purposes, was to extend over the whole territory of the United States. And it gave to each citizen rights and privileges outside of his State which he did not before possess, and placed him in every other State upon a perfect equality with its own citizens as to rights of person and rights of property; it made him a citizen of the United States.

It becomes necessary, therefore, to determine who were citizens of the several States when the Constitution was adopted. And in order to do this, we must recur to the Governments and institutions of the thirteen colonies, when they separated from Great Britain and formed new sovereignties, and took their places in the family of independent nations. We must inquire who, at that time, were recognized as the people or citizens of a State, whose rights and liberties had been outraged by the English Government; and who declared their independence, and assumed the powers of Government to defend their rights by force of arms.

In the opinion of the court, the legislation and histories of the times, and the language used in the Declaration of Independence, show, that neither the class of persons who had been imported as slaves, nor their descendants, whether they had become free or not, were then acknowledged as a part of the people, nor intended to be included in the general words used in that memorable instrument.

It is difficult at this day to realize the state of public opinion in relation to that unfortunate race, which prevailed in the civilized and enlightened portions of the world at the time of the Declaration of Independence, and when the Constitution of United States was framed and adopted. But the public history of every European nation displays it in a manner too plain to be mistaken.

They had for more than a century before been regarded as beings of an inferior order, and altogether unfit to associate with the white race, either in social or political relations; and so far inferior, that they had no rights which the white man was bound to respect; and that the Negro might justly and lawfully be reduced to slavery for his benefit. He was bought and sold, and treated as an ordinary article of merchandise and traffic, whenever a profit could be made by it. This opinion was at that time fixed and universal in the civilized portion of the white race. It was regarded as an axiom in morals as well as in politics, which no one thought of disputing or supposed to be open to dispute; and men in every grade and position in society daily and habitually acted upon it in their private pursuits, as well as in matters of public concern, without doubting for a moment the correctness of this opinion.

And in no nation was this opinion more firmly fixed or more uniformly acted upon than by the English Government and English people. They not only seized them on the coast of Africa, and sold them or held them in slavery for their own use; but they took them as ordinary articles of merchandise to every country where they could make a profit on them, and were far more extensively engaged in this commerce than any other nation in the world.

The opinion thus entertained and acted upon in England was naturally impressed upon the colonies they founded on this side of the Atlantic. And, accordingly, a Negro of the African race was regarded by them as an article of property and held, and bought and sold as such, in every one of the thirteen colonies which united in the Declaration of Independence, and afterwards formed the Constitution of the United States. The slaves were more or less numerous in the different colonies, as slave labor was found more or less profitable. But no one seems to have doubted the correctness of the prevailing opinion of the time....

The language of the Declaration of Independence is equally conclusive:

It begins by declaring that, "when in the course of human events it becomes necessary for one people to dissolve the political bonds which have connected them with another, and to assume among the powers of the earth the separate and equal station to which the laws of nature and nature's God entitle them, a decent respect for the opinions of mankind requires that they should declare the causes which impel them to the separation."

It then proceeds to say: "We hold these truths to be self-evident: that all men are created equal; that they are endowed by their Creator with certain unalienable rights; that among them is life, liberty, and the pursuit of happiness; that to secure these rights, Governments are instituted, deriving their just powers from the consent of the governed."

The general words above quoted would seem to embrace the whole human family, and if they were used in a similar instrument at this day would be so understood. But it is too clear for dispute, that the enslaved African race were not intended to be included, and formed no part of the people who framed and adopted this declaration; for if the language, as understood in that day, would embrace them, the conduct of the distinguished men who framed the Declaration of Independence would have been utterly and flagrantly inconsistent with the principles they asserted; and instead of the sympathy of mankind, to which they so confidently appealed, they would have deserved and received universal rebuke and reprobation.

Yet the men who framed this declaration were great men — high in literary acquirements — high in their sense of honor, and incapable of asserting principles inconsistent with those on which they were acting. They perfectly understood the meaning of the language they used, and how it would be understood by others; and they knew that it would not in any part of the civilized world be supposed to embrace the Negro race, which, by common consent, had been excluded from civilized Governments and the family of nations, and doomed to slavery. They spoke and acted according to the then established doctrines and principles, and in the ordinary language of the day, and no one misunderstood them. The unhappy black race were separated from the white by indelible marks, and laws long before established, and were never thought of or spoken of except as property, and when the claims of the owner or the profit of the trader were supposed to need protection.

This state of public opinion had undergone no change when the Constitution was adopted, as is equally evident from its provisions and language.

The brief preamble sets forth by whom it was formed, for what purposes, and for whose benefit and protection. It declares that it is formed by the people of the United States: that is to say, by those who were members of the different political communities in the several States; and its great object is declared to be to secure the blessings of liberty to themselves and their posterity. It speaks in general terms of the people of the United States, and of citizens of the several States, when it is providing for the exercise of the powers granted or the privileges accrued to the citizen. It does not define what description of persons are intended to be included under these terms, or who shall be regarded as a citizen and one of the people. It uses them as terms so well understood, that no further description or definition was necessary.

But there are two clauses in the Constitution which point directly and specifically to the negro race as a separate class of persons, and show clearly that they were not regarded as a portion of the people or citizens of the Government then formed.

One of these clauses reserves to each of the thirteen States the right to import slaves until the year 1808, if it thinks proper. And the importation which it thus sanctions was unquestionably of persons of the race of which we are speaking, as the traffic in slaves in the United States had always been confined to them. And by the other provision the States pledge themselves to each other to maintain the right of property of the master, by delivering up to him any slave who may have escaped from his service, and be found within their respective territories.... [These] two provisions show, conclusively, that neither the description of persons therein referred to, nor their descendants, were embraced in any of the other provisions of the Constitution; for certainly these two clauses were not intended to confer on them or their posterity the blessings of liberty, or any of the personal rights so carefully provided for the citizen....

[The] rights of property are united with the rights of person, and placed on the same ground by the fifth amendment to the Constitution, which provides that no person shall be deprived of life, liberty, and property, without due process of law. And an act of Congress which deprives a citizen of the United States of his liberty or property, merely because he came himself or brought his property into a particular Territory of the United States, and who had committed no offence against the laws, could hardly be dignified with the name of due process of law....

[And] if the Constitution recognizes the right of property of the master in a slave, and makes no distinction between that description of property and other property owned by a citizen, no tribunal, acting under the authority of the United States, whether it be legislative, executive, or judicial, has a right to draw such a distinction, or deny to it the benefit of the provisions and guarantees which have been provided for the protection of private property against the encroachments of the Government.

Now, as we have already said in an earlier part of this opinion, upon a different point, the right of property in a slave is distinctly and expressly affirmed in the Constitution. The right to traffic in it, like an ordinary article of merchandise and property, was guarantied to the citizens of the United States, in every State that might desire it, for twenty years. And the Government in express terms is pledged to protect it in all future time, if the slave escapes from his owner. This is done in plain words— too plain to be misunderstood. And no word can be found in the Constitution which gives Congress a greater power over slave property, or which entitles property of that kind to less protection than property of any other description. The only power conferred is the power coupled with the duty of guarding and protecting the owner in his rights.

Upon these considerations, it is the opinion of the court that the act of Congress which prohibited a citizen from holding and owning property of this kind in the territory of the United States north of the line therein mentioned, is not warranted by the Constitution, and is therefore void; and that neither Dred Scott himself, nor any of his family, were made free by being carried into this territory....

[All nine justices wrote opinions in *Dred Scott*, although Justice Taney's opinion spoke for the Court. Only Justices McLean and Curtis dissented.]

## *Note: The Slavery Debate after* Dred Scott

1. *Dred Scott* is among the most heavily criticized decisions of the Supreme Court, not just for its pro-slavery sentiment but also for its aggressive reaching out to decide issues—such as the constitutionality of the Missouri Compromise, and, by extension, other federal laws limiting slavery in the territories—that may not have been strictly necessary to decide the case. *See, e.g., Planned Parenthood v. Casey* (1992) (Scalia, J., dissenting) [*Supra.* Chapter 9] (comparing the majority's attempt to conclusively resolve the abortion question with *Dred Scott*'s assertedly similar attempt to resolve the slavery question); *Washington v. Glucksberg* (1997) (Souter, J., concurring in the judgment) [*Supra.* Chapter 10] (explaining how his understanding of substantive due process avoided the mistake of the *Dred Scott* Court).

2. *Dred Scott*'s invalidation of the Missouri Compromise strongly suggested that slavery was constitutionally protected in all federal territories. As such, it opened up the prospect of decisively tilting the political balance in favor of slaveholding interests. Northern opinion coalesced around opposition to expansion of slavery into the territories. A new party, the Republican Party, had first competed in the election of 1856 on a platform opposing the expansion of slavery. By 1860, it had become a leading party in the North. When its candidate, Abraham Lincoln, was elected President in 1860, a chain of events was triggered that culminated in the secession of eleven southern states, leading to the Civil War.

3. In the early years of the War, President Lincoln insisted that the war was not about slavery, but about preserving the union. (Part of this impetus was the fact that much of the northern electorate still did not strongly oppose slavery where it already existed, and part of it was because several slave states remained loyal.) Nevertheless, as the war dragged on anti-slavery sentiment grew. By the end of the war it was clear that a union victory would mean the end of slavery.

# B. Equal Protection and Race before 1937

## Note: The Early Post-Slavery Decades

1. The Thirteenth Amendment was enacted by Congress in January, 1865, and ratified in December of that year. That Amendment banned slavery, and gave Congress the power to enforce that prohibition. The year after, Congress used that enforcement power to enact the Civil Rights Act of 1866. That law was designed to combat the so-called "Black Codes," which the new southern state governments had quickly enacted. Those laws severely restricted the civil rights of the newly freed slaves, prohibiting them from activities such as traveling freely on their own, purchasing or owning land, or serving as jurors. The Civil Rights Act provided, among other things, that all Americans enjoyed "the same right ... to make or enforce contracts ... [and] to full and equal benefit of all laws and proceedings for the security of person and property" "as white citizens." While the Republican-controlled Congress overrode President Andrew Johnson's veto and enacted the bill, influential Republicans expressed concern that the Thirteenth Amendment did not authorize the law. Work began immediately on what became the Fourteenth Amendment, which ultimately included the now-familiar guarantee that "No state shall ... deny to any person within its jurisdiction the equal protection of the laws." The Fourteenth Amendment included a congressional enforcement provision similar to the one that appears in the Thirteenth Amendment.

2. Much of the early post-war caselaw governing racial equality arose in the context of federal legislation enacted to enforce the Fourteenth Amendment. Much of that caselaw reflected the spirit of *The Slaughter-House Cases*, 83 U.S. 36 (1873) [Note *supra.* Part III Introduction] — that is, concern about reading the Fourteenth Amendment (or congressional enforcement power) so broadly as to upset the federal-state balance. For example, in *Blyew v. United States*, 80 U.S. 581 (1872), the Court gave a very narrow reading to a provision of the Civil Rights Act that read as follows:

> ... [The] District Courts of the United States ... shall have, exclusively of the courts of the several States, cognizance of all crimes and offences committed against the provisions of this act, and also concurrently with the Circuit Courts of the United States, of all causes, civil and criminal, affecting persons who are denied, or cannot enforce in the courts ... of the State ... any of the rights secured to them by the first section of [this] act.

The Court held that the class of "affected persons" did not include persons who would function solely as witnesses. The Court also held that this provision did not authorize removal of a racially based murder case with African-Americans as the victims, on the ground that the victims were not "affected persons," since they had been killed.

3. In contrast to such narrow interpretations, the Court was sometimes willing to enforce federal equality legislation more aggressively. For example, in *Strauder v. West Virginia*, 100 U.S. 303 (1879), the Court upheld application of federal enforcement legislation that called for the removal of a case from state to federal court whenever the state proceeding would deny the litigant a federally-granted civil right. *Strauder* dealt with a situation where an African-American was tried on a criminal charge in a state that excluded African-Americans from service on grand or petit juries. Indeed, in *Ex parte Virginia*, 100 U.S. 339 (1879), the Court upheld the federal detention of a state court judge who violated federal law by excluding African-Americans from a jury.

4. Despite these occasional victories, as Reconstruction drew to a close in the late 1870s the Court became less and less hospitable to civil rights claims, just as Congress had become far less interested in enacting enforcement legislation. Instead, as discussed in Chapters 7 and 11, respectively, the Court began using the Fourteenth Amendment's Due Process and Equal Protection clauses as tools to review state regulation of business and economic relationships. As newly freed slaves lost political power in the south, "redeemer" southern governments began rebuilding a system of racial caste and segregation — a process the Court validated in 1896.

## Plessy v. Ferguson
### 163 U.S. 537 (1896)

MR. JUSTICE BROWN, after stating the case, delivered the opinion of the Court.

This case turns upon the constitutionality of an act of the General Assembly of the States of Louisiana, passed in 1890, providing for separate railway carriages for the white and colored races....

The petition for the writ of prohibition averred that petitioner was seven-eighths Caucasian and one eighth African blood; that the mixture of colored blood was not discernible in him, and that he was entitled to every right, privilege and immunity secured to citizens of the United States of the white race; and that, upon such theory, he took possession of a vacant seat in a coach where passengers of the white race were accommodated, and was ordered by the conductor to vacate said coach and take a seat in another assigned to persons of the colored race, and having refused to comply with such demand he was forcibly ejected with the aid of a police officer, and imprisoned in the parish jail to answer a charge of having violated the above act.

The constitutionality of this act is attacked upon the ground that it conflicts both with the thirteenth amendment of the constitution, abolishing slavery, and the fourteenth amendment, which prohibits certain restrictive legislation on the part of the states.

1. That it does not conflict with the thirteenth amendment, which abolished slavery and involuntary servitude, except as a punishment for crime, is too clear for argument. Slavery implies involuntary servitude, — a state of bondage; the ownership of mankind

as a chattel, or, at least, the control of the labor and services of one man for the benefit of another, and the absence of a legal right to the disposal of his own person, property, and services....

A statute which implies merely a legal distinction between the white and colored races—a distinction which is founded in the color of the two races, and which must always exist so long as white men are distinguished from the other race by color—has no tendency to destroy the legal equality of the two races, or re-establish a state of involuntary servitude....

2. By the fourteenth amendment, all persons born or naturalized in the United States, and subject to the jurisdiction thereof, are made citizens of the United States and of the state wherein they reside; and the states are forbidden from making or enforcing any law which shall abridge the privileges or immunities of citizens of the United States, or shall deprive any person of life, liberty, or property without due process of law, or deny to any person within their jurisdiction the equal protection of the laws....

The object of the [Fourteenth] amendment was undoubtedly to enforce the absolute equality of the two races before the law, but in the nature of things it could not have been intended to abolish distinctions based upon color, or to enforce social, as distinguished from political equality, or a commingling of the two races upon terms unsatisfactory to either. Laws permitting, and even requiring, their separation in places where they are liable to be brought into contact do not necessarily imply the inferiority of either race to the other, and have been generally, if not universally, recognized as within the competency of the state legislatures in the exercise of their police power. The most common instance of this is connected with the establishment of separate schools for white and colored children, which has been held to be a valid exercise of the legislative power even by courts of States where the political rights of the colored races have been longest and most earnestly enforced.

One of the earliest of these cases is that of *Roberts v. City of Boston*, 5 Cush. 198 (1849), in which the Supreme Judicial Court of Massachusetts held that the general school committee of Boston had power to make provision for the instruction of colored children in separate schools established exclusively for them, and to prohibit their attendance upon the other schools.... Similar laws have been enacted by Congress under its general power of legislation over the District of Columbia, as well as by the legislatures of many of the States, and have been generally, if not uniformly, sustained by the courts.

Laws forbidding the intermarriage of the two races may be said in a technical sense to interfere with the freedom of contract, and yet have been universally recognized as within the police power of the State....

It is claimed by the plaintiff in error that, in any mixed community, the reputation of belonging to the dominant race, in this instance the white race, is *property*, in the same sense that a right of action, or of inheritance, is property. Conceding this to be so, for the purposes of this case, we are unable to see how this statute deprives him of, or in any way affects his right to, such property. If he be a white man and assigned to a colored coach, he may have his action for damages against the company for being deprived of his so called property. Upon the other hand, if he be a colored man and be so assigned, he has been deprived of no property, since he is not lawfully entitled to the reputation of being a white man.

In this connection, it is also suggested by the learned counsel for the plaintiff in error that the same argument that will justify the state legislature in requiring railways to provide separate accommodations for the two races will also authorize them to require separate cars to be provided for people whose hair is of a certain color, or who are aliens, or who belong to certain nationalities, or to enact laws requiring colored people to walk upon one side of the street, and white people upon the other, or requiring white men's houses to be painted white, and colored men's black, or their vehicles or business signs to be of different colors, upon the theory that one side of the street is as good as the other, or that a house or vehicle of one color is as good as one of another color. The reply to all this is that every exercise of the police power must be reasonable, and extend only to such laws as are enacted in good faith for the promotion for the public good, and not for the annoyance or oppression of a particular class....

So far, then, as a conflict with the Fourteenth Amendment is concerned, the case reduces itself to the question whether the statute of Louisiana is a reasonable regulation, and with respect to this there must necessarily be a large discretion on the part of the legislature. In determining the question of reasonableness it is at liberty to act with reference to the established usages, customs and traditions of the people, and with a view of the promotion of their comfort, and the preservation of the public peace and good order. Gauged by this standard, we cannot say that a law which authorizes or even requires the separation of the two races in public conveyances is unreasonable, or more obnoxious to the Fourteenth Amendment than the acts of Congress requiring separate schools for colored children in the District of Columbia, the constitutionality of which does not seem to have been questioned, or the corresponding acts of state legislatures.

We consider the underlying fallacy of the plaintiff's argument to consist in the assumption that the enforced separation of the two races stamps the colored race with a badge of inferiority. If this be so, it is not by reason of anything found in the act, but solely because the colored race chooses to put that construction upon it. The argument necessarily assumes that if, as has been more than once the case, and is not unlikely to be so again, the colored race should become the dominant power in the state legislature, and should enact a law in precisely similar terms, it would thereby relegate the white race to an inferior position. We imagine that the white race, at least, would not acquiesce in this assumption. The argument also assumes that social prejudices may be overcome by legislation, and that equal rights cannot be secured to the Negro except by an enforced commingling of the two races. We cannot accept this proposition. If the two races are to meet upon terms of social equality, it must be the result of natural affinities, a mutual appreciation of each other's merits and a voluntary consent of individuals.... Legislation is powerless to eradicate racial instincts or to abolish distinctions based upon physical differences, and the attempt to do so can only result in accentuating the difficulties of the present situation. If the civil and political rights of both races be equal one cannot be inferior to the other civilly or politically. If one race be inferior to the other socially, the Constitution of the United States cannot put them upon the same plane.

It is true that the question of the proportion of colored blood necessary to constitute a colored person, as distinguished from a white person, is one upon which there is a difference of opinion in the different States, some holding that any visible admixture of black blood stamps the person as belonging to the colored race, others that it depends upon the preponderance of blood, and still others that the predominance of white blood must only be in the proportion of three fourths. But those are questions to be determined under the laws of each State and are not properly put in issue in this case. Under the allegations of his petition it may undoubtedly become a question of importance whether, under the laws of Louisiana, the petitioner belongs to the white or colored race.

MR. JUSTICE BREWER did not hear the argument or participate in the decision of this case.

MR. JUSTICE HARLAN dissenting....

It was said in argument that the statute of Louisiana does not discriminate against either race, but prescribes a rule applicable alike to white and colored citizens. But this argument does not meet the difficulty. Every one knows that the statute in question had its origin in the purpose, not so much to exclude white persons from railroad cars occupied by blacks, as to exclude colored people from coaches occupied by or assigned to white persons. Railroad corporations of Louisiana did not make discrimination among whites in the matter of accommodation for travellers. The thing to accomplish was, under the guise of giving equal accommodation for whites and blacks, to compel the latter to keep to themselves while travelling in railroad passenger coaches. No one would be so wanting in candor as to assert the contrary. The fundamental objection, therefore, to the statute is that it interferes with the personal freedom of citizens. "Personal liberty," it has been well said, "consists in the power of locomotion, of changing situation, or removing one's person to whatsoever places one's own inclination may direct, without imprisonment or restraint, unless by due course of law." If a white man and a black man choose to occupy the same public conveyance on a public highway, it is their right to do so, and no government, proceeding alone on grounds of race, can prevent it without infringing the personal liberty of each....

The white race deems itself to be the dominant race in this country. And so it is, in prestige, in achievements, in education, in wealth and in power. So, I doubt not, it will continue to be for all time, if it remains true to its great heritage and holds fast to the principles of constitutional liberty. But in view of the Constitution, in the eye of the law, there is in this country no superior, dominant, ruling class of citizens. There is no caste here. Our Constitution is color-blind, and neither knows nor tolerates classes among citizens. In respect of civil rights, all citizens are equal before the law. The humblest is the peer of the most powerful. The law regards man as man, and takes no account of his surroundings or of his color when his civil rights as guaranteed by the supreme law of the land are involved. It is, therefore, to be regretted that this high tribunal, the final expositor of the fundamental law of the land, has reached the conclusion that it is competent for a State to regulate the enjoyment by citizens of their civil rights solely upon the basis of race.

In my opinion, the judgment this day rendered will, in time, prove to be quite as pernicious as the decision made by this tribunal in the *Dred Scott* case. It was adjudged in that case that the descendants of Africans who were imported into this country and sold as slaves were not included nor intended to be included under the word "citizens" in the Constitution, and could not claim any of the rights and privileges which that instrument provided for and secured to citizens of the United States; that at the time of the adoption of the Constitution they were "considered as a subordinate and inferior class of beings, who had been subjugated by the dominant race, and, whether emancipated or not, yet remained subject to their authority, and had no rights or privileges but such as those who held the power and the government might choose to grant them." The recent amendments of the constitution, it was supposed, had eradicated these principles from our institutions. But it seems that we have yet, in some of the states, a dominant race, — a superior class of citizens, — which assumes to regulate the enjoyment of civil rights, common to all citizens, upon the basis of race.... Sixty millions of whites are in no danger from the presence here of eight millions of blacks. The destinies of the two races, in this country, are indissolubly linked together, and the interests of both require that the common government of all shall not permit the seeds of race hate to be planted under the sanction of law. What can more certainly arouse race hate, what more certainly create and perpetuate a feeling of distrust between these races, than state enactments, which, in fact, proceed on the ground that colored citizens are so inferior and degraded that they cannot be allowed to sit in public coaches occupied by white citizens? That, as all will admit, is the real meaning of such legislation as was enacted in Louisiana....

There is a race so different from our own that we do not permit those belonging to it to become citizens of the United States. Persons belonging to it are, with few exceptions, absolutely excluded from our country. I allude to the Chinese race. But by the statute in question, a Chinaman can ride in the same passenger coach with white citizens of the United States, while citizens of the black race in Louisiana, many of whom, perhaps, risked their lives for the preservation of the Union, who are entitled, by law, to participate in the political control of the State and nation, who are not excluded, by law or by reason of their race, from public stations of any kind, and who have all the legal rights that belong to white citizens, are yet declared to be criminals, liable to imprisonment, if they ride in a public coach occupied by citizens of the white race. It is scarcely just to say that a colored citizen should not object to occupying a public coach assigned to his own race. He does not object, nor, perhaps, would he object to separate coaches for his race, if his rights under the law were recognized. But he objects, and ought never to cease objecting to the proposition, that citizens of the white and black races can be adjudged criminals because they sit, or claim the right to sit, in the same public coach on a public highway.

The arbitrary separation of citizens, on the basis of race, while they are on a public highway, is a badge of servitude wholly inconsistent with the civil freedom and the equality before the law established by the Constitution. It cannot be justified upon any legal grounds.

If evils will result from the commingling of the two races upon public highways established for the benefit of all, they will be infinitely less than those that will surely come from state legislation regulating the enjoyment of civil rights upon the basis of race. We boast of the freedom enjoyed by our people above all other peoples. But it is difficult to reconcile that boast with a state of the law which, practically puts the brand of servitude and degradation upon a large class of our fellow-citizens, our equals before the law. The thin disguise of "equal" accommodations for passengers in railroad coaches will not mislead any one, nor atone for the wrong this day done....

### *Note: Separate but Equal before* Brown

1. *Plessy* placed the Supreme Court's stamp of approval on what eventually became known as "separate but equal" or "Jim Crow" (the name given to the entire regime of segregated facilities and services). To be sure, as *Plessy* noted, northern courts had often upheld racial segregation in schools. More significantly, the Thirty-Ninth Congress (which enacted the Fourteenth Amendment) provided for segregated education in District of Columbia schools. And even the Court itself had previously approved of racial segregation statutes, most notably the practice of punishing illicit sexual relations more severely when the persons involved were of different races. *Pace v. Alabama*, 106 U.S. 583 (1883). Nevertheless, *Plessy*'s approval of forced segregation of railroad cars helped cement a regime of statutes segregating many—sometimes essentially all—aspects of public life, from transportation to bathrooms to theaters and other public amusements. Indeed, statutes were enacted providing that court witnesses be sworn in on different Bibles, depending on the race of the witness.

2. It was only on rare occasions that the Court—and courts more generally—took seriously the "equal" part of "separate but equal." One such rare example was in *McCabe v. Atchison, Topeka & Santa Fe RR*, 235 U.S. 151 (1914). In *McCabe* several black plaintiffs challenged Oklahoma's separate but equal law governing rail transport, as applied to the availability of luxury rail accommodations. The railroad argued that it should not have to provide such accommodations to blacks, given the extremely low demand for that service. The Court did not formally reach the merits of the case because of a procedural flaw. However, five Justices suggested in *dicta* that the plaintiffs did have a right to demand such service, because their Fourteenth Amendment rights to equal (if separate) accommodations were "personal" rights.

Despite such rare suggestions that the "equal" part of "separate but equal" really meant something, as a practical matter the segregated facilities provided blacks were significantly inferior to those provided whites. Throughout the period of Jim Crow, for example, black schoolchildren received on a per capita basis far less education funding than their white counterparts.

3. Separate but equal remained firmly in place for the first third of the Twentieth century. In 1927, for example, the Court was able to remark casually that the legal status of segregated education had been "many times decided" in favor of its constitutionality. *Gong Lum v. Rice*, 275 U.S. 78 (1927). Starting in the 1930s, however, the National Association for the Advancement of Colored People (NAACP) began to challenge educational segregation. In *Missouri ex rel. Gaines v. Canada*, 305 U.S. 337 (1938), the Court invalidated Missouri's practice (replicated in other southern and border states) of not providing graduate and professional schools for blacks but instead paying tuition for black graduate students to attend school out of state. Seven justices of the Court, speaking through Chief Justice Hughes, reasoned that if Missouri provided white students with a graduate school opportunity, it had to afford an equal opportunity to black students. Citing *McCabe*, it rejected the state's argument that the small black student demand for such education justified its failure to establish graduate schools open to black students.

*Gaines* reflected the thinking of the leadership of the NAACP, in particular, Charles Hamilton Houston and Thurgood Marshall, that graduate school-student claims would force states to integrate, given the financial impossibility of establishing graduate schools solely for the small number of black students who in the 1930s would be qualified to enroll. After World War II, the NAACP continued to press for graduate program education, winning victories in *Sipuel v. Board of Regents*, 332 U.S. 631 (1948) (Oklahoma's failure to provide black students with a legal education); *Sweatt v. Painter*, 339 U.S. 629 (1950) (Texas's failure to provide black students with a legal education); and *McLaurin v. Oklahoma*, 339 U.S. 637 (1950).

*McLaurin* is noteworthy because Oklahoma allowed the black student (pursuing a doctorate in education) to attend the university whites attended, but segregated him by, among other things, assigning him a particular desk in the library and seat in the cafeteria, and forcing him to sit outside the door of the classrooms where his classes were taught. Citing, among cases, *Sweatt* (which was decided the same day), the Court held that those conditions deprived him of the opportunity to an equal education.

4. These postwar victories suggested that primary and secondary school segregation might also be constitutionally vulnerable. Nevertheless, obstacles remained. In particular, the post-graduate cases rested on factors that might not translate easily into claims that segregated childhood education was similarly unequal. Most notably, in *Sweatt* the Court had rejected Texas's argument that the black law school it established was equal to the University of Texas Law School to which Herman Sweatt sought admission, observing that the latter school—the state's flagship institution—provided both tangible and intangible benefits that the new school for black law students did not. Moreover, as pressure for racial equality mounted after 1945, southern states had embarked on tentative steps toward equalizing funding of black and white schools, or at least mitigating the worst inequalities.

5. At the same time, the Court was changing. Reflecting the nation's World War II commitment to destroying an explicitly racist Nazi regime, the Justices had gone

on record as insisting that racial discrimination was presumptively unconstitutional when it impaired persons' civil rights. Ironically, it made that commitment in the context of an opinion that upheld the internment of Japanese-Americans during World War II. Also, recall from Chapter 12's note on the Court's race jurisprudence during this era that the Court soon equivocated on that statement. Nevertheless, it was clear that the Court was rethinking its attitude toward racial discrimination.

# C. Dismantling Jim Crow

## 1. The Run-Up to *Brown*

### Korematsu v. United States

323 U.S. 214 (1944)

MR. JUSTICE BLACK delivered the opinion of the Court.

The petitioner, an American citizen of Japanese descent, was convicted in a federal district court for remaining in San Leandro, California, a Military Area, contrary to Civilian Exclusion Order No. 34 of the Commanding General of the Western Command, U.S. Army, which directed that after May 9, 1942, all persons of Japanese ancestry should be excluded from that area. No question was raised as to petitioner's loyalty to the United States. The Circuit Court of Appeals affirmed, and the importance of the constitutional question involved caused us to grant certiorari.

It should be noted, to begin with, that all legal restrictions which curtail the civil rights of a single racial group are immediately suspect. That is not to say that all such restrictions are unconstitutional. It is to say that courts must subject them to the most rigid scrutiny. Pressing public necessity may sometimes justify the existence of such restrictions; racial antagonism never can....

It is said that we are dealing here with the case of imprisonment of a citizen in a concentration camp solely because of his ancestry, without evidence or inquiry concerning his loyalty and good disposition towards the United States. Our task would be simple, our duty clear, were this a case involving the imprisonment of a loyal citizen in a concentration camp because of racial prejudice. Regardless of the true nature of the assembly and relocation centers—and we deem it unjustifiable to call them concentration camps with all the ugly connotations that term implies—we are dealing specifically with nothing but an exclusion order. To cast this case into outlines of racial prejudice, without reference to the real military dangers which were presented, merely confuses the issue. Korematsu was not excluded from the Military Area because of hostility to him or his race. He *was* excluded because we are at war with the Japanese Empire, because the properly constituted military authorities feared an invasion of our West Coast and felt constrained to take proper security measures, because they decided that the military urgency of the situation demanded that all citizens of Japanese ancestry be segregated from the West Coast temporarily, and finally, because Congress, reposing its confidence in this time of war in our military leader—as inevitably it must — determined that they should have the power to do just this. There was evidence of disloyalty on the part of some, the military authorities considered that the need for action was great, and time was short. We cannot — by availing ourselves of the calm perspective of hindsight — now say that at that time these actions were unjustified.

MR. JUSTICE FRANKFURTER, concurring. [omitted]

MR. JUSTICE ROBERTS, dissenting. [omitted]

MR. JUSTICE MURPHY, dissenting.

This exclusion of "all persons of Japanese ancestry, both alien and non-alien," from the Pacific Coast area on a plea of military necessity in the absence of martial law ought not to be approved. Such exclusion goes over "the very brink of constitutional power" and falls into the ugly abyss of racism.

In dealing with matters relating to the prosecution and progress of a war, we must accord great respect and consideration to the judgments of the military authorities who are on the scene and who have full knowledge of the military facts. The scope of their discretion must, as a matter of necessity and common sense, be wide. And their judgments ought not to be overruled lightly by those whose training and duties ill-equip them to deal intelligently with matters so vital to the physical security of the nation.

At the same time, however, it is essential that there be definite limits to military discretion, especially where martial law has not been declared. Individuals must not be left impoverished of their constitutional rights on a plea of military necessity that has neither substance nor military support. Thus, like other claims conflicting with the asserted constitutional rights of the individual, the military claim must subject itself to the judicial process of having its reasonableness determined and its conflicts with other interests reconciled. . . .

The judicial test of whether the Government, on a plea of military necessity, can validly deprive an individual of any of his constitutional rights is whether the deprivation is reasonably related to a public danger that is so "immediate, imminent, and impending" as not to admit of delay and not to permit the intervention of ordinary constitutional processes to alleviate the danger. Civilian Exclusion Order No. 34, banishing from a prescribed area of the Pacific Coast "all persons of Japanese ancestry, both alien and non-alien," clearly does not meet that test. Being an obvious racial discrimination, the order deprives all those within its scope of the equal protection of the laws as guaranteed by the Fifth Amendment. It further deprives these individuals of their constitutional rights to live and work where they will, to establish a home where they choose and to move about freely. In excommunicating them without benefit of hearings, this order also deprives them of all their constitutional rights to procedural due process. Yet no reasonable relation to an 'immediate, imminent, and impending' public danger is evident to support this racial restriction which is one of the most sweeping and complete deprivations of constitutional rights in the history of this nation in the absence of martial law.

It must be conceded that the military and naval situation in the spring of 1942 was such as to generate a very real fear of invasion of the Pacific Coast, accompanied by fears of sabotage and espionage in that area.... In adjudging the military action taken in light of the then apparent dangers, we must not erect too high or too meticulous standards; it is necessary only that the action have some reasonable relation to the removal of the dangers of invasion, sabotage and espionage. But the exclusion, either temporarily or permanently, of all persons with Japanese blood in their veins has no such reasonable relation. And that relation is lacking because the exclusion order necessarily must rely for its reasonableness upon the assumption that *all* persons of Japanese ancestry may have a dangerous tendency to commit sabotage and espionage and to aid our Japanese enemy in other ways. It is difficult to believe that reason, logic or experience could be marshalled in support of such an assumption....

Justification for the exclusion is sought ... upon questionable racial and sociological grounds not ordinarily within the realm of expert military judgment, supplemented by certain semi-military conclusions drawn from an unwarranted use of circumstantial evidence. Individuals of Japanese ancestry are condemned because they are said to be "a large, unassimilated, tightly knit racial group, bound to an enemy nation by strong ties of race, culture, custom and religion."[4] They are claimed to be given to "emperor worshipping ceremonies" and to "dual citizenship." Japanese language schools and allegedly pro-Japanese organizations are cited as evidence of possible group disloyalty, together with facts as to certain persons being educated and residing at length in Japan. It is intimated that many of these individuals deliberately resided "adjacent to strategic points," thus enabling them "to carry into execution a tremendous program of sabotage on a mass scale should any considerable number of them have been inclined to do so." The need for protective custody is also asserted. The report refers without identity to "numerous incidents of violence" as well as to other admittedly unverified or cumulative incidents. From this, plus certain other events not shown to have been connected with the Japanese Americans, it is concluded that the "situation was fraught with danger to the Japanese population itself" and that the general public "was ready to take matters into its own hands." Finally, it is intimated, though not directly charged or proved, that persons of Japanese ancestry were responsible for three minor isolated shelling and bombings of the Pacific Coast area, as well as for unidentified radio transmissions and night signalling.

The main reasons relied upon by those responsible for the forced evacuation, therefore, do not prove a reasonable relation between the group characteristics of Japanese Americans and the dangers of invasion, sabotage and espionage. The reasons appear, instead, to be largely an accumulation of much of the misinformation, half-truths and insinuations that for years have been directed against Japanese Americans by people with racial and economic prejudices—the same people who have been among

---

4. To the extent that assimilation is a problem, it is largely the result of certain social customs and laws of the American general public. Studies demonstrate that persons of Japanese descent are readily susceptible to integration in our society if given the opportunity. The failure to accomplish an ideal status of assimilation, therefore, cannot be charged to the refusal of these persons to become Americanized or to their loyalty to Japan.

the foremost advocates of the evacuation.[12] A military judgment based upon such racial and sociological considerations is not entitled to the great weight ordinarily given the judgments based upon strictly military considerations. Especially is this so when every charge relative to race, religion, culture, geographical location, and legal and economic status has been substantially discredited by independent studies made by experts in these matters.

The military necessity which is essential to the validity of the evacuation order thus resolves itself into a few intimations that certain individuals actively aided the enemy, from which it is inferred that the entire group of Japanese Americans could not be trusted to be or remain loyal to the United States. No one denies, of course, that there were some disloyal persons of Japanese descent on the Pacific Coast who did all in their power to aid their ancestral land. Similar disloyal activities have been engaged in by many persons of German, Italian and even more pioneer stock in our country. But to infer that examples of individual disloyalty prove group disloyalty and justify discriminatory action against the entire group is to deny that under our system of law individual guilt is the sole basis for deprivation of rights. Moreover, this inference, which is at the very heart of the evacuation orders, has been used in support of the abhorrent and despicable treatment of minority groups by the dictatorial tyrannies which this nation is now pledged to destroy. To give constitutional sanction to that inference in this case, however well-intentioned may have been the military command on the Pacific Coast, is to adopt one of the cruelest of the rationales used by our enemies to destroy the dignity of the individual and to encourage and open the door to discriminatory actions against other minority groups in the passions of tomorrow....

I dissent, therefore, from this legalization of racism. Racial discrimination in any form and in any degree has no justifiable part whatever in our democratic way of life. It is unattractive in any setting but it is utterly revolting among a free people who have embraced the principles set forth in the Constitution of the United States. All residents of this nation are kin in some way by blood or culture to a foreign land. Yet they are primarily and necessarily a part of the new and distinct civilization of the United States. They must accordingly be treated at all times as the heirs of the American experiment and as entitled to all the rights and freedoms guaranteed by the Constitution.

---

12. Special interest groups were extremely active in applying pressure for mass evacuation. Mr. Austin E. Anson, managing secretary of the Salinas Vegetable Grower-Shipper Association, has frankly admitted that "We're charged with wanting to get rid of the Japs for selfish reasons. * * * We do. It's a question of whether the white man lives on the Pacific Coast or the brown men. They came into this valley to work, and they stayed to take over. * * * They undersell the white man in the markets. * * * They work their women and children while the white farmer has to pay wages for his help,. If all the Japs were removed tomorrow, we'd never miss them in two weeks, because the white farmers can take over and produce everything the Jap grows. And we don't want them back when the war ends, either." Quoted by Taylor in his article 'The People Nobody Wants,' 214 *Sat. Eve. Post* 24 (May 9, 1942).

MR. JUSTICE JACKSON, dissenting....

Much is said of the danger to liberty from the Army program for deporting and detaining these citizens of Japanese extraction. But a judicial construction of the due process clause that will sustain this order is a far more subtle blow to liberty than the promulgation of the order itself. A military order, however unconstitutional, is not apt to last longer than the military emergency.... But once a judicial opinion rationalizes such an order to show that it conforms to the Constitution, or rather rationalizes the Constitution to show that the Constitution sanctions such an order, the Court for all time has validated the principle of racial discrimination in criminal procedure and of transplanting American citizens. The principle then lies about like a loaded weapon ready for the hand of any authority that can bring forward a plausible claim of an urgent need. Every repetition imbeds that principle more deeply in our law and thinking and expands it to new purposes. All who observe the work of courts are familiar with what Judge Cardozo described as "the tendency of a principle to expand itself to the limit of its logic." A military commander may overstep the bounds of constitutionality, and it is an incident. But if we review and approve, that passing incident becomes the doctrine of the Constitution. There it has a generative power of its own, and all that it creates will be in its own image. Nothing better illustrates this danger than does the Court's opinion in this case....

I should hold that a civil court cannot be made to enforce an order which violates constitutional limitations even if it is a reasonable exercise of military authority. The courts can exercise only the judicial power, can apply only law, and must abide by the Constitution, or they cease to be civil courts and become instruments of military policy.

Of course the existence of a military power resting on force, so vagrant, so centralized, so necessarily heedless of the individual, is an inherent threat to liberty. But I would not lead people to rely on this Court for a review that seems to me wholly delusive. The military reasonableness of these orders can only be determined by military superiors. If the people ever let command of the war power fall into irresponsible and unscrupulous hands, the courts wield no power equal to its restraint. The chief restraint upon those who command the physical forces of the country, in the future as in the past, must be their responsibility to the political judgments of their contemporaries and to the moral judgments of history.

My duties as a justice as I see them do not require me to make a military judgment as to whether General DeWitt's evacuation and detention program was a reasonable military necessity. I do not suggest that the courts should have attempted to interfere with the Army in carrying out its task. But I do not think they may be asked to execute a military expedient that has no place in law under the Constitution. I would reverse the judgment and discharge the prisoner.

## Note: The Political and Social Backdrop to Brown

1. The NAACP's victories in the graduate school cases of the late 1940s, when combined with *Korematsu's* strong rhetorical commitment to racial equality, provided

a seemingly attractive foundation for the attack on primary and secondary school segregation. At the same time, larger political and cultural forces were moving in the same direction. President Truman had desegregated the armed forces in 1948. A year before, Jackie Robinson became the first black major league baseball player when he started for the Brooklyn Dodgers. More broadly, during the 1930s and especially after the start of World War II, eugenics theories purporting to show racial differences in intelligence and morality fell into scientific and public disrepute.

The world scene also appeared favorable to a ruling against segregation. With the onset of the Cold War and the start of European decolonization came an intense competition between the United States and the Soviet Union for influence in what became known as the Third World. American diplomats often fretted that official government segregation was hindering their efforts to win the battle. Indeed, the State Department submitted an *amicus* brief in *Brown* urging the Court to strike down segregation exactly for this reason.

2. This is not to say that by the end of World War II the nation had reached a consensus rejecting segregation. Separate-but-equal remained firmly entrenched in southern and border states. In 1948 segregationist Democrats broke off from the national party and ran their own presidential candidate, South Carolina governor Strom Thurmond. His party—informally known as the "Dixiecrats"—won nearly 1.2 million votes and carried four states.

3. The Court originally heard the cases consolidated in *Brown* in the 1952–53 term. The historical record of the Justices' deliberations suggests that they were severely divided on the outcome, with one prominent historian suggesting that there were four votes to strike down the segregation, two votes to uphold it, and three Justices who were ambivalent. *See* Michael Klarman, *From Jim Crow to Civil Rights* 298 (2004). Justice Felix Frankfurter apparently suggested that the Court set the cases over for reargument on the question of the original meaning of the Fourteenth Amendment. Soon thereafter, Chief Justice Fred Vinson (who Professor Klarman suggests would have reaffirmed *Plessy*) died, and was replaced by Earl Warren, who took his seat in time for the reargument.

## 2. *Brown* and Its Implementation

### Brown v. Board of Education ("Brown I")

347 U.S. 483 (1954)

MR. CHIEF JUSTICE WARREN delivered the opinion of the Court.

These cases come to us from the States of Kansas, South Carolina, Virginia, and Delaware. They are premised on different facts and different local conditions, but a common legal question justifies their consideration together in this consolidated opinion.

In each of the cases, minors of the Negro race, through their legal representatives, seek the aid of the courts in obtaining admission to the public schools of their community on a nonsegregated basis. In each instance, they had been denied admission to schools attended by white children under laws requiring or permitting segregation according to race. This segregation was alleged to deprive the plaintiffs of the equal protection of the laws under the Fourteenth Amendment. In each of the cases other than the Delaware case, a three-judge federal district court denied relief to the plaintiffs on the so-called "separate but equal" doctrine announced by this Court in *Plessy v. Ferguson* (1896) [*Supra.* this chapter]. Under that doctrine, equality of treatment is accorded when the races are provided substantially equal facilities, even though these facilities be separate. In the Delaware case, the Supreme Court of Delaware adhered to that doctrine, but ordered that the plaintiffs be admitted to the white schools because of their superiority to the Negro schools.

The plaintiffs contend that segregated public schools are not "equal" and cannot be made "equal," and that hence they are deprived of the equal protection of the laws. Because of the obvious importance of the question presented, the Court took jurisdiction. Argument was heard in the 1952 Term, and reargument was heard this Term on certain questions propounded by the Court.

Reargument was largely devoted to the circumstances surrounding the adoption of the Fourteenth Amendment in 1868. It covered exhaustively consideration of the Amendment in Congress, ratification by the states, then existing practices in racial segregation, and the views of proponents and opponents of the Amendment. This discussion and our own investigation convince us that, although these sources cast some light, it is not enough to resolve the problem with which we are faced. At best, they are inconclusive. The most avid proponents of the post-War Amendments undoubtedly intended them to remove all legal distinctions among "all persons born or naturalized in the United States." Their opponents, just as certainly, were antagonistic to both the letter and the spirit of the Amendments and wished them to have the most limited effect. What others in Congress and the state legislatures had in mind cannot be determined with any degree of certainly.

An additional reason for the inconclusive nature of the Amendment's history, with respect to segregated sensors, is the status of public education at that time. In the South, the movement toward free common schools, supported by general taxation, had not yet taken hold. Education of white children was largely in the hands of private groups. Education of Negroes was almost non-existent, and practically all of the race were illiterate. In fact, any education of Negroes was forbidden by law in some states. Today, in contrast, many Negroes have achieved outstanding success in the arts and sciences as well as in the business and professional world. It is true that public school education at the time of the Amendment had advanced further in the North, but the effect of the Amendment on Northern States was generally ignored in the congressional debates. Even in the North, the conditions of public education did not approximate those existing today. The curriculum was usually rudimentary; ungraded schools were common in rural areas; the school term was but three months a year in many states; and compulsory school attendance was virtually unknown. As a consequence, it is not surprising that there should be so little in the history of the Fourteenth Amendment relating to its intended effect on public education....

In approaching this problem, we cannot turn the clock back to 1868 when the Amendment was adopted, or even to 1896 when *Plessy v. Ferguson* was written. We must consider public education in the light of its full development and its present place in American life throughout the Nation. Only in this way can it be determined if segregation in public schools deprives these plaintiffs of the equal protection of the laws.

Today, education is perhaps the most important function of state and local governments. Compulsory school attendance laws and the great expenditures for education both demonstrate our recognition of the importance of education to our democratic society. It is required in the performance of our most basic public responsibilities, even service in the armed forces. It is the very foundation of good citizenship. Today it is a principal instrument in awakening the child to cultural values, in preparing him for later professional training, and in helping him to adjust normally to his environment. In these days, it is doubtful that any child may reasonably be expected to succeed in life if he is denied the opportunity of an education. Such an opportunity, where the state has undertaken to provide it, is a right which must be made available to all on equal terms.

We come then to the question presented: Does segregation of children in public schools solely on the basis of race, even though the physical facilities and other "tangible" factors may be equal, deprive the children of the minority group of equal educational opportunities? We believe that it does. In *Sweatt v. Painter*, 339 U.S. 629 (1950) [Note *supra.* this chapter], in finding that a segregated law school for Negroes could not provide them equal educational opportunities, this Court relied in large part on 'those qualities which are incapable of objective measurement but which make for greatness in a law school.'... Such considerations apply with added force to children in grade and high schools. To separate them from others of similar age and qualifications solely because of their race generates a feeling of inferiority as to their status in the community that may affect their hearts and minds in a way unlikely ever to be undone. The effect of this separation on their educational opportunities was well stated by a finding in the Kansas case by a court which nevertheless felt compelled to rule against the Negro plaintiffs:

> Segregation of white and colored children in public schools has a detrimental effect upon the colored children. The impact is greater when it has the sanction of the law; for the policy of separating the races is usually interpreted as denoting the inferiority of the Negro group. A sense of inferiority affects the motivation of a child to learn. Segregation with the sanction of law, therefore, has a tendency to [retard] the educational and mental development of negro children and to deprive them of some of the benefits they would receive in a racially integrated school system.

Whatever may have been the extent of psychological knowledge at the time of *Plessy v. Ferguson*, this finding is amply supported by modern authority.[11] Any language in *Plessy v. Ferguson* contrary to this finding is rejected.

We conclude that in the field of public education the doctrine of "separate but equal" has no place. Separate educational facilities are inherently unequal. Therefore, we hold that the plaintiffs and others similarly situated for whom the actions have been brought are, by reason of the segregation complained of, deprived of the equal protection of the laws guaranteed by the Fourteenth Amendment. This disposition makes unnecessary any discussion whether such segregation also violates the Due Process Clause of the Fourteenth Amendment.

Because these are class actions, because of the wide applicability of this decision, and because of the great variety of local conditions, the formulation of decrees in these cases presents problems of considerable complexity. On reargument, the consideration of appropriate relief was necessarily subordinated to the primary question—the constitutionality of segregation in public education. We have now announced that such segregation is a denial of the equal protection of the laws. In order that we may have the full assistance of the parties in formulating decrees, the cases will be restored to the docket, and the parties are requested to present further argument on Questions 4 and 5 previously propounded by the Court for the reargument this Term.[*] The Attorney General of the United States is again invited to participate. The Attorneys General of the states requiring or permitting segregation in public education will also be permitted to appear as *amici curiae* upon request to do so by September 15, 1954, and submission of briefs by October 1, 1954.

## Bolling v. Sharpe

### 347 U.S. 497 (1954)

MR. CHIEF JUSTICE WARREN delivered the opinion of the Court.

This case challenges the validity of segregation in the public schools of the District of Columbia.... We have this day held that the Equal Protection Clause of the Fourteenth Amendment prohibits the states from maintaining racially segregated public schools. The legal problem in the District of Columbia is somewhat different, however. The Fifth Amendment, which is applicable in the District of Columbia, does not contain an equal protection clause as does the Fourteenth Amendment which applies only to the states. But the concepts of equal protection and due process, both stem-

---

11. K. B. Clark, *Effect of Prejudice and Discrimination on Personality Development* (Midcentury White House Conference on Children and Youth, 1950); Witmer and Kotinsky, *Personality in the Making* (1952), c. VI; Deutscher and Chein, "The Psychological Effects of Enforced Segregation: A Survey of Social Science Opinion," 26 *J.Psychol.* 259 (1948); Chein, "What are the Psychological Effects of Segregation Under Conditions of Equal Facilities?," 3 *Int. J. Opinion and Attitude Res.* 229 (1949); Brameld, "Educational Costs," in *Discrimination and National Welfare* (MacIver, ed., 1949), 44–48; Frazier, *The Negro in the United States* (1949), 674–681. And see generally Myrdal, *An American Dilemma* (1944).

* [Ed. Note: See footnote 2 of the next excerpted case for these questions.]

ming from our American ideal of fairness, are not mutually exclusive. The "equal protection of the laws" is a more explicit safeguard of prohibited unfairness than "due process of law," and, therefore, we do not imply that the two are always interchangeable phrases. But, as this Court has recognized, discrimination may be so unjustifiable as to be violative of due process.

Classifications based solely upon race must be scrutinized with particular care, since they are contrary to our traditions and hence constitutionally suspect.[3] As long ago as 1896, this Court declared the principle "that the Constitution of the United States, in its present form, forbids, so far as civil and political rights are concerned, discrimination by the General Government, or by the States, against any citizen because of his race." And in *Buchanan v. Warley*, 245 U.S. 60 (1917), the Court held that a statute which limited the right of a property owner to convey his property to a person of another race was, as an unreasonable discrimination, a denial of due process of law.

Although the Court has not assumed to define "liberty" with any great precision, that term is not confined to mere freedom from bodily restraint. Liberty under law extends to the full range of conduct which the individual is free to pursue, and it cannot be restricted except for a proper governmental objective. Segregation in public education is not reasonably related to any proper governmental objective, and thus it imposes on Negro children of the District of Columbia a burden that constitutes an arbitrary deprivation of their liberty in violation of the Due Process Clause.

In view of our decision that the Constitution prohibits the states from maintaining racially segregated public schools, it would be unthinkable that the same Constitution would impose a lesser duty on the Federal Government. We hold that racial segregation in the public schools of the District of Columbia is a denial of the due process of law guaranteed by the Fifth Amendment to the Constitution....

## *Note:* Brown v. Board of Education

1. The decision in *Brown* is thought to be one of the most significant in the history of the Supreme Court. But it is short. (The excerpt this book reprints includes over 80% of the Court's full opinion.) Are you surprised by its terseness? In particular, what do you make of the opinion's focus on the importance of education, and the absence of any assertion (let alone justification for) a general rule against racial segregation? As you'll see in the next sub-section, the Court eventually cited *Brown* for the proposition that racial segregation more generally is unconstitutional. But *Brown* itself did not take that step, even though cases like *Korematsu* could have been cited to support that rule. Does *Brown*'s focus on education detract from the impact the opinion could otherwise have had? Based on what you've read already, do you think there might have been a reason for Chief Justice Warren to have written the opinion the way he did?

2. *Brown* remains relevant for jurisprudential debates today. As you'll see in the last case in this chapter, *Parents Involved in Community Schools v. Seattle School District*

---

3. *Korematsu v. United States* (1944) [*Supra.* this chapter].

*No.1*, 551 U.S. 701 (2007), the justices continue today to debate what *Brown* "really meant." The debate in *Parents Involved* centered on the constitutionality of race-conscious government action that was defended as benign, and, indeed, as a remedy for past racial segregation. After this chapter considers the implementation of *Brown* and *Brown*'s immediate implications, the rest of this chapter will consider claims that such race consciousness violates the Fourteenth Amendment. *Brown* will cast a long shadow on that debate.

3. *Brown* also matters for legal theory. It is commonly assumed that no Supreme Court nominee could be confirmed today if she expressed doubts about *Brown*'s correctness. It is also often said that no theory of constitutional interpretation is legitimate if application of that theory would cast similar doubt. But today an important interpretive theory, called "originalism," stands in some tension, if not with the result in *Brown* than at least with the approach Chief Justice Warren took. Recall that Chief Justice Warren wrote that "we cannot turn the clock back to 1868 when the [Fourteenth] Amendment was adopted." He said that for a reason: recall that the Court ordered reargument in *Brown* in order to consider the original understanding of the Fourteenth Amendment as it related to public education. The difficulty is that the same Congress that drafted and passed the Fourteenth Amendment and sent it to the states for ratification also provided for segregated schools in the District of Columbia. (That *federal* segregation was struck down in *Bolling v. Sharpe*, excerpted above.) Congress's provision for segregated education even while enacting the Fourteenth Amendment raises serious concerns that a theory such as originalism, which seeks to interpret the Constitution according to the original understanding of a given provision, would necessarily lead a judge to vote the other way in a case like *Brown*. To be sure, prominent originalists contest this understanding of this history. *See, e.g.*, Michael McConnell, "Originalism and the Segregation Decision," 81 *Va. L. Rev.* 347 (1995). Regardless of who is correct on this question, the larger point is that *Brown*'s importance spans practicalities for American public education, the constitutionality of race conscious government action more generally, and American constitutional theory.

4. *Brown*'s methodology is also controversial. Footnote 11, reprinted in the excerpt above, refers to what the opinion describes as "modern" "psychological knowledge" about the effects of segregation on black schoolchildren. The most famous of the studies Footnote 11 referenced, "the doll study," involved giving young black children a black doll and a white doll, and asking them which doll they preferred: the researchers found black children preferred the white doll. Some scholars and judges have critiqued the Court's reliance on such psychological theory as inappropriate for a court. Indeed, some have critiqued the studies themselves as methodologically flawed. What do you think about the Court's reliance on such information?

5. *Bolling*, decided the same day as *Brown*, attracts somewhat less attention. But it raises problems of its own. Recall that there is no equal protection clause binding on the federal government; thus, the Court had to employ the Due Process Clause of the Fifth Amendment to strike down segregation in District of Columbia schools.

Ironically, it was only in *Bolling* that the Court cited *Korematsu* and its presumptive rule against race classifications. But note that the Court had to cast that statement in the context of deprivations of rights—after all, the Due Process Clause is generally understood as a protection for rights, not a general guarantee of equality, like the Equal Protection Clause. Does the Court persuasively argue why school segregation violates due process? Regardless of your answer to that question, consider the pressure the Court was under in *Bolling*: if the *United States* Supreme Court was going to require *states* to abandon school segregation, could it have done anything less with regard to the federal government's *own* schools? Can you find a hint of this imperative in *Bolling*?

# Brown v. Board of Education ("Brown II")

### 349 U.S. 294 (1955)

MR. CHIEF JUSTICE WARREN delivered the opinion of the Court.

These cases were decided on May 17, 1954. The opinions of that date, declaring the fundamental principle that racial discrimination in public education is unconstitutional, are incorporated herein by reference. All provisions of federal, state, or local law requiring or permitting such discrimination must yield to this principle. There remains for consideration the manner in which relief is to be accorded. Because these cases arose under different local conditions and their disposition will involve a variety of local problems, we requested further argument on the question of relief.[2] ...

Full implementation of these constitutional principles may require solution of varied local school problems. School authorities have the primary responsibility for educating, assessing, and solving these problems; courts will have to consider whether the action of school authorities constitutes good faith implementation of the governing

---

2. Further argument was requested on the following questions, previously propounded by the Court:

'4. Assuming it is decided that segregation in public schools violates the Fourteenth Amendment

'(a) would a decree necessarily follow providing that, within the limits set by normal geographic school districting, Negro children should forthwith be admitted to schools of their choice, or

'(b) may this Court, in the exercise of its equity powers, permit an effective gradual adjustment to be brought about from existing segregated systems to a system not based on color distinctions?

'5. On the assumption on which questions 4(a) and (b) are based, and assuming further that this Court will exercise its equity powers to the end described in question 4(b),

'(a) should this Court formulate detailed decrees in these cases;

'(b) if so, what specific issues should the decrees reach;

'(c) should this Court appoint a special master to hear evidence with a view to recommending specific terms for such decrees;

'(d) should this Court remand to the courts of first instance with directions to frame decrees in these cases, and if so what general directions should the decrees of this Court include and what procedures should the courts of first instance follow in arriving at the specific terms of more detailed decrees?'

constitutional principles. Because of their proximity to local conditions and the possible need for further hearings, the courts which originally heard these cases can best perform this judicial appraisal. Accordingly, we believe it appropriate to remand the cases to those courts.

In fashioning and effectuating the decrees, the courts will be guided by equitable principles. Traditionally, equity has been characterized by a practical flexibility in shaping its remedies and by a facility for adjusting and reconciling public and private needs. These cases call for the exercise of these traditional attributes of equity power. At stake is the personal interest of the plaintiffs in admission to public schools as soon as practicable on a nondiscriminatory basis. To effectuate this interest may call for elimination of a variety of obstacles in making the transition to school systems operated in accordance with the constitutional principles set forth in our May 17, 1954, decision. Courts of equity may properly take into account the public interest in the elimination of such obstacles in a systematic and effective manner. But it should go without saying that the vitality of these constitutional principles cannot be allowed to yield simply because of disagreement with them.

While giving weight to these public and private considerations, the courts will require that the defendants make a prompt and reasonable start toward full compliance with our May 17, 1954, ruling. Once such a start has been made, the courts may find that additional time is necessary to carry out the ruling in an effective manner. The burden rests upon the defendants to establish that such time is necessary in the public interest and is consistent with good faith compliance at the earliest practicable date. To that end, the courts may consider problems related to administration, arising from the physical condition of the school plant, the school transportation system, personnel, revision of school districts and attendance areas into compact units to achieve a system of determining admission to the public schools on a nonracial basis, and revision of local laws and regulations which may be necessary in solving the foregoing problems. They will also consider the adequacy of any plans the defendants may propose to meet these problems and to effectuate a transition to a racially nondiscriminatory school system. During this period of transition, the courts will retain jurisdiction of these cases.

The judgments below, except that in the Delaware case, are accordingly reversed and the cases are remanded to the District Courts to take such proceedings and enter such orders and decrees consistent with this opinion as are necessary and proper to admit to public schools on a racially nondiscriminatory basis with all deliberate speed the parties to these cases. The judgment in the Delaware case—ordering the immediate admission of the plaintiffs to schools previously attended only by white children—is affirmed on the basis of the principles stated in our May 17, 1954, opinion, but the case is remanded to the Supreme Court of Delaware for such further proceedings as that Court may deem necessary in light of this opinion.

## Note: *Resistance to* Brown

1. Americans greeted *Brown* with ambivalence. Surveys taken soon after the Court's decision found that slightly over half of Americans approved the decision, while ap-

proximately 40% disapproved of it. To be sure, attitudes varied significantly based on region, with a majority of white southerners disapproving.

2. *Brown* elicited a political response from southern leaders. In March, 1956, 82 Representatives and 19 Senators signed the "Southern Manifesto," a document expressing opposition to *Brown*. This group was comprised solely of legislators from formerly confederate states, and included the entire congressional delegations of Alabama, Arkansas, Georgia, Louisiana, Mississippi, South Carolina, and Virginia. It states, in its entirety, as follows:

### "DECLARATION OF CONSTITUTIONAL PRINCIPLES"

"The unwarranted decision of the Supreme Court in the public school cases is now bearing the fruit always produced when men substitute naked power for established law.

The Founding Fathers gave us a Constitution of checks and balances because they realized the inescapable lesson of history that no man or group of men can be safely entrusted with unlimited power. They framed this Constitution with its provisions for change by amendment in order to secure the fundamentals of government against the dangers of temporary popular passion or the personal predilections of public officeholders.

We regard the decisions of the Supreme Court in the school cases as a clear abuse of judicial power. It climaxes a trend in the Federal Judiciary undertaking to legislate, in derogation of the authority of Congress, and to encroach upon the reserved rights of the States and the people.

The original Constitution does not mention education. Neither does the 14th Amendment nor any other amendment. The debates preceding the submission of the 14th Amendment clearly show that there was no intent that it should affect the system of education maintained by the States.

The very Congress which proposed the amendment subsequently provided for segregated schools in the District of Columbia.

When the amendment was adopted in 1868, there were 37 States of the Union....

Every one of the 26 States that had any substantial racial differences among its people, either approved the operation of segregated schools already in existence or subsequently established such schools by action of the same law-making body which considered the 14th Amendment.

As admitted by the Supreme Court in the public school case (Brown v. Board of Education), the doctrine of separate but equal schools "apparently originated in Roberts v. City of Boston (1849), upholding school segregation against attack as being violative of a State constitutional guarantee of equality." This constitutional doctrine began in the North, not in the South, and it was followed not only in Massachusetts, but in Connecticut, New York, Illinois, Indiana, Michigan, Minnesota, New Jersey, Ohio, Pennsylvania and other northern states until they, exercising their rights as states through the constitutional processes of local self-government, changed their school systems.

In the case of Plessy v. Ferguson in 1896 the Supreme Court expressly declared that under the 14th Amendment no person was denied any of his rights if the States provided separate but equal facilities. This decision has been followed in many other cases. It is notable that the Supreme Court, speaking through Chief Justice Taft, a former President of the United States, unanimously declared in 1927 in Lum v. Rice that the "separate but equal" principle is "within the discretion of the State in regulating its public schools and does not conflict with the 14th Amendment."

This interpretation, restated time and again, became a part of the life of the people of many of the States and confirmed their habits, traditions, and way of life. It is founded on elemental humanity and commonsense, for parents should not be deprived by Government of the right to direct the lives and education of their own children.

Though there has been no constitutional amendment or act of Congress changing this established legal principle almost a century old, the Supreme Court of the United States, with no legal basis for such action, undertook to exercise their naked judicial power and substituted their personal political and social ideas for the established law of the land.

This unwarranted exercise of power by the Court, contrary to the Constitution, is creating chaos and confusion in the States principally affected. It is destroying the amicable relations between the white and Negro races that have been created through 90 years of patient effort by the good people of both races. It has planted hatred and suspicion where there has been heretofore friendship and understanding.

Without regard to the consent of the governed, outside mediators are threatening immediate and revolutionary changes in our public schools systems. If done, this is certain to destroy the system of public education in some of the States.

With the gravest concern for the explosive and dangerous condition created by this decision and inflamed by outside meddlers:

We reaffirm our reliance on the Constitution as the fundamental law of the land.

We decry the Supreme Court's encroachment on the rights reserved to the States and to the people, contrary to established law, and to the Constitution.

We commend the motives of those States which have declared the intention to resist forced integration by any lawful means.

We appeal to the States and people who are not directly affected by these decisions to consider the constitutional principles involved against the time when they too, on issues vital to them may be the victims of judicial encroachment.

Even though we constitute a minority in the present Congress, we have full faith that a majority of the American people believe in the dual system of government which has enabled us to achieve our greatness and will in time demand that the reserved rights of the States and of the people be made secure against judicial usurpation.

We pledge ourselves to use all lawful means to bring about a reversal of this decision which is contrary to the Constitution and to prevent the use of force in its implementation.

In this trying period, as we all seek to right this wrong, we appeal to our people not to be provoked by the agitators and troublemakers invading our States and to scrupulously refrain from disorder and lawless acts."

## Note: The Struggle to Implement Brown

1. *Brown II* reflected the Court's awareness of the real-world difficulty of desegregating public schools in areas where separate-but-equal was mandated by law. The difficulty arose less from the bureaucratic challenges involved in creating race-neutral policies than from the political and social resistance to desegregated education. An earlier vote noted the political strength of the segregationist "Dixiecrat" Party in the 1948 elections; the note immediately previous to this one noted the near-unanimous opposition to *Brown* from senators and representatives from the southern states.

2. The Court's fears were confirmed by the violent response to the first attempts at desegregation in the late 1950s and early 1960s. Recall from Chapter 1 *Cooper v. Aaron*, 358 U.S. 1 (1958), which involved Little Rock officials' refusal to obey *Brown II*'s mandate to begin desegregating the city's high schools. Such refusals became known as "massive resistance." The scale of that resistance was such that *Brown* remained essentially a nullity in many parts of the South.

Some districts, sometimes prodded by court orders, did begin halting efforts to comply with *Brown*. But these efforts often took the form of half-hearted measures, such as so-called "freedom of choice" plans that formally dissolved race-based student assignments but left attendance decisions to private choice. In the context of regions that had always been segregated, and where the threat of violence always lurked just below the surface, such plans led to private decision-making that recreated the previously segregated system. The result was that segregation remained the rule in the South: according to various studies, a decade after *Brown* over 90% of southern black schoolchildren and southern white schoolchildren attended schools where 90% or more of the students were of their own race. Some studies put the percentage even higher.

3. By the late 1960s the Court had become impatient with the slow pace of change. In *Green v. School Board of New Kent County, Virginia*, 391 U.S. 430 (1968), the Court rejected yet another freedom of choice plan, and highlighted the district's affirmative duty to act so as to establish a unitary school system. The Court made its impatience clear, noting that the district in that case had waited eleven years after *Brown* even to institute its (inadequate) freedom of choice plan. After recounting that history, the Court repeated what it had said four years earlier in a different desegregation case: "the time for mere 'deliberate speed' [had] run out."

Three years after *Green*, in *Swann v. Charlotte-Mecklenburg Board of Education*, 402 U.S. 1 (1971), the Court took the next logical step, by delineating the tools district courts possessed to implement *Green*'s mandate of desegregation "that promises realistically to work, and promises realistically to work now." In *Swann* a unanimous Court authorized district courts to supervise a wide variety of school board decisions, including student and teacher assignment, facilities equalization, school siting, and student transportation, in pursuit of desegregation.

4. *Swann* was the high-water mark of the Court's aggressiveness in enforcing *Brown*. Political opposition to desegregation increased as desegregation disputes spread to the North and West on the heels of the Court's 1973 decision opening for judicial remedy districts that had never engaged in *de jure* segregation (*i.e.*, segregation explicitly required by law.) *Keyes v. School District Number 1, Denver, Colorado*, 413 U.S. 189 (1973). Desegregation in the North quickly became a heated issue; most notably, violent desegregation clashes in Boston made national headlines in 1974.

The same year as *Keyes*, a 5–4 majority in *San Antonio Independent School District v. Rodriguez*, 411 U.S. 1 (1973) (Note *supra*. Chapter 12), rejected the argument that Texas's property tax financing method for public schools, and the unequal resources thereby provided schools in wealthy and poor districts, violated the Equal Protection Clause. In declining to second-guess the practice of unequal school financing, *Rodriguez* increased the attractiveness of newly formed, wealthier, suburban districts.

Those suburban districts became even more attractive when the Court blocked lower-court injunctions that involved them in desegregation remedies. Those lower courts had begun concluding that for some urban districts effective desegregation would sometimes require the involvement of their suburban neighbors, as white flight from the cities made urban districts less diverse and thus less capable of meaningful desegregation. But in *Milliken v. Bradley*, 418 U.S. 717 (1974), the Court rejected a district court's involvement of suburban Detroit districts in the court's plan to integrate Detroit schools, holding that the suburban districts were innocent of any illegal conduct and thus beyond the reach of the court's remedial powers. Two years later, in *Pasadena City Board of Education v. Spangler*, 427 U.S. 424 (1976), the Court rejected a district court's continued imposition of requirements governing the racial mix of a previously segregated school district, on the ground that the district had achieved the required racial mix for one year, and had thus achieved unitary status with regard to that feature of the district's operation.

5. *Milliken* and *Spangler* were watersheds, limiting, respectively, the geographic and temporal reach of desegregation remedies. Given the extraordinary complexity of and political controversy surrounding school desegregation, it was perhaps inevitable that the imposition of these limits would lead to incomplete desegregation. Perhaps just as importantly, courts' inability to complete the job would yield impatience with continued federal judicial oversight of local school districts. Starting in 1991 with *Board of Education of Oklahoma City Public Schools v. Dowell*, 498 U.S. 237 (1991), and continuing with *Freeman v. Pitts*, 503 U.S. 467 (1992) and *Missouri v. Jenkins*, 515 US. 70 (1995), the Court spoke of desegregation "to the extent practicable." That formula allowed, respectively, dissolution of an injunction when the school board had complied in good faith with a desegregative decree, despite the existence of vestiges of the segregated system; the freeing of a district from judicial supervision with respect to the parts of its operations that had achieved unitary status, despite the continued existence of dual system attributes in other of the district's operations; and the imposition of a requirement that judicial remedies be limited to the offending district, even if that limitation would make it impossible to eliminate all vestiges of the prior dual system.

6. Some scholars have concluded that these latter decisions focus as much on the practical capabilities of courts as on formal issues of liability and remedy. Implicit in that understanding is a sense that the Court was concerned about the practical limitations lower courts face when attempting to supervise for an indefinite period an institution as massive, complex, and important as a public school system. Other scholars have found in these opinions a sense of the Court's concern about other priorities, most notably its federalism-based interest in returning schools to local control as soon as possible. On this latter view, value choices (the Court's interest in returning schools to local control) played as much, or more, of a role in these cases as concerns about judges' institutional management capabilities.

## 3. The Implications of *Brown*

### *Note:* Naim *and the* Per Curiams

1. *Brown*'s focus on education — its importance in modern society and the effect of segregation on schoolchildren — suggests that that case did not have to be read as enunciating a broad rule presumptively invalidating all racial classifications. (For that matter, neither did *Korematsu*: recall that Justice Black referred to "legal restrictions *which curtail the civil rights* of a single racial group" (emphasis added); even Justice Murphy's dissent noted the substantive liberty deprivation the exclusion order accomplished.)

2. The *Brown* Court's caution in focusing on education was repeated the following year in a case that raised an even more difficult issue. In 1955 a case raising the question of state bans on interracial marriage reached the Court through its mandatory docket (that is, through a method that did not give it complete discretion over the decision whether to hear it). In *Naim v. Naim*, 350 U.S. 985 (1956), a Chinese man and a white woman, both residents of Virginia, married in North Carolina. After returning to Virginia the wife sought an annulment based on Virginia's ban on interracial marriages. When the state courts granted the annulment and that decision was appealed to the Supreme Court, the Court was faced with the question whether to confront the interracial marriage question only a year after *Brown*. After much internal discussion, the Court remanded the case to the Virginia courts for clarification of the record. The state courts simply asserted that the record was clear as it was; in response to that implicit defiance, the Court dismissed the appeal. The Court did not return to the interracial marriage issue for another twelve years.

3. In other areas implicating Jim Crow, however, the Court moved aggressively after *Brown*. What follows after this Note are a series of very short opinions, which scholars refer to as "the *per curiams*." "*Per curiam*," the Latin term for "by the Court," refers generally to opinions that are not attributed to a particular justice, but instead to the Court more generally. The particular *per curiams* at issue here struck down segregation in a wide range of government facilities, from parks (*Muir* and *Detiege*) to beaches (*Dawson*), golf courses (*Holmes*), city busses (*Gayle*), restaurants in public facilities (*Turner*), and courthouses (*Johnson*). They're notable for the extreme brevity of their

legal analysis, and, when one traces the cases they cite, for their ultimate foundation in *Brown*. Thus, even though *Brown* appeared to be cautious, and limited to the unique context of education, the Court soon used *Brown* to undo segregation more generally. (Eventually, these cases provided the foundation for a broader rule against racial discrimination that the Court finally used in 1967 to strike down the remaining anti-miscegenation laws. *See Loving v. Virginia* (1967), excerpted later in this chapter.) Consider whether the Court's use of *Brown* in that way is logically defensible.

## Muir v. Louisville Park Theatrical Association
### 347 U.S. 971 (1954)

PER CURIAM.

The Petition for writ of certiorari is granted. The judgment is vacated and the case remanded for consideration in the light of the Segregation Cases decided May 17, 1954, *Brown v. Board of Education* (1954) [*Supra.* this chapter] and conditions that now prevail.

## Mayor and City Council of Baltimore v. Dawson
### 350 U.S. 877 (1955)

PER CURIAM.

The motion to affirm is granted and the judgment is affirmed.

## Holmes v. City of Atlanta
### 350 U.S. 879 (1955)

PER CURIAM.

The petition for writ of certiorari is granted, the judgments both of the Court of Appeals and the District Court are vacated and the case is remanded to the District Court with directions to enter a decree for petitioners in conformity with *Mayor & City Council of Baltimore City v. Dawson* (1955) [*Supra.* this chapter].

## Gayle v. Browder
### 352 U.S. 903 (1956)

PER CURIAM.

The motion to affirm is granted and the judgment is affirmed. *Brown v. Board of Education* (1954); *Mayor and City Council of Baltimore v. Dawson* (1955); *Holmes v. Atlanta* (1955) [All *supra.* this chapter].

## New Orleans City Park Improvement Association v. Detiege
### 358 U.S. 54 (1958)

PER CURIAM.

The judgment is affirmed.

# Turner v. City of Memphis

## 369 U.S. 350 (1962)

PER CURIAM.

Appellant, a Negro refused nonsegregated service in the Memphis Municipal Airport restaurant operated by appellee Dobbs Houses, Inc., under a lease from appellee City of Memphis, instituted this action on behalf of himself and other Negroes similarly situated seeking an injunction against such discrimination.... Although the complaint alleged that appellees acted under color of state law, it did not identify any particular state statutes or regulations being challenged. But appellees' answers, in addition to asserting that the restaurant was a private enterprise to which the Fourteenth Amendment did not apply, invoked Tenn.Code Ann. §§ 53-2120, 53-2121, and Regulation No. R-18(L). The statutes as now phrased authorize the Division of Hotel and Restaurant Inspection of the State Department of Conservation to issue 'such rules and regulations * * * as may be necessary pertaining to the safety and/or sanitation of hotels and restaurants * * *' and make violations of such regulations a misdemeanor. The regulation, promulgated by the Division, provides that 'Restaurants catering to both white and negro patrons should be arranged so that each race is properly segregated.'... The City of Memphis alleged further that unless and until the regulation was declared unconstitutional, the city would be bound to object to desegregation of the restaurant by Dobbs Houses as a violation of Tennessee law and of the lease. Dobbs Houses alleged that desegregation by it of the restaurant would therefore subject it to forfeiture of the lease....

... Since, as was conceded by Dobbs Houses at the bar of this Court, the Dobbs Houses restaurant was subject to the strictures of the Fourteenth Amendment under *Burton v. Wilmington Parking Authority*, 365 U.S. 715 (1961), the statutes and regulation invoked by appellees could have furnished a defense to the action only insofar as they expressed an affirmative state policy fostering segregating in publicly operated facilities. But our decisions have foreclosed any possible contention that such a statute or regulation may stand consistently with the Fourteenth Amendment. *Brown v. Board of Education* (1954); *Mayor & City Council of Baltimore City v. Dawson* (1955); *Holmes v. City of Atlanta* (1955); *Gayle v. Browder* (1956); *New Orleans City Park Improvement Ass'n v. Detiege* (1958) [All *supra*. this chapter]....

... [We] see no reason why disposition of the case should await decision of the appeal by the Court of Appeals. On the merits, no issue remains to be resolved. This is clear under prior decisions and the undisputed facts of the case.... The petition is granted ... and the case is remanded to the District Court with directions to enter a decree granting appropriate injunctive relief against the discrimination complained of.

Mr. Justice WHITTAKER did not participate in the decision of this case.

# Johnson v. Virginia

## 373 U.S. 61 (1963)

PER CURIAM.

… The petitioner, Ford T. Johnson, Jr., was convicted of contempt of the Traffic Court of the City of Richmond, Virginia, and appealed his conviction to the Hustings Court, where he was tried without a jury and again convicted. The Supreme Court of Appeals of Virginia refused to grant a writ of error on the ground that the judgment appealed from was 'plainly right,' but the Chief Justice of that court stayed execution of the judgment pending disposition of this petition for certiorari.

The evidence at petitioner's trial in the Hustings Court is summarized in an approved statement of facts. According to this statement, the witnesses for the State testified as follows: The petitioner, a Negro, was seated in the Traffic Court in a section reserved for whites, and when requested to move by the bailiff, refused to do so. The judge then summoned the petitioner to the bench and instructed him to be seated in the right-hand section of the courtroom, the section reserved for Negroes. The petitioner moved back in front of the counsel table and remained standing with his arms folded, stating that he preferred standing and indicating that he would not comply with the judge's order. Upon refusal to obey the judge's further direction to be seated, the petitioner was arrested for contempt. At no time did he behave in a boisterous or abusive manner, and there was no disorder in the courtroom. The State, in its Brief in Opposition filed in this Court, concedes that in the section of the Richmond Traffic Court reserved for spectators, seating space 'is assigned on the basis of racial designation, the seats on one side of the aisle being for use of Negro citizens and the seats on the other side being for the use of white citizens.'

It is clear from the totality of circumstances, and particularly the fact that the petitioner was peaceably seated in the section reserved for whites before being summoned to the bench, that the arrest and conviction rested entirely on the refusal to comply with the segregated seating requirements imposed in this particular courtroom. Such a conviction cannot stand, for it is no longer open to question that a State may not constitutionally require segregation of public facilities. See, e.g., *Brown v. Board of Education* (1954); *Mayor and City Council of Baltimore v. Dawson* (1955); *Turner v. Memphis* (1962) [All *supra.* this chapter]. State-compelled segregation in a court of justice is a manifest violation of the State's duty to deny no one the equal protection of its laws. Reversed and remanded.

# Loving v. Virginia

## 388 U.S. 1 (1967)

MR. CHIEF JUSTICE WARREN delivered the opinion of the Court.

This case presents a constitutional question never addressed by this Court: whether a statutory scheme adopted by the State of Virginia to prevent marriages between persons solely on the basis of racial classifications violates the Equal Protection and

Due Process Clauses of the Fourteenth Amendment. For reasons which seem to us to reflect the central meaning of those constitutional commands, we conclude that these statutes cannot stand consistently with the Fourteenth Amendment....

Virginia is now one of 16 States which prohibit and punish marriages on the basis of racial classifications. Penalties for miscegenation arose as an incident to slavery and have been common in Virginia since the colonial period. The present statutory scheme dates from the adoption of the Racial Integrity Act of 1924, passed during the period of extreme nativism which followed the end of the First World War. The central features of this Act, and current Virginia law, are the absolute prohibition of a "white person" marrying other than another "white person," a prohibition against issuing marriage licenses until the issuing official is satisfied that the applicants' statements as to their race are correct, certificate of "racial composition" to be kept by both local and state registrars, and the carrying forward of earlier prohibitions against racial intermarriage.

## I

In upholding the constitutionality of these provisions in the decision below, the Supreme Court of Appeals of Virginia referred to its 1955 decision in *Naim v. Naim*, 197 Va. 80 (1955) [Note *supra.* this chapter], as stating the reasons supporting the validity of these laws. In *Naim*, the state court concluded that the State's legitimate purposes were 'to preserve the racial integrity of its citizens,' and to prevent 'the corruption of blood,' 'a mongrel breed of citizens,' and 'the obliteration of racial pride,' obviously an endorsement of the doctrine of White Supremacy. The court also reasoned that marriage has traditionally been subject to state regulation without federal intervention, and, consequently, the regulation of marriage should be left to exclusive state control by the Tenth Amendment.

While the state court is no doubt correct in asserting that marriage is a social relation subject to the State's police power, the State does not contend in its argument before this Court that its powers to regulate marriage are unlimited notwithstanding the commands of the Fourteenth Amendment. Nor could it do so in light of *Meyer v. Nebraska*, (1923) [*Supra.* Chapter 8], and *Skinner v. Oklahoma*, 316 U.S. 535 (1942) [Note *supra.* Chapter 8]. Instead, the State argues that the meaning of the Equal Protection Clause, as illuminated by the statements of the Framers, is only that state penal laws containing an interracial element as part of the definition of the offense must apply equally to whites and Negroes in the sense that members of each race are punished to the same degree....

Because we reject the notion that the mere 'equal application' of a statute containing racial classifications is enough to remove the classifications from the Fourteenth Amendment's proscription of all invidious racial discriminations, we do not accept the State's contention that these statutes should be upheld if there is any possible basis for concluding that they serve a rational purpose. The mere fact of equal application does not mean that our analysis of these statutes should follow the approach we have taken in cases involving no racial discrimination where the Equal Protection Clause has been arrayed against a statute discriminating between the kinds of advertising which may be displayed on trucks in New York City, *Railway Express Agency, Inc. v. People of the State of New York* (1949) [*Supra*. Chapter 11], or an exemption in Ohio's ad valorem tax for merchandise owned by a non-resident in a storage warehouse, *Allied Stores of Ohio, Inc. v. Bowers*, 358 U.S. 522 (1959). In these cases, involving distinctions not drawn according to race, the Court has merely asked whether there is any rational foundation for the discriminations, and has deferred to the wisdom of the state legislatures. In the case at bar, however, we deal with statutes containing racial classifications, and the fact of equal application does not immunize the statute from the very heavy burden of justification which the Fourteenth Amendment has traditionally required of state statutes drawn according to race.

The State argues that statements in the Thirty-ninth Congress about the time of the passage of the Fourteenth Amendment indicate that the Framers did not intend the Amendment to make unconstitutional state miscegenation laws.... While these statements have some relevance to the intention of Congress in submitting the Fourteenth Amendment, it must be understood that the pertained to the passage of specific statutes and not to the broader, organic purpose of a constitutional amendment. As for the various statements directly concerning the Fourteenth Amendment, we have said in connection with a related problem, that although these historical sources 'cast some light' they are not sufficient to resolve the problem; 'at best, they are inconclusive. The most avid proponents of the post-War Amendments undoubtedly intended them to remove all legal distinctions among 'all persons born or naturalized in the United States.' Their opponents, just as certainly, were antagonistic to both the letter and the spirit of the Amendments and wished them to have the most limited effect.' *Brown v. Board of Education* (1954) [*Supra*. this chapter]. We have rejected the proposition that the debates in the Thirty-ninth Congress or in the state legislatures which ratified the Fourteenth Amendment supported the theory advanced by the State, that the requirement of equal protection of the laws is satisfied by penal laws defining offenses based on racial classifications so long as white and Negro participants in the offense were similarly punished. *McLaughlin v. State of Florida*, 379 U.S. 184 (1964)....

There can be no question but that Virginia's miscegenation statutes rest solely upon distinctions drawn according to race. The statutes proscribe generally accepted conduct if engaged in by members of different races. Over the years, this Court has consistently repudiated 'distinctions between citizens solely because of their ancestry' as being 'odious to a free people whose institutions are founded upon the doctrine of equality.' At the very least, the Equal Protection Clause demands that racial classifications, especially suspect in criminal statutes, be subjected to the 'most rigid scrutiny,' *Korematsu v. United States* (1944) [*Supra*. this chapter], and, if they are ever to be upheld, they must be shown to be necessary to the accomplishment of some permissible state objective, independent of the racial discrimination which it was the object of the Fourteenth Amendment to eliminate....

There is patently no legitimate overriding purpose independent of invidious racial discrimination which justifies this classification. The fact that Virginia prohibits only interracial marriages involving white persons demonstrates that the racial classifications must stand on their own justification, as measures designed to maintain White Supremacy.[11] We have consistently denied the constitutionality of measures which restrict the rights of citizens on account of race. There can be no doubt that restricting the freedom to marry solely because of racial classifications violates the central meaning of the Equal Protection Clause.

II

These statutes also deprive the Lovings of liberty without due process of law in violation of the Due Process Clause of the Fourteenth Amendment. The freedom to marry has long been recognized as one of the vital personal rights essential to the orderly pursuit of happiness by free men.

Marriage is one of the 'basic civil rights of man,' fundamental to our very existence and survival. *Skinner*. To deny this fundamental freedom on so unsupportable a basis as the racial classifications embodied in these statutes, classifications so directly subversive of the principle of equality at the heart of the Fourteenth Amendment, is surely to deprive all the State's citizens of liberty without due process of law. The Fourteenth Amendment requires that the freedom of choice to marry not be restricted by invidious racial discriminations. Under our Constitution, the freedom to marry or not marry, a person of another race resides with the individual and cannot be infringed by the State.

These convictions must be reversed. It is so ordered.

Justice Stewart, concurring. [omitted]

# D. Can Race Be a Benign Criterion?

## *Note: An Introduction to "Affirmative Action"*

1. Whether fortuitous or not, the *Loving* Court's final destruction of official Jim Crow occurred at approximately the same time that government began serious consideration of using race as a classification tool in order to ensure equal opportunity and counteract past discrimination. To be sure, earlier periods had witnessed race-conscious government action. For example, some Reconstruction-era legislation, such as the Freedmen's Bureau Act, was aimed primarily at ameliorating the conditions faced by black former slaves. Much more recently, the *Brown II* Court presumably

---

11. Appellants point out that the State's concern in these statutes, as expressed in the words of the 1924 Act's title, 'An Act to Preserve Racial Integrity,' extends only to the integrity of the white race. While Virginia prohibits whites from marrying any nonwhite (subject to the exception for the descendants of Pocahontas), Negroes, Orientals, and any other racial class may intermarry without statutory interference. Appellants contend that this distinction renders Virginia's miscegenation statutes arbitrary and unreasonable even assuming the constitutional validity of an official purpose to preserve 'racial integrity.' We need not reach this contention because we find the racial classifications in these statutes repugnant to the Fourteenth Amendment, even assuming an even-handed state purpose to protect the 'integrity' of all races.

contemplated that lower courts would enforce *Brown I* through court orders that were explicitly race-conscious, even if those orders were intended to create school districts where race no longer mattered.

Starting in the 1960s, federal and then state legislatures and executives began using race as well. Apparently the first use of the term "affirmative action" in this context was in a 1961 Executive Order from the Kennedy White House, which required that federal government contracts provide that the "contractor will take affirmative action to ensure that applicants are employed, and that employees are treated during employment, without regard to their race, creed, color or national origin." In 1965 President Johnson gave the commencement address at Howard University, where he said "You do not take a person who, for years, has been hobbled by chains and liberate him, bring him up to the starting line of a race and then say, 'you are free to compete with all the others,' and still justly believe that you have been completely fair."

2. State governments soon began experimenting with using race for a variety of purposes that were described as distinct from—indeed, antithetical to—the oppressive use of race that the Court had struck down in cases such as *Loving*. Two of the main battlegrounds over the constitutionality of such race-conscious action were government contracting and higher education.

3. The first "affirmative action" or "reverse discrimination" case to reach the Court was *DeFunis v. Odergaard*, 416 U.S. 312 (1974). In that case, an unsuccessful white applicant to the University of Washington School of Law sued the university, challenging the law school's affirmative action admissions program. Because the trial court had ruled in his favor and ordered his admission to the law school, and because by the time his case reached the Court he was enrolled in his last quarter and the school had indicated that he would be allowed to complete that quarter and thus graduate, five justices of the Court held the case to be moot. (This part of the opinion is excerpted in the mootness materials in Chapter 1.) The Court did not reach the merits of a constitutional challenge to an affirmative action program until 1978.

## Regents of the University of California v. Bakke
### 438 U.S. 265 (1978)

Justice Powell announced the Court's judgment and filed an opinion, in Parts I, III-A and V-C of which White, J., joined; and in which Parts I and V-C of which Brennan, Marshall, and Blackmun, JJ, joined.*

[The University of California-Davis Medical School adopted a special admissions program whereby candidates who self-identified as "disadvantaged" were eligible for admission either under the school's general admission program or a special admission program for which 16 out of a total of 100 class seats were reserved. Alan Bakke, a

---

* [Ed note: Given this line-up only Parts I and V-C of Justice Powell's opinion commanded a majority of the Court.]

white male, applied for admission under the general admission program in both 1973 and 1974, and was rejected in both years. For the 1974 admitted class, the admissions committee considered only "disadvantaged" applicants who self-identified on the application form as "Blacks," "Chicanos," "Asians," or "American Indians."

After his 1974 rejection Bakke sued. The state trial court ruled in his favor on the ground that the special admissions program was racial discrimination prohibited by the state constitution, the Fourteenth Amendment, and Title VI, a federal law that prohibited racial discrimination in any program funded by the federal government. The California Supreme Court affirmed the lower court's decision solely on the Fourteenth Amendment ground, and ordered the school to admit Bakke.

In Part II of the opinion, in which Justice Powell wrote only for himself, he concluded that "Title VI must be held to proscribe only those racial classifications that would violate the Equal Protection Clause or the Fifth Amendment."]

### III

### A

... The guarantees of the Fourteenth Amendment extend to all persons. Its language is explicit: "No State shall ... deny to any person within its jurisdiction the equal protection of the laws." It is settled beyond question that the "rights created by the first section of the Fourteenth Amendment are, by its terms, guaranteed to the individual. The rights established are personal rights." The guarantee of equal protection cannot mean one thing when applied to one individual and something else when applied to a person of another color. If both are not accorded the same protection, then it is not equal.

Nevertheless, petitioner argues that the court below erred in applying strict scrutiny to the special admissions program because white males, such as respondent, are not a "discrete and insular minority" requiring extraordinary protection from the majoritarian political process. *United States v. Carolene Products* (1938) [*Supra.* chapter 12]. This rationale, however, has never been invoked in our decisions as a prerequisite to subjecting racial or ethnic distinctions to strict scrutiny. Nor has this Court held that discreteness and insularity constitute necessary preconditions to a holding that a particular classification is invidious.[28] See, e.g., *Skinner v. Oklahoma*, 316 U.S. 535 (1942) [Note *supra.* Chapter 8]. These characteristics may be relevant in deciding whether or not to add new types of classifications to the list of "suspect" categories or whether a particular classification survives close examination. See, e.g., *Massa-*

---

28. After *Carolene Products*, the first specific reference in our decisions to the elements of "discreteness and insularity" appears in *Minersville School District v. Gobitis* (1940) (Stone, J., dissenting) [Note *supra.* Chapter 12]. The next does not appear until 1970. *Oregon v. Mitchell*, 400 U.S. 112 (1970) (STEWART, J., concurring in part and dissenting in part). These elements have been relied upon in recognizing a suspect class in only one group of cases, those involving aliens. E.g., *Graham v. Richardson* (1971) [Note *supra.* Chapter 12].

chusetts Board of Retirement v. Murgia (1976) (age) [*Supra*. Chapter 12]; *San Antonio Independent School Dist. v. Rodriquez*, 411 U.S. 1 (1973) (wealth) [Note *supra*. Chapter 12]; *Graham v. Richardson*, 403 U.S. 365 (1971) (aliens) [Note *supra*. Chapter 12]. Racial and ethnic classifications, however, are subject to stringent examination without regard to these additional characteristics. We declared as much in the first cases explicitly to recognize racial distinctions as suspect:

> "Distinctions between citizens solely because of their ancestry are by their very nature odious to a free people whose institutions are founded upon the doctrine of equality." *Hirabayashi v. United States*, 320 U.S. 81 (1943).

> "All legal restrictions which curtail the civil rights of a single racial group are immediately suspect. That is not to say that all such restrictions are unconstitutional. It is to say that courts must subject them to the most rigid scrutiny." *Korematsu v. United States* (1944) [*Supra*. this chapter].

The Court has never questioned the validity of those pronouncements. Racial and ethnic distinctions of any sort are inherently suspect and thus call for the most exacting judicial examination.

## B

This perception of racial and ethnic distinctions is rooted in our Nation's constitutional and demographic history. The Court's initial view of the Fourteenth Amendment was that its "one pervading purpose" was "the freedom of the slave race, the security and firm establishment of that freedom, and the protection of the newly-made freeman and citizen from the oppressions of those who had formerly exercised dominion over him." *Slaughter-House Cases* (1873) [Note *supra*. Part III Introduction]. The Equal Protection Clause, however, was "virtually strangled in infancy by post-civil-war judicial reactionism." It was relegated to decades of relative desuetude while the Due Process Clause of the Fourteenth Amendment, after a short germinal period, flourished as a cornerstone in the Court's defense of property and liberty of contract. See, e.g., *Allgeyer v. Louisiana*, 165 U.S. 578 (1897) [Note *supra*. Chapter 7]; *Lochner v. New York* (1905) [*Supra*. Chapter 7]. In that cause, the Fourteenth Amendment's "one pervading purpose" was displaced. See, e.g., *Plessy v. Ferguson* (1896) [*Supra*. this chapter]. It was only as the era of substantive due process came to a close, see, e.g., *Nebbia v. New Nebbia v. New York* (1934); *West Coast Hotel v. Parrish* (1937) [Both *supra*. Chapter 7], that the Equal Protection Clause began to attain a genuine measure of vitality, see, e.g., *Carolene Products*; *Skinner*.

By that time it was no longer possible to peg the guarantees of the Fourteenth Amendment to the struggle for equality of one racial minority. During the dormancy of the Equal Protection Clause, the United States had become a Nation of minorities. Each had to struggle — and to some extent struggles still — to overcome the prejudices not of a monolithic majority, but of a "majority" composed of various minority groups of whom it was said — perhaps unfairly in many cases — that a shared characteristic was a willingness to disadvantage other groups. As the Nation filled with the stock of many lands, the reach of the Clause was gradually extended to all ethnic groups seeking protection from official discrimination. See *Strauder v. West Virginia*, 100 U.S. 303 (1880) (Celtic Irishmen) (dictum) [Note *supra*. this chapter]; *Yick Wo v. Hopkins*, 118 U.S. 356 (1886) (Chinese); *Truax v. Raich* (1915) [Note *supra*. Chapter 12] (Austrian resident aliens); *Korematsu* (Japanese); *Hernandez v. Texas*, 347 U.S. 475 (1954) (Mexican-Americans). The guarantees of equal protection, said the Court in *Yick Wo*, "are universal in their application, to all persons within the territorial jurisdiction, without regard to any differences of race, of color, or of nationality; and the equal protection of the laws is a pledge of the protection of equal laws." ...

Over the past 30 years, this Court has embarked upon the crucial mission of interpreting the Equal Protection Clause with the view of assuring to all persons "the protection of equal laws," *Yick Wo*, in a Nation confronting a legacy of slavery and racial discrimination. See, e.g., *Brown v. Board of Education* (1954) [*Supra*. this chapter]. Because the landmark decisions in this area arose in response to the continued exclusion of Negroes from the mainstream of American society, they could be characterized as involving discrimination by the "majority" white race against the Negro minority. But they need not be read as depending upon that characterization for their results. It suffices to say that "over the years, this Court has consistently repudiated 'distinctions between citizens solely because of their ancestry' as being 'odious to a free people whose institutions are founded upon the doctrine of equality.'"

Petitioner urges us to adopt for the first time a more restrictive view of the Equal Protection Clause and hold that discrimination against members of the white "majority" cannot be suspect if its purpose can be characterized as "benign."[34] The clock of our liberties, however, cannot be turned back to 1868. *Brown*. It is far too late to argue that the guarantee of equal protection to all persons permits the recognition of special

---

34. In the view of Mr. JUSTICE BRENNAN, Mr. JUSTICE WHITE, Mr. JUSTICE MARSHALL, and Mr. JUSTICE BLACKMUN, the pliable notion of "stigma" is the crucial element in analyzing racial classifications. The Equal Protection Clause is not framed in terms of "stigma." Certainly the word has no clearly defined constitutional meaning. It reflects a subjective judgment that is standardless. *All* state-imposed classifications that rearrange burdens and benefits on the basis of race are likely to be viewed with deep resentment by the individuals burdened. The denial to innocent persons of equal rights and opportunities may outrage those so deprived and therefore may be perceived as invidious. These individuals are likely to find little comfort in the notion that the deprivation they are asked to endure is merely the price of membership in the dominant majority and that its imposition is inspired by the supposedly benign purpose of aiding others. One should not lightly dismiss the inherent unfairness of, and the perception of mistreatment that accompanies, a system of allocating benefits and privileges on the basis of skin color and ethnic origin. Moreover, Mr. JUSTICE BRENNAN, Mr. JUSTICE WHITE, Mr. JUSTICE MARSHALL, and Mr. JUSTICE BLACKMUN offer no principle for deciding whether preferential classifications reflect a benign remedial purpose or a malevolent stigmatic classification, since they are willing in this case to accept mere *post hoc* declarations by an isolated state entity—a medical school faculty—unadorned by particularized findings of past discrimination, to establish such a remedial purpose

wards entitled to a degree of protection greater than that accorded others.[35] "The Fourteenth Amendment is not directed solely against discrimination due to a 'two-class
theory'—that is, based upon differences between 'white' and Negro." *Hernandez.*

Once the artificial line of a "two-class theory" of the Fourteenth Amendment is
put aside, the difficulties entailed in varying the level of judicial review according to
a perceived "preferred" status of a particular racial or ethnic minority are intractable.
The concepts of "majority" and "minority" necessarily reflect temporary arrangements
and political judgments. As observed above, the white "majority" itself is composed
of various minority groups, most of which can lay claim to a history of prior discrimination at the hands of the State and private individuals. Not all of these groups
can receive preferential treatment and corresponding judicial tolerance of distinctions
drawn in terms of race and nationality, for then the only "majority" left would be a
new minority of white Anglo-Saxon Protestants. There is no principled basis for deciding which groups would merit "heightened judicial solicitude" and which would
not.[36] Courts would be asked to evaluate the extent of the prejudice and consequent

---

35. Professor Bickel noted the self-contradiction of that view:

"The lesson of the great decisions of the Supreme Court and the lesson of contemporary history
have been the same for at least a generation: discrimination on the basis of race is illegal, immoral,
unconstitutional, inherently wrong, and destructive of democratic society. Now this is to be unlearned
and we are told that this is not a matter of fundamental principle but only a matter of whose ox is
gored. Those for whom racial equality was demanded are to be more equal than others. Having found
support in the Constitution for equality, they now claim support for inequality under the same Constitution." A. Bickel, *The Morality of Consent* (1975).

36. As I am in agreement with the view that race may be taken into account as a factor in an admissions program, I agree with my Brothers BRENNAN, WHITE, MARSHALL, and BLACKMUN
that the portion of the judgment that would proscribe all consideration of race must be reversed. See
Part V, *infra.* But I disagree with much that is said in their opinion.

They would require as a justification for a program such as petitioner's, only two findings: (i) that
there has been some form of discrimination against the preferred minority groups by "society at large"
(it being conceded that petitioner had no history of discrimination), and (ii) that "there is reason to
believe" that the disparate impact sought to be rectified by the program is the "product" of such discrimination:

"If it was reasonable to conclude—as we hold that it was—that the failure of minorities to qualify
for admission at Davis under regular procedures was due principally to the effects of past
discrimination, then there is a reasonable likelihood that, but for pervasive racial discrimination, respondent would have failed to qualify for admission even in the absence of Davis' special admissions
program."

The breadth of this hypothesis is unprecedented in our constitutional system. The first step is
easily taken. No one denies the regrettable fact that there has been societal discrimination in this
country against various racial and ethnic groups. The second step, however, involves a speculative
leap: but for this discrimination by society at large, Bakke "would have failed to qualify for admission"
because Negro applicants—nothing is said about Asians—would have made better scores. Not one
word in the record supports this conclusion, and the authors of the opinion offer no standard for
courts to use in applying such a presumption of causation to other racial or ethnic classifications.
This failure is a grave one, since if it may be concluded *on this record* that each of the minority groups
preferred by the petitioner's special program is entitled to the benefit of the presumption, it would

harm suffered by various minority groups. Those whose societal injury is thought to exceed some arbitrary level of tolerability then would be entitled to preferential classifications at the expense of individuals belonging to other groups. Those classifications would be free from exacting judicial scrutiny. As these preferences began to have their desired effect, and the consequences of past discrimination were undone, new judicial rankings would be necessary. The kind of variable sociological and political analysis necessary to produce such rankings simply does not lie within the judicial competence — even if they otherwise were politically feasible and socially desirable.

Moreover, there are serious problems of justice connected with the idea of preference itself. First, it may not always be clear that a so-called preference is in fact benign. Courts may be asked to validate burdens imposed upon individual members of a particular group in order to advance the group's general interest. Nothing in the Constitution supports the notion that individuals may be asked to suffer otherwise impermissible burdens in order to enhance the societal standing of their ethnic groups. Second, preferential programs may only reinforce common stereotypes holding that certain groups are unable to achieve success without special protection based on a factor having no relationship to individual worth. Third, there is a measure of inequity in forcing innocent persons in respondent's position to bear the burdens of redressing grievances not of their making.

By hitching the meaning of the Equal Protection Clause to these transitory considerations, we would be holding, as a constitutional principle, that judicial scrutiny of classifications touching on racial and ethnic background may vary with the ebb and flow of political forces. Disparate constitutional tolerance of such classifications well may serve to exacerbate racial and ethnic antagonisms rather than alleviate them. Also, the mutability of a constitutional principle, based upon shifting political and social judgments, undermines the chances for consistent application of the Constitution from one generation to the next, a critical feature of its coherent interpretation. In expounding the Constitution, the Court's role is to discern "principles sufficiently absolute to give them roots throughout the community and continuity over significant periods of time, and to lift them above the level of the pragmatic political judgments of a particular time and place."

If it is the individual who is entitled to judicial protection against classifications based upon his racial or ethnic background because such distinctions impinge upon personal rights, rather than the individual only because of his membership in a particular group, then constitutional standards may be applied consistently. Political judgments regarding the necessity for the particular classification may be weighed in the constitutional balance, *Korematsu*, but the standard of justification will remain constant. This is as it should be, since those political judgments are the product of rough compromise struck by contending groups within the democratic process. When they touch upon an individual's race or ethnic background, he is entitled to a judicial

---

seem difficult to determine that any of the dozens of minority groups that have suffered "societal discrimination" cannot also claim it, in any area of social intercourse. See Part IV-B, infra.

determination that the burden he is asked to bear on that basis is precisely tailored to serve a compelling governmental interest. The Constitution guarantees that right to every person regardless of his background.

C

Petitioner contends that on several occasions this Court has approved preferential classifications without applying the most exacting scrutiny. Most of the cases upon which petitioner relies are drawn from three areas: school desegregation, employment discrimination, and sex discrimination. Each of the cases cited presented a situation materially different from the facts of this case.

The school desegregation cases are inapposite. Each involved remedies for clearly determined constitutional violations. E.g., *Swann v. Charlotte-Mecklenburg Board of Education*, 402 US 1 (1971). Racial classifications thus were designed as remedies for the vindication of constitutional entitlement. Moreover, the scope of the remedies was not permitted to exceed the extent of the violations. E.g., *Milliken v. Bradley*, 418 U.S. 717 (1974). Here, there was no judicial determination of constitutional violation as a predicate for the formulation of a remedial classification.

The employment discrimination cases also do not advance petitioner's cause. For example, in *Franks v. Bowman Transportation Co.*, 424 U.S. 747 (1976), we approved a retroactive award of seniority to a class of Negro truckdrivers who had been the victims of discrimination—not just by society at large, but by the respondent in that case.... But we have never approved preferential classifications in the absence of proved constitutional or statutory violations.

Nor is petitioner's view as to the applicable standard supported by the fact that gender-based classifications are not subjected to this level of scrutiny. E.g., *Craig v. Boren* (1976) [*Supra.* Chapter 12]. Gender-based distinctions are less likely to create the analytical and practical problems present in preferential programs premised on racial or ethnic criteria. With respect to gender there are only two possible classifications. The incidence of the burdens imposed by preferential classifications is clear.... The resolution of these same questions in the context of racial and ethnic preferences presents far more complex and intractable problems than gender-based classifications. More importantly, the perception of racial classifications as inherently odious stems from a lengthy and tragic history that gender-based classifications do not share. In sum, the Court has never viewed such classification as inherently suspect or as comparable to racial or ethnic classifications for the purpose of equal protection analysis....

IV

We have held that in "order to justify the use of a suspect classification, a State must show that its purpose or interest is both constitutionally permissible and substantial, and that its use of the classification is 'necessary ... to the accomplishment' of its purpose or the safeguarding of its interest." *Griffiths.* The special admissions program purports to serve the purposes of: (i) "reducing the historic deficit of traditionally disfavored minorities in medical schools and in the medical profession"; (ii) countering the effects of societal discrimination; (iii) increasing the number of physicians who will practice in communities currently underserved; and (iv) obtaining the educational benefits that flow from an ethnically diverse student body. It is necessary to decide which, if any, of these purposes is substantial enough to support the use of a suspect classification.

## A

If petitioner's purpose is to assure within its student body some specified percentage of a particular group merely because of its race or ethnic origin, such a preferential purpose must be rejected not as insubstantial but as facially invalid. Preferring members of any one group for no reason other than race or ethnic origin is discrimination for its own sake. This the Constitution forbids. E.g., *Brown*.

## B

The State certainly has a legitimate and substantial interest in ameliorating, or eliminating where feasible, the disabling effects of identified discrimination. The line of school desegregation cases, commencing with *Brown*, attests to the importance of this state goal and the commitment of the judiciary to affirm all lawful means toward its attainment. In the school cases, the States were required by court order to redress the wrongs worked by specific instances of racial discrimination. That goal was far more focused than the remedying of the effects of "societal discrimination," an amorphous concept of injury that may be ageless in its reach into the past.

We have never approved a classification that aids persons perceived as members of relatively victimized groups at the expense of other innocent individuals in the absence of judicial, legislative, or administrative findings of constitutional or statutory violations. After such findings have been made, the governmental interest in preferring members of the injured groups at the expense of others is substantial, since the legal rights of the victims must be vindicated. In such a case, the extent of the injury and the consequent remedy will have been judicially, legislatively, or administratively defined. Also, the remedial action usually remains subject to continuing oversight to assure that it will work the least harm possible to other innocent persons competing for the benefit. Without such findings of constitutional or statutory violations, it cannot be said that the government has any greater interest in helping one individual than in refraining from harming another. Thus, the government has no compelling justification for inflicting such harm.

Petitioner does not purport to have made, and is in no position to make, such findings....

Hence, the purpose of helping certain groups whom the faculty of the Davis Medical School perceived as victims of "societal discrimination" does not justify a classification that imposes disadvantages upon persons like respondent, who bear no responsibility for whatever harm the beneficiaries of the special admissions program are thought to have suffered. To hold otherwise would be to convert a remedy heretofore reserved for violations of legal rights into a privilege that all institutions throughout the Nation could grant at their pleasure to whatever groups are perceived as victims of societal discrimination. That is a step we have never approved.

## C

Petitioner identifies, as another purpose of its program, improving the delivery of health-care services to communities currently underserved. It may be assumed that in some situations a State's interest in facilitating the health care of its citizens is sufficiently compelling to support the use of a suspect classification. But there is virtually no evidence in the record indicating that petitioner's special admissions program is either needed or geared to promote that goal. The court below addressed this failure of proof:

> The University concedes it cannot assure that minority doctors who entered under the program, all of whom expressed an 'interest' in practicing in a disadvantaged community, will actually do so. It may be correct to assume that some of them will carry out this intention, and that it is more likely they will practice in minority communities than the average white doctor. Nevertheless, there are more precise and reliable ways to identify applicants who are genuinely interested in the medical problems of minorities than by race. An applicant of whatever race who has demonstrated his concern for disadvantaged minorities in the past and who declares that practice in such a community is his primary professional goal would be more likely to contribute to alleviation of the medical shortage than one who is chosen entirely on the basis of race and disadvantage. In short, there is no empirical data to demonstrate that any one race is more selflessly socially oriented or by contrast that another is more selfishly acquisitive.

Petitioner simply has not carried its burden of demonstrating that it must prefer members of particular ethnic groups over all other individuals in order to promote better health-care delivery to deprived citizens. Indeed, petitioner has not shown that its preferential classification is likely to have any significant effect on the problem.

## D

The fourth goal asserted by petitioner is the attainment of a diverse student body. This clearly is a constitutionally permissible goal for an institution of higher education. Academic freedom, though not a specifically enumerated constitutional right, long has been viewed as a special concern of the First Amendment. The freedom of a university to make its own judgments as to education includes the selection of its student body....

The atmosphere of "speculation, experiment and creation"—so essential to the quality of higher education—is widely believed to be promoted by a diverse student body. As the Court noted in *Keyishian v. Board of Regents*, 385 U.S. 589 (1967), it is not too much to say that the "nation's future depends upon leaders trained through wide exposure" to the ideas and mores of students as diverse as this Nation of many peoples.

Thus, in arguing that its universities must be accorded the right to select those students who will contribute the most to the "robust exchange of ideas," petitioner invokes a countervailing constitutional interest, that of the First Amendment. In this light, petitioner must be viewed as seeking to achieve a goal that is of paramount importance in the fulfillment of its mission.

It may be argued that there is greater force to these views at the undergraduate level than in a medical school where the training is centered primarily on professional competency. But even at the graduate level, our tradition and experience lend support to the view that the contribution of diversity is substantial....

Ethnic diversity, however, is only one element in a range of factors a university properly may consider in attaining the goal of a heterogeneous student body. Although a university must have wide discretion in making the sensitive judgments as to who should be admitted, constitutional limitations protecting individual rights may not be disregarded. Respondent urges — and the courts below have held — that petitioner's dual admissions program is a racial classification that impermissibly infringes his rights under the Fourteenth Amendment. As the interest of diversity is compelling in the context of a university's admissions program, the question remains whether the program's racial classification is necessary to promote this interest.

V

A

It may be assumed that the reservation of a specified number of seats in each class for individuals from the preferred ethnic groups would contribute to the attainment of considerable ethnic diversity in the student body. But petitioner's argument that this is the only effective means of serving the interest of diversity is seriously flawed. In a most fundamental sense the argument misconceives the nature of the state interest that would justify consideration of race or ethnic background. It is not an interest in simple ethnic diversity, in which a specified percentage of the student body is in effect guaranteed to be members of selected ethnic groups, with the remaining percentage an undifferentiated aggregation of students. The diversity that furthers a compelling state interest encompasses a far broader array of qualifications and characteristics of which racial or ethnic origin is but a single though important element. Petitioner's special admissions program, focused *solely* on ethnic diversity, would hinder rather than further attainment of genuine diversity....

The experience of other university admissions programs, which take race into account in achieving the educational diversity valued by the First Amendment, demonstrates that the assignment of a fixed number of places to a minority group is not a necessary means toward that end. An illuminating example is found in the Harvard College program:

> In recent years Harvard College has expanded the concept of diversity to include students from disadvantaged economic, racial and ethnic groups. Harvard College now recruits not only Californians or Louisianans but also blacks and Chicanos and other minority students....

> In practice, this new definition of diversity has meant that race has been a factor in some admission decisions. When the Committee on Admissions reviews the large middle group of applicants who are 'admissible' and deemed capable of doing good work in their courses, the race of an applicant may tip the balance in his favor just as geographic origin or a life spent on a farm

may tip the balance in other candidates' cases. A farm boy from Idaho can bring something to Harvard College that a Bostonian cannot offer. Similarly, a black student can usually bring something that a white person cannot offer....

In Harvard College admissions the Committee has not set target-quotas for the number of blacks, or of musicians, football players, physicists or Californians to be admitted in a given year.... But that awareness [of the necessity of including more than a token number of black students] does not mean that the Committee sets a minimum number of blacks or of people from west of the Mississippi who are to be admitted. It means only that in choosing among thousands of applicants who are not only 'admissible' academically but have other strong qualities, the Committee, with a number of criteria in mind, pays some attention to distribution among many types and categories of students.

In such an admissions program, race or ethnic background may be deemed a "plus" in a particular applicant's file, yet it does not insulate the individual from comparison with all other candidates for the available seats. The file of a particular black applicant may be examined for his potential contribution to diversity without the factor of race being decisive when compared, for example, with that of an applicant identified as an Italian-American if the latter is thought to exhibit qualities more likely to promote beneficial educational pluralism. Such qualities could include exceptional personal talents, unique work or service experience, leadership potential, maturity, demonstrated compassion, a history of overcoming disadvantage, ability to communicate with the poor, or other qualifications deemed important. In short, an admissions program operated in this way is flexible enough to consider all pertinent elements of diversity in light of the particular qualifications of each applicant, and to place them on the same footing for consideration, although not necessarily according them the same weight. Indeed, the weight attributed to a particular quality may vary from year to year depending upon the "mix" both of the student body and the applicants for the incoming class.

This kind of program treats each applicant as an individual in the admissions process. The applicant who loses out on the last available seat to another candidate receiving a "plus" on the basis of ethnic background will not have been foreclosed from all consideration for that seat simply because he was not the right color or had the wrong surname. It would mean only that his combined qualifications, which may have included similar nonobjective factors, did not outweigh those of the other applicant. His qualifications would have been weighed fairly and competitively, and he would have no basis to complain of unequal treatment under the Fourteenth Amendment.[52]

It has been suggested that an admissions program which considers race only as one factor is simply a subtle and more sophisticated—but no less effective—means of ac-

---

52. The denial to respondent of this right to individualized consideration without regard to his race is the principal evil of petitioner's special admissions program. Nowhere in the opinion of Mr. JUSTICE BRENNAN, Mr. JUSTICE WHITE, Mr. JUSTICE MARSHALL, and Mr. JUSTICE BLACKMUN is this denial even addressed.

cording racial preference than the Davis program. A facial intent to discriminate, however, is evident in petitioner's preference program and not denied in this case. No such facial infirmity exists in an admissions program where race or ethnic background is simply one element—to be weighed fairly against other elements—in the selection process.... And a court would not assume that a university, professing to employ a facially nondiscriminatory admissions policy, would operate it as a cover for the functional equivalent of a quota system. In short, good faith would be presumed in the absence of a showing to the contrary in the manner permitted by our cases.

### B

In summary, it is evident that the Davis special admissions program involves the use of an explicit racial classification never before countenanced by this Court. It tells applicants who are not Negro, Asian, or Chicano that they are totally excluded from a specific percentage of the seats in an entering class. No matter how strong their qualifications, quantitative and extracurricular, including their own potential for contribution to educational diversity, they are never afforded the chance to compete with applicants from the preferred groups for the special admissions seats. At the same time, the preferred applicants have the opportunity to compete for every seat in the class.

The fatal flaw in petitioner's preferential program is its disregard of individual rights as guaranteed by the Fourteenth Amendment. Such rights are not absolute. But when a State's distribution of benefits or imposition of burdens hinges on ancestry or the color of a person's skin, that individual is entitled to a demonstration that the challenged classification is necessary to promote a substantial state interest. Petitioner has failed to carry this burden. For this reason, that portion of the California court's judgment holding petitioner's special admissions program invalid under the Fourteenth Amendment must be affirmed.

### C

In enjoining petitioner from ever considering the race of any applicant, however, the courts below failed to recognize that the State has a substantial interest that legitimately may be served by a properly devised admissions program involving the competitive consideration of race and ethnic origin. For this reason, so much of the California court's judgment as enjoins petitioner from any consideration of the race of any applicant must be reversed....

Opinion of Mr. Justice BRENNAN, Mr. Justice WHITE, Mr. Justice MARSHALL, and Mr. Justice BLACKMUN, concurring in the judgment in part and dissenting in part.

The Court today, in reversing in part the judgment of the Supreme Court of California, affirms the constitutional power of Federal and State Governments to act affirmatively to achieve equal opportunity for all. The difficulty of the issue presented—whether government may use race-conscious programs to redress the continuing effects of past discrimination—and the mature consideration which each of our Brethren has brought to it have resulted in many opinions, no single one speaking for the Court. But this should not and must not mask the central meaning of today's opinions: Government may take race into account when it acts not to demean or insult any racial group, but to remedy disadvantages cast on minorities by past racial prejudice, at least when appropriate findings have been made by judicial, legislative, or administrative bodies with competence to act in this area....

... Since we conclude that the affirmative admissions program at the Davis Medical School is constitutional, we would reverse the judgment below in all respects. Mr. JUS-TICE POWELL agrees that some uses of race in university admissions are permissible and, therefore, he joins with us to make five votes reversing the judgment below insofar as it prohibits the University from establishing race-conscious programs in the future.

I

Our Nation was founded on the principle that "all Men are created equal." Yet candor requires acknowledgment that the Framers of our Constitution, to forge the 13 Colonies into one Nation, openly compromised this principle of equality with its antithesis: slavery. The consequences of this compromise are well known and have aptly been called our "American Dilemma." Still, it is well to recount how recent the time has been, if it has yet come, when the promise of our principles has flowered into the actuality of equal opportunity for all regardless of race or color.

The Fourteenth Amendment, the embodiment in the Constitution of our abiding belief in human equality, has been the law of our land for only slightly more than half its 200 years. And for half of that half, the Equal Protection Clause of the Amendment was largely moribund so that, as late as 1927, Mr. Justice Holmes could sum up the importance of that Clause by remarking that it was the "last resort of constitutional arguments." *Buck v. Bell*, 274 U.S. 200 (1927) [Note *supra.* Chapter 8]. Worse than desuetude, the Clause was early turned against those whom it was intended to set free, condemning them to a "separate but equal" status before the law, a status always separate but seldom equal. Not until 1954—only 24 years ago—was this odious doctrine interred by our decision in *Brown* and its progeny,[3] which proclaimed that separate schools and public facilities of all sorts were inherently unequal and forbidden under our Constitution. Even then inequality was not eliminated with "all deliberate speed." *Brown v. Board of Education* [*Brown II*] (1955) [*Supra.* this chapter]. In 1968 and again in 1971, for example, we were forced to remind school boards of their obligation to eliminate racial discrimination root and branch. And a glance at our docket and at dockets of lower courts will show that even today officially sanctioned discrimination is not a thing of the past.

Against this background, claims that law must be "color-blind" or that the datum of race is no longer relevant to public policy must be seen as aspiration rather than as description of reality. This is not to denigrate aspiration; for reality rebukes us that race has too often been used by those who would stigmatize and oppress minorities.

---

3. *New Orleans City Park Improvement Assn. v. Detiege* (1958); *Muir v. Louisville Park Theatrical Assn.* (1954); *Mayor of Baltimore v. Dawson* (1955); *Holmes v. Atlanta* (1955); *Gayle v. Browder* (1956) [All *supra.* this chapter].

Yet we cannot—and, as we shall demonstrate, need not under our Constitution or Title VI, which merely extends the constraints of the Fourteenth Amendment to private parties who receive federal funds—let color blindness become myopia which masks the reality that many "created equal" have been treated within our lifetimes as inferior both by the law and by their fellow citizens....

III

A

The assertion of human equality is closely associated with the proposition that differences in color or creed, birth or status, are neither significant nor relevant to the way in which persons should be treated. Nonetheless, the position that such factors must be "constitutionally an irrelevance," *Edwards v. California*, 314 U.S. 160 (1941) (Jackson, J., concurring), summed up by the shorthand phrase "our Constitution is color-blind," *Plessy* (Harlan, J., dissenting), has never been adopted by this Court as the proper meaning of the Equal Protection Clause. Indeed, we have expressly rejected this proposition on a number of occasions.

Our cases have always implied that an "overriding statutory purpose" could be found that would justify racial classifications. See, e.g., *Korematsu*. More recently, in *McDaniel v. Barresi* (1971), this Court unanimously reversed the Georgia Supreme Court which had held that a desegregation plan voluntarily adopted by a local school board, which assigned students on the basis of race, was *per se* invalid because it was not color-blind. And in *North Carolina Board of Education v. Swann* we held, again unanimously, that a statute mandating color-blind school-assignment plans could not stand "against the background of segregation," since such a limit on remedies would "render illusory the promise of *Brown I.*" 402 U.S. 43 (1971).

We conclude, therefore, that racial classifications are not *per se* invalid under the Fourteenth Amendment. Accordingly, we turn to the problem of articulating what our role should be in reviewing state action that expressly classifies by race.

B

... Unquestionably we have held that a government practice or statute which restricts "fundamental rights" or which contains "suspect classifications" is to be subjected to "strict scrutiny" and can be justified only if it furthers a compelling government purpose and, even then, only if no less restrictive alternative is available.[30] But no fundamental right is involved here. Nor do whites as a class have any of the "traditional indicia of suspectness: the class is not saddled with such disabilities, or subjected to such a history of purposeful unequal treatment, or relegated to such a position of political powerlessness as to command extraordinary protection from the majoritarian political process." See *Carolene Products* n. 4.[31]

---

30. We do not pause to debate whether our cases establish a "two-tier" analysis, a "sliding scale" analysis, or something else altogether. It is enough for present purposes that strict scrutiny is applied at least in some cases.

31. Of course, the fact that whites constitute a political majority in our Nation does not necessarily mean that active judicial scrutiny of racial classifications that disadvantage whites is inappropriate.

Moreover, if the University's representations are credited, this is not a case where racial classifications are "irrelevant and therefore prohibited." Nor has anyone suggested that the University's purposes contravene the cardinal principle that racial classifications that stigmatize—because they are drawn on the presumption that one race is inferior to another or because they put the weight of government behind racial hatred and separatism—are invalid without more.[33]

On the other hand, the fact that this case does not fit neatly into our prior analytic framework for race cases does not mean that it should be analyzed by applying the very loose rational-basis standard of review that is the very least that is always applied in equal protection cases. "'The mere recitation of a benign, compensatory purpose is not an automatic shield which protects against any inquiry into the actual purposes underlying a statutory scheme.'" *Califano v. Webster*, 430 U.S. 313 (1977), quoting *Weinberger v. Wiesenfeld*, 420 U.S. 636 (1975) [Note *supra.* Chapter 12]. Instead, a number of considerations—developed in gender-discrimination cases but which carry even more force when applied to racial classifications—lead us to conclude that racial classifications designed to further remedial purposes "'must serve important governmental objectives and must be substantially related to achievement of those objectives.'" *Califano*, quoting *Craig v. Boren*.[35]

First, race, like, "gender-based classifications too often [has] been inexcusably utilized to stereotype and stigmatize politically powerless segments of society." While a carefully tailored statute designed to remedy past discrimination could avoid these vices, see *Schlesinger v. Ballard*, 419 U.S. 498 (1975); *Kahn v. Shevin*, 416 U.S. 351 (1974) [Both note *supra.* Chapter 12], we nonetheless have recognized that the line between honest and thoughtful appraisal of the effects of past discrimination and paternalistic stereotyping is not so clear and that a statute based on the latter is patently capable of stigmatizing all women with a badge of inferiority. Cf. *Schlesinger.* State

---

33. Indeed, even in *Plessy v. Ferguson* the Court recognized that a classification by race that presumed one race to be inferior to another would have to be condemned.

35. We disagree with our Brother POWELL's suggestion that the presence of "rival groups which can claim that they, too, are entitled to preferential treatment" distinguishes the gender cases or is relevant to the question of scope of judicial review of race classifications. We are not asked to determine whether groups other than those favored by the Davis program should similarly be favored. All we are asked to do is to pronounce the constitutionality of what Davis has done.

But, were we asked to decide whether any given rival group—German-Americans for example—must constitutionally be accorded preferential treatment, we do have a "principled basis" for deciding this question, one that is well established in our cases: The Davis program expressly sets out four classes which receive preferred status. The program clearly distinguishes whites, but one cannot reason from this a conclusion that German-Americans, as a national group, are singled out for invidious treatment. And even if the Davis program had a differential impact on German-Americans, they would have no constitutional claim unless they could prove that Davis intended invidiously to discriminate against German-Americans. If this could not be shown, then "the principle that calls for the closest scrutiny of distinctions in laws *denying* fundamental rights ... is inapplicable," and the only question is whether it was rational for Davis to conclude that the groups it preferred had a greater claim to compensation than the groups it excluded. Thus, claims of rival groups, although they may create thorny political problems, create relatively simple problems for the courts.

programs designed ostensibly to ameliorate the effects of past racial discrimination obviously create the same hazard of stigma, since they may promote racial separatism and reinforce the views of those who believe that members of racial minorities are inherently incapable of succeeding on their own.

Second, race, like gender and illegitimacy, see *Weber v. Aetna Casualty & Surety Co.*, 406 U.S. 164 (1972) [Note *supra.* Chapter 12], is an immutable characteristic which its possessors are powerless to escape or set aside. While a classification is not *per se* invalid because it divides classes on the basis of an immutable characteristic, see *Weber*, it is nevertheless true that such divisions are contrary to our deep belief that "legal burdens should bear some relationship to individual responsibility or wrongdoing," *Weber*; *Frontiero v. Richardson* (1973) (opinion of BRENNAN, WHITE, and MARSHALL, JJ.) [*Supra.* Chapter 12], and that advancement sanctioned, sponsored, or approved by the State should ideally be based on individual merit or achievement, or at the least on factors within the control of an individual.

Because this principle is so deeply rooted it might be supposed that it would be considered in the legislative process and weighed against the benefits of programs preferring individuals because of their race. But this is not necessarily so: The "natural consequence of our governing process [may well be] that the most 'discrete and insular' of whites ... will be called upon to bear the immediate, direct costs of benign discrimination." Moreover, it is clear from our cases that there are limits beyond which majorities may not go when they classify on the basis of immutable characteristics. See, e.g., *Weber*. Thus, even if the concern for individualism is weighed by the political process, that weighing cannot waive the personal rights of individuals under the Fourteenth Amendment.

In sum, because of the significant risk that racial classifications established for ostensibly benign purposes can be misused, causing effects not unlike those created by invidious classifications, it is inappropriate to inquire only whether there is any conceivable basis that might sustain such a classification. Instead, to justify such a classification an important and articulated purpose for its use must be shown. In addition, any statute must be stricken that stigmatizes any group or that singles out those least well represented in the political process to bear the brunt of a benign program. Thus, our review under the Fourteenth Amendment should be strict—not "'strict' in theory and fatal in fact," because it is stigma that causes fatality—but strict and searching nonetheless.

## IV

Davis' articulated purpose of remedying the effects of past societal discrimination is, under our cases, sufficiently important to justify the use of race-conscious admissions programs where there is a sound basis for concluding that minority underrepresentation is substantial and chronic, and that the handicap of past discrimination is impeding access of minorities to the Medical School.

## A

At least since *Green v. County School Board*, 391 U.S. 430 (1968), it has been clear that a public body which has itself been adjudged to have engaged in racial discrimination cannot bring itself into compliance with the Equal Protection Clause simply by ending its unlawful acts and adopting a neutral stance. Three years later, *Swann v. Charlotte-Mecklenburg Board of Education*, 402 U.S. 1 (1971) ... reiterated that racially neutral remedies for past discrimination were inadequate where consequences of past discriminatory acts influence or control present decisions. And the Court further held both that courts could enter desegregation orders which assigned students and faculty by reference to race, and that local school boards could *voluntarily* adopt desegregation plans which made express reference to race if this was necessary to remedy the effects of past discrimination. Moreover, we stated that school boards, even in the absence of a judicial finding of past discrimination, could voluntarily adopt plans which assigned students with the end of creating racial pluralism by establishing fixed ratios of black and white students in each school. In each instance, the creation of unitary school systems, in which the effects of past discrimination had been "eliminated root and branch," *Green*, was recognized as a compelling social goal justifying the overt use of race.

Finally, the conclusion that state educational institutions may constitutionally adopt admissions programs designed to avoid exclusion of historically disadvantaged minorities, even when such programs explicitly take race into account, finds direct support in our cases construing congressional legislation designed to overcome the present effects of past discrimination. Congress can and has outlawed actions which have a disproportionately adverse and unjustified impact upon members of racial minorities and has required or authorized race-conscious action to put individuals disadvantaged by such impact in the position they otherwise might have enjoyed. See *Franks v. Bowman Transportation Co.* Such relief does not require as a predicate proof that recipients of preferential advancement have been individually discriminated against; it is enough that each recipient is within a general class of persons likely to have been the victims of discrimination....

These cases cannot be distinguished simply by the presence of judicial findings of discrimination, for race-conscious remedies have been approved where such findings have not been made. *McDaniel; Schlesinger; Kahn.* Indeed, the requirement of a judicial determination of a constitutional or statutory violation as a predicate for race-conscious remedial actions would be self-defeating. Such a requirement would severely undermine efforts to achieve voluntary compliance with the requirements of law. And our society and jurisprudence have always stressed the value of voluntary efforts to further the objectives of the law. Judicial intervention is a last resort to achieve cessation of illegal conduct or the remedying of its effects rather than a prerequisite to action.

Nor can our cases be distinguished on the ground that the entity using explicit racial classifications itself had violated § 1 of the Fourteenth Amendment or an antidiscrimination regulation, for again race-conscious remedies have been approved where this is not the case. Moreover, the presence or absence of past discrimination by universities or employers is largely irrelevant to resolving respondent's constitutional claims. The claims of those burdened by the race-conscious actions of a university or employer who has never been adjudged in violation of an antidiscrimination law are not any more or less entitled to deference than the claims of the burdened non-minority workers in *Franks v. Bowman Transportation Co.*, in which the employer had violated Title VII, for in each case the employees are innocent of past discrimination....

Thus, our cases under Title VII of the Civil Rights Act have held that, in order to achieve minority participation in previously segregated areas of public life, Congress may require or authorize preferential treatment for those likely disadvantaged by societal racial discrimination. Such legislation has been sustained even without a requirement of findings of intentional racial discrimination by those required or authorized to accord preferential treatment, or a case-by-case determination that those to be benefited suffered from racial discrimination. These decisions compel the conclusion that States also may adopt race-conscious programs designed to overcome substantial, chronic minority underrepresentation where there is reason to believe that the evil addressed is a product of past racial discrimination....

... We therefore conclude that Davis' goal of admitting minority students disadvantaged by the effects of past discrimination is sufficiently important to justify use of race-conscious admissions criteria.

B

Properly construed, therefore, our prior cases unequivocally show that a state government may adopt race-conscious programs if the purpose of such programs is to remove the disparate racial impact its actions might otherwise have and if there is reason to believe that the disparate impact is itself the product of past discrimination, whether its own or that of society at large. There is no question that Davis' program is valid under this test.

Certainly, on the basis of the undisputed factual submissions before this Court, Davis had a sound basis for believing that the problem of underrepresentation of minorities was substantial and chronic and that the problem was attributable to handicaps imposed on minority applicants by past and present racial discrimination....

Moreover, Davis had very good reason to believe that the national pattern of underrepresentation of minorities in medicine would be perpetuated if it retained a single admissions standard. For example, the entering classes in 1968 and 1969, the years in which such a standard was used, included only 1 Chicano and 2 Negroes out of the 50 admittees for each year. Nor is there any relief from this pattern of underrepresentation in the statistics for the regular admissions program in later years.

Davis clearly could conclude that the serious and persistent underrepresentation of minorities in medicine depicted by these statistics is the result of handicaps under which minority applicants labor as a consequence of a background of deliberate, purposeful discrimination against minorities in education and in society generally, as well as in the medical profession. From the inception of our national life, Negroes have been subjected to unique legal disabilities impairing access to equal educational opportunity. Under slavery, penal sanctions were imposed upon anyone attempting to educate Negroes. After enactment of the Fourteenth Amendment the States continued to deny Negroes equal educational opportunity, enforcing a strict policy of segregation that itself stamped Negroes as inferior, *Brown I*, that relegated minorities to inferior educational institutions, and that denied them intercourse in the mainstream of professional life necessary to advancement....

Moreover, we need not rest solely on our own conclusion that Davis had sound reason to believe that the effects of past discrimination were handicapping minority applicants to the Medical School, because the Department of Health, Education, and Welfare, the expert agency charged by Congress with promulgating regulations enforcing Title VI of the Civil Rights Act of 1964, has also reached the conclusion that race may be taken into account in situations where a failure to do so would limit participation by minorities in federally funded programs, and regulations promulgated by the Department expressly contemplate that appropriate race-conscious programs may be adopted by universities to remedy unequal access to university programs caused by their own or by past societal discrimination....

C

The second prong of our test—whether the Davis program stigmatizes any discrete group or individual and whether race is reasonably used in light of the program's objectives—is clearly satisfied by the Davis program.

It is not even claimed that Davis' program in any way operates to stigmatize or single out any discrete and insular, or even any identifiable, nonminority group. Nor will harm comparable to that imposed upon racial minorities by exclusion or separation on grounds of race be the likely result of the program....

Nor was Bakke in any sense stamped as inferior by the Medical School's rejection of him. Indeed, it is conceded by all that he satisfied those criteria regarded by the school as generally relevant to academic performance better than most of the minority members who were admitted. Moreover, there is absolutely no basis for concluding that Bakke's rejection as a result of Davis' use of racial preference will affect him throughout his life in the same way as the segregation of the Negro schoolchildren in *Brown I* would have affected them. Unlike discrimination against racial minorities, the use of racial preferences for remedial purposes does not inflict a pervasive injury upon individual whites in the sense that wherever they go or whatever they do there is a significant likelihood that they will be treated as second-class citizens because of their color. This distinction does not mean that the exclusion of a white resulting from the preferential use of race is not sufficiently serious to require justification; but it does mean that the injury inflicted by such a policy is not distinguishable from disadvantages caused by a wide range of government actions, none of which has ever been thought impermissible for that reason alone.

In addition, there is simply no evidence that the Davis program discriminates intentionally or unintentionally against any minority group which it purports to benefit. The program does not establish a quota in the invidious sense of a ceiling on the number of minority applicants to be admitted. Nor can the program reasonably be regarded as stigmatizing the program's beneficiaries or their race as inferior. The Davis program does not simply advance less qualified applicants; rather, it compensates applicants, who it is uncontested are fully qualified to study medicine, for educational disadvantages which it was reasonable to conclude were a product of state-fostered discrimination. Once admitted, these students must satisfy the same degree requirements as regularly admitted students; they are taught by the same faculty in the same classes; and their performance is evaluated by the same standards by which regularly admitted students are judged. Under these circumstances, their performance and degrees must be regarded equally with the regularly admitted students with whom they compete for standing. Since minority graduates cannot justifiably be regarded as less well qualified than nonminority graduates by virtue of the special admissions program, there is no reasonable basis to conclude that minority graduates at schools using such programs would be stigmatized as inferior by the existence of such programs.

## D

We disagree with the lower courts' conclusion that the Davis program's use of race was unreasonable in light of its objectives. First, as petitioner argues, there are no practical means by which it could achieve its ends in the foreseeable future without the use of race-conscious measures. With respect to any factor (such as poverty or family educational background) that may be used as a substitute for race as an indicator of past discrimination, whites greatly outnumber racial minorities simply because whites make up a far larger percentage of the total population and therefore far outnumber minorities in absolute terms at every socioeconomic level.... Moreover, while race is positively correlated with differences in GPA and MCAT scores, economic disadvantage is not. Thus, it appears that economically disadvantaged whites do not score less well than economically advantaged whites, while economically advantaged blacks score less well than do disadvantaged whites. These statistics graphically illustrate that the University's purpose to integrate its classes by compensating for past discrimination could not be achieved by a general preference for the economically disadvantaged or the children of parents of limited education unless such groups were to make up the entire class.

Second, the Davis admissions program does not simply equate minority status with disadvantage. Rather, Davis considers on an individual basis each applicant's personal history to determine whether he or she has likely been disadvantaged by racial discrimination. The record makes clear that only minority applicants likely to have been isolated from the mainstream of American life are considered in the special program; other minority applicants are eligible only through the regular admissions program.... A case-by-case inquiry into the extent to which each individual applicant has been affected, either directly or indirectly, by racial discrimination, would seem to be, as a practical matter, virtually impossible, despite the fact that there are excellent reasons for concluding that such effects generally exist. When individual measurement is impossible or extremely impractical, there is nothing to prevent a State from using categorical means to achieve its ends, at least where the category is closely related to the goal....

E

Finally, Davis' special admissions program cannot be said to violate the Constitution simply because it has set aside a predetermined number of places for qualified minority applicants rather than using minority status as a positive factor to be considered in evaluating the applications of disadvantaged minority applicants. For purposes of constitutional adjudication, there is no difference between the two approaches. In any admissions program which accords special consideration to disadvantaged racial minorities, a determination of the degree of preference to be given is unavoidable, and any given preference that results in the exclusion of a white candidate is no more or less constitutionally acceptable than a program such as that at Davis.... There is no sensible, and certainly no constitutional, distinction between, for example, adding a set number of points to the admissions rating of disadvantaged minority applicants as an expression of the preference with the expectation that this will result in the admission of an approximately determined number of qualified minority applicants and setting a fixed number of places for such applicants as was done here.

The "Harvard" program, as those employing it readily concede, openly and successfully employs a racial criterion for the purpose of ensuring that some of the scarce places in institutions of higher education are allocated to disadvantaged minority students. That the Harvard approach does not also make public the extent of the preference and the precise workings of the system while the Davis program employs a specific, openly stated number, does not condemn the latter plan for purposes of Fourteenth Amendment adjudication. It may be that the Harvard plan is more acceptable to the public than is the Davis "quota." If it is, any State, including California, is free to adopt it in preference to a less acceptable alternative, just as it is generally free, as far as the Constitution is concerned, to abjure granting any racial preferences in its admissions program. But there is no basis for preferring a particular preference program simply because in achieving the same goals that the Davis Medical School is pursuing, it proceeds in a manner that is not immediately apparent to the public.

V

Accordingly, we would reverse the judgment of the Supreme Court of California holding the Medical School's special admissions program unconstitutional and directing respondent's admission, as well as that portion of the judgment enjoining the Medical School from according any consideration to race in the admissions process.

Separate opinion of Mr. JUSTICE WHITE. [omitted]

Mr. JUSTICE MARSHALL.

I agree with the judgment of the Court only insofar as it permits a university to consider the race of an applicant in making admissions decisions. I do not agree that petitioner's admissions program violates the Constitution. For it must be remembered that, during most of the past 200 years, the Constitution as interpreted by this Court did not prohibit the most ingenious and pervasive forms of discrimination against the Negro. Now, when a State acts to remedy the effects of that legacy of discrimination, I cannot believe that this same Constitution stands as a barrier.

## I
### A

Three hundred and fifty years ago, the Negro was dragged to this country in chains to be sold into slavery. Uprooted from his homeland and thrust into bondage for forced labor, the slave was deprived of all legal rights. It was unlawful to teach him to read; he could be sold away from his family and friends at the whim of his master; and killing or maiming him was not a crime. The system of slavery brutalized and dehumanized both master and slave....

### B

The status of the Negro as property was officially erased by his emancipation at the end of the Civil War. But the long-awaited emancipation, while freeing the Negro from slavery, did not bring him citizenship or equality in any meaningful way. Slavery was replaced by a system of "laws which imposed upon the colored race onerous disabilities and burdens, and curtailed their rights in the pursuit of life, liberty, and property to such an extent that their freedom was of little value." *Slaughter-House Cases* (1873) [Note *supra.* Part III Introduction]. Despite the passage of the Thirteenth, Fourteenth, and Fifteenth Amendments, the Negro was systematically denied the rights those Amendments were supposed to secure. The combined actions and inactions of the State and Federal Governments maintained Negroes in a position of legal inferiority for another century after the Civil War....

The Court's ultimate blow to the Civil War Amendments and to the equality of Negroes came in *Plessy*. In upholding a Louisiana law that required railway companies to provide "equal but separate" accommodations for whites and Negroes, the Court held that the Fourteenth Amendment was not intended "to abolish distinctions based upon color, or to enforce social, as distinguished from political equality, or a commingling of the two races upon terms unsatisfactory to either." Ignoring totally the realities of the positions of the two races, the Court remarked:

> We consider the underlying fallacy of the plaintiff's argument to consist in the assumption that the enforced separation of the two races stamps the colored race with a badge of inferiority. If this be so, it is not by reason of anything found in the act, but solely because the colored race chooses to put that construction upon it.

Mr. Justice Harlan's dissenting opinion recognized the bankruptcy of the Court's reasoning. He noted that the "real meaning" of the legislation was "that colored citizens are so inferior and degraded that they cannot be allowed to sit in public coaches occupied by white citizens." He expressed his fear that if like laws were enacted in other States, "the effect would be in the highest degree mischievous." Although slavery would have disappeared, the States would retain the power "to interfere with the full enjoyment of the blessings of freedom; to regulate civil rights, common to all citizens, upon the basis of race; and to place in a condition of legal inferiority a large body of American citizens…."

The fears of Mr. Justice Harlan were soon to be realized. In the wake of *Plessy*, many States expanded their Jim Crow laws, which had up until that time been limited primarily to passenger trains and schools. The segregation of the races was extended to residential areas, parks, hospitals, theaters, waiting rooms, and bathrooms. There were even statutes and ordinances which authorized separate phone booths for Negroes and whites, which required that textbooks used by children of one race be kept separate from those used by the other, and which required that Negro and white prostitutes be kept in separate districts….

Nor were the laws restricting the rights of Negroes limited solely to the Southern States. In many of the Northern States, the Negro was denied the right to vote, prevented from serving on juries, and excluded from theaters, restaurants, hotels, and inns. Under President Wilson, the Federal Government began to require segregation in Government buildings; desks of Negro employees were curtained off; separate bathrooms and separate tables in the cafeterias were provided; and even the galleries of the Congress were segregated….

The enforced segregation of the races continued into the middle of the 20th century….

## II

The position of the Negro today in America is the tragic but inevitable consequence of centuries of unequal treatment. Measured by any benchmark of comfort or achievement, meaningful equality remains a distant dream for the Negro….

In light of the sorry history of discrimination and its devastating impact on the lives of Negroes, bringing the Negro into the mainstream of American life should be a state interest of the highest order. To fail to do so is to ensure that America will forever remain a divided society.

## III

I do not believe that the Fourteenth Amendment requires us to accept that fate. Neither its history nor our past cases lend any support to the conclusion that a university may not remedy the cumulative effects of society's discrimination by giving consideration to race in an effort to increase the number and percentage of Negro doctors.

## A

… It is plain that the Fourteenth Amendment was not intended to prohibit measures designed to remedy the effects of the Nation's past treatment of Negroes. The Congress that passed the Fourteenth Amendment is the same Congress that passed the 1866 Freedmen's Bureau Act, an Act that provided many of its benefits only to Negroes. Although the Freedmen's Bureau legislation provided aid for refugees, thereby including white persons within some of the relief measures, the bill was regarded, to the dismay of many Congressmen, as "solely and entirely for the freedmen, and to the exclusion of all other persons...." ... The bill's supporters defended it — not by rebutting the claim of special treatment — but by pointing to the need for such treatment....

Since the Congress that considered and rejected the objections to the 1866 Freedmen's Bureau Act concerning special relief to Negroes also proposed the Fourteenth Amendment, it is inconceivable that the Fourteenth Amendment was intended to prohibit all race-conscious relief measures. It "would be a distortion of the policy manifested in that amendment, which was adopted to prevent state legislation designed to perpetuate discrimination on the basis of race or color," to hold that it barred state action to remedy the effects of that discrimination. Such a result would pervert the intent of the Framers by substituting abstract equality for the genuine equality the Amendment was intended to achieve....

## IV

While I applaud the judgment of the Court that a university may consider race in its admissions process, it is more than a little ironic that, after several hundred years of class-based discrimination against Negroes, the Court is unwilling to hold that a class-based remedy for that discrimination is permissible. In declining to so hold, today's judgment ignores the fact that for several hundred years Negroes have been discriminated against, not as individuals, but rather solely because of the color of their skins. It is unnecessary in 20th-century America to have individual Negroes demonstrate that they have been victims of racial discrimination; the racism of our society has been so pervasive that none, regardless of wealth or position, has managed to escape its impact. The experience of Negroes in America has been different in kind, not just in degree, from that of other ethnic groups. It is not merely the history of slavery alone but also that a whole people were marked as inferior by the law. And that mark has endured. The dream of America as the great melting pot has not been realized for the Negro; because of his skin color he never even made it into the pot.

These differences in the experience of the Negro make it difficult for me to accept that Negroes cannot be afforded greater protection under the Fourteenth Amendment where it is necessary to remedy the effects of past discrimination. In the *Civil Rights Cases*, 109 U.S. 3 (1883), the Court wrote that the Negro emerging from slavery must cease "to be the special favorite of the laws." We cannot in light of the history of the last century yield to that view. Had the Court in that decision and others been willing to "do for human liberty and the fundamental rights of American citizenship, what it did ... for the protection of slavery and the rights of the masters of fugitive slaves," *id.* (Harlan, J., dissenting), we would not need now to permit the recognition of any "special wards."

Most importantly, had the Court been willing in 1896, in *Plessy*, to hold that the Equal Protection Clause forbids differences in treatment based on race, we would not be faced with this dilemma in 1978. We must remember, however, that the principle that the "Constitution is color-blind" appeared only in the opinion of the lone dissenter. The majority of the Court rejected the principle of color-blindness, and for the next [58] years, from *Plessy* to *Brown I*, ours was a Nation where, *by law*, an individual could be given "special" treatment based on the color of his skin.

It is because of a legacy of unequal treatment that we now must permit the institutions of this society to give consideration to race in making decisions about who will hold the positions of influence, affluence, and prestige in America. For far too long, the doors to those positions have been shut to Negroes. If we are ever to become a fully integrated society, one in which the color of a person's skin will not determine the opportunities available to him or her, we must be willing to take steps to open those doors. I do not believe that anyone can truly look into America's past and still find that a remedy for the effects of that past is impermissible....

I fear that we have come full circle. After the Civil War our Government started several "affirmative action" programs. This Court in the *Civil Rights Cases* and *Plessy* destroyed the movement toward complete equality. For almost a century no action was taken, and this nonaction was with the tacit approval of the courts. Then we had *Brown I* and the Civil Rights Acts of Congress, followed by numerous affirmative-action programs. *Now*, we have this Court again stepping in, this time to stop affirmative-action programs of the type used by the University of California.

Mr. JUSTICE BLACKMUN.

I participate fully, of course, in the opinion that bears the names of my Brothers BRENNAN, WHITE, MARSHALL, and myself. I add only some general observations that hold particular significance for me, and then a few comments on equal protection.

I

At least until the early 1970's, apparently only a very small number, less than 2%, of the physicians, attorneys, and medical and law students in the United States were members of what we now refer to as minority groups. In addition, approximately three-fourths of our Negro physicians were trained at only two medical schools. If ways are not found to remedy that situation, the country can never achieve its professed goal of a society that is not race conscious.

I yield to no one in my earnest hope that the time will come when an "affirmative action" program is unnecessary and is, in truth, only a relic of the past. I would hope that we could reach this stage within a decade at the most. But the story of *Brown I*, decided almost a quarter of a century ago, suggests that that hope is a slim one. At some time, however, beyond any period of what some would claim is only transitional inequality, the United States must and will reach a stage of maturity where action along this line is no longer necessary. Then persons will be regarded as persons, and discrimination of the type we address today will be an ugly feature of history that is instructive but that is behind us.

The number of qualified, indeed highly qualified, applicants for admission to existing medical schools in the United States far exceeds the number of places available.... This inescapable fact is brought into sharp focus here because Allan Bakke is not himself charged with discrimination and yet is the one who is disadvantaged, and because the Medical School of the University of California at Davis itself is not charged with historical discrimination....

It is somewhat ironic to have us so deeply disturbed over a program where race is an element of consciousness, and yet to be aware of the fact, as we are, that institutions of higher learning, albeit more on the undergraduate than the graduate level, have given conceded preferences up to a point to those possessed of athletic skills, to the children of alumni, to the affluent who may bestow their largess on the institutions, and to those having connections with celebrities, the famous, and the powerful.

Programs of admission to institutions of higher learning are basically a responsibility for academicians and for administrators and the specialists they employ. The judiciary, in contrast, is ill-equipped and poorly trained for this.... For me, therefore, interference by the judiciary must be the rare exception and not the rule.

## II

I, of course, accept the propositions that (a) Fourteenth Amendment rights are personal; (b) racial and ethnic distinctions where they are stereotypes are inherently suspect and call for exacting judicial scrutiny; (c) academic freedom is a special concern of the First Amendment; and (d) the Fourteenth Amendment has expanded beyond its original 1868 concept and now is recognized to have reached a point where, as Mr. JUSTICE POWELL states..., it embraces a "broader principle."

This enlargement does not mean for me, however, that the Fourteenth Amendment has broken away from its moorings and its original intended purposes. Those original aims persist. And that, in a distinct sense, is what "affirmative action," in the face of proper facts, is all about. If this conflicts with idealistic equality, that tension is original Fourteenth Amendment tension, constitutionally conceived and constitutionally imposed, and it is part of the Amendment's very nature until complete equality is achieved in the area. In this sense, constitutional equal protection is a shield.

I emphasize in particular that the decided cases are not easily to be brushed aside. Many, of course, are not precisely on point, but neither are they off point. Racial factors have been given consideration in the school desegregation cases [and] in the employment cases. To be sure, some of these may be "distinguished" on the ground that victimization was directly present. But who is to say that victimization is not present for some members of today's minority groups, although it is of a lesser and perhaps different degree....

I am not convinced, as Mr. JUSTICE POWELL seems to be, that the difference between the Davis program and the one employed by Harvard is very profound or constitutionally significant. The line between the two is a thin and indistinct one. In each, subjective application is at work....

I add these only as additional components on the edges of the central question as to which I join my Brothers BRENNAN, WHITE, and MARSHALL in our more general approach. It is gratifying to know that the Court at least finds it constitutional for an academic institution to take race and ethnic background into consideration as one factor, among many, in the administration of its admissions program. I presume that that factor always has been there, though perhaps not conceded or even admitted. It is a fact of life, however, and a part of the real world of which we are all a part. The sooner we get down the road toward accepting and being a part of the real world, and not shutting it out and away from us, the sooner will these difficulties vanish from the scene.

I suspect that it would be impossible to arrange an affirmative-action program in a racially neutral way and have it successful. To ask that this be so is to demand the impossible. In order to get beyond racism, we must first take account of race. There is no other way. And in order to treat some persons equally, we must treat them differently. We cannot — we dare not — let the Equal Protection Clause perpetuate racial supremacy....

Mr. JUSTICE STEVENS, with whom THE CHIEF JUSTICE, Mr. JUSTICE STEWART, and Mr. JUSTICE REHNQUIST join, concurring in the judgment in part and dissenting in part.

[Justice Stevens, joined by three other justices, concluded that the Davis program violated Title VI. Given that conclusion he did not reach the constitutional issue.]

## Note: The Debate in Bakke

*Bakke* is the first case where the modern Court deeply engaged the question whether race conscious government action could ever be upheld as benign. In answering that question, the opinions of Justices Powell, Brennan, Marshall, and Blackmun raise fundamental issues about the nature and history of the Equal Protection Clause, the role of political process analysis, and the permissible (and impermissible) reasons for state officials to use race in their decision-making. Who do you find most persuasive, and why?

As you saw in *Bakke*, the Court's answers to these questions were highly fractured. They were also incomplete, given that four justices refrained from reaching the constitutional issue. Moreover, the uniqueness of the university admissions context made it even clearer that that case would not conclusively resolve the constitutionality of race-based affirmative action. It would take another decade before a (narrow) majority would coalesce to answer that question, and more than yet another decade before that consensus would be tested in the higher education context.

## Note: From Bakke to Croson

1. The Court's splintered decision in *Bakke* presaged a decade where the Court struggled to arrive at a majority position on the appropriate level of judicial review of government uses of race defended as benign. After *Bakke* the focus shifted away from university admissions and toward other contexts, but in no context was it able to produce a majority view.

2. In *Fullilove v. Klutznick*, 448 U.S. 448 (1980), the Court upheld a provision in a federal law allocating money to states for construction projects which required that a certain percentage of those contracts be set aside for minority business enterprises.

Six justices voted to uphold the set-aside, but spoke in a series of three opinions, none of which commanded more than three votes. *Fullilove* is discussed more in a note after the next excerpted case.

3. *Wygant v. Jackson Board of Education*, 476 U.S. 267 (1986), considered a contract signed by a board of education with a teacher's union which provided for a seniority rule in allocating layoffs, but with the proviso that minority teachers could not comprise a greater percentage of those laid off than their percentage in the overall teaching corps. Four justices rejected the conclusion of the district court that the layoff provision was a constitutionally valid effort to combat societal discrimination by ensuring that minority schoolchildren had minority teacher role models. They concluded that the plan did not satisfy the strict scrutiny required of such race-conscious government action. Justice White provided the fifth vote for the result, but concurred only in the judgment. He wrote:

> Whatever the legitimacy of hiring goals or quotas may be, the discharge of white teachers to make room for blacks, none of whom has been shown to be a victim of any racial discrimination, is quite a different matter. I cannot believe that in order to integrate a work force, it would be permissible to discharge whites and hire blacks until the latter comprised a suitable percentage of the work force. None of our cases suggest that this would be permissible under the Equal Protection Clause.... The layoff policy in this case—laying off whites who would otherwise be retained in order to keep blacks on the job—has the same effect and is equally violative of the Equal Protection Clause.

4. In *United States v. Paradise*, 480 U.S. 149 (1987), the Court was called on to judge the constitutionality of a district court's order, entered in response to a finding that a state police force had unconstitutionally discriminated in hiring and promoting black troopers, ordering the patrol for "a limited period of time" to promote one black trooper for every white trooper it promoted, as long as qualified black troopers were available and subject to other conditions.

Writing for four justices, Justice Brennan stated that it was "well established that government bodies, including courts, may constitutionally employ racial classifications essential to remedy unlawful treatment of racial or ethnic groups subject to discrimination." But he also acknowledged that the Court "has yet to reach consensus on the appropriate constitutional analysis" of such use of race. Nevertheless, he concluded that the Court did not have to reach that question, since the court's use of a race-conscious remedial order satisfied even strict scrutiny. Justice Stevens concurred in the judgment, concluding that the court order was constitutional on the authority of Court decisions authorizing race-conscious school desegregation remedies when a school district, like the state police in this case, was found to have engaged in unconstitutional discrimination. Chief Justice Rehnquist and Justices White, O'Connor and Scalia dissented.

# City of Richmond v. J.A. Croson Co.

## 488 U.S. 469 (1989)

JUSTICE O'CONNOR announced the judgment of the Court and delivered the opinion of the Court with respect to Parts I, III-B, and IV, an opinion with respect to Part II, in which THE CHIEF JUSTICE and JUSTICE WHITE join, and an opinion with respect to Parts III-A and V, in which THE CHIEF JUSTICE, JUSTICE WHITE, and JUSTICE KENNEDY join.

In this case, we confront once again the tension between the Fourteenth Amendment's guarantee of equal treatment to all citizens, and the use of race-based measures to ameliorate the effects of past discrimination on the opportunities enjoyed by members of minority groups in our society....

## I

On April 11, 1983, the Richmond City Council adopted the Minority Business Utilization Plan (the Plan). The Plan required prime contractors to whom the city awarded construction contracts to subcontract at least 30% of the dollar amount of the contract to one or more Minority Business Enterprises (MBE's).... The Plan defined an MBE as "[a] business at least fifty-one (51) percent of which is owned and controlled ... by minority group members." "Minority group members" were defined as "citizens of the United States who are Blacks, Spanish-speaking, Orientals, Indians, Eskimos, or Aleuts." There was no geographic limit to the Plan; an otherwise qualified MBE from anywhere in the United States could avail itself of the 30% set-aside. The Plan declared that it was "remedial" in nature, and enacted "for the purpose of promoting wider participation by minority business enterprises in the construction of public projects." ...

## III

## A

The Equal Protection Clause of the Fourteenth Amendment provides that "no State shall ... deny to *any person* within its jurisdiction the equal protection of the laws" (emphasis added). As this Court has noted in the past, the "rights created by the first section of the Fourteenth Amendment are, by its terms, guaranteed to the individual. The rights established are personal rights." The Richmond Plan denies certain citizens the opportunity to compete for a fixed percentage of public contracts based solely upon their race. To whatever racial group these citizens belong, their "personal rights" to be treated with equal dignity and respect are implicated by a rigid rule erecting race as the sole criterion in an aspect of public decisionmaking.

Absent searching judicial inquiry into the justification for such race-based measures, there is simply no way of determining what classifications are "benign" or "remedial" and what classifications are in fact motivated by illegitimate notions of racial inferiority or simple racial politics. Indeed, the purpose of strict scrutiny is to "smoke out" illegitimate uses of race by assuring that the legislative body is pursuing a goal important enough to warrant use of a highly suspect tool. The test also ensures that the means chosen "fit" this compelling goal so closely that there is little or no possibility that the motive for the classification was illegitimate racial prejudice or stereotype.

Classifications based on race carry a danger of stigmatic harm. Unless they are strictly reserved for remedial settings, they may in fact promote notions of racial inferiority and lead to a politics of racial hostility. We thus reaffirm the view expressed by the plurality in *Wygant v. Jackson Board of Education*, 476 U.S. 267 (1986), [Note *supra.* this chapter] that the standard of review under the Equal Protection Clause is not dependent on the race of those burdened or benefited by a particular classification....

Even were we to accept a reading of the guarantee of equal protection under which the level of scrutiny varies according to the ability of different groups to defend their interests in the representative process, heightened scrutiny would still be appropriate in the circumstances of this case. One of the central arguments for applying a less exacting standard to "benign" racial classifications is that such measures essentially involve a choice made by dominant racial groups to disadvantage themselves. If one aspect of the judiciary's role under the Equal Protection Clause is to protect "discrete and insular minorities" from majoritarian prejudice or indifference, some maintain that these concerns are not implicated when the "white majority" places burdens upon itself.

In this case, blacks constitute approximately 50% of the population of the city of Richmond. Five of the nine seats on the city council are held by blacks. The concern that a political majority will more easily act to the disadvantage of a minority based on unwarranted assumptions or incomplete facts would seem to militate for, not against, the application of heightened judicial scrutiny in this case....

B

... Like the "role model" theory employed in *Wygant*, a generalized assertion that there has been past discrimination in an entire industry provides no guidance for a legislative body to determine the precise scope of the injury it seeks to remedy. It "has no logical stopping point." "Relief" for such an ill-defined wrong could extend until the percentage of public contracts awarded to MBE's in Richmond mirrored the percentage of minorities in the population as a whole.

Appellant argues that it is attempting to remedy various forms of past discrimination that are alleged to be responsible for the small number of minority businesses in the local contracting industry. Among these the city cites the exclusion of blacks from skilled construction trade unions and training programs. This past discrimination has prevented them "from following the traditional path from laborer to entrepreneur." The city also lists a host of nonracial factors which would seem to face a member of any racial group attempting to establish a new business enterprise, such as deficiencies in working capital, inability to meet bonding requirements, unfamiliarity with bidding procedures, and disability caused by an inadequate track record.

While there is no doubt that the sorry history of both private and public discrimination in this country has contributed to a lack of opportunities for black entrepreneurs, this observation, standing alone, cannot justify a rigid racial quota in the awarding of public contracts in Richmond, Virginia. Like the claim that discrimination in primary and secondary schooling justifies a rigid racial preference in medical school admissions, an amorphous claim that there has been past discrimination in a particular industry cannot justify the use of an unyielding racial quota.

It is sheer speculation how many minority firms there would be in Richmond absent past societal discrimination, just as [in *Bakke*] it was sheer speculation how many minority medical students would have been admitted to the medical school at Davis absent past discrimination in educational opportunities. Defining these sorts of injuries as "identified discrimination" would give local governments license to create a patchwork of racial preferences based on statistical generalizations about any particular field of endeavor.

These defects are readily apparent in this case. The 30% quota cannot in any realistic sense be tied to any injury suffered by anyone. The District Court relied upon five predicate "facts" in reaching its conclusion that there was an adequate basis for the 30% quota: (1) the ordinance declares itself to be remedial; (2) several proponents of the measure stated their views that there had been past discrimination in the construction industry; (3) minority businesses received 0.67% of prime contracts from the city while minorities constituted 50% of the city's population; (4) there were very few minority contractors in local and state contractors' associations; and (5) in 1977, Congress made a determination that the effects of past discrimination had stifled minority participation in the construction industry nationally.

None of these "findings," singly or together, provide the city of Richmond with a "strong basis in evidence for its conclusion that remedial action was necessary." ... There is nothing approaching a prima facie case of a constitutional or statutory violation by *anyone* in the Richmond construction industry.

The District Court accorded great weight to the fact that the city council designated the Plan as "remedial." But the mere recitation of a "benign" or legitimate purpose for a racial classification is entitled to little or no weight....

Finally, the city and the District Court relied on Congress' finding in connection with the set-aside approved in *Fullilove v. Klutznick*, 448 U.S. 448 (1980) [Note *supra*. this chapter], that there had been nationwide discrimination in the construction industry. The probative value of these findings for demonstrating the existence of discrimination in Richmond is extremely limited. By its inclusion of a waiver procedure in the national program addressed in *Fullilove*, Congress explicitly recognized that the scope of the problem would vary from market area to market area....

In sum, none of the evidence presented by the city points to any identified discrimination in the Richmond construction industry.... To accept Richmond's claim that past societal discrimination alone can serve as the basis for rigid racial preferences would be to open the door to competing claims for "remedial relief" for every disadvantaged group. The dream of a Nation of equal citizens in a society where race is irrelevant to personal opportunity and achievement would be lost in a mosaic of shifting preferences based on inherently unmeasurable claims of past wrongs. "Courts would be asked to evaluate the extent of the prejudice and consequent harm suffered by various minority groups. Those whose societal injury is thought to exceed some arbitrary level of tolerability then would be entitled to preferential classifications...." *Bakke* (Powell, J.). We think such a result would be contrary to both the letter and spirit of a constitutional provision whose central command is equality.

The foregoing analysis applies only to the inclusion of blacks within the Richmond set-aside program. There is *absolutely no evidence* of past discrimination against Spanish-speaking, Oriental, Indian, Eskimo, or Aleut persons in any aspect of the Richmond construction industry. The District Court took judicial notice of the fact that the vast majority of "minority" persons in Richmond were black. It may well be that Richmond has never had an Aleut or Eskimo citizen. The random inclusion of racial groups that, as a practical matter, may never have suffered from discrimination in the construction industry in Richmond suggests that perhaps the city's purpose was not in fact to remedy past discrimination.

If a 30% set-aside was "narrowly tailored" to compensate black contractors for past discrimination, one may legitimately ask why they are forced to share this "remedial relief" with an Aleut citizen who moves to Richmond tomorrow? The gross overinclusiveness of Richmond's racial preference strongly impugns the city's claim of remedial motivation.

IV

As noted by the court below, it is almost impossible to assess whether the Richmond Plan is narrowly tailored to remedy prior discrimination since it is not linked to identified discrimination in any way. We limit ourselves to two observations in this regard.

First, there does not appear to have been any consideration of the use of race-neutral means to increase minority business participation in city contracting. Many of the barriers to minority participation in the construction industry relied upon by the city to justify a racial classification appear to be race neutral. If MBE's disproportionately lack capital or cannot meet bonding requirements, a race-neutral program of city financing for small firms would, *a fortiori*, lead to greater minority participation. The principal opinion in *Fullilove* found that Congress had carefully examined and rejected race-neutral alternatives before enacting the MBE set-aside. There is no evidence in this record that the Richmond City Council has considered any alternatives to a race-based quota.

Second, the 30% quota cannot be said to be narrowly tailored to any goal, except perhaps outright racial balancing. It rests upon the "completely unrealistic" assumption that minorities will choose a particular trade in lockstep proportion to their representation in the local population....

V

Nothing we say today precludes a state or local entity from taking action to rectify the effects of identified discrimination within its jurisdiction. If the city of Richmond had evidence before it that nonminority contractors were systematically excluding minority businesses from subcontracting opportunities, it could take action to end the discriminatory exclusion. Where there is a significant statistical disparity between the number of qualified minority contractors willing and able to perform a particular service and the number of such contractors actually engaged by the locality or the locality's prime contractors, an inference of discriminatory exclusion could arise. Under such circumstances, the city could act to dismantle the closed business system by taking appropriate measures against those who discriminate on the basis of race or other illegitimate criteria. In the extreme case, some form of narrowly tailored racial preference might be necessary to break down patterns of deliberate exclusion.

Nor is local government powerless to deal with individual instances of racially motivated refusals to employ minority contractors. Where such discrimination occurs, a city would be justified in penalizing the discriminator and providing appropriate relief to the victim of such discrimination. Moreover, evidence of a pattern of individual discriminatory acts can, if supported by appropriate statistical proof, lend support to a local government's determination that broader remedial relief is justified.

Even in the absence of evidence of discrimination, the city has at its disposal a whole array of race-neutral devices to increase the accessibility of city contracting opportunities to small entrepreneurs of all races. Simplification of bidding procedures, relaxation of bonding requirements, and training and financial aid for disadvantaged entrepreneurs of all races would open the public contracting market to all those who have suffered the effects of past societal discrimination or neglect. Many of the formal barriers to new entrants may be the product of bureaucratic inertia more than actual necessity, and may have a disproportionate effect on the opportunities open to new minority firms. Their elimination or modification would have little detrimental effect on the city's interests and would serve to increase the opportunities available to minority business without classifying individuals on the basis of race. The city may also act to prohibit discrimination in the provision of credit or bonding by local suppliers and banks. Business as usual should not mean business pursuant to the unthinking exclusion of certain members of our society from its rewards.

In the case at hand, the city has not ascertained how many minority enterprises are present in the local construction market nor the level of their participation in city construction projects. The city points to no evidence that qualified minority contractors have been passed over for city contracts or subcontracts either as a group or in any individual case. Under such circumstances, it is simply impossible to say that the city has demonstrated "a strong basis in evidence for its conclusion that remedial action was necessary."

Proper findings in this regard are necessary to define both the scope of the injury and the extent of the remedy necessary to cure its effects. Such findings also serve to assure all citizens that the deviation from the norm of equal treatment of all racial and ethnic groups is a temporary matter, a measure taken in the service of the goal of equality itself. Absent such findings, there is a danger that a racial classification is merely the product of unthinking stereotypes or a form of racial politics.... Because the city of Richmond has failed to identify the need for remedial action in the awarding of its public construction contracts, its treatment of its citizens on a racial basis violates the dictates of the Equal Protection Clause....

JUSTICE STEVENS, concurring in part and concurring in the judgment.

A central purpose of the Fourteenth Amendment is to further the national goal of equal opportunity for all our citizens. In order to achieve that goal we must learn from our past mistakes, but I believe the Constitution requires us to evaluate our policy decisions — including those that govern the relationships among different racial and ethnic groups — primarily by studying their probable impact on the future. I therefore do not agree with the premise that seems to underlie today's decision, ... that a governmental decision that rests on a racial classification is never permissible except as a remedy for a past wrong. I do, however, agree with the Court's explanation of why the Richmond ordinance cannot be justified as a remedy for past discrimination, and therefore join Parts I, III-B and IV of its opinion and judgment....

JUSTICE KENNEDY, concurring in part and concurring in the judgment. [omitted]

JUSTICE SCALIA, concurring in the judgment.

I agree with much of the Court's opinion, and, in particular, with JUSTICE O'CONNOR's conclusion that strict scrutiny must be applied to all governmental classification by race, whether or not its asserted purpose is "remedial" or "benign." I do not agree, however, with JUSTICE O'CONNOR's dictum suggesting that, despite the Fourteenth Amendment, state and local governments may in some circumstances discriminate on the basis of race in order (in a broad sense) "to ameliorate the effects of past discrimination." ...

In my view there is only one circumstance in which the States may act *by race* to "undo the effects of past discrimination": where that is necessary to eliminate their own maintenance of a system of unlawful racial classification. If, for example, a state agency has a discriminatory pay scale compensating black employees in all positions at 20% less than their nonblack counterparts, it may assuredly promulgate an order raising the salaries of "all black employees" to eliminate the differential. This distinction explains our school desegregation cases, in which we have made plain that States and localities sometimes have an obligation to adopt race-conscious remedies. While there is no doubt that those cases have taken into account the continuing "effects" of previously mandated racial school assignment, we have held those effects to justify a race-conscious remedy only because we have concluded, in that context, that they perpetuate a "dual school system." ...

A State can, of course, act "to undo the effects of past discrimination" in many permissible ways that do not involve classification by race. In the particular field of state contracting, for example, it may adopt a preference for small businesses, or even for new businesses — which would make it easier for those previously excluded by discrimination to enter the field. Such programs may well have racially disproportionate impact, but they are not based on race. And, of course, a State may "undo the effects of past discrimination" in the sense of giving the identified victim of state discrimination that which it wrongfully denied him — for example, giving to a previously rejected black applicant the job that, by reason of discrimination, had been awarded to a white applicant, even if this means terminating the latter's employment. In such a context, the white jobholder is not being selected for disadvantageous treatment because of his race, but because he was wrongfully awarded a job to which another is entitled. That is worlds apart from the system here, in which those to be disadvantaged are identified solely by race.

I agree with the Court's dictum that a fundamental distinction must be drawn between the effects of "societal" discrimination and the effects of "identified" discrimination, and that the situation would be different if Richmond's plan were "tailored" to identify those particular bidders who "suffered from the effects of past discrimination by the city or prime contractors." In my view, however, the reason that would make a difference is not, as the Court states, that it would justify race-conscious action — but rather that it would enable race-neutral remediation. Nothing prevents Richmond from according a contracting preference to identified victims of discrimination. While most of the beneficiaries might be black, neither the beneficiaries nor those disadvantaged by the preference would be identified *on the basis of their race*. In other words, far from justifying racial classification, identification of actual victims of discrimination makes it less supportable than ever, because more obviously unneeded.

In his final book, Professor Bickel wrote:

> "A racial quota derogates the human dignity and individuality of all to whom it is applied; it is invidious in principle as well as in practice. Moreover, it can easily be turned against those it purports to help. The history of the racial quota is a history of subjugation, not beneficence. Its evil lies not in its name, but in its effects: a quota is a divider of society, a creator of castes, and it is all the worse for its racial base, especially in a society desperately striving for an equality that will make race irrelevant." Alexander Bickel, *The Morality of Consent* (1975).

Those statements are true and increasingly prophetic. Apart from their societal effects, however, which are "in the aggregate disastrous," it is important not to lose sight of the fact that even "benign" racial quotas have individual victims, whose very real injustice we ignore whenever we deny them enforcement of their right not to be disadvantaged on the basis of race. As Justice Douglas observed: "A DeFunis who is white is entitled to no advantage by virtue of that fact; nor is he subject to any disability, no matter what his race or color. Whatever his race, he had a constitutional right to have his application considered on its individual merits in a racially neutral manner." When we depart from this American principle we play with fire, and much more than an occasional DeFunis, Johnson, or Croson burns.[*]

It is plainly true that in our society blacks have suffered discrimination immeasurably greater than any directed at other racial groups. But those who believe that racial preferences can help to "even the score" display, and reinforce, a manner of

---

* [Ed. note: *DeFunis* and *Johnson* were plaintiffs in earlier affirmative action cases.]

thinking by race that was the source of the injustice and that will, if it endures within our society, be the source of more injustice still. The relevant proposition is not that it was blacks, or Jews, or Irish who were discriminated against, but that it was individual men and women, "created equal," who were discriminated against. And the relevant resolve is that that should never happen again. Racial preferences appear to "even the score" (in some small degree) only if one embraces the proposition that our society is appropriately viewed as divided into races, making it right that an injustice rendered in the past to a black man should be compensated for by discriminating against a white. Nothing is worth that embrace....

JUSTICE MARSHALL, with whom JUSTICE BRENNAN and JUSTICE BLACKMUN join, dissenting.

It is a welcome symbol of racial progress when the former capital of the Confederacy acts forthrightly to confront the effects of racial discrimination in its midst. In my view, nothing in the Constitution can be construed to prevent Richmond, Virginia, from allocating a portion of its contracting dollars for businesses owned or controlled by members of minority groups. Indeed, Richmond's set-aside program is indistinguishable in all meaningful respects from — and in fact was patterned upon — the federal set-aside plan which this Court upheld in *Fullilove*.

A majority of this Court holds today, however, that the Equal Protection Clause of the Fourteenth Amendment blocks Richmond's initiative. The essence of the majority's position is that Richmond has failed to catalog adequate findings to prove that past discrimination has impeded minorities from joining or participating fully in Richmond's construction contracting industry. I find deep irony in second-guessing Richmond's judgment on this point. As much as any municipality in the United States, Richmond knows what racial discrimination is; a century of decisions by this and other federal courts has richly documented the city's disgraceful history of public and private racial discrimination. In any event, the Richmond City Council *has* supported its determination that minorities have been wrongly excluded from local construction contracting. Its proof includes statistics showing that minority-owned businesses have received virtually no city contracting dollars and rarely if ever belonged to area trade associations; testimony by municipal officials that discrimination has been widespread in the local construction industry; and the same exhaustive and widely publicized federal studies relied on in *Fullilove*, studies which showed that pervasive discrimination in the Nation's tight-knit construction industry had operated to exclude minorities from public contracting. These are precisely the types of statistical and testimonial evidence which, until today, this Court had credited in cases approving of race-conscious measures designed to remedy past discrimination.

More fundamentally, today's decision marks a deliberate and giant step backward in this Court's affirmative-action jurisprudence. Cynical of one municipality's attempt to redress the effects of past racial discrimination in a particular industry, the majority launches a grapeshot attack on race-conscious remedies in general. The majority's unnecessary pronouncements will inevitably discourage or prevent governmental entities, particularly States and localities, from acting to rectify the scourge of past discrimination. This is the harsh reality of the majority's decision, but it is not the Constitution's command.

I

As an initial matter, the majority takes an exceedingly myopic view of the factual predicate on which the Richmond City Council relied when it passed the Minority Business Utilization Plan. The majority analyzes Richmond's initiative as if it were based solely upon the facts about local construction and contracting practices adduced during the city council session at which the measure was enacted. In so doing, the majority downplays the fact that the city council had before it a rich trove of evidence that discrimination in the Nation's construction industry had seriously impaired the competitive position of businesses owned or controlled by members of minority groups. It is only against this backdrop of documented national discrimination, however, that the local evidence adduced by Richmond can be properly understood. The majority's refusal to recognize that Richmond has proved itself no exception to the dismaying pattern of national exclusion which Congress so painstakingly identified [in its findings in the statute upheld in *Fullilove*] infects its entire analysis of this case....

The members of the Richmond City Council were well aware of these exhaustive congressional findings, a point the majority, tellingly, elides. The transcript of the session at which the council enacted the local set-aside initiative contains numerous references to the 6-year-old congressional set-aside program, to the evidence of nationwide discrimination barriers described above, and to the *Fullilove* decision itself.

The city council's members also heard testimony that, although minority groups made up half of the city's population, only 0.67% of the $24.6 million which Richmond had dispensed in construction contracts during the five years ending in March 1983 had gone to minority-owned prime contractors. They heard testimony that the major Richmond area construction trade associations had virtually no minorities among their hundreds of members. Finally, they heard testimony from city officials as to the exclusionary history of the local construction industry. As the District Court noted, not a single person who testified before the city council denied that discrimination in Richmond's construction industry had been widespread. So long as one views Richmond's local evidence of discrimination against the backdrop of systematic nationwide racial discrimination which Congress had so painstakingly identified in this very industry, this case is readily resolved.

II

... My view has long been that race-conscious classifications designed to further remedial goals "must serve important governmental objectives and must be substantially related to achievement of those objectives" in order to withstand constitutional scrutiny. *Bakke* (joint opinion of BRENNAN, WHITE, MARSHALL, and BLACKMUN, JJ.); see also *Wygant* (MARSHALL, J., dissenting); *Fullilove* (MARSHALL, J., concurring in judgment). Analyzed in terms of this two-pronged standard, Richmond's set-aside, like the federal program on which it was modeled, is "plainly constitutional."

## A

### 1

Turning first to the governmental interest inquiry, Richmond has two powerful interests in setting aside a portion of public contracting funds for minority-owned enterprises. The first is the city's interest in eradicating the effects of past racial discrimination. It is far too late in the day to doubt that remedying such discrimination is a compelling, let alone an important, interest....

Richmond has a second compelling interest in setting aside, where possible, a portion of its contracting dollars. That interest is the prospective one of preventing the city's own spending decisions from reinforcing and perpetuating the exclusionary effects of past discrimination.

The majority pays only lipservice to this additional governmental interest. But our decisions have often emphasized the danger of the government tacitly adopting, encouraging, or furthering racial discrimination even by its own routine operations....

### 2

The remaining question with respect to the "governmental interest" prong of equal protection analysis is whether Richmond has proffered satisfactory proof of past racial discrimination to support its twin interests in remediation and in governmental non-perpetuation....

No one, of course, advocates "blind judicial deference" to the findings of the city council or the testimony of city leaders. The majority's suggestion that wholesale deference is what Richmond seeks is a classic straw-man argument. But the majority's trivialization of the testimony of Richmond's leaders is dismaying in a far more serious respect. By disregarding the testimony of local leaders and the judgment of local government, the majority does violence to the very principles of comity within our federal system which this Court has long championed. Local officials, by virtue of their proximity to, and their expertise with, local affairs, are exceptionally well qualified to make determinations of public good "within their respective sphere of authority." The majority, however, leaves any traces of comity behind in its headlong rush to strike down Richmond's race-conscious measure.

Had the majority paused for a moment on the facts of the Richmond experience, it would have discovered that the city's leadership is deeply familiar with what racial discrimination is. The members of the Richmond City Council have spent long years witnessing multifarious acts of discrimination, including, but not limited to, the deliberate diminution of black residents' voting rights, resistance to school desegregation, and publicly sanctioned housing discrimination. Numerous decisions of federal courts chronicle this disgraceful recent history....

## B

In my judgment, Richmond's set-aside plan also comports with the second prong of the equal protection inquiry, for it is substantially related to the interests it seeks to serve in remedying past discrimination and in ensuring that municipal contract procurement does not perpetuate that discrimination. The most striking aspect of the city's ordinance is the similarity it bears to the "appropriately limited" federal set-aside provision upheld in *Fullilove*. Like the federal provision, Richmond's is limited to five years in duration, and was not renewed when it came up for reconsideration in 1988. Like the federal provision, Richmond's contains a waiver provision freeing from its subcontracting requirements those nonminority firms that demonstrate that they cannot comply with its provisions. Like the federal provision, Richmond's has a minimal impact on innocent third parties. While the measure affects 30% of *public* contracting dollars, that translates to only 3% of overall Richmond area contracting.

Finally, like the federal provision, Richmond's does not interfere with any vested right of a contractor to a particular contract; instead it operates entirely prospectively. Richmond's initiative affects only future economic arrangements and imposes only a diffuse burden on nonminority competitors—here, businesses owned or controlled by nonminorities which seek subcontracting work on public construction projects....

## III

\* \* \*

### A

Today, for the first time, a majority of this Court has adopted strict scrutiny as its standard of Equal Protection Clause review of race-conscious remedial measures. This is an unwelcome development. A profound difference separates governmental actions that themselves are racist, and governmental actions that seek to remedy the effects of prior racism or to prevent neutral governmental activity from perpetuating the effects of such racism....

In concluding that remedial classifications warrant no different standard of review under the Constitution than the most brutal and repugnant forms of state-sponsored racism, a majority of this Court signals that it regards racial discrimination as largely a phenomenon of the past, and that government bodies need no longer preoccupy themselves with rectifying racial injustice. I, however, do not believe this Nation is anywhere close to eradicating racial discrimination or its vestiges. In constitutionalizing its wishful thinking, the majority today does a grave disservice not only to those victims of past and present racial discrimination in this Nation whom government has sought to assist, but also to this Court's long tradition of approaching issues of race with the utmost sensitivity.

### B

I am also troubled by the majority's assertion that, even if it did not believe generally in strict scrutiny of race-based remedial measures, "the circumstances of this case" require this Court to look upon the Richmond City Council's measure with the strictest scrutiny. The sole such circumstance which the majority cites, however, is the fact that blacks in Richmond are a "dominant racial group" in the city. In support of this characterization of dominance, the majority observes that "blacks constitute approximately 50% of the population of the city of Richmond" and that "five of the nine seats on the City Council are held by blacks."

While I agree that the numerical and political supremacy of a given racial group is a factor bearing upon the level of scrutiny to be applied, this Court has never held that numerical inferiority, standing alone, makes a racial group "suspect" and thus entitled to strict scrutiny review. Rather, we have identified *other* "traditional indicia of suspectness": whether a group has been "saddled with such disabilities, or subjected to such a history of purposeful unequal treatment, or relegated to such a position of political powerlessness as to command extraordinary protection from the majoritarian political process."

It cannot seriously be suggested that nonminorities in Richmond have any "history of purposeful unequal treatment." Nor is there any indication that they have any of the disabilities that have characteristically afflicted those groups this Court has deemed suspect. Indeed, the numerical and political dominance of nonminorities within the State of Virginia and the Nation as a whole provides an enormous political check against the "simple racial politics" at the municipal level which the majority fears. If the majority really believes that groups like Richmond's nonminorities, which constitute approximately half the population but which are outnumbered even marginally in political fora, are deserving of suspect class status for these reasons alone, this Court's decisions denying suspect status to women, see *Craig v. Boren* (1976) [*Supra.* Chapter 12], and to persons with below-average incomes stand on extremely shaky ground....

## IV

The majority today sounds a full-scale retreat from the Court's longstanding solicitude to race-conscious remedial efforts "directed toward deliverance of the century-old promise of equality of economic opportunity." *Fullilove.* The new and restrictive tests it applies scuttle one city's effort to surmount its discriminatory past, and imperil those of dozens more localities. I, however, profoundly disagree with the cramped vision of the Equal Protection Clause which the majority offers today and with its application of that vision to Richmond, Virginia's, laudable set-aside plan. The battle against pernicious racial discrimination or its effects is nowhere near won. I must dissent.

Justice Blackmun, with whom Justice Brennan joins, dissenting.

I join Justice Marshall's perceptive and incisive opinion revealing great sensitivity toward those who have suffered the pains of economic discrimination in the construction trades for so long.

I never thought that I would live to see the day when the city of Richmond, Virginia, the cradle of the Old Confederacy, sought on its own, within a narrow confine, to lessen the stark impact of persistent discrimination. But Richmond, to its great credit, acted. Yet this Court, the supposed bastion of equality strikes down Richmond's efforts as though discrimination had never existed or was not demonstrated in this particular litigation. Justice Marshall convincingly discloses the fallacy and the shallowness of that approach. History is irrefutable, even though one might sympathize with those who—though possibly innocent in themselves—benefit from the wrongs of past decades....

## *Note: A Different Standard for Race-Conscious Federal Action?*

1. *Bakke, Croson* and many of the other race-conscious government action cases of the 1980s considered the actions of states and state governmental units (such as the university board of regents in *Bakke*). Over these cases there hovered the question whether a different, more lenient, standard should govern *federal* race-conscious action.

2. In the modern era this question first arose in *Fullilove v. Klutznick*, 448 U.S. 448 (1980). *Fullilove* considered a challenge to a federal law providing funds to states to engage in certain types of construction projects. A part of that law provided that no federal funding would be provided to contracts unless the applicant state assured the federal disbursing authority that at least 10% of the value of the construction contracts would be let out to "minority business enterprises" (MBEs).

By a 6–3 vote the Court upheld the constitutionality of the MBE set-aside provision. Writing for himself and Justices White and Powell, Chief Justice Burger wrote that "a program that employs racial or ethnic criteria ... calls for close examination; yet we are bound to approach our task with appropriate deference to the Congress." Later in his opinion, he wrote:

> For its part, the Congress must proceed only with programs narrowly tailored to achieve its objectives, subject to continuing evaluation and reassessment; administration of the programs must be vigilant and flexible; and, when such a program comes under judicial review, courts must be satisfied that the legislative objectives and projected administration give reasonable assurance that the program will function within constitutional limitations.

He concluded his opinion as follows:

> Any preference based on racial or ethnic criteria must necessarily receive a most searching examination to make sure that it does not conflict with constitutional guarantees. This case is one which requires, and which has received, that kind of examination. This opinion does not adopt, either expressly or implicitly, the formulas of analysis articulated in such cases as *Bakke*. However, our analysis demonstrates that the MBE provision would survive judicial review under either "test" articulated in the several *Bakke* opinions.

Justice Powell wrote a concurring opinion, stating that he would have "placed greater emphasis than the Chief Justice on the need to articulate judicial standards of review in conventional terms." Nevertheless, he concluded that the Chief Justice's opinion was "substantially in accord" with his own views. While he applied his analysis in *Bakke* to the MBE set-aside, he also wrote that "unlike the Regents of the University of California, Congress properly may—and indeed must—address directly the problems of discrimination in our society." After discussing cases that construed statutes enacted under the Commerce Clause, he then wrote that "in addition, Congress has been given the unique constitutional power of legislating to enforce the provisions of the Thirteenth, Fourteenth, and Fifteenth Amendments." Considering that latter power, he wrote:

I conclude, therefore, that the Enforcement Clauses of the Thirteenth and Fourteenth Amendments confer upon Congress the authority to select reasonable remedies to advance the compelling state interest in repairing the effects of discrimination. But that authority must be exercised in a manner that does not erode the guarantees of these Amendments. The Judicial Branch has the special responsibility to make a searching inquiry into the justification for employing a race-conscious remedy. Courts must be sensitive to the possibility that less intrusive means might serve the compelling state interest equally as well. I believe that Congress' choice of a remedy should be upheld, however, if the means selected are equitable and reasonably necessary to the redress of identified discrimination. Such a test allows the Congress to exercise necessary discretion but preserves the essential safeguard of judicial review of racial classifications.

Justice Marshall, writing for himself and Justices Brennan and Blackmun, would have upheld the MBE set-aside based on his separate opinion in *Bakke*. In a footnote, he stated the following: "In *Bakke*, the issue was whether a special minority admissions program of a state medical school violated the Equal Protection Clause of the Fourteenth Amendment. In the present case, the issue is whether the minority set-aside provision violates the equal protection component of the Due Process Clause of the Fifth Amendment. As noted in *Bakke*, equal protection analysis in the Fifth Amendment area is the same as that under the Fourteenth Amendment."

Justice Stewart, joined by Justice Rehnquist, dissented. He wrote:

The equal protection standard of the Constitution has one clear and central meaning—it absolutely prohibits invidious discrimination by government. That standard must be met by every State under the Equal Protection Clause of the Fourteenth Amendment. And that standard must also be met by the United States itself under the Due Process Clause of the Fifth Amendment.

Appended to that last sentence was a footnote which read in its entirety (except for a citation): "Equal protection analysis in the Fifth Amendment area is the same as that under the Fourteenth Amendment."

Justice Stevens dissented separately, without addressing the federal power issue.

3. Even though *Croson* dealt with a city's contracting set-aside, several justices used that occasion to comment on whether federal race conscious action was appropriately reviewed under a different standard than analogous state action. Justice O'Connor's lead opinion in that case, for herself, Chief Justice Rehnquist and Justice White, said the following about that issue, when distinguishing *Fullilove*:

Appellant and its supporting amici rely heavily on *Fullilove* for the proposition that a city council, like Congress, need not make specific findings of discrimination to engage in race-conscious relief.... What appellant ignores is that Congress, unlike any State or political subdivision, has a specific constitutional mandate to enforce the dictates of the Fourteenth Amendment. The power to "enforce" may at times also include the power to define situations which *Congress* determines threaten principles of equality and to adopt prophylactic rules to deal with those situations. The Civil War Amendments themselves worked a dramatic change in the balance between congressional and state power over matters of race....

That Congress may identify and redress the effects of society-wide discrimination does not mean that, *a fortiori*, the States and their political subdivisions are free to decide that such remedies are appropriate. Section 1 of the Fourteenth Amendment is an explicit *constraint* on state power, and the States must undertake any remedial efforts in accordance with that provision. To hold otherwise would be to cede control over the content of the Equal Protection Clause to the 50 state legislatures and their myriad political subdivisions. The mere recitation of a benign or compensatory purpose for the use of a racial classification would essentially entitle the States to exercise the full power of Congress under § 5 of the Fourteenth Amendment and insulate any racial classification from judicial scrutiny under § 1. We believe that such a result would be contrary to the intentions of the Framers of the Fourteenth Amendment, who desired to place clear limits on the States' use of race as a criterion for legislative action, and to have the federal courts enforce those limitations. See *Associated General Contractors of Cal. v. City and Cty. of San Francisco*, 813 F.2d 922 (9th Cir. 1987) (Kozinski, J.) ("The city is not just like the federal government with regard to the findings it must make to justify race-conscious remedial action"); see also Days, "*Fullilove*," 96 *Yale L.J.* 453 (1987) ("*Fullilove* clearly focused on the constitutionality of a *congressionally* mandated set-aside program") (emphasis in original); Bohrer, "*Bakke, Weber,* and *Fullilove*: Benign Discrimination and Congressional Power to Enforce the Fourteenth Amendment," 56 *Ind. L.J.* 473 (1981) ("Congress may authorize, pursuant to section 5, state action that would be foreclosed to the states acting alone").

We do not, as Justice MARSHALL's dissent suggests, find in § 5 of the Fourteenth Amendment some form of federal pre-emption in matters of race. We simply note what should be apparent to all—§ 1 of the Fourteenth Amendment stemmed from a distrust of state legislative enactments based on race; § 5 is, as the dissent notes, "a positive grant of legislative power" to Congress. Thus, our treatment of an exercise of congressional power in *Fullilove* cannot be dispositive here....

Justice Scalia concurred in the judgment, writing the following about federal power to engage in race-conscious action:

As Justice O'CONNOR acknowledges..., it is one thing to permit racially based conduct by the Federal Government—whose legislative powers concerning matters of race were explicitly enhanced by the Fourteenth Amendment—and quite another to permit it by the precise entities against whose conduct in matters of race that Amendment was specifically directed. As we said in *Ex parte Virginia*, 100 U.S. 339 (1879) [Note *supra*. this chapter], the

Civil War Amendments were designed to "take away all possibility of oppression by law because of race or color" and "to be … limitations on the power of the States and enlargements of the power of Congress." Thus, without revisiting what we held in *Fullilove* (or trying to derive a rationale from the three separate opinions supporting the judgment, none of which commanded more than three votes), I do not believe our decision in that case controls the one before us here.

A sound distinction between federal and state (or local) action based on race rests not only upon the substance of the Civil War Amendments, but upon social reality and governmental theory. It is a simple fact that what Justice Stewart described in *Fullilove* as "the dispassionate objectivity [and] the flexibility that are needed to mold a race-conscious remedy around the single objective of eliminating the effects of past or present discrimination"—political qualities already to be doubted in a national legislature—are substantially less likely to exist at the state or local level. The struggle for racial justice has historically been a struggle by the national society against oppression in the individual States.… What the record shows … is that racial discrimination against any group finds a more ready expression at the state and local than at the federal level. To the children of the Founding Fathers, this should come as no surprise. An acute awareness of the heightened danger of oppression from political factions in small, rather than large, political units dates to the very beginning of our national history. As James Madison observed in support of the proposed Constitution's enhancement of national powers:

> "The smaller the society, the fewer probably will be the distinct parties and interests composing it; the fewer the distinct parties and interests, the more frequently will a majority be found of the same party; and the smaller the number of individuals composing a majority, and the smaller the compass within which they are placed, the more easily will they concert and execute their plan of oppression. Extend the sphere and you take in a greater variety of parties and interests; you make it less probable that a majority of the whole will have a common motive to invade the rights of other citizens; or if such a common motive exists, it will be more difficult for all who feel it to discover their own strength and to act in unison with each other." *The Federalist* No. 10.

Justice Kennedy joined Justice O'Connor's opinion except as it addressed the federal-state differential issue. On that issue he stated the following:

Part II [of Justice O'Connor's opinion] examines our case law upholding congressional power to grant preferences based on overt and explicit classification by race. See *Fullilove*. With the acknowledgment that the summary in Part II is both precise and fair, I must decline to join it. The process by which a law that is an equal protection violation when enacted by a State becomes transformed to an equal protection guarantee when enacted by Congress poses a difficult proposition for me; but as it is not before us, any reconsideration of that issue must await some further case.

Justice Marshall, writing for the four dissenters in *Croson*, criticized the implications of Justice O'Connor's and Justice Scalia's differential standard in the course of arguing for more relaxed review of Richmond's set-aside:

> To the degree that [the majority's requirement that state race-conscious set-asides need to be based on prima facie findings of actual legal violations] is grounded on a view that either § 1 or § 5 of the Fourteenth Amendment substantially disempowered States and localities from remedying past racial discrimination, the majority is seriously mistaken. With respect, first, to § 5, our precedents have never suggested that this provision ... was meant to preempt or limit state police power to undertake race-conscious remedial measures. To the contrary, in *Katzenbach v. Morgan*, 384 U.S. 641 (1966), we held that § 5 "is a *positive* grant of legislative power authorizing Congress to exercise its discretion in determining whether and what legislation is needed to secure the guarantees of the Fourteenth Amendment." Indeed, we have held that Congress has this authority even where no constitutional violation has been found. Certainly *Fullilove* did not view § 5 either as limiting the traditionally broad police powers of the States to fight discrimination, or as mandating a zero-sum game in which state power wanes as federal power waxes....

4. One year after *Croson*, in *Metro Broadcasting, Inc. v. FCC*, 497 U.S. 547 (1990), the Court on a 5–4 vote upheld Federal Communications Commission regulations granting advantages to minority-owned entities that sought broadcast licenses. Writing for the three *Croson* dissenters plus Justices White and Stevens, Justice Brennan addressed the federal-state standard differential as follows:

> It is of overriding significance in these cases that the [FCC's] minority ownership programs have been specifically approved — indeed mandated — by Congress. In *Fullilove*, Chief Justice Burger, writing for himself and two other Justices, observed that although "a program that employs racial or ethnic criteria ... calls for close examination," when a program employing a benign racial classification is adopted by an administrative agency at the explicit direction of Congress, we are "bound to approach our task with appropriate deference to the Congress, a co-equal branch charged by the Constitution with the power to 'provide for the ... general Welfare of the United States' and 'to enforce, by appropriate legislation,' the equal protection guarantees of the Fourteenth Amendment." *See also id.* (Powell, J., concurring); *id.* (MARSHALL, J., concurring in judgment). We explained that deference was appropriate in light of Congress' institutional competence as the National Legislature, see *id.* (opinion of Burger, C.J.); *id.* (Powell, J., concurring), as well as Congress' powers under the Commerce Clause, see *id.* (opinion of Burger, C.J.); *id.* (Powell, J., concurring), the Spending Clause, see *id.* (opinion of Burger, C.J.), and the Civil War Amendments, see *id.* (opinion of Burger, C.J.); *id.* (Powell, J., concurring).

He continued:

> A majority of the Court in *Fullilove* did not apply strict scrutiny to the race-based classification at issue.... We hold that benign race-conscious measures mandated by Congress—even if those measures are not "remedial" in the sense of being designed to compensate victims of past governmental or societal discrimination—are constitutionally permissible to the extent that they serve important governmental objectives within the power of Congress and are substantially related to achievement of those objectives.

Justice Stevens joined the majority opinion, but also wrote separately on an issue not implicating the federal-state differential.

Justice O'Connor, joined by Chief Justice Rehnquist and Justices Scalia and Kennedy, dissented. Citing cases including *Bolling v. Sharpe* (1954) (*Supra.* this chapter), she insisted that "The Constitution's guarantee of equal protection binds the Federal Government as it does the States, and no lower level of scrutiny applies to the Federal Government's use of race classifications." Two paragraphs later, however, she wrote the following:

> Congress has considerable latitude, presenting special concerns for judicial review, when it exercises its "unique remedial powers ... under §5 of the Fourteenth Amendment," see *Croson* (opinion of O'CONNOR, J.), but this case does not implicate those powers.

She thus argued that *Metro Broadcasting* was distinguishable from *Fullilove* in part on the ground that the challenged FCC regulations did not implicate Congress's enforcement power.

Justice Kennedy, joined by Justice Scalia, also wrote a separate dissent. Addressing the differential issue, he stated: "The approach taken to congressional measures under §5 of the Fourteenth Amendment in *Fullilove*, even assuming its validity, *see Croson* (opinion of KENNEDY, J.), is not applicable to this case."

5. *Metro Broadcasting* was short-lived. Five years later, in *Adarand v. Pena*, 515 U.S. 200 (1995), the Court, by a 5–4 vote, overruled it, and held that federal race-conscious action was subject to the same scrutiny as analogous action by states. *Adarand* considered, and held unconstitutional, a race-based contracting set-aside provision in the federal highway construction program. Describing *Metro Broadcasting* as "a surprising turn," Justice O'Connor, writing for the Court, insisted that the same standard be applied to federal and state race-conscious actions.

Dissenting for four justices, Justice Stevens criticized the majority's rejection of differential standards of review for federal and state race-conscious laws:

> These differences have been identified repeatedly and consistently both in opinions of the Court and in separate opinions authored by Members of today's majority. Thus, in *Metro Broadcasting* ... we identified the special "institutional competence" of our National Legislature. "It is of overriding significance in these cases," we were careful to emphasize, "that the FCC's

minority ownership programs have been specifically approved—indeed, mandated—by Congress." ... We recalled that the opinions of Chief Justice Burger and Justice Powell in *Fullilove* had "explained that deference was appropriate in light of Congress' institutional competence as the National Legislature, as well as Congress' powers under the Commerce Clause, the Spending Clause, and the Civil War Amendments."

Justice Stevens then quoted from the *Croson* excerpts presented from item 3, above, where Justices O'Connor and Scalia, who rejected a federal-state differential in *Adarand*, suggested that such a differential might in fact be appropriate. In response to that critique, Justice O'Connor wrote the following:

> It is true that various Members of this Court have taken different views of the authority § 5 of the Fourteenth Amendment confers upon Congress to deal with the problem of racial discrimination, and the extent to which courts should defer to Congress' exercise of that authority. See, e.g., *Metro Broadcasting* (O'CONNOR, J., dissenting); *Croson* (opinion of O'CONNOR, J., joined by REHNQUIST, C.J., and White, J.); *id.* (KENNEDY, J., concurring in part and concurring in judgment); *id.* (SCALIA, J., concurring in judgment); *Fullilove* (opinion of Burger, C.J.); *id.* (Powell, J., concurring); *id.* (Stewart, J., dissenting). We need not, and do not, address these differences today. For now, it is enough to observe that JUSTICE STEVENS' suggestion that any Member of this Court has repudiated in this case his or her previously expressed views on the subject is incorrect.

6. *Adarand*, in addition to deciding the federal-state differential issue, also resolved the question of the scrutiny required of contracting and other employment and economic set-asides. But race-conscious government action in education—and in particular higher education—remained an open question, given *Bakke*'s combination of Justice's Powell's analysis and the analysis of the four justice group that called for relatively more relaxed scrutiny of race-conscious admissions decisions in state educational institutions. That issue resurfaced in 2003.

## Grutter v. Bollinger

539 U.S. 306 (2003)

JUSTICE O'CONNOR delivered the opinion of the Court.

This case requires us to decide whether the use of race as a factor in student admissions by the University of Michigan Law School (Law School) is unlawful.

### I

### A

The Law School ranks among the Nation's top law schools. It receives more than 3,500 applications each year for a class of around 350 students. Seeking to "admit a group of students who individually and collectively are among the most capable," the Law School looks for individuals with "substantial promise for success in law school" and "a strong likelihood of succeeding in the practice of law and contributing in diverse ways to the well-being of others." ... More broadly, the Law School seeks "a mix of students with varying backgrounds and experiences who will respect and learn from each other." ...

The hallmark of [the law school] policy is its focus on academic ability coupled with a flexible assessment of applicants' talents, experiences, and potential "to contribute to the learning of those around them." The policy requires admissions officials to evaluate each applicant based on all the information available in the file, including a personal statement, letters of recommendation, and an essay describing the ways in which the applicant will contribute to the life and diversity of the Law School.... The policy stresses that "no applicant should be admitted unless we expect that applicant to do well enough to graduate with no serious academic problems."

The policy makes clear, however, that even the highest possible score does not guarantee admission to the Law School. Nor does a low score automatically disqualify an applicant. Rather, the policy requires admissions officials to look beyond grades and test scores to other criteria that are important to the Law School's educational objectives.... So-called " 'soft' variables" such as "the enthusiasm of recommenders, the quality of the undergraduate institution, the quality of the applicant's essay, and the areas and difficulty of undergraduate course selection" are all brought to bear in assessing an "applicant's likely contributions to the intellectual and social life of the institution."

The policy aspires to "achieve that diversity which has the potential to enrich everyone's education and thus make a law school class stronger than the sum of its parts." The policy does not restrict the types of diversity contributions eligible for "substantial weight" in the admissions process, but instead recognizes "many possible bases for diversity admissions." The policy does, however, reaffirm the Law School's longstanding commitment to "one particular type of diversity," that is, "racial and ethnic diversity with special reference to the inclusion of students from groups which have been historically discriminated against, like African-Americans, Hispanics and Native Americans, who without this commitment might not be represented in our student body in meaningful numbers." By enrolling a " 'critical mass' of [underrepresented] minority students," the Law School seeks to "ensure their ability to make unique contributions to the character of the Law School."

The policy does not define diversity "solely in terms of racial and ethnic status." Nor is the policy "insensitive to the competition among all students for admission to the Law School." Rather, the policy seeks to guide admissions officers in "producing classes both diverse and academically outstanding, classes made up of students who promise to continue the tradition of outstanding contribution by Michigan Graduates to the legal profession." ...

### B

Petitioner Barbara Grutter is a white Michigan resident who applied to the Law School in 1996 with a 3.8 GPA and 161 LSAT score. The Law School initially placed petitioner on a waiting list, but subsequently rejected her application. In December 1997, petitioner filed suit.... Petitioner alleged that respondents discriminated against her on the basis of race in violation of the Fourteenth Amendment; Title VI of the Civil Rights Act of 1964 ... and ... 42 U.S.C. § 1981.

Petitioner further alleged that her application was rejected because the Law School uses race as a "predominant" factor, giving applicants who belong to certain minority groups "a significantly greater chance of admission than students with similar credentials from disfavored racial groups." ... Petitioner also alleged that respondents "had no compelling interest to justify their use of race in the admissions process." ...

We granted certiorari ... to resolve the disagreement among the Courts of Appeals on a question of national importance: Whether diversity is a compelling interest that can justify the narrowly tailored use of race in selecting applicants for admission to public universities.

## II
## A

We last addressed the use of race in public higher education over 25 years ago. In the landmark *Board of Regents v. Bakke* case (1978) [*Supra.* this chapter] we reviewed a racial set-aside program that reserved 16 out of 100 seats in a medical school class for members of certain minority groups. The decision produced six separate opinions, none of which commanded a majority of the Court. Four Justices would have upheld the program against all attack on the ground that the government can use race to "remedy disadvantages cast on minorities by past racial prejudice." Four other Justices avoided the constitutional question altogether and struck down the program on statutory grounds. Justice Powell provided a fifth vote not only for invalidating the set-aside program, but also for reversing the state court's injunction against any use of race whatsoever. The only holding for the Court in *Bakke* was that a "State has a substantial interest that legitimately may be served by a properly devised admissions program involving the competitive consideration of race and ethnic origin." Thus, we reversed that part of the lower court's judgment that enjoined the university "from any consideration of the race of any applicant."

Since this Court's splintered decision in *Bakke*, Justice Powell's opinion announcing the judgment of the Court has served as the touchstone for constitutional analysis of race-conscious admissions policies. Public and private universities across the Nation have modeled their own admissions programs on Justice Powell's views on permissible race-conscious policies. We therefore discuss Justice Powell's opinion in some detail.

Justice Powell began by stating that "the guarantee of equal protection cannot mean one thing when applied to one individual and something else when applied to a person of another color. If both are not accorded the same protection, then it is not equal." In Justice Powell's view, when governmental decisions "touch upon an individual's race or ethnic background, he is entitled to a judicial determination that the burden he is asked to bear on that basis is precisely tailored to serve a compelling governmental interest." Under this exacting standard, only one of the interests asserted by the university survived Justice Powell's scrutiny.

First, Justice Powell rejected an interest in "reducing the historic deficit of traditionally disfavored minorities in medical schools and in the medical profession" as an unlawful interest in racial balancing. Second, Justice Powell rejected an interest in remedying societal discrimination because such measures would risk placing unnecessary burdens on innocent third parties "who bear no responsibility for whatever harm the beneficiaries of the special admissions program are thought to have suffered." Third, Justice Powell rejected an interest in "increasing the number of physicians who will practice in communities currently underserved," concluding that even if such an interest could be compelling in some circumstances the program under review was not "geared to promote that goal."

Justice Powell approved the university's use of race to further only one interest: "the attainment of a diverse student body." ... Justice Powell grounded his analysis in the academic freedom that "long has been viewed as a special concern of the First Amendment." Justice Powell emphasized that nothing less than the " 'nation's future depends upon leaders trained through wide exposure' to the ideas and mores of students as diverse as this Nation of many peoples." ... In seeking the "right to select those students who will contribute the most to the 'robust exchange of ideas,' " a university seeks "to achieve a goal that is of paramount importance in the fulfillment of its mission." Both "tradition and experience lend support to the view that the contribution of diversity is substantial."

Justice Powell was, however, careful to emphasize that in his view race "is only one element in a range of factors a university properly may consider in attaining the goal of a heterogeneous student body." For Justice Powell, "it is not an interest in simple ethnic diversity, in which a specified percentage of the student body is in effect guaranteed to be members of selected ethnic groups," that can justify the use of race. Rather, "the diversity that furthers a compelling state interest encompasses a far broader array of qualifications and characteristics of which racial or ethnic origin is but a single though important element." ...

We do not find it necessary to decide whether Justice Powell's opinion is binding ... [For] for the reasons set out below, today we endorse Justice Powell's view that student body diversity is a compelling state interest that can justify the use of race in university admissions.

B

The Equal Protection Clause provides that no State shall "deny to any person within its jurisdiction the equal protection of the laws." Because the Fourteenth Amendment "protects *persons*, not *groups*," all "governmental action based on race—a *group* classification long recognized as in most circumstances irrelevant and therefore prohibited—should be subjected to detailed judicial inquiry to ensure that the *personal* right to equal protection of the laws has not been infringed." *Adarand v. Pena*, 515 U.S. 200 (1995) [Note *supra*. this chapter]. We are a "free people whose institutions are founded upon the doctrine of equality." It follows from that principle that "government may treat people differently because of their race only for the most compelling reasons." *Id.*

We have held that all racial classifications imposed by government "must be analyzed by a reviewing court under strict scrutiny." This means that such classifications are constitutional only if they are narrowly tailored to further compelling governmental interests.... We apply strict scrutiny to all racial classifications to "'smoke out' illegitimate uses of race by assuring that [government] is pursuing a goal important enough to warrant use of a highly suspect tool." *Richmond v. J.A. Croson Co.* (1989) [*Supra.* this chapter].

Strict scrutiny is not "strict in theory, but fatal in fact." *Adarand.* Although all governmental uses of race are subject to strict scrutiny, not all are invalidated by it. As we have explained, "whenever the government treats any person unequally because of his or her race, that person has suffered an injury that falls squarely within the language and spirit of the Constitution's guarantee of equal protection." But that observation "says nothing about the ultimate validity of any particular law; that determination is the job of the court applying strict scrutiny." When race-based action is necessary to further a compelling governmental interest, such action does not violate the constitutional guarantee of equal protection so long as the narrow-tailoring requirement is also satisfied....

### III
### A

With these principles in mind, we turn to the question whether the Law School's use of race is justified by a compelling state interest. Before this Court, as they have throughout this litigation, respondents assert only one justification for their use of race in the admissions process: obtaining "the educational benefits that flow from a diverse student body." In other words, the Law School asks us to recognize, in the context of higher education, a compelling state interest in student body diversity.

We first wish to dispel the notion that the Law School's argument has been foreclosed, either expressly or implicitly, by our affirmative-action cases decided since *Bakke.* It is true that some language in those opinions might be read to suggest that remedying past discrimination is the only permissible justification for race-based governmental action. See, e.g., *Croson.* But we have never held that the only governmental use of race that can survive strict scrutiny is remedying past discrimination. Nor, since *Bakke,* have we directly addressed the use of race in the context of public higher education. Today, we hold that the Law School has a compelling interest in attaining a diverse student body.

The Law School's educational judgment that such diversity is essential to its educational mission is one to which we defer. The Law School's assessment that diversity will, in fact, yield educational benefits is substantiated by respondents and their *amici.* Our scrutiny of the interest asserted by the Law School is no less strict for taking into account complex educational judgments in an area that lies primarily within the expertise of the university. Our holding today is in keeping with our tradition of giving a degree of deference to a university's academic decisions, within constitutionally prescribed limits.... Our conclusion that the Law School has a compelling interest in a diverse student body is informed by our view that attaining a diverse student body is at the heart of the Law School's proper institutional mission, and that "good faith" on the part of a university is "presumed" absent "a showing to the contrary."

As part of its goal of "assembling a class that is both exceptionally academically qualified and broadly diverse," the Law School seeks to "enroll a 'critical mass' of minority students." The Law School's interest is not simply "to assure within its student body some specified percentage of a particular group merely because of its race or ethnic origin." *Bakke.* That would amount to outright racial balancing, which is patently unconstitutional. Rather, the Law School's concept of critical mass is defined by reference to the educational benefits that diversity is designed to produce.

These benefits are substantial. As the District Court emphasized, the Law School's admissions policy promotes "cross-racial understanding," helps to break down racial stereotypes, and "enables [students] to better understand persons of different races."....

These benefits are not theoretical but real, as major American businesses have made clear that the skills needed in today's increasingly global marketplace can only be developed through exposure to widely diverse people, cultures, ideas, and viewpoints. Brief for 3M et al.; Brief for General Motors Corp. What is more, high-ranking retired officers and civilian leaders of the United States military assert that, "based on [their] decades of experience," a "highly qualified, racially diverse officer corps ... is essential to the military's ability to fulfill its principle mission to provide national security." ...

Moreover, universities, and in particular, law schools, represent the training ground for a large number of our Nation's leaders. *Sweatt v. Painter*, 339 U.S. 629 (1950) [Note *supra.* this chapter] (describing law school as a "proving ground for legal learning and practice"). Individuals with law degrees occupy roughly half the state governorships, more than half the seats in the United States Senate, and more than a third of the seats in the United States House of Representatives....

In order to cultivate a set of leaders with legitimacy in the eyes of the citizenry, it is necessary that the path to leadership be visibly open to talented and qualified individuals of every race and ethnicity. All members of our heterogeneous society must have confidence in the openness and integrity of the educational institutions that provide this training. As we have recognized, law schools "cannot be effective in isolation from the individuals and institutions with which the law interacts." See *Sweatt*.... Access to legal education (and thus the legal profession) must be inclusive of talented and qualified individuals of every race and ethnicity, so that all members of our heterogeneous society may participate in the educational institutions that provide the training and education necessary to succeed in America.

The Law School does not premise its need for critical mass on "any belief that minority students always (or even consistently) express some characteristic minority viewpoint on any issue." To the contrary, diminishing the force of such stereotypes is both a crucial part of the Law School's mission, and one that it cannot accomplish with only token numbers of minority students. Just as growing up in a particular region or having particular professional experiences is likely to affect an individual's views, so too is one's own, unique experience of being a racial minority in a society, like our own, in which race unfortunately still matters. The Law School has determined, based on its experience and expertise, that a "critical mass" of underrepresented minorities is necessary to further its compelling interest in securing the educational benefits of a diverse student body.

B

Even in the limited circumstance when drawing racial distinctions is permissible to further a compelling state interest, government is still "constrained in how it may pursue that end: The means chosen to accomplish the [government's] asserted purpose must be specifically and narrowly framed to accomplish that purpose." The purpose of the narrow tailoring requirement is to ensure that "the means chosen 'fit' the compelling goal so closely that there is little or no possibility that the motive for the classification was illegitimate racial prejudice or stereotype." *Croson* (plurality opinion).

Since *Bakke*, we have had no occasion to define the contours of the narrow-tailoring inquiry with respect to race-conscious university admissions programs. That inquiry must be calibrated to fit the distinct issues raised by the use of race to achieve student body diversity in public higher education. Contrary to JUSTICE KENNEDY's assertions, we do not "abandon strict scrutiny." Rather, as we have already explained, we adhere to *Adarand*'s teaching that the very purpose of strict scrutiny is to take such "relevant differences into account."

To be narrowly tailored, a race-conscious admissions program cannot use a quota system—it cannot "insulate each category of applicants with certain desired qualifications from competition with all other applicants." *Bakke* (opinion of Powell, J.). Instead, a university may consider race or ethnicity only as a "'plus' in a particular applicant's file," without "insulating the individual from comparison with all other candidates for the available seats." *Id.* In other words, an admissions program must be "flexible enough to consider all pertinent elements of diversity in light of the particular qualifications of each applicant, and to place them on the same footing for consideration, although not necessarily according them the same weight." *Id....*

We are satisfied that the Law School's admissions program, like the Harvard plan described by Justice Powell, does not operate as a quota. Properly understood, a "quota" is a program in which a certain fixed number or proportion of opportunities are "reserved exclusively for certain minority groups." ... In contrast, "a permissible goal ... requires only a good-faith effort ... to come within a range demarcated by the goal itself," and permits consideration of race as a "plus" factor in any given case while still ensuring that each candidate "compete[s] with all other qualified applicants."

Justice Powell's distinction between the medical school's rigid 16-seat quota and Harvard's flexible use of race as a "plus" factor is instructive. Harvard certainly had minimum *goals* for minority enrollment, even if it had no specific number firmly in mind. What is more, Justice Powell flatly rejected the argument that Harvard's program was "the functional equivalent of a quota" merely because it had some " 'plus' " for race, or gave greater "weight" to race than to some other factors, in order to achieve student body diversity.

The Law School's goal of attaining a critical mass of underrepresented minority students does not transform its program into a quota. As the Harvard plan described by Justice Powell recognized, there is of course "some relationship between numbers and achieving the benefits to be derived from a diverse student body, and between numbers and providing a reasonable environment for those students admitted." "Some attention to numbers," without more, does not transform a flexible admissions system into a rigid quota. Nor, as JUSTICE KENNEDY posits, does the Law School's consultation of the "daily reports," which keep track of the racial and ethnic composition of the class (as well as of residency and gender), "suggest there was no further attempt at individual review save for race itself" during the final stages of the admissions process.... Moreover, as JUSTICE KENNEDY concedes, between 1993 and 1998, the number of African-American, Latino, and Native-American students in each class at the Law School varied from 13.5 to 20.1 percent, a range inconsistent with a quota....

That a race-conscious admissions program does not operate as a quota does not, by itself, satisfy the requirement of individualized consideration. When using race as a "plus" factor in university admissions, a university's admissions program must remain flexible enough to ensure that each applicant is evaluated as an individual and not in a way that makes an applicant's race or ethnicity the defining feature of his or her application. The importance of this individualized consideration in the context of a race-conscious admissions program is paramount.

Here, the Law School engages in a highly individualized, holistic review of each applicant's file, giving serious consideration to all the ways an applicant might contribute to a diverse educational environment.... Like the Harvard plan, the Law School's admissions policy "is flexible enough to consider all pertinent elements of diversity in light of the particular qualifications of each applicant, and to place them on the same footing for consideration, although not necessarily according ... them the same weight." *Bakke.*

We also find that, like the Harvard plan Justice Powell referenced in *Bakke*, the Law School's race-conscious admissions program adequately ensures that all factors that may contribute to student body diversity are meaningfully considered alongside race in admissions decisions. With respect to the use of race itself, all underrepresented minority students admitted by the Law School have been deemed qualified. By virtue of our Nation's struggle with racial inequality, such students are both likely to have experiences of particular importance to the Law School's mission, and less likely to be admitted in meaningful numbers on criteria that ignore those experiences....

Petitioner and the United States argue that the Law School's plan is not narrowly tailored because race-neutral means exist to obtain the educational benefits of student body diversity that the Law School seeks. We disagree. Narrow tailoring does not require exhaustion of every conceivable race-neutral alternative....

We agree with the Court of Appeals that the Law School sufficiently considered workable race-neutral alternatives. The District Court took the Law School to task for failing to consider race-neutral alternatives such as "using a lottery system" or "decreasing the emphasis for all applicants on undergraduate GPA and LSAT scores." But these alternatives would require a dramatic sacrifice of diversity, the academic quality of all admitted students, or both....

We acknowledge that "there are serious problems of justice connected with the idea of preference itself." *Bakke*. Narrow tailoring, therefore, requires that a race-conscious admissions program not unduly harm members of any racial group. Even remedial race-based governmental action generally "remains subject to continuing oversight to assure that it will work the least harm possible to other innocent persons competing for the benefit." To be narrowly tailored, a race-conscious admissions program must not "unduly burden individuals who are not members of the favored racial and ethnic groups." ...

We agree that, in the context of its individualized inquiry into the possible diversity contributions of all applicants, the Law School's race-conscious admissions program does not unduly harm nonminority applicants. We are mindful, however, that "a core purpose of the Fourteenth Amendment was to do away with all governmentally imposed discrimination based on race." Accordingly, race-conscious admissions policies must be limited in time. This requirement reflects that racial classifications, however compelling their goals, are potentially so dangerous that they may be employed no more broadly than the interest demands. Enshrining a permanent justification for racial preferences would offend this fundamental equal protection principle. We see no reason to exempt race-conscious admissions programs from the requirement that all governmental use of race must have a logical end point. The Law School, too, concedes that all "race-conscious programs must have reasonable durational limits." ...

We take the Law School at its word that it would "like nothing better than to find a race-neutral admissions formula" and will terminate its race-conscious admissions program as soon as practicable. It has been 25 years since Justice Powell first approved the use of race to further an interest in student body diversity in the context of public higher education. Since that time, the number of minority applicants with high grades and test scores has indeed increased. We expect that 25 years from now, the use of racial preferences will no longer be necessary to further the interest approved today....

JUSTICE GINSBERG, with whom JUSTICE BREYER joins, concurring.

... It is well documented that conscious and unconscious race bias, even rank discrimination based on race, remain alive in our land, impeding realization of our highest values and ideals. As to public education, data for the years 2000–2001 show that 71.6% of African-American children and 76.3% of Hispanic children attended a school in which minorities made up a majority of the student body. See E. Frankenberg, C. Lee & G. Orfield, *A Multiracial Society with Segregated Schools: Are We Losing the Dream?* (Jan. 2003). And schools in predominantly minority communities lag far behind others measured by the educational resources available to them.

However strong the public's desire for improved education systems may be, it remains the current reality that many minority students encounter markedly inadequate and unequal educational opportunities. Despite these inequalities, some minority students are able to meet the high threshold requirements set for admission to the country's finest undergraduate and graduate educational institutions. As lower school education in minority communities improves, an increase in the number of such students may be anticipated. From today's vantage point, one may hope, but not firmly forecast, that over the next generation's span, progress toward nondiscrimination and genuinely equal opportunity will make it safe to sunset affirmative action.

JUSTICE SCALIA, with whom JUSTICE THOMAS joins, dissenting. [omitted]

JUSTICE THOMAS, with whom JUSTICE SCALIA joins as to Parts I–VII, concurring in part and dissenting in part.

Frederick Douglass, speaking to a group of abolitionists almost 140 years ago, delivered a message lost on today's majority:

> In regard to the colored people, there is always more that is benevolent, I perceive, than just, manifested towards us. What I ask for the negro is not benevolence, not pity, not sympathy, but simply *justice*. The American people have always been anxious to know what they shall do with us.... I have had but one answer from the beginning. Do nothing with us! Your doing with us has already played the mischief with us. Do nothing with us! If the apples will not remain on the tree of their own strength, if they are worm-eaten at the core, if they are early ripe and disposed to fall, let them fall! ... And if the negro cannot stand on his own legs, let him fall also. All I ask is, give him a chance to stand on his own legs! Let him alone! ... Your interference is doing him positive injury.

*What the Black Man Wants: An Address Delivered in Boston, Massachusetts, on 26 January 1865,* reprinted in 4 THE FREDERICK DOUGLASS PAPERS (emphasis in original).

Like Douglass, I believe blacks can achieve in every avenue of American life without the meddling of university administrators. Because I wish to see all students succeed whatever their color, I share, in some respect, the sympathies of those who sponsor the type of discrimination advanced by the University of Michigan Law School (Law School). The Constitution does not, however, tolerate institutional devotion to the status quo in admissions policies when such devotion ripens into racial discrimination. Nor does the Constitution countenance the unprecedented deference the Court gives to the Law School, an approach inconsistent with the very concept of "strict scrutiny."

No one would argue that a university could set up a lower general admission standard and then impose heightened requirements only on black applicants. Similarly, a university may not maintain a high admission standard and grant exemptions to favored races. The Law School, of its own choosing, and for its own purposes, maintains an exclusionary admissions system that it knows produces racially disproportionate results. Racial discrimination is not a permissible solution to the self-inflicted wounds of this elitist admissions policy.

The majority upholds the Law School's racial discrimination not by interpreting the people's Constitution, but by responding to a faddish slogan of the cognoscenti. Nevertheless, I concur in part in the Court's opinion. First, I agree with the Court insofar as its decision, which approves of only one racial classification, confirms that further use of race in admissions remains unlawful. Second, I agree with the Court's holding that racial discrimination in higher education admissions will be illegal in 25 years. I respectfully dissent from the remainder of the Court's opinion and the judgment, however, because I believe that the Law School's current use of race violates the Equal Protection Clause and that the Constitution means the same thing today as it will in 300 months.

I

... The Constitution abhors classifications based on race, not only because those classifications can harm favored races or are based on illegitimate motives, but also because every time the government places citizens on racial registers and makes race relevant to the provision of burdens or benefits, it demeans us all. "Purchased at the price of immeasurable human suffering, the equal protection principle reflects our Nation's understanding that such classifications ultimately have a destructive impact on the individual and our society." *Adarand* (Thomas, J., concurring in part and concurring in the judgment).

II

Unlike the majority, I seek to define with precision the interest being asserted by the Law School before determining whether that interest is so compelling as to justify racial discrimination. The Law School maintains that it wishes to obtain "educational benefits that flow from student body diversity." This statement must be evaluated carefully, because it implies that both "diversity" and "educational benefits" are components of the Law School's compelling state interest. Additionally, the Law School's refusal to entertain certain changes in its admissions process and status indicates that the compelling state interest it seeks to validate is actually broader than might appear at first glance.

Undoubtedly there are other ways to "better" the education of law students aside from ensuring that the student body contains a "critical mass" of underrepresented minority students. Attaining "diversity," whatever it means, is the mechanism by which the Law School obtains educational benefits, not an end of itself. The Law School, however, apparently believes that only a racially mixed student body can lead to the educational benefits it seeks. How, then, is the Law School's interest in these allegedly unique educational "benefits" *not* simply the forbidden interest in "racial balancing" that the majority expressly rejects? ...

One must also consider the Law School's refusal to entertain changes to its current admissions system that might produce the same educational benefits. The Law School adamantly disclaims any race-neutral alternative that would reduce "academic selectivity," which would in turn "require the Law School to become a very different institution, and to sacrifice a core part of its educational mission." In other words, the Law School seeks to improve marginally the education it offers without sacrificing too much of its exclusivity and elite status.

The proffered interest that the majority vindicates today, then, is not simply "diversity." Instead the Court upholds the use of racial discrimination as a tool to advance the Law School's interest in offering a marginally superior education while maintaining an elite institution. Unless each constituent part of this state interest is of pressing public necessity, the Law School's use of race is unconstitutional. I find each of them to fall far short of this standard.

### III

\* \* \*

### B

Under the proper standard, there is no pressing public necessity in maintaining a public law school at all and, it follows, certainly not an elite law school. Likewise, marginal improvements in legal education do not qualify as a compelling state interest.

### 1

While legal education at a public university may be good policy or otherwise laudable, it is obviously not a pressing public necessity when the correct legal standard is applied.... The fact that some fraction of the States reject a particular enterprise ... creates a presumption that the enterprise itself is not a compelling state interest. In this sense, the absence of a public, American Bar Association (ABA) accredited, law school in Alaska, Delaware, Massachusetts, New Hampshire, and Rhode Island provides further evidence that Michigan's maintenance of the Law School does not constitute a compelling state interest.

### 2

As the foregoing makes clear, Michigan has no compelling interest in having a law school at all, much less an *elite* one. Still, even assuming that a State may, under appropriate circumstances, demonstrate a cognizable interest in having an elite law school, Michigan has failed to do so here....

The only cognizable state interests vindicated by operating a public law school are ... the education of that State's citizens and the training of that State's lawyers.... The Law School today, however, does precious little training of those attorneys who will serve the citizens of Michigan. In 2002, graduates of the Law School made up less than 6% of applicants to the Michigan bar, even though the Law School's graduates constitute nearly 30% of all law students graduating in Michigan. Less than 16% of the Law School's graduating class elects to stay in Michigan after law school....

### IV

The interest in remaining elite and exclusive that the majority thinks so obviously critical requires the use of admissions "standards" that, in turn, create the Law School's "need" to discriminate on the basis of race. The Court validates these admissions standards by concluding that alternatives that would require "a dramatic sacrifice of … the academic quality of all admitted students" need not be considered before racial discrimination can be employed. In the majority's view, such methods are not required by the "narrow tailoring" prong of strict scrutiny because that inquiry demands, in this context, that any race-neutral alternative work "about as well." … The Court never explicitly holds that the Law School's desire to retain the status quo in "academic selectivity" is itself a compelling state interest, and, as I have demonstrated, it is not. Therefore, the Law School should be forced to choose between its classroom aesthetic and its exclusionary admissions system—it cannot have it both ways.…

## B

### 1

The Court's deference to the Law School's conclusion that its racial experimentation leads to educational benefits will, if adhered to, have serious collateral consequences. The Court relies heavily on social science evidence to justify its deference. The Court never acknowledges, however, the growing evidence that racial (and other sorts) of heterogeneity actually impairs learning among black students. See, e.g., Flowers & Pascarella, "Cognitive Effects of College Racial Composition on African American Students After 3 Years of College," 40 *J. of College Student Development* 669 (1999) (concluding that black students experience superior cognitive development at Historically Black Colleges (HBCs) and that, even among blacks, "a substantial diversity moderates the cognitive effects of attending an HBC").…

## C

… Today … the majority ignores the "experience" of those institutions that have been forced to abandon explicit racial discrimination in admissions. The sky has not fallen at Boalt Hall at the University of California, Berkeley, for example. Prior to Proposition 209's adoption of Cal. Const., Art. 1, § 31(a), which bars the State from "granting preferential treatment … on the basis of race … in the operation of … public education," Boalt Hall enrolled 20 blacks and 28 Hispanics in its first-year class for 1996. In 2002, without deploying express racial discrimination in admissions, Boalt's entering class enrolled 14 blacks and 36 Hispanics. Total underrepresented minority student enrollment at Boalt Hall now exceeds 1996 levels. Apparently the Law School cannot be counted on to be as resourceful. The Court is willfully blind to the very real experience in California and elsewhere, which raises the inference that institutions with "reputations for excellence" rivaling the Law School's have satisfied their sense of mission without resorting to prohibited racial discrimination.

## V

Putting aside the absence of any legal support for the majority's reflexive deference, there is much to be said for the view that the use of tests and other measures to "predict" academic performance is a poor substitute for a system that gives every applicant a chance to prove he can succeed in the study of law. The rallying cry that in the absence of racial discrimination in admissions there would be a true meritocracy ignores the fact that the entire process is poisoned by numerous exceptions to "merit." For example, in the national debate on racial discrimination in higher education admissions, much has been made of the fact that elite institutions utilize a so-called "legacy" preference to give the children of alumni an advantage in admissions. This, and other, exceptions to a "true" meritocracy give the lie to protestations that merit admissions are in fact the order of the day at the Nation's universities. The Equal Protection Clause does not, however, prohibit the use of unseemly legacy preferences or many other kinds of arbitrary admissions procedures. What the Equal Protection Clause does prohibit are classifications made on the basis of race. So while legacy preferences can stand under the Constitution, racial discrimination cannot. I will not twist the Constitution to invalidate legacy preferences or otherwise impose my vision of higher education admissions on the Nation. The majority should similarly stay its impulse to validate faddish racial discrimination the Constitution clearly forbids....

## VI

The absence of any articulated legal principle supporting the majority's principal holding suggests another rationale. I believe what lies beneath the Court's decision today are the benighted notions that one can tell when racial discrimination benefits (rather than hurts) minority groups, and that racial discrimination is necessary to remedy general societal ills. This Court's precedents supposedly settled both issues, but clearly the majority still cannot commit to the principle that racial classifications are *per se* harmful and that almost no amount of benefit in the eye of the beholder can justify such classifications.

Putting aside what I take to be the Court's implicit rejection of *Adarand*'s holding that beneficial and burdensome racial classifications are equally invalid, I must contest the notion that the Law School's discrimination benefits those admitted as a result of it. The Court spends considerable time discussing the impressive display of *amicus* support for the Law School in this case from all corners of society. But nowhere in any of the filings in this Court is any evidence that the purported "beneficiaries" of this racial discrimination prove themselves by performing at (or even near) the same level as those students who receive no preferences.

The silence in this case is deafening to those of us who view higher education's purpose as imparting knowledge and skills to students, rather than a communal, rubber-stamp, credentialing process. The Law School is not looking for those students who, despite a lower LSAT score or undergraduate grade point average, will succeed in the study of law. The Law School seeks only a façade — it is sufficient that the class looks right, even if it does not perform right....

Beyond the harm the Law School's racial discrimination visits upon its test subjects, no social science has disproved the notion that this discrimination "engenders attitudes of superiority or, alternatively, provokes resentment among those who believe that they have been wronged by the government's use of race." "These programs stamp minorities with a badge of inferiority and may cause them to develop dependencies or to adopt an attitude that they are 'entitled' to preferences."

It is uncontested that each year, the Law School admits a handful of blacks who would be admitted in the absence of racial discrimination. Who can differentiate between those who belong and those who do not? The majority of blacks are admitted to the Law School because of discrimination, and because of this policy all are tarred as undeserving. This problem of stigma does not depend on determinacy as to whether those stigmatized are actually the "beneficiaries" of racial discrimination. When blacks take positions in the highest places of government, industry, or academia, it is an open question today whether their skin color played a part in their advancement. The question itself is the stigma—because either racial discrimination did play a role, in which case the person may be deemed "otherwise unqualified," or it did not, in which case asking the question itself unfairly marks those blacks who would succeed without discrimination. Is this what the Court means by "visibly open"? . . .

Finally, the Court's disturbing reference to the importance of the country's law schools as training grounds meant to cultivate "a set of leaders with legitimacy in the eyes of the citizenry," through the use of racial discrimination deserves discussion. As noted earlier, the Court has soundly rejected the remedying of societal discrimination as a justification for governmental use of race. *Wygant v. Jackson Board of Education*, 476 U.S. 267 (1986) [Note *supra.* this chapter]; *Croson.* For those who believe that every racial disproportionality in our society is caused by some kind of racial discrimination, there can be no distinction between remedying societal discrimination and erasing racial disproportionalities in the country's leadership caste. And if the lack of proportional racial representation among our leaders is not caused by societal discrimination, then "fixing" it is even less of a pressing public necessity. . . .

CHIEF JUSTICE REHNQUIST, with whom JUSTICE SCALIA, JUSTICE KENNEDY, and JUSTICE THOMAS join, dissenting.

I agree with the Court that, "in the limited circumstance when drawing racial distinctions is permissible," the government must ensure that its means are narrowly tailored to achieve a compelling state interest. I do not believe, however, that the University of Michigan Law School's (Law School) means are narrowly tailored to the interest it asserts. The Law School claims it must take the steps it does to achieve a "'critical mass'" of underrepresented minority students. But its actual program bears no relation to this asserted goal. Stripped of its "critical mass" veil, the Law School's program is revealed as a naked effort to achieve racial balancing. . . .

Before the Court's decision today, we consistently applied the same strict scrutiny analysis regardless of the government's purported reason for using race and regardless of the setting in which race was being used. We rejected calls to use more lenient review in the face of claims that race was being used in "good faith" because "more than good motives should be required when government seeks to allocate its resources by way of an explicit racial classification system." *Adarand.* We likewise rejected calls to apply more lenient review based on the particular setting in which race is being used. . . . Although the Court recites the language of our strict scrutiny analysis, its application of that review is unprecedented in its deference. . . .

Respondents' asserted justification for the Law School's use of race in the admissions process is "obtaining 'the educational benefits that flow from a diverse student body.'"...

In practice, the Law School's program bears little or no relation to its asserted goal of achieving "critical mass." Respondents explain that the Law School seeks to accumulate a "critical mass" of *each* underrepresented minority group. But the record demonstrates that the Law School's admissions practices with respect to these groups differ dramatically and cannot be defended under any consistent use of the term "critical mass."

From 1995 through 2000, the Law School admitted between 1,130 and 1,310 students. Of those, between 13 and 19 were Native American, between 91 and 108 were African-Americans, and between 47 and 56 were Hispanic. If the Law School is admitting between 91 and 108 African-Americans in order to achieve "critical mass," thereby preventing African-American students from feeling "isolated or like spokespersons for their race," one would think that a number of the same order of magnitude would be necessary to accomplish the same purpose for Hispanics and Native Americans. Similarly, even if all of the Native American applicants admitted in a given year matriculate, which the record demonstrates is not at all the case, how can this possibly constitute a "critical mass" of Native Americans in a class of over 350 students? In order for this pattern of admission to be consistent with the Law School's explanation of "critical mass," one would have to believe that the objectives of "critical mass" offered by respondents are achieved with only half the number of Hispanics and one-sixth the number of Native Americans as compared to African-Americans. But respondents offer no race-specific reasons for such disparities. Instead, they simply emphasize the importance of achieving "critical mass," without any explanation of why that concept is applied differently among the three underrepresented minority groups.

These different numbers, moreover, come only as a result of substantially different treatment among the three underrepresented minority groups, as is apparent in an example offered by the Law School and highlighted by the Court: The school asserts that it "frequently accepts nonminority applicants with grades and test scores lower than underrepresented minority applicants (and other nonminority applicants) who are rejected."...

Review of the record reveals only 67 such individuals. Of these 67 individuals, 56 were Hispanic, while only 6 were African-American, and only 5 were Native American. This discrepancy reflects a consistent practice....

These statistics have a significant bearing on petitioner's case. Respondents have *never* offered any race-specific arguments explaining why significantly more individuals from one underrepresented minority group are needed in order to achieve "critical mass" or further student body diversity. They certainly have not explained why Hispanics, who they have said are among "the groups most isolated by racial barriers in our country," should have their admission capped out in this manner....

Only when the "critical mass" label is discarded does a likely explanation for these numbers emerge. The Court states that the Law School's goal of attaining a "critical mass" of underrepresented minority students is not an interest in merely "'assuring within its student body some specified percentage of a particular group merely because of its race or ethnic origin.'" (quoting *Bakke*). The Court recognizes that such an interest "would amount to outright racial balancing, which is patently unconstitutional." The Court concludes, however, that the Law School's use of race in admissions, consistent with Justice Powell's opinion in *Bakke*, only pays "some attention to numbers."

But the correlation between the percentage of the Law School's pool of applicants who are members of the three minority groups and the percentage of the admitted applicants who are members of these same groups is far too precise to be dismissed as merely the result of the school paying "some attention to [the] numbers." As the tables below show,[*] from 1995 to 2000 the percentage of admitted applicants who were members of these minority groups closely tracked the percentage of individuals in the school's applicant pool who were from the same groups.... The tight correlation between the percentage of applicants and admittees of a given race ... must result from careful race based planning by the Law School....

I do not believe that the Constitution gives the Law School such free rein in the use of race. The Law School has offered no explanation for its actual admissions practices and, unexplained, we are bound to conclude that the Law School has managed its admissions program, not to achieve a "critical mass," but to extend offers of admission to members of selected minority groups in proportion to their statistical representation in the applicant pool. But this is precisely the type of racial balancing that the Court itself calls "patently unconstitutional."

Finally, I believe that the Law School's program fails strict scrutiny because it is devoid of any reasonably precise time limit on the Law School's use of race in admissions. We have emphasized that we will consider "the planned duration of the remedy" in determining whether a race-conscious program is constitutional....

The Court suggests a possible 25-year limitation on the Law School's current program. Respondents, on the other hand, remain more ambiguous, explaining that "the Law School of course recognizes that race-conscious programs must have reasonable durational limits, and the Sixth Circuit properly found such a limit in the Law School's resolve to cease considering race when genuine race-neutral alternatives become available." These discussions of a time limit are the vaguest of assurances. In truth, they permit the Law School's use of racial preferences on a seemingly permanent basis. Thus, an important component of strict scrutiny—that a program be limited in time—is casually subverted.

The Court, in an unprecedented display of deference under our strict scrutiny analysis, upholds the Law School's program despite its obvious flaws. We have said that when it comes to the use of race, the connection between the ends and the means used to attain them must be precise. But here the flaw is deeper than that; it is not

---

* [Ed. Note: The tables Justice Rehnquist referred to are omitted from this excerpt.]

merely a question of "fit" between ends and means. Here the means actually used are forbidden by the Equal Protection Clause of the Constitution.

JUSTICE KENNEDY, dissenting.

The separate opinion by Justice Powell in *Bakke* is based on the principle that a university admissions program may take account of race as one, nonpredominant factor in a system designed to consider each applicant as an individual, provided the program can meet the test of strict scrutiny by the judiciary. This is a unitary formulation. If strict scrutiny is abandoned or manipulated to distort its real and accepted meaning, the Court lacks authority to approve the use of race even in this modest, limited way. The opinion by Justice Powell, in my view, states the correct rule for resolving this case. The Court, however, does not apply strict scrutiny. By trying to say otherwise, it undermines both the test and its own controlling precedents....

To be constitutional, a university's compelling interest in a diverse student body must be achieved by a system where individual assessment is safeguarded through the entire process. There is no constitutional objection to the goal of considering race as one modest factor among many others to achieve diversity, but an educational institution must ensure, through sufficient procedures, that each applicant receives individual consideration and that race does not become a predominant factor in the admissions decisionmaking. The Law School failed to comply with this requirement, and by no means has it carried its burden to show otherwise by the test of strict scrutiny....

The Court, in a review that is nothing short of perfunctory, accepts the University of Michigan Law School's (Law School) assurances that its admissions process meets with constitutional requirements. The majority fails to confront the reality of how the Law School's admissions policy is implemented. The dissenting opinion by THE CHIEF JUSTICE, which I join in full, demonstrates beyond question why the concept of critical mass is a delusion used by the Law School to mask its attempt to make race an automatic factor in most instances and to achieve numerical goals indistinguishable from quotas. An effort to achieve racial balance among the minorities the school seeks to attract is, by the Court's own admission, "patently unconstitutional." It remains to point out how critical mass becomes inconsistent with individual consideration in some more specific aspects of the admissions process.

About 80% to 85% of the places in the entering class are given to applicants in the upper range of Law School Admissions Test scores and grades. An applicant with these credentials likely will be admitted without consideration of race or ethnicity. With respect to the remaining 15% to 20% of the seats, race is likely outcome determinative for many members of minority groups. That is where the competition becomes tight and where any given applicant's chance of admission is far smaller if he or she lacks minority status. At this point the numerical concept of critical mass has the real potential to compromise individual review.

The Law School has not demonstrated how individual consideration is, or can be, preserved at this stage of the application process given the instruction to attain what it calls critical mass. In fact the evidence shows otherwise. There was little deviation among admitted minority students during the years from 1995 to 1998. The percentage of enrolled minorities fluctuated only by 0.3%, from 13.5% to 13.8%. The number of minority students to whom offers were extended varied by just a slightly greater magnitude of 2.2%, from the high of 15.6% in 1995 to the low of 13.4% in 1998.

The District Court relied on this uncontested fact to draw an inference that the Law School's pursuit of critical mass mutated into the equivalent of a quota.... The narrow fluctuation band raises an inference that the Law School subverted individual determination, and strict scrutiny requires the Law School to overcome the inference.... At the very least, the constancy of admitted minority students and the close correlation between the racial breakdown of admitted minorities and the composition of the applicant pool, discussed by THE CHIEF JUSTICE, require the Law School either to produce a convincing explanation or to show it has taken adequate steps to ensure individual assessment. The Law School does neither....

If universities are given the latitude to administer programs that are tantamount to quotas, they will have few incentives to make the existing minority admissions schemes transparent and protective of individual review. The unhappy consequence will be to perpetuate the hostilities that proper consideration of race is designed to avoid. The perpetuation, of course, would be the worst of all outcomes. Other programs do exist which will be more effective in bringing about the harmony and mutual respect among all citizens that our constitutional tradition has always sought. They, and not the program under review here, should be the model, even if the Court defaults by not demanding it.

It is regrettable the Court's important holding allowing racial minorities to have their special circumstances considered in order to improve their educational opportunities is accompanied by a suspension of the strict scrutiny which was the predicate of allowing race to be considered in the first place. If the Court abdicates its constitutional duty to give strict scrutiny to the use of race in university admissions, it negates my authority to approve the use of race in pursuit of student diversity. The Constitution cannot confer the right to classify on the basis of race even in this special context absent searching judicial review. For these reasons, though I reiterate my approval of giving appropriate consideration to race in this one context, I must dissent in the present case.

## *Note:* Gratz v. Bollinger

1. The same day the Court decided *Grutter* it also decided *Gratz v. Bollinger*, 539 U.S. 244 (2003). *Gratz* considered the University of Michigan's *undergraduate* admissions process. That process used a numerical selection index on which an applicant could score a maximum 150 points, and awarded applicants from an "underrepresented racial or ethnic minority group" an automatic 20 points. Two white plaintiffs who were denied admission sued the university, alleging that the 20-point bonus violated the Equal Protection Clause.

2. By a 6–3 vote, the Court agreed. Writing for five justices, Chief Justice Rehnquist acknowledged *Grutter*'s holding that ensuring a diverse entering class constituted a compelling government interest that a university could assert when using race as a

factor in admissions decisions. However, he concluded that the university's flat 20-point bonus violated Justice Powell's insistence in *Bakke* that the use of admissions in race ensure an individualized consideration of each candidate.

Justice Thomas joined the Court's opinion, but wrote separately to note his continued disagreement with allowing universities to employ race at all in admissions decisions. Justice O'Connor also joined the Court's opinion, and wrote separately to reiterate the Court's point about the lack of individualized consideration. Justice Breyer joined Justice O'Connor's opinion but not the majority opinion; he also joined Part I of Justice Ginsburg's dissent, which argued that government should have more latitude to use race when seeking to undo the effects of past discrimination.

3. Justice Souter, joined in part by Justice Ginsburg, dissented, arguing that the university's admissions process did not operate as a quota, since non-minority applicants could outscore minority applicants and thus obtain admission, and also because the university's process gave point bonuses for other factors, such as Michigan residency. Justice Ginsburg, joined by Justice Souter and in part by Justice Breyer, also wrote a dissent. She argued that states should enjoy more latitude to use race to undo past discrimination, and that the university's point system had the benefit of using race in a transparent way, rather than through camouflaged means.

# E. Race Consciousness Today

## Parents Involved in Community Schools v. Seattle School District No. 1

### 551 U.S. 701 (2007)

Chief Justice ROBERTS announced the judgment of the Court, and delivered the opinion of the Court with respect to Parts I, II, III-A, and III-C, and an opinion with respect to Parts III-B and IV, in which Justices SCALIA, THOMAS and ALITO join.

[School districts in Seattle, Washington and Louisville, Kentucky adopted student assignment plans that used the race of the student as a tie-breaker in determining the school to which the student would be assigned. The Seattle district was never the subject of a judicial holding that it segregated students by race; the Louisville district had been adjudged to segregate, in violation of *Brown v. Board of Education* (1954) (*Supra.* this chapter), but in 2000 the district court had dissolved the desegregation decree, concluding that the district "had achieved unitary status by eliminating 'to the greatest extent practicable' the vestiges of its prior policy of segregation." Parents in each district sued, alleging that the districts' voluntary use of race as an assignment tool violated the Equal Protection Clause.]

### III

### A

It is well established that when the government distributes burdens or benefits on the basis of individual racial classifications, that action is reviewed under strict scrutiny.

*Grutter v. Bollinger* (2003) [*Supra*. this chapter]; *Adarand Constructors v. Pena*, 515 U.S. 200 (1995) [Note *supra*. this chapter]. As the Court recently reaffirmed, "racial classifications are simply too pernicious to permit any but the most exact connection between justification and classification." *Gratz v. Bollinger* (2003) [Note *supra*. this chapter]. In order to satisfy this searching standard of review, the school districts must demonstrate that the use of individual racial classifications in the assignment plans here under review is "narrowly tailored" to achieve a "compelling" government interest. *Adarand.*

Without attempting in these cases to set forth all the interests a school district might assert, it suffices to note that our prior cases, in evaluating the use of racial classifications in the school context, have recognized two interests that qualify as compelling. The first is the compelling interest of remedying the effects of past intentional discrimination. Yet the Seattle public schools have not shown that they were ever segregated by law, and were not subject to court-ordered desegregation decrees. The Jefferson County [Louisville] public schools were previously segregated by law and were subject to a desegregation decree entered in 1975. In 2000, the District Court that entered that decree dissolved it, finding that Jefferson County had "eliminated the vestiges associated with the former policy of segregation and its pernicious effects" and thus had achieved "unitary" status. Jefferson County accordingly does not rely upon an interest in remedying the effects of past intentional discrimination in defending its present use of race in assigning students.

Nor could it. We have emphasized that the harm being remedied by mandatory desegregation plans is the harm that is traceable to segregation, and that "the Constitution is not violated by racial imbalance in the schools, without more." *Milliken v. Bradley*, 418 U.S. 717 (1974). Once Jefferson County achieved unitary status, it had remedied the constitutional wrong that allowed race-based assignments. Any continued use of race must be justified on some other basis.

The second government interest we have recognized as compelling for purposes of strict scrutiny is the interest in diversity in higher education upheld in *Grutter....* The diversity interest was not focused on race alone but encompassed "all factors that may contribute to student body diversity." ...

In the present cases, by contrast, race is not considered as part of a broader effort to achieve "exposure to widely diverse people, cultures, ideas, and viewpoints;" race, for some students, is determinative standing alone.... Like the University of Michigan undergraduate plan struck down in *Gratz,* the plans here "do not provide for a meaningful individualized review of applicants" but instead rely on racial classifications in a "nonindividualized, mechanical" way....

Prior to *Grutter,* the courts of appeals rejected as unconstitutional attempts to implement race-based assignment plans—such as the plans at issue here—in primary and secondary schools. After *Grutter,* however, the two Courts of Appeals in these cases, and one other, found that race-based assignments were permissible at the elementary and secondary level, largely in reliance on that case.

In upholding the admissions plan in *Grutter* ... this Court relied upon consider-ations unique to institutions of higher education, noting that in light of "the expansive freedoms of speech and thought associated with the university environment, univer-sities occupy a special niche in our constitutional tradition." ... The present cases are not governed by *Grutter*.

B

Perhaps recognizing that reliance on *Grutter* cannot sustain their plans, both school districts assert additional interests, distinct from the interest upheld in *Grutter,* to justify their race-based assignments. In briefing and argument before this Court, Seattle contends that its use of race helps to reduce racial concentration in schools and to ensure that racially concentrated housing patterns do not prevent nonwhite students from having access to the most desirable schools. Jefferson County has ar-ticulated a similar goal, phrasing its interest in terms of educating its students "in a racially integrated environment."[12] Each school district argues that educational and broader socialization benefits flow from a racially diverse learning environment, and each contends that because the diversity they seek is racial diversity — not the broader diversity at issue in *Grutter* — it makes sense to promote that interest directly by relying on race alone.

The parties and their *amici* dispute whether racial diversity in schools in fact has a marked impact on test scores and other objective yardsticks or achieves intangible socialization benefits. The debate is not one we need to resolve, however, because it is clear that the racial classifications employed by the districts are not narrowly tailored to the goal of achieving the educational and social benefits asserted to flow from racial diversity. In design and operation, the plans are directed only to racial balance, pure and simple, an objective this Court has repeatedly condemned as illegitimate.

The plans are tied to each district's specific racial demographics, rather than to any pedagogic concept of the level of diversity needed to obtain the asserted educa-tional benefits.... The districts offer no evidence that the level of racial diversity nec-essary to achieve the asserted educational benefits happens to coincide with the racial demographics of the respective school districts....

This working backward to achieve a particular type of racial balance, rather than working forward from some demonstration of the level of diversity that provides the purported benefits, is a fatal flaw under our existing precedent. We have many times over reaffirmed that "racial balance is not to be achieved for its own sake." *Grutter* itself reiterated that "outright racial balancing" is "patently unconstitutional."

---

12. Jefferson County also argues that it would be incongruous to hold that what was constitutionally required of it one day — race-based assignments pursuant to the desegregation decree — can be con-stitutionally prohibited the next. But what was constitutionally required of the district prior to 2000 was the elimination of the vestiges of prior segregation — not racial proportionality in its own right. See *Freeman v. Pitts,* 503 U.S. 467 (1992). Once those vestiges were eliminated, Jefferson County was on the same footing as any other school district, and its use of race must be justified on other grounds.

Accepting racial balancing as a compelling state interest would justify the imposition of racial proportionality throughout American society, contrary to our repeated recognition that "at the heart of the Constitution's guarantee of equal protection lies the simple command that the Government must treat citizens as individuals, not as simply components of a racial, religious, sexual or national class."....

The principle that racial balancing is not permitted is one of substance, not semantics. Racial balancing is not transformed from "patently unconstitutional" to a compelling state interest simply by relabeling it "racial diversity." While the school districts use various verbal formulations to describe the interest they seek to promote — racial diversity, avoidance of racial isolation, racial integration — they offer no definition of the interest that suggests it differs from racial balance.

Jefferson County phrases its interest as "racial integration," but integration certainly does not require the sort of racial proportionality reflected in its plan. Even in the context of mandatory desegregation, we have stressed that racial proportionality is not required, and here Jefferson County has already been found to have eliminated the vestiges of its prior segregated school system....

## C

The districts assert, as they must, that the way in which they have employed individual racial classifications is necessary to achieve their stated ends. The minimal effect these classifications have on student assignments, however, suggests that other means would be effective. Seattle's racial tiebreaker results, in the end, only in shifting a small number of students between schools.... While we do not suggest that *greater* use of race would be preferable, the minimal impact of the districts' racial classifications on school enrollment casts doubt on the necessity of using racial classifications.... The districts have also failed to show that they considered methods other than explicit racial classifications to achieve their stated goals....

## IV

Justice BREYER's dissent takes a different approach to these cases, one that fails to ground the result it would reach in law. Instead, it selectively relies on inapplicable precedent and even *dicta* while dismissing contrary holdings, alters and misapplies our well-established legal framework for assessing equal protection challenges to express racial classifications, and greatly exaggerates the consequences of today's decision....

This Court has recently reiterated ... that "*all* racial classifications [imposed by government] ... must be analyzed by a reviewing court under strict scrutiny." Justice BREYER nonetheless relies on the good intentions and motives of the school districts, stating that he has found "no case that ... repudiated this constitutional asymmetry between that which seeks to *exclude* and that which seeks to *include* members of minority races." We have found many. Our cases clearly reject the argument that motives affect the strict scrutiny analysis. See *Adarand v. Pena*, 515 U.S. 200 (1995) [Note *supra.* this chapter] (rejecting idea that "benign" racial classifications may be held to "different standard"); *City of Richmond v. J.A. Croson Co.* (1989) [*Supra.* this chapter]

("Racial classifications are suspect, and that means that simple legislative assurances of good intention cannot suffice")....

If the need for the racial classifications embraced by the school districts is unclear, even on the districts' own terms, the costs are undeniable. "Distinctions between citizens solely because of their ancestry are by their very nature odious to a free people whose institutions are founded upon the doctrine of equality." *Adarand*. Government action dividing us by race is inherently suspect because such classifications promote "notions of racial inferiority and lead to a politics of racial hostility," *Croson*, "reinforce the belief, held by too many for too much of our history, that individuals should be judged by the color of their skin," and "endorse race-based reasoning and the conception of a Nation divided into racial blocs, thus contributing to an escalation of racial hostility and conflict." As the Court explained in *Rice v. Cayetano*, 528 U.S. 495 (2000), "one of the principal reasons race is treated as a forbidden classification is that it demeans the dignity and worth of a person to be judged by ancestry instead of by his or her own merit and essential qualities."

All this is true enough in the contexts in which these statements were made — government contracting, voting districts, allocation of broadcast licenses, and electing state officers — but when it comes to using race to assign children to schools, history will be heard. In *Brown I*, we held that segregation deprived black children of equal educational opportunities regardless of whether school facilities and other tangible factors were equal, because government classification and separation on grounds of race themselves denoted inferiority. It was not the inequality of the facilities but the fact of legally separating children on the basis of race on which the Court relied to find a constitutional violation in 1954. The next Term, we accordingly stated that "full compliance" with *Brown I* required school districts "to achieve a system of determining admission to the public schools *on a nonracial basis.*" *Brown v. Board of Education*, 349 U.S. 294 (1955) ("*Brown II*").

The parties and their *amici* debate which side is more faithful to the heritage of *Brown*, but the position of the plaintiffs in *Brown* was spelled out in their brief and could not have been clearer: "The Fourteenth Amendment prevents states from according differential treatment to American children on the basis of their color or race." Brief for Appellants in Nos. 1, 2, and 4 and for Respondents in No. 10 on Reargument in *Brown I*, O.T.1953, p. 15 (Summary of Argument). What do the racial classifications at issue here do, if not accord differential treatment on the basis of race? As counsel who appeared before this Court for the plaintiffs in *Brown* put it: "We have one fundamental contention which we will seek to develop in the course of this argument, and that contention is that no State has any authority under the equal-protection clause of the Fourteenth Amendment to use race as a factor in affording educational opportunities among its citizens." Tr. of Oral Arg. in *Brown I*, p. 7 (Robert L. Carter, Dec. 9, 1952). There is no ambiguity in that statement. And it was that position that prevailed in this Court, which emphasized in its remedial opinion that what was "at stake is the personal interest of the plaintiffs in admission to public schools as soon as practicable *on a nondiscriminatory basis,*" and what was required was "determining admission to the public schools *on a nonracial basis." Brown II.* What do the racial classifications do in these cases, if not determine admission to a public school on a racial basis?

Before *Brown*, schoolchildren were told where they could and could not go to school based on the color of their skin. The school districts in these cases have not carried the heavy burden of demonstrating that we should allow this once again — even for very different reasons. For schools that never segregated on the basis of race, such as Seattle, or that have removed the vestiges of past segregation, such as Jefferson County, the way "to achieve a system of determining admission to the public schools on a nonracial basis," *Brown II*, is to stop assigning students on a racial basis. The way to stop discrimination on the basis of race is to stop discriminating on the basis of race....

Justice Thomas, concurring.

Today, the Court holds that state entities may not experiment with race-based means to achieve ends they deem socially desirable. I wholly concur in The Chief Justice's opinion. I write separately to address several of the contentions in Justice Breyer's dissent (hereinafter the dissent). Contrary to the dissent's arguments, re-segregation is not occurring in Seattle or Louisville; these school boards have no present interest in remedying past segregation; and these race-based student-assignment programs do not serve any compelling state interest. Accordingly, the plans are unconstitutional. Disfavoring a color-blind interpretation of the Constitution, the dissent would give school boards a free hand to make decisions on the basis of race — an approach reminiscent of that advocated by the segregationists in *Brown v. Board of Education.* This approach is just as wrong today as it was a half-century ago. The Constitution and our cases require us to be much more demanding before permitting local school boards to make decisions based on race.

## I

The dissent repeatedly claims that the school districts are threatened with resegregation and that they will succumb to that threat if these plans are declared unconstitutional. It also argues that these plans can be justified as part of the school boards' attempts to "eradicate earlier school segregation." Contrary to the dissent's rhetoric, neither of these school districts is threatened with resegregation, and neither is constitutionally compelled or permitted to undertake race-based remediation. Racial imbalance is not segregation, and the mere incantation of terms like resegregation and remediation cannot make up the difference....

## II

Lacking a cognizable interest in remediation, neither of these plans can survive strict scrutiny because neither plan serves a genuinely compelling state interest. The dissent avoids reaching that conclusion by unquestioningly accepting the assertions of selected social scientists while completely ignoring the fact that those assertions are the subject of fervent debate. Ultimately, the dissent's entire analysis is corrupted by the considerations that lead it initially to question whether strict scrutiny should apply at all. What emerges is a version of "strict scrutiny" that combines hollow assurances of harmlessness with reflexive acceptance of conventional wisdom. When it comes to government race-based decisionmaking, the Constitution demands more.

## A

... Even supposing it mattered to the constitutional analysis, the race-based student-assignment programs before us are not as benign as the dissent believes. "Racial paternalism and its unintended consequences can be as poisonous and pernicious as any other form of discrimination." As these programs demonstrate, every time the government uses racial criteria to "bring the races together," someone gets excluded, and the person excluded suffers an injury solely because of his or her race. The petitioner in the Louisville case received a letter from the school board informing her that her *kindergartener* would not be allowed to attend the school of petitioner's choosing because of the child's race.... This type of exclusion, solely on the basis of race, is precisely the sort of government action that pits the races against one another, exacerbates racial tension, and "provokes resentment among those who believe that they have been wronged by the government's use of race." Accordingly, these plans are simply one more variation on the government race-based decisionmaking we have consistently held must be subjected to strict scrutiny....

## III

Most of the dissent's criticisms of today's result can be traced to its rejection of the colorblind Constitution. The dissent attempts to marginalize the notion of a color-blind Constitution by consigning it to me and Members of today's plurality. But I am quite comfortable in the company I keep. My view of the Constitution is Justice Harlan's view in *Plessy*: "Our Constitution is color-blind, and neither knows nor tolerates classes among citizens." *Plessy v. Ferguson* (1896) (dissenting opinion) [*Supra*. this chapter]. And my view was the rallying cry for the lawyers who litigated *Brown*. See, *e.g.*, Brief for Appellants in *Brown v. Board of Education*, O.T.1953, Nos. 1, 2, and 4 p. 65 ("That the Constitution is color blind is our dedicated belief"); Brief for Appellants in *Brown v. Board of Education*, O.T.1952, No. 1, p. 5 ("The Fourteenth Amendment precludes a state from imposing distinctions or classifications based upon race and color alone").

The dissent appears to pin its interpretation of the Equal Protection Clause to current societal practice and expectations, deference to local officials, likely practical consequences, and reliance on previous statements from this and other courts. Such a view was ascendant in this Court's jurisprudence for several decades. It first appeared in *Plessy*, where the Court asked whether a state law providing for segregated railway cars was "a reasonable regulation." ...

The segregationists in *Brown* embraced the arguments the Court endorsed in *Plessy* ... See, *e.g.*, Brief for Appellees on Reargument in *Briggs v. Elliott*, O.T.1953, No. 2, p. 76 ("A State has power to establish a school system which is capable of efficient administration, taking into account local problems and conditions")....

The similarities between the dissent's arguments and the segregationists' arguments do not stop there. Like the dissent, the segregationists repeatedly cautioned the Court to consider practicalities and not to embrace too theoretical a view of the Fourteenth Amendment. And just as the dissent argues that the need for these programs will lessen over time, the segregationists claimed that reliance on segregation was lessening and might eventually end.

What was wrong in 1954 cannot be right today.[27] ...

Justice KENNEDY, concurring in part and concurring in the judgment.

... I ... join Parts I and II of the Court's opinion. I also join Parts III-A and III-C for reasons provided below. My views do not allow me to join the balance of the opinion by THE CHIEF JUSTICE, which seems to me to be inconsistent in both its approach and its implications with the history, meaning, and reach of the Equal Protection Clause. JUSTICE BREYER's dissenting opinion, on the other hand, rests on what in my respectful submission is a misuse and mistaken interpretation of our precedents. This leads it to advance propositions that, in my view, are both erroneous and in fundamental conflict with basic equal protection principles. As a consequence, this separate opinion is necessary to set forth my conclusions in the two cases before the Court....

## II

Our Nation from the inception has sought to preserve and expand the promise of liberty and equality on which it was founded. Today we enjoy a society that is remarkable in its openness and opportunity. Yet our tradition is to go beyond present achievements, however significant, and to recognize and confront the flaws and injustices that remain. This is especially true when we seek assurance that opportunity is not denied on account of race. The enduring hope is that race should not matter; the reality is that too often it does.

This is by way of preface to my respectful submission that parts of the opinion by THE CHIEF JUSTICE imply an all-too-unyielding insistence that race cannot be a factor in instances when, in my view, it may be taken into account. The plurality opinion is too dismissive of the legitimate interest government has in ensuring all people have equal opportunity regardless of their race. The plurality's postulate that "the way to

---

27. It is no answer to say that these cases can be distinguished from *Brown* because *Brown* involved invidious racial classifications whereas the racial classifications here are benign. How does one tell when a racial classification is invidious? The segregationists in *Brown* argued that their racial classifications were benign, not invidious. See Tr. of Oral Arg. in *Briggs v. Elliott*, O.T.1953, No. 2, p. 83 ("[South Carolina] is confident of its good faith and intention to produce equality for all of its children of whatever race or color. It is convinced that the happiness, the progress and the welfare of these children is best promoted in segregated schools"); Brief for Appellees on Reargument in *Davis v. County School Board*, O.T.1953, No. 3, p. 82–83 ("Our many hours of research and investigation have led only to confirmation of our view that segregation by race in Virginia's public schools at this time not only does not offend the Constitution of the United States but serves to provide a better education for living for the children of both races"); Tr. of Oral Arg. in *Davis v. County School Board*, O.T.1952, No. 3, p. 71 ("To make such a transition, would undo what we have been doing, and which we propose to continue to do for the uplift and advancement of the education of both races. It would stop this march of progress, this onward sweep"). It is the height of arrogance for Members of this Court to assert blindly that their motives are better than others.

stop discrimination on the basis of race is to stop discriminating on the basis of race," is not sufficient to decide these cases. Fifty years of experience since *Brown v. Board of Education* should teach us that the problem before us defies so easy a solution. School districts can seek to reach *Brown*'s objective of equal educational opportunity. The plurality opinion is at least open to the interpretation that the Constitution requires school districts to ignore the problem of *de facto* resegregation in schooling. I cannot endorse that conclusion. To the extent the plurality opinion suggests the Constitution mandates that state and local school authorities must accept the status quo of racial isolation in schools, it is, in my view, profoundly mistaken.

The statement by Justice Harlan that "our Constitution is color-blind" was most certainly justified in the context of his dissent in *Plessy*. The Court's decision in that case was a grievous error it took far too long to overrule. *Plessy*, of course, concerned official classification by race applicable to all persons who sought to use railway carriages. And, as an aspiration, Justice Harlan's axiom must command our assent. In the real world, it is regrettable to say, it cannot be a universal constitutional principle.

In the administration of public schools by the state and local authorities it is permissible to consider the racial makeup of schools and to adopt general policies to encourage a diverse student body, one aspect of which is its racial composition. If school authorities are concerned that the student-body compositions of certain schools interfere with the objective of offering an equal educational opportunity to all of their students, they are free to devise race-conscious measures to address the problem in a general way and without treating each student in different fashion solely on the basis of a systematic, individual typing by race.

School boards may pursue the goal of bringing together students of diverse backgrounds and races through other means, including strategic site selection of new schools; drawing attendance zones with general recognition of the demographics of neighborhoods; allocating resources for special programs; recruiting students and faculty in a targeted fashion; and tracking enrollments, performance, and other statistics by race. These mechanisms are race conscious but do not lead to different treatment based on a classification that tells each student he or she is to be defined by race, so it is unlikely any of them would demand strict scrutiny to be found permissible. Executive and legislative branches, which for generations now have considered these types of policies and procedures, should be permitted to employ them with candor and with confidence that a constitutional violation does not occur whenever a decisionmaker considers the impact a given approach might have on students of different races. Assigning to each student a personal designation according to a crude system of individual racial classifications is quite a different matter; and the legal analysis changes accordingly....

In the cases before us it is noteworthy that the number of students whose assignment depends on express racial classifications is limited. I join Part III-C of the Court's opinion because I agree that in the context of these plans, the small number of assignments affected suggests that the schools could have achieved their stated ends through different means. These include the facially race-neutral means set forth above or, if necessary, a more nuanced, individual evaluation of school needs and student characteristics that might include race as a component. The latter approach would be informed by *Grutter,* though of course the criteria relevant to student placement would differ based on the age of the students, the needs of the parents, and the role of the schools.

### III

The dissent rests on the assumptions that these sweeping race-based classifications of persons are permitted by existing precedents; that its confident endorsement of race categories for each child in a large segment of the community presents no danger to individual freedom in other, prospective realms of governmental regulation; and that the racial classifications used here cause no hurt or anger of the type the Constitution prevents. Each of these premises is, in my respectful view, incorrect.

### A

The dissent's reliance on this Court's precedents to justify the explicit, sweeping, classwide racial classifications at issue here is a misreading of our authorities that, it appears to me, tends to undermine well-accepted principles needed to guard our freedom. And in his critique of that analysis, I am in many respects in agreement with The Chief Justice. The conclusions he has set forth in Part III-A of the Court's opinion are correct, in my view, because the compelling interests implicated in the cases before us are distinct from the interests the Court has recognized in remedying the effects of past intentional discrimination and in increasing diversity in higher education. As the Court notes, we recognized the compelling nature of the interest in remedying past intentional discrimination in *Freeman v. Pitts,* 503 U.S. 467 (1992), and of the interest in diversity in higher education in *Grutter.* At the same time, these compelling interests, in my view, do help inform the present inquiry. And to the extent the plurality opinion can be interpreted to foreclose consideration of these interests, I disagree with that reasoning.

As to the dissent, the general conclusions upon which it relies have no principled limit and would result in the broad acceptance of governmental racial classifications in areas far afield from schooling. The dissent's permissive strict scrutiny (which bears more than a passing resemblance to rational-basis review) could invite widespread governmental deployment of racial classifications....

### B

To uphold these programs the Court is asked to brush aside two concepts of central importance for determining the validity of laws and decrees designed to alleviate the hurt and adverse consequences resulting from race discrimination. The first is the difference between *de jure* and *de facto* segregation; the second, the presumptive invalidity of a State's use of racial classifications to differentiate its treatment of individuals....

Our cases recognized a fundamental difference between those school districts that had engaged in *de jure* segregation and those whose segregation was the result of other factors. School districts that had engaged in *de jure* segregation had an affirmative constitutional duty to desegregate; those that were *de facto* segregated did not. The distinctions between *de jure* and *de facto* segregation extended to the remedies available to governmental units in addition to the courts.... The Court's decision in *Croson* reinforced the difference between the remedies available to redress *de facto* and *de jure* discrimination:

> To accept a claim that past societal discrimination alone can serve as the basis for rigid racial preferences would be to open the door to competing claims for 'remedial relief' for every disadvantaged group. The dream of a Nation of equal citizens in a society where race is irrelevant to personal opportunity and achievement would be lost in a mosaic of shifting preferences based on inherently unmeasurable claims of past wrongs.

From the standpoint of the victim, it is true, an injury stemming from racial prejudice can hurt as much when the demeaning treatment based on race identity stems from bias masked deep within the social order as when it is imposed by law. The distinction between government and private action, furthermore, can be amorphous both as a historical matter and as a matter of present-day finding of fact. Laws arise from a culture and vice versa. Neither can assign to the other all responsibility for persisting injustices.

Yet, like so many other legal categories that can overlap in some instances, the constitutional distinction between *de jure* and *de facto* segregation has been thought to be an important one.... The distinction ought not to be altogether disregarded ... when we come to that most sensitive of all racial issues, an attempt by the government to treat whole classes of persons differently based on the government's systematic classification of each individual by race....

The cases here were argued upon the assumption, and come to us on the premise, that the discrimination in question did not result from *de jure* actions. And when *de facto* discrimination is at issue our tradition has been that the remedial rules are different. The State must seek alternatives to the classification and differential treatment of individuals by race, at least absent some extraordinary showing not present here.

C

The dissent refers to an opinion filed by Judge Kozinski in one of the cases now before us, and that opinion relied upon an opinion filed by Chief Judge Boudin in a case presenting an issue similar to the one here. Though this may oversimplify the matter a bit, one of the main concerns underlying those opinions was this: If it is legitimate for school authorities to work to avoid racial isolation in their schools, must they do so only by indirection and general policies? Does the Constitution mandate this inefficient result? Why may the authorities not recognize the problem in candid fashion and solve it altogether through resort to direct assignments based on student racial classifications? So, the argument proceeds, if race is the problem, then perhaps race is the solution.

The argument ignores the dangers presented by individual classifications, dangers that are not as pressing when the same ends are achieved by more indirect means. When the government classifies an individual by race, it must first define what it means to be of a race. Who exactly is white and who is nonwhite? To be forced to live under a state-mandated racial label is inconsistent with the dignity of individuals in our society. And it is a label that an individual is powerless to change. Governmental classifications that command people to march in different directions based on racial typologies can cause a new divisiveness. The practice can lead to corrosive discourse, where race serves not as an element of our diverse heritage but instead as a bargaining chip in the political process. On the other hand race-conscious measures that do not rely on differential treatment based on individual classifications present these problems to a lesser degree.

The idea that if race is the problem, race is the instrument with which to solve it cannot be accepted as an analytical leap forward. And if this is a frustrating duality of the Equal Protection Clause it simply reflects the duality of our history and our attempts to promote freedom in a world that sometimes seems set against it. Under our Constitution the individual, child or adult, can find his own identity, can define her own persona, without state intervention that classifies on the basis of his race or the color of her skin....

With this explanation I concur in the judgment of the Court.

Justice STEVENS, dissenting.

While I join Justice BREYER's eloquent and unanswerable dissent in its entirety, it is appropriate to add these words.

There is a cruel irony in THE CHIEF JUSTICE's reliance on our decision in *Brown*. The first sentence in the concluding paragraph of his opinion states: "Before *Brown*, schoolchildren were told where they could and could not go to school based on the color of their skin." This sentence reminds me of Anatole France's observation: "The majestic equality of the law, forbids rich and poor alike to sleep under the bridges, to beg in the streets, and to steal their bread." THE CHIEF JUSTICE fails to note that it was only black schoolchildren who were so ordered; indeed, the history books do not tell stories of white children struggling to attend black schools. In this and other ways, THE CHIEF JUSTICE rewrites the history of one of this Court's most important decisions.

THE CHIEF JUSTICE rejects the conclusion that the racial classifications at issue here should be viewed differently than others, because they do not impose burdens on one race alone and do not stigmatize or exclude. The only justification for refusing to ac-knowledge the obvious importance of that difference is the citation of a few recent opinions—none of which even approached unanimity—grandly proclaiming that all racial classifications must be analyzed under "strict scrutiny." See, *e.g., Adarand*.... The Court's misuse of the three-tiered approach to Equal Protection analysis merely reconfirms my own view that there is only one such Clause in the Constitution....

Justice BREYER, with whom Justice STEVENS, Justice SOUTER, and Justice GINSBURG join, dissenting.

These cases consider the longstanding efforts of two local school boards to integrate their public schools. The school board plans before us resemble many others adopted in the last 50 years by primary and secondary schools throughout the Nation. All of those plans represent local efforts to bring about the kind of racially integrated education that *Brown v. Board of Education* long ago promised—efforts that this Court has repeatedly required, permitted, and encouraged local authorities to undertake. This Court has recognized that the public interests at stake in such cases are "compelling." We have approved of "narrowly tailored" plans that are no less race-conscious than the plans before us. And we have understood that the Constitution *permits* local communities to adopt desegregation plans even where it does not *require* them to do so.

The plurality pays inadequate attention to this law, to past opinions' rationales, their language, and the contexts in which they arise. As a result, it reverses course and reaches the wrong conclusion. In doing so, it distorts precedent, it misapplies the relevant constitutional principles, it announces legal rules that will obstruct efforts by state and local governments to deal effectively with the growing resegregation of public schools, it threatens to substitute for present calm a disruptive round of race-related litigation, and it undermines *Brown*'s promise of integrated primary and secondary education that local communities have sought to make a reality. This cannot be justified in the name of the Equal Protection Clause....

## II
### *The Legal Standard*

A longstanding and unbroken line of legal authority tells us that the Equal Protection Clause permits local school boards to use race-conscious criteria to achieve positive race-related goals, even when the Constitution does not compel it. Because of its importance, I shall repeat what this Court said about the matter in *Swann v. Charlotte-Mecklenberg Board of Education*, 402 U.S. 1 (1971). Chief Justice Burger, on behalf of a unanimous Court in a case of exceptional importance, wrote:

School authorities are traditionally charged with broad power to formulate and implement educational policy and might well conclude, for example, that in order to prepare students to live in a pluralistic society each school should have a prescribed ratio of Negro to white students reflecting the proportion for the district as a whole. To do this as an educational policy is within the broad discretionary powers of school authorities.

The statement was not a technical holding in the case. But the Court set forth in *Swann* a basic principle of constitutional law—a principle of law that has found "wide acceptance in the legal culture." ... These statements nowhere suggest that this freedom is limited to school districts where court-ordered desegregation measures are also in effect....

The view that a more lenient standard than "strict scrutiny" should apply in the present context would not imply abandonment of judicial efforts carefully to determine the need for race-conscious criteria and the criteria's tailoring in light of the need. And the present context requires a court to examine carefully the race-conscious program at issue....

But unlike the plurality, such a judge would also be aware that a legislature or school administrators, ultimately accountable to the electorate, could *nonetheless* properly conclude that a racial classification sometimes serves a purpose important enough to overcome the risks they mention, for example, helping to end racial isolation or to achieve a diverse student body in public schools. Where that is so, the judge would carefully examine the program's details to determine whether the use of race-conscious criteria is proportionate to the important ends it serves....

### III
#### *Applying the Legal Standard*
##### A
#### *Compelling Interest*

The principal interest advanced in these cases to justify the use of race-based criteria goes by various names. Sometimes a court refers to it as an interest in achieving racial "diversity." Other times a court, like the plurality here, refers to it as an interest in racial "balancing." I have used more general terms to signify that interest, describing it, for example, as an interest in promoting or preserving greater racial "integration" of public schools. By this term, I mean the school districts' interest in eliminating school-by-school racial isolation and increasing the degree to which racial mixture characterizes each of the district's schools and each individual student's public school experience....

##### B
#### *Narrow Tailoring*

I next ask whether the plans before us are "narrowly tailored" to achieve these "compelling" objectives....

First, the race-conscious criteria at issue only help set the outer bounds of *broad* ranges. They constitute but one part of plans that depend primarily upon other, non-racial elements. To use race in this way is not to set a forbidden "quota." ...

Second, broad-range limits on voluntary school choice plans are less burdensome, and hence more narrowly tailored, than other race-conscious restrictions this Court has previously approved. Indeed, the plans before us are *more narrowly tailored* than the race-conscious admission plans that this Court approved in *Grutter*. Here, race becomes a factor only in a fraction of students' non-merit-based assignments—not in large numbers of students' merit-based applications....

Third, the manner in which the school boards developed these plans itself reflects "narrow tailoring." Each plan was devised to overcome a history of segregated public schools. Each plan embodies the results of local experience and community consultation. Each plan is the product of a process that has sought to enhance student choice, while diminishing the need for mandatory busing. And each plan's use of race-conscious elements is *diminished* compared to the use of race in preceding integration plans....

### VI
#### *Conclusions*

... The plans before us satisfy the requirements of the Equal Protection Clause....

Four basic considerations have led me to this view. *First,* the histories of Louisville and Seattle reveal complex circumstances and a long tradition of conscientious efforts by local school boards to resist racial segregation in public schools.... The plans under review—which are less burdensome, more egalitarian, and more effective than prior plans—continue in that tradition....

*Second,* since this Court's decision in *Brown,* the law has consistently and unequivocally approved of both voluntary and compulsory race-conscious measures to combat segregated schools. The Equal Protection Clause, ratified following the Civil War, has always distinguished in practice between state action that excludes and thereby subordinates racial minorities and state action that seeks to bring together people of all races....

*Third,* the plans before us, subjected to rigorous judicial review, are supported by compelling state interests and are narrowly tailored to accomplish those goals....

*Fourth,* the plurality's approach risks serious harm to the law and for the Nation. Its view of the law rests either upon a denial of the distinction between exclusionary and inclusive use of race-conscious criteria in the context of the Equal Protection Clause, or upon such a rigid application of its "test" that the distinction loses practical significance. Consequently, the Court's decision today slows down and sets back the work of local school boards to bring about racially diverse schools....

And what of respect for democratic local decisionmaking by States and school boards? For several decades this Court has rested its public school decisions upon *Swann's* basic view that the Constitution grants local school districts a significant degree of leeway where the inclusive use of race-conscious criteria is at issue. Now localities will have to cope with the difficult problems they face (including resegregation) deprived of one means they may find necessary....

And what of the long history and moral vision that the Fourteenth Amendment itself embodies? The plurality cites in support those who argued in *Brown* against segregation, and Justice THOMAS likens the approach that I have taken to that of segregation's defenders. But segregation policies did not simply tell schoolchildren "where they could and could not go to school based on the color of their skin;" they perpetuated a caste system rooted in the institutions of slavery and 80 years of legalized subordination. The lesson of history is not that efforts to continue racial segregation are constitutionally indistinguishable from efforts to achieve racial integration. Indeed, it is a cruel distortion of history to compare Topeka, Kansas, in the 1950's to Louisville and Seattle in the modern day—to equate the plight of Linda Brown (who was ordered to attend a Jim Crow school) to the circumstances of Joshua McDonald (whose request to transfer to a school closer to home was initially declined). This is not to deny that there is a cost in applying "a state-mandated racial label." But that cost does not approach, in degree or in kind, the terrible harms of slavery, the resulting caste system, and 80 years of legal racial segregation.

Finally, what of the hope and promise of *Brown?* For much of this Nation's history, the races remained divided. It was not long ago that people of different races drank from separate fountains, rode on separate buses, and studied in separate schools. In this Court's finest hour, *Brown v. Board of Education* challenged this history and helped to change it. For *Brown* held out a promise. It was a promise embodied in three Amendments designed to make citizens of slaves. It was the promise of true racial equality—not as a matter of fine words on paper, but as a matter of everyday life in the Nation's cities and schools. It was about the nature of a democracy that must work for all Americans. It sought one law, one Nation, one people, not simply as a matter of legal principle but in terms of how we actually live.

Not everyone welcomed this Court's decision in *Brown*. Three years after that decision was handed down, the Governor of Arkansas ordered state militia to block the doors of a white schoolhouse so that black children could not enter. The President of the United States dispatched the 101st Airborne Division to Little Rock, Arkansas, and federal troops were needed to enforce a desegregation decree. See *Cooper v. Aaron* (1958) [*Supra.* Chapter 1]. Today, almost 50 years later, attitudes toward race in this Nation have changed dramatically. Many parents, white and black alike, want their children to attend schools with children of different races. Indeed, the very school districts that once spurned integration now strive for it. The long history of their efforts reveals the complexities and difficulties they have faced. And in light of those challenges, they have asked us not to take from their hands the instruments they have used to rid their schools of racial segregation, instruments that they believe are needed to overcome the problems of cities divided by race and poverty. The plurality would decline their modest request.

The plurality is wrong to do so. The last half-century has witnessed great strides toward racial equality, but we have not yet realized the promise of *Brown*. To invalidate the plans under review is to threaten the promise of *Brown*. The plurality's position, I fear, would break that promise. This is a decision that the Court and the Nation will come to regret. I must dissent.

### Note: Race Consciousness Today

1. What is the current state of the law governing race-conscious government action? At one level, the answer to that question is simple: ever since the 1990s the Court has consistently stated that *any* government use of race is subject to strict scrutiny. But strict scrutiny can mean different things. Is the strict scrutiny used in *Croson* different from that employed in *Grutter*? Do the differing factual contexts (respectively, government contracting and university admissions) explain the difference? Or are the *Grutter* dissenters correct that the majority watered down strict scrutiny?

2. Are you persuaded that the same standard should be applied to *state* and *federal* uses of race? The note on that question presents contrasting perspectives on this question. Which side do you find more persuasive?

3. At least since *Croson*, affirmative action cases have been decided on very close (usually 5–4) votes. This fact gives the swing justice (first, Justice O'Connor, and later, Justice Kennedy) an enormous amount of influence over the law. Consider Justice Kennedy's opinion in *Parents Involved*. He attempted to stake out middle ground between the four-Justice coalitions on either side of him. How does his approach allow government to consider race? How does it forbid such consideration?

Is his approach coherent, or is it a green light for government to use race, as long as it doesn't admit it?

4. Note that in *Parents Involved* both Chief Justice Roberts and Justice Breyer claimed the mantle of *Brown v. Board of Education*. Which side has the better claim to being the true successor to *Brown*?

# Chapter 14

# The Intent Requirement

### Note: An Introduction to the Intent Requirement

This chapter examines the requirement, announced by the Court in 1976, that an equal protection plaintiff must prove that the challenged government action was motivated by an intent to classify on the allegedly-unconstitutional ground. For example, a plaintiff alleging unconstitutional race discrimination must show that the government actor (*e.g.*, the legislature or the town council) intended to classify based on race, rather than simply showing that, regardless of intent, the challenged action affected persons differently depending on their race. (The latter phenomenon is sometimes called "disparate impact," and stands in contrast to "discriminatory intent.")

In one sense, it may seem surprising that the Court took until 1976 to resolve such a foundational issue. But remember the history up that point: it was only a decade earlier, in *Loving v. Virginia* (1967) (*Supra.* Chapter 13), that the Court struck down the last vestige of official Jim Crow legislation—that is, legislation that explicitly treated people differently based on their race. Recall also from Chapter 12 that it was only in the 1970s that the Court began giving serious consideration to other types of discrimination, for example, based on sex and legitimacy. Once we realize these facts, it becomes less surprising that the discriminatory intent question had not been conclusively resolved in the first 108 years of the Fourteenth Amendment's existence.

This is not to say that before 1976 the Court never had opportunities to speak about the requirement that a plaintiff demonstrate discriminatory intent. As a note later in this chapter will show, the Court did in fact decide cases that spoke to the issue. But it was not until 1976 that the Court faced the question squarely.

### Washington v. Davis

426 U.S. 229 (1976)

MR. JUSTICE WHITE delivered the opinion of the Court.

This case involves the validity of a qualifying test administered to applicants for positions as police officers in the District of Columbia Metropolitan Police Department. The test was sustained by the District Court but invalidated by the Court of Appeals. We are in agreement with the District Court and hence reverse the judgment of the Court of Appeals.

## I

This action began on April 10, 1970, when two Negro police officers filed suit against the then Commissioner of the District of Columbia, the Chief of the District's Metropolitan Police Department, and the Commissioners of the United States Civil Service Commission. An amended complaint, filed December 10, alleged that the promotion policies of the Department were racially discriminatory and sought a declaratory judgment and an injunction. The respondents Harley and Sellers were permitted to intervene, their amended complaint asserting that their applications to become officers in the Department had been rejected, and that the Department's recruiting procedures discriminated on the basis of race against black applicants by a series of practices including, but not limited to, a written personnel test which excluded a disproportionately high number of Negro applicants. These practices were asserted to violate respondents' rights "under the due process clause of the Fifth Amendment to the United States Constitution, under 42 U.S.C. § 1981, and under D.C. Code § 1-320." ...

According to the findings and conclusions of the District Court, to be accepted by the Department and to enter an intensive 17-week training program, the police recruit was required to satisfy certain physical and character standards, to be a high school graduate or its equivalent, and to receive a grade of at least 40 out of 80 on "Test 21," which is "an examination that is used generally throughout the federal service," which "was developed by the Civil Service Commission, not the Police Department," and which was "designed to test verbal ability, vocabulary, reading and comprehension."

The validity of Test 21 was the sole issue before the court on the motions for summary judgment. The District Court noted that there was no claim of "an intentional discrimination or purposeful discriminatory acts" but only a claim that Test 21 bore no relationship to job performance and "has a highly discriminatory impact in screening out black candidates." Respondents' evidence, the District Court said, warranted three conclusions: "(a) The number of black police officers, while substantial, is not proportionate to the population mix of the city. (b) A higher percentage of blacks fail the Test than whites. (c) The Test has not been validated to establish its reliability for measuring subsequent job performance." This showing was deemed sufficient to shift the burden of proof to the defendants ... but the court nevertheless concluded that on the undisputed facts respondents were not entitled to relief. ...

## II

... As the Court of Appeals understood Title VII,[*] employees or applicants proceeding under it need not concern themselves with the employer's possibly discriminatory purpose but instead may focus solely on the racially differential impact of the challenged hiring or promotion practices. This is not the constitutional rule. We have never held that the constitutional standard for adjudicating claims of invidious racial discrimination is identical to the standards applicable under Title VII, and we decline to do so today.

---

* [Ed. Note: Title VII of the Civil Rights Act of 1964 prohibits, among other things, racial discrimination in employment.]

The central purpose of the Equal Protection Clause of the Fourteenth Amendment is the prevention of official conduct discriminating on the basis of race. It is also true that the Due Process Clause of the Fifth Amendment contains an equal protection component prohibiting the United States from invidiously discriminating between individuals or groups. But our cases have not embraced the proposition that a law or other official act, without regard to whether it reflects a racially discriminatory purpose, is unconstitutional *solely* because it has a racially disproportionate impact....

Almost 100 years ago, *Strauder v. West Virginia* (1880) [Note *supra.* Chapter 13], established that the exclusion of Negroes from grand and petit juries in criminal proceedings violated the Equal Protection Clause, but the fact that a particular jury or a series of juries does not statistically reflect the racial composition of the community does not in itself make out an invidious discrimination forbidden by the Clause. "A purpose to discriminate must be present which may be proven by systematic exclusion of eligible jurymen of the proscribed race or by unequal application of the law to such an extent as to show intentional discrimination." *Akins v. Texas*, 325 U.S. 398 (1945)....

The school desegregation cases have also adhered to the basic equal protection principle that the invidious quality of a law claimed to be racially discriminatory must ultimately be traced to a racially discriminatory purpose. That there are both predominantly black and predominantly white schools in a community is not alone violative of the Equal Protection Clause. The essential element of *de jure* segregation is "a current condition of segregation resulting from intentional state action." "The differentiating factor between *de jure* segregation and so-called *de facto* segregation ... is *purpose* or *intent* to segregate." ...

This is not to say that the necessary discriminatory racial purpose must be express or appear on the face of the statute, or that a law's disproportionate impact is irrelevant in cases involving Constitution-based claims of racial discrimination. A statute, otherwise neutral on its face, must not be applied so as invidiously to discriminate on the basis of race. It is also clear from the cases dealing with racial discrimination in the selection of juries that the systematic exclusion of Negroes is itself such an "unequal application of the law ... as to show intentional discrimination." *Akins.* A prima facie case of discriminatory purpose may be proved as well by the absence of Negroes on a particular jury combined with the failure of the jury commissioners to be informed of eligible Negro jurors in a community, or with racially non-neutral selection procedures. With a prima facie case made out, "the burden of proof shifts to the State to rebut the presumption of unconstitutional action by showing that permissible racially neutral selection criteria and procedures have produced the monochromatic result."

Necessarily, an invidious discriminatory purpose may often be inferred from the totality of the relevant facts, including the fact, if it is true, that the law bears more heavily on one race than another. It is also not infrequently true that the discriminatory impact—in the jury cases for example, the total or seriously disproportionate exclusion of Negroes from jury venires—may for all practical purposes demonstrate unconstitutionality because in various circumstances the discrimination is very difficult to explain on nonracial grounds. Nevertheless, we have not held that a law, neutral on its face and serving ends otherwise within the power of government to pursue, is invalid under the Equal Protection Clause simply because it may affect a greater proportion of one race than of another. Disproportionate impact is not irrelevant, but it is not the sole touchstone of an invidious racial discrimination forbidden by the Constitution. Standing alone, it does not trigger the rule that racial classifications are to be subjected to the strictest scrutiny and are justifiable only by the weightiest of considerations....

As an initial matter, we have difficulty understanding how a law establishing a racially neutral qualification for employment is nevertheless racially discriminatory and denies "any person ... equal protection of the laws" simply because a greater proportion of Negroes fail to qualify than members of other racial or ethnic groups. Had respondents, along with all others who had failed Test 21, whether white or black, brought an action claiming that the test denied each of them equal protection of the laws as compared with those who had passed with high enough scores to qualify them as police recruits, it is most unlikely that their challenge would have been sustained. Test 21, which is administered generally to prospective Government employees, concededly seeks to ascertain whether those who take it have acquired a particular level of verbal skill; and it is untenable that the Constitution prevents the Government from seeking modestly to upgrade the communicative abilities of its employees rather than to be satisfied with some lower level of competence, particularly where the job requires special ability to communicate orally and in writing. Respondents, as Negroes, could no more successfully claim that the test denied them equal protection than could white applicants who also failed. The conclusion would not be different in the face of proof that more Negroes than whites had been disqualified by Test 21. That other Negroes also failed to score well would, alone, not demonstrate that respondents individually were being denied equal protection of the laws by the application of an otherwise valid qualifying test being administered to prospective police recruits.

Nor on the facts of the case before us would the disproportionate impact of Test 21 warrant the conclusion that it is a purposeful device to discriminate against Negroes and hence an infringement of the constitutional rights of respondents as well as other black applicants. As we have said, the test is neutral on its face and rationally may be said to serve a purpose the Government is constitutionally empowered to pursue. Even agreeing with the District Court that the differential racial effect of Test 21 called for further inquiry, we think the District Court correctly held that the affirmative efforts of the Metropolitan Police Department to recruit black officers, the changing racial composition of the recruit classes and of the force in general, and the relationship of the test to the training program negated any inference that the Department discriminated on the basis of race or that "a police officer qualifies on the color of his skin rather than ability."

Under Title VII, Congress provided that when hiring and promotion practices disqualifying substantially disproportionate numbers of blacks are challenged, discriminatory purpose need not be proved, and that it is an insufficient response to demonstrate some rational basis for the challenged practices. It is necessary, in addition, that they be "validated" in terms of job performance in any one of several ways, perhaps by ascertaining the minimum skill, ability, or potential necessary for the position at issue and determining whether the qualifying tests are appropriate for the selection of qualified applicants for the job in question. However this process proceeds, it involves a more probing judicial review of, and less deference to, the seemingly reasonable acts of administrators and executives than is appropriate under the Constitution where special racial impact, without discriminatory purpose, is claimed. We are not disposed to adopt this more rigorous standard for the purposes of applying the Fifth and the Fourteenth Amendments in cases such as this.

A rule that a statute designed to serve neutral ends is nevertheless invalid, absent compelling justification, if in practice it benefits or burdens one race more than another would be far reaching and would raise serious questions about, and perhaps invalidate, a whole range of tax, welfare, public service, regulatory, and licensing statutes that may be more burdensome to the poor and to the average black than to the more affluent white.

Given that rule, such consequences would perhaps be likely to follow. However, in our view, extension of the rule beyond those areas where it is already applicable by reason of statute, such as in the field of public employment, should await legislative prescription ...

JUSTICE STEVENS, concurring.

While I agree with the Court's disposition of this case, I add these comments on the constitutional issue discussed in Part II ... of the Court's opinion.

The requirement of purposeful discrimination is a common thread running through the cases summarized in Part II. These cases include criminal convictions which were set aside because blacks were excluded from the grand jury, a reapportionment case in which political boundaries were obviously influenced to some extent by racial considerations, a school desegregation case, and a case involving the unequal administration of an ordinance purporting to prohibit the operation of laundries in frame buildings. Although it may be proper to use the same language to describe the constitutional claim in each of these contexts, the burden of proving a prima facie case may well involve differing evidentiary considerations. The extent of deference that one pays to the trial court's determination of the factual issue, and indeed, the extent to which one characterizes the intent issue as a question of fact or a question of law, will vary in different contexts.

Frequently the most probative evidence of intent will be objective evidence of what actually happened rather than evidence describing the subjective state of mind of the actor. For normally the actor is presumed to have intended the natural consequences of his deeds. This is particularly true in the case of governmental action which is frequently the product of compromise, of collective decisionmaking, and of mixed motivation. It is unrealistic, on the one hand, to require the victim of alleged discrimination to uncover the actual subjective intent of the decisionmaker or, conversely, to invalidate otherwise legitimate action simply because an improper motive affected the deliberation of a participant in the decisional process. A law conscripting clerics should not be invalidated because an atheist voted for it.

My point in making this observation is to suggest that the line between discriminatory purpose and discriminatory impact is not nearly as bright, and perhaps not quite as critical, as the reader of the Court's opinion might assume. I agree, of course, that a constitutional issue does not arise every time some disproportionate impact is shown. On the other hand, when the disproportion is as dramatic as in *Gomillion v. Lightfoot*, 364 U.S. 339 (1960) or *Yick Wo v. Hopkins*, 118 U.S. 356 (1886), it really does not matter whether the standard is phrased in terms of purpose or effect. Therefore, although I accept the statement of the general rule in the Court's opinion, I am not yet prepared to indicate how that standard should be applied in the many cases which have formulated the governing standard in different language....

JUSTICE BRENNAN, with who JUSTICE MARSHALL joins, dissenting.

[Justice Brennan focused on the statutory issue in the case and did not address the constitutional question.]

## Note: "The Arlington Heights *Factors*"

In addition to establishing the discriminatory intent requirement, *Washington v. Davis* also suggested how that requirement should be applied. The year after *Davis* the Court was more explicit about that factors relevant to that inquiry.

*Village of Arlington Heights v. Metropolitan Housing Development Corporation*, 429 U.S. 252 (1977), considered a claim that a municipality's zoning decision unconstitutionally discriminated on the basis of race, by denying a permit for the construction of a low-income housing complex that was expected to be racially integrated. (Chapter 1 of this book discussed one part of the Court's opinion, dealing with whether the plaintiffs had standing.)

Writing for the Court, Justice Powell explained the discriminatory intent inquiry as follows:

> Determining whether invidious discriminatory purpose was a motivating factor demands a sensitive inquiry into such circumstantial and direct evidence of intent as may be available. The impact of the official action — whether it "bears more heavily on one race than another," *Davis* — may provide an important starting point. Sometimes a clear pattern, unexplainable on grounds other than race, emerges from the effect of the state action even when the governing legislation appears neutral on its face. *Yick Wo v. Hopkins*, 118 U.S. 356 (1886); *Gomillion v. Lightfoot*, 364 U.S. 339 (1960). The evidentiary inquiry is then relatively easy. But such cases are rare. Absent a pattern as stark as that in *Gomillion* or *Yick Wo*, impact alone is not determinative, and the Court must look to other evidence.[15]

---

15. In many instances, to recognize the limited probative value of disproportionate impact is merely to acknowledge the "heterogeneity" of the Nation's population.

The historical background of the decision is one evidentiary source, particularly if it reveals a series of official actions taken for invidious purposes. The specific sequence of events leading up the challenged decision also may shed some light on the decisionmaker's purposes. For example, if the property involved here always had been zoned R-5 but suddenly was changed to R-3 when the town learned of MHDC's plans to erect integrated housing, we would have a far different case. Departures from the normal procedural sequence also might afford evidence that improper purposes are playing a role. Substantive departures too may be relevant, particularly if the factors usually considered important by the decisionmaker strongly favor a decision contrary to the one reached.

The legislative or administrative history may be highly relevant, especially where there are contemporary statements by members of the decisionmaking body, minutes of its meetings, or reports. In some extraordinary instances the members might be called to the stand at trial to testify concerning the purpose of the official action, although even then such testimony frequently will be barred by privilege.[18]

The foregoing summary identifies, without purporting to be exhaustive, subjects of proper inquiry in determining whether racially discriminatory intent existed. With these in mind, we now address the case before us.

After concluding that the plaintiffs had failed to carry their burden of establishing that race had been "a motivating factor" in the zoning decision, the Court then said the following, in footnote 21:

Proof that the decision by the Village was motivated in part by a racially discriminatory purpose would not necessarily have required invalidation of the challenged decision. Such proof would, however, have shifted to the Village the burden of establishing that the same decision would have resulted even had the impermissible purpose not been considered. If this were established, the complaining party in a case of this kind no longer fairly could attribute the injury complained of to improper consideration of a discriminatory purpose. In such circumstances, there would be no justification for judicial interference with the challenged decision.

### Note: "Because of, not in spite of"

An important gloss on the discriminatory intent inquiry was provided in 1979 when the Court considered an equal protection challenge to a state's civil service preference for veterans. *Personnel Administrator of Massachusetts v. Feeney*, 442 U.S. 256 (1979). In *Feeney*, a woman challenged that preference as unconstitutional sex dis-

---

18. This Court has recognized, ever since *Fletcher v. Peck*, 6 Cranch 87 (1810), that judicial inquiries into legislative or executive motivation represent a substantial intrusion into the workings of other branches of government. Placing a decisionmaker on the stand is therefore "usually to be avoided."

crimination, acknowledging that the law did not facially draw a sex line, but arguing, among other things, that the legislature had to know that the preference would benefit men more than women, given the far larger participation of men than women in the armed forces.

The Court rejected the discriminatory intent argument. Writing for seven justices, Justice Stewart wrote the following:

> When a statute gender-neutral on its face is challenged on the ground that its effects upon women are disproportionably adverse, a twofold inquiry is ... appropriate. The first question is whether the statutory classification is indeed neutral in the sense that it is not gender-based. If the classification itself, covert or overt, is not based upon gender, the second question is whether the adverse effect reflects invidious gender-based discrimination....

> The appellee's ultimate argument rests upon the presumption, common to the criminal and civil law, that a person intends the natural and foreseeable consequences of his voluntary actions. Her position was well stated in the concurring opinion in the District Court:

>> "Conceding ... that the goal here was to benefit the veteran, there is no reason to absolve the legislature from awareness that the means chosen to achieve this goal would freeze women out of all those state jobs actively sought by men. To be sure, the legislature did not wish to harm women. But the cutting-off of women's opportunities was an inevitable concomitant of the chosen scheme—as inevitable as the proposition that if tails is up, heads must be down. Where a law's consequences are *that* inevitable, can they meaningfully be described as unintended?"

> This rhetorical question implies that a negative answer is obvious, but it is not. The decision to grant a preference to veterans was of course "intentional." So, necessarily, did an adverse impact upon nonveterans follow from that decision. And it cannot seriously be argued that the Legislature of Massachusetts could have been unaware that most veterans are men. It would thus be disingenuous to say that the adverse consequences of this legislation for women were unintended, in the sense that they were not volitional or in the sense that they were not foreseeable.

> "Discriminatory purpose," however, implies more than intent as volition or intent as awareness of consequences. It implies that the decisionmaker, in this case a state legislature, selected or reaffirmed a particular course of action at least in part "because of," not merely "in spite of," its adverse effects upon an identifiable group. Yet nothing in the record demonstrates that this preference for veterans was originally devised or subsequently re-enacted because it would accomplish the collateral goal of keeping women in a stereotypic and predefined place in the Massachusetts Civil Service.

Justice Stevens, joined by Justice White, joined the majority but wrote the following concurrence.

While I concur in the Court's opinion, I confess that I am not at all sure that there is any difference between the two questions posed *ante*. If a classification is not overtly based on gender, I am inclined to believe the question whether it is covertly gender based is the same as the question whether its adverse effects reflect invidious gender-based discrimination. However the question is phrased, for me the answer is largely provided by the fact that the number of males disadvantaged by Massachusetts' veterans' preference (1,867,000) is sufficiently large—and sufficiently close to the number of disadvantaged females (2,954,000)—to refute the claim that the rule was intended to benefit males as a class over females as a class.

Justice Marshall, joined by Justice Brennan, dissented, writing as follows:

… [Since] reliable evidence of subjective intentions is seldom obtainable, resort to inference based on objective factors is generally unavoidable. To discern the purposes underlying facially neutral policies, this Court has therefore considered the degree, inevitability, and foreseeability of any disproportionate impact as well as the alternatives reasonably available.

In the instant case, the impact of the Massachusetts statute on women is undisputed.… Because less than 2% of the women in Massachusetts are veterans, the absolute-preference formula has rendered desirable state civil service employment an almost exclusively male prerogative.

As the District Court recognized, this consequence follows foreseeably, indeed inexorably, from the long history of policies severely limiting women's participation in the military.… Where the foreseeable impact of a facially neutral policy is so disproportionate, the burden should rest on the State to establish that sex-based considerations played no part in the choice of the particular legislative scheme. Clearly, that burden was not sustained here.…

### Note: When Does Impact Matter?

1. The intent requirement stands in contrast to an approach in which "mere" discriminatory impact triggers heightened judicial scrutiny. But, as both *Davis* and *Arlington Heights* recognized, discriminatory impact remains relevant to the intent analysis. As Justice Stevens noted in his *Davis* concurrence, the line between discriminatory intent and disparate impact may not be as sharp as it appears at first glance. A look at cases both before and after *Davis* and *Arlington Heights* illustrates Justice Stevens' point.

2. In *Yick Wo v. Hopkins*, 118 U.S. 356 (1886), the Court considered a San Francisco ordinance requiring official approval before a laundry could be established. The plaintiff, a Chinese national, argued, among other things, that the local officials approved the vast majority of applications made by white persons, but rejected most applications made by Chinese. The Court found in the operation of the law an equal protection violation, based on a combination of the unlimited discretion the officials enjoyed to approve or deny an application, and the fact that that discretion appeared to have been used in a racially discriminatory way:

In the present cases, we are not obliged to reason from the probable to the actual, and pass upon the validity of the ordinances complained of, as tried merely by the opportunities which their terms afford, of unequal and unjust discrimination in their administration. For the cases present the ordinances in actual operation, and the facts shown establish an administration directed so exclusively against a particular class of persons as to warrant and require the conclusion, that, whatever may have been the intent of the ordinances as adopted, they are applied by the public authorities charged with their administration, and thus representing the State itself, with a mind so unequal and oppressive as to amount to a practical denial by the State of that equal protection of the laws which is secured to the petitioners, as to all other persons, by the broad and benign provisions of the Fourteenth Amendment to the Constitution of the United States. Though the law itself be fair on its face and impartial in appearance, yet, if it is applied and administered by public authority with an evil eye and an unequal hand, so as practically to make unjust and illegal discriminations between persons in similar circumstances, material to their rights, the denial of equal justice is still within the prohibition of the Constitution.

3. Three-quarters of a century later, in *Gomillion v. Lightfoot*, 364 U.S. 339 (1960), the Court considered the constitutionality of the State of Alabama's redrawing of the municipal boundaries of the city of Tuskegee. That redrawing converted the city's geographical shape, in the Court's words, "from a square to an uncouth twenty-eight-sided figure" that removed from the city "all but four or five of its 400 Negro voters while not removing a single white voter or resident." The Court had no difficulty concluding that the allegations in the complaint, if true, made out a violation of the Fifteenth Amendment's prohibition on racial discrimination in voting. It did not even consider arguments that the state did not have a discriminatory motivation, focusing instead on arguments that this sort of local government power was largely immune from judicial scrutiny.

4. A decade after *Davis* and *Arlington Heights* the Court again had a chance to consider the relationship between intent and impact. In *McCleskey v. Kemp*, 481 U.S. 279 (1987), the Court confronted a claim that statistical disparities in the imposition of the death penalty created inequalities that violated both the Equal Protection Clause and the Eighth Amendment's prohibition on cruel and unusual punishment. While the latter issue is technically distinct from the equal protection issue, the Court's analysis of that latter issue has close connections with the former.

## McCleskey v. Kemp

### 481 U.S. 279 (1987)

JUSTICE POWELL delivered the opinion of the Court.

This case presents the question whether a complex statistical study that indicates a risk that racial considerations enter into capital sentencing determinations proves that petitioner McCleskey's capital sentence is unconstitutional under the Eighth or Fourteenth Amendment.

I

McCleskey, a black man, was convicted of two counts of armed robbery and one count of murder in the Superior Court of Fulton County, Georgia, on October 12, 1978. McCleskey's convictions arose out of the robbery of a furniture store and the killing of a white police officer during the course of the robbery.... In making its decision whether to impose the death sentence, the jury considered the mitigating and aggravating circumstances.... McCleskey offered no mitigating evidence. The jury recommended that he be sentenced to death on the murder charge and to consecutive life sentences on the armed robbery charges. The court followed the jury's recommendation and sentenced McCleskey to death....

... McCleskey ... filed a petition for a writ of habeas corpus in the Federal District Court for the Northern District of Georgia. His petition raised 18 claims, one of which was that the Georgia capital sentencing process is administered in a racially discriminatory manner in violation of the Eighth and Fourteenth Amendments to the United States Constitution. In support of his claim, McCleskey proffered a statistical study performed by Professors David C. Baldus, Charles Pulaski, and George Woodworth (the Baldus study) that purports to show a disparity in the imposition of the death sentence in Georgia based on the race of the murder victim and, to a lesser extent, the race of the defendant. The Baldus study is actually two sophisticated statistical studies that examine over 2,000 murder cases that occurred in Georgia during the 1970's. The raw numbers collected by Professor Baldus indicate that defendants charged with killing white persons received the death penalty in 11% of the cases, but defendants charged with killing blacks received the death penalty in only 1% of the cases. The raw numbers also indicate a reverse racial disparity according to the race of the defendant: 4% of the black defendants received the death penalty, as opposed to 7% of the white defendants.

Baldus also divided the cases according to the combination of the race of the defendant and the race of the victim. He found that the death penalty was assessed in 22% of the cases involving black defendants and white victims; 8% of the cases involving white defendants and white victims; 1% of the cases involving black defendants and black victims; and 3% of the cases involving white defendants and black victims. Similarly, Baldus found that prosecutors sought the death penalty in 70% of the cases involving black defendants and white victims; 32% of the cases involving white defendants and white victims; 15% of the cases involving black defendants and black victims; and 19% of the cases involving white defendants and black victims.

Baldus subjected his data to an extensive analysis, taking account of 230 variables that could have explained the disparities on nonracial grounds. One of his models concludes that, even after taking account of 39 nonracial variables, defendants charged with killing white victims were 4.3 times as likely to receive a death sentence as defendants charged with killing blacks. According to this model, black defendants were 1.1 times as likely to receive a death sentence as other defendants. Thus, the Baldus study indicates that black defendants, such as McCleskey, who kill white victims have the greatest likelihood of receiving the death penalty....

## II

McCleskey's first claim is that the Georgia capital punishment statute violates the Equal Protection Clause of the Fourteenth Amendment. He argues that race has infected the administration of Georgia's statute in two ways: persons who murder whites are more likely to be sentenced to death than persons who murder blacks, and black murderers are more likely to be sentenced to death than white murderers. As a black defendant who killed a white victim, McCleskey claims that the Baldus study demonstrates that he was discriminated against because of his race and because of the race of his victim. In its broadest form, McCleskey's claim of discrimination extends to every actor in the Georgia capital sentencing process, from the prosecutor who sought the death penalty and the jury that imposed the sentence, to the State itself that enacted the capital punishment statute and allows it to remain in effect despite its allegedly discriminatory application. We agree with the Court of Appeals, and every other court that has considered such a challenge, that this claim must fail.

## A

... To prevail under the Equal Protection Clause, McCleskey must prove that the decisionmakers in *his* case acted with discriminatory purpose. He offers no evidence specific to his own case that would support an inference that racial considerations played a part in his sentence. Instead, he relies solely on the Baldus study. McCleskey argues that the Baldus study compels an inference that his sentence rests on purposeful discrimination. McCleskey's claim that these statistics are sufficient proof of discrimination, without regard to the facts of a particular case, would extend to all capital cases in Georgia, at least where the victim was white and the defendant is black.

The Court has accepted statistics as proof of intent to discriminate in certain limited contexts. First, this Court has accepted statistical disparities as proof of an equal protection violation in the selection of the jury venire in a particular district. Although statistical proof normally must present a "stark" pattern to be accepted as the sole proof of discriminatory intent under the Constitution, *Arlington Heights v. Metropolitan Housing Dev. Corp.* (1977) [Note *supra.* this chapter], "because of the nature of the jury-selection task, ... we have permitted a finding of constitutional violation even when the statistical pattern does not approach [such] extremes." Second, this Court has accepted statistics in the form of multiple-regression analysis to prove statutory violations under Title VII of the Civil Rights Act of 1964.

But the nature of the capital sentencing decision, and the relationship of the statistics to that decision, are fundamentally different from the corresponding elements in the venire-selection or Title VII cases. Most importantly, each particular decision to impose the death penalty is made by a petit jury selected from a properly constituted venire. Each jury is unique in its composition, and the Constitution requires that its decision rest on consideration of innumerable factors that vary according to the characteristics of the individual defendant and the facts of the particular capital offense.

Thus, the application of an inference drawn from the general statistics to a specific decision in a trial and sentencing simply is not comparable to the application of an inference drawn from general statistics to a specific venire-selection or Title VII case. In those cases, the statistics relate to fewer entities, and fewer variables are relevant to the challenged decisions.

Another important difference between the cases in which we have accepted statistics as proof of discriminatory intent and this case is that, in the venire-selection and Title VII contexts, the decisionmaker has an opportunity to explain the statistical disparity. Here, the State has no practical opportunity to rebut the Baldus study. "Controlling considerations of ... public policy" dictate that jurors "cannot be called ... to testify to the motives and influences that led to their verdict." Similarly, the policy considerations behind a prosecutor's traditionally "wide discretion" suggest the impropriety of our requiring prosecutors to defend their decisions to seek death penalties, "often years after they were made." Moreover, absent far stronger proof, it is unnecessary to seek such a rebuttal, because a legitimate and unchallenged explanation for the decision is apparent from the record: McCleskey committed an act for which the United States Constitution and Georgia laws permit imposition of the death penalty.

Finally, McCleskey's statistical proffer must be viewed in the context of his challenge. McCleskey challenges decisions at the heart of the State's criminal justice system. "One of society's most basic tasks is that of protecting the lives of its citizens and one of the most basic ways in which it achieves the task is through criminal laws against murder." Implementation of these laws necessarily requires discretionary judgments. Because discretion is essential to the criminal justice process, we would demand exceptionally clear proof before we would infer that the discretion has been abused. The unique nature of the decisions at issue in this case also counsels against adopting such an inference from the disparities indicated by the Baldus study. Accordingly, we hold that the Baldus study is clearly insufficient to support an inference that any of the decisionmakers in McCleskey's case acted with discriminatory purpose.

### B

McCleskey also suggests that the Baldus study proves that the State as a whole has acted with a discriminatory purpose. He appears to argue that the State has violated the Equal Protection Clause by adopting the capital punishment statute and allowing it to remain in force despite its allegedly discriminatory application. But "discriminatory purpose ... implies more than intent as volition or intent as awareness of consequences. It implies that the decisionmaker, in this case a state legislature, selected or reaffirmed a particular course of action at least in part 'because of,' not merely 'in spite of,' its adverse effects upon an identifiable group." *Personnel Administrator of Massachusetts v. Feeney*, 442 U.S. 256 (1979) [Note *supra*. this chapter]. For this claim to prevail, McCleskey would have to prove that the Georgia Legislature enacted or maintained the death penalty statute *because of* an anticipated racially discriminatory effect. In *Gregg v. Georgia*, 428 U.S. 153 (1976), this Court found that the Georgia capital sentencing system could operate in a fair and neutral manner. There was no evidence then, and there is none now, that the Georgia Legislature enacted the capital punishment statute to further a racially discriminatory purpose.[20]

Nor has McCleskey demonstrated that the legislature maintains the capital punishment statute because of the racially disproportionate impact suggested by the Baldus study. As legislatures necessarily have wide discretion in the choice of criminal laws and penalties, and as there were legitimate reasons for the Georgia Legislature to adopt and maintain capital punishment, we will not infer a discriminatory purpose on the part of the State of Georgia. Accordingly, we reject McCleskey's equal protection claims.

### III

McCleskey also argues that the Baldus study demonstrates that the Georgia capital sentencing system violates the Eighth Amendment. [The Court then considered, and rejected, his argument that the statistical racial disparity in capital sentences rendered application of the death penalty law arbitrary and capricious, and thus a violation of the Eighth Amendment.]

Justice BRENNAN, with whom Justice Marshall joins, and with whom Justice Blackmun and Justice Stevens join in all but Part I, dissenting. [Justice Brennan's opinion is discussed in the note following this excerpt.].

Justice BLACKMUN, with whom Justice MARSHALL and Justice STEVENS join, and with whom Justice BRENNAN joins in all but Part IV-B, dissenting....

Justice BRENNAN has thoroughly demonstrated that, if one assumes that the statistical evidence presented by petitioner McCleskey is valid, as we must in light of the Court of Appeals' assumption, there exists in the Georgia capital sentencing scheme a risk of racially based discrimination that is so acute that it violates the Eighth Amendment.... Yet McCleskey's case raises concerns that are central not only to the principles underlying the Eighth Amendment, but also to the principles underlying the Fourteenth Amendment. Analysis of his case in terms of the Fourteenth Amendment is consistent with this Court's recognition that racial discrimination is fundamentally at odds with our constitutional guarantee of equal protection....

### II

#### A

A criminal defendant alleging an equal protection violation must prove the existence of purposeful discrimination. *Washington v. Davis* (1976) [*Supra.* this chapter]. He may establish a prima facie case of purposeful discrimination "by showing that the

---

20. McCleskey relies on "historical evidence" to support his claim of purposeful discrimination by the State. This evidence focuses on Georgia laws in force during and just after the Civil War. Of course, the "historical background of the decision is one evidentiary source" for proof of intentional discrimination. *Arlington Heights.* But unless historical evidence is reasonably contemporaneous with the challenged decision, it has little probative value. Cf. *Hunter v. Underwood*, 471 U.S. 222 (1985) (relying on legislative history to demonstrate discriminatory motivation behind state statute). Although the history of racial discrimination in this country is undeniable, we cannot accept official actions taken long ago as evidence of current intent.

totality of the relevant facts gives rise to an inference of discriminatory purpose." Once the defendant establishes a prima facie case, the burden shifts to the prosecution to rebut that case. "The State cannot meet this burden on mere general assertions that its officials did not discriminate or that they properly performed their official duties." The State must demonstrate that the challenged effect was due to "permissible racially neutral selection criteria." ...

B

... The Baldus study demonstrates that black persons are a distinct group that are singled out for different treatment in the Georgia capital sentencing system. The Court acknowledges, as it must, that the raw statistics included in the Baldus study and presented by petitioner indicate that it is much less likely that a death sentence will result from a murder of a black person than from a murder of a white person....

... Recognizing that additional factors can enter into the decisionmaking process that yields a death sentence, the authors of the Baldus study collected data concerning the presence of other relevant factors in homicide cases in Georgia during the time period relevant to McCleskey's case. They then analyzed the data in a manner that would permit them to ascertain the independent effect of the racial factors....

McCleskey produced evidence concerning the role of racial factors at the various steps in the decisionmaking process, focusing on the prosecutor's decision as to which cases merit the death sentence. McCleskey established that the race of the victim is an especially significant factor at the point where the defendant has been convicted of murder and the prosecutor must choose whether to proceed to the penalty phase of the trial and create the possibility that a death sentence may be imposed or to accept the imposition of a sentence of life imprisonment.... Petitioner submitted the deposition of Lewis R. Slaton, who, as of the date of the deposition, had been the District Attorney for 18 years in the county in which McCleskey was tried and sentenced.... He testified that during his years in the office, there were no guidelines informing the Assistant District Attorneys who handled the cases how they should proceed at any particular stage of the prosecution.... Slaton's deposition proves that, at every stage of a prosecution, the Assistant District Attorney exercised much discretion. The only guidance given was "on-the-job training." ...

In addition to this showing that the challenged system was susceptible to abuse, McCleskey presented evidence of the history of prior discrimination in the Georgia system. Justice BRENNAN has reviewed much of this history in detail in his dissenting opinion, including the history of Georgia's racially based dual system of criminal justice.[*] This historical background of the state action challenged "is one evidentiary source" in this equal protection case. *Arlington Heights v. Metropolitan Housing De-*

---

\* [Ed. Note: Justice Brennan's Eighth Amendment analysis is discussed in the note following this case.]

*velopment Corp.* (1977) [Note *supra.* this chapter]. Although I would agree that evidence of "official actions taken long ago" could not alone establish that the current system is applied in an unconstitutionally discriminatory manner, I disagree with the Court's statement that such evidence is now irrelevant, *ante.* n.20.

The above-described evidence, considered in conjunction with the other record evidence outlined by Justice BRENNAN ... gives rise to an inference of discriminatory purpose.... The burden, therefore, shifts to the State to explain the racial selections. It must demonstrate that legitimate racially neutral criteria and procedures yielded this racially skewed result.

In rebuttal, the State's expert suggested that if the Baldus thesis was correct then the aggravation level in black-victim cases where a life sentence was imposed would be higher than in white-victim cases.... The State did not test its hypothesis to determine if white-victim and black-victim cases at the same level of aggravating circumstances were similarly treated. McCleskey's experts, however, performed this test on their data. They demonstrated that the racial disparities in the system were not the result of the differences in the average aggravation levels between white-victim and black-victim cases. The State's meager and unsophisticated evidence cannot withstand the extensive scrutiny given the Baldus evidence. Here ... the State did not "demonstrate that when the factors were properly organized and accounted for there was no significant disparity" between the death sentences imposed on defendants convicted of killing white victims and those imposed on defendants convicted of killing black victims.... In sum, McCleskey has demonstrated a clear pattern of differential treatment according to race that is "unexplainable on grounds other than race." *Arlington Heights....*

JUSTICE STEVENS, with whom JUSTICE BLACKMUN joins, dissenting. [omitted]

## Note: The Eighth Amendment, Disparate Impact, and Inequality

1. In *McCleskey* the prisoner added to his equal protection claim an argument that Georgia's capital sentencing system violated the Eighth Amendment's prohibition on "cruel and unusual punishment," in part because it was applied arbitrarily — that is, based on inappropriate factors such as the race of the defendant or the victim. The Court rejected this claim, relying heavily on the fact that our criminal sentencing system relies heavily on the discretion juries possess to impose death or spare the defendant's life. The Court explained that its Eighth Amendment jurisprudence focused heavily on ensuring the fairness of the process that culminated in the jury's use of that discretion. But it concluded:

> Where the discretion that is so fundamental to our criminal process is involved, we decline to assume that what is unexplained is invidious. In light of the safeguards designed to minimize racial bias in the process, the fundamental value of jury trial in our criminal justice system, and the benefits that discretion affords to criminal defendants, we hold that the Baldus study does not demonstrate a constitutionally significant risk of racial bias affecting the Georgia capital sentencing process.

2. Justice Brennan, joined by the three justices who also dissented on the equal protection issue excerpted above, dissented on the Eighth Amendment issue. In the part of his opinion joined by all three other dissenters, he wrote as follows:

## II

At some point in this case, Warren McCleskey doubtless asked his lawyer whether a jury was likely to sentence him to die. A candid reply to this question would have been disturbing. First, counsel would have to tell McCleskey that few of the details of the crime or of McCleskey's past criminal conduct were more important than the fact that his victim was white. Furthermore, counsel would feel bound to tell McCleskey that defendants charged with killing white victims in Georgia are 4.3 times as likely to be sentenced to death as defendants charged with killing blacks. In addition, frankness would compel the disclosure that it was more likely than not that the race of McCleskey's victim would determine whether he received a death sentence: 6 of every 11 defendants convicted of killing a white person would not have received the death penalty if their victims had been black, while, among defendants with aggravating and mitigating factors comparable to McCleskey's, 20 of every 34 would not have been sentenced to die if their victims had been black. Finally, the assessment would not be complete without the information that cases involving black defendants and white victims are more likely to result in a death sentence than cases featuring any other racial combination of defendant and victim. The story could be told in a variety of ways, but McCleskey could not fail to grasp its essential narrative line: there was a significant chance that race would play a prominent role in determining if he lived or died.

The Court today holds that Warren McCleskey's sentence was constitutionally imposed. It finds no fault in a system in which lawyers must tell their clients that race casts a large shadow on the capital sentencing process. The Court arrives at this conclusion by stating that the Baldus study cannot "*prove* that race enters into any capital sentencing decisions or that race was a factor in McCleskey's particular case." Since, according to Professor Baldus, we cannot say "to a moral certainty" that race influenced a decision, we can identify only "a likelihood that a particular factor entered into some decisions," and "a discrepancy that appears to correlate with race." This "likelihood" and "discrepancy," holds the Court, is insufficient to establish a constitutional violation....

## III

* * *

## B

The Baldus study indicates that, after taking into account some 230 nonracial factors that might legitimately influence a sentencer, the jury *more likely than not* would have spared McCleskey's life had his victim been black. The study distinguishes between those cases in which (1) the jury exercises virtually no discretion because the strength or weakness of aggravating factors usually suggests that only one outcome is appropriate, and (2) cases reflecting an "intermediate" level of aggravation, in which the jury has considerable discretion in choosing a sentence. McCleskey's case falls into the intermediate range. In such cases, death is imposed in 34% of white-victim crimes and 14% of black-victim crimes, a difference of 139% in the rate of imposition of the death penalty. In other words, just under 59%—almost 6 in 10—of defendants comparable to McCleskey would not have received the death penalty if their victims had been black.

Furthermore, even examination of the sentencing system as a whole, factoring in those cases in which the jury exercises little discretion, indicates the influence of race on capital sentencing. For the Georgia system as a whole, race accounts for a six percentage point difference in the rate at which capital punishment is imposed. Since death is imposed in 11% of all white-victim cases, the rate in comparably aggravated black-victim cases is 5%. The rate of capital sentencing in a white-victim case is thus 120% greater than the rate in a black-victim case. Put another way, over half—55%—of defendants in white-victim crimes in Georgia would not have been sentenced to die if their victims had been black. Of the more than 200 variables potentially relevant to a sentencing decision, race of the victim is a powerful explanation for variation in death sentence rates—as powerful as nonracial aggravating factors such as a prior murder conviction or acting as the principal planner of the homicide.

These adjusted figures are only the most conservative indication of the risk that race will influence the death sentences of defendants in Georgia. Data unadjusted for the mitigating or aggravating effect of other factors show an even more pronounced disparity by race. The capital sentencing rate for all white-victim cases was almost *11 times* greater than the rate for black-victim cases. Furthermore, blacks who kill whites are sentenced to death at nearly *22 times* the rate of blacks who kill blacks, and more than *7 times* the rate of whites who kill blacks. In addition, prosecutors seek the death penalty for 70% of black defendants with white victims, but for only 15% of black defendants with black victims, and only 19% of white defendants with black victims. Since our decision upholding the Georgia capital sentencing system in *Gregg,* the State has executed seven persons. All of the seven were convicted of killing whites, and six of the seven executed were black. Such execution figures are especially striking in light of the fact that, during the period encompassed by the Baldus study, only 9.2% of Georgia homicides involved black defendants and white victims, while 60.7% involved black victims.

McCleskey's statistics have particular force because most of them are the product of sophisticated multiple-regression analysis. Such analysis is designed precisely to identify patterns in the aggregate, even though we may not be able to reconstitute with certainty any individual decision that goes to make up that pattern. Multiple-regression analysis is particularly well suited to identify the influence of impermissible considerations in sentencing, since it is able to control for permissible factors that may explain an apparent arbitrary pattern....

The statistical evidence in this case thus relentlessly documents the risk that McCleskey's sentence was influenced by racial considerations. This evidence shows that there is a better than even chance in Georgia that race will influence the decision to impose the death penalty: a majority of defendants in white-victim crimes would not have been sentenced to die if their victims had been black....

## C

Evaluation of McCleskey's evidence cannot rest solely on the numbers themselves. We must also ask whether the conclusion suggested by those numbers is consonant with our understanding of history and human experience. Georgia's legacy of a race-conscious criminal justice system, as well as this Court's own recognition of the persistent danger that racial attitudes may affect criminal proceedings, indicates that McCleskey's claim is not a fanciful product of mere statistical artifice.

For many years, Georgia operated openly and formally precisely the type of dual system the evidence shows is still effectively in place. The criminal law expressly differentiated between crimes committed by and against blacks and whites, distinctions whose lineage traced back to the time of slavery. During the colonial period, black slaves who killed whites in Georgia, regardless of whether in self-defense or in defense of another, were automatically executed.

By the time of the Civil War, a dual system of crime and punishment was well established in Georgia....

This Court has invalidated portions of the Georgia capital sentencing system three times over the past 15 years. The specter of race discrimination was acknowledged by the Court in striking down the Georgia death penalty in [1972] ...

History and its continuing legacy ... buttress the probative force of McCleskey's statistics. Formal dual criminal laws may no longer be in effect, and intentional discrimination may no longer be prominent. Nonetheless, ... "subtle, less consciously held racial attitudes" continue to be of concern, and the Georgia system gives such attitudes considerable room to operate. The conclusions drawn from McCleskey's statistical evidence are therefore consistent with the lessons of social experience....

## V

At the time our Constitution was framed 200 years ago this year, blacks "had for more than a century before been regarded as beings of an inferior order, either in social or political relations; and so far inferior, that they had no rights which the white man was bound to respect." *Dred Scott v. Sandford* (1857) [*Supra.* this chapter]. Only 130 years ago, this Court relied on these observations to deny American citizenship to blacks. A mere three generations ago, this Court sanctioned "racial segregation," stating that "if one race be inferior to the other socially, the Constitution of the United States cannot put them upon the same plane." *Plessy v. Ferguson* (1896) [*Supra.* Chapter 13].

In more recent times, we have sought to free ourselves from the burden of this history. Yet it has been scarcely a generation since this Court's first decision striking down racial segregation, and barely two decades since the legislative prohibition of racial discrimination in major domains of national life [were lifted]. These have been honorable steps, but we cannot pretend that in three decades we have completely escaped the grip of a historical legacy spanning centuries. Warren McCleskey's evidence confronts us with the subtle and persistent influence of the past. His message is a disturbing one to a society that has formally repudiated racism, and a frustrating one to a Nation accustomed to regarding its destiny as the product of its own will. Nonetheless, we ignore him at our peril, for we remain imprisoned by the past as long as we deny its influence in the present....

## Note: The Intent Requirement

1. Should there be a discriminatory intent requirement? Recall Justice Kennedy's opinion from the last race case from Chapter 13, *Parents Involved v. Seattle School Dist. No. 1*, 551 U.S. 701 (2007). In that opinion he wrote that "an injury stemming from racial prejudice can hurt as much when the demeaning treatment based on race identity stems from bias masked deep within the social order as when it is imposed by law." Thus, he seems to say, if one understands equal protection from the victim's perspective, the harm from discrimination is the same regardless of whether it is intentional or not. On the other hand, intent requirements are deeply embedded in our law: for example, premeditated murder is a more serious crime than negligent manslaughter, and the intentional non-lethal harming of someone can be prosecuted as assault, while negligent harming is sometimes considered only a tort. If we adopt the victim's perspective in these areas, are these distinctions inappropriate?

Consider also the practicalities. In *Washington v. Davis* Justice White concludes the Court's opinion by noting that many laws — most notably, those that have differing impacts based on income or wealth — will inevitably have disparate racial impacts, given the undeniable truth that in America racial minorities tend to be poorer than whites. Would dispensing with the intent requirement mean that entry fees to national parks and state-college tuition charges should be subject to strict scrutiny because they have disparate racial impacts?

If you were designing a constitutional system for modern America, would you include an intent requirement in your equality provision? In every case? Never? In some cases (and if so, which ones)? Why?

2. Now, assume an intent requirement. To what extent should that requirement be satisfied by statistics — that is, by "mere" disparate impact? Consider *McCleskey*. Leave aside the difficulties posed by the facts that a different jury makes every distinct sentencing decision, and that jury decisions are considered immune from judicial second-guessing. In other words, assume that a centralized office subject to judicial review made sentencing decisions in Georgia capital cases. Wouldn't the statistical disparities the Baldus study revealed strongly suggest some type of discriminatory "intent"? Recall the old saying that "where there's smoke, there's fire." Isn't there an enormous amount of "smoke" in *McCleskey*?

3. Finally, consider the uniqueness of the jury system that produced the sentences challenged in *McCleskey*. If you were a legislator or judge confronted with the Baldus study, but if you also understood that jury decisions could not be legitimately questioned, how would you attempt to mitigate the disparate effects of that system? Can you design a criminal justice system that retains this role for the jury but nevertheless is structured so as to prevent the results uncovered by the Baldus study? In other words, can you design a system whose *inputs* help mitigate racially disparate *outputs*?

# Chapter 15

# Equal Protection Analysis Today

### Note: "A Bare ... Desire to Harm a Politically Unpopular Group"

1. The cases excerpted in this chapter all date from the era when suspect class analysis was losing favor at the Court. To be sure, several caveats need to be made to this statement. First, the Court has continued to employ standards of scrutiny developed in part based on suspect class analysis. *See, e.g., Clark v. Jeter* (1988) (*Supra.* Chapter 12) (applying intermediate scrutiny to legitimacy classifications). Second, suspect class analysis has never been officially disowned by the Court, a fact that has allowed that analysis to continue in lower federal courts, as well as in state courts interpreting state constitutional equality provisions. Finally, the first of the cases excerpted below, *City of Cleburne v. Cleburne Living Center*, applies suspect class analysis, but concludes that the intellectually disabled do not qualify for suspect-class status. Nevertheless, the fact remains that the Supreme Court's dissatisfaction with suspect class analysis—a dissatisfaction that is clearly reflected in *City of Cleburne*—has made it necessary for the Court to consider another approach to equal protection.

2. In searching for that new approach, the Court has relied heavily on a case that dates, perhaps ironically, from the very early part of the suspect class era. In *Department of Agriculture v. Moreno*, 413 U.S. 528 (1973), the Court considered a challenge to an amendment to the federal food stamp law. That law determines eligibility for food stamps on a "household" basis. The challenged amendment redefined "household" in a way that excluded groups of unrelated persons who shared living expenses. The challenge was brought by several plaintiffs, all of whom lived in homes that had taken in unrelated persons, including a young girl from a neighboring home, and an older, ill woman who pooled her income with her hosts in exchange for home care.

The Court, speaking through Justice Brennan, began by noting that the statute's "household" definition did not further either of the food stamp law's overall purposes—alleviating hunger and stimulating the agricultural economy by stimulating demand. Examining the legislative history of the household definition provision, he observed that the "sparse" legislative history that existed "indicates that that amendment was intended to prevent so-called 'hippies' and 'hippie communes' from participating in the food stamp program." After this statement, he immediately continued as follows:

> The challenged classification clearly cannot be sustained by reference to this congressional purpose. For if the constitutional conception of 'equal protec-

tion of the laws' means anything, it must at the very least mean that a bare congressional desire to harm a politically unpopular group cannot constitute a *legitimate* governmental interest. As a result, a purpose to discriminate against hippies cannot, in and of itself and without reference to [some independent] considerations in the public interest, justify the 1971 amendment. [Brackets and italics in original.]

Investigating further, he rejected the government's proffered explanations that unrelated households were more likely to commit food stamp fraud, and were more unstable and thus more difficult to police for fraud. Justice Douglas concurred on a different ground, while Justice Rehnquist, joined by Chief Justice Burger, dissented.

3. *Moreno*'s statement that "a bare ... desire to harm a politically unpopular group cannot constitute a *legitimate* governmental interest" ultimately proved to be the foundation of a different approach to equal protection, which the Court began to turn to once it began to turn away from political process-based suspect class analysis.

## City of Cleburne v. Cleburne Living Center
### 473 U.S. 432 (1985)

Justice WHITE delivered the opinion of the Court.

A Texas city denied a special use permit for the operation of a group home for the mentally retarded, acting pursuant to a municipal zoning ordinance requiring permits for such homes. The Court of Appeals for the Fifth Circuit held that mental retardation is a "quasi-suspect" classification and that the ordinance violated the Equal Protection Clause because it did not substantially further an important governmental purpose. We hold that a lesser standard of scrutiny is appropriate, but conclude that under that standard the ordinance is invalid as applied in this case.

I

In July 1980, respondent Jan Hannah purchased a building at 201 Featherston Street in the city of Cleburne, Texas, with the intention of leasing it to Cleburne Living Center, Inc. (CLC), for the operation of a group home for the mentally retarded.... The city informed CLC that a special use permit would be required for the operation of a group home at the site, and CLC accordingly submitted a permit application. In response to a subsequent inquiry from CLC, the city explained that under the zoning regulations applicable to the site, a special use permit, renewable annually, was required for the construction of "hospitals for the insane or feebleminded, or alcoholic [*sic*] or drug addicts, or penal or correctional institutions." ... After holding a public hearing on CLC's application, the City Council voted 3 to 1 to deny a special use permit.

CLC then filed suit in Federal District Court against the city and a number of its officials, alleging, *inter alia*, that the zoning ordinance was invalid on its face and as applied because it discriminated against the mentally retarded in violation of the equal protection rights of CLC and its potential residents. The District Court found that "if the potential residents of the Featherston Street home were not mentally retarded, but the home was the same in all other respects, its use would be permitted under the city's zoning ordinance," and that the City Council's decision "was motivated primarily by the fact that the residents of the home would be persons who are mentally retarded." Even so, the District Court held the ordinance and its application constitutional. Concluding that no fundamental right was implicated and that mental retardation was neither a suspect nor a quasi-suspect classification, the court employed the minimum level of judicial scrutiny applicable to equal protection claims. The court deemed the ordinance, as written and applied, to be rationally related to the city's legitimate interests in "the legal responsibility of CLC and its residents, ... the safety and fears of residents in the adjoining neighborhood," and the number of people to be housed in the home.

The Court of Appeals for the Fifth Circuit reversed, determining that mental retardation was a quasi-suspect classification and that it should assess the validity of the ordinance under intermediate-level scrutiny. Because mental retardation was in fact relevant to many legislative actions, strict scrutiny was not appropriate. But in light of the history of "unfair and often grotesque mistreatment" of the retarded, discrimination against them was "likely to reflect deep-seated prejudice." In addition, the mentally retarded lacked political power, and their condition was immutable. The court considered heightened scrutiny to be particularly appropriate in this case, because the city's ordinance withheld a benefit which, although not fundamental, was very important to the mentally retarded. Without group homes, the court stated, the retarded could never hope to integrate themselves into the community. Applying the test that it considered appropriate, the court held that the ordinance was invalid on its face because it did not substantially further any important governmental interests. The Court of Appeals went on to hold that the ordinance was also invalid as applied.... We granted certiorari....

## II

The Equal Protection Clause of the Fourteenth Amendment commands that no State shall "deny to any person within its jurisdiction the equal protection of the laws," which is essentially a direction that all persons similarly situated should be treated alike. *Plyler v. Doe* (1982) [Note *supra*. Chapter 12]. Section 5 of the Amendment empowers Congress to enforce this mandate, but absent controlling congressional direction, the courts have themselves devised standards for determining the validity of state legislation or other official action that is challenged as denying equal protection. The general rule is that legislation is presumed to be valid and will be sustained if the classification drawn by the statute is rationally related to a legitimate state interest. *United States Railroad Retirement Board v. Fritz* (1980) [*Supra*. Chapter 11]. When social or economic legislation is at issue, the Equal Protection Clause allows the States wide latitude, *Fritz*, and the Constitution presumes that even improvident decisions will eventually be rectified by the democratic processes.

The general rule gives way, however, when a statute classifies by race, alienage, or national origin. These factors are so seldom relevant to the achievement of any legitimate state interest that laws grounded in such considerations are deemed to reflect prejudice and antipathy—a view that those in the burdened class are not as worthy or deserving as others. For these reasons and because such discrimination is unlikely to be soon rectified by legislative means, these laws are subjected to strict scrutiny and will be sustained only if they are suitably tailored to serve a compelling state interest. *McLaughlin v. Florida*, 379 U.S. 184 (1964); *Graham v. Richardson* (1971) [Note *supra.* Chapter 12]. Similar oversight by the courts is due when state laws impinge on personal rights protected by the Constitution. *Skinner v. Oklahoma*, 316 U.S. 545 (1942) [Note *supra.* Chapter 8].

Legislative classifications based on gender also call for a heightened standard of review. That factor generally provides no sensible ground for differential treatment. "What differentiates sex from such nonsuspect statuses as intelligence or physical disability … is that the sex characteristic frequently bears no relation to ability to perform or contribute to society." *Frontiero v. Richardson* (1973) (plurality opinion) [*Supra.* Chapter 12]. Rather than resting on meaningful considerations, statutes distributing benefits and burdens between the sexes in different ways very likely reflect outmoded notions of the relative capabilities of men and women. A gender classification fails unless it is substantially related to a sufficiently important governmental interest. *Mississippi University for Women v. Hogan* (1982) [Note *supra.* Chapter 12]; *Craig v. Boren* (1976) [*Supra.* Chapter 12]. Because illegitimacy is beyond the individual's control and bears "no relation to the individual's ability to participate in and contribute to society," *Mathews v. Lucas* (1976) [*Supra.* Chapter 12], official discriminations resting on that characteristic are also subject to somewhat heightened review. Those restrictions "will survive equal protection scrutiny to the extent they are substantially related to a legitimate state interest."

We have declined, however, to extend heightened review to differential treatment based on age:

> "While the treatment of the aged in this Nation has not been wholly free of discrimination, such persons, unlike, say, those who have been discriminated against on the basis of race or national origin, have not experienced a 'history of purposeful unequal treatment' or been subjected to unique disabilities on the basis of stereotyped characteristics not truly indicative of their abilities." *Massachusetts Board of Retirement v. Murgia* (1976) [*Supra.* Chapter 12].

The lesson of *Murgia* is that where individuals in the group affected by a law have distinguishing characteristics relevant to interests the State has the authority to implement, the courts have been very reluctant, as they should be in our federal system and with our respect for the separation of powers, to closely scrutinize legislative choices as to whether, how, and to what extent those interests should be pursued. In such cases, the Equal Protection Clause requires only a rational means to serve a legitimate end.

## III

Against this background, we conclude for several reasons that the Court of Appeals erred in holding mental retardation a quasi-suspect classification calling for a more exacting standard of judicial review than is normally accorded economic and social legislation. First, it is undeniable, and it is not argued otherwise here, that those who are mentally retarded have a reduced ability to cope with and function in the everyday world. Nor are they all cut from the same pattern: as the testimony in this record indicates, they range from those whose disability is not immediately evident to those who must be constantly cared for. They are thus different, immutably so, in relevant respects, and the States' interest in dealing with and providing for them is plainly a legitimate one. How this large and diversified group is to be treated under the law is a difficult and often a technical matter, very much a task for legislators guided by qualified professionals and not by the perhaps ill-informed opinions of the judiciary. Heightened scrutiny inevitably involves substantive judgments about legislative decisions, and we doubt that the predicate for such judicial oversight is present where the classification deals with mental retardation.

Second, the distinctive legislative response, both national and state, to the plight of those who are mentally retarded demonstrates not only that they have unique problems, but also that the lawmakers have been addressing their difficulties in a manner that belies a continuing antipathy or prejudice and a corresponding need for more intrusive oversight by the judiciary. Thus, the Federal Government has not only outlawed discrimination against the mentally retarded in federally funded programs, but it has also provided the retarded with the right to receive "appropriate treatment, services, and habilitation" in a setting that is "least restrictive of [their] personal liberty." Developmental Disabilities Assistance and Bill of Rights Act. In addition, the Government has conditioned federal education funds on a State's assurance that retarded children will enjoy an education that, "to the maximum extent appropriate," is integrated with that of nonmentally retarded children. Education of the Handicapped Act. The Government has also facilitated the hiring of the mentally retarded into the federal civil service by exempting them from the requirement of competitive examination. The State of Texas has similarly enacted legislation that acknowledges the special status of the mentally retarded by conferring certain rights upon them, such as "the right to live in the least restrictive setting appropriate to [their] individual needs and abilities," including "the right to live ... in a group home." Mentally Retarded Persons Act of 1977.

Such legislation thus singling out the retarded for special treatment reflects the real and undeniable differences between the retarded and others. That a civilized and decent society expects and approves such legislation indicates that governmental consideration of those differences in the vast majority of situations is not only legitimate but also desirable. It may be, as CLC contends, that legislation designed to benefit, rather than disadvantage, the retarded would generally withstand examination under a test of heightened scrutiny. The relevant inquiry, however, is whether heightened scrutiny is constitutionally mandated in the first instance. Even assuming that many of these laws could be shown to be substantially related to an important governmental purpose, merely requiring the legislature to justify its efforts in these terms may lead it to refrain from acting at all. Much recent legislation intended to benefit the retarded also assumes the need for measures that might be perceived to disadvantage them. The Education of the Handicapped Act, for example, requires an "appropriate" education, not one that is equal in all respects to the education of nonretarded children; clearly, admission to a class that exceeded the abilities of a retarded child would not be appropriate. Similarly, the Developmental Disabilities Assistance Act and the Texas Act give the retarded the right to live only in the "least restrictive setting" appropriate to their abilities, implicitly assuming the need for at least some restrictions that would not be imposed on others. Especially given the wide variation in the abilities and needs of the retarded themselves, governmental bodies must have a certain amount of flexibility and freedom from judicial oversight in shaping and limiting their remedial efforts.

Third, the legislative response, which could hardly have occurred and survived without public support, negates any claim that the mentally retarded are politically powerless in the sense that they have no ability to attract the attention of the lawmakers. Any minority can be said to be powerless to assert direct control over the legislature, but if that were a criterion for higher level scrutiny by the courts, much economic and social legislation would now be suspect.

Fourth, if the large and amorphous class of the mentally retarded were deemed quasi-suspect for the reasons given by the Court of Appeals, it would be difficult to find a principled way to distinguish a variety of other groups who have perhaps immutable disabilities setting them off from others, who cannot themselves mandate the desired legislative responses, and who can claim some degree of prejudice from at least part of the public at large. One need mention in this respect only the aging, the disabled, the mentally ill, and the infirm. We are reluctant to set out on that course, and we decline to do so.

Doubtless, there have been and there will continue to be instances of discrimination against the retarded that are in fact invidious, and that are properly subject to judicial correction under constitutional norms. But the appropriate method of reaching such instances is not to create a new quasi-suspect classification and subject all governmental action based on that classification to more searching evaluation. Rather, we should look to the likelihood that governmental action premised on a particular classification is valid as a general matter, not merely to the specifics of the case before us. Because mental retardation is a characteristic that the government may legitimately take into account in a wide range of decisions, and because both State and Federal Governments have recently committed themselves to assisting the retarded, we will not presume that any given legislative action, even one that disadvantages retarded individuals, is rooted in considerations that the Constitution will not tolerate.

Our refusal to recognize the retarded as a quasi-suspect class does not leave them entirely unprotected from invidious discrimination. To withstand equal protection review, legislation that distinguishes between the mentally retarded and others must be rationally related to a legitimate governmental purpose. This standard, we believe, affords government the latitude necessary both to pursue policies designed to assist the retarded in realizing their full potential, and to freely and efficiently engage in activities that burden the retarded in what is essentially an incidental manner. The State may not rely on a classification whose relationship to an asserted goal is so attenuated as to render the distinction arbitrary or irrational. See *United States Dept. of Agriculture v. Moreno*, 413 U.S. 528 (1973) [Note *supra.* this chapter]. Furthermore, some objectives—such as "a bare ... desire to harm a politically unpopular group," *id.*—are not legitimate state interests. Beyond that, the mentally retarded, like others, have and retain their substantive constitutional rights in addition to the right to be treated equally by the law.

IV

We turn to the issue of the validity of the zoning ordinance insofar as it requires a special use permit for homes for the mentally retarded.... The constitutional issue is clearly posed. The city does not require a special use permit in an R-3 zone for apartment houses, multiple dwellings, boarding and lodging houses, fraternity or sorority houses, dormitories, apartment hotels, hospitals, sanitariums, nursing homes for convalescents or the aged (other than for the insane or feebleminded or alcoholics or drug addicts), private clubs or fraternal orders, and other specified uses. It does, however, insist on a special permit for the Featherston home, and it does so, as the District Court found, because it would be a facility for the mentally retarded. May the city require the permit for this facility when other care and multiple-dwelling facilities are freely permitted?

It is true, as already pointed out, that the mentally retarded as a group are indeed different from others not sharing their misfortune, and in this respect they may be different from those who would occupy other facilities that would be permitted in an R-3 zone without a special permit. But this difference is largely irrelevant unless the Featherston home and those who would occupy it would threaten legitimate interests of the city in a way that other permitted uses such as boarding houses and hospitals would not. Because in our view the record does not reveal any rational basis for believing that the Featherston home would pose any special threat to the city's legitimate interests, we affirm the judgment below insofar as it holds the ordinance invalid as applied in this case.

The District Court found that the City Council's insistence on the permit rested on several factors. First, the Council was concerned with the negative attitude of the majority of property owners located within 200 feet of the Featherston facility, as well as with the fears of elderly residents of the neighborhood. But mere negative attitudes, or fear, unsubstantiated by factors which are properly cognizable in a zoning proceeding, are not permissible bases for treating a home for the mentally retarded differently from apartment houses, multiple dwellings, and the like. It is plain that the electorate as a whole, whether by referendum or otherwise, could not order city action violative of the Equal Protection Clause, and the city may not avoid the strictures of that Clause by deferring to the wishes or objections of some fraction of the body politic. "Private biases may be outside the reach of the law, but the law cannot, directly or indirectly, give them effect." *Palmore v. Sidoti*, 466 U.S. 429 (1984).

Second, the Council had two objections to the location of the facility. It was concerned that the facility was across the street from a junior high school, and it feared that the students might harass the occupants of the Featherston home. But the school itself is attended by about 30 mentally retarded students, and denying a permit based on such vague, undifferentiated fears is again permitting some portion of the community to validate what would otherwise be an equal protection violation. The other objection to the home's location was that it was located on "a five hundred year flood plain." This concern with the possibility of a flood, however, can hardly be based on a distinction between the Featherston home and, for example, nursing homes, homes for convalescents or the aged, or sanitariums or hospitals, any of which could be located on the Featherston site without obtaining a special use permit. The same may be said of another concern of the Council-doubts about the legal responsibility for actions which the mentally retarded might take. If there is no concern about legal responsibility with respect to other uses that would be permitted in the area, such as boarding and fraternity houses, it is difficult to believe that the groups of mildly or moderately mentally retarded individuals who would live at 201 Featherston would present any different or special hazard.

Fourth, the Council was concerned with the size of the home and the number of people that would occupy it. The District Court found, and the Court of Appeals repeated, that "if the potential residents of the Featherston Street home were not mentally retarded, but the home was the same in all other respects, its use would be permitted under the city's zoning ordinance." Given this finding, there would be no restrictions on the number of people who could occupy this home as a boarding house, nursing home, family dwelling, fraternity house, or dormitory. The question is whether it is rational to treat the mentally retarded differently. It is true that they suffer disability not shared by others; but why this difference warrants a density regulation that others need not observe is not at all apparent. At least this record does not clarify how, in this connection, the characteristics of the intended occupants of the Featherston home rationally justify denying to those occupants what would be permitted to groups occupying the same site for different purposes.... In the words of the Court of Appeals, "the City never justifies its apparent view that other people can live under such 'crowded' conditions when mentally retarded persons cannot."

In the courts below the city also urged that the ordinance is aimed at avoiding concentration of population and at lessening congestion of the streets. These concerns obviously fail to explain why apartment houses, fraternity and sorority houses, hospitals and the like, may freely locate in the area without a permit. So, too, the expressed worry about fire hazards, the serenity of the neighborhood, and the avoidance of danger to other residents fail rationally to justify singling out a home such as 201 Featherston for the special use permit, yet imposing no such restrictions on the many other uses freely permitted in the neighborhood.

The short of it is that requiring the permit in this case appears to us to rest on an irrational prejudice against the mentally retarded, including those who would occupy the Featherston facility and who would live under the closely supervised and highly regulated conditions expressly provided for by state and federal law.

The judgment of the Court of Appeals is affirmed insofar as it invalidates the zoning ordinance as applied to the Featherston home. The judgment is otherwise vacated, and the case is remanded.

Justice STEVENS, with whom THE CHIEF JUSTICE joins, concurring.

The Court of Appeals disposed of this case as if a critical question to be decided were which of three clearly defined standards of equal protection review should be applied to a legislative classification discriminating against the mentally retarded.[1] In fact, our cases have not delineated three—or even one or two—such well-defined standards.[2] Rather, our cases reflect a continuum of judgmental responses to differing classifications which have been explained in opinions by terms ranging from "strict scrutiny" at one extreme to "rational basis" at the other. I have never been persuaded that these so-called "standards" adequately explain the decisional process. Cases involving classifications based on alienage, illegal residency, illegitimacy, gender, age, or—as in this case—mental retardation, do not fit well into sharply defined classifications.

"I am inclined to believe that what has become known as the [tiered] analysis of equal protection claims does not describe a completely logical method of deciding cases, but rather is a method the Court has employed to explain decisions that actually apply a single standard in a reasonably consistent fashion." *Craig* (STEVENS, J., concurring). In my own approach to these cases, I have always asked myself whether I could find a "rational basis" for the classification at issue. The term "rational," of course, includes a requirement that an impartial lawmaker could logically believe

---

1. The three standards—"rationally related to a legitimate state interest," "somewhat heightened review," and "strict scrutiny" are briefly described *ante*.

2. In *United States RR Retirement Board v. Fritz*, after citing 11 cases applying the rational-basis standard, the Court stated [in footnote 10]: "The most arrogant legal scholar would not claim that all of these cases applied a uniform or consistent test under equal protection principles." Commenting on the intermediate standard of review in his dissent in *Craig v. Boren*, Justice REHNQUIST wrote:

> I would think we have had enough difficulty with the two standards of review which our cases have recognized—the norm of 'rational basis,' and the 'compelling state interest' required where a 'suspect classification' is involved—so as to counsel weightily against the insertion of still another 'standard' between those two. How is this Court to divine what objectives are important? How is it to determine whether a particular law is 'substantially' related to the achievement of such objective, rather than related in some other way to its achievement? Both of the phrases used are so diaphanous and elastic as to invite subjective judicial preferences or prejudices relating to particular types of legislation, masquerading as judgments whether such legislation is directed at 'important' objectives or, whether the relationship to those objectives is 'substantial' enough.

that the classification would serve a legitimate public purpose that transcends the harm to the members of the disadvantaged class.[4] Thus, the word "rational"—for me at least—includes elements of legitimacy and neutrality that must always characterize the performance of the sovereign's duty to govern impartially.

The rational-basis test, properly understood, adequately explains why a law that deprives a person of the right to vote because his skin has a different pigmentation than that of other voters violates the Equal Protection Clause. It would be utterly irrational to limit the franchise on the basis of height or weight; it is equally invalid to limit it on the basis of skin color. None of these attributes has any bearing at all on the citizen's willingness or ability to exercise that civil right. We do not need to apply a special standard, or to apply "strict scrutiny," or even "heightened scrutiny," to decide such cases.

In every equal protection case, we have to ask certain basic questions. What class is harmed by the legislation, and has it been subjected to a "tradition of disfavor" by our laws?[6] What is the public purpose that is being served by the law? What is the characteristic of the disadvantaged class that justifies the disparate treatment? In most cases the answer to these questions will tell us whether the statute has a "rational basis." The answers will result in the virtually automatic invalidation of racial classifications and in the validation of most economic classifications, but they will provide differing results in cases involving classifications based on alienage,[8] gender,[9] or illegitimacy.[10] But that is not because we apply an "intermediate standard of review" in

---

4. "I therefore believe that we must discover a correlation between the classification and either the actual purpose of the statute or a legitimate purpose that we may reasonably presume to have motivated an impartial legislature. If the adverse impact on the disfavored class is an apparent aim of the legislature, its impartiality would be suspect. If, however, the adverse impact may reasonably be viewed as an acceptable cost of achieving a larger goal, an impartial lawmaker could rationally decide that that cost should be incurred." *Fritz* (STEVENS, J., concurring in judgment).

6. The Court must be especially vigilant in evaluating the rationality of any classification involving a group that has been subjected to a "tradition of disfavor [for] a traditional classification is more likely to be used without pausing to consider its justification than is a newly created classification. Habit, rather than analysis, makes it seem acceptable and natural to distinguish between male and female, alien and citizen, legitimate and illegitimate; for too much of our history there was the same inertia in distinguishing between black and white. But that sort of stereotyped reaction may have no rational relationship—other than pure prejudicial discrimination—to the stated purpose for which the classification is being made." *Mathews v. Lucas* (1976) (STEVENS, J., dissenting) [*Supra.* chapter 12].

8. ... Compare *Sugarman v. Dougall* (1973) [striking down alienage classification as applied to various government employees] [*Supra.* Chapter 12], and *In re Griffiths*, 413 U.S. 717 (1973) [striking down alienage classification governing admission to a state bar] [Note *supra.* Chapter 12], with *Ambach v. Norwick*, 441 U.S. 68 (1979) [upholding alienage classification as applied to eligibility to be a schoolteacher], and *Foley v. Connelie*, 435 U.S. 291 (1978) [upholding alienage classification as applied to eligibility to be a state police officer] [both note *supra.* Chapter 12].

9. Compare *Reed v. Reed*, 404 U.S. 71 (1971) [Note *supra.* Chapter 12] with *Personnel Administrator of Mass. v. Feeney*, 442 U.S. 256 (1979) [Note *supra.* Chapter 14].

10. Compare *Lalli v. Lalli*, 439 U.S. 259 (1978) [upholding illegitimacy classification], with *Trimble v. Gordon*, 430 U.S. 762 (1977) [striking down illegitimacy classification].

these cases; rather it is because the characteristics of these groups are sometimes relevant and sometimes irrelevant to a valid public purpose, or, more specifically, to the purpose that the challenged laws purportedly intended to serve.

Every law that places the mentally retarded in a special class is not presumptively irrational. The differences between mentally retarded persons and those with greater mental capacity are obviously relevant to certain legislative decisions. An impartial lawmaker—indeed, even a member of a class of persons defined as mentally retarded—could rationally vote in favor of a law providing funds for special education and special treatment for the mentally retarded. A mentally retarded person could also recognize that he is a member of a class that might need special supervision in some situations, both to protect himself and to protect others. Restrictions on his right to drive cars or to operate hazardous equipment might well seem rational even though they deprived him of employment opportunities and the kind of freedom of travel enjoyed by other citizens. "That a civilized and decent society expects and approves such legislation indicates that governmental consideration of those differences in the vast majority of situations is not only legitimate but also desirable." *Ante.*

Even so, the Court of Appeals correctly observed that through ignorance and prejudice the mentally retarded "have been subjected to a history of unfair and often grotesque mistreatment." The discrimination against the mentally retarded that is at issue in this case is the city's decision to require an annual special use permit before property in an apartment house district may be used as a group home for persons who are mildly retarded. The record convinces me that this permit was required because of the irrational fears of neighboring property owners, rather than for the protection of the mentally retarded persons who would reside in respondent's home.

Although the city argued in the Court of Appeals that legitimate interests of the neighbors justified the restriction, the court unambiguously rejected that argument. In this Court, the city has argued that the discrimination was really motivated by a desire to protect the mentally retarded from the hazards presented by the neighborhood. Zoning ordinances are not usually justified on any such basis, and in this case, for the reasons explained by the Court, I find that justification wholly unconvincing. I cannot believe that a rational member of this disadvantaged class could ever approve of the discriminatory application of the city's ordinance in this case.

Accordingly, I join the opinion of the Court.

Justice MARSHALL, with whom Justice BRENNAN and Justice BLACKMUN join, concurring in the judgment in part and dissenting in part.

The Court holds that all retarded individuals cannot be grouped together as the "feebleminded" and deemed presumptively unfit to live in a community. Underlying this holding is the principle that mental retardation *per se* cannot be a proxy for depriving retarded people of their rights and interests without regard to variations in individual ability. With this holding and principle I agree. The Equal Protection Clause requires attention to the capacities and needs of retarded people as individuals.

I cannot agree, however, with the way in which the Court reaches its result or with the narrow, as-applied remedy it provides for the city of Cleburne's equal protection violation. The Court holds the ordinance invalid on rational-basis grounds and disclaims that anything special, in the form of heightened scrutiny, is taking place. Yet Cleburne's ordinance surely would be valid under the traditional rational-basis test applicable to economic and commercial regulation. In my view, it is important to articulate, as the Court does not, the facts and principles that justify subjecting this zoning ordinance to the searching review—the heightened scrutiny—that actually leads to its invalidation. [Because] I cannot accept the Court's disclaimer that no "more exacting standard" than ordinary rational-basis review is being applied, I write separately.

I

At the outset, two curious and paradoxical aspects of the Court's opinion must be noted. First, because the Court invalidates Cleburne's zoning ordinance on rational-basis grounds, the Court's wide-ranging discussion of heightened scrutiny is wholly superfluous to the decision of this case. This "two for the price of one" approach to constitutional decisionmaking—rendering two constitutional rulings where one is enough to decide the case—stands on their head traditional and deeply embedded principles governing exercise of the Court's Article III power. Just a few weeks ago, the Court "called to mind two of the cardinal rules governing the federal courts: One, never to anticipate a question of constitutional law in advance of the necessity of deciding it; the other never to formulate a rule of constitutional law broader than is required by the precise facts to which it is to be applied." ... The Court offers no principled justification for departing from these principles....

Second, the Court's heightened-scrutiny discussion is even more puzzling given that Cleburne's ordinance is invalidated only after being subjected to precisely the sort of probing inquiry associated with heightened scrutiny. To be sure, the Court does not label its handiwork heightened scrutiny, and perhaps the method employed must hereafter be called "second order" rational-basis review rather than "heightened scrutiny." But however labeled, the rational basis test invoked today is most assuredly not the rational-basis test of *Williamson v. Lee Optical of Oklahoma, Inc.*, 348 U.S. 483 (1955) [Note *supra.* Chapter 7], *Allied Stores of Ohio, Inc. v. Bowers*, 358 U.S. 522 (1959), and their progeny.

The Court, for example, concludes that legitimate concerns for fire hazards or the serenity of the neighborhood do not justify singling out respondents to bear the burdens of these concerns, for analogous permitted uses appear to pose similar threats. Yet under the traditional and most minimal version of the rational-basis test, "reform may take one step at a time, addressing itself to the phase of the problem which seems most acute to the legislative mind." *Williamson v. Lee Optical.* The "record" is said not to support the ordinance's classifications, but under the traditional standard we do not sift through the record to determine whether policy decisions are squarely supported by a firm factual foundation. Finally, the Court further finds it "difficult to believe" that the retarded present different or special hazards inapplicable to other groups. In normal circumstances, the burden is not on the legislature to convince the Court that the lines it has drawn are sensible; legislation is presumptively constitutional, and a State "is not required to resort to close distinctions or to maintain a precise, scientific uniformity with reference" to its goals. *Allied Stores of Ohio, Inc. v. Bowers.*

I share the Court's criticisms of the overly broad lines that Cleburne's zoning ordinance has drawn. But if the ordinance is to be invalidated for its imprecise classifications, it must be pursuant to more powerful scrutiny than the minimal rational-basis test used to review classifications affecting only economic and commercial matters. The same imprecision in a similar ordinance that required opticians but not optometrists to be licensed to practice, see *Williamson v. Lee Optical* ... would hardly be fatal to the statutory scheme.

The refusal to acknowledge that something more than minimum rationality review is at work here is, in my view, unfortunate in at least two respects. The suggestion that the traditional rational-basis test allows this sort of searching inquiry creates precedent for this Court and lower courts to subject economic and commercial classifications to similar and searching "ordinary" rational-basis review—a small and regrettable step back toward the days of *Lochner v. New York* (1905) [*Supra.* Chapter 7]. Moreover, by failing to articulate the factors that justify today's "second order" rational-basis review, the Court provides no principled foundation for determining when more searching inquiry is to be invoked. Lower courts are thus left in the dark on this important question, and this Court remains unaccountable for its decisions employing, or refusing to employ, particularly searching scrutiny. Candor requires me to acknowledge the particular factors that justify invalidating Cleburne's zoning ordinance under the careful scrutiny it today receives.

## II

I have long believed the level of scrutiny employed in an equal protection case should vary with "the constitutional and societal importance of the interest adversely affected and the recognized invidiousness of the basis upon which the particular classification is drawn." *San Antonio Independent School District v. Rodriguez*, 411 U.S. 1 (1973) (MARSHALL, J., dissenting) [Note *supra.* Chapter 12]. When a zoning ordinance works to exclude the retarded from all residential districts in a community, these two considerations require that the ordinance be convincingly justified as substantially furthering legitimate and important purposes.

First, the interest of the retarded in establishing group homes is substantial. The right to "establish a home" has long been cherished as one of the fundamental liberties embraced by the Due Process Clause. See *Meyer v. Nebraska* (1923) [*Supra.* Chapter 8]....

Second, the mentally retarded have been subject to a "lengthy and tragic history," *University of California Regents v. Bakke* (1978) (opinion of POWELL, J.) [*Supra.* Chapter 13], of segregation and discrimination that can only be called grotesque.

During much of the 19th century, mental retardation was viewed as neither curable nor dangerous and the retarded were largely left to their own devices. By the latter part of the century and during the first decades of the new one, however, social views of the retarded underwent a radical transformation. Fueled by the rising tide of Social Darwinism, the "science" of eugenics, and the extreme xenophobia of those years, leading medical authorities and others began to portray the "feeble minded" as a "menace to society and civilization ... responsible in a large degree for many, if not all, of our social problems." A regime of state-mandated segregation and degradation soon emerged that in its virulence and bigotry rivaled, and indeed paralleled, the worst excesses of Jim Crow. Massive custodial institutions were built to warehouse the retarded for life; the aim was to halt reproduction of the retarded and "nearly extinguish their race." Retarded children were categorically excluded from public schools, based on the false stereotype that all were ineducable and on the purported need to protect nonretarded children from them. State laws deemed the retarded "unfit for citizenship."

Segregation was accompanied by eugenic marriage and sterilization laws that extinguished for the retarded one of the "basic civil rights of man"—the right to marry and procreate. *Skinner v. Oklahoma*, 316 U.S. 545 (1942) [Note *supra.* Chapter 8]. Marriages of the retarded were made, and in some States continue to be, not only voidable but also often a criminal offense....

Prejudice, once let loose, is not easily cabined. As of 1979, most States still categorically disqualified "idiots" from voting, without regard to individual capacity and with discretion to exclude left in the hands of low-level election officials. Not until Congress enacted the Education of the Handicapped Act, were "the doors of public education" opened wide to handicapped children. But most important, lengthy and continuing isolation of the retarded has perpetuated the ignorance, irrational fears, and stereotyping that long have plagued them.[16]

In light of the importance of the interest at stake and the history of discrimination the retarded have suffered, the Equal Protection Clause requires us to do more than review the distinctions drawn by Cleburne's zoning ordinance as if they appeared in a taxing statute or in economic or commercial legislation. The searching scrutiny I would give to restrictions on the ability of the retarded to establish community group homes leads me to conclude that Cleburne's vague generalizations for classifying the "feeble-minded" with drug addicts, alcoholics, and the insane, and excluding them where the elderly, the ill, the boarder, and the transient are allowed, are not substantial or important enough to overcome the suspicion that the ordinance rests on impermissible assumptions or outmoded and perhaps invidious stereotypes.

---

16. See generally G. Allport, *The Nature of Prejudice* (1958) (separateness among groups exaggerates differences).

## III

In its effort to show that Cleburne's ordinance can be struck down under no "more exacting standard ... than is normally accorded economic and social legislation," the Court offers several justifications as to why the retarded do not warrant heightened judicial solicitude. These justifications, however, find no support in our heightened-scrutiny precedents and cannot withstand logical analysis.

The Court downplays the lengthy "history of purposeful unequal treatment" of the retarded by pointing to recent legislative action that is said to "belie a continuing antipathy or prejudice." Building on this point, the Court similarly concludes that the retarded are not "politically powerless" and deserve no greater judicial protection than "any minority" that wins some political battles and loses others. The import of these conclusions, it seems, is that the only discrimination courts may remedy is the discrimination they alone are perspicacious enough to see. Once society begins to recognize certain practices as discriminatory, in part because previously stigmatized groups have mobilized politically to lift this stigma, the Court would refrain from approaching such practices with the added skepticism of heightened scrutiny.

Courts, however, do not sit or act in a social vacuum. Moral philosophers may debate whether certain inequalities are absolute wrongs, but history makes clear that constitutional principles of equality, like constitutional principles of liberty, property, and due process, evolve over time; what once was a "natural" and "self-evident" ordering later comes to be seen as an artificial and invidious constraint on human potential and freedom. Compare *Plessy v. Ferguson* (1896) [*Supra.* Chapter 13], and *Bradwell v. Illinois*, 16 Wall. 130 (Bradley, J., concurring in judgment) [Note *supra.* Chapter 12], with *Brown v. Board of Education* (1954) [*Supra.* Chapter 13], and *Reed v. Reed*. Shifting cultural, political, and social patterns at times come to make past practices appear inconsistent with fundamental principles upon which American society rests, an inconsistency legally cognizable under the Equal Protection Clause. It is natural that evolving standards of equality come to be embodied in legislation. When that occurs, courts should look to the fact of such change as a source of guidance on evolving principles of equality. In an analysis the Court today ignores, the Court reached this very conclusion when it extended heightened scrutiny to gender classifications and drew on parallel legislative developments to support that extension:

> "Over the past decade, Congress has itself manifested an increasing sensitivity to sex-based classifications.... Thus, Congress itself has concluded that classifications based upon sex are inherently invidious, and this conclusion of a coequal branch of Government is not without significance to the question presently under consideration." *Frontiero v. Richardson.*

Moreover, even when judicial action *has* catalyzed legislative change, that change certainly does not eviscerate the underlying constitutional principle. The Court, for example, has never suggested that race-based classifications became any less suspect once extensive legislation had been enacted on the subject.

For the retarded, just as for Negroes and women, much has changed in recent years, but much remains the same; outdated statutes are still on the books, and irrational fears or ignorance, traceable to the prolonged social and cultural isolation of the retarded, continue to stymie recognition of the dignity and individuality of retarded people. Heightened judicial scrutiny of action appearing to impose unnecessary barriers to the retarded is required in light of increasing recognition that such barriers are inconsistent with evolving principles of equality embedded in the Fourteenth Amendment.

The Court also offers a more general view of heightened scrutiny, a view focused primarily on when heightened scrutiny does *not* apply as opposed to when it does apply. Two principles appear central to the Court's theory. First, heightened scrutiny is said to be inapplicable where *individuals* in a group have distinguishing characteristics that legislatures properly may take into account in some circumstances. Heightened scrutiny is also purportedly inappropriate when many legislative classifications affecting the *group* are likely to be valid. We must, so the Court says, "look to the likelihood that governmental action premised on a particular classification is valid as a general matter, not merely to the specifics of the case before us," in deciding whether to apply heightened scrutiny.

If the Court's first principle were sound, heightened scrutiny would have to await a day when people could be cut from a cookie mold. Women are hardly alike in all their characteristics, but heightened scrutiny applies to them because legislatures can rarely use gender itself as a proxy for these other characteristics. Permissible distinctions between persons must bear a reasonable relationship to their *relevant* characteristics, and gender *per se* is almost never relevant. Similarly, that some retarded people have reduced capacities in some areas does not justify using retardation as a proxy for reduced capacity in areas where relevant individual variations in capacity do exist.

The Court's second assertion—that the standard of review must be fixed with reference to the number of classifications to which a characteristic would validly be relevant—is similarly flawed. Certainly the assertion is not a logical one; that a characteristic may be relevant under some or even many circumstances does not suggest any reason to presume it relevant under other circumstances where there is reason to suspect it is not. A sign that says "men only" looks very different on a bathroom door than a courthouse door.

Our heightened-scrutiny precedents belie the claim that a characteristic must virtually always be irrelevant to warrant heightened scrutiny. *Plyler v. Doe*, 457 U.S. 202 (1982) [Note *supra.* Chapter 12], for example, held that the status of being an undocumented alien is not a "constitutional irrelevancy," and therefore declined to review with strict scrutiny classifications affecting undocumented aliens. While *Frontiero* stated that gender "frequently" and "often" bears no relation to legitimate legislative aims, it did not deem gender an impermissible basis of state action in all circumstances. Indeed, the Court has upheld some gender-based classifications. *Rostker v. Goldberg*, 453 U.S. 57 (1981); *Michael M. v. Superior Court of Sonoma County*, 450 U.S. 464 (1981) [Both note *supra.* Chapter 12]. Heightened but not strict scrutiny is considered appropriate in areas such as gender, illegitimacy, or alienage because the Court views the trait as relevant under some circumstances but not others. That view—indeed the very concept of heightened, as opposed to strict, scrutiny—is flatly inconsistent with the notion that heightened scrutiny should not apply to the retarded because "mental retardation is a characteristic that the government may legitimately take into account in a wide range of decisions." *Ante*. Because the government also may not take this characteristic into account in many circumstances, such as those presented here, careful review is required to separate the permissible from the invalid in classifications relying on retardation.

The fact that retardation may be deemed a constitutional irrelevancy in *some* circumstances is enough, given the history of discrimination the retarded have suffered, to require careful judicial review of classifications singling out the retarded for special burdens....

That more searching inquiry, be it called heightened scrutiny or "second order" rational-basis review, is a method of approaching certain classifications skeptically, with judgment suspended until the facts are in and the evidence considered. The government must establish that the classification is substantially related to important and legitimate objectives, see, e.g., *Craig v. Boren*, so that valid and sufficiently weighty policies actually justify the departure from equality. Heightened scrutiny does not allow courts to second-guess reasoned legislative or professional judgments tailored to the unique needs of a group like the retarded, but it does seek to assure that the hostility or thoughtlessness with which there is reason to be concerned has not carried the day. By invoking heightened scrutiny, the Court recognizes, and compels lower courts to recognize, that a group may well be the target of the sort of prejudiced, thoughtless, or stereotyped action that offends principles of equality found in the Fourteenth Amendment. Where classifications based on a particular characteristic have done so in the past, and the threat that they may do so remains, heightened scrutiny is appropriate....

## IV

In light of the scrutiny that should be applied here, Cleburne's ordinance sweeps too broadly to dispel the suspicion that it rests on a bare desire to treat the retarded as outsiders, pariahs who do not belong in the community....

## V

The Court's opinion approaches the task of principled equal protection adjudication in what I view as precisely the wrong way. The formal label under which an equal protection claim is reviewed is less important than careful identification of the interest at stake and the extent to which society recognizes the classification as an invidious one. Yet in focusing obsessively on the appropriate label to give its standard of review, the Court fails to identify the interests at stake or to articulate the principle that classifications based on mental retardation must be carefully examined to assure they do not rest on impermissible assumptions or false stereotypes regarding individual ability and need. No guidance is thereby given as to when the Court's freewheeling, and potentially dangerous, "rational-basis standard" is to be employed, nor is attention directed to the invidiousness of grouping all retarded individuals together.... I therefore concur in the judgment in part and dissent in part.

### *Note:* Cleburne, *Suspect Class Analysis and Rational Basis Review*

1. *Cleburne* was a watershed case. It marked the last time the Court seriously considered whether a group should be granted suspect class status. Recall that Chapter 12 presented cases performing similar analyses — recall also that by the end of the 1970s the Court was encountering difficulties with suspect class analysis.

Those difficulties fully manifested in *Cleburne*. Justice White's majority and Justice Marshall's partial dissent clashed over several fundamental aspects of suspect class analysis, including the significance of the fact that the intellectually disabled had won several legislative victories, and the fact that some differential treatment of that group was unquestionably appropriate. Perhaps even more notably, Justice White concluded his suspect class analysis (in the paragraph in Part III beginning "Fourth") by essentially conceding that the intellectually disabled satisfied at least some of the criteria for suspect class status, but refusing to grant it because *other* similarly-situated groups might then be able to claim that same status. What do you think of a doctrinal approach (like suspect class analysis) that leads the Court to reject its logical implications because those implications are undesirable?

Note also that earlier in his opinion Justice White worried that granting suspect class status might be problematic because courts applying heightened scrutiny to intellectual disability classifications might find it difficult to evaluate claims that particular types of differential treatment (*e.g.*, special education) constituted invidious, not appropriate, discrimination. Is it appropriate for a court to employ such practical considerations when deciding whether a group is a suspect (or quasi-suspect) class? What does the Court's anxiety suggest about what it is really saying when in *Cleburne* it denies that status to the intellectually disabled? We will return to this issue in Chapter 17, when we consider Congress's power to enforce the Equal Protection Clause.

Note also Justice Stevens' general critique of the entire enterprise of suspect class/ tiered scrutiny analysis. Recall Chapter 12's materials that dealt with that same jurisprudence. Now that you've seen those materials and Justice Stevens' critique, what is your ultimate verdict on *Carolene Products*-based suspect class analysis?

2. Consider now what came next in the majority opinion — the Court's decision that the city's action failed the rational basis test. As you saw in Chapter 11, traditional rational basis analysis is exceptionally deferential. Is *Cleburne*'s rational basis analysis similarly deferential? Can you find hints in the opinion suggesting that it's not? Why do you think the Court scrutinized the city's decision the way it did?

3. Ultimately, the Court concluded that the city's action was infected with animus. How does the Court understand that concept? How do you think it reached that con-

clusion? Didn't the city offer legitimate justifications for its decision? Why do you think the Court rejected those justifications?

## Romer v. Evans

### 517 U.S. 620 (1996)

Justice KENNEDY delivered the opinion of the Court.

One century ago, the first Justice Harlan admonished this Court that the Constitution "neither knows nor tolerates classes among citizens." *Plessy v. Ferguson* (1896) (dissenting opinion) [*Supra.* Chapter 13]. Unheeded then, those words now are understood to state a commitment to the law's neutrality where the rights of persons are at stake. The Equal Protection Clause enforces this principle and today requires us to hold invalid a provision of Colorado's Constitution.

I

The enactment challenged in this case is an amendment to the Constitution of the State of Colorado, adopted in a 1992 statewide referendum. The parties and the state courts refer to it as "Amendment 2," its designation when submitted to the voters. The impetus for the amendment and the contentious campaign that preceded its adoption came in large part from ordinances that had been passed in various Colorado municipalities. For example, the cities of Aspen and Boulder and the city and County of Denver each had enacted ordinances which banned discrimination in many transactions and activities, including housing, employment, education, public accommodations, and health and welfare services. What gave rise to the statewide controversy was the protection the ordinances afforded to persons discriminated against by reason of their sexual orientation. Amendment 2 repeals these ordinances to the extent they prohibit discrimination on the basis of "homosexual, lesbian or bisexual orientation, conduct, practices or relationships."

Yet Amendment 2, in explicit terms, does more than repeal or rescind these provisions. It prohibits all legislative, executive or judicial action at any level of state or local government designed to protect the named class, a class we shall refer to as homosexual persons or gays and lesbians. The amendment reads:

> No Protected Status Based on Homosexual, Lesbian or Bisexual Orientation. Neither the State of Colorado, through any of its branches or departments, nor any of its agencies, political subdivisions, municipalities or school districts, shall enact, adopt or enforce any statute, regulation, ordinance or policy whereby homosexual, lesbian or bisexual orientation, conduct, practices or relationships shall constitute or otherwise be the basis of or entitle any person or class of persons to have or claim any minority status, quota preferences, protected status or claim of discrimination. This Section of the Constitution shall be in all respects self-executing.

Soon after Amendment 2 was adopted, this litigation to declare its invalidity and enjoin its enforcement was commenced in the District Court for the City and County of Denver.... Although Governor Romer had been on record opposing the adoption of Amendment 2, he was named in his official capacity as a defendant, together with the Colorado Attorney General and the State of Colorado.

The trial court granted a preliminary injunction to stay enforcement of Amendment 2, and an appeal was taken to the Supreme Court of Colorado. Sustaining the interim injunction and remanding the case for further proceedings, the State Supreme Court held that Amendment 2 was subject to strict scrutiny under the Fourteenth Amendment because it infringed the fundamental right of gays and lesbians to participate in the political process.... On remand, the State advanced various arguments in an effort to show that Amendment 2 was narrowly tailored to serve compelling interests, but the trial court found none sufficient. It enjoined enforcement of Amendment 2, and the Supreme Court of Colorado, in a second opinion, affirmed the ruling. We granted certiorari, and now affirm the judgment, but on a rationale different from that adopted by the State Supreme Court.

II

The State's principal argument in defense of Amendment 2 is that it puts gays and lesbians in the same position as all other persons. So, the State says, the measure does no more than deny homosexuals special rights. This reading of the amendment's language is implausible. We rely not upon our own interpretation of the amendment but upon the authoritative construction of Colorado's Supreme Court. The state court, deeming it unnecessary to determine the full extent of the amendment's reach, found it invalid even on a modest reading of its implications. The critical discussion of the amendment, set out in *Evans I*, is as follows:

> The immediate objective of Amendment 2 is, at a minimum, to repeal existing statutes, regulations, ordinances, and policies of state and local entities that barred discrimination based on sexual orientation.... The 'ultimate effect' of Amendment 2 is to prohibit any governmental entity from adopting similar, or more protective statutes, regulations, ordinances, or policies in the future unless the state constitution is first amended to permit such measures.

Sweeping and comprehensive is the change in legal status effected by this law.... Homosexuals, by state decree, are put in a solitary class with respect to transactions and relations in both the private and governmental spheres. The amendment withdraws from homosexuals, but no others, specific legal protection from the injuries caused by discrimination, and it forbids reinstatement of these laws and policies.

The change Amendment 2 works in the legal status of gays and lesbians in the private sphere is far reaching, both on its own terms and when considered in light of the structure and operation of modern anti discrimination laws. That structure is well illustrated by contemporary statutes and ordinances prohibiting discrimination by providers of public accommodations. "At common law, innkeepers, smiths, and others who 'made profession of a public employment,' were prohibited from refusing, without good reason, to serve a customer." The duty was a general one and did not specify protection for particular groups. The common-law rules, however, proved insufficient in many instances.... In consequence, most States have chosen to counter discrimination by enacting detailed statutory schemes.

Colorado's state and municipal laws typify this emerging tradition of statutory protection and follow a consistent pattern. The laws first enumerate the persons or entities subject to a duty not to discriminate. The list goes well beyond the entities covered by the common law. The Boulder ordinance, for example, has a comprehensive definition of entities deemed places of "public accommodation." They include "any place of business engaged in any sales to the general public and any place that offers services, facilities, privileges, or advantages to the general public or that receives financial support through solicitation of the general public or through governmental subsidy of any kind." The Denver ordinance is of similar breadth, applying, for example, to hotels, restaurants, hospitals, dental clinics, theaters, banks, common carriers, travel and insurance agencies, and "shops and stores dealing with goods or services of any kind."

These statutes and ordinances also depart from the common law by enumerating the groups or persons within their ambit of protection. Enumeration is the essential device used to make the duty not to discriminate concrete and to provide guidance for those who must comply. In following this approach, Colorado's state and local governments have not limited antidiscrimination laws to groups that have so far been given the protection of heightened equal protection scrutiny under our cases. Rather, they set forth an extensive catalog of traits which cannot be the basis for discrimination, including age, military status, marital status, pregnancy, parenthood, custody of a minor child, political affiliation, physical or mental disability of an individual or of his or her associates—and, in recent times, sexual orientation.

Amendment 2 bars homosexuals from securing protection against the injuries that these public-accommodations laws address. That in itself is a severe consequence, but there is more. Amendment 2, in addition, nullifies specific legal protections for this targeted class in all transactions in housing, sale of real estate, insurance, health and welfare services, private education, and employment.

Not confined to the private sphere, Amendment 2 also operates to repeal and forbid all laws or policies providing specific protection for gays or lesbians from discrimination by every level of Colorado government. The State Supreme Court cited two examples of protections in the governmental sphere that are now rescinded and may not be reintroduced. The first is Colorado Executive Order D0035 (1990), which forbids employment discrimination against "all state employees, classified and exempt on the basis of sexual orientation." Also repealed, and now forbidden, are "various provisions prohibiting discrimination based on sexual orientation at state colleges." The repeal of these measures and the prohibition against their future reenactment demonstrate that Amendment 2 has the same force and effect in Colorado's governmental sector as it does elsewhere and that it applies to policies as well as ordinary legislation.

Amendment 2's reach may not be limited to specific laws passed for the benefit of gays and lesbians. It is a fair, if not necessary, inference from the broad language of the amendment that it deprives gays and lesbians even of the protection of general laws and policies that prohibit arbitrary discrimination in governmental and private settings. See, e.g., Colo.Rev.Stat. §24-4-106(7) (1988) (agency action subject to judicial review under arbitrary and capricious standard); §18-8-405 (making it a criminal offense for a public servant knowingly, arbitrarily, or capriciously to refrain from performing a duty imposed on him by law); §10-3-1104(1)(f) (prohibiting "unfair discrimination" in insurance); 4 Colo.Code of Regulations 801-1, Policy 11-1 (1983) (prohibiting discrimination in state employment on grounds of specified traits or "other non-merit factor"). At some point in the systematic administration of these laws, an official must determine whether homosexuality is an arbitrary and, thus, forbidden basis for decision. Yet a decision to that effect would itself amount to a policy prohibiting discrimination on the basis of homosexuality, and so would appear to be no more valid under Amendment 2 than the specific prohibitions against discrimination the state court held invalid.

If this consequence follows from Amendment 2, as its broad language suggests, it would compound the constitutional difficulties the law creates. The state court did not decide whether the amendment has this effect, however, and neither need we. In the course of rejecting the argument that Amendment 2 is intended to conserve resources to fight discrimination against suspect classes, the Colorado Supreme Court made the limited observation that the amendment is not intended to affect many anti discrimination laws protecting nonsuspect classes. In our view that does not resolve the issue. In any event, even if, as we doubt, homosexuals could find some safe harbor in laws of general application, we cannot accept the view that Amendment 2's prohibition on specific legal protections does no more than deprive homosexuals of special rights. To the contrary, the amendment imposes a special disability upon those persons alone. Homosexuals are forbidden the safeguards that others enjoy or may seek without constraint. They can obtain specific protection against discrimination only by enlisting the citizenry of Colorado to amend the State Constitution or perhaps, on the State's view, by trying to pass helpful laws of general applicability. This is so no matter how local or discrete the harm, no matter how public and widespread the injury. We find nothing special in the protections Amendment 2 withholds. These are protections taken for granted by most people either because they already have them or do not need them; these are protections against exclusion from an almost limitless number of transactions and endeavors that constitute ordinary civic life in a free society.

### III

The Fourteenth Amendment's promise that no person shall be denied the equal protection of the laws must coexist with the practical necessity that most legislation classifies for one purpose or another, with resulting disadvantage to various groups or persons. *Personnel Administrator of Mass. v. Feeney*, 442 U.S. 256 (1979) [Note *supra.* Chapter 14]; *F.S. Royster Guano Co. v. Virginia*, 253 U.S. 412 (1920). We have attempted to reconcile the principle with the reality by stating that, if a law neither burdens a fundamental right nor targets a suspect class, we will uphold the legislative classification so long as it bears a rational relation to some legitimate end.

Amendment 2 fails, indeed defies, even this conventional inquiry. First, the amendment has the peculiar property of imposing a broad and undifferentiated disability on a single named group, an exceptional and, as we shall explain, invalid form of legislation. Second, its sheer breadth is so discontinuous with the reasons offered for it that the amendment seems inexplicable by anything but animus toward the class it affects; it lacks a rational relationship to legitimate state interests.

Taking the first point, even in the ordinary equal protection case calling for the most deferential of standards, we insist on knowing the relation between the classification adopted and the object to be attained. The search for the link between classification and objective gives substance to the Equal Protection Clause; it provides guidance and discipline for the legislature, which is entitled to know what sorts of laws it can pass; and it marks the limits of our own authority. In the ordinary case, a law will be sustained if it can be said to advance a legitimate government interest, even if the law seems unwise or works to the disadvantage of a particular group, or if the rationale for it seems tenuous. See *Williamson v. Lee Optical of Okla., Inc.*, 348 U.S. 483 (1955) [Note *supra*. Chapter 7] (assumed health concerns justified law favoring optometrists over opticians); *Railway Express Agency, Inc. v. New York* (1949) [*Supra*. Chapter 11] (potential traffic hazards justified exemption of vehicles advertising the owner's products from general advertising ban). The laws challenged in the cases just cited were narrow enough in scope and grounded in a sufficient factual context for us to ascertain some relation between the classification and the purpose it served. By requiring that the classification bear a rational relationship to an independent and legitimate legislative end, we ensure that classifications are not drawn for the purpose of disadvantaging the group burdened by the law. See *Railroad Retirement Bd. v. Fritz* (1980) [*Supra*. Chapter 11] (STEVENS, J., concurring) ("If the adverse impact on the disfavored class is an apparent aim of the legislature, its impartiality would be suspect").

Amendment 2 confounds this normal process of judicial review. It is at once too narrow and too broad. It identifies persons by a single trait and then denies them protection across the board. The resulting disqualification of a class of persons from the right to seek specific protection from the law is unprecedented in our jurisprudence. The absence of precedent for Amendment 2 is itself instructive; "discriminations of an unusual character especially suggest careful consideration to determine whether they are obnoxious to the constitutional provision." *Louisville Gas & Elec. Co. v. Coleman*, 277 U.S. 32 (1928).

It is not within our constitutional tradition to enact laws of this sort. Central both to the idea of the rule of law and to our own Constitution's guarantee of equal protection is the principle that government and each of its parts remain open on impartial terms to all who seek its assistance. "Equal protection of the laws is not achieved through indiscriminate imposition of inequalities." *Sweatt v. Painter*, 339 U.S. 629

(1950) [Note *supra.* Chapter 13]. Respect for this principle explains why laws singling out a certain class of citizens for disfavored legal status or general hardships are rare. A law declaring that in general it shall be more difficult for one group of citizens than for all others to seek aid from the government is itself a denial of equal protection of the laws in the most literal sense. " 'The guaranty of 'equal protection of the laws is a pledge of the protection of equal laws.' " *Skinner v. Oklahoma*, 316 U.S. 545 (1942) [Note *supra.* Chapter 8] (quoting *Yick Wo v. Hopkins*, 118 U.S. 356 (1886) [Note *supra.* chapter 14]).

*Davis v. Beason*, 133 U.S. 333 (1890), not cited by the parties but relied upon by the dissent, is not evidence that Amendment 2 is within our constitutional tradition, and any reliance upon it as authority for sustaining the amendment is misplaced. In *Davis*, the Court approved an Idaho territorial statute denying Mormons, polygamists, and advocates of polygamy the right to vote and to hold office because, as the Court construed the statute, it "simply excludes from the privilege of voting, or of holding any office of honor, trust or profit, those who have been convicted of certain offences, and those who advocate a practical resistance to the laws of the Territory and justify and approve the commission of crimes forbidden by it." To the extent *Davis* held that persons advocating a certain practice may be denied the right to vote, it is no longer good law. To the extent it held that the groups designated in the statute may be deprived of the right to vote because of their status, its ruling could not stand without surviving strict scrutiny, a most doubtful outcome. To the extent *Davis* held that a convicted felon may be denied the right to vote, its holding is not implicated by our decision and is unexceptionable.

A second and related point is that laws of the kind now before us raise the inevitable inference that the disadvantage imposed is born of animosity toward the class of persons affected. "If the constitutional conception of 'equal protection of the laws' means anything, it must at the very least mean that a bare ... desire to harm a politically unpopular group cannot constitute a *legitimate* governmental interest." *Department of Agriculture v. Moreno* (1973) [Note *supra.* this chapter]. Even laws enacted for broad and ambitious purposes often can be explained by reference to legitimate public policies which justify the incidental disadvantages they impose on certain persons. Amendment 2, however, in making a general announcement that gays and lesbians shall not have any particular protections from the law, inflicts on them immediate, continuing, and real injuries that outrun and belie any legitimate justifications that may be claimed for it. We conclude that, in addition to the far-reaching deficiencies of Amendment 2 that we have noted, the principles it offends, in another sense, are conventional and venerable; a law must bear a rational relationship to a legitimate governmental purpose, and Amendment 2 does not.

The primary rationale the State offers for Amendment 2 is respect for other citizens' freedom of association, and in particular the liberties of landlords or employers who have personal or religious objections to homosexuality. Colorado also cites its interest in conserving resources to fight discrimination against other groups. The breadth of the amendment is so far removed from these particular justifications that we find it impossible to credit them. We cannot say that Amendment 2 is directed to any identifiable legitimate purpose or discrete objective. It is a status-based enactment divorced from any factual context from which we could discern a relationship to legitimate state interests; it is a classification of persons undertaken for its own sake, something the Equal Protection Clause does not permit. "Class legislation ... [is] obnoxious to the prohibitions of the Fourteenth Amendment...." *Civil Rights Cases*, 109 U.S. 3 (1883).

We must conclude that Amendment 2 classifies homosexuals not to further a proper legislative end but to make them unequal to everyone else. This Colorado cannot do. A State cannot so deem a class of persons a stranger to its laws. Amendment 2 violates the Equal Protection Clause, and the judgment of the Supreme Court of Colorado is affirmed.

Justice SCALIA, with whom THE CHIEF JUSTICE and Justice THOMAS join, dissenting.

The Court has mistaken a Kulturkampf[*] for a fit of spite. The constitutional amendment before us here is not the manifestation of a "'bare ... desire to harm'" homosexuals, *ante*, but is rather a modest attempt by seemingly tolerant Coloradans to preserve traditional sexual mores against the efforts of a politically powerful minority to revise those mores through use of the laws. That objective, and the means chosen to achieve it, are not only unimpeachable under any constitutional doctrine hitherto pronounced (hence the opinion's heavy reliance upon principles of righteousness rather than judicial holdings); they have been specifically approved by the Congress of the United States and by this Court.

In holding that homosexuality cannot be singled out for disfavorable treatment, the Court contradicts a decision, unchallenged here, pronounced only 10 years ago, see *Bowers v. Hardwick*, 478 U.S. 186 (1986) [Note *supra.* Chapter 10], and places the prestige of this institution behind the proposition that opposition to homosexuality is as reprehensible as racial or religious bias. Whether it is or not is *precisely* the cultural debate that gave rise to the Colorado constitutional amendment (and to the preferential laws against which the amendment was directed). Since the Constitution of the United States says nothing about this subject, it is left to be resolved by normal democratic means, including the democratic adoption of provisions in state constitutions. This Court has no business imposing upon all Americans the resolution favored by the elite class from which the Members of this institution are selected, pronouncing that "animosity" toward homosexuality, *ante*, is evil. I vigorously dissent.

I

Let me first discuss Part II of the Court's opinion, its longest section, which is devoted to rejecting the State's arguments that Amendment 2 "puts gays and lesbians in the same position as all other persons," and "does no more than deny homosexuals

---

\* [Ed. Note: The term "kulturkampf" refers to the efforts of a 19th century German prime minister to reduce the importance of Catholicism in Germany, by leading an anti-Catholic movement.]

special rights.". The Court concludes that this reading of Amendment 2's language is "implausible" under the "authoritative construction" given Amendment 2 by the Supreme Court of Colorado.

In reaching this conclusion, the Court considers it unnecessary to decide the validity of the State's argument that Amendment 2 does not deprive homosexuals of the "protection [afforded by] general laws and policies that prohibit arbitrary discrimination in governmental and private settings." I agree that we need not resolve that dispute, because the Supreme Court of Colorado has resolved it for us. In the case below, the Colorado court stated:

> It is significant to note that Colorado law currently proscribes discrimination against persons who are not suspect classes, including discrimination based on age, marital or family status, veterans' status, and for any legal, off-duty conduct such as smoking tobacco. *Of course Amendment 2 is not intended to have any effect on this legislation, but seeks only to prevent the adoption of antidiscrimination laws intended to protect gays, lesbians, and bisexuals* (emphasis added).

The Court utterly fails to distinguish this portion of the Colorado court's opinion. Colorado Rev. Stat. § 24-34-402.5, which this passage authoritatively declares *not* to be affected by Amendment 2, was respondents' primary example of a generally applicable law whose protections would be unavailable to homosexuals under Amendment 2. The clear import of the Colorado court's conclusion that it is not affected is that "general laws and policies that prohibit arbitrary discrimination" would continue to prohibit discrimination on the basis of homosexual conduct as well. This analysis, which is fully in accord with (indeed, follows inescapably from) the text of the constitutional provision, lays to rest such horribles, raised in the course of oral argument, as the prospect that assaults upon homosexuals could not be prosecuted. The amendment prohibits *special treatment* of homosexuals, and nothing more. It would not affect, for example, a requirement of state law that pensions be paid to all retiring state employees with a certain length of service; homosexual employees, as well as others, would be entitled to that benefit. But it would prevent the State or any municipality from making death-benefit payments to the "life partner" of a homosexual when it does not make such payments to the long-time roommate of a nonhomosexual employee. Or again, it does not affect the requirement of the State's general insurance laws that customers be afforded coverage without discrimination unrelated to anticipated risk. Thus, homosexuals could not be denied coverage, or charged a greater premium, with respect to auto collision insurance; but neither the State nor any municipality could require that distinctive health insurance risks associated with homosexuality (if there are any) be ignored.

Despite all of its hand wringing about the potential effect of Amendment 2 on general antidiscrimination laws, the Court's opinion ultimately does not dispute all this, but assumes it to be true. The only denial of equal treatment it contends homosexuals have suffered is this: They may not obtain *preferential* treatment without amending the State Constitution. That is to say, the principle underlying the Court's opinion is that one who is accorded equal treatment under the laws, but cannot as readily as others obtain *preferential* treatment under the laws, has been denied equal protection of the laws. If merely stating this alleged "equal protection" violation does not suffice to refute it, our constitutional jurisprudence has achieved terminal silliness.

The central thesis of the Court's reasoning is that any group is denied equal protection when, to obtain advantage (or, presumably, to avoid disadvantage), it must have recourse to a more general and hence more difficult level of political decision-making than others. The world has never heard of such a principle, which is why the Court's opinion is so long on emotive utterance and so short on relevant legal citation. And it seems to me most unlikely that any multilevel democracy can function under such a principle....

II

I turn next to whether there was a legitimate rational basis for the substance of the constitutional amendment—for the prohibition of special protection for homosexuals. It is unsurprising that the Court avoids discussion of this question, since the answer is so obviously yes. The case most relevant to the issue before us today is not even mentioned in the Court's opinion: In *Bowers*, we held that the Constitution does not prohibit what virtually all States had done from the founding of the Republic until very recent years—making homosexual conduct a crime. That holding is unassailable, except by those who think that the Constitution changes to suit current fashions.... If it is constitutionally permissible for a State to make homosexual conduct criminal, surely it is constitutionally permissible for a State to enact other laws merely *disfavoring* homosexual conduct.... And *a fortiori* it is constitutionally permissible for a State to adopt a provision *not even* disfavoring homosexual conduct, but merely prohibiting all levels of state government from bestowing *special protections* upon homosexual conduct. Respondents (who, unlike the Court, cannot afford the luxury of ignoring inconvenient precedent) counter *Bowers* with the argument that a greater-includes-the-lesser rationale cannot justify Amendment 2's application to individuals who do not engage in homosexual acts, but are merely of homosexual "orientation." Some Courts of Appeals have concluded that, with respect to laws of this sort at least, that is a distinction without a difference. The Supreme Court of Colorado itself appears to be of this view. See 882 P.2d, at 1349–1350 ("Amendment 2 targets this class of persons based on four characteristics: sexual orientation; conduct; practices, and relationships. Each characteristic provides a potentially different way of identifying that class of persons who are gay, lesbian, or bisexual. These four characteristics are not truly severable from one another because each provides nothing more than a different way of identifying *the same class of persons*") (emphasis added).

But assuming that, in Amendment 2, a person of homosexual "orientation" is someone who does not engage in homosexual conduct but merely has a tendency or desire to do so, *Bowers* still suffices to establish a rational basis for the provision. If it is rational to criminalize the conduct, surely it is rational to deny special favor and protection to those with a self-avowed tendency or desire to engage in the conduct....

## III

The foregoing suffices to establish what the Court's failure to cite any case remotely in point would lead one to suspect: No principle set forth in the Constitution, nor even any imagined by this Court in the past 200 years, prohibits what Colorado has done here. But the case for Colorado is much stronger than that. What it has done is not only unprohibited, but eminently reasonable, with close, congressionally approved precedent in earlier constitutional practice.

First, as to its eminent reasonableness. The Court's opinion contains grim, disapproving hints that Coloradans have been guilty of "animus" or "animosity" toward homosexuality, as though that has been established as un-American. Of course it is our moral heritage that one should not hate any human being or class of human beings. But I had thought that one could consider certain conduct reprehensible — murder, for example, or polygamy, or cruelty to animals — and could exhibit even "animus" toward such conduct. Surely that is the only sort of "animus" at issue here: moral disapproval of homosexual conduct, the same sort of moral disapproval that produced the centuries-old criminal laws that we held constitutional in *Bowers*. The Colorado amendment does not, to speak entirely precisely, prohibit giving favored status to people who are *homosexuals*; they can be favored for many reasons — for example, because they are senior citizens or members of racial minorities. But it prohibits giving them favored status *because of their homosexual conduct* — that is, it prohibits favored status *for homosexuality*.

But though Coloradans are, as I say, *entitled* to be hostile toward homosexual conduct, the fact is that the degree of hostility reflected by Amendment 2 is the smallest conceivable. The Court's portrayal of Coloradans as a society fallen victim to pointless, hate-filled "gay-bashing" is so false as to be comical. Colorado not only is one of the 25 States that have repealed their antisodomy laws, but was among the first to do so. But the society that eliminates criminal punishment for homosexual acts does not necessarily abandon the view that homosexuality is morally wrong and socially harmful; often, abolition simply reflects the view that enforcement of such criminal laws involves unseemly intrusion into the intimate lives of citizens.

There is a problem, however, which arises when criminal sanction of homosexuality is eliminated but moral and social disapprobation of homosexuality is meant to be retained. The Court cannot be unaware of that problem; it is evident in many cities of the country, and occasionally bubbles to the surface of the news, in heated political disputes over such matters as the introduction into local schools of books teaching that homosexuality is an optional and fully acceptable "alternative life style." The problem (a problem, that is, for those who wish to retain social disapprobation of homosexuality) is that, because those who engage in homosexual conduct tend to reside in disproportionate numbers in certain communities, and, of course, care about homosexual-rights issues much more ardently than the public at large, they possess political power much greater than their numbers, both locally and statewide. Quite understandably, they devote this political power to achieving not merely a grudging social toleration, but full social acceptance, of homosexuality.

By the time Coloradans were asked to vote on Amendment 2, their exposure to homosexuals' quest for social endorsement was not limited to newspaper accounts of happenings in places such as New York, Los Angeles, San Francisco, and Key West. Three Colorado cities — Aspen, Boulder, and Denver — had enacted ordinances that listed "sexual orientation" as an impermissible ground for discrimination, equating the moral disapproval of homosexual conduct with racial and religious bigotry. The phenomenon had even appeared statewide: The Governor of Colorado had signed an executive order pronouncing that "in the State of Colorado we recognize the diversity in our pluralistic society and strive to bring an end to discrimination in any form," and directing state agency-heads to "ensure non-discrimination" in hiring and promotion based on, among other things, "sexual orientation." I do not mean to be critical of these legislative successes; homosexuals are as entitled to use the legal system for reinforcement of their moral sentiments as is the rest of society. But they are subject to being countered by lawful, democratic countermeasures as well.

That is where Amendment 2 came in. It sought to counter both the geographic concentration and the disproportionate political power of homosexuals by (1) resolving the controversy at the statewide level, and (2) making the election a single-issue contest for both sides. It put directly, to all the citizens of the State, the question: Should homosexuality be given special protection? They answered no. The Court today asserts that this most democratic of procedures is unconstitutional. Lacking any cases to establish that facially absurd proposition, it simply asserts that it must be unconstitutional, because it has never happened before.

> [Amendment 2] identifies persons by a single trait and then denies them protection across the board. The resulting disqualification of a class of persons from the right to seek specific protection from the law is unprecedented in our jurisprudence. The absence of precedent for Amendment 2 is itself instructive....

> It is not within our constitutional tradition to enact laws of this sort. Central both to the idea of the rule of law and to our own Constitution's guarantee of equal protection is the principle that government and each of its parts remain open on impartial terms to all who seek its assistance.

As I have noted above, this is proved false every time a state law prohibiting or disfavoring certain conduct is passed, because such a law prevents the adversely affected group — whether drug addicts, or smokers, or gun owners, or motorcyclists — from changing the policy thus established in "each of [the] parts" of the State....

But there is a much closer analogy, one that involves precisely the effort by the majority of citizens to preserve its view of sexual morality statewide, against the efforts of a geographically concentrated and politically powerful minority to undermine it. The Constitutions of the States of Arizona, Idaho, New Mexico, Oklahoma, and Utah *to this day* contain provisions stating that polygamy is "forever prohibited." Polygamists, and those who have a polygamous "orientation," have been "singled out" by these provisions for much more severe treatment than merely denial of favored status; and that treatment can only be changed by achieving amendment of the state constitutions. The Court's disposition today suggests that these provisions are unconstitutional, and that polygamy must be permitted in these States on a state-legislated, or perhaps even local-option, basis—unless, of course, polygamists for some reason have fewer constitutional rights than homosexuals....

I cannot say that this Court has explicitly approved any of these state constitutional provisions; but it has approved a territorial statutory provision that went even further, depriving polygamists of the ability even to achieve a constitutional amendment, by depriving them of the power to vote. In *Davis v. Beason*, Justice Field wrote for a unanimous Court:

> In our judgment, § 501 of the Revised Statutes of Idaho Territory, which provides that 'no person ... who is a bigamist or polygamist or who teaches, advises, counsels, or encourages any person or persons to become bigamists or polygamists, or to commit any other crime defined by law, or to enter into what is known as plural or celestial marriage, or who is a member of any order, organization or association which teaches, advises, counsels, or encourages its members or devotees or any other persons to commit the crime of bigamy or polygamy, or any other crime defined by law ... is permitted to vote at any election, or to hold any position or office of honor, trust, or profit within this Territory,' *is not open to any constitutional or legal objection* (emphasis added).

... This Court cited *Beason* with approval as recently as 1993, in an opinion authored by the same Justice who writes for the Court today.... Has the Court concluded that the perceived social harm of polygamy is a "legitimate concern of government," and the perceived social harm of homosexuality is not?

### IV

I strongly suspect that the answer to the last question is yes, which leads me to the last point I wish to make: The Court today, announcing that Amendment 2 "defies ... conventional [constitutional] inquiry," and "confounds [the] normal process of judicial review," employs a constitutional theory heretofore unknown to frustrate Colorado's reasonable effort to preserve traditional American moral values. The Court's stern disapproval of "animosity" towards homosexuality might be compared with what an earlier Court (including the revered Justices Harlan and Bradley) said in *Murphy v. Ramsey*, 114 U.S. 15 (1885), rejecting a constitutional challenge to a United States statute that denied the franchise in federal territories to those who engaged in polygamous cohabitation:

> Certainly no legislation can be supposed more wholesome and necessary in the founding of a free, self-governing commonwealth, fit to take rank as one of the co-ordinate States of the Union, than that which seeks to establish it on the basis of the idea of the family, as consisting in and springing from the union for life of one man and one woman in the holy estate of matrimony; the sure foundation of all that is stable and noble in our civilization; the best

guaranty of that reverent morality which is the source of all beneficent progress in social and political improvement.

I would not myself indulge in such official praise for heterosexual monogamy, because I think it no business of the courts (as opposed to the political branches) to take sides in this culture war.

But the Court today has done so, not only by inventing a novel and extravagant constitutional doctrine to take the victory away from traditional forces, but even by verbally disparaging as bigotry adherence to traditional attitudes. To suggest, for example, that this constitutional amendment springs from nothing more than "'a bare ... desire to harm a politically unpopular group,'" *ante*, quoting *Department of Agriculture v. Moreno*, is nothing short of insulting. (It is also nothing short of preposterous to call "politically unpopular" a group which enjoys enormous influence in American media and politics, and which, as the trial court here noted, though composing no more than 4% of the population had the support of 46% of the voters on Amendment 2).

When the Court takes sides in the culture wars, it tends to be with the knights rather than the villeins—and more specifically with the Templars, reflecting the views and values of the lawyer class from which the Court's Members are drawn. How that class feels about homosexuality will be evident to anyone who wishes to interview job applicants at virtually any of the Nation's law schools. The interviewer may refuse to offer a job because the applicant is a Republican; because he is an adulterer; because he went to the wrong prep school or belongs to the wrong country club; because he eats snails; because he is a womanizer; because she wears real-animal fur; or even because he hates the Chicago Cubs. But if the interviewer should wish not to be an associate or partner of an applicant because he disapproves of the applicant's homosexuality, *then* he will have violated the pledge which the Association of American Law Schools requires all its member schools to exact from job interviewers: "assurance of the employer's willingness" to hire homosexuals. Bylaws of the Association of American Law Schools. This law-school view of what "prejudices" must be stamped out may be contrasted with the more plebeian attitudes that apparently still prevail in the United States Congress, which has been unresponsive to repeated attempts to extend to homosexuals the protections of federal civil rights laws, and which took the pains to exclude them specifically from the Americans with Disabilities Act of 1990.

\* \* \*

Today's opinion has no foundation in American constitutional law, and barely pretends to. The people of Colorado have adopted an entirely reasonable provision which does not even disfavor homosexuals in any substantive sense, but merely denies them preferential treatment. Amendment 2 is designed to prevent piecemeal deterioration of the sexual morality favored by a majority of Coloradans, and is not only an appropriate means to that legitimate end, but a means that Americans have employed before. Striking it down is an act, not of judicial judgment, but of political will. I dissent.

### *Note: Justice O'Connor's Concurrence in* Lawrence v. Texas

1. Justice Scalia's dissent in *Romer* relied heavily on *Bowers v. Hardwick*, 478 U.S. 186 (1986) (Note *supra.* Chapter 10), which upheld, against a substantive due process challenge, Georgia's sodomy statute. The Georgia law was sex-neutral; that is, it prohibited both opposite- and same-sex couples from engaging in sodomy. In *Lawrence v. Texas* (2003) (*Supra.* Chapter 10), the Court overruled *Bowers* and struck down, on substantive due process grounds, Texas's sodomy law, which criminalized only same-sex sexual activity.

2. Justice O'Connor joined the *Bowers* majority. In *Lawrence*, she wrote a separate opinion, declining to vote to overrule *Bowers* and instead relying on equal protection to strike down the Texas law. She wrote as follows:

> The Equal Protection Clause of the Fourteenth Amendment "is essentially a direction that all persons similarly situated should be treated alike." *Cleburne v. Cleburne Living Center, Inc.* (1985) [*Supra.* this chapter]. Under our rational basis standard of review, "legislation is presumed to be valid and will be sustained if the classification drawn by the statute is rationally related to a legitimate state interest." *Cleburne*; see also *Department of Agriculture v. Moreno* (1973) [Note *supra.* this chapter]; *Romer v. Evans* (1996) [*Supra.* this chapter]; *Nordlinger v. Hahn* (1992) [Note *supra.* Chapter 11].
>
> Laws such as economic or tax legislation that are scrutinized under rational basis review normally pass constitutional muster, since "the Constitution presumes that even improvident decisions will eventually be rectified by the democratic processes." *Cleburne*; *Williamson v. Lee Optical*, 348 U.S. 483 (1955) [Note *supra.* Chapter 7]. We have consistently held, however, that some objectives, such as "a bare ... desire to harm a politically unpopular group," are not legitimate state interests. *Moreno.* See also *Cleburne*; *Romer.* When a law exhibits such a desire to harm a politically unpopular group, we have applied a more searching form of rational basis review to strike down such laws under the Equal Protection Clause.
>
> We have been most likely to apply rational basis review to hold a law unconstitutional under the Equal Protection Clause where, as here, the challenged legislation inhibits personal relationships. In *Moreno*, for example, we held that a law preventing those households containing an individual unrelated to any other member of the household from receiving food stamps violated equal protection because the purpose of the law was to "discriminate against hippies." The asserted governmental interest in preventing food stamp fraud was not deemed sufficient to satisfy rational basis review. In *Eisenstadt v. Baird* (1972) [Note *supra.* Chapter 9], we refused to sanction a law that discriminated between married and unmarried persons by prohibiting the distribution of contraceptives to single persons. Likewise, in *Cleburne*, we held that it was irrational for a State to require a home for the mentally disabled to obtain a special use permit when other residences—like fraternity houses and apart-

ment buildings—did not have to obtain such a permit. And in *Romer*, we disallowed a state statute that "impos[ed] a broad and undifferentiated disability on a single named group"—specifically, homosexuals.

The statute at issue here makes sodomy a crime only if a person "engages in deviate sexual intercourse with another individual of the same sex." Sodomy between opposite-sex partners, however, is not a crime in Texas. That is, Texas treats the same conduct differently based solely on the participants. Those harmed by this law are people who have a same-sex sexual orientation and thus are more likely to engage in behavior prohibited by § 21.06 [the Texas law].

The Texas statute makes homosexuals unequal in the eyes of the law by making particular conduct—and only that conduct—subject to criminal sanction. It appears that prosecutions under Texas' sodomy law are rare. This case shows, however, that prosecutions under § 21.06 *do* occur....

Texas attempts to justify its law, and the effects of the law, by arguing that the statute satisfies rational basis review because it furthers the legitimate governmental interest of the promotion of morality. In *Bowers*, we held that a state law criminalizing sodomy as applied to homosexual couples did not violate substantive due process. We rejected the argument that no rational basis existed to justify the law, pointing to the government's interest in promoting morality. The only question in front of the Court in *Bowers* was whether the substantive component of the Due Process Clause protected a right to engage in homosexual sodomy. *Bowers* did not hold that moral disapproval of a group is a rational basis under the Equal Protection Clause to criminalize homosexual sodomy when heterosexual sodomy is not punished.

This case raises a different issue than *Bowers*: whether, under the Equal Protection Clause, moral disapproval is a legitimate state interest to justify by itself a statute that bans homosexual sodomy, but not heterosexual sodomy. It is not. Moral disapproval of this group, like a bare desire to harm the group, is an interest that is insufficient to satisfy rational basis review under the Equal Protection Clause. See, e.g., *Moreno*; *Romer*. Indeed, we have never held that moral disapproval, without any other asserted state interest, is a sufficient rationale under the Equal Protection Clause to justify a law that discriminates among groups of persons.

Moral disapproval of a group cannot be a legitimate governmental interest under the Equal Protection Clause because legal classifications must not be "drawn for the purpose of disadvantaging the group burdened by the law." *Romer*. Texas' invocation of moral disapproval as a legitimate state interest proves nothing more than Texas' desire to criminalize homosexual sodomy. But the Equal Protection Clause prevents a State from creating "a classification of persons undertaken for its own sake." *Id.* And because Texas so rarely enforces its sodomy law as applied to private, consensual acts, the law serves more as a statement of dislike and disapproval against homosexuals than as a tool to stop criminal behavior. The Texas sodomy law "raises the inevitable inference that the disadvantage imposed is born of animosity toward the class of persons affected." *Id.* ...

A State can of course assign certain consequences to a violation of its criminal law. But the State cannot single out one identifiable class of citizens for punishment that does not apply to everyone else, with moral disapproval as the only asserted state interest for the law. The Texas sodomy statute subjects homosexuals to "a lifelong penalty and stigma. A legislative classification that threatens the creation of an underclass ... cannot be reconciled with" the Equal Protection Clause. *Plyler v. Doe* (1982) (Powell, J., concurring) [Note *supra.* Chapter 12]

Whether a sodomy law that is neutral both in effect and application, see *Yick Wo v. Hopkins* (1886) [Note *supra.* Chapter 14], would violate the substantive component of the Due Process Clause is an issue that need not be decided today. I am confident, however, that so long as the Equal Protection Clause requires a sodomy law to apply equally to the private consensual conduct of homosexuals and heterosexuals alike, such a law would not long stand in our democratic society. In the words of Justice Jackson:

> The framers of the Constitution knew, and we should not forget today, that there is no more effective practical guaranty against arbitrary and unreasonable government than to require that the principles of law which officials would impose upon a minority be imposed generally. Conversely, nothing opens the door to arbitrary action so effectively as to allow those officials to pick and choose only a few to whom they will apply legislation and thus to escape the political retribution that might be visited upon them if larger numbers were affected." *Railway Express Agency, Inc. v. New York* (1949) (concurring opinion) [*Supra.* Chapter 11].

That this law as applied to private, consensual conduct is unconstitutional under the Equal Protection Clause does not mean that other laws distinguishing between heterosexuals and homosexuals would similarly fail under rational basis review. Texas cannot assert any legitimate state interest here, such as national security or preserving the traditional institution of marriage. Unlike the moral disapproval of same-sex relations — the asserted state interest in this case — other reasons exist to promote the institution of marriage beyond mere moral disapproval of an excluded group.

A law branding one class of persons as criminal based solely on the State's moral disapproval of that class and the conduct associated with that class runs contrary to the values of the Constitution and the Equal Protection Clause, under any standard of review. I therefore concur in the Court's judgment that Texas' sodomy law banning "deviate sexual intercourse" between consenting adults of the same sex, but not between consenting adults of different sexes, is unconstitutional.

3. In addition to dissenting from the *Lawrence* majority's due process analysis, Justice Scalia, again joined by Chief Justice Rehnquist and Justice Thomas, also disagreed with Justice O'Connor's equal protection analysis. He wrote, in relevant part:

> Justice O'CONNOR simply decrees application of "a more searching form of rational basis review" to the Texas statute. The cases she cites do not recognize such a standard, and reach their conclusions only after finding, as required by conventional rational-basis analysis, that no conceivable legitimate state interest supports the classification at issue. See *Romer*; *Cleburne*; *Moreno*. Nor does Justice O'CONNOR explain precisely what her "more searching form" of rational-basis review consists of. It must at least mean, however, that laws exhibiting "a desire to harm a politically unpopular group" are invalid *even though* there may be a conceivable rational basis to support them.
>
> This reasoning leaves on pretty shaky grounds state laws limiting marriage to opposite-sex couples. Justice O'CONNOR seeks to preserve them by the conclusory statement that "preserving the traditional institution of marriage" is a legitimate state interest. But "preserving the traditional institution of marriage" is just a kinder way of describing the State's *moral disapproval* of same-sex couples. Texas's interest in § 21.06 could be recast in similarly euphemistic terms: "preserving the traditional sexual mores of our society." In the jurisprudence Justice O'CONNOR has seemingly created, judges can validate laws by characterizing them as "preserving the traditions of society" (good); or invalidate them by characterizing them as "expressing moral disapproval" (bad).

4. Justice Scalia closed his *Lawrence* dissent with the following:

> One of the benefits of leaving regulation of this matter to the people rather than to the courts is that the people, unlike judges, need not carry things to their logical conclusion. The people may feel that their disapprobation of homosexual conduct is strong enough to disallow homosexual marriage, but not strong enough to criminalize private homosexual acts — and may legislate accordingly. The Court today pretends that it possesses a similar freedom of action, so that we need not fear judicial imposition of homosexual marriage, as has recently occurred in Canada.... At the end of its opinion — after having laid waste the foundations of our rational-basis jurisprudence — the Court says that the present case "does not involve whether the government must give formal recognition to any relationship that homosexual persons seek to enter." Do not believe it. More illuminating than this bald, unreasoned disclaimer is the progression of thought displayed by an earlier passage in the Court's opinion, which notes the constitutional protections afforded to "personal decisions relating to *marriage*, procreation, contraception, family relationships, child rearing, and education," and then declares that "persons in a homosexual relationship may seek autonomy for these purposes, just as

heterosexual persons do" (emphasis added). Today's opinion dismantles the structure of constitutional law that has permitted a distinction to be made between heterosexual and homosexual unions, insofar as formal recognition in marriage is concerned. If moral disapprobation of homosexual conduct is "no legitimate state interest" for purposes of proscribing that conduct, *ante*; and if, as the Court coos (casting aside all pretense of neutrality), "when sexuality finds overt expression in intimate conduct with another person, the conduct can be but one element in a personal bond that is more enduring," what justification could there possibly be for denying the benefits of marriage to homosexual couples exercising "the liberty protected by the Constitution," *id.*? Surely not the encouragement of procreation, since the sterile and the elderly are allowed to marry. This case "does not involve" the issue of homosexual marriage only if one entertains the belief that principle and logic have nothing to do with the decisions of this Court. Many will hope that, as the Court comfortingly assures us, this is so.

The matters appropriate for this Court's resolution are only three: Texas's prohibition of sodomy neither infringes a "fundamental right" (which the Court does not dispute), nor is unsupported by a rational relation to what the Constitution considers a legitimate state interest, nor denies the equal protection of the laws. I dissent.

## *Note:* United States v. Windsor

1. In 1996, when the first same-sex marriage litigation (in Hawaii) was showing signs of success, Congress enacted the Defense of Marriage Act (DOMA). Among other things, DOMA restricted the effect one state's same-sex marriage decision would have on marriage rights in other states. In addition, Section 3 of the law defined marriage for federal purposes (*e.g.*, Social Security survivor's benefits) as exclusively between a man and a woman, regardless of whether the couple had been validly married according to a state's law.

2. In 2013, litigation reached the Supreme Court challenging Section 3. *United States v. Windsor*, 133 S.Ct. 2675 (2013) concerned a federal estate tax liability Edie Windsor was said to have owed the federal government when her same-sex spouse, Thea Spyer, passed away. Windsor and Spyer, New York residents, had married in Canada, and New York recognized their Canadian marriage. Windsor challenged the federal tax liability, which would have been much lower had the federal government recognized her as married. The Justice Department agreed with her on the merits, but the Court found a justiciable controversy when Congress intervened to defend Section 3 of DOMA.

3. In *Windsor*, five justices struck down Section 3 as violating the equal protection principles of the Fifth Amendment. Writing for those justices, Justice Kennedy noted the long history of federal reliance on state law for the determination of marital status for purposes of federal law. While he recognized that Congress had the power to define marriage for federal law purposes, he also noted that Section 3 of DOMA was

a comprehensive federal definition of marriage, rather than one more particularized to a given regulatory area, such as immigration or taxation. He then continued:

> Against this background [of traditional state authority to define marriage] DOMA rejects the long-established precept that the incidents, benefits, and obligations of marriage are uniform for all married couples within each State, though they may vary, subject to constitutional guarantees, from one State to the next. Despite these considerations, it is unnecessary to decide whether this federal intrusion on state power is a violation of the Constitution because it disrupts the federal balance. The State's power in defining the marital relation is of central relevance in this case quite apart from principles of federalism. Here the State's decision to give this class of persons the right to marry conferred upon them a dignity and status of immense import. When the State used its historic and essential authority to define the marital relation in this way, its role and its power in making the decision enhanced the recognition, dignity, and protection of the class in their own community. DOMA, because of its reach and extent, departs from this history and tradition of reliance on state law to define marriage. "'Discriminations of an unusual character especially suggest careful consideration to determine whether they are obnoxious to the constitutional provision.'" *Romer v. Evans* (1996) [*Supra*. this chapter] (quoting *Louisville Gas & Elec. Co. v. Coleman*, 277 U.S. 32 (1928)).

> The Federal Government uses this state-defined class for the opposite purpose—to impose restrictions and disabilities. That result requires this Court now to address whether the resulting injury and indignity is a deprivation of an essential part of the liberty protected by the Fifth Amendment. What the State of New York treats as alike the federal law deems unlike by a law designed to injure the same class the State seeks to protect. . . .

> The States' interest in defining and regulating the marital relation, subject to constitutional guarantees, stems from the understanding that marriage is more than a routine classification for purposes of certain statutory benefits. Private, consensual sexual intimacy between two adult persons of the same sex may not be punished by the State, and it can form "but one element in a personal bond that is more enduring." *Lawrence v. Texas* (2003) [*Supra*. Chapter 10]. By its recognition of the validity of same-sex marriages performed in other jurisdictions and then by authorizing same-sex unions and same-sex marriages, New York sought to give further protection and dignity to that bond. For same-sex couples who wished to be married, the State acted to give their lawful conduct a lawful status. This status is a far-reaching legal acknowledgment of the intimate relationship between two people, a relationship deemed by the State worthy of dignity in the community equal with all other marriages. It reflects both the community's considered perspective on the historical roots of the institution of marriage and its evolving understanding of the meaning of equality.

## IV

DOMA seeks to injure the very class New York seeks to protect. By doing so it violates basic due process and equal protection principles applicable to the Federal Government. See U.S. Const., Amdt. 5; *Bolling v. Sharpe* (1954) [*Supra.* Chapter 13]. The Constitution's guarantee of equality "must at the very least mean that a bare congressional desire to harm a politically unpopular group cannot" justify disparate treatment of that group. *Department of Agriculture v. Moreno* (1973) [Note *supra.* this chapter]. In determining whether a law is motived by an improper animus or purpose, "discriminations of an unusual character" especially require careful consideration. DOMA cannot survive under these principles. The responsibility of the States for the regulation of domestic relations is an important indicator of the substantial societal impact the State's classifications have in the daily lives and customs of its people. DOMA's unusual deviation from the usual tradition of recognizing and accepting state definitions of marriage here operates to deprive same-sex couples of the benefits and responsibilities that come with the federal recognition of their marriages. This is strong evidence of a law having the purpose and effect of disapproval of that class. The avowed purpose and practical effect of the law here in question are to impose a disadvantage, a separate status, and so a stigma upon all who enter into same-sex marriages made lawful by the unquestioned authority of the States.

The history of DOMA's enactment and its own text demonstrate that interference with the equal dignity of same-sex marriages, a dignity conferred by the States in the exercise of their sovereign power, was more than an incidental effect of the federal statute. It was its essence. The House Report announced its conclusion that "it is both appropriate and necessary for Congress to do what it can to defend the institution of traditional heterosexual marriage.... H.R. 3396 is appropriately entitled the 'Defense of Marriage Act.' The effort to redefine 'marriage' to extend to homosexual couples is a truly radical proposal that would fundamentally alter the institution of marriage." H.R.Rep. No. 104-664, pp. 12–13 (1996). The House concluded that DOMA expresses "both moral disapproval of homosexuality, and a moral conviction that heterosexuality better comports with traditional (especially Judeo-Christian) morality." *Id.* The stated purpose of the law was to promote an "interest in protecting the traditional moral teachings reflected in heterosexual-only marriage laws." *Id.* Were there any doubt of this far-reaching purpose, the title of the Act confirms it: The Defense of Marriage.

The arguments put forward by BLAG [the congressional intervenor] are just as candid about the congressional purpose to influence or interfere with state sovereign choices about who may be married. As the title and dynamics of the bill indicate, its purpose is to discourage enactment of state same-sex marriage laws and to restrict the freedom and choice of couples married under those laws if they are enacted. The congressional goal was "to put a thumb on the scales and influence a state's decision as to how to shape its own marriage laws." The Act's demonstrated purpose is to ensure that if any State decides to recognize same-sex marriages, those unions will be treated as second-class marriages for purposes of federal law. This raises a most serious question under the Constitution's Fifth Amendment.

DOMA's operation in practice confirms this purpose. When New York adopted a law to permit same-sex marriage, it sought to eliminate inequality; but DOMA frustrates that objective through a system-wide enactment with no identified connection to any particular area of federal law. DOMA writes inequality into the entire United States Code. The particular case at hand concerns the estate tax, but DOMA is more than a simple determination of what should or should not be allowed as an estate tax refund. Among the over 1,000 statutes and numerous federal regulations that DOMA controls are laws pertaining to Social Security, housing, taxes, criminal sanctions, copyright, and veterans' benefits.

DOMA's principal effect is to identify a subset of state-sanctioned marriages and make them unequal. The principal purpose is to impose inequality, not for other reasons like governmental efficiency. Responsibilities, as well as rights, enhance the dignity and integrity of the person. And DOMA contrives to deprive some couples married under the laws of their State, but not other couples, of both rights and responsibilities. By creating two contradictory marriage regimes within the same State, DOMA forces same-sex couples to live as married for the purpose of state law but unmarried for the purpose of federal law, thus diminishing the stability and predictability of basic personal relations the State has found it proper to acknowledge and protect. By this dynamic DOMA undermines both the public and private significance of state-sanctioned same-sex marriages; for it tells those couples, and all the world, that their otherwise valid marriages are unworthy of federal recognition. This places same-sex couples in an unstable position of being in a second-tier marriage. The differentiation demeans the couple, whose moral and sexual choices the Constitution protects, see *Lawrence*, and whose relationship the State has sought to dignify. And it humiliates tens of thousands of children now being raised by same-sex couples. The law in question makes it even more difficult for the children to understand the integrity and closeness of their own family and its concord with other families in their community and in their daily lives.

Under DOMA, same-sex married couples have their lives burdened, by reason of government decree, in visible and public ways. By its great reach, DOMA touches many aspects of married and family life, from the mundane to the profound. It prevents same-sex married couples from obtaining government healthcare benefits they would otherwise receive. It deprives them of the Bankruptcy Code's special protections for domestic-support obligations. It forces them to follow a complicated procedure to file their state and federal taxes jointly. It prohibits them from being buried together in veterans' cemeteries.... DOMA also brings financial harm to children of same-sex couples....

\* \* \*

The power the Constitution grants it also restrains. And though Congress has great authority to design laws to fit its own conception of sound national policy, it cannot deny the liberty protected by the Due Process Clause of the Fifth Amendment.

What has been explained to this point should more than suffice to establish that the principal purpose and the necessary effect of this law are to demean those persons who are in a lawful same-sex marriage. This requires the Court to hold, as it now does, that DOMA is unconstitutional as a deprivation of the liberty of the person protected by the Fifth Amendment of the Constitution.

4. Justice Scalia, joined by Chief Justice Roberts and Justices Thomas and Alito, dissented. He argued that the federal government had a rational basis for enacting Section 3 in its desire to avoid the federal law complexities that might arise if a married same-sex couple's activities, such as land ownership, spanned both states that recognized same-sex marriage and those that did not. Chief Justice Roberts and Justice Alito each wrote separate dissents.

5. Recall from Chapter 10 that in 2015 the Court overturned *state* bans on same-sex marriage. In that case, *Obergefell v. Hodges*, the Court relied primarily on due process reasoning, but added in aspects of equal protection analysis. The concluding part of the next Chapter considers this aspect of *Obergefell*.

## Note: The Animus "Doctrine" (?)

1. The quotation marks around the word "doctrine" and the question mark to the title of this note are intended to draw attention to the under-theorized nature of the Supreme Court's use of animus as a justification for holding that a law violates the Equal Protection Clause. Consider the following questions.

2. How is animus supposed to be uncovered? In all of these cases the Court found animus lurking only after examining the challenged law more carefully than is normally called for under standard equal protection review. This is most clearly visible in *Cleburne*, where the Court insisted on evidence in the record supporting the government's asserted legitimate justification for its housing permit denial. As Justice Marshall pointed out in his separate opinion in *Cleburne*, putting the burden on the government to show affirmative support for its decision reverses the normal burden of proof courts impose when performing rational basis review. Is there some unstated, unacknowledged, step the Court takes before looking for animus as carefully as it does? What might that step be?

3. *Romer* is in some ways a more straightforward application of this same style of judicial review. The Court expressed concern at the breadth of Amendment 2, decided

that the law is so broad that Colorado's legitimate justifications (law enforcement re-source conservation and protection for other persons' associational rights) simply could not justify the law, and then concluded, almost by a process of elimination, that there was no other possible justification for the law except animus. But since when is a law's overbreadth fatal for equal protection purposes under the rational basis standard? Or does that overbreadth itself provide evidence of what Coloradans must have been thinking of when they pulled the lever for Amendment 2?

4. Consider the implications of an animus conclusion. In her *Lawrence* concurrence, Justice O'Connor wrote that "When a law exhibits ... a desire to harm a politically unpopular group, we have applied a more searching form of rational basis review to strike down such laws under the Equal Protection Clause." This sentence could either be read to mean that "when a law exhibits ... a desire to harm a politically unpopular group," it will be automatically struck down as violating equal protection. Or it could be read to mean that such a law triggers "a more searching form of rational basis review," and might (or might not) be struck down.

This distinction may strike you as trivial. But if the first interpretation is correct, then animus would seem to be a *per se* violation of equal protection—once a court detects animus, the law is struck down: game over. If the second interpretation is correct, then (at least theoretically), it could still survive. Thus, under this second reading a court could say that a law is in fact motivated by animus, but is nevertheless constitutional. Is that even possible? Shouldn't "a bare desire to harm a politically unpopular group" automatically render a law unconstitutional?

Note that Justice O'Connor wrote this sentence artfully enough to leave this fundamental question undecided. This is a nice example of careful (or, some might say, deliberately ambiguous) writing that leaves important questions unanswered.

5. Finally, return to first principles. Our discussion of equal protection began with a discussion of the "class legislation" concept prevalent in the Nineteenth and early Twentieth centuries. Recall from cases such as *Barbier v. Connolly* (1884) (*Supra.* Chapter 11) that class legislation jurisprudence sought to distinguish between laws that classified in pursuit of legitimate government purposes and those that classified simply to confer benefits or impose burdens on particular groups. Does that venerable idea echo *Moreno*'s concern about laws that "exhibit a desire to harm a politically un-popular group?" If so, then recall the fate of class legislation jurisprudence. In particular, recall how courts ultimately realized they could not distinguish between statutory distinctions pursuing legitimate public goals and statutory distinctions that were imposed for illegitimate, private, reasons. Recall also that the *Carolene Products* Court reacted to that realization by planting the seeds of what eventually became suspect class analysis. And finally, recall that animus doctrine began to flower exactly when suspect class analysis itself began to falter. As you survey the state of equal protection today, are we back to where we started from?

# Chapter 16

# Equal Protection
# Fundamental Rights

So far our discussion of equal protection has focused on the constitutionality of government classifications, or "discrimination," without reference to the importance of the interest the government is withholding. (Recall that Justice Marshall often called for equal protection analysis to focus on *both* the classification *and* the nature of the benefit that was being distributed unequally—but in standard equal protection cases he was never able to convince a majority of the Court to embrace that approach.) However, a strand of equal protection law focuses exactly on the importance of the interest—*i.e.*, it requires that unequal government distribution of particularly important interests be justified by more than simply a rational basis. The following case provides an example of such an analysis, written, perhaps tellingly, by Justice Marshall.

## Zablocki v. Redhail

434 U.S. 374 (1978)

Mr. Justice MARSHALL delivered the opinion of the Court.

At issue in this case is the constitutionality of a Wisconsin statute, Wis.Stat. §§ 245.10(1), (4), (5), which provides that members of a certain class of Wisconsin residents may not marry, within the State or elsewhere, without first obtaining a court order granting permission to marry. The class is defined by the statute to include any "Wisconsin resident having minor issue not in his custody and which he is under obligation to support by any court order or judgment." The statute specifies that court permission cannot be granted unless the marriage applicant submits proof of compliance with the support obligation and, in addition, demonstrates that the children covered by the support order "are not then and are not likely thereafter to become public charges." No marriage license may lawfully be issued in Wisconsin to a person covered by the statute, except upon court order; any marriage entered into without compliance with § 245.10 is declared void; and persons acquiring marriage licenses in violation of the section are subject to criminal penalties.

After being denied a marriage license because of his failure to comply with § 245.10, appellee brought this class action ... challenging the statute as violative of the Equal Protection and Due Process Clauses of the Fourteenth Amendment and seeking declaratory and injunctive relief. The United States District Court for the Eastern District of Wisconsin held the statute unconstitutional under the Equal Protection Clause and enjoined its enforcement. We noted probable jurisdiction, and we now affirm.

I

Appellee Redhail is a Wisconsin resident who, under the terms of § 245.10, is unable to enter into a lawful marriage in Wisconsin or elsewhere so long as he maintains his Wisconsin residency. The facts, according to the stipulation filed by the parties in the District Court, are as follows. In January 1972, when appellee was a minor and a high school student, a paternity action was instituted against him in Milwaukee County Court, alleging that he was the father of a baby girl born out of wedlock on July 5, 1971. After he appeared and admitted that he was the child's father, the court entered an order on May 12, 1972, adjudging appellee the father and ordering him to pay $109 per month as support for the child until she reached 18 years of age. From May 1972 until August 1974, appellee was unemployed and indigent, and consequently was unable to make any support payments.

On September 27, 1974, appellee filed an application for a marriage license with appellant Zablocki, the County Clerk of Milwaukee County, and a few days later the application was denied on the sole ground that appellee had not obtained a court order granting him permission to marry, as required by § 245.10. Although appellee did not petition a state court thereafter, it is stipulated that he would not have been able to satisfy either of the statutory prerequisites for an order granting permission to marry. First, he had not satisfied his support obligations to his illegitimate child, and as of December 1974 there was an arrearage in excess of $3,700. Second, the child had been a public charge since her birth, receiving benefits under the Aid to Families with Dependent Children program. It is stipulated that the child's benefit payments were such that she would have been a public charge even if appellee had been current in his support payments....

II

In evaluating §§ 245.10(1), (4), (5) under the Equal Protection Clause, "we must first determine what burden of justification the classification created thereby must meet, by looking to the nature of the classification and the individual interests affected." Since our past decisions make clear that the right to marry is of fundamental importance, and since the classification at issue here significantly interferes with the exercise of that right, we believe that "critical examination" of the state interests advanced in support of the classification is required.

The leading decision of this Court on the right to marry is *Loving v. Virginia* (1967) [*Supra*. Chapter 13]. In that case, an interracial couple who had been convicted of violating Virginia's miscegenation laws challenged the statutory scheme on both equal protection and due process grounds. The Court's opinion could have rested solely on the ground that the statutes discriminated on the basis of race in violation of the Equal Protection Clause. But the Court went on to hold that the laws arbitrarily deprived the couple of a fundamental liberty protected by the Due Process Clause, the freedom to marry....

Although *Loving* arose in the context of racial discrimination, prior and subsequent decisions of this Court confirm that the right to marry is of fundamental importance for all individuals. Long ago, in *Maynard v. Hill*, 125 U.S. 190 (1888), the Court characterized marriage as "the most important relation in life," and as "the foundation of the family and of society, without which there would be neither civilization nor progress." In *Meyer v. Nebraska* (1923) [*Supra.* Chapter 8], the Court recognized that the right "to marry, establish a home and bring up children" is a central part of the liberty protected by the Due Process Clause, and in *Skinner v. Oklahoma*, 316 U.S. 535 (1942) [Note *supra.* Chapter 8], marriage was described as "fundamental to the very existence and survival of the race."

More recent decisions have established that the right to marry is part of the fundamental "right of privacy" implicit in the Fourteenth Amendment's Due Process Clause. In *Griswold v. Connecticut* (1965) [*Supra.* Chapter 9], the Court observed:

> We deal with a right of privacy older than the Bill of Rights — older than our political parties, older than our school system. Marriage is a coming together for better or for worse, hopefully enduring, and intimate to the degree of being sacred. It is an association that promotes a way of life, not causes; a harmony in living, not political faiths; a bilateral loyalty, not commercial or social projects. Yet it is an association for as noble a purpose as any involved in our prior decisions.

Cases subsequent to *Griswold* and *Loving* have routinely categorized the decision to marry as among the personal decisions protected by the right of privacy....

It is not surprising that the decision to marry has been placed on the same level of importance as decisions relating to procreation, childbirth, child rearing, and family relationships. As the facts of this case illustrate, it would make little sense to recognize a right of privacy with respect to other matters of family life and not with respect to the decision to enter the relationship that is the foundation of the family in our society. The woman whom appellee desired to marry had a fundamental right to seek an abortion of their expected child, see *Roe v. Wade* (1973) [*Supra.* Chapter 10], or to bring the child into life to suffer the myriad social, if not economic, disabilities that the status of illegitimacy brings, see *Weber v. Aetna Casualty & Surety Co.*, 406 U.S. 164 (1972) [Note *supra.* Chapter 12]. Surely, a decision to marry and raise the child in a traditional family setting must receive equivalent protection. And, if appellee's right to procreate means anything at all, it must imply some right to enter the only relationship in which the State of Wisconsin allows sexual relations legally to take place.

By reaffirming the fundamental character of the right to marry, we do not mean to suggest that every state regulation which relates in any way to the incidents of or prerequisites for marriage must be subjected to rigorous scrutiny. To the contrary, reasonable regulations that do not significantly interfere with decisions to enter into the marital relationship may legitimately be imposed. The statutory classification at issue here, however, clearly does interfere directly and substantially with the right to marry.

Under the challenged statute, no Wisconsin resident in the affected class may marry in Wisconsin or elsewhere without a court order, and marriages contracted in violation of the statute are both void and punishable as criminal offenses. Some of those in the affected class, like appellee, will never be able to obtain the necessary court order, because they either lack the financial means to meet their support obligations or cannot prove that their children will not become public charges. These persons are absolutely prevented from getting married. Many others, able in theory to satisfy the statute's requirements, will be sufficiently burdened by having to do so that they will in effect be coerced into forgoing their right to marry. And even those who can be persuaded to meet the statute's requirements suffer a serious intrusion into their freedom of choice in an area in which we have held such freedom to be fundamental.

## III

When a statutory classification significantly interferes with the exercise of a fundamental right, it cannot be upheld unless it is supported by sufficiently important state interests and is closely tailored to effectuate only those interests. Appellant asserts that two interests are served by the challenged statute: the permission-to-marry proceeding furnishes an opportunity to counsel the applicant as to the necessity of fulfilling his prior support obligations; and the welfare of the out-of-custody children is protected. We may accept for present purposes that these are legitimate and substantial interests, but, since the means selected by the State for achieving these interests unnecessarily impinge on the right to marry, the statute cannot be sustained.

There is evidence that the challenged statute, as originally introduced in the Wisconsin Legislature, was intended merely to establish a mechanism whereby persons with support obligations to children from prior marriages could be counseled before they entered into new marital relationships and incurred further support obligations.... The statute actually enacted, however, does not expressly require or provide for any counseling whatsoever, nor for any automatic granting of permission to marry by the court, and thus it can hardly be justified as a means for ensuring counseling of the persons within its coverage. Even assuming that counseling does take place — a fact as to which there is no evidence in the record — this interest obviously cannot support the withholding of court permission to marry once counseling is completed.

With regard to safeguarding the welfare of the out-of-custody children, appellant's brief does not make clear the connection between the State's interest and the statute's requirements. At argument, appellant's counsel suggested that, since permission to marry cannot be granted unless the applicant shows that he has satisfied his court-determined support obligations to the prior children and that those children will not become public charges, the statute provides incentive for the applicant to make support payments to his children. This "collection device" rationale cannot justify the statute's broad infringement on the right to marry.

First, with respect to individuals who are unable to meet the statutory requirements, the statute merely prevents the applicant from getting married, without delivering any money at all into the hands of the applicant's prior children. More importantly, regardless of the applicant's ability or willingness to meet the statutory requirements, the State already has numerous other means for exacting compliance with support obligations, means that are at least as effective as the instant statute's and yet do not impinge upon the right to marry. Under Wisconsin law, whether the children are from a prior marriage or were born out of wedlock, court-determined support obligations may be enforced directly via wage assignments, civil contempt proceedings, and criminal penalties. And, if the State believes that parents of children out of their custody should be responsible for ensuring that those children do not become public charges, this interest can be achieved by adjusting the criteria used for determining the amounts to be paid under their support orders.

There is also some suggestion that § 245.10 protects the ability of marriage applicants to meet support obligations to prior children by preventing the applicants from incurring new support obligations. But the challenged provisions of § 245.10 are grossly underinclusive with respect to this purpose, since they do not limit in any way new financial commitments by the applicant other than those arising out of the contemplated marriage. The statutory classification is substantially overinclusive as well: Given the possibility that the new spouse will actually better the applicant's financial situation, by contributing income from a job or otherwise, the statute in many cases may prevent affected individuals from improving their ability to satisfy their prior support obligations. And, although it is true that the applicant will incur support obligations to any children born during the contemplated marriage, preventing the marriage may only result in the children being born out of wedlock, as in fact occurred in appellee's case. Since the support obligation is the same whether the child is born in or out of wedlock, the net result of preventing the marriage is simply more illegitimate children.

The statutory classification created by §§ 245.10(1), (4), (5) thus cannot be justified by the interests advanced in support of it. The judgment of the District Court is, accordingly, Affirmed.

Mr. Chief Justice BURGER, concurring. [omitted]

Mr. Justice STEWART, concurring in the judgment.

I cannot join the opinion of the Court. To hold, as the Court does, that the Wisconsin statute violates the Equal Protection Clause seems to me to misconceive the meaning of that constitutional guarantee. The Equal Protection Clause deals not with substantive rights or freedoms but with invidiously discriminatory classifications. The paradigm of its violation is, of course, classification by race. *McLaughlin v. Florida*, 379 U.S. 184 (1964); *Loving* (concurring opinion).

Like almost any law, the Wisconsin statute now before us affects some people and does not affect others. But to say that it thereby creates "classifications" in the equal protection sense strikes me as little short of fantasy. The problem in this case is not one of discriminatory classifications, but of unwarranted encroachment upon a constitutionally protected freedom. I think that the Wisconsin statute is unconstitutional because it exceeds the bounds of permissible state regulation of marriage, and invades the sphere of liberty protected by the Due Process Clause of the Fourteenth Amendment....

## II

… The Court is understandably reluctant to rely on substantive due process. But to embrace the essence of that doctrine under the guise of equal protection serves no purpose but obfuscation. "Couched in slogans and ringing phrases," the Court's equal protection doctrine shifts the focus of the judicial inquiry away from its proper concerns, which include "the nature of the individual interest affected, the extent to which it is affected, the rationality of the connection between legislative means and purpose, the existence of alternative means for effectuating the purpose, and the degree of confidence we may have that the statute reflects the legislative concern for the purpose that would legitimately support the means chosen."

To conceal this appropriate inquiry invites mechanical or thoughtless application of misfocused doctrine. To bring it into the open forces a healthy and responsible recognition of the nature and purpose of the extreme power we wield when, in invalidating a state law in the name of the Constitution, we invalidate *pro tanto* the process of representative democracy in one of the sovereign States of the Union.

Mr. Justice POWELL, concurring in the judgment.

I concur in the judgment of the Court that Wisconsin's restrictions on the exclusive means of creating the marital bond, erected by Wis.Stat. §§ 245.10(1), (4), and (5) (1973), cannot meet applicable constitutional standards. I write separately because the majority's rationale sweeps too broadly in an area which traditionally has been subject to pervasive state regulation. The Court apparently would subject all state regulation which "directly and substantially" interferes with the decision to marry in a traditional family setting to "critical examination" or "compelling state interest" analysis. Presumably, "reasonable regulations that do not significantly interfere with decisions to enter into the marital relationship may legitimately be imposed." *Ante.* The Court does not present, however, any principled means for distinguishing between the two types of regulations. Since state regulation in this area typically takes the form of a prerequisite or barrier to marriage or divorce, the degree of "direct" interference with the decision to marry or to divorce is unlikely to provide either guidance for state legislatures or a basis for judicial oversight.

## I

On several occasions, the Court has acknowledged the importance of the marriage relationship to the maintenance of values essential to organized society. "This Court has long recognized that freedom of personal choice in matters of marriage and family life is one of the liberties protected by the Due Process Clause of the Fourteenth Amendment." Our decisions indicate that the guarantee of personal privacy or autonomy secured against unjustifiable governmental interference by the Due Process Clause "has some extension to activities relating to marriage…." "While the outer limits of this aspect of privacy have not been marked by the Court, it is clear that among the decisions that an individual may make without unjustified government interference are personal decisions relating to marriage…."

Thus, it is fair to say that there is a right of marital and familial privacy which places some substantive limits on the regulatory power of government. But the Court has yet to hold that all regulation touching upon marriage implicates a "fundamental right" triggering the most exacting judicial scrutiny.

The principal authority cited by the majority is *Loving.* Although Loving speaks of the "freedom to marry" as "one of the vital personal rights essential to the orderly pursuit of happiness by free men," the Court focused on the miscegenation statute before it. Mr. Chief Justice Warren stated:

> Marriage is one of the 'basic civil rights of man,' fundamental to our very existence and survival. *Skinner.* To deny this fundamental freedom on so unsupportable a basis as the racial classifications embodied in these statutes classifications so directly subversive of the principle of equality at the heart of the Fourteenth Amendment, is surely to deprive all the State's citizens of liberty without due process of law. The Fourteenth Amendment requires that the freedom of choice to marry not be restricted by invidious racial discriminations. Under our Constitution, the freedom to marry, or not marry, a person of another race resides with the individual and cannot be infringed by the State.

Thus, *Loving* involved a denial of a "fundamental freedom" on a wholly unsupportable basis — the use of classifications "directly subversive of the principle of equality at the heart of the Fourteenth Amendment...." It does not speak to the level of judicial scrutiny of, or governmental justification for, "supportable" restrictions on the "fundamental freedom" of individuals to marry or divorce.

In my view, analysis must start from the recognition of domestic relations as "an area that has long been regarded as a virtually exclusive province of the States."...

## II

State power over domestic relations is not without constitutional limits. The Due Process Clause requires a showing of justification "when the government intrudes on choices concerning family living arrangements" in a manner which is contrary to deeply rooted traditions. *Moore v. City of East Cleveland, Ohio* (1977) (plurality opinion) [*Supra.* Chapter 10]. Due process constraints also limit the extent to which the State may monopolize the process of ordering certain human relationships while excluding the truly indigent from that process. Furthermore, under the Equal Protection Clause the means chosen by the State in this case must bear "'a fair and substantial relation'" to the object of the legislation. *Reed v. Reed*, 404 U.S. 71 (1971) [Note *supra.* Chapter 12]; *Craig v. Boren* (1976) (Powell, J., concurring) [*Supra.* Chapter 12].

The Wisconsin measure in this case does not pass muster under either due process or equal protection standards. Appellant identifies three objectives which are supposedly furthered by the statute in question: (i) a counseling function; (ii) an incentive to satisfy outstanding support obligations; and (iii) a deterrent against incurring further obligations. The opinion of the Court amply demonstrates that the asserted counseling objective bears no relation to this statute. No further discussion is required here.

The so-called "collection device" rationale presents a somewhat more difficult question. I do not agree with the suggestion in the Court's opinion that a State may never condition the right to marry on satisfaction of existing support obligations simply because the State has alternative methods of compelling such payments. To the extent this restriction applies to persons who are able to make the required support payments but simply wish to shirk their moral and legal obligation, the Constitution interposes no bar to this additional collection mechanism. The vice inheres, not in the collection concept, but in the failure to make provision for those without the means to comply with child-support obligations....

The third justification, only obliquely advanced by appellant, is that the statute preserves the ability of marriage applicants to support their prior issue by preventing them from incurring new obligations. The challenged provisions of § 245.10 are so grossly underinclusive with respect to this objective, given the many ways that additional financial obligations may be incurred by the applicant quite apart from a contemplated marriage, that the classification "does not bear a fair and substantial relation to the object of the legislation." *Craig*; cf. *Moore* (plurality opinion).

The marriage applicant is required by the Wisconsin statute not only to submit proof of compliance with his support obligation, but also to demonstrate — in some unspecified way — that his children "are not then and are not likely thereafter to become public charges." This statute does more than simply "fail to alleviate the consequences of differences in economic circumstances that exist wholly apart from any state action." *Griffin v. Illinois*, 351 U.S. 12 (1956) (Harlan, J., dissenting) [Note *supra*. Chapter 12]. It tells the truly indigent, whether they have met their support obligations or not, that they may not marry so long as their children are public charges or there is a danger that their children might go on public assistance in the future. Apparently, no other jurisdiction has embraced this approach as a method of reducing the number of children on public assistance. Because the State has not established a justification for this unprecedented foreclosure of marriage to many of its citizens solely because of their indigency, I concur in the judgment of the Court.

Mr. Justice STEVENS, concurring in the judgment. [omitted]

Mr. Justice REHNQUIST, dissenting.

I substantially agree with my Brother POWELL's reasons for rejecting the Court's conclusion that marriage is the sort of "fundamental right" which must invariably trigger the strictest judicial scrutiny. I disagree with his imposition of an "intermediate" standard of review, which leads him to conclude that the statute, though generally valid as an "additional collection mechanism" offends the Constitution by its "failure to make provision for those without the means to comply with child-support obligations." For similar reasons, I disagree with my Brother STEWART's conclusion that the statute is invalid for its failure to exempt those persons who "simply cannot afford to meet the statute's financial requirements." I would view this legislative judgment in the light of the traditional presumption of validity. I think that under the Equal Protection Clause the statute need pass only the "rational basis test," *Dandridge v. Williams*, 397 U.S. 471 (1970) [Note *supra.* Chapter 12], and that under the Due Process Clause it need only be shown that it bears a rational relation to a constitutionally permissible objective. *Ferguson v. Skrupa* (1963) (Harlan, J., concurring) [*Supra.* Chapter 7]. The statute so viewed is a permissible exercise of the State's power to regulate family life and to assure the support of minor children, despite its possible imprecision in the extreme cases envisioned in the concurring opinions....

## *Note: Identifying Equal Protection Fundamental Rights*

In one sense, *Zablocki* presented an easy case for the Court: prior precedent had clearly recognized marriage as a fundamental right. That fact made it easier for Justice Marshall to insist on presumptive equal access to it. But in other cases, the ambiguous status of the interest at issue has caused the Court to fracture.

Recall *San Antonio Independent School District v. Rodriguez*, 411 U.S. 1 (1973), discussed as part of Chapter 12's examination of the Court's attitude to wealth as a possibly suspect class. After rejecting the plaintiffs' claim that Texas's school financing system unconstitutionally discriminated based on wealth, Justice Powell, writing for the five-justice majority, then considered their argument that the right to education was fundamental for equal protection purposes, and that the unequal school funding the Texas scheme produced was unconstitutional.

He rejected that argument as well. He acknowledged that education was important—and, indeed, that *Brown v. Board of Education* (1954) (*Supra.* Chapter 13) had explained the importance of education to full participation in civic life. "But," he continued, "the importance of a service performed by the State does not determine whether it must be regarded as fundamental for purposes of examination under the Equal Protection Clause." After considering a number of cases, he concluded as follows:

> The lesson of these cases in addressing the question now before the Court is plain. It is not the province of this Court to create substantive constitutional rights in the name of guaranteeing equal protection of the laws. Thus, the key to discovering whether education is "fundamental" is not to be found in comparisons of the relative societal significance of education as opposed to subsistence or housing. Nor is it to be found by weighing whether education is as important as the right to travel. Rather, the answer lies in assessing whether there is a right to education explicitly or implicitly guaranteed by the Constitution.

He concluded that, as important as education was (including in making explicit guarantees such as freedom of speech, and rights such as the right to vote, more effectively exercised), it was itself not a constitutional right.

Justice Marshall's dissent took issue with the majority's conclusion on this point. He wrote that "the fundamental importance of education is amply indicated by the prior decisions of this Court, by the unique status accorded public education by our society, and by the close relationship between education and some of our most basic constitutional values." He cited *Brown* as support for the first criterion, noted, in support of the second, that "in 48 of our 50 States the provision of public education is mandated by the state constitution," and noted the close connection between education and effective use of rights such as free speech and voting.

Obviously, the identification of fundamental rights for equal protection purposes is related to the analogous process of identifying fundamental rights for purposes of the Due Process Clause. Should there be any difference at all in those processes? What should be the effect of the fact that, if a state chose, it could simply refrain from providing public education at all? Does that make it any less of a fundamental right if the state *does* choose to provide it, but then does so unequally?

## Note: The Current Status of the Fundamental Rights Strand of Equal Protection

As one might expect from the term, the fundamental rights strand of equal protection protects rights the Court has deemed especially important. Of course, one would expect that such rights would also be protected by the Due Process Clause, which provides substantive protection for "fundamental" rights by insisting that deprivations of such rights satisfy strict scrutiny. As illustrated by comparing the majority opinion in *Zablocki* with Justice Stewart's concurrence, the same law might be understood as violating both the fundamental rights strand of equal protection and the Due Process Clause.

Some rights, however, have become especially identified with the fundamental right strand. In part this identification with equal protection arises from the fact that the state is not constitutionally obligated to provide the right in question, but when it does, the Court believes it to be sufficiently important as to presumptively require that it be provided equally to all. For example, the Court has held that, while a state may fill certain offices or make decisions by election or otherwise, if it chooses election then citizens of that jurisdiction have an equal right to vote—including the right to have their vote counted equally. *See, e.g., Bush v. Gore*, 531 U.S. 98, 104 (2000) ("The individual citizen has no federal constitutional right to vote for electors for the President of the United States unless and until the state legislature chooses a statewide election as the means to implement its power to appoint members of the electoral college.... When the state legislature vests the right to vote for President in its people, the right to vote as the legislature has prescribed is fundamental; and one source of its fundamental nature lies in the equal weight accorded to each vote and the equal dignity owed to each voter.").

Other rights primarily subject to equal protection analysis include electoral candidates' access to ballots and would-be litigants' access to the judicial process. *See, e.g., Williams v. Rhodes*, 393 U.S. 23 (1968) (ballot access); *M.L.B. v. S.L.J.*, 519 U.S. 102 (1996) (recognizing that "most decisions" in the area of indigent persons' access to judicial processes, such as appeals, "rest on an equal protection framework ... for due process does not independently require that the State provide a right to appeal."). Another right, the right to interstate travel, was at one point partially grounded in the fundamental rights strand, but more recently has been at least partially regrounded in the Fourteenth Amendment's Privileges or Immunities Clause. *See Shapiro v. Thompson*, 394 U.S. 618 (1969) (fundamental rights strand); *Saenz v. Roe*, 526 U.S. 489 (1999) (Privileges or Immunities Clause).

## *Note: Liberty and Equality Today*

As this chapter has made clear, liberty and equality co-exist in a tight, yet ambiguous relationship. In recent years, this relationship has taken the form of explicit cross-fertilization of each doctrine with elements of the other.

Consider the following excerpt from *Lawrence v. Texas*, the 2003 case (excerpted in Chapter 10) in which Justice Kennedy used the Due Process Clause to invalidate Texas's same-sex sodomy law:

> As an alternative argument in this case, counsel for the petitioners and some amici contend that *Romer v. Evans* (1996) [*Supra.* Chapter 15], provides the basis for declaring the Texas statute invalid under the Equal Protection Clause. That is a tenable argument, but we conclude the instant case requires us to address whether *Bowers v. Hardwick*, 478 U.S. 186 (1986) [Note *supra.* Chapter 10], itself has continuing validity. Were we to hold the statute invalid under the Equal Protection Clause some might question whether a prohibition would be valid if drawn differently, say, to prohibit the conduct both between same-sex and different-sex participants.

> Equality of treatment and the due process right to demand respect for conduct protected by the substantive guarantee of liberty are linked in important respects, and a decision on the latter point advances both interests. If protected conduct is made criminal and the law which does so remains unexamined for its substantive validity, its stigma might remain even if it were not enforceable as drawn for equal protection reasons. When homosexual conduct is made criminal by the law of the State, that declaration in and of itself is an invitation to subject homosexual persons to discrimination both in the public and in the private spheres. The central holding of *Bowers* has been brought in question by this case, and it should be addressed. Its continuance as precedent demeans the lives of homosexual persons.

Consider now this excerpt from *United States v. Windsor*, the 2013 case (discussed in a note in Chapter 15) where the Court, again speaking through Justice Kennedy, used equal protection reasoning to invalidate the federal Defense of Marriage Act's provision defining marriage for federal law purposes as existing solely between a man and a woman:

> DOMA seeks to injure the very class New York [the state that recognized the same-sex marriage at issue] seeks to protect. By doing so it violates basic due process and equal protection principles applicable to the Federal Government.

The Constitution's guarantee of equality "must at the very least mean that a bare congressional desire to harm a politically unpopular group cannot" justify disparate treatment of that group. *Department of Agriculture v. Moreno* (1973) [*Supra*. Chapter 15].... DOMA cannot survive under these principles. The responsibility of the States for the regulation of domestic relations is an important indicator of the substantial societal impact the State's classifications have in the daily lives and customs of its people. DOMA's unusual deviation from the usual tradition of recognizing and accepting state definitions of marriage here operates to deprive same-sex couples of the benefits and responsibilities that come with the federal recognition of their marriages. This is strong evidence of a law having the purpose and effect of disapproval of that class. The avowed purpose and practical effect of the law here in question are to impose a disadvantage, a separate status, and so a stigma upon all who enter into same-sex marriages made lawful by the unquestioned authority of the States.

The history of DOMA's enactment and its own text demonstrate that interference with the equal dignity of same-sex marriages, a dignity conferred by the States in the exercise of their sovereign power, was more than an incidental effect of the federal statute. It was its essence....

DOMA's principal effect is to identify a subset of state-sanctioned marriages and make them unequal. The principal purpose is to impose inequality, not for other reasons like governmental efficiency. Responsibilities, as well as rights, enhance the dignity and integrity of the person. And DOMA contrives to deprive some couples married under the laws of their State, but not other couples, of both rights and responsibilities....

The liberty protected by the Fifth Amendment's Due Process Clause contains within it the prohibition against denying to any person the equal protection of the laws. While the Fifth Amendment itself withdraws from Government the power to degrade or demean in the way this law does, the equal protection guarantee of the Fourteenth Amendment makes that Fifth Amendment right all the more specific and all the better understood and preserved....

Finally, consider the following language from *Obergefell v. Hodges*, the 2015 case (excerpted in Chapter 10) striking down same-sex marriage bans in the states:

It cannot be denied that this Court's cases describing the right to marry presumed a relationship involving opposite-sex partners ... Still, there are other, more instructive precedents. This Court's cases have expressed constitutional principles of broader reach. In defining the right to marry these cases have identified essential attributes of that right based in history, tradition, and other constitutional liberties inherent in this intimate bond....

This analysis compels the conclusion that same-sex couples may exercise the right to marry. The four principles and traditions to be discussed demonstrate that the reasons marriage is fundamental under the Constitution apply with equal force to same-sex couples.

A first premise of the Court's relevant precedents is that the right to personal choice regarding marriage is inherent in the concept of individual autonomy ... This is true for all persons, whatever their sexual orientation. See *Windsor*. There is dignity in the bond between two men or two women who seek to marry and in their autonomy to make such profound choices.

A second principle in this Court's jurisprudence is that the right to marry is fundamental because it supports a two-person union unlike any other in its importance to the committed individuals.... As this Court held in *Lawrence*, same-sex couples have the same right as opposite-sex couples to enjoy intimate association....

A third basis for protecting the right to marry is that it safeguards children and families and thus draws meaning from related rights of childrearing, procreation, and education.... As all parties agree, many same-sex couples provide loving and nurturing homes to their children....

Fourth and finally, this Court's cases and the Nation's traditions make clear that marriage is a keystone of our social order.... There is no difference between same- and opposite-sex couples with respect to this principle. Yet by virtue of their exclusion from that institution, same-sex couples are denied the constellation of benefits that the States have linked to marriage. This harm results in more than just material burdens. Same-sex couples are consigned to an instability many opposite-sex couples would deem intolerable in their own lives. As the State itself makes marriage all the more precious by the significance it attaches to it, exclusion from that status has the effect of teaching that gays and lesbians are unequal in important respects. It demeans gays and lesbians for the State to lock them out of a central institution of the Nation's society. Same-sex couples, too, may aspire to the transcendent purposes of marriage and seek fulfillment in its highest meaning.

The limitation of marriage to opposite-sex couples may long have seemed natural and just, but its inconsistency with the central meaning of the fundamental right to marry is now manifest. With that knowledge must come the recognition that laws excluding same-sex couples from the marriage right impose stigma and injury of the kind prohibited by our basic charter....

The right of same-sex couples to marry that is part of the liberty promised by the Fourteenth Amendment is derived, too, from that Amendment's guarantee of the equal protection of the laws. The Due Process Clause and the Equal Protection Clause are connected in a profound way, though they set forth independent principles. Rights implicit in liberty and rights secured by equal protection may rest on different precepts and are not always coextensive, yet in some instances each may be instructive as to the meaning and reach of the other. In any particular case one Clause may be thought to capture the essence of the right in a more accurate and comprehensive way, even as the two Clauses may converge in the identification and definition of the right. This interrelation of the two principles furthers our understanding of what freedom is and must become....

... It is now clear that the challenged laws burden the liberty of same-sex couples, and it must be further acknowledged that they abridge central precepts of equality. Here the marriage laws enforced by the respondents are in essence unequal: same-sex couples are denied all the benefits afforded to opposite-sex couples and are barred from exercising a fundamental right. Especially against a long history of disapproval of their relationships, this denial to same-sex couples of the right to marry works a grave and continuing harm. The imposition of this disability on gays and lesbians serves to disrespect and subordinate them. And the Equal Protection Clause, like the Due Process Clause, prohibits this unjustified infringement of the fundamental right to marry.

These considerations lead to the conclusion that the right to marry is a fundamental right inherent in the liberty of the person, and under the Due Process and Equal Protection Clauses of the Fourteenth Amendment couples of the same-sex may not be deprived of that right and that liberty. The Court now holds that same-sex couples may exercise the fundamental right to marry. No longer may this liberty be denied to them. *Baker v. Nelson* must be and now is overruled, and the State laws challenged by Petitioners in these cases are now held invalid to the extent they exclude same-sex couples from civil marriage on the same terms and conditions as opposite-sex couples.

In all of these cases, the Court connects liberty and equality, but in different ways. At times it appears to suggest that its decision in the given case could be grounded on either due process or equal protection, while at other times it seems to suggest that either due process draws its meaning from equal protection concepts, or vice-versa.

These excerpts are from the three of the most important recent Fourteenth Amendment cases. Given these statements, what would you say about the current meaning of Fourteenth Amendment rights?

# Part V

# General Fourteenth Amendment Issues

Part V considers issues that are common to both the Due Process and Equal Protection Clauses. Chapter 17 examines Congress's power to enforce the provisions of the Fourteenth Amendment. The Enforcement Clause provides Congress with an important tool for regulating states; however, the Court has disagreed about the meaning of the requirement that such legislation be "appropriate."

Chapter 18 considers the requirement that a plaintiff bringing a due process or equal protection claim demonstrate "state action" — *i.e.*, conduct by the state. As straightforward as this requirement appears at first blush, it raises difficult conceptual and practical questions.

# Chapter 17

# Congressional Power to Enforce the Fourteenth Amendment

When we think of the Fourteenth Amendment, we usually think of court cases where a plaintiff alleges that the government-defendant has directly violated the plaintiff's due process or equal protection rights. However, Section 5 of the Fourteenth Amendment states that "The Congress shall have the power to enforce, by appropriate legislation, the provisions of [the Amendment]." In recent years, the Enforcement Clause has taken on new importance, since after *Seminole Tribe of Florida v. Florida*, 517 U.S. 44 (1996) (*Supra.* Chapter 6), the Interstate Commerce Power has been understood as not giving Congress the power to make states liable for retrospective relief such as damages. Because the "Enforcement Power" (sometimes also called the "Section 5 power") does allow Congress to impose such retrospective relief, it has become an important tool for Congress when it seeks to force states to comply with a federal mandate.

## Note: The Enforcement Power before City of Boerne v. Flores

1. An early version of the proposal that became the Fourteenth Amendment consisted simply of a grant of congressional power to protect persons' due process and equal protection rights from state infringement, rather than the current combination of a judicially-enforceable prohibition (in Section 1) and a grant of congressional enforcement power (in Section 5). This structure was criticized by those who foresaw the day that southern states would be readmitted to the Union and once again represented in Congress, at which time it was feared that federal legislation enacted pursuant to that grant of power would be repealed. As explained by Justice Kennedy in *City of Boerne*, below, some Reconstruction-era members of Congress also expressed concern that this structure gave Congress too much power to intrude into matters previously left to the states.

After a series of proposals and changes, the amendment took the form we know today, with Section 1 a self-executing, judicially-enforceable prohibition on state infringements of a set of rights (including due process and equal protection), and Section 5 a grant of congressional authority to "enforce" that amendment. (Sections 2–4 deal with matters that have largely (though not completely) faded from relevance today.)

2. The fate of the Enforcement Clause mirrored the fate of Reconstruction. As congressional interest in enacting enforcement legislation waned, the Court, mirroring

969

society's increasing disinterest in Reconstruction, interpreted the Enforcement Clause narrowly. The most important Enforcement Clause decision of the era, a decision that is often seen as the final chapter in Reconstruction, was the *Civil Rights Cases*, 109 U.S. 3 (1883). As implied by the title, the opinion decided several cases brought under the Civil Rights Act of 1875, which prohibited racial discrimination in places of public accommodation, such as theaters and hotels. In those cases the Court held that Congress exceeded its enforcement authority in enacting the statute, since the Fourteenth Amendment prohibited only state action, while the statute regulated private conduct. Justice Harlan was the sole dissenter. He argued that non-discriminatory access to public accommodations was a civil right that Congress had the power to protect.

3. After the *Civil Rights Cases* the Enforcement Clause fell into desuetude, as Congress lost interest in protecting civil rights. It was only with the advent of the Civil Rights Movement of the mid-Twentieth century that attention again returned to the Clause, as Congress again took up the challenge of guaranteeing civil rights.

Starting in 1957, Congress began enacting a series of civil rights bills. But not until the early 1960s, with congressional consideration of what became the Civil Rights Act of 1964, did Enforcement Clause doctrine come under new scrutiny. A key element of the 1964 law was a prohibition on discrimination in public accommodations analogous to the one that had been struck down in 1875. When considering that part of the bill, legal advisers in the Kennedy and Johnson Administrations and in Congress considered basing that prohibition on the Enforcement Clause. It was thought that doctrinal developments over the prior several decades had undercut the *Civil Rights Cases*, and that the Supreme Court would be receptive to an argument that the Enforcement Clause authorized prohibitions on public accommodation discrimination. Ultimately, however, it was decided to base and defend the law primarily as an exercise of Congress's power under the Interstate Commerce Clause. The cases upholding this part of the Civil Rights Act based on the commerce power, *Heart of Atlanta Motel v. United States*, 379 U.S. 241 (1964) and *Katzenbach v. McClung*, 379 U.S. 294 (1964), are discussed in a note in Chapter 4.

4. The modern Court's first consideration of the Enforcement Clause occurred in *Katzenbach v. Morgan*, 384 U.S. 641 (1966). *Morgan* considered a challenge to a provision of the Voting Rights Act of 1965 which prohibited states—in this case, New York—from using English literacy tests to disqualify voters that had been educated in Spanish in a Puerto Rican school. The case was complicated by the fact that several years before *Morgan*, the Court had held in *Lassiter v. Northampton County Board of Elections*, 360 U.S. 45 (1959), that English-literacy tests did not necessarily violate the Constitution.

By a 7–2 vote the Court upheld the statute. Justice Brennan, writing for the majority, offered two theories for why the statute was a valid enforcement of Puerto Ricans' equal protection rights. First, he noted that voting power translates into political clout, which in turn ensures responsiveness to a community's needs. He thus saw the voting protection granted Puerto Ricans as a means of ensuring broader equality in obtaining governmental services and benefits.

More controversially, Justice Brennan also concluded that the Court should defer to Congress's judgments about the meaning of equal protection. Thus, while the Court itself had concluded in *Lassiter* that literacy tests did not constitute invidious discrimination, he argued that the Court should defer to a congressional determination that at least some such tests were in fact constitutionally invidious.

Justice Harlan, joined by Justice Stewart, dissented. He challenged the Court's deference to Congress on matters of constitutional interpretation. He noted that while in this case Congress had embraced a broader understanding of constitutional rights, under the majority's theory nothing stopped Congress from interpreting the Fourteenth Amendment more narrowly than the Court had. Justice Brennan replied that the congressional power to re-interpret constitutional rights only extended to interpretations that expanded rights. In turn, Justice Harlan criticized what became known as this "one-way ratchet," describing it as unprincipled.

5. In 1997, the Court took a very different, and more limited, approach to the Enforcement Clause. The case, *City of Boerne v. Flores*, 521 U.S. 507 (1997), arose out of a challenge to the Religious Freedom Restoration Act (RFRA). RFRA was enacted in response to the Court's decision in *Employment Division v. Smith*, 494 U.S. 872 (1990). In *Smith*, the Court embraced a reading of the Free Exercise Clause of the First Amendment that protected religious exercise only from legislation that singled out religious practice. In other words, *Smith* embraced a rule in which legislation that imposed a generally-applicable restriction on conduct would not be struck down simply because it burdened religious conduct. For example, under *Smith* a state law imposing a general restriction on the consumption of wine would not be struck down as infringing Roman Catholics' rights to exercise their religion simply because the consumption of wine was part of ritual Catholic religious exercise.

The public reaction to *Smith* was quite negative. Within a few years, Congress overwhelmingly enacted RFRA, citing its authority to enforce the Due Process Clause, which, as discussed in Chapter 8, has incorporated the Free Exercise Clause. RFRA imposed severe limits on states' ability to burden religious conduct through such generally-applicable laws. *City of Boerne* arose when a Roman Catholic diocese in Texas used RFRA to challenge a city's refusal to permit the diocese to enlarge a church building that was located within a historic district.

## City of Boerne v. Flores

### 521 U.S. 507 (1997)

Justice KENNEDY delivered the opinion of the Court.*

A decision by local zoning authorities to deny a church a building permit was challenged under the Religious Freedom Restoration Act of 1993 (RFRA or Act), 42 U.S.C. § 2000bb et seq. The case calls into question the authority of Congress to enact RFRA. We conclude the statute exceeds Congress' power.

---

\* Justice SCALIA joins all but Part III-A-1 of this opinion.

## I

Situated on a hill in the city of Boerne, Texas, some 28 miles northwest of San Antonio, is St. Peter Catholic Church. Built in 1923, the church's structure replicates the mission style of the region's earlier history. The church seats about 230 worshippers, a number too small for its growing parish.... In order to meet the needs of the congregation the Archbishop of San Antonio gave permission to the parish to plan alterations to enlarge the building.

A few months later, the Boerne City Council passed an ordinance authorizing the city's Historic Landmark Commission to prepare a preservation plan with proposed historic landmarks and districts. Under the ordinance, the commission must preapprove construction affecting historic landmarks or buildings in a historic district.

Soon afterwards, the Archbishop applied for a building permit so construction to enlarge the church could proceed. City authorities, relying on the ordinance and the designation of a historic district (which, they argued, included the church), denied the application. The Archbishop brought this suit challenging the permit denial in the United States District Court for the Western District of Texas.

The complaint contained various claims, but to this point the litigation has centered on RFRA and the question of its constitutionality. The Archbishop relied upon RFRA as one basis for relief from the refusal to issue the permit. The District Court concluded that by enacting RFRA Congress exceeded the scope of its enforcement power under § 5 of the Fourteenth Amendment. The court certified its order for interlocutory appeal and the Fifth Circuit reversed, finding RFRA to be constitutional. We granted certiorari, and now reverse.

## II

Congress enacted RFRA in direct response to the Court's decision in *Employment Div., Dept. of Human Resources of Oregon v. Smith*, 494 U.S. 872 (1990) [Note *supra.* this chapter]. There we considered a Free Exercise Clause claim brought by members of the Native American Church who were denied unemployment benefits when they lost their jobs because they had used peyote. Their practice was to ingest peyote for sacramental purposes, and they challenged an Oregon statute of general applicability which made use of the drug criminal. In evaluating the claim, we declined to apply the balancing test set forth in *Sherbert v. Verner*, 374 U.S. 398 (1963), under which we would have asked whether Oregon's prohibition substantially burdened a religious practice and, if it did, whether the burden was justified by a compelling government interest.... *Smith* held that neutral, generally applicable laws may be applied to religious practices even when not supported by a compelling governmental interest.

Four Members of the Court disagreed. They argued the law placed a substantial burden on the Native American Church members so that it could be upheld only if the law served a compelling state interest and was narrowly tailored to achieve that end....

These points of constitutional interpretation were debated by Members of Congress in hearings and floor debates. Many criticized the Court's reasoning, and this disagreement resulted in the passage of RFRA. Congress announced:

"(1) The framers of the Constitution, recognizing free exercise of religion as an unalienable right, secured its protection in the First Amendment to the Constitution;

"(2) laws 'neutral' toward religion may burden religious exercise as surely as laws intended to interfere with religious exercise;

"(3) governments should not substantially burden religious exercise without compelling justification;

"(4) *in Employment Division v. Smith*, 494 U.S. 872 (1990), the Supreme Court virtually eliminated the requirement that the government justify burdens on religious exercise imposed by laws neutral toward religion; and

"(5) the compelling interest test as set forth in prior Federal court rulings is a workable test for striking sensible balances between religious liberty and competing prior governmental interests." 42 U.S.C. §2000bb(a).

The Act's stated purposes are:

"(1) to restore the compelling interest test as set forth in *Sherbert v. Verner*, 374 U.S. 398 ... and to guarantee its application in all cases where free exercise of religion is substantially burdened; and

"(2) to provide a claim or defense to persons whose religious exercise is substantially burdened by government." §2000bb(b).

RFRA prohibits "government" from "substantially burdening" a person's exercise of religion even if the burden results from a rule of general applicability unless the government can demonstrate the burden "(1) is in furtherance of a compelling governmental interest; and (2) is the least restrictive means of furthering that compelling governmental interest." §2000bb-1. The Act's mandate applies to any "branch, department, agency, instrumentality, and official (or other person acting under color of law) of the United States," as well as to any "State, or ... subdivision of a State." §2000bb-2(1). The Act's universal coverage is confirmed in §2000bb-3(a), under which RFRA "applies to all Federal and State law, and the implementation of that law, whether statutory or otherwise, and whether adopted before or after [RFRA's enactment]." In accordance with RFRA's usage of the term, we shall use "state law" to include local and municipal ordinances.

### III

### A

Under our Constitution, the Federal Government is one of enumerated powers. *M'Culloch v. Maryland* (1819) [*Supra.* Chapters 3 & 4]. The judicial authority to determine the constitutionality of laws, in cases and controversies, is based on the premise that the "powers of the legislature are defined and limited; and that those limits may not be mistaken, or forgotten, the constitution is written." *Marbury v. Madison* (1803) [*Supra.* Chapter 1].

Congress relied on its Fourteenth Amendment enforcement power in enacting the most far-reaching and substantial of RFRA's provisions, those which impose its requirements on the States. See Religious Freedom Restoration Act of 1993, S.Rep. No. 103-111, pp. 13–14 (1993) (Senate Report); H.R.Rep. No. 103-88, p. 9 (1993) (House Report). The Fourteenth Amendment provides, in relevant part:

> "Section 1.... No State shall make or enforce any law which shall abridge the privileges or immunities of citizens of the United States; nor shall any State deprive any person of life, liberty, or property, without due process of law, nor deny to any person within its jurisdiction the equal protection of the laws.
>
> ....
>
> "Section 5. The Congress shall have power to enforce, by appropriate legislation, the provisions of this article."

The parties disagree over whether RFRA is a proper exercise of Congress' § 5 power "to enforce" by "appropriate legislation" the constitutional guarantee that no State shall deprive any person of "life, liberty, or property, without due process of law" nor deny any person "equal protection of the laws."

In defense of the Act, respondent the Archbishop contends, with support from the United States, that RFRA is permissible enforcement legislation. Congress, it is said, is only protecting by legislation one of the liberties guaranteed by the Fourteenth Amendment's Due Process Clause, the free exercise of religion, beyond what is necessary under *Smith*. It is said the congressional decision to dispense with proof of deliberate or overt discrimination and instead concentrate on a law's effects accords with the settled understanding that § 5 includes the power to enact legislation designed to prevent, as well as remedy, constitutional violations. It is further contended that Congress' § 5 power is not limited to remedial or preventive legislation.

All must acknowledge that § 5 is "a positive grant of legislative power" to Congress, *Katzenbach v. Morgan*, 384 U.S. 641 (1966) [Note *supra.* this chapter]. In *Ex parte Virginia*, 100 U.S. 339 (1879) [Note *supra.* Chapter 13], we explained the scope of Congress' § 5 power in the following broad terms:

> Whatever legislation is appropriate, that is, adapted to carry out the objects the amendments have in view, whatever tends to enforce submission to the prohibitions they contain, and to secure to all persons the enjoyment of perfect equality of civil rights and the equal protection of the laws against State denial or invasion, if not prohibited, is brought within the domain of congressional power.

Legislation which deters or remedies constitutional violations can fall within the sweep of Congress' enforcement power even if in the process it prohibits conduct which is not itself unconstitutional and intrudes into "legislative spheres of autonomy previously reserved to the States." *Fitzpatrick v. Bitzer* (1976) [*Supra.* Chapter 6]. For example, the Court upheld a suspension of literacy tests and similar voting requirements under Congress' parallel power to enforce the provisions of the Fifteenth Amendment, see U.S. Const., Amdt. 15, § 2, as a measure to combat racial discrimination in voting, *South Carolina v. Katzenbach*, 383 U.S. 301 (1966), despite the facial constitutionality of the tests under *Lassiter v. Northampton County Bd. of Elec-*

*tions*, 360 U.S. 45 (1959) [Note *supra.* this chapter]. We have also concluded that other measures protecting voting rights are within Congress' power to enforce the Fourteenth and Fifteenth Amendments, despite the burdens those measures placed on the States. *South Carolina v. Katzenbach* (upholding several provisions of the Voting Rights Act of 1965); *Katzenbach v. Morgan* (upholding ban on literacy tests that prohibited certain people schooled in Puerto Rico from voting); *Oregon v. Mitchell*, 400 U.S. 112 (1970) (upholding 5-year nationwide ban on literacy tests and similar voting requirements for registering to vote); *City of Rome v. United States*, 446 U.S. 156 (1980) (upholding 7-year extension of the Voting Rights Act's requirement that certain jurisdictions preclear any change to a "standard, practice, or procedure with respect to voting").

It is also true, however, that "as broad as the congressional enforcement power is, it is not unlimited." *Oregon v. Mitchell* (opinion of Black, J.). In assessing the breadth of §5's enforcement power, we begin with its text. Congress has been given the power "to enforce" the "provisions of this article." We agree with respondent, of course, that Congress can enact legislation under §5 enforcing the constitutional right to the free exercise of religion. The "provisions of this article," to which §5 refers, include the Due Process Clause of the Fourteenth Amendment. Congress' power to enforce the Free Exercise Clause follows from our holding in *Cantwell v. Connecticut*, 310 U.S. 296 (1940), that the "fundamental concept of liberty embodied in [the Fourteenth Amendment's Due Process Clause] embraces the liberties guaranteed by the First Amendment."

Congress' power under §5, however, extends only to "enforcing" the provisions of the Fourteenth Amendment. The Court has described this power as "remedial," *South Carolina v. Katzenbach.* The design of the Amendment and the text of §5 are inconsistent with the suggestion that Congress has the power to decree the substance of the Fourteenth Amendment's restrictions on the States. Legislation which alters the meaning of the Free Exercise Clause cannot be said to be enforcing the Clause. Congress does not enforce a constitutional right by changing what the right is. It has been given the power "to enforce," not the power to determine what constitutes a constitutional violation. Were it not so, what Congress would be enforcing would no longer be, in any meaningful sense, the "provisions of [the Fourteenth Amendment]."

While the line between measures that remedy or prevent unconstitutional actions and measures that make a substantive change in the governing law is not easy to discern, and Congress must have wide latitude in determining where it lies, the distinction exists and must be observed. There must be a congruence and proportionality between the injury to be prevented or remedied and the means adopted to that end. Lacking such a connection, legislation may become substantive in operation and effect. History and our case law support drawing the distinction, one apparent from the text of the Amendment.

1

The Fourteenth Amendment's history confirms the remedial, rather than substantive, nature of the Enforcement Clause. The Joint Committee on Reconstruction of the 39th Congress began drafting what would become the Fourteenth Amendment in January 1866. The objections to the Committee's first draft of the Amendment, and the rejection of the draft, have a direct bearing on the central issue of defining Congress' enforcement power. In February, Republican Representative John Bingham of Ohio reported the following draft Amendment to the House of Representatives on behalf of the Joint Committee:

> "The Congress shall have power to make all laws which shall be necessary and proper to secure to the citizens of each State all privileges and immunities of citizens in the several States, and to all persons in the several States equal protection in the rights of life, liberty, and property." Cong. Globe, 39th Cong., 1st Sess., 1034 (1866).

The proposal encountered immediate opposition.... Members of Congress from across the political spectrum criticized the Amendment, and the criticisms had a common theme: The proposed Amendment gave Congress too much legislative power at the expense of the existing constitutional structure. E.g., id., at 1063–1065 (statement of Rep. Hale); id., at 1082 (statement of Sen. Stewart); id., at 1095 (statement of Rep. Hotchkiss); id., at App. 133–135 (statement of Rep. Rogers). Democrats and conservative Republicans argued that the proposed Amendment would give Congress a power to intrude into traditional areas of state responsibility, a power inconsistent with the federal design central to the Constitution....

As a result of these objections having been expressed from so many different quarters, the House voted to table the proposal until April. The congressional action was seen as marking the defeat of the proposal. See The Nation, Mar. 8, 1866, p. 291 ("The postponement of the amendment ... is conclusive against the passage of [it]"). The measure was defeated "chiefly because many members of the legal profession s[aw] in [it] ... a dangerous centralization of power," The Nation, supra, at 291, and "many leading Republicans of the House [of Representatives] would not consent to so radical a change in the Constitution," Cong. Globe, 42d Cong., 1st Sess., App., at 151 (statement of Rep. Garfield). The Amendment in its early form was not again considered. Instead, the Joint Committee began drafting a new article of Amendment, which it reported to Congress on April 30, 1866.

Section 1 of the new draft Amendment imposed self-executing limits on the States. Section 5 prescribed that "the Congress shall have power to enforce, by appropriate legislation, the provisions of this article." Under the revised Amendment, Congress' power was no longer plenary but remedial. Congress was granted the power to make the substantive constitutional prohibitions against the States effective. Representative Bingham said the new draft would give Congress "the power ... to protect by national law the privileges and immunities of all the citizens of the Republic ... whenever the same shall be abridged or denied by the unconstitutional acts of any State." Representative Stevens described the new draft Amendment as "allowing Congress to correct the unjust legislation of the States." The revised Amendment proposal did not raise the concerns expressed earlier regarding broad congressional power to prescribe uniform national laws with respect to life, liberty, and property. See, e.g., Cong. Globe,

42d Cong., 1st Sess., at App. 151 (statement of Rep. Garfield) ("The [Fourteenth Amendment] limited but did not oust the jurisdiction of the States"). After revisions not relevant here, the new measure passed both Houses and was ratified in July 1868 as the Fourteenth Amendment.

The significance of the defeat of the Bingham proposal was apparent even then. During the debates over the Ku Klux Klan Act only a few years after the Amendment's ratification, Representative James Garfield argued there were limits on Congress' enforcement power, saying "unless we ignore both the history and the language of these clauses we cannot, by any reasonable interpretation, give to [§ 5] ... the force and effect of the rejected [Bingham] clause." *Ibid.* Scholars of successive generations have agreed with this assessment. See H. Flack, The Adoption of the Fourteenth Amendment 64 (1908); Bickel, The Voting Rights Cases, 1966 *S.Ct. Rev.* 79.

The design of the Fourteenth Amendment has proved significant also in maintaining the traditional separation of powers between Congress and the Judiciary. The first eight Amendments to the Constitution set forth self-executing prohibitions on governmental action, and this Court has had primary authority to interpret those prohibitions. The Bingham draft, some thought, departed from that tradition by vesting in Congress primary power to interpret and elaborate on the meaning of the new Amendment through legislation.... While this separation-of-powers aspect did not occasion the widespread resistance which was caused by the proposal's threat to the federal balance, it nonetheless attracted the attention of various Members. See Cong. Globe, 39th Cong., 1st Sess., at 1064 (statement of Rep. Hale) (noting that Bill of Rights, unlike the Bingham proposal, "provides safeguards to be enforced by the courts, and not to be exercised by the Legislature"); id., at App. 133 (statement of Rep. Rogers) (prior to Bingham proposal it "was left entirely for the courts ... to enforce the privileges and immunities of the citizens"). As enacted, the Fourteenth Amendment confers substantive rights against the States which, like the provisions of the Bill of Rights, are self-executing. The power to interpret the Constitution in a case or controversy remains in the Judiciary.

## 2

The remedial and preventive nature of Congress' enforcement power, and the limitation inherent in the power, were confirmed in our earliest cases on the Fourteenth Amendment. In the *Civil Rights Cases*, 109 U.S. 3 (1883) [Note *supra.* this chapter], the Court invalidated sections of the Civil Rights Act of 1875 which prescribed criminal penalties for denying to any person "the full enjoyment of" public accommodations and conveyances, on the grounds that it exceeded Congress' power by seeking to regulate private conduct. The Enforcement Clause, the Court said, did not authorize Congress to pass "general legislation upon the rights of the citizen, but corrective legislation, that is, such as may be necessary and proper for counteracting such laws as the States may adopt or enforce, and which, by the amendment, they are prohibited from making or enforcing...." The power to "legislate generally upon" life, liberty, and property, as opposed to the "power to provide modes of redress" against offensive state action, was "repugnant" to the Constitution. Id. Although the specific holdings of these early cases might have been superseded or modified, see, e.g., *Heart of Atlanta Motel, Inc. v. United States*, 379 U.S. 241 (1964) [Note *supra.* Chapter 4]; *United States v. Guest*, 383 U.S. 745 (1966), their treatment of Congress' § 5 power as corrective or preventive, not definitional, has not been questioned....

3

Any suggestion that Congress has a substantive, non-remedial power under the Fourteenth Amendment is not supported by our case law....

There is language in our opinion in *Katzenbach v. Morgan* which could be interpreted as acknowledging a power in Congress to enact legislation that expands the rights contained in § 1 of the Fourteenth Amendment. This is not a necessary interpretation, however, or even the best one. In *Morgan*, the Court considered the constitutionality of § 4(e) of the Voting Rights Act of 1965, which provided that no person who had successfully completed the sixth primary grade in a public school in, or a private school accredited by, the Commonwealth of Puerto Rico in which the language of instruction was other than English could be denied the right to vote because of an inability to read or write English. New York's Constitution, on the other hand, required voters to be able to read and write English. The Court provided two related rationales for its conclusion that § 4(e) could "be viewed as a measure to secure for the Puerto Rican community residing in New York nondiscriminatory treatment by government." Under the first rationale, Congress could prohibit New York from denying the right to vote to large segments of its Puerto Rican community, in order to give Puerto Ricans "enhanced political power" that would be "helpful in gaining nondiscriminatory treatment in public services for the entire Puerto Rican community." Section 4(e) thus could be justified as a remedial measure to deal with "discrimination in governmental services." The second rationale, an alternative holding, did not address discrimination in the provision of public services but "discrimination in establishing voter qualifications." The Court perceived a factual basis on which Congress could have concluded that New York's literacy requirement "constituted an invidious discrimination in violation of the Equal Protection Clause." Both rationales for upholding § 4(e) rested on unconstitutional discrimination by New York and Congress' reasonable attempt to combat it. As Justice Stewart explained in *Oregon v. Mitchell*, interpreting *Morgan* to give Congress the power to interpret the Constitution "would require an enormous extension of that decision's rationale."

If Congress could define its own powers by altering the Fourteenth Amendment's meaning, no longer would the Constitution be "superior paramount law, unchangeable by ordinary means." It would be "on a level with ordinary legislative acts, and, like other acts, ... alterable when the legislature shall please to alter it." *Marbury*. Under this approach, it is difficult to conceive of a principle that would limit congressional power. Shifting legislative majorities could change the Constitution and effectively circumvent the difficult and detailed amendment process contained in Article V.

We now turn to consider whether RFRA can be considered enforcement legislation under § 5 of the Fourteenth Amendment.

## B

Respondent contends that RFRA is a proper exercise of Congress' remedial or preventive power. The Act, it is said, is a reasonable means of protecting the free exercise of religion as defined by *Smith*. It prevents and remedies laws which are enacted with the unconstitutional object of targeting religious beliefs and practices. To avoid the difficulty of proving such violations, it is said, Congress can simply invalidate any law which imposes a substantial burden on a religious practice unless it is justified by a compelling interest and is the least restrictive means of accomplishing that interest. If Congress can prohibit laws with discriminatory effects in order to prevent racial discrimination in violation of the Equal Protection Clause, see *Fullilove v. Klutznick*, 448 U.S. 448 (1980) (plurality opinion) [Note *supra*. Chapter 13]; *City of Rome*, then it can do the same, respondent argues, to promote religious liberty.

While preventive rules are sometimes appropriate remedial measures, there must be a congruence between the means used and the ends to be achieved. The appropriateness of remedial measures must be considered in light of the evil presented. See *South Carolina v. Katzenbach*. Strong measures appropriate to address one harm may be an unwarranted response to another, lesser one.

A comparison between RFRA and the Voting Rights Act is instructive. In contrast to the record which confronted Congress and the Judiciary in the voting rights cases, RFRA's legislative record lacks examples of modern instances of generally applicable laws passed because of religious bigotry. The history of persecution in this country detailed in the hearings mentions no episodes occurring in the past 40 years. See, e.g., Religious Freedom Restoration Act of 1991, Hearings on H.R. 2797 before the Subcommittee on Civil and Constitutional Rights of the House Committee on the Judiciary, 102d Cong., 2d Sess., 331–334 (1993) (statement of Douglas Laycock) (House Hearings). The absence of more recent episodes stems from the fact that, as one witness testified, "deliberate persecution is not the usual problem in this country." House Hearings 334 (statement of Douglas Laycock). Rather, the emphasis of the hearings was on laws of general applicability which place incidental burdens on religion. Much of the discussion centered upon anecdotal evidence of autopsies performed on Jewish individuals and Hmong immigrants in violation of their religious beliefs, and on zoning regulations and historic preservation laws (like the one at issue here), which, as an incident of their normal operation, have adverse effects on churches and synagogues. It is difficult to maintain that they are examples of legislation enacted or enforced due to animus or hostility to the burdened religious practices or that they indicate some widespread pattern of religious discrimination in this country. Congress' concern was with the incidental burdens imposed, not the object or purpose of the legislation. See House Report 2; Senate Report 4–5; House Hearings 64 (statement of Nadine Strossen); id., at 117–118 (statement of Rep. Stephen J. Solarz); 1990 House Hearing 14 (statement of Rep. Stephen J. Solarz). This lack of support in the legislative record, however, is not RFRA's most serious shortcoming. Judicial deference, in most cases, is based not on the state of the legislative record Congress compiles but "on due regard for the decision of the body constitutionally appointed to decide."

As a general matter, it is for Congress to determine the method by which it will reach a decision.

Regardless of the state of the legislative record, RFRA cannot be considered remedial, preventive legislation, if those terms are to have any meaning. RFRA is so out of proportion to a supposed remedial or preventive object that it cannot be understood as responsive to, or designed to prevent, unconstitutional behavior. It appears, instead, to attempt a substantive change in constitutional protections. Preventive measures prohibiting certain types of laws may be appropriate when there is reason to believe that many of the laws affected by the congressional enactment have a significant likelihood of being unconstitutional. See *City of Rome* (since "jurisdictions with a demonstrable history of intentional racial discrimination ... create the risk of purposeful discrimination," Congress could "prohibit changes that have a discriminatory impact" in those jurisdictions). Remedial legislation under §5 "should be adapted to the mischief and wrong which the [Fourteenth] Amendment was intended to provide against." *Civil Rights Cases*.

RFRA is not so confined. Sweeping coverage ensures its intrusion at every level of government, displacing laws and prohibiting official actions of almost every description and regardless of subject matter. RFRA's restrictions apply to every agency and official of the Federal, State, and local Governments. RFRA applies to all federal and state law, statutory or otherwise, whether adopted before or after its enactment. RFRA has no termination date or termination mechanism. Any law is subject to challenge at any time by any individual who alleges a substantial burden on his or her free exercise of religion.

The reach and scope of RFRA distinguish it from other measures passed under Congress' enforcement power, even in the area of voting rights. In *South Carolina v. Katzenbach*, the challenged provisions were confined to those regions of the country where voting discrimination had been most flagrant, and affected a discrete class of state laws, i.e., state voting laws. Furthermore, to ensure that the reach of the Voting Rights Act was limited to those cases in which constitutional violations were most likely (in order to reduce the possibility of overbreadth), the coverage under the Act would terminate "at the behest of States and political subdivisions in which the danger of substantial voting discrimination has not materialized during the preceding five years." The provisions restricting and banning literacy tests, upheld in *Katzenbach v. Morgan* ... attacked a particular type of voting qualification, one with a long history as a "notorious means to deny and abridge voting rights on racial grounds." In *City of Rome*, the Court rejected a challenge to the constitutionality of a Voting Rights Act provision which required certain jurisdictions to submit changes in electoral practices to the Department of Justice for preimplementation review. The requirement was placed only on jurisdictions with a history of intentional racial discrimination in voting. Like the provisions at issue in *South Carolina v. Katzenbach*, this provision permitted a covered jurisdiction to avoid preclearance requirements under certain conditions and, moreover, lapsed in seven years. This is not to say, of course, that §5 legislation requires termination dates, geographic restrictions, or egregious predicates. Where, however, a congressional enactment pervasively prohibits constitutional state action in an effort to remedy or to prevent unconstitutional state action, limitations of this kind tend to ensure Congress' means are proportionate to ends legitimate under § 5.

The stringent test RFRA demands of state laws reflects a lack of proportionality or congruence between the means adopted and the legitimate end to be achieved. If an objector can show a substantial burden on his free exercise, the State must demonstrate a compelling governmental interest and show that the law is the least restrictive means of furthering its interest. Claims that a law substantially burdens someone's exercise of religion will often be difficult to contest. Requiring a State to demonstrate a compelling interest and show that it has adopted the least restrictive means of achieving that interest is the most demanding test known to constitutional law. If " 'compelling interest' really means what it says ... many laws will not meet the test.... [The test] would open the prospect of constitutionally required religious exemptions from civic obligations of almost every conceivable kind." *Smith*. Laws valid under *Smith* would fall under RFRA without regard to whether they had the object of stifling or punishing free exercise. We make these observations not to reargue the position of the majority in *Smith* but to illustrate the substantive alteration of its holding attempted by RFRA. Even assuming RFRA would be interpreted in effect to mandate some lesser test, say, one equivalent to intermediate scrutiny, the statute nevertheless would require searching judicial scrutiny of state law with the attendant likelihood of invalidation. This is a considerable congressional intrusion into the States' traditional prerogatives and general authority to regulate for the health and welfare of their citizens.

The substantial costs RFRA exacts, both in practical terms of imposing a heavy litigation burden on the States and in terms of curtailing their traditional general regulatory power, far exceed any pattern or practice of unconstitutional conduct under the Free Exercise Clause as interpreted in *Smith*. Simply put, RFRA is not designed to identify and counteract state laws likely to be unconstitutional because of their treatment of religion. In most cases, the state laws to which RFRA applies are not ones which will have been motivated by religious bigotry. If a state law disproportionately burdened a particular class of religious observers, this circumstance might be evidence of an impermissible legislative motive. Cf. *Washington v. Davis* (1976) [*Supra*. Chapter 14]. RFRA's substantial-burden test, however, is not even a discriminatory effects or disparate-impact test. It is a reality of the modern regulatory state that numerous state laws, such as the zoning regulations at issue here, impose a substantial burden on a large class of individuals. When the exercise of religion has been burdened in an incidental way by a law of general application, it does not follow that the persons affected have been burdened any more than other citizens, let alone burdened because of their religious beliefs. In addition, the Act imposes in every case a least restrictive means requirement—a requirement that was not used in the pre-*Smith* jurisprudence RFRA purported to codify—which also indicates that the legislation is broader than is appropriate if the goal is to prevent and remedy constitutional violations.

When Congress acts within its sphere of power and responsibilities, it has not just the right but the duty to make its own informed judgment on the meaning and force of the Constitution. This has been clear from the early days of the Republic. In 1789, when a Member of the House of Representatives objected to a debate on the constitutionality of legislation based on the theory that "it would be officious" to consider the constitutionality of a measure that did not affect the House, James Madison explained that "it is incontrovertibly of as much importance to this branch of the Government as to any other, that the constitution should be preserved entire. It is our duty." 1 Annals of Congress 500 (1789). Were it otherwise, we would not afford Congress the presumption of validity its enactments now enjoy.

Our national experience teaches that the Constitution is preserved best when each part of the Government respects both the Constitution and the proper actions and determinations of the other branches. When the Court has interpreted the Constitution, it has acted within the province of the Judicial Branch, which embraces the duty to say what the law is. *Marbury v. Madison* (1803) (*Supra.* Chapter 1). When the political branches of the Government act against the background of a judicial interpretation of the Constitution already issued, it must be understood that in later cases and controversies the Court will treat its precedents with the respect due them under settled principles, including stare decisis, and contrary expectations must be disappointed. RFRA was designed to control cases and controversies, such as the one before us; but as the provisions of the federal statute here invoked are beyond congressional authority, it is this Court's precedent, not RFRA, which must control.

It is for Congress in the first instance to "determine whether and what legislation is needed to secure the guarantees of the Fourteenth Amendment," and its conclusions are entitled to much deference. *Katzenbach v. Morgan.* Congress' discretion is not unlimited, however, and the courts retain the power, as they have since *Marbury v. Madison*, to determine if Congress has exceeded its authority under the Constitution. Broad as the power of Congress is under the Enforcement Clause of the Fourteenth Amendment, RFRA contradicts vital principles necessary to maintain separation of powers and the federal balance. The judgment of the Court of Appeals sustaining the Act's constitutionality is reversed.

Justice STEVENS, concurring. [omitted].

Justice SCALIA, with whom Justice STEVENS joins, concurring in part.

[Justice Scalia responded to Justice O'Connor's attack on the Court's reasoning in *Smith*, the case to which RFRA was intended to respond.]

Justice O'CONNOR, with whom Justice BREYER joins except as to the first paragraph of Part I, dissenting.

… I remain of the view that *Smith* was wrongly decided, and I would use this case to reexamine the Court's holding there. …

I

I agree with much of the reasoning set forth in Part III-A of the Court's opinion. Indeed, if I agreed with the Court's standard in *Smith*, I would join the opinion.

As the Court's careful and thorough historical analysis shows, Congress lacks the "power to decree the substance of the Fourteenth Amendment's restrictions on the States." *Ante.* Rather, its power under § 5 of the Fourteenth Amendment extends only to enforcing the Amendment's provisions. In short, Congress lacks the ability independently to define or expand the scope of constitutional rights by statute. Accordingly, whether Congress has exceeded its § 5 powers turns on whether there is a "congruence and proportionality between the injury to be prevented or remedied and the means adopted to that end." *Ante.* This recognition does not, of course, in any way diminish Congress' obligation to draw its own conclusions regarding the Constitution's meaning. Congress, no less than this Court, is called upon to consider the requirements of the Constitution and to act in accordance with its dictates. But when it enacts legislation in furtherance of its delegated powers, Congress must make its judgments consistent with this Court's exposition of the Constitution and with the limits placed on its legislative authority by provisions such as the Fourteenth Amendment.

The Court's analysis of whether RFRA is a constitutional exercise of Congress' § 5 power, set forth in Part III-B of its opinion, is premised on the assumption that *Smith* correctly interprets the Free Exercise Clause. This is an assumption that I do not accept. I continue to believe that *Smith* adopted an improper standard for deciding free exercise claims....

Justice SOUTER, dissenting.

To decide whether the Fourteenth Amendment gives Congress sufficient power to enact the Religious Freedom Restoration Act of 1993, the Court measures the legislation against the free-exercise standard of *Employment Div., Dept. of Human Resources of Oregon v. Smith....* [I] have serious doubts about the precedential value of the *Smith* rule and its entitlement to adherence.... But without briefing and argument on the merits of that rule ... I am not now prepared to join Justice O'CONNOR in rejecting it or the majority in assuming it to be correct. In order to provide full adversarial consideration, this case should be set down for reargument permitting plenary reexamination of the issue. Since the Court declines to follow that course, ... the constitutionality of the Act of Congress to enforce the free-exercise right cannot now be soundly decided. I would therefore dismiss the writ of certiorari as improvidently granted, and I accordingly dissent from the Court's disposition of this case.

Justice BREYER, dissenting.

I agree with Justice O'CONNOR that the Court should direct the parties to brief the question whether *Smith* was correctly decided, and set this case for reargument. I do not, however, find it necessary to consider the question whether, assuming *Smith* is correct, § 5 of the Fourteenth Amendment would authorize Congress to enact the legislation before us. Thus, while I agree with some of the views expressed in the first paragraph of Part I of Justice O'CONNOR's dissent, I do not necessarily agree with all of them. I therefore join Justice O'CONNOR's dissent, with the exception of the first paragraph of Part I.

## *Note:* City of Boerne v. Flores

1. Justice Kennedy's Enforcement Clause analysis in *City of Boerne* was broadly accepted by the Court. Six justices signed onto all or most of the opinion. Among the three dissenters, Justice O'Connor explicitly agreed with the Court's Enforcement Clause analysis, and took issue only with the underlying question of how far the free religious exercise right should be understood; Justice Breyer approved of at least part of Justice O'Connor's agreement with the majority's Enforcement Clause analysis; and Justice Souter, also disagreeing with the scope of the underlying right, did not reach the Enforcement Clause issue. Thus, *City of Boerne* enjoyed a level of consensus that was (and remains) rare for such a high-stakes constitutional law case. What do you think explains that consensus?

2. As exemplified in *City of Boerne*, the Court's analysis of enforcement legislation under the "congruence and proportionality" standard entails two steps. First, the Court identifies the constitutional right at issue, and the degree to which that right is being violated. Second, it compares that right to the scope of the enforcement legislation, to determine whether that legislation is "congruent and proportional" to the right it seeks to enforce. This step includes considering both whether Congress has uncovered evidence of a pattern of state violations of the underlying constitutional rule, and the breadth of the enforcement legislation. In *City of Boerne* the Court concluded that RFRA's broad protection for religious exercise was disproportionate to the underlying constitutional violation it sought to deter—the singling out of religious exercise for disfavored treatment.

3. As noted above, justices on both sides of the political spectrum joined *City of Boerne*. However, rifts soon developed in its application. The two following cases reflect those rifts, which have continued into the present. They also reveal the crucial role the congruence and proportionality test accords to the constitutional status of the underlying right, as identified by the Court itself. The importance of that judicial analysis of the underlying right Congress seeks to protect underscores the important role the Court plays—not just directly but also indirectly—in determining the scope of Congress's power under the Enforcement Clause.

## Board of Trustees of the University of Alabama v. Garrett
### 531 U.S. 356 (2001)

Chief Justice REHNQUIST delivered the opinion of the Court.

We decide here whether employees of the State of Alabama may recover money damages by reason of the State's failure to comply with the provisions of Title I of the Americans with Disabilities Act of 1990 (ADA or Act), 42 U.S.C. §§ 12111–12117. We hold that such suits are barred by the Eleventh Amendment.

The ADA prohibits certain employers, including the States, from "discriminating against a qualified individual with a disability because of the disability of such individual in regard to job application procedures, the hiring, advancement, or discharge of employees, employee compensation, job training, and other terms, conditions, and privileges of employment." To this end, the Act requires employers to "make reasonable accommodations to the known physical or mental limitations of an otherwise qualified individual with a disability who is an applicant or employee, unless [the employer] can demonstrate that the accommodation would impose an undue hardship on the operation of the [employer's] business." ...

Respondent Patricia Garrett, a registered nurse, was employed as the Director of Nursing, OB/Gyn/Neonatal Services, for the University of Alabama in Birmingham Hospital. In 1994, Garrett was diagnosed with breast cancer and subsequently underwent a lumpectomy, radiation treatment, and chemotherapy. Garrett's treatments required her to take substantial leave from work. Upon returning to work in July 1995, Garrett's supervisor informed Garrett that she would have to give up her Director position. Garrett then applied for and received a transfer to another, lower paying position as a nurse manager. See ibid.

Respondent Milton Ash worked as a security officer for the Alabama Department of Youth Services (Department). Upon commencing this employment, Ash informed the Department that he suffered from chronic asthma and that his doctor recommended he avoid carbon monoxide and cigarette smoke, and Ash requested that the Department modify his duties to minimize his exposure to these substances. Ash was later diagnosed with sleep apnea and requested, again pursuant to his doctor's recommendation, that he be reassigned to daytime shifts to accommodate his condition. Ultimately, the Department granted none of the requested relief. Shortly after Ash filed a discrimination claim with the Equal Employment Opportunity Commission, he noticed that his performance evaluations were lower than those he had received on previous occasions.

Garrett and Ash filed separate lawsuits in the District Court, both seeking money damages under the ADA. Petitioners moved for summary judgment, claiming that the ADA exceeds Congress' authority to abrogate the State's Eleventh Amendment immunity. In a single opinion disposing of both cases, the District Court agreed with petitioners' position and granted their motions for summary judgment. The cases were consolidated on appeal to the Eleventh Circuit. The Court of Appeals reversed....

We granted certiorari to resolve a split among the Courts of Appeals on the question whether an individual may sue a State for money damages in federal court under the ADA.

I

The Eleventh Amendment provides:

> The Judicial power of the United States shall not be construed to extend to any suit in law or equity, commenced or prosecuted against one of the United States by Citizens of another State, or by Citizens or Subjects of any Foreign State.

Although by its terms the Amendment applies only to suits against a State by citizens of another State, our cases have extended the Amendment's applicability to suits by citizens against their own States. See *Kimel v. Florida Bd. of Regents*, 528 U.S.

62 (2000); *College Savings Bank v. Florida Prepaid Postsecondary Ed. Expense Bd.*, 527 U.S. 666 (1999); *Seminole Tribe of Fla. v. Florida* (1996) [*Supra.* Chapter 6]; *Hans v. Louisiana*, 134 U.S. 1 (1890) [Note *supra.* Chapter 6]. The ultimate guarantee of the Eleventh Amendment is that nonconsenting States may not be sued by private individuals in federal court.

We have recognized, however, that Congress may abrogate the States' Eleventh Amendment immunity when it both unequivocally intends to do so and "acts pursuant to a valid grant of constitutional authority." The first of these requirements is not in dispute here. See 42 U.S.C. § 12202 ("A State shall not be immune under the eleventh amendment to the Constitution of the United States from an action in a Federal or State court of competent jurisdiction for a violation of this chapter"). The question, then, is whether Congress acted within its constitutional authority by subjecting the States to suits in federal court for money damages under the ADA.

Congress may not, of course, base its abrogation of the States' Eleventh Amendment immunity upon the powers enumerated in Article I. See *Seminole Tribe* ("The Eleventh Amendment restricts the judicial power under Article III, and Article I cannot be used to circumvent the constitutional limitations placed upon federal jurisdiction"); *Alden v. Maine* (1999) [*Supra.* Chapter 6]. In *Fitzpatrick v. Bitzer* (1976) [*Supra.* Chapter 6], however, we held that "the Eleventh Amendment, and the principle of state sovereignty which it embodies, are necessarily limited by the enforcement provisions of § 5 of the Fourteenth Amendment." As a result, we concluded, Congress may subject nonconsenting States to suit in federal court when it does so pursuant to a valid exercise of its § 5 power.... Accordingly, the ADA can apply to the States only to the extent that the statute is appropriate § 5 legislation.

Section 1 of the Fourteenth Amendment provides, in relevant part:

> No State shall make or enforce any law which shall abridge the privileges or immunities of citizens of the United States; nor shall any State deprive any person of life, liberty, or property, without due process of law; nor deny to any person within its jurisdiction the equal protection of the laws.

Section 5 of the Fourteenth Amendment grants Congress the power to enforce the substantive guarantees contained in § 1 by enacting "appropriate legislation." See *City of Boerne v. Flores* (1997) [*Supra.* this chapter]. Congress is not limited to mere legislative repetition of this Court's constitutional jurisprudence. "Rather, Congress' power 'to enforce' the Amendment includes the authority both to remedy and to deter violation of rights guaranteed thereunder by prohibiting a somewhat broader swath of conduct, including that which is not itself forbidden by the Amendment's text." *Kimel*; *City of Boerne*.

*City of Boerne* also confirmed, however, the long-settled principle that it is the responsibility of this Court, not Congress, to define the substance of constitutional guarantees. Accordingly, § 5 legislation reaching beyond the scope of § 1's actual guarantees must exhibit "congruence and proportionality between the injury to be prevented or remedied and the means adopted to that end."

## II

The first step in applying these now familiar principles is to identify with some precision the scope of the constitutional right at issue. Here, that inquiry requires us to examine the limitations § 1 of the Fourteenth Amendment places upon States' treatment of the disabled. As we did last Term in *Kimel*, we look to our prior decisions under the Equal Protection Clause dealing with this issue.

In *Cleburne v. Cleburne Living Center, Inc.* (1985) [*Supra.* Chapter 15], we considered an equal protection challenge to a city ordinance requiring a special use permit for the operation of a group home for the mentally retarded. The specific question before us was whether the Court of Appeals had erred by holding that mental retardation qualified as a "quasi-suspect" classification under our equal protection jurisprudence. We answered that question in the affirmative, concluding instead that such legislation incurs only the minimum "rational-basis" review applicable to general social and economic legislation.[4] In a statement that today seems quite prescient, we explained that

> if the large and amorphous class of the mentally retarded were deemed quasi-suspect for the reasons given by the Court of Appeals, it would be difficult to find a principled way to distinguish a variety of other groups who have perhaps immutable disabilities setting them off from others, who cannot themselves mandate the desired legislative responses, and who can claim some degree of prejudice from at least part of the public at large. One need mention in this respect only the aging, the disabled, the mentally ill, and the infirm. We are reluctant to set out on that course, and we decline to do so.

Under rational-basis review, where a group possesses "distinguishing characteristics relevant to interests the State has the authority to implement," a State's decision to act on the basis of those differences does not give rise to a constitutional violation. "Such a classification cannot run afoul of the Equal Protection Clause if there is a rational relationship between the disparity of treatment and some legitimate governmental purpose." *Heller v. Doe*, 509 U.S. 312 (1993). Moreover, the State need not articulate its reasoning at the moment a particular decision is made. Rather, the burden is upon the challenging party to negative "any reasonably conceivable state of facts that could provide a rational basis for the classification." *Heller*.

Justice BREYER suggests that *Cleburne* stands for the broad proposition that state decisionmaking reflecting "negative attitudes" or "fear" necessarily runs afoul of the Fourteenth Amendment. See *post* (dissenting opinion) (quoting *Cleburne*). Although such biases may often accompany irrational (and therefore unconstitutional) dis-

---

4. Applying the basic principles of rationality review, *Cleburne* struck down the city ordinance in question. The Court's reasoning was that the city's purported justifications for the ordinance made no sense in light of how the city treated other groups similarly situated in relevant respects. Although the group home for the mentally retarded was required to obtain a special use permit, apartment houses, other multiple-family dwellings, retirement homes, nursing homes, sanitariums, hospitals, boarding houses, fraternity and sorority houses, and dormitories were not subject to the ordinance.

crimination, their presence alone does not a constitutional violation make. As we noted in *Cleburne*: "Mere negative attitudes, or fear, unsubstantiated by factors which are properly cognizable in a zoning proceeding, are not permissible bases for treating a home for the mentally retarded differently...." This language, read in context, simply states the unremarkable and widely acknowledged tenet of this Court's equal protection jurisprudence that state action subject to rational-basis scrutiny does not violate the Fourteenth Amendment when it "rationally furthers the purpose identified by the State." *Massachusetts Bd. of Retirement v. Murgia* (1976) (per curiam) [*Supra.* Chapter 12].

Thus, the result of *Cleburne* is that States are not required by the Fourteenth Amendment to make special accommodations for the disabled, so long as their actions toward such individuals are rational. They could quite hardheadedly—and perhaps hardheartedly—hold to job-qualification requirements which do not make allowance for the disabled. If special accommodations for the disabled are to be required, they have to come from positive law and not through the Equal Protection Clause.[5]

## III

Once we have determined the metes and bounds of the constitutional right in question, we examine whether Congress identified a history and pattern of unconstitutional employment discrimination by the States against the disabled. Just as § 1 of the Fourteenth Amendment applies only to actions committed "under color of state law," Congress' § 5 authority is appropriately exercised only in response to state transgressions. See *Kimel* ("Congress never identified any pattern of age discrimination by the States, much less any discrimination whatsoever that rose to the level of constitutional violation"). The legislative record of the ADA, however, simply fails to show that Congress did in fact identify a pattern of irrational state discrimination in employment against the disabled.

Respondents contend that the inquiry as to unconstitutional discrimination should extend not only to States themselves, but to units of local governments, such as cities and counties. All of these, they say, are "state actors" for purposes of the Fourteenth Amendment. This is quite true, but the Eleventh Amendment does not extend its immunity to units of local government. These entities are subject to private claims for damages under the ADA without Congress' ever having to rely on § 5 of the Fourteenth Amendment to render them so. It would make no sense to consider constitutional violations on their part, as well as by the States themselves, when only the States are the beneficiaries of the Eleventh Amendment.

---

5. It is worth noting that by the time that Congress enacted the ADA in 1990, every State in the Union had enacted such measures. At least one Member of Congress remarked that "this is probably one of the few times where the States are so far out in front of the Federal Government, it's not funny." Hearing on Discrimination Against Cancer Victims and the Handicapped before the Subcommittee on Employment Opportunities of the House Committee on Education and Labor, 100th Cong., 1st Sess., 5 (1987). A number of these provisions, however, did not go as far as the ADA did in requiring accommodation.

Congress made a general finding in the ADA that "historically, society has tended to isolate and segregate individuals with disabilities, and, despite some improvements, such forms of discrimination against individuals with disabilities continue to be a serious and pervasive social problem." 42 U.S.C. § 12101(a)(2). The record assembled by Congress includes many instances to support such a finding. But the great majority of these incidents do not deal with the activities of States.

Respondents in their brief cite half a dozen examples from the record that did involve States. A department head at the University of North Carolina refused to hire an applicant for the position of health administrator because he was blind; similarly, a student at a state university in South Dakota was denied an opportunity to practice teach because the dean at that time was convinced that blind people could not teach in public schools. A microfilmer at the Kansas Department of Transportation was fired because he had epilepsy; deaf workers at the University of Oklahoma were paid a lower salary than those who could hear. The Indiana State Personnel Office informed a woman with a concealed disability that she should not disclose it if she wished to obtain employment.[6]

Several of these incidents undoubtedly evidence an unwillingness on the part of state officials to make the sort of accommodations for the disabled required by the ADA. Whether they were irrational under our decision in *Cleburne* is more debatable, particularly when the incident is described out of context. But even if it were to be determined that each incident upon fuller examination showed unconstitutional action on the part of the State, these incidents taken together fall far short of even suggesting the pattern of unconstitutional discrimination on which § 5 legislation must be based. Congress, in enacting the ADA, found that "some 43,000,000 Americans have one or more physical or mental disabilities." 42 U.S.C. § 12101(a)(1). In 1990, the States alone employed more than 4.5 million people. It is telling, we think, that given these large numbers, Congress assembled only such minimal evidence of unconstitutional state discrimination in employment against the disabled.

Justice BREYER maintains that Congress applied Title I of the ADA to the States in response to a host of incidents representing unconstitutional state discrimination in employment against persons with disabilities. A close review of the relevant materials, however, undercuts that conclusion. Justice BREYER's Appendix C consists not of legislative findings, but of unexamined, anecdotal accounts of "adverse, disparate treatment by state officials." *Post.* Of course, as we have already explained, "adverse, disparate treatment" often does not amount to a constitutional violation where rational-basis scrutiny applies. These accounts, moreover, were submitted not directly to Congress but to the Task Force on the Rights and Empowerment of Americans

---

6. The record does show that some States, adopting the tenets of the eugenics movement of the early part of this century, required extreme measures such as sterilization of persons suffering from hereditary mental disease. These laws were upheld against constitutional attack 70 years ago in *Buck v. Bell*, 274 U.S. 200 (1927) [Note *supra.* Chapter 8]. But there is no indication that any State had persisted in requiring such harsh measures as of 1990 when the ADA was adopted.

with Disabilities, which made no findings on the subject of state discrimination in employment.[7] See the Task Force's Report entitled From ADA to Empowerment (Oct. 12, 1990). And, had Congress truly understood this information as reflecting a pattern of unconstitutional behavior by the States, one would expect some mention of that conclusion in the Act's legislative findings. There is none. Although Justice BREYER would infer from Congress' general conclusions regarding societal discrimination against the disabled that the States had likewise participated in such action, the House and Senate committee reports on the ADA flatly contradict this assertion. After describing the evidence presented to the Senate Committee on Labor and Human Resources and its subcommittee (including the Task Force Report upon which the dissent relies), the Committee's Report reached, among others, the following conclusion: "Discrimination still persists in such critical areas as employment in the private sector, public accommodations, public services, transportation, and telecommunications." The House Committee on Education and Labor, addressing the ADA's employment provisions, reached the same conclusion: "After extensive review and analysis over a number of Congressional sessions, … there exists a compelling need to establish a clear and comprehensive Federal prohibition of discrimination on the basis of disability in the areas of employment in the private sector, public accommodations, public services, transportation, and telecommunications." Thus, not only is the inference Justice BREYER draws unwarranted, but there is also strong evidence that Congress' failure to mention States in its legislative findings addressing discrimination in employment reflects that body's judgment that no pattern of unconstitutional state action had been documented.

Even were it possible to squeeze out of these examples a pattern of unconstitutional discrimination by the States, the rights and remedies created by the ADA against the States would raise the same sort of concerns as to congruence and proportionality as were found in *City of Boerne*. For example, whereas it would be entirely rational (and therefore constitutional) for a state employer to conserve scarce financial resources by hiring employees who are able to use existing facilities, the ADA requires employers to "make existing facilities used by employees readily accessible to and usable by individuals with disabilities." The ADA does except employers from the "reasonable accommodation" requirement where the employer "can demonstrate that the accommodation would impose an undue hardship on the operation of the business of such covered entity." However, even with this exception, the accommodation duty far exceeds what is constitutionally required in that it makes unlawful a range of alternative responses that would be reasonable but would fall short of im-

7. Only a small fraction of the anecdotes Justice BREYER identifies in his Appendix C relate to state discrimination against the disabled in employment. At most, somewhere around 50 of these allegations describe conduct that could conceivably amount to constitutional violations by the States, and most of them are so general and brief that no firm conclusion can be drawn. The overwhelming majority of these accounts pertain to alleged discrimination by the States in the provision of public services and public accommodations, which areas are addressed in Titles II and III of the ADA.

posing an "undue burden" upon the employer. The Act also makes it the employer's duty to prove that it would suffer such a burden, instead of requiring (as the Constitution does) that the complaining party negate reasonable bases for the employer's decision.

The ADA also forbids "utilizing standards, criteria, or methods of administration" that disparately impact the disabled, without regard to whether such conduct has a rational basis. Although disparate impact may be relevant evidence of racial discrimination, see *Washington v. Davis* (1976) [*Supra.* Chapter 14], such evidence alone is insufficient even where the Fourteenth Amendment subjects state action to strict scrutiny. See, e.g., *ibid*. ("Our cases have not embraced the proposition that a law or other official act, without regard to whether it reflects a racially discriminatory purpose, is unconstitutional solely because it has a racially disproportionate impact").

The ADA's constitutional shortcomings are apparent when the Act is compared to Congress' efforts in the Voting Rights Act of 1965 to respond to a serious pattern of constitutional violations. In *South Carolina v. Katzenbach*, 383 U.S. 301 (1966), we considered whether the Voting Rights Act was "appropriate" legislation to enforce the Fifteenth Amendment's protection against racial discrimination in voting. Concluding that it was a valid exercise of Congress' enforcement power under § 2 of the Fifteenth Amendment,[8] we noted that "before enacting the measure, Congress explored with great care the problem of racial discrimination in voting."

In that Act, Congress documented a marked pattern of unconstitutional action by the States. State officials, Congress found, routinely applied voting tests in order to exclude African-American citizens from registering to vote. Congress also determined that litigation had proved ineffective and that there persisted an otherwise inexplicable 50-percentage-point gap in the registration of white and African-American voters in some States. Congress' response was to promulgate in the Voting Rights Act a detailed but limited remedial scheme designed to guarantee meaningful enforcement of the Fifteenth Amendment in those areas of the Nation where abundant evidence of States' systematic denial of those rights was identified.

The contrast between this kind of evidence, and the evidence that Congress considered in the present case, is stark. Congressional enactment of the ADA represents its judgment that there should be a "comprehensive national mandate for the elimination of discrimination against individuals with disabilities." Congress is the final authority as to desirable public policy, but in order to authorize private individuals to recover money damages against the States, there must be a pattern of discrimination by the States which violates the Fourteenth Amendment, and the remedy imposed by Congress must be congruent and proportional to the targeted violation. Those requirements are not met here, and to uphold the Act's application to the States would

---

8. Section 2 of the Fifteenth Amendment is virtually identical to § 5 of the Fourteenth Amendment.

allow Congress to rewrite the Fourteenth Amendment law laid down by this Court in *Cleburne*.[9] Section 5 does not so broadly enlarge congressional authority. The judgment of the Court of Appeals is therefore

Reversed.

Justice KENNEDY, with whom Justice O'CONNOR joins, concurring.

Prejudice, we are beginning to understand, rises not from malice or hostile animus alone. It may result as well from insensitivity caused by simple want of careful, rational reflection or from some instinctive mechanism to guard against people who appear to be different in some respects from ourselves. Quite apart from any historical documentation, knowledge of our own human instincts teaches that persons who find it difficult to perform routine functions by reason of some mental or physical impairment might at first seem unsettling to us, unless we are guided by the better angels of our nature. There can be little doubt, then, that persons with mental or physical impairments are confronted with prejudice which can stem from indifference or insecurity as well as from malicious ill will.

One of the undoubted achievements of statutes designed to assist those with impairments is that citizens have an incentive, flowing from a legal duty, to develop a better understanding, a more decent perspective, for accepting persons with impairments or disabilities into the larger society. The law works this way because the law can be a teacher. So I do not doubt that the Americans with Disabilities Act of 1990 will be a milestone on the path to a more decent, tolerant, progressive society.

It is a question of quite a different order, however, to say that the States in their official capacities, the States as governmental entities, must be held in violation of the Constitution on the assumption that they embody the misconceived or malicious perceptions of some of their citizens. It is a most serious charge to say a State has engaged in a pattern or practice designed to deny its citizens the equal protection of the laws, particularly where the accusation is based not on hostility but instead on the failure to act or the omission to remedy. States can, and do, stand apart from the citizenry. States act as neutral entities, ready to take instruction and to enact laws when their citizens so demand. The failure of a State to revise policies now seen as incorrect under a new understanding of proper policy does not always constitute the purposeful and intentional action required to make out a violation of the Equal Protection Clause. See *Washington v. Davis*.

---

9. Our holding here that Congress did not validly abrogate the States' sovereign immunity from suit by private individuals for money damages under Title I does not mean that persons with disabilities have no federal recourse against discrimination. Title I of the ADA still prescribes standards applicable to the States. Those standards can be enforced by the United States in actions for money damages, as well as by private individuals in actions for injunctive relief under *Ex parte Young*, 209 U.S. 123 (1908) [Note *supra*. Chapter 6]. In addition, state laws protecting the rights of persons with disabilities in employment and other aspects of life provide independent avenues of redress. See n. 5, *supra*.

For the reasons explained by the Court, an equal protection violation has not been shown with respect to the several States in this case. If the States had been transgressing the Fourteenth Amendment by their mistreatment or lack of concern for those with impairments, one would have expected to find in decisions of the courts of the States and also the courts of the United States extensive litigation and discussion of the constitutional violations. This confirming judicial documentation does not exist. That there is a new awareness, a new consciousness, a new commitment to better treatment of those disadvantaged by mental or physical impairments does not establish that an absence of state statutory correctives was a constitutional violation.

It must be noted, moreover, that what is in question is not whether the Congress, acting pursuant to a power granted to it by the Constitution, can compel the States to act. What is involved is only the question whether the States can be subjected to liability in suits brought not by the Federal Government (to which the States have consented, see *Alden v. Maine*, but by private persons seeking to collect moneys from the state treasury without the consent of the State. The predicate for money damages against an unconsenting State in suits brought by private persons must be a federal statute enacted upon the documentation of patterns of constitutional violations committed by the State in its official capacity. That predicate, for reasons discussed here and in the decision of the Court, has not been established. With these observations, I join the Court's opinion.

Justice BREYER, with whom Justice STEVENS, Justice SOUTER, and Justice GINSBURG join, dissenting.

Reviewing the congressional record as if it were an administrative agency record, the Court holds the statutory provision before us, 42 U.S.C. § 12202, unconstitutional. The Court concludes that Congress assembled insufficient evidence of unconstitutional discrimination, that Congress improperly attempted to "rewrite" the law we established in *Cleburne*, and that the law is not sufficiently tailored to address unconstitutional discrimination.

Section 5, however, grants Congress the "power to enforce, by appropriate legislation," the Fourteenth Amendment's equal protection guarantee. U.S. Const., Amdt. 14, § 5. As the Court recognizes, state discrimination in employment against persons with disabilities might "'run afoul of the Equal Protection Clause'" where there is no "'rational relationship between the disparity of treatment and some legitimate governmental purpose.'" In my view, Congress reasonably could have concluded that the remedy before us constitutes an "appropriate" way to enforce this basic equal protection requirement. And that is all the Constitution requires.

I

The Court says that its primary problem with this statutory provision is one of legislative evidence. It says that "Congress assembled only ... minimal evidence of unconstitutional state discrimination in employment." In fact, Congress compiled a vast legislative record documenting "'massive, society-wide discrimination'" against persons with disabilities. S.Rep. No. 101-116, pp. 8–9 (1989) (quoting testimony of Justin Dart, chairperson of the Task Force on the Rights and Empowerment of Americans with Disabilities). In addition to the information presented at 13 congressional hearings (see Appendix A, *infra*), and its own prior experience gathered over 40 years during which it contemplated and enacted considerable similar legislation (see Appendix B, *infra*), Congress created a special task force to assess the need for comprehensive legislation. That task force held hearings in every State, attended by more than 30,000 people, including thousands who had experienced discrimination first hand. See From ADA to Empowerment, Task Force on the Rights and Empowerment of Americans with Disabilities 16 (Oct. 12, 1990) (hereinafter Task Force Report). The task force hearings, Congress' own hearings, and an analysis of "census data, national polls, and other studies" led Congress to conclude that "people with disabilities, as a group, occupy an inferior status in our society, and are severely disadvantaged socially, vocationally, economically, and educationally." 42 U.S.C. § 12101(a)(6). As to employment, Congress found that "two-thirds of all disabled Americans between the age of 16 and 64 [were] not working at all," even though a large majority wanted to, and were able to, work productively. S.Rep. No. 101-116, at 9. And Congress found that this discrimination flowed in significant part from "stereotypic assumptions" as well as "purposeful unequal treatment." 42 U.S.C. § 12101(a)(7).

The powerful evidence of discriminatory treatment throughout society in general, including discrimination by private persons and local governments, implicates state governments as well, for state agencies form part of that same larger society. There is no particular reason to believe that they are immune from the "stereotypic assumptions" and pattern of "purposeful unequal treatment" that Congress found prevalent. The Court claims that it "makes no sense" to take into consideration constitutional violations committed by local governments. But the substantive obligation that the Equal Protection Clause creates applies to state and local governmental entities alike....

In any event, there is no need to rest solely upon evidence of discrimination by local governments or general societal discrimination. There are roughly 300 examples of discrimination by state governments themselves in the legislative record. See, e.g., Appendix C, *infra*. I fail to see how this evidence "falls far short of even suggesting the pattern of unconstitutional discrimination on which § 5 legislation must be based." *Ante.*

The congressionally appointed task force collected numerous specific examples, provided by persons with disabilities themselves, of adverse, disparate treatment by state officials. They reveal, not what the Court describes as "half a dozen" instances of discrimination, but hundreds of instances of adverse treatment at the hands of state officials—instances in which a person with a disability found it impossible to obtain a state job, to retain state employment, to use the public transportation that was readily available to others in order to get to work, or to obtain a public education, which is often a prerequisite to obtaining employment. State-imposed barriers also frequently made it difficult or impossible for people to vote, to enter a public building, to access important government services, such as calling for emergency assistance, and to find a place to live due to a pattern of irrational zoning decisions similar to the discrimination that we held unconstitutional in *Cleburne*. See Appendix C.

As the Court notes, those who presented instances of discrimination rarely provided additional, independent evidence sufficient to prove in court that, in each instance, the discrimination they suffered lacked justification from a judicial standpoint. Perhaps this explains the Court's view that there is "minimal evidence of unconstitutional state discrimination." But a legislature is not a court of law. And Congress, unlike courts, must, and does, routinely draw general conclusions—for example, of likely motive or of likely relationship to legitimate need—from anecdotal and opinion-based evidence of this kind, particularly when the evidence lacks strong refutation. In reviewing § 5 legislation, we have never required the sort of extensive investigation of each piece of evidence that the Court appears to contemplate. Compare *ante* with *Katzenbach v. Morgan*, 384 U.S. 641 (1966) [Note *supra.* this chapter] (asking whether Congress' likely conclusions were reasonable, not whether there was adequate evidentiary support in the record). Nor has the Court traditionally required Congress to make findings as to state discrimination, or to break down the record evidence, category by category. Compare *ante* (noting statements in two congressional Reports that mentioned state discrimination in public services and transportation but not in employment), with *Morgan* (considering what Congress "might" have concluded); id. (holding that likely discrimination against Puerto Ricans in areas other than voting supported statute abolishing literacy test as qualification for voting).

Regardless, Congress expressly found substantial unjustified discrimination against persons with disabilities. 42 U.S.C. § 12101(9) (finding a pattern of "unnecessary discrimination and prejudice" that "costs the United States billions of dollars in unnecessary expenses resulting from dependency and nonproductivity"). Moreover, it found that such discrimination typically reflects "stereotypic assumptions" or "purposeful unequal treatment." 42 U.S.C. § 12101(7). In making these findings, Congress followed our decision in *Cleburne*, which established that not only discrimination against persons with disabilities that rests upon "'a bare ... desire to harm a politically unpopular group,'" 473 U.S., at 447 (quoting *Department of Agriculture v. Moreno*, 413 U.S. 528 (1973) [Note *supra.* Chapter 15]), violates the Fourteenth Amendment, but also discrimination that rests solely upon "negative attitudes," "fear," or "irrational prejudice," *id.* Adverse treatment that rests upon such motives is unjustified discrimination in *Cleburne*'s terms.

The evidence in the legislative record bears out Congress' finding that the adverse treatment of persons with disabilities was often arbitrary or invidious in this sense, and thus unjustified. For example, one study that was before Congress revealed that "most ... governmental agencies in [one State] discriminated in hiring against job applicants for an average period of five years after treatment for cancer," based in part on coworkers' misguided belief that "cancer is contagious." 2 Leg. Hist. 1619–1620 (testimony of Arlene B. Mayerson). A school inexplicably refused to exempt a deaf teacher, who taught at a school for the deaf, from a "listening skills" requirement.

Government's Lodging 1503. A State refused to hire a blind employee as director of an agency for the blind—even though he was the most qualified applicant. Id., at 974. Certain state agencies apparently had general policies against hiring or promoting persons with disabilities. Id., at 1159, 1577. A zoo turned away children with Downs Syndrome "because [the zookeeper] feared they would upset the chimpanzees." S.Rep. No. 101-116, at 7. There were reports of numerous zoning decisions based upon "negative attitudes" or "fear," *Cleburne*, such as a zoning board that denied a permit for an obviously pretextual reason after hearing arguments that a facility would house "'deviants'" who needed "'room to roam,'" Government's Lodging 1068. A complete listing of the hundreds of examples of discrimination by state and local governments that were submitted to the task force is set forth in Appendix C, infra. Congress could have reasonably believed that these examples represented signs of a widespread problem of unconstitutional discrimination.

## II

The Court's failure to find sufficient evidentiary support may well rest upon its decision to hold Congress to a strict, judicially created evidentiary standard, particularly in respect to lack of justification. Justice KENNEDY's empirical conclusion—which rejects that of Congress—rests heavily upon his failure to find "extensive litigation and discussion of the constitutional violations," in "the courts of the United States." And the Court itself points out that, when economic or social legislation is challenged in court as irrational, hence unconstitutional, the "burden is upon the challenging party to negative any reasonably conceivable state of facts that could provide a rational basis for the classification." ... Imposing this special "burden" upon Congress, the Court fails to find in the legislative record sufficient indication that Congress has "negatived" the presumption that state action is rationally related to a legitimate objective.

The problem with the Court's approach is that neither the "burden of proof" that favors States nor any other rule of restraint applicable to judges applies to Congress when it exercises its §5 power. "Limitations stemming from the nature of the judicial process ... have no application to Congress." *Oregon v. Mitchell*, 400 U.S. 112 (1970) (Brennan, White, and Marshall, JJ., concurring in part and dissenting in part). Rational-basis review—with its presumptions favoring constitutionality—is "a paradigm of *judicial* restraint." *FCC v. Beach Communications, Inc.*, 508 U.S. 307 (1993) (emphasis added). And the Congress of the United States is not a lower court.

Indeed, the Court in *Cleburne* drew this very institutional distinction.... Our invocation of judicial deference and respect for Congress was based on the fact that "§5 of the [Fourteenth] Amendment empowers Congress to enforce [the equal protection] mandate." *Cleburne*. Indeed, we made clear that the absence of a contrary congressional finding was critical to our decision to apply mere rational-basis review to disability discrimination claims—a "congressional direction" to apply a more stringent standard would have been "controlling." *Ibid*. In short, the Court's claim that "to uphold the Act's application to the States would allow Congress to rewrite the

Fourteenth Amendment law laid down by this Court in *Cleburne*" is repudiated by *Cleburne* itself.

There is simply no reason to require Congress, seeking to determine facts relevant to the exercise of its §5 authority, to adopt rules or presumptions that reflect a court's institutional limitations. Unlike courts, Congress can readily gather facts from across the Nation, assess the magnitude of a problem, and more easily find an appropriate remedy. Cf. *Cleburne* (addressing the problems of the "large and diversified group" of persons with disabilities "is a difficult and often a technical matter, very much a task for legislators guided by qualified professionals and not by the perhaps ill-informed opinions of the judiciary"). Unlike courts, Congress directly reflects public attitudes and beliefs, enabling Congress better to understand where, and to what extent, refusals to accommodate a disability amount to behavior that is callous or unreasonable to the point of lacking constitutional justification. Unlike judges, Members of Congress can directly obtain information from constituents who have firsthand experience with discrimination and related issues.

Moreover, unlike judges, Members of Congress are elected.... To apply a rule designed to restrict courts as if it restricted Congress' legislative power is to stand the underlying principle—a principle of judicial restraint—on its head. But without the use of this burden of proof rule or some other unusually stringent standard of review, it is difficult to see how the Court can find the legislative record here inadequate. Read with a reasonably favorable eye, the record indicates that state governments subjected those with disabilities to seriously adverse, disparate treatment. And Congress could have found, in a significant number of instances, that this treatment violated the substantive principles of justification—shorn of their judicial-restraint-related presumptions—that this Court recognized in *Cleburne*.

### III

The Court argues in the alternative that the statute's damages remedy is not "congruent" with and "proportional" to the equal protection problem that Congress found. The Court suggests that the Act's "reasonable accommodation" requirement, 42 U.S.C. §12112(b)(5)(A), and disparate-impact standard, §12112(b)(3)(A), "far exceed what is constitutionally required." But we have upheld disparate-impact standards in contexts where they were not "constitutionally required."

And what is wrong with a remedy that, in response to unreasonable employer behavior, requires an employer to make accommodations that are reasonable? Of course, what is "reasonable" in the statutory sense and what is "unreasonable" in the constitutional sense might differ. In other words, the requirement may exceed what is necessary to avoid a constitutional violation. But it is just that power—the power to require more than the minimum that §5 grants to Congress, as this Court has repeatedly confirmed....

The Court's more recent cases have professed to follow the longstanding principle of deference to Congress. See *Kimel* ("Congress' §5 power is not confined to the enactment of legislation that merely parrots the precise wording of the Fourteenth Amendment." Rather, Congress can prohibit a "somewhat broader swath of conduct, including that which is not itself forbidden by the Amendment's text"); *Florida Prepaid* ("Congress must have wide latitude") *City of Boerne* (Congress' "conclusions are entitled to much deference"). And even today, the Court purports to apply, not to depart from, these standards. But the Court's analysis and ultimate conclusion deprive its declarations of practical significance....

## IV

The Court's harsh review of Congress' use of its § 5 power is reminiscent of the similar (now-discredited) limitation that it once imposed upon Congress' Commerce Clause power. Compare *Carter v. Carter Coal Co.*, 298 U.S. 238 (1936) [Note *supra.* Chapter 4], with *United States v. Darby* (1941) [*Supra.* Chapter 4] (rejecting *Carter Coal*'s rationale). I could understand the legal basis for such review were we judging a statute that discriminated against those of a particular race or gender, see *United States v. Virginia* (1996) [*Supra.* Chapter 12], or a statute that threatened a basic constitutionally protected liberty such as free speech. The legislation before us, however, does not discriminate against anyone, nor does it pose any threat to basic liberty. And it is difficult to understand why the Court, which applies "minimum 'rational-basis' review" to statutes that burden persons with disabilities, *ante*, subjects to far stricter scrutiny a statute that seeks to help those same individuals.

I recognize nonetheless that this statute imposes a burden upon States in that it removes their Eleventh Amendment protection from suit, thereby subjecting them to potential monetary liability. Rules for interpreting § 5 that would provide States with special protection, however, run counter to the very object of the Fourteenth Amendment. By its terms, that Amendment prohibits States from denying their citizens equal protection of the laws. Hence "principles of federalism that might otherwise be an obstacle to congressional authority are necessarily overridden by the power to enforce the Civil War Amendments 'by appropriate legislation.'"...

[The Appendices to Justice Breyer's opinion are omitted.]

## Nevada Dept of Human Resources v. Hibbs
### 538 U.S. 721 (2003)

Chief Justice REHNQUIST delivered the opinion of the Court.

The Family and Medical Leave Act of 1993 (FMLA or Act) entitles eligible employees to take up to 12 work weeks of unpaid leave annually for any of several reasons, including the onset of a "serious health condition" in an employee's spouse, child, or parent. The Act creates a private right of action to seek both equitable relief and money damages "against any employer (including a public agency) in any Federal or State court of competent jurisdiction," should that employer "interfere with, restrain, or deny the exercise of" FMLA rights. We hold that employees of the State of Nevada may recover money damages in the event of the State's failure to comply with the family-care provision of the Act.

Petitioners include the Nevada Department of Human Resources (Department) and two of its officers. Respondent William Hibbs (hereinafter respondent) worked for the Department's Welfare Division. In April and May 1997, he sought leave under the FMLA to care for his ailing wife, who was recovering from a car accident and neck surgery. The Department granted his request for the full 12 weeks of FMLA leave and authorized him to use the leave intermittently as needed between May and December 1997.... In October 1997, the Department informed respondent that he had exhausted his FMLA leave, that no further leave would be granted, and that he must report to work by November 12, 1997. Respondent failed to do so and was terminated.

Respondent sued petitioners in the United States District Court seeking damages and injunctive and declaratory relief.... The District Court awarded petitioners summary judgment on the grounds that the FMLA claim was barred by the Eleventh Amendment and that respondent's Fourteenth Amendment rights had not been violated. Respondent appealed.... The Ninth Circuit reversed.

We granted certiorari to resolve a split among the Courts of Appeals on the question whether an individual may sue a State for money damages in federal court for violation of § 2612(a)(1)(C).

For over a century now, we have made clear that the Constitution does not provide for federal jurisdiction over suits against nonconsenting States. *Board of Trustees of Univ. of Ala. v. Garrett* (2001) [*Supra.* this chapter]; *Kimel v. Florida Bd. of Regents*, 528 U.S. 62 (2000); *College Savings Bank v. Florida Prepaid Postsecondary Ed. Expense Bd.*, 527 U.S. 666 (1999); *Seminole Tribe of Fla. v. Florida* (1996) [*Supra.* Chapter 6]; *Hans v. Louisiana*, 134 U.S. 1 (1890) [Note *supra.* Chapter 6].

Congress may, however, abrogate such immunity in federal court if it makes its intention to abrogate unmistakably clear in the language of the statute and acts pursuant to a valid exercise of its power under § 5 of the Fourteenth Amendment. See *Garrett.* The clarity of Congress' intent here is not fairly debatable. The Act enables employees to seek damages "against any employer (including a public agency) in any Federal or State court of competent jurisdiction," and Congress has defined "public agency" to include both "the government of a State or political subdivision thereof" and "any agency of ... a State, or a political subdivision of a State." ... This case turns, then, on whether Congress acted within its constitutional authority when it sought to abrogate the States' immunity for purposes of the FMLA's family-leave provision.

In enacting the FMLA, Congress relied on two of the powers vested in it by the Constitution: its Article I commerce power and its power under § 5 of the Fourteenth Amendment to enforce that Amendment's guarantees.[1] Congress may not abrogate the States' sovereign immunity pursuant to its Article I power over commerce. *Seminole*

---

1. Compare 29 U.S.C. § 2601(b)(1) ("It is the purpose of this Act ... to balance the demands of the workplace with the needs of families, to promote the stability and economic security of families, and to promote national interests in preserving family integrity") with § 2601(b)(5) ("to promote the goal of equal employment opportunity for women and men, pursuant to [the Equal Protection] Clause") and § 2601(b)(4) ("to accomplish [the Act's other purposes] in a manner that, consistent with the Equal Protection Clause..., minimizes the potential for employment discrimination on the basis of sex"). See also S.Rep. No. 103-3, p. 16 (1993), U.S.Code Cong. & Admin.News 1993, pp. 3, 18 (the FMLA "is based not only on the Commerce Clause, but also on the guarantees of equal pro-

*Tribe.* Congress may, however, abrogate States' sovereign immunity through a valid exercise of its § 5 power, for "the Eleventh Amendment, and the principle of state sovereignty which it embodies, are necessarily limited by the enforcement provisions of § 5 of the Fourteenth Amendment." *Fitzpatrick v. Bitzer* (1976) [*Supra.* Chapter 6]. See also *Garrett.*

Two provisions of the Fourteenth Amendment are relevant here: Section 5 grants Congress the power "to enforce" the substantive guarantees of § 1 — among them, equal protection of the laws — by enacting "appropriate legislation." Congress may, in the exercise of its § 5 power, do more than simply proscribe conduct that we have held unconstitutional. "Congress' power 'to enforce' the Amendment includes the authority both to remedy and to deter violation of rights guaranteed thereunder by prohibiting a somewhat broader swath of conduct, including that which is not itself forbidden by the Amendment's text." *Garrett; City of Boerne v. Flores* (1997) [*Supra.* this chapter]; *Katzenbach v. Morgan,* 384 U.S. 641 (1966) [Note *supra.* this chapter]. In other words, Congress may enact so-called prophylactic legislation that proscribes facially constitutional conduct, in order to prevent and deter unconstitutional conduct.

*City of Boerne* also confirmed, however, that it falls to this Court, not Congress, to define the substance of constitutional guarantees. "The ultimate interpretation and determination of the Fourteenth Amendment's substantive meaning remains the province of the Judicial Branch." *Kimel.* Section 5 legislation reaching beyond the scope of § 1's actual guarantees must be an appropriate remedy for identified constitutional violations, not "an attempt to substantively redefine the States' legal obligations." We distinguish appropriate prophylactic legislation from "substantive redefinition of the Fourteenth Amendment right at issue," *id.,* by applying the test set forth in *City of Boerne*: Valid § 5 legislation must exhibit "congruence and proportionality between the injury to be prevented or remedied and the means adopted to that end."

The FMLA aims to protect the right to be free from gender-based discrimination in the workplace.[2] We have held that statutory classifications that distinguish between males and females are subject to heightened scrutiny. See, e.g., *Craig v. Boren* (1976) [*Supra.* Chapter 12]. For a gender-based classification to withstand such scrutiny, it must "serve important governmental objectives," and "the discriminatory means employed [must be] substantially related to the achievement of those objectives." *United States v. Virginia* (1996) [*Supra.* Chapter 12]. The State's justification for such a classification "must not rely on overbroad generalizations about the different talents, ca-

---

tection and due process embodied in the 14th Amendment"); H.R.Rep. No. 103-8, pt. 1, p. 29 (1993) (same).

2. The text of the Act makes this clear. Congress found that, "due to the nature of the roles of men and women in our society, the primary responsibility for family caretaking often falls on women, and such responsibility affects the working lives of women more than it affects the working lives of men." 29 U.S.C. § 2601(a)(5). In response to this finding, Congress sought "to accomplish the [Act's other] purposes ... in a manner that ... minimizes the potential for employment discrimination on the basis of sex by ensuring generally that leave is available ... on a gender-neutral basis, and to promote the goal of equal employment opportunity for women and men" §§ 2601(b)(4) and (5).

pacities, or preferences of males and females." We now inquire whether Congress had evidence of a pattern of constitutional violations on the part of the States in this area.

The history of the many state laws limiting women's employment opportunities is chronicled in—and, until relatively recently, was sanctioned by—this Court's own opinions.... Until our decision in *Reed v. Reed*, 404 U.S. 71 (1971) [Note *supra*. Chapter 12], "it remained the prevailing doctrine that government, both federal and state, could withhold from women opportunities accorded men so long as any basis in reason could be conceived for the discrimination."

Congress responded to this history of discrimination by abrogating States' sovereign immunity in Title VII of the Civil Rights Act of 1964, and we sustained this abrogation in *Fitzpatrick*. But state gender discrimination did not cease.... According to evidence that was before Congress when it enacted the FMLA, States continue to rely on invalid gender stereotypes in the employment context, specifically in the administration of leave benefits.... The long and extensive history of sex discrimination prompted us to hold that measures that differentiate on the basis of gender warrant heightened scrutiny; here, as in *Fitzpatrick*, the persistence of such unconstitutional discrimination by the States justifies Congress' passage of prophylactic § 5 legislation.

As the FMLA's legislative record reflects, a 1990 Bureau of Labor Statistics (BLS) survey stated that 37 percent of surveyed private-sector employees were covered by maternity leave policies, while only 18 percent were covered by paternity leave policies. The corresponding numbers from a similar BLS survey the previous year were 33 percent and 16 percent, respectively. While these data show an increase in the percentage of employees eligible for such leave, they also show a widening of the gender gap during the same period. Thus, stereotype-based beliefs about the allocation of family duties remained firmly rooted, and employers' reliance on them in establishing discriminatory leave policies remained widespread.[3]

Congress also heard testimony that "parental leave for fathers ... is rare. Even ... where child-care leave policies do exist, men, both in the public and private sectors, receive notoriously discriminatory treatment in their requests for such leave." Joint Hearing 147 (Washington Council of Lawyers).... This and other differential leave policies were not attributable to any differential physical needs of men and women, but rather to the pervasive sex-role stereotype that caring for family members is women's work.

Finally, Congress had evidence that, even where state laws and policies were not facially discriminatory, they were applied in discriminatory ways....

---

3. While this and other material described leave policies in the private sector, a 50-state survey also before Congress demonstrated that "[t]he proportion and construction of leave policies available to public sector employees differs little from those offered private sector employees." The Parental and Medical Leave Act of 1986: Joint Hearing before the Subcommittee on Labor-Management Relations and the Subcommittee on Labor Standards of the House Committee on Education and Labor, 99th Cong., 2d Sess., 33 (1986) (hereinafter Joint Hearing) (statement of Meryl Frank, Director of the Yale Bush Center Infant Care Leave Project).

In sum, the States' record of unconstitutional participation in, and fostering of, gender-based discrimination in the administration of leave benefits is weighty enough to justify the enactment of prophylactic § 5 legislation.

We reached the opposite conclusion in *Garrett* and *Kimel*. In those cases, the § 5 legislation under review responded to a purported tendency of state officials to make age- or disability-based distinctions. Under our equal protection case law, discrimination on the basis of such characteristics is not judged under a heightened review standard, and passes muster if there is "a rational basis for doing so at a class-based level, even if it 'is probably not true' that those reasons are valid in the majority of cases." Thus, in order to impugn the constitutionality of state discrimination against the disabled or the elderly, Congress must identify, not just the existence of age- or disability-based state decisions, but a "widespread pattern" of irrational reliance on such criteria. We found no such showing with respect to the ADEA and Title I of the Americans with Disabilities Act of 1990(ADA). *Kimel*; *Garrett*.

Here, however, Congress directed its attention to state gender discrimination, which triggers a heightened level of scrutiny. See, e.g., *Craig*. Because the standard for demonstrating the constitutionality of a gender-based classification is more difficult to meet than our rational-basis test — it must "serve important governmental objectives" and be "substantially related to the achievement of those objectives" — it was easier for Congress to show a pattern of state constitutional violations....

The impact of the discrimination targeted by the FMLA is significant. Congress determined:

> "Historically, denial or curtailment of women's employment opportunities has been traceable directly to the pervasive presumption that women are mothers first, and workers second. This prevailing ideology about women's roles has in turn justified discrimination against women when they are mothers or mothers-to-be." Joint Hearing 100.

Stereotypes about women's domestic roles are reinforced by parallel stereotypes presuming a lack of domestic responsibilities for men. Because employers continued to regard the family as the woman's domain, they often denied men similar accommodations or discouraged them from taking leave. These mutually reinforcing stereotypes created a self-fulfilling cycle of discrimination that forced women to continue to assume the role of primary family caregiver, and fostered employers' stereotypical views about women's commitment to work and their value as employees. Those perceptions, in turn, Congress reasoned, lead to subtle discrimination that may be difficult to detect on a case-by-case basis.

We believe that Congress' chosen remedy, the family-care leave provision of the FMLA, is "congruent and proportional to the targeted violation," *Garrett*. Congress had already tried unsuccessfully to address this problem through Title VII and the amendment of Title VII by the Pregnancy Discrimination Act. Here, as in *Katzenbach*, Congress again confronted a "difficult and intractable problem," where previous legislative attempts had failed. Such problems may justify added prophylactic measures in response.

By creating an across-the-board, routine employment benefit for all eligible employees, Congress sought to ensure that family-care leave would no longer be stigmatized as an inordinate drain on the workplace caused by female employees, and that employers could not evade leave obligations simply by hiring men. By setting a minimum standard of family leave for all eligible employees, irrespective of gender, the FMLA attacks the formerly state-sanctioned stereotype that only women are responsible for family caregiving, thereby reducing employers' incentives to engage in discrimination by basing hiring and promotion decisions on stereotypes.

The dissent characterizes the FMLA as a "substantive entitlement program" rather than a remedial statute because it establishes a floor of 12 weeks' leave. In the dissent's view, in the face of evidence of gender-based discrimination by the States in the provision of leave benefits, Congress could do no more in exercising its § 5 power than simply proscribe such discrimination. But this position cannot be squared with our recognition that Congress "is not confined to the enactment of legislation that merely parrots the precise wording of the Fourteenth Amendment," but may prohibit "a somewhat broader swath of conduct, including that which is not itself forbidden by the Amendment's text."....

Unlike the statutes at issue in *City of Boerne*, *Kimel*, and *Garrett*, which applied broadly to every aspect of state employers' operations, the FMLA is narrowly targeted at the faultline between work and family—precisely where sex-based overgeneralization has been and remains strongest—and affects only one aspect of the employment relationship....

For the above reasons, we conclude that § 2612(a)(1)(C) is congruent and proportional to its remedial object, and can "be understood as responsive to, or designed to prevent, unconstitutional behavior." *City of Boerne*.

The judgment of the Court of Appeals is therefore Affirmed.

Justice SOUTER, with whom Justice GINSBURG and Justice BREYER join, concurring.

Even on this Court's view of the scope of congressional power under § 5 of the Fourteenth Amendment, see *Garrett*; *Kimel*; *Florida Prepaid*, the Family and Medical Leave Act of 1993 is undoubtedly valid legislation, and application of the Act to the States is constitutional; the same conclusions follow *a fortiori* from my own understanding of § 5, see *Garrett* (BREYER, J., dissenting); *Kimel* (STEVENS, J., dissenting); *Florida Prepaid* (STEVENS, J., dissenting); see also *Katzenbach v. Morgan*. I join the Court's opinion here without conceding the dissenting positions just cited or the dissenting views expressed in *Seminole Tribe* (SOUTER, J., dissenting).

Justice STEVENS, concurring in the judgment. [omitted]

Justice SCALIA, dissenting.

I join Justice KENNEDY's dissent, and add one further observation: The constitutional violation that is a prerequisite to "prophylactic" congressional action to "enforce" the Fourteenth Amendment is a violation by the State against which the enforcement action is taken. There is no guilt by association, enabling the sovereignty of one State to be abridged under § 5 of the Fourteenth Amendment because of violations by another State, or by most other States, or even by 49 other States.…

Justice KENNEDY, with whom Justice SCALIA and Justice THOMAS join, dissenting.

The Family and Medical Leave Act of 1993 makes explicit the congressional intent to invoke § 5 of the Fourteenth Amendment to abrogate state sovereign immunity and allow suits for money damages in federal courts. The specific question is whether Congress may impose on the States this entitlement program of its own design, with mandated minimums for leave time, and then enforce it by permitting private suits for money damages against the States. This in turn must be answered by asking whether subjecting States and their treasuries to monetary liability at the insistence of private litigants is a congruent and proportional response to a demonstrated pattern of unconstitutional conduct by the States. If we apply the teaching of these and related cases, the family leave provision of the Act, in my respectful view, is invalid to the extent it allows for private suits against the unconsenting States.

Congress does not have authority to define the substantive content of the Equal Protection Clause; it may only shape the remedies warranted by the violations of that guarantee. *City of Boerne.* This requirement has special force in the context of the Eleventh Amendment, which protects a State's fiscal integrity from federal intrusion by vesting the States with immunity from private actions for damages pursuant to federal laws. The Commerce Clause likely would permit the National Government to enact an entitlement program such as this one; but when Congress couples the entitlement with the authorization to sue the States for monetary damages, it blurs the line of accountability the State has to its own citizens. These basic concerns underlie cases such as *Garrett* and *Kimel*, and should counsel far more caution than the Court shows in holding § 2612(a)(1)(C) is somehow a congruent and proportional remedy to an identified pattern of discrimination.

The Court is unable to show that States have engaged in a pattern of unlawful conduct which warrants the remedy of opening state treasuries to private suits. The inability to adduce evidence of alleged discrimination, coupled with the inescapable fact that the federal scheme is not a remedy but a benefit program, demonstrates the lack of the requisite link between any problem Congress has identified and the program it mandated.

\* \* \*

The relevant question, as the Court seems to acknowledge, is whether, notwithstanding the passage of Title VII and similar state legislation, the States continued to engage in widespread discrimination on the basis of gender in the provision of family leave benefits. If such a pattern were shown, the Eleventh Amendment would not bar Congress from devising a congruent and proportional remedy. The evidence to substantiate this charge must be far more specific, however, than a simple recitation of a general history of employment discrimination against women. When the federal statute seeks to abrogate state sovereign immunity, the Court should be more careful to insist on adherence to the analytic requirements set forth in its own precedents. Persisting overall effects of gender-based discrimination at the workplace must not be ignored; but simply noting the problem is not a substitute for evidence which identifies some real discrimination the family leave rules are designed to prevent.

Respondents fail to make the requisite showing....

As the Court seems to recognize, the evidence considered by Congress concerned discriminatory practices of the private sector, not those of state employers....

The Court seeks to connect the evidence of private discrimination to an alleged pattern of unconstitutional behavior by States through inferences drawn from two sources. The first is testimony by Meryl Frank, Director of the Infant Care Leave Project, Yale Bush Center in Child Development and Social Policy, who surveyed both private and public employers in all 50 States and found little variation between the leave policies in the two sectors. *Ante* (citing The Parental and Medical Leave Act of 1986: Joint Hearing before the Subcommittee on Labor-Management Relations and the Subcommittee on Labor Standards of the House Committee on Education and Labor, 99th Cong., 2d Sess., 33 (1986) (hereinafter Joint Hearing)). The second is a view expressed by the Washington Council of Lawyers that even "'where child-care leave policies do exist, men, both in the public and private sectors, receive notoriously discriminatory treatment in their requests for such leave.'" *Ante* (quoting Joint Hearing 147).

Both statements were made during the hearings on the proposed 1986 national leave legislation, and so preceded the Act by seven years. The 1986 bill, which was not enacted, differed in an important respect from the legislation Congress eventually passed. That proposal sought to provide parenting leave, not leave to care for another ill family member. The testimony on which the Court relies concerned the discrimination with respect to the parenting leave. Even if this isolated testimony could support an inference that private sector's gender-based discrimination in the provision of parenting leave was parallel to the behavior by state actors in 1986, the evidence would not be probative of the States' conduct some seven years later with respect to a statutory provision conferring a different benefit....

The Court's reliance on evidence suggesting States provided men and women with the parenting leave of different length suffers from the same flaw. This evidence concerns the Act's grant of parenting leave, §§ 2612(a)(1)(A), (B), and is too attenuated to justify the family leave provision....

The Court maintains the evidence pertaining to the parenting leave is relevant because both parenting and family leave provisions respond to "the same gender stereotype: that women's family duties trump those of the workplace." This sets the contours of the inquiry at too high a level of abstraction. The question is not whether the family leave provision is a congruent and proportional response to general gender-based stereotypes in employment which "have historically produced discrimination in the hiring and promotion of women," *ante*; the question is whether it is a proper remedy to an alleged pattern of unconstitutional discrimination by States in the grant of family leave. The evidence of gender-based stereotypes is too remote to support the required showing....

Stripped of the conduct which exhibits no constitutional infirmity, the Court's "extensive and specific ... record of unconstitutional state conduct," *ante*, boils down to the fact that three States, Massachusetts, Kansas, and Tennessee, provided parenting leave only to their female employees, and had no program for granting their employees (male or female) family leave. As already explained, the evidence related to the parenting leave is simply too attenuated to support a charge of unconstitutional discrimination in the provision of family leave....

Considered in its entirety, the evidence fails to document a pattern of unconstitutional conduct sufficient to justify the abrogation of States' sovereign immunity. The few incidents identified by the Court "fall far short of even suggesting the pattern of unconstitutional discrimination on which § 5 legislation must be based." *Garrett*....

Our concern with gender discrimination, which is subjected to heightened scrutiny, as opposed to age- or disability-based distinctions, which are reviewed under rational standard, does not alter this conclusion. The application of heightened scrutiny is designed to ensure gender-based classifications are not based on the entrenched and pervasive stereotypes which inhibit women's progress in the workplace. *Ante.* This consideration does not divest respondents of their burden to show that "Congress identified a history and pattern of unconstitutional employment discrimination by the States." *Garrett.* The Court seems to reaffirm this requirement. In my submission, however, the Court does not follow it. Given the insufficiency of the evidence that States discriminated in the provision of family leave, the unfortunate fact that stereotypes about women continue to be a serious and pervasive social problem would not alone support the charge that a State has engaged in a practice designed to deny its citizens the equal protection of the laws. *Garrett.*

The paucity of evidence to support the case the Court tries to make demonstrates that Congress was not responding with a congruent and proportional remedy to a perceived course of unconstitutional conduct. Instead, it enacted a substantive entitlement program of its own....

It has been long acknowledged that federal legislation which "deters or remedies constitutional violations can fall within the sweep of Congress' enforcement power even if in the process it prohibits conduct which is not itself unconstitutional." *City of Boerne.* The Court has explained, however, that Congress may not "enforce a constitutional right by changing what the right is." *Ibid.* The dual requirement that Congress identify a pervasive pattern of unconstitutional state conduct and that its remedy be proportional and congruent to the violation is designed to separate permissible exercises of congressional power from instances where Congress seeks to enact a substantive entitlement under the guise of its § 5 authority ...

It bears emphasis that, even were the Court to bar unconsented federal suits by private individuals for money damages from a State, individuals whose rights under the Act were violated would not be without recourse. The Act is likely a valid exercise of Congress' power under the Commerce Clause, and so the standards it prescribes will be binding upon the States. The United States may enforce these standards in actions for money damages; and private individuals may bring actions against state officials for injunctive relief under *Ex parte Young*, 209 U.S. 123 (1908) [Note *supra.* Chapter 6]. What is at issue is only whether the States can be subjected, without consent, to suits brought by private persons seeking to collect moneys from the state treasury. Their immunity cannot be abrogated without documentation of a pattern of unconstitutional acts by the States, and only then by a congruent and proportional remedy. There has been a complete failure by respondents to carry their burden to establish each of these necessary propositions. I would hold that the Act is not a valid abrogation of state sovereign immunity and dissent with respect from the Court's conclusion to the contrary.

## Note: The Role of Suspect Class Analysis in Congruence and Proportionality Review

There is a remarkable difference in tone between the majority's analyses in *Garrett* and *Hibbs*. What are the differences in the Court's treatment of the ADA and the FMLA? What accounts for the level of deference the Court accords the FMLA in *Hibbs*? Why isn't that same deference accorded in *Garrett*? In considering that question, recall *City of Cleburne v. Cleburne Living Center*, 473 U.S. 432 (1985), excerpted in Chapter 15. How does the *Garrett* Court understand *Cleburne*? Do you agree with that understanding? Does *Cleburne* really state the constitutional rule to which the ADA had to be congruent and proportional? Or did the *Cleburne* Court reach its suspect class decision based on more pragmatic concerns about judicial competence? If the latter reading of *Cleburne* is correct, then how would you describe the constitutional rule *Cleburne* announced, and thus the rule which furnishes the correct focal point for a congruence and proportionality analysis of the ADA?

## Note: The Enforcement Clause after Garrett and Hibbs

1. The template set in *Garrett* and *Hibbs* has largely continued until recent years. In performing congruence and proportionality review, the Court has continued to rely heavily on its own estimate of the constitutional significance of the right at issue, which it then compares to the breadth of the rights conferred in the statute. As with *Garrett* and *Hibbs*, this approach has led to fractured opinions at the Court.

2. In *Tennessee v. Lane*, 541 U.S. 509 (2004), the Court considered an Enforcement Clause challenge to the public services provisions of the Americans With Disabilities Act. (*Garrett* had considered the employment provisions of that statute.) *Lane* involved two disabled plaintiffs who were unable to access parts of state courthouses because the buildings were not disabled-accessible, and who then sued the state under the ADA.

Writing for a five-Justice majority consisting of the four *Garrett* dissenters plus Justice O'Connor, Justice Stevens ruled in favor of the plaintiffs. Justice Stevens viewed the case not as involving the ADA's public services provisions in general, but rather simply as applied to the plaintiffs' claims of courthouse access. In so doing, he was able to characterize the underlying constitutional right sought to be enforced as the due process right to access state judicial processes, rather than the equal protection right against disability discrimination in general. This narrower focus allowed Justice Stevens to characterize the right Congress sought to enforce as quite significant, because settled due process law viewed access to state courts as a fundamental right.

Given the importance of the underlying right to judicial access, Justice Stevens found the ADA a "congruent and proportional" enforcement of that right. He noted that the ADA required "reasonable accommodations" for the disabled, a term he found similar to the due process requirement that "'within the limits of practicability, a State must afford to all individuals a meaningful opportunity to be heard' in its courts." *Lane* (quoting *Boddie v. Connecticut*, 401 U.S. 371 (1971)).

Chief Justice Rehnquist dissented for three Justices. He took issue with the majority's "as-applied" analysis of the ADA, arguing that the Court should have considered the constitutionality of the ADA's public services provisions as a whole. He accused the majority of "rigging the congruence and proportionality test by artificially constricting the scope of the statute to closely mirror a recognized constitutional right."

Justice Scalia dissented separately. He announced that he was abandoning the congruence and proportionality test, which he described as "malleable" and "flabby," and which he compared to tests that "have a way of turning into vehicles for the implementation of individual judges' policy preferences." In its place, he announced that in the future he would vote to allow Congress only to proscribe or punish actual violations of the Fourteenth Amendment. He stated: "Nothing in § 5 allows Congress to go *beyond* the provisions of the Fourteenth Amendment to proscribe, prevent, or 'remedy' conduct that does not *itself* violate any provision of the Fourteenth Amendment. So-called 'prophylactic legislation' is reinforcement rather than enforcement." He made an exception to this rule for legislation enforcing the right to racial equality, citing the long line of precedent allowing Congress to enact enforcement legislation such as the Voting Rights Act.

3. The *Garrett-Hibbs-Lane* template, in which the level of judicial scrutiny of enforcement legislation mirrored the protected status of the right the legislation sought to enforce, started to erode in 2012. In *Coleman v. Court of Appeals*, 132 S.Ct. 1327 (2012), the Court considered the enforcement power foundation of another provision of the Family and Medical Leave Act (FMLA). In *Hibbs* the Court had upheld the FMLA's family care provisions as valid enforcement legislation, noting that, because sex discrimination triggered heightened judicial scrutiny, "it was easier for Congress to show a pattern of state constitutional violations" justifying enforcement legislation. *Coleman* considered a separate provision of the FMLA, one that provided leave time for *personal* medical reasons.

Writing for four justices, Justice Kennedy found the self-care provision to exceed the enforcement power. The plaintiff had argued, among other things, that the self-care leave benefit helped counteract the perceived skew in leave in favor of women. The theory was that FMLA family care leave, even if available on a sex-neutral basis, would likely be taken more by women (and would be perceived by employers as more of a women's benefit). Thus, the theory went, it was necessary to add to that benefit a leave provision that would be perceived as more generally-applicable to men and women alike. Otherwise, the theory concluded, FMLA family care leave would *harm* women by giving employers another reason to prefer male job applicants.

Justice Kennedy rejected that argument, calling it "overly complicated" and "unconvincing." He also noted that it contradicted the plaintiff's earlier argument, which turned on a claim that women took more personal care leave than men, and thus needed FMLA leave to equalize their attractiveness as employees. He nowhere mentioned the "easier" task *Hibbs* stated that Congress faced when legislating to protect the equal protection right to sex equality. Justice Thomas joined the plurality opinion but also wrote separately.

Justice Scalia concurred in the judgment striking down the self-care provision. However, he repeated the criticism of the congruence and proportionality test that he had leveled in his dissent in *Lane*. (See item 2, *supra*.) Further criticizing what he believed to be that test's malleability, he observed that Justice Kennedy's and Justice Ginsburg's application of the test both seemed plausible to him.

Justice Ginsburg dissented for four justices. In relevant part, she agreed with the plaintiff's argument recounted above. After evaluating that argument, she wrote:

> Congress therefore had good reason to conclude that the self-care provision — which men no doubt would use — would counter employers' impressions that the FMLA would otherwise install female leave. Providing for self-care would thus reduce employers' corresponding incentive to discriminate against women in hiring and promotion. In other words, "the availability of self-care leave to men serves to blunt the force of stereotypes of women as primary caregivers by increasing the odds that men and women will invoke the FMLA's leave provisions in near-equal numbers."

### Note: The State Action Requirement and the Enforcement Clause

1. As explained earlier in this chapter, in the *Civil Rights Cases* the Court held that the Enforcement Clause did not authorize Congress to prohibit private conduct, for example, racial discrimination in privately-owned public accommodations such as theaters. However, by the mid-twentieth century, that holding had come under some pressure, as private parties engaged in violence, sometimes tolerated or even encouraged by states, designed to prevent African-Americans from enjoying their Fourteenth Amendment rights, for example, to non-segregated schools. Chapter 18, which considers the "state action" doctrine, examines when state involvement in private conduct becomes so significant that the private conduct becomes, for constitutional purposes, attributable to the state. This Note considers that issue from the perspective of Congress's power under the Enforcement Clause.

2. In *United States v. Guest*, 383 U.S. 745 (1966), the Court considered an indictment alleging a conspiracy to violate a citizen's federal civil rights. In an opinion for the Court upholding the indictments, Justice Stewart did not reach the question of

whether the Enforcement Clause empowered Congress to punish a conspiracy comprised of purely private action, as he found that a local sheriff had plotted with the private parties to violate the citizen's rights. Writing for three Justices, Justice Brennan rejected the rule from the *Civil Rights Cases*, and argued that any conspiracy—even a purely private one—to deny individuals their Fourteenth Amendment rights could be punished as appropriate "enforcement" of the Amendment. Justice Clark, writing for three other Justices, expressed agreement with Justice Brennan's view. Justice Brennan noted Justice Clark's opinion, and observed that between these two separate opinions six Justices agreed with this proposition.

3. In *United States v. Morrison*, 529 U.S. 598 (2000), the Court rejected the implications of the Brennan and Clark opinions in *Guest*. *Morrison* dealt with the Violence Against Women Act (VAWA), a federal statute that gave victims of gender-motivated violence a federal-law cause of action against their attackers. In *Morrison* the Court struck down this provision of VAWA, holding that it exceeded Congress's powers under both the Interstate Commerce Clause (as discussed in a note in Chapter 4) and the Enforcement Clause.

Chief Justice Rehnquist's opinion for five Justices returned to the *Civil Rights Cases*'s requirement that Enforcement Clause legislation must target some unconstitutional conduct by the state. It described Justice Brennan's and Justice Clark's analyses as *dicta*, noting that both Justice Stewart's and Justice Clark's opinions recognized that the sheriff's connivance in the conspiracy established state action. According to Justice Rehnquist, these facts thereby made any further analysis of the scope of the Enforcement Clause unnecessary to the holding, and thus reduced the number of actual votes to overrule *The Civil Rights Cases* to the three associated with Justice Brennan's opinion.

Of the two dissenting opinions in *Morrison*, only Justice Breyer's touched on the Enforcement Clause issue. (Justice Souter's dissent focused solely on the Commerce Clause issue.) Because Justice Breyer argued that VAWA was constitutional under Commerce Clause, he concluded that he did not need to decide the Enforcement Clause issue. However, he did express doubts about the majority's reasoning. In an opinion joined by Justice Stevens, Justice Breyer conceded that the Enforcement Clause authorized Congress only to remedy state conduct. But he argued that VAWA's provision of a private right-of-action did in fact remedy the conduct of state actors: "namely, those States which, through discriminatory design or the discriminatory conduct of their officials, failed to provide adequate (or any) state remedies for women injured by gender-motivated violence—a failure that the States, and Congress, documented in depth." He argued that the *Civil Rights Cases* did not face this sort of issue, and therefore did not serve as precedent for rejecting the government's argument on this point. He also argued that the provision of the private right-of-action was a congruent and proportional response to the problem of states' failure to protect women, since, among other things, the federal law merely imposed liability for the violation of rights that state law already recognized.

# Chapter 18

# The Problem of "State Action"

### Note: The State Action Issue

1. This chapter considers the problem posed by the general rule that, for the most part, only government entities (not private parties) are required to comply with constitutional requirements. That statement is not completely accurate: most notably, the Thirteenth Amendment's ban on slavery applies to both government and private parties. But most other constitutional provisions—and, most importantly for our purposes, the Fourteenth Amendment's set of rights and liberties—apply only against government action. Constitutional doctrine calls this limitation the "state action" requirement—but note that in this case "state" refers to government as a general matter, and thus refers to both the federal government and the states.

2. The "state action" requirement is generally thought to date to *The Civil Rights Cases*, 109 U.S. 3 (1883). That case, discussed in a note in Chapter 17, dealt with a federal law that sought to enforce the Equal Protection Clause by, among other things, prohibiting discrimination in places of public accommodation, such as restaurants and theaters. In holding that the statute exceeded Congress's enforcement power, the Court concluded that the Fourteenth Amendment restricted only the actions of state governments. Speaking for the Court, Justice Bradley wrote the following:

> The first section of the Fourteenth Amendment..., after declaring who shall be citizens of the United States, and of the several States, is prohibitory in its character, and prohibitory upon the States. It declares that: 'no State shall make or enforce any law which shall abridge the privileges or immunities of citizens of the United States; nor shall any State deprive any person of life, liberty, or property without due process of law; nor deny to any person within its jurisdiction the equal protection of the laws.
>
> It is State action of a particular character that is prohibited. Individual invasion of individual rights is not the subject-matter of the amendment. It has a deeper and broader scope. It nullifies and makes void all State legislation, and State action of every kind, which impairs the privileges and immunities of citizens of the United States, or which injures them in life, liberty, or property without due process of law, or which denies to any of them the equal protection of the laws. It not only does this, but, in order that the national will, thus declared, may not be a mere brutum fulmen, the last section of the amendment invests Congress with power to enforce it by appropriate legislation. To enforce what? To enforce the prohibition. To adopt appropriate

legislation for correcting the effects of such prohibited State law and State acts, and thus to render them effectually null, void, and innocuous.

3. Despite the seeming straightforwardness of the idea that the Fourteenth Amendment only applies to state government, the state action prohibition implicates a fundamental difficulty in constitutional law. That difficulty arises when one realizes that the state is often involved in the private action that is ostensibly beyond the scope of the Fourteenth Amendment. For example, while the state could not itself eject persons from a government office building because of those persons' race, it could, at least conceivably, offer its assistance to a private property owner who wished to keep his facilities segregated. (This example assumes the absence of statutory law banning such segregation.) Would police enforcement of a trespass law at the behest of a segregationist property owner constitute "state action"? Of course, in a basic way it would—literally, the "state" is "acting" through its police force. Should that count as "state action"? What if a state court enforced a private contract between a landlord and a tenant, requiring the tenant to maintain the property in a segregated condition? *Shelley v. Kraemer*, 335 U.S. 1 (1948), excerpted later in this chapter, confronts this latter question.

4. One way of approaching these questions is by conceding that, in one way or another, "states" "act" in a very large number of contexts. Under this approach to the "state action" question, a court would not ask simply whether the "state" is "acting;" instead, it would investigate the character of that "state action." For example, is the state requiring private parties to perform certain actions that, if the state itself performed, would violate the Constitution? Is the state expressing its approval of such private action, without requiring it? Or is it simply authorizing such action? Under this approach to the issue, the key question for courts is whether state conduct of these types implicates the state so much that the state itself can be said to have engaged in it.

5. This chapter begins its consideration of the state action issue by separating out three distinct analytical strands as they were developed in foundational cases. First, it considers cases where the private actor is the functional equivalent of the government. The most obvious example of this situation is where a private actor maintains what, for all intents and purposes, constitutes a municipality. *Marsh v. Alabama*, the first case excerpted below, considers just such a "company town." The note after *Marsh* examines how far that logic could and should extend. Second, this chapter considers situations where government is "entangled" with private conduct, such that the private conduct—*e.g.*, racial discrimination—should be attributed to the state. Third, this chapter considers the special cases of judicial enforcement of private agreements and legislative approval of private conduct. With these basics established, the chapter concludes by examining more recent cases, to uncover how the Court's thinking on the state action issue has evolved.

# A. Government Functions

## Marsh v. Alabama

### 326 U.S. 501 (1946)

Mr. Justice BLACK delivered the opinion of the Court.

In this case we are asked to decide whether a State, consistently with the First and Fourteenth Amendments, can impose criminal punishment on a person who undertakes to distribute religious literature on the premises of a company-owned town contrary to the wishes of the town's management. The town, a suburb of Mobile, Alabama, known as Chickasaw, is owned by the Gulf Shipbuilding Corporation. Except for that it has all the characteristics of any other American town. The property consists of residential buildings, streets, a system of sewers, a sewage disposal plant and a 'business block' on which business places are situated. A deputy of the Mobile County Sheriff, paid by the company, serves as the town's policeman. Merchants and service establishments have rented the stores and business places on the business block and the United States uses one of the places as a post office from which six carriers deliver mail to the people of Chickasaw and the adjacent area. The town and the surrounding neighborhood, which can not be distinguished from the Gulf property by anyone not familiar with the property lines, are thickly settled, and according to all indications the residents use the business block as their regular shopping center. To do so, they now, as they have for many years, make use of a company-owned paved street and sidewalk located alongside the store fronts in order to enter and leave the stores and the post office. Intersecting company-owned roads at each end of the business block lead into a four-lane public highway which runs parallel to the business block at a distance of thirty feet. There is nothing to stop highway traffic from coming onto the business block and upon arrival a traveler may make free use of the facilities available there. In short the town and its shopping district are accessible to and freely used by the public in general and there is nothing to distinguish them from any other town and shopping center except the fact that the title to the property belongs to a private corporation.

Appellant, a Jehovah's Witness, came onto the sidewalk we have just described, stood near the post-office and undertook to distribute religious literature. In the stores the corporation had posted a notice which read as follows: 'This Is Private Property, and Without Written Permission, No Street, or House Vendor, Agent or Solicitation of Any Kind Will Be Permitted.' Appellant was warned that she could not distribute the literature without a permit and told that no permit would be issued to her. She protested that the company rule could not be constitutionally applied so as to prohibit her from distributing religious writings. When she was asked to leave the sidewalk and Chickasaw she declined. The deputy sheriff arrested her and she was charged in the state court with violating Title 14, Section 426 of the 1940 Alabama Code which makes it a crime to enter or remain on the premises of another after having been warned not to do so. Appellant contended that to construe the state statute as applicable to her activities would abridge her right to freedom of press and religion contrary to the First and Fourteenth Amendments to the Constitution. This contention was rejected and she was convicted....

Had the title to Chickasaw belonged not to a private but to a municipal corporation and had appellant been arrested for violating a municipal ordinance rather than a ruling by those appointed by the corporation to manage a company-town it would have been clear that appellant's conviction must be reversed. Under our decision in *Lovell v. Griffin*, 303 U.S. 444 (1938), and others which have followed that case, neither a state nor a municipality can completely bar the distribution of literature containing religious or political ideas on its streets, sidewalks and public places or make the right to distribute dependent on a flat license tax or permit to be issued by an official who could deny it at will.... From these decisions it is clear that had the people of Chickasaw owned all the homes, and all the stores, and all the streets, and all the sidewalks, all those owners together could not have set up a municipal government with sufficient power to pass an ordinance completely barring the distribution of religious literature. Our question then narrows down to this: Can those people who live in or come to Chickasaw be denied freedom of press and religion simply because a single company has legal title to all the town? For it is the state's contention that the mere fact that all the property interests in the town are held by a single company is enough to give that company power, enforceable by a state statute, to abridge these freedoms.

We do not agree that the corporation's property interests settle the question. The State urges in effect that the corporation's right to control the inhabitants of Chickasaw is coextensive with the right of a homeowner to regulate the conduct of his guests. We can not accept that contention. Ownership does not always mean absolute dominion. The more an owner, for his advantage, opens up his property for use by the public in general, the more do his rights become circumscribed by the statutory and constitutional rights of those who use it. Thus, the owners of privately held bridges, ferries, turnpikes and railroads may not operate them as freely as a farmer does his farm. Since these facilities are built and operated primarily to benefit the public and since their operation is essentially a public function, it is subject to state regulation....

We do not think it makes any significant constitutional difference as to the relationship between the rights of the owner and those of the public that here the State, instead of permitting the corporation to operate a highway, permitted it to use its property as a town, operate a 'business block' in the town and a street and sidewalk on that business block. Whether a corporation or a municipality owns or possesses the town the public in either case has an identical interest in the functioning of the community in such manner that the channels of communication remain free. As we have heretofore stated, the town of Chickasaw does not function differently from any other town. The 'business block' serves as the community shopping center and is freely accessible and open to the people in the area and those passing through. The managers appointed by the corporation cannot curtail the liberty of press and religion of these people consistently with the purposes of the Constitutional guarantees, and a state statute, as the one here involved, which enforces such action by criminally punishing those who attempt to distribute religious literature clearly violates the First and Fourteenth Amendments to the Constitution.

Many people in the United States live in company-owned towns. These people, just as residents of municipalities, are free citizens of their State and country. Just as all other citizens they must make decisions which affect the welfare of community and nation. To act as good citizens they must be informed. In order to enable them to be properly informed their information must be uncensored. There is no more reason for depriving these people of the liberties guaranteed by the First and Fourteenth Amendments than there is for curtailing these freedoms with respect to any other citizen.

When we balance the Constitutional rights of owners of property against those of the people to enjoy freedom of press and religion, as we must here, we remain mindful of the fact that the latter occupy a preferred position.... In our view the circumstance that the property rights to the premises where the deprivation of liberty, here involved, took place, were held by others than the public, is not sufficient to justify the State's permitting a corporation to govern a community of citizens so as to restrict their fundamental liberties and the enforcement of such restraint by the application of a State statute. Insofar as the State has attempted to impose criminal punishment on appellant for undertaking to distribute religious literature in a company town, its action cannot stand. The case is reversed and the cause remanded for further proceedings not inconsistent with this opinion.

Mr. Justice JACKSON took no part in the consideration or decision of this case.

Mr. Justice FRANKFURTER, concurring. [omitted]

Mr. Justice REED [joined by THE CHIEF JUSTICE and JUSTICE BURTON], dissenting....

A state does have the moral duty of furnishing the opportunity for information, education and religious enlightenment to its inhabitants, including those who live in company towns, but it has not heretofore been adjudged that it must commandeer, without compensation, the private property of other citizens to carry out that obligation. Heretofore this Court has sustained the right of employees, under an appropriate statute, protecting full freedom of employee organization, to solicit union membership in nonworking time on the property of an employer and against his express prohibition. This is because the prohibition is an impediment to the right of organization which is protected by a statute which governs a relation between employers and employees if and when the latter are admitted to the employers' premises as licensees. It was recognized in the opinion that the freedom of solicitation was the result of a regulatory statute and was not a Constitutional right. In the area which is covered by the guarantees of the First Amendment, this Court has been careful to point out that the owner of property may protect himself against the intrusion of strangers....

Our Constitution guarantees to every man the right to express his views in an orderly fashion. An essential element of 'orderly' is that the man shall also have a right to use the place he chooses for his exposition. The rights of the owner, which the

Constitution protects as well as the right of free speech, are not outweighed by the interests of the trespasser, even though he trespasses in behalf of religion or free speech. We cannot say that Jehovah's Witnesses can claim the privilege of a license, which has never been granted, to hold their meetings in other private places, merely because the owner has admitted the public to them for other limited purposes. Even though we have reached the point where this Court is required to force private owners to open their property for the practice there of religious activities or propaganda distasteful to the owner, because of the public interest in freedom of speech and religion, there is no need for the application of such a doctrine here. Appellant, as we have said, was free to engage in such practices on the public highways, without becoming a trespasser on the company's property.

## Note: Shopping Centers as State Actors

1. While company towns have largely faded in importance in contemporary American society, another species of privately owned property—the shopping center—has emerged as a competitor to traditional publicly owned streets. During the 1960s and 1970s the Court considered whether shopping centers were the functional equivalent of company towns.

2. In *Amalgamated Food Employees Union v. Logan Valley Plaza, Inc.*, 391 U.S. 308 (1968), the Court held that a shopping center was a state actor. *Logan Valley* considered a claim by a union that sought to picket an employer on the shopping center grounds. Analogizing the shopping center to the company owned town in *Marsh*, the Court held that the picketers had a First Amendment right to enter the property for that purpose. Justice Marshall wrote the majority opinion; separate dissents were written by Justices White, Harlan and Black (the latter being the author of *Marsh*).

3. Four years later the Court reached a different result in *Lloyd Corp. v. Tanner*, 407 U.S. 551 (1972). *Lloyd* involved anti-Vietnam War picketing at a shopping center. A five-justice majority rejected the picketers' argument that the shopping center was a state actor. The Court distinguished *Logan Valley* on the ground that the picketing in that case—labor picketing directed at a particular store in the shopping center—required, for it to be effective, that the picketers have access to the privately owned property. By contrast, Justice Powell said for the majority in *Lloyd*, "The handbilling by respondents in the malls of Lloyd Center had no relation to any purpose for which the center was built and being used." Justice Marshall, the author of *Logan Valley*, dissented, joined by Justices Douglas, Brennan, and Stewart, all of who had either joined Justice Marshall's opinion or written a concurring opinion.

4. Again four years later, the Court in *Hudgens v. NLRB*, 424 U.S. 507 (1976), faced a situation analogous to that in *Logan Valley*: labor picketing of a store located in a shopping center. The Court, however, reached a different result. Writing for the majority, Justice Stewart, who had joined the *Logan Valley* opinion and dissented in *Lloyd*, concluded that *Lloyd* had effectively overruled *Logan Valley*, with the result that shopping center owners do not have to comply with constitutional requirements, such as the First Amendment, otherwise applicable only to states.

# B. Government Entanglement

## *Note: Radio Programs on Streetcars*

1. An early case, *Public Utilities Commission v. Pollack*, 343 U.S. 451 (1952), illustrates the myriad ways in which a private party might be subject to constitutional requirements otherwise applicable only to government. *Pollack* considered a First Amendment challenge to the decision of a Washington, D.C., streetcar company to broadcast music on its streetcars. The company, Capital Transit, was a private corporation; nevertheless, the Court held that it was subject to the requirements of the First Amendment. Writing for six justices, Justice Burton wrote the following:

> We find in the reasoning of the court below a sufficiently close relation between the Federal Government and the radio service to make it necessary for us to consider those Amendments. In finding this relation we do not rely on the mere fact that Capital Transit operates a public utility on the streets of the District of Columbia under authority of Congress. Nor do we rely upon the fact that, by reason of such federal authorization, Capital Transit now enjoys a substantial monopoly of street railway and bus transportation in the District of Columbia. We do, however, recognize that Capital Transit operates its service under the regulatory supervision of the Public Utilities Commission of the District of Columbia which is an agency authorized by Congress. We rely particularly upon the fact that that agency, pursuant to protests against the radio program, ordered an investigation of it and, after formal public hearings, ordered its investigation dismissed on the ground that the public safety, comfort and convenience were not impaired thereby.

Thus, government approval—at least its implicit approval—of the company's decision sufficiently implicated the state in that decision as to trigger First Amendment scrutiny. How far such an entanglement theory should extend has been heavily litigated ever since.

2. If the thought of a bus or subway company piping in music strikes you as irksome, consider the fact that Justice Frankfurter recused himself from the case because of his dislike of that practice. He wrote: "My feelings are so strongly engaged as a victim of the practice in controversy that I had better not participate in judicial judgment upon it."

## Burton v. Wilmington Parking Authority
### 365 U.S. 715 (1961)

Mr. Justice CLARK delivered the opinion of the Court.

In this action for declaratory and injunctive relief it is admitted that the Eagle Coffee Shoppe, Inc., a restaurant located within an off-street automobile parking building in Wilmington, Delaware, has refused to serve appellant food or drink solely because he is a Negro. The parking building is owned and operated by the Wilmington Parking Authority, an agency of the State of Delaware, and the restaurant is the Authority's lessee. Appellant claims that such refusal abridges his rights under the Equal Protection Clause of the Fourteenth Amendment to the United States Constitution. The Supreme Court of Delaware has held that Eagle was acting in 'a purely private capacity' under its lease; that its action was not that of the Authority and was not, therefore, state action within the contemplation of the prohibitions contained in that Amendment.... On the merits we have concluded that the exclusion of appellant under the circumstances shown to be present here was discriminatory state action in violation of the Equal Protection Clause of the Fourteenth Amendment.

The Authority was created by the City of Wilmington.... It is 'a public body corporate and politic, exercising public powers of the State as an agency thereof.' Its statutory purpose is to provide adequate parking facilities for the convenience of the public and thereby relieve the 'parking crisis, which threatens the welfare of the community * * *.' To this end the Authority is granted wide powers including that of constructing or acquiring by lease, purchase or condemnation, lands and facilities, and that of leasing 'portions of any of its garage buildings or structures for commercial uses by the lessee, where, in the opinion of the Authority, such leasing is necessary and feasible for the financing and operation of such facilities.'...

The first project undertaken by the Authority was the erection of a parking facility on Ninth Street in downtown Wilmington.... Before it began actual construction of the facility, the Authority was advised by its retained experts that the anticipated revenue from the parking of cars and proceeds from sale of its bonds would not be sufficient to finance the construction costs of the facility. Moreover, the bonds were not expected to be marketable if payable solely out of parking revenues. To secure additional capital needed for its 'debt-service' requirements, and thereby to make bond financing practicable, the Authority decided it was necessary to enter long-term leases with responsible tenants for commercial use of some of the space available in the projected 'garage building.' The public was invited to bid for these leases.

In April 1957 such a private lease, for 20 years and renewable for another 10 years, was made with Eagle Coffee Shoppe, Inc., for use as a 'restaurant, dining room, banquet hall, cocktail lounge and bar and for no other use and purpose.' The multi-level space of the building which was let to Eagle, although 'within the exterior walls of the structure, has no marked public entrance leading from the parking portion of the facility into the restaurant proper * * * (whose main entrance) is located on Ninth Street.' In its lease the Authority covenanted to complete construction expeditiously, including completion of 'the decorative finishing of the leased premises and utilities therefor, without cost to Lessee,' including necessary utility connections, toilets, hung acoustical tile and plaster ceilings; vinyl asbestos, ceramic tile and concrete floors; connecting stairs and wrought iron railings; and wood-floored show windows. Eagle spent some $220,000 to make the space suitable for its operation and, to the extent such improvements were so attached to realty as to become part thereof, Eagle to the same extent enjoys the Authority's tax exemption....

The *Civil Rights Cases*, 109 U.S. 3 (1883) [Note *supra.* this chapter], 'embedded in our constitutional law' the principle 'that the action inhibited by the first section

(Equal Protection Clause) of the Fourteenth Amendment is only such action as may fairly be said to be that of the States. That Amendment erects no shield against merely private conduct, however discriminatory or wrongful.'... It is clear, as it always has been since the *Civil Rights Cases*, that 'Individual invasion of individual rights is not the subject-matter of the amendment,' *id.*, and that private conduct abridging individual rights does no violence to the Equal Protection Clause unless to some significant extent the State in any of its manifestations has been found to have become involved in it. Because the virtue of the right to equal protection of the laws could lie only in the breadth of its application, its constitutional assurance was reserved in terms whose imprecision was necessary if the right were to be enjoyed in the variety of individual-state relationships which the Amendment was designed to embrace. For the same reason, to fashion and apply a precise formula for recognition of state responsibility under the Equal Protection Clause is an 'impossible task' which 'This Court has never attempted.' Only by sifting facts and weighing circumstances can the nonobvious involvement of the State in private conduct be attributed its true significance.

... In this connection the Delaware Supreme Court seems to have placed controlling emphasis on its conclusion, as to the accuracy of which there is doubt, that only some 15% of the total cost of the facility was 'advanced' from public funds; that the cost of the entire facility was allocated three-fifths to the space for commercial leasing and two-fifths to parking space; that anticipated revenue from parking was only some 30.5% of the total income, the balance of which was expected to be earned by the leasing; that the Authority had no original intent to place a restaurant in the building, it being only a happenstance resulting from the bidding; that Eagle expended considerable moneys on furnishings; that the restaurant's main and marked public entrance is on Ninth Street without any public entrance direct from the parking area; and that 'the only connection Eagle has with the public facility * * * is the furnishing of the sum of $28,700 annually in the form of rent which is used by the Authority to defray a portion of the operating expense of an otherwise unprofitable enterprise.' While these factual considerations are indeed validly accountable aspects of the enterprise upon which the State has embarked, we cannot say that they lead inescapably to the conclusion that state action is not present. Their persuasiveness is diminished when evaluated in the context of other factors which must be acknowledged.

The land and building were publicly owned. As an entity, the building was dedicated to 'public uses' in performance of the Authority's 'essential governmental functions.' The costs of land acquisition, construction, and maintenance are defrayed entirely from donations by the City of Wilmington, from loans and revenue bonds and from the proceeds of rentals and parking services out of which the loans and bonds were payable. Assuming that the distinction would be significant, the commercially leased areas were not surplus state property, but constituted a physically and financially integral and, indeed, indispensable part of the State's plan to operate its project as a self-sustaining unit. Upkeep and maintenance of the building, including necessary repairs, were responsibilities of the Authority and were payable out of public funds. It cannot be doubted that the peculiar relationship of the restaurant to the parking facility in which it is located confers on each an incidental variety of mutual benefits. Guests of the restaurant are afforded a convenient place to park their automobiles, even if they cannot enter the restaurant directly from the parking area. Similarly, its convenience for diners may well provide additional demand for the Authority's parking facilities. Should any improvements effected in the leasehold by Eagle become part of the realty, there is no possibility of increased taxes being passed on to it since the fee is held by a tax-exempt government agency. Neither can it be ignored, especially in view of Eagle's affirmative allegation that for it to serve Negroes would injure its business, that profits earned by discrimination not only contribute to, but also are indispensable elements in, the financial success of a governmental agency.

Addition of all these activities, obligations and responsibilities of the Authority, the benefits mutually conferred, together with the obvious fact that the restaurant is operated as an integral part of a public building devoted to a public parking service, indicates that degree of state participation and involvement in discriminatory action which it was the design of the Fourteenth Amendment to condemn. It is irony amounting to grave injustice that in one part of a single building, erected and maintained with public funds by an agency of the State to serve a public purpose, all persons have equal rights, while in another portion, also serving the public, a Negro is a second-class citizen, offensive because of his race, without rights and unentitled to service, but at the same time fully enjoys equal access to nearby restaurants in wholly privately owned buildings. As the [state court] pointed out, in its lease with Eagle the Authority could have affirmatively required Eagle to discharge the responsibilities under the Fourteenth Amendment imposed upon the private enterprise as a consequence of state participation. But no State may effectively abdicate its responsibilities by either ignoring them or by merely failing to discharge them whatever the motive may be. It is of no consolation to an individual denied the equal protection of the laws that it was done in good faith.... By its inaction, the Authority, and through it the State, has not only made itself a party to the refusal of service, but has elected to place its power, property and prestige behind the admitted discrimination. The State has so far insinuated itself into a position of interdependence with Eagle that it must be recognized as a joint participant in the challenged activity, which, on that account, cannot be considered to have been so 'purely private' as to fall without the scope of the Fourteenth Amendment.

Because readily applicable formulae may not be fashioned, the conclusions drawn from the facts and circumstances of this record are by no means declared as universal truths on the basis of which every state leasing agreement is to be tested. Owing to the very 'largeness' of government, a multitude of relationships might appear to some to fall within the Amendment's embrace, but that, it must be remembered, can be determined only in the framework of the peculiar facts or circumstances present. Therefore respondents' prophecy of nigh universal application of a constitutional precept so peculiarly dependent for its invocation upon appropriate facts fails to take into account 'Differences in circumstances [which] beget appropriate differences in law.' Specifically defining the limits of our inquiry, what we hold today is that when a State leases public property in the manner and for the purpose shown to have been the case here, the proscriptions of the Fourteenth Amendment must be complied with by the lessee as certainly as though they were binding covenants written into the agreement itself....

Mr. Justice STEWART, concurring.

I agree that the judgment must be reversed, but I reach that conclusion by a route much more direct than the one traveled by the Court. In upholding Eagle's right to deny service to the appellant solely because of his race, the Supreme Court of Delaware relied upon a statute of that State which permits the proprietor of a restaurant to refuse to serve 'persons whose reception or entertainment by him would be offensive to the major part of his customers * * *.' There is no suggestion in the record that the appellant as an individual was such a person. The highest court of Delaware has thus construed this legislative enactment as authorizing discriminatory classification based exclusively on color. Such a law seems to me clearly violative of the Fourteenth Amendment. I think, therefore, that the appeal was properly taken, and that the statute, as authoritatively construed by the Supreme Court of Delaware, is constitutionally invalid.

Mr. Justice HARLAN, with whom Mr. Justice WHITTAKER joins, dissenting. [omitted]

Mr. Justice FRANKFURTER, dissenting. [omitted]

## *Note:* Moose Lodge No. 107 v. Irvis

Beginning in the 1970s, the arrival of new justices at the Supreme Court heralded a more restrictive approach to the state action requirement. One of the earliest examples of this evolution is *Moose Lodge No. 107 v. Irvis*, 407 U.S. 163 (1972). *Moose Lodge* involved a lawsuit by an African-American against a private fraternal organization, alleging that the organization discriminated against him by refusing him service in its bar. The plaintiff alleged that there was state action because of the involvement of the state liquor authority in licensing the bar.

Writing for six Justices, Justice Rehnquist rejected the state action argument. He began his analysis with cautionary language:

> The Court has never held ... that discrimination by an otherwise private entity would be violative of the Equal Protection Clause if the private entity receives any sort of benefit or service at all from the State, or if it is subject to state regulation in any degree whatever. Since state-furnished services include such necessities of life as electricity, water, and police and fire protection, such a holding would utterly emasculate the distinction between private as distinguished from state conduct set forth in *The Civil Rights Cases*, 109 U.S. 3 (1883) [Note *supra.* this chapter], and adhered to in subsequent decisions.

After a lengthy quotation from *Burton v. Wilmington Parking Authority*, the Court then distinguished that case:

> Here there is nothing approaching the symbiotic relationship between lessor and lessee that was present in *Burton*, where the private lessee obtained the

benefit of locating in a building owned by the state-created parking authority, and the parking authority was enabled to carry out its primary public purpose of furnishing parking space by advantageously leasing portions of the building constructed for that purpose to commercial lessees such as the owner of the Eagle Restaurant. Unlike *Burton*, the Moose Lodge building is located on land owned by it, not by any public authority. Far from apparently holding itself out as a place of public accommodation, Moose Lodge quite ostentatiously proclaims the fact that it is not open to the public at large. Nor is it located and operated in such surroundings that although private in name, it discharges a function or performs a service that would otherwise in all likelihood be performed by the State. In short, while Eagle was a public restaurant in a public building, Moose Lodge is a private social club in a private building.

The Court then considered, and rejected, the argument that state action was present because of the state's regulation of drinking establishments. In particular, it considered the plaintiff's argument that the state had effectively created a monopoly over liquor service by limiting the number of licenses that would be given out in a given municipality.

> However detailed this type of regulation may be in some particulars, it cannot be said to in any way foster or encourage racial discrimination. Nor can it be said to make the State in any realistic sense a partner or even a joint venturer in the club's enterprise. The limited effect of the prohibition against obtaining additional club licenses when the maximum number of retail licenses allotted to a municipality has been issued, when considered together with the availability of liquor from hotel, restaurant, and retail licensees, falls far short of conferring upon club licensees a monopoly in the dispensing of liquor in any given municipality or in the State as a whole.

The Court then conceded that in one respect it might be possible, on remand, for the plaintiff to demonstrate state action:

> The District Court found that the regulations of the Liquor Control Board adopted pursuant to statute affirmatively require that 'every club licensee shall adhere to all of the provisions of its Constitution and By-Laws.' ... The effect of this particular regulation on Moose Lodge under the provisions of the constitution placed in the record in the court below would be to place state sanctions behind its discriminatory membership rules.... Even though the Liquor Control Board regulation in question is neutral in its terms, the result of its application in a case where the constitution and bylaws of a club required racial discrimination would be to invoke the sanctions of the State to enforce a concededly discriminatory private rule. State action, for purposes of the Equal Protection Clause, may emanate from rulings of administrative and regulatory agencies as well as from legislative or judicial action. [Application] of state sanctions to enforce such a rule would violate the Fourteenth Amendment. Although the record before us is not as clear as one would like,

appellant has not persuaded us that the District Court should have denied any and all relief.

Justice Douglas, joined by Justice Marshall, dissented, finding state action to be more prevalent than indicated by the majority. He relied heavily on the fact that in the area where the parties were located the state-mandated quota for liquor licenses had long been filled. Thus, he concluded, the board's action in licensing Moose Lodge had the result of denying African-Americans their right to congregate and drink.

Justice Brennan, also joined by Justice Marshall, wrote a separate dissent, stressing the comprehensiveness of the state's regulation of alcohol sales. He concluded, "It would be difficult to find a more pervasive interaction of state authority with personal conduct."

# Jackson v. Metropolitan Edison Co.
## 419 U.S. 345 (1974)

Mr. Justice REHNQUIST delivered the opinion of the Court.

Respondent Metropolitan Edison Co. is a privately owned and operated Pennsylvania corporation which holds a certificate of public convenience issued by the Pennsylvania Public Utility Commission empowering it to deliver electricity to a service area which includes the city of York, Pa. As a condition of holding its certificate, it is subject to extensive regulation by the Commission. Under a provision of its general tariff filed with the Commission, it has the right to discontinue service to any customer on reasonable notice of nonpayment of bills.

[After non-payment of an electricity bill the utility terminated service to the customer-petitioner.] Petitioner then filed suit against Metropolitan in the United States District Court for the Middle District of Pennsylvania under the Civil Rights Act of 1871 seeking damages for the termination and an injunction requiring Metropolitan to continue providing power to her residence until she had been afforded notice, a hearing, and an opportunity to pay any amounts found due. She urged that under state law she had an entitlement to reasonably continuous electrical service to her home and that Metropolitan's termination of her service for alleged nonpayment, action allowed by a provision of its general tariff filed with the Commission, constituted 'state action' depriving her of property in violation of the Fourteenth Amendment's guarantee of due process of law.

The District Court granted Metropolitan's motion to dismiss petitioner's complaint on the ground that the termination did not constitute state action.... On appeal, the United States Court of Appeals for the Third Circuit affirmed.... We granted certiorari to review this judgment.

The Due Process Clause of the Fourteenth Amendment provides: 'Nor shall any State deprive any person of life, liberty, or property, without due process of law.' In 1883, this Court in *The Civil Rights Cases*, 109 U.S. 3 (1883) [Note *supra.* this chapter], affirmed the essential dichotomy set forth in that Amendment between deprivation by the State, subject to scrutiny under its provisions, and private conduct, 'however discriminatory or wrongful,' against which the Fourteenth Amendment offers no shield. *Shelley v. Kraemer*, 335 U.S. 1 (1948).

We have reiterated that distinction on more than one occasion since then. See, e.g., *Moose Lodge No. 107 v. Irvis*, 407 U.S. 163 (1972) [Note *supra.* this chapter]; *Evans v. Abney*, 396 U.S. 435 (1970). While the principle that private action is immune from the restrictions of the Fourteenth Amendment is well established and easily stated, the question whether particular conduct is 'private,' on the one hand, or 'state action,' on the other, frequently admits of no easy answer. *Burton v. Wilmington Parking Authority* (1961) [*Supra.* this chapter]; *Moose Lodge No. 107.*

Here the action complained of was taken by a utility company which is privately owned and operated, but which in many particulars of its business is subject to extensive state regulation. The mere fact that a business is subject to state regulation does not by itself convert its action into that of the State for purposes of the Fourteenth Amendment. Nor does the fact that the regulation is extensive and detailed, as in the case of most public utilities, do so. *Public Utilities Comm'n v. Pollak*, 343 U.S. 451 (1952) [Note *supra.* this chapter]. It may well be that acts of a heavily regulated utility with at least something of a governmentally protected monopoly will more readily be found to be 'state' acts than will the acts of an entity lacking these characteristics. But the inquiry must be whether there is a sufficiently close nexus between the State and the challenged action of the regulated entity so that the action of the latter may be fairly treated as that of the State itself. *Moose Lodge No. 107.* The true nature of the State's involvement may not be immediately obvious, and detailed inquiry may be required in order to determine whether the test is met. *Burton.*

Petitioner advances a series of contentions which, in her view, lead to the conclusion that this case should fall on the *Burton* side of the line drawn in *The Civil Rights Cases*, rather than on the *Moose Lodge* side of that line. We find none of them persuasive.

Petitioner first argues that 'state action' is present because of the monopoly status allegedly conferred upon Metropolitan by the State of Pennsylvania. As a factual matter, it may well be doubted that the State ever granted or guaranteed Metropolitan a monopoly.[8] But assuming that it had, this fact is not determinative in considering whether Metropolitan's termination of service to petitioner was 'state action' for purposes of the Fourteenth Amendment. In *Pollak*, where the Court dealt with the activities of the District of Columbia Transit Co., a congressionally established monopoly, we expressly disclaimed reliance on the monopoly status of the transit authority. Similarly, although certain monopoly aspects were presented in *Moose Lodge No. 107*, we

---

8. ... There is nothing in either Metropolitan's certificate or in the statutes under which it was issued indicating that the State has granted or guaranteed to Metropolitan monopoly status. In fact Metropolitan does face competition within portions of its service area from another private utility company and from municipal utility companies.... As petitioner admits, such public utility companies are natural monopolies created by the economic forces of high threshold capital requirements and virtually unlimited economy of scale. Regulation was superimposed on such natural monopolies as a substitute for competition and not to eliminate it....

found that the Lodge's action was not subject to the provisions of the Fourteenth Amendment. In each of those cases, there was insufficient relationship between the challenged actions of the entities involved and their monopoly status. There is no indication of any greater connection here.

Petitioner next urges that state action is present because respondent provides an essential public service required to be supplied on a reasonably continuous basis by Pa.Stat.Ann., Tit. 66, § 1171, and hence performs a 'public function.' We have, of course, found state action present in the exercise by a private entity of powers traditionally exclusively reserved to the State. See, e.g., *Nixon v. Condon*, 286 U.S. 73 (1932) (election); *Terry v. Adams*, 345 U.S. 461 (1953) (election); *Marsh v. Alabama* (1946) (company town) [*Supra.* this chapter]; *Evans v. Newton*, 382 U.S. 296 (1966) (municipal park). If we were dealing with the exercise by Metropolitan of some power delegated to it by the State which is traditionally associated with sovereignty, such as eminent domain, our case would be quite a different one. But while the Pennsylvania statute imposes an obligation to furnish service on regulated utilities, it imposes no such obligation on the State. The Pennsylvania courts have rejected the contention that the furnishing of utility services is either a state function or a municipal duty.

Perhaps in recognition of the fact that the supplying of utility service is not traditionally the exclusive prerogative of the State, petitioner invites the expansion of the doctrine of this limited line of cases into a broad principle that all businesses 'affected with the public interest' are state actors in all their actions.

We decline the invitation for reasons stated long ago in *Nebbia v. New York* (1934) [*Supra.* Chapter 7], in the course of rejecting a substantive due process attack on state legislation:

> It is clear that there is no closed class or category of businesses affected with a public interest.... The phrase 'affected with a public interest' can, in the nature of things, mean no more than that an industry, for adequate reason, is subject to control for the public good. In several of the decisions of this court wherein the expressions 'affected with a public interest,' and 'clothed with a public use,' have been brought forward as the criteria ... it has been admitted that they are not susceptible of definition and form an unsatisfactory test....

Doctors, optometrists, lawyers, Metropolitan, and Nebbia's upstate New York grocery selling a quart of milk are all in regulated businesses, providing arguably essential goods and services, 'affected with a public interest.' We do not believe that such a status converts their every action, absent more, into that of the State.

We also reject the notion that Metropolitan's termination is state action because the State 'has specifically authorized and approved' the termination practice. In the instant case, Metropolitan filed with the Public Utility Commission a general tariff—a provision of which states Metropolitan's right to terminate service for nonpayment. This provision has appeared in Metropolitan's previously filed tariffs for many years and has never been the subject of a hearing or other scrutiny by the Commission. Although the Commission did hold hearings on portions of Metropolitan's general tariff relating to a general rate increase, it never even considered the reinsertion of this provision in the newly filed general tariff. The provision became effective 60 days after filing when not disapproved by the Commission.

As a threshold matter, it is less than clear under state law that Metropolitan was even required to file this provision as part of its tariff or that the Commission would have had the power to disapprove it. The District Court observed that the sole connection of the Commission with this regulation was Metropolitan's simple notice filing with the Commission and the lack of any Commission action to prohibit it.

The case most heavily relied on by petitioner is *Public Utilities Comm'n v. Pollak*. There the Court dealt with the contention that Capital Transit's installation of a piped music system on its buses violated the First Amendment rights of the bus riders. It is not entirely clear whether the Court alternatively held that Capital Transit's action was action of the 'State' for First Amendment purposes, or whether it merely assumed, arguendo, that it was and went on to resolve the First Amendment question adversely to the bus riders. In either event, the nature of the state involvement there was quite different than it is here. The District of Columbia Public Utilities Commission, on its own motion, commenced an investigation of the effects of the piped music, and after a full hearing concluded not only that Capital Transit's practices were 'not inconsistent with public convenience, comfort, and safety,' but also that the practice 'in fact, through the creation of better will among passengers, … tends to improve the conditions under which the public ride.' Here, on the other hand, there was no such imprimatur placed on the practice of Metropolitan about which petitioner complains. The nature of governmental regulation of private utilities is such that a utility may frequently be required by the state regulatory scheme to obtain approval for practices a business regulated in less detail would be free to institute without any approval from a regulatory body. Approval by a state utility commission of such a request from a regulated utility, where the commission has not put its own weight on the side of the proposed practice by ordering it, does not transmute a practice initiated by the utility and approved by the commission into 'state action.' At most, the Commission's failure to overturn this practice amounted to no more than a determination that a Pennsylvania utility was authorized to employ such a practice if it so desired. Respondent's exercise of the choice allowed by state law where the initiative comes from it and not from the State, does not make its action in doing so 'state action' for purposes of the Fourteenth Amendment.

We also find absent in the instant case the symbiotic relationship presented in *Burton v. Wilmington Parking Authority*. There where a private lessee, who practiced racial discrimination, leased space for a restaurant from a state parking authority in a publicly owned building, the Court held that the State had so far insinuated itself into a position of interdependence with the restaurant that it was a joint participant in the enterprise. We cautioned, however, that while 'a multitude of relationships might appear to some to fall within the Amendment's embrace,' differences in circumstances beget differences in law, limiting the actual holding to lessees of public property.

Metropolitan is a privately owned corporation, and it does not lease its facilities from the State of Pennsylvania. It alone is responsible for the provision of power to its customers. In common with all corporations of the State it pays taxes to the State, and it is subject to a form of extensive regulation by the State in a way that most other business enterprises are not. But this was likewise true of the appellant club in *Moose Lodge No. 107*, where we said:

> However detailed this type of regulation may be in some particulars, it cannot be said to in any way foster or encourage racial discrimination. Nor can it be said to make the State in any realistic sense a partner or even a joint venturer in the club's enterprise.

All of petitioner's arguments taken together show no more than that Metropolitan was a heavily regulated, privately owned utility, enjoying at least a partial monopoly in the providing of electrical service within its territory, and that it elected to terminate service to petitioner in a manner which the Pennsylvania Public Utility Commission found permissible under state law. Under our decision this is not sufficient to connect the State of Pennsylvania with respondent's action so as to make the latter's conduct attributable to the State for purposes of the Fourteenth Amendment....

Mr. Justice DOUGLAS, dissenting.

I reach the opposite conclusion from that reached by the majority on the state-action issue....

In *Burton* we said: 'Only by sifting facts and weighing circumstances can the nonobvious involvement of the State in private conduct be attributed its true significance.' A particularized inquiry into the circumstances of each case is necessary in order to determine whether a given factual situation falls within 'the variety of individual-state relationships which the [Fourteenth] Amendment was designed to embrace.' *Id.* As our subsequent discussion in Burton made clear, the dispositive question in any state-action case is not whether any single fact or relationship presents a sufficient degree of state involvement, but rather whether the aggregate of all relevant factors compels a finding of state responsibility. *Id.* See generally *Moose Lodge No. 107*.

It is not enough to examine seriatim each of the factors upon which a claimant relies and to dismiss each individually as being insufficient to support a finding of state action. It is the aggregate that is controlling.

It is said that the mere fact of respondent's monopoly status, assuming arguendo that that status is state conferred or state protected, 'is not determinative in considering whether Metropolitan's termination of service to petitioner was 'state action' for purposes of the Fourteenth Amendment.' *Ante.* Even so, a state-protected monopoly status is highly relevant in assessing the aggregate weight of a private entity's ties to the State.

It is said that the fact that respondent's services are 'affected with a public interest' is not determinative. I agree that doctors, lawyers, and grocers are not transformed into state actors simply because they provide arguably essential goods and services and are regulated by the State. In the present case, however, respondent is not just one person among many; it is the only public utility furnishing electric power to the city. When power is denied a householder, the home, under modern conditions, is likely to become unlivable.

Respondent's procedures for termination of service may never have been subjected to the same degree of state scrutiny and approval, whether explicit or implicit, that was present in *Public Utilities Comm'n v. Pollak*. Yet in the present case the State is heavily involved in respondent's termination procedures, getting into the approved tariff a requirement of 'reasonable notice.' Pennsylvania has undertaken to regulate numerous aspects of respondent's operations in some detail, and a 'hands-off' attitude of permissiveness or neutrality toward the operations in this case is at war with the state agency's functions of supervision over respondent's conduct in the area of servicing householders, particularly where (as here) the State would presumably lend its weight and authority to facilitate the enforcement of respondent's published procedures.

In the aggregate, these factors depict a monopolist providing essential public services as a licensee of the State and within a framework of extensive state supervision and control. The particular regulations at issue, promulgated by the monopolist, were authorized by state law and were made enforceable by the weight and authority of the State. Moreover, the State retains the power of oversight to review and amend the regulations if the public interest so requires. Respondent's actions are sufficiently intertwined with those of the State, and its termination-of-service provisions are sufficiently buttressed by state law to warrant a holding that respondent's actions in terminating this householder's service were 'state action' for the purpose of giving federal jurisdiction over respondent under 42 U.S.C. § 1983. Though the Court pays lip service to the need for assessing the totality of the State's involvement in this enterprise, its underlying analysis is fundamentally sequential rather than cumulative. In that perspective, what the Court does today is to make a significant departure from our previous treatment of state-action issues....

Mr. Justice BRENNAN, dissenting.

I do not think that a controversy existed between petitioner and respondent entitling petitioner to be heard in this action....

Mr. Justice MARSHALL, dissenting.

I agree with my Brother BRENNAN that this case is a very poor vehicle for resolving the difficult and important questions presented today.... Since the Court has disposed of the case by finding no state action, however, I think it appropriate to register my dissent on that point.

I

The Metropolitan Edison Co. provides an essential public service to the people of York, Pa. It is the only entity public or private, that is authorized to supply electric service to most of the community. As a part of its charter to the company, the State imposes extensive regulations, and it cooperates with the company in myriad ways. Additionally, the State has granted its approval to the company's mode of service termination—the very conduct that is challenged here. Taking these factors together, I have no difficulty finding state action in this case. As the Court concluded in *Burton*, the State has sufficiently 'insinuated itself into a position of interdependence with [the company] that it must be recognized as a joint participant in the challenged activity.'

Our state-action cases have repeatedly relied on several factors clearly presented by this case: a state-sanctioned monopoly; an extensive pattern of cooperation between the 'private' entity and the State; and a service uniquely public in nature. Today the Court takes a major step in repudiating this line of authority and adopts a stance that is bound to lead to mischief when applied to problems beyond the narrow sphere of due process objections to utility terminations.

## A

When the State confers a monopoly on a group or organization, this Court has held that the organization assumes many of the obligations of the State. Even when the Court has not found state action based solely on the State's conferral of a monopoly, it has suggested that the monopoly factor weighs heavily in determining whether constitutional obligations can be imposed on formally private entities. Indeed, in *Moose Lodge No. 107*, the Court was careful to point out that the Pennsylvania liquor-licensing scheme 'falls far short of conferring upon club licensees a monopoly in the dispensing of liquor in any given municipality or in the State as a whole.'

The majority distinguishes this line of cases with a cryptic assertion that public utility companies are 'natural monopolies.' *Ante*, at n.8. The theory behind the distinction appears to be that since the State's purpose in regulating a natural monopoly is not to aid the company but to prevent its charging monopoly prices, the State's involvement is somehow less significant for state-action purposes. I cannot agree that so much should turn on so narrow a distinction. Initially, it is far from obvious that an electric company would not be subject to competition if the market were unimpeded by governmental restrictions....

The difficulty inherent in this kind of economic analysis counsels against excusing natural monopolies from the reach of state-action principles. To invite inquiry into whether a particular state-sanctioned monopoly might have survived without the State's express approval grounds the analysis in hopeless speculation. Worse, this approach ignores important implications of the State's policy of utilizing private monopolies to provide electric service. Encompassed within this policy is the State's determination not to permit governmental competition with the selected private company, but to cooperate with and regulate the company in a multitude of ways to ensure that the company's service will be the functional equivalent of service provided by the State.

## B

The pattern of cooperation between Metropolitan Edison and the State has led to significant state involvement in virtually every phase of the company's business. The majority, however, accepts the relevance of the State's regulatory scheme only to the extent that it demonstrates state support for the challenged termination procedure. Moreover, after concluding that the State in this case had not approved the company's termination procedures, the majority suggests that even state authorization and approval would not be sufficient: the State would apparently have to order the termination practice in question to satisfy the majority's state-action test.

I disagree with the majority's position on three separate grounds. First, the suggestion that the State would have to 'put its own weight on the side of the proposed practice by ordering it' seems to me to mark a sharp departure from our previous state-action cases. From *The Civil Rights Cases* to *Moose Lodge*, we have consistently indicated that state authorization and approval of 'private' conduct would support a finding of state action.

Second, I question the wisdom of giving such short shrift to the extensive interaction between the company and the State, and focusing solely on the extent of state support for the particular activity under challenge. In cases where the State's only significant involvement is through financial support or limited regulation of the private entity, it may be well to inquire whether the State's involvement suggests state approval of the objectionable conduct. But where the State has so thoroughly insinuated itself into the operations of the enterprise, it should not be fatal if the State has not affirmatively sanctioned the particular practice in question.

Finally, it seems to me in any event that the State has given its approval to Metropolitan Edison's termination procedures. The State Utility Commission approved a tariff provision under which the company reserved the right to discontinue its service on reasonable notice for nonpayment of bills.

The majority attempts to make something of the fact that the tariff provision was not challenged in the most recent Utility Commission hearings, and that it had apparently not been challenged before. But the provision had been included in a tariff required to be filed and approved by the State pursuant to statute. That it was not seriously questioned before approval does not mean that it was not approved. It suggests, instead, that the Commission was satisfied to permit the company to proceed in the termination area as it had done in the past. The majority's test puts potential plaintiffs in a difficult position: if the Commission approves the tariff without argument or a hearing, the State has not sufficiently demonstrated its approval and support for the company's practices. If, on the other hand, the State challenges the tariff provision on the ground, for example, that the 'reasonable notice' does not meet the standards of fairness that it expects of the utility, then the State has not put its weight behind the termination procedure employed by the company, and again there is no state action. Apparently, authorization and approval would require the kind of hearing that was held in *Pollak*, where the Public Utilities Commission expressly stated that the bus company's installation of radios in buses and streetcars was not inconsistent with the public convenience, safety, and necessity. I am afraid that the majority has in effect restricted *Pollak* to its facts if it has not discarded it altogether.

## C

The fact that the Metropolitan Edison Co. supplies an essential public service that is in many communities supplied by the government weighs more heavily for me than for the majority. The Court concedes that state action might be present if the activity in question were 'traditionally associated with sovereignty,' but it then undercuts that point by suggesting that a particular service is not a public function if the State in question has not required that it be governmentally operated. This reads the 'public function' argument too narrowly. The whole point of the 'public function' cases is to look behind the State's decision to provide public services through private parties. See *Evans v. Newton*; *Terry v. Adams*; *Marsh v. Alabama*. In my view, utility service is traditionally identified with the State through universal public regulation or ownership to a degree sufficient to render it a 'public function.'

I agree with the majority that it requires more than a finding that a particular business is 'affected with the public interest' before constitutional burdens can be imposed on that business. But when the activity in question is of such public importance that the State invariably either provides the service itself or permits private companies to act as state surrogates in providing it, much more is involved than just a matter of public interest. In those cases, the State has determined that if private companies wish to enter the field, they will have to surrender many of the prerogatives normally associated with private enterprise and behave in many ways like a governmental body. And when the State's regulatory scheme has gone that far, it seems entirely consistent to impose on the public utility the constitutional burdens normally reserved for the State.

Private parties performing functions affecting the public interest can often make a persuasive claim to be free of the constitutional requirements applicable to governmental institutions because of the value of preserving a private sector in which the opportunity for individual choice is maximized.... In the due process area, a similar value of diversity may often be furthered by allowing various private institutions the flexibility to select procedures that fit their particular needs. But it is hard to imagine any such interests that are furthered by protecting privately owned public utility companies from meeting the constitutional standards that would apply if the companies were state owned. The values of pluralism and diversity are simply not relevant when the private company is the only electric company in town....

## III

What is perhaps most troubling about the Court's opinion is that it would appear to apply to a broad range of claimed constitutional violations by the company. The Court has not adopted the notion, accepted elsewhere, that different standards should apply to state action analysis when different constitutional claims are presented. Thus, the majority's analysis would seemingly apply as well to a company that refused to extend service to Negroes, welfare recipients, or any other group that the company preferred, for its own reasons, not to serve. I cannot believe that this Court would hold that the State's involvement with the utility company was not sufficient to impose upon the company an obligation to meet the constitutional mandate of nondiscrimination. Yet nothing in the analysis of the majority opinion suggests otherwise. I dissent.

### Note: Government Authorization and Cooperation

The cases in this section reflect how fact-intensive the state action inquiry can be. Nevertheless, are there consistent principles that can derived from these cases? Or are the methodologies in these cases fundamentally inconsistent?

Why does Justice Rehnquist say in *Jackson v. Metropolitan Edison* that the facts of that case "fall on the *Burton* side of the [state action] line ... rather than on the *Moose Lodge* side of that line"? Why does Justice Marshall, dissenting in *Jackson*, accuse the majority of both not following the law set down in *Moose Lodge* and reading *Pollak* so narrowly as to either confine it to its particular facts or "discard" it? Both of these justices argue that their side is the one consistent with precedent. Is one of them right, or does it depend on how you read that precedent? Or is that precedent simply too narrow to provide guidance in future cases?

# C. Judicial Enforcement and Legislative Authorization

One subset of government "entanglement" with private actors consists of situations where either courts enforce private agreements that, if entered into by the government itself, would violate the Constitution, or legislatures authorize—and hence are held to have approved—of such private actions. This latter set of situations overlaps considerably with the situations covered in the materials in the previous subsection— for example, in *Jackson*, where the justices debate the extent of Pennsylvania's approval of the utility's service termination procedures. Nevertheless, legislative (as well as judicial) approval of private conduct can be understood as a particular species of situations justifying its own analysis. As the cases below demonstrate, this category of state action presents difficult problems.

### Shelley v. Kraemer
#### 334 U.S. 1 (1948)

Mr. Chief Justice VINSON delivered the opinion of the Court.

These cases present for our consideration questions relating to the validity of court enforcement of private agreements, generally described as restrictive covenants, which have as their purpose the exclusion of persons of designated race or color from the ownership or occupancy of real property. Basic constitutional issues of obvious importance have been raised.

The first of these cases comes to this Court on certiorari to the Supreme Court of Missouri. On February 16, 1911, thirty out of a total of thirty-nine owners of property fronting both sides of Labadie Avenue between Taylor Avenue and Cora Avenue in the city of St. Louis, signed an agreement, which was subsequently recorded, providing in part:

> * * * the said property is hereby restricted to the use and occupancy for the term of Fifty (50) years from this date, so that it shall be a condition all the time and whether recited and referred to as (sic) not in subsequent conveyances and shall attach to the land, as a condition precedent to the sale of the same, that hereafter no part of said property or any portion thereof shall be, for said term of Fifty-years, occupied by any person not of the Caucasian race, it being intended hereby to restrict the use of said property for said period of time against the occupancy as owners or tenants of any portion of said property for resident or other purpose by people of the Negro or Mongolian Race.

The entire district described in the agreement included fifty-seven parcels of land. The thirty owners who signed the agreement held title to forty-seven parcels, including the particular parcel involved in this case. At the time the agreement was signed, five of the parcels in the district were owned by Negroes. One of those had been occupied by Negro families since 1882, nearly thirty years before the restrictive agreement was executed. The trial court found that owners of seven out of nine homes on the south side of Labadie Avenue, within the restricted district and 'in the immediate vicinity' of the premises in question, had failed to sign the restrictive agreement in 1911. At the time this action was brought, four of the premises were occupied by Negroes, and had been so occupied for periods ranging from twenty-three to sixty-three years. A fifth parcel had been occupied by Negroes until a year before this suit was instituted.

On August 11, 1945, pursuant to a contract of sale, petitioners Shelley, who are Negroes, for valuable consideration received from one Fitzgerald a warranty deed to the parcel in question. The trial court found that petitioners had no actual knowledge of the restrictive agreement at the time of the purchase.

On October 9, 1945, respondents, as owners of other property subject to the terms of the restrictive covenant, brought suit in Circuit Court of the city of St. Louis praying that petitioners Shelley be restrained from taking possession of the property and that judgment be entered divesting title out of petitioners Shelley and revesting title in the immediate grantor or in such other person as the court should direct. The trial court denied the requested relief on the ground that the restrictive agreement, upon which respondents based their action, had never become final and complete because it was the intention of the parties to that agreement that it was not to become effective until signed by all property owners in the district, and signatures of all the owners had never been obtained.

The Supreme Court of Missouri sitting en banc reversed and directed the trial court to grant the relief for which respondents had prayed. That court held the agreement effective and concluded that enforcement of its provisions violated no rights guaranteed to petitioners by the Federal Constitution. At the time the court rendered its decision, petitioners were occupying the property in question.

The second of the cases under consideration comes to this Court from the Supreme Court of Michigan. The circumstances presented do not differ materially from the Missouri case....

Petitioners have placed primary reliance on their contentions, first raised in the state courts, that judicial enforcement of the restrictive agreements in these cases has violated rights guaranteed to petitioners by the Fourteenth Amendment of the Federal Constitution and Acts of Congress passed pursuant to that Amendment. Specifically, petitioners urge that they have been denied the equal protection of the laws, deprived of property without due process of law, and have been denied privileges and immunities of citizens of the United States. We pass to a consideration of those issues.

## I.

Whether the equal protection clause of the Fourteenth Amendment inhibits judicial enforcement by state courts of restrictive covenants based on race or color is a question which this Court has not heretofore been called upon to consider....

It cannot be doubted that among the civil rights intended to be protected from discriminatory state action by the Fourteenth Amendment are the rights to acquire, enjoy, own and dispose of property. Equality in the enjoyment of property rights was regarded by the framers of that Amendment as an essential pre-condition to the realization of other basic civil rights and liberties which the Amendment was intended to guarantee....

It is likewise clear that restrictions on the right of occupancy of the sort sought to be created by the private agreements in these cases could not be squared with the requirements of the Fourteenth Amendment if imposed by state statute or local ordinance. We do not understand respondents to urge the contrary....

But the present cases ... do not involve action by state legislatures or city councils. Here the particular patterns of discrimination and the areas in which the restrictions are to operate, are determined, in the first instance, by the terms of agreements among private individuals. Participation of the State consists in the enforcement of the restrictions so defined. The crucial issue with which we are here confronted is whether this distinction removes these cases from the operation of the prohibitory provisions of the Fourteenth Amendment.

Since the decision of this Court in *The Civil Rights Cases*, 109 U.S. 3 (1883) [Note *supra.* this chapter], the principle has become firmly embedded in our constitutional law that the action inhibited by the first section of the Fourteenth Amendment is only such action as may fairly be said to be that of the States. That Amendment erects no shield against merely private conduct, however discriminatory or wrongful.

We conclude, therefore, that the restrictive agreements standing alone cannot be regarded as a violation of any rights guaranteed to petitioners by the Fourteenth Amendment. So long as the purposes of those agreements are effectuated by voluntary adherence to their terms, it would appear clear that there has been no action by the State and the provisions of the Amendment have not been violated.

But here there was more. These are cases in which the purposes of the agreements were secured only by judicial enforcement by state courts of the restrictive terms of the agreements. The respondents urge that judicial enforcement of private agreements does not amount to state action; or, in any event, the participation of the State is so attenuated in character as not to amount to state action within the meaning of the Fourteenth Amendment. Finally, it is suggested, even if the States in these cases may be deemed to have acted in the constitutional sense, their action did not deprive petitioners of rights guaranteed by the Fourteenth Amendment. We move to a consideration of these matters.

## II.

That the action of state courts and of judicial officers in their official capacities is to be regarded as action of the State within the meaning of the Fourteenth Amendment, is a proposition which has long been established by decisions of this Court. That principle was given expression in the earliest cases involving the construction of the terms of the Fourteenth Amendment.... In *The Civil Rights Cases*, this Court pointed out that the Amendment makes void 'state action of every kind' which is inconsistent with the guaranties therein contained, and extends to manifestations of 'state authority in the shape of laws, customs, or judicial or executive proceedings.' Language to like effect is employed no less than eighteen times during the course of that opinion.

Similar expressions, giving specific recognition to the fact that judicial action is to be regarded as action on the State for the purposes of the Fourteenth Amendment, are to be found in numerous cases which have been more recently decided....

But the examples of state judicial action which have been held by this Court to violate the Amendment's commands are not restricted to situations in which the judicial proceedings were found in some manner to be procedurally unfair. It has been recognized that the action of state courts in enforcing a substantive common-law rule formulated by those courts, may result in the denial of rights guaranteed by the Fourteenth Amendment, even though the judicial proceedings in such cases may have been in complete accord with the most rigorous conceptions of procedural due process. Thus, in *American Federation of Labor v. Swing*, 312 U.S. 321 (1941), enforcement by state courts of the common-law policy of the State, which resulted in the restraining of peaceful picketing, was held to be state action of the sort prohibited by the Amendment's guaranties of freedom of discussion....

The short of the matter is that from the time of the adoption of the Fourteenth Amendment until the present, it has been the consistent ruling of this Court that the action of the States to which the Amendment has reference, includes action of state courts and state judicial officials. Although, in construing the terms of the Fourteenth Amendment, differences have from time to time been expressed as to whether particular types of state action may be said to offend the Amendment's prohibitory provisions, it has never been suggested that state court action is immunized from the operation of those provisions simply because the act is that of the judicial branch of the state government.

## III.

Against this background of judicial construction, extending over a period of some three-quarters of a century, we are called upon to consider whether enforcement by state courts of the restrictive agreements in these cases may be deemed to be the acts of those States; and, if so, whether that action has denied these petitioners the equal protection of the laws which the Amendment was intended to insure.

We have no doubt that there has been state action in these cases in the full and complete sense of the phrase. The undisputed facts disclose that petitioners were willing purchasers of properties upon which they desired to establish homes. The owners of the properties were willing sellers; and contracts of sale were accordingly consummated. It is clear that but for the active intervention of the state courts, supported by the full panoply of state power, petitioners would have been free to occupy the properties in question without restraint.

These are not cases, as has been suggested, in which the States have merely abstained from action, leaving private individuals free to impose such discriminations as they see fit. Rather, these are cases in which the States have made available to such individuals the full coercive power of government to deny to petitioners, on the grounds of race or color, the enjoyment of property rights in premises which petitioners are willing and financially able to acquire and which the grantors are willing to sell. The difference between judicial enforcement and nonenforcement of the restrictive covenants is the difference to petitioners between being denied rights of property available to other members of the community and being accorded full enjoyment of those rights on an equal footing.

The enforcement of the restrictive agreements by the state courts in these cases was directed pursuant to the common-law policy of the States as formulated by those courts in earlier decisions.... The judicial action in each case bears the clear and unmistakable imprimatur of the State. We have noted that previous decisions of this Court have established the proposition that judicial action is not immunized from the operation of the Fourteenth Amendment simply because it is taken pursuant to the state's common-law policy. Nor is the Amendment ineffective simply because the particular pattern of discrimination, which the State has enforced, was defined initially by the terms of a private agreement. State action, as that phrase is understood for the purposes of the Fourteenth Amendment, refers to exertions of state power in all forms. And when the effect of that action is to deny rights subject to the protection of the Fourteenth Amendment, it is the obligation of this Court to enforce the constitutional commands.

We hold that in granting judicial enforcement of the restrictive agreements in these cases, the States have denied petitioners the equal protection of the laws and that, therefore, the action of the state courts cannot stand....

For the reasons stated, the judgment of the Supreme Court of Missouri and the judgment of the Supreme Court of Michigan must be reversed.

Mr. Justice REED, Mr. Justice JACKSON, and Mr. Justice RUTLEDGE took no part in the consideration or decision of these cases.

# Reitman v. Mulkey

387 U.S. 369 (1967)

Mr. Justice WHITE delivered the opinion of the Court.

The question here is whether Art. I, § 26, of the California Constitution denies 'to any person * * * the equal protection of the laws' within the meaning of the Fourteenth Amendment of the Constitution of the United States. Section 26 of Art. I, an initiated measure submitted to the people as Proposition 14 in a statewide ballot in 1964, provides in part as follows:

> Neither the State nor any subdivision or agency thereof shall deny, limit or abridge, directly or indirectly, the right of any person, who is willing or desires to sell, lease or rent any part or all of his real property, to decline to sell, lease or rent such property to such person or persons as he, in his absolute discretion, chooses....

The issue arose in two separate actions in the California courts, *Mulkey v. Reitman* and *Prendergast v. Snyder*.... [The California Supreme Court] ... held that Art. I, § 26, was invalid as denying the equal protection of the laws guaranteed by the Fourteenth Amendment....

We affirm the judgments of the California Supreme Court. We first turn to the opinion of that court in *Reitman*, which quite properly undertook to examine the constitutionality of § 26 in terms of its 'immediate objective,' its 'ultimate effect' and its 'historical context and the conditions existing prior to its enactment'....

First, the court considered whether § 26 was concerned at all with private discriminations in residential housing. This involved a review of past efforts by the California Legislature to regulate such discriminations. The Unruh Act, on which respondents based their cases, was passed in 1959. The Hawkins Act ... followed and prohibited discriminations in publicly assisted housing. In 1961, the legislature enacted proscriptions against restrictive covenants. Finally, in 1963, came the Rumford Fair Housing Act, superseding the Hawkins Act and prohibiting racial discriminations in the sale or rental of any private dwelling containing more than four units. That act was enforceable by the State Fair Employment Practice Commission.

It was against this background that Proposition 14 was enacted. Its immediate design and intent, the California court said, were 'to overturn state laws that bore on the right of private sellers and lessors to discriminate,' the Unruh and Rumford Acts, and 'to forestall future state action that might circumscribe this right.' This aim was successfully achieved: the adoption of Proposition 14 'generally nullifies both the Rumford and Unruh Acts as they apply to the housing market,' and establishes 'a purported constitutional right to privately discriminate on grounds which admittedly would be unavailable under the Fourteenth Amendment should state action be involved.'

Second, the court conceded that the State was permitted a neutral position with respect to private racial discriminations and that the State was not bound by the Federal Constitution to forbid them. But, because a significant state involvement in private discriminations could amount to unconstitutional state action, *Burton v. Wilmington Parking Authority* (1961) [*Supra.* this chapter], the court deemed it necessary to determine whether Proposition 14 invalidly involved the State in racial discriminations in the housing market. Its conclusion was that it did.

To reach this result, the state court examined certain prior decisions in this Court in which discriminatory state action was identified. Based on these cases, it concluded that a prohibited state involvement could be found 'even where the state can be charged with only encouraging,' rather than commanding discrimination. Also of particular interest to the court was Mr. Justice Stewart's concurrence in *Burton*, where it was said that the Delaware courts had construed an existing Delaware statute as 'authorizing' racial discrimination in restaurants and that the statute was therefore invalid. To the California court 'the instant case presents an undeniably analogous situation' wherein the State had taken affirmative action designed to make private discriminations legally possible. Section 26 was said to have changed the situation from one in which discrimination was restricted 'to one wherein it is encouraged, within the meaning of the cited decisions'; §26 was legislative action 'which authorized private discrimination' and made the State 'at least a partner in the instant act of discrimination * * *.' The court could 'conceive of no other purpose for an application of section 26 aside from authorizing the perpetration of a purported private discrimination * * *.' The judgment of the California court was that §26 unconstitutionally involves the State in racial discriminations and is therefore invalid under the Fourteenth Amendment.

There is no sound reason for rejecting this judgment. Petitioners contend that the California court has misconstrued the Fourteenth Amendment since the repeal of any statute prohibiting racial discrimination, which is constitutionally permissible, may be said to 'authorize' and 'encourage' discrimination because it makes legally permissible that which was formerly proscribed. But, as we understand the California court, it did not posit a constitutional violation on the mere repeal of the Unruh and Rumford Acts. It did not read either our cases or the Fourteenth Amendment as establishing an automatic constitutional barrier to the repeal of an existing law prohibiting racial discriminations in housing; nor did the court rule that a State may never put in statutory form an existing policy of neutrality with respect to private discriminations. What the court below did was first to reject the notion that the State was required to have a statute prohibiting racial discriminations in housing. Second, it held the intent of §26 was to authorize private racial discriminations in the housing market, to repeal the Unruh and Rumford Acts and to create a constitutional right to discriminate on racial grounds in the sale and leasing of real property. Hence, the court dealt with §26 as though it expressly authorized and constitutionalized the private right to discriminate. Third, the court assessed the ultimate impact of §26 in the California environment and concluded that the section would encourage and significantly involve the State in private racial discrimination contrary to the Fourteenth Amendment.

The California court could very reasonably conclude that §26 would and did have wider impact than a mere repeal of existing statutes. Section 26 mentioned neither the Unruh nor Rumford Act in so many words. Instead, it announced the constitutional right of any person to decline to sell or lease his real property to anyone to whom he did not desire to sell or lease. Unruh and Rumford were thereby *pro tanto* repealed. But the section struck more deeply and more widely. Private discriminations in housing were now not only free from Rumford and Unruh but they also enjoyed a far different status than was true before the passage of those statutes. The right to discriminate, including the right to discriminate on racial grounds, was now embodied in the State's basic charter, immune from legislative, executive, or judicial regulation at any level of the state government. Those practicing racial discriminations need no longer rely solely on their personal choice. They could now invoke express constitutional authority, free from censure or interference of any kind from official sources. All individuals, partnerships, corporations and other legal entities, as well as their agents and representatives, could now discriminate with respect to their residential real property, which is defined as any interest in real property of any kind or quality, 'irrespective of how obtained or financed,' and seemingly irrespective of the relationship of the State to such interests in real property....

This Court has never attempted the 'impossible task' of formulating an infallible test for determining whether the State 'in any of its manifestations' has become significantly involved in private discriminations. 'Only by sifting facts and weighing circumstances' on a case-by-case basis can a 'nonobvious involvement of the State in private conduct be attributed its true significance.' *Burton*. Here the California court, armed as it was with the knowledge of the facts and circumstances concerning the passage and potential impact of §26, and familiar with the milieu in which that provision would operate, has determined that the provision would involve the State in private racial discriminations to an unconstitutional degree. We accept this holding of the California court.

The assessment of §26 by the California court is similar to what this Court has done in appraising state statutes or other official actions in other contexts. In *McCabe v. Atchison, Topeka & Santa Fe R. Co.*, 235 U.S. 151 (1914) [Note *supra*. Chapter 13], the Court dealt with a statute which, as construed by the Court, authorized carriers to provide cars for white persons but not for Negroes. Though dismissal of the complaint on a procedural ground was affirmed, the Court made it clear that such a statute was invalid under the Fourteenth Amendment because a carrier refusing equal service to Negroes would be 'acting in the matter under the authority of a state law.' This was nothing less than considering a permissive state statute as an authorization to discriminate and as sufficient state action to violate the Fourteenth Amendment in the context of that case. Similarly, in *Nixon v. Condon*, 286 U.S. 73 (1932), the Court was faced with a statute empowering the executive committee of a political party to prescribe the qualifications of its members for voting or for other participation, but containing no directions with respect to the exercise of that power. This was authority which the committee otherwise might not have had and which was used by the committee to bar Negroes from voting in primary elections. Reposing this power in the executive committee was said to insinuate the State into the self-regulatory, decision-making scheme of the voluntary association; the exercise of the power was viewed as an expression of state authority contrary to the Fourteenth Amendment.

In *Burton*, the operator-lessee of a restaurant located in a building owned by the State and otherwise operated for public purposes, refused service to Negroes. Although the State neither commanded nor expressly authorized or encouraged the discriminations, the State had 'elected to place its power, property and prestige behind the admitted discrimination' and by 'its inaction * * * has * * * made itself a party to the refusal of service * * *' which therefore could not be considered the purely private choice of the restaurant operator.

In *Peterson v. City of Greenville*, 373 U.S. 244 (1963), and in *Robinson v. State of Florida*, 378 U.S. 153 (1964), the Court dealt with state statutes or regulations requiring, at least in some respects, segregation in facilities and services in restaurants. These official provisions, although obviously unconstitutional and unenforceable, were deemed in themselves sufficient to disentitle the State to punish, as trespassers, Negroes who had been refused service in the restaurants. In neither case was any proof required that the restaurant owner had actually been influenced by the state statute or regulation. Finally, in *Lombard v. State of Louisiana*, 373 U.S. 267 (1963), the Court interpreted public statements by New Orleans city officials as announcing that the city would not permit Negroes to seek desegregated service in restaurants. Because the statements were deemed to have as much coercive potential as the ordinance in the *Peterson* case, the Court treated the city as though it had actually adopted an ordinance forbidding desegregated service in public restaurants.

None of these cases squarely controls the case we now have before us. But they do illustrate the range of situations in which discriminatory state action has been identified. They do exemplify the necessity for a court to assess the potential impact of official action in determining whether the State has significantly involved itself with invidious discriminations. Here we are dealing with a provision which does not just repeal an existing law forbidding private racial discriminations. Section 26 was intended to authorize, and does authorize, racial discrimination in the housing market. The right to discriminate is now one of the basic policies of the State. The California Supreme Court believes that the section will significantly encourage and involve the State in private discriminations. We have been presented with no persuasive considerations indicating that these judgments should be overturned.

Mr. Justice DOUGLAS, concurring.

While I join the opinion of the Court, I add a word to indicate the dimensions of our problem.

This is not a case as simple as the one where a man with a bicycle or a car or a stock certificate or even a log cabin asserts the right to sell it to whomsoever he pleases, excluding all others whether they be Negro, Chinese, Japanese, Russians, Catholics, Baptists, or those with blue eyes. We deal here with a problem in the realm of zoning, similar to the one we had in *Shelley v. Kraemer* (1948) [*Supra*. this chapter], where we struck down restrictive covenants.

Those covenants are one device whereby a neighborhood is kept 'while' or 'Caucasian' as the dominant interests desire. Proposition 14 in the setting of our modern housing problem is only another device of the same character....

Zoning is a state and municipal function. When the State leaves that function to private agencies or institutions which are licensees and which practice racial discrimination and zone our cities into white and black belts or white and black ghettoes, it suffers a governmental function to be performed under private auspices in a way the State itself may not act....

Leaving the zoning function to groups which practice racial discrimination and are licensed by the States constitutes state action in the narrowest sense in which *Shelley* can be construed....

Under California law no person may 'engage in the business, act in the capacity of, advertise or assume to act as a real estate broker or a real estate salesman within this State without first obtaining a real estate license.'... There is no difference, as I see it, between a State authorizing a licensee to practice racial discrimination and a State, without any express authorization of that kind nevertheless launching and countenancing the operation of a licensing system in an environment where the whole weight of the system is on the side of discrimination. In the latter situation the State is impliedly sanctioning what it may not do specifically.

If we were in a domain exclusively private, we would have different problems. But urban housing is in the public domain as evidenced not only by the zoning problems presented but by the vast schemes of public financing with which the States and the Nation have been extensively involved in recent years. Urban housing is clearly marked with the public interest. Urban housing, like restaurants, inns, and carriers or like telephone companies, drugstores, or hospitals, is affected with a public interest in the historic and classical sense....

Since the real estate brokerage business is one that can be and is state-regulated and since it is state-licensed, it must be dedicated, like the telephone companies and the carriers and the hotels and motels to the requirements of service to all without discrimination—a standard that in its modern setting is conditioned by the demands of the Equal Protection Clause of the Fourteenth Amendment....

Mr. Justice HARLAN, whom Mr. Justice BLACK, Mr. Justice CLARK, and Mr. Justice STEWART join, dissenting.

I consider that this decision, which cuts deeply into state political processes, is supported neither by anything 'found' by the Supreme Court of California nor by any of our past cases decided under the Fourteenth Amendment. In my view today's holding, salutary as its result may appear at first blush, may in the long run actually serve to handicap progress in the extremely difficult field of racial concerns. I must respectfully dissent.

The facts of this case are simple and undisputed. The legislature of the State of California has in the last decade enacted a number of statutes restricting the right of private landowners to discriminate on the basis of such factors as race in the sale or rental of property. These laws aroused considerable opposition, causing certain groups to organize themselves and to take advantage of procedures embodied in the California Constitution permitting a 'proposition' to be presented to the voters for a constitutional amendment. 'Proposition 14' was thus put before the electorate in the 1964 election and was adopted by a vote of 4,526,460 to 2,395,747. The Amendment, Art. I, § 26, of the State Constitution, reads in relevant part as follows:

> Neither the State nor any subdivision or agency thereof shall deny, limit or abridge, directly or indirectly, the right of any person, who is willing or desires to sell, lease or rent any part or all of his real property, to decline to sell, lease or rent such property to such person or persons as he, in his absolute discretion, chooses.

I am wholly at a loss to understand how this straight forward effectuation of a change in the California Constitution can be deemed a violation of the Fourteenth Amendment....

The Equal Protection Clause of the Fourteenth Amendment ... does not undertake to control purely personal prejudices and predilections, and individual acting on their own are left free to discriminate on racial grounds if they are so minded, *Civil Rights Cases*. By the same token the Fourteenth Amendment does not require of States the passage of laws preventing such private discrimination, although it does not of course disable them from enacting such legislation if they wish.

In the case at hand California, acting through the initiative and referendum, has decided to remain 'neutral' in the realm of private discrimination affecting the sale or rental of private residential property; in such transactions private owners are now free to act in a discriminatory manner previously forbidden to them. In short, all that has happened is that California has effected a *pro tanto* repeal of its prior statutes forbidding private discrimination. This runs no more afoul of the Fourteenth Amendment than would have California's failure to pass any such antidiscrimination statutes in the first instance. The fact that such repeal was also accompanied by a constitutional prohibition against future enactment of such laws by the California Legislature cannot well be thought to affect, from a federal constitutional standpoint, the validity of what California has done. The Fourteenth Amendment does not reach such state constitutional action any more than it does a simple legislative repeal of legislation forbidding private discrimination.

I do not think the Court's opinion really denies any of these fundamental constitutional propositions. Rather it attempts to escape them by resorting to arguments which appear to me to be entirely ill-founded.

## I.

The Court attempts to fit § 26 within the coverage of the Equal Protection Clause by characterizing it as in effect an affirmative call to residents of California to discriminate. The main difficulty with this viewpoint is that it depends upon a characterization of § 26 that cannot fairly be made. The provision is neutral on its face, and it is only by in effect asserting that this requirement of passive official neutrality is camouflage that the Court is able to reach its conclusion. In depicting the provision as tantamount to active state encouragement of discrimination the Court essentially relies on the fact that the California Supreme Court so concluded. It is said that the findings of the highest court of California as to the meaning and impact of the enactment are entitled to great weight. I agree, of course, that findings of fact by a state court should be given great weight, but this familiar proposition hardly aids the Court's holding in this case.

There is no disagreement whatever but that § 26 was meant to nullify California's fair-housing legislation and thus to remove from private residential property transactions the state-created impediment upon freedom of choice.... The Court declares that the California court 'held the intent of § 26 was to authorize private racial discriminations in the housing market * * *,' but there is no supporting fact in the record for this characterization. Moreover, the grounds which prompt legislators or state voters to repeal a law do not determine its constitutional validity. That question is decided by what the law does, not by what those who voted for it wanted it to do, and it must not be forgotten that the Fourteenth Amendment does not compel a State to put or keep any particular law about race on its books. The Amendment only forbids a State to pass or keep in effect laws discriminating on account of race. California has not done this.

A state enactment, particularly one that is simply permissive of private decision-making rather than coercive and one that has been adopted in this most democratic of processes, should not be struck down by the judiciary under the Equal Protection Clause without persuasive evidence of an invidious purpose or effect. The only 'factual' matter relied on by the majority of the California Supreme Court was the context in which Proposition 14 was adopted, namely, that several strong antidiscrimination acts had been passed by the legislature and opposed by many of those who successfully led the movement for adoption of Proposition 14 by popular referendum. These circumstances, and these alone, the California court held, made § 26 unlawful under this Court's cases interpreting the Equal Protection Clause.... Accepting all the suppositions under which the state court acted, I cannot see that its conclusion is entitled to any special weight in the discharge of our own responsibilities. Put in another way, I cannot transform the California court's conclusion of law into a finding of fact that the State through the adoption of § 26 is actively promoting racial discrimination. It seems to me manifest that the state court decision rested entirely on what that court conceived to be the compulsion of the Fourteenth Amendment, not on any fact-finding by the state courts.

## II.

There is no question that the adoption of § 26, repealing the former state antidiscrimination laws and prohibiting the enactment of such state laws in the future, constituted 'state action' within the meaning of the Fourteenth Amendment. The only issue is whether this provision impermissibly deprives any person of equal protection of the laws. As a starting point, it is clear that any statute requiring unjustified discriminatory treatment is unconstitutional. E.g., *Brown v. Board of Education* (1954) [*Supra.* Chapter 13], *Peterson v. City of Greenville*. And it is no less clear that the Equal

Protection Clause bars as well discriminatory governmental administration of a statute fair on its face. E.g., *Yick Wo v. Hopkins*, 118 U.S. 356 (1886) [Note *supra*. Chapter 14]. This case fits within neither of these two categories: Section 26 is by its terms inoffensive, and its provisions require no affirmative governmental enforcement of any sort. A third category of equal-protection cases, concededly more difficult to characterize, stands for the proposition that when governmental involvement in private discrimination reaches a level at which the State can be held responsible for the specific act of private discrimination, the strictures of the Fourteenth Amendment come into play. In dealing with this class of cases, the inquiry has been framed as whether the State has become 'a joint participant in the challenged activity, which, on that account, cannot be considered to have been so 'purely private' as to fall without the scope of the Fourteenth Amendment.' *Burton v. Wilmington Parking Authority*.

Given these latter contours of the equal-protection doctrine, the assessment of particular cases is often troublesome, as the Court itself acknowledges. However, the present case does not seem to me even to approach those peripheral situations in which the question of state involvement gives rise to difficulties. The core of the Court's opinion is that § 26 is offensive to the Fourteenth Amendment because it effectively encourages private discrimination. By focusing on 'encouragement' the Court, I fear, is forging a slippery and unfortunate criterion by which to measure the constitutionality of a statute simply permissive in purpose and effect, and inoffensive on its face.

It is true that standards in this area have not been definitely formulated, and that acts of discrimination have been included within the compass of the Equal Protection Clause not merely when they were compelled by a state statute or other governmental pressures, but also when they were said to be 'induced' or 'authorized' by the State. Most of these cases, however, can be approached in terms of the impact and extent of affirmative state governmental activities, e.g., the action of a sheriff, *Lombard v. Louisiana*; the official supervision over a park, *Evans v. Newton*, 382 U.S. 296 (1966); a joint venture with a lessee in a municipally owned building, *Burton v. Wilmington Parking Authority*. In situations such as these the focus has been on positive state co-operation or partnership in affirmatively promoted activities, an involvement that could have been avoided. Here, in contrast, we have only the straight-forward adoption of a neutral provision restoring to the sphere of free choice, left untouched by the Fourteenth Amendment, private behavior within a limited area of the racial problem. The denial of equal protection emerges only from the conclusion reached by the Court that the implementation of a new policy of governmental neutrality, embodied in a constitutional provision and replacing a former policy of antidiscrimination, has the effect of lending encouragement to those who wish to discriminate. In the context of the actual facts of the case, this conclusion appears to me to state only a truism: people who want to discriminate but were previously forbidden to do so by state law are now left free because the State has chosen to have no law on the subject at all. Obviously whenever there is a change in the law it will have resulted from the concerted activity of those who desire the change, and its enactment will allow those supporting the legislation to pursue their private goals.

A moment of thought will reveal the far-reaching possibilities of the Court's new doctrine, which I am sure the Court does not intend. Every act of private discrimination is either forbidden by state law or permitted by it. There can be little doubt that such permissiveness—whether by express constitutional or statutory provision, or implicit in the common law—to some extent 'encourages' those who wish to discriminate to do so. Under this theory 'state action' in the form of laws that do nothing more than passively permit private discrimination could be said to tinge all private discrimination with the taint of unconstitutional state encouragement.

This type of alleged state involvement, simply evincing a refusal to involve itself at all, is of course very different from that illustrated in such cases as *Lombard*, *Peterson*, *Evans* and *Burton*, where the Court found active involvement of state agencies and officials in specific acts of discrimination. It is also quite different from cases in which a state enactment could be said to have the obvious purpose of fostering discrimination. I believe the state action required to bring the Fourteenth Amendment into operation must be affirmative and purposeful, actively fostering discrimination. Only in such a case is ostensibly 'private' action more properly labeled 'official.' I do not believe that the mere enactment of § 26, on the showing made here, falls within this class of cases.

### III.

I think that this decision is not only constitutionally unsound, but in its practical potentialities short-sighted. Opponents of state antidiscrimination statutes are now in a position to argue that such legislation should be defeated because, if enacted, it may be unrepealable. More fundamentally, the doctrine underlying this decision may hamper, if not preclude, attempts to deal with the delicate and troublesome problems of race relations through the legislative process. The lines that have been and must be drawn in this area, fraught as it is with human sensibilities and frailties of whatever race or creed, are difficult ones. The drawing of them requires understanding, patience, and compromise, and is best done by legislatures rather than by courts. When legislation in this field is unsuccessful there should be wide opportunities for legislative amendment, as well as for change through such processes as the popular initiative and referendum. This decision, I fear, may inhibit such flexibility. Here the electorate itself overwhelmingly wished to overrule and check its own legislature on a matter left open by the Federal Constitution. By refusing to accept the decision of the people of California, and by contriving a new and ill-defined constitutional concept to allow federal judicial interference, I think the Court has taken to itself powers and responsibilities left elsewhere by the Constitution.

I believe the Supreme Court of California misapplied the Fourteenth Amendment, and would reverse its judgments, and remand the case for further appropriate proceedings.

## Note: Government Neutrality, Government Approval, and "State Action"

1. *Shelley* and *Reitman* illustrate one of the basic facts about the "state action" doctrine—the state is almost always involved, in some way, in the actions of private par-

ties. But that fact by itself does not mean that the challenged action satisfies the "state action" requirement.

2. Consider *Shelley*. At one level, Chief Justice Vinson's analysis is unassailable: The state court in question was an arm of the "state," and thus, when it "acted," the state action requirement was satisfied. But, as commentators have pointed out ever since 1948, that analysis proves too much. What if private parties A and B contract, and then A sues B, claiming a breach? If the court enforces the contract, or orders B to pay damages, does that mean that the private agreement between A and B is now state action? What if the contract required B, the tenant, to keep persons of a particular race off the property of A, the owner? If A's successful attempt to enforce that provision against B constitutes "state action," then can parties ever make enforceable contracts requiring conduct that a state could not itself perform? Put another way, if this hypothetical constitutes state action, then are all contractual relationships subject to the Fourteenth Amendment? For example, what if property owner A required as part of a lease that tenant B could not keep a gun on the premises? Would that violate the Second Amendment? Re-read *Shelley*, and see if you can discern something about the facts of the case that makes its implications less extreme than these hypotheticals might suggest.

3. *Reitman* is similarly vexing. Justice Harlan's dissent vociferously protests that the result in that case means that a state that enacts a non-discrimination law can never repeal it. Indeed, he goes farther, and implies that under the Court's approach a state that *never even enacts* such a law might be guilty of unconstitutional discrimination. Is he correct? After all, in all three situations the result is the same: there's no anti-discrimination law on the books. Is there a way to find "state action" in one (or two) of these situations, but not the other(s)? Is it enough to say that Proposition 14 "encouraged" Californians to discriminate in a way not done by a simple repeal of an anti-discrimination law or a failure to enact such a law in the first place? Is there anything in the particular context of Proposition 14's enactment that persuades you that the majority is correct?

# D. Cross-Cutting State Action Issues

## Rendell-Baker v. Kohn

### 457 U.S. 830 (1982)

Chief Justice BURGER delivered the opinion of the Court.

We granted certiorari to decide whether a private school, whose income is derived primarily from public sources and which is regulated by public authorities, acted under color of state law when it discharged certain employees.

I

A

Respondent Kohn is the director of the New Perspectives School, a nonprofit institution located on privately owned property in Brookline, Massachusetts. The school was founded as a private institution and is operated by a board of directors, none of whom are public officials or are chosen by public officials. The school specializes in dealing with students who have experienced difficulty completing public high schools; many have drug, alcohol, or behavioral problems, or other special needs. In recent years, nearly all of the students at the school have been referred to it by the Brookline or Boston School Committees, or by the Drug Rehabilitation Division of the Massachusetts Department of Mental Health. The school issues high school diplomas certified by the Brookline School Committee.

When students are referred to the school by Brookline or Boston under Chapter 766 of the Massachusetts Acts of 1972, the School Committees in those cities pay for the students' education. The school also receives funds from a number of other state and federal agencies. In recent years, public funds have accounted for at least 90%, and in one year 99%, of respondent school's operating budget. There were approximately 50 students at the school in those years and none paid tuition.

To be eligible for tuition funding under Chapter 766, the school must comply with a variety of regulations, many of which are common to all schools. The State has issued detailed regulations concerning matters ranging from recordkeeping to student-teacher ratios. Concerning personnel policies, the Chapter 766 regulations require the school to maintain written job descriptions and written statements describing personnel standards and procedures, but they impose few specific requirements.

The school is also regulated by Boston and Brookline as a result of its Chapter 766 funding. By its contract with the Boston School Committee, which refers to the school as a "contractor," the school must agree to carry out the individualized plan developed for each student referred to the school by the Committee. The contract specifies that school employees are not city employees.

The school also has a contract with the State Drug Rehabilitation Division. Like the contract with the Boston School Committee, that agreement refers to the school as a "contractor." It provides for reimbursement for services provided for students referred to the school by the Drug Rehabilitation Division, and includes requirements concerning the services to be provided. Except for general requirements, such as an equal employment opportunity requirement, the agreement does not cover personnel policies.

While five of the six petitioners were teachers at the school, petitioner Rendell-Baker was a vocational counselor hired under a grant from the federal Law Enforcement Assistance Administration, whose funds are distributed in Massachusetts through the State Committee on Criminal Justice. As a condition of the grant, the Committee on Criminal Justice must approve the school's initial hiring decisions. The purpose of this requirement is to insure that the school hires vocational counselors who meet the qualifications described in the school's grant proposal to the Committee; the Committee does not interview applicants for counselor positions.

### B

Rendell-Baker was discharged by the school in January 1977, and the five other petitioners were discharged in June 1978.... They brought suit against the school and its directors in December 1978...., alleging that their rights under the First, Fifth, and Fourteenth Amendments had been violated.

### C

On April 16, 1980, the District Court for the District of Massachusetts granted the defendant's motion for summary judgment in the suit brought by Rendell-Baker.... Noting that, although the State regulated the school in many ways, it imposed few conditions on the school's personnel policies, the District Court concluded that the nexus between the school and the State was not sufficiently close so that the action of the school in discharging Rendell-Baker could be considered action of the Commonwealth of Massachusetts.

Nine days earlier, on April 7, 1980, a different judge of the District Court for the District of Massachusetts had reached a contrary conclusion on the same question in the case brought by the other five petitioners....

### D

The Court of Appeals for the First Circuit consolidated the two actions. It ... concluded that the District Court ... in the action brought by the five teachers had erred in concluding that the defendants acted under color of state law.

### II

### A

Petitioners ... allege that respondents violated 42 U.S.C. § 1983, by discharging them because of their exercise of their First Amendment right of free speech and without the process due them under the Fourteenth Amendment.... [Section] 1983, which was enacted pursuant to the authority of Congress to enforce the Fourteenth Amendment, prohibits interference with federal rights under color of state law.

In *United States v. Price*, 383 U.S. 787 (1966), the Court stated:

> In cases under § 1983, 'under color' of law has consistently been treated as the same thing as the 'state action' required under the Fourteenth Amendment....

... The core issue presented in this case is not whether petitioners were discharged because of their speech or without adequate procedural protections, but whether the school's action in discharging them can fairly be seen as state action.[6] If the action of the respondent school is not state action, our inquiry ends.

---

6. The Court has concluded that the acts of a private party are fairly attributable to the state on certain occasions when the private party acted in concert with state actors. For example, in *Adickes v. S. H. Kress & Co.*, 398 U.S. 144 (1970), the issue was whether a restaurant violated [42 U.S.C.] § 1983 by refusing service to a white teacher who was in the company of six Negro students; the town sheriff arrested the white teacher for vagrancy as a result of her request to be served lunch in their

B

In *Blum v. Yaretsky*, 457 U.S. 991 (1982),[*] the Court analyzed the state action requirement of the Fourteenth Amendment. The Court considered whether certain nursing homes were state actors for the purpose of determining whether decisions regarding transfers of patients could be fairly attributed to the State, and hence be subjected to Fourteenth Amendment due process requirements. The challenged transfers primarily involved decisions, made by physicians and nursing home administrators, to move patients from "skilled nursing facilities" to less expensive "health related facilities." Like the New Perspectives School, the nursing homes were privately owned and operated. Relying on *Flagg Brothers*; *Jackson v. Metropolitan Edison Co.* (1974) [*Supra.* this chapter]; *Moose Lodge No. 107 v. Irvis*, 407 U.S. 163 (1972) [Note *supra.* this chapter]; and *Adickes*, the Court held that, "a State normally can be held responsible for a private decision only when it has exercised coercive power or has provided such significant encouragement, either overt or covert, that the choice must in law be deemed to be that of the State." In determining that the transfer decisions were not actions of the State, the Court considered each of the factors alleged by petitioners here to make the discharge decisions of the New Perspectives School fairly attributable to the State.

---

company. The Court concluded that the restaurant acted under color of state law because it conspired with the sheriff, a state actor, in depriving the white teacher of federal rights.

Similarly, *Flagg Brothers, Inc. v. Brooks*, 436 U.S. 149 (1978), and *Lugar v. Edmondson Oil Co.*, 457 U.S. 922 (1982), illustrate the relevance of whether action was taken in concert with a state actor. The issue in *Flagg Brothers* was whether a warehouseman could be sued under § 1983 because it sought to execute a lien by selling goods in its possession pursuant to § 7-210 of the New York Uniform Commercial Code. While the sale was authorized by a state statute, and hence appeared to be threatened under color of state law, the Court did not reach that issue. Instead, it concluded that the warehouseman's decision to threaten to sell the goods was not "properly attributable to the State of New York," since no state actor was involved. Since the respondent in *Flagg Brothers* claimed that the warehouseman violated her Fourteenth Amendment rights to due process and equal protection, and the Fourteenth Amendment is only offended by action of the state, we held that no claim for relief had been stated.

In *Lugar*, a lessee obtained an *ex parte* writ of attachment pursuant to a state statute, which was executed by a sheriff. The Court held that § 1983 applied because the involvement of the sheriff distinguished the case from *Flagg Brothers*. The lessee thus acted under color of state law and the sheriff's involvement satisfied the state action requirement.

The limited role played by the Massachusetts Committee on Criminal Justice in the discharge of Rendell-Baker is not comparable to the role played by the public officials in *Adickes* and *Lugar*. The uncontradicted evidence presented by the school showed that the Committee had the power only initially to review the qualifications of a counselor selected by the school to insure that the counselor met the requirements described in the school's grant application. The Committee had no power to hire or discharge a counselor who had the qualifications specified in the school's grant application. Moreover, the Committee did not take any part in discharging Rendell-Baker; on the contrary, it attempted to use leverage to aid her. It requested an explanation for her discharge from the school and stated that it would not approve the appointment of a successor unless a grievance committee considered Rendell-Baker's case. As the Court of Appeals correctly concluded, there is no evidence that the Committee had any authority to take even those steps.

 *   [Ed. Note: *Blum* was decided the same day as *Rendell-Baker*.]

First, the nursing homes, like the school, depended on the State for funds; the State subsidized the operating and capital costs of the nursing homes, and paid the medical expenses of more than 90% of the patients. Here the Court of Appeals concluded that the fact that virtually all of the school's income was derived from government funding was the strongest factor to support a claim of state action. But in *Blum v. Yaretsky*, we held that the similar dependence of the nursing homes did not make the acts of the physicians and nursing home administrators acts of the State, and we conclude that the school's receipt of public funds does not make the discharge decisions acts of the State.

The school, like the nursing homes, is not fundamentally different from many private corporations whose business depends primarily on contracts to build roads, bridges, dams, ships, or submarines for the government. Acts of such private contractors do not become acts of the government by reason of their significant or even total engagement in performing public contracts.

The school is also analogous to the public defender found not to be a state actor in *Polk County v. Dodson*, 454 U.S. 312 (1981). There we concluded that, although the State paid the public defender, her relationship with her client was "identical to that existing between any other lawyer and client." Here the relationship between the school and its teachers and counselors is not changed because the State pays the tuition of the students.

A second factor considered in *Blum* was the extensive regulation of the nursing homes by the State. There the State was indirectly involved in the transfer decisions challenged in that case because a primary goal of the State in regulating nursing homes was to keep costs down by transferring patients from intensive treatment centers to less expensive facilities when possible. Both state and federal regulations encouraged the nursing homes to transfer patients to less expensive facilities when appropriate. The nursing homes were extensively regulated in many other ways as well. The Court relied on *Jackson*, where we held that state regulation, even if "extensive and detailed," did not make a utility's actions state action.

Here the decisions to discharge the petitioners were not compelled or even influenced by any state regulation. Indeed, in contrast to the extensive regulation of the school generally, the various regulators showed relatively little interest in the school's personnel matters. The most intrusive personnel regulation promulgated by the various government agencies was the requirement that the Committee on Criminal Justice had the power to approve persons hired as vocational counselors. Such a regulation is not sufficient to make a decision to discharge, made by private management, state action. See n. 6, *supra*.

The third factor asserted to show that the school is a state actor is that it performs a "public function." However, our holdings have made clear that the relevant question is not simply whether a private group is serving a "public function." We have held that the question is whether the function performed has been "traditionally the *exclusive* prerogative of the State." *Jackson* (quoted in *Blum*) (emphasis added). There can be no doubt that the education of maladjusted high school students is a public function, but that is only the beginning of the inquiry. Chapter 766 of the Massachusetts Acts of 1972 demonstrates that the State intends to provide services for such students at public expense. That legislative policy choice in no way makes these services the exclusive province of the State. Indeed, the Court of Appeals noted that until recently the State had not undertaken to provide education for students who could not be served by traditional public schools. That a private entity performs a function which serves the public does not make its acts state action.

Fourth, petitioners argue that there is a "symbiotic relationship" between the school and the State similar to the relationship involved in *Burton v. Wilmington Parking Authority* (1961) [*Supra*. this chapter]. Such a claim is rejected in *Blum*, and we reject it here. In *Burton*, the Court held that the refusal of a restaurant located in a public parking garage to serve Negroes constituted state action. The Court stressed that the restaurant was located on public property and that the rent from the restaurant contributed to the support of the garage. In response to the argument that the restaurant's profits, and hence the State's financial position, would suffer if it did not discriminate, the Court concluded that this showed that the State profited from the restaurant's discriminatory conduct. The Court viewed this as support for the conclusion that the State should be charged with the discriminatory actions. Here the school's fiscal relationship with the State is not different from that of many contractors performing services for the government. No symbiotic relationship such as existed in Burton exists here.

C

We hold that petitioners have not stated a claim for relief under 42 U.S.C. § 1983; accordingly, the judgment of the Court of Appeals for the First Circuit is Affirmed.

Justice WHITE, concurring in the judgments.

The issue in *Blum v. Yaretsky* is whether a private nursing home's decision to discharge or transfer a Medicaid patient satisfies the state-action requirement of the Fourteenth Amendment. To satisfy this requirement, respondents must show that the transfer or discharge is made on the basis of some rule of decision for which the State is responsible. It is not enough to show that the State takes certain actions in response to this private decision. The rule of decision implicated in the actions at issue [in *Blum*] appears to be nothing more than a medical judgment. This is the clear import of the majority's conclusion [in *Blum*] that the "decisions ultimately turn on medical judgments made by private parties according to professional standards that are not established by the State," with which I agree.

Similarly, the allegations of the petitioners in [this case] fail to satisfy the state-action requirement. In this case, the question of state action focuses on an employment decision made by a private school that receives most of its funding from public sources and is subject to state regulation in certain respects. For me, the critical factor is the absence of any allegation that the employment decision was itself based upon some rule of conduct or policy put forth by the State. As the majority states, "in contrast to the extensive regulation of the school generally, the various regulators showed relatively little interest in the school's personnel matters." The employment decision remains, therefore, a private decision not fairly attributable to the State.

Accordingly, I concur in the judgments.

Justice MARSHALL, with whom Justice BRENNAN joins, dissenting.

Petitioners in these consolidated cases, former teachers and a counselor at the New Perspectives School in Brookline, Mass., were discharged by the school's administrators when they criticized certain school policies. They commenced actions under 42 U.S.C. § 1983, claiming that they had been discharged in violation of the First, Fifth, and Fourteenth Amendments. The Court today holds that their suits must be dismissed because the school did not act "under color" of state law. According to the majority, the decision of the school to discharge petitioners cannot fairly be regarded as a decision of the Commonwealth of Massachusetts.

In my view, this holding simply cannot be justified. The State has delegated to the New Perspectives School its statutory duty to educate children with special needs. The school receives almost all of its funds from the State, and is heavily regulated. This nexus between the school and the State is so substantial that the school's action must be considered state action. I therefore dissent....

## II

The decisions of this Court clearly establish that where there is a symbiotic relationship between the State and a privately owned enterprise, so that the State and a privately owned enterprise are participants in a joint venture, the actions of the private enterprise may be attributable to the State. "Conduct that is formally 'private' may become so entwined with governmental policies or so impregnated with a governmental character" that it can be regarded as governmental action. See *Burton*; see also *Jackson*; *Moose Lodge No. 107*. The question whether such a relationship exists "can be determined only in the framework of the peculiar facts or circumstances present." *Burton*. Here, an examination of the facts and circumstances leads inexorably to the conclusion that the actions of the New Perspectives School should be attributed to the State; it is difficult to imagine a closer relationship between a government and a private enterprise.

The New Perspectives School receives virtually all of its funds from state sources. This financial dependence on the State is an important indicium of governmental involvement. The school's very survival depends on the State. If the State chooses, it may exercise complete control over the school's operations simply by threatening to withdraw financial support if the school takes action that it considers objectionable.

The school is heavily regulated and closely supervised by the State. This fact provides further support for the conclusion that its actions should be attributed to the State. The school's freedom of decisionmaking is substantially circumscribed by the Massachusetts Department of Education's guidelines and the various contracts with state agencies. For example, the school is required to develop and comply with written rules for hiring and dismissal of personnel. Almost every decision the school makes is substantially affected in some way by the State's regulations.[1]

The fact that the school is providing a substitute for public education is also an important indicium of state action. The provision of education is one of the most important tasks performed by government: it ranks at the very apex of the function of a State. Of course, as the majority emphasizes, performance of a public function is by itself sufficient to justify treating a private entity as a state actor only where the function has been "traditionally the exclusive prerogative of the State." *Jackson*. See *Marsh v. Alabama* (1946) [*Supra*. this chapter]. But the fact that a private entity is performing a vital public function, when coupled with other factors demonstrating a close connection with the State, may justify a finding of state action.

The school's provision of a substitute for public education deserves particular emphasis because of the role of Chapter 766. Under this statute, the State is required to provide a free education to all children, including those with special needs. Clearly, if the State had decided to provide the service itself, its conduct would be measured against constitutional standards. The State should not be permitted to avoid constitutional requirements simply by delegating its statutory duty to a private entity. In my view, such a delegation does not convert the performance of the duty from public to private action when the duty is specific and the private institution's decisionmaking authority is significantly curtailed.

When an entity is not only heavily regulated and funded by the State, but also provides a service that the State is required to provide, there is a very close nexus with the State. Under these circumstances, it is entirely appropriate to treat the entity as an arm of the State. Here, since the New Perspectives School exists solely to fulfill the State's obligations under Chapter 766, I think it fully reasonable to conclude that the school is a state actor....

The majority repeatedly compares the school to a private contractor that "depends primarily on contracts to build roads, bridges, dams, ships, or submarines for the government." The New Perspectives School can be readily distinguished, however. Although shipbuilders and dambuilders, like the school, may be dependent on government funds, they are not so closely supervised by the government. And unlike most private contractors, the school is performing a statutory duty of the State.

The majority also focuses on the fact that the actions at issue here are personnel decisions. It would apparently concede that actions directly affecting the students could be treated as under color of state law, since the school is fulfilling the State's

---

1. The majority argues that the fact that the school receives almost all of its funds from the state is not enough, by itself, to justify a finding of state action. It also contends that the fact that the school is closely supervised and heavily regulated is not enough, by itself, to justify such a finding. I am in general agreement with both propositions. However, when these two factors are present in the same case, and when other indicia of state action are also present, a finding of state action may very well be justified. By analyzing the various indicia of state action separately, without considering their cumulative impact, the majority commits a fundamental error.

obligations to those children under Chapter 766. It suggests, however, that the State has no interest in personnel decisions. As I have suggested, I do not share this narrow view of the school's obligations; the personnel decisions challenged here are related to the provision of Chapter 766 education. In any event, since the school is funded almost entirely by the State, is closely supervised by the State, and exists solely to perform the State's statutory duty to educate children with special needs—since the school is really just an arm of the State—its personnel decisions may appropriately be considered state action.

III

Even though there are myriad indicia of state action in this case, the majority refuses to find that the school acted under color of state law when it discharged petitioners. The decision in this case marks a return to empty formalism in state action doctrine. Because I believe that the state action requirement must be given a more sensitive and flexible interpretation than the majority offers, I dissent.

## Brentwood Academy v.
## Tennessee Secondary School Athletic Association
### 531 U.S. 288 (2001)

Justice SOUTER delivered the opinion of the Court.

The issue is whether a statewide association incorporated to regulate interscholastic athletic competition among public and private secondary schools may be regarded as engaging in state action when it enforces a rule against a member school. The association in question here includes most public schools located within the State, acts through their representatives, draws its officers from them, is largely funded by their dues and income received in their stead, and has historically been seen to regulate in lieu of the State Board of Education's exercise of its own authority. We hold that the association's regulatory activity may and should be treated as state action owing to the pervasive entwinement of state school officials in the structure of the association, there being no offsetting reason to see the association's acts in any other way....

I

[The Association penalized Brentwood, a member school, for a recruiting violation. When Brentwood sued the Association, alleging a violation of its Fourteenth Amendment rights, the Association responded that it was not a state actor and thus not subject to the Fourteenth Amendment.]

II

A

Our cases try to plot a line between state action subject to Fourteenth Amendment scrutiny and private conduct (however exceptionable) that is not. *Jackson v. Metropolitan Edison Co.* (1974) [*Supra.* this chapter]. The judicial obligation is not only to "preserve an area of individual freedom by limiting the reach of federal law and avoid the imposition of responsibility on a State for conduct it could not control," but also to assure that constitutional standards are invoked "when it can be said that the State is responsible for the specific conduct of which the plaintiff complains." If the Fourteenth Amendment is not to be displaced, therefore, its ambit cannot be a simple line between States and people operating outside formally governmental organizations, and the deed of an ostensibly private organization or individual is to be treated sometimes as if a State had caused it to be performed. Thus, we say that state action may be found if, though only if, there is such a "close nexus between the State and the challenged action" that seemingly private behavior "may be fairly treated as that of the State itself." *Jackson*.

What is fairly attributable is a matter of normative judgment, and the criteria lack rigid simplicity. From the range of circumstances that could point toward the State behind an individual face, no one fact can function as a necessary condition across the board for finding state action; nor is any set of circumstances absolutely sufficient, for there may be some countervailing reason against attributing activity to the government. See *Polk County v. Dodson*, 454 U.S. 312 (1981).

Our cases have identified a host of facts that can bear on the fairness of such an attribution. We have, for example, held that a challenged activity may be state action when it results from the State's exercise of "coercive power," *Blum v. Yaretsky*, 457 U.S. 991 (1982), when the State provides "significant encouragement, either overt or covert," *id.*, or when a private actor operates as a "willful participant in joint activity with the State or its agents." We have treated a nominally private entity as a state actor when it is controlled by an "agency of the State," *Pennsylvania v. Board of Directors of City Trusts of Philadelphia*, 353 U.S. 230 (1957) (per curiam), when it has been delegated a public function by the State, when it is "entwined with governmental policies," or when government is "entwined in [its] management or control.".

Amidst such variety, examples may be the best teachers, and examples from our cases are unequivocal in showing that the character of a legal entity is determined neither by its expressly private characterization in statutory law, nor by the failure of the law to acknowledge the entity's inseparability from recognized government officials or agencies. *Lebron v. National Railroad Passenger Corporation*, 513 U.S. 374 (1995), held that Amtrak was the Government for constitutional purposes, regardless of its congressional designation as private; it was organized under federal law to attain governmental objectives and was directed and controlled by federal appointees. *Pennsylvania v. Board of Directors of City Trusts of Philadelphia* held the privately endowed Girard College to be a state actor and enforcement of its private founder's limitation of admission to whites attributable to the State, because, consistent with the terms of the settlor's gift, the college's board of directors was a state agency established by state law. Ostensibly the converse situation occurred in *Evans v. Newton*, 382 U.S. 296 (1966), which held that private trustees to whom a city had transferred a park were nonetheless state actors barred from enforcing racial segregation, since the park served the public purpose of providing community recreation, and "the municipality remained entwined in [its] management [and] control." ...

B

... [The] "necessarily fact-bound inquiry" leads to the conclusion of state action here. The nominally private character of the Association is overborne by the pervasive entwinement of public institutions and public officials in its composition and workings, and there is no substantial reason to claim unfairness in applying constitutional standards to it.

The Association is not an organization of natural persons acting on their own, but of schools, and of public schools to the extent of 84% of the total.... Although the findings and prior opinions in this case include no express conclusion of law that public school officials act within the scope of their duties when they represent their institutions, no other view would be rational, the official nature of their involvement being shown in any number of ways. Interscholastic athletics obviously play an integral part in the public education of Tennessee, where nearly every public high school spends money on competitions among schools. Since a pickup system of interscholastic games would not do, these public teams need some mechanism to produce rules and regulate competition. The mechanism is an organization overwhelmingly composed of public school officials who select representatives (all of them public officials at the time in question here), who in turn adopt and enforce the rules that make the system work. Thus, by giving these jobs to the Association, the 290 public schools of Tennessee belonging to it can sensibly be seen as exercising their own authority to meet their own responsibilities. Unsurprisingly, then, the record indicates that half the council or board meetings documented here were held during official school hours, and that public schools have largely provided for the Association's financial support. A small portion of the Association's revenue comes from membership dues paid by the schools, and the principal part from gate receipts at tournaments among the member schools. Unlike mere public buyers of contract services, whose payments for services rendered do not convert the service providers into public actors, see *Rendell-Baker v. Kohn* (1982) [*Supra.* this chapter], the schools here obtain membership in the service organization and give up sources of their own income to their collective association. The Association thus exercises the authority of the predominantly public schools to charge for admission to their games; the Association does not receive this money from the schools, but enjoys the schools' moneymaking capacity as its own.

In sum, to the extent of 84% of its membership, the Association is an organization of public schools represented by their officials acting in their official capacity to provide an integral element of secondary public schooling....

To complement the entwinement of public school officials with the Association from the bottom up, the State of Tennessee has provided for entwinement from top down. State Board members are assigned ex officio to serve as members of the board of control and legislative council, and the Association's ministerial employees are treated as state employees to the extent of being eligible for membership in the state retirement system....

The entwinement down from the State Board is therefore unmistakable, just as the entwinement up from the member public schools is overwhelming. Entwinement will support a conclusion that an ostensibly private organization ought to be charged with a public character and judged by constitutional standards; entwinement to the degree shown here requires it.

C

Entwinement is also the answer to the Association's several arguments offered to persuade us that the facts would not support a finding of state action under various criteria applied in other cases. These arguments are beside the point, simply because the facts justify a conclusion of state action under the criterion of entwinement, a conclusion in no sense unsettled merely because other criteria of state action may not be satisfied by the same facts.

The Association places great stress, for example, on the application of a public function test, as exemplified in *Rendell-Baker*. There, an apparently private school provided education for students whose special needs made it difficult for them to finish high school. The record, however, failed to show any tradition of providing public special education to students unable to cope with a regular school, who had historically been cared for (or ignored) according to private choice. It was true that various public school districts had adopted the practice of referring students to the school and paying their tuition, and no one disputed that providing the instruction aimed at a proper public objective and conferred a public benefit. But we held that the performance of such a public function did not permit a finding of state action on the part of the school unless the function performed was exclusively and traditionally public, as it was not in that case. The Association argues that application of the public function criterion would produce the same result here, and we will assume, arguendo, that it would. But this case does not turn on a public function test, any more than *Rendell-Baker* had anything to do with entwinement of public officials in the special school.

For the same reason, it avails the Association nothing to stress that the State neither coerced nor encouraged the actions complained of. "Coercion" and "encouragement" are like "entwinement" in referring to kinds of facts that can justify characterizing an ostensibly private action as public instead. Facts that address any of these criteria are significant, but no one criterion must necessarily be applied. When, therefore, the relevant facts show pervasive entwinement to the point of largely overlapping identity, the implication of state action is not affected by pointing out that the facts might not loom large under a different test.

D

This is not to say that all of the Association's arguments are rendered beside the point by the public officials' involvement in the Association, for after application of the entwinement criterion, or any other, there is a further potential issue, and the Association raises it. Even facts that suffice to show public action (or, standing alone, would require such a finding) may be outweighed in the name of some value at odds with finding public accountability in the circumstances. In *Polk County* a defense lawyer's actions were deemed private even though she was employed by the county and was acting within the scope of her duty as a public defender. Full-time public employment would be conclusive of state action for some purposes, but not when the employee is doing a defense lawyer's primary job; then, the public defender does "not act on behalf of the State; he is the State's adversary." *Polk County*. The state-action doctrine does not convert opponents into virtual agents.

The assertion of such a countervailing value is the nub of each of the Association's two remaining arguments, neither of which, however, persuades us. The Association suggests, first, that reversing the judgment here will somehow trigger an epidemic of unprecedented federal litigation. Even if that might be counted as a good reason for a *Polk County* decision to call the Association's action private, the record raises no reason for alarm here. Save for the Sixth Circuit, every Court of Appeals to consider a statewide athletic association like the one here has found it a state actor.... No one, however, has pointed to any explosion of § 1983 cases against interscholastic athletic associations in the affected jurisdictions....

Nor do we think there is anything to be said for the Association's contention that there is no need to treat it as a state actor since any public school applying the Association's rules is itself subject to suit under § 1983 or Title IX of the Education Amendments of 1972. If Brentwood's claim were pushing at the edge of the class of possible defendant state actors, an argument about the social utility of expanding that class would at least be on point, but because we are nowhere near the margin in this case, the Association is really asking for nothing less than a dispensation for itself....

The judgment of the Court of Appeals for the Sixth Circuit is reversed, and the case is remanded for further proceedings consistent with this opinion.

Justice THOMAS, with whom THE CHIEF JUSTICE, Justice SCALIA, and Justice KENNEDY join, dissenting.

We have never found state action based upon mere "entwinement." Until today, we have found a private organization's acts to constitute state action only when the organization performed a public function; was created, coerced, or encouraged by the government; or acted in a symbiotic relationship with the government. The majority's holding—that the Tennessee Secondary School Athletic Association's (TSSAA) enforcement of its recruiting rule is state action—not only extends state-action doctrine beyond its permissible limits but also encroaches upon the realm of individual freedom that the doctrine was meant to protect. I respectfully dissent....

I

* * *

A

... [Common] sense dictates that the TSSAA's actions cannot fairly be attributed to the State, and thus cannot constitute state action. The TSSAA was formed in 1925 as a private corporation to organize interscholastic athletics and to sponsor tournaments among its member schools. Any private or public secondary school may join the TSSAA by signing a contract agreeing to comply with its rules and decisions. Although public schools currently compose 84% of the TSSAA's membership, the TSSAA does not require that public schools constitute a set percentage of its membership, and, indeed, no public school need join the TSSAA. The TSSAA's rules are enforced not by a state agency but by its own board of control, which comprises high school principals, assistant principals, and superintendents, none of whom must work at a public school. Of course, at the time the recruiting rule was enforced in this case, all of the board members happened to be public school officials. However, each board member acts in a representative capacity on behalf of all the private and public schools in his region of Tennessee, and not simply his individual school.

The State of Tennessee did not create the TSSAA. The State does not fund the TSSAA and does not pay its employees.[1] In fact, only 4% of the TSSAA's revenue comes from the dues paid by member schools; the bulk of its operating budget is derived from gate receipts at tournaments it sponsors. The State does not permit the TSSAA to use state-owned facilities for a discounted fee, and it does not exempt the TSSAA from state taxation. No Tennessee law authorizes the State to coordinate interscholastic athletics or empowers another entity to organize interscholastic athletics on behalf of the State. The only state pronouncement acknowledging the TSSAA's existence is a rule providing that the State Board of Education permits public schools to maintain membership in the TSSAA if they so choose.

Moreover, the State of Tennessee has never had any involvement in the particular action taken by the TSSAA in this case: the enforcement of the TSSAA's recruiting rule prohibiting members from using "undue influence" on students or their parents or guardians "to secure or to retain a student for athletic purposes." There is no indication that the State has ever had any interest in how schools choose to regulate recruiting ...

B

... The TSSAA has not performed a function that has been "traditionally exclusively reserved to the State." *Jackson.* The organization of interscholastic sports is neither a traditional nor an exclusive public function of the States. Widespread organization and administration of interscholastic contests by schools did not begin until the 20th century.... The TSSAA no doubt serves the public, particularly the public schools, but the mere provision of a service to the public does not render such provision a traditional and exclusive public function. See *Rendell-Baker.*

It is also obvious that the TSSAA is not an entity created and controlled by the government for the purpose of fulfilling a government objective, as was Amtrak in

---

1. Although the TSSAA's employees, who typically are retired teachers, are allowed to participate in the state retirement system, the State does not pay any portion of the employer contribution for them. The TSSAA is one of three private associations, along with the Tennessee Education Association and the Tennessee School Boards Association, whose employees are statutorily permitted to participate in the state retirement system.

*Lebron.* Indeed, no one claims that the State of Tennessee played any role in the creation of the TSSAA as a private corporation in 1925....

In addition, the State of Tennessee has not "exercised coercive power or ... provided such significant encouragement [to the TSSAA], either overt or covert," *Blum*, that the TSSAA's regulatory activities must in law be deemed to be those of the State. The State has not promulgated any regulations of interscholastic sports, and nothing in the record suggests that the State has encouraged or coerced the TSSAA in enforcing its recruiting rule.... Likewise, even if the TSSAA were dependent on state funding to the extent of 90%, as was the case in *Blum*, instead of less than 4%, mere financial dependence on the State does not convert the TSSAA's actions into acts of the State. See *Blum*; *Rendell-Baker*. Furthermore, there is no evidence of "joint participation" between the State and the TSSAA in the TSSAA's enforcement of its recruiting rule. The TSSAA's board of control enforces its recruiting rule solely in accordance with the authority granted to it under the contract that each member signs.

Finally, there is no "symbiotic relationship" between the State and the TSSAA. *Moose Lodge No. 107 v. Irvins*, 407 U.S. 163 (1972) [Note *supra.* this chapter]; cf. *Burton*. Contrary to the majority's assertion, the TSSAA's "fiscal relationship with the State is not different from that of many contractors performing services for the government." *Rendell-Baker*. The TSSAA provides a service—the organization of athletic tournaments—in exchange for membership dues and gate fees, just as a vendor could contract with public schools to sell refreshments at school events. Certainly the public school could sell its own refreshments, yet the existence of that option does not transform the service performed by the contractor into a state action. Also, there is no suggestion in this case that, as was the case in *Burton*, the State profits from the TSSAA's decision to enforce its recruiting rule.

Because I do not believe that the TSSAA's action of enforcing its recruiting rule is fairly attributable to the State of Tennessee, I would affirm.

## II

Although the TSSAA's enforcement activities cannot be considered state action as a matter of common sense or under any of this Court's existing theories of state action, the majority presents a new theory. Under this theory, the majority holds that the combination of factors it identifies evidences "entwinement" of the State with the TSSAA, and that such entwinement converts private action into state action. The majority does not define "entwinement," and the meaning of the term is not altogether clear. But whatever this new "entwinement" theory may entail, it lacks any support in our state-action jurisprudence. Although the majority asserts that there are three examples of entwinement analysis in our cases, there is no case in which we have rested a finding of state action on entwinement alone....

Because the majority never defines "entwinement," the scope of its holding is unclear. If we are fortunate, the majority's fact-specific analysis will have little bearing beyond this case. But if the majority's new entwinement test develops in future years, it could affect many organizations that foster activities, enforce rules, and sponsor extracurricular competition among high schools—not just in athletics, but in such diverse areas as agriculture, mathematics, music, marching bands, forensics, and cheerleading. Indeed, this entwinement test may extend to other organizations that are composed of, or controlled by, public officials or public entities, such as firefighters, policemen, teachers, cities, or counties. I am not prepared to say that any private organization that permits public entities and public officials to participate acts as the State in anything or everything it does, and our state-action jurisprudence has never reached that far. The state-action doctrine was developed to reach only those actions that are truly attributable to the State, not to subject private citizens to the control of federal courts hearing § 1983 actions.

I respectfully dissent.

## Note: The State Action Puzzle

The cases in this chapter provide only a sampling of the many cases the Court has decided that raise difficult state action issues. Is there any logic to these cases, or to state action analysis more generally? To be sure, the Court often warns that state action cases are highly fact- and context-dependent. But by itself, that warning degenerates into an admission that the doctrine is utterly *ad hoc*. Can you derive any principles from these cases? If you can't, then how would you advise the Court to decide state action cases?

# Index